The Greek Islands

written and researched by

Marc Dubin, Mark Ellingham, John Fisher and Natania Jansz

additional accounts by

Andrew Benson, John Bozman, Lance Chilton, Nick Edwards, Geoff Garvey and Samantha Stenzel

www.roughguides.com

ROUGH GUIDES

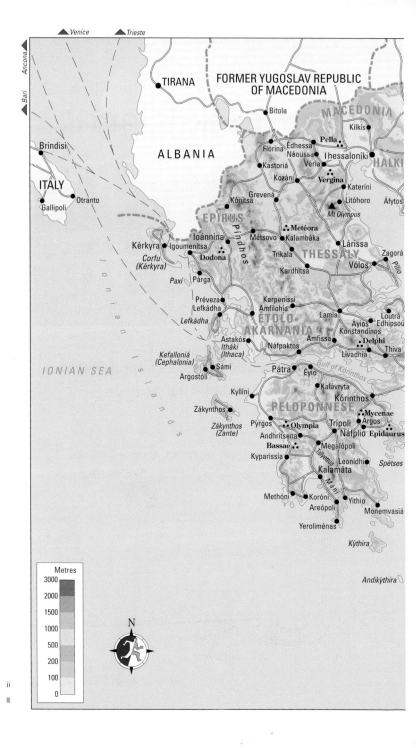

Venice   Trieste

Ancona   Bari

TIRANA   FORMER YUGOSLAV REPUBLIC
OF MACEDONIA

Bitola

MACEDONIA

Kilkís

Pélla

ALBANIA   Flórina   Édhessa
Náoussa   Ihessaloníki   HALKI
Kastoriá   Véria
Kozáni   Vergina   Katéríni

Brindísi

ITALY   Grevená   Litóhoro   Áfytos
Otranto   Kónitsa   Mt Olympus
Gallipoli

EPIRUS   Métoora

Ioánnina   Métsovo   Kalambáka   Lárissa
Kérkyra   Igoumenítsa   Trikala   THESSALY   Zagorá
Corfu   Dodona   Kardhítsa   Vólos
(Kérkyra)   Pilio

Paxí   Párga

Préveza   Karpeníssi
Lefkádha   Amfilohía   Lamía   Loutrá
Lefkádha   Áyios   Edhipsoú
ETOLO-   Konstandínos
AKARNANÍA   Amfissa   Delphi
Astakós   Náfpaktos   Thiva
Itháki   Livadhiá
(Ithaca)   Gulf of Kórinthos

Kefallonía   Pátra   Éyio
(Cephalonia)   Sámi
Argostóli   Kalávryta   Kórinthos

Kyllíni   PELOPONNESE   Mycenae
Zákynthos   Argos
Pýrgos   Olympia   Trípoli   Epidaurus
Zákynthos   Andhrítsena   Náfplio
(Zante)   Bassae   Megalópoli
Kyparissía   Leonídhi   Spétses
Kalamáta

Methóni   Koróni   Yíthio
Areópoli   Monemvasiá
Yeroliménas

Kýthira

IONIAN SEA

Ionian Islands

Andikýthira

Metres
3000
2000
1500
1000
500
200
100
0

N

ii

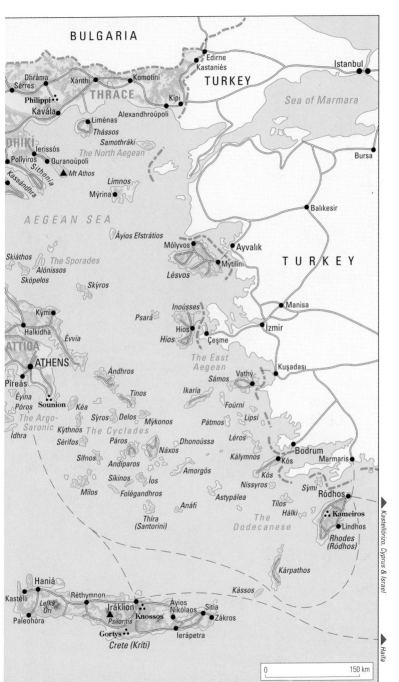

BULGARIA

TURKEY

Edirne
Kastaniés
Istanbul

Dhráma
Sérres
Xánthi
Komotiní
THRACE
Kipi
Philippi
Kavála
Alexandhroúpoli

Sea of Marmara

Liménas
Thássos
Samothráki
The North Aegean

DHIKI
Ierissós
Políyiros
Ouranoúpoli
Sithonía
Mt Athos
Kassándhra

Bursa

AEGEAN SEA

Límnos
Mýrina

Balıkesir

Áyios Efstrátios

Skíathos
The Sporades
Alónissos
Skópelos
Skýros

Mólyvos
Mytilíni
Ayvalık
Lésvos

TURKEY

Kými
Halkídha
Évvia

Inoússes
Psará
Hios
Híos
Çeşme

Manisa

İzmir

ATTICA
ATHENS
Pireás
Éyina
Póros
Sounion
Kéa
Ándhros
Tínos
Sýros Delos
Mýkonos
Ikaría
Foúrni
Sámos
Vathý
Lipsí
Pátmos
Kuşadası

The East
Aegean

The Argo-Saronic
Ídhra
Kýthnos
Sérifos
The Cyclades
Páros
Sífnos
Andíparos
Síkinos
Mílos
Folégandhros
Íos
Anáfi
Thíra
(Santorini)

Dhonoússa
Náxos
Amorgós
Astypálea
Léros
Kálymnos
Kós
Kós
Nissyros
Tílos
Hálki
Sými
Ródhos
Bodrum
Marmaris

The Dodecanese

Kameiros
Líndhos
Rhodes
(Ródhos)

Kárpathos

Haniá
Kastélli
Lefká Óri
Paleohóra
Réthymnon
Iráklion
Psilorítis
Knossos
Gortys
Crete (Kríti)
Áyios Nikólaos
Sitía
Zákros
Ierápetra

Kássos

0   150 km

Kastellórizo, Cyprus & Israel

Haifa

iii

Introduction to

The Greek Islands

It would take a lifetime of island-hopping to really get to know the more than 160 permanently inhabited Greek islands, let alone the countless smaller gull-roosts which dot the Aegean and Ionian seas. At the right time of year or day, they conform remarkably well to their fantastic travel-poster image; any tourist board would give its eye-teeth for the commonplace vision of purple-shadowed island silhouettes floating on a cobalt-and-rose horizon.

Closer to hand, island **beaches** come in all shapes, sizes and consistencies, from discrete crescents framed by tree-fringed cliffs straight out of a Japanese screen painting, to deserted, mile-long gifts deposited by small streams, where you could imagine enacting Crusoe scenarios among the dunes. But inland there is always civilization, whether the tiny cubist villages of the remoter outposts or burgeoning resorts as cosmopolitan – and brazen – as any in the Mediterranean.

What amazes most first-time visitors is the islands' relative **lack of pollution**. If you're used to the murky waters of the open Mediterranean as sampled in Spain, Israel or southern France, the Aegean will come as a revelation, with forty-foot visibility the norm, and all manner of sea creatures

Fact file

- Greece is currently the eastern-most member of the EU, with a surface area of 131,957 square kilometres (50,949 square miles) divided into 51 provinces. No other country, with the obvious exceptions of Indonesia and the Philippines, has so many islands, though they form only about ten percent of Greece's total territory. The population is overwhelmingly Greek-speaking and 96 percent are Greek Orthodox in religious affiliation, with noticeable Catholic, Sunni Muslim, Jewish and evangelical Christian minorities, plus (mostly on the mainland) pockets of Turkish-, Romany- and Macedonian-speakers. Around one million live out on the islands, and nearly half of these live in towns of over five thousand people.

- Per "native" population of roughly 10.4 million, Greece has the highest proportion of immigrants in Europe – estimated at 800,000 to 1.1 million, most of these Albanian.

- Since 1974 Greece has been a parliamentary republic, with the president as head of state and a 300-seat, single-chamber parliament led by a prime minister. At present PASOK, the (approximately) social democratic ruling party, is enjoying its third consecutive term in office, something hitherto unheard of in the perennially unstable – and historically rightist – Greek political world.

- Tourism is the country's main foreign-currency earner, with over ten million visitors from overseas in a good year. Shipping, which used to occupy second place, is in crisis and has been replaced by agricultural products, especially olive oil and olives, citrus, raisins and wine.

visible, from starfish and octopuses on the bottom to vast schools of fish.

The sea is also a **watersports** paradise: the joys of snorkelling and kayaking are on offer to novices, and some of the best windsurfing areas in the world beckon. Yacht charter, whether bare-boat or skippered, is big business, particularly out of Rhodes, Kálymnos, Lefkádha, Póros and Pireás; indeed, the Greek islands are rated on a par with the Caribbean for quality sailing itineraries. And during the months when the sea is too cold or the weather too blustery, many islands – not necessarily the largest ones – offer superb **hiking** on surviving mule-trails between hill villages, or up the highest summits.

Although more protected than the Greek mainland from invasions, the various archipelagos have been subject to a staggering variety of **foreign influences**. Romans, Arabs, Byzantines, crusading Knights of Saint John, Genoese, Venetians, French, English, Italians and Ottomans have all controlled different islands since the time of Alexander the Great. The high tide of empire has left behind countless **monuments**: frescoed Byzantine churches and monasteries, the fortified Venetian towns of the Cyclades and the Ionians, the more conventional castles of the Genoese and Knights in the northeast Aegean and Dodecanese, Ottoman bridges and mosques, and the Art Deco or mock-Renaissance edifices of the Italian Fascist administration.

Constructions from many of these eras are often juxtaposed with – or even superimposed on – the cities and temples of ancient Greece, which provide the foundation in all senses for claims of an enduring Hellenic **cultural identity** down the centuries; museums, particularly on Crete, Rhodes, Sámos, Híos, Lésvos and Límnos, amply document the archeological evidence. But it was medieval Greek peasants, fishermen and shepherds, working without an indigenous ruling class or formal Renaissance to impose models of taste or patronize the arts, who most tangibly contributed to our idea of Greekness with their songs and dances, costumes, weaving and vernacular architecture. Much of this has vanished in recent decades, replaced by an avalanche of *bouzoúki*-instrumental cassettes, "genuine museum copies" and tacky souvenir shops, but enough remains in isolated pockets for visitors to marvel at Greek popular culture's combination of form and function.

Of course, most Greek-island visits are devoted to more hedonistic pursuits: going lightly dressed, swimming in balmy waters at dusk, talking and drinking under the stars until 3am. Such pleasures amply compensate for certain enduring weaknesses in the Greek **tourism "product"**: don't go expecting orthopedic mattresses, state-of-the-art plumbing, Cordon-Bleu cuisine or attentive service. Except at a limited number of upmarket facilities in new or restored buildings, hotel and pension rooms can be box-like, campsites tend to be of the rough-and-ready sort, and the food at its best is fresh and simply presented.

Boatyards

Even in the more touristed islands, a remarkable number of traditional boatyards (*karnáyia*) still survive. Small craft are built in the time-honoured way, with the keel and framework assembled first from seasoned pine, which abounds in Greek coastal regions, and then overlaid with planking. You can often spot *karnáyia* from some distance by the bright-orange *mínio*, or red-lead paint, applied to the exposed wood – long illegal in most of the EU but still the preservative of choice in Greece.

The Greek islanders

To attempt an understanding of the islanders, it's useful to realize how recent and traumatic were the events that created the modern Greek state and **national character** – the latter a blend of extroversion and pessimism not entirely due to Greece's strategic position between the West and the Middle East.

Until the early 1900s, Crete, the east Aegean and the Dodecanese – nearly half the islands described in this book – remained in Ottoman or Italian hands. Meanwhile, many people from these "unredeemed" territories lived in Asia Minor, Egypt, western Europe or the northern Balkans. The Balkan Wars of 1912–13, the Greco-Turkish war of 1919–22, Greece's 1917–18 World War I involvement and the organized **population exchanges** which followed each of these conflicts had profound, brutal effects. Orthodox refugees from Turkey suddenly made up a noticeable proportion of the population of Crete and the northeast Aegean (especially Thássos and Lésvos), and with the forced or voluntary departure of their Levantines, Muslims and (during World War II) Jews, these islands gradually lost their multicultural traits.

Even before the last war, the Italian occupation of the Dodecanese was characterized by progressively stricter suppression of Greek Orthodox identity, but in general the war years in most other island groups were not quite so dire as on the mainland. Neither was the 1946–49 civil war that followed, nor the 1967–74 dictatorship, so keenly felt out in the Aegean, though benign neglect was about the best many islands could expect until the 1960s. Given the chance to emigrate to Australia, Canada or Africa, many entrepreneurial islanders did so, continuing a trend of **depopulation** which ironically had accelerated earlier in the twentieth century, following political union of the

northeast Aegean and Dodecanese with the Greek mainland. The uncomfortably close memory of catastrophe, continuing misrule and scarce opportunity at home spurred yet another diaspora.

The advent of **tourism** in the 1960s arguably saved a number of islands from complete desolation, though local attitudes towards this deliverance have been decidedly ambivalent. It galls local pride to have become a class of seasonal service personnel, and the encounter between outsiders and villagers has often been corrosive to a deeply conservative rural society. Though younger Greeks are happily adaptable as they rake in the proceeds at resort areas, tourists still need to be sensitive in their behaviour towards the older generation. The mind boggles imagining the reaction of black-clad elders to nude bathing, or even scanty apparel, in a country where – despite being increasingly out of step with majority sentiment – the Orthodox Church remains an all-but-established faith and self-appointed guardian of national identity. In the presence of Italian-style espresso bars, internet cafés and cash dispensers, it's easy to be lulled into thinking that Greece became thoroughly European the moment it joined the EU – until a flock of sheep is paraded along the main street at high noon, and the 1pm ferry shows up at 3pm, or not at all.

Where to go

here is no such thing as a "typical" Greek island; each has its distinctive personality, history, architecture, flora – even a unique tourist clientele.

Wayside shrines

Throughout Greece you'll see, by the side of the road, small shrines, or *ikonostáses*, which usually hold a saint's icon, an oil lamp, a few floatable wicks

and a box of matches. Unlike in Latin America, they don't necessarily mark the spot where someone met their end in a motoring accident (though just occasionally they do); typically they were erected by one family or even one individual in fulfilment of a vow, or *támma*, to a particular saint to reciprocate for favours granted. *Ikonostáses* come in various sizes and designs, from spindly, derrick-like metal constructions to sumptuous, gaily painted models of small cathedrals in marble and plaster which you can practically walk into. Often they indicate the presence of a larger but less convenient (and often locked) church off in the countryside nearby, dedicated to the same saint, and act as a substitute shrine where the devout wayfarer can reverence the icon it contains.

The Evil Eye

Belief in the Evil Eye is pan-Mediterranean and goes at least as far back as Roman times, but nowhere has it hung on so tenaciously as in Greece (and neighbouring coastal Turkey). In a nutshell, whenever something attractive, valuable or unusual – an infant, a new car, a prized animal – becomes suddenly, inexplicably indisposed, it is assumed to be *matisméno*, or "eyed". Blue-eyed individuals are thought most capable of casting this spell, always unintentionally or at least unconsciously (unlike *máyia*, or wilful black magic). The diagnosis is confirmed by discreet referral to a "wise woman", who is also versed in the proper counter-spell. But prevention is always better than cure, and this involves two main strategies. When admiring something or someone, the admirer – blue-eyed or otherwise – must mock-spit ("*phtoo, phtoo, phtoo!*") to counteract any stirrings of envy which, according to anthropologists, are the root-cause of the Eye. And the proud owners or parents will protect the object of admiration in advance with a blue amulet, hung about the baby's/animal's neck or the car's rear-view mirror, or even painted directly onto a boat's bow.

Landscapes vary from the lush cypress-and-olive-swathed Ionians to the bare, wind-scoured ridges of the Cyclades and Dodecanese, by way of subtle gradations between these extremes in the Sporades and northeast Aegean. Setting aside the scars from a few unfortunate man-made developments, it would be difficult to single out an irredeemably ugly island; all have their adherents and individual appeal, described in the chapter introductions.

Perhaps the best strategy for initial visits is to sample assorted islands from contiguous archipelagos – Crete, the Dodecanese, the Cyclades and the northeast Aegean are all reasonably well connected with each other, though the Sporades, Argo-Saronic and Ionian groups offer limited (or no) possibilities for island-hopping, and usually involve a long traipse across the mainland to get to. If time and money are short, the best place to visit is well-preserved **Ídhra** in the Argo-Saronic, just a short ride from Pireás (the main port of Athens), but an utterly different place once the day-cruises have gone; neighbouring **Spétses** has similar architectural charm and more accessible beaches. Of the Sporades, **Skýros** and **Skópelos** remain the most traditional and aesthetic, with forests, pale-sand beaches and well-preserved capitals. Among the Cyclades, cataclysmically volcanic **Thíra (Santoríni)** and **Mýkonos** with its perfectly preserved harbour town rank as must-see spectacles, but fertile, mountainous **Náxos** and gently rolling **Sífnos** have life more independent of cruise-ship tourism and seem more amenable to long stays. For true aficionados, dramatically cliff-girt **Amorgós** or **Folégandhros**, rocky **Sýros** with its UNESCO-recognized harbour town, artistic **Tínos** or lonely **Anáfi** and its balmy, south-facing beaches are less obvious but equally satisfying choices. **Crete** could (and does) fill an entire Rough Guide to itself, but the highlights have to be **Knossos** and the nearby **archeological museum** in Iráklion, the other Minoan palaces at **Festós** and **Ayía Triádha**, and the west in general – **Réthymnon** with its intact old town, the proud city of **Haniá**, with its hinterland extending to the relatively unspoiled southwest coast, reachable via the fabled **Samarian gorge**. **Rhodes**, with its unique old town, is capital of the Dodecanese, but picturesque, Neoclassical **Sými** opposite and austere **Pátmos**, the island of Revelation, are far more manageable. **Kárpathos**, marooned between Rhodes and Crete, has some of the best beaches and walking in the Dodecanese, while **Léros** and **Níssyros** will appeal to those looking for characterful, unspoilt islands that don't necessarily have superb coastline. From Pátmos or Léros, it's easy to continue north via **Sámos**, still one of the most attractive islands despite recent fires, and **Híos**, with striking medieval architecture – to balmy, olive-cloaked **Lésvos**, perhaps the most traditional of all islands in way of life. The Ionian islands are, probably more than any other area except Crete and Rhodes, package-holiday territory, but if you're exiting Greece towards Italy by all means stop in at **Corfu** to at least savour the Venetian-style main town, which along with neighbouring **Paxí** islet survived severe 1953 earthquake damage. Little **Itháki**, again easiest reached from the mainland, is relatively untouristed, given a lack of beaches, though big brother **Kefalloniá** is now well and truly in the spotlight owing to spectacular scenery – and exposure in Louis de Bernière's blockbuster novel, *Captain Corelli's Mandolin*.

When to go

M ost islands and their inhabitants are far more agreeable, and resolutely Greek, outside the **busiest period** of early July to late August, when crowds of foreigners or locals, soaring temperatures and the effects of the infamous

meltémi can detract considerably from enjoyment. The *meltémi* is a cool, fair-weather wind which originates in high-pressure systems over the far north Aegean, gathering momentum as it travels southwards and assuming near-gale magnitude by the time it reaches Crete. North-facing coasts there, and throughout the Cyclades and Dodecanese, bear the full brunt; its howling is less pronounced in the north or east Aegean, where continental landmasses provide some shelter for the islands just offshore.

You won't miss out on **warm weather** if you come between late May and mid-June – when a wide variety of garden produce and fish is still available – or in September, when the sea is warmest for swimming, though at these times you'll find little activity on the northernmost islands of Thássos and Samothráki. During October you'll probably hit a week's stormy spell, but for much of that month the "little summer of Áyios Dhimítrios", the Greek equivalent of **Indian summer**, prevails. While autumn choice in restaurants and nightlife can be limited, the light is softer, and going out at midday becomes a pleasure rather than an ordeal. The most reliable venues for late-autumn or early-winter breaks are Rhodes and relatively balmy southeastern Crete, where swimming in December is not unheard of.

December to March are the **coldest** and least comfortable months, particularly on the Ionian islands, historically the rainiest patch in Greece from November onwards (though lately suffering, like most of the country, from prolonged drought). The high peaks of northerly or lofty islands wear a brief mantle of **snow** around the turn of the year, with Crete's mountainous spine staying partly covered (global warming permitting) into April. Between January and April the glorious lowland wildflowers start to bloom, beginning in the southeast Aegean. April weather is notoriously unreliable, though the air is crystal-clear and the landscape **green** – a photographer's dream. May is more settled, though the sea is still a bit cool for prolonged dips.

Other factors that affect the timing of a Greek-island visit have to do with the level of tourism and the related **amenities** provided. Service standards,

particularly in tavernas, invariably slip under peak-season pressure, and room rates are at their highest from July to September. If you can only visit during midsummer, reserve a package well in advance, or plan an itinerary off the beaten track. Between November and April, you have to contend with pared-back ferry schedules (and almost non-existent hydrofoil or catamaran departures), plus skeletal facilities when you arrive. However, you will find fairly adequate services to the more populated islands, and at least one hotel and taverna open in the port or main town of all but the tiniest isles.

Average temperatures (°F) and rainfall (days)

	Jan		March		May		July		Sept		Nov	
	Max	Min	Max	Min	Max	Min	Max	Min	Max	Min	Max	Min
Crete (Haniá)	60	46	64	48	76	56	86	68	82	64	70	54
rainfall	17		11		5		0		3		10	
Cyclades (Mýkonos)	58	50	62	52	72	62	82	72	78	68	66	58
rainfall	14		8		5		0.5		1		9	
Ionian (Corfu)	56	44	62	46	74	58	88	70	82	64	66	52
rainfall	13		10		6		2		5		12	
Dodecanese (Rhodes)	58	50	62	48	74	58	86	70	82	72	68	60
rainfall	15		7		2		0		1		7	
Sporades (Skiáthos)	55	45	58	47	71	58	82	71	75	64	62	53
rainfall	12		10		3		0		8		12	
East Aegean (Lésvos)	54	42	60	46	76	60	88	70	82	66	64	50
rainfall	11		7		6		2		2		9	

30

things not to miss

It's not possible to see everything that the Greek islands have to offer in one trip – and we don't suggest you try. What follows is a selective taste of the islands' highlights: outstanding buildings, superb ancient sites and natural wonders. They're arranged alphabetically in five colour-coded categories, which you can browse through to find the very best things to see and experience. All highlights have a page reference to take you straight to the guide, where you can find out more.

01 **Lindos acropolis, Rhodes** Page **299** ● From the Hellenistic acropolis of Lindos, high above the modern village, you look north along the length of Rhodes island.

02 **Windsurfing off Vassilikí, Lefkádha** Page **504** • Located in a vast, cliff-flanked bay, Vassilikí is one of Europe's biggest windsurf centres.

03 **Mountain vineyards, Sámos** Page **367** • Despite recent fires, Sámos remains arguably the most verdant and beautiful of the east Aegean islands.

04 **Khryssopiyís monastery, Sífnos** Page **130** • Spectacularly sited Khryssopiyís monastery sits atop a sea-washed spit of land on Sifnos's southeast coast.

05 Knossós palace, Crete

Page 219 • The most restored, vividly coloured and ultimately most exciting of Crete's Minoan palaces.

06 Monastery of Saint John, Pátmos

Page 356 • Built in honour of Saint John the Divine, this huge monastery is a warren of interconnecting courtyards, chapels, stairways, arcades, galleries and roof terraces.

07 Égina: Temple of Aphaia

Page 96 • The beautiful fifth-century BC Temple of Aphaia is one of the most complete and visually complex ancient buildings in Greece.

08 Loggerhead sea turtle
Page **525** • The Ionian islands harbour one of the Mediterranean's main concentrations of the endangered loggerhead sea turtle.

09 Volcano floor, Níssyros
Page **325** • No stay on Níssyros would be complete without a visit to the island's dormant volcano.

10 Dovecotes on Tínos
Page **142** • Distinctive, ornate dovecotes, introduced by the Venetians, punctuate the island of Tínos.

11 Hozoviotíssas monastery, Amorgós Page 181 •

With its vast walls gleaming white at the base of a sheer orange cliff, the Hozoviotíssas monastery is a dramatic sight.

12 Ídhra Page 103 •

Ídhra's perfect horseshoe-shaped harbour is surrounded by grand eighteenth-century mansions.

13 Art Deco cinema, Lakkí, Léros Page 349 •

The wide boulevards of Léros's main port, Lakkí, are lined with marvellous Italian Art Deco buildings.

14 **Hikers in the Gorge of Samariá, Crete** Page **266** •
The magnificent Gorge of Samariá is the longest in Europe.

15 **Village weaver, near Lasíthi Plateau** Page **236** •
Traditional crafts, such as weaving and embroidery, still flourish in parts of Crete.

16 **Vaï beach, Crete** Page **244** • A superb beach, fringed with palm trees – claimed to be Europe's only indigenous wild date-palm grove.

17 Tomatoes drying, Híos Page **394** ● Strings of sun-drying tomatoes are a common sight in autumn in Híos's mastic villages.

18 Kérkyra (Corfu) old town Page **479** ● With its elegant Venetian architecture and fine museums, Corfu's capital is the cultural heart of the Ionians.

19 Longós, Paxí

Page **499** • The prettiest coastal village on verdant, largely unspoiled Paxí.

20 Kárpathos: view south from Ólymbos village

Page **287** • The view south from windswept, remote Ólymbos gives a good idea of the rugged coast of northern Kárpathos.

21 Naoússa harbour, Páros

Page **162** • Páros's second port, Naoússa is still very much a traditional, working harbour.

22 Melissáni Cave, Kefalloniá

Page **510** • Take a boat trip to the underwater Melissáni cave, and admire the rock formations and play of light on the cave walls.

23 View over Firá

Page **192** • This island capital is one of several villages that teeter at the edge of Thíra's (Santoríni's) caldera cliff.

24 Harbour, Sými

Page **312** • The mansions of Sými's picturesque harbour, built with wealth from the sponge trade, are part of an architecturally protected area.

25 Skýros
Page **457** •
Only "discovered"
by tourism in the
early 1990s, Skýros
remains one of the
most traditional
islands in the
Aegean.

26 Mólyvos, Lésvos
Page **414** • The castle-crowned village of Mólyvos ranks as one of the most beautiful on Lésvos.

27 Paradise beach, Mykonos
Page **151** • The golden sand of Paradise beach attracts numerous holiday-makers in summer.

28 **Ápella beach, Kárpathos** Page 287 • One of the most scenic of Kárpathos's east-coast beaches.

29 **Haniá old town waterfront, Crete** Page 261 • Haniá displays haunting vestiges of its Venetian and Ottoman past.

30 **Chapel of Metamórfosis, Dhíkeos peak, Kós** Page 334 • A hike up 846-metre Dhíkeos peak to the Metamórfosis chapel rewards you with excellent panoramic views.

contents

Using the Rough Guide

We've tried to make this Rough Guide a good read and easy to use. The book is divided into six main sections, and you should be able to find whatever you want in one of them.

front section

The front colour section offers a quick tour of the Greek Islands. The **introduction** aims to give you a feel for the islands, with suggestions on where to go. We also tell you what the weather is like and include a basic country fact file. Next, our authors round up their favourite aspects of the Greek Islands in the **things not to miss** section – whether it's great festivals, amazing sights or a special hotel. Right after this comes the Rough Guide's full **contents** list.

basics

You've decided to go and the basics section covers all the pre-departure nitty-gritty to help you plan your trip. This is where to find out which airlines fly to your destination, what to do about money and insurance, about internet access, food, security, public transport, car rental – in fact just about every piece of **general practical information** you might need.

guide

This is the heart of the Rough Guide, divided into user-friendly chapters, each of which covers a specific island group. Every chapter starts with a list of highlights and an introduction that helps you to decide where to go, depending on your time and budget. Likewise, introductions to the various towns and smaller areas within each chapter should help you plan your itinerary. We start most town accounts with information on arrival and accommodation, followed by a tour of the sights, and finally reviews of places to eat and drink, and details of nightlife. Longer accounts also have a directory of practical listings. Each chapter concludes with **public transport** details for that region.

contexts

Read contexts to get a deeper understanding of how Greece ticks. We include a brief history, articles about music and wildlife, together with a detailed further reading section that reviews dozens of books relating to Greece and the islands.

language

This is a brief introduction to the Greek language and contains advice on the best language-learning materials available. You'll also find a list of basic Greek words and phrases, common food and drink terms and a **glossary** of words and phrases that recur throughout the guide.

index + small print

Apart from a full index, which includes maps as well as places, this section covers publishing information, credits and acknowledgements, and also has our contact details in case you want to send in updates and corrections to the book – or suggestions as to how we might improve it.

contents ▶

basics ▶

guide ▶

1 The Argo-Saronic

2 The Cyclades

3 Crete

4 The Dodecanese

5 The east and north Aegean

6 The Sporades and Évvia

7 The Ionian islands

contexts ▶

language ▶

index ▶

chapter map of **the Greek Islands**

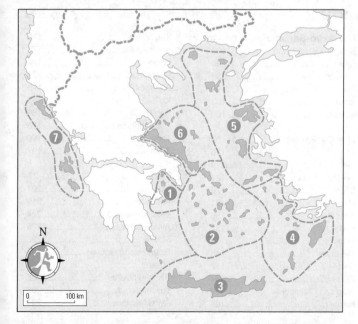

contents

colour section

Greece and islands map ....ii–iii
Greek islanders.....................................viii
Where to go ix

When to go..xi
Things not to miss xiv

basics

Getting there 9
Departure points: Athens, Pireás
    and main ports 25
Visas and red tape 29
Insurance 30
Health matters 32
Costs, money and banks 34
Information, maps and websites 38
Getting around 42
Accommodation 52
Eating and drinking 56
Communications: post, phones
    and internet 63

The media 67
Opening hours and public holidays 69
Festivals and cultural events 70
Sports and outdoor pursuits 74
Finding work 75
Trouble, crime and sexual
    harassment 77
Travellers with disabilities 79
Senior travellers 81
Gay and lesbian travellers 82
Travelling with children 83
Directory 84

guide

❶ **The Argo-Saronic** 89–110
    Salamína 93
    Égina 94
    Angístri 98
    Póros 100
    Ídhra 103
    Spétses 106

❷ **The Cyclades** 111–201
    Kéa 116
    Kýthnos 119
    Sérifos 122
    Sífnos 126
    Mílos 131
    Kímolos 136
    Ándhros 137
    Tínos 142
    Mýkonos 146
    Delos 152
    Sýros 154
    Páros and Andíparos 159
    Náxos 166

    Koufoníssi 175
    Skhinoússa 177
    Iráklia 178
    Dhonoússa 179
    Amorgós 179
    Íos 183
    Síkinos 186
    Folégandhros 188
    Thíra 190
    Anáfi 197

❸ **Crete** 203–274
    Iráklion 207
    Knossós 219
    Festós (Phaestos) 224
    Ayía Triádha 225
    Mátala 226
    Goúrnes and Goúves 228
    Mália 230
    Sísi and Mílatos 232
    Lasíthi plateau 236
    Áyios Nikólaos 237

Sitía 242
Ierápetra 246
Réthymnon 248
Haniá 257
The Samarian Gorge 266
Kastélli 270

④ The Dodecanese 275–362
Kássos 279
Kárpathos 282
Rhodes 288
Hálki 307
Kastellórizo 309
Sými 312
Tílos 318
Níssyros 322
Kós 326
Psérimos 337
Astypálea 337
Kálymnos 342
Léros 348
Pátmos 352
Lipsí 358
Arkí 359
Maráthi 359
Agathónissi 359

**⑤ The east and north
Aegean** 363–440
Sámos 367
Ikaría 381

Foúrni 387
Híos 388
Psará 400
Inoússes 401
Lésvos 402
Límnos 418
Áyios Efstrátios 424
Samothráki 425
Thássos 430

**⑥ The Sporades
and Évvia** 441–473
Skiáthos 444
Skópelos 449
Alónissos and minor islets 453
Skýros 457
Évvia 462

⑦ The Ionian islands 475–527
Corfu 479
Mathráki 497
Othoní 497
Eríkoussa 497
Paxí and Andípaxi 497
Lefkádha 500
Kefalloniá 507
Itháki 516
Zákynthos 520
Kýthira 528
Andikýthira 535

contexts
537–609

Historical framework 539
Mythology 567
Music 577

Wildlife 584
Books 594

language
611–627

Learning basic Greek 613
The Greek alphabet 614
Greek words and phrases 615
A food and drink glossary 619

Katharévoussa, dhimotikí and
  dialects 622
A glossary of recurrent words
  and terms 624

index and small print
630–646

Full index 630
Twenty years of Rough Guides 643
Rough Guide credits........................644
Publishing information 644

Help us update 644
Acknowledgements 645
Readers' letters...............................645
Photo credits...................................646

map symbols

maps are listed in the full index using coloured text

┅┅┅	International boundary	ᵚ	Marshland
┄┄┄	Chapter division boundary	⬓	Waterfall
▬▬▬	Motorway	ᨆ	Spring/spa
═══	Major paved road	⌂	Cave
═══	Minor paved road	⊙	Statue/memorial
━━━	Unpaved road	⚡	Ski area
⋯⋯⋯	Road under construction	⬠	Refuge
▬▬▬	Pedestrianized street	⚠	Campsite
┄┄┄	Footpath	◉	Accommodation
⫿⫿⫿	Steps	■	Restaurant
▬♦▬	Railway	✕	Airport
─ ─ ─	Ferry route	₽	Parking
═══	Waterway	Ⓜ	Metro station
🕌	Mosque	★	Bus/taxi stop
✡	Synagogue	☦	Lighthouse
⬦	Church	ⓘ	Information office
⛪	Monastery or convent	⊠	Post office
∴	Archeological site	©	Telephone
♜	Castle	▬	Building
⫻	Hill	➕	Church
▲	Peak	⊞	Christian cemetery
〱	Mountains	▦	Park
ᨆ	Viewpoint	▨	Beach

basics

basics

Getting there 9

Departure points: Athens, Pireás and main ports 25

Visas and red tape 29

Insurance 30

Health matters 32

Costs, money and banks 34

Information, maps and websites 38

Getting around 42

Accommodation 52

Eating and drinking 56

Communications: post, phones and internet 63

The media 67

Opening hours and public holidays 69

Festivals and cultural events 70

Sports and outdoor pursuits 74

Finding work 75

Trouble, crime and sexual harassment 77

Travellers with disabilities 79

Senior travellers 81

Gay and lesbian travellers 82

Travelling with children 83

Directory 84

Getting there

It's 2000 miles (or more) from the UK and Ireland to many points in Greece, so for most north European visitors flying is the only viable option. There are direct flights to a variety of Greek destinations from all the major British airports; flying time is three and a half to four and a half hours, depending on your start point and Greek destination. Road or rail alternatives from the UK take a minimum of three days, and are only worth considering if you plan to visit Greece as part of an extended trip through Europe. The most popular route is down through Italy, then across to Greece by ferry. The old overland route through former Yugoslavia will remain impractical for the foreseeable future, but a much longer route via Hungary, Romania and Bulgaria is still possible.

Only two carriers currently fly direct to Greece from North America, so most North Americans travel to a gateway European city, and pick up an onward connecting flight with an associated airline. You may discover that it's cheaper to arrange the final Greece-bound leg of the journey yourself, in which case your only criterion will be finding a suitable, good-value North America–Europe flight; such onward flights from the UK are detailed on p.11–13.

It's fairly easy to track down flights from Australia to Athens, less so from New Zealand. But given most people's travel plans, you might be better off with a Round-the-World (RTW) ticket that includes Greece. If London is your first destination in Europe, and you've picked up a reasonably good deal on a flight there, it's probably best to wait until you reach the UK before arranging your onward travel to Greece.

Airfares to Greece from Europe and North America always depend on the **season**, with the highest in effect from June to August (plus Easter week), when the weather is best; fares drop during the "shoulder" seasons – April/May and September/October – and you'll get the best prices during the low season, November to March (excluding Christmas and New Year weeks when prices are hiked up and seats are at a premium). Note also that flying on weekends from North America ordinarily adds $50 or so to the round-trip fare; price ranges quoted below assume midweek travel. Australian and New Zealand fares have their low season from mid-January to the end of February and October/November; high season is mid-

May to August, plus December to mid-January; and shoulder season the rest of the year.

You can often cut costs by going through a **specialist flight agent** – either a consolidator, who buys up blocks of tickets from the airlines and sells them at a discount, or a **discount agent**, who in addition to dealing with discounted flights may also offer special student and youth fares and a range of other travel-related services such as travel insurance, rail passes, car rentals, tours and the like. Some UK agents specialize in **charter flights**, which may be cheaper than anything available on a scheduled flight, but again departure dates are fixed and withdrawal penalties are high. For Greece, you may even find it more cost-effective (especially from the UK) to pick up a **package deal**, with accommodation included, from one of the tour operators listed below.

Booking flights online

Many airlines and discount travel websites offer you the opportunity to book your tickets online, cutting out the costs of agents and middlemen. Good deals can often be found through discount or auction sites, as well as through the airlines' own websites. Even if you don't end up actually buying your ticket online, the websites are worth a visit to clue you up on what the prevailing published economy fares are; however, these sites often don't have the really inexpensive, transient deals. The cheapest of the airlines' published fares is an APEX (Advance Purchase Excursion) ticket, which has certain restrictions. You may be expected to book – and pay – at least 14–21 days before departure, keep to a minimum/maximum limit on your stay (typically 30 or 60 days), and be liable to penalties (including total loss of ticket value) if you change your schedule. Some airlines also issue "student" tickets to those under 26, often extending the maximum stay to a year. There is also a number of "Senior" or "Golden" fares available for those over 60. When exploring a quoted fare on a website, always click the "Rules" link – all conditions will be spelled out in small print. Any reputable site will have a secure, encrypted facility for making credit-card payments – if it doesn't, you're probably better off not using the site to purchase.

Online booking agents and general travel sites

Ⓦwww.etn.nl/discount.htm A hub of consolidator and discount agent web links, maintained by the non-profit European Travel Network.

Ⓦwww.princeton.edu/Main/air800.html Has an extensive list of airline toll-free numbers and websites.

Ⓦwww.flyaow.com Online air travel info and reservations site.

Ⓦwww.smilinjack.com/airlines.htm Lists an up-to-date compilation of airline website addresses.

Ⓦhttp://travel.yahoo.com Incorporates a lot of Rough Guide material in its coverage of destination countries and cities across the world, with information about places to eat and sleep etc.

Ⓦwww.cheaptickets.com or www.cheaptickets.co.uk Discount flight specialists.

Ⓦwww.cheapflights.com Flight deals, travel agents, plus links to other travel sites.

Ⓦwww.lastminute.com Offers good last-minute holiday package and flight-only deals.

Ⓦwww.deckchair.com Bob Geldof's online venture, drawing on a wide range of airlines.

Ⓦwww.expedia.com or www.expedia.co.uk Discount airfares, all-airline search engine and daily deals.

Ⓦwww.travelocity.co.uk Destination guides, hot web fares and best deals for car rental, accommodation and lodging as well as fares. Provides access to the travel agent system SABRE, the most comprehensive central reservations system in the US.

Ⓦwww.travelselect.com Useful, fairly easy-to-use site without most of the guff and banner adverts of the better-known sites. Linked to walk-in travel agency in the UK (London storefront) and the US (2 premises) if you want to talk to a human.

Ⓦwww.hotwire.com Bookings from the US only. Last-minute savings of up to forty percent on regular published fares. Travellers must be at least 18 and there are no refunds, transfers or changes allowed. Log-in required.

Surviving Athens airport

Athens' **new airport**, Eleftherios Venizelos, opened on 28 March 2001, replacing the old, cramped but undeniably convenient one at Ellinikó, south of town. The new terminal has made itself widely unpopular with travellers for its distance east of Athens (26km), its (thus far) indirect public transport connections into town, its battery-farm architecture and enormous size (claimed third largest in the world), this last factor making **missed connections** a distinct possibility. Poor marking makes mad dashes down nightmarishly endless concourses and up escalators (there are a few lifts for luggage trolleys) doubly stressful. Printed airport rules stipulate a **minimum of 55 minutes** between your incoming flight's arrival and onward flight's departure, but some airlines – for example Olympic – are insisting on a minimum leeway of **90 minutes**. Given Olympic's habitual lateness, the presence of security checks even for transfer passengers and the fact that all aircraft for domestic flights are parked a very long shuttle-coach-ride distant on the runway, prudence would dictate observing this rule when buying fares. Some, but not all, ticketing systems won't let you book an itinerary if the layover is too short.

Now, the good news: the departure concourse **shops are excellent**, and eating opportunities are fairly abundant, though seats are in short supply (as they are in all departure lounges). Best of all – and the only conspicuous advantage of the new unified terminal – you can have your **luggage checked through to your final domestic destination**, even if your international- and domestic-leg airlines are different. Do this at the outset as a precaution, and even if your inbound flight is hideously late, you stand a good chance of getting yourself and your carry-on to the end of your itinerary as planned, even if your luggage only shows up the next day.

Ⓦwww.priceline.com or
www.priceline.co.uk Bookings from the US/UK
only. Name-your-own-price website that has deals
at around forty percent off standard fares. You
cannot specify flight times (although you do
specify dates) and the tickets are non-refundable,
non-transferable and non-changeable.

Ⓦwww.skyauction.com Bookings from the US
only. Auctions tickets and travel packages using a
"second bid" scheme. The best strategy is to bid
the maximum you're willing to pay, since if you
win you'll pay just enough to beat the runner-up
regardless of your maximum bid.

Ⓦ www.travel.com.au Australian website with a
good range of discounted air fares; no-nonsense,
easy to use and interpret.

Ⓦwww.travelshop.com.au Australian website
offering discounted flights, packages, insurance
and online bookings.

Domestic airlines

Aegean-Cronus City centre ☎010/99 44
444, 99 88 414 or countrywide ☎08010/20
000; airport ☎010/35 34 294 or ☎010/35
30 101.
Axon City centre ☎010/68 00 063; airport:
☎010/35 32 533.
Olympic Airways City centre ☎010/96 66
666 or countrywide ☎08010/44 444; airport ☎010/93 65 529.

Flights from the UK and Ireland

Most of the cheaper flights from Britain and
Ireland to Greece are **charters**, which are
sold either with a package holiday or (less
commonly) as a flight-only option. The flights
have fixed and unchangeable outward and
return dates, and usually a maximum stay of
four weeks.

For longer stays or more flexibility, or if
you're travelling out of season (when few
charters are available), you'll need a
scheduled flight. As with charters, these
are offered under a wide variety of fares,
and are again often sold off at a discount
by agents. Useful advertisements for discounted flights are found in the weekend-
supplement travel sections of newspapers
like *The Independent*, *The Guardian*, *The
Observer* and *The Sunday Times*, as well

as weekly listings magazines such as *Time
Out*.

Although **Athens** remains the prime destination for cheap fares, there are also direct
flights from Britain to **Thessaloníki**,
Kalamáta, **Kavála** and **Préveza (Áktio)** on
the Greek mainland (all of these are either
ports for various islands, or close to such),
and to the islands themselves of **Crete**,
Rhodes, **Kós**, **Corfu**, **Mýkonos**,
Zákynthos, **Kefaloniá**, **Skiáthos**, **Sámos**,
Lésvos and **Límnos**. And with any flight to
Athens, you can buy a **domestic connecting flight** (on the national carrier, Olympic, or
its rivals Axon and Aegean-Cronus) to one of
three dozen or so additional Greek mainland
and island airports.

Charter flights

Travel agents throughout Britain sell **charter
flights** to Greece, which usually operate
from late April or May to late October or mid-
November (depending on destination); late-
night departures and early-morning arrivals
are common, though you may have a choice
of more civilized hours. Even the high-street
chains frequently promote "flight-only" deals,
or discount all-inclusive holidays, when their
parent companies need to offload their seat
allocations. Charter airlines include Air 2000,
Flying Colours, Britannia, JMC and Monarch,
but you can only book tickets on these
through their designated agents (see
pp.13–14), and you may find that flight-only
deals are rare indeed at peak season.

Charter flights to Athens are reasonable –
sample return fares to Athens from London
in midsummer start from around £160
(Manchester £180, Glasgow £200), but
there are always bargains to be had. You
generally pay dearly for the convenience of a
direct flight to the holiday island of your
choice, skipping Athens: sample high-
season fares range from £210 (Gatwick to
Rhodes or Corfu) up to a hefty £300
(Manchester to Zákynthos or Kefaloniá).
Sámos is particularly outrageous at around
£350 – you may well find scheduled services
via Athens are cheaper.

The greatest variety of **flight destinations** tends to be from London (Heathrow
or Gatwick) and Manchester. In summer, if
you book in advance, you should have a
choice of most of the Greek regional airports listed above. Flying from elsewhere in

Britain (Birmingham, Bristol, Cardiff, East Midlands, Luton, Stansted, Glasgow or Newcastle), or looking for last-minute discounts, you'll find options more limited, most commonly to Athens, Corfu, Rhodes, Kós and Crete.

Summer charters operate **from Dublin and Belfast** to Athens and there are additional services to Mýkonos, Rhodes, Crete and Corfu. A high-season charter from Dublin to Athens costs upwards of €317 return, while a week's package on one of the above islands costs from €635 per person for two weeks.

It's worth noting that **non-EU nationals** who buy charter tickets to Greece must buy a round-trip ticket, to return after no fewer than three days and no more than four weeks, and must accompany it with an accommodation voucher for at least the first few nights of their stay – check that the ticket satisfies these conditions or you could be refused entry. In practice, the "accommodation voucher" has become a formality; it has to name an existing hotel, but you're not expected to use it (and probably won't be able to if you try).

The other important condition regards **travel to Turkey** (or any other neighbouring country). If you travel to Greece on a charter flight, you may visit another country only as a day-trip; if you stay overnight, you will possibly invalidate your ticket. This rule is justified by the Greek authorities because they subsidize charter airline landing fees, and are therefore reluctant to see tourists spending their money outside Greece. Whether you go along with that rationale or not, there is no way around it, since the Turkish authorities clearly stamp all passports, and the Greeks usually check them. We have, however, had reports of charter-flight-only patrons flying to Kós, happily spending a week in Turkish Bodrum, and then returning without incident, but it would be wise to double-check if the rule is still in effect.

Student/youth charters can be sold as one-way flights only. By combining two one-way charters you can, therefore, stay for over a month. Student/youth charter tickets are available to anyone under 26, and to all card-carrying full-time students under 32.

Finally, remember that **reconfirmation** of return charter flights is vital and should be

done at least 72 hours before departure. If you've travelled out with a package company, this service will usually be included as part of the rep's duties, but you should not assume that it has been done. Personal visits to the airline's representative office are best, as phone numbers given on ticket wallets are typically engaged.

Scheduled flights

The advantages of **scheduled flights** are that they can be booked well in advance, have longer ticket validities (30, 60, 90 or even 180 days), involve fewer or none of the typical restrictions applicable to charters, and often leave at more social hours. However, many of the cheaper, shorter-duration fares do have advance-purchase and/or minimum-stay requirements, and also severe restrictions on date changes or refunds. As with charters, discount fares on scheduled flights are available from most high-street travel agents, as well as from a number of specialist flight and student /youth agencies – though it's always well worth contacting the airlines direct, using the telephone numbers listed below. Like charters, they must be reconfirmed within 72 hours of the return leg (in practice, 36 hours is usually enough).

Scheduled airlines

Aer Lingus in Republic of Ireland ☎01/705 3333 or 844 4777, ☻www.aerlingus.ie.
British Airways ☎0845/773 3377, in Republic of Ireland ☎1-800/626747, ☻www.britishairways.com.
British Midland ☎0870/607 0555, in Northern Ireland ☎0845/755 4554, in Republic of Ireland ☎01/283 8833, ☻www.flybmi.com.
Cronus Airlines ☎020/7580 3500, ☻www.cronus.gr.
EasyJet ☎0870/600 0000, ☻www.easyjet.com.
Olympic Airways ☎0870/606 0460, in Republic of Ireland ☎01/608 0090, ☻www.olympic-airways.gr.
Ryanair ☎0870/156 9569, in Republic of Ireland ☎01/609 7800, ☻www.ryanair.com.

The widest choice of scheduled flights from the **UK to Greece** is with the Greek national carrier **Olympic Airways** and with **British Airways**, who both fly from London Heathrow to Athens (twice daily on BA, three times daily on Olympic), mostly direct, but on Olympic stopping four times weekly in Thessaloníki. In addition, Olympic has three weekly flights to Athens from Manchester. BA also offers one daily Athens service from Gatwick, but nothing to Thessaloníki. Both airlines have a range of special fares, and even in July and August, discount flight agents or websites can come up with deals, valid for sixty days away, for as low as £200 return, including tax; more realistically, you'll pay around £250 return during high season from London, £300 from Manchester. It may be worth avoiding absolutely rock-bottom fares, as Olympic in particular no longer allows changes to your return date on tickets of under ninety-days' validity. In the spring or autumn, return fares to Athens run to about £180 including taxes, and in winter dip to about £150. As this route is common-rated between these airlines, you'll also be able to book onward connections simultaneously to domestic Greek airports, though discounts will apply only if using Olympic on all legs of the journey.

Cronus Airlines, so far the only private Greek airline to challenge Olympic on international routes to Britain, offers daily late-evening services to Athens from London Heathrow, arriving at dawn the next day. Any advertised fares to Thessaloníki all currently go via Athens, with a two-hour layover; direct services have yet to materialize consistently. Fares to either city weigh in at about £170 low season, tax included, or £250 high season.

Note that flights from British regional airports route through Heathrow in the first instance, with a supplement applicable. Olympic has a code-sharing partnership with British Midland, which should ease the pain (and possibly the cost) of connections from Scotland and the north of England in particular.

Potentially the cheapest, no-frills service is provided by **EasyJet**, out of London Luton to Athens only; fares vary from £49 to £159 one way, tax included, with the exact amount depending on the season, how far in advance you book and availability for the particular flight – a last-minute booking for three weeks from the end of August will probably result in a combined return fare of £210. Departures also vary with time of year, but typically there are two flights daily,

in the early afternoon and quite late in the evening. The cheaper tickets are obviously very restrictive, and there's no on-board meal service. On the plus side, EasyJet usually offers special train fares from central London (Waterloo, West Hampstead, King's Cross) to Luton Parkway (free shuttle bus thence to airport) in co-operation with Thameslink.

Irish travellers will find year-round scheduled services with Aer Lingus and British Airways operating from both **Dublin** and **Belfast via Heathrow** to Athens, or from Dublin via Heathrow on British Midland and Olympic, but you'll find them pricey compared to charters. Youth and student fares are offered by USIT Now (see p.14 for contact details).

Travelling to London and buying a separate ticket there is an alternative if direct flights from Ireland are in short supply, and may sometimes save you a little money, but on the whole it's rarely worth the time and effort. For the record, budget flights to London are offered by British Midland, Aer Lingus and Ryanair.

Flight and travel agents in the UK and Republic of Ireland

Air 2000 ☎0870/750 0001, ⊛www.firstchoice.co.uk. Flight-only division (charters) of First Choice Holidays.

Aran Travel International Galway ☎091/562 595, ℱ564 581, ⊛www.iol.ie/~aran/aranmain.htm. Good-value flights to all parts of the world.

Argo Holidays 100 Wigmore St, London W1H 9DR ☎020/7331 7000. Designated consolidator for Olympic, BA and Virgin Atlantic; consistently does some of the lowest fares, and offers better service than the airlines concerned.

Avro Vantage House, 1 Weir Rd, London SW19 8UX ☎020/8715 4440, ⊛www.avro.co.uk. Seat-only sales of all Monarch charter flights to Athens, Corfu, Iráklion (Crete) and Rhodes from a selection amongst Gatwick, Luton, Manchester and Glasgow.

CIE Tours International Dublin ☎01/703 1888, ⊛www.cietours.ie. General flight and tour agent.

Co-op Travel Care Belfast ☎028/9047 1717, ℱ471 339. Flights and holidays around the world.

Cosmos ☎0870/908 4299, ⊛www.cosmos-holidays.co.uk. Offers flight-only arrangements on Monarch from Manchester, Gatwick and Birmingham to a variety of holiday islands.

Greece & Cyprus Travel Centre 44 Birmingham

Rd, Sutton Coldfield, West Midlands B72 1QQ ☎0121/355 6955, ⓦwww.greece-cyprus.co.uk. Flight consolidator and general Greek packages specialist.

JMC ☎0870/758 0194, ⓦwww.jmc.com. Good selection of flights only to Ketalloniá, Zákynthos, Áktio (Préveza-Lefkádha), Kós, Skiáthos, Sámos and Rhodes from a half-dozen UK airports.

Joe Walsh Tours Dublin ☎01/872 2555 or 676 3053, Cork ☎021/427 7959, ⓦwww.joewalshtours.ie. General budget fares agent.

Lee Travel Cork ☎021/427 7111, ⓦwww.leetravel.ie. Flights and holidays worldwide.

Liffey Travel Dublin ☎01/878 8322 or 878 8063. Package-tour specialists.

The London Flight Centre ☎020/7244 6411, ⓦwww.topdecktravel.co.uk. Long-established agent dealing in discount flights.

Mondial Travel 8 Moscow Rd, London W2 4BT ☎020/7792 3333. Good consolidator agent for scheduled flights to Greece; can nearly match EasyJet prices on the major airlines.

North South Travel Moulsham Mill Centre, Parkway, Chelmsford, Essex CM2 7PX ☎01245/608291, ⓦwww.nstravel.demon.uk. Friendly, competitive flight agency, offering discounted fares worldwide – profits are used to support projects in the developing world, especially the promotion of sustainable tourism.

Rosetta Travel Belfast ☎028/9064 4996, ⓦwww.rosettatravel.com. Flight and holiday agent.

STA Travel ☎0870/160 6070, ⓦwww.statravel.co.uk. Worldwide specialists in low-cost flights and tours for students and under-26s, though other customers welcome. A dozen branches across England, especially on or near university campuses.

Student & Group Travel Dublin ☎01/677 7834. Student and group specialists to Europe.

Sunset Air Fares Sunset Business Centre, Manchester Road, Bolton BL4 8RT ☎0870/607 5085. Flight-only and fly-drive deals from regional airports to Kalamáta, Áktio (Préveza-Lefkádha) and Kavála (for Thássos) in addition to the usual destinations; typically on Flying Colours.

Thomson ☎0870/550 2555, ⓦwww .thomson-holidays.com. Limited flight-only deals on Britannia to Corfu, Rhodes, Iráklion (Crete), Thessaloníki, Zákynthos, Kós, Sámos, Kefalloniá, Skiáthos and Kavála (for Thássos) on Britannia Airways.

Trailfinders ☎020/7628 7628, in Republic of Ireland ☎01/677 7888, ⓦwww.trailfinders.com.

One of the best-informed and most efficient agents for independent travellers; for scheduled flights only; all branches (there's at least one in all the UK's largest cities, plus Dublin) open daily until 6pm, Thurs until 7pm.

usit CAMPUS ☎0870/240 1010, ⓦwww.usitcampus.co.uk. Student/youth travel specialists, offering discount flights, with town branches in London, Birmingham, Bristol, Cambridge, Edinburgh, Manchester and Oxford, as well as a presence in all YHA shops and many university campuses across Britain.

usit NOW Belfast ☎028/9032 7111, Dublin ☎01/602 1777 or 677 8117, Cork ☎021/427 0900, Derry ☎028/7137 1888, ⓦwww.usitnow.ie. Student and youth specialists for flights and trains.

Packages and tours

Virtually every British **tour operator** includes Greece in its programme, though with many of the larger, cheap-and-cheerful outfits you'll find choices limited to the established resorts – notably the islands of Rhodes, Kós, Crete, Skiáthos, Zákynthos and Corfu. If you buy one of these at a last-minute discount, especially in spring or autumn, you may find it costs little more than a flight – and you can use the accommodation included as much or as little as you want.

For a more low-key and genuinely "Greek" resort, however, it's better to book your holiday through one of the **specialist agencies** listed opposite. Most of these are fairly small-scale operations, providing competitively priced packages with flights (unless otherwise stated) and often more traditional village-based accommodation. They also make an effort to offer islands without overdeveloped tourist resorts. Such agencies tend to divide into two types: those which, like the major chains, contract a block of accommodation and flight seats (or even their own plane) for a full season, and an increasing number of bespoke agencies which tailor holidays at your request, making all transport and accommodation arrangements on the spot. These can work out somewhat more expensive, but the quality of flights and lodging is often correspondingly higher.

The **walking** holiday operators listed on p.16 either run trekking groups of ten to fifteen people plus an experienced guide, or provide customers with a printed, self-guiding itinerary, and arranged accommodation at the end of each day. Walks tend to be day-long hikes from one or more bases, or point-to-point treks staying in village accommodation en route. Camping out is not usually involved.

Sailing holidays usually involve small flotillas of four- to eight-berth yachts, taking in different anchorages each night, or are shore-based, with instruction in small-craft handling. All levels of experience are catered for. Prices start at around £520 per person, flights included, in a group of four on a two-week flotilla. Alternatively, confident sailors can simply arrange to charter a yacht from a broker; the Greek National Tourist Organization has lists of companies.

Specialist package operators

VILLA OR VILLAGE ACCOMMODATION

Argo Holidays 100 Wigmore St, London W1H 9DR ☎020/7331 7070, ⊛www.argo-holidays .com. Packages to luxury hotels and top villas on about twenty islands; special strengths are the Argo-Saronic, northeast Aegean and Dodecanese (including "Winter Sun" on Rhodes).

Cachet Travel First Floor, Coomb House, 7 St Johns Rd, Isleworth, Middlesex TW7 6NH ☎020/8768 1818, ⊛www.cachet-travel.co.uk. Attractive range of villas and apartments, in the more unspoilt south and west of Crete.

CV Travel 43 Cadogan St, London SW3 2PR ☎0870/606 0013, ⊛www.cvtravel.co.uk. Quality villas, mostly on Corfu and Paxí but also Itháki, Spétses, Pátmos, Alónissos, Crete and Thíra.

Direct Greece Granite House, 31–33 Stockwell St, Glasgow G1 4RY ☎0141/559 7111; Manchester ☎0161/236 2838; London ☎020/8785 4000; ℻0141/553 1752. Moderately priced villas, apartments and restored houses on Rhodes, Hálki, Kálymnos, Kefalloniá, Lésvos, Corfu and Crete.

Elysian Holidays 16 High St, Tenterden, Kent TN30 6AP ☎01580/766599, ⊛www.elysianholidays.co.uk. Began as Híos restored-house specialists, now have a wide programme of quality premises on a dozen islands, including Páros, Skýros, Spétses, Mýkonos, Pátmos and the Candili Estate on Évvia.

Greek Islands Club 10–12 Upper Square, Old Isleworth, Middlesex TW7 7BJ ☎020/8232 9780, ⊛www.greekislandsclub.com. Extremely high-quality villas throughout the Ionian and Sporades islands; also Pátmos, Thíra and Crete.

Greek Sun Holidays 1 Bank St, Sevenoaks, Kent TN13 1UW ☎01732/740317, ⊛www.greeksun.co.uk. Good-value package

holidays, including some fly-drive options, in the Dodecanese, northeast Aegean and Cyclades; also tailor-made island-hopping itineraries.

Hidden Greece ☎020/7839 2553, ℻7839 4327, ⊜hiddengreece@ntours.co.uk. A bespoke agency running for forty-plus years now, arranging accommodation on and transport to thirty less-visited islands, mostly in the Cyclades and Dodecanese.

Island Wandering 51a London Rd, Hurst Green, Sussex TN19 7QP ☎01580/860733, ⊛www.islandwandering.com. Tailor-made island-hopping itineraries between most Greek archipelagos; deals range from pre-booked accommodation only (this tends to be on the basic side) to mini-tours, with local ferry or air transfers arranged.

Laskarina Holidays St Marys Gate, Wirksworth, Derbyshire DE4 4DQ ☎01629/822203, ⊛www.laskarina.co.uk. Top-end villas, quality hotels and restored houses on Spétses, Skópelos, Alónissos, Hálki, Sými, Tilos, Kálymnos, Télendhos, Léros, Lipsí, Pátmos, Ikaría and Sámos; scores consistently high marks for customer service.

Pure Crete 79 George St, Croydon CR10 1LD ☎020/8760 0879, ⊛www.pure.crete.com. Characterful, converted cottages and farmhouses in western Crete.

Simply Simon Holidays 1/45 Nevern Square, London SW5 9PF ☎020/7373 1933, ⊛www.simplysimon.co.uk. Cyclades specialist, focusing on small hotels and studios; direct charters to Mýkonos.

Simply Travel Kings House, Wood St, Kingston-upon-Thames, Surrey KT1 1UG ⊛www .simply-travel.com. Administers Simply Ionian ☎020/8541 2202 for the entire Ionian island chain; and Simply Crete ☎020/8541 2201. Offers high-quality apartments, villas and small hotels for each area.

Sunvil Holidays Sunvil House, 7–8 Upper Square, Old Isleworth, Middlesex TW7 7BJ ☎020/8568 4499, ⊛www.sunvil.co.uk/greece. Durable and consistently high-quality outfit specializing in upmarket hotels and villas in the Ionian islands, the Sporades, select Cyclades, western Crete, Límnos, Sámos, Ikaría, Pátmos and Sývota.

Tapestry Holidays 24 Chiswick High Rd, London W4 1TE ☎020/8235 7788, ⊛www.tapestryholidays.com. Top-rated Turkey specialists now branched out into quality villas, hotels and restoration inns on Kefalloniá.

Travel à la Carte First Floor, 32 High St, Thatcham, Berks RG19 3JD ☎01635/863030, ⊛www.travelalacarte.co.uk. Established Corfu specialist, now branched out to beach and rural villas on Alónissos, Hálki, Paxí, Skiáthos, Skópelos and Sými as well.

Travelux 40 High St, Tenterden, Kent TN30 6AR ☎01580/765000, ⓦ www.travelux.co.uk. Long-established Lefkádha villa specialists.

WALKING AND HORSE-RIDING HOLIDAYS

ATG Oxford ☎01865/315678, ⓦ www.atg-oxford .co.uk. Somewhat pricey but high-standard guided walks on Ándhros and Náxos.

Exodus 9 Weir Rd, London SW12 0LT ☎020/8675 5550, ⓦ www.exodus.co.uk. One-week treks on Évvia/Skýros, or the White Mountains of Crete; also sail-walk two-week tours through the Cyclades.

Explore Worldwide 1 Frederick St, Aldershot, Hampshire GU11 1LQ ☎01252/760 1000, ⓦ www.exploreworldwide.com. Treks on Crete; also island-wanderer trips, mostly in the Cyclades, mixing kaïki-sailing with light walking ashore.

Headwater 146 London Rd, Northwich, Cheshire CW9 5HH ☎01606/813367, ⓦ www.headwater-holidays.co.uk. Treks on Amorgós island; "Best of Ionian" eight-day holiday taking in Itháki and Kefalloniá.

Ramblers Holidays Longcroft House, Fretherne Rd, Welwyn Garden City, Herts AL8 6PQ ☎01707/331133, ⓦ www.ramblersholidays.co.uk. An outfit which has shed its former fusty image, actively courts a younger clientele and now offers fairly challenging treks in Crete; also easier outings on Sámos, Pátmos, Náxos, Sérifos, Kýthnos and Amorgós.

Waymark Holidays 44 Windsor Rd, Slough SL1 2EJ ☎01753/516477, ⓦ www.waymarkholidays.co. Spring and autumn walking holidays (10–14 days) on Sámos, Mílos and Crete's White Mountains.

NATURE AND WILDLIFE

Limosa ☎01263/578143. Springtime birding on Lésvos.

Marengo Guided Walks 17 Bernard Crescent, Hunstanton PE36 6ER ☎01485/532710, ⓦ www.marengo.supanet.com. Annually changing programme of easy walks guided by ace botanist Lance Chilton; past one-week offerings have included Sámos, Sými, northern Lésvos, Crete and Thássos.

SAILING HOLIDAYS

The Moorings Bradstowe House, Middle Wall, Whitstable, Kent CT5 1BF ☎01227/776677, ⓦ www.moorings.com. Operates bareboat charters out of Athens, Corfu, Skiáthos and Kós Town.

Nautilus Yachting 4 Church St, Edenbridge, Kent TN8 5BD ☎01732/867445, ⓦ www .nautilus-yachting.co.uk. Bareboat yacht charter out of Athens, Corfu, Lefkádha, Kós, Rhodes and Skiáthos; also flotilla holidays from Lefkádha and Póros.

Seafarer Cruising & Sailing Albatross House, 14 New Hythe Lane, Larkfield, Kent ME20 6AB ☎01732/229900, ⓦ www.seafarercruises.com. UK agent for Vernicos Yachts (Greece), with shareboat/flotillas out of Póros and bareboats out of Athens, Rhodes, Corfu, Skiáthos, Kós, Sámos and Mýkonos.

Setsail Holidays ☎01737/764443, ⓦ www.setsail.co.uk. Bareboat charters from Póros and sail/land-stay combinations.

Sportif ☎01273/844919, ⓦ www.sportif-uk.com. Windsurfing packages on Kós, Rhodes, Kárpathos, Lefkádha and Náxos. Instruction clinics in conjunction with nearby accommodation.

Sunsail The Port House, Port Solent, Portsmouth, Hampshire PO6 4TH ☎02392/222222, ⓦ www.sunsail.com. Resort-based tuition in dinghy sailing, yachting and windsurfing at five locations in Greece; one- or two-week flotilla sailings northwards out of Kós Town, Lefkádha, Kefalloniá and the Sporades. Good facilities for non-sailing children.

MIND AND BODY

Skyros Centre 92 Prince of Wales Rd, London NW5 3NE ☎020/7267 4424, ⓦ www.skyros.com. Holistic health, fitness, crafts and "personal growth" holidays at two centres on the island of Skýros, as well as prestigious writers' workshops tutored by big names.

By rail from the UK, Ireland and the rest of Europe

Travelling **by train** from Britain or Ireland to Greece takes three and a half to four and a half days and fares work out much more expensive than flights. However, with a regular ticket, stopovers are possible – in France, Switzerland and Italy – while with an InterRail or Eurail pass you can take in Greece as part of a wider train trip around Europe.

Routes

The most practical route from Britain crosses France, Switzerland and Italy before embarking on the ferry from Bari or Brindisi to Pátra (Patras). Book seats well in advance, especially in summer (for ferry information, see box on pp.20–1).

Until 1990, the route through **former Yugoslavia** was the most popular; for obvious reasons this is a non-starter for the foreseeable future, recent developments in Serbia notwithstanding. A more roundabout alternative from Budapest runs via **Bucharest** and **Sofia** to **Thessaloníki**, which is advised as your first Greek stop, since Athens is six to seven hours further on the train.

Standard tickets

Regular train tickets from Britain to Greece are not good value; London to Athens costs at least £400 return, undiscounted second-class. If you are under 26, you can get a youth ticket, discounting these fares by around 25 percent; these are available through usit CAMPUS and Connex. Both regular and youth tickets have two-months' return validity, or can be purchased as one-ways, and the Italy routes include the ferry crossing. The tickets also allow for stopovers, so long as you stick to the route prescribed.

Rail passes

Better value by far is to buy an **InterRail pass**, which offers unlimited travel (except for express-train supplements and reservation fees) on a zonal basis with 28 European rail networks. These passes are only available to **European residents**, and you will be asked to provide proof of residency before being allowed to purchase one. The passes come in over-26 and (cheaper) under-26 versions; they're available for 22 days (one zone only), or one month, and you can purchase up to three zones, or a global pass covering all zones. You may save a bit by booking via the InterRail website ⓦ www.inter-rail.co.uk

To reach Greece from the UK you'll need a pass valid for at least two zones; Greece falls in Zone G, together with Italy, Turkey and Slovenia, plus most of the Brindisi-Igoumenítsa ferries. To reach Italy from Britain, you'll need to purchase a Zone E pass to cross France; to reach northern Greece via central Europe, you'll need so many other zones (C, D and H) that you'll be obliged to buy an all-zone pass. InterRail

passes do not allow free travel between Britain and the continent, although InterRail Pass holders are eligible for discounts on rail travel in Britain and Northern Ireland, the cross-Channel ferries, and the London–Paris Eurostar service.

Finally, anyone over 60 and holding a British Rail Senior Citizen Railcard, can buy a **Rail Europe Senior Card** (£5 for a year). This gives up to thirty percent reductions on rail fares throughout Europe and thirty percent off sea crossings.

For **North Americans, Australians and New Zealanders, a Eurail Pass** is not likely to pay for itself if you're planning to stick to Greece. This pass, which must be purchased before arrival in Europe, allows unlimited free first-class train travel in Greece and sixteen other countries, and is available in increments of fifteen days, twenty-one days, one month, two months and three months. If you're under 26, you can save money with a Eurail Youthpass, which is valid for second-class travel or, if you're travelling with one to four other companions, a joint Eurail Saverpass, both of which are available in the same increments as the Eurail Pass. You stand a better chance of getting your money's worth out of a Eurail Flexipass, which is good for ten- or fifteen-days' travel within a two-month period. This, too, comes in first-class, under-26/second-class (Eurorail Youth Flexipass) and group (Eurail Saver Flexipass) versions.

In addition, a scaled-down version of the Flexipass, the **Europass**, is available which allows first-class and youth (second-class) travel in France, Germany, Italy, Spain and Switzerland for any five, six, eight, ten or fifteen days within two months. Up to four "associate" countries (Austria/Hungary, Benelux, Greece, Portugal) can be included for an additional fee. The Europass Saverpass is a version of the Europass for people travelling in groups of two or more that offers a saving of fifteen percent per person on the regular fare. Details of prices for all these passes can be found on ⓦ www.raileurope.com, and the passes can be purchased from one of the agents listed below.

Rail contacts

In the UK and Ireland

Connex ☎ 0870/001 0174. International enquiries and reservations.

Iarnród Éireann Dublin ☎ 01/836 6222,
Ⓦ www.irishrail.ie.
Northern Ireland Railways ☎ 028/9089/9411,
Ⓦ www.nirailways.co.uk.
Rail Europe (SNCF French Railways) ☎ 0870/584
8848, Ⓦ www.raileurope.co.uk.
Standard as well as discounted rail fares for under-
26s on a variety of European routes; also agents for
InterRail, Eurostar and Eurodomino.
usit CAMPUS ☎ 0870/240 1010,
Ⓦ www.usitcampus.co.uk. Books student/youth
discount train tickets and sells passes.

In North America

CIT Rail ☎ 1-800/223-7987, 1-800/CIT-TOUR or
212/730-2400, in Canada ☎ 1-800/361-7799,
Ⓦ www.fs-on-line.com. Eurail and Europass.
DER Travel ☎ 1-888/337-7350,
Ⓦ www.dertravel.com/Rail. Eurail, Europass and
many individual country passes.
European Rail Services Canada ☎ 1-800/205-
5800 or 416/695-1211,
Ⓦ www.europeanrailservices.com. Eurail, Europass
and many individual country passes.
Europrail International Inc Canada ☎ 1-
888/667-9734, Ⓦ www.europrail.net. Eurail,
Europass and many individual country passes.
Online Travel ☎ 1-800/660-5300 or 847/318-
8890, Ⓦ www.eurorail.com. Eurail Pass, Europass
and individual country passes for Austria, Britain,
Bulgaria, Czech Republic, Germany, Greece, Holland,
Italy, Norway and Spain.
Rail Europe ☎ 1-800/438-7245, Canada ☎ 1-
800/361-7245, Ⓦ www.raileurope.com/us. Official
North American Eurail Pass agent; also sells
Europass, multinational passes and most single-
country passes.

In Australia and New Zealand

CIT World Travel Australia ☎ 02/9267 1255,
Ⓦ www.cittravel.com.au. Eurail, Europass and
Italian rail passes.
Rail Plus Australia ☎ 1300/555 003 or 03/9642
8644, Ⓔ info@railplus.com.au; New Zealand
☎ 09/303 2484. Sells Eurail and Europass.
Trailfinders Australia ☎ 02/9247 7666,
Ⓦ www.trailfinder.com.au. All European passes.

By car from the UK and Ireland

If you have the time and inclination, **driving
to Greece** can be a pleasant proposition.
Realistically, though, it's really only worth
considering if you have at least a month to

spare, are going to stay in Greece for an
extended period, or want to take advantage
of various stopovers en route. The most
popular **route** is down through France and
Italy to catch one of the Adriatic ferries. A
longer alternative through eastern Europe
(Hungary, Romania and Bulgaria) is just
about feasible.

The fastest way to get across **to the
continent** is the **Eurotunnel** service via the
Channel Tunnel; the alternative is one of
the time-honoured **ferry** crossings (see
opposite). Eurotunnel operates shuttle
trains 24 hours a day, for cars, motorcy-
cles, buses and their passengers. The
service runs continuously between
Folkestone and Coquelles, near Calais,
with up to four departures per hour (only
one per hour midnight–6am) and takes
35min (45min for some night departure
times), though you must arrive at least
30min before departure. It is possible to
turn up and buy your ticket at the toll
booths (after exiting the M20 at junction
11a), though at busy times booking is
advisable. **Rates** depend on the time of
year, time of day and length of stay; it's
cheaper to travel between 10pm and 6am,
while the highest fares are reserved for
weekend departures and returns in July
and August. For current information, contact the **Eurotunnel Customer Services
Centre** at ☎ 0870/535 3535, Ⓦ www
.eurotunnel.com.

The traditional cross-Channel options for
most travellers are the **ferry or hovercraft**
links between Dover and Calais or Boulogne
(the quickest and cheapest routes),
Ramsgate and Dunkerque, or Newhaven
and Dieppe. Irish drivers will prefer routes
bypassing Britain, direct to Roscoff or
Cherbourg, or from the southwest of
England to St-Malo or Caen.

Ferry **prices** vary according to the time
of year and, for motorists, the size of your
car. The Dover–Calais/Boulogne runs, for
example, start at about £245–340 open
return for a car with up to five passengers,
though this range can nearly double in
peak season.

Ferries crossing the Channel and the Irish Sea

Brittany Ferries ☎ 0870/901 2400, Republic of

Ireland ☎021/277705, ℻277262,
ⓦwww.brittanyferries.co.uk. Poole to Cherbourg;
Portsmouth to Caen and St-Malo; Plymouth to
Roscoff (March–Nov/Dec); Cork to Roscoff
(March–Oct only).

Hoverspeed ☎0870/524 0241,
ⓦwww.hoverspeed.co.uk. Twenty-four daily
departures. Dover to Calais and Ostend; Newhaven
to Dieppe.

Irish Ferries ☎0870/517 1717, Republic of
Ireland ☎1890/313131, ⓦwww.irishferries.com.
Dublin to Holyhead; Rosslare to Pembroke,
Cherbourg and Roscoff. Continental services
March to end Sept.

P&O European Ferries ☎0870/242 4999,
ⓦwww.poportsmouth.com. Portsmouth to
Cherbourg and Le Havre.

P&O Irish Sea ☎0870/242 4777, Republic of
Ireland ☎01/800 409 049,
ⓦwww.poirishsea.com. Larne to Cairnryan or
Fleetwood; Dublin to Liverpool.

P&O Stena Line ☎0870/600 0600,
ⓦwww.posl.com. Dover to Calais.

Sea France ☎0870/571 1711,
ⓦwww.seafrance.com. Dover to Calais.

Stena Line ☎0870/570 7070, Republic of Ireland
☎01/204 7777, ⓦwww.stenaline.co.uk. Rosslare
to Fishguard; Dun Laoghaire or Dublin to Holyhead;
Belfast to Stranraer.

Swansea Cork Ferries ☎01792/456116, in
Republic of Ireland ☎021/427 1166,
ⓔ reservations scferries@aol.com. Cork to
Swansea (no sailings Nov 7 to March 11).

Via Italy

For motorists heading for western Greece
or the Ionian islands, it has always made
most sense to drive **via Italy** – and whatever your final destination, taking a ferry on
the final leg makes for a more relaxed journey. Initial routes down to Italy through
France and **Switzerland** are very much a
question of personal taste. One of the
most direct is Calais–Reims–Geneva–Milan
and then down the Adriatic coast to the
Italian port of your choice. Even on the
quickest autoroutes (with their accompanying tolls), the journey will involve two
overnight stops.

Once in **Italy**, you've a choice of five
ports. Regular car and passenger ferries link
Ancona, **Bari** and **Brindisi** with
Igoumenítsa (the port of Epirus in western
Greece) and/or **Pátra** (at the northwest tip of

the Peloponnese and the closest port to
Athens). Most sail via the island of **Corfu**,
and a bare handful of companies link other
Ionian islands such as **Paxí** or **Kefalloniá** en
route to Pátra from mid-July (east-bound) to
mid-September (west-bound) only; you can
stop over at no extra charge if you get these
halts specified on your ticket. Generally,
these ferries run year round, but services are
greatly reduced out of season. Ferries also
sail regularly from **Venice** and less frequently
from **Trieste**. For more details see the box
on pp.20–1.

The crossing to Igoumenítsa is usually, but
not always, substantially cheaper than to
Pátra; the **cheapest** of all the crossings is
from Brindisi to Igoumenítsa. However, drivers will discover that the extra cost in Italian
motorway tolls and fuel offsets the Brindisi or
Bari Brindisi's savings over those from Ancona,
Trieste or Venice; the shipping companies
are well aware of this and set their prices
accordingly.

In summer, it is essential to **book tickets** a
few days ahead, especially in the peak
July–August season. During the winter you
can usually just turn up at the main ports
(Brindisi, Trieste and Venice have the most
reliable departures at that time of year), but
it's still wise to book in advance, certainly if
you are taking a car or want a cabin. A few
phone calls or internet searches before leaving home are, in any case, advisable, as the
range of fares and operators (from Brindisi
especially) is considerable; if you do just turn
up at the port, it's worth spending some time
shopping around the agencies.

Via Hungary, Romania and Bulgaria

Avoiding former Yugoslavia involves a pretty substantial diversion through Hungary,
Romania and Bulgaria. Too exhausting and
too problematic at the best of times, this is
not a drive to contemplate unless you
actively want to see some of the countries
en route. However, it's all simpler than it
was, with visas easier to obtain at the borders, if you haven't fixed them in advance.

From **Budapest**, the quickest route
through Romania is via Timişoara, then on
towards Sofia in Bulgaria and across the Rila
mountains to the border at Kulata. Once at
the Greek border, you have a three- to four-
hour drive to Thessaloníki or Kavála. Bear in

Italy–Greece ferries

Note: all timings are approximate.

From Ancona ANEK and Minoan to Pátra (24–26hr), usually via Igoumenítsa (16–19hr); 5 weekly Jan–May, 6 weekly May–Oct with ANEK; 6 weekly year-round on Minoan except mid-Jan to mid-Feb. Blue Star daily Oct–March to Igoumenítsa (15hr) and Pátra (21hr). Also Superfast direct to Igoumenítsa (15hr) or Pátra (19hr) almost daily year round. Most sailings at 7–10pm, but there are a number of early-afternoon departures on ANEK and Blue Star.

From Bari Ventouris to Pátra direct (17hr 30min), 3–4 weekly June–Dec; Igoumenítsa (11hr 30min) via Corfu (10hr), 3 weekly April–June & mid-Sept to Dec, 6 weekly July to mid-Sept; Marlines to Igoumenítsa (12hr) 4 weekly late June to mid-Oct, July–Sept calls at Corfu once weekly; Superfast heads almost daily year-round for Igoumenítsa (9hr 30min) and Pátra (15hr 30min). Most sailings at 7–10pm.

From Brindisi Agoudimos to Igoumenítsa at least 4 weekly April–Dec, daily late June–early Sept (9hr). Blue Star almost daily year-round to Corfu (7hr) and Igoumenítsa (8hr 30min). Fragline to Corfu/Igoumenítsa (9hr) almost daily late March–early Oct. Med Link Lines, daily year-round to Pátra (10hr direct); via Kefalloniá (11hr) 4–6 weekly mid-July to mid-Aug, via

Igoumenítsa sporadically mid-June to mid-Aug. Minoan, almost daily late May–late Sept to Corfu (7hr) and Igoumenítsa (8hr 30min). Ventouris, conventional ferry 6 weekly to Corfu (7hr) and Igoumenítsa (8hr 30min) late June–early Sept; high-speed craft daily late April to mid-Sept to Corfu (3hr) and Igoumenítsa (4hr), 3 daily Fri–Sun late June to mid-Sept, calling at Paxí (5hr) once daily late July–early Sept.

There's a fairly even division between late-morning and -evening departures, with high-speed craft doing daytime crossings. Agoudimos, Fragline, Med Link and Ventouris in August all depart 7–9.30pm, while Minoan and Ventouris in other months leave at 11am. The Ventouris high-speed craft departs at 3pm in spring, and in summer at 8.30am, 2pm and 7pm; Blue Star leaves at 10.30am all year.

From Trieste ANEK to Igoumenítsa (24hr), 5 weekly Jan–April, daily April–Oct; most days continues to Pátra (31hr). Usually departs 2pm.

From Venice Blue Star, 4 weekly year-round to Igoumenítsa (26hr) and Pátra (33hr); Minoan daily April–Oct to the same ports (25hr & 35hr respectively), also stopping at Corfu. Departures at about 7pm.

Sample fares

Prices below are one-way high/low season fares; port taxes (€5–8 per person and per car in each direction) are not included. Substantial reductions apply on many lines for both InterRail or Eurail pass-holders, and for those under 26. Discounts of 30–50 percent are usually available on return tickets, even in peak season. Many companies allow you to sleep in your van on board, sparing you the cost of a cabin berth; ask about reduced "camping" fares.

mind that road conditions are often poor and border formalities extensive. Contact the relevant embassies and the AA for more advice

Flights from North America

The Greek national airline, Olympic Airways, flies out of New York (JFK), Boston, Montréal and Toronto. The airline – and also its domestic competitors Axon and Aegean-Cronus – can offer reasonably priced add-on flights within Greece, especially to the Greek

islands. Delta is the only North American carrier currently offering any direct service to Athens, though American Airlines, TWA and USAir have code-sharing agreements with Olympic, and in conjunction with Olympic they quote through fares to/from Chicago, Dallas/Fort Worth, Denver, LA, Miami, Ottawa, Quebec, SF, Seattle, Tampa, Vancouver, and Washington DC.

Another option to consider is picking up any suitable flight to Europe and making your way to Greece by train, in which case a Eurail Pass makes a reasonable investment – details are given on p.17.

Igoumenítsa from Bari or Brindisi: deck class €40–47/€22–32; car from €46–51/€26–32. Superfast fares are €51/42 (deck) and €58/39 (car), also valid all the way to Pátra. The Ventouris high-speed craft work out at €65/56 for a seat, €59/35 per car to Igoumenítsa or Corfu; Paxí is a considerably dearer destination.

Pátra from Ancona: conventional ferry deck class €63/37; car from €86/47. Superfast

fares to Igoumenítsa or Ancona are €78/56 (deck) and €104/71 (car). Blue Star is cheaper for comparable speed at €62/41 deck, €85/52 car.

Pátra from Brindisi: deck class €44/29; car from €47/28.

Pátra from Trieste: deck class €71/54; car from €103/66.

Pátra from Venice: deck class €62–72/43–57; car from €103–106/55–67.

Italian agents

The dialling code for Italy is ☎ 39.

Agoudimos c/o Hellas Ferry Lines, Corso Garibaldi 81, Brindisi ☎0831/529091, ℱ529217.

ANEK Ancona: Stazione Marittima ☎071/205959; Trieste, Stazione Marittima ☎040/322 0604, ℱ322 0142.

Blue Star Brindisi: ☎0831/548115; Ancona: Stazione Marittima ☎071/207 1068, ℱ207 0874; Venice: Stazione Marittima 103 ☎041/277 0559, ℱ277 0367.

Fragline Via Spalato 31, Brindisi ☎0831/548534, ℱ540147.

Marlines c/o Pier Paolo Santelia, Stazione Marittima, Bari ☎080/523 1824, ℱ523 0287.

Med Link Lines c/o Discovery Shipping, Costa Morena, Brindisi ☎ & ℱ0831/548116.

Minoan Lines Ancona: Via Astagno 1 ☎071/201708, ℱ201933; Brindisi, c/o Euromare, Corso Garibaldi 102–104 ☎0831/562936, ℱ562952; Venice, Santa Marta (San Basilio) Magazzino 17 ☎041/271 2345, ℱ521 2929.

Superfast Ferries Ancona: Via XXIX Settembre 2/0 ☎071/202033, ℱ202219; Bari, Corso A. de Tullio 6 ☎080/521 1416, ℱ572 0427.

Ventouris Bari: c/o P. Lorusso & Co, Stazione Marittima Booths 18–20 ☎080/521 7609, ℱ521 7734; Brindisi, c/o Venmare, Corso Garibaldi 56 ☎0831/521 614, ℱ521 654.

Ferries on the internet

All of the shipping companies have websites, as given below. Viamare Travel Ltd (☎020/7431 4560, ⓦwww.viamare.com) is the UK agent for most of these companies.

Agoudimos Lines ⓦwww.agoudimos-lines.com
ANEK ⓦwww.anek.gr
Blue Star ⓦwww.bluestarferries.com
Fragline ⓦwww.fragline.gr

Marlines ⓦwww.marlines.com
Med Link Lines ⓦwww.mll.gr
Minoan Lines ⓦwww.minoan.gr
Superfast ⓦwww.superfast.com
Ventouris ⓦwww.ventouris.gr

Useful airlines in North America

Air Canada ☎1-888/247–2262, ⓦwww.aircanada.ca.
Air France ☎1-800/237-2747, in Canada ☎1-800/667-2747, ⓦwww.airfrance.com.
Alitalia ☎1-800/223-5730, in Canada ☎1-800/361-8336, ⓦwww.alitalia.com.
American Airlines ☎1-800/433-7300, ⓦwww.aa.com.
British Airways ☎1-800/247-9297, ⓦwww.british-airways.com.
Canadian Airlines ☎1-888/247-2262, ⓦwww.aircanada.ca.

Continental Airlines domestic ☎1-800/523-3273, international ☎1-800/231-0856, ⓦwww.continental.com.
Delta Air Lines domestic ☎1-800-221-1212, international ☎1-800/241-4141, ⓦwww.delta.com.
Iberia ☎1-800/772-4642, ⓦwww.iberia.com.
KLM/Northwest US domestic ☎1-800/225-2525, international ☎1-800/447-4747, in Canada ☎514/397-0775, ⓦwww.klm.com.
Lufthansa ☎1-800/645-3880, in Canada ☎1-800/563-5954, ⓦwww.lufthansa-ca.com.
Olympic Airways ☎1-800/223-1226 or 212/735-0200, ⓦwww.olympic-airways.gr.

Swissair ☎1-800/221-4750,
ⓦwww.swissair.com.
TWA domestic ☎1-800/221-2000, international
☎1-800/892-4141, ⓦwww.twa.com.
US Airways domestic ☎1-800/428-4322,
international ☎1-800/622-1015,
ⓦwww.usairways.com.
Virgin Atlantic Airways ☎1-800/862-8621,
ⓦwww.virgin-atlantic.com.

Discount travel companies

Air Brokers International ☎1-800/883-3273 or
415/397-1383, ⓦwww.airbrokers.com.
Consolidator and specialist in RTW and Circle-Pacific
tickets.
Airhitch ☎1-800/326-2009 or 212/864-2000,
ⓦwww.airhitch.org. Standby seat broker: for a set
price, they guarantee to get you on a flight as
close to your preferred Western European
destination as possible, within a week. Costs are
currently $165 (plus taxes and a $29 processing
fee) from or to the East Coast region; $233 (plus
tax & $29 reg. fee) from/to the West Coast or
(when available) the Pacific Northwest; $199 (plus
tax & $29 reg. fee) from/to the Midwest; and $177
(plus tax & $29 reg. fee) from/to the southeast.
(Taxes for all Europe itineraries are $16 eastbound
and $46 westbound.)
Airtech ☎212/219-7000, ⓦwww.airtech.com.
Standby seat broker; also deals in consolidator fares
and courier flights.
Council Travel ☎1-800/226-8624 or 617/528-
2091, ⓦwww.counciltravel.com. Nationwide (60
branches) organization that mostly, but by no
means exclusively, specializes in student/budget
travel.
Educational Travel Center ☎1-800/747-5551
or 608/256-5551, ⓦwww.edtrav.com.
Student/youth discount agent.
High Adventure Travel ☎1-800/350-0612 or
415/912-5600, ⓦwww.airtreks.com. RTW and
Circle-Pacific tickets. The website features an
interactive database that lets you build and price
your own RTW itinerary
New Frontiers/Nouvelles Frontières ☎1-
800/677-0720 or 212/986-6006,
ⓦwww.NewFrontiers.com. French discount-travel
firm. Other branches in LA, San Francisco and
Québec City.
Skylink US ☎1-800/AIR-ONLY or 212/573-8980,
Canada ☎1-800/SKY-LINK. Consolidator.
STA Travel ☎1-800/777-0112 or 1-800/781-
4040, ⓦwww.sta-travel.com. Worldwide specialists
in independent travel; also student IDs, travel
insurance, car rental, rail passes, etc.

Student Flights ☎1-800/255-8000 or 480/951-
1177, ⓦwww.isecard.com. Student/youth fares,
student IDs.
TFI Tours International ☎1-800/745-8000 or
212/736-1140. Consolidator.
Travac ☎1-800/872-8800,
ⓦwww.thetravelsite.com. Consolidator and charter
broker, with another office in Orlando.
Travelers Advantage Cendant Membership
Services, Inc ☎1-877/259-2691,
ⓦwww.travelersadvantage.com. Discount travel
club; annual membership fee required (currently $1
for 3 months' trial).
Travel Avenue ☎1-800/333-3335,
ⓦwww.travelavenue.com. Full-service travel agent
that offers discounts in the form of rebates.
Travel Cuts in Canada ☎1-800/667 2887, in US
☎416/979 2406, ⓦwww.travelcuts.com.
Canadian student-travel organization.
Worldtek Travel ☎1/800-243-1723,
ⓦwww.worldtek.com. Discount travel agency for
worldwide travel.
Worldwide Discount Travel Club ☎305/534-
2642. Discount travel club.

Flights from the US and Canada

The daily non-stop flights **to Athens out of
New York JFK and Boston** (1 stop) on
Olympic start at around US$700 round trip
in winter, rising to around $1400 in summer
for a maximum thirty-day stay with seven-
day advance purchase. Delta has several
weekly direct services from New York JFK to
Athens, but high-season published discount
fares are vastly overpriced at close to $2000;
you can save a bit by changing in Paris to
Axon Airlines for the final leg. In general,
one-stop flights are less expensive; at the
time of writing, Alitalia was offering the
cheapest summer fares New York–Athens
(via Rome) at just over $1000, less than half
that in winter. Travelling during the May and
October "shoulder seasons" will also yield
significant savings.

Common-rating (ie price-fixing) and marketing agreements between the various airlines means that fares to **Athens from the
Mid-West, Deep South or the West
Coast** are little different; from Chicago,
Miami, Dallas, Seattle or Los Angeles you're
looking at $1700–1900 high season,
$500–600 in winter, something in between
at shoulder season. These tickets typically
involve the use of American Airlines, Air
France, Alitalia, Iberia, KLM, Sabena and

Swissair, via their European gateway cities. With little to distinguish these itineraries price-wise, you might examine the stopover times at their respective European hubs, as these can sometimes be overnight. You may be better off getting a domestic add-on to New York and heading directly to Athens from there.

As with the US, air fares **from Canada to Athens** vary depending on where you start your journey, and whether you take a direct service. Olympic flies non-stop out of Montréal and Toronto four times weekly for a scheduled return fare of about CDN$1400 in winter, climbing to nearly CDN$3000 in summer. Indirect flights on Air Canada and British Airways (both via London Heathrow), or KLM, Air France, Sabena or Swissair will cost about CDN$500 less in summer, though in winter their fares are little different from Olympic; frequencies via the European hubs are daily or nearly so. From Calgary or Vancouver, there are no direct flights; expect to pay CDN$2800–3000 during summer, on such combinations as Air Canada/Lufthansa or Air Canada/KLM.

European–Greek regional connections

There are direct scheduled flights (some summer only), mostly with Olympic or Cronus, to:

Thessaloníki from Amsterdam, Belgrade, Berlin, Brussels, Bucharest, Budapest, Dusseldorf, Frankfurt, Larnaca, London, Milan, Moscow, Munich, Paris, Prague, Stuttgart, Vienna, Zurich.
Iráklion (Crete) from Helsinki, Larnaca, Paris, Stuttgart.

Specialist tour operators: North America

Adventures Abroad Canada ☎1-800/665-3998 or 604/303-1099, ⊛www.adventures-abroad.com. Offers a twenty-day "Poetic Greek Isles" tour in spring or autumn, about $2000 land-only.
BCT Scenic Walking ☎1-800/473-1210, ⊛www.bctwalk.com. Offers an eight-day "Ancient Isle of Crete" tour, spring and fall, with a mix of gorge-walking and archeological sites.
Brendan Tours ☎1-800/421-8446, ⊛www.brendantours.com. Cruises from $1500, plus a few island-specific packages.

Caravan Tours ☎1-888/227-2826, ⊛www.caravantours.com. Rather rushed eighteen-day land-and-sea tour, taking in mainland highlights and a cruise of select islands; six departures annually May–Oct.
Classic Adventures ☎1-800/935-5000, ⊛www.classicadventures.com. Cycle through the archeological sites and medieval towns of Crete in twelve days for about $2400, land-only.
Cloud Tours ☎1-800/223-7880, ⊛www.cloudtours.com. Arranges island-hopping itineraries between the big names (Crete, Rhodes, Thíra); uses expensive hotels.
Hellenic Adventures ☎1-800/851-6349, ⊛www.hellenicadventures.com. Small-group, human-scale tours, led by an enthusiastic Greek-American; the five hiking-and-sailing itineraries are much better than average, taking in unusual highlights such as Híos and Límnos. The website is fun and easy to use, too.
Himalayan Travel ☎1-800/225-2380 or 203/743-2349, ⊛www.gorp.com/himtravel.htm. The widest array of Greek walking tours, self-guiding and hotel/inn-based unless otherwise indicated: Kefalloniá–Itháki (8 days, $1000); Crete's southwest coast (8 days, $1050).
Insight International Tours ☎1-800/582-8380, ⊛www.inusa.insightvacations.com. Offers "Grecian Delights" tour, fifteen days for $1500, with a four-day cruise tacked on, passing through the more famous "postcard" isles.
IST Cultural Tours ☎1-800/833-2111, ⊛www.ist-tours.com. Their "Historic Greece and Turkey" tour runs to sixteen days, nine of it cruising; fairly upmarket, and divided evenly between Greece and Turkey.
Samodyssey ☎ & ⊕773/472-765, ✉Samodyssey@aol.com. Twice-yearly small-group tours of about three weeks' duration put together by Hellenophile Sam Stenzel, who lived in Athens for decades; includes a changing selection from the islands, plus the Turkish coast.
Valef Yachts ☎1-800/223-3845, ⊛www.valefyachts.com. Offers a choice of fixed, eight-day motor-yacht cruises in the Dodecanese or the Ionian islands; a bit rushed, but affordable at $900–1150 per person. Also very expensive bareboat charter (sailing or motor yacht); pick your craft from the online brochure.

Flights from Australia and New Zealand

With the huge Greek-emigrant community in Australia, Olympic does a fair job of providing direct links to Greece, although they're seldom the cheapest option. The airline offers three weekly flights to Athens from Sydney, and two from Melbourne, via Bangkok, with onward connections to other Greek destinations. There are no direct flights from New Zealand – you'll have to get yourself to Australia, Southeast Asia or a nearby European hub for onward travel.

Tickets purchased direct from the airlines tend to be expensive; travel agents or Australia-based websites offer much better deals on fares and have the latest information on limited specials, Round-the-World (RTW) fares and stopovers. Some of the best discounts are through Flight Centres, Trailfinders and STA, who can also advise on visa regulations.

If Greece is only one stop on a longer journey, you might want to consider buying a RTW fare. Some travel agents can sell you an "off-the-shelf" **RTW ticket** that will have you touching down in about half a dozen cities (Athens is on many itineraries); others will have to assemble one for you, which can be tailored to your needs but is apt to be more expensive. Figure on A$2250/2600 low/high season for a RTW ticket including Greece, on Star Alliance airlines. In the past, Qantas and British Airways have also offered RTW fares, dubbed the "Global Explorer". RTW fares from any point in Australia are usually common-rated, ie the price is the same from whichever Australian airport you commence travel. From New Zealand, allow over NZ$3500 for the same programmes.

For a **simple return fare**, you may have to buy an add-on internal flight to reach the international gateways of Sydney or Melbourne. Because of the way Australians travel, most tickets are **valid for one year**; at the time of writing, **high-season** departures could be had for A$1770 (one-stop flight on PIA and Qantas) to A$1900 on Olympic, the latter valid all the way to any domestic airport in Greece. Cheaper multi-stop fares on Egyptair (A$1500), Emirates ($1720) or Gulf Air (A$1800) tend to be reserved for students or over-60s. Leaving at **low season** means fares of A$1460 (Olympic) to A$1520 (combination of United, Lufthansa and Singapore Airlines); students can try Egyptair (A$1360), while seniors currently have Gulf Air (A$1410). Other airlines which in the past have had advantageous fares to Greece include Aeroflot (via Singapore and Moscow),

Alitalia (via Rome or Milan), Royal Jordanian (via Amman), and Thai Airways (via Bangkok).

From New Zealand, the usual routes to Athens are either westbound several times weekly via Bangkok, Sydney or Singapore, on Thai Airways, Singapore Airlines or Air New Zealand, or eastbound almost daily via Los Angeles with Air New Zealand. Published return fares are currently edging up to NZ$3500, and even discount outlet tickets close to NZ$3000, so a RTW fare as described above may be your best option.

Airlines

Aeroflot Australia ℡02/9262 2233, ⓦwww.aeroflot.com.
Air New Zealand Australia ℡13 2476, New Zealand ℡0800/737 000 or 09/357 3000, ⓦwww.airnz.com.
Several flights weekly to Athens via LA or Bangkok from major Australian and New Zealand cities (in partnership with the "Star Alliance" and other code-share arrangements).
Alitalia Australia ℡02/9244 2400, New Zealand ℡09/ 302 1452, ⓦwww.alitalia.it.
British Airways Australia ℡02/8904 8800, New Zealand ℡09/356 8690, ⓦwww.british-airways.com.
Egyptair Australia ℡02/9267 6979, ⓦwww.egyptair.com.
Gulf Air Australia ℡02/9244 2199, New Zealand ℡09/308 3366, ⓦwww.gulfairco.com.
Lufthansa Australia ℡1300/655 727 or 02/9367 3887, New Zealand ℡09/303 1529 or 0800/945 220, ⓦwww.lufthansa.com.
Olympic Airways Australia ℡1800/221 663 or 02/9251 2044, ⓦwww.olympic-airways.com.
Qantas Australia ℡13/13 13, New Zealand ℡09/357 8900 or 0800/808 767, ⓦwww.qantas.com.au.
Royal Jordanian Airlines Australia ℡02/9244 2701; New Zealand agent: Innovative Travel ℡03/365 3910; ⓦwww.rja.com.jo.
Singapore Airlines Australia ℡13/10 11 or 02/9350 0262, New Zealand ℡09/303 2129 or 0800/808 909, ⓦwww.singaporeair.com.
Thai Airways Australia ℡1300/651 960, New Zealand ℡09/377 3886; ⓦwww.thaiair.com.

Travel agents

Anywhere Travel Australia ℡02/9663 0411 or 018 401 014, ℮anywhere@ozemail.com.au.
Budget Travel New Zealand ℡09/366 0061 or 0800/808 040.

Destinations Unlimited New Zealand ☏ 09/373 4033.

Flight Centre Australia ☏ 02/9235 3522 or for nearest branch ☏ 13 1600, New Zealand ☏ 09/358 4310, ⊛ www.flightcentre.com.au.

Northern Gateway Australia ☏ 08/8941 1394, ⊜ oztravel@norgate.com.au

STA Travel Australia ☏ 13 1776 or 1300/360 960, New Zealand ☏ 09/309 0458 or 366 6673, ⊛ www.statravel.com.au.

Student Uni Travel Australia ☏ 02/9232 8444, ⊜ Australia@backpackers.net.

Thomas Cook Australia ☏ 13 1771 or 1800/801 002, New Zealand ☏ 09/379 3920, ⊛ www.thomascook.com.au.

Trailfinders Australia ☏ 02/9247 7666.

usit BEYOND New Zealand ☏ 09/379 4224 or 0800/788 336, ⊛ www.usitbeyond.co.nz.

Specialist agents and tour operators

Adventure Travel Company ☏ 09/379 9755, ⊜ advakl@hot.co.nz. New Zealand agent for Peregrine Adventures (see below).

Australians Studying Abroad ☏ 03/9509 1955 or 1800/645 755, ⊛ www.asatravinfo.com.au. Their "Hellenic Heritage" study tour takes a relatively leisurely 23 days to cover most of the major ancient/medieval sites on the islands, with Istanbul thrown in; fairly pricey at A$7000 land only.

House of Holidays Australia ☏ 1800/335 084, ⊛ www.houseofholidays.com.au. Offers various tours for four to fourteen days' duration.

Kompas Holidays Australia ☏ 07/3222 3333 or 1800/269 968, ⊛ www.kompasholidays.com.au. Scores for its Greek island-hopping programme, covering eleven of the better-known islands; they arrange hotels (3-day minimum stay per island) and all ferry transfers.

Peregrine Adventures Australia ☏ 03/9662 2700 or 1300/655 433, ⊛ www.peregrine.net.au. Exclusive Antipodean reps for Exodus (UK), selling their eight-day walking expedition around Tínos.

Sun Island Tours Australia ☏ 02/9283 3840, ⊛ www.sunislandtours.com.au. An assortment of island-hopping, fly-drives, cruises and guided land-tour options.

Departure points: Athens, Pireás and main ports

As detailed in the "Getting There" section, you may well find yourself travelling to the islands via Athens. This is not necessarily a hardship. The Greek capital is, admittedly, no holiday resort, with its concrete architecture and air pollution, but it has modern excitements of its own, as well as superlative ancient sites. A couple of nights' stopover will allow you to take in the Acropolis, the ancient agora and major museums, wander around the old quarter of Pláka and the bazaar area, and sample some of the country's best restaurants and clubs. And a morning arrival in Athens would allow you time to take a look at the Acropolis and Pláka, before heading down to the port of Pireás (Piraeus) to catch one of the overnight ferries to Crete or the Dodecanese.

Not all the islands are accessible from Pireás, so we've given brief accounts of other useful mainland ports below.

Athens

Athens' new **airport**, "Eleftherios Venizelos", at Spáta some 26km east of the city, opened in March 2001, replacing the far

more convenient (if tiny) one south of town at Ellinikó. There are ample banking facilities in the arrivals hall, including several cash dispensers. As yet, there are no light-rail or underground links the whole way into town (foreseen for 2003 at the earliest); the best you can do is take the E94 express bus (every 16 min 6am–8.30pm, half-hourly 8.30pm–midnight) from outside the arrivals hall to the current last metro stop, Ethnikí Ámyna, and then continue into the centre. Otherwise there's the E95 express bus all the way to central Syndagma square (every 25min 6am–7.50pm; every 35 min otherwise), incidentally, your only option from midnight to 6am. There is also the **E96 express bus to Pireás (Piraeus) port** (every 20 min 5am–7pm, half-hourly 7pm–8.30pm, every 40min 8.30pm–5am), going via the beach suburbs. All three services cost €3, but for the price you automatically get a "one-day" travelcard valid on all Athens public transport. Tickets should be bought from a booth beside the stops, or, if this is closed, can be purchased on the bus; make sure you have small change. A taxi to Pireás should cost no more than €24 – at most times of the day your driver will find it quicker to imitate the E-bus by heading southwest to Vári and Voúla and then north through the southerly beach suburbs rather than struggle through traffic in the northern suburbs. This amount should include a €1.20 airport surcharge and €0.15 for each item of luggage, but make sure the meter is working (fares begin at €0.70, minimum fare €1.50) and visible from the start – double or even quintuple overcharging of newcomers is the norm.

For those who have stopped off in Athens for the day or overnight, it's about 9km from the city centre **to** the ferry port of **Pireás**. The easiest way to get there is by **taxi**, which should cost around €4.50–6, depending on your start-point and how many bags you have. You may find that you have fellow passengers in the cab: this is permitted, and each drop-off will pay the full fare. Otherwise, Line 1 of the metro (Kifissiá-Pireás) will get you there easily, passing through Omónia and Monastiráki stations and depositing you, at the port, within moderate walking distance of many boat-berths.

All international **trains** arrive at the Stathmós Laríssis, just to the northwest of the city centre. You can take yellow trolley bus (#1) or the metro immediately outside to reach Sýndagma square.

Accommodation and eating

Finding **accommodation** in Athens is not a problem except during midsummer – though it's always best to phone ahead. A small selection of places is listed below, ranging from hostels to fairly comfortable hotels.

For a quick stay, **Pláka**, the oldest quarter of the city, is the obvious area. It spreads south of Sýndagma square, lies within easy walking range of the Acropolis and has lots of outdoor restaurants and cafés. It's possible to stay in the port of Pireás, too, though there's no real need, and you might as well make the most of your time in Athens. All the listings below are in Pláka, except for *Marble House* and *Art Gallery*, which are just south in Veïkoú/Koukáki district, and the *Tempi* which is just north of Monastiráki square and station.

Hostels and budget inns

Festos Youth and Student Guesthouse Filellínon 18 ☎010/32 32 455. €10 a bunk, €22 doubles.
John's Place Patróöu 5, Pláka ☎010/32 29 719. €27 double; also multi-bed rooms.
Kouros Kódrou 11 ☎010/32 27 431. ❸
Marble House Pension in a quiet alley off Anastasíou Zínni 35, Koukáki ☎010/92 34 058. ❷
Phaedra Herefóndos 16, Pláka ☎010/32 38 641. ❷
Student and Travellers' Inn Kydhathinéon 16 ☎010/32 44 808. ❸
Tempi Eólou 29 ☎010/32 13 175. ❷
Thisseus Inn Thisséos 10 ☎010/32 45 960. €12 each in quads, €27 doubles.

Mid-range hotels

Acropolis House Kódrou 6–8 ☎010/32 22 344. ❹
Adonis Kódrou 3 ☎010/324 9737. ❹
Art Gallery Pension Erekhthíou 5, Veïkoú ☎010/92 38 376. ❹
Nefeli Iperídhou 16, Pláka ☎010/32 25 800. ❹

Pláka is bursting with touristy **restaurants**, most of them very pleasantly situated but poor value. Three with nice sites *and* good food are *Iy Ipiros*, actually on Platía Ayíou Filíppou in the Monastiráki flea market, for *mayireftá*; *O Thanasis*, nearby at Mitropóleos 69, for dynamite souvláki and kebabs; and *Kafenio Dhioskouri*, Dhioskoúron, for seafood snacks with an unbeatable view of the ancient agora. *Eden*, at Liossíou 12, is one of the city's few vegetarian restaurants.

The city and sights

Central Athens is a compact, easily walkable area. Its hub is **Sýndagma square** (Platía Syndágmatos), flanked by the Parliament building, banks and airline offices. Pretty much everything you'll want to see in a fleeting visit – the Acropolis, Pláka, the major museums – lies within 20–30 minutes' walk of here. Just east of the square, too, are the **National Gardens** – the nicest spot in town for a siesta.

Walk south from Sýndagma, along Níkis or Filellínon streets, and then briefly west, and you'll find yourself in Pláka, the surviving area of the nineteenth-century, pre-Independence village. Largely pedestrianized, it is a delightful area just to wander around – and it is the approach to the Acropolis. For a bit of focus to your walk, take in the fourth-century BC **Monument of Lysikrates**, used as a study by Byron, to the east, and the Roman-era **Tower of the Winds** (Aéridhes), to the west. The latter adjoins the Roman Forum. Climb north from the Tower of the Winds and you reach **Anafiótika**, with its whitewashed Cycladic-style cottages (built by workers from the island of Anáfi) and the eclectic **Kanellópoulos Museum** (Tues–Sun 8am–2.30pm; €2.40).

Head north from the Roman Forum (Tues–Sun 8am–3pm; €1.50), along Athinás or Eólou streets, and you come to an equally characterful part of the city – the **bazaar** area, which shows Athens in its Near Eastern lights. **Monastiráki square** is worth a look, too, with its Ottoman mosque (now a museum of ceramics). On Sundays a genuine **flea market** sprawls to its west, out beyond the tourist shops promoted as "Athens Flea Market".

Even with a few hours to spare between flight and ferry, you can take in a visit to the **Acropolis** (summer Mon 11am–6.30pm, Tues–Sun 8am–6.30pm; may close 2.30pm in winter; €6). The complex of temples, rebuilt by Pericles in the "Golden Age" of the fifth century BC, is focused on the famed Parthenon. This, and the smaller Athena Nike and Erechtheion temples are given context by a small museum housing some of the original relief art left behind by Lord Elgin.

If you have more time, make your way down to the **Theatre of Dionysos**, on the south slope (Tues–Sun 8.30am–2.30pm; may open longer July & Aug; €1.50), and/or to the Ancient (Classical Greek era) **agora** (southeastern entrance down the path from the Areopagus; northern entrance on Adhrianoú; Tues–Sun 8.30am–3pm; €3), presided over by the Doric **Thiseíon**, or Temple of Hephaestus.

Athens' major museum is the **National Archeological Museum** (Patissíon 28; summer Mon 12.30–7pm, Tues–Sun 8am–7pm; winter Mon 10.30am–5pm, Tues–Sun 8.30am–2.45pm; €6). Its highlights include the Mycenaean (*Odyssey*-era) treasures, Classical sculpture and, upstairs, the brilliant Minoan frescoes from Thíra (Thíra).

Two other superb museums are the **Benáki** (Mon, Wed, Fri, Sat 9am–5pm; Thurs 9am–midnight; Sun 9am–3pm; closed Tues; €6), a fascinating personal collection of ancient and folk treasures, and the **Goulandris Museum of Cycladic and Ancient Greek Art** (Mon–Fri 10am–4pm, Sat 10am–3pm; €3), with its wonderful display of figurines from the Cycladic island civilization of the third millennium BC.

Pireás

Pireás (Piraeus), the port of Athens, is the southwesternmost stop on Line 1 of the **metro** which you can board at Platía Viktorías, Omónia or Monastiráki squares. The journey takes about 25 minutes – trains run from 6am to midnight – with a flat fare of €0.60 (€0.75 if you've used Line 2 or Line 3 as well). If you're travelling **by rail** from Pátra, the train continues through Athens down to Pireás.

You can buy **ferry and catamaran tickets** from agencies at the harbour in Pireás, or in central Athens (there are several outlets on Lefóros Amalías, which runs south of Sýndagma square). Wherever you buy tickets, make sure you ask around the agencies and get a ferry that makes a reasonably direct run to your island destination. There may be little choice to obscure islands, but ferries to the Cyclades and Dodecanese can take very different routes.

For the Argo-Saronic islands, you will probably take a "Hellas Flying Dolphin" **hydrofoil** from the Zéa Marina (except for Égina services and the Saronic Dolphins to Ídhra and Spétses which depart from Aktí Tzelépi) – a taxi ride (or bus #8) from the metro. These are twice as fast and around twice the cost, but conventional ferries to the islands beyond Égina are scarce. Tickets can be bought in advance in Athens – worth doing in high season – or an hour before departure at the quay.

Other mainland ports

Although Pireás has a wide choice of ferry, catamaran and hydrofoil connections, certain islands can (or must) be reached from other ports on the mainland. Below is a quick run-through of the more important and useful.

Note also that there are two islands – **Évvia** (northeast of Athens) and **Lefkádha** in the Ionian islands – that require no ferry, and can be reached by bus, and in Évvia's case also by train.

Alexandhróupoli

The third northern port (6hr by bus from Thessaloníki) has regular ferries and summer-only hydrofoils to Samothráki. It's a somewhat unenticing place to stay, though if you get stuck the *Lido* at Paleológou 15 (℡05510/28 808) represents by far the best budget-hotel value.

Igoumenítsa

Many ferries from Italy call at Igoumenítsa, stopping at Corfu en route. There are regular shuttles across to **Corfu**, to both the main town and also Lefkími in the south, plus once-daily service to **Paxí**. Hotel vacancies are plentiful as nobody stays more than a night; the *Stavrodhromi* (℡06650/22 343) is a reliable, friendly cheapie, 500m inland at Soulíou 14.

Kavála

The second port of northern Greece (3hr by bus from Thessaloníki) offers fast access to **Thássos**, either direct by hydrofoil, or from the nearby ro-ro shuttle point at Keramotí. There are also links to **Límnos** and other **northeast Aegean** islands, as well as (sporadically in summer) to **Samothráki**. The city has a line of good tavernas in the old quarter below the castle, but pleasant, affordable hotels are in short supply. In ascending order of comfort and price, try the *Akropolis* (℡0510/223 543) at Venizélou 29, the *Panorama* (℡0510/224 205) at Venizélou 32/c or the *Esperia* (℡0510/229 621) at Erythroú Stavroú 42, opposite the archeological museum.

Kyllíni

This small port, south of Pátra (buses), is the main departure point for the Ionian island of Zákynthos, and in summer has boats to Kefalloniá. Little point in staying, if you time things right.

Kými

This is technically an island port – on Évvia (see Chapter 6) – but is mentioned here as it is the main port for **Skýros** in the Sporades. Kými can be reached from Athens by bus, which should be timed to dovetail with ferry departures. If you miss the connection, staying options are limited to two fairly expensive hotels.

Lávrio

This tiny port, south of Athens (and reachable by bus from the Mavromatéon terminal; 1hr 15min) has daily ferries to **Kéa**, the closest of the Cyclades, and less often to **Kýthnos**, Kéa's neighbour.

Neápoli

A small, undistinguished port at the southern foot of the Peloponnese, with ferry and hydrofoil connections to **Kýthira**, and local boats to the islet of **Elafónissos**. It can be reached by hydrofoil in summer from Pireás.

Párga and Astakós

These two small ports, south of Igoumenítsa, have daily ferries to, respectively, **Paxí** and **Kefalloniá** in the Ionian. Párga is a popular, crowded resort, more pleasant (and with more accommodation vacancies, mostly studios) off-season; Astakós is rarely busy but has few places to stay – buses from Athens tend to dovetail with ferry departures, currently just once daily, that sometimes call at **Itháki** too.

Pátra (Patras)

Pátra is the major port of the Peloponnese, and the main jump-off for Italy and most of the **Ionian islands**. Easiest access from Athens is on the train (Stathmós Peloponíssou terminal; 4hr), since the Pátra station is right by the boat terminals. The city itself is uninteresting, so plan on moving out the same day, if possible. Reasonable budget hotels include the *El Greco*, Ayíou

Andhréou 145 (☎0610/272 931) or the *Ayios Georgios* at Ayíou Andhréou 73 (☎0610/225 092).

Ráfina

Another small port near Athens (again reachable by bus from the Mavromatéon terminal; 40min). Connections are to the **Cyclades**, **northeast Aegean** and nearby **Évvia**.

Thessaloníki

The northern capital is a busy mainland port. There are useful long-haul **ferries** to Kós and Rhodes via Sámos; to the northeastern Aegean islands; and to Crete via select Sporades and Cyclades. There are also useful hydrofoils to **Skíathos**, **Skópelos** and **Alónissos** in the Sporades. It's worth exploring the Byzantine churches, especially the Áyios Yeóryios Rotónda and tiny Óssios Davídh, as well as the Archeological Museum. Hotels are plentiful if mostly uninspiring, noisy and often vastly overpriced; worthwhile exceptions include the *Tourist* on Mitropóleos 21 (☎0310/276 335); the *Nea Mitropolis* at Syngroú 22 (☎0310/525 540); the *Bill* at Syngroú 29, corner Amvrossíou (☎0310/537 666); and the *Orestias Castorias* at Agnóstou Stratiótou 14 (☎0310/276 517).

Vólos and Áyios Konstandínos

Vólos is a large port city – modern and rather grim – in Thessaly, in central Greece. It is easiest reached from Athens by bus (Mavromatéon terminal; 4hr), though there's also a couple of through express trains daily, via Lárissa. Ferries and hydrofoils run regularly to the Sporades – **Skiáthos**, **Skópelos** and **Alónissos**. Try to complete your journey the same day; failing that, pleasantly situated budget hotels include the *Roussas* (☎04210/21 732) at Iatroú Tzánou, 1km east of the dock, or the *Iasson* right by the dock (☎04210/26 075). **Áyios Konstandínos** is an alternative, less busy, port for the **Sporades**, again with buses from Athens (Mavromatéon terminal; 2hr 30min).

Yíthio

This elegant Peloponnese town has ferries most days to the isolated island of **Kýthira**, plus a few times weekly to Kíssamos in western Crete. It's a 5–6hr haul here by bus (Kifissóu 100 terminal) from Athens, changing at Spárti. Budget hotels or pensions in town include the *Kondoyannis*, Vassiléos Pávlou 19 (☎07330/22 518); the *Saga* on Tzanetáki, opposite Kranae islet (☎07330/23 220); and the *Kranae*, Vassiléos Pávlou 15 (☎07330/22 011).

Visas and red tape

UK and all other EU nationals (plus those of Norway and Iceland) need only a valid passport for entry to Greece; you are no longer stamped in on arrival or out upon departure, and in theory at least enjoy uniform civil rights with Greek citizens. US, Australian, New Zealand, Canadian and most non-EU Europeans receive mandatory entry and exit stamps in their passports and can stay, as tourists, for ninety days. Note that such nationals arriving by flight or boat from another EU state may not be stamped in routinely at minor ports, so it's best to make sure this is done in order to avoid unpleasantness on exit.

If you are planning to **travel overland**, you should check current visa requirements for Hungary, Romania and Bulgaria at their closest consulates; transit visas for most of these territories are at present issued at the borders, though at a higher price than if obtained in advance at a local consulate.

Visa extensions

If you wish to remain in Greece for longer than three months, as a non-EU/EFTA national you should officially apply for an extension. This can be done in the larger cities like Athens, Thessaloníki, Pátra, Rhodes and Iráklion through the *Ypiresía Allodhapón* (Aliens' Bureau); prepare yourself for concerted bureaucracy. In other locations you visit the local police station, where the staff are apt to be more cooperative.

Unless of Greek descent, visitors from **non-EU** countries are currently allowed only one six-month extension to a tourist visa, for which a hefty fee is charged – up to €150. In theory, EU nationals are allowed to stay indefinitely but, to be sure of avoiding any problems, it's best to get a resident visa and (if appropriate) a work permit – see "Finding work", p.75. In either case, the procedure should be set in motion at least four weeks before your time runs out. If you don't already have a work permit, you will be required to present pink, personalized bank **exchange receipts** totalling at least €1500 for the preceding three months, as proof that you are importing sufficient funds to support yourself without working. Possession of unexpired credit cards, a Greek **savings account passbook** or travellers' cheques can to some extent substitute for the pink receipts; the pages of the passbook in par-

ticular should be photocopied and given to the police.

Certain individuals get around the law by leaving Greece every three months and re-entering a few days later, ideally via a different frontier post, for a new, ninety-day tourist stamp. However, with the recent flood of Albanian and Eastern European refugees into the country, all looking for work, security and immigration personnel don't always look very kindly on this practice.

If you **overstay** your time and then leave under your own power – ie are not deported – you'll be hit with a huge spot fine upon departure, effectively a double-priced retroactive visa extension; no excuses will be entertained except perhaps a doctor's certificate stating you were immobilized in hospital. It cannot be overemphasized just how exigent Greek immigration officials often are on this issue.

Greek embassies abroad

Australia 9 Turrana St, Yarralumla, Canberra, ACT 2600 ℡02/6273 3011.
Britain 1a Holland Park, London W11 3TP ℡020/7221 6467, ⊛www.greekembassy.org.uk.
Canada 80 Maclaren St, Ottawa, ON K2P 0K6 ℡613/238-6271.
Ireland 1 Upper Pembroke St, Dublin 2 ℡01/676 7254.
New Zealand 5–7 Willeston St, Wellington ℡04/473 7775.
USA 2221 Massachusetts Ave, NW, Washington DC 20008 ℡202/939-5800, ⊛www.greekembassy.org.

Insurance

Even though EU healthcare privileges apply in Greece (see below for details), you'd do well to take out an insurance policy before travelling to cover against theft, loss, illness or injury. Before paying for a whole new policy, however, it's worth checking whether you are already covered: some all-risks homeowners' or renters' insurance policies *may* cover your possessions when overseas, and many private medical schemes (such as BUPA or PPP in the UK) offer coverage extensions for abroad.

In Canada, provincial health plans usually provide partial cover for medical mishaps overseas, while holders of official student/teacher/youth cards in Canada and the US are entitled to meagre accident coverage and hospital in-patient benefits. **Students** will often find that their student health coverage extends during the vacations and for one term beyond the date of last enrolment. Most **credit-card issuers** also offer some sort of vacation insurance, which is often automatic if you pay for the holiday with their card. However, it's vital to check just what these policies cover – frequently only death or dismemberment in the UK.

After exhausting the possibilities above, you might want to contact a **specialist travel insurance** company, or consider the travel insurance deal we offer (see box below). A typical travel insurance policy usually provides cover for the **loss** of baggage, tickets and – up to a certain limit – cash, cards or cheques, as well as **cancellation** or curtailment of your journey. Most of them exclude so-called **dangerous sports** unless an extra premium is paid: in the Greek islands this means motorbiking, windsurfing and possibly sailing, with most visitors engaging in one or the other at some point. Many policies can be chopped and changed to exclude coverage you don't need – for example, sickness and accident benefits can often be excluded or included at will. If you do take medical coverage, ascertain whether benefits will be paid as treatment proceeds or only after return home, whether there is a **24-hour medical emergency number**, and how much the deductible is (sometimes negotiable). When securing baggage cover, make sure that the **per-article limit** – typically under £500 in the UK – will cover your most valuable possession. Travel agents and tour operators in the UK are likely to **require travel insurance** when you book a package holiday, though after a change in the UK law in late 1998 they can no longer insist that you buy their own – however, you will be required to sign a declaration saying that you have a policy with a particular company.

If you need to make a **medical claim**, you should keep receipts for medicines and treatment, and in the event you have anything stolen or lost, you must obtain an **official statement** from the police or the airline which lost your bags. In the wake of growing numbers of fraudulent claims, most insurers won't even entertain one unless you have a police report. There is usually also a **time limit** for submitting claims after the end of your journey.

Rough Guide travel insurance

Rough Guides offers its own travel insurance, customized for our readers by a leading UK broker and backed by a Lloyds underwriter. It's available for anyone, of any nationality, travelling anywhere in the world.

There are two main Rough Guide insurance plans: **Essential**, for basic, no-frills cover; and **Premier** – with more generous and extensive benefits. Alternatively, you can take out **annual multitrip insurance**, which covers you for any number of trips throughout the year (with a maximum of 60 days for any one trip). Unlike many policies, the Rough Guides schemes are calculated by the day, so if you're travelling for 27 days rather than a month, that's all you pay for. If you intend to be away for the whole year, the Adventurer policy will cover you for 365 days. Each plan can be supplemented with a "Hazardous Activities Premium" if you plan to indulge in sports considered dangerous, such as scuba-diving or trekking. Rough Guides also does good deals for older travellers, and will insure you up to any age, at prices comparable to Saga's.

For a policy quote, call the Rough Guide Insurance Line toll-free on ☏ 0800/015 0906 (in the UK); on ☏ 1-866/220-5588 (in the USA); or, if you're calling from elsewhere ☏ +44 1243/621046. Alternatively, get an online quote at ⓦ www.roughguides.com/insurance.

Health matters

British and other EU nationals are officially entitled to free medical care in Greece upon presentation of an E111 form, available from most post offices. "Free", however, means admittance only to the lowest grade of state hospital (known as a *yenikó nosokomío*), and does not include nursing care, special tests or the cost of medication. If you need prolonged medical care, you should make use of private treatment, which is as expensive as anywhere in western Europe – this is where your travel insurance policy (see above) comes in handy. The US, Canada, Australia and New Zealand have no formal healthcare agreements with Greece (other than allowing for free emergency trauma treatment).

There are no required **inoculations** for Greece, though it's wise to ensure that you are up to date on tetanus and polio. The **water** is safe pretty much everywhere, though you will come across shortages or brackish supplies on some of the drier and more remote islands. Bottled water is widely available if you're feeling cautious.

Specific hazards

The main health problems experienced by visitors have to do with **overexposure to the sun**, and the odd nasty from the sea. To combat the former, don't spend too long in the sun, cover up limbs, wear a hat and drink plenty of fluids in the hot months to avoid any danger of **sunstroke**; remember that even hazy sun can burn. For sea-gear, goggles or a dive mask for swimming and footwear for walking over wet or rough rocks are useful.

Hazards of the deep

In the sea, you may have the bad luck to meet an armada of **jellyfish** (*tsoúkhtres*), especially in late summer; they come in various colours and sizes ranging from purple "pizzas" to invisible, minute creatures. Various over-the-counter remedies for jellyfish stings are sold in resort pharmacies; baking soda or diluted ammonia also help to lessen the sting. The welts and burning usually subside of their own accord within a few hours; there are no deadly man-of-war species in Greek waters.

Less vicious but more common are black, spiky **sea urchins** (*ahini*), which infest rocky shorelines year-round; if you step on or graze one, a sewing needle (you can crudely sterilize it by heat from a cigarette lighter) and olive oil are effective for removing spines; if you don't extract them they'll fester. You can take your revenge by eating the roe of the reddish–purple ones, which is served as a delicacy in a few seafood restaurants.

The worst maritime danger – fortunately very rare – is the **weever fish** (*dhrákena*) which buries itself in shallow-water sand with just its poisonous dorsal and gill spines protruding. If you tread on one, the sudden pain is excruciating, and the exceptionally potent venom can cause permanent paralysis of the affected area. Imperative first aid is to immerse your foot in water as hot as you can stand, which degrades the toxin and relieves the swelling of joints and attendant pain, but you should still seek medical attention as soon as possible.

Somewhat more common are **stingrays and skates** (Greek names include *platý*, *seláhi*, *vátos* or *trígona*), which mainly frequent bays with sandy bottoms where they can camouflage themselves. Though shy, they can give you a nasty lash with their tail if trodden on, so shuffle your feet a bit when entering the water.

When snorkelling in deeper water, especially around Crete, the Dodecanese or the east Aegean, you may happen upon a brightly coloured **moray eel** (*smérna*) sliding back and forth out of its rocky lair. Keep a respectful distance – their slightly comical air and clown-colours belie an irritable temper and the ability to inflict nasty bites or even sever fingers.

Sandflies, dogs and mosquitoes

If you are sleeping on or near a **beach**, it's wise to use insect repellent, either lotion or wrist/ankle bands, and/or a tent with a screen to guard against **sandflies**. Their bites are potentially dangerous, as these flies spread leishmaniasis, a parasitic infection characterized by chronic fever, listlessness and weight loss. It's difficult to treat, requiring long courses of medication.

In Greece, the main reservoirs for leishmaniasis are **dogs**. Transmission of the disease to humans by fleas has not been proven, but it's wisest not to befriend strays as they also carry echinococcosis, a debilitating liver fluke. In humans these form nodules and cysts which can only be removed surgically.

Mosquitoes (*kounóupia*) in Greece carry nothing worse than a vicious bite, but they can be infuriating. One solution is to burn pyrethrum incense coils (*spíres* or *fidhákia*), which are widely and cheaply available, if pungently malodorous. Better, if you can get them, are the small electrical devices (trade names Vape-Net or Bay-Vap) that vaporize an odourless insecticide tablet; many accommodation proprietors supply them routinely. Insect repellents such as Autan are available from most general stores and kiosks.

Creepy-crawlies

Adders (*ohiés*) and **scorpions** (*skorpií*) are found throughout Greece; both creatures are shy, but take care when climbing over drystone walls where snakes like to sun themselves, and don't put hands or feet in places, like shoes, where you haven't looked first. The wiggly, fast-moving **centipedes** which look like a rubber toy from Hong Kong should also be treated with respect, as they pack a nasty bite.

The number of annual deaths from **snakebite** in Europe is very small. Many snakes will bite if threatened, whether they are venomous or not. If a bite injects venom, then swelling will normally occur within thirty minutes. If this happens, get medical attention; keep the bitten part still; and make sure all body movements are as gentle as possible. If medical attention is not nearby then bind the limb firmly to slow the blood circulation, but not so tightly as to stop the blood flow.

Many reptiles, including snakes, can harbour *Salmonella* bacteria, so should be handled cautiously and preferably not at all. This applies particularly to tortoises.

In addition to munching its way through a fair fraction of Greece's surviving pine forests, the **pine processionary caterpillar** – taking this name from the long, nose-to-tail convoys which individuals form at certain points in their life cycle – sports highly irritating hairs, with a poison worse than a scorpion's. If you touch one, or even a tree-trunk they've been on recently, you'll know all about it for a week, and the welts may require antihistamine to heal.

Pharmacies, drugs and contraception

For **minor complaints** it's enough to go to the local *farmakío*. Greek pharmacists are highly trained and dispense a number of medicines which elsewhere could only be prescribed by a doctor. In the larger towns and resorts there'll usually be one who speaks good English. Pharmacies are usually closed evenings and Saturday mornings, but all should have a monthly schedule (in both English and Greek) on their door showing the complete roster of night and week-end duty pharmacists in town.

Greeks are famously hypochondriac, so pharmacies are veritable Aladdin's caves of **arcane drugs and sundry formulas** – just about everything available in North America and northern Europe is here, and then some. **Homeopathic** and **herbal** remedies are quite widely available, too, and the largest towns have dedicated homeopathic pharmacies, identified by the characteristic green cross. There is a large homeopathic centre in Athens at Nikosthénous 8, Platía Plastíra, Pangráti ☎010/70 98 199; the Centre of Homeopathic Medicine is at Perikléous 1, Maroússi ☎010/80 52 671.

If you regularly use any form of **prescription drug**, you should bring along a copy of the prescription, together with the generic name of the drug; this will help should you need to replace it, and also avoids possible problems with customs officials. In this regard, it's worth being aware that **codeine is banned** in Greece. If you import any you might find yourself in serious trouble, so check labels carefully; it's the core ingredient of Panadeine, Veganin, Solpadeine, Codis and Empirin-Codeine, to name just a few common compounds.

Hayfever sufferers should be prepared for the early Greek pollen season, at its height from April to June. If you are taken by surprise, you'll be able to get tablets and creams at a pharmacy, but it's cheaper to come prepared. Commercial antihistamines like Triludan are difficult to find in smaller towns, and local brands can be overpriced.

Contraceptive pills are more readily available every year, but don't count on getting these – or spermicidal jelly/foam – outside of a few large island towns, over-the-counter at the larger *farmakía*; Greek women tend not to use any sort of birth control systematically, and have an average of four abortions during their adult life. **Condoms**, however, are inexpensive and ubiquitous – just ask for *profylaktiká* (the slangy terms *plastiká* or slightly vulgar *kapótes* are even better understood) at any pharmacy or corner *períptero* (kiosk).

Women's hygienic supplies are sold in pharmacies or in supermarkets near the toilet paper and diapers. Napkins ("Always" brand) are ubiquitous; tampons can be trickier to find in remoter spots, especially on the smaller islands.

Doctors and hospitals

You'll find English-speaking **doctors** in any of the bigger towns or resorts; the tourist police, hotel staff or even your consulate should be able to come up with some names if you have any difficulty.

For an **ambulance**, phone ☎166. In **emergencies** – cuts, broken bones, etc – treatment is given free in **state hospitals**, though you will only get the most basic level of nursing care. Greek families routinely take in food and bedding for relatives, so as a tourist you'll be at a severe disadvantage. Somewhat better are the ordinary state-run **out-patient clinics** (*yiatría*) attached to most public hospitals and also found in rural locales. These operate on a first-come, first-served basis, so go early; usual hours are 8am to noon, though it's sometimes possible to get seen by someone between 1 and 5pm.

Costs, money and banks

The cost of living in Greece has spiralled during the years of EU membership: the days of renting an island house for a monthly pittance are long gone, and food prices at corner shops now differ little from those of other member countries. However, outside the established resorts, travel between and around the islands remains reasonably priced, with the cost of restaurant meals, short-term accommodation and public transport still cheaper than anywhere in northern or western Europe except parts of Portugal.

Prices depend on where and when you go. Island capitals and the trendier small islands (such as Sými, Sífnos, Paxí and Pátmos) are more expensive, and costs everywhere increase sharply in July, August and at Christmas, New Year or Easter. **Students** with an International Student Identity Card (ISIC) can get discounted (sometimes free) admission at many archeological sites and museums; those **over 60** can rely on site-admission discounts of 25 to 30 percent, as well as similar discounts for transport. These, and other occasional discounts, tend to be more readily available to EU nationals.

Some basic costs

On most islands a **daily per-person budget** of £23–27/US$32–38 will get you basic accommodation, breakfast, picnic lunch, a short ferry or bus ride and a simple evening meal, as one of a couple. Camping would cut costs marginally. On £35–38/$49–54 a day you could be living quite well, plus sharing the cost of renting a large motorbike or small car.

Inter-island **ferries**, a main unavoidable expense, are reasonably priced, subsidized by the government in an effort to preserve remote island communities. To give you some idea of prices, the cheapest cabin for the overnight journey from Athens to Sámos, an eleven-hour trip, costs about €37, while a deck-class ticket for the four-hour trip from Rhodes to Kós costs about €11. For €4–7 you can catch a short-hop ferry to the numerous small islands that lie closer to Rhodes, Kós and Sámos, the most likely touchdown points if you're flying to the Dodecanese or east Aegean on a direct charter; a cheap cabin from Pireás to Rhodes, one of the longest single ferry journeys in Greece, will set you back €47. Local ferries in the Cyclades are a bit pricier for the sea miles travelled; Páros or Náxos to Thíra in the Cyclades runs at about €9.

The simplest double **room** generally costs around €20.50–26.50 a night, depending on the location and the plumbing arrangements. Bona fide single rooms are rare, and cost about seventy percent of double rates. Organized **campsites** are little more than €4 per person, with similar charges per tent and perhaps 25 percent more for a camper van. With discretion you can camp for free in the more remote, rural areas.

A basic taverna **meal** with local wine can be had for around €9–10 a head. Add a better bottle of wine, seafood or more careful cooking, and it could be up to €20 a head; you'll rarely pay more than that. Sharing seafood, Greek salads and dips is a good way to keep costs down in the better restaurants, and even in the most developed of resorts, with inflated "international" menus, you'll often be able to find a more earthy but decent taverna where the locals eat.

Youth and student discounts

Various official and quasi-official **youth/student ID cards** soon pay for themselves in savings. Full-time students are eligible for the International Student ID Card (ISIC), which entitles the bearer to special air, rail and ferry fares and discounts at museums, theatres and other attractions. For Americans there's also a health benefit, providing up to $3000 in emergency medical coverage and $100 a day for 60 days in the hospital, plus a 24-hour hotline to call in the event of a medical, legal or financial emergency. The card costs $22 for Americans; CAN$16 for Canadians; AUS$16.50 for Australians; NZ$21 for New Zealanders; and £6 in the UK.

You only have to be 26 or younger to qualify for the **International Youth Travel Card**, which costs US$22/£7 and carries the same benefits. Teachers qualify for the **International Teacher Identity Card (ITIC)**, offering similar discounts and costing £6, US$22, Can$16, AUS$16.50 and NZ$21. All these cards are available in the US from Council Travel, STA, Travel CUTS and, in Canada, Hostelling International (see p.22 for addresses); in Australia and New Zealand from STA or Campus Travel; and in the UK from CTS Travel (ⓦ www.ctstravel.co.uk).

Several other travel organizations and accommodation groups also sell their own cards, good for various discounts. A university photo ID might open some doors, but is not as easily recognizable as the ISIC cards, although the latter are often not accepted as valid proof of age.

Banks and exchange

Greek **banks** are normally open Monday to Thursday 8.30am–2pm, Friday 8.30am–1.30pm. Certain branches in the major towns or tourist centres are open extra hours in the evenings and on Saturday mornings for exchanging money. Always take your passport with you as proof of identity and be prepared for at least one long line.

Outside these times, the largest hotels and travel agencies can often provide this service, albeit sometimes with hefty commissions. On small islands with no full-service bank, "authorized" bank agents will charge yet another extra fee (1–2 percent) to cover the cost of posting a travellers' cheque to the main branch.

The safest, though most expensive, way to carry money is as **travellers' cheques**. These can be obtained from banks (even if you don't have an account) or from offices of Thomas Cook and American Express; you'll

The euro

Greece is one of twelve European Union countries which have changed over to a single currency, the **euro** (€). The transition period, which began on January 1, 1999, was lengthy, however: euro notes and coins were not issued until January 1, 2002, with the Greek drachma (*dhrakhmí*, the oldest currency in Europe) remaining in place for cash transactions, at a fixed rate of 340.75 drachmas to 1 euro, until they were scrapped entirely on 28 February, 2002. You will be able to exchange any leftover drachma coins into euros until March 2004, and any old drachma paper notes until March 2012, at branches of the Bank of Greece. For the most up-to-date **exchange rates** of the US dollar or the pound sterling against the euro, consult the very useful currency speculators' website, ⓦ www.oanda.com. Rates at the time of research are: £1 = €1.60, US$1 = €1.08, Aus$1 = €0.53. You should not be charged commission for changing euro-denomination travellers' cheques in any of the twelve countries within the euro zone (also known as "Euroland").

All local prices in this book are given in euros. Amounts were derived from the last known drachma price of late 2001, and usually rounded up – as the Greeks will almost certainly do, if the experience of decimalization in the UK is anything to go by. Also judging by past practice, Greek shopkeepers are unlikely to bother much with shortfalls of 10 cents or less, whether in their favour or yours.

Euro notes exist in **denominations** of 5, 10, 20, 50, 100, 200 and 500 euros, and coins in denominations of 1, 2, 5, 10, 20 and 50 cents and 1 and 2 euros.

usually pay a commission of between one and two percent, though it pays to be aware of any special commission-free deals from your travel agent or your home bank. You can cash the cheques at most banks, though rarely elsewhere. Each travellers' cheque encashment in Greece will incur a minimum commission charge of €1.20–2.40, depending on the bank, for amounts of up to €60 equivalent, so you won't want to make too many small-value transactions. For greater amounts, a set percentage will apply. Make sure you keep the purchase agreement and a record of cheque serial numbers safe and separate from the cheques themselves. In the event that cheques are lost or stolen, the issuing company will expect you to report the loss forthwith; most companies claim to replace lost or stolen cheques within 24 hours.

Small-denomination **foreign bank notes** are also extremely useful, and relatively unlikely to be stolen in Greece. Since the freeing up of all remaining currency controls in 1994, a number of authorized brokers for exchanging foreign cash have emerged in Athens and other major tourist centres. When changing small amounts, choose those bureaux that charge a flat percentage commission (usually one percent) rather than a high minimum. There's also a small number of 24-hour automatic **foreign-note-changing machines** in a few resorts, but again a high minimum commission tends to be deducted.

In 1998, the Greek **post office** largely abandoned the business of changing money – a nuisance, as many tiny islands have a post office but no bank. If you have a UK-based Girobank account, you may still be able to use your chequebook to get money at some remote post offices. You may also find that main post offices (in provincial capitals) are the designated receiving points for Western Union money transfers (see opposite).

Finally, there is no need to **purchase euros** before arrival unless you're coming in at some ungodly hour to one of the remoter land or sea frontier posts, or on a Sunday. Airport arrival lounges will always have an exchange booth or cash dispenser for passengers on incoming international flights.

Credit cards and cash dispensers

Major **credit cards** are not usually accepted by cheaper tavernas or hotels, but they're almost essential for renting cars, for buying Olympic Airways tickets and for expensive souvenirs. Major travel agents may also claim to accept them, though note that a **three-percent surcharge** is often levied on the purchase of ferry (as opposed to air) tickets.

Credit/debit cards are also handy for withdrawing money from the growing network of Greek **cash dispensers** (ATMs); you'll just need to know the PIN numbers for your cards. Larger airports (such as Athens,

Crete, Rhodes, Corfu and Thessaloníki) have at least one cash dispenser in the arrivals hall, and almost any town or island with a population larger than a few thousand (or a substantial tourist traffic) also has them. The best distributed are those of the National Bank/Ethniki Trapeza, the Bank of Piraeus /Trapeza Pireos, and the Commercial Bank/Emboriki Trapeza, which happily and interchangeably accept Visa, MasterCard, Visa Electron, Plus and Cirrus cards; those of the equally widespread Alpha Bank/Alfa Trapeza and its subsidiary the Ionian Bank/Ioniki Trapeza are somewhat more restrictive, accepting only American Express and Visa-affiliated cards.

Cash-dispenser transactions with **debit cards** linked to a cheque account via the Plus/Cirrus systems attract charges of 2.25 percent on the sterling/dollar transaction value, subject to a minimum of £1.75, making them the **least expensive** way of getting money in Greece as long as you withdraw more than £80 equivalent in euros (about €130). By contrast, using **credit cards** at a cash dispenser is one of the **dearest** ways of obtaining cash: a cash advance per-transaction fee of £1.50 minimum typically applies in the UK, plus a "foreign transaction" surcharge of up to 2.75 percent on the total, depending on the card issuer.

Wiring money

All told, learning and using the PIN numbers for any debit or credit cards you have is the quickest and least expensive way of securing moderate amounts of funds from abroad. In an emergency, however, you can arrange to have more substantial amounts of **money wired** from your home **bank to a bank** in Greece. Receiving funds by SWIFT transfer takes a minimum of two working days and up to ten. From the UK, a bank charge of 0.03 percent, with a minimum of £17, maximum £35, is typically levied for two-day service; some building societies charge a £20 flat fee irrespective of the amount. If you choose this route, your home bank will need the address and (ideally) the branch number of the bank where you want to pick up the money. It's unwise to transfer more than the equivalent of €10,000 (currently about US$8500 or £6000); above that limit, as part of measures to combat money-laundering and organized crime, the receiving Greek bank will begin asking awkward questions and imposing punitive commissions.

Having money wired from home using one of the **companies** listed below is never convenient – local affiliate offices other than the post office are thin on the ground in Greece – and is even more expensive than using a bank, and should be considered as a last resort. However, unlike with banks, the funds should be available for collection at Amex's, Thomas Cook's or Western Union's local representative office within hours of being sent.

Money-wiring companies

In the UK and Ireland
Moneygram ☎0800/018 0104, ⓦwww.moneygram.com.
Thomas Cook ☎01733/318922, Belfast ☎028/9055 0030, Dublin ☎01/677 1721.
Western Union Money Transfer ☎0800/833 833, ⓦwww.westernunion.com.

In North America
American Express Moneygram ☎1-800/926-9400, ⓦwww.moneygram.com.
Thomas Cook US ☎1-800/287-7362, Canada ☎1-888 /8234-7328, ⓦwww.us.thomascook.com.
Western Union ☎1-800/325-6000, ⓦwww.westernunion.com.

In Australia
American Express Moneygram ☎1800/230 100, ⓦwww.moneygram.com.
Western Union ☎1800/649 565, ⓦwww.westernunion.com.

In New Zealand
American Express Moneygram ☎09/379 8243 or 0800/262 263, ⓦwww.moneygram.com.
Western Union ☎09/270 0050, ⓦwww.westernunion.com.

Information, maps and websites

The National Tourist Organization of Greece (Ellinikós Organismós Tourismoú, or EOT; GNTO abroad, ⓦ www.gnto.gr) maintains offices in most European capitals, plus major cities in North America and Australia (see below for addresses). It publishes an impressive array of free, glossy, regional pamphlets, which are good for getting an idea of where you want to go, even if the actual text should sometimes be taken with an occasional spoonful of salt. Also available from the EOT are a reasonable fold-out map of the country and a large number of brochures on special interests and festivals.

Tourist offices

In Greece, you will find official **EOT offices** in many of the larger towns and resorts. The principal Athens office is at Amerikís 2, just up from Stadhíou. Here, in addition to the usual leaflets, you can find weekly **schedules** for the inter-island **ferries** – hardly a hundred-percent reliable, but useful as a guideline. EOT staff should be able to advise on current opening hours for local sites and museums, and occasionally can give assistance with accommodation.

Where there is no EOT office, you can get information (and often a range of leaflets) from **municipally run** tourist offices, for example those in Kós and Mólyvos – these are often highly motivated and better than the EOT branches. In the absence of any of these, you can visit the **Tourist Police**, essentially a division (often just a single delegate) of the local police. They can sometimes provide you with lists of rooms to let, which they regulate, but they're really where you go if you have a **serious complaint** about an accommodation or eating establishment.

Greek national tourist offices abroad

Australia 51 Pitt St, Sydney, NSW 2000
☎ 02/9241 1663, ⓔ hto@tpg.com.au.
Canada 91 Scollard St, 2nd Floor, Toronto M5R 1GR, Ontario ☎ 416/968-2220,
ⓔ grnto.tor@sympatico.ca.
Israel 5 Shalom Aleichem Street, Tel Aviv 61262
☎ 03/5170501, ⓔ hellenic@netvision.net.il.
Netherlands Kerkstraat 61, 1017 GC Amsterdam
☎ 20/6254212, ⓔ gnot@planet.nl.

UK 4 Conduit St, London W1R 0DJ ☎ 020/7734 5997, ⓔ EOT-greektouristoffice@btinternet.com.
USA 645 Fifth Ave, New York, NY 10022
☎ 212/421-5777.

The GNTO website lists a dozen more non-English-speaking countries with full tourist offices. If your home country isn't listed there, apply to the embassy. There are no Greek tourist offices in Ireland, South Africa or New Zealand.

Maps

No authoritative, authentic maps . . . . Well, isn't that as it should be? Why does anybody need maps? If an individual wants them he's a spy. If a country needs maps it's moribund. A well-mapped country is a dead country. A complete survey is a burial shroud. A life with maps is a tyranny!

That extract from Alan Sillitoe's unjustly neglected 1971 satire, *Travels in Nihilon*, pretty much sums up the prevailing attitude towards **maps** in Greece, which are an endless source of confusion and often outright misinformation. Each cartographic company seems to have its own peculiar system of transcribing Greek letters into the Roman alphabet – and these, as often as not, do not match the semi-official transliterations on the road signs.

The most reliable **general touring maps** of the Greek islands are those published by the Athens-based Road Editions (ⓦ www.road.gr) and Emvelia Editions (ⓦ www.emvelia.gr). **Road Editions** products are widely available in Greece at selected bookstores, including their own retail outlet in Athens at Ippokrátous 65, and at a surprising number of filling stations and general tourist shops. In Britain they are found at Stanfords (see p.40) and the Hellenic Book Service; in case of difficulty, contact (in Britain) Portfolio, Unit 1C, West Ealing Business Centre, Alexandria Road, London W13 0NJ (☎020/8579 7748). In the US, they're sold exclusively through Map Link (see address on p.40) or Omni Resources, PO Box 2096, Burlington NC 27216 (☎910/227-8300, ⓦwww.omnimap.com). Much newer **Emvelia** currently has just one retail outlet in Athens – Ellinoekdhotiki, at Navarínou 12 – and very sporadic sales points overseas – notably the Hellenic Book Service in London, UK – but this situation is bound to improve.

Having extensively field-tested both brands, we can give no clear answer as to **which is better**. Road Editions products are more intelligently folded and easier to read, but often lack detail; Emvelia tends to show more villages in a busier format. Both are somewhat out-of-date in the matter of current road surfaces. In short, neither is anywhere near perfect, but, based on large-scale military maps not usually available to the public, they're the best you will find. To date their island products include Crete at 1:250,000, plus a steadily growing number of titles for smaller ones, among them Rhodes, Kós, Sýros, Corfu, Thíra, Kéa, Milos, Zákynthos, Ándhros, Sámos, Náxos, Páros, Mýkonos, Kefallonia-Itháki, Kýthira, Paxí and Lefkádha.

If Road products are unavailable, reliable second choices are the growing new series published by **Anavasi**, better known for their mainland mountaineering maps; at present they cover a random selection of isles, including the Sporades and some of the Cyclades.

A good alternative are the **GeoCenter** maps *Greece and the Islands* and *Greek Islands/Aegean Sea*, which together cover the country at a scale of 1:300,000. The single-sided fold-up Freytag-Berndt 1:650,000, with an index, is very nearly as good, and easier to use when driving. Despite mid-1990s revisions and updating, Michelin #980 remains a fourth choice. All these are widely available in Britain and North America, though less easily in Greece. **Freytag-Berndt** also publishes a series of more detailed maps on various regions of Greece, such as the Cyclades and the northeast Aegean islands (in two sheets); these are best bought overseas from specialist outlets, though in Greece they are re-jacketed and distributed by Efstathiadis.

Hiking/topographical maps

Hiking/topographical maps are gradually improving in quality and availability, with a number of companies having a go at loosening the stranglehold which the army has long excercised on detailed information. Most of these commercial products (issued by Road, Korfes magazine or Anavisi) are understandably devoted only to mainland mountain areas and are based on the older maps of the **Yeografikí Ipiresía Stratoú** (Army Geographical Service, or YIS). If you want to obtain these for islands, visit the **YIS** at Evelpídhon 4, north of Aréos Park in Athens, on Monday, Wednesday or Friday from 8am to noon only. All foreigners must leave their passport with the gate guard; EU citizens may proceed directly to the sales hall, where efficient, computerized transactions take just a few minutes. Other nationals will probably have to go upstairs for a vetting interview; if you don't speak reasonably good Greek, it's best to have a Greek friend get them for you.

As of writing, YIS maps covering Crete, the Dodecanese, the east Aegean, Skýros, most of Corfu and much of Epirus, Macedonia and Thrace are still off-limits to all foreigners, as well as Greeks. With matters unsettled across the Balkans, previous plans to lift such restrictions have been shelved indefinitely. A German company, **Harms**, has released a series of five maps at 1:80,000 scale which cover Crete from west to east and show, with about fifty percent accuracy, many hiking routes; despite these defects, they're invaluable until and unless the YIS declassifies this area, and they are available overseas at specialist map outlets.

Finally, for hiking in particular areas of Crete, Corfu, Sámos, Rhodes, Sými, Párga, Pílio, Thássos and Lésvos, maps-with-guide-booklets published by **Marengo Publications** in England also prove very useful. Stanfords keeps a good stock of these, or order from Marengo direct at 17 Bernard Crescent, Hunstanton PE36 6ER ☎01485/532710, ⓦwww.marengo.supanet .com.

Map outlets

UK and Ireland

Blackwell's Map and Travel Shop, 53 Broad St, Oxford OX1 3BQ ☎01865/792792, ⊛www.bookshop.blackwell.co.uk.

Easons Bookshop, 40 O'Connell St, Dublin 1 ☎01/873 3811, ⊛www.eason.ie.

Heffers Map and Travel, 20 Trinity St, Cambridge, CB2 1TJ ☎01223/568568, ⊛www.heffers.co.uk.

Hodges Figgis Bookshop, 56–58 Dawson St, Dublin 2 ☎01/677 4754, ⊛www.hodgesfiggis.com.

James Thin Melven's Bookshop, 29 Union St, Inverness IV1 1QA ☎01463/233500, ⊛www.jthin.co.uk.

John Smith and Sons, 26 Colquhoun Ave, Glasgow, G52 4PJ ☎0141/552 3377, ⊛www.johnsmith.co.uk.

The Map Shop, 30a Belvoir St, Leicester, LE1 6QH ☎0116/2471400.

National Map Centre, 22–24 Caxton St, London SW1H 0QU ☎020/7222 2466, ⊛www.mapsnmc.co.uk.

Newcastle Map Centre, 55 Grey St, Newcastle upon Tyne NE1 6EF ☎0191/261 5622, ⊛www.traveller.ltd.uk.

Ordnance Survey of Northern Ireland, Colby House, Stranmillis Ct, Belfast BT9 5BJ ☎028/9066 1244, ⊛www.osni.gov.uk.

Ordnance Survey Service, Phoenix Park, Dublin 8 ☎01/820 6100, ⊛www.irlgov.ie/osi/.

Stanfords, 12–14 Long Acre, London WC2E 9LP ☎020/7836 1321, ⊛www.stanfords.co.uk; maps by mail or phone order are available on this number and via ⊜sales@stanfords.co.uk. Other branches within British Airways offices at 156 Regent St, W1R 5TA ☎020/7434 4744, and 29 Corn St, Bristol BS1 1HT ☎0117/929 9966.

The Travel Bookshop, 13–15 Blenheim Crescent, London W11 2EE ☎020/7229 5260, ⊛www.thetravelbookshop.co.uk.

US and Canada

Adventurous Traveler Bookstore, PO Box 64769, Burlington, VT 05406 ☎1-800/282-3963, ⊛www.AdventurousTraveler.com.

Book Passage, 51 Tamal Vista Blvd, Corte Madera, CA 94925 ☎415/927-0960, ⊛www.bookpassage.com.

Elliot Bay Book Company, 101 S Main St, Seattle, WA 98104 ☎206/624-6600 or 1-800/962-5311, ⊛www.elliotbaybook.com.

Forsyth Travel Library, 226 Westchester Ave, White Plains, NY 10604 ☎1-800/367-7984, ⊛www.forsyth.com.

Globe Corner Bookstore, 28 Church St, Cambridge, MA 02138 ☎1-800/358-6013, ⊛www.globecorner.com.

GORP Adventure Library online only ☎1-800/754-8229, ⊛www.gorp.com.

Map Link Inc., 30 S La Patera Lane, Unit 5, Santa Barbara, CA 93117 ☎805/692-6777, ⊛www.maplink.com.

Open Air Books and Maps, 25 Toronto St, Toronto ON M5C 2R1 ☎416/363-0719.

Phileas Fogg's Travel Center, #87 Stanford Shopping Center, Palo Alto, CA 94304 ☎1-800/533-3644, ⊛www.foggs.com.

Rand McNally, 444 N Michigan Ave, Chicago, IL 60611 ☎312/321-1751, ⊛www.randmcnally.com; 150 E 52nd St, New York, NY 10022 ☎212/758-7488; 595 Market St, San Francisco, CA 94105 ☎415/777-3131; around thirty stores across the US – call ☎1-800/333-0136 ext 2111 or check the website for the nearest store.

Travel Books & Language Center, 4437 Wisconsin Ave, Washington, DC 20016 ☎1-800/220-2665, ⊛www.bookweb.org/bookstore/travellers.

The Travel Bug Bookstore, 2667 West Broadway, Vancouver V6K 2G2 ☎604/737-1122, ⊛www.swifty.com/tbug.

Traveler's Choice Bookstore, 22 W 52nd St, New York, NY 10019 ☎212/664-0995, ⊜tvlchoice@aol.com.

Ulysses Travel Bookshop, 4176 St-Denis, Montréal, PQ H2W 2M5 ☎514/843-9447, ⊛www.ulysses.ca.

World of Maps, 118 Holland Ave, Ottawa, Ontario K1Y 0X6 ☎613/724-6776, ⊛www.itmb.com.

World Wide Books and Maps, 1247 Granville St, Vancouver V6Z 1G3 ☎604/687-3320, ⊛www.worldofmaps.com.

Australia and New Zealand

The Map Shop, 6 Peel St, Adelaide ☎08/8231 2033, ⊛www.mapshop.net.au.

Mapland, 372 Little Bourke St, Melbourne ☎03/9670 4383, ⊛www.mapland.com.au.

Mapworld, 173 Gloucester St, Christchurch ☎03/374 5399, ⊕03/374 5633, ⊛www.mapworld.co.nz.

Perth Map Centre, 1/884 Hay St, Perth ☎08/9322 5733, ⊛www.perthmap.com.au.

Specialty Maps, 46 Albert St, Auckland ☎09/307 2217, ⊛www.ubd-online.co.nz/maps.

Travel Bookshop, Shop 3, 175 Liverpool St, Sydney ☎02/9261 8200.

Worldwide Maps & Guides, 187 George St, Brisbane ☎07/3221 4330.

Greece on the internet

Greece is strongly represented on the **internet**, with many bilingual English–Greek websites offering information on nearly every conceivable subject. Some of it, however, is little more than propaganda – anything to do with Macedonia, for example, is liable to be pretty over-the-top. Almost every well-visited island will have its own website, though some of these, in bizarre dialects of "Gringlish", are barely readable, while others – mastered by expatriate residents – are fluent enough but rather vague on specifics so as to avoid raising local hackles. Country-wide and regional sites recommended below are reasonably useful, balanced and literate.

ⓦwww.greektravel.com
A subjective, North-American-oriented but highly useful site maintained by North Carolinan Matt Barrett, who's been visiting Greece for over three decades. It contains lots of recommendations, destination thumbnails, tricks and shortcuts, plus hundreds of links to affiliated sites.

ⓦhttp://forecast.uoa.gr
An excellent one-stop site for the temperature, wind direction and rainfall country-wide, maintained by the University of Athens physics faculty. Pick a specific island for an all-parameters report; an English option is available.

ⓦwww.poseidon.ncmr.gr
A Greek oceanographer's site maintained by the National Centre for Marine Research which profiles Aegean weather meticulously, including groovy graphics of sea currents and surface winds, based on satellite imaging. It's slowish but sophisticated, good for yachties and reports one topic (rain, temperature, etc) at a time.

ⓦwww.culture.gr
The Greek Ministry of Culture's website. The best bit is its alphabetical gazetteer to monuments, archeological sites and museums. It's not complete, and the opening hours are probably unreliable, but it does have a lot of info about the more obscure sites.

ⓦwww.athensnews.gr
The online edition of the *Athens News*, Greece's longest-running, quality English-language newspaper, with the day's top stories. It's a bit slow, but easy to find your way around.

ⓦwww.eKathimerini.com/news/news.asp
The online edition of the abridged English translation of *Kathemerini*, one of Greece's most respected dailies. It's fully archived for years back, and has an excellent search facility.

ⓦwww.hellenicbooks.com
The website of the UK's premier Greek bookstore. It posts full, opinionated reviews of its stock, offers the possibility of buying online and has witty descriptions of every island compiled by proprietor Stelios Jackson and his assistant Markos Stefanou.

ⓦwww.ktel.org/frontpage.shtml
Bilingual website of the KTEL, or national bus syndicate. It posts fairly reliable schedules; the main problem is that many areas (including most of the Aegean islands) are not covered.

ⓦwww.gtp.gr
The website of *Greek Travel Pages*, the fat (and expensive) printed manual on every Greek travel agent's desk. It's mostly resorted to for its ferry schedules (also kept on a separate site, ⓦwww.gtpweb.com). It was completely revamped in 2001, though is still not a hundred-percent reliable.

ⓦwww.west-crete.com
Cretophiles' favourite site, with all travel/cultural topics (even a naturists' page) – and not restricted to the west of the island.

ⓦhttp://stigmes.gr/br
An English-summary online edition of what's claimed to be Crete's leading monthly magazine; plus it has lots of links to other Crete-related sites.

ⓦwww.kalymnos-isl.gr
The island's official website, with the English pages edited by expatriate radio journalist and author Faith Warn. The news pages are meaty and current, tourism specifics a bit anodyne.

ⓦwww.lesvos.com
An excellent overview of Lésvos, compiled by Matt Barrett (see above). The restaurant recommendations are particularly reliable – since he's only here a few months of the year, the author can say what he likes.

ⓦwww.symivisitor.com
Current news for aficionados, a range of accommodation, restaurant and beach profiles, presented by the publishers of the monthly island newspaper.

Getting around

Island-hopping is an essential feature of a Greek holiday; the ferry network – supplemented in season by hydrofoils – is extensive, and will eventually get you to any of the 166 inhabited isles. Planes are relatively expensive, at three to four times the cost of a deck-class ferry ticket and almost twice as much as the cheapest cabin berth. They are, however, useful for saving time at the start or finish of a visit, providing critical links between smaller islands and Athens, Thessaloníki, Rhodes and Crete. On the islands themselves, buses provide skeletal connections, which most tourists choose to supplement by renting a scooter, motorbike or car.

Sea transport

Four different types of vessel operate in the Greek islands: medium-sized to large **ordinary ferries** (which operate the main services); **high-speed catamarans**, also medium-sized to large, which match hydrofoils in speed but carry a certain number of cars; **hydrofoils**, which carry only passengers; and local **kaïkia** (small boats which do short hops and excursions in season). Costs are very reasonable on the longer journeys, though proportionately more expensive for shorter, inter-island connections. Short-haul

---

The wreck of the Express Samina – and beyond

September 27, 2000, was a sort of Judgement Day for the Greek domestic ferry industry. Around midnight in gale conditions, the *Express Samina* (née the *Golden Vergina*), the oldest ship in the domestic fleet, slammed full speed into the Pórtes rocks outside Páros harbour in the Cyclades, and sank within minutes. The bridge was unstaffed by senior officers, all of whom were elsewhere watching a football match on television. The British and Greek navies, exercising in the area, plus swarms of fishing boats from Páros, together plucked most of the 500-plus aboard from the water, including numerous foreign tourists, but 82 passengers drowned. It was the worst maritime disaster in Greece since the ferry *Iraklion* went down in December 1966, with 226 casualties.

Skipper Vassilis Yiannakis and the first mate were quickly charged with manslaughter and criminal negligence, and are still on remand, awaiting trial. Once the furore had died down, the pair – especially the captain, who had been involved in two prior collisions – seemed on reflection to be easy scapegoats. The boat had previously been owned by Agapitos Lines, one of several shipping companies swallowed up by Minoan Flying Dolphins in its several-year drive to acquire eighty-percent dominance of the Greek passenger-ferry industry (among larger companies, only ANEK, NEL and DANE have escaped their grasp) – and a near-monopoly on sailings to the Cyclades and the Dodecanese. In this they had been assisted by a previous merchant-marine minister in the PASOK government, who also became a focus of opprobrium, along with Minoan Flying Dolphins management (one of whom, general manager Pandelis Sfinias, committed suicide on November 30 by jumping from the sixth floor of his Pireás headquarters).

It also emerged that the 34-year-old *Express Samina* was the worst but by no means the only rustbucket in the Greek domestic fleet well past its scrap-by date. EU regulations normally require ships to be retired after 27 years of service, but Greek shipping interests had wheedled an extension to 35 years from Brussels – in much the same way that Minoan Flying Dolphins had cajoled the Greek government ministry into granting it, rather than any remaining smaller competitors, licences for any route, profitable or otherwise. With an effective monopoly and regulated fares, there was little incentive (as there is on the Greece–Italy lines) to keep boats up to date. Greek newspapers quickly tallied eighteen ferries 29 years old or older. The age of the *Express Samina* was a critical factor in her rapid sinking; newer craft have multiple airtight compartments, so that a single breach in the hull will not be fatal, but the

lines with monopolies – for example on the Alexandhroúpoli–Samothráki and Kými–Skýros runs – are invariably overpriced.

We've indicated most of the **ferry, catamaran and hydrofoil connections**, both on the maps (see pp.86–87 for a general pattern) and in the "Travel Details" at the end of each chapter. Don't take our listings as exhaustive or wholly reliable, however, as schedules are notoriously erratic, and must be verified each year; details given are essentially for departures between late June and mid-September. **Out-of-season** departure frequencies are severely reduced, with many islands connected only once or twice a week. However, in spring or autumn those ferries that do operate are often compelled by the transport ministry to call at extra or unusual islands, making possible some interesting connections.

The most reliable, up-to-date information is available from the local **port police** (*limenarhío*), which maintains offices at Pireás (☎010/42 26 000) and on or near the harbours of all fair-sized islands. Smaller places may only have a *limenikós stathmós* (marine station), often just a single room with a VHF radio. Their officers rarely speak much English, but keep complete schedules posted – and, meteorological report in hand, are the final arbiters of whether a ship will sail or not in stormy weather conditions. *Apagorevtikó*, or obligatory halt of all seaborne traffic, is applied for weather in excess of force 7 on the Beaufort scale; hydrofoils tend to be confined to port at force 6 or above, with catamarans falling somewhere in between. There are, however, exceptions to this system depending on the direction of the wind (southerlies are considered exceptionally dangerous) and since the sinking of the *Express Samina* (see box) the port police have been erring on the side of caution.

Few ferry companies produce regular **schedule** sheets. The only attempt at an all-inclusive Greek ferry guide is the yearly *Greek Travel Routes, Domestic Sea*

Express Samina had just a single compartment, and was effectively doomed the moment the rocks tore a three-metre gash in her side (though the crew having left bulkhead doors open did not help). Most lifesaving equipment, from the ancient, cork-buoyed lifejackets to the snail-slow lifeboats, was inadequate or scarcely used at the critical hour. Only the year before, an inspection engineer had resigned in protest that his verdict on the boat as unseaworthy was being ignored by Minoan.

The government had to be seen to be doing something, and so made a show of granting some minor routes to Minoan's competitors during the weeks following the sinking, and pushed for a three-year limit on service time for boats in early 2001. It's in the medium term, however, that the fallout from the disaster has had most effect. The oldest members of the domestic fleet were instantly confined to port, pending safety inspections – which several did not pass, leaving a shortfall. Those ships which could be brought into compliance with EU standards were refitted, but clean bills of health were often issued in an arbitrary and biased manner; a loophole in the law allows substandard craft to continue operating if their destination is a non-EU country. As a result, much of 2001 saw very skeletal connections to certain remoter islands; Kastellórizo and Tílos were particularly hard hit, losing their catamaran schedule at mid-season when the boat in question switched to more lucrative ports. In the prevailing climate of protecting profits (and one's legal behind) before service, matters are likely to get worse before they get better. Only a few newly commissioned ferries – such as NEL's high-speed catamarans *Aeolos Express*, *Aeolos Kenderis* and *Aelos Express II* – have taken to the water since the wreck. Investigation of the disaster is still under way, and Minoan Flying Dolphins remains the target of a vast number of civil suits for wrongful death, and a criminal investigation as well – not, perhaps, unrelated to the directors' July 2001 decision to rechristen the company Hellas Flying Dolphins. Terrified of another public-relations disaster in the run-up to Greece's hosting of the 2004 Olympics, the port police have become far stricter about confining boats to port in marginal weather conditions, compounding the effect of already sparse departure frequencies.

The *Rough Guide* authors apologize, therefore, if travel details for ferry routes seem incomplete or pessimistic. Schedules only stabilized (relatively speaking) from July 2001 onward, and the route of the *Express Samina* in particular was not adequately substituted by another craft – for the first time in over half a century, there was no connection from Páros and Náxos to Sámos, and nobody was venturing any guesses as to prevailing conditions in 2002.

Schedules, co-produced by the GNTO and the Greek travel agents' manual the GTP; be prepared to master an array of bewildering abbreviations for ports and shipping companies. The printed guide is available at GNTO/EOT offices, but you'll find a sporadically updated version at ⓦ www.gtpnet.com.

Regular ferries

On most **ferry** routes, your only consideration will be getting a boat that leaves on the day, and for the island, that you want. However, when sailing from **Pireás**, the main port of Athens, to the Cyclades or Dodecanese islands, you should have a choice of at least two, often three, sailings and may want to bear in mind a few of the factors below.

Routes taken and the speed of the boats can vary enormously. A journey from Pireás to Thíra (Thíra), for instance, can take anything from nine to fourteen hours. Prior to buying a ticket it's wise to establish how many stops there will be before your island, and the estimated time of arrival. Many agents act just for one specific boat (they'll blithely tell you that theirs is the only available service), so you may have to ask around to uncover alternatives. Especially in high season, early arrival is critical in getting what may be a very limited stock of accommodation.

Since the *Express Samina* disaster (see box on pp.42–3), a few of the most elderly craft have been consigned to the scrap heap or dumped overseas. Though spanking-new **boats** are still a rarity, you will more often than not be surprised to encounter a former English Channel or Scandinavian fjord ferry, rechristened and enjoying a new lease of life in the Aegean.

Regular ferry **tickets** are, in general, best bought on the day of departure, unless you need to reserve a cabin berth or space for a car. Buying tickets in advance will tie you down to a particular craft at a particular time – and innumerable factors can make you regret that. Most obviously there's bad weather, which, particularly off-season, can play havoc with the schedules, causing some small boats to remain at anchor and others to alter their routes drastically. (The ticket price is refunded if a boat fails to sail.) There are only three periods of the year – March 23–25, the week before and after

Easter, and most of August – when ferries need to be booked at least a couple of days in advance.

Following cases in 1996 of captains loading ferrles to double their rated capacity, **obligatory advance ticketing** was universally introduced in 1998. Staff at the gangway will bar you from embarking if you don't have a ticket, and tickets are absolutely no longer available on board. In many cases there may not even be a last-minute sales booth at the quayside. **Fares** for each route are currently set by the transport ministry and should not differ among ships or agencies, though curiously, tickets for journeys towards Athens are marginally more expensive than those in the opposite direction. There is usually a twenty-percent discount on round-trip fares.

The cheapest class of ticket, which you'll probably automatically be sold, is **deck class**, variously called *tríti* or *gámma thési*. This gives you the run of most boats except for the upper-class restaurant and bar. On the shorter, summer journeys the best place to be, in any case, is on deck – space best staked out as soon as you get on board. However, boats acquired recently seem, with their glaring overhead lights and moulded-plastic bucket seats, expressly designed to frustrate those attempting to sleep on deck. In such cases it's well worth the few extra euros for a **cabin bunk**, especially if you can share with friends (cabins are usually quadruple, occasionally triple or double). Class consciousness is the rule, so deck-class passengers may find themselves firmly locked out of second-class facilities at night to prevent them from crashing on the plush sofas, and may have to make do with pullman-type seats. **First-class** cabins usually cost scarcely less than a plane flight and are not terrific value – the main difference between first and second being the presence of a bathroom in the cabin, and a better location. Most cabins, incidentally, are overheated or overchilled, and pretty airless; ask for an *exoterikí* (outer) cabin if you want a porthole (though these are always bolted shut).

All bookings are now computerized, and supposedly have accurate space allocations that preclude **overbookings**, but occasionally you may be sold a cabin berth at an intermediate port only to find that they are "full" when the boat arrives. Pursers will usually not refund you the difference between a cabin and third class. Your first- or second-class fare entitles you to a bunk, and this is clearly stated (in Greek) on the verso of your ticket. Make a scene if necessary until you are accommodated – there are often cabins in the bilge, set aside for the crew but generally unused, where you can sleep.

Motorbikes and cars get issued extra tickets, in the latter case four to five times the passenger deck-class fare, depending on size. Car fees are roughly proportionate to distance: Sámos–Ikaría is €26–29.50 depending on port and direction, while Sámos–Pireás is about €73.50. This obviously limits the number of islands you'll want to drag a car to – it's really only worth it for the larger ones like Crete, Rhodes, Híos, Lésvos, Sámos, Corfu or Kefalloniá. Even with these, unless you're planning a stay of more than four days, you may find it cheaper to leave your car on the mainland and rent another on arrival. Technically, written permission is required to take rental motorbikes and cars on ferries, though in practice few crew will bother to quiz you on this.

Some ferries sell a limited range of **food on board**, though it tends to be overpriced and mediocre. Honourable exceptions are the meals served by DANE, NEL and all ferries to Crete on their overnight sailings. On the short, daytime hops between the various islands of the Argo-Saronic, Cyclades and Sporades, it's a good idea to stock up beforehand with your own provisions; most ferries on these lines offer nothing other than biscuits, greasy, pre-fab pizzas, coffee and soft drinks.

Hydrofoils and catamarans

Hydrofoils – commonly known as *dhelfínia* or "Flying Dolphins" – are roughly twice as fast (and at least twice as expensive) as ordinary ferries. However, they're a useful alternative to regular ferries if you are pushed for time, and their network can also neatly fill gaps in ferry scheduling. Their main drawback (aside from frequent engine breakdowns) is that they were originally designed for cruising on placid Russian or Polish rivers, and are quite literally out of their depth on the open sea; thus they are extremely sensitive to bad weather, and even in moderate seas are not for the seasick-prone. Most of these services don't operate – or are heavily reduced – from October to June and

are prone to arbitrary cancellation if not enough passengers turn up. Following the *Express Samina* sinking, hydrofoils are no longer allowed to carry scooters or bicycles as in the past.

At present, hydrofoils operate among the **Argo-Saronic** islands close to Athens, among the northern **Sporades** (Évvia, Skiáthos, Skópelos and Alónissos), between Thessaloníki and certain resorts on **Halkidhikí**, between Kavála and Thássos, between Alexandhroúpoli and **Samothráki**, among certain of the **Cyclades** (Ándros, Tínos, Mýkonos, Páros, Náxos, Amorgós, the minor islets, Íos, Thíra), and in the **Dodecanese** and east Aegean among Rhodes, Kós, Kálymnos, Léros and Pátmos, with regular forays up to Sámos, Ikaría and Foúrni, or over to Tílos and Níssyros. Services beyond Sámos to **Híos** and **Lésvos** sputter along unreliably in high season, if at all. The principal mainland ports are Zéa and Flísvos marinas in Pireás, Rafína, Vólos, Áyios Konstandínos and Thessaloníki, as well as Kavála and Alexandhroúpoli. Services in the Argo-Saronic are run by Hellas Flying Dolphins, Saronic Dolphins and Sea Falcon; in the Cyclades by Dolphin Sea Lines and Minoan; and in the Dodecanese or east Aegean by Kiriakoulis Maritime. You may see craft with other livery, but we have excluded them, as they are chartered by tour agencies and do not offer scheduled services controlled by the ministry of transport.

Catamarans have been a prominent feature of Greek maritime life since the late 1990s, attempting to combine the speed of hydrofoils with the (relative) reliability and vehicle-carrying capacity of larger ferries. The fact that they are new and sleek, purpose-built in France or Scandinavia, does not prevent numerous breakdowns, since they are constantly playing catch-up to fill in weather-cancelled itineraries and thus miss necessary maintenance. **Inside** they are rather soulless: ruthlessly air-conditioned, with no deck seating to take the air and the most banal Greek TV blaring at you from numerous aeroplane-type screens. Indeed the whole experience has been likened to **riding on a plane**, right down to the seat type. Cabins are non-existent and food facilities even more minimal than on conventional ferries – after all, you'll be at your destination within six hours, the longest trajectory at present. Car fare rates are normal, though passenger **tickets** are at least double a comparable ferry journey, ie similar to hydro-foil rates.

Small ferries, kaïkia and taxi boats

In season **kaïkia** (caiques) and **small ferries** of a few hundred tonnes' displacement sail between adjacent islands and to a few of the more obscure ones. These can be extremely useful and often very pleasant, but are no cheaper than mainline services. In fact, if they're classified as tourist agency charters, and not passenger lines controlled by the transport ministry, they tend to be quite expensive, with pressure to buy return fares (one-ways are almost always available). The more consistent kaïki links are summarized in the "Travel Details" section of each chapter, though inevitably departures depend on the whims of local boat-owners, so the only firm information is to be had on the quay-side. Kaïkia and small ferries, despite appearances, have a good safety record; indeed it's the larger car-ferries, like the *Iraklion* and the *Express Samina*, that have in the past run into trouble. EU regulations being what they are, however, it seems that many of these smaller boats are doomed for trivial reasons, such as not having a second lavatory. Likely to survive are the swarms of **taxi boats** which are a feature of Sými and Itháki, among other spots; these exist to shuttle clients on set routes to remote beaches or ports which can be only be reached arduously, if at all, overland. Costs on these are generally reasonable, usually per person but occasionally per boat.

Domestic flights

Olympic Airways and its subsidiary Olympic Aviation (ⓦwww.olympic-airways.gr) at present operate most of the **domestic flights** within Greece. They cover a fairly wide network of islands and larger mainland towns, though most routes are to and from Athens or Thessaloníki. Airline operation has been officially deregulated in Greece since 1993, but the only private airlines to have successfully challenged the state-run carrier are the recently merged Aegean-Cronus Airlines (ⓦwww.aegeanair.com and/or ⓦwww.cronus.gr), and newcomer Axon. Aegean-Cronus has cherry-picked the high-volume, high-profit routes between Crete (Haniá and Iráklio), Thíra, Mytilíni, Rhodes, Corfu, Kavála, Ioánnina, Athens and Thessaloníki; Axon, newly appeared in 2001, currently links Athens or Thessaloníki with Sámos, Mýkonos, Thíra, Rhodes and Crete (Haniá and Iráklio), though their Embraor jets are the sleekest and fastest things going domestically. **Tickets** for all three airlines are most easily obtained from travel agents (their own high-street outlets are thin on the ground). Axon and Aegean-Cronus often undercut Olympic price-wise, and surpass it service-wise, though flight frequencies tend to be sparse. This, of course, could change drastically if financially troubled Olympic goes under, as is perennially threatened, and a successor state carrier offers inevitably reduced service.

For the moment, Olympic **schedules** can be picked up at their offices abroad (see "Getting There") or through their branch offices and representatives in Greece, which are maintained in almost every town or island of any size; Greek-only small booklets appear twice yearly (typically October and June), while English-language books geared more for an international readership are published twice yearly (April and October). There are often long gaps in availability, when you'll have to consult the website or closest sales office. Aegean-Cronus has historically produced two booklets per year, in spring and late autumn.

Fares for flights to and between the islands, including the domestic airport tax of about €10, work out around three to four times the cost of a ferry journey, but on certain inter-island hauls that are poorly served by boat (Rhodes–Kastellórizo or Kárpathos–Kássos, for example), you should consider this time well bought. For obscure reasons, flights between Athens and Mílos or Kýthira are slightly better value per air mile, so take advantage.

Island flights are often full in peak season; if they're an essential part of your plans, it is worth trying to make a **reservation** at least a week to ten days in advance. If a flight you've set your heart on is full, **waiting lists** exist – and are worth signing onto at the airport check-in counter; experience has shown that there are almost always one or two no-shows or cancellations. Domestic air tickets are non-refundable, but you can change your flight, space permitting, without penalty as late as a couple of hours before your original departure.

Incidentally, the only surviving Olympic-run **shuttle buses** between the main town and the airport are on Kós, Límnos and Kastellórizo; others have long since been axed as a cost-cutting exercise. In other places (Híos, Rhodes), municipally run services have picked up the slack, but otherwise you're at the mercy of the taxi-drivers who congregate outside the arrivals gate.

Like ferries, flights are subject to **cancellation** in bad weather, since many services are on small, 50- or 68-seat ATR turbo-prop planes, or even tinier Dornier 18-seaters, none of which will fly in strong winds or (depending on the destination airport) after dark. Despite these uncertainties, a flight on a Dornier puddle-jumper is a highly recommended experience. You can watch the crew, who are often on first-name terms with passengers, flicking switches in the cockpit; virtually every seat has a view, and you fly low enough to pick out every island feature – you might even select beaches in advance.

Size restrictions also mean that the 15-kilo baggage weight limit can be fairly strictly enforced, especially on the Dorniers; if, however, you've just arrived from overseas or purchased your ticket outside Greece, you are allowed the 20–23-kilo standard international limit. All services operated on the domestic network are **non-smoking**.

Island ground transport

Most islands have some kind of bus service, but many visitors prefer to rent a two- or four-wheeler. Even if you just do this for a day, you can get the measure of a small or medium-sized island and work out where you'd like to be based.

Buses

Bus services on the **major routes** are highly efficient and frequent. On **secondary roads** they're less regular, with long gaps, but even the remotest villages will be connected – at least on weekdays – by a school or market bus to the island capital. As these often leave shortly after dawn, an alarm clock can be a useful travel aid. Coming in the opposite direction, these local buses usually leave the county town at about 2pm. There are usually buses to connect the port and main town for ferry arrivals or departures.

The network is nationally run by a single syndicate known as the **KTEL** (*Kratikó Tamío Ellinikón Leoforíon*). However, even in medium-sized towns there can be several scattered terminals for services in different directions, so make sure you have the right station for your departure.

Buses are amazingly **prompt** as a rule, so be there in plenty of time for scheduled departures. On small island routes, it's generally first come, first served, with some standing allowed, and tickets dispensed on the spot by an *ispráktoros* or conductor. However, these tickets tend to be issued only up to the next major town, where you'll have to alight briefly and purchase an onward fare (there is always enough time for this).

Motorbikes, scooters and bicycles

The cult of the **motorcycle** is highly developed in Greece, presided over by a jealous deity apparently requiring regular human sacrifice. Accidents among both foreign and local bikers are routine occurrences, with annual fatalities edging into two figures on the busier islands. Some package companies have even taken to warning clients in print against renting motorbikes (thereby making a bit extra on organized overland excursions), but with caution and common sense – and an eye to increasingly enforced regulations – riding a two-wheeler through a resort should be a lot safer than piloting one through London or New York.

Many tourists come to grief on rutted dirt tracks or astride mechanically dodgy machines. In other cases **accidents** are due to attempts to cut corners, in all senses, or by riding two to an underpowered scooter simply not designed to propel such a load. Don't be tempted by this apparent economy – you won't regret getting two separate scooters, or one powerful 100cc bike to share – and remember that you're likely to be charged an exorbitant sum for any repairs if you do have a wipeout. Also, verify that your travel insurance policy covers motorcycle accidents.

One worthwhile precaution is to wear a **crash helmet** (*kránio*); many rental outfits will offer you one, and some will make you sign a waiver of liability if you refuse it. Helmet-wearing is in fact required by law, but few riders (except army conscripts) wear them – though compliance is increasing as police set up random roadblocks to catch offenders. Reputable establishments demand a full motorcycle driving licence for any engine over 90cc (the law actually stipulates "over 50cc"), and you will usually have to leave your passport as security. For smaller models, any driving licence will do.

Small **motor scooters** with automatic transmission, known in Greek as *papákia* (little ducks) after their characteristic noise, are good transport for all but the hilliest islands. They're available for rent on many islands for €11.80–17.80. This specimen rate-range can be bargained down out of peak season, or if you negotiate for a longer period of rental.

Before riding off, make sure you check the bike's **mechanical state**, since many are only cosmetically maintained. Bad brakes and worn or oil-fouled spark plugs are the most common defects; dealers often keep the front brakes far too loose, with the commendable intention of preventing you going over the handlebars. If you break down it's your responsibility to return the machine, so take down the phone number of the rental agency in case it gives out in the middle of nowhere. Better outlets often offer a free retrieval service.

There are vanishingly few true **mopeds** – motor-driven pedal-cycles – remaining in Greece; one or two models are still sold, but none is rented.

As far as **scooters** go, the Piaggio Vespa or Peugeot were always more comfortable than mopeds for long trips, but still aren't very stable on unpaved surfaces. The latest generation of these models is ultra-trendy and practical enough, but thirsty on fuel; a few still don't have kick-starts as backups to the battery. Bungee cords (a *khtapódi* or "octopus" in slang) for tying down bundles are supplied on request, while capacious baskets are also often a feature.

In the family of true **motorbikes** with manual transmissions, the favourite workhorses, in descending order of reliability, are the Honda 50, Yamaha Townmate and Suzuki FB Birdie; gears are shifted with an easy-to-learn left-foot pedal action, and (very important) these can all be push-started if the starting crank fails. They can carry two, though if you have a choice, the Honda Cub 70–90cc series give more power at nominal extra cost, as does the Yamaha 80

Townmate. Best of all is the attractive, 1997-premiered Honda Astrea 100 and its rival-brand clones, very powerful but scarcely bigger than older models.

Cycling

Cycling in Greece is not such hard going as you might imagine (except in midsummer), especially on one of the mountain bikes that are rapidly supplanting the old bone-shakers at rental outfits; they rarely cost more than €6 a day. You do, however, need steady nerves, as roads are generally narrow with no verges or bike lanes (except on Kós), and many Greek drivers consider cyclists a lower form of life, on a par with the snakes regularly found run over.

If you have your own mountain or touring bike (the latter not rented in Greece), you might consider taking it along by **train** or **plane** (it's free if within your 20–23kg international air allowance). Once in Greece you should be able to take a bike for free on most of the ferries, in the guard's van on most trains (for a small fee – it goes on a later goods train otherwise), and with a little persuasion in the luggage bays of buses. Any small spare parts you might need, however, are best brought along, since specialist bike shops are only found in the largest island towns.

Driving and car rental

Automobiles have obvious advantages for getting to the more inaccessible parts of larger islands, but this is one of the more expensive countries in Europe to **rent a car**. If you drive **your own vehicle** to and through Greece, via EU member states, you no longer require a Green Card. In accordance with a 1998 directive, insurance contracted in any EU member state is valid in any other, but in many cases this is only third-party cover – the statutory legal minimum. Competition in the industry is so intense, however, that many UK insurers will throw in full, pan-European cover for free or for a nominal sum, up to sixty days; shop around if necessary.

EU citizens bringing their own cars should no longer get a carnet stamp in their passport, and the car is in theory free to circulate in the country for six months, or until its home-based road tax or insurance expires, whichever comes first. In practice, drivers of **EU cars** are rarely quizzed no matter how long they've been in the country, but if you call attention to yourself, by having an accident for example, the customs has the power to impound the car immediately until or unless you can prove it's been in Greece for less than six months (the ticket for any ferry you may have arrived on from Turkey or Italy is considered sufficient). The **fines** for overstaying are horrendous – effectively triple-priced retroactive road tax – and **import duties**, while beaten down recently, are still likely to be around half the actual value of the vehicle. If you're resident and don't officially import your car, you're only allowed to use a car for six-month periods each year (you choose the time period); the customs affixes a seal between the steering wheel and pedals to enforce "down time", and the vehicle must be kept off-road in your absence.

Other nationalities will get a **non-EU** car entered in their passport; the carnet normally allows you to keep a vehicle in Greece for up to six months, exempt from road tax. It is difficult, though not impossible, to leave the country without the vehicle; the nearest customs post will seal it for you (while you fly back home for a family emergency, for example) but you must find a Greek national to act as your **guarantor**, and possibly pay storage if you don't have access to off-street parking. This person will assume ownership of the car should you ultimately abandon it; you will also need a guarantor for the single, **nine-month extension** you're allowed until the vehicle has to remain under seal for six months, as described above.

Car rental

Car rental on the islands starts at €271–291 a week in high season for the smallest, A-group vehicle from a one-off outlet or local chain, including unlimited mileage, tax and insurance. Overseas tour operators' and international chains' brochures threaten alarming rates of €353–391 for the same period but, except in August, no rental company expects to fetch that price for a car. Outside peak season, at the smaller local outfits, you can sometimes get terms of about €36 per day, all inclusive, with even better rates for three days or more. **Comparison shopping**

among agencies in the larger resorts can yield a variation in quotes of up to twenty percent for the same conditions over a four-to-seven-day period; the most negotiable variable is whether or not kilometres in excess of one hundred per day (a common hidden catch) are free. Open **jeeps**, an increasingly popular extravagance, begin at about €82 per day, rising to as much as €97 at busy times and places.

Note that brochure prices in Greece almost never include tax, **collision damage waiver** (CDW) and personal insurance. CDW in particular is absolutely vital, as the coverage included by law in the basic rental fee is generally inadequate, so check the fine print on your contract. Be careful of the hammering that cars get on dirt tracks; tyres, windshield and the underside of the vehicle are almost always excluded from even supplementary insurance policies. All agencies will want either a **credit card** or a large **cash deposit** up front; minimum age requirements vary from 21 to 23. **Driving licences** issued by any European Union state are honoured, but in theory (and increasingly, in practice) an International Driving Licence is required by all other drivers, including Australians, New Zealanders and North Americans. This must be arranged before departure, as ELPA (the Greek motoring association) no longer issues IDLs to foreign nationals.

In peak season, you may get a better price through one of the **overseas booking companies** that deals with local firms than if you negotiate for rental in Greece itself; this may also be the only way to get hold of a car, at any price, at such times. Competitive companies in Britain include Autos Abroad, Holiday Autos and Transhire (see above). Autorent, Payless, European, Kosmos, National/Alamo, Reliable, Eurodollar and Just are dependable Greek, or smaller international, chains with branches in many towns; all are considerably cheaper than the biggest international operators Budget, Europcar, Hertz and Avis. Specific local recommendations, mostly based on author experience, are given in the guide.

In terms of **models**, many of them unfamiliar to UK/US drivers, the more competitive companies tend to offer the Subaru M80 or Vivio, the Fiat Cinquecento or Seisento and the Suzuki Swift 1000 as A-group cars, and Opel (Vauxhall) Corsa 1.2, Fiat Uno/Punto, Peugeot 106, Hyundai Atos, Citroën Saxo,

Renault Clio or Nissan Micra in the B group. Any more than two adults, with luggage, will generally require B category. The badly designed, underpowered Suzuki Alto 600 or 800, Fiat Panda 750/900 and Seat Marbella should be avoided if at all possible as A-group cars, and indeed have been phased out by the more reputable agencies. The standard four-wheel-drive option is a Suzuki jeep (1.3- or 1.6-litre), mostly open – great for bashing down rutted tracks to remote beaches.

Car-rental agencies

In the UK and Ireland

Autos Abroad ☎0870/066 7788,
🖰www.autosabroad.com.
Avis ☎0870/606 0100, Republic of Ireland
☎01/605 7555, 🖰www.avisworld.com.
Budget ☎0800/181181, 🖰www.go-budget
.co.uk, Republic of Ireland ☎01/878 7814,
🖰www.budget.ie.
Europcar ☎0845/722 2525,
🖰www.europcar.co.uk, Republic of Ireland
☎01/614 2800, 🖰www.europcar.ie.
Hertz ☎0870/844 8844, Republic of Ireland
01/813 3416, 🖰www.hertz.co.uk.
Holiday Autos ☎0870/400 0000,
🖰www.holidayautos.com, Republic of Ireland
☎01/872 9366, 🖰www.holidayautos.ie.
National ☎0870/536 5365,
🖰www.nationalcar.com.
Thrifty ☎01494/751600, Northern Ireland
☎028/9445 2565, 🖰www.thrifty.co.uk.
Transhire ☎01923/834910.

In North America

Alamo ☎1-800/522-9696,
🖰www.alamo.com.
Auto Europe US ☎1-800/223-5555, Canada
☎1-888/223-5555, 🖰www.autoeurope.com.
Avis US ☎1-800/331-1084, Canada ☎1-
800/272-5871, 🖰www.avis.com.
Budget ☎1-800/527-0700,
🖰www.budgetrentacar.com.
Europe by Car ☎1-800/223-1516,
🖰www.europebycar.com.
Hertz US ☎1-800/654-3001, Canada ☎1-
800/263-0600, 🖰www.hertz.com.
Kemwel Holiday Autos ☎1-800/422-7737,
🖰www.kemwel.com.
National ☎1-800/227-7368,
🖰www.nationalcar.com.
Thrifty ☎1-800/367-2277, 🖰www.thrifty.com.

In Australia

Avis ☎13 6333, 🖰www.avis.com.
Budget ☎1300/362 848, 🖰www.budget.com.
Hertz ☎1800/550 067, 🖰www.hertz.com.
National ☎13/1908.
Thrifty ☎1300/367 227, 🖰www.thrifty.com.au.

In New Zealand

Avis ☎09/526 5231 or 0800/655 111,
🖰www.avis.com.
Budget ☎0800/652 227 or 09/375 2270,
🖰www.budget.com.
Hertz ☎09/309 0989 or 0800/655 955,
🖰www.hertz.com.
National ☎09/537 2582.
Thrifty ☎09/309 0111, 🖰www.thrifty.com.nz.

Motoring organizations

In the UK and Ireland

AA ☎0800/444500, 🖰www.theaa.co.uk.
AA Travel Dublin ☎01/617 9988,
🖰www.aaireland.ie.
RAC ☎0800/550055, 🖰www.rac.co.uk.

In North America

American Automobile Association (AAA)
Each state has its own branch of this club –
check the phone book for local address and
phone number (or call ☎1-800/222-4357,
🖰www.aaa.com).
Canadian Automobile Association (CAA)
☎613/247-0117, 🖰www.caa.com. Again, each
region has its own club – check the phone book
for local address and phone number.

In Australia and New Zealand

Australian Automobile Association ☎02/6247
7311.
New Zealand Automobile Association
☎09/377 4660.

Driving in Greece

Greece has the highest **accident rate** in the European Union after Portugal, and on or the larger tourist islands it's easy to see why. Driving habits amongst locals can be atrocious: overtaking is erratic, tailgating and barging out heedlessly from side-roads are preferred pastimes, lane lines and turn signals may as well not exist, and motorbikes hog the road or weave from side to side. **Drunk driving** is also a major problem; Sunday afternoons in rural areas are particularly bad, and for the same reason you should avoid driving late at night at weekends or holidays.

Matters are made worse by poor **road conditions**: signposting is absent or badly placed, pavement markings are faded, asphalt can turn into a one-lane surface or a dirt track without warning on secondary routes, and you're heavily dependent on magnifying mirrors at blind intersections in congested villages. Uphill drivers insist on their **right of way**, as do those first to approach a one-lane bridge; **flashed headlights** usually mean the opposite of what they do in the UK or North America, here signifying that the other driver insists on coming through or overtaking.

Wearing a **seatbelt** is compulsory, as is keeping a first-aid kit in the boot (some rental companies skimp on this), and children under the age of 10 are not allowed to sit in the front seats. It's illegal to drive away from any kind of accident, and you can be held at a police station for up to 24 hours. If this happens, you have the right to ring your consulate immediately to summon a lawyer; don't make a statement to anyone who doesn't speak, and write, very good English. In practice, once police are informed that there was no personal injury, they rarely come out to investigate.

Tourists with proof of AA/RAC/AAA membership are given free road assistance from ELPA, the Greek equivalent, which runs **breakdown services** on several of the larger islands; in an emergency ring their road assistance service on ☎104. Many car-rental companies have an agreement with ELPA's equally widespread competitors Hellas Service and Express Service, which also have three-digit nationwide numbers; however, you will always get a faster response if you dial the local number for the area you're stranded in (ask for these in advance). Any breakdown service is prohibitively expensive to summon on your own – over €120 to enrol as an "instant member" for a year.

Running a vehicle

Petrol/gasoline currently costs €0.76–0.90 per litre for either regular unleaded (amólyvdhi) or super unleaded; leaded four-star will be unavailable after January 1, 2002, with little bottles of additives available for those engines that can't easily digest super unleaded. It is easy to run out of fuel after dark or on weekends in both rural and urban areas; most stations close at 8pm sharp, and nearly as many are shut all day Sunday. There will always be at least one pump per district open on a rota basis, but it's not always apparent which one it is. So always fill up, or insist on full rental vehicles at the outset, and if you've brought your own car, keep a full jerrycan at all times. Some stations which claim to be open around the clock are in fact automated only after-hours – you will have to use bill-taking machines, which don't give change. If you fill your tank without having exhausted your credit, punch the button for a receipt and get change the next day during attended hours (assuming you're still in the area).

Petrol stations run by international companies (BP, Mobil, Shell and Texaco) often take **credit cards**; Greek chains like EKO, Mamidhakis, Jetoil, Revoil and Elinoil usually don't (except in tourist areas). The tiny, generic-petrol stations of the EP chain are always the cheapest around.

Incidentally, a few retro scooters still consume "**mix**" – a red- or green-tinted fuel dispensed from a transparent cylindrical device. This contains a minimum of three percent two-stroke oil by volume; when unavailable, you brew it up yourself by adding to super-grade fuel the necessary amount of separately bottled two-stroke oil (ládhi dhýo trohón in Greek). It's wise to err on the generous side – say five percent – or you risk the engine seizing up.

In terms of **maintenance**, the easiest car models to have serviced and buy parts for in Greece are VWs (including combi and Transporter vans), Mercedes, BMWs, Audis, Opels, Ladas, Skodas and virtually all French, Italian, Korean and Japanese makes. British models are a bit more difficult, but you should be fine as long as you haven't brought anything too esoteric like a Hillman Minx – the Mini is, for example, still very popular in Greece, Fords are present (though not common), and the Opel is of course the continental brand of Vauxhall.

In general, both mechanics' **workshops** and **parts retailers** are clustered at the approach and exit roads of all major towns, usually prominently signposted. For the commonest makes, emergency spares like fan belts and cables are often found at surprisingly remote service stations, so don't hesitate to ask at an unlikely-looking spot. Rural mechanics are okay for quick patch-up jobs like snapped clutch cables, but for major problems it's best to limp into the nearest sizable town to find a mechanic who is factory-trained for your make.

Hitching

Hitching carries the usual risks and dangers, and is inadvisable for women travelling alone, but, overall, Greece is one of the safer countries in which to do it. It's fairly reliable, too, as a means of getting around in remote areas, so long as you're not overly concerned about time; lifts are fairly frequent but tend to be short.

Hitching is easiest in remote areas of the larger islands; at its best, hitching is a useful way of picking up some Greek. While you'll often get lifts from Greeks eager to display or practise their English, there will be as many where to communicate you're forced to try the language. In the more thinly populated rural areas, you'll see numbers of elderly Greeks waving down a ride – you'll be doing a useful service by picking them up, and reciprocating in some small way for the hospitality which is still often the rule in isolated regions.

Taxis

Greek **taxis** are among the cheapest in western Europe – so long as you get an honest driver who switches the meter on and does not use high-tech devices to doctor the reading. Use of the meter is mandatory within city or town limits, where Tariff "1" applies, while in rural areas or between midnight and 5am, Tariff "2" is in effect. On certain islands, such as Kálymnos and Léros, set rates apply on specific fixed routes for "collective" taxis – these only depart when full. Otherwise, throughout Greece the meter starts at €0.75, though the minimum fare is €1.50; any baggage not actually on your lap is charged at €0.15 apiece. Additionally, there are surcharges of €0.90 for leaving or entering an airport, and €0.60 for leaving a harbour area. If you summon a taxi by phone on spec, there's a €1.50 charge, while a pre-arranged rendevous is €1.80 extra; in either case the meter starts running from the moment the driver begins heading towards you. All categories of supplemental charges must be set out on a card affixed to the dashboard. For a week or so before and after Orthodox Easter, and Christmas, a *filodhórima* or gratuity of about ten percent is levied. Any or all of these extras will legitimately bump up the basic meter reading of about €4 per ten rural kilometres.

Accommodation

There are huge numbers of beds for tourists in Greece, so most of the year you can rely on turning up pretty much anywhere and finding a room – if not in a hotel, then in a private house or block of rooms (the standard island accommodation). Only from early July to early September, and around Easter, the country's high season, are you likely to experience problems. At these times, if you don't have accommodation reserved well in advance, you'd be wise to keep well off the main tourist trails, turning up at each new place early in the day and taking whatever is available – you may be able to exchange it for something better later on.

Out of season, you face a slightly different problem: most private rooms – and campsites – operate only from late April or early

May to October, leaving hotels your only option. During winter you may have no choice but to stay in the main towns or ports. There will often be very little life out-side these places anyway, with all the sea-sonal beach bars and restaurants closed. On many smaller islands, you will often find just one hotel – and perhaps one taverna – staying open year-round. Be warned also that any resort or harbour hotels which do operate through the winter are likely to have a certain number of **prostitutes** as long-term guests; licensed prostitution is legal in Greece, and the management reckons this is the most painless way to keep the bills paid.

Hotels

Hotels in the larger resorts are often con-tracted out on a seasonal basis by foreign package-holiday companies, though there are often vacancies available (especially in spring or autumn) for walk-in trade. The tourist police set official **categories** for hotels, which range from "L" (Luxury) down to the rarely encountered "E" class; all except the top category have to keep with-in set price limits. There is talk of replacing the letter system with a star grading sys-tem as in other countries. While they last, letter ratings are supposed to correspond to **facilities** available, though in practice categorization often depends on location within a resort, number of rooms and "influence" with the tourism authorities – there are so-called E-class hotels with under nine rooms which are plusher than nearby C-class outfits. It is mandatory for D-class hotels to have at least some rooms with attached baths; C-class must addi-tionally have a bar or designated breakfast area. The presence of a pool and/or tennis court will attract a B-class rating, while A-category hotels should have a restaurant, bar and extensive common areas. Often these, and the L outfits (essentially self-contained complexes), back onto a quasi-private beach.

In terms of **food**, C-class hotels are required only to provide the most rudimenta-ry of continental breakfasts – you may choose not to take, or pay, for it – while B-class and above will usually offer some sort of buffet breakfast including cheese, cold cuts, sausages, eggs and so on. With some outstanding exceptions, noted in the *guide*, lunch or supper at hotel-affiliated restaurants is bland and poor value.

Hot water

A key variable in both rooms and hotels is the type of water heating. Rooftop **solar units** (*iliaká*), with their nonexistent running costs, are more popular than electric **immersion heaters** (*thermosífona*). Under typical high-season demand, however, solar-powered tanks tend to run out of hot water with the post-beach shower crunch at 6pm, with no more available until the next day. A heater, either as a backup or primary source, is more reliable; proprietors may either jealously guard the boiler controls or entrust you with its workings, which involves either a circuit breaker or a rotary switch turned to "I" for fifteen minutes. You should never shower with a *thermosífono* powered up (look for the glow-lamp indica-tor on the tank) – besides the risk of shock from badly earthed plumbing, it would be fairly easy to empty smaller tanks and burn out the heating element.

Private rooms

The most common island-resort accommo-dation is **privately let rooms** (*dhomátia*). Like hotels, these are regulated and officially divided into three classes (A down to C), according to facilities. These days the bulk of them are in new, purpose-built, low-rise buildings, but a few are still actually in peo-ple's homes, where you'll occasionally be treated to disarming hospitality.

Rooms are almost always scrupulously clean, whatever their other amenities. At their (now all-but-vanished) **simplest**, you'll get a bare, concrete-floored room, with a hook on the back of the door and toilet facil-ities outside in the courtyard. At the **fancier** end of the scale, they are modern, fully fur-nished places with an en-suite bathroom and a fully equipped kitchen shared by guests. Between these extremes there will be a choice of rooms at various prices – owners will usually show you the most expensive first. Some of the cheap places will also have more expensive rooms with en-suite facilities – and vice versa, with rare singles often tucked under stairways or in other less desirable corners of the building. Price and quality are not necessarily directly linked, so always ask to see the room before agreeing to take it.

Accommodation price codes

Throughout the book we've categorized accommodation according to the following **price codes**, which denote the cheapest available double room in high season. All prices are for the room only, except where otherwise indicated in accounts. Many hotels, especially those in category ④ and over, include breakfast in the price; you'll need to check this when booking. During low season, rates can drop by more than fifty percent, especially if you are staying for three or more nights. Exceptions are during the Christmas and Easter weeks when you'll pay high-season prices. Single rooms, where available, cost around seventy percent of the price of a double.

① Up to €24
② €24–33
③ €34–42

④ €43–58
⑤ €59–72
⑥ €73 and upwards

Note: Youth hostels typically charge €7–9 for a dormitory bed.

Areas to **look for rooms**, along with recommendations of the best places, are included in the *guide*. As often as not, however, the rooms find you: owners descend on ferry or bus arrivals to fill any space they have, sometimes waving photos of the premises. In smaller places you'll often see rooms advertised, sometimes in German (*Zimmer*); the Greek signs to look out for are "ENIKIAZÓMENA DHOMÁTIA" or "ENIKIÁZONTEH DHOMÁTIA". In the more developed island resorts, where package holidaymakers predominate, *dhomátia* owners will often require you to stay for at least three days, or even a week.

It has become standard practice for rooms proprietors, like hotel staff, to ask to keep your **passport** – ostensibly "for the tourist police", who do require customer particulars – but in reality to prevent you skipping out with an unpaid bill. Some owners may be satisfied with just taking down your details, as is done in hotels, and they'll almost always return the documents once you get to know them, or if you need them for another purpose.

If you are **stranded**, or arrive very late in a remote island village, you may very well find that there is someone with an unlicensed room prepared to earn extra money by putting you up. This should not be counted on, but things work out more often than not. Otherwise, the most polite course is to have a meal or drink at the taverna or kafenío and then, especially in summer, enquire as to the possibility of sleeping either in the vacant schoolhouse or in a spare room at the *kinotikó grafío* (community records office).

Old-fashioned, 1970s-vintage rooms on the remoter islets, occasionally still without private bath, tend to fall into the ① price category. Standard, en-suite rooms without cooking facilities weigh in at ②; newer, well-amenitied rooms and self-catering studios occupy the top end of the ③ niche, along with the more modest C-class hotels, the better among these edging into ④. The top half of ④ corresponds fairly well to the better-value B-class hotels and the humbler designer inns in popular centres like the trendier Cyclades, while ⑤ tallies with most of B-class and the really state-of-the-art restoration projects. ⑥ means A- and L-class, and the sky's the limit here – €150 is by no means unheard of these days.

Prices in any establishment should by law be displayed on the back of the door of your room, or over the reception desk. If you feel you're being overcharged at a place which is officially registered, threaten to report it to the tourist office or police, who will generally adopt your side in such cases. A hotelier is free to offer a room at any amount under the official rate, but it's an offence to charge one euro-cent over the permitted price for the **current season**. Depending on location, there are up to three of these: typically October to May (low), June to mid-July, and September (mid) and mid-July through August (high). Small amounts over the posted price may be legitimately explained by municipal tax or out-of-date forms. More commonly you will find that you have bargained so well, or arrived so far out of high season, that you are actually paying far less than the maximum prices – which are in any case optimistically pitched for a few high-traffic days in the year.

In **winter**, officially from November 1 until early April, private rooms – except in Ródhos Old Town and the biggest towns of Crete – are closed pretty much across the board to keep the few open hotels in business. There's no point in traipsing about hoping to find exceptions; most owners obey the system very strictly. If they don't, the room-owners will find you themselves and, watching out for hotel rivals, guide you back to their place.

Villas and long-term rentals

The easiest – and usually most economical – way to arrange a **villa rental** is through one of the package-holiday companies detailed on p.15. They represent some superb places, from fairly simple to luxurious, and costs can be very reasonable, especially if shared between a few people. Several of the companies we list will arrange "**multi-centre**" stays on two islands over two weeks.

On the islands, a few local travel agents arrange villa rentals, though they are often places the overseas companies gave a miss on or could not fill. **Out of season**, you can sometimes get a good deal on villa or apartment rental for a month or more by asking around locally, though in these days of EU convergence and the increasing desirability of the islands as year-round residences, "good deal" means anything under €160 per month for a large studio (*garsoniéra*) or €205 for a small one-bedroom flat.

Hostels and monasteries

The Greek islands are not exactly packed with **youth hostels** (*xenón neótitos* in the singular), – just a few on Thíra, Rhodes and Crete, mostly not officially recognized by the IYHF. Of those that do exist the majority tend to be pretty run-down and/or filthy, and thus a far cry from similar north European institutions. Competition from unofficial "student hostels" (see below) and inexpensive rooms means that they are not as cost-effective as elsewhere in Europe. It's best to have a valid IYHF card, but you can often buy one on the spot, or maybe just pay a little extra for your bed. Dorms tend to have three to six beds; most hostels have a curfew at 11pm or midnight, and many places only open in spring and summer.

The tradition of offering hospitality to travellers (of the appropriate sex) at Greek **monasteries** and **convents** is more common on the mainland than on the islands, so you should always ask locally before heading out to one for the night. Also, dress modestly – shorts for men and women, and short skirts are total anathema – and try to arrive early in the evening, not later than 8pm or sunset (whichever is earlier).

Camping

Officially recognized campsites range from ramshackle compounds to highly organized and rather soulless complexes, formerly run by EOT prior to privatization. Most places cost just under €4 a night per person, slightly less per tent and €7.50 per camper van, but at the fanciest sites, rates for two people plus a tent can add up to the price of a basic room. Generally, you don't have to worry about leaving tents or other equipment unattended at wardened campsites; Greeks are very honest. The main risk, alas, comes from other campers. The Panhellenic Camping Association publishes an annual booklet covering most officially recognized Greek campsites and the facilities they offer; it's available from many EOT offices.

Camping rough – outside authorized campsites – is such an established element of Greek travel that few people realize that it's officially illegal. Since 1977 "freelance" camping, as EOT calls it, has actually been forbidden by a law originally enacted to harass gypsies, and regulations are increasingly enforced. Another drawback is the increased prevalence of theft in rural areas, often by bands of refugees from Albania and other north Balkan states. All told, you will feel less vulnerable inside a tent, camper van or even a rock-cave – not that rain is likely during the long Greek summer, but some protection is essential from wind, sun, insects (see "Health", p.32) and stray animals raiding your food. You will always need at least a light sleeping bag, since even summer nights can get cool and damp; a foam pad is also recommended for pitching on harder ground.

If you do camp rough, it's vital to exercise sensitivity and discretion. Police will crack down on people camping (and especially littering) around popular tourist beaches, particularly when a large community of campers develops. Off the beaten track, however, nobody is very bothered, though it is always best to ask permission locally in the village taverna or café. During high season, when everything – even the authorized campsites – may be full, attitudes towards camping rough are more relaxed, even in the most touristed places. At such times the best strategy is to find a sympathetic taverna, which in exchange for regular patronage will probably be willing to guard small valuables and let you use their facilities.

Eating and drinking

Greeks spend a lot of time socializing outside their homes, and sharing a meal is one of the chief ways of doing it. The atmosphere is always relaxed and informal, and pretensions (and expense-account prices) are rare outside of the more chi-chi parts of Athens and certain major resorts. Greeks are not prodigious drinkers – tippling is traditionally meant to accompany food – though since the mid-1990s a whole range of bars and pubs has sprung up, both in tourist resorts and as pricey music halls at the outskirts of the major towns.

Breakfasts, picnic fare and snacks

Greeks don't generally eat **breakfast**, so the only egg-and-bacon kind of places are in resorts where foreigners congregate, or where there are returned North American or Australian Greeks. Such spots can some-times be fairly good value (€4.50–6.50 for the works, maybe even with "French" filter coffee), especially if there's competition. More indigenous alternatives are yoghurts at a *galaktopolío* (milk bar), or cheese pies and pretzel rings from a bakery (see "Snacks", opposite).

Picnic fare

Picnic fare is good, cheap and easily available at bakeries and *manávika* (fruit-and-veg stalls). **Bread**, alas, is often of minimal nutritional value and inedible within a day of purchase. It's worth paying extra at the bakery (*foúrnos* or *psomádhiko*) for *olikís* (wholemeal), *sikalísio* (rye bread), *oktásporo* (eight-grain) or even *enneásporo* (nine-grain), the latter types most commonly baked where large numbers of Germans or Scandinavians are about. When buying **olives**, go for the fat Kalamáta or Ámfissa ones; they're more expensive, but tastier. However, locally gathered olives – especially the slightly shrivelled *hamádhes* or fully ripened, ground-gathered olives – often have a distinctive nutty taste, compensating for large kernels. The best **honey** is reckoned to be the pure-thyme variety from the more barren islands (such as Límnos, Náxos and Astypálea), although it's about double the price of ordinary honeys.

Honey is an ideal topping for the famous local **yoghurt**, which is not confined to the bland Fage-brand stuff of the UK supermarket. All of the larger island towns have at least one dairy shop where locally produced yoghurts are sold in plastic or (better) clay containers of various sizes. Sheep-milk yoghurt is richer and sweeter, scarcely requiring honey; cow-milk yoghurt is tarter but more widely available. Side by side with these will be *krémes* (custards) and *ryzógala* (rice puddings) in one-serving plastic containers.

Feta cheese is ubiquitous – sometimes, ironically, imported from Holland or Denmark, though this is being clamped down on, and local brands are usually better and not much more expensive. The goat's-milk variety can be very dry and salty, so ask for a taste before buying. If you have access to a fridge, leaving the cheese overnight in a plastic container filled with water will solve both problems, though if left too long like this the cheese simply dissolves. This sampling advice goes for other indigenous cheeses as well, the most palatable of which are the expensive gruyère-type *graviéra*.

Despite membership of the EU, plus growing personal incomes and exotic tastes, Greece imports very little garden produce from abroad, aside from bananas and a few mangoes. **Fruit** in particular is relatively expensive and available only by season, though in the more cosmopolitan spots it is possible to find such things as avocados (light-green ones from Crete are excellent) for much of the year. Reliable picnic fruits include *yiarmádhes*, a variety of giant peach available during August and September; *krystália*, tiny, hard green pears that ripen a month or two later and are heavenly; and the *himoniátiko* melon (called casava in North America) which appears at the same time, in its yellow, puckered skin with green flecks. Greece also has a burgeoning kiwi industry, and while the first crop in October coincides with the end of the tourist season, availability carries over into the following May. Less portable, but succulent, are **figs** (*sýka*); there's a crop of large fruits in May, followed by smaller ones in August. Salad **vegetables** are more reasonably priced; besides the famous, enormous tomatoes (June to September), there is a bewildering variety of springtime greens, including rocket, dill, enormous spring onions and lettuces. Useful expressions for shopping are *éna tétarto* (250g) and *misó kiló* (500g).

Snacks

Traditional **snacks** can be one of the distinctive pleasures of Greek eating, though they are being increasingly edged out by an obsession with *tóst* (toasted sandwiches) and other Western junk/fast food at nationwide chains such as Goody's (burgers), Everest and Grigoris Mikroyevmata (assorted), Roma Pizza and Theios Vanias (baked pastries) – somewhat less insipid for being homegrown. However, independently produced kebabs (*souvlákia*) are widely available, and in most larger resorts and towns you'll find *yíros* – doner kebab with garnish in thick, doughy *píta* bread that's closer to Indian naan bread.

Other common snacks include *tyrópites* (cheese pies) and *spanokópites* (spinach pies), which can usually be found at the

baker's, as can *kouloúria* (crispy pretzel rings sprinkled with sesame seeds) and *voutímata* (dark biscuits heavy on the molasses, cinnamon and butter).

Restaurants

Greek cuisine and **restaurants** are simple and straightforward. There's usually no snobbery about eating out; everyone does it regularly, and it's still reasonable – typically €9–13 per person for a substantial (non-seafood) meal with a measure of house wine. Even if the cooking is simple, you should expect it to be wholesome; Greeks are fussy about freshness and provenance and do not willingly or knowingly like to eat frozen New Zealand lamb chops, farmed fish or pre-fried chips.

That said, there's a lot of **lazy cooking** about – especially in resorts, where menus are dominated by pizza, spaghetti and chops. Amongst seasoned Greek travellers, the term "tourist moussaká" – the dish heavy with cheap potato slices, and nary a crumb of mince – is shorthand for this kind of low-grade culinary fraud. Sending unacceptable food back is the only potential way to raise the standard of resort dining.

Of late you find growing numbers of what the Greeks call "**kultúra**" restaurants, often pretentious attempts at Greek nouvelle cuisine with speciality wine lists, which tend to be long on airs and graces, and (at €17.50–23.50 a head) short on value. The exceptions which succeed have been singled out in the text.

When choosing a restaurant, the usual best strategy is to go where the Greeks go. And they go late: 2pm to 3.30pm for **lunch**, 9pm to 11pm for **supper**. You can eat earlier, but you're likely to get indifferent service and cuisine if you frequent establishments catering to the tourist schedule. Chic appearance is not a reliable guide to quality; often the more ramshackle, traditional outfits represent the best value. One good omen is the waiter bringing a carafe of refrigerated water, unbidden, rather than pushing you to order bottled stuff.

In busy resort areas, it's wise to keep a wary eye on the **waiters**, who are inclined to urge you into ordering more than you want, then bring things you haven't ordered. Although cash-register receipts are required in all establishments, these are often only for the grand total, and itemized **bills** will be in totally illegible Greek script. Where prices are printed on menus, you'll be paying the right-hand (higher) of the two columns, inclusive of all taxes and usually service charge, although a small extra tip of about ten per-cent directly to the waiter is hugely appreci-ated – and usually not expected.

Bread costs extra, but consumption is not obligatory; unless it is assessed as part of the cover charge, you have the right to send it back without paying for it. You'll be consid-ered deviant for refusing it, but so much Greek bread is inedible sawdust that there's little point in paying extra unless you actually want to use it as a scoop for dips.

Children are always welcome, day or night, at family tavernas, and Greeks don't mind in the slightest if they play tag between the tables or chase the **cats** running in men-dicant packs – which you should not feed, as signs often warn you They are wild and pretty desperate, and you'll need a doctor's visit and tetanus jab if they whack at a dan-gled bit of food and claw your hand instead.

Estiatória

There are two basic types of restaurant: the *estiatório* and the **taverna**. Distinctions between the two are slight, though the for-mer is more commonly found in large towns and tends to have the slightly more compli-cated dishes termed *mayireftá* (literally, "cooked"). With their long hours, old-fashioned-tradesmen's clientele and tiny profit margins, *estiatória* are, alas, something of a vanishing breed.

An *estiatório* will generally feature a variety of such oven-baked casserole dishes as *moussakás*, *pastítsio*, meat or game stews like *kokinistó* and *stifádho*, *yemistá* (stuffed tomatoes or peppers), the oily vegetable casseroles called *ladherá* and oven-baked meat and fish. Usually you go into the kitchen and point at the desired steam trays to choose these dishes.

Batches are cooked in the morning and then left to stand, which is why this *mayireftá* food is often **lukewarm** or even cold. Greeks don't mind this (most actually believe that hot food is bad for you), and dishes like *yemistá* are actually enhanced by being allowed to cool off and stand in their own juice. Similarly, you have to specify if you want your food with little or no oil (*horís*

ládhi), but once again you will be considered a little strange since Greeks regard olive oil as essential to digestion (and indeed it is the healthiest of the vegetable oils, even in large quantities).

Desserts (*epidhórpia* in formal Greek) of the pudding-and-pie variety don't exist at *estiatória*, and yoghurt or cheese only occa-sionally. Fruit, however, is always available in season; watermelon (often on the house), melon and grapes are the summer stan-dards. Autumn treats worth asking after include *kydhóni* or *akhládhi stó foúrno*, baked quince or pear with some sort of syrup or nut topping.

Tavernas and psistariés

Tavernas range from the glitzy and fashion-able to rough-and-ready ones with seating under a reed canopy, behind a beach. Really primitive ones have a very limited (often unwritten) menu, but the more established will offer some of the main *mayireftá* dishes mentioned above, as well as the standard taverna fare. This essentially means **mezé-dhes** (hors-d'oeuvres) or *orektiká* (appetiz-ers) and *tís óras* (meat and fish, fried or grilled to order).

Psistariés or grill-houses serve spit-roasted lamb, pork or goat (generically termed *kon-dosoúvli*), grilled chicken (*kotópoulo skáras*) or *kokorétsi* (grilled offal roulade). They will usually have a limited selection of mezédhes and salads (*salátes*), but no *mayireftá* at all.

Since the idea of courses is foreign to Greek cuisine, starters, main dishes and sal-ads often arrive together unless you request otherwise. The best thing is to order a selec-tion of *mezédhes* and salads to share, in true Greek fashion. Waiters encourage you to take the *horiátiki saláta* – the so-called Greek **salad**, including feta cheese – because it is the most expensive. If you only want tomato, or tomato and cucumber, ask for *domato-saláta* or *angourodomáta*. *Láhano-karóto* (cabbage-carrot) and *maroúli* (lettuce) are the typical winter and spring salads respec-tively.

The most interesting **mezédhes** are *tzatzíki* (yoghurt, garlic and cucumber dip), *melitzanosaláta* (aubergine/eggplant dip), *kolokythákia tiganitá* (courgette/zucchini slices fried in batter) or *melitzánes tiganités* (aubergine/eggplant slices fried in batter), *yígandes* (white haricot beans in vinaigrette or hot tomato sauce), *tyropitákia* or *spanakópites* (small cheese and spinach pies), *revythókeftedhes* or *pittaroúdhia* (chickpea patties similar to falafel), *okhtapódhi* (octopus) and *mavromátika* (black-eyed peas).

Among **meats**, *souvláki* (shish kebab) and *brizóles* (chops) are reliable choices, often locally produced. In both cases, pork (*hirinó*) is usually better and cheaper than veal (*moskharísio*). The best *souvláki*, though not often available, is lamb (*arnísio*). At *psistariés*, meaty lamb shoulder chops (*kopsídha*) are more substantial than the scrawny rib chops called *païdhákia*; roast lamb (*arní psitó*) and roast kid (*katsíki stó fournó*) are considered *estiatório* fare. *Keftédhes* (breadcrumbed meatballs), *biftékia* (similar, but meatier) and the spicy, home-made, coarsegrain sausages called *loukánika* are cheap and good. *Kotópoulo* (chicken), especially grilled, is widely available but typically battery-farmed in Epirus or on Évvia. Other dishes worth trying are stewed goat (*gídha vrastí*) or baked goat (*katsíki stó foúrno*) – goat in general is a wonderfully healthy meat, typically free-range, undosed with antibiotics or hormones.

As in *estiatória*, traditional tavernas offer fruit rather than sticky **desserts**, though nowadays these are often available, along with coffee, in tavernas frequented by foreigners.

Fish and seafood

Seaside *psarotavérnes* offer **fish**, though for the inexperienced, ordering can be fraught with peril. Summer visitors get a relatively poor choice of fish, most of it frozen, farmed or imported from Egypt and North Africa. Drag-net-trawling is prohibited from the end of May until the beginning of October, when only lamp-lure (*grí-grí*), trident, "doughnut" trap (*kýrtos*) and multi-hook line (*paragádhi*) methods are allowed. During these warmer months, such few fish as are caught tend to be smaller and dry-tasting, and are served with butter sauce. Taverna owners often comply only minimally with the requirement to indicate when seafood is **frozen** (look for the abbreviation "kat.", "k" or just an asterisk on the Greek-language side of the menu).

Given these considerations, it's often best to set your sights on the **humbler**, seasonally migrating or perennially local species. The cheapest consistently available fish are *gópes* (bogue), *atherína* (sand smelts) and *marídhes* (picarel), eaten head and all, best rolled in salt and sprinkled with lemon juice. In the Dodecanese, *yermanós* (same as Australian leatherback) is a good frying fish which appears in spring; *gávros* (anchovy) and *sardhélles* (sardines) are late summer treats, at their best in the northeast Aegean. In the north Aegean or around Pílio, *pandelís* or *sykiós* (Latin *Corvina nigra*, in French "corb") is caught in early summer, and is highly esteemed since it's a rock-dweller not a bottom feeder – and therefore a bit pricier than the preceding. In autumn especially you may encounter *psarósoupa* (fish broth) or *kakaviá* (a bouillabaisse-like stew).

The **choicer** varieties, such as *barboúni* (red mullet), *tsipoúra* (gilt-head bream), *lavráki* (seabass) or *fangrí* (common bream), will be expensive if wild – anywhere from €26.50–41 per kilo, depending on what the market will bear. If the price seems too good to be true, it's almost certainly **farmed**. Prices are usually quoted by the kilo, and should be not much more than double the street-market rate, so if a type of bream is €14.70 a kilo at the fishmonger's, expect it to be not more than €30 at the taverna. Standard procedure is to go to the glass-fronted cooler and pick your own specimen, and have it weighed (cleaned) in your presence.

Vegetarians

If you are **vegetarian**, you may be in for a hard time, and will often have to assemble a meal from various *mezédhes*. Even the excellent standbys of yoghurt with honey, *tzatzíki* and Greek salad begin to pall after a while, and many of the supposed "vegetable" dishes on menus are cooked in stock and have pieces of meat added to liven them up. Wholly or largely vegetarian restaurants, however, are slowly on the increase in touristy areas; this guide highlights them where appropriate.

Cheaper **seafood** (*thalassiná*) such as *kalamarákia* (fried baby squid, usually frozen) and *okhtapódhi* (octopus) are a summer staple of most seaside tavernas, and occasionally *mýdhia* (mussels), *kydhónia* (cockles) and *garídhes* (small prawns) will be on offer at reasonable prices. Keep an eye out, however, to freshness and season – mussels in particular are a common cause of stomach upsets or even mild poisoning.

As the more favoured species have become overfished, **unusual seafoods**, formerly the exclusive province of the poor, are putting in a greater appearance on menus. Ray or skate (variously known as *platý*, *seláhi*, *trígona* or *vátos*) can be fried or used in soup, and is even dried for decoration. Sea urchins (*ahiní*) are also a humble (and increasingly rare) favourite, being split and emptied for the sake of their (reputedly aphrodisiac) roe that's eaten raw. Only the reddish ones are gravid; special shears are sold for opening them if you don't fancy a hand full of spines. Many a quiet beach is littered with their halved carapaces, evidence of an instant Greek picnic.

Wines

Both *estiatória* and tavernas will usually offer you a choice of bottled **wines**, and many still have their own house variety: kept in barrels, sold in bulk by the quarter-, half- or full litre, and served either in glass flagons or the brightly coloured tin "monkey-cups" called *kantária*. Not as many tavernas stock their own wine as once did, but it's worth asking whether they have wine *varelísio* (barrelled) or *hýma* (in bulk). You should expect to pay €3.50–5 per litre, with smaller measures priced proportionately. Non-resinated wine is almost always more than decent. **Retsina** – pine-resinated wine, a slightly acquired taste – is also available straight from the barrel, though the bottled brands Yeoryiadhi from Thessaloníki, Malamatina from central Greece (often cut with soda water), and Cambas from near Athens, are all excellent and likely to be more consistent in quality.

Among the **bottled wines** available **nationwide**, Cambas Attikos, Boutari Lac des Roches, any white from Zítsa and the Rhodian CAIR products (especially the Moulin range) are good, inexpensive whites, while Boutari Naoussa and Kourtakis Apelia are decent, mid-range reds. If you want a better but still moderately priced red, go for the Merlot of either Boutari and Tsantali, or Averof Katoï from Epirus.

If you're travelling around **wine-producing islands**, however, you may as well go for **local bottlings**; the best available guide to the emerging Greek domaines and vintners is Nico Manessis' *The Illustrated Greek Wine Book* (see p.599 in *Contexts* for ordering information). Almost anything produced on Límnos is decent; the Alexandrine muscat is now used for whites, the local *límnio* grape for reds and rosés. Thíra, another volcanic island, has a number of premium white products such as Ktima Arghyrou and Boutari Nykhteri, and the Gentilini Robola white of Kefalloniá is justly esteemed. Páros (Moraïtis) and Náxos also both have acceptable local vintages, while Crete is now beginning to have labels superior to the bog-standard Logado, such as Economou (Sitía) and Lyrakis (Iráklio). On Rhodes, Alexandhris products from Émbonas are well thought of, as is the Emery label with its Villaré white, and CAIR's dry white "2400".

Curiously, island red wines (except for Rhodes's CAIR Moulin and Emery Cava) are almost uniformly mediocre; in this respect you're better off choosing **reds from the mainland**. Carras from Halkidhikí does the excellent Porto Carras, while Ktima Tselepou offers a very palatable Cabernet-Merlot blend. Antonopoulos Yerontoklima (Pátra), Ktima Papaïoannou Nemea (Peloponnese), and Tsantali Rapsani (Thessaly) are all superb, velvety reds – and likely to be found only in the better *kultúra* tavernas or *káves* (bottle shops). Antonopoulos, Tselepos (Mantinia domaine) and Papaïoannou also do excellent **mainland whites**.

The other **premium micro-wineries** on the mainland whose products have long been fashionable, in both red and white, include the vastly overrated Hatzimihali (Atalánti, central Greece), Spyropoulos (central Peloponnese), Athanasiadhi (central Greece), Skouras (Argolid) and the two rival Lazaridhi vintners (Dhráma, east Macedonia), especially their superb Merlots. For any of these you can expect to pay €7–10 per bottle in a shop, double that at a taverna.

Last but not least, CAIR on Rhodes makes its very own "**champagne**" ("naturally sparkling wine fermented en boteille", says the label), in both brut and demi-sec versions. It's not Moët & Chandon quality by any means, but at less than €6 per bottle, who's complaining...

Cafés, cake shops and bars

The Greek eating and drinking experience encompasses a variety of other places beyond restaurants. Most importantly, there is the institution of the **kafenío**, found in every town, village and hamlet in the country. In addition, you'll come across **ouzerís**, *zaharoplastía* (Greek patisseries) and *barákia*.

The kafenío

The **kafenío** (plural "kafenía") is the traditional Greek coffee shop or café. Although its main business is "Greek" (Middle Eastern) coffee – prepared *skéto* or *pikró* (unsweetened), *métrio* (medium) or *glykó* (sweet) – it also serves spirits such as oúzo (see below), brandy (usually Metaxa or Botrys brand, in three grades), beer, tea (either sage-based tea known as *alisfakiá*, or British-style) and soft drinks. Another refreshing drink sold in cafés is *kafés frappé*, iced, jigger-shaken instant coffee with or without milk and sugar, which is uniquely Greek despite its French-sounding name. Like Greek coffee, it is always accompanied by a welcome glass of cold water. Standard fizzy soft drinks are also sold in all kafenía.

Usually the only **edibles** available are "spoon sweets" or *glyká koutalioú* (sticky, syrupy preserves of quince, grape, fig, citrus fruit or cherry) and the traditional but now-vanishing *ipovrýhio*, a piece of mastic submerged in a glass of water like a submarine – which is what the word means in Greek.

Like tavernas, kafenía range from the plastic, chrome and sophisticated to the old-fashioned, spit-on-the-floor or mock-retro variety, with marble or brightly painted metal tables and straw-bottomed chairs. An important institution anywhere in Greece, they form the pivot of life in the country villages. You get the impression that many men spend most of their waking hours there. Greek women are rarely to be seen in the more traditional places – and foreign women may sometimes feel uneasy or unwelcome in these establishments. Even in holiday resorts, you will find that there is at least one coffeehouse that the local men have reserved for themselves.

Some kafenía close at siesta time, but many remain open from early in the morning until late at night. The chief summer socializing time is 6–8pm, immediately after the siesta. This is the time to take your pre-dinner oúzo, as the sun begins to sink and the air cools down.

Oúzo, mezédhes, ouzerís and mezedhopolía

Oúzo and *tsikoudhiá* (Crete) are simple spirits of up to 48 percent alcohol, distilled from grape-mash residue left over from wine-making, and then usually flavoured with herbs such as anise or fennel. There are nearly thirty name brands of oúzo, with the best reckoned to be from Lésvos and Sámos; inferior ones are either weak (such as the Rhodian Fokiali, at forty percent) or spiked with molasses or grain alcohol to "boost" them.

When you order, you will be served two glasses: one with the oúzo, and one full of water to be tipped into your oúzo until it turns a milky white. You can drink it straight, but the strong, burning taste is hardly refreshing if you do. It is increasingly common to add **ice cubes** (*pagáki*), a bowl of which will be provided upon request. The next measure up from a glass is a *karafáki* – a deceptively small 200ml vial.

A much smoother variant of oúzo is **soúma**, found chiefly on Rhodes and Sámos, but in theory anywhere grapes are grown. The smoothness is deceptive – two or three glasses of it and you had better not have any other firm plans for the afternoon.

Until the 1980s, every oúzo you ordered was automatically accompanied by a small plate of **mezédhes** on the house: bits of cheese, cucumber, tomato, a few olives, sometimes octopus or even a couple of small fish. Unfortunately, these days "oúzo mezédhes" is a separate, more expensive option on a price list. Often, however, they are not featured on any formal menu, but if you order a *karafáki* you will automatically be offered a small selection of snacks.

Though they are confined to the better resorts and select neighbourhoods of the larger islands and towns, one kind of drinking establishment specializes in oúzo and mezédhes. These are called **ouzerí** (same in the Greek plural, we've added 's' to the hybrid). In some towns you may also come across *mezedhopolía*, basically a bigger, more upmarket kind of ouzerí. Ouzerís are well worth trying for the marvellous variety of mezédhes they serve (though lately numbers of mediocre tavernas have counterfeited the name). At the genuine article, several plates of mezédhes plus drinks will effectively substitute for a more involved meal at a taverna (though it usually works out more expensive if you have a healthy appetite). Faced with an often bewilderingly varied menu, you might opt for the *pikilía* (medley, assortment) available in several sizes, the largest and most expensive one usually heavy on the seafood. At other ouzerís the language barrier may be overcome by the waiter wielding an enormous *dhískos* or tray laden with all the current cold offerings – you pick the ones you like the look of.

Sweets, breakfast and western coffee

Similar to the kafenío is the *zaharoplastío*, a cross between café and patisserie, serving coffee, alcohol, yoghurt with honey and sticky cakes.

The better establishments offer an amazing variety of pastries, cream-and-chocolate confections, honey-soaked Greco–Turkish sweets like *baklavás*, *kataïfi* (honey-drenched "shredded wheat"), *loukoumádhes* (deep-fried batter puffs dusted with cinnamon and dipped in syrup), *galaktoboúreko* (custard pie) and so on.

If you want a stronger slant towards the dairy products and away from the pure sugar, seek out a *galaktopolío*, where you'll often find *ryzógalo* (rice pudding – rather better than the English canned variety), *kréma* (custard) and locally made *yiaoúrti* (yoghurt), best if it's *próvio* (from sheep's milk).

Ice cream, sold principally at the gelaterie which have swept over Greece of late (*Dhodhoni* is the posh chain), can be very good and almost indistinguishable from Italian prototypes. A scoop (*baláki*) costs €0.90–1.30; you'll be asked if you want it in a cup (*kypelláki*) or a cone (*konáki*), and whether you want toppings like *santí* (whipped cream) or nuts. By contrast, the mass-produced brands like Delta or Evga are pretty average, with the exception of Skandalo and Nirvana labels; Häagen-Dazs is also widely available and identical to its north European profile. A sign reading "PAGOTÓ POLÍTIKO" or "KAÏMÁKI" means

that the shop concerned makes its own Turkish-style ice cream – as good as or better than the usual Italian version – and the proprietors are probably of Asia Minor or Constantinopolitan descent.

Both *zaharoplastía* and *galaktopolía* are more family-oriented places than the kafenío, and many also serve a basic **continental breakfast** of *méli me voútyro* (honey poured over a pat of butter) or jam (all kinds are called *marmeládha* in Greek; ask for *portokáli* – orange – if you want proper marmalade) with fresh bread or *friganiés* (melba-toast-type slivers). You are also more likely to find proper (*evropaïkó*) tea and non-Greek coffee.

"Nes"(café) has become the generic term for all instant **coffee**, regardless of brand; it's generally pretty vile, and since the mid-1990s there's been a nation-wide reaction against it. Even in the smallest provincial capital or resort there will be at least one trendy café which does a range of foreign-style coffees – filter, dubbed *fíltros* or *gallikós* (French), cappuccino and espresso – at overseas prices.

Bars – and beer

Bars (*barákia* in the plural), once confined to towns, cities and holiday resorts, are now found all over Greece. They range from clones of Parisian cafés or Spanish bodegas to seaside cocktail bars, with music or TV running all day. At their most sophisticated, however, they are well-executed theme venues in ex-industrial premises or Neoclassical houses that can hold their own against close equivalents in Spain or London, with western (currently techno, dub or ambient) soundtracks.

For this and other reasons, drinks are invariably more expensive than in a café. Bars are, however, most likely to stock a range of **beers**, mostly foreign labels made locally under licence at just one or two breweries on the central mainland. However, since 1996 several genuinely **local new formulae** have appeared: Mythos, a smooth lager in a green bottle, put out by the Boutari vintners; Pils Hellas, a sharp pilsner; and last but not least, the resurrected Fix, for years until its demise in 1980 Greece's only beer, though not (according to those who remember) much better the second time around than the first. Kronenberg 1664 and Kaiser are two of the more common quality **foreign-licence** varieties, with the latter available in both light and dark. Bland, inoffensive Amstel and the increasingly rare, yeasty Henninger are the two cheapies; the Dutch themselves claim that Amstel is better than the one available in Holland, and Amstel also makes a very palatable, strong (seven percent) **bock**. Heineken, still referred to as a "*prássini*" by bar and taverna staff after its green bottle, despite the advent of Mythos, is too harshly sharp for many. Since 1993 a tidal wave of even pricier, genuinely imported German beers, such as Bitburger, Fisher and Warstein (plus a few British ones), has washed over the fancier resorts. A curiosity – confined to Corfu and Paxí – is *tsitsibýra* (ginger beer), a holdover from the nineteenth-century British occupation of the Ionian islands; cloudy, greyish-white and fizzy, it tastes vaguely of lemon and the sour beginnings of fermentation in its little bottle.

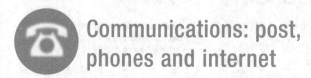

Communications: post, phones and internet

Postal services

Post offices are open Monday to Friday from 7.30am to 2pm, though certain main branches have hours until the evening and on Saturday morning.

Airmail letters from the mainland take three to seven days to reach the rest of Europe, five to twelve days to get to North America, and a bit longer for Australia and New Zealand. Generally, the larger the island (and the planes serving its airport), the quicker the service. Postal rates for up to 20g fall within the normal EU range: €0.60 for postcards or letters to Europe, North America or Australasia. For a modest fee (about €3) you can shave a day or two off delivery time to any destination by using the **express service** (*katepígonda*). **Registered** (*systiméno*) delivery is also available for a similar amount, but proves quite slow unless coupled with express service. If you are sending large purchases or excess baggage home, note that **parcels** should and often can only be handled in the main provincial or county capitals. This way, your bundle will be in Athens, and on an international flight, within a day. Always present your box open for inspection, and come prepared with tape, twine and scissors – most post offices will sell cardboard boxes, but nothing to actually close the package.

For a simple letter or card, a stamp (*grammatósimo*) can also be purchased at a *períptero* (kiosk). However, the proprietors charge ten percent commission on the cost of the stamp, and never seem to know the current international rates.

Ordinary **post boxes** are bright yellow, express boxes dark red, but it's best to use only those by the door of an actual post office, since days may pass between collections at other street-corner or wall-mounted boxes. If you are confronted by two slots, "ESOTERIKÓ" is for domestic mail, "EXOTERIKÓ" for overseas. Often there are more: one box or slot for mail into Athens and suburbs, one for your local province, one for "other" parts of Greece, and one for overseas; if in doubt, ask someone.

The **poste-restante** system is reasonably efficient, especially at the post offices of larger towns. Mail should be clearly addressed and marked "poste restante", with your surname underlined, to the main post office of whichever town you choose. It will be held for a month and you'll need your passport to collect it.

Phones

Making **telephone calls** is relatively straightforward, though the **OTE** (Organismós Tiliepikinoníon tís Elládhos, the state-run telecom) has historically provided some of the worst service in the EU. However, since the mid-1990s this has improved drastically,

Useful phone codes and numbers

Phoning Greece from abroad

Dial the international access code (given below) + 30 (country code) + area code (minus initial 0) + number

Australia ☎ 0011   Canada ☎ 011   Ireland ☎ 010   New Zealand ☎ 00   UK ☎ 00   US ☎ 011

Phoning abroad from Greece

Dial the country code (given below) + area code (minus any initial 0) + number

Australia ☎ 0061   Canada ☎ 001   Ireland ☎ 00353   New Zealand ☎ 0064   UK ☎ 0044   US ☎ 001

Greek phone codes

Athens ☎ 010

Corfu ☎ 06610

Iráklion ☎ 0810

Kefalloniá ☎ 06710 (west), ☎ 06740 (east)

Kós ☎ 02420

Mýkonos ☎ 02890

Páros ☎ 02840

Pátra ☎ 0610

Rhodes ☎ 02410

Thíra ☎ 02860

Skiáthos ☎ 04270

Thessaloníki ☎ 0310

Zákynthos ☎ 06950

Local call rate (like UK's ☎ 0845) ☎ 0801

Mobiles ☎ 093, ☎ 094, ☎ 095, ☎ 097

Toll-free/Freefone ☎ 0800

Useful Greek telephone numbers

Ambulance ☎ 166

ELPA Road Service ☎ 104

Fire brigade, urban ☎ 199

Forest fire reporting ☎ 191

Operator ☎ 132 (Domestic)

Operator ☎ 161 (International)

Police/Emergency ☎ 100

Speaking clock ☎ 141

Tourist police ☎ 171 (Athens); ☎ 01-171 (elsewhere)

Phone charge-card operator access numbers from Greece

AT&T USA Direct ☎ 00 800 1311

Australia ☎ 00 800 6111

Australia (Optus) ☎ 00 800 6121

Bell Atlantic ☎ 00 800 1821

Bell South ☎ 00 800 1721

British Telecom ☎ 00 800 4411

Canada Direct ☎ 00 800 1611

MCI ☎ 00 800 1211

NTL (ex-Cable and Wireless) ☎ 00 800 4422

Sprint ☎ 00 800 1411

---

and rates have dropped dramatically, under the twin threats of privatization and competition from thriving local mobile networks.

All land-line exchanges are supposed to become **digital** (*psifiakó*) by the year 2002, but until this project is complete you may still encounter a few **pulse-analogue** (*palmikó*) exchanges. When ringing long-distance on such circuits, you must wait for a critical series of six electrical crunches on the line after dialling the country or Greek area code, before proceeding.

Call boxes, poorly maintained and invariably sited at the noisiest street corners, work only with phone cards; these come in four sizes – 100 units, 200 units, 500 units and 1000 units – and are available from kiosks and newsagents. Not surprisingly, the more expensive cards are the best value in terms of euros per unit. Despite numbers hopefully scribbled

on the appropriate tabs, call boxes cannot be rung back; however, green, countertop card phones kept by many hotels can be rung.

If you won't be around long enough to use up a phonecard (the cheapest is about €3), it's probably easier to make **local calls** from a *períptero* or **street kiosk**. Here the phone may be connected to a meter (if not, there'll be a sign saying *móno topikó*, "local only"), and you pay after you have made the call. Local, one-unit calls are reasonable enough (about €0.15 for the first three minutes), but long-distance ones add up quickly.

Other options for calling include a bare handful of **counter coin-op phones** in bars, kafenía and hotel lobbies; these should take small euro coins – probably five-cent, ten-cent, twenty-cent and fifty-cent denominations – and, unlike kerbside phone boxes, can be rung back. Most of them are made in northern Europe and bear instructions in English. You'll probably want to avoid making long-distance calls **from hotel rooms**, as a minimum one hundred percent surcharge will be slapped on – we've heard tales of triple and quadruple markups, and since hotels apparently have the legal right to do this, complaining to the tourist police is unlikely to get you anywhere.

For **international** (*exoterikó*) **calls**, it's again best to use kerbside card-phones. You can no longer make metered calls from Greek telecoms offices (the OTE) themselves – most keep daytime hours only and offer at most a quieter card-phone or two. Like BT Phoneshops in the UK, they are mainly places to get Greece-based service (including OTE's own mobile network Cosmote), pay your bills, and buy one of an array of phones and fax machines for sale. **Faxes** are best sent from post offices and some travel agencies – at a price; receiving a fax may also incur a small charge.

Overseas phone calls with a 100-unit card will **cost**, approximately, €0.40 per minute to all EU countries and much of the rest of central Europe, North America and Australia – versus €0.28 per minute on a private subscriber line. There is no particular cheap rate for overseas calls to these destinations, and dialling countries with problematic phone systems like Russia, Israel or Egypt is obviously rather more. **Within Greece**, undiscounted **rates** are €0.16 per minute on a subscriber line, rather more from

Changes to Greek phone codes

As we go to press, we are advised that all **area codes** in Greece are set to change in early 2002, owing to the Greek telecoms running out of land lines. A "0" is to be added to the end of each area code (thus Athens will become 010, Pátra 0610, Ioánnina 06510, etc). In anticipation of this change, we have amended area codes accordingly throughout the *Guide*. It is also anticipated that callers will be obliged to dial all digits (code plus subscriber number) whether they're in the same area code or not, as in France. In effect this means that there will be no more area codes in Greece, merely ten-digit numbers, though this could not be absolutely confirmed at the time of research.

a card-phone; a twenty percent discounted rate applies daily from 10pm to 8am, and from 10pm Saturday until 8am Monday.

Charge-card call services from Greece back to the home country are provided in the UK by British Telecom (☏0800/345144, 📧www.chargecard.bt.com), and NTL (ex-Cable & Wireless, ☏0500/100505); in North America, Canada Direct, AT&T (☏0800/890 011, then 888 641 6123 when you hear the AT&T prompt to be transferred to the 24-hr Florida Call Centre), MCI and Sprint; in Australia, Optus (☏1300/300 937) or Telstra (☏1800/038 000), and in New Zealand Telecom NZ (☏04/801 9000). There are now a few local-dial numbers with some providers (given in the box opposite) which enable you to connect to the international network for the price of a one-unit call, and then charge the call to your home number – usually cheaper than the alternatives.

Mobile phones

Mobile phones are an essential fashion accessory in Greece, which has the highest per-capita usage in Europe outside of Italy – in a population of roughly 11 million, there are claimed to be 6.5 million mobile handsets in use. There are three **networks** at present: Panafon-Vodafon, Telestet and Cosmote. Calling any of them from Britain, you will find that costs are exactly the same as calling a fixed phone – so you won't need to worry about ringing them when given as alternative numbers for accommodation – though of course such numbers are pricey when rung locally. **Coverage** country-wide is fairly good, though there is a number of "dead" zones on really remote islets. **Pay-as-you-go**, contract-free plans are heavily promoted in Greece (such as Telestet B-Free and Panafon-Vodafon À La Carte), and if you're going to be around for a while – for example, studying, or working for a season in the tourist industry – an outlay of €90 or less will see you to a decent apparatus and your first calling card (though you can spend up to €200 for flash models). This lasts up to a year – even if you use up your talk time you'll still have an incoming number, along with a voice-mail service. Top-up calling cards – predicted to be in denominations of €6, €15 and €18 depending on the network – are available at all *períptera*.

If you want to use your **home-based mobile abroad**, you'll need to check with your phone provider whether it will work. North American users will only be able to use tri-band rigs in Greece. Any GSM mobile from the UK, Australia or New Zealand should work fine in Greece.

In the UK, for all but the very top-of-the-range packages, you'll have to inform your service network before going abroad to get international access ("**roaming**") switched on. You may get charged extra for this depending on the terms of your package and where you are travelling to. You are also likely to be charged extra for **incoming calls** when abroad, as the people calling you will be paying the usual rate; discount plans are available to reduce the cost of forwarding the call to you overseas by as much as seventy percent. If you want to **retrieve messages** while you're away, you'll have to ask your provider for a new access number, as your home one (or one-stroke "mail" key) is unlikely to work abroad.

In terms of **call charges**, experience (and examining UK-based bills) has shown that the local network that you select out of the three local networks makes little difference: depending on the length of the call, chat back to the UK (including voice-mail retrieval) works out at £0.49–55 per minute; ringing land-lines within Greece is £0.23–0.26 per minute; and calling Greek mobiles ranges from £0.30 to 0.43 per minute – all significantly more than using a card-phone, but worth it to most for the convenience and privacy.

Email and internet

Email and internet use has caught on in a big way in Greece; electronic addresses or websites are given in this guide for the growing number of travel companies and hotels that have them. For your own email needs, you're best off using the various **internet cafés** which have sprung up in the larger towns – street addresses are given where appropriate. Rates tend to be about €4.50 per hour maximum, often less.

Ideally you should sign up in advance for a free **internet email address** that can be accessed from anywhere, for example YahooMail or Hotmail – accessible through ⓦ www.yahoo.com and ⓦ www.hotmail .com. Once you've set up an account, you can use these sites to pick up and send mail from any internet café, or hotel with internet access.

Alternatively, you can lug **your own laptop** around, not such a burden as they get progressively lighter. You will need about 2m of North American-standard cable (UK ones will *not* work), lightweight and easily purchasable in Greece, with RJ-11 male terminals at each end. The Greek **dial tone** is discontinuous and thus not recognized by most modems – instruct it to "ignore dial tone". Many newer hotel rooms have RJ-11 **sockets**, but some older ones still have their phones hard-wired into the wall. You can get around this problem with a female-female **adaptor**, either RJ-11- or 6P6C-configured, available at better electrical retailers. They weigh and cost next to nothing, so carry both (one is sure to work) for making a splice between your cable and the RJ-11 end of the cable between the wall and phone (which you simply unplug). You will usually have to dial an initial "9" or "0" to get around the hotel's central switchboard for a proper external dial tone.

Compuserve and AOL definitely have **points of presence** in Greece, but more obscure ISPs may also have a reciprocal agreement with Greek-based ISPs like forth-net.gr and otenet.gr, so ask your provider for a list of any available dial-up numbers. **Piggybacking charges** tend to be fairly high, but for a modest number of minutes per day, still work out rather less than patronizing an internet café.

The media

Although the Greek press and airwaves have been relatively free since the fall of the colonels' dictatorship in 1974, nobody would ever propose the Greek media as a paradigm of responsible or objective journalism. Papers are almost uniformly sensational, state-run radio and TV often biased in favour of the ruling party, and private channels imitative of the worst American programming. Most visitors will tune all this out, however, seeking solace in the music of private radio stations, or the limited number of English-language publications.

British **newspapers** are fairly widely available in Greece at a cost of €2–2.50 for dailies, or €3.50–4.20 for Sunday editions. You'll find one-to-two-day-old copies of *The Times*, *The Telegraph*, *The Independent* and *The Guardian*'s European edition, plus a few of the tabloids, in all the resorts as well as in major towns. American and international alternatives include the turgid *USA Today* and the slightly more readable *International Herald Tribune*, the latter including as a major bonus a free though somewhat abridged English translation of the respected Greek daily *Kathimerini* (online at ⓦwww.eKathimerini.com; see also below). Among numerous foreign **magazines**, *Time* and *Newsweek* are also widely available.

There are relatively few surviving **locally produced** English-language magazines or papers. The late lamented **magazine** *The Athenian* folded in 1997 after 23 years, with a rather sloppy successor, *Atlantis*, rising less than phoenix-like from the ashes. Marginally better is the expensive, glossy *Odyssey*, produced every other month by and for wealthy diaspora Greeks, and little different from the average in-flight magazine. By far the best of the English-language **newspapers** is the four-colour *Athens News* (daily except Monday, online at ⓦwww.athensnews.gr; €1.50) in colour with good features and Balkan news, plus entertainment and arts listings on Friday, available in most resorts.

Before setting out from the **UK**, there are two **Greece-specific periodicals** well worth consulting. One is the *Anglo-Hellenic Review* (£2), published twice yearly by the Anglo-Hellenic League; it has excellent essays by renowned scholars, and good reviews of recently issued books on Greek topics.

Obtain it either from the Hellenic Book Service (see p.600) or The Hellenic Centre, 16/18 Paddington St, London W1M 4AS. The other is the Greek London Embassy's almost monthly newsletter, *Greece: Background-News-Information*. Though it's clearly pro-government to the point of verging on propaganda, it's well written (even humorous), giving a lively overview of events in the country over the past few weeks. To register on their mailing list (free), contact them on ☎020/7727 3071, ⓕ7727 8960 or email ⓔofficepress@compuserve.com.

Greek publications

Many papers have ties (including funding) with specific **political groups**, which bias tends to decrease the already low quality of Greek dailies. Among these, only the **centrist** *Kathemerini* – whose former proprietress Helen Vlahos attained heroic status for her defiance of the junta – approaches the standards of a major European newspaper. *Eleftherotypia*, once a PASOK mouthpiece, now aspires to more independence, and has links with Britain's *The Guardian*; *Avriani* has taken its place as the PASOK cheerleading section. *Ta Nea* is a highly popular, MOR tabloid, vaguely similar to London's *The Evening Standard* and much loved for its extensive small ads. On the far **Left**, *Avyi* is the Eurocommunist/Synaspismós forum with literary leanings, while *Rizospastis* acts as the organ of the KKE (unreconstructed Communists). *Ethnos* became notorious some years back for receiving covert funding from the KGB to act as a disinformation bulletin. At the other end of the political spectrum, *Apoyevmatini* generally supports the **centre-right** Néa

Dhimokratía party, while *Estía's* no-photo format and reactionary politics are both stuck somewhere at the beginning of the twentieth century. The ultra-nationalist, lunatic fringe is staked out by paranoid *Stohos* ("Our Goal: Greater Greece; Our Capital: Constantinople").

Among **magazines** that are not merely translations of overseas titles, *Takhydhromos* is the respectable news-and-features weekly, *Ena* is more sensationalist, *Klik* a crass rip-off of Britain's *The Face*, while *To Pondiki* (The Mouse) is a satirical weekly revue in the same vein as Britain's *Private Eye*; its famous covers are spot-on and accessible to anyone with minimal Greek. More specialized niches are occupied by low-circulation titles such as *Adhesmatos Typos* (a slightly rightist, muckraking journal) and *Andí*, an intelligent bi-weekly somewhat in the mould of Britain's *New Statesman and Society*.

Radio

If you have a **radio** on your personal stereo, playing dial roulette can be rewarding. Greek music programmes are always accessible (if variable in quality), and since abolition of the government's former monopoly of wavelengths, regional stations have mushroomed; indeed the airwaves are now positively cluttered as every island town sets up its own studio and transmitter. The two state-run channels are ER1 (a mix of news, talk and popular music) and ER 2 (strictly popular music).

On heavily touristed islands like Rhodes, Corfu and Crete, there will usually be at least one station on the FM band trying its luck at English-moderated programming by and for foreigners. The Turkish state radio's Third Channel is also widely (if somewhat unpatriotically) listened to on border islands for its classical, jazz and blues programmes. The **BBC World Service** broadcasts on short wave throughout Greece; 6.18, 9.41, 15.07 and 12.09 MHz are the most common frequencies. However, it has been announced that short-wave services are to be phased out in many parts of the world, so if you can't live without them consult Ⓦ www.bbc.co.uk/worldservice, which lists all their global frequencies. The **Voice of America**, with its transmitters on Rhodes, can be picked up in most of the Dodecanese on medium wave.

Television

Television first appeared in Greece in 1965, but it only became dominant during the 1967–74 junta, with the ruling colonels using it as a means of social control and to purvey anodyne variety revues, sports events and so on. As in many countries, it transformed the Greeks from a nation of live performers and coffee-house habitués to introverted stay-at-homes, which dovetailed nicely with the junta's "family values".

Greece's centralized, government-controlled **TV stations**, ET1, NET and (out of Thessaloníki) ET3, nowadays lag behind private, mostly rather right-wing channels – Antenna, Star, Alpha and Makedonia TV – in the ratings. Mega is the one possible exception to the rule of private dross, recently taken on by the Boutos family and improved beyond recognition. On NET, news summaries in English are broadcast daily at 6pm. Programming on all stations has evolved little since junta days, tending to be a mix of soaps (especially Italian, Spanish and Latin American), game shows, westerns, B-movies and sports. All foreign films and serials are broadcast in their original language, with Greek subtitles. Except for the nearly-round-the-clock channels Mega, Star, Alpha and Antenna, most channels broadcast from around noon until the small hours. Numerous **cable and satellite** channels are received, including CNN, MTV, Filmnet, Euronews (in English), French TV5 and Italian Rai Due. The range available depends on the area (and hotel) you're in.

Opening hours and public holidays

It is virtually impossible to generalize about Greek **opening hours**, except to say that they change constantly. The traditional timetable starts at a relatively civilized hour, with shops opening between 8.30 and 9.30am, then runs through until lunchtime, when there is a long break for the hottest part of the day. Most places, except banks and government offices, may then reopen in the mid- to late afternoon.

Tourist areas tend to adopt a slightly more northern European timetable, with shops and offices, as well as the most important archeological sites and museums, usually open throughout the day.

Business and shopping hours

Most **government agencies** are open to the public on weekdays from 8am to 2pm. In general, however, you'd be optimistic to show up after 1pm expecting to be served the same day, as queues can be long. Private businesses, or anyone providing a service, frequently operate a straight 9am-to-5/6pm schedule. If someone is actually selling something, then they are more likely to follow a split shift as detailed below.

Shopping hours during the hottest months are theoretically Monday, Wednesday and Saturday from approximately 9am to 2.30pm, and Tuesday, Thursday and Friday from 8.30am to 2pm and 6 to 9pm. During the cooler months the morning schedule shifts slightly forward, the evening session a half or even a full hour back. There are, however, many exceptions to these rules by virtue of holidays and professional idiosyncrasy, so it's best not to count on getting anything done except from Monday to Friday, between 9.30am and 1pm. It's worth noting that **delis** and **butchers** are not allowed to sell fresh meat during summer afternoons (though some flout this rule); similarly **fishmongers** are only open in the morning until they sell out (usually by noon), as are **pharmacies**, which additionally are shut on Saturday (except for the duty pharmacist).

Ancient sites and monasteries

All the major **ancient sites** are now fenced off and, like most **museums**, charge **admission fees** ranging from a token €1.50 to a whopping €6, with an average fee of around €2.40. At most of them reductions of twenty-five to thirty percent apply to senior citizens, and fifty percent to students with proper identification – students from the EU with proper ID will often get in free. In addition, entrance to all state-run sites and museums is **free** to all EU nationals on Sundays and public holidays from November to March – non-EU nationals are unlikely to be detected as such unless they go out of their way to advertise the fact.

Opening hours vary from site to site. As far

Public holidays

January 1
January 6
March 25
First Monday of Lent (variable Feb/March; see below)
Easter weekend (variable April/May; see below)
May 1
Pentecost or Whit Monday (50 days after Easter; see below)
August 15
October 28
December 25 and 26

Variable religious feasts

Lenten Monday
| 2002 | March 18 |
| 2003 | March 10 |

Easter Sunday
| 2002 | May 5 |
| 2003 | April 27 |

Whit Monday
| 2002 | June 24 |
| 2003 | June 16 |

as possible, individual times are quoted in the text, but bear in mind that these change with exasperating frequency, and at smaller sites may be subject to the whim of a local *fýlakas* or site guard. Unless specified, the times quoted are generally summer hours, in effect from around late May to the end of September. Reckon on similar days but later opening and earlier closing in winter. Note also that the **last admission ticket** is typically sold fifteen or twenty minutes before the cited closing time.

Along with your ticket, most sites and museums will provide a little colour **folding pamphlet** prepared by the *Tamío Arheoloyikón Porón* (Archeological Receipts Fund); they usually include an accurate if potted history and site or gallery plan, and we've found them to be uniformly excellent, in stark contrast to the often miserable labelling of the sites or galleries themselves.

Serious students will therefore want to invest in **site guides** or **museum catalogues**, which have often been expertly compiled by the excavating archeologists or curators.

Smaller sites generally close for a long lunch and **siesta** (even where they're not supposed to), as do **monasteries**. The latter are generally open from 9am to 1pm and 5 to 8pm (3.30 to 6.30pm in winter) for limited visits. Most monasteries impose a fairly strict **dress code** for visitors: no shorts on either sex, with women expected to cover their arms and wear skirts; the necessary wraps are sometimes provided on the spot.

It's free to take **photos** of open-air sites, though museum photography and the use of videos or tripods anywhere requires an extra fee and written permit. This usually has to be arranged in writing from the nearest Department of Antiquities (*Eforía Arheotíton*). It's also worth knowing that Classical studies students can get a free annual pass to all Greek museums and sites by presenting themselves at the office on the rear corner (Tossítsa/Bouboulínas) of the National Archeological Museum in Athens – take documentation, two passport-sized photographs and be prepared to say you're a teacher.

Festivals and cultural events

Many of the big Greek popular festivals have a religious basis, so they're observed in accordance with the Orthodox calendar. Give or take a few saints, this is similar to the regular Catholic liturgical year, except for Easter, which can fall as many as five (but usually one or two) weeks to either side of the western festival – in 2001 the two coincided (a very rare event). Other festivals are cultural in nature, with the highlight for most people being to catch a performance of Classical drama in one of the country's ancient theatres. There's also a full programme of cinema and modern theatre, with something on offer in even the smallest town at some point during the year.

Easter

Easter is by far the most important festival of the Greek year – infinitely more so than Christmas – and taken much more seriously than it is anywhere in western Europe, aside from Spain. From Wednesday of Holy Week until the following Monday, the state radio and TV networks are given over solely to religious programmes.

The **festival** is an excellent time to be in

Greece, both for its beautiful religious ceremonies and for the days of feasting and celebration that follow. The mountainous island of **Ídhra** with its alleged 360 churches and monasteries is the prime Easter resort, but unless you plan well in advance you have no hope of finding accommodation at that time. Other famous Easter celebrations are held at Corfu, Pyrgí on Híos, Ólymbos on Kárpathos and St John's monastery on Pátmos.

The first great public ceremony takes place on **Good Friday** evening as the Descent from the Cross is lamented in church. At dusk the *Epitáfios*, Christ's funeral bier, lavishly decorated by the women of the parish (in large villages there will be more than one, from each church), leaves the sanctuary and is paraded solemnly through the streets. In many places, Crete especially, this is accompanied by the burning of effigies of Judas Iscariot.

Late **Saturday** evening sees the climax in a majestic *Anástasis* Mass to celebrate Christ's triumphant return. At the stroke of midnight all the lights in every crowded church are extinguished, and the congregation plunged into the darkness which envelops Christ as He passes through the underworld. Then there's a faint glimmer of light behind the altar screen before the priest appears, holding aloft a lighted taper and chanting "*Avtó to Fós . . .* " (This is the Light of the World). Stepping down to the level of the parishioners, he touches his flame to the unlit candles of the nearest worshippers, intoning "*Dévteh, léveteh Fós*" (Come, take the Light). Those at the front of the congregation and on the aisles do the same for their neighbours until the entire church – and the outer courtyard, standing room only for latecomers – is ablaze with burning candles and the miracle reaffirmed.

Even the most committed agnostic is likely to find this moving. The traditional greeting, as fireworks explode all around you in the street, is "*Khristós anésti*" (Christ is risen), to which the response is "*Alithós anésti*" (Truly He is risen). In the week up to Easter Sunday you should wish people "*Kaló Páskha*" (Happy Easter); on or after the day, you say "*Khrónia pollá*" (Many happy returns).

Worshippers then take the burning **candles** home through the streets; they are said to bring good fortune to the house if they arrive still burning. On reaching the front door it is common practice to make the sign of the cross on the lintel with the flame, leaving a black smudge visible for the rest of the year. The forty-day **Lenten fast** – still observed by the devout and in rural areas – is traditionally broken early on Sunday morning with a meal of *mayerítsa*, a soup made from lamb tripe, rice, dill and lemon. The rest of the lamb will be roasted on a spit for Sunday lunch, and festivities often take place through the rest of the day.

The Greek equivalent of **Easter eggs** are hard-boiled eggs (painted red on Holy Thursday), which are baked into twisted, sweet bread-loaves (*tsouréki*) or distributed on Easter Sunday. People rap their eggs against their friends' eggs, and the owner of the last uncracked egg is considered lucky.

The festival calendar

Most of the other Greek festivals are celebrations of one or other of a multitude of **saints**; the most important are detailed below. A village or church bearing the saint's name is a fair guarantee of some sort of observance – sometimes right across the town or island, otherwise quiet, local and consisting of little more than a special liturgy and banners adorning the chapel in question. Saints' days are also celebrated as **name days**; if you learn that it's an acquaintance's name day, you wish them "*Khrónia pollá*" ("Many years", as in "Many happy returns"). Also listed are a few more secular holidays, most enjoyable of which are the pre-Lenten carnivals.

In addition to the specific dates mentioned, there are literally scores of **local festivals**, or *paniyíria*, celebrating the patron saint of the main village church. With hundreds of possible name-saints' days (calendars list two or three, often obscure, for each day) you're unlikely to travel around Greece for long without stumbling on something.

It is important to remember the concept of the *paramoní*, or **eve of the festival**. Most of the events listed below are celebrated on the night before, so if you show up on the morning of the date given you will very probably have missed any music, dancing or drinking.

January 1
New Year's Day (*Protokhroniá*) in Greece is the feast day of Áyios Vassílios (Saint Basil), and is celebrated with church services and the baking of a special loaf, the *vassilópitta*, in which a coin is baked which brings its finder good luck throughout the year. The traditional New Year greeting is "*Kalí khroniá*".

January 6
Epiphany (*Ayía Theofánia*, or *Fóta* for short), when the *kalikántzari* (hobgoblins) who run riot on earth during the twelve days of Christmas are rebanished to the nether world by various rites of the Church. The most important of these is the

blessing of baptismal fonts and all outdoor bodies of water. At lakeside, seaside or riverside locations, the priest traditionally casts a crucifix into the deep, with local youths competing for the privilege of recovering it.

Pre-Lenten carnivals

These – known in Greek as *Apokriátika* – span three weeks, climaxing during the seventh weekend before Easter. *Katharí Dheftéra* (Lenten Monday) of the first carnival week is always seven weeks before Easter Sunday. Pátra Carnival, with a chariot parade and costume parties, is one of the largest and most outrageous in the Mediterranean; on the last Sunday before Lent there's a grand parade, with the city's large gay population in conspicuous participation. The Ionian islands, especially Kefalloniá, are also noted for carnival, while the outrageous Goat Dance is enacted on Skýros in the Sporades.

March 25

Independence Day and the feast of the Annunciation (*Evangelismós* in Greek) is both a religious and a national holiday, with, on the one hand, military parades and dancing to celebrate the beginning of the revolt against Turkish rule in 1821, and on the other church services to honour the news given to Mary that she was to become the Mother of Christ. There are major festivities on Tínos, Ídhra (Hydra) and any locality with a monastery or church named Evangelístria or Evangelismós.

April 23

The feast of Áyios Yeóryios (Saint George), the patron of shepherds, is a big rural celebration, with much feasting and dancing at associated shrines and towns. Good venues include the island of Skýros, of which George is patron saint. If April 23 falls before Easter, ie during Lent, the festivities are postponed until the Monday after Easter.

May 1

May Day (*Protomayiá*) is the great urban holiday when townspeople traditionally make for the countryside to picnic, returning with bunches of wild flowers. Wreaths are hung on their doorways or balconies until they are burnt in bonfires on Saint John's Eve (June 23). There are also large demonstrations by the Left, claiming the *Ergatikí Protomayiá* (Working-Class First of May) as their own.

May 21

The feast of Áyios Konstandínos (Saint

Constantine) and his mother, Ayía Eléni (Saint Helen), the first pro-Orthodox Byzantine rulers. It's widely celebrated as the name day for two of the more popular Christian names in Greece.

May/June

The Monday of Áyio Pnévma (the Holy Spirit, Whit Monday in UK) marks the descent of same to the assembled disciples, fifty days after Easter. Usually a modest liturgy is celebrated at rural chapels of the Holy Spirit, gaily decked out with pennants.

June 29–30

The joint feast of Áyios Pétros and Áyios Pávlos (Saints Peter and Paul), two of the more widely celebrated name days, is on the 29th. Celebrations often run together with that for the Gathering of (all) the Holy Apostles (Áyii Apóstoli), on the 30th.

July 17

The feast of Ayía Marína: a big event in rural areas, as she's an important protector of crops. The eponymous port town on Léros will be en fête, as will Ayía Marína village on Kássos. Between mid-July and mid-September there are religious festivals every few days, especially in the rural areas, and what with these, the summer heat and a mass exodus from the big cities, ordinary business slows or even halts.

July 20

The feast of Profítis Ilías (the Prophet Elijah) is widely celebrated at the countless hill- or mountain-top shrines of Profítis Ilías.

July 26

Ayía Paraskeví is celebrated in parishes or villages bearing that name.

August 6

Metamórfosis toú Sotíros (Transfiguration of the Saviour) provides another excuse for celebrations, particularly at Khristós Ráhon village on Ikaría, and at Plátanos on Léros.

August 15

Apokímisis tís Panayías (Assumption or Dormition of the Blessed Virgin Mary). This is the day when people traditionally return to their home village, and in most places there will be no accommodation available on any terms. Even some Greeks will resort to sleeping in the streets. There is a great pilgrimage to Tínos, and major festivities at Páros, at Ayiássos on Lésvos, on Lipsí and at Ólymbos on Kárpathos.

August 29
Apokefálisis toú Prodhrómou (Beheading of John the Baptist). Popular pilgrimages and celebrations at Vrykoúnda on Kárpathos.

September 8
Yénnisis tís Panayías (Birth of the Virgin Mary) sees special services in churches dedicated to the event, and a double cause for rejoicing on Spétses where they also celebrate the anniversary of the battle of the straits of Spétses, which took place on September 8, 1822. A re-enactment of the battle takes place in the harbour, followed by fireworks and feasting well into the night. Elsewhere, a lively festival at Vourliótes, Sámos, and a pilgrimage of childless women to the monastery at Tsambíka, Rhodes.

September 14
A last major summer festival, the **Ípsosis toú Stavroú** (Exaltation of the Cross).

September 24
The feast of **Áyios Ioánnis Theológos** (Saint John the Divine), observed on Níssyros and Pátmos.

October 26
The feast of **Áyios Dhimítrios** (Saint Demetrius), another popular name day, particularly celebrated in Thessaloníki, of which he is the patron saint. In rural areas the new wine is traditionally broached on this day, a good excuse for general inebriation.

October 28
Óhi Day, the year's major patriotic shindig – a national holiday with parades, folk-dancing and speeches to commemorate Metaxas's apocryphal one-word reply to Mussolini's 1940 ultimatum: "*Ohi!*" (No!).

November 8
Another popular name day, the feast of the **Archangels Michael and Gabriel** (Mihaïl and Gavríïl, or *tón Taxiárhon*), marked by rites at the numerous churches named after them, particularly at the rural monastery of Taxiárhis on Sými, and the big monastery of Mandamádhos, Lésvos.

December 6
The feast of **Áyios Nikólaos** (Saint Nicholas), the patron of seafarers, who has many chapels dedicated to him.

December 25
A much less festive occasion than Greek Easter, **Christmas** (*Khristoúyenna*) is still an important

religious feast celebrating the birth of Christ, and in recent years it has started to take on more of the trappings of the western Christmas, with decorations, Christmas trees and gifts. December 26 is not Boxing Day as in England but the **Sýnaxis tís Panayías**, or Gathering of the Virgin's Entourage.

December 31
New Year's Eve (*Paramoní Protokhroniá*), when, as on the other twelve days of Christmas, a few children still go door-to-door singing the traditional *kálanda* (carols), receiving money in return. Adults tend to sit around playing cards, often for money. The *vassilópitta* is cut at midnight (see January 1).

Cultural festivals

As well as religious festivals, Greece has a full range of **cultural festivals,** including a few on the more popular islands. A leaflet entitled *Greek Festivals*, available from GNTO offices abroad, includes details of these smaller, local festivals of music, drama and dance. The most durable are listed below:

Itháki Music Festival (July)
Ippokrateia Festival, Kós (July–Aug)
Manolis Kalomíris Festival, Sámos (July–Aug)
Réthymnon Renaissance Festival (July–Aug)
Sými Festival (July–Sept)
Lefkádha Arts Jamboree (Aug)
Makrinítsa/Vólos Festival (Aug)
Ioánnina Folk Festival (mid-July to mid-Aug)
Iráklion Festival (early Aug)
Thíra Music Festival (Aug–Sept)
Rhodes Festival (Aug–Oct)

Cinema

Greek **cinemas** show a large number of American and British movies, always in the original soundtrack with Greek subtitles, though fly-posters tend to be Greek-only. **Indoor** screenings are highly affordable, currently €5–7 depending on location and plushness of facilities; they shut from mid-May to late September unless they have air-conditioning or a roll-back roof. Accordingly in summer vast numbers of outdoor cinemas operate; an outdoor movie (marginally cheaper) is worth catching at least once for the experience alone, though it's best to opt for the early screening (about 9pm) since the sound on the 11pm show gets turned down or even off to avoid complaints of noise from adjacent residences.

Sports and outdoor pursuits

The Greek seashore offers endless scope for watersports, with windsurfing-boards for rent in most resorts and, less reliably, waterskiing and parasailing facilities. On land, the greatest attraction lies in hiking; often the smaller, less developed islands are better for this than the larger ones criss-crossed by roads.

In terms of spectating, the twin Greek obsessions are **football** (soccer) and **basketball**, with **volleyball** a close third in popularity.

Watersports

The years since the mid-1980s have seen a massive growth in the popularity of **windsurfing** in Greece. The country's bays and coves are ideal for beginners, and boards can be rented in literally hundreds of resorts. Particularly good areas, with established schools, include Vassilikí on Lefkádha island, Kéfalos on Kós, Zákynthos, western Náxos, Kokkári on Sámos, several spots on Lésvos, Corfu's west coast, numerous locales on Crete (especially Paleohóra), and Methóni in the Peloponnese. You can almost always pay for an initial period of instruction, if you've not tried the sport previously. Board rental rates are very reasonable – about €10 an hour.

Waterskiing is available at a number of the larger resorts, and a fair few of the smaller ones too. By the crippling rental standards of the ritzier parts of the Mediterranean it is a bargain, with twenty minutes' instruction often available for around €13–16. At many resorts, parasailing (*parapént* in Greek) is also possible; rates start at €18 a go.

A combination of steady winds, appealing seascapes and numerous natural harbours have long made Greece a tremendous place for **sailing**. Holiday companies offer all sorts of packaged and tailor-made cruises (see pp.16 & 23 in "Getting There"). In Greece, small boats and motorized dinghies are rented out by the day at many resorts. Spring and autumn are the most pleasant and least expensive seasons; *meltémi* winds make for pretty nauseous sailing between late June and early September, and summer rates for the same craft can be three times as high as shoulder-season prices. For more details,

pick up the informative though now somewhat dated brochure *Sailing the Greek Sea* from GNTO offices, or contact the Hellenic Yachting Federation, Aktí Navárhou Koundourióti 7, 185 34 Pireás (℡010/41 37 351, ℻41 31 119).

Because of the potential for pilfering submerged antiquities, **scuba-diving** is severely restricted, its legal practice confined to certain coasts around Attica, Kálymnos, Kalamáta, Préveza, Rhodes, Skiáthos, Corfu, Zákynthos and Mýkonos. For more information and an update on new, approved sites, contact the Union of Greek Diving Centres (℡010/92 29 532 or 41 18 909), or request the sporadically available information sheet *Regulations Concerning Underwater Activities* from the nearest branch of the GNTO/EOT.

Walking

Young urban Greeks have only recently become used to the notion that anyone should want to **walk** for pleasure, yet if you have the time and stamina it is probably the single best way to see the quieter islands; for more detail, you may want to acquire specific hiking guidebooks; see p.599 in *Contexts*. See also p.39 for details of hiking maps available, and pp.16, 23 and 25 for details of companies offering walking holidays on the islands.

Football and basketball

Football (soccer) is far and away the most popular sport in Greece – both in terms of participating and watching. The most important (and most heavily sponsored) teams are Panathanaïkós and AEK of Athens, Olympiakós of Pireás and PAOK of Thessaloníki. The only major team on the islands is the Cretan Ofí. If you're interested, matches (usually played on Wednesday nights and Sunday afternoons) are easy enough to catch from September to May. In mid-autumn you might even see one of the Greek teams playing European competition. The Greek national team qualified for the 1994 World Cup in some style, and then proceeded to lose all their three games heavily and returned from the US without scoring a goal.

The nation's **basketball** team is one of the continent's strongest and won the European Championship in 1987 – cheered all the way with enormous enthusiasm. At private-club level, many of the football teams maintain basketball squads – Panathanaïkós and Olympiakós were European champions in 1996 and 1997 respectively.

Finding work

Since Greece's full accession to the European Union in early 1993, a citizen of any EU state has (in theory) the right to work in Greece. In practice, however, there are a number of bureaucratic hurdles to overcome. Formerly, the most common job for foreigners was teaching English in the numerous private cramming academies (*frondistíria*), but lately severe restrictions have been put on the availability of such positions for non-Greeks, and you'll probably have more luck finding something in the commercial or leisure-oriented trade. Similarly, that other long-standing fallback of long-haul backpackers, picking fruit or greenhouse vegetables, is now the exclusive province of Albanian males.

Short-term work

EU membership notwithstanding, short-term work in Greece is always on an unofficial basis and for this reason it will generally be where you can't be seen by the police or you're badly paid – or, more often, both. The influx, since 1990, of between 800,000 and 1.1 million (estimates vary) Albanians, Ukrainians, Bulgarians, Pakistanis, Moldavians, Russians, Somalis, Filipinos and others has resulted in a surplus of unskilled labour and severely depressed wages. **Youth hostels** are still a good source of information on temporary work – indeed a few may even offer you a job themselves, if you turn up at the right time.

Tourism-related work

Most women working casually in Greece find jobs in **bars** or **restaurants** around the main resorts. Men, unless they are "trained" chefs, will be edged out by Albanians even when it comes to washing up.

If you're waiting or serving, most of your wages will probably have to come from tips but you may well be able to get a deal that includes free food and lodging; evening-only hours can be a good shift, leaving you a lot of free time. The main drawback may be the machismo and/or chauvinist attitudes of your employer. (Ads in the local press for "girl bar staff" are certainly best ignored; see "Sexual Harassment" on p.78)

Corfu, with its big British slant, is an obvious choice for bar work; Rhodes, Kós, Crete, Skiáthos, Páros, Íos and Thíra are also promising. Start looking, if you can, around April or May; you'll get better rates at this time if you're taken on for a season.

On a similar, unofficial level you might be able to get a sales job in **tourist shops** on Corfu, Ídhra, Rhodes or Crete, or (if you've the expertise) helping out at one of the **windsurfing** schools that have sprung up all around the coast. **Yacht marinas** can also prove good hunting-grounds though less for the romantic business of crewing, than scrubbing down and repainting. Again, the best possibilities are likely to be on Rhodes, Corfu or Kálymnos; the Zéa port at Pireás is actually the biggest marina, but non-Greek owners don't tend to rest up there for long.

Perhaps the best type of tourism-related work, however, is that of courier/greeter/group co-ordinator for a **package holiday company**. All you need is EU nationality and language proficiency compatible with the clientele, though knowledge of Greek is a big plus. English-only speakers are pretty well restricted to places with a big British package trade, namely Crete, Rhodes, Skiáthos and the Ionian islands.

Many such staff are recruited through ads in newspapers issued outside Greece, but it's by no means unheard of to be hired on the spot in April or May. A big plus, however you're taken on, is that you're usually guaranteed about six months of steady work, often with use of a car thrown in, and that if things work out you may be re-employed the following season with contract and foreign-currency wages from the home company, not from the local affiliate.

Selling and busking

You may do better by working for yourself. Travellers report rich pickings during the tourist season from **selling jewellery** on island beaches, or on boats – craftware from Asia is especially popular with Greeks. Once you've managed to get the stuff past the customs officials (who will be sceptical, for instance, that all those trinkets are presents for friends), there rarely seem to be problems with the local police, though it probably pays to be discreet.

Busking can also be quite lucrative. Playing on the Athens metro or the city's streets, it's possible to make up to €9 in a two-hour session, though in the new metro extension the practice is likely to be strictly banned.

Documentation for long-term employment

If you plan to work professionally for someone else, you first visit the nearest Department of Employment and collect two forms: one an **employment application** which you fill in, the other for the formal offer of work by your prospective employer. Once these are vetted, and revenue stamps (*hartósima*, purchased at kiosks) applied, you take them to the Aliens' Bureau (*Ypiresía Allodhapón*) or, in its absence, the central police station, to support your application for a **residence permit** (*ádhia paramonís*). For this, you will also need to bring your passport, six photographs, more *hartósima* and a stable address (not a hotel). Permits are given for terms of one year (green triptych booklets), or five years (white booklets) if they've become well acquainted with you.

You should allow four to six weeks for all the formalities to be completed; the bottleneck is usually the required **health examination** at the nearest public hospital. There you will be chest-X-rayed for signs of TB, blood-tested for hepatitis B & C, HIV and a couple of other nasties, and have a (farcical) evaluation by a neurologist or psychiatrist for signs of mental disorder; this is all done at a reasonable cost. Usually some crucial consultant is on holiday, delaying the proceedings; once you've assembled all the results, you'll have to trot these over yourself to the local public health office, where a periodic (once weekly at best) meeting of its administrative council will vet and endorse these, and issue you with a certificate of approval. Finally you take this to the local police or Aliens' Bureau, which should have your permit ready, free of charge other than for a few more *hartósima*, within three working days.

As a **self-employed professional**, you must satisfy the requirements of the Greek state with equivalent qualifications to native Greeks plying the same trade. You should also befriend a good accountant, who will advise you on which of the several varieties of incorporation are to your advantage; trading under a fictitious name is vastly more expensive tax-wise than doing business as a private person. You will need to sign on with **TEBE**, the Greek National Insurance scheme for self-employed people (analogous to Class 4 National Insurance contributions in the UK). If you are continuing to contribute to a social insurance scheme in a country which has reciprocal agreements with Greece (all EU states do), this must be proved in writing – a tedious and protracted process.

Once you're square with TEBE, visit the tax office or *eforía* to be issued a **tax number** (abbreviated "ah-fi-mi" in Greek, similar to a UK Schedule D number) which must be cited in all transactions. To be issued one of these, you need to bring a birth certificate which shows the full unmarried names of *both* your parents. You will be required to prepare receipt and invoice books with your tax number professionally printed on them, or have a rubber stamp made up for applying that number to every sheet. The tax office will also determine which rate of **VAT** (the "fi-pi-ah") you should pay for each kind of transaction; VAT returns must be filed every two months, which is where a friendly accountant comes in handy again.

The self-employed tend to be issued five-year residence permits. **EU nationals** who do not intend to work in Greece but still need a residence permit (such as second-property-owners needing to set up a bank account) will still get a "white" pass fairly easily, but must present evidence of financial solvency; personalized pink exchange receipts, travellers' cheques or credit cards are all considered valid proofs.

At present, undocumented **non-EU nationals** who wish to work in Greece do so surreptitiously, with the ever-present risk of denunciation to the police and instant deportation. Having been forced to accept large numbers of EU citizens looking for jobs in a climate of rising unemployment, Greek immigration authorities are cracking down hard on any suitable targets, be they Albanian, African, Swiss or North American. That old foreigners' standby, teaching English, is now available only to holders of TEFL certificates – preferably Greeks, non-EU nationals of Greek descent and EU nationals in that order. If you are a non-EU foreign national of Greek descent, you are termed *omólogos* (returned Greek diaspora member) and in fact have tremendous employment, taxation and residence rights and privileges – you can, for example, open your very own *frondistírio* without any qualifications, something starkly evident in the often abysmal quality of language instruction in Greece.

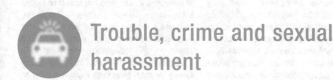

Trouble, crime and sexual harassment

As in the past, Greece remains one of Europe's safest countries, with a low crime rate and a deserved reputation for honesty. If you leave a bag or wallet at a café, you'll most likely find it scrupulously looked after, pending your return. Similarly, Greeks are relatively relaxed about leaving possessions unlocked or unattended on the beach, in rooms or on campsites. The biggest hazards on beaches, oddly, are free-ranging goats – who will eat just about anything left accessible – and the wake of passing cruise ships or ferries, which can wash all your possessions out to sea with little or no warning.

In recent years, however, there has been a large increase in **theft** and **crimes against persons** (blamed largely on Albanian and Romanian refugees) in towns, remote villages and resorts, so it's wise to lock things up and treat Greece like any other European destination. Following are also a few pointers on offences that might get you into trouble locally, and some advice on sexual harassment – still a lingering fact of life given the classically Mediterranean machismo of Greek culture.

Specific offences

The most common causes of a brush with authority are nude bathing or sunbathing, and camping outside an authorized site.

Nude bathing is legal on only a very few beaches (most famously on Mýkonos), and is deeply offensive to the more traditional Greeks – exercise considerable sensitivity to local feeling and the kind of place you're in. It is, for example, very bad etiquette to swim or sunbathe nude within sight of a church, of which there are many along the Greek coast. Generally, if a beach has become fairly well established as naturist, or is well secluded, it's highly unlikely that the police are going to come charging in. Where they do get bothered is if they feel a place is turning into a "hippie beach" or nudity is getting too overt on mainstream tourist stretches.

Most of the time, the only action will be a warning, but you can officially be arrested straight off – facing up to three days in jail and a stiff fine.

Topless (sun)bathing for women is technically legal nationwide, but specific locales often opt out of the "liberation" by posting signs, which should be heeded.

Very similar guidelines apply to **camping rough**, which has been theoretically illegal nationwide since 1977 (see "Accommodation", p.55). Even for this you're still unlikely to incur anything more than a warning to move on. The only real risk of arrest is if you are told to clear off and fail to do so. In either of the above cases, even if the police do take any action against you, it's more likely to be a brief spell in their cells than any official prosecution.

Incidentally, any sort of **disrespect** towards the Greek state or Orthodox Church in general, or Greek civil servants in particular, may be construed as offences in the most literal sense, so it's best to keep your comments on how things are working (or not) to yourself. Every year a few foreign louts find themselves in deep trouble over a drunken indiscretion. This is a society where verbal injuries count, with a consistent backlog of court cases dealing with the alleged public utterance of *malákas* (wanker).

In the non-verbal field, ripped or soiled clothes and untucked-in shirts are considered nearly as insulting. Don't expect a uniformly civil reception if dressed in **grunge attire**, since Greeks will interpret this in one of two possible ways, neither reflecting well on you. Poverty is an uncomfortably close memory for many, and they may consider that you're making light of hard times. More to the point, the cult of *la bella figura* is developed to near-Italian levels in Greece; if you clearly have so little self-respect as to appear slovenly and dishevelled in public, why should any Greek respect you?

Drug offences are treated as major crimes, particularly since there's a mushrooming local use and addiction problem. The maximum penalty for "causing the use of drugs by someone under 18", for example, is life imprisonment and an astronomical fine. Theory is by no means practice, but foreigners caught in possession of even small amounts of grass do get long jail sentences if there's evidence that they've been supplying the drug to others. Moreover, you could

be inside for well over a year awaiting a trial date, with little or no chance of bail being granted.

In an **emergency**, dial ☎ 100 for the police; ☎ 171 for the tourist police in Athens, ☎ 01-171 outside of it; ☎ 166 for an ambulance; ☎ 191 to report a forest fire; and ☎ 199 for the urban fire brigade. These calls should all be toll-free from a card-phone.

If you get arrested for any offence, you have a right to contact your **consulate**, who will arrange a lawyer for your defence. Beyond this, there is little they can, or in most cases will, do. There are honorary British consulates on Rhodes, Crete and Corfu.

Sexual harassment

Thousands of women travel independently in Greece without being **harassed** or feeling intimidated. Greek machismo, however, remains strong, if less upfront than in, for example, southern Italy. With the recent sea-change in local mores – specifically, a vast increase in the "availability" of young Greek women to young local men, up to and including living together before marriage – much of the impetus for trying one's luck with foreign girls has faded. Any hassle you do get is likely to be from a dwindling minority of professionally single Greek men, known as *kamákia* (fish harpoons), who migrate in summer to the beach bars and discos of the main resorts and towns, specifically in pursuit of "liberated, fun-loving" tourists.

Indigenous Greeks, who become increasingly protective of you as you become more of a fixture in any one place, treat these outsiders with contempt; their obvious stakeouts are waterfront cafés, beach bars and dance clubs. Words worth remembering as unambiguous responses include "*pápsteh*" (stop it), "*afístemeh*" (leave me alone) and "*fíyeteh*" (go away), the latter intensified if followed by "*dhrómo!*" (road, as in "Hit the road!").

Hitching is not advisable for lone women travellers, but **camping** is generally not a problem, though away from recognized sites it is often wise to attach yourself to a local family by making arrangements to use nearby private land. In the remoter islands you may feel more uncomfortable travelling alone. The intensely traditional Greeks may have trouble understanding why you are unaccompanied, and might not welcome your presence in their exclusively male kafenía – often the only place where you can get a drink. Travelling with a man, you're more likely to be treated as a *xéni*, a word meaning both (female) stranger and guest.

Lone men need to be aware of one long-established racket in the largest island ports. You may be approached by dubious gents asking the time, or your origins, and then offering to take you for a drink in a nearby bar. This is invariably staffed with hostesses (who may also be on the game), whose main job is to convince you to treat them to drinks. At the end of the night you'll be landed with an outrageous bill, some of which goes towards the hostess's "commission"; physical threats are brought to bear on reluctant payers.

Consumer protection on holiday

In a tourist industry as developed as in Greece there are inevitably a number of cowboys and shady characters amongst the taxi-drivers, hoteliers and car-rental agencies in particular. **EKPIZO**, the **Greek Consumers' Association**, has established a "Legal Information and Assistance for Tourists" programme, to be run yearly from June to September. Their main branch is in Athens ☏ 010/33 04 444, with offices also in Pátra and Crete. EKPI-ZO issues a pamphlet about holidaymakers' rights, available in airports and tourist offices. They are prepared to pursue serious cases, by friendly persuasion or court action if necessary.

Travellers with disabilities

It is all too easy to wax lyrical over the attractions of Greece: the stepped, narrow alleys, the ease of travel by bus and ferry, the thrill of clambering around the great archeological sites. It is almost impossible, on the other hand, for the able-bodied travel writer to see these attractions as potential hazards for anyone who has difficulty in walking, is wheelchair-bound or suffers from some other disability.

However, don't be discouraged. It is possible to enjoy an inexpensive and trauma-free holiday in Greece if some time is devoted to gathering **information** before arrival. Much existing or readily available information is out of date – you should always try to double-check. A number of addresses of contact organizations are published below. The Greek National Tourist Office is a good first step as long as you have specific questions to put to them; they publish a useful questionnaire which you could send to hotels or owners of apartment/villa accommodation.

Contacts for travellers with disabilities

In the UK and Ireland

Access Travel, 6 The Hillock, Astley, Lancashire M29 7GW ☏ 01942/888844, ⊛ www.access-travel.co.uk. A tour operator that can arrange flights, transfer and accommodation. This is a small business, personally checking out places before recommendation. They can guarantee accommodation standards on Rhodes in particular. ATOL bonded, established seven years.
Disability Action Group, 2 Annadale Ave, Belfast

BT7 3JH ☎ 028/9049 1011. Provides information about access for disabled travellers abroad.

Holiday Care, 2nd floor, Imperial Building, Victoria Rd, Horley, Surrey RH6 7PZ ☎ 01293/774535, Minicom ☎ 01293/776943, ⓦ www.holidaycare.org.uk. Provides free lists of accessible accommodation abroad – European, American and long-haul destinations – plus a list of accessible attractions in the UK. Information on financial help for holidays available.

Irish Wheelchair Association, Blackheath Drive, Clontarf, Dublin 3 ☎ 01/833 8241, ⓕ 833 3873, ⓔ iwa@iol.ie. Useful information provided on travelling abroad with a wheelchair.

Tripscope, Alexandra House, Albany Rd, Brentford, Middlesex TW8 0NE ☎ 08457/585 641, ⓦ www.justmobility.co.uk/tripscope. This registered charity provides a national telephone information service offering free advice on UK and international transport for those with a mobility problem.

In the US and Canada

Access-Able ⓦ www.access-able.com. Online resource for travellers with disabilities.

Directions Unlimited, 123 Green Lane, Bedford Hills, NY 10507 ☎ 1-800/533-5343 or 914/241-1700. Tour operator specializing in custom tours for people with disabilities.

Mobility International USA, 451 Broadway, Eugene, OR 97401 Voice and TDD ☎ 541/343-1284, ⓦ www.miusa.org. Information and referral services, access guides, tours and exchange programmes. Annual membership $35 (includes quarterly newsletter).

Society for the Advancement of Travelers with Handicaps (SATH), 347 5th Ave, New York, NY 10016 ☎ 212/447-7284, ⓦ www.sath.org. A non-profit educational organization that has actively represented travellers with disabilities since 1976.

Travel Information Service ☎ 215/456-9600. Telephone-only information and referral service.

Twin Peaks Press, Box 129, Vancouver, WA 98661 ☎ 360/694-2462 or 1-800/637-2256, ⓔ twinpeak@pacifier.com. Publisher of the *Directory of Travel Agencies for the Disabled* ($19.95), listing more than 370 agencies worldwide; *Travel for the Disabled* ($19.95); the *Directory of Accessible Van Rentals* ($12.95); and *Wheelchair Vagabond* ($19.95), loaded with personal tips.

Wheels Up! ☎ 1-888/389-4335, ⓦ www.wheelsup.com. Provides discounted airfare, tour and cruise prices for disabled travellers, also publishes a free monthly newsletter and has a comprehensive website.

In Australia and New Zealand

ACROD (Australian Council for Rehabilitation of the Disabled), PO Box 60, Curtin, ACT 2605 ☎ 02 6282 4333; 24 Cabarita Rd, Cabarita, NSW 2137 ☎ 02/9743 2699. Provides lists of travel agencies and tour operators for people with disabilities.

Disabled Persons Assembly, 4/173–175 Victoria St, Wellington, New Zealand ☎ 04/801 9100. Resource centre with lists of travel agencies and tour operators for people with disabilities.

Planning a holiday

There are **organized tours** and **holidays** specifically for people with disabilities; many companies in Britain will advise on the suitability of holidays or villas advertised in their brochures. If you want to be more independent, it's perfectly possible, provided that you do not leave home with the vague hope that things will turn out all right, and that "people will help out" when you need assistance. This cannot be relied on. You must either be completely confident that you can manage alone, or travel with an able-bodied friend (or two).

It's important to become an authority on where you must be self-reliant and where you may expect help, especially regarding transport and accommodation. For example, while the new Athens airport has lifts between arrivals and the departures concourse, and the Athens metro also has lifts for wheelchairs in every station, you cannot assume that every express bus between the arrivals exit and the first metro stop will be of a "kneeling" design.

It is also vital to **be honest** – with travel agencies, insurance companies, companions and, above all, with yourself. Know your limits and make sure others know them. If you do not use a wheelchair all the time but your walking capabilities are limited, remember that you are likely to need to cover greater distances while travelling (often over tougher terrain and in hotter weather) than you are used to. If you use a wheelchair, it's advisable to have it serviced before you go, and carry a repair kit.

Read your **travel insurance** small print carefully to make sure that people with a pre-existing medical condition are not excluded. And use your travel agent to make your journey simpler: **airlines** or bus companies can cope better if they are expecting you, with a wheelchair provided at airports and staff primed to help. A **medical certificate** of your fitness to travel, provided by your doctor, is also extremely useful; some airlines or insurance companies may insist on it.

Make a **list** of all the facilities that will make your life easier while you are away. You may want a ground-floor room, or access to a large elevator; you may have special dietary requirements, or need level ground to enable you to reach shops, beaches, bars and places of interest. You should also keep track of all your other special needs, making sure, for example, that you have extra supplies of drugs – carried with you if you fly – and a prescription including the generic name in case of emergency. Carry spares of any kind of drug, clothing or equipment that might be hard to find in Greece; if there's an association representing people with your disability, contact them early in the planning process.

Senior travellers

Travellers over sixty are accorded every respect in Greece; you are, for example, rather less likely to be grumbled or shouted at by the famously irate Athens bus drivers or harbour officials. Seniors are entitled to discounts at state-run attractions of twenty-five to thirty percent; long-term bus passes in the major cities are similarly discounted; and, without making much effort to publicize the fact, Olympic Airways (and quite possibly its new private competitors) also offer discounts off full fares on domestic flights. Keep proof of age to hand for all these benefits.

Contacts for senior travellers

In the UK

Saga Holidays ☎01303/771111, ⓦwww.sagaholidays.com. The country's biggest and most established specialist in tours and holidays aimed at older people.

In the US

American Association of Retired Persons, 601 E St, NW Washington, DC 20049 ☎1-800/424-3410, membership hotline ☎1-800/515-2299 or 202/434-2277, ⓦwww.aarp.org. Can provide discounts on accommodation and vehicle rental. Membership open to US and Canadian residents aged 50 or over for an annual fee of US $10 or $27 for three years. Canadian residents only have the annual option.

Elderhostel, 75 Federal St, Boston, MA 02110 ☎1-877-426-8056, ⓦwww.elderhostel.com. Runs an extensive worldwide network of educational and activity programmes, cruises and homestays for people over 60 (companions may be younger). Programmes generally last a week or more and costs are in line with those of commercial tours.

Saga Holidays, 222 Berkeley St, Boston, MA 02116 ☎1-877/265-6862, ⓦwww.sagaholidays.com. Specializes in worldwide group travel for seniors. Saga's Smithsonian Odyssey Tours, which include Greece, have a more educational slant.

Vantage Travel ☎1-800/322-6677, ⓦwww.vantagetravel.com. Specializes in worldwide group travel for seniors.

Gay and lesbian travellers

The term "Greek love" may still evoke titters from those educated in British public schools of a classicizing persuasion, but in modern Greece overtly **gay behaviour** in public remains **taboo** for men in **rural areas.** There is, however, a fairly sizable **gay contingent** at certain resorts like Ídhra, Rhodes or Mýkonos, still the most popular European gay resort after Ibiza in Spain. Skála Eressoú on Lésvos, the birthplace of Sappho, is (appropriately) an international mecca for **lesbians.** Homosexuality is legal over the age of 17, and (male) bisexual behaviour common but rarely admitted. Greek men are terrible flirts, but cruising them is a semiotic minefield and definitely at your own risk – references in gay guides to "known" male cruising grounds should be treated sceptically. "Out" gay Greeks are rare, and "out" local lesbians rarer still; foreign same-sex couples will be regarded in the provinces with some bemusement but accorded the standard courtesy as foreigners. The gay movement in Greece is represented by Akoe Amphi, PO Box 26022, 10022 Athens ☎010/77 19 221.

Contacts for gay and lesbian travellers

In the UK

ⓦwww.gaytravel.co.uk Online gay and lesbian travel agent, offering good deals on all types of holiday. Also lists gay- and lesbian-friendly hotels around the world.
Dream Waves, Redcot High St, Child Okeford, Blandford, DT22 8ET ☎01258/861149, ⓔDreamwaves@aol.com. Specializes in exclusively gay holidays, including summer sun packages.
Madison Travel, 118 Western Rd, Hove, East Sussex NN3 1DB ☎01273/202532, ⓦwww.madisontravel.co.uk. Established travel agents specializing in packages to gay- and lesbian-friendly mainstream destinations, and also to gay/lesbian destinations.
Respect Holidays, 74 Haverstock Hill, London NW3 2BE ☎020/7485 8855, ⓦwww .respect-holidays.co.uk. Offers exclusively gay packages to all popular European resorts.
Also check out adverts in the weekly papers *Boyz* and *Pink Paper*, handed out free in gay venues.

In the US and Canada

Damron Company, PO Box 422458, San Francisco, CA 94142 ☎1-800/462-6654 or 415/255-0404, ⓦwww.damron.com. Publisher of the *Men's Travel Guide*, a pocket-sized yearbook full of listings of hotels, bars, clubs and resources for gay men; the *Women's Traveler*, which

provides similar listings for lesbians; and *Damron Accommodations*, which provides detailed listings of over 1000 accommodations for gays and lesbians worldwide. All of these titles are offered at a discount on the website. No specific city guides – everything is incorporated in the yearbooks.
Ferrari Publications, PO Box 37887, Phoenix, AZ 85069 ☎1-800/962-2912 or 602/863-2408, ⓦwww.ferrariguides.com. Publishes *Ferrari Gay Travel A to Z*, a worldwide gay and lesbian guide; *Inn Places*, a worldwide accommodation guide; the guides *Men's Travel in Your Pocket*; and *Women's Travel in Your Pocket*, and the quarterly *Ferrari Travel Report*.
International Gay/Lesbian Travel Association, 4331 N Federal Hwy, Suite 304, Ft Lauderdale, FL 33308 ☎1-800/448-8550, ⓦwww.iglta.org. Trade group that can provide a list of gay- and lesbian-owned or friendly travel agents, accommodation and other travel businesses.

In Australia and New Zealand

Gay and Lesbian Travel ⓦwww.galta.com.au. Directory and links for gay and lesbian travel in Australia and worldwide.
Gay Travel ⓦwww.gaytravel.com. The site for trip planning, bookings and general information about international travel.
Parkside Travel, 70 Glen Osmond Rd, Parkside, SA 5063 ☎08/8274 1222 or 1800/888 501, ⓔhwtravel@senet.com.au. Gay travel agent associated with local branch of Hervey World

Travel; all aspects of gay and lesbian travel worldwide.

Pinkstay ⊛ www.pinkstay.com. Everything from visa information to finding accommodation and work around the world.

Silke's Travel, 263 Oxford St, Darlinghurst, NSW 2010 ☏ 02/9380 6244 or 1800/807 860,

⊜ silba@magna.com.au. Long-established gay and lesbian specialist, with the emphasis on women's travel.

Tearaway Travel, 52 Porter St, Prahan, VIC 3181 ☏ 03/9510 6344, ⊜ tearaway@bigpond.com. Gay-specific business dealing with international and domestic travel.

Travelling with children

Children are worshipped and indulged in Greece, arguably to excess, and present few problems when travelling. As elsewhere in the Mediterranean, they are not segregated from adults at meal times and early on in life are inducted into the typical late-night routine. So you'll see plenty of kids at tavernas, expected to eat (and up to their capabilities, talk) like adults. Outside of certain all-inclusive resorts, however (see "Contacts" below) there are very few amusements specifically for kids – certainly nothing like Disney World Paris.

Most ferry-boat lines and airlines in Greece offer some sort of **discount** for children, ranging from fifty to hundred percent depending on their age; hotels and rooms won't charge extra for infants, and levy a modest surcharge for "third" beds which the child occupies by him/herself.

Baby foods and nappies/diapers are ubiquitous and reasonably priced; private rooms establishments and luxury hotels are more likely to offer some kind of **babysitting** service than the mid-range, C-class hotels.

Contacts for travellers with children

In the UK and Ireland

Club Med ☏ 0700/258 2633, ⊛ www.clubmed.com. Specializes in purpose-built holiday resorts, with kids' club, entertainment and

sports facilities on site; has villages on Corfu, Évvia and Kós.

Mark Warner Holidays ☏ 020/7761 7000, ⊛ www.markwarner.co.uk. Holiday villages with children's entertainment and childcare laid on.

Simply Travel ☏ 020/8541 2280, ⊛ www.simply-travel.com. Upmarket tour company offering villas and hotels in the less touristy parts of Greece. May be able to provide qualified, English-speaking nannies to come to your villa and look after the children.

In the US

Travel With Your Children, 40 5th Ave, New York, NY 10011 ☏ 212/477 5524 or 1-888/822-4388. Publish a regular newsletter, *Family Travel Times* ⊛ www.familytraveltimes.com, as well as a series of books on travel with children including *Great Adventure Vacations With Your Kids*.

Directory

ADDRESSES In Greece streets are cited in the genitive case, usually with no tag like "Street" or "Avenue"; the number always follows. Thus something described as 36 Venizelos Avenue in Roman-alphabet letterhead comes out at Venizélou 36, and it's this convention which we've adopted throughout the book. Postcodes are five-digit, nationwide, and precede the municipality concerned, eg 83100 Sámos.

BARGAINING This isn't a regular feature of touristic life, though you'll find it possible with private rooms and certain hotels out of season. Similarly, you should be able to negotiate discounted rates for vehicle rental, especially for longer periods. Services such as shoe, watch and camera repair don't have iron-clad rates, so use common sense when assessing charges (advance written estimates are not routine practice).

DEPARTURE TAX This is levied on all international ferries – currently €4.50–6 per person and per car or motorbike, usually (but not always) included within the quoted price of the ticket. To non-EU states (eg Turkey, Croatia and Israel), it's €11.80–14.70 per person, sometimes arbitrarily levied twice (on entry and exit). There's also an airport departure tax of £6.50 equivalent (currently €10.50) for destinations less than 750 miles away, roughly double that if it's further, but this is always included in the price of the ticket – there's no collection at the airport itself. This tax, nicknamed the *spatósima* locally, was supposedly for funding construction of the new Athens airport at Spáta, but since this opened in March 2001, it hasn't been abolished . . . .

ELECTRICITY Voltage is 220 volt AC throughout the country. Wall outlets – rarely abundant enough – take double round-pin plugs as in the rest of continental Europe. Three-to-two-pin adapters should be purchased beforehand in the UK, as they can be difficult to find locally; standard 5-, 6- or 7-amp models permit operation of a hair dryer or travel iron. If necessary, you can change the fuse to a higher rating back in the UK; beware, they're physically smaller than the 13-amp ones popped into all three-prong plugs, and you may have to go to a specialist electrical dealer for them. Unless they're dual voltage, North American appliances will require both a step-down transformer and a plug adapter (the latter easy to find in Greece).

FILMS Fuji and Kodak print films are reasonably priced and easy to have processed – you practically trip over "One Hour Foto" places in resorts. APS film is also widely sold and processed. Kodak and Fuji slide films can be purchased, again at UK prices or better, in larger towns, but the only place on the islands where you can get them processed is Iráklion, so you'll probably have to wait till you get home.

GREEK-LANGUAGE COURSES The longest established outlet is The Athens Centre, Arhimídhous 48, Méts, 116 36 Athens ☎010/70 12 268, ℱ70 18 603, ℮athenscr@compulink.gr. One to try on Crete is Lexis, 48 Dhaskaloyiánni, 731 00 Haniá ☎ & ℱ08210/55 673, ℮lexis-glacc@cha.forthnet.gr.

LAUNDRIES *Plindíria*, as they're known in Greek, are prominent in the main resort towns; sometimes an attended service wash is available for little or no extra charge over the basic cost of €5–5.50 per wash and dry. Self-catering villas or *dhomátia* will usually be furnished with a drying line and a selection of plastic wash-tubs (*skáfes*) or a bucket (*kouvás*). In hotels, laundering should be done in a more circumspect manner; management can freak out if you use bathroom washbasins (Greek wall-mounting being what it is) or do more than a few socks and undies. It's best to use the flat pans of showers for both washing and hanging to dry; if you haven't come with a universal flat plug, wadded-up toilet paper can be quite effective in stopping the drain hole.

PERÍPTERA These are street-corner kiosks, or sometimes a hole-in-the-wall shopfront. They sell everything from pens to disposable razors, stationery to soap, sweets to condoms, cigarettes to plastic crucifixes, yoghurts to milk-in-cartons – and are often open when nothing else is.

TIME As throughout the EU, Greek summer time begins at 2am on the last Sunday in March, when the clocks go forward one hour, and ends at 2am the last Sunday in October when they go back. Be alert to this, as the change is not well publicized, leading scores of visitors to miss planes and ferries every year. Greek time is thus always two hours ahead of Britain. For North America, the difference is seven hours for Eastern Standard Time, ten hours for Pacific Standard Time, with an extra hour plus or minus for those weeks in April and October when one place is on daylight saving and the other isn't. A recorded time message (in distinctly slow Greek, 24-hour convention) is available by dialling ⓣ141.

TOILETS Public toilets are usually in parks or squares, often subterranean; otherwise try a bus station. Except in areas frequented by tourists, public toilets tend to be pretty filthy – it's best to use those in restaurants and bars. Remember that throughout Greece, you drop paper in the adjacent wastebins, *not* in the bowl.

USEFUL THINGS TO BRING A high-quality, porcelain-lined canteen or drinking-water bottle; a small alarm clock for early buses and ferries; a flashlight if you're camping out; sunscreen of high SPF (25 or above, tricky to find and/or expensive in Greece); pocket knife (Swiss Army type or similar), with tweezers, mini-screwdriver and other similar accessories (these are now widely sold in Greece at hunting/fishing shops); ear plugs for noisy ferries or hotels; and good-quality tea bags.

GREEK FERRIES, CATAMARANS & HYDROFOILS

Shading of lines indicates
frequency of sailings in summer

Daily

4 to 6 per week

1 to 3 per week

Adapted from an original drawing by Phil Green

GREECE

Corfu Town
Igoumenítsa
Lefkími
Páxi
Párga
Vassilikí (Lefkádha)
Nydhrí (Lefkádha)
Astakós
Fiskárdho
Sámi
Kefalloniá
Argostóli
Pessádha
Áyios Nikólaos
Zákynthos
Zákynthos Town
Kyllíni
Póros
Itháki
Pátra
Rio
Andírio
Évyo
Áyios Konstandínos
Vólos
Tríkeri
Thessaloníki
Alónissos
Skópelos
Skáthos
Skýros
Péfki
Kými

ATHENS

PIREÁS
Rafína
Lávrio
Kéa
Kýthnos
Sérifos
Sífnos
Kímolos
Mílos
Síkinos
Folégandhros
Thírassía
Thíra
Anáfi
Angístri
Méthana
Éyina
Póros
Idhra
Spétses
Pórto Héli
Náfplio
Ermióni
Leonídhi
Kyparíssi
Yérakas
Monemvasía
Neápoli
Kýthira
Andikýthira
Elafónisos
Výthio
Kastélli

TURKEY

Alexandhroúpoli
Keramotí
Kavála
Néa Péramos
Thássos
Samothráki
Límnos
Áyios Efstrátios
Lésvos
Híos
Sámos
Ikaría
Foúrni
Mýkonos
Tínos
Ándhros
Sýros
Páros
Náxos
Íos
Dhonoússa
Skhinoússa
Iráklia
Koufoníssi
Amorgós
Astypálea
Níssyros
Agathoníssi
Lípsi
Léros
Pátmos
Kálymnos
Kós
Tílos
Sými
Háliki
Rhodes
Kárpathos
Kássos
Sitía
Kastellórizo

CRETE

Áyios Nikólaos
Iráklion
Réthymnon
Haniá
Hóra Sfakíon
Gávdhos
Paleohóra

guide

guide

1 The Argo-Saronic 89–110

2 The Cyclades 111–201

3 Crete 203–274

4 The Dodecanese 275–362

5 The east and north Aegean 363–440

6 The Sporades and Évvia 441–473

7 The Ionian islands 475–527

1

The Argo-Saronic

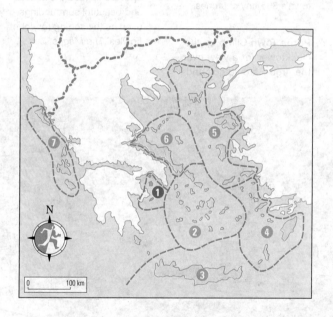

CHAPTER 1   # Highlights

✱ **Temple of Aphaia, Égina**
The best preserved Archaic temple on any island, set on a pretty pine-wooded hill. See p.94

✱ **Paleohóra, Égina** Explore some of the now deserted town's 365 tiny churches. See p.96

✱ **Póros Town** Climb up the clocktower for a view over the Argo-Saronic gulf and the Peloponnese. See p.100

✱ **Ídhra Town** A perfect horse-shoe-shaped harbour surrounded by grand 18th-century mansions. See p.103

✱ **Spétses** Admire the house and beautiful surroundings used as the setting for John Fowles' *The Magus*. See p.106

The Argo-Saronic

The rocky, volcanic chain of **Argo-Saronic** islands, most of them barely an olive's throw from the Argolid, differs to a surprising extent not just from the mainland but from one another. Less surprising – given their proximity to the mainland – is their massive popularity, with Égina (Aegina) almost becoming an Athenian suburb at weekends. Ídhra (Hydra), Póros and Spétses (Spetsai) are not far behind in summer, though their visitors tend to be predominantly cruise- and package-tourists. More than any other group, these islands are at their best out of season, when populations fall dramatically and the port towns return to a quieter, more provincial life.

Égina, important in antiquity and more or less continually inhabited since then, is the most fertile of the group, famous for its pistachio nuts, as well as for one of the finest ancient temples in Greece. Its main problem – the crowds – can be escaped by avoiding weekends, or taking the time to explore its satellite isle, **Angístri**.

The three southerly islands, **Spétses**, **Ídhra** and **Póros**, are pine-cloaked and comparatively infertile. They were not extensively settled until medieval times, when refugees from the mainland – principally Albanian Christians – established themselves here. In response to the barrenness of their new homes the islanders adopted piracy as a livelihood. The seamanship and huge fleets thus acquired were placed at the disposal of the Greek nation during the War of Independence. Today, foreigners and Athenians have replaced locals in the rapidly depopulating harbour towns; windsurfers and sailboats are faint echoes of the massed warships and kaïkia once at anchor.

Accommodation price codes

Throughout the book we've categorized accommodation according to the following **price codes**, which denote the cheapest available double room in high season. All prices are for the room only, except where otherwise indicated. Many hotels, especially those in category ❹ and over, include breakfast in the price; you'll need to check this when booking. During low season, rates can drop by more than fifty percent, especially if you are staying for three or more nights. Exceptions are during the Christmas and Easter weeks when you'll pay high-season prices. Single rooms, where available, cost around seventy percent of the price of a double.

❶ Up to €24
❷ €24–33
❸ €34–42

❹ €43–58
❺ €59–72
❻ €73 and upwards

Note: Youth hostels typically charge €7–9 for a dormitory bed.
For more accommodation details, see pp.52–54.

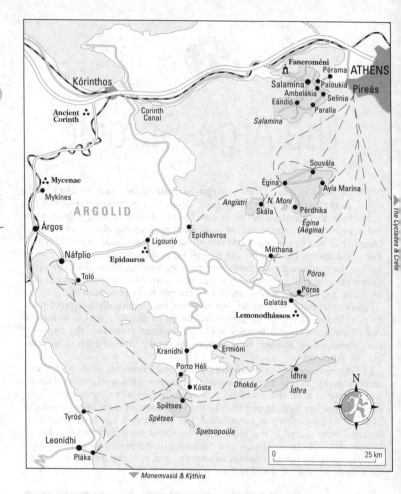

The Cyclades & Crete

▼ Monemvasiá & Kýthira

Ferry routes and schedules

Details of ferry routes, together with approximate journey times and frequencies, are to be found at the end of each chapter in the "Travel details" section. Please note that these are for general guidance only. Ferry schedules change with alarming regularity and the only information to be relied upon is that provided by the port police in each island harbour. Ferry agents in Pireás and on the islands are helpful, of course, but keep in mind that they often represent just one ferry line and won't necessarily inform you of the competition. Be aware, too, that ferry services to the smaller islands tend to be pretty skeletal from mid-September through to April.

In many island groups, ferries are supplemented by catamarans and hydrofoils which tend to take half the time and be twice the price. Most of the major hydrofoil routes are operated from May to early September, with lesser ones sometimes running in July and August only.

The closest island of the Argo-Saronic group, **Salamína**, is virtually a suburb of Pireás, just over a kilometre offshore to its east, and almost touches the industrial city of Mégara to the west. It is frequented by Athenian weekenders or is a base for commuting to the capital, but sees very few foreign visitors. Despite its proximity to the metropolis, it is noted for its distinct folk dances and costumes.

Salamína (Salamis)

Salamína is the quickest possible island hop from Athens. Take the Kifissiá–Pireás train to the end of the line in Pireás and then one of the green buses marked Pérama to the shipyard port of Pérama, just west of Pireás, and a ferry (daily 5am–midnight; €0.40) will whisk you across to the little port of Paloukía in a matter of minutes. The ferry crosses the narrow strait where, in 480 BC, the Greek navy trounced the Persian fleet, despite being outnumbered three to one; this battle is said by some to be more significant than the battle of Marathon, ten years earlier. Alternatively, ferries run from Pireás, next to the Argo-Saronic Flying Dolphins berth (every 30min, 8am–5pm; 45min; €1.05), calling en route at Ambelákia. On arrival in Paloukía, you won't be rewarded by desirable or isolated beaches – the pollution of Pireás and Athens is a little too close for comfort, although the water has much improved in recent years – but you may escape the capital's smog and city pace.

Paloukía, Salamína Town and Selínia

By the ferry dock in **PALOUKÍA** is a bus station, with services to the contiguous capital Salamína Town (3km) and beyond, though the large selection of signed destinations can be confusing.

SALAMÍNA TOWN (also known as Kouloúri) is home to 18,000 of the island's 23,000 population. It's a depressing place, with a couple of banks, a fish market and motorway-like traffic. Pretty much uniquely for an island town – and emphasizing the absence of tourists – there is no bike or scooter rental outlet, and also no hotel (not that you'd want to stay). Bus services link most points on the island, though information about them is scanty. **Iliaktí beach** is pleasant enough, some 5km to the west.

Buses marked **FANEROMÉNI** run to the port at the northwest tip of the island, the **Voudóro peninsula**, where there are ferries across to Lákki Kalomírou, near Mégara on the Athens–Kórinthos road. En route it passes close by the frescoed seventeenth-century **monastery of Faneroméni** (6km from Salamína), rather majestically sited above the gulf.

Around 6km to the south of Paloukía is a third island port, **SELÍNIA**, which has connections direct to the Pireás ferry dock (winter 9.30am, summer five crossings daily between 8am and 2.30pm; 30min; €1.10). It can also be reached direct by bus from Paloukía. This is the main summer resort, with a pleasant waterfront, a bank, several tavernas and two inexpensive hotels, the *Akroyali* (☎010/46 73 263; ❷) and *Votsalakia* (☎010/46 71 334; ❷).

Eándio and the south

South from Salamína Town, the road edges the coast towards Eándio (6km; regular buses). There are a few tavernas along the way, but the sea vistas are not inspiring. **EÁNDIO**, however, is quite a pleasant village, with a little pebble beach and the island's best **hotel**, the *Gabriel* (☎010/46 62 275; ❸), which overlooks the bay, whose waters are said to be returning to health, although the Salamína waterfront opposite can be less than sweet-smelling.

Two roads continue from Eándio. The one to the southeast runs to the unassuming village resorts of Peráni and Paralía (both around 4km from Eándio). The more interesting route is southeast towards Kanákia (8km from Eándio; two buses daily), over the island's pine-covered mountain, and passing (at around 5km) a monastery – dedicated, like most Salamína churches, to Áyios Nikólaos. At the monastery, turn off left to the harbour and small-scale resort of Peristéria (5km). This is a much more attractive settlement than the littered beach and scruffy huts of Kanákia itself.

Égina (Aegina)

Égina was a major power in Classical times, rivalling Athens. It carried trade to the limits of the known world, maintained a sophisticated silver coinage system (the first in Greece) and had prominent athletes and craftsmen. During the fifth century BC, however, the islanders made the political mistake of siding with their fellow Dorians, the Spartans. Athens seized on this as an excuse to act on a long-standing jealousy; her fleets defeated those of the islanders in two separate sea battles and, after the second, the population was expelled and replaced by more tractable colonists.

Subsequent history was less distinguished, with the pattern of occupation familiar to central Greece – by Romans, Franks, Venetians, Catalans and Turks – before the War of Independence brought a brief period as seat of government for the fledgling Greek nation. For a time it was a prison island and only comparatively recently has it shaken off the consequent unfavourable reputation. The grim Égina prison still stands behind the stadium, but is currently used as a stray-dog shelter. These days, the island is most famous for its **pistachio orchards**, whose thirsty trees lower the water table several feet annually – hence the notices warning you of the perennial water crisis.

Athenians regard Égina as a beach annexe for their city, being the closest place to the capital most of them would swim at, though for tourists it has a monument as fine as any in the Aegean in its beautiful fifth-century BC **Temple of Aphaia**. This is located on the east coast, close to the port of **Ayía Marína**, and if it is your primary goal, you'd do best to take one of the ferries or hydrofoils which run directly there in season. Hydrofoils are more frequent than ferries, run from the same quay in Pireás as the conventional boats, and cost hardly any more. If you plan to stay, then make sure your boat docks at **Égina Town**, the island capital. Ferries and hydrofoils also stop at **Souvála**, a Greek weekend retreat between the two ports devoid of interest to outsiders.

Égina Town

A solitary column of the Temple of Apollo beckons as your ferry or hydrofoil steams around the point into the harbour at **ÉGINA TOWN**. The island's capital, it makes an attractive base, with some grand old buildings from the time (1826–28) when it served as the first capital of Greece during the War of Independence. And for somewhere so close to Athens, it isn't especially overrun by foreign tourists, although accommodation prices are high, particularly at weekends.

The **long harbour** waterfront combines the workaday with the picturesque, but is nonetheless appealing: fishermen talk and tend their nets, and kaïkia selling produce from the mainland bob at anchor. North of the port, behind the small town beach, a lone column on a low hill, known, logically enough, as

Kolóna (Column) marks the remains of the temple of Apollo and the ancient acropolis. Near the entrance to the ruins (Tues–Sun 8.30am–3pm; €1.50), a small but worthwhile **archeology museum** has finds from the extensive excavations that have revealed five thousand years and ten layers of settlement; a free pamphlet gives a history and explains the objects on display. On the north flank of Kolóna hill there's an attractive bay with a very small, sandy **beach** – the best spot for swimming in the immediate vicinity of the town.

The town's other sights include the restored **Markéllos Tower**, seat of the first Greek government, uphill from the middle of the harbour, near the large **Church of Áyios Nikólaos**. The frescoed thirteenth-century church of **Ómorfi Ekklisía** is a fifteen-minute walk east of the port. In the suburb of Livádhi, just to the north, a plaque marks the residence of **Nikos Kazantzakis**, when he was writing his most celebrated book, *Zorba the Greek*.

Arrival and accommodation

The **bus station** is on the spacious Platía Ethneyersías, just north of the ferry arrival point, with excellent services to most villages; buy your tickets before you get on the bus. Horse buggies and taxis are found nearby. The **post office** is across the square, and the **tourist police** post (☎02970/23 333) is immediately behind it in the same building as the regular police. Several offices on and behind the main waterfront rent cars, scooters, motorbikes and mountain bikes – Égina is large and hilly enough to make a motor worthwhile for anything other than a pedal to the beaches towards Pérdhika. Four **banks** line the main waterfront. Aegina Island Holidays (☎02970/26 430) on the waterfront near the church, offers excursions to the Epidaurus theatre festival, handles tickets for the hydrofoils to Souvála and Ayía Marína, and books accommodation.

Good inexpensive **accommodation** can be found in the *Electra* rooms (☎02970/23 360, ☞26 715; ②) on Leonárdhou Ladhá, above the square. On the seafront between the square and the Kolóna are the *Avra* (☎02970/22 303, ☞23

917; ●) and the friendly *Plaza Hotel* (☎02970/25 600; ●), where seaview rooms may be a bit noisy. The pleasantly situated *House of Peace* on the corner of Kanari and Aphroditi is under new management and has rooms and apartments (☎02970/23 790, ⓕ28 818, ⓔthe_house_of_peace@yahoo.com). Up above the Markéllos Tower is the attractively restored *Traditional Pension* (*Eyinitiko Arhondiko*; ☎02970/24 968, ⓕ24 156; ●) and on the other side of the church the *Stone House* (*To Petrino Spiti*, ☎ 02970/23 827) has pleasant studios for three (●). Aegina Island Holidays can book air-conditioned doubles with private facilities (●).

Eating and entertainment

There are enough reasonable **tavernas** in the town: directly behind the fish market on P. Irióti is *Psarotaverna Agora*, particularly good for inexpensive seafood and with outdoor seating on the cobbles in summer; near the *Avra* hotel, the small *Lekkas* is excellent for no-nonsense meat grills by the waterside; and nearby *Flisvos* offers charcoal-grilled food by the sea. Further south along the main quay, near the Ionian Bank, the *Estiatorinon Economou* serves good traditional food, while a couple of kilometres south, in the suburbs, the *Stratigos* serves straightforward but well-prepared food overlooking the little harbour at Fáros. Self-caterers will find good prices and a large selection at the Kritikou supermarket on the Ayía Marína road, just beyond the stadium and prison.

In terms of **nightlife**, Égina Town boasts two summer **cinemas**: the Olympia near the football grounds before the *Miranda* hotel, and the new Akroyiali at the south end of the harbour on the Pérdhika road, which shows quality foreign films; the winter cinema, the Titina, is by the park of the medieval tower-house, a block below the OTE. The young and lively might try the *Apocalypse* or *Perdiotika* **bars**, or Petros' *Tropic* all-night café. The well-heeled can sample genuine live *bouzoúki* at Athenian prices at *Kanellas*, also on the waterfront. Most **discos** are across the island in Ayía Marína, but the vast *Vareladiko* disco is in Fáros, just beyond the *Stratigos* taverna.

The free *Essential Aegina* is a useful **listings** booklet, updated regularly during the summer season and available from tourist offices, and some hotels and restaurants.

The Temple of Aphaia

The Doric **Temple of Aphaia** (Mon–Fri 8am–7pm, Sat & Sun 8am–3pm; €2.40) lies 12km east of Égina Town, among pines that are tapped to flavour the local retsina, and beside a less aesthetic radio mast. It is one of the most complete and visually complex ancient buildings in Greece, its superimposed arrays of columns and lintels evocative of an Escher drawing. Built in the fifth century BC to replace a destroyed sixth-century original, it slightly predates the Parthenon. The dedication is unusual: Aphaia was a Cretan nymph who had fled from the lust of King Minos, and seems to have been worshipped almost exclusively on Égina. As recently as two centuries ago the temple's pediments were intact and virtually perfect, depicting two battles at Troy. However, like the Elgin marbles they were "purchased" from the Turks – this time by Ludwig I of Bavaria, which explains their current residence in Munich's Glyptothek museum.

Buses from Égina Town to Ayía Marína stop at the temple, or you could walk from Ayía Marína along the path that takes up where Kolokotróni leaves off, but rented transport allows you to stop at the monastery of Áyios Nektários and at the island's former capital of Paleohóra (see opposite).

Áyios Nektários and Paleohóra

Áyios Nektários, a whitewashed modern convent situated around halfway to the Temple of Afaia, was named in honour of the Greek Orthodox Church's most recent and controversial saint, Anastasios Kefalas, a rather high-living monk who died in 1920 and was canonized in 1962. An oversized church – the largest in Greece – was recently completed on the main road below. Opposite the convent car park a partly paved road leads up into the hills towards the seventeenth-century convent of Khryssoleóndissa – primarily worth seeing for its views.

Paleohóra, a kilometre or so further east, was built in the ninth century as protection against piracy, but failed singularly in this capacity during Barbarossa's 1537 raid. Abandoned in 1827 following Greek independence, Paleohóra is now utterly deserted, but possesses the romantic appeal of a ghost village. You can drive right up to the site: take the turning left after passing the new large church and keep going about 400m. Some twenty of Paleohóra's reputed 365 churches and monasteries – one for every saint's day – remain in a recognizable state, and can be visited, but only those of Episkopí (locked), Áyios Yeóryios and Metamórfosis (on the lower of the two trails) retain frescoes of any merit or are in any state of preservation. Little remains of the town itself; when the islanders left, they simply abandoned their houses and moved to Égina Town.

The east: Ayía Marína and Pórtes

The island's major package resort of **AYÍA MARÍNA**, 15km from Égina Town, lies on the east coast of the island, south of the Afaía temple ridge. The concentrated tackiness of its jam-packed high street rivals anything found on Corfu: signs abound for Guinness and cider, burger bars and salaciously named cocktails. The beach is packed and overlooked by constantly sprouting, half-built hotels, and the water is not clean. It's really only worth coming here for connections to Pireás. There are around five ferries a day in season, with departures in the morning and late in the afternoon.

Beyond the resort, the paved road continues south 8km to **PÓRTES**, a low-key shore hamlet. Among the uneasy mix of new summer villas-in-progress (no short-term accommodation) and old basalt cottages are scattered a few tiny fish **tavernas** and snack bars, with a functional beach between the two fishing anchorages. The road climbs to the village of Anitséou, just below a major saddle on the flank of Mount Óros, and then forges west towards the scenic village of **Pahiá Ráhi**, almost entirely rebuilt in traditional style by foreign owners. From here, a sharp, winding descent leads to the main west-coast road at Marathónas (see below), or a longer, paved and tree-lined route heads back to Égina Town.

Mount Óros

Just south of the saddle between Pahiá Ráhi and Anitséou, mentioned above, are the foundations of the shrine of **Ellaníou Dhiós**, with the monastery of Taxiárhis squatting amid the massive masonry. The 532-metre summit cone of **Mount Óros**, an hour's walk from the highest point of the road, is capped by the modern chapel of Análipsi (the Ascension) and has views across the entire island and much of the Argo-Saronic Gulf.

Gerald Thompson's *A Walking Guide to Aegina*, available locally, describes in detail a series of walks across the range of mountains and wooded valleys between Mount Óros and the Afaía temple and down to the port of Souvála, all avoiding main roads.

The west: Marathónas, Pérdhika and Moní islet

The road due south of Égina Town running along the west coast of the island is served by regular buses (8–10 daily). Small but sprawling **MARATHÓNAS**,

5km from Égina, has the biggest of the west coast's small and rather scruffy sand beaches, and is tolerable enough, with a scattering of rooms, tavernas and cafés along the shore.

PÉRDHIKA, 9km along at the end of the coastal road, scenically set on its little bay, is the most pleasant and picturesque village on the island and certainly has the best range of nonpackaged **accommodation** outside Égina Town. There are rooms on the main road, and just off it, immediately before the waterfront, is the well-priced *Hotel Hippocampus* (℡02970/61 363; ❸). On first sight the elongated village can appear characterless; however, further exploration reveals a relaxed, seaside-holiday atmosphere, very different from the rest of the island. On the attractive, pedestrianized waterfront esplanade, overlooking a panorama of Moní islet and the Peloponnese, are a dozen **tavernas** and cafés; probably the best food is at *O Nondas*.

The only other diversion at Pérdhika is a trip to the pale-limestone offshore islet of **Moní** (10min; several departures daily; €1.50 one way). There are no facilities on the island and most of it is fenced off as a nature conservation area. It's really only worth the trip for a swim in wonderfully clear water, as Pérdhika bay itself is of questionable cleanliness and has very small beach areas.

Angístri

Angístri, fifteen minutes by catamaran from Égina, is small enough to be overlooked by most island-hoppers, though it is now in many foreign holiday brochures. The island fosters an uneasy coexistence between Athenian and German old-timers, who bought property here years ago, and British newcomers on package trips. Beaches, however, remain better and less crowded than on Égina, and out of season the pine-covered island succumbs to a leisurely village pace, with many islanders still making a living from fishing and farming. Headscarves worn by the old women indicate the islanders' Albanian ancestry, and until recently they still spoke Arvanítika – a dialect of medieval Albanian with Greek accretions – amongst themselves.

The Angístri dock in Égina Town is immediately south of the main harbour. **Boats and catamarans** from Égina and Pireás call at Skála, and possibly at Mýlos. **From Pireás**, a direct ferry runs at least twice daily in season, once a day out of season, taking two hours; the fast catamaran three times a day, via Égina, takes one hour. A water taxi is based in Angístri, but will be more expensive.

Skála and Mýlos

The essentially modern resort of **SKÁLA** is dominated by many new apartment buildings and hotels with little to distinguish them, spreading west halfway along the north shore of the island. The popular town beach, Angístri's only sandy one, nestles against the protected south shore of this headland, below the big white church. Just inland of the ferry dock is the attractive hotel *Yana* (℡02970/91 228; ❷), sharing a pool with the *Alter Ego* self-catering apartments; both are run by the helpful Nektarios (Nick) Panou of Skala Travel (℡02970/91 356, ℻91 342, ✉nik.panou@otenet.gr), who can also arrange reservations for other **accommodation**. On summer weekends you would be well advised to reserve ahead. For **food**, there's the *Neptune* taverna in Skála and *Alter Ego* serves excellent crepes; in Mýlos the *Sailor* and *Konaki* are recommended.

Both **scooters** and **mountain bikes** are available for rent; Limenária, near the end of the trans-island road, is less than 8km distant, so in cooler weather

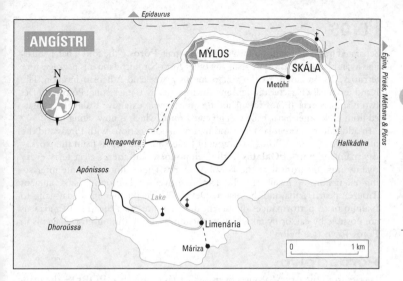

you can comfortably cross Angístri on foot or by bike. A road to the left of the
harbour leads within fifteen minutes to the *Angistri Club*, with a disco-bar on
the rocks above the sea, and the nearby *Alkyoni* taverna. From there, it's another ten-minutes' walk to the secluded **Halikádha** pebble beach backed by
crumbling cliffs and pine-covered hills; along with Dhragonéra (see below), this
is the best that the island has to offer, and is clothing-optional.

   Metóhi, the hillside hamlet just above Skála, was once the main village, and
in recent years has been completely bought up and restored by foreigners
and Athenians; there are no facilities.

   Ever-spreading Skála threatens in the future to merge with **MÝLOS**
(Megalohóri), just 1.5km west along the north coast. Once you penetrate a
husk of new construction, you find an attractive, traditional Argo-Saronic-style
village centre. Although there's no decent beach nearby, it makes an alternative
base to Skála, with plenty of rented **rooms** and some **hotels**. The *Milos Hotel*
(T02970/91 241; ❷) is a good, well-positioned choice.

The rest of the island

A regular bus service, designed to dovetail with the ferry schedule, connects
Skála and Mýlos with Limenária on the far side of the island – or you could
hike from Metóhi along a winding dirt road through the pine forest, with
views across to Égina and the Peloponnese. The paved west-coast road takes
you past the turning for **Dhragonéra**, a broad pebble beach with a dramatic
panorama across to the mainland.

   LIMENÁRIA is a small farming community set at the edge of a fertile
plateau in the southeast corner of the island, and still largely unaffected by
tourism. There are two tavernas – *Tasos* is very good – and a few rooms. A sign
points to a misleadingly named "beach", really just a spot, often monopolized
by male naturists, where you can swim off the rocks. A half-hour walk west of
Limenária, on the old path which parallels the road, will bring you past a shallow salt lake, to a seasonal taverna overlooking the tiny islet of Apónissos and
larger Dhoroússa beyond.

Póros

Separated from the mainland by a 450-metre strait, **Póros** ("the ford") barely qualifies as an island, and far more than any other Argo-Saronic island it is package-tour territory. Its proximity to Pireás also means a weekend Athenian invasion. The island town has character though, and the topography is interesting: Póros is in fact two islands, **Sferiá** (Póros Town) and the much more extensive **Kalávria**, separated from each other by a shallow engineered canal, which is now silting up.

In addition to its regular ferry and hydrofoil connections with Pireás and the other Argo-Saronics, Póros has frequent boats shuttling across from the workaday mainland port of **Galatás** in the Peloponnese, and there's a car ferry every twenty minutes from near the Naval Academy. These allow for some interesting excursions – locally to the lemon groves of Lemonodhássos, ancient Troezen near Trizína, and the nearby Devil's Bridge. Further afield, day-trips to Náfplio or to performances of ancient drama at the great theatre of Epidaurus are possible by car, or by taking an excursion, available through travel agents in Póros Town (see below).

Póros Town

Ferries from the Argo-Saronics or from Galatás drop you at **PÓROS**, the main town on the island, which rises steeply on three sides of the tiny volcanic Sferiá. The harbour and town are picturesque, and the cafés and waterfront lively. Fishermen sell their catches direct from the boat and it is possible to arrange fishing trips. Particular sights are the hilltop clocktower and a small, well-labelled **archeological museum** (Mon–Sat 9am–3pm; free), with items from the mainland site of Troezen and elsewhere.

Near the main ferry dock is the helpful Family Tours (☎02980/23 743, ℻24 480) which has a variety of rooms available. Also on the waterfront are three other **travel agents**: Marinos Tours (☎02980/23 423), sole agents for Hellas Flying Dolphin hydrofoils and with well-priced local maps, Hellenic Sun

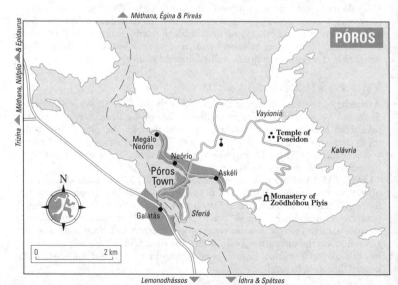

△ Póros harbour

Travel (℡02980/25 901) and Saronic Gulf Travel (℡02980/24 555). All these agencies **exchange** money, arrange **accommodation** in rented rooms and handle **tours** off the island. If you want to look around on your own, quieter places to stay are up on the hill behind the clocktower, although prices are generally on the high side. To the right of the road to Kalávria you'll find two reasonable hotels: *Dimitra* (℡02980/22 697, ℻25 653; ❷) and *Latsi* (℡02980/22 392; ❷). Most of the other hotels are across the canal on Kalávria. Camping is not encouraged anywhere on the island and the nearest official campsite, *Kyrayelo*, is just west of Galatás.

Down on the quayside, among the cafés, bars, creperies and souvenir shops facing Galatás, good-value **restaurants** include *Grill Oasis* and *Mouragio*, at the far end away from the ferry dock. *Moskhoyiannis* has traditional Greek food in the souvenir lane which runs between the Alpha Bank and the post office square. A well-signed lane, between the *Latsi* and the school, leads gently up, past the police station and the Ergani weaving shop, to the upper square. Here, by the Áyios Yeóryios cathedral are a cluster of good tavernas: *Platanos*, *Perasma*, *Dimitris* – the last run by a local butcher, so offers excellent meat – and, just beyond, the *Kipos* (*Garden*). The *Lithos* bar is nearby and the *Korali* and *Sirocco* **discos** provide nightlife, with both Greek and foreign music.

Additional facilities around the waterfront include **scooter** and **bicycle** rental outlets (you can take either across on boats to the mainland), four **banks**, a **post office**, the summer-only Diana **cinema** and the helpful **tourist police** (℡02980/22 462; mid-May to Sept).

Kalávria

Most of Póros's **hotels** are to be found on Kalávria, the main body of the island, just across the canal beyond the Naval Cadets' Training School. They stretch for a couple of kilometres on either side of the bridge, with some of those to the west in Neório ideally situated to catch the dawn chorus – the Navy's marching band. If you'd rather sleep in, head beyond the first bay where the fishing boats tie up. Two kilometres from the bridge, in **Megálo Neório**, is the pleasant *Pavlou* hotel (℡02980/22 734, ℻22 735; ❺–❻), a larger beach and a watersports centre.

Alternatively, turn right through **Askélli**, where posh hotels and villas face good clear water. Two **bus** routes run half-hourly from Poros Town waterfront to Askéli and Zoödhóhou Piyís, and to Neório.

The monastery of Zoödhóhou Piyís and Temple of Poseidon

At the end of the four-kilometre stretch of road through Askéli lies the eighteenth-century **monastery of Zoödhóhou Piyís** ("Life-giving Spring") whose monks have fled the tourists and have been replaced by a caretaker. It's a pretty spot, with a couple of summer tavernas at the beach below.

From here you can either walk up across to the northern side of the island through the pines, or bike along the road. Initially, Kalávria appears to be mostly pine forest, but the far side has fertile plateaus, olive terraces, small deserted beaches in narrow inlets and magnificent panoramic views. Foot or bike routes lead you to a saddle in the hills and the few columns and ruins that make up the sixth-century BC **Temple of Poseidon**. Keep your eyes open or you may miss them; look for a small blue caretaker's hut. It was here that Demosthenes, fleeing from the Macedonians after taking part in the last-ditch resistance of the Athenians, took poison rather than surrender. The road leads on, back down in a circular route to the canal and Sferiá.

Ídhra (Hydra)

The port and town of **Ídhra**, with tiers of substantial greystone mansions and white-walled, red-tiled houses climbing up from a perfect horseshoe harbour, are a beautiful spectacle. The whole island is treated as a national monument, blessedly free of traffic – except for an occasional garbage lorry – making it one of the most peaceful and refreshing destinations in Greece. Unfortunately, thousands of others think so too, so the town's busy from Easter until September. In summer, especially with the midday crush of cruise-ship day-trippers and the weekend invasion of Athenians, it's packed to the gills; the front becomes one long outdoor café and souvenir stall, the hotels are full and the discos flourish. Once a fashionable artists' colony, established in the 1960s as people restored the grand old houses, it has experienced a predictable metamorphosis into one of the more popular (and expensive) resorts in Greece. Good beaches are also notably scarce. But this acknowledged, a visit is still recommended, especially out of peak season and during the week.

Ídhra Town

The waterfront of **ÍDHRA TOWN** is lined with mansions, most of them built during the eighteenth century, on the accumulated wealth of a remarkable merchant fleet of 160 ships which traded as far afield as America and, during the Napoleonic Wars, broke the British blockade to sell grain to France. Fortunes were made and the island also enjoyed a special relationship with the Turkish Porte, governing itself and paying no tax, but providing sailors for the sultan's navy. These conditions naturally attracted Greek immigrants from the less-privileged mainland, and by the 1820s the town's population was nearly 20,000 – an incredible figure when you reflect that today it is under 3000. During the War of Independence, Hydriot merchants provided many of the ships for the Greek forces and consequently many of the commanders.

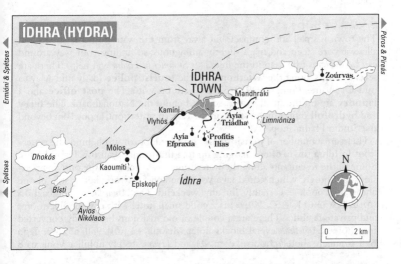

Ídhra festivals

On the second or third weekend in June, Ídhra Town celebrates the **Miaoulia**, in honour of Admiral Andreas Miaoulis whose **fire boats**, packed with explosives, were set adrift upwind of the Turkish fleet during the War of Independence. The highlight of the celebrations is the burning of a boat at sea as a tribute to the sailors who risked their lives in this dangerous enterprise.

On an altogether more peaceful note, the **International Puppet Theatre Festival** takes place here at the end of July and appeals to children of all ages.

Easter is a particularly colourful and moving experience here. Ídhra's prosperity allows for grand celebrations, with a special emphasis on performances of choral music. Reservations must be made well ahead of time for all of these festivals.

The **mansions** (*arhóndika*) of these merchant families, designed by Venetian and Genoese architects, are still the great monuments of the town. A town map is available locally, if you are interested in seeking them out – some are labelled at the entrance with "*Oikía*" (home) and the family name. On the western waterfront, and the hill behind, are the **Voulgaris** mansion, with its interesting interior, and the **Tombazis** mansion, used as a holiday hostel for arts students. Set among pines above the restored windmill on the western point, the **Koundouriotis** mansion was the home of George Koundouriotis, a wealthy shipowner who fought in the War of Independence and whose great grandson, Pavlos Koundouriotis, was president of republican Greece in the 1920s. It is being refurbished as a museum with EU funding. On the eastern waterfront are the **Kriezis** mansion, the **Spiliopoulos** mansion and the **Tsamados** mansion – now the national merchant navy college which you can sometimes visit between lectures. The **historical archives museum** is also on the eastern waterfront (Tues–Sun 9am–2.30pm; €3).

Ídhra is also reputedly hallowed by no fewer than 365 churches – a total claimed by many a Greek island, but here with some justice. The most important is the church of **Panayía Mitropóleos**, set in a monastic courtyard by the port, with a distinctive clocktower and a **Byzantine museum** of uncertain opening hours.

Practicalities

The town is small and compact, but away from the waterfront the streets and alleyways are steep and maps slightly ambiguous, so finding your way around can be difficult (the map in the free *This Summer in Hydra* will help). There are several **banks** along the waterfront, and the **tourist police** (daily mid-May to mid-Oct 9am–10pm; ☎02980/52 205) are on Vótsi. The **post office** and a **laundry** are on the small market square, behind the National bank. The **ferry** and **hydrofoil** offices are upstairs on the eastern waterfront, about 10m beyond the Studio Hydra shop.

There are a number of **pensions** and **hotels** along, or just behind, the waterfront in Ídhra town, often charging up to a third more than usual island rates. Some of the restaurants along the waterfront act as agents for the outlying pensions and hotels, which could save you time and footwork; better still, phone ahead and book – certainly for any weekend. The *Amarillis* at Tombázi 15 (☎02980/53 611, ℗52 249; ◍) is a good small hotel with comfortable rooms and private facilities. There are a couple of old mansions beautifully converted into hotels: *Angelica*, several blocks up at Miaoúli 42 (☎02980/53 202, ℗53 698, ✉angelicahotel@hotmail.com; ◍), and *Hydra*, steeply uphill at Voulgari 8

(☎ & ℻ 02980/52 102, ✉hydrahotel@aig.forthnet.gr; ❹). Of the pensions, try the *Erofili*, further up Tombázi (☎02980/54 049; ❷).

There's no shortage of **restaurants** and cafés around the waterfront, but for good tavernas you would do better to head a little inland. The *Garden* taverna, known for tasty meat dishes, is on the road heading up from the hydrofoil dock, with the equally good *Xeri Elia* down the narrow street outside the *Garden*'s wall. Above the *Amarillis Hotel* is the small *Barba Dimas* taverna, which has wonderful mezédhes, snails and fish. Further up on the same road, *To Kryfo Limani* (supper only) is a pleasant taverna in a small garden, while further yet will bring you excellent home cooking at the *Yeitoniko* (also known as *Manolis & Christina's*), which has tables on its roof and a small veranda. For light snacks and breakfast, try the small and friendly *Pigadi* café, downhill from the *Amarillis*.

For **nightlife** you might start at a portside bar: try the *Pirate* or *To Roloi*. Or hike up the hill west of town to *Heaven*, a disco favoured by the younger set. A few minutes further west on the way to Kamíni you'll have no trouble locating the *Scirocco* disco, if it's open.

Beaches around Ídhra Town

The town's only sandy beach is at **MANDHRÁKI**, 1.5km east of the harbour along a concrete road; it's the private domain of the *Miramare Hotel* (☎02980/52 300; ❻), although the windsurfing centre is open to all.

On the opposite side of the harbour, to the southwest, a broad coastal path leads around to **KAMÍNI**, about a twenty-minute walk. Just as you reach Kamíni on the right is a small pension, *Antonia* (☎02980/52 481; ❸) On the left, across the street, Eléni Petrolékka has a popular rival pension and apartments (☎02980/52 701; ❸). Also on the left is the *Kondylenia* restaurant, with fresh fish and wonderful views of the sunset. About 50m up the dry, paved streambed to the left is *Christina's*, a fine traditional Greek fish taverna.

Thirty-minutes' walk beyond Kamíni (or a boat ride from the port) will bring you to **VLYHÓS**, a small hamlet with three tavernas, rooms, a small beach and a restored nineteenth-century bridge. The *Iliovasilema* taverna enjoys sunset views from the water's edge, near the small jetty, while just beyond are the attractive *Antigone* rooms (☎02980/53 228, ℻53 042; ❹) and café. Any of these establishments can call a water taxi to whisk you back to town. **Camping** is tolerated here (though nowhere else closer to town) and the swimming in the lee of an offshore islet is good. Further out is the steep-sided island of **Dhokós**, large but only seasonally inhabited by goatherds and people tending their olives.

The rest of the island

There are no motor vehicles on Ídhra, except for a few lorries to cart away rubble and rubbish, and no surfaced roads away from the port; the island is mountainous and its interior accessible only by foot or hoof. The net result is that most tourists don't venture beyond the town, so by a little walking you can find yourself in a dramatically different kind of island. The pines devastated by forest fires in 1985 are fortunately now growing back.

Following the streets of the town upwards and inland behind the *Angelica* you reach a path which winds up the mountain for about an hour's walk to the **monastery of Profítis Ilías** and the **convent of Ayía Efpraxía**. Both are beautifully situated; the nuns at the convent (the lower of the two) offer hand-woven fabrics for sale. A path continues behind Profítis Ilías to a saddle overlooking the south coast and a steeply descending *kalderími* onwards to scattered houses and chapels near the sea. From the saddle, a faint path climbs to the right for twenty minutes to the 588-metre summit of Mount Éros, the Argo-Saronic islands' highest viewpoint. To the east of Profítis Ilías are four more monasteries, the nearest to town being **Ayía Triádha**, occupied by a few monks (no women admitted). From here a path continues east for two more hours to the cloister of **Zourvás** in the extreme east of the island.

A dirt road continues west of Vlyhós, past a busy boat-repair yard, to **Episkopí**, a high plateau planted with olives and vineyards and dotted by a scattering of homes (no facilities), and then climbs above Mólos Bay, the property of an Athenian hospital owner, and closed to the public. From Episkopí itself, vague tracks lead to the southwestern extreme of the island, on either side of which the bays of **Bísti** and **Áyios Nikólaos** offer solitude and good swimming. Bísti has a pebble beach with rocks for swimming off at one side; Áyios Nikólaos has a small sand beach.

The best cove of the many on the south coast is **Limnióniza** (beyond Ayía Triádha), with a pebble beach and pine trees; the overland access path is long (1hr 15min from town) though well-marked and obvious.

Points on the coast can be reached much more easily by **water taxis**, which will drop you off and then pick you up again at any time you arrange.

Spétses (Spetsai)

Spétses was the island where the author John Fowles once lived and which he used, thinly disguised as Phraxos, as the setting for *The Magus*. It is today very popular with well-to-do Athenians and with foreigners, and seems to have risen above the bad 1980s reputation earned by an unhealthy proportion of cheap package tours and lager louts. The architecture of Spétses Town is distinct and distinguished, though less photogenic than that of Ídhra. Lacking any dramatic topography, and despite a bout of forest-fire devastation in 1990, hints of the landscape described by Fowles are still to be seen: "away from its inhab-

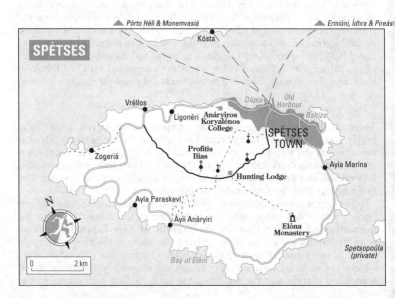

ited corner [it is] truly haunted . . . its pine forests uncanny". Remarkably, at Áyii Anáryiri, Spétses' best beach, development has been restrained to a scattering of holiday villas.

Spétses Town

SPÉTSES TOWN is the island's port – and its only settlement. It shares with Ídhra the same history of late eighteenth-century mercantile adventure and prosperity, and the same leading role in the War of Independence, which made its foremost citizens the aristocrats of the newly independent Greek state. Pebble-mosaic courtyards and streets sprawl between 200-year-old mansions, whose architecture is quite distinct from the Peloponnesian styles across the water. Though homeowners may bring private cars onto the island, their movement inside the town limits is prohibited. A few taxis supplement the horse-drawn buggies, whose bells ring cheerfully night and day along the long waterfront, though animal welfare activists are justifiably worried by the condition of some of the horses by summer's end. Motorbikes, scooters and noisy three-wheel mini-trucks are the preferred mode of transport, and career continuously through the town streets, making life almost as difficult for pedestrians as if cars had been allowed.

The sights are principally the majestic old houses and gardens, the grandest of which is the magnificent Mexis family mansion, built in 1795 and now used as the **local museum** (Tues–Sun 8.30am–2.15pm; €1.50), housing displays of relics from the War of Independence that include the bones of the Spetsiot admiral-heroine Laskarina Bouboulina. One of Bouboulina's homes, to the rear of the cannon-studded main harbour known as the **Dápia**, has been made into a **museum** (daily morning and late afternoon; €3) by her descendants and is well worth visiting. Guided tours (30min) are given in English several times a day.

Just outside the town, Fowles aficionados will notice **Anáryiros Koryalénos College**, a curious Greek re-creation of an English public school where the author was employed and set part of his tale; it is now vacant, save for the occasional conference or kids' holiday programme. Like the massive waterfront **Hotel Posidonion,** where kings and presidents once slept, the college was endowed by Sotirios Anaryiros, the island's great nineteenth-century benefactor. An enormously rich self-made man, he was also responsible for replanting the pine forest that now covers the island. His former residence, behind the *Hotel Roumani*, is a Pharaonic monument to bad taste.

Walking east from the Dápia, you pass the **Old Harbour** inlet, still a well-protected mooring, and the church of **Áyios Nikólaos** with its graceful belfry, "Freedom or Death" memorial and some giant pebble mosaics. At the end of the road you reach the **Baltíza** inlet where, among the sardine-packed yachts, half a dozen boatyards continue to build kaïkia in the traditional manner; it was one of these that re-created the *Argo* for Tim Severin's re-enactment of the "Jason Voyage". An extensive new housing development behind Baltíza will probably edge local prices even higher.

Practicalities

A good way to get around the island is by bike, and, despite the hills, you can reach most points or make the 25km circuit without too much exertion. Several reliable **bike** and **scooter** rental outlets are scattered through town.

All kinds of **accommodation** are available in Spétses Town, but be warned that prices are inflated in high season, although the town is smaller and less steep than Ídhra, so hunting around for a good deal is not such hard work. If you don't fancy pounding the streets yourself, try Alasia Travel (☎02980/74 098), Melédon Tourist and Travel Agency (☎02980/74 497) or Pine Island Tours (☎02980/72 464), all by the Dápia. Simple but comfortable hotels include *Faros* (☎02980/72 613, ⓕ72 614; ❸) on Platía Oroloyíou ("Clocktower Square"), *Stelios* (☎02980/72 971; ❸) on the waterfront, and *Star* (☎02980/72 214, ⓕ27 872; ❺), which is quieter because its pebble-mosaic pavement makes it off-limits to vehicles. A few hotels – the *Faros* (see above), the *Alexandris* (☎02980/72 211; ❸), above the petrol station, and the waterfront *Klimis* (☎02980/72 334; ❹) – stay open all winter. Inland a few blocks from the ferry landing the *Villa Christina* (☎02980/72 218; ❹), an old villa in its own quiet garden, has doubles and studios with a fridge, some with views of the harbour. You might even want to spring for the recently renovated *Posidonion* (☎02980/72 308, ⓕ72 209; ❺).

In Spétses Town, **food** and **drink** tend to be overpriced. Among the better options are *Roussos*, 300m east of the Dápia, just beyond the *Klimis*; or the *Lazaros* taverna, about 400m up from the Dápia, which are better-priced and have good food. For fish, go to the *Bouboulina* ouzerí opposite the fish market, which is before *Klimis*, or the long-established *Patralis* near the water in Kounoupítsa, west towards the *Spetses* hotel. The *Bakery Restaurant*, above the popular bakery just up from the ferry landing, offers more updated fare, including a fine artichoke moussaka. The ouzerí *Byzantino* is popular, characterful, but expensive, as are many other places around the Old Harbour.

By day, *To Kafenio*, near the Flying Dolphin office at the Dápia, remains steadfastly traditional, with drinks and lunchtime mezédhes – a good place to watch and wait for your ferry. By night, clubbers head for *Figaro*, in the Old Harbour, and the places at the other end of town around Kounoupítsa. Few of these places shut until the fishermen are setting out.

The **post office** is near the *Roussos* taverna, while a couple of **banks** are behind the Dápia, near the *Roumani* hotel. There's also a **laundry** behind Platía Oroloyíou.

Around the island

For **swimming** you need to get clear of the town. Beaches within walking distance are at **Ayía Marína** (twenty minutes east, with the very pleasant *Paradise* restaurant), at various spots beyond the Old Harbour, and several other spots half an hour away in either direction. The tempting smaller isle of **Spetsopoúla**, just offshore from Ayía Marína, is off-limits: it's the private property of the heirs of shipping magnate Stavros Niarchos.

For heading further afield, you'll need to hire a **bike** or **scooter**, or use the **kaïkia** rides from the Dápia, which run to beaches around the island in summer. A very expensive alternative are **water taxis**, though they can take up to ten people. **Walkers** might want to go over the top of the island to Áyii Anáryiri; forest fire has ravaged much of the southern side's pines between Ayía Marína and Áyii Anáryiri, though happily they are growing back. There is a **bus** service to Áyii Anáryiri from near the *Roussos* taverna, running several times a day in season. Routes out of town start from beyond the *Lazaros* taverna, and pass the forest service firewatch tower. Brave the precariously attached steps and you're rewarded with the island's highest and best viewpoint.

West from Spétses Town

Heading west from the Dápia around the coast, the road is paved or in good condition almost all around the island. The forest that survived the fires stretches from the central hills right down to the western shores and makes for a beautiful coastline with little coves and rocky promontories, all shaded by trees. *Panas Taverna* at Ligonéri, run by a Greek-American woman, provides wonderful respite from the bustle of town. You can swim below and then have lunch or dinner under the pines. A regular bus service runs to Ligonéri in season from in front of the *Hotel Posidonion*. A (not always reliable) timetable is posted at the stop.

Vréllos is the next place you come to, at the mouth of a wooded valley known locally as "Paradise", which would be a fairly apt description, except that, like so many of the beaches, it becomes littered every year with windblown rubbish. However, the entire shore is dotted with coves and in a few places there are small, seasonal tavernas – there's a good one at **Zogeriá**, for instance, where the scenery and rocks more than make up for the small beach.

Working your way anticlockwise around the coast towards Áyii Anáryiri you reach **Áyia Paraskeví** with its small church and beach – one of the most beautiful coves on Spétses and an alternate stop on some of the kaïki runs. There's a basic beach café and watersports here in summer. On the hill behind is the house John Fowles used as the setting for *The Magus*, the **Villa Yasemiá**, available for rent to Fowles aficionados; contact Pine Island Tours (℡02980/72 464, ℻73 255).

Áyii Anáryiri

Áyii Anáryiri, on the south side of the island, is the best, if also the most popular, beach: a beautiful, long, sheltered bay of fine sand. Gorgeous first thing in the morning, it fills up later in the day with bathers, windsurfers and, at one corner, speedboats driving waterskiers. On the right-hand side of the bay, looking out to sea, there's a sea cave, which you can walk or swim to and explore, if you're not discouraged by the ominous rockfall on the access steps. There's a good seafront taverna and another, *Tassos*, just behind, run by one of the island's great eccentrics.

Travel details

Ferries

From the central harbour at Pireás at least 4 boats daily run to Ayía Marína (1hr) and 11 to Égina (1hr 30min); 1–2 daily to Skála and Mýlos (2hr); 4 daily to Póros (3hr 30min); 1–2 daily to Ídhra (4hr 30min) and Spétses (5hr 30min). About 4 connections daily between Égina and Póros; 4–5 daily between Égina and Angístri; from Angístri about 4 weekly to Paleá Epídhavros, far less frequently to Póros and Méthana.

Most of the ferries stop on the Peloponnesian mainland at Méthana (between Égina and Póros) and Ermióni (between Ídhra and Spétses); it is possible to board them here. Some continue from Spétses to Pórto Héli. There are also constant boats between Póros and Galatás (10min) from dawn until late at night, boat-taxis between Spétses and Pórto Héli, and 4 daily ferries between Spétses and Kósta.

NB there are more ferries at weekends and fewer out of season (although the service remains good); for Égina and Póros they leave Pireás most frequently between 7.30am and 9am, 2pm and 4pm. Do not buy a return ticket as it saves no money and limits you to one specific boat. The larger landing-craft ferries are generally less expensive, but the smaller regular boats are somewhat faster. A schedule is posted at the small Port Police kiosk on the quay, and tickets can be purchased at nearby stalls. The general information number for the Argo-Saronic ferries is ℡010/41 75 382.

Flying Dolphin hydrofoils

Approximately hourly services from Aktí Tselépi at Pireás to Égina only 6am–8pm in season, 7am–7pm out of season (40min).

Most hydrofoils going beyond Égina leave from

the Zéa Marina: 4–15 times daily to Póros (1hr), Ídhra (1hr 40min) and Spétses (2hr–2hr 30min) but there are also several more convenient services daily from Aktí Tselépi, run by Saronic Dolphins (both on far Southeast quay). All these times depend upon the stops en route, and frequencies vary with the season.

Égina is connected with Méthana and Póros 1–3 times a day; Póros, Ídhra and Spétses with each other 5–7 times daily. Some hydrofoils also stop at Méthana and Ermióni and most of those to Spétses continue to Porto Héli (15min more). This is a junction of the hydrofoil route – in season there is usually one a day onwards to Toló and Náfplio (and vice versa; 30 and 45min) and another to Monemvasía (2hr). The Monemvasía hydrofoil continues 2–4 days a week (Fri–Sun) to the island of Kýthira.

NB Services are heavily reduced out of season, though all the routes between Pórto Héli and Pireás still run. Hydrofoils are usually twice as fast and twice as expensive as ordinary boats, though to Égina the price is little different. You can now buy round-trip tickets to destinations in the Argo-Saronic Gulf. In season, it's not unusual for departures to be fully booked for a day or so at a time.

Details and tickets available from the Hellas Flying Dolphins office in Athens at 2 Vas. Konstandinou (☎010/75 20 540) or in Pireás at Ákti Themistokléous 8 (☎010/41 99 000). Tickets can be bought at the departure quays on Aktí Tselépi in Pireás and at Zéa Marina.

2

The Cyclades

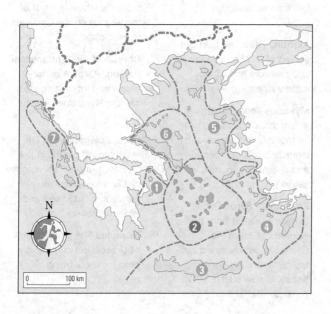

CHAPTER 2 # Highlights

✳ **Delos** The Cyclades' sacred centre and holiest ancient site, birthplace of Apollo and Artemis. See p.152

✳ **Caldera of Thíra** A spectacular geographical wonder, this crater left by a colossal volcanic explosion averages five miles in diameter. See p.190

✳ **Akrotíri, Thíra** The best preserved of all Minoan cities, and possibly part of legendary Atlantis. See p.196

✳ **Mýkonos Town** Charming labyrinthine lanes filled with restaurants, boutiques and nightlife but is overpriced and overrun by tourists in season. See p.146

✳ **Ermoúpoli, Sýros** Once Greece's busiest port, the elegant capital of the Cyclades, with arcaded central platía and an opera house, is now a UNESCO heritage site. See p.154

✳ **Boat tour around Mílos** Take in the geological diversity of this volcanic island, with swimming and a late lunch on nearby Kímolos. See p.132

✳ **Tragéa, Náxos** This fertile inland plain, covered with orchards, shelters most of the villages on the Cyclades' largest island. See p.173

✳ **Church of Ekatondapylianí, Paríkia, Páros** A picturesque and interesting sixth-century Byzantine church. See p.160

✳ **Hóra, Folégandhros** The least spoiled capital in the Cyclades, atop a spectacular cliff and free of traffic, with a handsome old *kástro* and white churches. See p.189

✳ **Hóra, Íos** The party capital of Greece, yet surprisingly pretty and charming. See p.185

2

The Cyclades

N amed after the circle they form around the sacred island of Delos, the **Cyclades** (Kykládhes) is the most satisfying Greek archipelago for island-hopping. On no other group do you get quite such a strong feeling of each island as a microcosm, each with its own distinct traditions, customs and path of modern development. Most of these self-contained realms are compact enough to walk around in a few days, giving you a sense of completeness and identity impossible on, say, Crete or most of the Ionian islands.

The islands do share some features, with the majority of them (Ándhros, Náxos, Sérifos and Kéa excepted) being arid and rocky; most also share the "Cycladic" style of brilliant-white, cubist architecture. The extent and impact of tourism, though, is markedly haphazard, so that although some English is spoken on most islands, a slight detour from the beaten track – from Íos to Síkinos, for example – can have you groping for your Greek phrasebook.

But whatever the level of tourist development, there are only two islands where it has come completely to dominate their character: **Íos**, the original hippie-island and still a paradise for hard-drinking backpackers, and **Mýkonos**, by far the most popular of the group, with its teeming old town, selection of nude beaches and sophisticated clubs and gay bars. After these two, **Páros**, **Sífnos**, **Náxos** and **Thíra** (Santoríni) are currently the most popular, with their beaches and main towns drastically overcrowded at the height of the season. To avoid the hordes altogether – except in August, when nearly everywhere is overrun and escape is impossible – the most promising islands are

Accommodation price codes

Throughout the book we've categorized accommodation according to the following **price codes**, which denote the cheapest available double room in high season. All prices are for the room only, except where otherwise indicated. Many hotels, especially those in category ❹ and over, include breakfast in the price; you'll need to check this when booking. During low season, rates can drop by more than fifty percent, especially if you are staying for three or more nights. Exceptions are during the Christmas and Easter weeks when you'll pay high-season prices. Single rooms, where available, cost around seventy percent of the price of a double.

❶ Up to €24	❹ €43–58
❷ €24–33	❺ €59–72
❸ €34–42	❻ €73 and upwards

Note: Youth hostels typically charge €7–9 for a dormitory bed.
For more accommodation details, see pp.52–54.

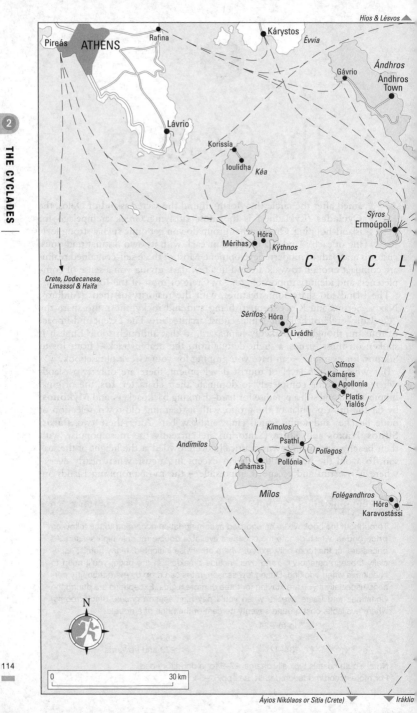

Pireás

ATHENS

Rafina

Kárystos

Évvia

Gávrio

Ándhros

Ándhros
Town

Lávrio

Korissía

Ioulidha Kéa

Crete, Dodecanese,
Limassol & Haifa

Hóra

Mérihas Kýthnos

Sýros
Ermoúpoli

C Y C L

Sérifos Hóra

Livádhi

Sífnos
Kamáres
Apollonía

Platís
Yialós

Kímolos

Andímilos

Psathí

Políegos

Adhámas

Pollónia

Mílos

Folégandhros

Hóra
Karavostássi

N

114

0   30 km

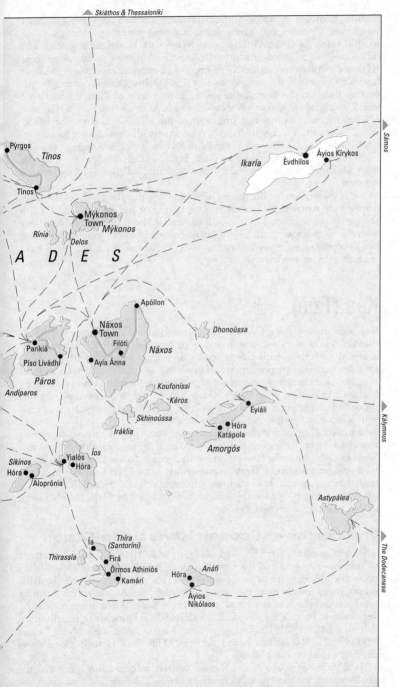

Skiáthos & Thessaloníki

Pýrgos

Tínos

Tínos

Ikaría   Évdhilos   Áyios Kírykos

Sámos

Mýkonos
Town
Mýkonos

Rínia

Delos

A   D   E   S

Apóllon

Dhonoússa

Náxos
Town
Filóti

Parikiá

Píso Livádhi

Náxos

Ayía Ánna

Páros

Koufoníssi

Andíparos

Kéros

Skhinoússa

Eyiáli

Kálymnos

Iráklia

Hóra
Katápola

Amorgós

Íos

Síkinos

Yialós

Hóra

Hóra

Astypálea

Aloprónia

Ía

Thíra
(Santoríni)

The Dodecanese

Thirassía

Firá

Órmos Athiniós

Hóra   Anáfi

Kamári

Áyios
Nikólaos

(Crete)

Síkinos, Kímolos or Anáfi, or the minor islets around Náxos. For a different view of the Cyclades, visit **Tínos** and its imposing pilgrimage church, a major spiritual centre of Greek Orthodoxy, or **Sýros** with its elegant townscape and (like Tínos) large Catholic minority. Due to their closeness to Athens, adjacent **Kýthnos** and **Kéa** are predictably popular – and relatively expensive – weekend havens for Greeks. The one major ancient site is **Delos** (Dhílos), certainly worth making time for: the commercial and religious centre of the Classical Greek world, it's visited most easily on a day-trip, by kaïki or jet boat from Mýkonos.

When it comes to **moving on**, many of the islands – in particular Mílos, Páros, Náxos and Thíra – are handily connected with Crete (easier in season), while from Tínos, Mýkonos, Sýros, Páros, Náxos, Thíra or Amorgós you can reach many of the Dodecanese by direct boat. Similarly, you can regularly get from Mýkonos, Náxos, Sýros and Páros to Ikaría and Sámos (in the eastern Aegean).

One consideration for the timing of your visit is that the Cyclades often get frustratingly **stormy**, particularly in early spring or late autumn, and it's also the group worst affected by the *meltémi*, which blows sand and tables about with ease throughout much of July and August. Delayed or cancelled ferries are not uncommon, so if you're heading back to Athens to catch a flight leave yourself a day or two's leeway.

Kéa (Tziá)

Kéa is the closest of the Cyclades to the mainland and is extremely popular in summer, and at weekends year-round, with Athenians. Their impact is mostly confined to certain small coastal resorts, leaving most of the interior quiet, although there is a preponderance of expensive apartments and villas and not as many good tavernas as you might expect because so many visitors self-cater. Midweek or outside peak season, Kéa is a more enticing destination, with its rocky, forbidding perimeter and inland oak and almond groves. It's an excellent destination for those who enjoy a rural ramble.

As ancient Keos, the island and its strategic, well-placed harbour supported four cities – a pre-eminence that continued until the nineteenth century when Sýros became the main Greek port. Today, tourists account for the sea traffic with regular (in season) **ferry connections** with Lávrio on the mainland (only a ninety-minute bus ride from Athens), plus useful hydrofoils and ferries to and from Pireás, Sýros and Kýthnos; there may also be Mega Dolphin services to and from Zéa (near Pireás).

The northwest coast: Korissía to Otziás

The small northern ferry and hydrofoil port of **KORISSÍA** has fallen victim to uneven expansion and has little beauty to lose; if you don't like its looks upon disembarking, try to get a bus to Písses (16km), Otziás (6km) or Ioulídha (6km). Buses usually meet the boats; during July and August there's a regular fixed schedule around the island, but at other times public transport can be very elusive. There are a few **taxis** on Kéa, and two motorbike rental outfits: Adonis (☎02880/21 097), close to the *Karthea* hotel, and Moto Center (☎02880/21 844), a little inland near the OTE, both of them being more expensive than on most islands.

There's a list of rooms in the seafront **tourist information** office, and the kindly agents for the Flying Dolphin hydrofoils (To Stegadhi bookshop), sell

maps and guides, and can phone around in search of **accommodation**. The best choices are the *Nikitas* pension (℡02880/21 193; ❷), open all year and very friendly; *Hotel Korissia* (℡02880/21 484; ❸–❹), well inland along the stream bed; *Hotel Tzia Mas* (℡02880/21 305; ❷–❹), right behind the east end of the otherwise uninspiring port beach; and the somewhat noisy *Karthea* (℡02880/21 204; ❹), which does, however, boast single rooms and year-round operation, a cameo appearance in recent Greek history: when the junta fell in July 1974, the colonels were initially imprisoned for some weeks in the then-new hotel, while the recently restored civilian government pondered what to do with them; Kéa was then so remote and unvisited that the erstwhile tyrants were safely out of reach of a vengeful populace. For **eating**, *Iy Akri* and *Angyrovoli* near the *Karthea* hotel have standard fare, while near the jetty *Apothiki* seems more popular than its smarter neighbour, *Lagoudera*. There's good swimming at **Yialiskári**, a small, eucalyptus-fringed beach between Korissía and Vourkári; the *Yialiskari* rooms (℡02880/21 197; ❷) enjoy a good view.

VOURKÁRI, a couple of kilometres to the north, is more compact and arguably more attractive than Korissía, serving as the favourite hangout of the yachting set; there's no real beach or accommodation here. Three fairly expensive and indistinguishable **tavernas** serve up good seafood dishes, and there's a very good ouzerí – *Strofi tou Mimi* – located where the road cuts inland towards Otziás. The few **bars** include *Vourkariani*, popular with an older crowd, and the slightly more happening *Kokko Cafe* and *Emage*.

Another 4km to the east, **OTZIÁS** has a small beach that's a bit better than that at Korissía, though more exposed to prevailing winds; facilities are limited to a couple of tavernas and a fair number of apartments for rent. Kéa's only functioning monastery, the eighteenth-century **Panayía Kastrianí**, is an hour's walk along a dirt road from Otziás. Although more remarkable for its fine setting on a high bluff than for any intrinsic interest, the hostel at the monastery (T02880/21 348) is the cheapest accommodation deal on the island, albeit rather basic, isolated and not dependably open. From here you can take the pleasant walk on to the island capital, Ioulídha, in another two hours.

Ioulídha

IOULÍDHA (ancient Ioulis), aka Hóra, was the birthplace of the renowned early fifth-century BC poets Simonides and Bacchylides. With its numerous red-tiled roofs, Neoclassical buildings and winding flagstoned paths, it is by no means a typical Cycladic village, but, beautifully situated in an amphitheatric fold in the hills, it is architecturally the most interesting settlement on the island, and the best base for exploring it. Accordingly Ioulídha has "arrived" in recent years, with numerous trendy bars and bistros much patronized at weekends, but during the week it's quiet, its narrow lanes excluding vehicles. The **archeological museum** (Tues–Sun 8.30am–3pm; free) displays finds from the four ancient city-states of Kéa, although the best items were long ago spirited away to Athens. The lower reaches of the town stretch across a spur to the **Kástro**, a tumbledown Venetian fortress incorporating stones from an ancient temple of Apollo. Fifteen-minutes' walk northeast, on the path toward Panayía Kastrianí, you pass the **Lion of Kea**, a sixth-century BC sculpture carved out of an outcrop of rock, six metres long and three metres high. There are steps right down to the lion, but the effect is most striking from a distance.

There are a couple of **pensions** in Ioulídha: the somewhat pokey *Filoxenia* (T02880/22 057; ❷), perched above a shoeshop in the middle of town, with no en-suite plumbing and saggy beds; and the more comfortable *Ioulis* (T02880/22 177; ❸), which has its own terrace restaurant, up in the *kástro*.

You're spoiled for choice when it comes to **eating** and **drinking** though, with quality generally higher here than in Korissía. *Iy Piatsa*, just as you enter the lower town from the car park, has a variety of tasty dishes, while *Iy Dafni*, reached by a path from the bus stop, and *To Kalofagadhon*, up on the platía, both enjoy great views, the latter being the best place for a full-blown meat feast. Further up there is good standard fare on the terrace of *To Steki tis Tzias*. The aptly named *Panorama* serves up pastries and coffee and is a good place to watch the sun set, while after-dark action seems to oscillate between such bars as *Kamini*, *Leon* and, best of all, *Mylos*. *Ta Pedhia Pezi* (which means "the guys are playing"), is a lively hangout a few kilometres out of town off the road towards Písses and is terrific for a full-on *bouzoúki* night. A **post office** and **bank agent** round up the list of amenities.

The south

About 8km southwest of Ioulídha, reached via a mix of tracks and paths, or by mostly paved road, the crumbling Hellenistic watchtower of **Ayía Marína** sprouts dramatically from the grounds of a small nineteenth-century monastery.

Beyond, the paved main road twists around the startling scenic head of the lovely agricultural valley at **PÍSSES**, emerging at a large and little-developed beach. There are two tavernas, plus a pleasant **campsite**, *Camping Kea*, which has good turfy ground and also runs the studios (☎02880/31 302) further inland. Of the tavernas, the best is *To Akroyiali*, with a good range of dishes and excellent rosé wine, as well as rooms to rent upstairs (☎02880/31 301 or 31 327; ❷).

Beyond Písses, the asphalt – and the bus service – peters out along the 5km road south to **KOÚNDOUROS**, a sheltered, convoluted bay popular with yachters; there's a taverna behind the largest of several sandy coves, none cleaner or bigger than the beach at Písses. The luxury *Kea Beach* hotel (☎02880/31 230; ❹–❺) sits out on its own promontory with tennis courts, pool, and a hamlet of dummy windmills built as holiday homes. At the south end of the bay, *St George Bungalows* (☎02880 31 277; ❸) has smart rooms at very reasonable prices, as well as its own taverna which is recommended. A further 2km south at **Kambí**, there's a nice little beach and a good taverna, *To Kambi*.

Besides the very scant ruins of ancient Poiessa near Písses, the only remains of any real significance from Kéa's past are fragments of a temple of Apollo at **ancient Karthaia**, tucked away on the southeastern edge of the island above Póles Bay, with an excellent deserted twin beach that's easiest reached by boat. Otherwise, it's a good three-hour round-trip walk from the hamlet of Stavroudháki, some way off the lower road linking Koúndouros, Hávouna and Káto Meriá. Travelling by motorbike, the upper road, which plies more directly between Písses and Káto Meriá, is worth following as an alternative return along the island's summit to Ioulídha; it's paved between Ioulídha and Káto Meriá, and the entire way affords fine views over the thousands of magnificent oaks which are Kéa's most distinctive feature.

Kýthnos (Thermiá)

Though perhaps the dullest and certainly the most barren of the Cyclades, a short stay on **Kýthnos** is a good antidote to the exploitation likely to be encountered elsewhere. Few foreigners bother to visit and the island is much quieter than Kéa. It's a place where Athenians come to buy land for villas, go spear-fishing and sprawl on generally mediocre beaches without having to jostle for space. You could use it as a first or, better, last island stop; in season there are several **ferry connections** a week with Kéa and Lávrio, a frequent ferry and hydrofoil service to and from Sérifos, Sífnos and Pireás, plus further direct ferry and hydrofoil connections with Mílos and Kímolos.

Mérihas and around

In good weather boats dock on the west coast at **MÉRIHAS**, a rather functional ferry and fishing port with most of the island's facilities. This fact almost obliges you to stay here, and makes Mérihas something of a relative tourist ghetto, but it's redeemed by proximity to the island's best beaches. The closest beach of any repute is **Episkopí**, a 500-metre stretch of averagely clean grey sand with a single taverna, thirty-minutes' walk north of the town; you can shorten this considerably by sticking to coast-hugging trails and tracks below the road. Far better are the adjacent beaches of **Apókroussi**, which has a canteen, and **Kolóna**, the latter essentially a sandspit joining the islet of Áyios Loukás to Kýthnos. These lie about an hour's walk northwest of Episkopí, and are easiest reached by boat-trip from the harbour. Camping is generally toler-

ated, even on Martinákia beach, the nearest to Mérihas, which has an eponymous taverna.

Owners of **accommodation** often meet the ferries in high season. There are
numerous rooms to let, but they tend to be large and equipped for visiting
families, so they can be on the expensive side – although with some opportunity for bargaining during the week. Out of season, owners are often not on
the premises, but a contact phone number is usually posted up. Few places have
sea views, one exception being the *Kythnos Hotel* (℡02810/32 247; ❷), near
the ferry dock, which has the added bonus of being open all year round. A little inland, behind the small bridge on the seafront, *Panayiota* (℡02810/32 268;
❸) is a decent choice; and there are plenty of other rooms and studios of similar price and quality along the same road. The Milos Express agency may be
able to help you find a room (℡02810/32 104, ℱ32 291).

The best **restaurants** are *To Kandouni*, furthest from the ferry, a tasty grill
with tables right by the water and specialities like *sfougáto*; and *Kissos*, a little
inland from the middle of the harbour, where you pay for the food rather than
the setting. There's also a bakery on the road to Dhryopída. Among purveyors
of a modest nightlife, by far the friendliest and liveliest place is *To Vyzantio*.
Remezzo behind the beach plays good popular music, while eclectic Greek folk

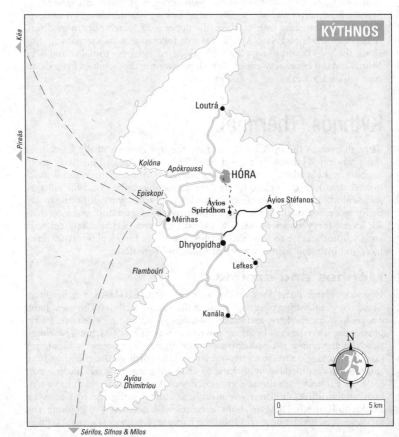

can be heard at the modern *New Corner*, 100m along the road to Dhryopídha. The latest addition of any significance is *Akrotiri Club*, perched up on the headland above the south end of the harbour, playing that popular island blend of summer hits and Greek music.

The **bus service**, principally to Loutrá, Hóra, Dhryopídha and Kanála, is reasonably reliable, in season at least; the only motorbike rental is through the main Milos Express agency and is noticeably more expensive than on many islands. The Cava Kythnos shop doubles as the official **National Bank** outlet (exchange all day, credit cards accepted for a €3 fee), and is the agent for hydrofoil tickets and the boat to Kéa.

Hóra and Loutrá

HÓRA lies 6km northeast of Mérihas, set in the middle of the island. Tilting south off an east–west ridge, and laid out to an approximate grid plan, it's an awkward blend of Kéa-style gabled roofs, Cycladic churches with dunce-cap cupolas, and concrete monsters. Hóra supports a **post office** (open only until noon); the closest accommodation at present is at Loutrá (see below). You can **eat** at *To Kentro* taverna run by Maria Tzoyiou near the small square, or at *To Steki* grill; *Paradisos*, on the approach road from Mérihas is another reasonable option. As well as a rather sophisticated kafenío on the square, there is a very pleasant bar, *Apokalypsi*, a little further up, with outdoor seating.

The much-vaunted resort of **LOUTRÁ** (3km north of Hóra and named after its thermal baths) is scruffy, its nineteenth-century spa long since replaced by a sterile modern construction. The best **taverna**, *Katerini*, is a little out on a limb in the neighbouring bay to the west. Otherwise there are a few seafront bars and tavernas offering basic services, such as showers, to yachting crews. There is no shortage of places to sleep: **pensions** such as *Delfíni* (℡02810/31 430; ❷), the *Meltemi* (℡02810/31 271; ❷, furnished apartments ❹–❺) and *Porto Klaras* (℡02810/31 276; ❸) are acceptable choices. You can also stay in the state-run *Xenia* baths complex (℡02810/31 217; ❸), where a twenty-minute bath plus basic check-up – blood pressure, heart rate and weight – costs about €3. The small bay of Ayía Iríni, just a kilometre east of Loutrá, is a more pleasant place to swim and boasts the decent *Trehandiri* taverna on the hill above the bay.

Dhryopídha and the south

You're handily placed in Hóra to tackle the most interesting thing to do on Kýthnos: the beautiful **walk** south to Dhryopídha. It takes about ninety minutes, initially following the old cobbled way that leaves Hóra heading due south; critical junctions in the first few minutes are marked by red paint dots. The only reliable water is a well in the valley bottom, reached after thirty minutes, just before a side trail to the triple-naved **chapel of Áyios Spyrídhon** which has recycled Byzantine columns. Just beyond this, you collide with a bulldozed track between Dhryopídha and Áyios Stéfanos, but purists can avoid it by bearing west towards some ruined ridgetop windmills and picking up secondary paths for the final forty minutes of the hike.

More appealing than Hóra by virtue of spanning a ravine, **DHRYOPÍDHA**, with its pleasing tiled roofs, is reminiscent of Spain or Tuscany. A surprisingly large place, it was once the island's capital, built around a famous cave, the Katafíki, at the head of a well-watered valley. Tucked away behind the cathedral is a tiny **folklore museum** that opens erratically in high season. Beside the cathedral is a cheap *psistariá*, *To Steki*, and a good local ouzerí called *O*

Apithanos ("the unbelievable guy"). Some people let rooms in their houses, but the nearest official accommodation is 6km south at Kanála.

KANÁLA is a good alternative to Loutrá. There are some rooms in the older settlement up on the promontory and a good taverna, *Louloudhas*, with a huge terrace overlooking the larger western beach, **Megáli Ámmos**, which also has rooms and a combination snack bar and taverna. Two adjacent **pensions** on the beach are *Anna* (☎02810/32 035; ②) and the B&B *Margarita* (☎02810/32 265; ②–④), with the latter warmly recommended for its home-like atmosphere.

From Kanála, a succession of small coves extends up the east coast as far as **ÁYIOS STÉFANOS**, a small coastal hamlet with two high-season tavernas opposite a chapel-crowned islet linked by a causeway to the body of the island. Southwest of Dhryopídha, reached by a turning off the road to Kanála, **Flamboúri** is the most presentable beach on the west coast. The extension of the asphalted road southwards makes the double bay of **Ayíou Dhimitríou** more accessible than before; although not too exciting, there are a couple of tavernas and rooms to rent in high season.

Sérifos

Sérifos has long languished outside the mainstream of history and modern tourism. Little has happened here since the legendary Perseus returned with Medusa's head, in time to save his mother, Danaë, from being ravished by the local king Polydectes – turning him, his court and the green island into stone. Many would-be visitors are deterred by the apparently barren, hilly interior which, with the stark, rocky coastline, makes Sérifos appear uninhabited until the ferry turns into Livádhi bay. The island is recommended for serious **walkers**, who can head for several small villages in the little-explored interior, plus some isolated coves. Modern Serifots love seclusion, and here, more than anywhere else in the Cyclades, you will find farmsteads miles from anywhere, with only a donkey path to their door. Many people still keep livestock and produce their own wines, and many also cultivate the wild narcissus for export.

Few islanders speak much English; even a few select words of amateur Greek will come in handy and will be warmly received. American yachties drop anchor here in some numbers as well, to take on fresh water which, despite appearances, Sérifos has in abundance.

Livádhi and the main beaches

Most visitors stay in the port, **LIVÁDHI**, set in a wide greenery-fringed bay and handy for most of the island's beaches. The usually calm bay here is a magnet for island-hopping yachts, whose crews chug to and fro in dinghies all day and night. It's not the most attractive place on Sérifos and mosquitoes abound, but Livádhi and the neighbouring cove of Livadhákia are certainly the easiest places to find rooms and any amenities you might need, all of which are very scarce elsewhere.

Unfortunately, the long **beach** at Livádhi is nothing to write home about: the sand is hard-packed and muddy, and the water weedy and prone to intermittent jellyfish flotillas – only the far northeastern end is at all usable. Turn left up the main business street, or climb over the southerly headland from the cemetery, to reach the neighbouring, far superior **Livadhákia**. This golden-sand beach, shaded by tamarisk trees, offers snorkelling and other watersports, as well as an acceptable taverna. If you prefer more seclusion, five-minutes' stroll across the headland to the south brings you to the smaller **Karávi** beach, which is cleaner and almost totally naturist, but has no shade or facilities.

A slightly longer 45-minute walk north of the port along a bumpy track leads to **Psilí Ámmos**, a sheltered, white-sand beach considered the best on the island. Accordingly it's popular, with two rival tavernas which tend to be full in high season. Naturists are pointed – via a ten-minute walk across the headland – towards the larger and often deserted **Áyios Ioánnis** beach, but this is rather exposed with no facilities at all, and only the far south end is inviting. Both beaches are theoretically visited by kaïkia from Livádhi, as are two nearby sea caves, but don't count on it. Additionally, and plainly visible from arriving ferries, two more sandy coves hide at the far southeastern flank of the island opposite an islet; they are accessible on foot only, by a variation of the track to Psilí Ámmos. The more northerly of the two, **Áyios Sóstis**, has a well with fresh water and is the most commonly used beach for secluded camping.

Practicalities

The helpful Krinas Travel (℡02810/51 448, ℻51 073, €sertrav@otenet.gr), near the jetty, sells **hydrofoil** and **boat** tickets. The public **bus stop** and posted schedule are at the base of the yacht and fishing-boat jetty. You can rent a **bike** or **car** from Blue Bird next to the filling station on the main street or from Krinas Travel.

Accommodation proprietors don't always meet ferries, with the exception of the *Coralli Camping Bungalows*, which regularly sends a minibus, but in high season you'll have to step lively off the boat to get a decent bed. The most rewarding hunting grounds are on the headland above the ferry dock, or Livadhákia beach (see opposite); anything without a sea view will be a notch cheaper. Up on the headland, the *Pension Cristi* (℡02810/51 775; ❷) has an excellent, quiet position overlooking the bay; the nearby *Areti* (℡02810/51 479; ❷–❹) is a little smarter but less friendly. Alternatively, down in the flatlands, the inexpensive seafront rooms of *Anna* (℡02810/51 263; ❷) and *Fani* (℡02810/51 746; ❷) are friendly and spotlessly clean, though the rooms at the front get some traffic noise. The *Hotel Anna* (℡02810/51 666; ❸–❹), above the pizzeria by the yacht harbour, is another fall-back, while the cheapest

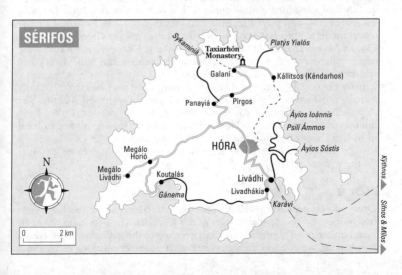

rooms in Livádhi are next to each other at the far end of the bay: *Margarita* (℡02810/51 321; ❶) and *Adonios Peloponnisos* (℡02810/51 113; ❶).

Livadhákia, ten- to fifteen-minutes' walk south, offers more nocturnal peace, choice and quality, though it has a more touristy feel and the mosquitoes are positively ferocious – bring insecticide coils or make sure your room is furnished with electric vapour pads. One of the oldest and largest complexes of rooms and apartments, close to the beach and with verdant views, is run by Vaso Stamataki (℡02810/51 346; ❷). Newer and higher-standard choices include the *Helios Pension* (℡02810/51 066; ❸), just above the road as you arrive at Livadhákia, and, further along, the *Medusa* (℡02810/51 127; ❸). Cheaper are the rooms in adjacent buildings just after *Helios*, run by two sisters, Yioryia (℡02810/51 336; ❷) and Mina (℡02810/51 545; ❷–❸) – the latter place has sea views. Further along are *Dhorkas* (℡02810/51 422; ❹) and, right by the beach above a restaurant, *O Alexandros* (℡02810/51 119; ❸). Near the built-up area, beside one of only two public access tracks to the beach and behind the best patch of sand, *Coralli Camping Bungalows* (℡02810/51 500, ⓦ www.coralli.gr; ❸–❹) has a restaurant, bar, shop and landscaped camping area.

A makeshift road runs the length of the Livádhi seafront, crammed with restaurants, clubs, shops, supermarkets, and a **cashpoint** at the Alpha Bank. Turn up the road across from the yacht jetty to reach the main street; the *Mylos* bakery – look for the windmill painted on its corner – has exceptionally good cheese pies and wholegrain bread, and there's a **pharmacy** up on the right.

Like most islands, **tavernas** near the quay tend to be slightly pricier, but *Mokkas* fish taverna is recommended nonetheless. Walk up the beach and meals get less expensive; the two best traditional tavernas are the busy *Perseus* and *Cyclades*. Another 500m brings you to *Stamatis*, a favourite with locals for inexpensive home-style food. At the extreme far northeast end of the beach, *Sklavenis* (aka *Margarita's*) has a homely feel and courtyard seating, but the food can be overly deep-fried and quite pricey. Closer to the yacht harbour, *Meltemi* is a good, if slightly expensive, ouzerí – something out of the ordinary for the island. For crepes and ice cream, try *Meli*, in the commercial centre by the port police.

Nightlife is surprisingly lively, and most of it's clustered in or near a minimall on the seafront just up from the yacht jetty, so you should be able to quickly find something to suit your taste. The *Roman Cafe Bar*, inside the mall, has a pool table and plays a sophisticated mix of jazz, blues, Latin and adventurous modern. *Alter Ego*, at the back, offers more typically Greek music while *Captain Hook*, upstairs, is louder and more rocking. *Vitamin C* and *Karnayio* are two popular bars next door, and further up the beach is the *Sérifos Yacht Club*, which is actually just a dolled-up kafenío.

Buses connect Livádhi with Hóra, 2km away, some ten times daily, but only manage one or two daily trips to Megálo Livádhya, Galaní and Kállitsos. You may well want to walk, if you're travelling light; it's a pleasant if steep forty minutes up a cobbled way to Hóra, with the *kalderími* leading off from a bend in the road about 300m out of Livádhia. By the beginning of October, you'll have no choice, since the bus – like nearly everything else – ceases operation for the winter.

Hóra

Quiet and atmospheric **HÓRA**, teetering precariously above the harbour, is one of the most spectacular villages of the Cyclades. The best sights are to be found on the town's borders: tiny churches cling to the cliff-edge, and there are breathtaking views across the valleys below. At odd intervals along its alleyways you'll find part of the old castle making up the wall of a house, or a marble statue leaning incongruously in one corner. A pleasant diversion is the hour-long **walk** down to **Psilí Ámmos**: start from beside Hóra's cemetery and aim for the lower of two visible pigeon towers, and then keep close to the phone wires, which will guide you towards the continuation of the double-walled path descending to a bend in the road just above the beach.

Among two or three **tavernas**, the nicest place is *Zorbas*, near the church on the upper square, serving local dishes such as wild fennel fritters; *Stavros*, just east of the bus-stop platía, is friendly and dependable and can arrange **rooms** too (☎02810/51 303; ❶). The island's **post office** is found in the lowest quarter, and a few more expensive rooms for rent lie about 200m north of town, on the street above the track to the cemetery.

The north

North of Hóra, the island's high water-table sometimes breaks the surface to run in delightful rivulets swarming with turtles and frogs, though in recent years many of the open streams seem to have dried up. Reeds, orchards and even the occasional palm tree still take advantage of the unexpected moisture, even if it's no longer visible. This is especially true at **KÁLLITSOS** (Kéndarhos), reached by a ninety-minute path from Hóra, marked by fading red paint splodges along a donkey track above the cemetery. Once at Kállitsos (no facilities), a paved road leads west for 3km to the fifteenth- to seventeenth-century **monastery of Taxiarhón**, designed for sixty monks but presently home only to one of the island's two parish priests – part of a dying breed of farmer-fisherman monks. If he's about, the priest will show you treasures in the monastic church, such as an ivory-inlaid bishop's throne, silver lamps from Egypt (to where many Serifots emigrated during the nineteenth century) and the finely carved *témblon*.

As you loop back towards Hóra from Kállitsos on the asphalt, the fine villages of Galaní and Panayía (named after its tenth-century church) make convenient stops. In **GALANÍ** you can sometimes get simple **meals** at the central store, which also sells excellent, tawny-pink, sherry-like wine; its small-scale production in the west of the island is highly uneconomic, so you'll find it at few other places on Sérifos. Below the village, trails lead to the remote and often windswept beach of **Sykaminiá**, with no facilities and no camping allowed; a better bet for a local swim is the more sheltered cove of **Platýs Yialós** at the extreme northern tip of the island, reached by a partly paved track (negotiable by scooter) that branches off just east of Taxiarhón. The neighbouring beach has a taverna, *Nikoulias*, with a couple of very basic rooms (☎02810/52 174; ❷), which nonetheless have great views. The church at **Panayiá** is usually locked, but comes alive on its feast day of Xilopanayía (August 16). Traditionally the first couple to dance around the adjacent olive tree would be the first to marry that year, but this led to unseemly brawls so the priest always goes first these days.

The southwest

A little way south of Panayía, you reach a junction in the road. Turn left to return to Hóra, or continue straight towards **Megálo Horió** – the site of ancient Sérifos, but with little else to recommend it. **Megálo Livádhi**, further on, is a remote and quiet beach resort 8km west of Hóra, with two lovely tavernas whose tables are practically on the beach. *Iy Mardhitsa* taverna has some simple rooms behind the beach (☎02810/51 003; ❶). Iron and copper ore were once exported from here, but cheaper African deposits sent the mines into decline and today most of the idle machinery rusts away, though some gravel-crushing still goes on. At the north end of the beach there's a monument to four workers killed during a protest against unfair conditions in 1916. An alternate turning just below Megálo Horió leads to the small mining and fishing port of **Koutalás**, a pretty sweep of bay with a church-tipped rock, and a long if narrow beach. It has become rather a ghost settlement and the workers' restaurants have all closed down, but there is one snack bar/taverna, catering mainly for yachting crews. The winding track above the village leads to Livádhi, and apart from the pleasant **Gánema** beach, which has a taverna of the same name, there are no places to rest or buy refreshments on the long journey back.

Sífnos

Sífnos is a more immediately appealing island than its northern neighbours since it's prettier, more cultivated and has some fine architecture. This means that it's also much more popular, and extremely crowded in July or August, when rooms are very difficult to find. Take any offered as you land, come armed with a reservation or, best of all, time your visit for spring or autumn, though bear in mind that most of the bars and the souvenir shops aren't likely to be open. In keeping with the island's somewhat upmarket clientele, freelance camping is forbidden, while nudism is tolerated only in isolated coves. The locals tend to be more cosmopolitan and aloof than on neighbouring islands, but in the more out-of-the-way places they're usually hospitable.

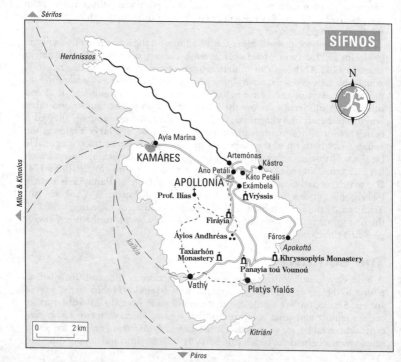

The island's modest size – no bigger than Kýthnos or Sérifos – makes it eminently explorable. The **bus service** is excellent, most of the roads quite decent, and there's a network of paths that are fairly easy to follow. Sífnos has a strong tradition of pottery and was long esteemed for its distinctive cuisine, although most tourist-oriented cooking is only a little above average. However, the island's shops and greengrocers are well stocked in season.

Ferry connections have improved in recent years, keeping pace with the island's increasing popularity. The *Express Milos* and *Express Dionysos* ply a regular shuttle via Kýthnos and Sérifos, then on to Mílos and Kímolos before heading east to Folégandros, Síkinos, Íos and Thíra, from where the course is reversed back to Pireás. Links with the central Cyclades are provided by the infrequent visits of the *Georgios Express* to Páros or Sýros and backed up by an almost daily hydrofoil service which also goes to Náxos and Mýkonos several times a week.

Kamáres

KAMÁRES, the island's port, is tucked away at the foot of high, bare cliffs in the west, which enclose a beach. A busy, fairly downmarket resort with concrete blocks of villas edging up to the base of the cliffs, Kamáres' seafront road is crammed with bars, travel agencies, ice-cream shops and fast-food places. You can store luggage at the Aegean Thesaurus **travel agency** while hunting for a room (proprietors tend not to meet boats); they also change money and can book accommodation throughout the island.

Accommodation is relatively expensive, though bargaining can be productive outside peak season. Try the reasonable *Hotel Stavros* (☎02840/31 641; ❷) or, further along above the town beach, the good but pricier *Boulis Hotel* (☎02840/32 122; ❸–❹), which has very friendly management. Above the *Boulis*, the welcoming *Makis* **campsite** (☎ & ☏02840/32 366) has good facilities and good-value air-conditioned rooms (❸). Continue past the *Makis* and turn right up from the end of the beach to find newer, quieter accommodation in Ayía Marína, including the *Mosha Pension* (☎02840/31 719; ❷), and the newly remodelled *Delphini Hotel* (☎02840/33 740; ❻), which has its own pool.

The best **restaurants** are the *Meropi*, ideal for a pre-ferry lunch, the *Boulis* (under the same management as the *Boulis Hotel*) with its collection of huge retsina barrels, the *Kamares* ouzerí and *Kira Margena* at the far end of the beach in Ayía Marína. Kamáres also has a little **nightlife**: the *Collage Bar*, good for a sunset cocktail, and *Folie-Folie*. The best place to **hire a scooter** is at Dionysos.

Apollonía and Artemónas

A steep twenty-minute bus ride (hourly service until late at night) takes you up to **APOLLONÍA**, the centre of Hóra, an amalgam of three hilltop villages which have merged over the years into one continuous community. With white buildings, flower-draped balconies, belfries and pretty squares, it is eminently scenic, though not self-consciously so. On the central platía itself, the **folk museum** (daily 9.30am–2pm & 6–10pm; €1) is worth a visit. As well as an interesting collection of textiles, lace, costumes and weaponry, there are paintings by Nikolaos Tselemendi, a celebrated cookery teacher.

Radiating out from the platía is a network of stepped marble footways and the main pedestrian street, flagstoned Odhós Styliánou Prókou, which leads off to the south, lined with shops, restaurants, bars and churches, including the cakebox cathedral, **Áyios Spyrídhon**, and the eighteenth-century church of **Panayía Ouranoforía**, which stands in the highest quarter of town, incorporating fragments of a seventh-century BC temple of Apollo and a relief of Áyios Yeóryios over the door. **Áyios Athanásios**, next to Platía Kleánthi Triandafýlou, has frescoes and a wooden *témblon*. Some 3km southeast, a short distance from the village of Exámbela, you'll find the active monastery of **Vrýssis** which dates from 1612 and is home to a good collection of religious artefacts and manuscripts.

ARTEMÓNAS, fifteen minutes south of Apollonía on foot, is worth a morning's exploration for its churches and elegant Venetian and Neoclassical houses alone. **Panayía Gourniá** (the key is kept next door) has vivid frescoes; the clustered-dome church of **Kohí** was built over an ancient temple of Artemis (also the basis of the village's name); and seventeenth-century **Áyios Yeóryios** contains fine icons. Artemónas is also the point of departure for **Herónissos**, an isolated hamlet with two tavernas and a few potteries behind a deeply indented, rather bleak bay at the northwestern tip of the island. There's a motorable dirt track there and occasional boat trips from Kamáres, though these are only worth the effort on calm days.

Practicalities

The **post office** and **bus stop** edge onto Apollonía's central platía. The **bank** and **police station** are located on the main road leading north out of town. There are rooms scattered all over the village, making them hard to find; however, there are some obvious choices along the road towards Fáros (thus a bit noisy), the *Margarita* (☏02840/31 032; ❷) being fairly representative. The *Hotel Sifnos* (☏02840/31 624, ☏33 067; ❸), on the main pedestrian street, is the most traditional in its architecture and furnishing, and is operated by the friendly Diareme family. All the central hotels are sure to be noisy when the nearby clubs are open during the summer, and if you want quieter premises with a better view, be prepared to pay more: *Margarita Kouki* (☏02840/33 152; ❷), above the luxurious *Hotel Petali* (☏02840/33 024; ❺–❻), north of the square on the pedestrian lane, is a welcome exception. Probably your best bet is to look on the square for the main branch of the excellent travel agency, Aegean Thesaurus (☏02840/31 151, ☏32 190, ✉aegean@thesaurus.gr), which can book you into rooms of all categories. They also sell a worthwhile package consisting of an accurate topographical map, bus/boat schedules and a short text on Sífnos for about €1.50.

There are a number of **restaurants** in Apollonía, including *Iy Orea Sifnos*, with good food despite its kitchy decor, on the central square; for excellent pizza and pasta find *Mama Mia* up the pedestrian lane to the north; and *Cafe Sifnos*, next to the *Hotel Sifnos* on the main pedestrian street, serves something for nearly every taste and is open all day. There are several tavernas up in the backstreets: *To Apostoli to Koutouki* is quite good for standard Greek fare and very reasonable; probably the best and most famous place to eat on the island, owing to its highly-rated chef, is *Liotrivi* (*Manganas*) on the square up in Artemónas, where there's also an excellent bakery.

Most of the **nightlife** can be found on the main pedestrian street south of the square, where you'll find *Isidora*, *Cafe Folie* and *Argo* – the biggest and loudest. The *Camel Club*, on the road to Fáros, is another popular place for late-night action. For *bouzoúki* there's the *Aloni*, just above the crossroad to *kástro*.

The east coast

Most of Sífnos's coastal settlements are along the less precipitous eastern shore, within a modest distance of Hóra and its surrounding cultivated plateau. These all have good bus services, and a certain amount of food and accommodation,

Kástro being far more appealing than the resorts of Platýs Yialós and Fáros which can get very overcrowded in July and August.

Kástro

An alternative east-coast base which seems the last place on Sífnos to fill up in season, **KÁSTRO** can be reached on foot from Apollonía in 35 minutes, all but the last ten on a clear path beginning at the fork in the road to Kástro, threading its way via Káto Petáli hamlet. Built on a rocky outcrop with an almost sheer drop to the sea on three sides, the ancient capital of the island retains much of its medieval character. Parts of its boundary walls survive, along with a full complement of sinuous, narrow streets graced by balconied, two-storey houses and some fine sixteenth- and seventeenth-century churches with ornamental floors. Venetian coats of arms and ancient wall-fragments can still be seen on some of the older dwellings; there are the remains of the ancient acropolis (including a ram's head sarcophagus by one of the medieval gates), as well as a small **archeological museum** (Tues–Sun 8am–2.30pm; free), which does not always stick closely to the official opening hours, installed in a for-mer Catholic church in the higher part of the village.

Among the several **rooms**, the modernized *Aris* apartments (T02840/31 161; ❷–❹) have something for most budgets and are open all year. More rooms are available at the lower end of the village, of which the friendly *Marianna* (T02840/33 681; ❷) is a good basic option. The *Star* and *Leonidas* are the obvi-ous **tavernas** to try out, while the *Cavos Sunrise* café-bar is laid-back and has a fantastic view. On the edge of town, the *Castello* disco-bar is a livelier hangout.

There's nothing approximating a beach in Kástro; for a swim you have to walk to the nearby rocky coves of **Serália** (to the southeast, and with more rooms) and **Paláti**. You can also hike – from the windmills on the approach road near Káto Petáli – to either the sixteenth-century monastery of **Khryssostómou**, or along a track opposite the cliff-face that overlooks the church of the **Eptá Martíres** (Seven Martyrs); nudists sun themselves and snorkel on and around the flat rocks below.

Platýs Yialós

From Apollonía there are almost hourly buses to the resort of **PLATÝS YIALÓS**, some 12km distant, near the southern tip of the island. Despite claims to be the longest beach in the Cyclades, the sand can get very crowd-ed. Diversions include a pottery workshop, but many are put off by the con-tinuous row of snack bars and rooms to rent, which line the entire stretch of beach, and the strong winds which plague it. **Rooms** are expensive, although the comfortable *Pension Angelaki* (T02840/71 288; ❸), near the bus stop, is more reasonably priced, while the *Hotel Efrossyni* (T02840/71 353; ❹) next door is comfortable, and breakfast is included in the price. The local **campsite** is rather uninspiring – a stiff hike inland, shadeless and on sloping, stony ground. Among several fairly pricey **tavernas** are the straightforward *To Steki* and *Bus Stop*, and there is *Mama Mia* for pizza and pasta.

A more rewarding walk uphill from Platýs Yialós brings you to the convent of **Panayía toú Vounoú** (though it's easy to get lost on the way without the locally sold map); the caretaker should let you in if she's about.

Fáros and around

Less crowded beaches are to be found just to the northeast of Platýs Yialós (though unfortunately not directly accessible along the coast). **FÁROS**, again with regular bus links to Apollonía, makes an excellent fall-back base if you don't strike it lucky elsewhere. A small and friendly resort, it has some of the cheapest **accommodation** on the island, as well as a couple of smarter places, including the recommended *Apéranto* guesthouse (⊤02840/71 473; ❸) at the far end of the bay. *To Kyma* is a pleasant seafront **taverna**, and the smart *On the Rocks*, perched on the headland at the far end of the beach, serves a tasty selection of snacks as well as full meals. The closest beaches are not up to much: the town strand itself is muddy, shadeless and crowded, and the one to the northeast past the headland is not much better. Head off in the opposite direction, however, through the older part of the village, and things improve at **Glyfó**, a longer, wider family beach about twenty minutes away.

Continuing from Glyfó, a fifteen-minute cliffside path leads to the beach of **Apokoftó**, with a couple of good tavernas, and, up an access road, to the *Hotel Flora* (⊤02840/71 278; ❷–❸), which has superb views. The shore itself tends to collect seaweed, however, and a rock reef must be negotiated to get into the water. Flanking Apokoftó to the south, marooned on a sea-washed spit and featuring on every OTE poster of the island, is the disestablished, seventeenth-century **Khryssopiyís monastery**, where until recently cells were rented out as tourist accommodation. According to legend, the cleft in the rock appeared when two village girls, fleeing to the spit to escape the attentions of menacing pirates, prayed to the Virgin to defend their virtue.

The interior and Vathý

Apollonía is a good base from which to start your explorations of remoter Sífnos. You can rent **bikes** at Moto Apollo, beside the petrol station on the road to Fáros, but the island is best explored on foot.

Taking the path out from Katavatí (the district south of Apollonía) you'll pass, after a few minutes, the beautiful empty **monastery of Firáyia** and – fifteen minutes along the ugly new road – the path climbing up to **Áyios Andhréas**, where you'll be rewarded with tremendous views over the islands of Sýros, Páros, Íos, Folégandhros and Síkinos. Just below the church is an enormous Bronze Age archeological site.

Even better is the all-trail walk to Vathý, around three hours from Katavatí and reached by bearing right at a signed junction in Katavatí. Part way along you can detour on a conspicuous side-trail to the **monastery of Profítis Ilías**, on the very summit of the island, with a vaulted refectory and extensive views.

Vathý

A fishing village on the shore of a stunning funnel-shaped bay, **VATHÝ** is the most attractive and remote base on the island. However, the highway there has been recently improved, so it's poised for development, with a new luxury hotel with a huge pool. There are an increasing number of **rooms**, the best deals probably being at *Manolis* taverna (⊤02840/71 111; ❷), or those attached to the tiny **monastery of the Archangel Gabriel**. Unusually, camping rough meets with little objection from the locals, a reflection of their friendly attitude towards outsiders. For **food**, *Manolis* does excellent grills and has a fascinating gyrating clay oven in the courtyard; *Iy Okeanidha* has good mezédhes such as chickpea balls and cheesy aubergine patties; while *To Tsikali* behind the monastery is cheaper but less varied.

Now that there are regular **buses** (8 daily in high season, 2 daily at other times) the kaïkia no longer run from Kamáres. It is possible to walk to Platýs Yíalos in ninety minutes, but the path is not well marked. At the far end of the bay a traditional pottery still functions.

Mílos

Volcanic **Mílos** boasts amazing geological diversity, weird rock formations, hot springs, good beaches and sensational views. Minoan settlers were attracted by obsidian, and other products of its volcanic soil made the island one of the most important of the Cyclades in the ancient world. Today the quarrying of barite, perlite and porcelain has left deep scars on the landscape but given the island a relative prosperity and independence. It hasn't had to tart itself up to court tourism – the main reason it's worth a stay of several days.

You get a good preview of the island's geological wonders as your ferry enters Mílos Bay, one of the world's most striking natural harbours, shaped by an ancient explosion. Off the north coast, accessible only by excursion boat, the Glaroníssia (Seagull Isles) are shaped like massed organ pipes, and there are more weird formations on the southwest coast at Kléftiko. Inland, too, you frequently come across strange, volcanic outcrops, and thermal springs burst forth.

Like most volcanic islands, Mílos is quite fertile: away from the summits of **Profítis Ilías** in the southwest and lower hills in the east, a gently undulating countryside is intensively cultivated to produce grain, hay and orchard fruits. The island's domestic architecture, with its lava-built, two-up-two-down houses, isn't as immediately impressive as its more pristine neighbours, but is charming nonetheless. There's an excellent free guide booklet, *Welcome to Mílos*, which can be picked up from tourist offices, hotels and restaurants.

Adhámas

The main port of **ADHÁMAS**, known as Adhámandas to locals, was founded by Cretan refugees fleeing a failed rebellion in 1841. With a handsome new marble-paved esplanade around its natural headland it's now among the most attractive ports in the Cyclades, lively enough, with all the requisite facilities.

Most **accommodation** is concentrated on the hill above the harbour and on or just off the main road to Pláka, and ranges from real cheapies with shared facilities, like that of Anna Gozadhinou (℡02870/22 364; ❶), to smart rooms with TV and all mod cons, like *Thalassitra* (℡02870/23 570; ❹). Best choices include the *Delfini* (℡02870/22 001; ❷–❸), one block behind the town beach to the left from the ferry landing, the smart, central, double-glazed *Portiani Hotel* (℡02870/22 940; ❸–❻) and the luxury *Santa Maria Village* (℡02870/21 949; ❹–❺), 300m behind the beach. During high season the highly organized **tourist office** opposite the ferry dock has a daily updated list of available rooms around the island, and a handy brochure with all the numbers at any given time. Until recently freelance **camping** went undisturbed at the small **Frangomnímata** beach, ten-minutes' walk northwest by the French war memorial, but with the arrival of the first official campsite at Hivadolímni beach (℡02870/31 410) things seem set to change. As is the case with many campsites in Greece, bungalows are also available (❹); a campsite minibus meets ferries.

Flisvos, near the jetty, is a good place to **eat**. Of the three adjacent tavernas along the seafront towards the long tamarisk-lined beach south of town, *Navagio* is the best value, although the service is slow. Just off the main street inland, *Ta Pitsounakia* is a good cheap *psistariá* with a pleasant courtyard. The local internet café (℡02870/28 011, ✉pmayros@yahoo.com) is up near the Ayía Triáda church. Apart from the obvious string of cafés along the main seafront drag, *Akri*, above the jetty, is a more hip **bar**, with a pleasant veranda. *Micro Cafe*, on the way to the first beach east of town, has an English-speaking owner who plays varied music and plays requests, and *Fuego*, above the far end of the beach, goes on until sunrise playing a mixture of summer hits and Greek pop.

On the quayside, several **travel agencies** sell ferry tickets and maps, have information about coastal boat-trips and rent motorbikes and cars. Dolfin Tours (℡02870/23 183, ℻23 409), near the Emboriko Bank, is particularly friendly and helpful, and sells tickets to Crete and the Dodecanese. There are also several **banks** and a **post office**. Adhámas is the hub of the island's **bus services**, which run hourly to Pláka, nine times daily in high season to Pollónia, seven times daily to Paleohóri via Zefiria and to Provatás. The taxi rank is nearby – call ℡02870/22 219 to book. Some visitors arrive by plane from Athens; most seats, however, are reserved by the local mining industry. The new, but already inadequate **airport** is 5km southeast of the port, close to Zefiria.

The **Mining Museum of Mílos** (daily 9.30am–1pm & 5–8pm; free), housed in a new building towards the south beach, charts the mining history of Mílos. Take a **boat tour** round the island on one of three boats; weather permitting, these normally leave at 9am and make several stops at inaccessible swimming spots like the magnificent Kléftiko, with a late lunch on Kímolos (see p.135 and p.136).

The northwestern villages and ancient Melos

The main appeal of Mílos is in an area that has been the island's focus of habitation since Classical times, where a cluster of villages huddle in the lee of a crag, four kilometres northwest of the harbour.

PLÁKA (MÍLOS) is the largest of these communities and the official capital of the island, with a hospital and **post office**. There is also a **motorbike rental** outfit near the archeological museum (see below). There are **rooms** available scattered around the village, with those on the west side offering spectacular views (there's a map and listing in *Welcome to Mílos*). Among the nicest of these are the pretty studios of Sotiria & Stavros Karamitsou (☎02870/23 820; ❹) and those of Stratis Vourakis (☎02870/21 702; ❹). Kaliopi Moraitou (☎02870/41 353; ❹) has newly refurbished rooms in the house where the Venus de Milo was allegedly hidden following its discovery (see p.134), and Maria Kentrota (☎02870/21 572; ❸) has a couple of charming, if basic, studios close to the archeological museum. There are also three or four blocks of modern accommodation overlooking the busy approach road. A number of ouzerís have opened up in recent years, making Pláka a real **eating** paradise: highly recommended are *Arhondoula*, *Dhiporto* and *To Kastro* up in the centre of the village, as well as *Plakiani Gonia* on the approach road. The *Utopia Cafe* is a fine place to stop for a coffee or a drink and take in the sensational view, especially at sunset.

Pláka boasts **two museums**. Behind the lower car park, at the top of the approach boulevard through the newer district, the **archeological museum** (Tues–Sun 8.30am–3pm; €1.50) contains numerous obsidian implements, plus a whole wing of finds from ancient Phylakope (see p.135) whose highlights include a votive lamp in the form of a bull and a rather Minoan-looking terracotta goddess. Labelling is scant, but isn't really needed for a plaster cast of the most famous statue in the world, the Venus de Milo, the original of which was found on the island in 1820 and appropriated by the French; her arms were knocked off in the melée surrounding her abduction. Up in a mansion of the old quarter, the **folk museum** (Tues–Sat 10am–2pm & 6–9pm; €1.50) offers room re-creations, but is otherwise a Greek-labelled jumble of impedimenta pertaining to milling, brewing, cheese-making, baking and weaving, rounded off by old engravings, photos and mineral samples.

A stairway beginning near the police station leads up to the old Venetian **Kástro**, its slopes clad in stone and cement to channel precious rainwater into cisterns. The enormous chapel of **Panayía Thalassítra** looms near the summit, where the ancient Melians made their last stand against the Athenians before the massacre of 416 BC. Today it offers one of the best views in the Aegean, particularly at sunset in clear conditions.

The attractive village of **TRYPITÍ** (meaning "perforated"), which takes its name from the cliffside tombs nearby and covers a long ridge a kilometre south of Pláka, is another good base if you're after a village environment. There are a few modest **rooms**, two of which are just down the steep street from the tiny platía below the main church. The best place to **eat** is *Ta Glaronisia*, on the main street and there's a nice little bar, *Konaki*, near the main square. From Trypití, it's a pleasant 45-minute walk down to Adhámas via Skinópi on the winding old *kalderími*, which begins on the saddle linking Trypití with the hamlet of Klimatovoúni.

TRIOVÁSSALOS and its twin **PÉRAN TRIOVÁSSALOS** are more workaday, less polished than Pláka or Trypití. There are "rooms to rent" signs out here as well, but they'll inevitably be noisier. Péran also offers the idiosyncratic taverna *O Hamos* (which means "a mess") and a naive pebble mosaic in the courtyard of **Áyios Yeóryios church** – created in 1880, it features assorted animal and plant motifs.

Local sites and the coast

From Pláka's archeological museum, signs point you towards the **early Christian catacombs** (Tues–Sun 8.30am–3pm; free), 1km south of Pláka and just 400m from Trypití village; steps lead down from the road to the inconspicuous entrance. Some 5000 bodies were buried in tomb-lined corridors stretching some 200m into the soft volcanic rock, but only the first 50m is illuminated and accessible by boardwalk. Don't miss the adjacent ruins of **ancient Melos**, extending down from Pláka almost to the sea. There are huge Dorian walls, the usual column fragments lying around and, best of all, a well-preserved Roman **amphitheatre** (unrestricted access) some 200m west of the catacombs by track, then trail. Only seven rows of seats remain intact, but these evocatively look out over Klíma to the bay. Between the catacombs and the theatre is the signposted spot where the Venus de Milo was found; promptly delivered to the French consul for "safekeeping" from the Turks, this was the last the Greeks saw of the statue until a copy was belatedly forwarded from the Louvre in Paris.

At the very bottom of the vale, **KLÍMA** is the most photogenic of several fishing hamlets on the island, with its picturesque boathouses tucked underneath the principal living areas. There's no beach to speak of, and only one place to stay – the impeccably sited, if a little basic *Panorama* (☎02870/21 623; ❷–❹), with an acceptable balcony taverna.

Pláthiena, 45-minutes' walk northwest of Pláka, is the closest proper beach, and thus is extremely popular in summer. There are no facilities, but the beach is fairly well protected and partly shaded by tamarisks. Head initially west from near the police station on the marked footpath towards **ARETÍ** and **FOURKOVOÚNI**, two more cliff-dug, boathouse-hamlets very much in the Klíma mould. Although the direct route to Pláthiena is signposted, it no longer goes via Fourkovoúni; both hamlets are reached by side-turnings off the main route, which becomes a jeep track as you approach Fourkovoúni. By scooter, access to Pláthiena is only from Plakés, the northernmost and smallest of the five northwestern villages.

The south

The main road to the south of the island splits at **Kánava junction**, a dreary place at first glance owing to the large power plant here. But opposite this, indicated by a rusty sign pointing seaward, is the first of Mílos's **hot springs**, which bubble up in the shallows and are much enjoyed by the locals.

Taking the left or easterly fork leads to **ZEFYRÍA**, hidden among olive groves below the bare hills; it was briefly the medieval capital until an eighteenth-century epidemic drove out the population. Much of the old town is still deserted, though some life has returned, and there's a magnificent seventeenth-century church.

South of here it's a further 8km down a winding road to the coarse-sand beach of **Paleohóri**. Actually a triple strand totalling 800m in length, it's indisputably the island's best; clothing's optional at the westerly cove, where steam vents heat both the shallow water and the rock overhangs onshore. There are a number of **places to stay**, such as the inland *Broutsos* (☎010/34 78 425; ❹), the purpose-built rooms at the *Artemis* restaurant (☎02870/31 221; ❹) nearer the beach, and Panayiota Vikelli's rooms (☎02870/31 228; ❹). The place to eat is *Pelagos*, which has a large raised patio.

The westerly road from Kánava junction leads past the airport gate to **Hivadholímni**, considered to be the best beach on Mílos bay itself. Not that this is saying much: Hivadholímni is north-facing and thus garbage-prone, with shallow sumpy water offshore, although there is a taverna, a disco-bar and a sizeable community of campers during the summer. It's better to veer south to **Provatás**, a short but tidy beach, closed off by colourful cliffs on the east. Being so easy to get to, it hasn't escaped some development: there are two **rooms** establishments plus, closer to the shore, a newer, luxury complex, *Golden Milos Beach* (☎02870/31 307; ④–⑥). The best value for food and accommodation is the *Maistrali* (☎02870/31 206; ③).

Some 2km west of Provatás, you'll see a highway sign for **Kípos**. Below and to the left of the road, a small **medieval chapel** dedicated to the Kímisis (Assumption) sits atop foundations far older – as evidenced by the early Christian reliefs stacked along the west wall and a carved, cruciform baptismal font in the *ieron* behind the altar screen. At one time a spring gushed from the low-tunnel cave beside the font – sufficiently miraculous in itself on arid Mílos. Several kilometres before Provatás, a road forks east through a dusty white quarry to the trendy and popular beach of **Firipláka**. Further east, **Tsigrádho** beach is accessible by boat, or by the novel means of a rope hanging down a crevice in the cliff-face.

For the most part **Hálakas**, the southwestern peninsula centred on the wilderness of 748-metre Profítis Ilías, is uninhabited and little built upon, with the exception of the **monastery of Sidherianós**. The roads are memorable, if a little tiring, and several spots are worth making the effort to see. **Emboriós** on the east side of the peninsula has a fine little beach and a great local taverna with a few cheap rooms (☎02870/21 389; ③). On the mostly rugged west coast, **Triádhes** is one of the finest and least spoilt beaches in the Cyclades, but you'll have to bring your own provisions. **Kléftiko** in the southwest corner is only reachable by boat, but repays the effort to get there with its stunning rock formations, semi-submerged rock tunnels and colourful coral.

The north coast

From either Adhámas or the Pláka area, good roads run roughly parallel to the **north coast** which, despite being windswept and largely uninhabited, is not devoid of interest. **Mandhrákia**, reached from Péran Triovássalos, is another boathouse settlement, and **Sarakíniko**, to the east, is a sculpted inlet with a sandy seabed and a summer beach café. About 8km from Adhámas, the little hamlet of **Páhena**, not shown on many maps, has a small beach and cluster of rooms – try *Terry's* (☎02870/22 640; ③). About a kilometre beyond this, the remains of three superimposed Neolithic settlements crown a small knoll at **Fylakopí** (ancient Phylakope); the site was important archeologically, but hasn't been maintained and is difficult to interpret. Just before the site is another one of Milos's coastal wonders: the deep-sea inlet of **Papáfranga**, set in a ravine and accessible through a gap in the cliffs.

Pollónia

POLLÓNIA, 12km northeast of Adhámas, must be the windiest spot on the island, hence the name of its longest-lived and best **bar**, *Okto Bofor* (meaning "Force 8 gales"), near the church. The second resort on Mílos after Adhámas, it is, not surprisingly, immensely popular with windsurfers, and a diving centre has further increased its popularity among watersports enthusiasts. Pollónia is essentially a small harbour protected by a storm-lashed spit of land on the northeast, where self-catering units are multiplying rapidly, fringed by a long but narrow, tamarisk-fringed beach to the rear, and closed off on the south by a smaller promontory on which the tiny original settlement huddles. Besides the town beach, the only other convenient, half-decent beach is at **Voúdhia**, 3km east, where you will find more of the island's hot springs, although it is effectively spoiled by its proximity to huge mining works, which lend it the desolate air of a *Mad Max* location.

On the quay are several **tavernas** and a couple of very mediocre café/snack bars. Inland and south of here you'll find a concentration of **accommodation**, more simple rooms and fewer apartments, most with the slight drawback of occasional noise and dust from quarry trucks. Among the highest-quality units here are the *Kapetan Tasos Studios* (℡02870/41 287;●), with good views of the straits between Mílos and Kímolos; *Flora* (℡02870/41 249; ●), on the road towards the spit, is a more reasonable option, as are *Efi* rooms (℡02870/41 396;●), above the far end of the beach; *Andreas* (℡02870/41 262;●) has triple studios with stunning views and easy access to the quiet neighbouring bay. Pollónia has no bank or post office, but the friendly Axios Rent A Car office (℡02870/41 442) can change money and advise you on accommodation matters. A **motorbike rental** place and a well-stocked **supermarket** complete the list of amenities. There is a huge map fixed on a metal frame near the bus stop, which shows all the facilities and gives telephone numbers.

Getting to Kímolos may be the main reason you're here. The *Tria Adhelfia* makes the trip daily year-round at 6.45am and 2pm, returning from Kímolos an hour later. During high season, there is also an open ferry boat, so that there are at least five crossings a day.

Kímolos

Of the three islets off the coast of Mílos, Andímilos is home to a rare species of chamois, Políegos has more ordinary goats, but only **Kímolos** has any human habitation. Volcanic like Mílos, with the same little lava-built rural cottages, it profits from its geology and used to export chalk (*kimolía* in Greek) until the supply was exhausted. Fuller's earth is still extracted locally, and the fine dust of this clay is a familiar sight on the island, where mining still outstrips fishing and farming as an occupation. Rugged and barren in the interior, it has some fertile land on the southeast coast where wells provide water, and this is where the population of about eight hundred is concentrated.

Kímolos is sleepy indeed from September to June, and even in August sees few visitors. This is probably just as well, since there are fewer than a hundred beds on the whole island, and little in the way of other amenities.

Psathí and Hóra

Whether you arrive by ferry, or by kaïki from Pollónia, you'll dock at the hamlet of **PSATHÍ**, pretty much a non-event except for the excellent *To Kyma* **taverna** midway along the beach. The laissez-faire attitude towards tourism is demonstrated by the fact that there are no rooms here. **Ferry tickets** are sold only outside the expensive café at the end of the jetty, an hour or so before the anticipated arrival of the boat; the *Tria Adhelfia* and another open ferry come and go from Pollónia on Mílos from the base of the jetty five times a day in summer. There is no bus on the island, but a licence has been obtained for a taxi, so now only a driver is required. The friendly locals will sometimes offer you a lift.

Around the bay there are a few old windmills and the dazzlingly white **HÓRA** perched on the ridge above them. Unsung – and neglected, although there are plans to reconstruct it and build government rooms – is the magnificent, two-gated sixteenth-century *kástro*, the best preserved of such fortresses built against marauding pirates in the Cyclades; the perimeter houses are intact and inhabited but its heart is a jumble of ruins. Just outside the *kástro* to the north stands the conspicuously unwhitewashed, late-sixteenth-century church of **Khryssóstomos**, the oldest and most beautiful on the island. It takes fifteen minutes to walk up to the surprisingly large town, passing the adequate *Villa Maria* (℡02870/51 392; ❷), about five minutes along the way and nearer to Psathí. Further accommodation is available in Hóra itself, where Margaro Petraki (℡02870/51 314; ❶), has rooms tucked away in the rather unglamorous maze of backstreets, as does Nikos Ventouris (℡02870/51 329; ❶) above his kafenío nearby. Sofia Ventouris (℡02870/51 219; ❸) has a few new studios with sea views, close to the church. The aptly named *Panorama*, near the east gate of the *kástro*, is the most elaborate and consistently open **taverna**. *Meltemi*, to the west of the village, is a good, new taverna which also has some rooms (℡02870/51 360; ❷). There are a couple of basic *psistariés*, as well as *1860*, a surprisingly sophisticated **café-bar**. Self-catering is an easy proposition – and may be a necessity before June or after August – with a well-stocked supermarket, produce stalls and a butcher. Finally, there are a couple of boat agencies, and a **post office** in the west of the village. The small **archeological museum** (Tues & Fri 8am–2pm, Wed, Thurs, Sat, Sun 8am–1pm), currently on the road into Hóra, is due to move to more spacious premises near the church; its collection comprises pottery from the Geometric to the Roman period.

Around the island

During summer at least, the hamlet of **ALYKÍ** on the south coast is a better bet for staying than Psathí and Hóra; it only takes about thirty minutes to walk there on the paved road that forks left just before the *Villa Maria*. Alykí is named after the salt pan which sprawls between a rather mediocre beach with no shade or shelter, and has a pair of **rooms** – *Sardis* (℡02870/51 458; ❸) and *Passamihalis* (℡02870/51 340; ❷) – and simple **tavernas**. You can stroll west one cove to **Bonátsa** for better sand and shallow water, though you won't escape the winds. Passing another cove you come to the even more attractive beach of Kalamítsi, with better shade and the good little taverna and rooms of *Ventouris* (❸). To the east, between Alykí and Psathí, the smaller, more secluded beach of **Skála** is better for camping.

The 700m coarse-sand beach of **Ellinká** is 45-minutes' walk west of Alykí: starting on the road, bear left – just before two chapels on a slope – onto a narrower track which runs through the fields at the bottom of the valley. Divided by a low bluff, the beach is bracketed by two capes and looks out over Dhaskalió islet; it tends to catch heavy weather in the afternoon, and there are no facilities here.

Another road leads northeast from Hóra to a beach and radioactive springs at **Prássa**, 7km away. The route takes in impressive views across the straits to Políegos, and there are several shady peaceful coves where it's possible to camp out. Innumerable goat tracks invite exploration of the rest of the island; in the far northwest, on Kímolos's summit, are the ruins of an imposing Venetian fortress known as **Paleókastro**. The local community has plans to open an official campsite at Klíma Bay 2km northeast of Hóra, once it has relocated the rubbish dump that currently befouls the place.

Ándhros

Ándhros, the second largest and northernmost of the Cyclades, has a number of fine features to offer the visitor and is a great place for serious walkers. Thinly populated but prosperous, its fertile, well-watered valleys have attracted scores of Athenian holiday villas whose red-tiled roofs and white walls stand out among the greenery. Some of the more recent of these have robbed many of the villages of life and atmosphere, turning them into scattered settlements with no nucleus, and creating a weekender mentality manifest in noisy Friday and Sunday evening traffic jams at the ferry dock. The island doesn't cater to independent travellers, and it can be difficult to find a bed during high season, especially at weekends. On the positive side, the permanent population is distinctly hospitable; traditionally working on ships, they are only too happy to try out their English on you. Together with some of the more idiosyncratic reminders of the Venetian period, such as the *peristereónes* (pigeon towers) and the *frákhtes* (dry-stone walls, here raised to the status of an art form), it is this friendliness that lends Ándhros its charm.

Ferries connect the island with Rafína on the mainland, only an hour from Athens on the bus, and you can loop back onto the central Cycladic routes via

Mýkonos, Tínos or Sýros. A bus usually meets arriving ferries and runs to Batsí and on to Hóra at least six times a day in the high season.

Northern and western Ándhros

All ferries and catamarans arrive at the main port, **GÁVRIO**, a moderately attractive holiday resort. Few venture onto the adjacent windswept beach; however, there are plenty more attractive alternatives just to the south, where you'll find some of the area's better accommodation. A converted dovecote houses a sporadically functioning **tourist office**, and there are half a dozen ferry **ticket agents**, a **bank**, and a **post office** on the waterfront.

The cheapest **accommodation** is in the basic *Galaxias* (☎02820/71 228; ❷), which serves as a late-arrival fall-back. There are more room and studio outfits along and above the main coastal road to Batsí: *Aktion* (☎02820/71 607; ❸) is fairly representative, while *Andros Holiday Hotel* (☎02820/71 384; ❻) is a good upmarket choice. **Restaurants** worth trying include the good if basic *estiatório*, *Tria Asteria*; the *Veggera* taverna 100m inland with its pleasant leafy courtyard; and the smart *Trehandiri* ouzerí opposite the catamaran dock. **Nightlife** revolves around a string of cafés and bars along the harbourfront, of which *Marlin* is a popular choice. Alternatively, there are one or two lively venues on Áyios Pétros beach several kilometres south, including *Marabou* taverna which frequently features live guitar music. Along the same stretch the excellent *Yiannouli* taverna is worth checking out for lunch.

The road north begins behind the *Hotel Gavrion Beach*. Around 3km northwest are two beaches named **Fellós**: one with holiday villas and a taverna, the other hidden beyond the headland and popular with freelance campers. Beyond Ápano Fellós, the countryside is empty except for a few hamlets inhabited by the descendants of Albanians who settled here and in southern Évvia several hundred years ago.

Most visitors head 8km south down the coast, past the lively Khryssí Ammos beach, and the *Perakkis Hotel* above it (☎02820/71 456; ❸), to **BATSÍ**, the island's main resort, with large hotels and bars around its fine natural harbour. The beautiful though often crowded beach curves round the port, and the sea is cold, calm and clean (except near the taxi park). **Hotels** range from the central, comfortable *Chryssi Akti* (☎02820/41 236; ❸) to the upmarket *Aneroussa Beach Hotel* (☎02820/41 045; ❸–❻), south of town past the Stivári area towards Áyia Marína beach – a picturesque cove with *Yiannoulis* fish taverna and studios (☎02820/41 963; ❸). Besides these there are plenty of other rooms, and good **food** can be had, especially at *To Akroyiali* and *Pizza Ritsa*. Other choices include *Stamatis*, an established taverna with a nice atmosphere, and *Ta Delfinia,* which has a pleasant, sheltered balcony. For something a little different have a shrimp feast at *Restaurant Sirocco*, on the inland path above the village. There are several café-bars, such as *Capriccio* and *Select*, a half a dozen or so loud indoor bars featuring the standard foreign/Greek musical mix, and even an outdoor cinema with a different movie every night in the summer. There are two banks, with cash dispensers. For information on walking tours, a free copy of the informative *Island of Andro*, or other travel needs go to Greek Sun Travel (☎02820/41 198, ⓕ41 239, ⓔgreeksun@traveling.gr), upstairs near the taxi park.

From Batsí you're within easy walking distance of some beautiful inland villages. At **KÁTO KATÁKILOS**, one hour inland, there are a couple of seasonal **tavernas** including *O Gregos*; a rough track leads to **ATÉNI**, a hamlet in a lush, remote valley. **ÁNO KATÁKILOS** has a couple of undervisited tavernas with fine views across the village. A right-hand turning out of Katákilos heads up the mountain to **ARNÍ**, whose lone taverna is often shrouded in mist. Another rewarding trip is to a well-preserved, twenty-metre-high tower at **Áyios Pétros**, a mystery even to locals, 5km from Gávrio or 9km coming from Batsí.

South of Batsí along the main road are **Káto** and **Áno Apróvato**. Káto has rooms, including *Galini* (℡02820/41 472; ❷), a taverna and a path to a quiet beach, while nearby is the largely unexplored archeological site of **Paleópolis**. Áno has the excellent taverna *To Balkoni tou Egeou*, which can be most easily visited on one of the "Mezédhes Nights" organized from Batsí by Greek Sun Travel and various hotels, though for a more authentic evening you may be better off making your own way there.

Hóra and around

A bus service links the west coast with **HÓRA**, aka **ÁNDHROS TOWN**, 35km from Gávrio. With its setting on a rocky spur cutting across a huge bay, the capital is the most attractive place on the island. Paved in marble and schist from the still-active local quarries, the buildings around the bus station are grand nineteenth-century affairs, and the squares with their ornate wall fountains and gateways are equally elegant. The hill quarters are modern and rather exclusive, while the small port on the west side of the headland has a yacht supply station and ferry landing. There are beaches on both sides of the headland, the better of which is Parapórti, to the east, though it's somewhat exposed to the *meltémi* winds in summer.

The few **hotels** in town are on the expensive side and tend to be busy with holidaying Greeks, although you could try the traditional *Aigli* (℡02820/22 303; ❷), opposite the big church on the main walkway. Most rooms are clustered behind the long **Nimbório** northwest of town, and range from cheap family guesthouses like *Firiou* (℡02820/22 921; ❶) and good clean rooms like those of *Villa Stella* (℡02820/22 471; ❸) to modern apartments such as the *Alkioni Inn* (℡02820/24 522; ❹). The *Paradise Hotel* (℡02820/22 187, Ⓔmarlos@mail.otenet.gr; ❺–❻), with its swimming pool and tennis court, is the most upmarket choice. For **eating**, most cafés are up in Hóra: *Plátanos* has a generous mezédhes selection which can be enjoyed with an oúzo under the plane trees; the appropriately named *O Stathmos* right by the bus station is good; and there's a decent *psistariá* on the main drag. The nicest taverna is *O Nonas*, tucked away at the town end of the beach behind the ugly *Xenia* hotel; *Nostos*, a smart new pizzeria nearby on the seafront, is another popular choice. Up in Hóra there's the *Rock Café* for a **drink**, but Nimboúrio beach is the epicentre of **nightlife** with the two-storey *Veggera*, a thumping disco halfway along, and the huge *Kavo* right at the end, which plays Greek music till after 4am. There's a post office and bank around town, a couple of travel agents and three motorbike rentals behind the beach.

From the square right at the end of town you pass through an archway and down to windswept **Platía Ríva**, with its statue of the unknown sailor scanning the sea. (This stolid bronze, a gift from the Soviet Union, was recently toppled and broken by a high wind, but locals plan to restore it.) Beyond lies the thirteenth-century Venetian *kástro*, precariously joined to the mainland by a narrow-arched bridge, which was damaged by German munitions in World War II. Don't be discouraged by the stark modern architecture of the **archeological museum** (Tues–Sun 8.30am–2.30pm; €1.50), on the main street; it proves to be well laid out and labelled, with instructive models. Its prize item is the fourth-century "Hermes of Ándros", reclaimed from a prominent position in the Athens archeological museum. Behind it, the **Modern Art Museum** (Wed–Mon 10am–2pm, also 6–8pm in summer; €3) has a sculpture garden and a permanent collection with works by Picasso, Matisse, Kandinsky, Chagall and others, as well as temporary shows.

Hiking is particularly inviting south and west from Ándhros, where there are lush little river valleys. One obvious destination is **MÉNITES**, a hill village just up a green valley choked with trees and straddled by stone walls. The church of the **Panayía** may have been the location of a temple of Dionysos, where water was turned into wine; water still flows continuously from the local rocks. Nearby is the medieval village of **MESSARIÁ**, with the deserted twelfth-century Byzantine church of **Taxiárhis** below and the pleasantly shady *Platanos* taverna. The finest monastery on the island, **Panakhrándou**, is only an hour's (steep) walk away, via the village of Falliká: reputedly tenth-century, it's still defended by massive walls but occupied these days by just three monks. It clings to an iron-stained cliff southwest of Hóra, to which you can return directly with a healthy two- to three-hour walk down the creek valley, guided by red dots.

Hidden by the ridge directly north of Hóra, the prosperous nineteenth-century village of **STENIÉS** was built by the vanguard of today's shipping magnates; just below, at Yiália, there's a small pebble beach with a taverna. Nearby on the road to Strapouriés is a wonderful taverna, *Bozakis*, which boasts a view all the way down to the coast and excellent food. Beyond Steniés is **APIKÍA**, a tidy little village which bottles Sariza-brand mineral water for a living; there are a few **tavernas**, including *O Tassos* which has a lovely garden setting and specialities such as goat and rabbit. There are a very limited number of **rooms** here, as well as the "luxury" hotel *Pigi Sariza* (☎02820/23 799 or 23 899; ❸–❺), which is getting a bit tatty around the edges. The road is now asphalted up to Vourkotí and even past this point is quite negotiable via Arní to the west coast. There are some stunning views all along this road but bike riders need to take care when the *meltémi* is blowing – it can get dangerously windy.

Southern Ándhros

On your way south, you might stop at **Zagorá**, a fortified Geometric town – unique in having never been built over – that was excavated in the early 1970s. Located on a desolate, flat-topped promontory with cliffs falling away on three sides, it's worth a visit for the view alone. With your own transport, the sheltered cove of Sinéti south of Hóra is also worth a detour.

The village of **KORTHÍ**, the end of the line, is a friendly place which is slowly waking up to its tourist potential. Set on a large sandy bay, cut off from the rest of the island by a high ridge and so relatively unspoiled, it is pleasant enough to merit spending the night at *Villa Aristidou* (☎02820/62 122; ❷) or at the austere-looking *Hotel Korthion* (☎02820/61 218; ❷–❸). There are also several good seafood **restaurants**, and a number of pleasant café-bars including *Erolo Cafe* on the seafront. You could also take in the nearby convent of **Zoödhóhou Piyís** (open to visitors before noon), with illuminated manuscripts and a disused weaving factory.

To the north is **PALEÓKASTRO**, a tumbledown village with a ruined Venetian castle and a legend about an old woman who betrayed the stronghold to the Turks, then jumped off the walls in remorse, landing on a rock now known as "Old Lady's Leap". In the opposite direction out of Korthí are **AÏDHÓNIA** and **KAPARIÁ**, dotted with pigeon towers (*peristereónes*) left by the Venetians.

Tínos

Tínos still feels one of the most Greek of the larger islands. A few foreigners have discovered its beaches and unspoiled villages, but most visitors are Greek, here to see the church of **Panayía Evangelístria**, a grandiose shrine erected on the spot where a miraculous icon with healing powers was found in 1822. A local nun, now canonized as Ayía Pelayía, was directed in a vision to unearth the relic just as the War of Independence was getting underway, a timely coincidence which served to underscore the links between the Orthodox Church and Greek nationalism. Today, there are two major annual pilgrimages, on March 25 and August 15, when, at 11am, the icon bearing the Virgin's image is carried in state down to the harbour over the heads of the faithful.

The Ottoman tenure here was the most fleeting in the Aegean. **Exóbourgo**, the craggy mount dominating southern Tínos and surrounded by most of the island's sixty-odd villages, is studded with the ruins of a Venetian citadel which defied the Turks until 1715, long after the rest of Greece had fallen. An enduring legacy of the long Venetian rule is a persistent **Catholic minority**, which accounts for almost half the population, and a sectarian rivalry said to be responsible for the numerous graceful belfries scattered throughout the island – Orthodox and Catholic parishes vying to build the tallest. The sky is pierced, too, by distinctive and ornate dovecotes, even more in evidence here than on Ándhros. Aside from all this, the inland village architecture is striking and there's a flourishing folk-art tradition which finds expression in the abundant local marble. The islanders have remained open and hospitable to the relatively few foreigners and the steady stream of Greek visitors who touch down here, and any mercenary inclinations seem to be satisfied by booming sales in religious paraphernalia to the faithful.

Tínos Town and the southern beaches

At **TÍNOS TOWN**, trafficking in devotional articles certainly dominates the streets leading up from the busy waterfront to the Neoclassical **church** (daily 8am–8pm) which towers above. Approached via a massive marble staircase, the famous **icon** inside is all but buried under a dazzling array of jewels; below is the crypt (where the icon was discovered) and a mausoleum for the sailors drowned when the Greek warship *Elli*, at anchor off Tínos during a pilgrimage, was torpedoed by an Italian submarine on August 15, 1940. Museums around the courtyard display more objects donated by the faithful (who inundate the island for the two big yearly festivals), as well as icons, paintings and work by local marble sculptors.

The shrine aside – and all the attendant stalls, shops and bustle – the port is none too exciting, with just scattered inland patches of nineteenth-century buildings. You might make time for the **Archeological Museum** (Tues–Sun 8.30am–3pm; €1.50) on the way up to the church, whose collection includes a fascinating sundial from the local Roman sanctuary of Poseidon and Amphitrite (see p.144).

Practicalities

Ferries dock at any of three different **jetties**; which one depends on weather conditions. There are at least two boats a day from Pireás and Sýros, and four from Rafína and Ándhros going on to Mýkonos, as well as a useful hydrofoil, and less-frequent ferry connections to Páros, Náxos and Thíra. When you're leaving, ask your ticket agent which jetty to head for. **Buses** leave from a small

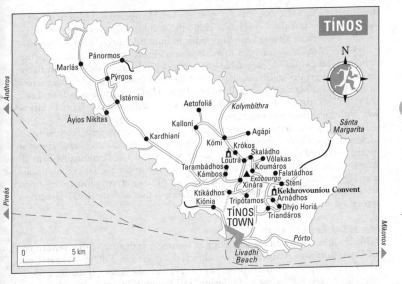

parking area in front of a cubbyhole-office on the quay, to Pánormos, Kalloní, Stení, Pórto and Kiónia (timetables available here; no buses after 7.30pm). A **motorbike** is perhaps a more reliable means of exploring – Vidalis at Zanáki Alavánou 16 is a good rental agency.

Windmills Travel (☎ & ⨍ 02830/23 398, ✉ tinos@windmills-travel.com), on the front towards the new jetty, can help with information as well as hotel and **tour bookings**; they even have a book exchange. In season an excursion boat does day-trips taking in Delos (see p.152) and Mýkonos (Tues–Sun; €15 round trip); this makes it possible to see Delos without the expense of staying overnight in Mýkonos, but only allows you two and a half hours at the site. The **tourist police** are located on the road to the west of the new jetty.

To have any chance of securing a reasonably priced **room** around the pilgrimage day of March 25 (August 15 is hopeless), you must arrive several days in advance. At other times there's plenty of choice, though you'll still be competing with out-of-season pilgrims, Athenian tourists and the ill and disabled seeking a miracle cure. Of the hotels, the *Eleana* (☎02830/22 561; ❷), east of the quay about 200m inland from the Commercial Bank and taxi stand, is a good budget option. Slightly pricier options include the *Avra* (☎02830/22 242; ❸), a Neoclassical relic on the waterfront, and the *Vyzantio* (☎02830/22 421; ❹), three blocks inland on the road to Pórto. The *Favie Suzanne* (☎02830/22 693, ⨍25 993; ❹), across the small square is probably a bit quieter, while the newly-renovated *Hotel Tinion* (☎02830/22 261; ⨍24 754; ❹), behind the post office, is a stylish 1920s hotel. The *Vyzantio* (above) and the *Meltémi* (☎02830/22 881; ❸) at Filipóti 7, near Megalohárıs, are the only places open out of season. Finally, there is a smart hotel, the *Aeolos Bay* (☎02830/23 410; ❹) with a swimming pool, near the beginning of the beach road east of the promontory. Otherwise, beat the crowds by staying at *Tinos Camping*, which also has a few nice rooms to let (☎02830/22 344; ❶); follow the signs and it's a ten-minute walk from the port.

As usual, most seafront **restaurants** are rather overpriced and indifferent, with the exception of a friendly *psitopolío* right opposite the bus station, and the smarter *Xinari* restaurant and pizzeria on Evangelístrias. About midway along the port near the *Leto Hotel*, behind the dolphin fountain, there are three excellent tavernas: *Kunilio*, with tasty pork in mustard sauce (*hirinó mé moustárda*); *Metaxi Mas*, a *mezedopolío* that has a remarkably varied menu, including delicious *hortokeftédhes* (vegetable croquettes); and *Palea Pallada*, justifiably proud of its grilled *loukániko*, sharp local feta and smooth house wine. Across from *Palea Pallada* there's a small bakery, *Psomi Horiatiko*, and across from both is the Palláda, the public square where every morning there's a farmer's **market** with local fruit and vegetables.

There are a few **bars**, mostly in a huddle near the new quay. *Fevgatos* has a pleasant atmosphere, *Koutsaros* on the corner plays rock music, and *Pyrsos* is pretty lively with a mixture of international hits and Greek music. At 3am all bars in Tínos Town close, but for those not ready to hit the sack, the *Paradise* and *Veggera* club duplex on the main road out of town to Amphitrite stay open until dawn, the former playing mainly Greek music and the latter favouring trance.

Nearby beaches

Kiónia, 3km northwest (hourly buses in summer), is the site of the **Sanctuary of Poseidon and Amphitrite** which was discovered in 1902; the excavations yielded principally columns (*kiónia* in Greek), but also a temple, baths, a fountain and hostels for the ancient pilgrims. The **beach** is functional enough, lined with rooms to rent and snack bars, but it's better to walk past the large *Tinos Beach Hotel* (T02830/22 626; ●), the last stop for the bus, and follow an unpaved road to a series of sandy coves beyond.

The beach beyond the headland east of town starts off rocky but improves if you walk 500m further along. Further east, **Pórto** (six buses daily) boasts two good beaches, with a couple of good tavernas as well as **rooms** at the reasonably priced restaurant belonging to *Akti Aegeou* (T02830/24 248; ●), on the first beach of Áyios Pandelímon, as well as the smart studios of *Porto Raphael* (T02830/22 403; ●), above Áyios Ioánnis. *Porto Tango* (T02830/24 410; ●) is an excellent upmarket hotel here, with a lovely pool setting.

Northern Tínos

A good beginning to a foray into the interior is to take the stone stairway – the continuation of Odhós Ayíou Nikoláou – that passes behind and to the left of the Evangelístria. This climbs for ninety minutes through appealing countryside to **KTIKÁDHOS**, a fine village with a good seaview taverna, *Iy Dhrosia*. You can either flag down a bus on the main road or stay with the trail until Xinára (see opposite).

Heading northwest from the junction flanked by Ktikádhos, Tripótamos and Xinára, there's little to stop for – except the fine dovecotes around Tarambádhos – until you reach **KARDHIANÍ**, one of the most strikingly set and beautiful villages on the island, with its views across to Sýros from amid a dense oasis. Nestled in the small sandy bay below is a fine little restaurant by the name of *Anemos*, which serves octopus stew and other dishes at good prices. Kardhianí has been discovered by wealthy Athenians and expatriates, and now offers the exotic *To Perivoli* taverna. **ISTÉRNIA**, just a little beyond, is not nearly so appealing but there is some accommodation on offer, including the *Lameras Hotel* (T02830/31 215; ●). The *Tavsternia* taverna commands stunning panoramic views and there are a few cafés, perched above the turning for **Órmos Isterníon,** a comparatively small but overdeveloped beach.

Five daily buses along this route finish up at **PÝRGOS**, a few kilometres further north and smack in the middle of the island's marble-quarrying district. A beautiful village, its local artisans are renowned throughout Greece for their skill in producing marble ornamentation; ornate fanlights and bas-relief plaques crafted here adorn houses throughout Tínos. Pýrgos is also home to the School of Arts, and the **Museum of Tinian Artists** (daily 11am–2pm & 5.30–6.30pm; €1) contains numerous representative works from some of the island's finest artists. There are two **kafenía** and a **snack bar** on the attractive shady platía, and one acceptable **taverna** opposite the bus station. Pýrgos is popular in summer, and if you want to stay there are some new **studios** for rent on the main road coming into the village; alternatively ask the locals on the platía.

The marble products were once exported from **PÁNORMOS** (Órmos) harbour, 4km northeast, with its tiny but commercialized beach; there's little reason to linger, but if you get stuck there are rooms and some tavernas.

Around Exóbourgo

The ring of villages around **Exóbourgo** mountain is the other focus of interest on Tínos. The fortified pinnacle itself (570m), with ancient foundations as well as the ruins of three Venetian churches and a fountain, is reached by steep steps from **XINÁRA** (near the island's major road junction), the seat of the island's Roman Catholic bishop. Most villages in north central Tínos have mixed populations, but Xinára and its immediate neighbours are purely Catholic; the inland villages also tend to have a more sheltered position, with better farmland nearby – the Venetians' way of rewarding converts and their descendants. Yet **TRIPÓTAMOS**, just south of Xinára, is a completely Orthodox village with possibly the finest architecture in this region – and has accordingly been pounced on by foreigners keen to restore its historic properties.

At **LOUTRÁ**, the next community north of Xinára, there's an Ursuline convent and a good **folk art museum** (summer only 10.30am–3.30pm; free) in the old Jesuit monastery; to visit, leave the bus at the turning for Skaládho. From Krókos, 1km northwest of Loutra, which has a scenically situated restaurant, *O Krokos*, it's a forty-minute walk to **VÓLAKAS** (Vólax), one of the most remote villages on the island, a windswept oasis surrounded by bony rocks. Here, half a dozen elderly Catholic basketweavers fashion some of the best examples in Greece. There is a small **folklore museum** (free) which you have to ask the lady living in the house opposite the entrance to open, and the charming outdoor **Fontaine Theatre** which in August hosts visiting theatre groups from all over Greece. Accommodation is hard to come by, but there are a couple of places to eat, including the recommended *O Rokos* taverna.

At Kómi, 5km beyond Krókos, you can take a detour for **KOLYMBÍTHRA**, a magnificent double beach: one part wild, huge and windswept (temporary residence to pink flamingos migrating to Africa during May), the other sheltered and with a couple of tavernas including *Kolibithra Beach* (⊕02830/51 213), which also has rooms (◐). The bus to Kallóni goes on to Kolymbíthra twice a day in season; out of season you'll have to get off at Kómi and walk 4km.

From either Skaládho or Vólakas you go on to Koúmaros, where another long stairway leads up to Exóbourgo, or skirt the pinnacle towards Stení and Falatádhos which appear as white speckles against the fertile Livádha valley. From Stení you can catch the bus back to the harbour (seven daily). On the way down, try and stop off at one of the beautiful settlements just below the important twelfth-century **convent of Kekhrovouníou**, where Ayía Pelayía had her vision. Particularly worth visiting are **DHÝO HORIÁ**, which has a fine main square where cave-fountains burble, and **TRIANDÁROS**, which has two reasonable **eating** places: *Iy Lefka* and *Eleni's* (a tiny place at the back of the village). If you have your own transport, there are quite wide and fairly negotiable tracks down to some lovely secluded bays on the east of the island from the area of Stení. One such is **Sánta Margaríta**; given the lack of tourist development here, it's a good idea to take something to drink.

This is hardly an exhaustive list of Tiniot villages; armed with a map and good walking shoes for tackling the many old trails that still exist, you could spend days within sight of Exóbourgo and never pass through the same hamlets twice. Take warm clothing out of season, especially if you're on a scooter, since the forbidding mountains behind Vólakas and the Livadhéri plain keep things noticeably cool.

Mýkonos

Originally visited only as a stop on the way to ancient Delos, **Mýkonos** has become easily the most popular (and the most expensive) of the Cyclades. Boosted by direct air links with Britain and domestic flights from Athens, it sees an incredible 800,000 tourists pass through in a good year, producing some spectacular overcrowding in high summer on Mýkonos's 75 square kilometres. But if you don't mind the crowds, or – and this is a much more attractive proposition – you come out of season, the prosperous capital is still one of the most beautiful of all island towns, its immaculately whitewashed houses concealing hundreds of little churches, shrines and chapels.

The sophisticated nightlife is pretty hectic, amply stimulated by Mýkonos's former reputation as *the* gay resort of the Mediterranean – a title shared in recent years with places like Ibiza and Sitges in Spain; whatever, the locals take this comparatively exotic clientele in their stride. Unspoiled it isn't, but the island does offer excellent (if crowded) beaches, picturesque windmills and a rolling arid interior. An unheralded Mýkonian quirk is the legality of scuba diving, a rarity in Greece, and dive centres have sprung up on virtually every beach.

Mýkonos Town

Don't let the crowds put you off exploring **MÝKONOS TOWN**, the archetypal postcard image of the Cyclades. Its sugar-cube buildings are stacked around a cluster of seafront fishermen's dwellings, with every nook and cranny scrubbed and shown off. Most people head out to the beaches during the day, so early morning or late afternoon are the best times to wander the maze of narrow streets. The labyrinthine design was intended to confuse the pirates who plagued Mýkonos in the eighteenth and early nineteenth centuries, and it still has the desired effect.

You don't need any maps or hints to explore the convoluted streets and alleys of town – getting lost is half the fun. There are, however, a few places worth seeking out. Coming from the ferry quay you'll pass the **Archeological Museum** (Tues–Sat 9am–3.30pm, Sun 10am–3pm; €1.50) on your way into town, which displays some good Delos pottery; the town also boasts a **Maritime Museum** displaying various nautical artefacts, including a lighthouse re-erected in the back garden (Tues–Sun 8.30am–3pm; €1).

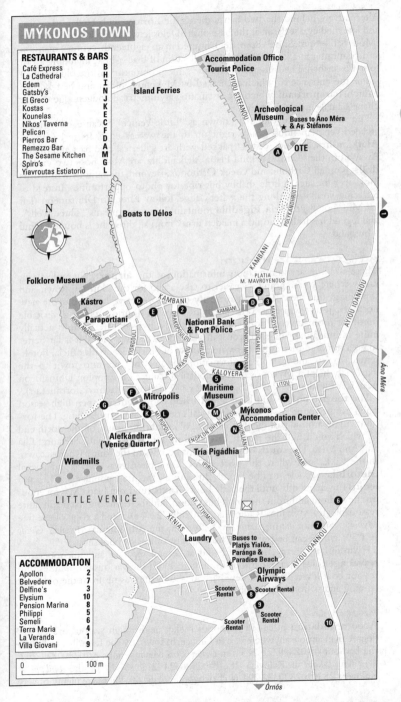

MÝKONOS TOWN

RESTAURANTS & BARS

Café Express	B
La Cathedral	H
Edem	I
Gatsby's	N
El Greco	J
Kostas	K
Kounelas	E
Nikos' Taverna	C
Pelican	F
Pierros Bar	D
Remezzo Bar	A
The Sesame Kitchen	M
Spiro's	G
Yiavroutas Estiatorio	L

Accommodation Office
Tourist Police

Island Ferries

Archeological Museum

Buses to Áno Méra & Ay. Stéfanos

OTE

Folklore Museum

Kástro
Paraportianí

KAMBANI

National Bank & Port Police

PLATIA M. MAVROYENOUS

KALOYERA

Maritime Museum

Mýkonos Accommodation Center

Mitrópolis

Alefkándhra ('Venice Quarter')

Tría Pigádhia

Windmills

LITTLE VENICE

Laundry

Buses to Platýs Yialós, Paránga & Paradise Beach

Olympic Airways

Scooter Rental

Scooter Rental

Scooter Rental

Boats to Délos

Áno Méra

Órnos

ACCOMMODATION

Apollon	2
Belvedere	7
Delfine's	3
Elysium	10
Pension Marina	8
Philippi	5
Semeli	6
Terra Maria	4
La Veranda	1
Villa Giovani	9

N

0   100 m

Alternatively, behind the two banks there's the **library**, with Hellenistic coins and late medieval seals, or, at the base of the Delos jetty, the **Folklore Museum** (Mon–Sat 4–8pm, Sun 5–8pm; free), housed in an eighteenth-century mansion and cramming in a larger-than-usual collection of bric-a-brac, including a vast four-poster bed. The museum shares the same promontory as the old Venetian *kástro*, the entrance to which is marked by Mýkonos's oldest and best-known church, **Paraportianí**, which is a fascinating asymmetrical hodgepodge of four chapels amalgamated into one.

The shore leads to the area known as "Little Venice" because of its high, arcaded Venetian houses built right up to the water's edge. Its real name is **Alefkándhra**, a trendy district packed with art galleries, chic bars and discos. Away from the seafront, behind Platía Alefkándhra, are Mýkonos's two **cathedrals**: Roman Catholic and Greek Orthodox. Beyond, the famous **windmills** look over the area, a little shabby but ripe for photo opportunities. Instead of retracing your steps along the water's edge, follow Énoplon Dhinaméon (left off Mitropóleos) to **Tría Pigádhia** fountain. The name means "Three Wells", and legend has it that should a maiden drink from all three she is bound to find a husband.

Arrival and information

There is some accommodation information at the **airport**, but unless you know where you're going it's easier to take a taxi for the 3km into town, and sort things out there. The vast majority of visitors arrive by boat at the new northern **jetty**, which is 1km north of town in Toúrlos, where a veritable horde of room-owners pounces on the newly arrived. The scene is actually quite intimidating, and so, if you can avoid the grasping talons, it is far better to go a hundred metres further where a row of offices deal with official hotels, rented rooms and camping information, or get the bus into town to the extremely helpful Mykonos Accommodation Centre on Énoplon Dhinaméon near Tría Pigádia (℡02890/23 160, ℻24 137, ✉mac@mac.myk.forthnet.gr).

The **tourist police** and local **accommodation centre** (open high season only) can be found up from the ferry stalls near the old ferry landing. The harbour curves around past the dull, central Polikandhrióti beach, off the north end of which you'll find the **north bus station**, for Toúrlos, Áyios Stéfanos, Elía and Áno Méra. The **south bus station**, for beaches to the south, is across town, in the Lákka area where the **post office**, Olympic Airways office and several **motorbike** agencies can be found. Buses to all the most popular beaches and resorts run frequently until the early hours. **Taxis** run from Platía Mavroyénous on the seafront and from the south bus station, and their rates are fixed and quite reasonable; try Mykonos Radio Taxi (℡02890/22 400). Find a copy of the free *Mykonos Summertime* magazine or, better yet, the Athinorama *Mykonos Guide* (€1.50) which can be purchased from tourist offices or bookshops.

Hydrofoil and ferry tickets are sold at several separate and uncooperative **travel agencies** on the harbour front. Check out the various possibilities, and if your boat leaves from the new harbour, catch the bus up from the old ferry landing across from the Eurobank.

Accommodation

Accommodation prices in Mýkonos rocket in the high season to a greater degree than almost anywhere else in Greece. In town, try the friendly *Apollon* on the harbour (℡02890/22 223; ❸), *Delfine's* on Mavroyénous (℡02890/22 292; ❻), *Terra Maria* at Kaloyéra 18 (℡02890/24 212; ❹–❻) or the *Philippi* at Kaloyéra 25 (℡02890/22 294, ✉chrico@otenet.gr; ❻). There are plenty of very expensive hotels like *Semeli Hotel* (☎02890/27 466, ⑰27 467; ⑨) above town on Ayíou Ioánnou, which has a pool, whirlpool and very tastefully decorated rooms, or the *Belvedere Hotel* (☎02890/25 122, ⓔbelvedere@myk.forthnet.gr; ⓞ) next door. *La Veranda* (☎02890/23 670; ⓞ) is a hidden gem, located on the hillside above town, with rooms set around a small pool. Unsurprisingly, most accommodation is extremely gay-friendly: *Elysium* (☎02890/23 952; ⑥) is almost exclusively gay. Two recommended **pensions** are on the south side of town above the bus station: *Villa Giovanni* (☎02890/22 485; ⑨) and *Pension Marina* (☎02890/24 960; ⑨) on Ayíou Ioánnou and Láka. There are two **campsites**: *Mykonos Camping* (☎02890/24 578) above Paránga beach is smaller and has a more pleasant setting than nearby *Paradise Camping* on Paradise beach (☎02890/22 852, ⓔPARADISE@paradise.myk.forthnet.gr); however, the latter also has bungalows (④). Both are packed in season, and dance music from the 24-hour bars on Paradise Beach makes sleep difficult. The overpriced campsite restaurants serving poor food are best avoided. Hourly bus services to Paránga and Paradise Beach continue into the early hours but can get very overcrowded.

Eating and nightlife

Even **light meals** and **snacks** are expensive in Mýkonos, but there are several bakeries, supermarkets and fruit stalls, some concentrated near the south bus station. For good *tyrópites* and *milópites* try Anemomilos (Karapis), on the right about fifty metres up Mavroyénous.

The area around Alefkándhra is a promising place to head for a full **meal**: *La Cathedral*, by the two cathedrals on the platía, has standard fare; *Pelican*, behind the cathedrals, is pricey but well sited; and *Kostas*, also nearby, has competitive prices, a good wine list including barrelled wine (not easily found on Mýkonos) and friendly service. Less than fifty metres further along Mitropóleos, the small *Yiavroutas Estiatorio* is probably the least expensive and

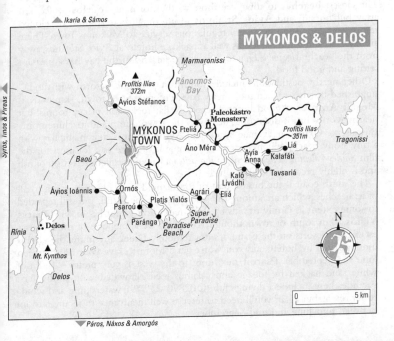

most authentically Greek place on the island, again with good barrelled wine. *Kounelas* is a good fish taverna with more reasonable prices than *Spiro's* on the seafront. *Edem*, close to Panakhrándou, offers poolside dining. *El Greco* at Tría Pigádhia is expensive but romantic, and *Gatsby's* on Tourlianís is a gay-friendly restaurant with an adventurous menu. *The Sesame Kitchen* on Énoplon Dhinaméon is an acceptable vegetarian restaurant; however, most of the smarter restaurants in Mýkonos do cater well for vegetarians anyway. Just behind the town hall is *Nikos' Taverna* – crowded, reasonable and recommended. For **late-night** snacks, most of the cafés on Kambani stay open until the small hours, and *Cafe Express* is open all night.

Nightlife in town is every bit as good as it's cracked up to be – and every bit as pricey. *Remezzo* (near the OTE) is one of the oldest bars, now a bit over the hill but a lively spot nonetheless, and a good place to have a drink before moving onto *Mercedes Club*; both are popular with young Athenians. *Skandinavian Bar-Disco* is a cheap-and-cheerful party spot, as is the nearby *Irish Bar*, and there are more sophisticated bars on Andhroníkou Matoyiánni and Énoplon Dhinaméon. *Katerina's*, *Caprice* and *Kastro*, in Little Venice, are ideal for sunset cocktails; the first serves delicious fresh fruit juices, and the latter plays classical music and is popular with an older gay crowd. Back (northeast) towards the harbour, *La Mer* is a popular disco/bar playing a lively mix of Greek and dance music, while *Porta* is a popular gay haunt near *Kounelas* restaurant. *Pierro's* and *Icarus* (upstairs), just off Platía Mavroyénous, become the focal point of gay activity later on, the latter having great drag shows and welcoming proprietors. *Cavo Paradiso*, near *Paradise Camping*, is the after-hours club where die-hard party animals of all persuasions come together.

The beaches

The closest **beaches** to town are those to the north, at **Toúrlos** (only 2km away but horrid) and **Áyios Stéfanos** (4km, much better), both developed resorts and connected by a very regular bus service to Mýkonos Town. There are tavernas and rooms to let (as well as package hotels) at Áyios Stéfanos, away from the beach; *Mocambo Lido* taverna at the far end of the bay has a pleasant setting and good food.

Other nearby destinations include southwest peninsula resorts, with undistinguished beaches tucked into pretty bays. The nearest to town, 1km away, is **Megáli Ámmos**, a good beach backed by flat rocks and pricey rooms, but nearby Kórfos bay is disgusting, thanks to the town dump and machine noise. Buses serve **Ornós**, an average beach, and **Áyios Ioánnis**, a dramatic bay with a tiny, stony beach, which achieved its moment of fame as a location for the film *Shirley Valentine*. The taverna *To Iliovasilema* has an excellent selection of fish and is highly recommended, if a little pricey.

The south coast is the busiest part of the island. Kaïkia ply from town to all of its beaches, which are among the straightest on the island, and still regarded to some extent as family strands by the Greeks. You might begin with **Platýs Yialós**, 4km south of town, though you won't be alone: one of the longest-established resorts on the island, it's not remotely Greek any more, the sand is monopolized by hotels, and you won't get a room to save your life between June and September. **Psaroú**, next door to the west, is very pretty – 150m of white sand backed by foliage and calamus reeds, crowded with sunbathers. Facilities here include a diving club (℡02890/23 579), waterskiing and windsurfer rental, but again you'll need to reserve well in advance to secure a room between mid-June and mid-September.

Just over the headland to the east of Platýs Yialós is **Paránga beach**, which is actually two beaches separated by a smaller headland. The highly recommended *Nicolas* taverna and rooms (☎02890/23 566; ④) on the first beach is worlds apart from its noisy neighbour which is home to a loud beach bar and *Mýkonos Camping*. A dusty footpath beyond Platýs Yialós crosses the fields and caves of the headland across the clifftops past Paranga, and drops down to **Paradise Beach**, a crescent of golden sand that is packed in season. Behind are the shops, self-service restaurants and noisy 24-hour beach bars of *Paradise Camping*. The next bay east contains **Super Paradise** (officially "Plindhrí") beach, accessible by footpath or by kaïki. One of the most fun beaches on the island, it has a decent taverna and two bars at opposite ends of the beach pumping out cheesy summer hits. One half of the beach is very mixed, getting progressively more gay as you walk away from where the kaïkia dock towards the beach bar perched in the hills, below which the beach is almost exclusively gay and nudist.

Probably the **best beach** on Mýkonos is **Eliá**, the last port of call for the kaïkia. A broad, sandy stretch with a verdant backdrop, it's the longest beach on the island, though split in two by a rocky area. It's gay-friendly, but also increasingly popular with families because of the proximity of Watermania (10am–midnight; adults €12, under 12s €6, under 5s free; there's a free daily bus from Mýkonos Town; ☎02890/71 685) the island's biggest **waterslide park**, and several restaurants, including the excellent *Matheos*. If the crowds have followed you this far, one last escape route is to follow the bare rock footpath over the spur (look for the white house) at the end of Eliá beach. This cuts upwards for grand views east and west and then winds down to **Kaló Livádhi** (seasonal bus service), a stunning beach adjoining an agricultural valley scattered with little farmhouses; even here there's a restaurant (a good one at that) at the far end of the beach. **Liá**, further on, is smaller but delightful, with bamboo windbreaks and clear water, plus another taverna.

East of Eliá, roughly 12km by road from the town, **Ayía Ánna** boasts a shingle beach and taverna, with the cliffs above granting some fine vistas. **Tarsaná**, on the other side of the isthmus, has a long, coarse-sand beach, with watersports, a taverna and smart bungalows on offer. **Kalafáti**, almost adjacent, is more of a tourist community, its white-sand beach supporting a few hotels, restaurants and a disco. There's a local bus service from here to Áno Méra (see below), or you can jump on an excursion boat to **Tragoníssi**, the islet just offshore, for spectacular coastal scenery, seals and wild birds. The rest of the east coast is difficult – often impossible – to reach: there are some small beaches, really only worth the effort if you crave solitude, and the region is dominated by the peak of Profítis Ilías, sadly spoiled by a huge radar dome and military establishment. The **north coast** suffers persistent battering from the *meltémi*, plus tar and litter pollution, and for the most part is bare, brown and exposed. **Pánormos Bay** is the exception to this – a lovely, relatively sheltered beach. Despite a good restaurant, a relaxed beach bar and the rather conspicuous *Albatros Club Hotel* (☎02890/25 130; ⑤), Pánormos remains one of the least crowded beaches on the island.

Áno Méra

From Pánormos Bay, it's an easy walk to the only other settlement of any size on the island, **ÁNO MÉRA**, where you should be able to find a **room**. The village prides itself on striving to maintain a traditional way of life, although the result is rather fake and wishy-washy: the so-called traditional kafenío has long since ditched Greek coffee for cappuccino and traditional sweets for "ice-cream special". There are, however, several acceptable **tavernas** on the platía, of which *Tou Apostoli to Koutouki* is most popular with locals, and a large **hotel** – Hotel Ano Mera (T02890/71 276; ⑨–⑧). The red-roofed church near the square is the sixteenth-century **monastery of Panayía Tourlianí**, where a collection of Cretan icons and the unusual eighteenth-century marble baptismal font are worth seeing. It's not far, either, to the late twelfth-century **Paleokástro monastery** (also known as Dárga), just north of the village, in a magnificent green setting on an otherwise barren slope. To the northwest are more of the same dry and wind-buffeted landscapes, though they do provide some enjoyable, rocky walking with expansive views across to neighbouring islands – head to Áyios Stéfanos for buses back to the harbour.

Delos (Dhílos)

The remains of **ancient Delos**, Pindar's "unmoved marvel of the wide world", though skeletal and swarming now with lizards and tourists, give some idea of the past grandeur of this sacred isle a few sea-miles west of Mýkonos. The ancient town (Tues–Sun 8.30am–3pm; €4.40) lies on the west coast on flat, sometimes marshy ground which rises in the south to **Mount Kýnthos**. From the summit – an easy walk – there's a magnificent view across the Cyclades: the name of the archipelago means "those [islands] around [Delos]".

The first excursion boats to Delos leave Mýkonos daily at 8.30am (€5.80 round trip), except Mondays when the site is closed. You have to return on the same boat, but in season each does the trip several times and you can choose what time you leave. The last return is usually about 3pm, and you'll need to arrive early if you want to make a thorough tour of the site. In season a daily kaïki makes return trips from the beaches (€9) with pick-up points at Platýs Yialós and Órnos, but only allows you three hours on the island. It's a good idea to bring your own food and drink as the tourist pavilion's snack bar is a rip-off.

Some history

Delos's ancient fame was due to the fact that Leto gave birth to the divine twins Artemis and Apollo on the island, although its fine harbour and central position did nothing to hamper development. When the Ionians colonized the island around 1000 BC it was already a cult centre, and by the seventh century BC it had become the commercial and religious centre of the **Amphictionic League**. Unfortunately Delos also attracted the attention of Athens, which sought dominion over this prestigious island; the wealth of the Delian Confederacy, founded after the Persian Wars to protect the Aegean cities, was harnessed to Athenian ends, and for a while Athens controlled the Sanctuary of Apollo. Athenian attempts to "purify" the island began with a decree that no one could die or give birth on Delos – the sick and the pregnant were taken to the islet of Rheneia – and culminated in the simple expedient of banishing the native population.

Delos reached its peak in the third and second centuries BC, after being declared a free port by its Roman overlords. In the end, though, its undefended wealth brought ruin: first Mithridates (88 BC), then Athenodorus (69 BC) plundered the treasures and the island never recovered. By the third century AD, Athens could not even sell it, and for centuries, every passing seafarer stopped to collect a few prizes.

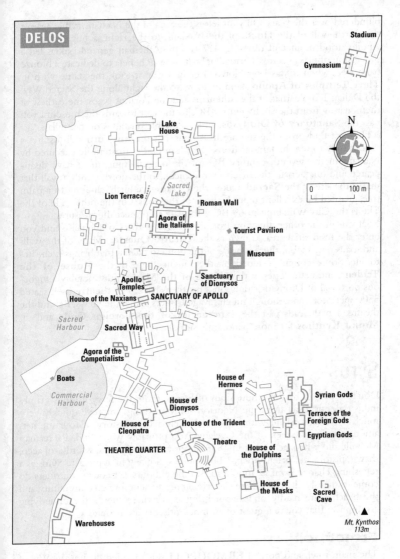

DELOS

Stadium

Gymnasium

Lake House

Sacred Lake

Lion Terrace

Roman Wall

Agora of the Italians

Tourist Pavilion

Museum

0   100 m

Apollo Temples

Sanctuary of Dionysos

House of the Naxians   SANCTUARY OF APOLLO

Sacred Harbour

Sacred Way

Agora of the Competialists

Boats

Commercial Harbour

House of Hermes

Syrian Gods

House of Dionysos

Terrace of the Foreign Gods

House of Cleopatra

House of the Trident

Egyptian Gods

THEATRE QUARTER

Theatre

House of the Dolphins

House of the Masks

Sacred Cave

Warehouses

Mt. Kynthos 113m

The site

As you land, the Sacred Harbour is on your left, the Commercial Harbour on your right and straight ahead is the **Agora of the Competialists**. Competialists were Roman merchants or freed slaves who worshipped the Lares Competales, the guardian spirits of crossroads; offerings to Hermes would once have been placed in the middle of the agora, their position now marked by a round and a square base. The **Sacred Way** leads north from the far left corner; it used to be lined with statues and the grandiose monuments of rival kings. Along it you reach three marble steps which lead into the **Sanctuary of Apollo**; much was lavished on the god, but the forest of offerings has been plundered over the years. On your left is the Stoa of the Naxians, while against the north wall of the House of the Naxians, to the right, a huge statue of Apollo stood in ancient times. In 417 BC the Athenian general Nikias led a procession of priests across a bridge of boats from Rheneia to dedicate a bronze palm tree; when it was later blown over in a gale it took the statue with it. Three **Temples of Apollo** stand in a row to the right along the Sacred Way: the Delian Temple, that of the Athenians and the Porinos Naos, the earliest of them, dating from the sixth century BC. To the east towards the museum you pass the **Sanctuary of Dionysos**, with its marble phalluses on tall pillars.

The best finds from the site are in Athens, but the **museum** still justifies a visit, if only to see the famous **lions**, their lean bodies masterfully executed by Naxians in the seventh century BC (of the original nine, three have disappeared and one adorns the Arsenale in Venice). To the north stands a wall that marks the site of the **Sacred Lake** where Leto gave birth, clinging to a palm tree, guarded by excellent reproductions of the lions. On the other side of the lake is the City Wall, built in 69 BC – too late to protect the treasures.

Set out in the other direction from the Agora of the Competialists and you enter the residential area, known as the **Theatre Quarter**. Many of the walls and roads remain, but there is none of the domestic detail that brings such sites to life. Some colour is added by the mosaics: one in the **House of the Trident**, and better ones in the **House of the Masks**, most notably a vigorous portrayal of Dionysos riding on a panther's back. The **theatre** itself seated 5500 spectators, and, though much ravaged, offers some fine views. Behind the theatre, a path leads past the **Sanctuaries of the Foreign Gods** and up **Mount Kýnthos** for more panoramic sightseeing.

Sýros

Don't be put off by first impressions of **Sýros**. From the ferry it looks grimly industrial, but away from the Neórion shipyard things improve quickly. Very much a working island with only a relatively recent history of tourism, it is among the most Greek of the Cyclades. You probably won't find, as Herman Melville did when he visited in 1856, shops full of "fez-caps, swords, tobacco, shawls, pistols, and orient finery", but you're still likely to appreciate Sýros as a refreshing change from its more touristic neighbours. Of course, outsiders do come to the island; in fact there's a thriving permanent foreign community, and the beaches are hardly undeveloped, but everywhere there's the underlying assumption that you're a guest of an inherently private people.

Ermoúpoli

The main town and port of **ERMOÚPOLI** was founded during the War of Independence by refugees from Psará and Híos, becoming Greece's chief port in the nineteenth century. Although Pireás outstripped it long ago, Ermoúpoli is still the largest town in the Cyclades, and the archipelago's capital. Medieval Sýros was largely a Catholic island, but an influx of Orthodox refugees during the War of Independence created two distinct communities; now almost equal in numbers, the two groups today still live in their respective quarters, occupying two hills that rise up from the sea.

Ermoúpoli itself, the **lower town**, is worth at least a night's stay, with grandiose buildings a relic of its days as a major port. The long, central **Platía Miaoúli** is named after an admiral of the revolution whose statue stands there, and in the evenings the population parades in front of its arcades, while the children ride the mechanical animals. Up the stairs to the left of the town hall is the small **Archeological Museum** (Tues–Sun 8.30am–3pm; free), with three rooms of finds from Sýros, Páros and Amorgós. To the left of the clocktower more stairs climb up to **Vrondádho**, the hill that hosts the Orthodox quarter. The wonderful church of the **Anástassi** stands atop the hill, with its domed roof and great views over Tínos and Mýkonos – if it's locked, ask for the key at the priest's house.

Up from the right of the square you'll find the **Apollon Theatre**, a copy of Milan's La Scala, which has recently undergone a major renovation and occasionally hosts performances. Up from it is the handsome Orthodox church of **Áyious Nikólaos**, and beyond it to the right is **Vapória**, where the island's wealthiest shipowners, merchants and bankers built their mansions.

On the taller hill to the left is the intricate medieval quarter of **Áno Sýros**, with a clutch of Catholic churches below the cathedral of St George. There are fine views of the town below, and, close by, the **Cappuchin monastery of St Jean**, founded in 1535 to do duty as a poorhouse. It takes about 45 minutes of tough walking up Omírou to reach this quarter, passing the Orthodox and Catholic cemeteries on the way – the former full of grand shipowners' mausoleums, the

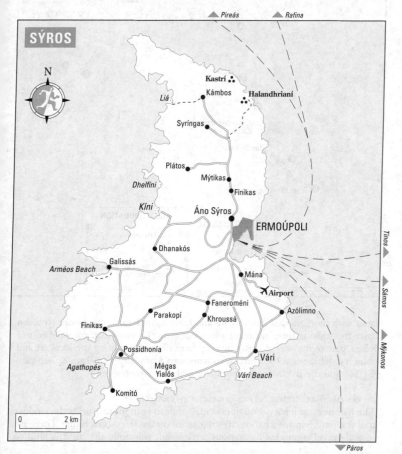

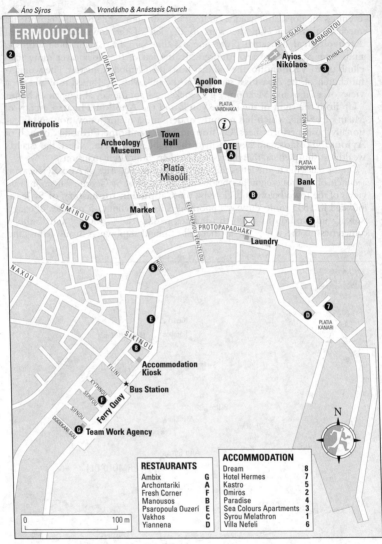

▲ Áno Sýros   ▲ Vrondádho & Anástasis Church

ERMOÚPOLI

Áyios Nikólaos

Apollon Theatre

PLATIA VARDHAKA

Mitrópolis

Archeology Museum

Town Hall

OTE

Platía Miaoúli

PLATIA TSIROPINA

Bank

Market

PROTOPAPADHAKI

Laundry

PLATIA KANARI

Accommodation Kiosk

★ Bus Station

Ferry Quay

Team Work Agency

N

RESTAURANTS	
Ambix	G
Archontariki	A
Fresh Corner	F
Manousos	B
Psaropoula Ouzerí	E
Vakhos	C
Yiannena	D

ACCOMMODATION	
Dream	8
Hotel Hermes	7
Kastro	5
Omiros	2
Paradise	4
Sea Colours Apartments	3
Syrou Melathron	1
Villa Nefeli	6

0 — 100 m

latter with more modest monuments and French and Italian inscriptions (you can halve the walking time by taking a shortcut onto the stair-street named Andhréa Kárga, part of the way along). Once up here it's worth visiting the local art and church exhibitions at the Vamvákeris **museum** (daily 10.30am–1pm & 7–10pm; €1.50), and the Byzantine museum attached to the monastery.

Arrival, facilities and accommodation

The harbour is still busy, though nowadays it deals with more tourists than indus-trial shipping; Sýros is a major crossover point on the ferry-boat routes. There are several **travel agencies** for various ferries and hydrofoils, the most helpful of which is TeamWork (☎02810/83 400, ℱ83 508, ✉teamwork@otenet.gr). Also on the harbourfront is the **bus station**, along with the **tourist police** and several **motorbike** rental places, of which Apollon on Andíparou, one block behind the seafront, is recommended. **Odhós Híou**, the market street, is especially lively on Saturday when people come in from the surrounding countryside to sell fresh produce.

Keeping step with a growing level of tourism, **rooms** have improved in quality and number in recent years; many are in garishly decorated, if crumbling, Neoclassical mansions. Good choices include *Kastro* rooms, Kalomenopóulou 12 (☎02810/88 064; ②), *Dream*, on the seafront near the bus station (☎02810/84 356; ③), and *Paradise*, Omírou 3 (☎02810/83 204; ③). Particularly recommended are the traditionally decorated rooms of *Villa Nefeli*, Parou 21 (☎02810/87 076; ③), and *Sea Colours Apartments* (☎02810/88 716; ④), located at Áyios Nikólaos beach, a quieter corner of town. A notch up in price and quality is the well-sited *Hotel Hermes* (☎02810/83 011; ⑤–⑥) on Platía Kanári, overlooking the port. A more stylish traditional hotel is the *Omiros* (☎02810/84 910, ℱ86 266; ④–⑤) or, for luxury, try the *Syrou Melathron* (☎02810/86 495, ℱ87 806; ⑥), beyond Áyios Nikólaos in Vapória. TeamWork agency (see above), on the waterfront, is a useful source of information and able to help with your accommodation needs. In the summer you might try the kiosk belonging to the Rooms and Apartments Association of Sýros (☎02810/87 360), also on the waterfront.

Eating, drinking and nightlife

Numerous shops sell *loukoúmia* (Turkish delight), *madoláta* (nougats) and *halvadhópita* (sweetmeat pie) for which the island is famed.

The most authentic and reasonably priced of the harbour **eateries** are the *Yiannena Estiatorio* on Platía Kanári and the popular *Psaropoula Ouzeri*. East of Platía Miaoúli, the *Manousos* taverna is a good traditional place, as is *Archontariki*, which serves delicious *patátes mé keséri* (fries with cheese). The most respected traditional taverna is *Vakhos*, near the market, with specialities like rabbit casserole and haddock in garlic sauce. *Ambix*, near where the ferries dock, is a good Italian restaurant; for snacks resist the glitzy *Goody's* hamburger-joint and have a *yíros* at the more authentic *Fresh Corner* nearby. In Áno Sýros, the *Thea* taverna, signposted in Greek from the car park, is fine and affords the views its name would suggest; *Iy Piatsa* ouzerí is also worth a try.

Sýros still honours its contribution to the development of **rebétika**; *bouzoúki*-great Markos Vamvakaris hailed from here, and a platía in Áno Sýros has been named after him. **Taverna–clubs** such as *Xanthomalis* (up in Áno Sýros) with music at weekends, now take their place beside a batch of more conventional disco-clubs down near the Apollon Theatre. There are several other (often expensive) *bouzoúki* bars scattered around the island, mostly strung along routes to beach resorts. The seafront has a rash of lively **bars**: the *Cotton Club* café seems to be the focal point of activity in this area. There's a more interesting cluster around the Platía Miaoúli: *Clearchos* piano bar is rather smooth, *Agora* has imaginative decor, good DJs and a lovely garden, and *Piramatiko* is heaving, playing a loud and varied mix from indie to house. The big venue for night-owls is *Rodo*, a huge club in a converted warehouse out past the Neórión shipyard opposite the turning to Vári. The *Aegean Casino* on the seafront features live music at the restaurant, and is open till 6am for those who have money to burn (and are sufficiently well-dressed). Above it, *Muses* has live music on Friday and Saturday nights; the €7.35 entrance includes your first drink.

Around the island

The main loop road (to Gallissás, Fínikas, Mégas Yialós, Vári and back), and the road west to Kíni, are good: **buses** ply the routes hourly in season, and run until late. Elsewhere, expect potholes – especially to the **north** where the land is barren and high, with few villages. The main route north from Áno Sýros has improved and is quite easily negotiable by bike; en route, the village of **Mýtikas** has a decent taverna just off the road. A few kilometres further on the road forks, with the left turn leading, after another left, to the small settlement of **Syríngas**, where there's an interesting cave to explore. Straight on leads to **Kámbos**, from where a path leads down to Liá Beach; the right fork eventually descends to the northeast coast after passing an excellent kafenío, *Sgouros*, with views across to Tínos.

The well-trodden route **south** offers more tangible and accessible rewards. Closest to the capital, fifteen minutes away by bus, is the twin-beach coastal settlement of **KÍNI**. Good accommodation includes the *Sunset Hotel* (T02810/71 211; ❸–❹), with the excellent *Zalounis* taverna just below and, just away from the seafront, the *Hotel Elpida* (T02810/71 224; ❷–❹). **Dhelfíni**, just to the north, is also a fine beach.

GALISSÁS, a few kilometres south, but reached by different buses, has developed along different lines. Fundamentally an agricultural village, it's been taken over since the mid-1980s by backpackers attracted by the island's only **campsites** – both have good facilities and send minibuses to all boats, but *Camping Yianna* (T02810/42 418) has the advantage over the newer *Two Hearts* (T02810/42 052) of being closer to the sea – and a very pretty beach, more protected than Kíni's. This new-found popularity has created a surplus of unaesthetic **rooms**, which at least makes bargaining possible, and six bona fide hotels, of which the cheapest are *O Petros* and *Semiramis* (T02810/42 067; both ❸–❹), though the *Benois* (T02810/42 833; ❸–❺) is decent value, with buffet breakfast included. Among the many **eating** choices, *Tò Iliovasilema*, next to *Benois*, is an acceptable fish taverna, and *Cavos*, part of a luxury complex, the *Dolphin Beach Hotel* (T02810/42 924; ❻), has great views overlooking the bay. Galissás's identity crisis is exemplified by the proximity of bemused, grazing dairy cattle, a heavy-metal music pub and upmarket handicrafts shops. Still, the people are welcoming, and if you feel the urge to escape, you can rent a scooter, or walk ten minutes past the headland to the nudist beach of **Armeós**, where there's fresh spring water. Note that buses out are erratically routed; to be sure of making your connection you must wait at the high-road stop, not down by the beach.

A pleasant forty-minute walk or a ten-minute bus ride south from Galissás brings you to the more mainstream resort of **FÍNIKAS**, purported to have been settled originally by the Phoenicians (although an alternative derivation could be from *fínikas*, meaning "palm tree" in Greek). The beach is narrow and gritty, right next to the road but protected to some extent by a row of tamarisk trees; the pick of the hotels is the *Cyclades* (T02810/42 255; ❹–❺), and there is an acceptable restaurant just in front, while the *Amaryllis* rooms (T02810/42 894; ❸) are slightly cheaper. The fish taverna *O Barpalias* on the seafront is recommended.

Fínikas is separated by a tiny headland from its neighbour **POSSIDHONÍA** (or Delagrazzia), a nicer spot with some idiosyncratically ornate mansions and a bright blue church right on the edge of the village. It's worth walking ten minutes further south, past the naval yacht club and its patrol boat to **Agathopés**, with a sandy beach and a little islet just offshore. Komitó, at the end of the unpaved track leading south from Agathopés, is nothing more than a stony beach fronting an olive grove. **Accommodation** around Possidhonía ranges from the smart *Possidonion* hotel (T02810/42 100; ❹–❺) on the seafront to basic rooms inland, while *Meltémi* is a good seafood taverna.

The road swings east to **MÉGAS YIALÓS**, a small resort below a hillside festooned with brightly painted houses. The long, narrow beach is lined with shady trees and there are pedal boats for hire. Of the **room** set-ups, *Mike and Bill's* (☏02810/43 531; ❷) is a reasonable deal, and the pricier *Alexandra Hotel* (☏02810/42 540; ❹–❺), on the bay, enjoys lovely views. **VÁRI** is more – though not much more – of a town, with its own small fishing fleet. Beach-goers are in a goldfish bowl, as it were, with tavernas and **rooms** looming right overhead, but it is the most sheltered of the island's bays, something to remember when the *meltémi* is up. The *Kamelo* hotel (☏02810/61 217; ❹) provides the best value and has TV in all the rooms. The adjacent cove of **AKHLÁDHI** is far more pleasant and boasts two small good-value hotels, including the *Emily* (☏02810/61 400; ❸–❹), on the seafront, and has one taverna.

Páros and Andíparos

Gently and undramatically furled around the single peak of Profítis Ilías, **Páros** has a little of everything one expects from a Greek island: old villages, monasteries, fishing harbours, a labyrinthine capital, and some of the best nightlife

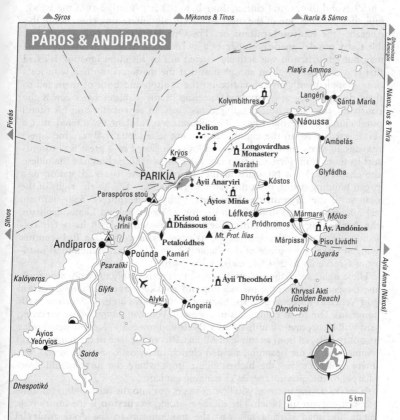

and beaches in the Aegean. Parikía, the hóra, is the major hub of interisland ferry services, so that if you wait long enough you can get to just about any island in the Aegean. However, the island is almost as touristy and expensive as Mýkonos – in peak season, it's touch-and-go when it comes to finding rooms and beach space. At such times, the attractive inland settlements or the satellite island of **Andíparos** handle the overflow. Incidentally, the August 15 festival here is one of the best such observances in Greece, with a parade of flare-lit fishing boats and fireworks delighting as many Greeks as foreigners, but it's a real feat to secure accommodation around this time.

Parikía and around

PARIKÍA sets the tone architecturally for the rest of Páros, with its ranks of typically Cycladic white houses punctuated by the occasional Venetian-style building and church domes. The busy waterfront is jam-packed with bars, restaurants, hotels and ticket agencies. Continue inland from the **windmill** past the tourist information office and taxi station to reach **Mavroyénous Square**, around which you'll find a maze of houses designed to thwart both the wind and pirates, and the telephone office, police station (and tourist police), banks and Olympic Airlines office.

Just beyond the central clutter, though, to the left (southeast) of the windmill, the town has one of the most architecturally interesting churches in the Aegean – the **Ekatondapilianí**, or "The One-Hundred-Gated". What's visible today was designed and supervised by Isidore of Miletus in the sixth century, but construction was actually carried out by his pupil Ignatius. It's said that it was so beautiful on completion that the master, consumed with jealousy, grappled with his apprentice on the rooftop and both of them fell to their deaths. They are portrayed kneeling at the column bases across the courtyard, the old master tugging at his beard in repentance and his rueful pupil clutching a broken head. The church was substantially altered after a severe earthquake in the eighth century, but its essentially Byzantine aspect remains, its shape an imperfect Greek cross. Enclosed by a great wall to protect its icons from pirates, it is in fact three interlocking churches; the oldest, the chapel of Áyios Nikólaos to the left of the apse, is an adaptation of a pagan building dating from the early fourth century BC. To the right of the courtyard, the **Byzantine Museum** (daily 9am–1pm & 5.30–9.30pm; €1.50, free on Tues) displays a collection of icons. Behind Ekatondapilianí, the **Archeological Museum** (Tues–Sun 8am–3pm; €1.50) has a fair collection of antique bits and pieces, its prize exhibits being a fifth-century winged Nike and a piece of the *Parian Chronicle*, a social and cultural history of Greece up to 264 BC engraved in marble.

These sights apart, the real attraction of Parikía is simply to wander the town itself, especially along the meandering **old market street**. Arcaded lanes lead past Venetian-influenced villas, traditional island dwellings and ornate wall-fountains. The town culminates in a seaward Venetian *kástro*, whose surviving east wall incorporates a fifth-century BC round tower and is constructed using masonry pillaged from a temple of Athena. Part of the base of the temple is still visible next to the beautiful, arcaded church of Áyios Konstandínos and Ayía Eléni which crowns the highest point, from where the fortified hill drops sharply to the quay in a series of hanging gardens.

If you're staying in town, you'll want to get out into the surroundings at some stage, if only to the beach. The most rewarding **excursion** is the hour's walk along the road starting just past the museum up to the **Áyii Anáryiri** monastery. Perched on the bluff above town, this makes a great picnic spot, with cypress groves, a gushing fountain and some splendid views.

There are **beaches** immediately north and south of the harbour, though none are particularly attractive when compared with Páros's best. In fact, you might prefer to avoid the northern stretch altogether and head **south** along the asphalt road instead. The first unsurfaced side-track you come to leads to a small, sheltered beach; fifteen minutes further on is **PARASPÓROS**, with an attractively landscaped and relatively quiet **campsite** (☎02840/21 100) and beach near the remains of an ancient temple to Asklepios (see p.332), the god of medicine and son of Apollo. Continuing for 45 minutes (or a short hop by bus) brings you to arguably the best of the bunch, **AYÍA IRÍNI**, with good sand and a taverna next to a farm and shady olive grove.

Off in the same direction, but a much longer two-hour haul each way, is **PETALOÚDHES**, the so-called "Valley of the Butterflies", a walled-in oasis where millions of Jersey tiger moths perch on the foliage during early summer (June–Sept 9am–8pm; €1.20). The trip pays more dividends when combined with a visit to the eighteenth-century nunnery of **Khristoú stoú Dhássous**, at the crest of a ridge twenty minutes to the north. Only women are allowed in the sanctuary, although men can get as far as the courtyard. The succession of narrow drives and donkey paths linking both places begins just south of Parikía. Petaloúdhes can be reached from Parikía by bus (in summer), by scooter or on an overpriced excursion by mule.

Arrival, information and accommodation

Ferries **dock** in Parikía by the windmill; the **bus stop** is 100m or so to the left. Bus routes extend to Náoussa in the north, Poúnda (for Andíparos) in the west, Alikí in the south and Dhrýos on the island's east coast (with another very useful service between Dhrýos and Náoussa). Buses to Náoussa carry on running hourly through the night, while other services stop around midnight. The **airport** is around 12km south of town, close to Alykí – from where ten daily buses run to Parikía.

Most of the island is flat enough for bicycle rides, but motorbikes are more common and are available for rent at several places in town; Forget-Me-Not, along the seafront west of the bus stop, offers a professional and friendly service. Polos Tours, left of the windmill, is one of the more together and friendly **travel agencies**, issuing air tickets when Olympic is shut, and acting as agents for virtually all the boats. Luggage can be left at Santorineos Travel, 50m beyond Polos Tours.

As for **accommodation**, Parikía is a pleasant and central base, but absolutely mobbed in summer. You'll be met off the ferry by locals offering rooms, even at the most unlikely hours; most rooms and hotels are to the left of the windmill, and some can be a long walk. One of the best deals to be had is at the *Pension Festos* on the backstreets inland, managed by young Brits (☎02840/21 635; €11.75 per person); it has beds in shared rooms, making it a good choice for single travellers. Of the hotels, the smart, family-run *Argonauta* (☎02840/21 440, ℱ23 442, ℮hotel@argonauta.gr; ❹), at the back of Mavroyénous Square near the National Bank, is highly recommended. Other acceptable hotels include the *Dina* (☎02840/21 325; ❸), further inland, in the market; the *Oasis* (☎02840/21 227; ❹), near the windmill; the small, family-run *Kypreou* (☎02840/21 383; ❹) across from Ekatondapilianí church; and the *Pension Antoine* (☎02840/24 435 ❶), also near the church. Irini Triandafilou (☎02840/23 022; ❸) has a few basic rooms within the *kástro*, some with good sea views. *Argonauta Appartments* (☎02840/23 888; ❹) have some smart accommodation in the Livádhia area in the north of town. *Koula Camping* (☎02840/22 081), along the seafront east of the bus stop, has good facilities but can get noisy. *Krios Camping* (☎02840/22 081), across the bay to the north has a nice beach.

Eating, drinking and nightlife

Most of the eating establishments in Parikía are along the waterfront to the right (south) of the windmill. Many are run by outsiders operating under municipal concession, so there is year-to-year variation in proprietors and quality. *Magic*, near the *kástro*, is a good place for breakfast, and *Hibiscus*, next to the Town Hall, offers generous-sized wood-oven-baked pizzas. Head inland for more substantial meals: *Koutouki Thanasis*, on a backstreet to the left of the Town Hall, serves oven food for locals and bold tourists; *Argonauta Restaurant*, near the hotel of the same name, across from the National Bank, is dependably good; and further back in the market is the popular taverna, *Garden of Dionysos*. *May Tey* serves average Chinese food at moderate mark-up, while Italian dishes can be found at *Cavo D'Oro* in the Livádhia area. *Trata*, behind the ancient cemetery left of the windmill, is recommended for fish; *Le Coq Fou*, in the Market near *Dionysos*, is a good breakfasting spot, serving excellent crepes; *Ragousis Bakery*, behind the National Bank, is a good place for sandwiches and pastries; and beyond it you'll find the *Happy Green Cow*, a nice vegetarian café. *Cookies Cyber Cafe* (ⓦwww.paroslink.com), about midway along the old market, is a friendly place that offers free internet access with the purchase of its snacks.

Parikía has a wealth of **pubs**, **bars** and low-key **discos**, not as pretentious as those on Mýkonos or as raucous as the scene on Íos, but certainly everything in between. The most popular cocktail bars extend along the seafront, mostly to the south of the windmill, tucked into a series of open squares and offering competing but staggered (no pun intended) "happy hours", so that you can drink cheaply for much of the evening. Beware of anything too cheap as some places still sell *bómba*, a local hooch that can get you really drunk fast and really sick afterwards. A rowdy crowd favours the conspicuous *Saloon D'Or*, while the *Pirate Bar*, behind the Town Hall, features jazz and blues. *Evinos* and *Pebbles* are more genteel, the latter pricey but with good sunset views and classical music. The "theme" pubs are a bit rough and ready for some – most outrageous is the *Dubliner/Paros Rock Complex*, comprising four bars, a snack section, disco and seating area.

Finally, a thriving cultural centre, Arhilohos (near Ekatondapilianí) caters mostly to locals, with occasional **film** screenings – there are also two open-air cinemas, Neo Rex and Paros, where foreign films are shown in season.

Náoussa and around

The second port of Páros, **NÁOUSSA** is a major resort town grown up around a charming little port. Modern concrete hotels and attendant trappings have all but swamped its original character, though down at the small harbour, fishermen still tenderize octopuses by thrashing them against the walls, and with a little patience you can still find some of its winding, narrow alleys and simple Cycladic houses. The local festivals – an annual Fish and Wine Festival on July 2, and an August 23 shindig celebrating an old naval victory over the Turks – are also still celebrated with enthusiasm; the latter tends to be brought forward to coincide with the August 15 festival of the Panayía. Most people are here for the local beaches (see opposite) and the relaxed nightlife; there's really only one sight, a **museum** (daily 9am–1.30pm & 7–9pm; free) in the monastery of Áyios Athanásios, with an interesting collection of Byzantine and post-Byzantine icons from the churches and monasteries around Náoussa.

Despite encroaching development, the town is noted for its nearby beaches and is a good place to head for as soon as you reach Páros. Because it's newer and more fashionable than Parikía, accommodation is more expensive. There is a helpful local council information centre just over the bridge, west from the harbour, and Nissiotissa Tours (☎02840/51 480, ℱ51 189), off the left side of the main square, which can help you find a room, though it specializes in transport. The *Sea House* (☎02840/52 198; ❹) on the rocks above Pipéri beach was the first place in Náoussa to let rooms and has one of the best locations. Out of season you should haggle for reduced prices at the *Madaki* (☎02840/51 475; ❹), just over the bridge west of the harbour, and at the basic, but well-located *Stella* (☎02840/52 198; ❸), several blocks inland from the old harbour. If you don't mind a five-minute climb, the friendly *Papadakis* (☎02840/52 504; ❺) has excellent views. There are two campsites in the vicinity: the relaxed and friendly *Naoussa* (☎02840/51 565), out of town towards Kolymbíthres (see below), and the newer *Surfing Beach* (☎02840/51 013) at Sánta Mariá, north-east of Náoussa; both run courtesy minibuses to and from Parikía.

Most of the harbour tavernas are surprisingly good, specializing in fresh fish and seafood; *O Barbarossas* ouzerí is the best of these. There are more places to eat along the main road leading inland from just beside the little bridge over the canal. *Glaros*, with good barrelled unresinated wine, and the *Vengera* opposite stay open until the early morning hours. Bars cluster around the old harbour: *Linardo* and *Agosta* play dance music, *Camaron* plays mainly Greek music, and *Café Sante*, inland, off the main drag, is a cool spot playing easy-listening, and mellower dance grooves. There are several big clubs up from the bus station, including *Nostos* and *Privilege,* popular with a younger late-night crowd.

Local beaches

Pipéri beach is a couple of minutes' walk west of Náoussa's harbour; there are other good-to-excellent beaches within walking distance, and a summer kaïki service to connect them. To the west, an hour's tramp brings you to Kolymbíthres ("Basins"), where there are three tavernas and the wind- and sea-sculpted rock formations from which the place draws its name. A few minutes beyond, Monastíri beach, below the abandoned Pródhromos monastery, is similarly attractive, and partly nudist. If you go up the hill after Monastíri onto the rocky promontory, the island gradually shelves into the sea via a series of flattish rock ledges, making a fine secluded spot for diving and snorkelling, as long as the sea is calm. Go northeast and the sands are better still, the barren headland spangled with good surfing beaches. Langéri is backed by dunes; the best surfing is at Sánta María, a trendy beach connected with Náoussa by road, which also has a couple of tavernas, including the pleasant *Aristofanes*; and Platiá Ámmos perches on the northeastern tip of the island.

The northeast coast and inland

AMBELÁS hamlet marks the start of a longer trek down the east coast. Ambelás itself has a good beach, a small taverna and some rooms and hotels, of which the *Hotel Christiana* (☎02840/51 573; ❸) is good value, with great fresh fish, local wine in the restaurant and extremely friendly proprietors. From here a rough track leads south, passing several undeveloped stretches on the way; after about an hour you reach Mólos beach, impressive and not particularly crowded. MÁRMARA, twenty minutes further on, has rooms to let and makes an attractive place to stay, though the marble that the village is built from and named after has largely been whitewashed over.

If Mármara doesn't appeal, then serene **MÁRPISSA**, just to the south, might – a maze of winding alleys and ageing archways overhung by floral balconies, all clinging precariously to the hillside. There are rooms here too: *Afendakis* (T02840/41 141; ②) has clean and modern rooms and furnished apartments (⑥), and you can while away a spare hour climbing up the conical Kéfalos hill, on whose fortified summit the last Venetian lords of Páros were overpowered by the Ottomans in 1537. Today the monastery of **Áyios Andónios** occupies the site, but the grounds are locked; to enjoy the views over eastern Páros and the straits of Náxos fully, pick up the key from the priest in Márpissa before setting out (ask in the minimarket of his whereabouts). On the shore nearby, **PÍSO LIVÁDHI** was once a quiet fishing village, but has been ruined by rampant construction in the name of package tourism. The main reason to visit is to catch a (seasonal) kaïki to Ayía Ánna on Náxos; if you need to **stay** overnight here, *Hotel Andromache* (T02840/41 387 or 42 565; ②–④) is a good place behind the beach, as is the *Akteon Hotel* (T02840/41 873; ②–⑤) at **Logarás beach** next door. The *Captain Kafkis Camping* (T02840/41 479) – a small quiet **campsite** – is out of town on the road up to Márpissa.

Inland

The road runs west from Píso Livádhi back to the capital. A medieval flag-stoned path once linked both sides of the island, and parts of it survive in the east between Mármara and the villages around Léfkes. **PRÓDHROMOS**, encountered first, is an old fortified farming settlement with defensive walls girding its nearby monastery, while **LÉFKES** itself, an hour up the track, is perhaps the most beautiful and unspoiled settlement on Páros. The town flourished from the seventeenth century on, its population swollen by refugees fleeing from coastal piracy; indeed it was the island's hóra during most of the Ottoman period. Léfkes's marbled alleyways and amphitheatrical setting are unparalleled and, despite the few rooms, a disco (*Akrovatis*), a taverna on the outskirts and the presence of two oversized hotels – the *Hotel Pantheon* (T02840/41 646; ②–④), a large 1970s hotel at the top of the village, and *Lefkes Village* (T02840/41 827 or 42 398; ④–⑥), a beautiful hotel on the outskirts, with stunning views – the area around the main square has steadfastly resisted change; the central kafenío and bakery observe their siestas religiously.

Thirty minutes further on, through olive groves, is **KÓSTOS**, a simple village and a good place for lunch in a taverna. Any traces of path disappear at **MARÁTHI**, on the site of the ancient marble quarries which once supplied much of Europe. Considered second only to Carrara marble, the last slabs were mined here by the French in the nineteenth century for Napoleon's tomb. From Maráthi, it's easy enough to pick up the bus on to Parikía, but if you want to continue hiking, strike south for the monastery of **Áyios Minás**, twenty minutes away. Various Classical and Byzantine masonry fragments are worked into the walls of this sixteenth-century foundation, and the friendly custodians can put you on the right path up to the convent of **Thapsaná**. From here, other paths lead either back to Parikía (two hours altogether from Áyios Minás), or on up to the island's summit for the last word in views over the Cyclades.

The south of the island

There's little to stop for south of Parikía until **POÚNDA**, 6km away, and then only to catch the ferry to Andíparos (see opposite). What used to be a sleepy hamlet is now a concrete jungle, and neighbouring **ALYKÍ** appears to be permanently under construction. The **airport** is close by, making for lots of unwelcome noise; the sole redeeming feature is an excellent beachside restaurant, by the large tamarisk tree. The end of the southern bus route is at Angeriá, about 3km inland of which is the **convent of Áyii Theodhóri**. Its nuns specialize in weaving locally commissioned articles and are further distinguished as *paleomeroloyítes*, or old-calendarites, meaning that they follow the medieval Orthodox (Julian) calendar, rather than the Gregorian one.

Working your way around the **south coast**, there are two routes east to Dhryós. Either retrace your steps to Angeriá and follow the (slightly inland) coastal road, which skirts a succession of isolated coves and small beaches, or keep on across the foothills from Áyii Theodhóri – a shorter walk. Aside from an abundant water supply (including a duck pond) and surrounding orchards, **DHRÝOS** village is mostly modern and characterless, lacking even a well-defined platía. Follow the lane signed "Dhrýos Beach", however, and things improve a bit.

Between here and Píso Livádhi to the north are several sandy coves – Khryssí Aktí ("Golden Beach"), Tzirdhákia, Mezádha, Poúnda and Logarás – prone to pummelling by the *meltémi*, yet all favoured to varying degrees by campers and by windsurfers making a virtue out of necessity. **KHRYSSÍ AKTÍ** is now thoroughly overrun with tavernas, room complexes and the whole range of watersports; there are also tavernas at Logarás, but other facilities are concentrated in Dhryós, which is still the focal point of this part of the island.

Andíparos

Andíparos was once quiet and unspoiled, but now the secret is definitely out. The waterfront is lined with new hotels and apartments, and in high season it can be full, though in recent years families seem to be displacing the young, international crowd. It has managed to hold on to much of its friendly small island atmosphere and still has a lot going for it, including good sandy beaches and an impressive cave, and the rooms and hotels are less expensive than on Páros.

Most of the population of eight hundred live in the large low-lying northern **village**, across the narrow straits from Páros, the new development on the outskirts concealing an attractive traditional settlement around the *kástro*. A long, flag-stoned pedestrian street forms its backbone, leading from the jetty to the Cycladic houses around the outer wall of the *kástro*, which was built by Leonardo Loredano in the 1440s as a fortified settlement safe from pirate raids – the Loredano coat of arms can still be seen on a house in the courtyard. The only way into the courtyard is through a pointed archway from the platía, where several cafés are shaded by a giant eucalyptus. Inside, more whitewashed houses surround two churches and a cistern built into the surviving base of the central tower.

Andíparos's **beaches** begin right outside town: **Psaralíki**, just to the south with golden sand and tamarisks for shade, is much better than Sifnéïko (aka "Sunset") on the opposite side of the island. Villa development is starting to follow the newly paved road down the east coast, but has yet to get out of hand. **Glýfa**, 4km down, is another good beach and, further south, **Sorós** has rooms and tavernas. On the west coast there are some fine small sandy coves at **Áyios Yeóryios**, the end of the road, and another long stretch of sand at **Kalóyeros**. Kaïki make daily trips round the island and, less frequently, to the uninhabited islet of Dhespotikó, opposite Áyios Yeóryios.

The great **cave** (summer daily 10.45am–3.45pm; €3) in the south of the island is the chief attraction for day-trippers. In these eerie chambers the Marquis de Nointel, Louis XIV's ambassador to Constantinople, celebrated Christmas Mass in 1673 while a retinue of five hundred, including painters, pirates, Jesuits and Turks, looked on; at the exact moment of midnight explosives were detonated to emphasize the enormity of the event. Although electric light and cement steps have diminished its mystery and grandeur, the cave remains impressive. Tour buses (€2.35 one-way) – buy a one-way fare so you can return on the first available bus – and public buses (€1.10 one-way) run from the port every hour in season; bus services and opening hours are reduced and in winter you'll have to fetch the key for the cave from the mayor or village council (℡02840/61 218).

Practicalities

To get here, you have a choice of **boats** from Parikía (hourly; 40min), arriving at the jetty opposite the main street, or the car ferry from Poúnda (every 30min; 10min), arriving 150m to the south. In season there's no need to use the car ferry unless you take a scooter over or miss the last boat back to Parikía; the car ferry keeps running until midnight. The service to Parikía is reduced out of season and runs only once a day in winter.

There are plenty of **hotels** along the waterfront, including *Anargyros* (℡02840/61 204; ❷), which has good, basic rooms. More upmarket places to the north of the jetty include *Mantalena* (℡02840/61 206; ❸–❺) and *Artemis* (℡02840/61 460; ❹–❻), while inland there are some cheaper rooms as well as the *Hotel Galini* (℡02840/61 420; ❷–❺) to the left of the main street. The popular **campsite** (℡02840/61 221) is a ten-minute walk northeast along a track, next to its own nudist beach; the water here is shallow enough for campers to wade across to the neighbouring islet of Dhipló. For peace and quiet with a degree of comfort try *Studios Delfini* (℡093/275 911; ❹) at Áyios Yeóryios, a long stretch of beach with several tavernas, of which *Captain Pipinos* is recommended.

The best of the waterfront **tavernas** is *Anargyros*, below the hotel of the same name. The main street leads up beside it, and *Klimataria*, 100m inland off to the left, has tables in a pleasant, shady garden. *The Corner Cafe*, also on the main street, has excellent coffee. *To Kastro* is one of the better restaurants outside the *kástro*, where you'll also find the excellent *To Kendro* sweetshop. There are plenty of **bars** around this eucalyptus-filled platía, where a festive atmosphere prevails at night. *Café Margarita* is a pleasant street-side hangout on the way up to this platía. For quiet music and views of the mountains try *Café Yam*, an outdoor café-bar near the *Klimataria*. A short-schedule **bank**, a **post office**, a cinema and several **travel agents** round up the list of amenities.

Náxos

Náxos is the largest and most fertile of the Cyclades, and, with its green and mountainous highland scenery, seems immediately distinct from many of its neighbours. The difference is accentuated by the **unique architecture** of many of the interior villages: the Venetian Duchy of the Aegean, which ruled from the thirteenth to the sixteenth century, left towers and fortified mansions scattered throughout the island, while medieval Cretan refugees bestowed a singular character upon Náxos's eastern settlements.

Today Náxos could easily support itself without tourists by relying on its production of potatoes, olives, grapes and lemons, but it has thrown in its lot with mass tourism, so that parts of the island are now almost as busy and commercialized as Páros in season. But the island certainly has plenty to see if you know

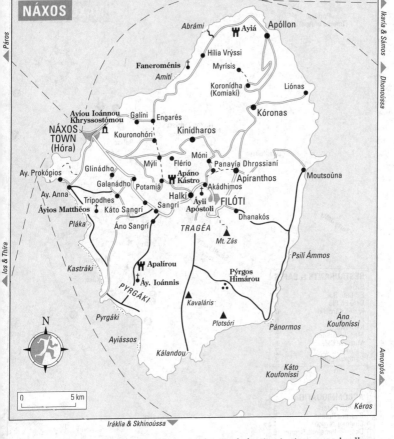

where to look: the highest mountains in the Cyclades, intriguing central valleys, a spectacular north coast and marvellously sandy beaches in the southwest.

Náxos Town

A long causeway, built to protect the harbour to the north, connects **NÁXOS TOWN** (or Hóra) with the islet of Palátia – the place where, according to legend, Theseus abandoned Ariadne on his way home from Crete. The famous stone **Portára** that has greeted visitors for 2500 years is the portal of a temple of Apollo, built on the orders of the tyrant Lygdamis in the sixth century BC, but never completed. Most of the town's life goes on down by the crowded port esplanade or just behind it; back streets and alleys behind the harbour lead up through low arches of the old town, Boúrgos, to the fortified *kástro*, from where Marco Sanudo and his successors ruled over the Cyclades. Only two of the *kástro*'s original seven towers remain, though the north gate (approached from Apóllonos) survives as a splendid example of a medieval fort entrance. The Venetians' Catholic descendants, now much declined in numbers, still live in the old mansions which encircle the site, many with ancient coats of arms above

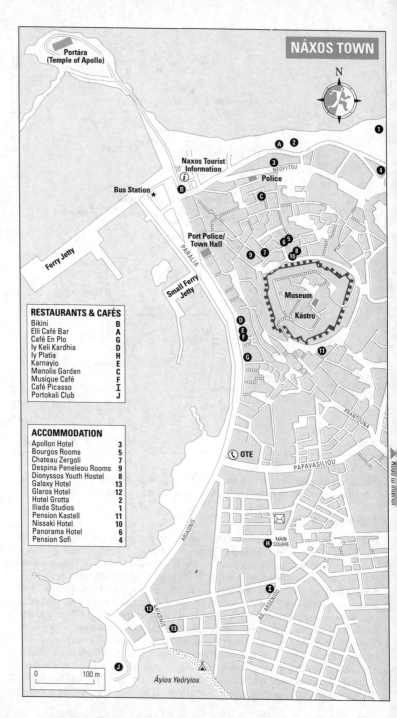

NÁXOS TOWN

Portára (Temple of Apollo)

N

1

A 2
Naxos Tourist Information
3
i
NEOFYTOU
Police
B
Bus Station ★
C

Ferry Jetty

Port Police/ Town Hall
6 5
9 7 8
PARALIA
10

Small Ferry Jetty

Museum
Kástro

D
E
F
G
11

PRANTOUNA

Road to interior

RESTAURANTS & CAFÉS

Bikini	B
Elli Café Bar	A
Café En Plo	G
Iy Keli Kardhia	D
Iy Platia	H
Karnayio	E
Manolis Garden	C
Musique Café	F
Café Picasso	I
Portokali Club	J

PAPAVASILIOU

OTE

ACCOMMODATION

Apollon Hotel	3
Bourgos Rooms	5
Chateau Zergoli	7
Despina Peneleou Rooms	9
Dionyssos Youth Hostel	8
Galaxy Hotel	13
Glaros Hotel	12
Hotel Grotta	2
Iliada Studios	1
Pension Kastell	11
Nissaki Hotel	10
Panorama Hotel	6
Pension Sofi	4

ARIADNIS

MAIN SQUARE
H

I
AG. ARSENIOU

ARIADNIS
12
13

J
0   100 m

Áyios Yeóryios

crumbling doorways. One of these, the **Domus Della-Rocca-Barozzi** (opening hours vary; €1.50), is open to the public; the tour even includes a tasting from the family's wine cellar. Other brooding relics survive in the same area: a seventeenth-century Ursuline convent and the Roman Catholic cathedral, restored in questionable taste in the 1950s, though still displaying a thirteenth-century crest inside. Nearby was one of Ottoman Greece's first schools, the French School; opened in 1627 for Catholic and Orthodox students alike, its pupils included, briefly, Nikos Kazantzakis. The school building now houses an excellent **archeological museum** (Tues–Sun 8.30am–2.30pm; €3), with finds from Náxos, Koufoníssi, Keros and Dhonoússa, including an important collection of Early Cycladic figurines. Archaic and Classical sculpture and pottery dating from Neolithic through to Roman times are also on display. On the roof terrace a Hellenistic mosaic floor shows a nereid surrounded by deer and peacocks.

As well as archeological treasures, Náxos has some very good sandal-makers – try the Markos store on Papavassilíou. The island is also renowned for its cheese – sharp *kefalotýri* and milder *graviéra* – wines and *kítron*, a sweet citron liqueur.

Arrival, transport and information

Large **ferries** dock along the northerly harbour causeway; all small boats and the very useful *Skopelitis* ferry use the jetty in the fishing harbour, not the main car-ferry dock. The **bus station** is at its landward end: buses run five times a day to Apóllon (€3.40), and one of the morning services to Apóllon takes the newly paved coastal road via Engarés and Abrámi, and is much quicker though not any cheaper. There are six buses a day to Apíranthos via Filóti, two of these going on to Moutsoúna on the east coast. Buses run (every 30min 8am–midnight) to Áyios Prokópios, Ayía Ánna and as far as the *Maragas* campsite on Pláka beach, and four times a day to Pirgáki. Printed timetables are available from the bus station. **Naxos Tourist Information** (☎02850/25 201, ℱ30 285), on the seafront near the jetty, is a wealth of information and also has details of rooms.

Accommodation

There's plenty of accommodation in Náxos and you should have no problem finding somewhere to stay. Once you've run the gauntlet of touts on the jetty, there are three basic areas to look for **rooms** in Náxos Town: in the old quarter near the *kástro*, where they are hard to find and relatively expensive; up to the left (north) of town in Grótta; and south of town near Áyios Yeóryios beach, where they are most abundant and less expensive, but with significant nighttime noise from clubs and discos. *Despina Panteleou* (☎02850/22 356; ❸), the newer *Bourgos Rooms* (☎02850/25 979; ❸) and *Pension Kastell* (☎02850/23 082, ℯpension.kastell@gmx.net; ❸) are good choices near the *kástro*, where you'll also find the *Dionyssos Youth Hostel* (☎02850/22 331; €14.70 dorm bed). In Grótta, try *Pension Sofi* (☎02850/25 582; ❸) or *Iliada Studios* (☎02850/23 303 or 24 277, ℯILIADA@naxos-island.com; ❹) on the cliff beyond, with good views over the town and out to sea.

Hotel choices near the *kástro* include the charming traditional *Chateau Zevgoli* (☎02850/22 993; ❻), with antique-furnished, air-conditioned rooms, and *Panorama* (☎02850/24 404; ❹). Across from the cathedral near the ancient agora you'll find one of the newest and best, the *Apollon* (☎02850/22 468, ℱ25 200, ℯapollon-hotel@naxos-island.com; ❹). Up in Grótta there's the friendly *Grotta* (☎02850/22 215; ❸–❹), while near Áyios Yeóryios beach there's the *Nissaki* (☎02850/25 710; ❹), with a pool; the *Glaros* (☎02850/23 101; ❸); and the more upscale *Galaxy* (☎02850/22 422; ❺–❻) further along, and plenty more to choose from.

Eating, drinking and nightlife

One of the best quayside breakfast bars is the *Bikini* creperie. Further along to the south are a string of relatively expensive but simple oven-food **tavernas** – *Iy Kali Kardhia* is typical, serving acceptable casserole dishes washed down with barrelled wine. *Iy Platia* on the main square, near Áyios Yeóryios beach, serves traditional fare and is popular with Greeks, while the nearby *Cafe Picasso* serves Mexican food (evenings only) to a mixed crowd. On the front *Karnayio* is a good, if a little pricey, fish taverna; *Cafe En Plo* and *Musique Café* are two reasonable places in the middle of the quay, both popular with locals. *Manolis Garden Taverna*, nearby the ancient agora, is one of the most pleasant of the Boúrgos tourist eateries. *Elli Cafe Bar Restaurant* behind Grótta beach is a little more expensive but serves imaginative food, and *Portokali Club* on the headland to the south of town is a club, café and restaurant with good views over Áyios Yeóryios bay. There's a good **bakery** about midway along the harbour front. For local cheese, wine, *kítron*, spices and other dried comestibles head for Tirokomika Proionia Naxou, a delightful old store on Papavassilíou.

Much of the evening action goes on at the south end of the waterfront, where you'll find *Day & Night, Cream, Veggera* and *Med*. The *Ocean Club Disco*, further south, above the near end of Áyios Yeóryios beach, is probably the hottest place for dancing to loud and lively pop. *Sugar Island*, also popular with the younger set, is near Grótta while *Lakridi*, behind the town hall, plays jazz and blues for those wanting something more sedate. There's also an open-air **cinema**, the Cine Astra, on the road to the airport at the southern end of town; it's a fair walk out, but the Ayía Ánna bus stops here.

The southwestern beaches

The **beaches** around Náxos Town are worth sampling. For some unusual swimming just to the **north** of the port, beyond the causeway, **Grótta** is easiest to reach. Besides the caves after which the place is named, the remains of submerged Cycladic buildings are visible, including some stones said to be the entrance to a tunnel leading to the unfinished temple of Apollo. The finest spots, though, are all **south** of town, the entire southwestern coastline boasting a series of excellent **beaches** accessible by regular bus. **ÁYIOS YEÓRYIOS**, a long sandy bay fringed by the southern extension of the hotel "colony", is within walking distance. There's a line of cafés and tavernas at the northern end of the beach, and a windsurfing school, plus the first of four **campsites**, whose touts you will no doubt have become acquainted with at the ferry jetty. This first campsite, *Camping Naxos* (℡02850/23 500), isn't recommended; *Maragas* and *Plaka* have far more attractive locations on Pláka beach (see p.172). A word of warning for campers: although this entire coast is relatively sheltered from the *meltémi*, the plains behind are boggy and you should bring along mosquito repellent.

Buses take you to **ÁYIOS PROKÓPIOS** beach, with plenty of reasonably priced hotels, rooms and basic tavernas, plus the relaxed *Apollon* campsite (℡02850/24 117) nearby. *Hotel Lianos Village* (℡02850/23 366, ⓔlianos-village@nax.forthnet.gr; ④–⑤) is an upmarket choice with a pleasant pool setting; of the restaurants *Pizzeria Promponas* has a varied menu and nice setting. Rapid development along this stretch means that this resort has blended into the next resort of **AYÍA ÁNNA** (habitually referred to as "Ayi'Ánna"), further along the busy road; here you will find accommodation of similar price and quality. The seaview *Hotel Ayia Anna* (℡02850/42 576; ③) and adjacent *Gorgona* taverna are recommended, as is *Bar Bagianni* on the road from Áyia Ánna to Áyios

△ Temple of Apollo, Náxos

Prokópios, a colourful and popular bar which serves vegetarian food. Moving along the coast, away from the built-up area, the beach here is nudist.

Beyond the headland stretch the five kilometres of **PLÁKA** beach, a vegetation-fringed expanse of white sand. Things are not so built up here, and parts of the beach are nudist (past *Plaka* campsite). There are two suitably laid-back and friendly **campsites** here: *Maragas* (T02850/24 552) which also has double rooms (●), and the newer *Plaka* campsite (T02850/42 700), a little further along, which is small and quiet with a few inexpensive bungalows (●); be aware, however, that it's 6km into town, and the camp's bus will not run at your convenience (they usually run in concurrence with the ferry service). The *Hotel Orkos Village* (T02850/75 321, E orkos@nax.forthnet.gr; ●) has apartments in an attractive location, on a hillside above the coast between Pláka beach and Mikrí Vígla.

For real isolation, go to the other side of Mikrí Vígla headland, along a narrow footpath across the cliff-edge, to **KASTRÁKI** beach; towards the middle of the beach *Areti* (T02850/75 292; ●) has apartments and a restaurant. A few people camp around the taverna on the small headland a little further down. In summer this stretch, all the way from Mikrí Vígla down to Pyrgáki, attracts camper-vans and windsurfers from all over Europe. On the Alíko promontory to the south of Kastráki there is a small nudist beach.

From Kastráki, it's a couple of hours' walk up to the Byzantine castle of **Apalírou** which held out for two months against the besieging Marco Sanudo. The fortifications are relatively intact and the views magnificent. **Pyrgáki** beach has a couple of tavernas and a few rooms; four kilometres further on is **Ayiássos** beach.

The rest of the **southern coast** – indeed, virtually the whole of the southeast of the island – is remote and mountain-studded; you'd have to be a dedicated and well-equipped camper/hiker to get much out of the region.

Central Náxos and the Tragéa

Although buses bound for Apóllon (in the north) link up the central Naxian villages, the core of the island – between Náxos Town and Apíranthos – is best explored by motorbike or on foot. Much of the region is well off the beaten track, and can be a rewarding excursion if you've had your fill of beaches; Christian Ucke's *Walking Tours on Naxos*, available from bookshops in Náxos town, is a useful guide for hikers.

Once out of Hóra, you quickly arrive at the neighbouring villages of **GLINÁDHO** and **GALANÁDHO**, forking respectively right and left. Both are scruffy market centres: Glinádho is built on a rocky outcrop above the Livádhi plain, while Galánadho displays the first of Náxos's fortified mansions and an unusual "double church". A combined Orthodox chapel and Catholic sanctuary separated by a double arch, the church reflects the tolerance both by the Venetians during their rule and by the locals to established Catholics afterwards. Continue beyond Glinádho to **TRÍPODHES** (ancient Biblos), 9km from Náxos Town. Noted by Homer for its wines, this old-fashioned agricultural village has nothing much to do, but you can enjoy a coffee at the shaded kafenío. The start of a long but rewarding walk is a rough road (past the parish church) which leads down the colourful Pláka valley, past an old watchtower and the Byzantine church of **Áyios Matthéos** ("mosaic pavement"), and ends at the glorious Pláka beach (see above).

To the east, the twin villages of **SANGRÍ**, on a vast plateau at the head of a long valley, can be reached by continuing to follow the left-hand fork past

Galanádho, a route which allows a look at the domed eighth-century church of **Áyios Mámas** (on the left), once the Byzantine cathedral of the island but neglected during the Venetian period and now a sorry sight. Either way, **KÁTO SANGRÍ** boasts the remains of a Venetian castle, while **ÁNO SANGRÍ** is a comely little place, all cobbled streets and fragrant courtyards. Thirty-minutes' stroll away, on a path leading south out of the village, are the partially reconstructed remains of a Classical temple of Demeter.

The Tragéa

From Sangrí the road twists northeast into the **Tragéa** region, scattered with olive trees and occupying a vast highland valley. It's a good jumping-off point for all sorts of exploratory rambling, and **HALKÍ** is a fine introduction to what is to come. Set high up, 16km from the port, it's a noble and silent town with some lovely churches. The **Panayía Protóthronis** church, with its eleventh-to thirteenth-century frescoes, and the romantic **Grazia (Frangopoulos) Pýrgos**, are open to visitors, but only in the morning. Tourists wanting to stay here are still something of a rarity, although you can usually get a room in someone's house by asking at the store. *Yiannis* taverna is the focal point of village activity and has a good selection of fresh *mezédhes* to enjoy with a glass of oúzo. Nearby is the distillery and shop of Vallindras Naxos Citron, whose charming proprietors explain the process of producing this speciality citrus liqueur (*kítron*), followed by a little tasting session. The olive and citrus plantations surrounding Halkí are crisscrossed by paths and tracks, the groves dotted with numerous Byzantine chapels and the ruins of fortified *pyrgi* or Venetian mansions. Between Halkí and Akadhimí, but closer to the latter, sits the peculiar twelfth-century "piggyback" church of **Áyii Apóstoli**, with a tiny chapel (where the ennobled donors worshipped in private) perched above the narthex; there are brilliant thirteenth-century frescoes as well.

The road from Halkí heads north to MONÍ. Just before the village, you pass the sixth-century monastery of **Panayía Dhrossianí**, a group of stark, grey-stone buildings with some excellent frescoes; the monks allow visits at any time, though you may have to contend with coach tours from Náxos Town. Moní itself enjoys an outstanding view of the Tragéa and surrounding mountains, and has four tavernas, plus some rooms. The main road leads on to Kinídharos, with an old marble quarry above the village; a few kilometres beyond, a signpost points you down a rough track to the left, to **FLÉRIO** (commonly called Melanés). The most interesting of the ancient marble quarries on Náxos, this is home to two famous **koúri**, dating from the sixth century BC, that were left recumbent and unfinished because of flaws in the material. Even so, they're finely detailed figures, over five metres in length. One of the statues lies in a private, irrigated orchard; the other is up a hillside some distance above, and you will need to seek local guidance to find it.

From Flério you could retrace your steps to the road and head back to Hóra via Mýli and the ruined Venetian castle at Kouronohóri, both pretty hamlets connected by footpaths. If you're feeling more adventurous, ask to be directed south to the footpath which leads over the hill to the Potamiá villages. The first of these, **ÁNO POTAMIÁ**, has a fine taverna and a rocky track back towards the Tragéa. Once past the valley the landscape becomes craggy and barren, the forbidding Venetian fortress of **Apáno Kástro** perched on a peak just south of the path. This is believed to have been Sanudo's summer home, but the fortified site goes back further, if the Mycenaean tombs found nearby are any indication. From the fort, paths lead back to Halkí in around an hour. Alternatively, you can continue further southwest down the Potamiá valley towards Hóra, passing first the ruined **Cocco Pýrgos** – said to be haunted by one Constantine Cocco, the victim of a seventeenth-century clan feud – on the way to **MÉSO POTAMIÁ**, joined by some isolated dwellings with its twin village **KÁTO POTAMIÁ**, nestling almost invisibly among the greenery flanking the creek.

At the far end of the gorgeous Tragéa valley, **FILÓTI**, the largest village in the region, lies on the slopes of Mount Zás (or Zeus) which, at 1000m, is the highest point in the Cyclades. Under the shade of the plane trees on the main platía are several pleasant kafenía, as well as *Babulas Grill-Restaurant* (☎02850/31 426; ❶), which has the best rooms in the village. To get an idea of the old village, climb the steps up the hill starting at the platía. A turning at the southern end of the village is signposted to the **Pýrgos Himárou**, a remote twenty-metre Hellenistic watchtower, and **Kalándou** beach on the south coast; beyond the turning the road is unpaved. There are no villages in this part of the island, so bring supplies if you're planning to camp. From the village, it's a round-trip walk of three to four hours to the summit of Zás, a climb which rewards you with an astounding panorama of virtually the whole of Náxos and its Cycladic neighbours. From the main Filóti–Apóllon road, take the sideroad towards Dhánakos until you reach a small chapel on the right, just beside the start of the waymarked final approach trail. (Save yourself the rather tedious walk along the tarmac road by taking the bus towards Apóllon and asking the driver to let you off at the Dhánakos turning. There is a sign before the turnoff to the Zas Cave, a pleasant place for a picnic, but not a good point from which to tackle the steep ascent to the summit.)

APÍRANTHOS, a hilly, winding 10km beyond, shows the most Cretan influence of all the interior villages. There are four small **museums** and two Venetian fortified mansions, while the square contains a miniature church with a three-tiered bell tower. Ask to be pointed to the start of the spectacular path up over the ridge behind; this ends either in Moní or Kalóxilos, depending on whether you fork right or left respectively at the top. Cafés and tavernas on the main street look out over a terraced valley below. Rooms are available but are not advertised – ask in the cafés or in the embroidery shop. Apíranthos is a good quiet place to stay for a few days, and being high in the mountains is noticeably cooler and greener than the coast.

Apíranthos has a beach annexe of sorts at **Moutsoúna**, 12km east. Emery mined near Apíranthos used to be transported here by means of an aerial funicular and then shipped out of the port. The industry collapsed in the 1980s, and the sandy cove beyond the dock now features a growing colony of holiday villas. An unpaved road heads south along the coast to a remote sandy beach at **Psilí Ámmos** – ideal for self-sufficient campers, but you must take enough water. From here a track carries on to **Pánormos** beach in the southeastern corner of the island.

Northern Náxos

The route through the mountains from Apíranthos to Apóllon is very scenic, and the road surface is in good condition all the way. Jagged ranges and hairpin bends confront you before reaching Kóronos, the halfway point, where a road off to the right threads through a wooded valley to **Liónas**, a tiny and very Greek port with a pebble beach. You'd do better to continue, past Skadhó, to the remote, emery-miners' village of **KOMIAKÍ** which is a pleasing, vine-covered settlement – the highest village in the island and the original home of *kítron* liqueur.

Back on the main road, a series of slightly less hairy bends leads down a long valley to **APÓLLON** (Apóllonas), a small resort with two beaches: a tiny and crowded stretch of sand backed by cafés and restaurants, and a longer and quieter stretch of shingle, popular mainly with Greek families. If you are staying, try the friendly rooms of *Maria* (℡02850/67 106; ❷) behind the harbour. The only major attraction is a **koúros**, approached by a path from the main road just above the village. Lying *in situ* at a former marble quarry, this largest of Náxos's abandoned stone figures is just over ten metres long, but, compared with those at Flério, disappointingly lacking in detail. Here since 600 BC, it serves as a singular reminder of the Naxians' traditional skill; the famous Delian lions (see p.154) are also made of Apollonian marble. Not surprisingly, bus tours descend upon the village during the day, and Apóllon is now quite a popular little place. The local festival, celebrated on August 28–29, is one of Náxos's best.

From Náxos town there is now a daily bus service direct to Apóllon (taking about an hour). It's easy to make a round trip of the north coast and inland villages by bus in either direction. The coastal road is spectacularly beautiful, going high above the sea for most of the way – it's more like parts of Crete or the mainland than other islands. Ten kilometres past the northern cape sprouts the beautiful **Ayiá** *pýrgos*, or tower, another foundation (in 1717) of the Cocco family. There's a tiny hamlet nearby, and, 7km further along, a track leads off to **Abrámi** beach, an idyllic spot with a highly recommended family-run taverna and **rooms** to let, *Pension and Restaurant Efthimios* (℡02850/63 244; ❷). Just beyond the hamlet of Hília Výssi is the abandoned **monastery of Faneroménis**, built in 1606. Carrying on along the coastal road you will reach Engarés valley, at the foot of which is another quiet beach, **Amití**, which can be reached via one of two dirt tracks, the most obvious being the one leading down from Galíni, only 6km from Hóra. On the final stretch back to the port you pass a unique eighteenth-century Turkish fountain-house and the fortified monastery of **Ayíou Ioánnou Khryssostómou**, where a couple of aged nuns are still in residence. A footpath from the monastery and the road below lead straight back to town.

Koufoníssi, Skhinoússa, Iráklia and Dhonoússa

In the patch of the Aegean between Náxos and Amorgós there is a chain of six small islands relatively neglected by tourists and by the majority of Greeks, few of whom have heard of them. **Kéros** – ancient Karos – is an important archeological site but has no permanent population, and **Káto Koufoníssi** is inhabited only by goatherds. However, the other four islands – **Áno Koufoníssi**, **Skhinoússa**, **Iráklia** and **Dhonoússa** – are all inhabited, served by ferry and can be visited. Now increasingly discovered by Greeks and foreigners alike, the islets' popularity has hastened the development of better facilities, but they're still a welcome break from the mass tourism of the rest of the Cyclades, especially during high season. If you want real peace and quiet – what the Greeks call *isykhía* – get there soon.

A few times weekly in summer a Pireás-based **ferry** – usually the *Express Adonis*, *Express Hermes* or the *Georgios Express* – calls at each of the islands, linking them with Náxos and Amorgós and (usually) Páros and Sýros. A small local ferry, the *Express Skopelitis*, is a reliable daily fixture, leaving the little ferry quay in Náxos in mid-afternoon for relatively civilized arrival times at all the islets.

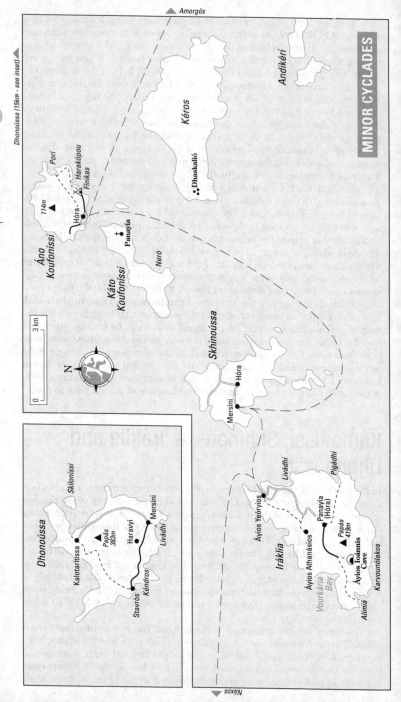

▲ *Amorgós*

MINOR CYCLADES

Dhonoússa (15km – see inset) ▲

PórI

Áno Koufoníssi

114m ▲

Hóra
Harakópou
Finíkas

Kéros

Andikéri

● *Dhaskalió*

Panayía ✝

Neró

Káto Koufoníssi

3 km

N

0   3 km

Skhinoússa

Hóra

Mersíni

Dhonoússa

Skíloníssi

Kalotarítissa

Papás
383m ▲

Haravyí

Mersíni

Stavrós
Kéndros

Livádhi

Livádhi

Áyios Yeóryios

Panayía (Hóra)

Pigádhi

Iráklia

Áyios Athanásios

Vourkária Bay

Papás
419m ▲

⊙ *Áyios Ioánnis Cave*

Karvoúniokas

Alimiá

Náxos ▼

Koufoníssi and Kéros

Áno Koufoníssi is the most populous island of the group; there is a reasonable living to be made from fishing and, with some of the best beaches in the Cyclades, it is attracting increasing numbers of Greek and foreign holidaymakers. Small enough to walk round in a morning, the island can actually feel overcrowded in July and August.

The old single-street village of **HÓRA**, on a low hill behind the harbour, is being engulfed by new room and hotel development, but still has a friendly, small-island atmosphere. A map by the jetty shows where to find all the island's **rooms**: *To Limani* (☎02850/71 851 or 71 450; ②) is a café with rooms near the harbour; the popular restaurant and pension *Melissa* (☎02850/71 454; ②) is another good choice. The most upmarket options include *Hotel Aegeon* (☎02850/74 050 or 74 051; ⑤), by the village beach, or *Ostria Village* (☎02850/71 671; ④), on the hillside to the east of the village. *Akroyiali* (☎02850/71 685; ③) is on the front just beyond the beach; Yeoryia Kouveou has beautifully situated rooms at *Hondros Kavos* (☎02850/71 707; ②), outside the village to the east; and the *Petros Club* (☎02850/71 728; ④) is in a quiet position inland, with excellent views.

Koufoníssi is noted for its fish **tavernas**; *To Nikitouri*, up in Hóra, has very personable Greek-American management, and the *Karnayio* ouzerí on the bay to the west of the harbour is cheaper than most and has a fine array of seafood. The nearby *To Steki Tis Marias* is a good breakfast place with a few rooms (②), and has views over the narrow channel to Káto Koufoníssi. The most popular nightspot is *Soroccos*, a lively café-bar on the front, while good alternatives include *Ta Kalamia*, with a quieter choice of music; *Nikitas*; and *Skholeio*, a creperie and bar. *To Palio Fanari*, to the west of the village, is the club favoured by locals, playing a mix of dance and Greek music. The OTE office and ticket agency are on the main street, and money, unusually of late, can be changed at the somewhat improvised "post office" (limited hours), north of the town hall.

All the good beaches are in the southeast of the island, getting better as you go east along a dirt path that skirts the coastline along the edge of low cliffs. **Fínikas**, a ten-minute walk from the village, is the first of four wide coves with gently shelving golden sand, where there are rooms and an acceptable taverna. Further east is **Harakópou**, which has a windswept **campsite** (☎02850/71 683) with cane shade and rather poor facilities on the headland before the next beach, **Thános**. Next is **Platiá Púnda**, where caves have been hollowed out of the cliffs. Further east, the path rounds a rocky headland to **Porí**, a much longer and wilder beach, backed by dunes and set in a deep bay. It can be reached more easily from the village by following a track heading inland through the low scrub-covered hills.

KÁTO KOUFONÍSSI, the uninhabited island to the southwest, has a seasonal taverna and some more secluded beaches; a kaïki shuttles people across until late in the evening. A festival is held here on August 15, at the church of the Panayía. The island of **Kéros** is harder to reach, but if there is a willing group of people keen to visit the ancient site, a boat and boatmen can be hired at around €45 for the day.

Skhinoússa

A little to the southwest, the island of **Skhinoússa** is just beginning to awaken to its tourist potential. Boats dock at the small port of Mersíni, which has one pension (☎02850/71 157; ④) and a couple of cafés; a road leads up to **HÓRA**, aka Panayía, the walk taking just over ten minutes. As you enter the village, the well-stocked "**Tourist Centre**" is one of the first buildings. Yiorgos

Grispos is a mine of information and is personally responsible for the island's map and postcards, as well as being the boat/hydrofoil agent, having a metred phone and selling Greek and foreign press.

Accommodation is mostly in fairly simple rooms, such as *Pension Meltemi* (☏02850/71 195; ❹), *Anesis* (☏02850/71180; ❷) and the pleasant *Provaloma* (☏02850/71 936; ❷), which also has a taverna. The rooms belonging to Anna (☏02850/71 161; ❷) are particularly recommended, as is the modern *Hotel Sunset* (☏02850/71 948; ❷–❹) which enjoys stunning views of the harbour. The main concentration of **restaurants**, cafés and bars is along the main thoroughfare, including the popular *Bar Ostria* and a lively ouzerí.

There are no fewer than sixteen **beaches** dotted around the island, accessible by a lacework of trails. **Tsigoúri** is a ten-minute walk southwest from Hóra; largely undeveloped except for the new *Tsigouri Beach Villas* (☏02850/71 175; ❸), which has a good taverna with great views. The only other beach with any refreshments is **Almyrós**, a half-hour southeast of Hóra, which has a simple canteen.

Iráklia

In an attempt to accommodate increasing visitor numbers, **Iráklia** (pronounced Irakliá by locals), the westernmost of the minor Cyclades, is losing its charm as the number of purpose-built rooms increases.

Ferries and hydrofoils call at **ÁYIOS YEÓRYIOS**, a small but sprawling settlement behind a sandy tamarisk-backed beach. Irini Koveou (☏02850/71 488; ❷) has a café-restaurant and rooms opposite the harbour, and more rooms and places to eat can be found along the old road to Livádhi beach. *Anna's Place* (☏02850/71 145; ❷) has rooms with shared cooking facilities, and *Mestrali* (☏02850/71 807; ❷) has newer rooms as well as its own café-cum-taverna. Theofanis Gavalas (☏02850/71 565; ❷), Dhimítrios Stefanídhis (☏02850/71 484; ❷), Alexandra Tournaki (☏02850/71 482; ❷) and Angelos Koveos (☏02850/71 486; ❷) all have rooms nearby. *O Pefkos* is a pleasant **taverna**, with tables shaded by a large pine tree, while the café/shop *Melissa* acts as the main ticket agency for ferries. The recommended *Perigiali* taverna also has a small shop selling maps showing the mule path to a fine **cave** of Ayíos Ioánnis on the west side of the island.

Livádhi, the best beach on the island, is a fifteen-minute walk southeast of town. There is shade, but bring refreshments, as the taverna might not be open. The village of Livádhi, deserted since 1940, stands on the hillside above, its houses ruined and overgrown; among the remains are Hellenistic walls incorporated into a later building, and fortifications from the time of Marco Sanudo. Marietta Markoyianni (☏02850/71 252; ❷) has the only rooms on the beach; *Zografos Rooms* (☏02850/71 946; ❹), above the road to Panayía, has fine views but is rather remote.

PANAYÍA or **HÓRA**, an unspoiled one-street village at the foot of Mount Papás, is another hour's walk inland along the paved road. It has a bakery/minimarket, two café/shops and the excellent and cheap *O Kritikos* ouzerí, but no rooms. A track to the east heads down to Pigádhi, a rocky beach with sea urchins, at the head of a narrow inlet. To the west a track from the near-deserted hamlet of **Áyios Athanásios** leads back to the port.

The **cave of Áyios Ioánnis** lies behind the mountain, at the head of a valley leading to Vourkária bay. From Panayía, follow a signposted track west before zigzagging up to a saddle well to the north of the summit, with views over Skhinoússa, Koufoníssi, Kéros, Náxos and Amorgós; the path drops down to the south around the back of the mountain. A painted red arrow on the left indicates the turning to the cave, just over an hour's walk from Panayía. A church bell hangs from a cypress tree above the whitewashed entrance; inside there's a shrine, and the cave opens up into a large chamber with stalactites and stalagmites. It can be explored to a depth of 120m and is thought to be part of a much larger cave system, yet to be opened up; a festival is held here every year on August 18.

The main trail continues beyond the cave to a small sandy beach at **Alimiá** but this can be reached more easily with the beach boat from Áyios Yeóryios. In season the boat sails daily to either Skhinoússa, Alimiá or the nearby pebble beach of Karvounólakos.

Dhonoússa

Dhonoússa is a little out on a limb compared with the other minor Cyclades, and ferries and hydrofoils call less frequently. Island life centres on the pleasant port settlement of **STAVRÓS**, spread out behind the harbour and the village beach.

Rooms, most without signs, tend to be booked up by Greek holiday-makers in August; try Mihalis Prasinos (℡02850/51 578; ❹ based on four people sharing), with rooms along a lane behind the church; Dhimitris Prasinos (℡02850/51 579; ❷), with rooms open year-round near the *Iliovasilema* restaurant; or Nikos Prasinos (℡02850/51 551; ❹), who has good new studios above the rocks west of the harbour. *Ta Kymata* is the most popular of the four **tavernas** but *Meltemi* is also good, as is the friendly *Aposperitis*, right on the village beach. Nikitas Roussos (℡02850/51 648) has a **ticket agency** above the harbour and can book rooms and change money – at high rates so you would be wise to bring enough with you.

The hills around Stavrós are low and barren and scarred by bulldozed tracks, but a little walking is repaid with dramatic scenery and a couple of fine beaches. Campers and nudists head for **Kéndros**, a long and attractive stretch of sand fifteen minutes to the east, although shade is limited and there are no facilities. A road has been built on the hillside above, replacing the donkey track to the farming hamlets of Haravyí and Mersíni; these have more hens and goats in the streets than people, and there are no cafés, shops or rooms. **Mersíni** is an hour's walk from Stavrós and has a welcome spring beneath a plane tree, the island's only running water. A nearby path leads down to Livádhi, an idyllic white-sand beach with tamarisks for shade. In July and August there's a daily beach boat from the port.

The road to **KALOTARÍTISSA**, on the northeast coast is now paved and no longer an especially attractive walk. You might want to head inland from Stavrós toward Papás, the island's highest point, from where a valley drops down rapidly to the tiny village with a simple **taverna** and one room to rent (℡02850/51 562; ❶). There are two small pebble beaches and a path that continues above the coast to Mersíni. It takes four to five hours to walk round the island.

Amorgós

Amorgós, with its dramatic mountain scenery and laid-back atmosphere, is attracting visitors in increasing numbers; most ferries and hydrofoils call at both Katápola in the southwest and Eyiáli in the northeast – with these destinations, rather than Amorgós, on schedules – and there is a regular bus service between both ports. The island can get extremely crowded in midsummer, the numbers swollen by French paying their respects to the film location of Luc Besson's *The Big Blue*, although few actually venture out to the wreck of the *Olympia*,

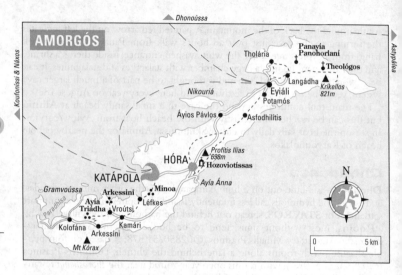

at the island's west end, which figured so prominently in the movie. In general it's a low-key, escapist clientele, happy to have found a relatively large, interesting and uncommercialized island with excellent walking.

The southwest

KATÁPOLA, set at the head of a deep bay, is actually three separate hamlets: **Katápola** proper on the south flank, **Rahídhi** on the ridge at the head of the gulf and **Xilokeratídhi** along the north shore. There is a beach in front of Rahídhi, but the beach to the west of Katápola is better, though not up to the standards of Eyiáli in the northeast. In season there is also a regular kaïki to nearby beaches at **Maltézi** and **Plákes** (€1.20 return) and a daily kaïki to the islet of **Gramvoússa** off the western end of Amorgós (€6 return).

There are plenty of small **hotels** and **pensions** and, except in high summer when rooms are almost impossible to find, proprietors tend to meet those boats arriving around sunset – though not necessarily those that show up in the small hours. A good clean place next to the beach at the western end of Katápola is *Eleni Rooms* (☏02850/71 543 or 71 628; ❹); *Dhimitri's Place* in Rahídhi (☏02850/71 309; ❶) is a compound of interconnecting buildings in an orchard with shared cooking facilities; on the same road, *Angeliki Rooms* (☏02850/71 280; ❷) is well run, friendly and good value; the smart traditional *Hotel Minoa* (☏02850/71 480; ❸–❺) on the waterfront may be a bit too noisy for some, who might try the *Valsamitis* (☏02850/71 148; ❷–❺), off the northeast corner of the port. *Panayiotis Rooms* (☏02850/71 890; ❷) in Xilokeratídhi is also good value and inland, south of the port you'll find the *Hotel Anna* (☏02850/71 218; ❷), with a lovely setting and basic cooking facilities. There are several similarly priced pensions further east, including *Big Blue* and *Sofia*. The **campsite** (☏02850/71 802) is well signed between Rahídhi and Xilokeratídhi.

In Katápola proper, *Mourayio* is the most popular **taverna** in town; alternatively try the *Akrogiali*. There are four tavernas near the campsite near Xilokeratídhi, of which the first is a friendly fish taverna, and of the others around the corner *Vitzentzos* is by far the best. What **nightlife** there is focuses on a handful of cafés and pubs. A bar called *Le Grand Bleu* in Xilokeratídhi regularly shows *The Big Blue* on video but there are other less obvious and less expensive places to drink, such as *The Moon Bar* next door or *45 Strofes*, a café and bar on the front at Rahídhi.

Prekas is the one-stop **boat ticket agency**, and there are several **motorbike rental** outlets including the friendly Corner Rentabike, though the local bus service is more than adequate and the walking trails are delightful.

Steps, and then a jeep track, lead south out of Katápola to the remains of **ancient Minoa**, which are apt to disappoint close up: some polygonal wall four or five courses high, the foundations of an Apollo temple, a crumbled Roman structure and bushels of unsorted pottery shards. The setting, however, with views encompassing Hóra and ancient Arkessíni, is memorable. Beyond Minoa the track dwindles to a trail, continuing within a few hours to Arkessíni (see p.182) via several hamlets – a wonderful **excursion** with the possibility of catching the bus back.

The **bus** shuttles almost hourly until 11pm between Katápola and Hóra, the island capital; several times daily it continues to Ayía Ánna via Hozoviotíssas monastery, and once a day (9.45am) out to the "Káto Meriá", made up of the hamlets of Kamári, Arkessíni and Kolofána. **HÓRA**, also accessible by an hourlong path beginning from behind the Rahídhi campsite, is one of the best-preserved settlements in the Cyclades, with a scattering of tourist shops, cafés, tavernas and rooms. Dominated by a rock plug wrapped with a chapel or two, the thirteenth-century Venetian fortifications look down on countless other bulbous churches – including Greece's smallest, **Áyios Fanoúrios**, which holds just three worshippers – and a line of decapitated windmills beyond. Of the half-dozen or so **places to stay**, *Pension O Ilias* (℡02850/71 277; ❷) is recommended. *Liotrivi* restaurant, down the steps from the bus stop, is probably the best place to **eat** in town. In addition to a pair of traditional tavernas, *Kastanis* and *Klimataria*, there are several noisy bistro/café/pubs, with *To Plateaki* in the upper plaza perennially popular in the late afternoon, and *Giulia Kafeneon*, near the bus stop, livelier later on. Also in the upper square is the island's main **post office**.

From the top of Hóra, near the upper satellite-dish tower, a wide cobbled *kalderími* drops down to two major attractions, effectively short-cutting the road and taking little longer than the bus to reach them. Bearing left at an inconspicuous fork after fifteen minutes, you'll come to the spectacular **monastery of Hozoviotíssas** (daily 8am–1pm; donation expected, modest dress required), which appears suddenly as you round a bend, its vast wall gleaming white at the base of a towering orange cliff. Only four monks occupy the fifty rooms now, but they are quite welcoming considering the number of visitors who file through; you can see the eleventh-century icon around which the monastery was founded, along with a stack of other treasures. Legend has it that during the Iconoclastic period a precious icon of the Virgin was committed to the sea by beleaguered monks at Hózova, in the Middle East, and it washed up safely at the base of the palisade here. The view from the *katholikón's* terrace overshadows all for most visitors, and to round off the experience, you are ushered into a comfy reception room and treated to a sugary lump of *loukoúmi*, a fiery shot of *kítron* and a cool glass of water.

The right-hand trail leads down, within forty minutes, to the pebble **beaches** at **Ayía Ánna**. Skip the first batch of tiny coves in favour of the path to the westernmost bay, where naturists cavort, almost in scandalous sight of the monastery far above. As yet there are no tavernas here, nor a spring, so bring food and water for the day.

For alternatives to Ayía Ánna, take the morning bus out toward modern Arkessíni, alighting at **Kamári** hamlet (where there's a single taverna) for the twenty-minute path down to the adjacent beaches of **Notiná**, **Moúros** and **Poulopódhi**. Like most of Amorgós's south-facing beaches, they're clean, with calm water, and here, too, a freshwater spring dribbles most of the year. The road is paved as far as **Kolofána**, where there is one place with **rooms**. From here unpaved roads lead to the western tip of the island, and remote beaches at Káto Kámbos and at Paradhísa, facing the islet of Gramvoússa.

Archeology buffs will want to head north from Kamári to Vroútsi, start of the overgrown hour-long route to **ancient Arkessíni**, a collection of tombs, six-metre-high walls and houses out on the cape of Kastrí. The main path from Minoa also passes through Vroútsi, ending next to the well-preserved Hellenistic fort known locally as the "Pýrgos", just outside modern **ARKESSÍNI**. The village has a single taverna with rooms, and, more importantly, an afternoon bus back to Hóra and Katápola.

The northeast

The energetically inclined can walk the four to five hours from Hóra to Eyiáli, either continuing on the faint trail just beyond Hozoviotíssas, or taking the scenic and sheltered valley track through Terláki and Rikhtí. The two routes, and the modern jeep road, more or less meet an hour out of Hóra. Along most of the way, you're treated to amazing views of **Nikouriá islet**, nearly joined to the main island, and in former times a leper colony. The only habitations en route are the summer hamlet of **Asfodhilítis**, with well water but little else for the traveller, and **Potamós**, a double village you encounter on the stroll down towards Eyiáli bay.

EYIÁLI (Órmos) is smaller than Katápola but more picturesque, so it's gaining in popularity. The road inland, behind the harbour, leads to a group of **hotels** of similar price and quality. *Nikitas* (℡02850/73 237; ❷) is the most pleasant, in that it stands on its own in a field, commanding unobstructed sea views. Above is a row of hotels including *Pension Christine* (℡02850/73 236; ❷), *Akrogiali* (℡02850/73 249; ❸) and *Hotel Pelagos* (℡02850/73 206; ❷). Above on the main road is *Poseidon Studios* (℡02850/73 453; ❹), which have fully equipped kitchens. Along the beach is the *Lakki* (℡02850/73 244; ❹) and behind this the pleasant *Pension Askas* (℡02850/73 333; ❹) – both of which have their own shaded tavernas. Next to *Pension Askas* there is a very friendly official **campsite**, *Amorgos Camping* (℡02850/73 500), usually less crowded than that in Katápola. Overlooking the bay on the road up to Tholária is a luxury hotel with a swimming pool, the *Egialis* (℡02850/73 393; ❹–❻). For **eating out**, try *To Limani* (aka *Katerina's*) on the single inland lane, packed until midnight by virtue of its excellent food and barrel wine. Other good options are the *Amorgialos* kafenío right by the harbour, which serves up octopus, and *Delear*, a smart beach bar with live music some evenings and rather pricey drinks. A few seasonal music **bars**, such as *Blé Café*, attempt to compete with *Katerina's*. The *Corte Club* at the *Egialis* hotel is a typical holiday resort disco playing northern European dance music and Greek pop. For a more active adventure you can take advantage of the new **diving** centre, Dive Ventures (℡02850/73 611), which organizes daily boat and shore dives.

The main Eyiáli **beach** is more than serviceable, getting less weedy and reefy as you stroll further north, the sand interrupted by the remains of a Roman building jutting into the sea. A trail here leads over various headlands to an array of clothing-optional bays: the first sandy, the second mixed sand and gravel, the last shingle. There are no facilities anywhere so bring along what you need.

There is a **bus service** up to each of the two villages visible above and east of Eyiáli, with eight departures daily up and down (a timetable is posted by the harbour bus stop), but it would be a shame to miss out on the beautiful **loop walk** linking them with the port. A path starting at the far end of the beach heads inland and crosses the road before climbing steeply to **THOLÁRIA**, named after vaulted Roman tombs found around Vígla, the site of ancient Eyiáli. Vígla is on a hill opposite the village but there is little to see beyond the bases of statues and traces of city walls incorporated into later terracing. Another path winds down behind the hill to a tiny pebble beach at Mikrí Vlihádha far below. There are a few **taverna-cafés**, including a handsome wooden-floored establishment near the church, and several places to stay, including some comfortable **rooms** (reserve through *Pension Lakki* in Eyiáli), the large and upmarket *Vigla* (T02850/73 288; ❸–❺) and the *Thalassino Oneiro* (T02850/73 345; ❷), which has a fine restaurant and an extremely friendly owner.

LANGÁDHA is another hour's walk along a path starting below Tholária; to the left of the trail is the chapel of Astrátios with an altar supported by the capital of a Corinthian column. Past here there are views down to the inlet of Megáli Vlihádha and, on a clear day, across to Ikaría in the north. The path descends through the village of Stroúmbos, abandoned apart from a few houses restored as holiday homes, and into a small gorge before climbing the steps up to Langádha. The place is home to a sizeable colony of expatriates – reflected in the German-Greek cooking at the beautifully located *Nikos'* **taverna** at the lower end of the village, which also runs the attached *Pagali* hotel (T02850/73 310; ❹). The *Loza* taverna, at the top of the village also owns a more straightforward pension with rooms (T02850/73 315; ❷).

Beyond Langádha, another rocky path leads around the base of the island's highest peak, the 821-metre-high **Kríkellos**, passing on the way the fascinating church of **Theológos**, with lower walls and ground plan dating to the fifth century. Somewhat easier to reach, by a slight detour off the main Tholária-Langádha trail, are the church and festival grounds of **Panayía Panohorianí** – not so architecturally distinguished but a fine spot nonetheless.

Íos

No other island is quite like **Íos**, nor attracts the same vast crowds of young people, although attempts are being made to move the island's tourism upmarket. Buildings are now painted white with blue trim, instead of garish psychedelic hues; camping rough is discouraged; and Greece's early closing laws (3am except Fri & Sat) are enforced, and bars no longer stay open all night. (There is still, however, a lingering problem with *bómba*, a cheap local drink that gets you drunk fast and then makes you sick. It might be worth resisting drinks that are suspiciously cheap.)

The only real villages – **Yialós**, **Hóra** and **Mylopótamos** – are in one small corner of the island, and until recently development elsewhere was restricted by poor roads. As a result there are still some very quiet beaches with just a few rooms to rent. Yialós has one of the best and safest natural harbours in the Cyclades, with a newly paved esplanade, and there is talk of building a new yacht marina.

Most visitors stay along the arc delineated by the port – at Yialós, where you'll arrive (there's no airport), in Hóra above it or at the beach at Mylopótamos; it's a small area, and you soon get to know your way around. **Buses** constantly shuttle between Koumbára, Yialós, Hóra and Mylopótamos, with a daily service running roughly from 8am to midnight; you should never have to wait more than fifteen minutes during high season, but at least once try the short walk up (or down) the stepped path between Yialós and Hóra. Various travel offices run their own buses to the beaches at Manganári and Ayía Theodhóti; they sell return tickets only and are a bit expensive. To rent your own transport, try Jacob's Car and Bike Rental (☎02860/91 047) in Yialós or Vangelis Bike Rental (☎02860/91 919) in Hóra; unlike most of the other islands, here you'll need a valid motorcycle license.

Despite its past popularity, **sleeping on the beach** on Íos is discouraged these days. Crime and police raids are becoming more frequent as the island strains under the sheer impact of increasing youth tourism, and the police have been known to turn nasty. They prefer you to sleep in the official campsites and, given the problem of theft, you should probably take their advice.

Yialós and Hóra

From **YIALÓS** quayside, **buses** turn around just to the left, while Yialós **beach** – surprisingly peaceful and uncrowded – is another five-minutes' walk in the same direction. You might be tempted to grab a room in Yialós as you arrive: owners meet the ferries, hustling the town's **accommodation**, and there are also a couple of kiosks by the jetty that will book rooms for you. In shoulder season you can bargain for prices considerably lower than those listed below, but the town won't be in full swing. *Hotel Mare Monte* (☎02860/91 585; ❹), about halfway down the beach, has clean modern rooms and a small pool; *Galini Rooms* (☎02860/91 115; ❹), down a lane behind the beach, is a good quiet choice, if a little out of the way. One of the best choices is the quiet family-owned *Golden Sun* (☎02860/91 110; ❹), about 300m up the road to Hóra, which has a large pool. There are more rooms on the stepped path from Yialós to Hóra although they can be noisy at night: the *Hotel-Bar Helios* (☎02860/91 500; ❹) has a few simple, older rooms, and smarter options near-

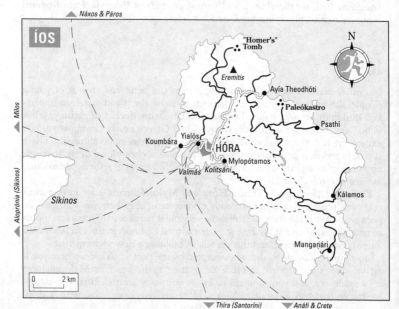

by include *Armadoras* (☎02860/91 201; ❹), with a pleasant pool and bar, and *Hotel Poseidon* (☎02860/91 091; ❹). *Ios Camping* (☎02860/91 329) is friendly and clean and has a rather luxurious swimming pool and café area. Yialós has other essentials, including a reasonable supermarket and a few **tavernas**. The *Octopus Tree*, a small kafenío by the fishing boats, serves cheap fresh seafood caught by the owner, while on the front heading towards the beach the *Waves Restaurant* does good Indian food. A twenty-minute stroll over the headland at **KOUMBÁRA**, there's a smaller and less-crowded beach, with a rocky islet to explore, and the *Polydoros* taverna, one of the better places to eat on Iós – well worth the walk or bus ride.

HÓRA (aka Iós Town), a twenty-minute walk up behind the port, is one of the most picturesque towns in the Cyclades, filled with meandering arcaded lanes and whitewashed chapels, though it's overwhelmed by crowds of young revellers in the high season. It divides naturally into two parts: the old town climbing the hillside to the left as you arrive, and the newer development to the right.

There are plenty of basic **rooms** in the old part, although the bars can make sleep difficult. Your best strategy for a modicum of quiet is to wend your way up to the left where you find several establishments, including *Francesco's* (☎02860/91 223; ❸). Lower down there's the *Hotel Filippou* (☎02860/91 290; ❸), above the National Bank and next to the cathedral, and Yannis Stratis (☎02860/91 494; ❷) has a few very simple rooms next door. Your best chances for affordable rest will be found in the newer quarter: *Markos Pension* (☎02860/91 059; ❹; ask for the ten percent discount for *Rough Guide* readers), with a poolside bar; *Lofos (The Hill) Pension* (☎02860/91 481: ❹), to the right up from the Rollan supermarket; *Katerina Rooms* (☎02860/91 997; ❹), just out of town down a path past the *Iós Club*; the new *Village Twins* (☎02860/92 211; ❹), up to the left before the *Scorpion Club*; and the friendly *Four Seasons Pension* (☎02860/91 308 or winter ☎02860/92 081; ❹), up from Vangelis Bike Rental.

Every evening in summer Hóra is the centre of the island's **nightlife**, its streets throbbing with music from ranks of competing discos and clubs – mostly free, or with a nominal entrance charge, though drinks tend to be expensive. Most of the smaller **bars** and pubs are tucked into the thronging narrow streets of the old village on the hill, offering something for everyone – unless you just want a quiet drink – and you'll have no trouble finding them. A welcome exception to the techno-pop dancing fodder can be found at the *Ios Club*, perched right up on the hill, which plays quieter music, has reasonable food and is a good place to watch the sunset. The larger **dancing clubs**, include the *Mojo*, which plays techno and trance music, *Scorpion* and *Cavos*, on the main road to Mylopótamos.

Eating is a secondary consideration but there are plenty of cheap and cheerful *psistariés* and takeaway joints: sound choices include the Italian restaurant *Pinocchio*, and the *Mezedhopolío Lord Byron* in an alley up to the left in the old quarter – it's open year round and tries hard to re-create a traditional atmosphere, with old rembétika music and some good, unusual Greek food.

Culturally things are improving with the recent opening of the **Archeological Museum of Ios** (Tues–Sun 8am–2pm; €1.50), on the second floor of the yellow town hall, which hopes to attract a more diverse range of visitors to the island. The outdoor theatre of Odysseus Elytis, behind the windmills, provides a beautiful setting in which to enjoy concerts and plays, details of which can be found at the travel agent/information booth next to the archeological museum.

Around the island

The most popular stop on the island's bus routes is **MYLOPÓTAMOS** (universally abbreviated to Mylópotas), the site of a magnificent beach and a mini-resort. Due to the large number of young travellers in Íos, **camping** is a popular option. *Far Out* (☎02860/91 468), the better of the campsites also has bungalows (❶); it has an attractive setting and excellent facilities, including an air-conditioned cafeteria, but it's very popular and can get noisy and crowded. *The Purple Pig* (☎02860/91 302, ✉purplpig@otenet.gr), a friendly Australian-run backpackers' complex, by the road up to Hóra, has clean bungalows ❶–❷, good camping facilities and plenty of other pleasurable distractions, including its own club and a poolside bar. Up the road at the far end of the beach, *Gorgona* (☎02860/91 307; ❹) and *Dracos* (☎02860/91 281 or 91 010; ❹) have reasonable rooms, and *Dracos* also has a good taverna on its own little quay, serving freshly caught fish. The *Far Out Hotel* (☎02860/91 446 or 91 702; ❹), on the road down from Hóra, and the luxurious *Ios Palace Hotel* (☎02860/91 269; ❺), above the near end of the beach, are the most upmarket choices. On the rocks, beyond the *Ios Palace*, the *Harmony Restaurant* is one of the better places to eat, serving pizzas and Mexican food. The restaurants and self-service cafés behind the beach are uninspiring, and only the *Faros Café* rates a mention for staying open through the night to cater for the crowds returning from Hóra in the early hours. Mylopótamos itself has surprisingly little in the way of nightlife.

From Yialós, daily boats depart at around 10am (returning in the late afternoon) to **Manganári** on the south coast, where there's a beach and a swanky hotel; you can also get there by scooter. There's an expensive speedboat (€12) from Yialós to Manganári, but most people go by private buses run by travel agencies (€5 return), which leave Yialós about 11am, calling at Hóra and Mylopótamos and return later in the afternoon. Predominantly nudist, Manganári is the beach to come to for serious tans, although there's more to see, and a better atmosphere at **Ayía Theodhóti** up on the east coast. There's a paved road across the island to Ayía Theodhóti – the daily excursion bus costs €3 return. A couple of kilometres south of Ayía Theodhóti is a ruined Venetian castle which encompasses the ruins of a marble-finished town and a Byzantine church. In the unlikely event that the beach – a good one and mainly nudist – is too crowded, try the one at **Psathí**, 14km to the southeast. Frequented by wealthy Athenians, this small resort has a couple of pricey tavernas, making it better for a day-trip than an extended stay. The road is very poor and not really safe for scooters, although there are plans to improve it. Another island beach is at **Kálamos**: get off the Manganári bus at the turning for Kálamos, which leaves you with a four-kilometre walk.

"**Homer's**" **tomb** can be reached by motorbike along a safe unpaved road (turning left from the paved road to Ayía Theódhoti 4.5km from Hóra). The town itself has long since slipped down the side of the cliff, but the rocky ruins of the entrance to a tomb remain, as well as some graves – one of which is claimed to be Homer's, but which in reality probably dates only to the Byzantine era.

Síkinos

Síkinos has so small a population that the mule ride or walk up from the port to the village was only replaced by a bus late in the 1980s and, until the new jetty was completed at roughly the same time, it was the last major Greek island

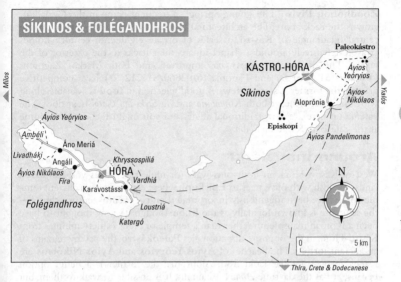

Thíra, Crete & Dodecanese

where ferry passengers were still taken ashore in launches. With no dramatic characteristics, nor any nightlife to speak of, few foreigners make the short trip over here from neighbouring Íos and Folégandhros or from sporadically connected Páros, Náxos or Thíra. There is no bank on the island, but there is a **post office** up in Kástro-Hóra, and you can sometimes change cash at the store in Aloprónia.

Aloprónia and Kástro-Hóra

Such tourist facilities as exist are concentrated in the little harbour of **ALOPRÓNIA**, with its long sandy beach and extended breakwater and jetty. More and more formal **accommodation** is being built here, but it's still possible to camp or just sleep out under the tamarisks behind the beach. For rooms, try *Flora* (✆02860/51 214; ❶), near the main road leading to Hóra, *Loukas* (✆02860/51 076; ❶–❹), which has rooms and studios around town to suit most budgets, or the recommended *The Rock* (✆02860/51 135; ❷), above the *Vrachos Pizzaria/Rock Cafe*; alternatively, the comfortable and traditional *Hotel Kamares* (✆02860/51 234; ❷) has a nicer setting than the conspicuous *Porto Sikinos* luxury complex (✆02860/51 247; ❹). *To Meltemi* **taverna** on the quay is the locals' hangout, while the fancier *Ostria* is affiliated with the *Hotel Kamares* and the *Loukas* provides standard fare. The *Rock Cafe* above the quay plays a more varied music selection than its name would suggest and attracts a good mix of people, while *Vengera* music bar on the opposite side of the bay is a smoother joint.

The double village of **KÁSTRO-HÓRA** is served by the single island bus, which shuttles regularly from early morning till quite late in the evening between the harbour and here, though the route should soon be extended to Episkopí with the completion of the new road. On the ride up, the scenery turns out to be less desolate than initial impressions suggest. Draped across a ridge overlooking the sea, Kástro-Hóra makes for a charming day-trip, and the lovely oil-press **museum** (July to mid-Sept 6.30–8.30pm; free), run privately by a Greek-American, is highly recommended. A partly ruined monastery,

Zoödhóhou Piyís ("Life-giving Spring", a frequent name in the Cyclades), crowns the rock above. The architectural highlight of the place, though, is the central quadrangle of **Kástro**, a series of ornate eighteenth-century houses arrayed defensively around a chapel square, their backs to the exterior of the village. The quality of **rooms** has improved, and both Markos Zagoreos (☎02860/51 263; ●) and Haroula (☎02860/51 212; ●) have competitive prices – the former has great views. A good selection of **food** is available, along with fine local wine, at both *Klimataria* and *To Steki tou Garbi* next door. The kafenía up here are very traditional affairs and you might feel more welcome at the café-bars *Kastro* or *Platía*.

Around the island

West of Kástro-Hóra, an hour-plus walk (or mule ride) takes you through a landscape lush with olive trees to **Episkopí**, where elements of an ancient temple-tomb have been ingeniously incorporated into a seventh-century church – the structure is known formally as the Iróön, though it's now thought to have been a Roman mausoleum rather than a temple of Hera. Ninety minutes from Kástro-Hóra, in the opposite direction, lies **Paleokástro**, the patchy remains of an ancient fortress. The beaches of **Áyios Yeóryios** and **Áyios Nikólaos** are reachable by a regular kaïki from Aloprónia; the former is a better option because it has the daytime *Almira* restaurant. It is possible to walk to them, but there is no real path at the later stages. A more feasible journey by foot is to the pebble beach at **Áyios Pandelímonas**: just under an hour's trail walk southwest of Aloprónia, it is the most scenic and sheltered on the island, and is also served by a kaïki in season.

Folégandhros

The cliffs of **Folégandhros** rise sheer in places over 300m from the sea – until the early 1980s as effective a deterrent to tourists as they always were to pirates. It was used as an island of political exile right up until 1974, but life in the high, barren interior has been eased since the junta years by the arrival of electricity and the construction of a lengthways road from the harbour to Hóra and beyond. Development has been given further impetus by the recent exponential increase in tourism and the mild commercialization this has brought.

A veritable explosion in accommodation for most budgets, and improvement in ferry arrival times, means there is no longer much need for – or local tolerance of – sleeping rough on the beaches. The increased wealth and trendiness of the heterogeneous clientele is reflected in fancy jewellery shops, an arty postcard gallery and a helipad. Yet away from the showcase Hóra and the beaches, the countryside remains mostly pristine, and is largely devoted to the spring and summer cultivation of barley, the mainstay of many of the Cyclades before the advent of tourism. Donkeys and donkey paths are also still very much in evidence, since the terrain on much of the island is too steep for vehicle roads.

Karavostássi and around

KARAVOSTÁSSI, the rather unprepossessing port whose name simply means "ferry stop", serves as a last-resort base; it has several **hotels** but little atmosphere. Best value if you do decide to stay is *Hotel Aeolos* (☎02860/41

205; ❷), while the *Poseidon* (☎02860/41 272; ❹) throws in breakfast at its decent restaurant *To Kati Allo*, which means "Something Else" and the new *Vrahos Hotel* (☎02860/41 304; ❹) has some nice rooms on the far side of the bay. *Iy Kali Kardhia* **taverna** above the harbour is recommended, and there are a couple of pleasant beach **bars** including the *Smyrna Ouzeri*, housed in a converted boathouse. There are many buses a day in summer to Hóra, three continuing to Áno Meriá; if you're feeling adventurous try Jimmy's motorbike rental (☎02860/41 448), which is cheaper than its counterparts in Hóra.

The closest **beach** is the smallish, but attractive enough, sand-and-pebble **Vardhiá**, signposted just north over the headland. Some twenty minutes' walk south lies **Loustriá**, a rather average beach with tamarisk trees and the island's official **campsite**, *Livadi Camping* (☎02860 41 304), which is good and friendly, although the hot water supply can be erratic.

Easily the most scenic beach on Folégandhros, a 300-metre stretch of peagravel with an offshore islet, is at **Katergó**, on the southeastern tip of the island. Most people visit on a boat excursion from Karavostássi or Angáli, but you can also get there on foot from the hamlet of Livádhi, a short walk inland from Loustriá. Be warned, though, that it's a rather arduous trek, with some nasty trail-less slithering in the final moments.

Hóra

The island's real character and appeal are to be found in the spectacular **HÓRA**, perched on a clifftop plateau some 45 minutes' walk from the dock; an hourly high-season **bus** service (6 daily spring/autumn) runs from morning until late at night. Locals and foreigners – hundreds of them in high season – mingle at the cafés and tavernas under the almond, flowering Judas and pepper trees of the two main platías, passing the time unmolested by traffic, which is banned from the village centre. Towards the cliff-edge, and entered through two arcades, the defensive core of the medieval *kástro* is marked by ranks of two-storey houses, whose repetitive, almost identical stairways and slightly recessed doors are very appealing.

From the square where the bus stops, a zigzag path with views down to both coastlines climbs to the cragtop, wedding-cake church of **Kímisis Theotókou**, nocturnally illuminated to grand effect. Beyond and below it hides the **Khryssospiliá**, a large cave with stalactites, accessible only to proficient climbers; the necessary steps and railings have crumbled away into the sea, although a minor, lower grotto can still be visited by kaïki from the port.

Practicalities

Hóra's **accommodation** seems slightly weighted to favour hotels over rooms, with concentrations around the bus plaza at the eastern entrance to the village and at the western edge. Many of the tavernas and shops advertise rooms in their windows; otherwise try the purpose-built complex run by Irini Dekavalla (☎02860/41 235; ❸), east of the bus stop. The nearby *Hotel Polikandia* (☎02860/41 322; ❹) has an engaging proprietress and lower rates off-season. The most luxurious facilities are at the cliff-edge *Anemomilos Apartments* (☎02860/41 309; ❺), immaculately appointed and with stunning views; the new *Meltemi* (☎02860/41 328; ❸), just opposite, has clean, comfortable rooms. The only hotel within Hóra is the traditional *Castro* (☎02860/41 230; ❸–❹), built in 1212 and fully renovated in 1992, with three rather dramatic rooms looking directly out on an alarming drop to the sea. At the western edge of Hóra near the police station, a dense cluster of rooms tend to block each other's views; the least claustrophobic is the recently renovated *Odysseas* (☎02860/41 276; ❸), which also manages some attractive apartments near the *Anemomilos*, the *Folgeandros Apartments* (☎02860/41 239; ❹). By the roadside on the way to Áno Meriá, the *Fani-Vevis* (☎02860/41 237; ❷–❹), in a Neoclassical mansion overlooking the sea, seems to function only in high season; 100m beyond are some smart new studios (☎02860/41 274; ❺) managed by *Iy Kali Kardhia* (see p.189).

Hóra's dozen or so **restaurants** are surprisingly varied. The *Folegandhros* ouzerí in water-cistern plaza, is fun, if a bit eccentrically run. Breakfast can be enjoyed on the adjacent Platía Kondaríni at *Iy Melissa*, which does good fruit and yogurt, omelettes and juices. *Iy Piatsa* has a nightly changing menu of well-executed Greek dishes, while their neighbour and local hangout *O Kritikos* is notable only for its grills. *Iy Pounda* near the bus stop is the most traditional place and has a small garden, while *Apanemo* at the far end of town has good food and a quieter setting, despite its proximity to the main bar area. Self-catering is an attractive option, with two well-stocked fruit shops and two supermarkets. Hóra is inevitably beginning to sprawl unattractively at the edges, but this at least means that the burgeoning **nightlife** – two dance bars and a number of music pubs and ouzerís – can be exiled to the north, away from most accommodation. *Avli* and *Greco* are two lively bars and both play up-to-date sounds, while *Kellari* is a rustic and charming wine bar where the atmosphere is more relaxed. A **post office** (no bank) completes the list of amenities, though the single **ferry agent** also does money exchange, as does the friendly and competent Italian-run Sottavento agency, which offers a wide range of services.

The rest of the island

Northwest of Hóra a narrow, paved road threads its way towards **ÁNO MERIÁ**, the other village of the island; after 4km you pass its first houses, clustered around the three churches of Áyios Pandelímonas, Áyios Yeóryios and Áyios Andhréas. Four **tavernas** operate in high season only: *Barba Kostas* is at the beginning of the village, *O Mimis* is about halfway along, *Iy Sinandisi* is at the turning for Áyios Yeóryios beach, while *Iliovasilema*, at the far end of the sprawling village, completes the list. Several **rooms** are also available, including *Stella's* (☎02860/41 329; ❶) and *Irini's* (☎02860/41 344; ❶).

Up to six times a day in high season a **bus** trundles out here to drop people off at the footpaths down to the various sheltered beaches on the southwest shore of the island. Busiest of these is **Angáli** (aka Vathý), with four rather basic rooms outfits including *Vangelis* (☎02860/41 105; ❶) and *Panagiotis* (☎02860/41 116; ❷) and two equally simple summer-only tavernas, reached by a fifteen-minute walk along a dirt road from the bus stop.

Nudists should take the paths which lead twenty minutes east or west to **Firá** or **Áyios Nikólaos** beaches respectively; the latter in particular, with its many tamarisks, coarse sand and view back over the island, is Katergó's only serious rival in the best-beach sweepstakes. At Áyios Nikólaos, a lone taverna operates up by the namesake chapel; Firá has no facilities at all. From the *Iliovasilema* taverna, a motorable track continues north to a point from where a 500-metre path takes you down to the pleasant little bay of **Ambéli**.

Thíra (Santoríni)

As the ferry manoeuvres into the great caldera of **Thíra**, the land seems to rise up and clamp around it. Gaunt, sheer cliffs loom hundreds of feet above, nothing grows or grazes to soften the awesome view, and the only colours are the reddish-brown, black and grey pumice striations layering the cliff-face. The landscape tells of a history so dramatic and turbulent that legend hangs as fact upon it.

From as early as 3000 BC the island developed as a sophisticated outpost of Minoan civilization, until sometime between 1647 and 1628 BC (according to latest estimates) when catastrophe struck: the volcano-island erupted, its heart sank below the sea leaving a crater (caldera) 10km in diameter, and earthquakes reverberated across the Aegean. Thíra was destroyed and the great Minoan civilization on Crete was dealt a severe blow. At this point the island's history became linked with legends of Atlantis, the "Happy Isles Submerged by Sea". Plato insisted that the legend was true, and Solon dated the cataclysm to 9000 years before his time – if you're willing to accept a mistake and knock off the final zero, a highly plausible date.

These apocalyptic events, though, scarcely concern modern tourists, who come here to take in the spectacular views, stretch out on the island's dark-sand beaches and absorb the peculiar, infernal atmosphere; as recently as a century

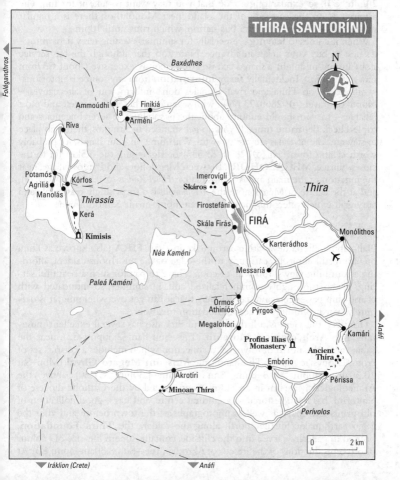

THÍRA (SANTORÍNI)

ago, Thíra was still reckoned to be infested with vampires. Though not nearly so predatory as the undead, current visitors have in fact succeeded in pretty much killing off most genuine island life, creating in its place a rather expensive and stagey playground.

Arrival and departure

Ferries dock at the somewhat grim port of **Órmos Athiniós**; **Skála Firás** and **Ía** in the north are reserved for local ferries, excursion kaïkia and cruise ships. **Buses**, astonishingly crammed, connect Athiniós with the island capital Firá, and, less frequently, with Ía and the main beaches at Kamári and Périssa. Disembark quickly and take whatever bus is going, if you want to avoid a long wait or a tedious hike up. You'll be accosted at Athiniós by people offering rooms all over the island; in the summer it might be a good idea to pay attention to them, given the scramble for beds, in Firá especially. From Skála Firás, you have the traditional route of 580 steps (about 45 minutes) up to Firá – not too difficult a walk, if you don't mind mule manure – or you can go by mule (€3, negotiable in off-season) or cable car (summer only 6.40am–10pm, every 20min; €3), so exhilarating a ride that you may want to take it for fun. The **airport** is on the east side of the island, near Monólithos; there is a regular shuttle-bus service to the Firá bus station, which runs until 10pm.

When it comes to **leaving** – especially for summer/evening ferry departures – it's best to buy your ticket in advance. Note, too, that although the bus service stops around midnight, a shared taxi isn't outrageously expensive (about €6 from Firá to Athiniós). Incidentally, **ferry information** from any source is notoriously unreliable on Thíra and rival agencies don't inform you of alternatives – Nomikos Travel (℡02860/23 660), with seven branches, is the largest and most reliable – so you should enquire about the possibilities at several agencies and triple-check departure times. If you do get stranded in Athiniós, there's no place to stay, and the tavernas are pretty awful. With time on your hands, it's probably worth calling for a taxi (℡02860/22 555) or zigzagging the 3.5km up to the closest village, **MEGALOHÓRI**. Between Megalohóri and Pýrgos village, near the junction of the main and Athiniós road, is *Hotel Zorbas* (℡02860/31 433; ●), and at the centre of Megalohóri, the *Yeromanolis* is a surprisingly reasonable and tasty grill which offers the increasingly rare home-made Santoríni wine.

Firá

Half-rebuilt after a devastating earthquake in 1956, **FIRÁ** (also known as Thíra or Hóra) still clings precariously to the edge of the enormous caldera, affording astonishing views. You will, of course, have to pay for such a beautiful setting. It's so thoroughly commercialized and, in summer, so inundated with cruise-ship passengers and day-trippers that it can get overwhelming; it is definitely worth phoning for accommodation in advance.

However, the view is still thrilling, and Firá also has several excellent museums. The **Archeological Museum** (Tues–Sun 8am–2.30pm; €3), near the cable car to the north of town, has a collection which includes a curious set of erotic Dionysiac figures. The handsome **Museum Megaro Ghyzi** (Mon–Sat 10.30am–1.30pm & 5–8pm, Sun 10.30am–4.30pm; €1.50) above the Archeological Museum in an old mansion owned by the Catholic diocese of Santoríni, has been restored as a cultural centre, and has a good collection of old prints and maps as well as photographs of the town before and after the 1956 earthquake. Further north along the caldera the **Thira Foundation**, housed in galleries carved into the cliffside, contains superb life-size 3D colour photo reproductions of the frescos of Akrotíri (Tues–Sun 8.30am–3pm; €3). At the other end of town, between the cathedral and bus station, the **Museum of Prehistoric Thira** (Tues–Sun 8.30am–3pm; free), a newly opened museum housed in a handsome building, has interesting displays of fossils, Cycladic art, and astonishing finds from Akrotíri.

Practicalities

For a caldera-view **hotel** in Firá consider the excellent *Loucas* (℡02860/22 480, ℱ24 882, ✉loucasason@ath.fortnet.gr; ❺–❻), a traditional hotel with barrel-ceilinged caves – to prevent collapse during an earthquake – carved into the cliffside, and a beautiful new pool; or the nearby *Kavalari* (℡02860/22 455, ℱ22 603; ❻). There are plenty of rooms without caldera views at the back of town. *Villa Haroula* (℡02860/24 226; ❺) is a good smart option on the road down to *Santorini Camping* (℡02860/22 944), the nearest **campsite**. (The newest and best campsite on the island is *Caldera View Camping* (℡02860/82 010) near Akrotíri village.) Along the same road *Pension Petros* (℡02860/22 573; ❹) and *Pension Soula* (℡02860/23 473; ❺) are two reasonable, if not very exciting, alternatives. There are two **youth hostels** north of the main square on the road to Ía, not far from each other: *Thira Youth Hostel* (℡02860/22 387) and *International Youth Hostel Kamares* (℡02860/24 472), both budget-priced (€6 per person) but noisy at night.

FIROSTEFÁNI, between Firá and Imerovígli, is the best bet for reasonably priced rooms with views over the caldera. Rooms in Firostefáni of varying prices and standards include *Apartments Gaby* (℡02860/22 057; ❺), *Hotel Mylos* (℡02860/23 884; ❹), *Kafieris Hotel* (℡02860/22 189; ❸–❹) and the rooms of Ioannis Roussos (℡02860/22 611 or 22 862; ❹). For something smarter, *Manos Apartments* (℡02860/23 202; ❺–❻) is highly recommended.

Another good location, where you don't have to pay for the (caldera) view, is **KARTERÁDHOS**, a small village about twenty-minutes' walk southeast of Firá, where you'll find pleasant *Hotel Albatross* (℡02860/23 435, ℱ23 431; ❺), the charming *Cyclades* (℡02860/24 543; ❺) and the welcoming *Pension George* (℡02860/22 351; ❸). Nomikos Travel can help you find a room (see below).

Firá's **restaurants** are primarily aimed at the tourist market, but for dependably good food with a sensational view find *Aris*, below the *Loucas Hotel*, or *Flame of the Volcano*, the last of the caldera-side restaurants north past the cable-car station (towards Firostefáni). On Erythroú Stavroú, the first street up from the main square, *Nikolas* is an old and defiantly traditional taverna, but it can be hard to get a table; the best budget choice is *Naoussa*, further north on the same street, upstairs on the right. Otherwise try *Koutouki* on 25-Martíou, the road to Ía, the welcoming *Mama's Cyclades*, a little further up on the same road, or *Aktaion* in Firostefáni. Most of the **nightlife** can be found northwest of the central square on Erythroú Stavroú: *Town Club*, *Amnesia*, *Murphy's* and, just above, *Enigma* and *Koo*. The best bars from which to admire the caldera are *Franco's*, a rather exclusive and pricey cocktail bar, and the more relaxed *Renaissance*, below the *Loucas Hotel*.

Nomikos Travel (℡02860/23 660) on 25-Martíou, opposite the OTE, is friendly and organizes excursions and trips to ancient Thíra and Thirassía in conjunction with Kamari Tours (℡02860/31 390). **Buses** leave Firá from just south of Platía Theotokopoúlou to Périssa, Perívolos, Kamári, Monólithos, Akrotíri, Órmos Athiniós and the airport. **Taxis** (℡02860/22 555) go from near the bus station. If you want to see the whole island in a couple of days a rented **motorbike** might do, though you must be very careful – especially since local drivers seem to enjoy antagonizing tourists on difficult and precipitous roads; try Moto Chris at the top of the road that leads down to *Santorini Camping*.

The north

Once outside Firá, the rest of Thíra comes as a nice surprise, although development is beginning to encroach. The volcanic soil is highly fertile, with every available space terraced and cultivated: wheat, tomatoes (most made into paste), pistachios and grapes are the main crops, all still harvested and planted by hand. The island's *vysándo* and *nikhtéri* wines are a little sweet for many tastes but are among the finest produced in the Cyclades.

A satisfying – if demanding – approach to Ía, 12km from Firá in the northwest of the island, is to walk the stretch from **IMEROVÍGLI**, 3km out of Firá, using a spectacular footpath along the lip of the caldera; the walk takes around two hours. Imerovígli is crowded with luxury, caldera-side **apartments** such as *Chromata* (☎02860/24 850; ◒) and *Astra* (☎02860/23 641; ◒), requiring reservations well in advance; *Katerina* (☎02860/22 708; ◒–◒) is a more moderately priced hotel, with caldera views from the large balcony/bar area only. Between the *Katerina* and *Chromata*, *Altana* is a small caldera-side **café** whose position and relaxed atmosphere make for a pleasing breakfast spot. Continuing to Ía, you'll pass Toúrlos, an old Venetian citadel on Cape Skáros.

ÍA, the most delightful village on the island, was once a major fishing port of the Aegean, but it has declined in the wake of economic depression, wars, earthquakes and depleted fish stocks. Partly destroyed in the 1956 earthquake, the town has been sympathetically reconstructed, its pristine white houses clinging to the cliff-face. Apart from the caldera and the village itself there are a couple of things to see, including the **Naval Museum** (daily except Tues 9am–1pm & 5–8pm) and the very modest remains of a Venetian castle. With a **post office**, a couple of travel agencies – Karvounis (☎02860/71 290, ℉71 291, ℮mkarvounis@otenet.gr), on the pedestrian street, is the older and more reliable – and several **bike-rental** offices (of which Motor Fun is particularly good), Ía is a fine, and quieter, alternative to Firá.

Much of the town's **accommodation** is in its restored old houses, including the traditional *Hotel Lauda* (☎02860/71 204; ◒–◒), the *Hotel Anemones* (☎02860/71 342; ◒–◒) and the *Hotel Fregata* (☎02860/71 221; ◒). Near the bus terminal, also reachable by the main road that continues round to the back end of the village, is an excellent hostel – the *Oia Youth Hostel* (☎02860/71 465), with a terrace and shady courtyard, a good bar, clean dormitories and breakfast included. Generally, the further you go along the central ridge towards the new end of Ía, the better value the **restaurants**: the *Anemomilos* and *Laokastri* are two such examples. The *Neptune*, near the church square, with good Greek dishes and vegetable specials, has a pleasant rooftop garden. **Nightlife** revolves around sunset-gazing, for which people are coached in from all over the island, creating traffic chaos; when this pales, there's *Petra* and *Alitana*, two bars on the road leading down to the youth hostel, both playing easy listening in pleasant garden surroundings.

Below the town, 200-odd steps switchback hundreds of metres down to two small harbours: **Ammoúdhi**, for the fishermen, and **Arméni**, where the excursion boats dock. Both have excellent fish tavernas. *Sunset* taverna at Ammoúdhi is recommended, and at Arméni there is a taverna which specializes in grilled octopus lunches. **FINIKIÁ**, 1km east of Ía, is a very quiet and traditional little village. *Lotza Rooms* (☎02860/71 051; ◒) are located in an old house in the middle of the village, while *Hotel Finikia* (☎02860/71 373; ◒), above the village near the main road, is a smarter option. Just north of Ía is **Baxédhes** beach, a quiet alternative to Kamári and Périssa (see opposite), with a few tavernas including the *Paradhisos*, which has good food and reasonable prices.

The east and south

Beaches on Thíra, to the east and south, are bizarre – long black stretches of volcanic sand which get blisteringly hot in the afternoon sun. They're no secret, and in the summer the crowds can be a bit overpowering. Closest to Firá, **MONÓLITHOS** has a couple of tavernas but is nothing special. Further south, **KAMÁRI** has surrendered lock, stock and barrel to the package-tour operators and there's not a piece of sand that isn't fronted by concrete villas. Nonetheless it's quieter and cleaner than most, with some beachfront **accommodation**, including *Hotel Nikolina* (℡02860/31 702; ➋), with basic but cheap rooms towards the southern end of the beach, as well as the *White House* (℡02860/31 441; ➍) and the friendly *Sea Side Rooms* (℡02860/33 403; ➋) further along the beach. *Rose Bay Hotel* (℡02860/33 650; ➎) is a far pricier option, with a pleasant pool setting, set back away from the noisy beach thoroughfare. *Kamari Camping* (℡02860/31 453), a fifteen-minute walk on the road out of Kamári, is a small municipal-run site with limited facilities and no points for a warm welcome.

Psistaria O Kritikos, a taverna-grill frequented by locals rather than tourists, is one of the best places to **eat** on the island. It's a long way out of Kamári on the road up to Messariá, and too far to walk, but the bus stops outside. There are plenty of cafés and restaurants behind the beach, though many are expensive or uninspired. *Saliveros*, in front of the *Hotel Nikolina*, has taverna food at reasonable prices, and *Almira*, next to *Sea Side Rooms*, is a smarter restaurant and only a little more expensive. Kamári is a family resort with little in the way of clubs and nightlife, but there is a good open-air **cinema** near the campsite, and in summer buses run until 1am, so there's no problem getting back to Firá after seeing a film.

Things are scruffier at **PÉRISSA**, around the cape. Because of its attractive situation and abundance of cheap rooms, it's noisy and crowded with backpackers. *Camping Perissa Beach* (℡02860/81 343) is right behind the beach and has plenty of shade but is also next to a couple of noisy late-night bars. There is also a youth hostel on the road into Périssa: *Anna* (℡02860/82 182; €10 per person) has dorm beds as well as a few simple studios closer to the beach. There are plenty of cheap rooms in the same area and some upmarket hotels behind the beach; the modern *Meltemi Hotel* (℡02860/81 325; ➋–➎) is a sensible choice. The beach itself extends almost 7km to the west, sheltered by the occasional tamarisk tree, with beach bars dotted along at intervals; *Wet Stories*, about ten-minutes' walk from Périssa village, has a fun atmosphere and a varied snack selection.

Kamári and Périssa are separated by the Mésa Vounó headland, on which stood **ancient Thíra** (Tues–Sun 9am–3pm), the post-eruption settlement dating from the ninth century BC. Excursion buses go up from Kamári (€15), staying two hours at the site (ask at Kamári Tours behind the beach) but you can walk the **cobbled path** starting from the square in Kamári by the Argo General Store. The path zigzags up to a whitewashed church by a **cave**, containing one of Thíra's few freshwater springs, before crossing over to meet the road and ending at a saddle between Mésa Vounó and Profítis Ilías, where a refreshments van sells expensive drinks. From here, the path to the site passes a chapel dating back to the fourth century AD before skirting round to the Temenos of Artemidoros with bas-relief carvings of a dolphin, eagle and lion representing Poseidon, Zeus and Apollo. Next, the trail follows the sacred way of the ancient city through the remains of the agora and past the theatre. Most of the ruins (dating mainly from Hellenistic and Roman times) are difficult to place, but the site is impressively large and the views are awesome. The site can also be reached by a path from Périssa, and either way it's less than an hour's walk.

Inland along the same mountain spine is the monastery of **Profítis Ilías**, now sharing its refuge with Greek radio and TV pylons and the antennae of a NATO station. With just one monk remaining to look after the church, the place only really comes to life for the annual Profítis Ilías festival, when the whole island troops up here to celebrate. The views are still rewarding, though, and from near the entrance to the monastery an old footpath heads across the ridge in about an hour to ancient Thíra. The easiest ascent is the thirty-minute walk from the village of Pýrgos.

PÝRGOS itself is one of the oldest settlements on the island, a jumble of old houses and alleys that still bear the scars of the 1956 earthquake. It climbs to another Venetian fortress crowned by several churches and you can clamber around the battlements for sweeping views over the entire island and its Aegean neighbours. By way of contrast **MESSARIÁ**, a thirty-minute stroll north, has a skyline consisting solely of massive church domes that lord it over the houses huddled in a ravine.

Akrotíri

Evidence of the Minoan colony that once thrived here has been uncovered at the other ancient site of **Akrotíri** (Tues–Sat 8.30am–3pm; €15), at the south-western tip of the island. Tunnels through the volcanic ash uncovered structures, two and three storeys high, first damaged by earthquake then buried by eruption; Professor Marinatos, the excavator and now an island hero, was killed by a collapsing wall and is also buried on the site. Only a small part of what was the largest Minoan city outside of Crete has been excavated thus far. Lavish frescoes adorned the walls, and Cretan pottery was found stored in a chamber; most of the frescoes are currently exhibited in Athens, though you can see excellent reproductions at the Thira Foundation in Firá (see p.192). Visit early to avoid crowds and heat.

Akrotíri itself can be reached by bus from Firá or Périssa; the excellent *Glaros* taverna, on the way to Kókkini Ámmos beach, has fine food and barrelled wine. Kókkini Ámmos is about 500m from the site and is quite spectacular with high reddish-brown cliffs above sand the same colour (the name means "red sand"). There's a drinks stall in a cave hollowed into the base of the cliff. It's a better beach than the one below the site, but gets crowded in season.

The Kaméni islets and Thirassía

From either Firá or Ía, boat excursions and local ferries run to the charred volcanic islets of **Paleá Kaméni** and **Néa Kaméni**, and on to the relatively unspoiled islet of Thirassía, which was once part of Thíra until shorn off by an eruption in the third century BC. At Paleá Kaméni you can swim from the boat to hot springs with sulphurous mud, and Néa Kaméni, with its own mud-clouded hot springs, features a demanding hike to a volcanically active crater.

The real attraction though, is **Thirassía**, the quietest island in the Cyclades. The views are as dramatic as any on Thíra, and tourism has little effect on island life. The downside is that there is no sandy beach, no nightlife and nowhere to change money.

Most tour boats head for **Kórfos**, a stretch of shingle backed by fishermen's houses and high cliffs. It has a few tavernas, including *Tonio* which stays open when the day-trippers have gone, but no rooms. From Kórfos a stepped path climbs up to **MANOLÁS**, nearly 200m above. Donkeys are still used for transport, and stables can be seen in both villages. Manolás straggles along the edge of the caldera, an untidy but attractive small island village that gives an idea of what Thíra was like before tourism arrived there. It has a bakery, a couple of shops and a few tavernas, including the friendly *Panorama*, that opens only for the midday rush; the **restaurant** at the *Hotel Cavo Mare* (☎02860/29 176; ❹) wins out by giving diners the use of the swimming pool. Dhimítrios Nomikós has **rooms** (☎02860/29 102; ❷) overlooking the village from the south.

The best **excursion** from Manolás is to follow the unmade road heading south; about halfway along you pass the church of Profítis Ilías on a hilltop to the left. From here an old and overgrown trail descends through the deserted caldera-side village of **Kerá**, before running parallel with the road to the **monastery of the Kímisis** above the southern tip of the island. Minoan remains were excavated in a pumice quarry to the west of here in 1867, several years before the first discoveries at Akrotíri, but there is nothing to be seen today.

Ferries run to Thirassía four times a week in season and three times a week through the winter. There is no problem taking a car or rental bike over, but fill up with petrol first. Day-trips take in Néa Kaméni and Paleá Kaméni but are quite expensive (€18) and only stay two or three hours on Thirassía.

Anáfi

A ninety-minute boat ride to the east of Thíra, **Anáfi** is the last stop for ferries and hydrofoils and something of a travellers' dead end, with no longer any high season ferries on to Crete or the Dodecanese. Not that this is likely to bother most of the visitors, who intentionally come here for weeks in midsummer, and take over the island's beaches with a vengeance.

At most other times the place seems idyllic, and indeed may prove too sleepy for some: there are no bona fide hotels, scooters, discos or organized excursions, and donkeys are still the main method of transport in the interior. Anáfi, though initially enchanting, is a harsh place, its mixed granite/limestone core overlaid by volcanic rock spewed out by Thíra's eruptions. Apart from the few olive trees and vines grown in the valleys, the only plants that seem to thrive are prickly pears.

The harbour and Hóra

The tiny harbour hamlet of **ÁYIOS NIKÓLAOS** has a single taverna, *To Akroyiali*, with a few rooms (☎02860/61 218; ❶), while *Dave's Cafe*, with straw umbrellas above the beach, is a colourful English-run drinking spot. Jeyzed Travel (☎02860/61 253, ☏61 352) can provide information as well as issue ferry tickets, change money and book rooms. In August there are enough Greek visitors to fill all the rooms on the island, so it's a good idea to book ahead. Most places to stay are in Hóra. In season a bus runs from the harbour every two hours or so, 9am to 11pm, to stops at both ends of the village.

HÓRA itself, adorning a conical hill overhead, is a stiff, 25-minute climb up the obvious old mule path which shortcuts the modern road. Exposed and blustery when the *meltémi* is blowing, Hóra can initially seem a rather forbidding ghost town. This impression is slowly dispelled as you discover the hospitable islanders taking their coffee in sheltered, south-facing terraces, or under the anti-earthquake barrel vaulting that features in domestic architecture here.

The modern, purpose-built **rooms** run by Kalliopi Halari (☎02860/61 271; ❶) and Voula Loudharou (☎02860/61 279; ❶), and those run by Margarita

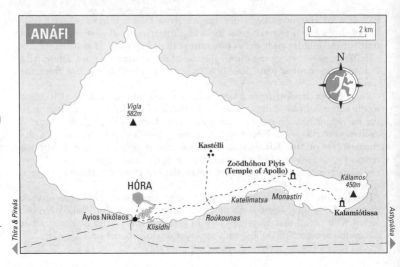

Kollídha (☎02860/61 292; ❷) at the east edge of the village, are about the most comfortable – and boast stunning views south to the islets of Ftená, Pahiá and Makriá, and the distinctive monolith at the southeastern corner of Anáfi. Evening **diners** seem to divide their custom between the simple, welcoming *To Steki*, with reasonable food and barrel wine served on its terrace, and the more upmarket *Alexandhra's* on the central walkway. *Armenaki* is a lively taverna/ouzerí which hosts regular *bouzoúki* nights. Otherwise nightlife revolves around the two bars: *Mylos*, in a converted windmill in the village, and *Mantres* on the main road between the port and Hóra. Several shops, a bakery and a **post office** round up the list of amenities.

East along the coast: beaches and monasteries

The glory of Anáfi is a string of south-facing beaches starting under the cliffs at Áyios Nikólaos. Freelance campers head for **KLISÍDHI**, a short walk to the east of the harbour, which has 200m of tan, gently shelving sand. Above the calamus-and-tamarisk oasis backing the beach there are two cafés and a taverna, including the *Kafestiatorion tis Margaritas*, with popular rooms (☎02860/61 237; ❷). The *Villa Apollon* on the hillside above has the island's most upmarket accommodation (☎02860/61 348; ❷). Klisídhi can be reached by road but it's quicker to take the clifftop path starting behind the power station at the harbour. East of here the beaches can only be reached by foot or boat.

From a point on the paved road just east of Hóra, the **main path** skirting the south flank of the island is signposted "Kastélli – Paleá Hóra – Roúkouna – Monastíri". The primary branch of this trail roller-coasts in and out of several agricultural valleys that provide most of Anáfi's produce and fresh water. Just under an hour along, beside a well, you veer down a side trail to **Roúkounas**, easily the island's best beach, with some 500m of broad sand rising to tamarisk-stabilized dunes, which provide welcome shade. A single taverna, *Tou Papa*, operates up by the main trail in season; the suggestively craggy hill of **Kastélli**, an hour's scramble above the taverna, is the site both of ancient Anáfi and a ruined Venetian castle.

Beyond Roúkounas, it's another half-hour on foot to the first of the exquisite half-dozen **Katelímatsa** coves, of all shapes and sizes, and 45 minutes to **Monastíri** beach – all without facilities, so come prepared. Nudism is banned on Monastíri, because of its proximity to the monasteries.

The monasteries

Between Katelímatsa and Kálamos, the main route keeps inland, past a rare spring, to arrive at the **monastery of Zoödhóhou Piyís**, some two hours out of Hóra. A ruined temple of Apollo is incorporated into the monastery buildings to the side of the main gate; according to legend, Apollo caused Anáfi to rise from the waves, pulling off a dramatic rescue of the storm-lashed Argonauts. The courtyard, with a welcome cistern, is the venue for the island's major festival, celebrated eleven days after Easter. A family of cheesemakers lives next door and can point you up the start of the spectacular onward path to **Kalamiótissa**, a little monastery perched atop the abrupt pinnacle at the extreme southeast of the island. It takes another hour to reach, but is eminently worthwhile for the stunning scenery and views over the entire south coast. Kalamiótissa comes alive only during its September 7–8 festival; at other times, you could haul a sleeping bag up here to witness the amazing sunsets and sunrises, with your vantage point often floating in a sea of cloud. There is no water up here, so bring enough with you. It's a full day's outing from Hóra to Kalamiótissa and back; you might wish to take advantage, in at least one direction, of the excursion **kaïki** that runs from Áyios Nikólaos to Monastíri (6 times daily in high season). There is also a slightly larger mail and supplies boat (currently Mon & Thurs 11am) which takes passengers to and from Thíra (Órmos Athiniós), supplementing the main-line ferries to Pireás.

Travel details

Ferries

Most of the Cyclades are served by main-line ferries from Pireás. Boats for Kéa depart from Lávrio, which will become increasingly important as work proceeds on the new highway to the new international airport at Spáta. There are daily services from Rafína to Ándhros, Tínos and Mýkonos, with less frequent sailings to Sýros, Páros, Náxos and Amorgós, and the north and east Aegean. All three ports are easily reached by bus from Athens. From June to September there are also a few weekly sailings from Thessaloníki to the most popular islands.

The frequency of sailings given below is intended to give an idea of services from April to October, when most visitors tour the islands. During the winter expect departures to be at or below the minimum level listed, with some routes cancelled entirely. Conversely, routes tend to be more comprehensive in spring and autumn, when the government obliges shipping companies to make extra stops to compensate for numbers of boats still in dry dock.

All agents are required to issue computerized

tickets, using a computerized booking system. This was designed to conform to EU regulations and prevent the overcrowding of ferries so common in the past. It means that, in high season, certain popular routes may be booked up days in advance, so if you're visiting a few islands it is important to check availability on arrival in Greece, and book your outward and final pre-flight tickets well ahead. There is not usually so much problem with space between islands as there is to and from Pireás.

Amorgós 6–8 ferries weekly to Náxos and Páros, one of these continuing to Rafína rather than Pireás; 3–4 weekly to Sýros; 2–3 weekly to Tínos and Mýkonos; 2–3 weekly to Ándhros, Koufoníssi, Skhinoússa, Iráklia and Dhonoússa; 2–3 weekly to Astypálea.

Anáfi 6–8 weekly to Pireás (12hr 30min), mostly via Thíra (1hr 30min), Íos, Náxos, Páros; 1 weekly to Sýros, Síkinos and Folégandhros; 2 weekly mail boats to Thíra (2hr).

Ándhros At least 3 daily to Rafína (2hr), Tínos (2hr) and Mýkonos; 4 weekly to Sýros; 2 weekly to

Amorgós and Náxos; 1–4 weekly to Paros.

Dhonoússa 3–4 weekly to Amorgós; 2–3 weekly to Náxos, Koufoníssi, Skhinoússa, Iráklia and Páros; 1 weekly to Pireás, Mýkonos, Tínos and Sýros; 2 weekly to Astypálea.

Íos At least 3 daily to Pireás (10hr), Páros (5hr), Náxos (3hr) and Thíra (several of which continue to Anáfi); 4–5 weekly to Síkinos and Folégandhros; 1 weekly to Crete; 1 weekly to Mílos, Kímolos, Sérifos and Sífnos; 2–3 weekly to Sýros and Kássos; daily to Mýkonos.

Kéa 1–3 daily to Lávrio (1hr 30min); 4 weekly to Kýthnos; 2 weekly to Sýros.

Kímolos 2 daily kaïkia to Mílos (Pollónia) year-round, 5 in summer; 2–5 weekly to Mílos (Adhámas), Sífnos, Sérifos, Kýthnos and Pireás (7hr); 2 weekly to Folégandhros, Síkinos and Thíra.

Koufoníssi, Skhinoússa, Iráklia 2–3 weekly to Náxos; 1–2 weekly to Páros, Sýros and Tínos and Mýkonos; 1 weekly to Dhonoússa, Amorgós and Pireás.

Kýthnos 4–12 weekly to Pireás (3hr 15min); 4–10 weekly to Sérifos, Sífnos, Kímolos and Mílos; 3–4 weekly to Thíra and Folégandhros; 1–2 weekly to Síkinos, Sýros, Íos and Kéa.

Mílos At least daily to Pireás (8hr); Thurs–Sat to Sífnos (2hr), Sérifos and Kýthnos; 2–5 daily kaïkia or 4–6 weekly ferries to Kímolos; 2–3 weekly to Folégandhros, Síkinos, Íos and Thíra; 2 weekly to Sýros; 2 weekly to Crete (Iráklion or Sitía); 2 weekly to Kássos and Kárpathos; 1 weekly to Hálki and Rhodes.

Mýkonos At least 2 daily to Pireás (5hr), Rafína (3hr 30min), Tínos (1hr), Ándhros (2hr 30min) and Sýros (2hr); 2–3 weekly to Amorgós; 2 weekly to Crete (Iráklion), Skiáthos and Thessaloníki; 1–2 weekly to Dhonoússa, Koufoníssi, Skhinoússa and Iráklia; 1 weekly to Pátmos and Foúrni; 3–4 weekly to Ikaría and Sámos; daily to Íos, Náxos and Páros; daily (except Mon) excursion boats to Delos.

Náxos At least 3 daily to Pireás (8hr), Páros (1hr), Íos and Thíra; 6–8 weekly to Sýros; 5–7 weekly to Amorgós; 3 weekly to Crete (Iráklion); 5–6 weekly to Amorgós; 4–5 weekly to Tínos; 5 weekly to Síkinos and Folégandhros; 2 weekly to Ándhros and Rafína; 3 weekly to Anáfi; 3–4 weekly to Rhodes; 2–4 weekly to Ikaría and Sámos; 4 weekly to Astypálea; 1–2 weekly to Kássos and Kárpathos; 1 weekly to Kós and Foúrni; 2–3 weekly to Skiáthos and Thessaloníki; 3–4 weekly to Iráklia, Skhinoússa, Koufoníssi and Dhonoússa.

Páros At least 3 daily to Pireás (7hr), Andíparos, Náxos, Íos, Thíra; 6–8 weekly to Sýros and Tínos; 4

weekly to Iráklion (Crete); 3–4 weekly to Ikaría and Sámos; 4–6 weekly to Síkinos, Folégandhros and Amorgós; 4 weekly to Rafína and Ándhros; 2–3 weekly to Skiáthos and Thessaloníki; daily to Rhodes; 4–6 weekly to Anáfi; 1–2 weekly to Foúrni, Kós, Kássos and Kárpathos; 4 weekly to Astypálea; 2–4 weekly to Koufoníssi, Iráklia and Dhonoússa; 1 weekly to Vólos; 1 weekly to Pátmos and Kálymnos; 3–6 weekly to Ikaría and Sámos; at least 1 daily to Mýkonos; at least hourly (from Pariklá) to Andíparos in summer, dropping to 3 weekly in winter. There is also a car ferry from Poúnda to Andíparos at least hourly throughout the year.

Sérifos and Sífnos 5–12 weekly to Pireás (4hr 30min), Kýthnos and each other; 5–10 weekly to Mílos; 2–5 weekly to Kímolos; 2–3 weekly to Folégandhros, Síkinos and Thíra; once weekly to Íos; 2 weekly to Sýros; 1–2 weekly to Crete from Sífnos only; twice weekly from Sífnos to Páros.

Síkinos and Folégandhros 6 weekly between each other, and to Pireás (10hr); 2 weekly to Sýros, Kýthnos, Sérifos, Sífnos, Mílos and Kímolos; 3–6 weekly to Íos, Thíra, Páros and Náxos.

Sýros At least 2 daily to Pireás (4hr), Tínos (1hr), Mýkonos (2hr), Náxos and Páros; at least 2 weekly to Rafína (3hr 30min) and Ándhros; 3 weekly to Amorgós and the islets behind Náxos; 2–4 weekly to Íos and Thíra; 1 weekly to Síkinos and Folégandhros; 3 weekly to Ikaría, Sámos and Astypálea; 2 weekly to Kéa, Kýthnos, Sérifos, Sífnos, Mílos and Kímolos; 1 weekly to Pátmos, Léros and Lipsí; 2–4 weekly to Skiáthos and Thessaloníki.

Thíra At least 3 daily to Pireás (10–12hr), Páros, Íos and Náxos; 5–6 weekly to Iráklion, Crete (5hr) and Thessaloníki; 6–8 weekly to Síkinos and Folégandhros; 4–6 weekly to Anáfi and Sífnos; daily to Mýkonos; 6–8 weekly to Sýros; 3–5 weekly to Tínos and Skiáthos; 2–4 weekly to Milos and Kímolos; 1–2 weekly to Kárpathos, Kássos and Sérifos; 2 weekly to Rhodes; 1 weekly to Vólos; 4–6 weekly to Thirassía (plus lots of expensive daily excursion boats in season); 2 weekly mail boats to Anáfi.

Tínos At least 2 daily to Pireás (5hr), Rafína (4hr), Ándhros, Sýros and Mýkonos; 3–4 weekly to Páros and Náxos; 3 weekly to Thíra and Iráklion (Crete); 2–4 weekly to Skiáthos and Thessaloníki; 3 weekly to Amorgós; 1 weekly to Íos, Koufoníssi, Skhinoússa, Iráklia and Dhonoússa; also excursion boats calling at Delos and Mýkonos, 1 daily except Mon.

Other services

To simplify the lists above, certain strategic hydrofoil and small-boat services have been omitted. Of these, the *Express Skopelitis* plies daily in season between Mýkonos and Amorgós, spending each night at the latter and threading through all of the minor isles between it and Náxos, as well as Náxos and Páros (Píso Livádhi), in the course of a week; however, it's unreliable and often overcrowded. The *Seajet* catamaran – a small-capacity (and expensive) jet-boat (☎ 010 41 41 250 for details) – operates daily during summer out of Rafína and connects Sýros, Ándhros, Tínos,

Mýkonos, Páros, Náxos and Thíra. Cycladic routes are pretty well mapped out by the three hydrofoil companies – Hellas Flying Dolphins, Speed Lines and Cruises (Santorini Dolphin) and Dolphin Sea Line, with regular services from Zéa (Pireás), Thíra and Rafína respectively. Hydrofoil travel is expensive; however, when time is an issue, or for more regular connections to some of the less commonly serviced routes such as the minor islets around Náxos, these handy flying machines are a welcome addition to the conventional fleet.

Flights

There are airports on Páros, Mýkonos, Thíra, Sýros, Mílos and Náxos. In season, or during storms when ferries are idle, you have little chance of getting a seat with Olympic Airways at less than three days' notice. Olympic's Athens–Milos route is probably the best value for money, but it's usually booked by the island's mining executives; the other destinations seem deliberately overpriced, in a usually unsuccessful attempt to keep passenger volume manageable. Axon & Aegean-Cronus have summer flights to Thíra and Mýkonos. Expect off-season (Oct–April) frequencies to drop by at least eighty percent.
Flights are on Olympic unless otherwise stated.

Athens–Mílos (1–2 daily; 45min)
Athens–Mýkonos (5–6 daily on Olympic; 2–3 daily on Axon; 45min)
Athens–Náxos (6 weekly; 45min)
Athens–Páros (3–4 daily; 45min)
Athens–Sýros (6 weekly on Olympic; 35min)
Athens–Thíra (5–6 daily on Olympic; 3 daily on Axon & Aegean-Cronus; 50min)
Mýkonos–Rhodes (2 weekly; 1hr)
Mýkonos–Thessaloníki (3 weekly; 1hr 15min)
Mýkonos–Thíra (3–7 weekly; 30min)
Thíra–Iráklion (Crete) (2 weekly; 40min)
Thíra–Rhodes (3–6 weekly; 1hr)
Thíra–Thessaloníki (3 weekly; 1hr 30min)

3

Crete

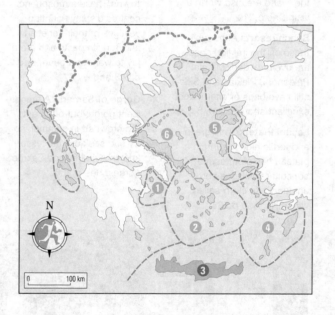

N

0   100 km

CHAPTER 3 # Highlights

* **Archeological Museum, Iráklion** The world's foremost Minoan museum. See p.213

* **Minoan Sites** Knossós is the most exciting, but Mália, Festós, Zákros and other archeological ruins across the island are also worth a visit. See p.219

* **Beach resorts** Although those on the Iráklion coast are overcrowded, Mátala, Paleohóra, Plakiás and Sitía still have bags of charm and excellent strands. See p.226

* **Lasíthi Plateau** This green and fertile high mountain plateau has picturesque agricultural villages and unique white cloth-sailed windmills. See p.236

* **The Dhiktean cave** Stunningly situated on the Lasíthi Plateau, and, like many Cretan caves, has ancient historical connections. See p.237

* **Haniá and Réthymnon old towns** These atmospheric centres display haunting vestiges of their Venetian and Turkish pasts and are a joy to wander around. See p.248 and p.257

* **Gorge of Samariá** A magnificent gorge, but often gets too crowded in summer, so try and seek out the lesser-known Ayía Iríni and Zákros gorges. See p.266

Crete

C rete (Kríti) is a great deal more than just another Greek island. In many places, especially in the cities or along the developed north coast, it doesn't feel like an island at all, but rather a substantial land in its own right – a mountainous, wealthy and surprisingly cosmopolitan one. But when you lose yourself among the mountains, or on the lesser-known coastal reaches of the south, it has everything you could want of a Greek island and more: great beaches, remote hinterlands and hospitable people.

In **history**, Crete is distinguished above all as the home of Europe's earliest civilization. It was only at the beginning of the twentieth century that the legends of King Minos and of a Cretan society that ruled the Greek world in prehistory were confirmed by excavations at **Knossós** and **Festós**. Yet the **Minoans** had a remarkably advanced society, the centre of a maritime trading empire as early as 2000 BC. The artworks produced on Crete at this time are unsurpassed anywhere in the ancient world, and it seems clear that life on Crete in those days was good. This apparently peaceful culture survived at least three major natural disasters. Each time the palaces were destroyed, and each time they were rebuilt on a grander scale. Only after the last destruction, probably the result of an eruption of Thíra (Santoríni) and subsequent tidal waves and earthquakes, do significant numbers of weapons begin to appear in the ruins. This, together with the appearance of the Greek language, has been interpreted to mean that Mycenaean Greeks had taken control of the island. Nevertheless, for nearly five-hundred years, by far the longest period of peace the island has seen, Crete was home to a culture well ahead of its time.

Accommodation price codes

Throughout the book we've categorized accommodation according to the following **price codes**, which denote the cheapest available double room in high season. All prices are for the room only, except where otherwise indicated. Many hotels, especially those in category ❹ and over, include breakfast in the price; you'll need to check this when booking. During low season, rates can drop by more than fifty percent, especially if you are staying for three or more nights. Exceptions are during the Christmas and Easter weeks when you'll pay high-season prices. Single rooms, where available, cost around seventy percent of the price of a double.

❶ Up to €24
❷ €24–33
❸ €34–42

❹ €43–58
❺ €59–72
❻ €73 and upwards

Note: Youth hostels typically charge €7–9 for a dormitory bed.
For more accommodation details, see pp.52–54.

The Minoans of Crete probably came originally from Anatolia; at their height they maintained strong links with Egypt and with the people of Asia Minor, and this position as meeting point and strategic fulcrum between east and west has played a major role in Crete's subsequent history. Control of the island passed from Greeks to Romans to Saracens, through the Byzantine empire to Venice, and finally to Turkey for more than two centuries. During World War II, the island was **occupied** by the Germans and attained the dubious distinction of being the first place to be successfully invaded by paratroops.

Today, with a flourishing **agricultural economy**, Crete is one of the few islands which could probably support itself without tourists. Nevertheless, **tourism** is heavily promoted. The northeast coast in particular is overdeveloped, and though there are parts of the south and west coasts that have not been spoiled, they are getting harder to find. By contrast, the high mountains of the interior are still barely touched, and one of the best things to do on Crete is to **rent a vehicle** and explore the remoter villages.

Where to go

Every part of Crete has its loyal devotees and it's hard to pick out highlights, but generally if you want to get away from it all you should head west, towards **Haniá** and the smaller, less well-connected places along the south and west coasts. It is in this part of the island that the White Mountains rise, while below them yawns the famous **Samarian Gorge**. The **far east**, around **Sitía**, is also relatively unscathed with a string of isolated beaches worth seeking out to the south of the over-popular **Väï beach**, which lures crowds attracted by its famous palm grove. However, Sitía's new international airport, currently under construction, could change things significantly here in the next few years.

Whatever you do, your first main priority will probably be to leave **Iráklion** (Heraklion) as quickly as possible, having paid the obligatory, and rewarding, visit to the **Archeological Museum** and nearby **Knossós**. The other great Minoan sites cluster around the middle of the island: **Festós** and **Ayía Triádha** to the south (with Roman **Górtys** to provide contrast), and **Mália** on the north coast. Almost wherever you go you'll find a reminder of the island's history, whether it's the town of **Gourniá** near the cosmopolitan resort of **Áyios Nikólaos**, the exquisitely sited palace of **Zákros** in the far east, or the lesser sites scattered around the west. Unexpected highlights include Crete's Venetian forts at **Réthymnon** and **Frangokástello**; its hundreds of frescoed Byzantine churches, most famously at **Kritsá**; and, at Réthymnon and Haniá, the cluttered old Venetian and Turkish quarters.

Climate

Crete has by far the longest summers in Greece, and you can get a decent tan here right into October and swim at least from May until November. The one seasonal blight is the *meltémi*, a northerly wind which regularly blows harder here and more continuously than anywhere else in Greece – the best of several reasons for avoiding an **August** visit if you can. It's far from an ill wind, however, as it also lowers humidity and makes the island's higher summer temperatures more bearable.

Iráklion, Knossós and central Crete

Many visitors to Crete arrive in the island's capital, **Iráklion** (Heraklion), but it's not an outstandingly beautiful city, nor one where you'll want to stay much longer than it takes to visit the **Archeological Museum** and nearby **Knossós**. Iráklion itself, though it has its good points – superb fortifications, a fine market, atmospheric old alleys and some interesting lesser museums – is for the most part an experience in survival: despite a recent makeover of central areas by the city hall it remains modern, raucous, traffic-laden and overcrowded.

The area immediately around the city is less touristy than you might expect, mainly because there are few decent beaches of any size on this central part of the coast. To the west, mountains drop straight into the sea virtually all the way to Réthymnon, with just two significant coastal settlements: **Ayía Pelayía**, a sizeable resort, and **Balí**, which is gradually becoming one. Eastwards, the main resorts are at least 30km away, at **Hersónissos** and beyond, although there is a string of rather unattractive developments all the way there. Inland, there's agricultural country, some of the richest on the island, a cluster of Crete's better vineyards, and a series of wealthy but rather dull villages. Directly behind the capital rises **Mount Ioúktas** with its characteristic profile of Zeus; to the west the Psilorítis massif spreads around the peak of **Mount Psilorítis** (Ídha) the island's highest mountain. On the south coast there are few roads and little development of any kind, except at **Ayía Galíni** in the southwest, a nominal fishing village long since swamped with tourists, and **Mátala**, which has thrown out the hippies that made it famous and is now crowded with package-trippers. **Léndas** has to some extent occupied Mátala's old niche.

Despite the lack of resorts, there seem constantly to be thousands of people trekking back and forth across the centre of the island. This is largely because of the superb archeological sites in the south: **Festós**, second of the Minoan palaces, with its attendant villa at **Ayía Triádha**, and **Górtys**, capital of Roman Crete.

Iráklion

The best way to approach **IRÁKLION** is by sea: that way you see the city as it should be seen, with Mount Ioúktas rising behind and the Psilorítis range to the west. As you get closer, it's the city walls that first stand out, still dominating and fully encircling the oldest part of town; finally you sail in past the great Venetian **fort** defending the harbour entrance. Unfortunately, big ships no longer dock in the old port but at great modern concrete wharves alongside, which neatly sums up Iráklion itself. Many of the old parts have been restored from the bottom up, but they're of no relevance to the bustle and noise that characterizes much of the city today. In recent times, however, Iráklion's administrators have been giving belated attention to dealing with some of the image problems, and large tracts of the centre – particularly the focal Platía Eleftherías – have been landscaped and refurbished with the aim of presenting a less daunting prospect to the visitor.

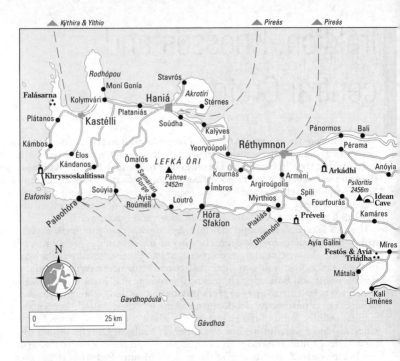

Orientation, arrival and information

Virtually everything you're likely to want to see in Iráklion lies within the walled city, and even here the majority falls into a relatively small sector – the northeastern corner. The most vital thoroughfare, **25-Avgoústou**, links the harbour with the commercial city centre. At the bottom it is lined with shipping and travel agencies and rental outlets, but further up these give way to banks, restaurants and stores. **Platía Venizélou** (or Fountain Square), off to the right, is crowded with cafés and restaurants; behind Venizélou lies **El Greco Park** (actually a rather cramped garden), with more bars, while on the opposite side of 25-Avgoústou are some of the more interesting of Iráklion's older buildings. Further up 25-Avgoústou, **Kalokerinoú** leads down to Haniá Gate and westwards out of the city; straight ahead, **Odhós–1821** is a major shopping street, and adjacent 1866 is given over to the animated **market**. To the left, Dhikeosínis heads for the city's main square, **Platía Eleftherías**, paralleled by the touristy pedestrian alley, Dedhálou, the direct link between the two squares. The newly revamped Eleftherías is very much the traditional centre of the city, both for traffic – which swirls around it constantly – and for life in general; it is ringed by more expensive tourist cafés and restaurants and comes alive in the evening with crowds of strolling locals.

Points of arrival

Iráklion **airport** is right on the coast, 4km east of the city. **Bus** #1 leaves for Platía Eleftherías every few minutes from the car park in front of the terminal; buy your ticket (€0.55) at the booth before boarding. There are also plenty of **taxis** outside (which you'll be forced to use when the buses stop at 11pm), and prices to major destinations are posted here and in the domestic departures hall

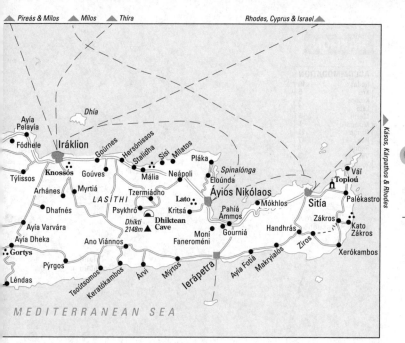

– it's about €4 to the centre of town. Get an agreement on the fare before taking a cab and beware if the driver extols the virtues of a particular place to stay and offers to drop you there – he'll usually be getting a kickback from the proprietors. To avoid such hassles ask to be dropped at the central Platía Eleftherías, from where everything is in easy walking distance.

There are three main **bus stations** and a small terminus. Services along the coastal highway to or from the **east** (Mália, Áyios Nikólaos, Ierápetra, Sitía and so on) use the terminal just off the main road between the ferry dock and the Venetian harbour; the #2 local bus to Knossós runs from the city bus stop, adjacent to the east bus station. Main road services **west** (Réthymnon and Haniá) leave from a terminal close to the east bus station on the other side of the road. Buses for the **southwest** (Festós, Mátala or Ayía Galíni) and along the inland roads west (Týlissos, Anóyia) operate out of a terminal just outside Haniá Gate, a very long walk from the centre along Kalokerinoú (or jump on any bus heading down this street). From the wharves where the **ferries** dock, the city rises directly ahead in steep tiers. If you're heading for the centre, for the archeological museum or the tourist office, cut straight up the stepped alleys behind the bus station onto Dhoúkos Bofór and to Platía Eleftherías; this will take about fifteen minutes. For accommodation though, and to get a better idea of the layout of Iráklion's main attractions, it's simplest to follow the main roads by a rather more roundabout route. Head west along the coast, past the major eastbound bus station and on by the Venetian harbour before cutting up towards the centre on 25-Avgoústou.

Information

Iráklion's **tourist office** has had its hours cut to weekdays only (Mon–Fri 8.30am–5pm; ☎0810/228 225, ℉226 020) and is located just below Platía

IRÁKLION

ACCOMMODATION
Hellas	10
Kris	5
Kronos	1
Lato	2
Marin	8
Mirabello	6
Olympic	11
Rea	7
Rodos	9
Vergina	3
Youth Hostel	4

S. VENIZELOU

SKORDHILON

ODHOS 1878

St Andrew's Bastion

Priouli Fountain

SAVATHIANON

SFAKION

MAKARIOU

DEDHIOHAKI

KALOKERINOU

AYION DHEKA

PLATIA EKATERINIS

Áyios Minas

Cathedral

Pantokratóros Bastion

Pórta Hanión

PLASTIRA

KARDIOTISSIS

South/West Bus Station

62 MARTYRON

TOMBAZI

YIANIKOU

THERISSOU

ROMANOU

PLASTIRA

THENON

Kazantzakis' Tomb

N

KONDILAKI

Martinengo Bastion

0   250 m

◄ Haniá & Festós

Haniá & Festós

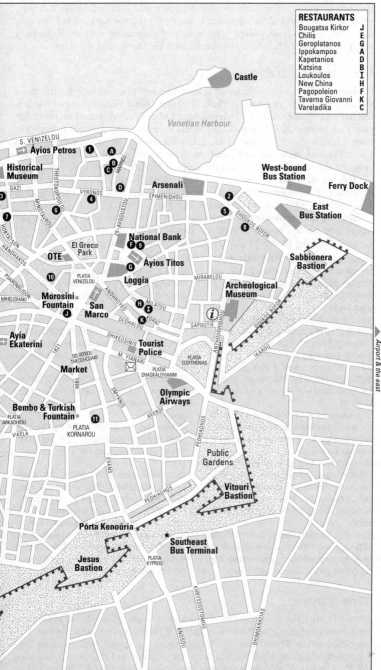

RESTAURANTS

Bougatsa Kirkor	**J**
Chilis	**E**
Geroplatanos	**G**
Ippokampos	**A**
Kapetanios	**D**
Katsina	**B**
Loukoulos	**I**
New China	**H**
Pagopoleion	**F**
Taverna Giovanni	**K**
Vareladika	**C**

Castle

Venetian Harbour

S. VENIZELOU

Áyios Petros ❶ Ⓐ

Historical Museum

GAZI

THEOTOKOPOULOU

MARINELI

Ⓑ
Ⓒ

VYRONOS

Ⓓ

Arsenáli

EPIMENIDHOU

❷

DHOUKOS BOFOR

West-bound Bus Station

Ferry Dock

East Bus Station

❺

❽

MINOTAVROU

MAVROU

HORTATSON

HANDHAKOS

25-AVGHOUSTOU

El Greco Park

OTE

PSAROMILIGON

MIHELIDHAKI

❶❷

National Bank

Ⓕ ❾

Áyios Títos

Ⓖ

Loggia

MIRABELOU

Sabbionera Bastion

Archeological Museum

Morosini Fountain

Ⓙ

San Marco

ANDHROVED

DEDHALOU

Ⓗ

Ⓚ

MILATOU

KORAI

ⓘ

SAPOUTIE

ANTHOUDHIDHOU

DHOUKOS BOFOR

Ayía Ekateríni

1821

OD. FOTIOU THEODHOSAKI

M. YIANARI

DHIKEOSINIS

Tourist Police

Market

1866

SMYRNIS

PLATIA DHASKALOYIANNI

PLATIA ELEFTHERIAS

IKAROU

Bembo & Turkish Fountain

PLATIA ARKADHIOU

VIKELA

❶❶

PLATIA KORNAROU

Olympic Airways

AVEROF

PEDHIADHOS

EVANS

Public Gardens

PEDHIADHOS

Vitouri Bastion

Pórta Kenoúria

★

Southeast Bus Terminal

PLATIA KYPROU

Jesus Bastion

KHRYSOSTOMOU

KNOSOU

DHIMOKRATIAS

Airport & the east

▼ *Knossós & Natural History Museum*

Eleftherías, opposite the Archeological Museum at Zanthoudhídhou 1. A sub-office at the **airport** (April–Sept daily 9am–9pm) is good for basic information and maps. The **tourist police** – more helpful than most – are at Dhikeosínis 10 (℡0810/283 190), halfway between Platía Eleftherías and the market.

Accommodation

Finding a **room** can be difficult in season. The best place to look for inexpensive rooms is in the area around Platía Venizélou, along Hándhakos and towards the harbour to the west of 25-Avgoústou. Other concentrations of affordable places are around El Greco park and in the streets above the Venetian harbour. Better hotels mostly lie closer to Platía Eleftherías, to the south of Platía Venizélou and near the east- and westbound bus stations. The dusty park between the main bus station and the harbour is often crowded with the sleeping bags of those who failed to find, or couldn't afford, a room; however, the police are far less tolerant to rough sleepers these days, and while crashing here is a possibility, a pleasant environment it certainly is not.

There are no **campsites** near Iráklion. The nearest sites both lie to the east of the city: *Creta Camping* at Káto Goúves (℡08970/41 400), 16km east, and *Caravan Camping* (℡08970/22 025) at Hersónissos, 28km east.

Hellas, Hándhakos 24 ℡0810/288 851, ℱ284 442. Hostel-type place with simple doubles, and dormitory rooms (€6 per bed) favoured by younger travellers. Also has a roof garden and snack bar. ❶

Kris, Dhoúkos Bofór 2, near the Venetian harbour ℡0810/223 944. Apartment-style rooms with kitchenette, fridge, great balcony views and friendly female proprietor. ❸

Kronos, Agaráthou 2, west of 25-Avgoústou ℡0810/282 240, ℱ285 853. Pleasant, friendly and modern hotel with sea view and baths in all rooms. ❷

Lato, Epomenídhou 15 ℡0810/228 103, ℱ240 350. Stylish and luxurious hotel where the air-con rooms have minibar, TV and sea view balcony with breakfast included. ❺

Marin, Dhoúkos Bofór 10 ℡0810/224 736, ℱ224 730. Comfortable and good-value rooms with bath, overlooking the Venetian harbour; get a balcony room at the front for a great view. Very convenient for the bus stations and the Archeological Museum. ❸

Mirabello, Theotokopoúlou 20 ℡0810/285 052, ℱ225 852, ℮mirabhot@otenet.gr. Good-value, family-run place with some rooms en-suite in a quiet street close to El Greco Park. ❷–❸

Olympic, Platía Kornárou ℡0810/288 861, ℱ222 512. Overlooking the busy platía and the famous Bembo and Turkish fountains. One of the many hotels built in the 1960s, but one of the few that has been refurbished; rates include breakfast. ❹

Rea, Kalimeráki 1 ℡0810/223 638, ℱ242 189. A friendly, comfortable and clean pension in a quiet street. Some rooms with washbasin, others with own shower. ❶

Pension Rodos, Platía Áyios Títos ℡0810/228 519. Homely and clean no-frills doubles and triples on a picturesque square with a great breakfast bar next door. ❶

Vergina, Hortátson 32 ℡0810/242 739. Basic but pleasant rooms with washbasins in a quiet street and set around a courtyard with a giant banana tree. ❶

Youth Hostel, Výronos 5 ℡0810/286 281, ℱ222 947. Formerly Iraklíon's official youth hostel, it has been stripped of its HI status. It is in fact a good place to stay, family run and very friendly and helpful. There's plenty of space and some beds (albeit illegal) on the roof if you fancy sleeping out under the stars. Private rooms (€13.50) as well as dormitories (€5.90 per bed); hot showers, breakfast and other meals available.

The Town

From the port, the town rises overhead, and you can cut up the stepped alleys for a direct approach to Platía Eleftherías (Liberty Square) and the Archeological Museum. The easiest way to the middle of things, though, is to head west along the coast road, past the main bus stations and the *arsenáli*, and then up 25-Avgoústou, which leads into Platía Venizélou. This is crowded with

Iraklian youth patronizing outdoor cafés (marginally cheaper than those on Eleftherías), and with travellers who've arranged to meet in "Fountain Square". The recently restored **Morosini Fountain** itself is not particularly spectacular at first glance, but on closer inspection is really a very beautiful work; it was built by Venetian governor Francesco Morosini in the seventeenth century, incorporating four lions which were some three hundred years old even then. From the platía you can strike up Dhedhálou, a pedestrianized street full of tourist shops and restaurants, or continue on 25-Avgoústou to a major traffic junction. To the right, Kalokerinoú leads west out of the city, the market lies straight ahead, and Platía Eleftherías is a short walk to the left up Dhikeosínis.

Platía Eleftherías and the Archeological Museum

The recently revamped **Platía Eleftherías**, with seats shaded by palms and eucalyptuses is very much the traditional heart of the city: traffic swirls around it constantly, and on summer evenings strolling hordes jam its expensive cafés and restaurants. Most of Iráklion's more expensive shops are in the streets leading off the platía.

The **Archeological Museum** (Mon noon–7pm, Tues–Sun 8am–7pm; €4.40) is nearby, directly opposite the OTE office. Almost every important prehistoric and Minoan find on Crete is included in this fabulous, if bewilderingly large, collection. The museum tends to be crowded, especially when a guided tour stampedes through, but it's worth taking time over. You can't hope to see everything, nor can we attempt to describe it all (several good museum guides are sold here; the best probably being the glossy one by J.A. Sakellarakis), but highlights include the **mosaics** in Room 2 (the galleries are arranged basically in chronological order), the famous **inscribed disc** from Festós in Room 3 (itself the subject of several books), most of Room 4, especially the magnificent bull's head **rhyton** (drinking vessel), the **jewellery** in Room 6 (and elsewhere) and the engraved **black vases** in Room 7. Save some of your time and energy for upstairs, where the **Hall of the Frescoes**, with intricately reconstructed fragments of the wall paintings from Knossós and other sites, is especially wonderful.

The Archeological Museum's renovation

A long-overdue **renovation** of the archeological museum is planned to begin in the near future which, once completed, should place it in the forefront of museum design in Greece. New buildings are planned to house the administration offices, freeing up more space for exhibits, and a new subterranean floor is to be excavated beneath the museum to stage special exhibitions.

Preliminary soundings for the latter section have – perhaps predictably – uncovered the remains of a **Roman villa**, a **Venetian aqueduct** as well as the remnants of a **Franciscan monastery**, all of which previously occupied the site at different times. These will need to be properly investigated before any work can begin, thus making any starting or completion dates difficult to forecast. A further brake on the timetable at the time of writing is a government freeze applied to all public expenditure not directly connected with the staging of the Olympics in 2004. When work does get under way and while it is in progress, there will inevitably be some frustration for visitors as rooms are closed and items moved around. All this means that our account may not be entirely accurate, but it should still be possible to identify the major exhibits in the collection without too much difficulty.

△ Archeological Museum, Iráklion, Crete

Walls and fortifications

The massive **Venetian walls**, in places up to fifteen metres thick, are the most obvious evidence of Iráklion's later history. Though their fabric is incredibly well preserved, access is virtually nonexistent. It is possible, just, to walk along them from St Andrew's Bastion over the sea in the west, as far as the Martinengo Bastion where lies the **tomb of Nikos Kazantzakis**, Cretan author of *Zorba the Greek*, whose epitaph reads: "I believe in nothing, I hope for nothing, I am free." At weekends, Iraklians gather here to pay their respects and enjoy a free view of the soccer matches played by one of the city's two team's in the stadium below. If the walls seem altogether too much effort, the **port fortifications** are very much easier to see. Stroll out along the jetty (crowded with courting couples after dark) and you can get inside the sixteenth-century **castle** (Tues–Sat 8.30am–3pm, Sun 10am–3pm; €1.50, students €0.60) at the harbour entrance, emblazoned with the Venetian Lion of St Mark. Standing atop this, you can begin to understand how Iráklion (or Candia as it was known until the seventeenth century) withstood a 22-year siege before finally falling to the Ottomans. On the landward side of the port, the Venetian **arsenáli** (arsenals) can also be seen, their arches rather lost amid the concrete road system all around.

Churches and other museums

From the harbour, 25-Avgoústou will take you up past most of the rest of what's interesting. The **church of Áyios Títos**, on the left as you approach Platía Venizélou, borders a pleasant little platía. Byzantine in origin but substantially rebuilt by the Venetians, it looks magnificent principally because, like most of the churches here, it was adapted by the Turks as a mosque and only reconsecrated in 1925; consequently it has been renovated on numerous occasions. On the top side of this platía, abutting 25-Avgoústou, is the Venetian **city hall** with its famous loggia, again almost entirely rebuilt. Just above this, facing Platía Venizélou, is the **church of San Marco**, its steps usually crowded with the overflow of people milling around in the platía. Neither of these last two buildings has found a permanent role in its refurbished state, but both are generally open to house some kind of exhibition or craft show.

Slightly away from the obvious city-centre circuit, but still within the bounds of the walls, there are a couple of lesser museums worth seeing if you have the time. First of these is the excellent collection of **icons** in the **church of Ayía Ekateríni** (Mon–Fri 9.30am–2.30pm; €1.50), an ancient building just below the undistinguished cathedral, off Kalokerinoú. The finest here are six large scenes by Mihaïl Damaskinos (a near-contemporary of El Greco) who fused Byzantine and Renaissance influences. Supposedly both Damaskinos and El Greco studied at Ayía Ekateríni in the sixteenth century, when it functioned as a sort of monastic art school.

The **Historical Museum** (Mon–Fri 9am–5pm, Sat 9am–2pm; €3) is some way from here, down near the waterfront opposite the stark *Xenia* hotel. Its display of folk costumes and jumble of local memorabilia includes the reconstructed studies of both Nikos Kazantzakis and Emanuel Tsouderos (the latter both Cretan statesman and former Greek prime minister). There's enough variety to satisfy just about anyone, including the only El Greco painting on Crete, *View of Mount Sinai and the Monastery of St Catherine*.

A new **Natural History Museum** (June–Sept daily 9am–7pm; Oct–May Mon–Fri 9am–3pm, Sun 10am–6pm; €4.40, concessions €1.50; ⓦ www.nhmc.uoc.gr) is definitely worth the trek out to visit it. Covering three floors, as well as the usual flora and fauna displays, it has exhibits detailing the island's geological evolution, the arrival of man and the environment as it would have appeared to the Minoans. The museum lies 2km south of the Pórta Kenoúria (a gate in the walls) along the road to Knossós. Bus #2 from Platía Eleftherías will drop you there (ask for the "Pagritio School" stop) or take a taxi (about €2.50).

The beaches

Iráklion's **beaches** are some way out, whether east or west of town. In either direction they're easily accessible by bus: #6 heads west from the stop outside the *Astoria* hotel in Platía Eleftherías; #7 east from the stop opposite this, under the trees in the centre of the platía.

Almyrós (or Ammoudhári) to the west has been subjected to a degree of development, comprising a campsite, several medium-size hotels and one giant one (the *Zeus Beach*, in the shadow of the power station at the far end), which makes the beach hard to get to without walking through or past something built up.

Amnissós, to the east, is the better choice, with several tavernas and the added amusement of planes swooping in immediately overhead to land. This is where most locals go on their afternoons off; the furthest of the beaches is the best, although new hotels are encroaching here, too. Little remains here to indicate the once-flourishing port of Knossós aside from a rather dull, fenced-in dig. If you're seriously into antiquities, however, you'll find a more rewarding site in the small Minoan villa, known as **Nírou Háni** (Tues–Sun 8.30am–3pm; free) at Háni Kokkíni, the first of the full-blown resort developments east of Iráklion.

Eating

Big city as it is, Iráklion disappoints when it comes to eating. The cafés and tavernas of platías **Venizélou** and **Eleftherías** are essential places to sit and watch the world pass, but their food is expensive and mediocre. One striking exception is *Bougatsa Kirkor*, by the Morosini fountain in Venizélou, where you can sample authentic Cretan *bougátsa* – a creamy cheese pie sprinkled with sugar and cinnamon; alternatively, try a plate of *loukoumádhes* (dough fritters), available from a number of cafés (*Aktarika* is good) near the junction of Dhikeosínis and 25-Avgoústou. The cafés and tavernas on **Dhedhálou**, the pedestrian alley linking the two main platías, are very run of the mill, with persistent waiters enticing you in with faded photographs of what appears to be food.

A more atmospheric option is to head for the little alley, **Fotíou Theodhosáki**, which runs through from the market to Odhós Evans. It is entirely lined with the tables of rival taverna owners, certainly authentic and catering for market traders and their customers as well as tourists. Compared with some, they often look a little grimy, but they are by no means cheap, which can come as a surprise.

A relaxed lunchtime venue in the **centre** of town is *Geroplatanos* with tables on the leafy Platía Ayíou Títou beside the church of the same name. Across from here is one of Iráklion's most stylish bars, *Pagopoleion* ("Ice Factory"), also good for lazy terrace breakfasts and snacks; the same place has now added an excellent restaurant and although medium priced, the food is consistently good – their recommended *mezedhákia* buffet (Sat & Sun 1–4pm) allows you to fill a plate for €4.50. *Pagopoleion* is the creation of photographic artist Chrissy Karelli, who has preserved a strident inscription on one wall, left by the Nazi occupiers who used local labour to run what was then Iráklion's only ice factory. Still near the centre, just off Eleftherías at **Platía Dhaskaloyiánni** (where the post office is), are some inexpensive and unexceptional tavernas; by day the platía is however a pleasant and relaxing venue, if not for a meal then to sit at one of its cafés, which transform themselves into more raucous and crowded music bars after dark. Nearer Venizélou, try exploring some of the backstreets to the east, off Dhedhálou and behind the loggia. The *Taverna Giovanni*, on the alley Koräï parallel to Dhedhálou, is one of the better tavernas in Iráklion, although the pricey food and an expensive wine list seem aimed more at Iráklion's smart set than the casual visitor. Should you have a craving for non-Greek food, there is Italian at the equally expensive *Loukoulos* and Chinese at the *New China Restaurant*, both with leafy courtyards and in the same street as the *Taverna Giovanni*. More reasonable prices are on offer at the very good new taverna-ouzerí *Vareladika*, Monís Agaráthou 13, close to the Venetian harbour which offers a wide range of Cretan specialities in a stylish setting. Mexican tacos and beers are on offer at *Chilis*, Hándhakos 71 on the west side of the central zone – an area with many lively bars and cafés.

The **waterfront** is dotted with fish tavernas with little to recommend them. Instead, turn left at the bottom of 25-Avgoústou and cross the road to *Ippokampos*, which specializes in excellent-value fish dishes and mezédhes at moderate prices. It is deservedly popular with locals and is often crowded late into the evening: you may have to wait in line or turn up earlier than the Greeks eat. Even if you see no space it is worth asking as the owner may suddenly disappear inside the taverna and emerge with yet another table to carry further down the pavement. For simple and cheap seafood mezédhes, slightly south from here, *Katsina* at Marineli 12 is a simple and friendly ouzerí with outdoor tables; this alley has a whole bunch of similar places popular with locals, ending with *Kapetanios*, opposite the pint-sized chapel of Áyios Dimítrios.

For **snacks** and **takeaways**, there's a whole group of *souvláki* stalls clustering around the top of 25-Avgoústou at the entrance to El Greco Park, which is handy if you need somewhere to sit and eat. For *tyrópita* and *spanakópita* (cheese or spinach pies) and other pastries, sweet or savoury, there are no shortage of *zaharoplastía* and places such as *Everest* – just north of the Morosini fountain – which does takeaways of these as well as a whole bunch of other savouries. If you want to buy your own food, the **market** on Odhós 1866 is the place to go; it's an attraction in itself, and does a great line in modestly priced Cretan herbs (including saffron) to take home.

Drinking, nightlife and entertainment

Iráklion is a bit of a damp squib as far as **nightlife** goes, certainly when compared with many other towns on the island. If you're determined, however, there are a few city-centre possibilities, and plenty of options if all you want to do is sit and **drink**. In addition, there are a number of **cinemas** scattered about: check the posters on the boards by the tourist police office.

Bars

The city's most animated **bars** are located around **Platía Koräï** behind Dhedhálou (up from the *Giovanni* restaurant listed above) and along the alley of the same name to the west. On summer nights these places are packed with Iráklion's younger set and you don't really need a guidebook to direct you. *Flash* and *To Avgo* are the most popular venues on the platía itself while along the alley are places such as *Rebels* and the glitzy new *Korais*, with plant-festooned terrace, movie-screens and music – currently *the* place to be seen. A little to the north, *Pagopoleion* beside the church of Áyios Títos is a less frenetic after-dark alternative with a DJ and laid-back Latin and modern Greek sounds. After ten at night a lively bar scene also fans out into the streets around Hándhakos; among a number of new-style places *Jasmin*, Ayiostefanitón 6, is tucked in an alley on the left, midway down Hándhakos, and serves a variety of teas (including the Cretan *dhíktamo* – a panacea used by the ancients) with easy jazz and rock as background music. Nearby, *Orianas* at Psaroníligon 15 is a new music and drinks bar on two floors which has a varied programme of live music at weekends including jazz, blues, reggae and rock acts.

In and around **Platía Venizélou** (Fountain Square), there are many bars, again some are very fashionable, with *Andromeda* and *Aktarika* being a couple of the most popular. These represent a new breed of kafenío emerging in Iráklion, attracting a younger crowd: the drinks are **cocktails** rather than *rakí*, the music is Western or modern Greek, and there are prices to match. There are similar bars along Kandanoléon, off El Greco Park, and on the east side of the park itself.

Clubs and discos

For **discos** and **clubs** proper, there is a large selection, even if they all play techno at the moment, interspersed with Greek music (not the type played for tourists). *Privilege* is the most popular, down towards the harbour at the bottom of Dhoúkos Bofór, below the Archeological Museum. The nearby *Yacht Club* provides it with competition, and along Ikarou, downhill from Platía Eleftherías, another group of clubs is gathered including *Minoica*, *Korus Club* and *Athina*, all playing similar music and popular with young Iraklians. *Aman*, at the junction of Odhós Ay. Títos and Idomeneos and just east of the Áyios Títos church, with cine screens around its dance floor and three bars, is another more central alternative.

Listings

Airlines Aegean, Dhimokratias 11 ☎0810/344 394; Axon, Ethinikís Andístasis 134 ☎0810/320 330; Cronus Air, Odhós-1821 10, near El Greco Park ☎0810/397 368; Olympic, Platía Eleftherías ☎0810/229 191. Charter airlines flying in to Iráklion mostly use local travel agents as their representatives.

Airport For airport information call ☎0810/245 644. Bus #1 runs from Platía Eleftherías to the airport every few minutes; buy a ticket (€0.45) from the booth outside the *Astoria Hotel* first.

Banks There are now 24hr cash dispensers all over town, but the main bank branches are on 25-Avgoústou.

Car and bike rental 25-Avgoústou is lined with rental companies, but you'll often find cheaper rates on the backstreets; it's always worth asking for discounts. Good places to start include: Blue Sea, Kosmá Zótou 7, near the bottom of 25-Avgoústou ☎0810/241 097, for cars and bikes, which gives a twenty percent discount to Rough Guide readers; Sun Rise, 25-Avgoústou 46 ☎0810/221 609, also does both cars and bikes. For cars: Reliable, Epimenidou 8 off the east side of the same street ☎0810/344 212; Motor Club, Platía Ánglon 1 at the bottom of 25-Avgoústou facing the port ☎0810/222 408; and Ritz in the *Hotel*

Rea, Kalimeráki 1 ☎0810/223 638, are other possibilities. All offer free delivery to hotels and airport.

Ferry tickets Available from Minoan Lines, 25-Avgoústou 78 ☎0810/229 646 (handles the islands and Athens), ANEK Lines, 25-Avgoústou 33 ☎0810/222 481 (Athens only), or any of the travel agents listed opposite. Another source for tickets and ferry information is the long-established Paleologus Travel, 25-Avgoústou 5 ☎0810/346 185; their comprehensive website, ⊛www.ferries.gr, is excellent.

Hospital Most central is the hospital on Apollónion, southwest of Platía Kornárou, between Albér and Moussoúrou.

Internet Iráklion now has a number of internet cafés located in and around the city centre. *Netcafé*, Odhós-1878 4 (daily 10am–midnight, near the sea to the west of the Historical Museum; €3.50 for 1hr; ⊛www.the-netcafe.net) is good; other central places with similar charges and hours are *Istos*, Malakoúti 2 near the Arsenali; *Gallery Games*, Korai 6; and *Konsova*, Dhikeosínis 25.

Laundry Washsalon, Hándhakos 18 (Mon–Sat 8am–8pm) is reliable and also does service washes (€5.90 for 6kg). Laundry Perfect at Malikoúti 32, north of the Archeological Museum, will do the same for €5.30 (Mon–Sat 9am–9pm).

Left luggage Offices in the eastbound and south-west bus stations (daily 6.30am–8pm; €0.90 per bag per day), as well as a commercial agency at Hándhakos 18 (daily 24hr; large locker €1.50 per day). You can also leave bags at the youth hostel (even if you don't stay there) for €1.50 per bag per day. If you want to leave your bag while you go off on a bike for a day or two, the rental company should be prepared to store it.

Newspapers and books For English-language newspapers and novels, as well as local guides and maps, Dhedhálou is the best bet, where Bibliopoleio (no. 6) stocks a wide selection of books in English. The excellent Planet International Bookstore, on four floors behind Platía Venizélou at the corner of Hándhakos and Kydhonías (☎0810/281 558), has the island's biggest stock of English-language titles and is a great place to browse; they also buy, sell and exchange second-hand books in English.

Pharmacies Plentiful on the main shopping streets – at least one is open 24hr on a rota basis; the others will have a sign on the door indicating which it is. There are traditional herbalists in the market.

Post office Main office in Platía Dhaskaloyiánnis, off Eleftherías (Mon–Fri 7.30am–8pm). There's also a temporary office (a van) at the entrance to El Greco Park (daily 7.30am–7pm).

Taxis Major taxi ranks in Platía Eleftherías and by the Morosini Fountain (Platía Venizélou), or call ☎0810/210 102 or 210 168. Prices displayed on boards at the taxi stands.

Telephones The OTE head office is on the west side of El Greco Park; it's open 8am–11pm, but most overseas destinations can now be phoned from street booths using a phone card (*telekárta*) obtainable from a *períptero* (street kiosk).

Toilets In El Greco Park and the public gardens near the cathedral, or at the bus stations and the Archeological Museum (no entrance charge).

Travel agencies Budget operators and student specialists include the extremely helpful Blavakis Travel, Platía Kallergón 8, just off 25-Avgoústou by the entrance to El Greco Park ☎0810/282 541, and Prince Travel, 25-Avgoústou 30 ☎0810/282 706. For excursions around the island, villa rentals and so on, the bigger operators are probably easier: Irman Travel, Dhedhálou 26 ☎0810/242 527, or Creta Travel Bureau, Epimenídhou 20–22 ☎0810/227 002. The latter is also the local American Express agent.

Knossós

KNOSSÓS, the largest of the **Minoan palaces**, reached its cultural peak more than three thousand years ago, though a town of some importance persisted here well into the Roman era. It lies on a low, largely man-made hill some 5km southeast of Iráklion; the surrounding hillsides are rich in lesser remains spanning 25 centuries, starting at the beginning of the second millennium BC.

Barely a hundred years ago the palace existed only in mythology. Knossós was the court of the legendary King Minos, whose wife Pasiphae bore the Minotaur, half-bull, half-man. Here the labyrinth was constructed by Daedalus to contain the monster, and youths were brought from Athens as human sacrifice until Theseus arrived to slay the beast and, with Ariadne's help, escape its lair. The discovery of the palace, and the interplay of these legends with fact, is among the most amazing tales of modern archeology. Heinrich Schliemann, the German excavator of Troy, suspected that a major Minoan palace lay under the various tumuli here, but was denied the necessary permission to dig by the local Ottoman authorities at the end of the nineteenth century. It was left for Sir Arthur Evans, whose name is indelibly associated with Knossós, to excavate the site, from 1900 onwards.

The #2 and #4 local **buses** set off every ten minutes from Iráklion's city bus stands (adjacent to the eastbound bus station), proceed up 25-Avgoústou (with a stop just south of Platía Venizélou) and out of town on Odhós-1821 and Evans. This is also the route you should also take if **driving** (follow the signs from Platía Eleftherías); a **taxi** from the centre will cost around €2.50. At Knossós, outside the fenced site, stands the *caravanserai* where ancient wayfarers

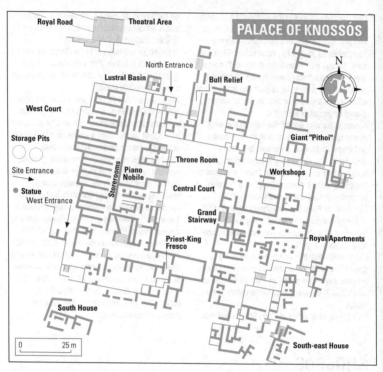

3

CRETE | Knossós

would rest and water their animals. Head out onto the road and you'll find no lack of watering holes for modern travellers either – a string of rather pricey tavernas and tacky souvenir stands. There are several **rooms** for rent here, and if you're really into Minoan culture, there's a lot to be said for staying out this way to get an early start. Be warned, though, that this zone is expensive and unashamedly commercial.

The site

As soon as you enter the **Palace of Knossós** (daily: April–Sept 8am–7pm; Oct–March 8.30am–3pm; €4.40) through the West Court, the ancient ceremonial entrance, it is clear how the legends of the labyrinth grew up around it. Even with a detailed plan, it's almost impossible to find your way around the site with any success. The best advice is not to try; wander around for long enough and you'll eventually stumble upon everything. If you're worried about missing the highlights, you can always tag along with one of the constant guided tours for a while, catching the patter and then backtracking to absorb the detail when the crowd has moved on. Outside the period December to February you won't get the place to yourself, whenever you come, but exploring on your own does give you the opportunity to appreciate individual parts of the palace in the brief lulls between groups.

Knossós was liberally "restored" by Evans, and these restorations have been the source of furious controversy among archeologists ever since. It has become clear that much of Evans's upper level – the so-called *piano nobile* – is pure conjecture. Even so, his guess as to what the palace might have looked like is certainly as good as anyone else's, and it makes the other sites infinitely more meaningful if you have seen Knossós first. Without the restorations, it would be almost impossible to imagine the grandeur of the multistorey palace or to see the ceremonial stairways, strange, top-heavy pillars and gaily painted walls that distinguish the site. For some idea of the size and complexity of the palace in its original state, take a look at the cutaway drawings (wholly imaginary but probably not too far off) on sale outside.

Royal Apartments

The superb **Royal Apartments** around the central staircase are not guess-work, and they are plainly the finest of the rooms at Knossós. The **Grand Stairway** itself is a masterpiece of design: not only a fitting approach to these sumptuously appointed chambers, but also an integral part of the whole plan, its large well bringing light into the lower storeys. Light wells such as these, usually with a courtyard at the bottom, are a constant feature of Knossós and a reminder just how important creature comforts were to the Minoans, and how skilled they were at providing them.

For evidence of this luxurious lifestyle you need look no further than the **Queen's Suite**, off the grand **Hall of the Colonnades** at the bottom of the staircase. Here, the main living room is decorated with the celebrated **dolphin fresco** (a reproduction; the original is now in the Iráklion archeological muse-um) and with running friezes of flowers and abstract spirals. On two sides it opens out onto courtyards that let in light and air; the smaller one would prob-ably have been planted with flowers. The room may have been scattered with cushions and hung with plush drapes, while doors and further curtains between the pillars would have allowed for privacy, and provided cool shade in the heat of the day. Remember, though, that all this is speculation and some of it is pure hype; the dolphin fresco, for example, was found on the courtyard floor, not in the room itself, and would have been viewed from an upper balcony as a sort of trompe l'oeil, like looking through a glass-bottomed boat. Whatever the truth, this is an impressive example of Minoan architecture, the more so when you follow the dark passage around to the queen's **bathroom**. Here is a clay tub, protected behind a low wall (and again probably screened by curtains when in use), and the famous "flushing" toilet (a hole in the ground with drains to take the waste away – it was flushed by throwing a bucket of water down).

The much perused **drainage system** was a series of interconnecting terra-cotta pipes running underneath most of the palace. Guides to the site never fail to point these out as evidence of the advanced state of Minoan civilization, and they are indeed quite an achievement, in particular the system of baffles and overflows to slow down the runoff and avoid any danger of flooding. Just how much running water there would have been, however, is another matter; the water supply was, and is, at the bottom of the hill, and even the combined efforts of rainwater catchment and hauling water up to the palace can hardly have been sufficient to supply the needs of more than a small elite.

Going up the Grand Stairway to the floor above the queen's domain, you come to a set of rooms generally regarded as the **King's Quarters**. These are chambers in a considerably sterner vein; the staircase opens into a grandiose reception chamber known as the **Hall of the Royal Guard**, its walls deco-rated in repeated shield patterns. Immediately off here is the **Hall of the Double Axes**, believed to be have been the ruler's personal chamber, a dou-ble room that would allow for privacy in one portion while audiences were held in the more public section. Its name comes from the double-axe symbol carved into every block of masonry.

The Throne Room and the rest of the palace

Continuing to the top of the Grand Stairway, you emerge onto the broad **Central Court**, a feature of all the Minoan palaces. Open now, this would once have been enclosed by the walls of the buildings all around. On the far side, in the northwestern corner of the courtyard, is the entrance to another of Knossós's most atmospheric survivals, the **Throne Room**. Here, a worn stone throne – with its hollowed shaping for the posterior – sits against the wall of a surprisingly small chamber; along the walls around it are ranged stone benches, suggesting a king ruling in council, and behind there's a reconstructed fresco of two griffins. In all probability in Minoan times this was the seat of a priestess rather than a ruler (there's nothing like it in any other Minoan palace), and its conversion into a throne room seems to have been a late innovation wrought by the invading Mycenaeans, during their short-lived domination prior to the palace's final destruction in the fourteenth century BC. The Throne Room is now closed off with a wooden gate, but you can lean over this for a good view, and in the antechamber there's a wooden copy of the throne on which everyone perches to have their picture taken.

The rest you'll see as you wander, contemplating the legends of the place which blur with reality. Try not to miss the giant *pithoi* in the northeast quadrant of the site, an area known as the palace workshops; the storage chambers which you see from behind the Throne Room, and the reproduced frescoes in the reconstructed room above it; the fresco of the Priest-King looking down on the south side of the central court, and the relief of a charging bull on its north side. This last would have greeted you if you entered the palace through its north door; you can see evidence here of some kind of gatehouse and a lustral bath, a sunken area perhaps used for ceremonial bathing and purification. Just outside this gate is the **theatral area**, an open space a little like a stepped amphitheatre, which may have been used for ritual performances or dances. From here the **Royal Road**, claimed as the oldest road in Europe, sets out. At one time, this probably ran right across the island; nowadays it ends after about a hundred yards in a brick wall beneath the modern road. Circling back around the outside of the palace, you get more idea of its scale by looking up at it; on the south side are a couple of small reconstructed Minoan houses which are worth exploring.

Beyond Knossós

If you have transport, the drive beyond Knossós can be an attractive and enjoyable one, taking minor roads through much greener country, with vineyards draped across low hills and flourishing agricultural communities. If you want specific things to seek out, head first for **MYRTIÁ**, an attractive village with the small **Kazantzákis Museum** (Mon, Wed, Sat & Sun 9am–1pm & 4–8pm, Tues & Fri 9am–1pm; €2.95) in a house where the writer's parents once lived. **ARHÁNES**, at the foot of Mount Ioúktas, is a much larger place that was also quite heavily populated in Minoan times. None of the three archeological sites here is open to the public, but **Anemospiliá**, 2km northwest of the town (directions from the archeological museum below), can be visited and has caused huge controversy since its excavation in the 1980s: many traditional views of the Minoans, particularly that of Minoan life as peaceful and idyllic, have had to be rethought in the light of the discovery of an apparent human sacrifice. Close to Arhánes' main square, an excellent new **archeological museum** (daily except Tues 8.30am–3pm; free) displays finds from here and other nearby excavations, including the strange ceremonial dagger seemingly used for human sacrifice. From Arhánes you can also drive (or walk with a couple of hours to spare) to the summit of Mount Ioúktas to see the imposing remains of a Minoan **peak sanctuary** and enjoy spectacular panoramic **views** towards Knossós (with which it was linked) and the northern coast beyond. At **VATHÝPETRO**, south of the mountain, is a **Minoan villa and vineyard** (Mon–Sat 8.30am–2pm; free), which once controlled the rich farmland south of Arhánes. Inside, a remarkable collection of farming implements was found, as well as a unique **wine press** which remains *in situ*. Substantial amounts of the farm buildings remain, and it's still surrounded by fertile vines (Arhánes is one of Crete's major wine-producing zones) three and a half thousand years later – making it probably the oldest still-functioning vineyard in Europe, if not the world.

Southwest from Iráklion: sites and beaches

If you take a **tour** from Iráklion (or one of the resorts), you'll probably visit the **Górtys**, **Festós** and **Ayía Triádha** sites in a day, with a lunchtime swim at **Mátala** thrown in. Doing it by public transport, you'll be forced into a rather more leisurely pace, but there's still no reason why you shouldn't get to all three and reach Mátala within the day; if necessary, it's easy enough to hitch the final stretch. **Bus services** to the Festós site are excellent, with some nine a day to and from Iráklion (fewer run on Sun), five of which continue to or come from Mátala; there are also services direct to Ayía Galíni. If you're arriving in the afternoon, plan to visit Ayía Triádha first, as it closes early.

The route to Áyii Dhéka

The road from Iráklion towards Festós is a pretty good one by the standards of Cretan mountain roads, albeit rather dull. The country you're heading towards is the richest agricultural land on the island, and right from the start the villages en route are large and businesslike. In the biggest of them, **Ayía Varvára**, there's a great rock outcrop known as the **Omphalos** (Navel) of Crete, supposedly the very centre of the island.

Past here, you descend rapidly to the fertile fields of the Messará plain, where the road joins the main route across the south near the village of **ÁYII DHÉKA**. For religious Cretans Áyii Dhéka is something of a place of pilgrimage; its name, "The Ten Saints", refers to ten early Christians martyred here under the Romans. The old Byzantine church in the centre of the village preserves the stone block on which they are supposed to have been decapitated and in a crypt below the modern church on the village's western edge you can see the martyrs' (now empty) tombs. It's an attractive village to wander around, with several places to eat and even some **rooms** along the main road.

Górtys

Within easy walking distance of Áyii Dhéka, either through the fields or along the main road, sprawls the site of **Górtys** (daily 8am–6pm; €2.40), ruined capital of the Roman province that included not only Crete but also much of North Africa. After a look at the plan of the extensive site at the entrance, cutting across the fields to the south of the road will give you some idea of the scale of this city, at its zenith in approximately the third century AD. An enormous variety of remains, including an impressive **theatre**, and a couple of

temples are strewn across your route and more spectacular discoveries are being unearthed by the archeologists who return to dig each summer. Even in Áyii Dhéka you'll see Roman pillars and statues lying around in people's yards or propping up their walls.

There had been a settlement here from the earliest times and evidence of a Minoan site has been enearthed on the acropolis, but the extant ruins date almost entirely from the Roman era. Only now is the site being systematically excavated by the Italian Archeological School. At the main entrance to the **fenced site**, to the north of the road, are the ruins of the still impressive **basilica of Áyios Títos**; the eponymous saint converted the island to Christianity and was its first bishop. Beyond this is the **odeion** which houses the most important discovery on the site, the **Law Code**. These great inscribed blocks of stone were incorporated by the Romans from a much earlier stage of the city's development; they're written in an obscure early Greek-Cretan dialect, and in a style known as *boustrophedon* (ox-ploughed), with the lines reading alternately in opposite directions like the furrows of a ploughed field. At ten metres by three metres, this is reputedly the largest Greek inscription ever found. The laws set forth reflect a strictly hierarchical society: five witnesses were needed to convict a free man of a crime, only one for a slave; raping a free man or woman carried a fine of a hundred staters, violating a serf only five. A small **museum** in a loggia (also within the fenced area) holds a number of large and finely worked sculptures found at Górtys, more evidence of the city's importance.

Míres

Some 20km west of Górtys, **MÍRES** is an important market town and focal point of transport for the fertile Messará plain: if you're switching buses to get from the beaches on the south coast to the archeological sites or the west, this is where you'll do it. There are good facilities including a **bank**, a few **restaurants** and a couple of **rooms**, though there's no particular reason to stay unless you are waiting for a bus or looking for work (it's one of the better places for agricultural jobs). A useful **internet** café, *Net Escape* (Ⓦwww.netescape.gr), near the bus stop will allow you to send a few emails while awaiting onward connections. Heading straight for Festós, there's usually no need to stop.

Festós (Phaestos)

The **Palace of Festós** (daily 8am–6pm; €3.55) was excavated by the Italian, Federico Halbherr (also responsible for the early work at Górtys), at almost exactly the same time as Evans was working at Knossós. The style of the excavations, however, could hardly have been more different. Here, to the approval of most traditional archeologists, reconstruction was kept to an absolute minimum – it's all bare foundations, and walls which rise at most a metre above ground level. This means that despite a magnificent setting overlooking the plain of Messará, the palace at Festós is not as immediately arresting as those at Knossós or Mália. Much of the site is fenced off and, except in the huge central court, it's almost impossible to get any sense of the place as it was; the plan is almost as complex as at Knossós, with none of the reconstruction to bolster the imagination.

It's interesting to speculate why the palace was built halfway up a hill rather than on the plain below – certainly not for defence, for this is in no way a good defensive position. Psychological superiority over the peasants or reasons of health are both possible, but it seems quite likely that it was simply the magnificent view that finally swayed the decision. The site looks over Psilorítis to the north and the huge plain, with the Lasíthi mountains beyond it, to the east.

Towards the top of Psilorítis you should be able to make out a small black smudge: the entrance to the Kamáres cave (see p.236).

On the ground closer at hand, you can hardly fail to notice the strong similarities between Festós and the other palaces: the same huge rows of storage jars, the great courtyard with its monumental stairway, and the theatral area. Unique to Festós, however, is the third courtyard, in the middle of which are the remains of a **furnace** used for metalworking. Indeed, this eastern corner of the palace seems to have been home to a number of craftsmen, including potters and carpenters. Oddly enough, Festós was much less ornately decorated than Knossós; there is no evidence, for example, of any of the dramatic Minoan wall-paintings.

The **tourist pavilion** near the entrance serves drinks and **food**, as well as the usual postcards, books and souvenirs. The nearby village of **ÁYIOS IOÁNNIS**, along the road towards Mátala, has economical **rooms**, including some at *Taverna Ayios Ioannis* (☎08920/42 006; ❶), which is also a good place to eat.

Ayía Triádha

Some of the finest artworks in the museum at Iráklion came from **Ayía Triádha** (daily 8.30am–3pm; €1.45), about a 45-minute walk (or a short drive) from Festós. No one is quite sure what this site is, but the most common theory has it as some kind of royal summer villa. It's smaller than the palaces, but if anything even more lavishly appointed and beautifully situated. In any event, it's an attractive place to visit, far less crowded than Festós, with a wealth of interesting little details. Look out in particular for the row of **stores** in front of what

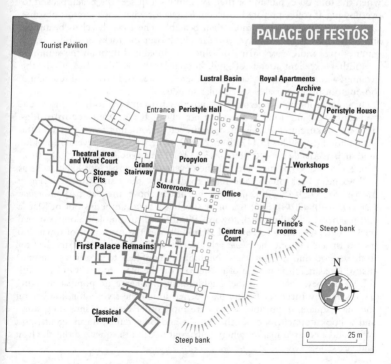

PALACE OF FESTÓS

Tourist Pavilion

Lustral Basin   Royal Apartments
Archive
Entrance Peristyle Hall
Peristyle House

Theatral area
and West Court   Propylon
Grand
Storage Stairway   Workshops
Pits
Storerooms
Office   Furnace

First Palace Remains   Central   Prince's   Steep bank
Court   rooms

N

Classical
Temple
0   25 m
Steep bank

was apparently a marketplace, although recent thinking tends towards the idea that these were constructed after the villa had declined, possibly in the Mycenaean period. The remains of a **paved road** that probably led down to a harbour on the Gulf of Messará can also be seen running alongside the royal villa. The sea itself looks invitingly close, separated from the base of the hill only by Timbáki airfield (mainly used for motor racing these days), but if you try to drive down there, it's almost impossible to find your way around the unmarked dust tracks. There's a fourteenth-century **church** – dedicated to Áyios Yeóryios – at the site, worth visiting in its own right for the remains of ancient frescoes.

Mátala

MÁTALA has by far the best-known **beach** in Iráklion province, widely promoted and included in tours mainly because of the famous **caves** cut into the cliffs above its beautiful sands. These are believed to be ancient **tombs** first used by Romans or early Christians, but more recently inhabited by a sizeable hippie community. You'll still meet people who will assure you that this is *the* travellers' beach on Crete. Not any more it isn't. Today, the town is full of package tourists and tries hard to present a respectable image. The caves have long since been cleared and cleaned up and these days are a fenced-off **archeological site** (April–Sept daily 10am–4pm; €1.50) and locked up every evening.

A few people still manage to evade the security, or sleep on the beach or in the adjacent campsite, but on the whole the place has changed entirely. The years since the early 1980s have seen the arrival of crowds and the development of hotels, restaurants and even a disco to service them; early afternoon, when the tour buses pull in for their swimming stop, sees the beach packed to overflowing. If you're prepared to accept Mátala for what it is – a resort of some size – you'll find the place more than bearable. The town beach is beautiful, and if the crowds get excessive, you can climb over the rocks in about twenty minutes (past more caves, many of which are inhabited through the summer) to another excellent stretch of sand, known locally as "Red Beach". In the evening, when the trippers have gone, there are waterside bars and restaurants looking out over invariably spectacular sunsets.

The chief problems concern prices and crowds: rooms are both expensive and oversubscribed, and food is good but not cheap. If you want **accommodation**, try looking up the little street to the left as you enter town, just after the *Zafiria* hotel (☎08920/45 112, ☎45 725; ❷), where there are several rooms for rent, such as *Matala View* (☎08920/45 114; ❶) and *Pension Nikos* (☎08920/42 375, ☎ 45 120; ❷). If these are full, then everywhere closer in is likely to be as well, so head back out on the main road, or try the **campsite**, *Camping of Matala* (☎08920/45 720), next to the beach above the car park; *Kommos Camping* (☎08920/45 596) is a nicer site, but a few kilometres out of Mátala and reached by heading back towards Pítsidia and turning left along a signed track. There are places to **eat and drink** all over the main part of town, and it's worth seeking out the *Skala* fish taverna on the south side of the bay for fresh seafood and a great view. Nightlife is confined to a solitary summer **disco**, *Kandari*, plus a couple of music bars on the main square. On the south side of the bay, *Odysea* and the neighbouring *Sea Horse* are popular drinking haunts. A new **internet** facility has opened inside the stylish *Kafeneio* bar on the main square. Impossible to miss are most other facilities, including stores and a bookshop, currency exchange, car and bike rental, travel agents, post office and a covered market where tourist tat has almost squeezed out the fruit and veg stalls.

One way to enjoy a bit more peace is to stay at **PITSÍDHIA**, about 5km inland. This has long been a well-used option, so it's not quite as cheap as you might expect, but there are plenty of rooms, lively places to eat and even music bars. If you decide to stay here, the beach at **KALAMÁKI** is an alternative to Mátala. Both beaches are approximately the same distance to walk, though there is a much better chance of a bus or a lift to Mátala. Kalamáki has developed somewhat, with a number of **rooms** – *Psiloritis* (☎08920/45 693, ⒡45 249; ❶) is a good bet – and a couple of tavernas, but it's still a rather unfinished, soulless little place. The beach stretches for miles, surprisingly wild and windswept, lashed by sometimes dangerously rough surf. At the southern end (more easily reached by a path off the Pitsídhia–Mátala road) lies **Kómmos**, once a Minoan port serving Festós and now the site of a major archeological excavation. It's not yet open to the public, but you can peer into the fenced-off area to see what's been revealed so far, which is pretty impressive: dwellings, streets, hefty stonework and even the ship sheds where repairs on the Minoan fleet were carried out.

Iráklion's south coast

South of the Messará plain are two more beach resorts, Kalí Liménes and Léndas, with numerous other little beaches along the coast in between, but nothing spectacular. **Public transport** is very limited indeed; you'll almost always have to travel via Míres (see p.224). If you have your own transport, the roads in these parts are all passable and newly sealed, but most are very slow going; the Kófinas hills, which divide the plain from the coast, are surprisingly precipitous.

Kalí Liménes

While Mátala itself was an important port under the Romans, the chief harbour for Górtys lay on the other side of Cape Líthinon at **KALÍ LIMÉNES**. Nowadays, this is once again a significant port – for oil tankers. This has rather spoiled its chances of becoming a major resort, and there are few proper facilities, but some people like Kalí Liménes: it's certainly off the beaten track and the constant procession of tankers gives you something to look at while beach lounging. There are a couple of places offering **rooms** – the best is the seafront *Taverna Panorama* (☎08920/97 517; ❶) which also has a decent **taverna** attached. The coastline is broken up by spectacular cliffs and, as long as there hasn't been a recent oil spill, the beaches are reasonably clean and totally empty.

Léndas

LÉNDAS, further east along the coast, is far more popular, with a couple of buses daily from Iráklion and a partly justified reputation for being peaceful (sullied by considerable summer crowds). Many people who arrive think they've come to the wrong place, as at first sight the village looks shabby, the beach is small, rocky and dirty, and the rooms are frequently all booked. A number of visitors leave without ever correcting that initial impression, but the attraction of Léndas is not the village at all but on the other (west) side of the headland. Here, there's a vast, excellent sandy beach, part of it usually taken over by nudists, and a number of taverna/bars overlooking it from the roadside. The beach is a couple of kilometres from Léndas, along a rough track; if you're walking, you can save time by cutting across the headland. A considerably more attractive prospect than staying in Léndas itself is **camping** on the beach to the west of the village, or with luck getting a **room** at one of the few beach tavernas – try *Villa Tsapakis* (☎08920/95 378, ℉95 377; ❶) with seaview rooms and reductions for longer stays. They will also change **money on a credit card** here (a useful service in this part of Crete where banks and cash-machines are nonexistent) and have their own **taverna**, *Odysseas*, nearby. After you've discovered the beach, even Léndas begins to look more welcoming, and at least it has most of the facilities you'll need, including a couple of minimarkets and the friendly Monza travel agency, both of which will change money, a single-screen **internet** café on the main square, and numerous places to **eat and drink**.

Once you've come to terms with the place, you can also explore some less good but quite deserted beaches eastwards, and the scrappy remains of **ancient Lebena** on a hilltop overlooking them. There was an important Asclepion (temple of the god Asclepius) here around some now-diverted warm springs, but only the odd broken column and fragments of mosaic survive in a fenced-off area on the village's northern edge.

East of Iráklion: the package-tour coast

East of Iráklion, the startling pace of **tourist development** in Crete is all too plain to see. The merest hint of a beach is an excuse to build at least one hotel, and these are outnumbered by the concrete shells of resorts-to-be. It's hard to find a room in this monument to the package-tour industry, and it can be expensive if you do.

Goúrnes and Goúves

As a general rule, the further you go, the better things get: when the road detours all too briefly inland, the more alluring Crete of olive groves and stark mountains asserts itself. You certainly won't see much of it at **GOÚRNES**, where an abandoned former US Air Force base is about to be transformed into a **giant sea aquarium** and visitor complex, or at nearby Káto Goúves, where there's a **campsite**, *Camping Creta* (☎08970/41 400), sharing a boundary with the former base. From here, however, you can head inland to the old village of **GOÚVES**, a refreshing contrast, and just beyond to the **Skotinó cave**, one of the largest and most spectacular on the island (about an hour's walk from the coast; open all hours; free).

Not far beyond Goúrnes is the turning for the direct route up to the Lasíthi plateau, and shortly after that you roll into the first of the big resorts, Hersónissos or, more correctly, Límin Hersoníssou; Hersónissos is the village in the hills just behind, also overrun by tourists.

Hersónissos (Límin Hersoníssou)

HERSÓNISSOS was once just a small fishing village; today it's the most popular of Crete's package resorts. If what you want is plenty of bars, tavernas, restaurants and Eurodisco nightlife, then this is the place to come. The resort has numerous small patches of sand beach between rocky outcrops, but a shortage of places to stay in peak season.

Hersonissos' focal main street, the two-kilometre long Odhós Elefthériou Venizélou, is a seemingly endless ribbon of bars, travel agents, tacky jewellery and beachwear shops, amusement arcades and – during the daytime at least – nose-to-tail traffic jams. North of here, along the modern seafront, a solid line of restaurants and bars is broken only by the occasional souvenir shop; in their midst you'll find a small pyramidal Roman **fountain** with broken mosaics of fishing scenes, the only real relic of the ancient town of Chersonesos. Around the headland above the harbour and in odd places along the seafront, you can see remains of Roman harbour installations, mostly submerged.

Beach and clubs excepted, the distractions of Hersónissos comprise **Lychnostatis Open-Air Museum** (Tues–Sun 9.30am–2pm; €3), a surprisingly rewarding "museum" of traditional Crete, on the coast at the eastern edge of the town; a small aquarium, **Aqua World** (April–Oct daily 10am–9pm; €4.40, children and students €2.90), just off the main road at the west end of town, up the road almost opposite the *Hard Rock Cafe*; the watersports paradise **Star Water Park** (daily June–Sept 10am–7pm; April & May 10am–6pm; €12.50 for a full day, or €9.50 half-day, reductions for under-12s) near the beach at the eastern end of the resort; and, a few kilometres inland, the competing **Aqua Splash Water Park** which has similar features and prices.

A short distance inland are the three **hill villages** of Koutoulafári, Piskopianó and "old" Hersónissos, which all have a good selection of tavernas, and are worth searching out for accommodation.

Practicalities

Hersónissos is well provided with all the back-up **services** you need to make a holiday go smoothly. Banks, bike and car rental and post office are all on or just off the main drag, as are the taxi ranks. A number of **internet** cafés have opened along the main street, the cheapest of which is *El Greco Palace*, Venizélou 109, at the eastern end. **Buses** running east and west leave every thirty minutes.

Finding somewhere to stay can verge on the impossible in July and August. Much of the **accommodation** here is allocated to package-tour operators and what remains for casual visitors is among the priciest on the island. To check for availability of accommodation generally, the quickest and best option is to enquire at one of the many travel agencies along the main street, Venizélou, such as Zakros Tours (☎08970/22 317) at no. 46. The town's most reasonably priced (for Hersónissos) central options include the *Nancy*, Ayías Paraskevís 15 (☎08970/22 212; ❸), and *Virginia*, Máchis Krítis 18 (☎ & ℱ 08970/22 455; ❸), but be prepared for a fair amount of noise. One place to try on the western edge as you enter the town is *Hotel Ilios* (☎08970/22 500; ℱ22 582; ❹), just back from the main road, which has a rooftop pool. There are two good **campsites**: one at the eastern end of town, *Caravan Camping* (☎08970/22 025), which also has several reed-roofed bungalows, and *Camping Hersonissos* (☎08970/22 902), just to the west of town. The well-run "paleo" (old) **youth hostel** is no longer affiliated to the main organization and charges €8.80 for a bed with use of kitchen; it's sited at the extreme eastern end of Venizélou (☎08970/23 674), a little beyond *Caravan Camping* (see above) and serves meals.

Despite the vast number of **eating places**, there are few in Hersónissos worth recommending, and the tavernas down on the harbourfront should be avoided. One of the few Greek tavernas that stands out is *Kavouri* along Arhéou Theátrou, but it's fairly expensive; a cheaper in-town alternative for some delicious and inexpensive Cretan cooking is *Taverna Creta Giannis*, Kaniadakí 4, just off the south side of Venizélou slightly east of the church. Nearby, and also definitely worth a try, is *Passage to India*, an authentic and extremely good Indian restaurant; it lies on Petrakis, another side street just off the main street near the church. Heading out of town on the Piskopianó road, near the junction to Koutoulafári, the friendly *Fegari* taverna also serves good Greek food at reasonable prices. Sitting at your table overlooking the street below you can view the steady trek of clubbers heading down the hill to the bars and night-clubs of Hersónissos. The hill villages have the greatest selection of tavernas, particularly Koutoulafári, where you can have a relaxed evening amongst the narrow streets and small platías.

Hersónissos is renowned for its **nightlife**, and there's certainly no shortage of it. A night's partying kicks off around the **bars** ringing the harbour, which is packed with promenaders and the overspill from countless noisy music bars from 10pm through to the early hours. After midnight, the larger **disco-clubs** and **pubs** in the streets leading up to and along Elefthériou Venizélou are the places to be seen. Currently the most popular music clubs are *Aria* (open July–Aug only), the island's largest, on the main road at the west end of town, *It After Dark*, also on Venizélou, and *Camelot* and *New York*, both near the harbour. The *Hard Rock Café*, close to *Aria* on Venizélou, has a terrace where clubbers chill out between venues. If you fancy a quiet drink then you've come to the wrong resort, but you could try *Kahluai Beach Cocktail Bar* or *Haris Ouzo & Raki Place* (beneath the *Hotel Virginia*). There is an open-air **cinema** showing original-version films at the *Creta Maris* hotel at the west end of the town and close to the beach.

Stalídha

STALÍDHA is a Cinderella town, sandwiched in between its two louder, brasher and some would say uglier sisters, Mália and Hersónissos, but it is nei-ther quiet or undeveloped. This rapidly expanding beach resort, with more than sixty tavernas and bars and a few discos, can offer the best of both worlds, with a friendlier and more relaxed setting, a better beach (and usual array of watersports) and very easy access to its two livelier neighbours. The town essentially consists of a single, relatively traffic-free street which rings the seafront for more than two miles, before the apartment blocks briefly become fewer and further, until the mass development of Mália begins.

Finding a place to stay can be difficult, since **accommodation** is almost entirely in studio and apartment blocks which are booked by package compa-nies in high season. Out of season, however, you may well be able to negotiate a very reasonable price for a studio apartment complete with swimming pool; ask in the central travel agencies first, as they will know what is available, and expect to pay at least €25 for two. Finding somewhere to **eat** is less difficult as there are plenty of rather ordinary tavernas, the best and most authentic being *Maria's* and the *Hellas Taverna*, both at the western end of the seafront.

Stalídha is completely overshadowed by its neighbours when it comes to **nightlife**, though you can dance at *Bells* disco, on the main coast road, or at *Rhythm*, on the beach; the music bars *Sea Wolf Cocktail Bar* and *Akti Bar* are near each other along the beach.

Mália

Along with the other resorts along this stretch of coast, much of **MÁLIA** is carved up by the package industry, so in peak season finding a place to stay is not always easy. The town's focus is a T-junction (where the **bus** drops you) and from where the Beach Road – a kilometre-long strip lined with bars, clubs, games arcades, tavernas and souvenir shops – heads north to the sea and beach-es. South of this junction the older village presents a slightly saner image of what Mália used to be, but even here rampant commercialism is making inroads.

The best **accommodation** options, especially if you want any sleep, are

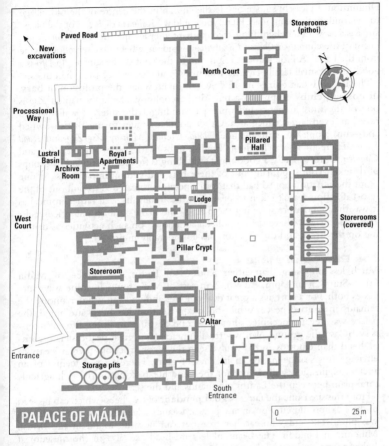

3

PALACE OF MÁLIA

Map labels:

Paved Road · New excavations · Storerooms (pithoi) · North Court · Processional Way · Pillared Hall · Lustral Basin · Royal Apartments · Archive Room · Lodge · Storerooms (covered) · West Court · Pillar Crypt · Storeroom · Central Court · Altar · Entrance · Storage pits · South Entrance

0   25 m

---

among the numerous **rooms** and **pensions** signposted in the old town, such as *Esperia* (☎08970/31 086; ❸), up a side road slightly east of the T-junction. Backtracking from the junction, along the main Iráklion road, there are a number of reasonably priced **pensions** on the left and right including *Hibiscus* (☎08970/31 313, ℱ32 042; ❷), which has rooms and studios with kitchenette and fridge around a pool in a garden behind. If you really want to be in the centre of things, try *Kostas* (☎08970/31 485; ❷), a family-run pension incongruously located behind the mini-golf at the end of the Beach Road. Otherwise, on arrival visit one of the travel companies along the main road – such as Stallion Travel, Venizélou 128 (☎08970/33 690) – to enquire about accommodation availability. All the other things you're likely to need – **banks** with cash machines, **post office** and food shops – are strung out along the main street near the junction, but the town's best **internet** access, *Internet Café*, is bang in the middle of the Beach Road madness (about a third of the way down on the right), but no less friendly or efficient for that.

Eating in Mália is unlikely to be a problem as **restaurants** jostle for your custom at every step, especially along the Beach Road. None is particularly good here, and a few are diabolical. The best places for a meal are around Platía Ayíou

Dhimitríou, a pleasant square beside the church in the centre of the old village to the south of the main road. Here, you could try *Kalimera* or *Petros*, or the pleasant *Kalesma* with a delightful terrace, perhaps after an aperitif at *Bar Yiannis* just north of the church or *Ouzeri Elizabeth* alongside it, where they serve local wine from the barrel. A little harder to find, and to the west of the square, *Apolafsi* is a good-quality small family taverna which is slightly less pricey than the others.

The Beach Road comes into its own at night, when the profusion of **bars**, **discos** and **clubs** erupt into a pulsating cacophony. The aptly named *Zoo* is one of the most frenetic, and once past midnight the internal walls part to reveal an even larger dance area. Other popular venues (many British-owned and -run) along the strip include *Cloud*, *Cosmos*, *Midway*, *Zig-Zag* and *Road House*. There are also a clutch of "English pubs" with names like *Newcastle* and *Camden*. Unfortunately, a good night's clubbing is frequently spoiled by groups of drunken youths pouring out of these bars and getting into brawls. At one point the situation got so bad that tour operators threatened to pull out of the resort if action wasn't taken to deal with the hooligans – all rather ironical as it was they who were shipping them in by the plane-load on cut-price packages. Recent years have seen a police clampdown on such activities as drinking on the street, and the situation has considerably improved.

The Palace of Mália

Much less imposing than either Knossós or Festós, the **Palace of Mália** (Tues–Sun 8.30am–3pm; €2.40), 2km east of Mália town, in some ways surpasses both. For a start, it's a great deal emptier and you can wander among the remains in relative peace. While no reconstruction has been attempted, the palace was never reoccupied after its second destruction in the fifteenth-century BC, so the ground plan is virtually intact. It's a great deal easier to comprehend than Knossós and, if you've seen the reconstructions there, it's easy to envisage this seaside palace in its days of glory. There's a real feeling of an ancient civilization with a taste for the good life, basking on the rich agricultural plain between the Lasíthi mountains and the sea.

From this site came the famous **gold pendant** of two bees (which can be seen in the Iráklion museum or on any postcard stand), allegedly part of a horde that was plundered and whose other treasures can now be found in the British Museum in London. The beautiful leopard-head axe, also in the museum at Iráklion, was another of the treasures found here. At the site, look out for the strange indented stone in the central court (which probably held ritual offerings), for the remains of ceremonial stairways and for the giant *pithoi* which stand like sentinels around the palace. To the north and west of the main site, archeological digs are still going on as the **large town** which surrounded the palace comes slowly to light, and part of this can now be viewed via an overhead walkway.

Any passing **bus** should stop at the site, or you could even rent a **bike** for a couple of hours as it's a pleasant, flat ride from Mália town. Leaving the archeological zone and turning immediately right, you can follow the road down to a lovely stretch of clean and relatively peaceful **beach**, backed by fields, scrubland and a single makeshift taverna, which serves good fresh fish. From here you can walk back along the shore to Mália or take a bus (every 30min in either direction) from the stop on the main road.

Sísi and Mílatos

Head **east** from the Palace of Mália, and it's not long before the road leaves the coast, climbing across the hills towards Áyios Nikólaos. If you want to escape the frenetic pace of all that has gone before, try continuing to **SÍSI** or

MÍLATOS. These little shore villages are bypassed by the main road as it cuts inland, and are still very much in the early stages of the tourist industry, though both have several **tavernas** – the seafront *Fisherman's Place* in Sísi is worth a try. The more developed of the two, Sísi, is charmingly situated around a small harbour overlooked by balcony bars and more tavernas. The resort has recently opened its first **disco bar** (*Faros*), a sure sign that more development is on the way, portended by a large holiday complex (*Kalimera Krita*) a couple of kilometres to the east; there's even a **post office**, confirming its resort status. Accommodation in both places is mainly in studios and apartments; it's best to ask in the travel agencies for details of availability. In Sísi there's also a small pension, *Elena* (no phone; ❸) just behind the harbour, and a shady **campsite** with pool and taverna (☎08410/71 247) signposted on the way in.

In quieter Mílatos, rooms can be found in the old village, 2km inland, but the seaside settlement – despite a rather pebbly beach – is more desirable. A number of the seafront tavernas let out rooms and, outside the peak season when there's little chance of a bed, the friendly *Taverna Socrates* (☎08410/81 375; ❶) is worth a try and does decent **food**. Despite their beaches, the resorts make for a refreshing change of pace, and there are some fine, deep aprons of sand in the rocky coves beyond the resort centres.

West of Iráklion: around Psilorítis

Most people heading west from Iráklion speed straight out on the **E75 coastal highway**, nonstop to Réthymnon. If you're in a hurry this is not such a bad plan; the road is fast and spectacular, hacked into the sides of mountains which for the most part drop straight to the sea, though there are no more than a couple of places where you might consider stopping. By contrast, the old roads inland are agonizingly slow, but they do pass through a whole string of **attractive villages** beneath the heights of the Psilorítis range. From here you can set out to explore the **mountains** and even walk across them to emerge in villages with views of the south coast.

The coastal route towards Réthymnon

Leaving the city, the **new highway** runs behind a stretch of highly developed coast, where the hotels compete for shore space with a cement works and power station. As soon as you reach the mountains, though, all this is left behind and there's only the clash of rock and sea to contemplate. As you start to climb, look out for **Paleókastro**, hovering beside a bridge which carries the road over a small cove; the castle is so weathered as to be almost invisible against the brownish face of the cliff.

Ayía Pelayía and Fódhele

Some 3km below the highway, as it rounds the first point, lies the resort of **AYÍA PELAYÍA**. It looks extremely attractive from above but, once there, you're likely to find the narrow, taverna-lined beach packed to full capacity; this is not somewhere to roll up in high season without reserved **accommodation**, although in quieter times *Zorba's Rooms* (☎ & ℱ 0810/256 072; ❷), along the nameless main street behind the beach, should have space. Opposite here, the Pangosmio travel agency (☎0810/811 402, ℱ811 424) may be able to come up with something, even at the last minute in high season. Out of season you might find a real bargain apartment and, despite the high-season crowds, the resort maintains a dignity long since lost in Mália and Hersónissos, and even a certain exclusivity; a couple of Crete's most luxurious hotels, including the enormous *Peninsula* (☎0810/811 313, ℉811 219, ⓦwww.peninsula.gr; ⓖ), nestle on the headlands just beyond the main town beach. There are plenty of **mini markets** for buying picnic food and **internet** access is available at *Netcafé Atlas*, next door to *Zorba's Rooms*.

Not far beyond Ayía Pelayía, there's a turning inland to the village of **FÓDHELE**, allegedly El Greco's birthplace. A plaque from the University of Valladolid (in Spain) acknowledges the claim and, true or not, the community has built a small tourist industry on that basis. There are a number of craft shops and some pleasant tavernas where you can sit outside along the river. A peaceful 1km walk (or drive) takes you to the spuriously titled (and rarely open) "El Greco's house" and the more worthwhile and picturesque fourteenth-century Byzantine **church of the Panayía** (Mon–Fri 9.30am–5pm; free) with frescoes, opposite. None of this amounts to very much but it is a pleasant, relatively unspoiled village if you simply want to sit in peace for a while. A couple of **buses** a day run here from Iráklion, and there's the odd tour; if you arrive on a direct bus, the walk back down to the highway (about 3km), where you can flag down a passing service, is not too strenuous.

Balí and Pánormos

BALÍ, on the coast approximately halfway between Iráklion and Réthymnon, also used to be tranquil and undeveloped, and by the standards of the north coast it still is in many ways. The village is built around a trio of small coves, some 2km from the highway (a hot walk from the bus), and is similar to Ayía Pelayía except that the beaches are not quite as good and there are no big hotels, just an ever-growing proliferation of studios, apartment buildings, rooms for rent and a number of "modest hotels" (brochure-speak). You'll have plenty of company here and it has to be said that Balí has become a package resort too popular for its own good. The third and best beach, known as "Paradise", no longer really deserves the name; it's a beautiful place to splash about, surrounded by mountains rising straight from the sea, but there's rarely a spare inch on the sand in high season.

Continuing along the coast, the last stop before you emerge on the flat stretch leading to Réthymnon is at **PÁNORMOS**. This makes a good stopover if you're in search of somewhere more peaceful and authentic. The small sandy beach can get crowded when boats bring day-trippers from Réthymnon, but most of the time the attractive village remains relatively unspoiled, and succeeds in clinging to its Cretan identity. There are several decent **tavernas** – try *Taverna Panorama* in the heart of the village – and **rooms** places, one large hotel and the very comfortable *Pension Lucy* (☎08340/51 212, ℉51 434; ❷), which has also sprung a seafront offshoot with balcony studio rooms and apartments.

Inland towards Mount Psilorítis

Of the **inland routes**, the old main road (via Márathos and Dhamásta) is not the most interesting. This, too, was something of a bypass in its day and there are few places of any size or appeal, though it's a very scenic drive. If you want to dawdle, you're better off on the road which cuts up to **Týlissos** and then goes via **Anóyia**. It's a pleasant ride through fertile valleys filled with olive groves and vineyards, a district (the Malevísi) renowned from Venetian times for the strong, sweet Malmsey wine.

Týlissos and Anóyia

TÝLISSOS has a significant archeological site (daily 8.30am–3pm; €1.20) where three Minoan houses were excavated; unfortunately, its reputation is based more on what was found here (many pieces in the Iráklion museum) and on its significance for archeologists than on anything which remains to be seen. Still, it's worth a look, if you're passing, for a glimpse of Minoan life away from the big palaces, and for the tranquillity of the pine-shaded remains.

ANÓYIA is a much more tempting place to stay, especially if the summer heat is becoming oppressive. Spilling prettily down a hillside close below the highest peaks of the mountains, it looks traditional, but closer inspection shows that most of the buildings are actually concrete; the village was destroyed during World War II and the local men rounded up and shot – one of the German reprisals for the abduction of General Kreipe by the Cretan Resistance. The town has a reputation as a **handicrafts** centre (especially for woven and woollen goods), skills acquired both through bitter necessity after most of the men had been killed, and in a conscious attempt to revive the town. At any rate it worked, for the place is thriving today – thanks, it seems, to a buoyant agricultural sector made rich by stockbreeding, and the number of elderly widows keen to subject any visitor to their terrifyingly aggressive sales techniques.

Quite a few people pass through Anóyia during the day, but not many of them stay, even though there are some good pensions and rented rooms in the upper half of the town, including the flower-bedecked *Aris* (☏08340/31 460, ℱ31 058; ❶) and the nearby *Aristea* (☏08340/31 459; ❷), which has en-suite rooms and spectacular views, and includes breakfast. The town has a very different, more traditional ambience at night, and the only problem is likely to be finding a **place to eat**: although there are plenty of snack bars and so-called tavernas, most have extremely basic menus, more or less limited to spit-barbecued lamb, which is the tasty local speciality served up by the grill places on the lower square. If you can face it, a steep hike to the top of the village will bring you to *Taverna Skalómata* with well-prepared taverna standards and a fine view.

Mount Psilorítis and its caves

Heading for the mountains, a smooth road ascends the 21km from Anóyia to an altitude of 1400m on the **Nídha plateau** at the base of Mount Psilorítis. Here, the *Taverna Nida* (☏08340/31 141; April–Sept daily; Sat & Sun only in winter) serves up hearty taverna standards and has a couple of **rooms** (❶), which makes it a good base for hikes in the surrounding mountains. A short path leads from the taverna to the celebrated **Idhéon Ándhron** (Idean cave), a rival of that on Mount Dhíkti (see p.237) for the title of Zeus's birthplace, and certainly associated from the earliest of times with the cult of Zeus. The remnants of a major archeological dig carried out inside – including a miniature railway used by archeologists to remove tonnes of rock and rubble – still litter the site giving the place a rather unattractive prospect. When you enter the cave down concrete steps into the depths, it turns out to be a rather shallow affair, devoid even of natural wonders. In short, there's not a great deal to see.

The taverna also marks the start of the way to the top of **Mount Psilorítis** (2456m), Crete's highest mountain, a climb that for experienced, properly shod hikers is not at all arduous. The route (now forming a stretch of the E4 Pan-European footpath) is well marked with the usual red dots, and it should be a six- to seven-hour return journey to the **chapel of Tímios Stavrós** ("Holy Cross") at the summit, although in spring, thick snow may slow you down.

If you're prepared to camp on the plateau (it's very cold, but there's plenty of available water) or find rooms at the taverna, you could continue on foot next day down to the southern slopes of the range. It's a beautiful hike and also relatively easy, four hours or so down a fairly clear path to **Vorízia** where there is no food or accommodation, although **KAMÁRES**, 4km west, has both: for **rooms**, the very cheap and basic *Hotel Psiloritis* (℡08920/43 290; ❶) should have a bed, and the best **place to eat** is the *Taverna Bournelis* at the village's western end. If you're still interested in **caves**, there's a more rewarding one above Kamáres, a climb of some five hours on a good, but aggressively steep path. The start of the route is just to the left of the *Taverna Bournelis* and the proprietors here can advise on the ascent (in Greek and German only). There is at least one daily **bus** from here down to Míres and alternate (more difficult) routes to the peak of Psilorítis if you want to approach from this direction.

Eastern Crete

Eastern Crete is dominated by **Áyios Nikólaos**, and while it is a highly developed resort, by no means all of the east is like this. Far fewer people venture beyond the road south to **Ierápetra** and into the eastern isthmus, where only **Sitía** and the famous beach at **Vái** ever see anything approaching a crowd. Inland, too, there's interest, especially on the extraordinary **Lasíthi** plateau, which is worth a night's stay if only to observe its abidingly rural life.

Inland to the Lasíthi plateau

Leaving the palace at Mália, the highway cuts inland towards **NEÁPOLI**, soon beginning a spectacular climb into the mountains. Set in a high valley, Neápoli is a market town little touched by tourism. There is one excellent **hotel** (*Neapolis*; ℡08410/33 966; ❷), some rooms, a modern church and a folk museum. Beyond the town, it's about twenty minutes before the bus suddenly emerges high above the Gulf of Mirabéllo and Áyios Nikólaos, the island's biggest resort. If you're stopping, Neápoli also marks the second point of access to the **Lasíthi Plateau**.

Scores of bus tours drive up here daily to view the "thousands of white-cloth-sailed windmills" which irrigate the high plain ringed by mountains, and most groups will be disappointed. There are very few working windmills left, and these operate only for limited periods (mainly in June), although most roadside tavernas seem to have adopted many of those made redundant as marketing features. This is not to say the trip is not justified, as it would be for the drive alone, and there are many other compensations. The plain is a fine example of rural Crete at work, every inch devoted to the cultivation of potatoes, apples, pears, figs, olives and a host of other crops; stay in one of the villages for a night or two and you'll see real life return as the tourists leave. There are plenty of easy rambles around the villages as well, through orchards and past the rusting remains of derelict windmills.

You'll find **rooms** in the main village of **TZERMIÁDHO**, where the *Hotel Kourites* (℡08440/22 194; ❷) is to be found on the eastern edge, **ÁYIOS**

YEÓRYIOS – where there's a **folk museum**, and the economical and friendly *Hotel Dias* (℡08440/31 207; ❶) – and **PSYKHRÓ**, where the *Hotel Zeus* (℡08440/31 284; ❷) lies close to the Dhiktean cave.

The Dhiktean cave

Psykhró is much the most visited village on the plateau, as it's the base for visiting Lasíthi's other chief attraction, the birthplace of Zeus, the **Dhiktean cave** (daily 8.30am–7pm, Oct–March closes at 3pm; €2.40). In legend, Zeus's father, the Titan Kronos, was warned that he would be overthrown by a son and accordingly ate all his offspring; however, when Rhea gave birth to Zeus in the cave, she fed Kronos a stone and left the child concealed, protected by the Kouretes, who beat their shields outside to disguise his cries. The rest, as they say, is history (or at least myth). There's an obvious path running up to the cave from Psykhró, near the start of which (beyond the car park) the mule handlers will attempt to persuade you the ascent is better done on one of their steeds (costing a hefty €6). In reality, it's hardly a particularly long or dauntingly steep hike to the cave entrance.

The cave has been made more "visitor-friendly" in recent years which has introduced concrete steps in place of slippery stones, and electric lighting instead of flashlamps and candles. Inevitably some of the magic and mystery has been lost and the "guides", who used to make the visit much more interesting with their hilarious and preposterous tales, have now been banned, presumably in the interests of accuracy and decorum. Thus you will now have to pick out for yourself the stalactites and stalagmites formed in the image of the breasts of Rhea where the infant Zeus was suckled, as well as the baby Zeus himself – a feat verging on the impossible for someone lacking a Cretan imagination.

One of the cave guardians, Petros Zarvakis, is also a wildlife expert and leads **guided wild-flower and bird-spotting hikes** (April–Sept) into the mountains surrounding the plain, and also to the summit of Mount Dhíkti; if he is not on duty at the cave entrance, he can be contacted at his home in the village (℡08440/31 316 for details). **Buses** run around the plateau to Psykhró direct from Iráklion and from Áyios Nikólaos via Neápoli. Both roads offer spectacular views, coiling through a succession of passes guarded by lines of ruined windmills.

Áyios Nikólaos and around

ÁYIOS NIKÓLAOS ("Ag Nik" to the majority of its British visitors) is set around a supposedly bottomless **salt lake**, now connected to the sea to form an inner harbour. It is supremely picturesque and has some style and charm, which it exploits to the full. There are no sights as such but the excellent **archeological museum** (Tues–Sun 8.30am–3pm; €1.45) and an interesting **folk museum** (daily except Sat 10am–1.30pm & 7–9.30pm; €0.90) are both worth seeking out. The lake and port are surrounded by restaurants and bars, which charge above the odds, and whilst the resort is still very popular, some tourists are distinctly surprised to find themselves in a place with no decent beach at all.

There are swimming opportunities further north however, where the pleasant low-key resort of **Eloúnda** is the gateway to the mysterious islet of **Spinalónga**, and some great backcountry to the north – perfect to explore on a scooter. Inland from Áyios Nikólaos, **Kritsá** with its famous frescoed church and textile sellers is a tour-bus haven, but just a couple of kilometres away, the imposing ruins of **ancient Lató** are usually deserted.

Áyios Nikólaos practicalities

The **tourist office** (April–Oct daily 8am–9.30pm; ☎08410/22 357, ℱ82 534), situated between the lake and the port, is one of the best on the island for information about accommodation. The greatest concentration of **stores** and **travel agents** are on the hill between the bridge and Platía Venizélou (along the streets 25-Martíou, Koundourou and 28-Oktovríou). The main **ferry agent** is Plora Travel (☎08410/26 465 or 23 090) on the corner of 28-Oktovríou and K. Sfakianáki. The **post office** (Mon–Sat 7.30am–2pm) is halfway up the newly pedestrianized 28-Oktovríou on the right. To **hire a motorbike**, **scooter** or **mountain bike** try the reliable Mike Manolis

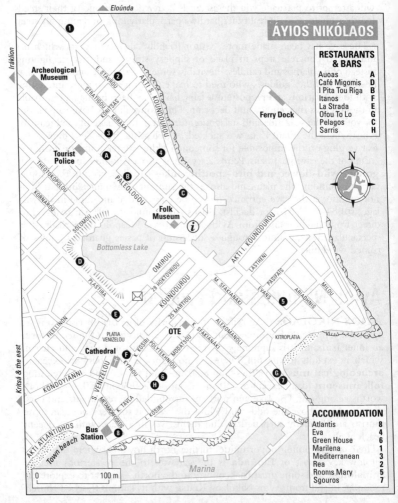

ÁYIOS NIKÓLAOS

▲ Eloúnda

◄ Iráklion

Archeological Museum

Tourist Police

Folk Museum
ⓘ

Bottomless Lake

◄ Kritsá & the east

Cathedral

OTE

PLATÍA VENIZÉLOU

Bus Station

AKTÍ ATLANTIDHOS

Town beach

Marina

Ferry Dock

N

RESTAURANTS & BARS

Auoas	A
Café Migomis	D
I Pita Tou Ríga	B
Itanos	F
La Strada	E
Ofou To Lo	G
Pelagos	C
Sarris	H

ACCOMMODATION

Atlantis	8
Eva	4
Green House	6
Marilena	1
Mediterranean	3
Rea	2
Rooms Mary	5
Sgouros	7

0 — 100 m

(☎08410/24 940), who has a pitch along Modatsou, just northeast of the OTE. Good **car rental** deals are available at Club Cars, 28-Oktovríou 24 (☎08410/25 868), near the post office. Various **boat trips** to points around the gulf (such as Spinalónga and Eloúnda; about €7.50) leave from the west side of the harbour. **Internet** cafés *Peripou*, 28-Oktovríou 25 (daily 9.30am–2am; €3 per hour), and *Café du Lac* at no. 17 on the same street are Áyios Nikólaos's most central places to pick up your emails.

Accommodation

The town is no longer packed solid with tourists, so it is much easier to find a place to stay, though in the peak season you won't have so much choice. One thing in your favour is that there are literally thousands of **rooms**, scattered all around town. The tourist office normally has a couple of boards with cards and brochures about hotels and rooms, including their prices. If the prices seem very reasonable it is because many are for the low season. There is no longer a youth hostel, and the nearest **campsite** is *Gournia Moon*, 17km away (see p.242).

(see p.242).

Atlantis, Metamorfoseos, one block east of the bus station ☎08410/28 964. Nothing special but handy for early or late buses; there's a snack bar below for breakfast. ❶

Hotel Eva, Stratigoú Kóraka 20 ☎08410/22 587. Decent simple rooms in a misnamed pension close to the centre. ❶

Green House, Modhátsou 15 ☎08410/22 025. Probably the best cheap place to stay in town; clean with shared facilities. ❶

Marilena, Érythrou Stavroú 14 ☎08410/22 681, ℉24 218. Not the bargain it once was, but it's still a pleasant place to stay; some rooms with sea view and balcony. ❸

Rooms Mary, Evans 13 near the Kitroplatía ☎08410/24 384. Very friendly place with en-suite balcony rooms (some with sea view); access to fridge and use of kitchen. Also has some apartments nearby costing slightly more. ❶

Mediterranean, S. Dhávaki 27 ☎08410/23 611. Clean, economical rooms without bath close to the lake. ❶

Hotel Rea, Marathónos 1 ☎08410/82 023, ℉28 324. Charming older hotel with stunning views from pleasant balcony rooms overlooking the Mirabéllo Gulf. ❸

Sgouros, Kitroplatía ☎08410/28 931, ℉25 568. Modern hotel overlooking one of the town's beaches, and close to plenty of tavernas. ❷

Eating

At least when it comes to eating there's no chance of missing out, even if some of the prices are fancier than the restaurants. There are tourist-oriented **tavernas** all around the lake and harbour and little to choose between them, apart from the different perspectives you get on the passing fashion show. Have a drink here perhaps, or a mid-morning coffee, and choose somewhere else to eat. The places around the Kitroplatía are generally fairer value, but again you are paying for the location.

Auoas, Paleológou 44. This taverna serves good, traditional Cretan dishes in and under a plant-covered trellised courtyard, where food and wine prices are among the lowest in town.

Café Migomis, Nikoláou Plastíra 22. Pleasant café high above the bottomless lake with a stunning view. Perfect place for breakfast, afternoon or evening drinks.

I Pita Tou Ríga, Paleológou 24, close to the lake. Excellent Lilliputian snack-bar/restaurant serving imaginative fare – salads, filled pitta breads and some Asian dishes; has a small terrace.

Itanos, Kýprou 1, off the east side of Platía Venizélou. Popular with locals, this taverna serves

Cretan food and wine and has a terrace across the road opposite.

La Strada, Nikoláou Plastíra 5, just below the west side of Platía Venizélou. Authentic and good-value pizza and pasta (although the meat dishes are pricey), should you fancy a change of cuisine.

Ofou To Lo, Kitroplatía. Best of the moderately priced places on the seafront here: the food is consistently good.

Pelagos, on Stratigoú Kóraka, just back off the lake behind the tourist office. A stylish fish taverna with garden, serving excellent food reflected in the prices.

Sarri's, Kíprou 15, off the east side of Platía Venizélou. Great little economical neighbourhood

café-diner especially good for breakfast fare and *souvláki*, all served on a leafy terrace.

Drinking and nightlife

After you've eaten you can get into the one thing which Áyios Nikólaos unde-niably does well: **bars and nightlife**. Not that you really need a guide to this – the bars are hard to avoid, and you can just follow the crowds to the most popular places centred around the harbour and 25-Martíou. For a more relaxed drink you could try *Hotel Alexandros* on Paleológou (behind the tourist office), with a rooftop cocktail bar overlooking the lake, which after dark metamor-phoses into a 1960s to 1980s period music bar. A similar pace rules at *Zygos* on the north side of the lake which serves low-priced cocktails and ices until the small hours. One curiosity worth a look in the harbour itself is *Armida*, a bar inside a beautifully restored century-old wooden trading vessel, serving cock-tails and simple *mezédhes*.

Quiet drinking, however, is not what it's all about in the **disco bars**. *Lipstick*, on the east side of the harbour is the only genuine full-blown dance club while the nearby *Studio* doesn't hit its stride until the small hours when the pubs and restaurants close. There are raucous music bars to try at the bottom of 25-Martíou ("Soho Street") where it heads up the hill – *Rififi*, *Royale*, *Tounel* and *Sant Maria* all get going at sunset; across the harbour *Aquarius*, *Charlie Chan*, *Lotus*, *Cellar* and *Roxy* are also very popular and you'll soon be accosted by their respective greeters as they each try to persuade you to help swell their takings.

The coast north of Áyios Nikólaos

North of Áyios Nikólaos, the swankier hotels are strung out along the coast road, with upmarket restaurants, discos and cocktail bars scattered between them. **ELOÚNDA**, a resort on a more acceptable scale, is about 8km out along this road. Buses run regularly, but if you feel like renting a scooter it's a spec-tacular ride, with impeccable views over a gulf dotted with islands and moored supertankers. Ask at the bookshop near the post office, on the central square facing the sea, about the attractive seaview *Delfinia Apartments* (☎08410/41 641, ℱ41 515; ❶–❹). Or you could try the friendly *Pension Oasis* (☎08410/41 076, ℱ41 128; ❷), which has rooms with kitchenette just off the square, behind the church; there are quite a few similar places along the same road. Alternatively, one of the many travel agents around the main square can help with finding a room or apartment; try the friendly Olous Travel (☎08410/41 324, ℱ41 132), which also gives out information and changes money or trav-ellers' cheques. For **eating**, *Britomares*, in a plum spot in the centre of the har-bour, is the town's best taverna, and more economical fish and *mezédhes* are to be had at the simple *Ouzerí Manos*, last in line on the north side of the har-bour. **Nightlife** tends to be generally low key, and centres around café terraces and cocktail bars. The *Hellas* café, on a backroad behind the beach, has live Greek music at weekends.

Just before the centre of the village, a road (signposted) leads downhill to a natural causeway leading to the ancient "sunken city" of **Oloús**. There are restored windmills, a short length of canal, Venetian salt pans and a well-pre-served dolphin **mosaic**, inside a former Roman basilica, but of the sunken city itself no trace beyond a couple of walls in about two feet of water. At any rate swimming is good, though watch out for sea urchins.

From Eloúnda, kaïkia run half-hourly in high season (about €6 return) to the fortress-rock of **Spinalónga**. As a bastion of the Venetian defence, this tiny islet withstood the Turkish invaders for 45 years after the mainland had fallen; in more recent decades, it served as a leper colony. As you watch the boat which brought you disappear to pick up another group, an unnervingly real sense of the desolation of those years descends. **PLÁKA**, back on the mainland, and 5km north of Eloúnda, used to be the colony's supply point; now it is a haven from the crowds, with a small pebble beach and a couple of ramshackle fish **tavernas**, one of which, *Taverna Spinalonga*, can arrange a boat to take you across to Spinalónga for about €4.50. There are boat trips daily from Áyios Nikólaos to Oloús, Eloúnda and Spinalónga (costing around €7.50–9), usually visiting at least one other island along the way.

Inland to Kritsá and Lató

The other excursion everyone takes from Áyios Nikólaos is to **KRITSÁ**, a "traditional" village about 10km inland. Buses run at least every hour from the bus station, and despite the commercialization it's still a good trip: the local **crafts** (weaving, ceramics and embroidery basically, though they sell almost everything here) are fair value, and it's also a welcome break from living in the fast lane at "Ag Nik". In fact, if you're looking for somewhere to stay around here, Kritsá has a number of advantages: chiefly availability of **rooms**, better prices and something at least approaching a genuinely Cretan atmosphere; try *Argyro* (☎08410/51 174; ❶), with pleasant rooms around a courtyard on your way in to the village. The small platía at the centre of the village is the focus of life and there are a number of decent places to eat here, too: *Taverna-Snack Bar Tzortzis*, just uphill from the platía and bus stop, is a good bet, or *Sygonos*, near the bus stop, for a meal or coffee and cake under one of the plane trees.

On the approach road, some 2km before Kritsá, is the lovely Byzantine **church of Panayía Kyrá** (April–Oct daily 8.30am–2.30pm; €2.40), inside which survives perhaps the most complete set of Byzantine frescoes in Crete. The fourteenth- and fifteenth-century works have been much retouched, but they're still worth the visit. Excellent (and expensive) reproductions are sold from a shop alongside. Just beyond the church, a surfaced road leads off for 3km to the archeological site of **Lató** (Tues–Sun 9am–3pm; closed first Sun of the month; free), where the substantial remains of a Doric city are coupled with a grand hilltop setting. The city itself is extensive, but largely neglected, presumably because visitors and archeologists on Crete are more concerned with the Minoan era. Ruins aside, you could come here just for the views: west over Áyios Nikólaos and beyond to the bay and Oloús (which was Lató's port), and inland to the Lasíthi mountains.

The eastern isthmus

The main road south and then east from Áyios Nikólaos is not a wildly exciting one, essentially a drive through barren hills sprinkled with villas and skirting above the occasional sandy cove. Five kilometres beyond a cluster of development at Kaló Hório, a track is indicated on the right for the **Moní Faneroméni**. The track (though partly asphalted) is a rough one and climbs dizzily skywards for 6km, giving spectacular views over the Gulf of Mirabéllo along the way. The **view** from the monastery over the gulf must be among the finest in Crete. To get into the rather bleak-looking monastery buildings, knock loudly. You will be shown up to the chapel, built into a cave sanctuary, and the frescoes – although late – are quite brilliant.

Gourniá, Pahiá Ámmos and Mókhlos

Back on the coast road, it's another 2km to the site of **Gourniá** (Tues–Sun 8.30am–3pm; €1.45), slumped in the saddle between two low peaks. The most completely preserved **Minoan town**, its narrow alleys and stairways intersect a throng of one-roomed houses (of which only the ground-floor walls survive – they would have had at least one upper floor) centred on a main square, and the rather grand house of what may have been a local ruler or governor. Although less impressive than the great palaces, the site is strong on revelations about the lives of the ordinary people – many of the dwellings housed crafts-men in wood, metal and clay, who left behind their tools and materials to be found by the excavators. Its desolation today (you are likely to be alone save for a dozing guard) only serves to heighten the contrast with what must have been a cramped and raucous community 3500 years ago.

It is tempting to cross the road here and take one of the paths through the wild thyme to the sea for a swim. Don't bother – the bay and others along this part of the coastline act as a magnet for every piece of floating detritus dumped off Crete's north coast. There is a larger beach (though with similar problems), and rooms to rent, in the next bay along at **PAHIÁ ÁMMOS**, about twenty-minutes' walk, where there is also an excellent fish taverna, *Aiolus*; in the other direction, there's the campsite of *Gournia Moon* (☎08420/93 243), with its own small cove and a swimming pool.

This is the narrowest part of the island, and from here a fast road cuts across the isthmus to Ierápetra (p.246) in the south. In the north though, the route on towards Sitía is one of the most exhilarating in Crete. Carved into cliffs and mountain-sides, the road teeters above the coast before plunging inland at Kavoúsi. Of the beaches you see below, only **MÓKHLOS** is at all accessible, some 5km below the main road. This sleepy seaside village has a few rooms, a hotel or two and a number of **tavernas** – *To Bogázi* is good – squatting along its tiny harbour; if you find yourself needing a **place to stay**, you could try the rooms at the clean and simple *Pension Hermes* (☎08430/97 074; ➊) behind the waterfront, which are the cheapest in the village, or there's *Hotel Sofia* (☎08430/94 738, ℻94 238; ➋) on the harbour itself for a bit more en-suite luxury. Nearer Sitía the familiar olive groves are interspersed with vineyards used for creating wine and sultanas, and in late summer the grapes, spread to dry in the fields and on rooftops, make an extraordinary sight in the varying stages of their slow change from green to gold to brown.

Sitía

SITÍA is the port and main town of the relatively unexploited eastern edge of Crete. It's a pleasantly scenic if unremarkable place, offering a plethora of water-side restaurants, a long sandy beach and a lazy lifestyle little affected even by the thousands of visitors in peak season. There's an almost Latin feel to the town, reflected in (or perhaps caused by) the number of French and Italian tourists, and it's one of those places that tends to grow on you, perhaps inviting a longer stay than intended. For entertainment there's the **beach**, providing good swimming and windsurfing, and in town a mildly entertaining **folklore museum** (Mon–Sat 9.30am–5pm; €1.45), a Venetian fort and Roman fish tanks to explore, plus an excellent **archeological museum** (July & Aug daily 8.30am–3pm; Sept–June Tues–Sun same hours; €1.45). As part of a government push to increase tourism at this end of the island, a new **international airport** (due to open in 2004) is being constructed on a plateau above the town, and will most likely have a big impact on Sitía itself as well as the surrounding area.

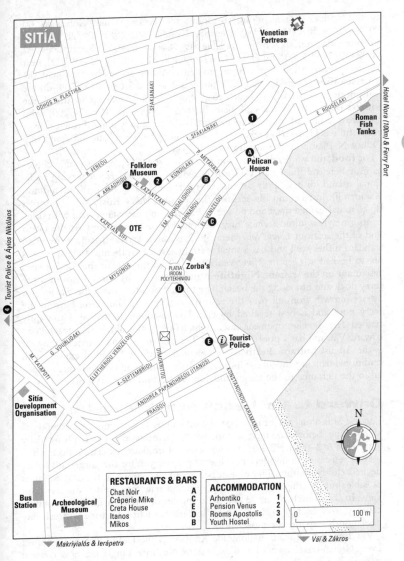

SITÍA

Venetian
Fortress

ODHOS N. PLASTIRA

SFAKIANAKI

I. SFAKIANAKI

E. ROUSELAKI

Roman
Fish
Tanks

R. FEREOU

Folklore
Museum

2

1

A
Pelican
House

Hotel Nora (100m) & Ferry Port

V. ARKADHIOU

N. KAZANTZAKI

I. KONDILAKI

P. METAXAKI

3

EM. LOUNDALIDHOU

B

V. KORNAROU

EL. VENIZELOU

C

KAPETAN SIFI

OTE

MYSONOS

PLATIA
IROON
POLYTEKHNIOU

Zorba's

D

Tourist Police & Áyios Nikólaos

G. VOURLIDAKI

ELEFTHERIOU VENIZELOU

DIMOKRITOU

E

i Tourist
Police

M. KATAPOTI

4-SEPTEMVRIOU

ANDHREA PAPANDHREOU (ITANOS)

PRAISOU

KONSTANDINOU KARAMANLI

Sitía
Development
Organisation

N

CRETE | The eastern isthmus

3

Bus
Station

Archeological
Museum

RESTAURANTS & BARS
Chat Noir   A
Crêperie Mike   C
Creta House   E
Itanos   D
Mikos   B

ACCOMMODATION
Arhontiko   1
Pension Venus   2
Rooms Apostolis   3
Youth Hostel   4

0   100 m

Makriyialós & Ierápetra

Váï & Zákros

Practicalities

The bus drops you at the new **bus station** (actually an office on the street) on the southwest fringe of the centre and close to the town's main **supermarket**, useful for stocking up on provisions. There are plenty of cheap pensions and **rooms** within easy walking distance, especially in the streets around the folklore museum and beyond here towards the ferry port. A good and friendly **youth hostel** (☎08430/22 693; dorm beds €4.40, rooms ❶) on the main road as it enters town from Áyios Nikólaos also has a few private rooms and a garden for tents; there's rarely any problem about sleeping on the beach (though it is worth going a little way out of town to avoid any danger of being roused by the police). For economical rooms, try *Pension Venus*, Kondiláki 60 (☏08430/24 307; ❶), or *Hotel Arhontiko*, Kondiláki 16 (☏08430/28 172; ❶); en-suite accommodation is available at *Rooms Apostolis*, Kazantzákis 27 (☏08430/22 993; ❷), and *Hotel Nora*, Rouseláki 31 (☏08430/23 017; ❷), near the ferry port. Should you have problems finding somewhere to stay, the **tourist office** (Mon–Fri 9am–2.30pm & 5–8.30pm; ☏08430/23 300) on the seafront at the start of the beach road should be able to help, or there's the **tourist police** at Mysónos 24 (daily 7.30am–2.30pm; ☏08430/24 200), who also provide limited tourist information; both can supply a good town map. A colourful weekly **market** takes place on Tuesdays between 7am and 2pm along Odhós N. Plastira to the northwest of the centre.

For **food**, the waterside places are relatively expensive; the best-value choices near here are the *Itanos Cafe* for mezédhes and *Creta House* serving traditional island dishes, both at the start of the beach road (Konstandínou Karamanlí). Just behind the seafront the popular *Mikos*, Kornárou 117, serves up charcoal-grilled meat and potent local wine, and the waiters run with dishes to a newly aquired terrace fifty metres away on the seafront. At the north end of the seafront *Chat Noir*, Metaxaki 2, is a new arrival that does the usual standard dishes well and has a small seafront terrace. Authentic Belgian crepes are to be had at *Creperie Mike*, Venizélou 162, to the east of the focal *Zorba's* restaurant on the seafront. **Nightlife** centres on a few bars and discos near the ferry dock and out along the beach. The town's monster disco-club, *Planitarion*, attracts crowds from all over the east. It's a couple of kilometres beyond the ferry port, and is best reached by taxi. The in-town alternative is the aptly named *Hot Summer* open-air disco, which lies 800m along the beach road towards Váï, and has a pool and gardens. The one major excitement of the year is the August **Sultana Festival** – a celebration of the big local export, with traditional dancing and all the locally produced wine you can consume included in the entrance to the fairground, located beyond the ferry port.

Onward to Váï Beach and Palékastro

Leaving Sitía along the beach, the Váï road climbs above a rocky, unexceptional coastline before reaching a fork to the **monastery of Toploú** (daily 9am–1pm & 2–6pm; €2.40). The monastery's forbidding exterior reflects a history of resistance to invaders, but doesn't prepare you for the gorgeous flower-decked cloister within. The blue-robed monks keep out of the way as far as possible, but in quieter periods their cells and refectory are left discreetly on view. In the church is one of the masterpieces of Cretan art, the eighteenth-century icon *Lord Thou Art Great* by Ioannis Kornaros. Outside you can buy enormously expensive reproductions.

Váï Beach itself features alongside Knossós or the Lasíthi plateau on almost every Cretan travel agent's list of excursions. Not surprisingly, it is now covered in sunbeds and umbrellas, though it is still a superb beach. Above all, it is famous for its palm trees, and the sudden appearance of the grove is indeed an exotic shock; lying on the fine sand in the early morning, the illusion is of a Caribbean island – a feature seized upon by countless TV-commercial makers seeking an exotic location on the cheap. As everywhere, notices warn that "camping is forbidden by law", and for once the authorities seem to mean it – most campers climb over the headlands to the south or north. If you do sleep out, watch your belongings, since this seems to be the one place on Crete with crime on any scale. There's a compulsory car park (€1.75), a café and an expensive taverna at the beach, plus toilets and showers. Because of its status as a nature reserve there is **no accommodation** here whatsoever; the nearest place offering a bed for the night is Palékastro (see below). By day you can find a bit more solitude by climbing the rocks or swimming to one of the smaller beaches which surround Váï. **Ítanos**, twenty minutes' walk north by an obvious trail, has a couple of tiny beaches and some modest ruins from the Classical era.

PALÉKASTRO, an attractive farming village some 9km south, makes a good place to stopover. Although its beaches can't begin to compare with those at Váï, you'll find several modest places with **rooms** – among them *Hotel Hellas* (℡08430/61 240, ℻61 340, ⓔhellas_h@otenet.gr; ❷), which offers en-suite facilities and food, and the good-value *Vai* (℡08430/61 287; ❶), with rooms above a taverna at the west end of the village, on the Sitía road. The extensive **beaches** provide plenty of space to **camp** out without the crowds, but you should respect local sensitivities, keeping away from the main strands and responsibly disposing of any rubbish. Add in a small **folk museum** (May–Oct Tues–Sun 8.30am–1pm; free), a number of reasonable **tavernas**, a few **bars** and even a **dance–club**, *Design*, and the place begins to seem positively throbbing. The sea is a couple of kilometres down a dirt track, effortlessly reached with a scooter hired from Motor Action (℡08430/61 276) next door to the *Hotel Hellas*. Palékastro is also the crossroads for the road south to Zákros and your own transport presents all kinds of beach and exploration possibilities.

Zákros

ÁNO ZÁKROS (Upper Zákros) lies a little under 20km from Palékastro. There are several tavernas and a simple hotel, the *Zakros* (℡08430/43 379, ℻93 379; ❶), which has some rooms with bath and great views from its rear rooms; it also offers guests a free minibus service to the Minoan palace and beach. The Minoan palace is actually at Káto ("lower") Zákros, 8km further down towards the sea. Most buses run only to the upper village, but in summer, a couple every day do run all the way to the site. Part way along you can, if on foot, take a short cut through an impressive **gorge** (the "Valley of the Dead", named for ancient tombs in its sides) but it's usually not difficult to hitch if your bus does leave you in the village.

The **Palace of Zákros** (Tues–Sun: April–Sept 8am–7pm; Oct–March 8am–3pm; €1.45) was an important find for archeologists; it had been occupied only once (between 1600 and 1450 BC), and was abandoned hurriedly and completely. Later, it was forgotten almost entirely and as a result was never plundered or even discovered by archeologists until very recently. The first major excavation began only in 1960; all sorts of everyday objects (tools, raw materials, food, pottery) were thus discovered intact among the ruins, and a great deal was learned from being able to apply modern techniques (and knowledge of the Minoans) to a major dig from the very beginning. None of this is especially evident when you're at the palace, except perhaps in a particularly simple ground plan, so it's as well that it is also a rewarding visit in terms of the setting. Although the site is set back from the sea, in places it is often marshy and waterlogged – partly the result of eastern Crete's slow subsidence, partly the fault of a spring which once supplied fresh water to a cistern beside the royal apartments, and whose outflow is now silted up. In wetter periods, among the remains of narrow streets and small houses of the town outside the palace and higher up, you can keep your feet dry and get an excellent view down over the central court and royal apartments. If you want a more detailed overview of the remains, buy the guide to the site on sale at the entrance.

The delightful village of **KÁTO ZÁKROS** is little more than a collection of tavernas, some of which rent out rooms around a peaceful beach and minuscule fishing anchorage. It's a wonderfully restful place, but is often unable to cope with the volume of visitors seeking accommodation in high season, and as rooms are rarely to be had on spec you'd be wise to ring ahead. You should also be aware that villagers are far more hostile these days to wild camping after years of problems, and you should be sensitive to their concerns. Reliable rooms can be found at *Poseidon* (℡08430/93 316; ❶), which has fine sea views, and the friendly *George Villas* (℡ & ℱ 08430/93 201; ❷), 600m behind the archeological site along a driveable track. Otherwise ask at the seafront *Poseidon* (℡08430/26 896) taverna which seems to act as an agent for many other room options.

Ierápetra and the southeast coast

From Sitía, the route south is a cross-country roller-coaster ride until it hits the south coast at **MAKRYIALÓS**. This little fishing village has one of the best beaches at this end of Crete, with fine sand which shelves so gently you feel you could walk the 320km to Africa. Unfortunately, since the early 1990s it has been heavily developed, so while still a very pleasant place to stop for a swim or a bite (the outstanding *Porfira* taverna on the sea is recommended), it's not somewhere you're likely to find cheap **rooms**. Outside of peak season you could try *Irini Rooms* (℡08430/51 422; ❷), on the main road through the village near where the bus drops you.

From here to Ierápetra there's little reason to stop; the few beaches are rocky and the coastal plain submerged under ranks of polythene-covered greenhouses. Beside the road leading into Ierápetra are long but exposed stretches of sand, including the appropriately named "Long Beach", where you'll find a **campsite**, *Camping Koutsounari* (℡08420/61 213), which offers plenty of shade and has a taverna and minimarket.

Ierápetra

IERÁPETRA itself is a bustling modern supply centre for the region's farmers. It also attracts a fair number of package tourists and not a few backpackers looking for work in the prosperous surrounding agricultural zone, especially out of season. The tavernas along the tree-lined seafront are scenic enough and the EU blue-flagged beach stretches a couple miles east. But as a town, most people find it pretty uninspiring, despite an ongoing modernization programme which has cleaned up the centre and revamped the seafront. Although there has been a port here since Roman times, only the **Venetian fort** guarding the harbour and a crumbling Turkish minaret remain as reminders of better days. What little else has been salvaged is in the one-room **Archeological Museum** (Tues–Sat 8am–3pm; €1.50) near the post office.

The town hall (*dhimarhío*) on the main square Platía Kanoupáki, or the library next door, should be able to provide a copy of the detailed town map (but not much else) which will help you find your way around. If you want to stay, head up Kazantzákis from the chaotic bus station, and you'll find a friendly welcome and good-value apartment-style **rooms** at *Rooms Popi* at no. 27 (℡08420/24 289; ❶), or equal comfort in the nearby *Cretan Villa*, Lakérdha 16 (℡ & ℱ 08420/28 522, ⓦwww.cretan-villa.com; ❷), a beautiful 180-year-old house. More central and economical is the *Hotel Ersi*, Platía Eleftherías 20

(☎08420/23 208; ❶), which will also rent you a seafront apartment nearby for not much more than the cost of a room. The cheapest rooms option is *Rent Rooms Nikos*, Ioannidou 4, in the old town (☎08420/23 208; ❶), close to the *Gorgona* taverna. You'll find places to **eat** and **drink** all along the waterfront, the better places such as *Taverna Napoleon* and *Gorgona* being towards the Venetian fort. **Nightlife** centres on a clutch of **clubs**, **bars** and fast-food places along central Kyrba, behind the promenade. Ierápetra's **internet café**, *Orfeas* (€3 per 30min), is at Koundourioútou 25, just north of the museum, and serves good breakfasts.

West from Ierápetra

Heading west from Ierápetra, the first stretch of coast is grey and dusty, the road jammed with trucks and lined with drab ribbon development. There are a number of small resorts along the beach, though little in the way of public transport. If travelling under your own steam, there is a scenic detour worth taking at Gría Liyiá: the road on the right for Anatolí climbs to Máles, a village clinging to the lower slopes of the **Dhíkti range**. Here would be a good starting point for **walking** through some stunning mountain terrain (the E4 Pan-European footpath which crosses the island from east to west passes just 3km north of here). Otherwise, the dirt road back down towards the coast (signposted Míthi) has spectacular views over the Libyan Sea, and eventually follows the Mírtos river valley down to Mírtos itself.

Mýrtos and Árvi

MÝRTOS, 18km west of Ierápetra, is the first resort that might actually tempt you to stop, and it's certainly the most accessible, just off the main road with numerous daily **buses** to Ierápetra and a couple direct to Iráklion. Although developed to a degree, it nonetheless remains tranquil and inexpensive, with lots of young travellers (many of whom often sleep on the beach, to the irritation of locals). There are plenty of **rooms** possibilities, amongst which you could try the central *Rooms Angelos* (☎08420/51 106; ❷) and *Nikos House* (☎08420/51 116; ❶), or the less expensive *Rooms Despina* (☎08420/51 343; ❶) at the back of the village near the bus stop. A useful travel agent, Magic Tours (☎08420/25 135, ℻28 809) on the central main street is a good source of **information**, **changes money**, rents **cars** and sells boat and plane tickets. Just off the road from Ierápetra a couple of kilometres east of the village (and signed) are a couple of excavated hilltop **Minoan villas** you might want to explore: Néa Mýrtos and Pírgos.

After Mýrtos the main road turns inland towards Áno Viánnos, then continues across the island towards Iráklion; several places on the coast are reached by a series of rough side-tracks. That hasn't prevented one of them, **ÁRVI**, from becoming a larger resort than Mýrtos. The beach hardly justifies it, but it's an interesting little excursion (with at least one bus a day) if only to see the bananas and pineapples grown here and to experience the microclimate – noticeably warmer than neighbouring zones, especially in spring or autumn – that encourages them. For rooms you could try the central *Pension Gorgona* (☎08950/71 211; ❶).

Beyond Árvi

Two more villages, Keratókambos and Tsoútsouros, look tempting on the map. **KERATÓKAMBOS** has a rather stony beach and a range of **rooms**, not easy to come by in August. Try the *Morning Star* taverna (☎08950/51 209; ❶) which has rooms with and without bath, or the comparable *Taverna Kriti*

(☎08950/51 231; ❶) next door; the **food** at both places is tasty too. Although popular with Cretan day-trippers, Keratókambos is a great place to escape the tourist grind for a spell.

TSOÚTSOUROS, 10km west as the crow flies and now linked by an asphalted road to the major highway further north, is similar to its neighbour with a line of tavernas, hotels and rooms places arching behind a seafront, to the east and west of which are a couple of decent if pebbly, grey-sand **beaches**. Not as popular as its neighbours, **rooms** may be available here when the other resorts are full. Try *Rooms Mihalis* (☎08910/92 250; ❶) near the centre of the seafront. There are no facilities for changing money at either place, although both have a couple of **supermarkets**, handy for gathering picnic ingredients.

If you hope to continue across the **south** of the island, be warned that there are no buses, despite completion of the road towards Míres after years of work. It's an enjoyable rural drive, but progress can be slow; there's very little traffic if you're trying to hitch.

Réthymnon and around

The relatively low, narrow section of Crete which separates the Psilorítis range from the White Mountains in the west seems at first a nondescript, even dull part of the island. Certainly in scenic terms it has few of the excitements that the west can offer; there are no major archeological sites and many of the villages seem modern and ugly. On the other hand, **Réthymnon** itself is an attractive and lively city, with some excellent beaches nearby. And on the south coast, in particular around **Plakiás**, there are beaches as fine as any Crete can offer, and as you drive towards them the scenery and villages improve by the minute.

Réthymnon

Since the early 1980s, **RÉTHYMNON** has seen a greater influx of tourists than perhaps anywhere else on Crete, with the development of a whole series of large hotels extending almost 10km along the beach to the east. For once, though, the middle of town has been spared, so that at its heart Réthymnon remains one of the most beautiful of Crete's major cities (only Haniá is a serious rival) with an enduringly provincial air. A wide sandy beach and palm-lined promenade border a labyrinthine tangle of Venetian and Turkish houses lining streets where ancient minarets lend an exotic air to the skyline. Dominating everything from the west is the superbly preserved outline of the **fortress** built by the Venetians after a series of pirate raids had devastated the town.

The town

With a **beach** right in the heart of town, it's tempting not to stir at all from the sands, but Réthymnon repays at least some gentle exploration. For a start, you could try checking out the further reaches of the beach itself. The waters protected by the breakwaters in front of town have their disadvantages – notably crowds and dubious hygiene – but less sheltered sands stretch for miles to the east, crowded at first but progressively less so if you're prepared to walk a bit.

Away from the beach, you don't have far to go for the most atmospheric part of town, immediately behind the **inner harbour**. Almost anywhere here, you'll find unexpected old buildings, wall fountains, overhanging wooden balconies, heavy, carved doors and rickety shops, many still with local craftsmen sitting out front, gossiping as they ply their trades. Look out especially for the **Venetian loggia**, which houses a shop selling high quality and expensive reproductions of Classical art; the **Rimóndi fountain**, another of the more elegant Venetian survivals; and the **Nerandzés mosque**, the best preserved in

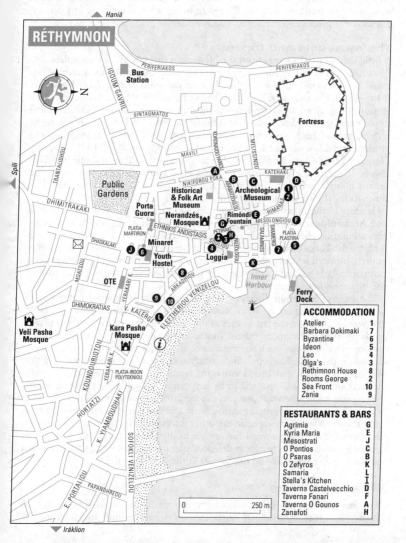

RÉTHYMNON

Haniá

Spíli

Iráklion

Bus Station

PERIFERIAKOS

PERIFERIAKOS

IGOUM GAVRIIL

SINTÁGMATOS

MÁVILI

KORONEOU PÁNOU

T. MELISSINOÚ

KATEHÁKI

Fortress

TRIANTALIDHOU

DHIMITRAKAKI

Public Gardens

NIKIFOROU FOKA

ARAMBATZOGLOU

A

B

C

D

Historical & Folk Art Museum

Archeological Museum

1
2

DHASKALAKI

MOÁTSOU

Porta Guora

PLATÍA MARTÍRON

Nerandzés Mosque

ETHNIKIS ANDISTASIS

PETIHÁKI

SOULIOU

Rimóndi Fountain

E

G

MESOLONGIOÚ

HIMÁRIS

F

PLATÍA PLÁSTIRA

DÁMVERGI

SALAMÍNOS

3
4

PALEOLÓGOU

Loggia

7

5

Minaret

J

6

H

Youth Hostel

K

OTE

8

Inner Harbour

DHIMOKRATÍAS

YERAKÁRI K.

9

ARKADHIOU

10

Ferry Dock

Veli Pasha Mosque

KOUNDOURIÓTOU

YERAKÁRI K.

Kara Pasha Mosque

V. KALÉRGI

ELEFTHERÍOU VENIZÉLOU

L

i

PLATÍA IROÓN POLYTEKNÍOU

HORTÁTZI

K. YIAMBOUDHÁKI

SOFOKLÍ VENIZÉLOU

E. PORTALIOU

PAPANDHRÉOU

N

0   250 m

ACCOMMODATION
Atelier	1
Barbara Dokimaki	7
Byzantine	6
Ideon	5
Leo	4
Olga's	3
Rethimnon House	8
Rooms George	2
Sea Front	10
Zania	9

RESTAURANTS & BARS
Agrimia	G
Kyria Maria	E
Mesostrati	J
O Pontios	C
O Psaras	B
O Zefyros	K
Samaria	I
Stella's Kitchen	L
Taverna Castelvecchio	D
Taverna Fanari	F
Taverna O Gounos	A
Zanafoti	H

249

Réthymnon but currently serving as a music school and closed to the public. When repairs are completed it should again be possible to climb the spiral staircase to the top of the **minaret** for a stunning view over the town. Simply by walking past these three, you'll have seen many of the liveliest parts of Réthymnon. Ethnikís Andistásis, the street leading straight up from the fountain, is also the town's **market** area.

The old city ends at the Porta Guora at the top of Ethnikís Andistásis, the only surviving remnant of the city walls. Almost opposite are the quiet and shady **public gardens**. These are always a soothing place to stroll, and in the latter half of July the **Réthymnon Wine Festival** is staged here. Though touristy, it's a thoroughly enjoyable event, with spectacular local dancing as the evening progresses and the barrels empty. The entrance fee includes all the wine you can drink, though you'll need to bring your own cup or buy one of the souvenir glasses and carafes on sale outside the gardens.

The museums and fortress

A little further up the street from the Nerandzés mosque at M.Vernárdhou 28, a beautifully restored seventeenth-century Venetian mansion is the home of the small but tremendously enjoyable **Historical and Folk Art Museum** (Mon–Fri 9.30am–2pm; €2.95, children and students €1.45). Gathered within four, cool, airy rooms are musical instruments, old photos, basketry, farm implements, an explanation of traditional ceramic and breadmaking techniques, smiths' tools, traditional costumes and jewellery, lace, weaving and embroidery (look out for a traditional-style tapestry made in 1941 depicting German parachutists landing at Máleme), pottery, knives and old wooden chests. It makes for a fascinating insight into a fast disappearing rural (and urban) lifestyle, which had often survived virtually unchanged from Venetian times to the 1960s, and is well worth a look.

Heading in the other direction from the fountain you'll come to the fortress and **Archeological Museum** (Tues–Sun 8.30am–3pm; €1.40), which occupies a building almost directly opposite the entrance to the fortress. This was built by the Turks as an extra defence, and later served as a prison, but it's now entirely modern inside: cool, spacious and airy. Unfortunately, the collection is not particularly exciting, and really only worth seeing if you're going to miss the bigger museums elsewhere on the island.

The massive **Venetian fortress** (Tues–Sun 8am–7pm; reduced hours out of season; €2.40) is a must, however. Said to be the largest Venetian castle ever built, this was a response, in the last quarter of the sixteenth century, to a series of **pirate raids** (by Barbarossa among others) that had devastated the town. Inside is now a vast open space dotted with the remains of all sorts of barracks, arsenals, officers' houses, earthworks and deep shafts, and at the centre a large domed building that was once a church and later a **mosque** (complete with a surviving but sadly defaced *mihrab*). It was designed to be large enough for the entire population to take shelter within the walls, and you can see that it probably was. Although much is ruined, it remains thoroughly atmospheric, and you can look out from the walls over the town and harbour, or in the other direction along the coast to the west. It's also worth walking around the outside of the fortress, preferably at sunset, to get an impression of its fearsome defences, plus great views along the coast and a pleasant resting point around the far side at the *Sunset* taverna.

Practicalities

The **bus station** in Réthymnon is by the sea to the west of town just off Periferiakós, the road which skirts the waterfront around the fortress. The

tourist office (April–Sept Mon–Fri 8am–7pm; ☎08310/56 350) backs onto the main town beach, close to the mobile **post office** (summer only). If you arrive by **ferry**, you'll be more conveniently placed, over at the western edge of the harbour. To access the **internet** and pick up emails head for the *Galero Internet Café* (€4.50 per hr), beside the Rimóndi fountain in the old town or *Café-Bar Internet*, Platía Martiron 4, near the Porta Guora on the south edge of the old town (€1.20 per 15min) or – between the two – User Computer Shop, Ethnikis Andistaseos 83, has similar rates.

Accommodation

There's a great number of places to stay in Réthymnon, and only at the height of the season are you likely to have difficulty finding somewhere, though you may get weary looking. The greatest concentration of **rooms** is in the tangled streets west of the inner harbour, between the Rimóndi fountain and the museums; there are also quite a few places on and around Arkadhíou and Platía Frakidháki.

The nearest **campsite**, *Camping Elizabeth* (☎08310/28 694), lies 4km east of town; take the bus for the hotels (marked *Scaleta/El Greco*) from the long-distance bus station to get there. It's a pleasant, large site on the beach, with all facilities.

Atelier, Himáras 32 ☎08310/24 440. Pleasant rooms close to *Rooms George*, run by a talented potter, who has her studio in the basement and sells her wares in a shop on the other side of the building. ❷

Barbara Dokimaki, Platía Plastíra 14 ☎08310/22 319, ℱ24 581. Strange warren of a rooms place, with one entrance at the above address, just off the seafront behind the *Ideon*, and another on Dambérgi; ask for the newly refurbished top-floor studio rooms, which have balconies and kitchenette. ❷

Byzantine, Vospórou 26 ☎08310/55 609. Excellent-value rooms in a renovated Byzantine palace. The tranquil patio bar is open to all, and breakfast is included in price. ❷

Rooms George, Makedhonías 32 ☎08310/50 965. Decent en-suite rooms (some with fridge), near the Archeological Museum. ❷

Ideon, Platía Plastíra 10 ☎08310/28 667, ℱ28 670. High-class hotel with a brilliant position just north of the ferry dock; little chance of space in season, though. ❺

Leo, Vafé 2 ☎08310/26 197. Good hotel with lots of wood and a traditional feel; the price includes breakfast, and there's a bar. ❷

Olga's Pension, Soulíou 57 ☎08310/54 896, ℱ29 851. The star attraction at this very friendly pension on one of Réthymnon's most touristy streets is the resplendent flower-filled roof garden. ❶

Rethimnon House, V. Kornárou 1 ☎08310/23 923. Very pleasant rooms of a high standard in an old building just off Arkadhíou. Bar downstairs. ❷

Sea Front, Arkádhiou 159 ☎08310/51 981, ℱ51 062, ℮elotia@ret.forthnet.gr. Rooms with sea views and balconies in an attractively refurbished mansion with ceiling fans and lots of wood. ❷

Youth hostel, Tombázi 41 ☎08310/22 848. The cheapest beds (€4.50) in town. Large, clean, and very friendly and popular, it has food, showers, clothes-washing facilities and a multilingual library.

Zania, Pávlou Vlástou 3 ☎08310/28 169. Pension right on the corner of Arkadhíou; a well-adapted old house, but only a few rooms. ❶

Eating and drinking

Immediately behind the town beach are arrayed the most touristy **restaurants**, the vast majority being overpriced and of dubious quality. One that maintains some integrity (and reasonable prices) is the *Samaria* taverna, almost opposite the tourist office. Around the inner **harbour** there's a second, rather more expensive, group of tavernas, specializing in fish, though as often as not the intimate atmosphere in these places is spoiled by the stench from the harbour itself; *O Zefyros* is one of the less outrageously pricey and maintains reasonable standards. Not far from here and slightly west of Platía Plastíra, *Taverna Fanari* at Makedhonías 5 is a good-value little restaurant serving up tasty lamb and chicken dishes. Another good option in this zone is *Taverna Castelvecchio*, Himáras 29, a long-established family taverna next to the fortress which has a pleasant terrace with view over the town and offers some vegetarian choices.

The cluster of kafenía and tavernas by the **Rimóndi fountain** and the newer places spreading into the surrounding streets generally offer considerably better value than the inner harbour, and a couple of the old-fashioned kafenía serve magnificent yogurt and honey. Places to try include *Kyria María* at Moskhovítou 20, tucked down an alley behind the fountain (after the meal, everyone gets a couple of María's delicious *tyropitákia* with honey on the house); *Agrimia*, a reliable standard on Platía Petiháki, slightly east of the fountain; and the *Zanfoti* kafenío overlooking the fountain which is relatively expensive, but a great place to people-watch over a coffee; and for a slightly cheaper option *O Psaras* (The Fisherman), a simple, friendly taverna by the church on the corner of Nikifórou Foká and Koronéou. A good lunchtime stop close to the Archeological Museum is *O Pontios*, Melissinoú 34, a simple place with tables outside and an enthusiastic female proprietor. Healthy, home-baked lunches can also be had at *Stella's Kitchen*, a simple café linked to *Olga's Pension* at Soulíou 55, where meals can be enjoyed up on the leafy roof garden. Tucked behind the church on Platía Martíron, *Mesostrati* is a pleasant little neighbourhood ouzerí/taverna serving well-prepared Cretan country dishes and has a small terrace. A noisier evening alternative is *Taverna O Gounos*, Koronéou 6 in the old town; the family who run it perform live *lyra* every night, and when things get really lively the dancing starts.

If you want takeaway food, there are numerous **souvláki** stalls, including a couple on Arkadhíou and Paleológou and another at Petikháki 52, or you can buy your own ingredients at the **market** stalls set up daily on Ethnikís Andistásis below the Porta Guora. There are small general stores scattered everywhere, particularly on Paleológou and Arkadhíou; east along the beach road you'll even find a couple of mini supermarkets. The **bakery** *I Gaspari* on Mesolongíou, just behind the Rimóndi fountain, sells the usual cheese pies, cakes and the like, and it also bakes excellent brown, black and rye bread. There's a good *zaharoplastío*, *N.A. Skartsilakos*, at Paleológou 36, just north of the fountain, and several more small cafés which are good for breakfast or a quick coffee.

Nightlife

Nightlife is concentrated in the same general areas as the tavernas. At the west end of Venizélou, in the streets behind the inner harbour, the overflow from a small cluster of noisy music bars – *Venetsianako*, *Dimman* and *Xtreme* – begins to spill out onto the pavement as partygoers gather for the nightly opening of the *Fortezza Disco* in the inner harbour itself, which is the glitziest in town, flanked by its competitors *Metropolis*, *NYC*, *Nitro* and the nearby *Opera Club* a little way down Salamínos. Heading up this street, a string of more subdued cocktail bars – *Petaloúda*, *Memphis*, *Santan* and *Pasodia* – cater for those in search of a quieter drink, as does *Notas*, at Himáras 27 near the *Fortezza* and facing the *Atelier* pension, which puts on live (acoustic) guitar and song every night. A new bar scene popular with the local student community has recently taken root around Platía Plastira, above the inner harbour, where music bars include *Karma*, *Art*, *Da Cappo* and *Enzzo*, all with expansive terraces.

Around Réthymnon

While some of Crete's most drastic resort development spreads ever eastwards out of Réthymnon, to the west a sandy coastline, not yet greatly exploited, runs all the way to the borders of Haniá province. But of all the short trips that can be made out of Réthymnon, the best known and still the most worthwhile is to the **monastery of Arkádhi**.

Southeast to Arkádhi

The **monastery of Arkádhi** (daily 8am–1.30pm & 3.30–8pm; entry to museum €1.45), some 25km southeast of the city and immaculately situated in the foothills of the Psilorítis range, is also something of a national Cretan shrine. During the 1866 rebellion against the Turks, the monastery became a rebel strongpoint in which, as the Turks gained the upper hand, hundreds of Cretan independence fighters and their families took refuge. Surrounded and, after two days of fighting, on the point of defeat, the defenders ignited a powder magazine just as the Turks entered. Hundreds (some sources claim thousands) were killed, Cretan and Turk alike, and the tragedy did much to promote international sympathy for the cause of Cretan independence. Nowadays, you can peer into the roofless vault where the explosion occurred and wander about the rest of the well-restored grounds. Outside the entrance a modern monument displays the skulls of many of the victims. The sixteenth-century **church** survived, and is one of the finest Venetian structures left on Crete; other buildings house a small **museum** devoted to the exploits of the defenders of the (Orthodox) faith. The monastery is easy to visit by public bus or on a tour.

West to Aryiroúpolis, Yeoryoúpoli and beyond

Leaving Réthymnon to the west, the main road climbs for a while above a rocky coastline before descending (after some 5km) to the sea, where it runs alongside sandy **beaches** for perhaps another 7km. An occasional hotel offers accommodation, but on the whole there's nothing but a line of straggly bushes between the road and the windswept sands. If you have your own vehicle, there are plenty of places you can stop at here for a swim, and rarely anyone else around – but beware of some very strong currents.

One worthwhile detour inland is to **ARYIROÚPOLIS**, a charming village perched above the Mousselás river valley and the seat of ancient Lappa, a Greek and Roman town of some repute. The village is famous for its **springs** which gush dramatically from the hillside and provide most of the city of Réthymnon's water supply. Among a number of **places to stay** try *Rooms Argiroupolis* (☎08310/81 148, ☏81 149; ❷), near the springs, or *Rooms Zografakis* (08310/81 269; ❶) and *Agnantema* (☎08310/81 172; ❶) in the upper village. For **places to eat**, you're spoilt for choice, with five tavernas at the springs and a bar (serving tasty mezédhes) in the upper village together with tavernas at the *Zografakis* and *Agnantema* rooms places, the latter enjoying a spectacular terrace view down the river valley. A shop under the arch in the main square, named Lappa Avocado and selling local products of the region including olive oil and avocado-based skin products, can provide a free **map** detailing a surprising number of churches, caves and ancient remains to see in and around the village, including an outstanding third-century **Roman mosaic**. An interesting **folklore museum** (daily 10am–7pm; free) – signed from the main square – is worth a look for its collection of tapestries, farm implements, photos and ephemera collected by the Zografakis family who have lived here for countless generations. There are numerous fine **walks** to be had in the surrounding hills, on which the proprietor of the Lappa Avocado shop, who speaks English, will advise. Although little over 20km from Réthymnon and easy to get to with your own transport, Aryiroúpolis is also served by **buses** from Réthymnon's bus station (Mon–Fri only) at 11.30am and 2.30pm, and in the reverse direction at 7.30am, 12.30pm and a late afternoon service at 4.45pm (May–Oct) or 3.30pm (rest of year).

Back on the coastal route, if you are looking for a place to relax for a while, probably the best base is **YEORYOÚPOLI** just across the provincial border in Haniá, where the beach is cleaner, wider and further from the road. There's been a distinct acceleration in the pace of development at Yeoryoúpoli over the last few years and it's now very much a resort, packed with rooms to rent, small hotels, apartment buildings, tavernas and travel agencies; there's even a small land train to transport visitors along the seafront and on short excursions. But everything remains on a small scale, and the undeniably attractive setting is untarnished, making it a very pleasant place to pass a few days, as long as you don't expect to find many vestiges of traditional Crete. Most of the better rooms, including *Rent Rooms Stelios* (☎08250/61 308; ❷), *Irene* (☎08250/61 278; ❷) and *Cretan Cactus* (☎08250/61 027; ❶), are away from the main platía along the road down towards the beach. More central possibilities include *Rooms Voula* (☎08250/61 359; ❶) above a gift shop to the east of the platía and the *Paradise Taverna* (☎08250/61 313; ❷) off the southeast corner of the platía, which has rooms and is a good place to eat.

Within walking distance inland – though it can also be visited on the tourist train from Yeoryoúpoli – is **Kournás**, Crete's only freshwater lake, set deep in a bowl of hills and almost constantly changing colour. There are a few tavernas with rooms to rent along the shore here (bring mosquito repellent), or you could try for a bed in the nearby hill village of **MATHÉS** where the *Villa Kapasa* (☎08250/61 050; ❷) has some very pleasant en-suite rooms around a garden. *Taverna Mathes*, the village taverna has great terrace views and good food. A few kilometres uphill from the lake in **KOURNÁS** village, the *Kali Kardia* taverna is another great place to sample the local lamb and sausages.

Beyond Yeoryoúpoli, the main road heads inland, away from a cluster of coastal villages beyond Vámos. It thus misses the Dhrápano peninsula, the setting for the film of *Zorba the Greek*, with some spectacular views over the sapphire Bay of Soúdha and several quiet beaches. **Kókkino Horió**, the movie location, and nearby **Pláka** are indeed postcard-picturesque (more so from a distance), but **Kefalás**, inland, outdoes both of them. On the exposed north coast there are good beaches at **Almyrídha** and **Kalýves**, and off the road between them. Both are fast developing into resorts in their own right; accommodation is mostly in apartments and rooms are scarce, although there are a few mid-range and more upmarket hotels, and a decent pension, *Katrina* (☎08250/31 366; ❶), a short walk uphill from the centre of Almyrídha. With a string of good fish tavernas (try *Dimitri's*) along the beach and a pleasantly refreshing sea breeze, Almyrídha also makes for an enjoyable lunch stop.

South from Réthymnon

There are a couple of alternative routes south from Réthymnon, but the main one heads straight out from the centre of town, an initially featureless road due south across the middle of the island towards **Ayía Galíni**. About 23km out, a turning cuts off to the right for **Plakiás** and **Mýrthios**, following the course of the spectacular Kourtaliótiko ravine.

Plakiás and the south coast

Since the late 1980s, **PLAKIÁS** has undergone a major boom and is no longer the pristine village all too many people arriving here expect. That said, it's still quite low key, and there's a satisfactory beach and a string of good tavernas around the dock. There are hundreds of **rooms**, but at the height of summer you'll need to arrive early if you hope to find one; the last to fill are generally those on the road leading inland, away from the waterside. For rooms try *Christos Taverna* (℡08320/31 472; ❶) or the nearby *Stefanakis Rooms* (℡08320/ 32 027; ❶) on the seafront, or the excellent balcony rooms at *Ippokambos* (℡08320/31 525; ❶) slightly inland on the road to the relaxed **youth hostel** (℡08320/31 306; €3.75 dorms), which is 500m inland and signed from the seafront.

Once you've found a room there's not a lot else to discover here. Every facility you're likely to need is strung out around the waterfront, including a temporary **post office** parked by the harbour, **bike rental**, **money exchange**, **supermarket** and even a **laundry**. Places to eat are plentiful too. The attractive **tavernas** on the waterfront in the centre are a little expensive; you'll eat cheaper further inland – seek out *Taverna Medusa* at the east end of town, reached up the road inland from the Monza Travel agency and then right. On the way to here you'll pass *Nikos Souvlaki* which dishes up the least expensive meals in town, often accompanied by live *bouzoúki* music in the evenings. Just around the corner from the *Christos* taverna (which is a good bet for fish) at the west end of the harbour you'll find a line of waterfront places facing west – *Sunset* and *Glaros* are worth a try.

Mýrthios

For a stay of more than a day or two, **MÝRTHIOS**, in the hills behind Plakiás, also deserves consideration. It's no longer a great deal cheaper, and its once-popular youth hostel which put it on the map with legions of younger travellers over the years sadly closed in 1999. But at least you'll find locals still outnumbering the tourists, and the friendly *Plateia Taverna* – which catered to many of the youth hostel's guests – has had a makeover and still serves up excellent food. They can also advise on places to stay in the village. The Plakiás bus will usually loop back through Mýrthios, but check; otherwise, it's less than five-minutes' walk from the junction. It takes twenty minutes to walk down to the beach at Plakiás, a little longer to Dhamnóni, and if you're prepared to walk for an hour or more, there are some entirely isolated coves to the west – ask for directions at the taverna.

Dhamnóni

Some of the most tempting **beaches** in central Crete hide just to the east of Plakiás, though unfortunately they're now a very poorly kept secret. These three splashes of yellow sand, divided by rocky promontories, are within easy walking distance and together go by the name **Dhamnóni**. At the first, Dhamnóni proper, there's a taverna with showers and a wonderfully long strip of sand, but there's also a lot of new development including a number of nearby rooms for rent and a huge and ugly Swiss-owned holiday village, which has colonized half of the main beach. At the far end, you'll generally find a few people who've dispensed with their clothes, while the little cove which shelters the middle of the three beaches (barely accessible except on foot) is entirely nudist. Beyond this, **Ammoúdhi** beach has another taverna, *Ammoudi* (℡08320/31 355; ❷), with good rooms for rent, and slightly more of a family atmosphere.

Préveli and "Palm Beach"

Next in line comes **PRÉVELI**, some 6km southeast of Lefkóyia. It takes its name from a **monastery** (daily 8am–1.30pm & 3.30–8pm; €2.60) high above the sea which, like every other in Crete, has a proud history of resistance, in this case accentuated by its role in World War II as a shelter for marooned Allied soldiers awaiting evacuation off the south coast. There are fine views and a monument commemorating the rescue operations, but little else to see. The evacuations took place from "**Palm Beach**", a sandy cove with a small date-palm grove and a solitary drink stand where a stream feeds a little oasis. The beach usually attracts a summer camping community and is now also the target of day-trip boats from Plakiás and Ayía Galíni. Sadly, these groups between them deposit heaps of rubbish, often leaving this lovely place filthy, and despite an ongoing clean-up campaign it seems barely worth the effort. The climb down from the monastery is steep, rocky and surprisingly arduous: it's a great deal easier to come here by boat.

Spíli and Ayía Galíni

Back on the main road south, the pleasant country town of **SPÍLI** lies about 30km from Réthymnon. A popular coffee break for coach tours passing this way, Spíli warrants time if you can spare it. Sheltered under a cliff are narrow alleys of ancient houses, all leading up from a platía with a famous 24-spouted **Venetian fountain**. If you have your own transport, it's a worthwhile place to stay, peacefully rural at night but with several good **rooms** for rent. Try the *Green Hotel* (☎08320/22 225; ❶) on the main road or the charming *Rooms Herakles* (☎08320/22 411; ❷; reductions for stays of more than one night) just behind, the eponymous proprietor of which can advise on some superb **walks** in the surrounding hills. *Rooms Herakles* also rents out **mountain bikes**, there are two **banks** along the main street (with cash dispensers) and **internet** access is possible at *Cafe Babis*, close to the Venetian fountain.

The ultimate destination of most people on this road is **AYÍA GALÍNI**. If heading here was your plan, maybe you should think again since this pictur-esque "fishing village" is so busy in high season that you can't see it for the tour buses, hotel billboards and British package tourists. It also has a beach much too small for the crowds that congregate here. Even so, there are a few saving graces – mainly some excellent restaurants and bars, plenty of rooms and a friendly atmosphere that survives and even thrives on all the visitors. Out of season, it can be quite enjoyable too, and from November to April the mild climate makes it an ideal spot to spend the winter. A lot of long-term travellers do just that, so it's a good place to find work packing tomatoes or polishing cucumbers. If you want somewhere to stay, start looking at the top end of town, around the main road: the economical *Hotel Minos* (☎08320/91 292; ❶), with superb views, is a good place to start, with the nearby *Hotel Hariklia* (☎08320/91 350, ☎91 257; ❷) as a backup, but there are dozens of possibili-ties, and usually something to be found even at the height of summer.

The coastal plain east of Ayía Galíni, hidden under acres of polythene green-houses and burgeoning concrete sprawl, must be among the ugliest regions in Crete, and **Timbáki** the dreariest town. Since this is the way to Festós and back to Iráklion, you may have no choice but to grin and bear it.

The Amári Valley

An alternative route south from Réthymnon, and a far less travelled one, is the road which turns off on the eastern fringe of town to run via the **Amári**

Valley. Very few buses go this way, but if you're driving it's well worth the extra time. There's little specifically to see or do (though hidden away are a number of richly frescoed Byzantine churches), but it's an impressive drive under the flanks of the mountains and a reminder of how, in places, rural Crete continues to exist regardless of visitors. The countryside here is delightfully green even in summer, with rich groves of olive and assorted fruit trees, and if you **stay** (there are rooms in Thrónos and Yerákari), you'll find the nights are cool and quiet. It may seem odd that many of the villages along the way are modern: they were systematically destroyed by the German army in reprisal for the 1944 kidnapping of General Kreipe.

Haniá and the west

The substantial attractions of Crete's westernmost quarter are all the more enhanced by its relative lack of visitors, and despite the now-rapid spread of tourist development, the west is likely to remain one of the emptier parts of the island. This is partly because there are no big sandy beaches to accommodate resort hotels, and partly because it's so far from the great archeological sites. But for mountains and empty (if often pebbly) beaches, it's unrivalled.

Haniá itself is an excellent reason to come here and, along with Réthymnon, is one of the two Cretan cities which could be described as enjoyable in itself. The immediately adjacent coast is relatively developed and not overly exciting; if you want beaches head for the south coast. **Paleohóra** is the only place which could really be described as a resort, and even this is on a thoroughly human scale; others are emptier still. **Ayía Rouméli** and **Loutró** can be reached only on foot or by boat; **Hóra Sfakíon** sees hordes passing through but few who stay; **Frangokástello**, nearby, has a beautiful castle and the first stirrings of development. Behind these lie the **Lefká Óri** (White Mountains) and, above all, the famed walk through the **Gorge of Samariá**.

Haniá

HANIÁ, as any of its residents will tell you, is spiritually the capital of Crete, even if the nominal title was passed back (in 1971) to Iráklion. For many, it is also by far the island's most attractive city, especially if you can catch it in spring, when the Lefká Óri's snowcapped peaks seem to hover above the roofs. Although it is for the most part a modern city, you might never know it as a tourist. Surrounding the small outer harbour is a wonderful jumble of half-derelict **Venetian streets** that survived the wartime bombardments, and it is here that life for the visitor is concentrated. Restoration and gentrification, consequences of the tourist boom, have made inroads of late, but it remains an atmospheric place.

Arrival, information and orientation

Large as it is, Haniá is easy to handle once you've reached the centre; you may get lost wandering among the narrow alleys of the old city but that's a rela-

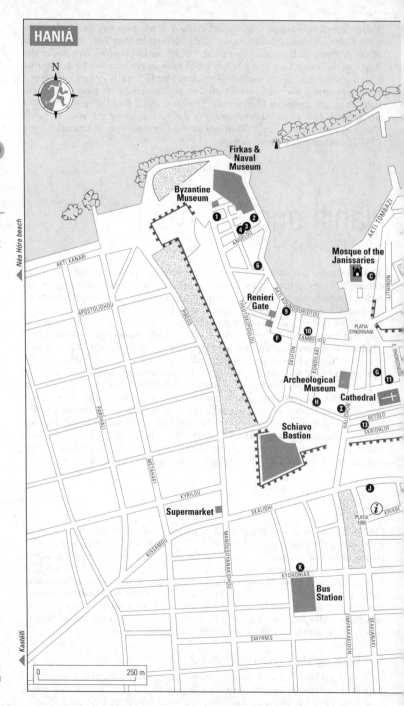

HANIÁ

N

Firkas &
Naval
Museum

Byzantine
Museum

1

2

4 3

ANGELOU

6

Mosque of the
Janissaries

C

AKTI TOMBAZI

LITHINON

Renieri
Gate

9

THEOTOKOPOULOU

AKTI KOUNDOURIOTOU

10

ZAMBELIOU

PLATIA
SYNDRIVANI

F

SKUFON

KONDILAKI

G

E. DHROTHEOU

Archeological
Museum

11

Cathedral

H

I

BETOLO

HALIDHON

13

SKRIDHLOF

Schiavo
Bastion

J

Supermarket

SKALIDHI

KRIARI

PLATIA
1866

i

KISSAMOU

MANOUSOYANAKIDHOU

PIREOS

PARHALI

METAHAKI

AKTI KANARI

APOSTOLIDHOU

KYRILOU

K

KYDHONIAS

Bus
Station

ZIMVRAKAKIDHON

SFAKIANAKI

SMYRNIS

0   250 m

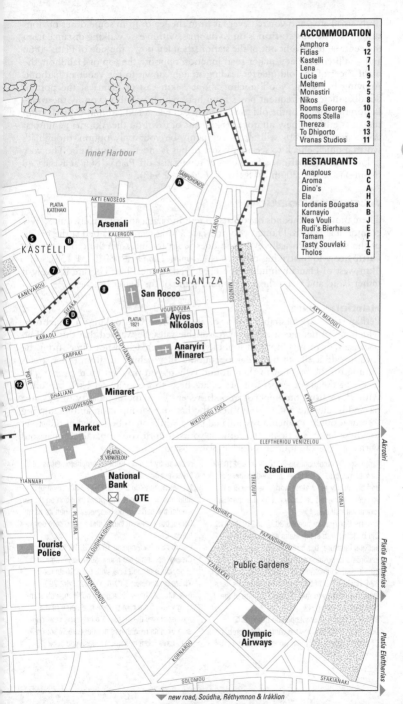

Inner Harbour

ACCOMMODATION

Amphora	6
Fidias	12
Kastelli	7
Lena	1
Lucia	9
Meltemi	2
Monastiri	5
Nikos	8
Rooms George	10
Rooms Stella	4
Thereza	3
To Dhiporto	13
Vranas Studios	11

RESTAURANTS

Anaplous	D
Aroma	C
Dino's	A
Ela	H
Iordanis Boúgatsa	K
Karnayio	B
Nea Vouli	J
Rudi's Bierhaus	E
Tamam	F
Tasty Souvlaki	I
Tholos	G

PLATIA KATEHAKI

AKTI ENOSEOS

SARPIDHONOS

IKAROU

Arsenali

KALERGON

KASTÉLLI

KANEVAROU

SIFAKA

SPIÁNTZA

MINOOS

AKTI MIAOULI

SIFAKA

San Rocco

VOURDOUBA

PLATIA 1821

Ayios Nikólaos

KARAOLI

DHASKALOYIANNIS

SARPAKI

Anaryíri Minaret

POTIE

DHALIANI

Minaret

NIKIFOROU FOKA

KYPROU

TSOUDHERON

Market

ELEFTHERIOU VENIZELOU

PLATIA S. VENIZELOU

YIANNARI

National Bank

OTE

N. PLASTIRA

ANOHREA

TAIKOUPI

Stadium

KORAI

Akrotíri

VELOUDHAKIDHON

PAPANDHREOU

Tourist Police

TZANAKAKI

Public Gardens

APIKOKONOU

Platía Eleftherías

KORNAROU

Olympic Airways

SOLOMOU

SFAKIANAKI

Platía Eleftherías

259

▼ new road, Soúdha, Réthymnon & Iráklion

tively small area, and you're never far from the sea or from some other obvious landmark. The **bus station** is on Kydhonías, within easy walking distance from the centre – turn right out of the station, then left down the side of Platía-1866 and you'll emerge at a major road junction opposite the top of Halídhon, the main street of the old quarter leading straight down to the Venetian harbour. Arriving by **ferry**, you'll anchor about 10km east of Haniá at the port of Soúdha: there are frequent buses from here which will drop you by the **market** on the fringes of the old town, or you can take a taxi (around €4.50). From the city's efficient new **airport** (15km east of town on the Akrotíri peninsula) taxis (around €8.80) will almost certainly be your only option, though it's worth a quick check to see if any sort of bus is meeting your flight. The very helpful **tourist office** is in the new town, just off Platía-1866 at Kriári 40 (Mon–Fri 8am–2.30pm ☎08210/92 624, ⓕ92 943).

Accommodation

There must be thousands of **rooms** to rent in Haniá and, unusually, quite a few comfortable **hotels**. Though you may face a long search for a bed at the height of the season, eventually everyone does seem to find something. The nearest **campsite** within striking distance is *Camping Hania* (☎08210/31 138), some 4km west of Haniá behind the beach, served by local bus. The site is lovely, if rather basic, and just a short walk from some of the better beaches.

Harbour area

Perhaps the most desirable rooms of all are those overlooking the **harbour**, which are sometimes available at reasonable rates: be warned that this is often because they're very noisy at night. Most are approached not direct from the harbourside itself but from Zambelíou, the alley behind, or from other streets leading off the harbour further around (where you may get more peace). The nicest of the more expensive places are here, too, equally set back but often with views from the upper storeys. In recent years the popularity of this area has led to anyone with a room near the harbour tarting it up and attempting to rent it out at a ridiculously inflated price. You'll often be touted in the street for these and it's wise not to commit yourself until you've made comparisons with some of the more reasonable places listed below.

Amphora, Theotokopoúlou 20 ☎ & ⓕ 08210/93 224. Large, traditional hotel in Venetian mansion, and beautifully renovated; worth the expense if you get a view, but probably not for the cheaper rooms without one. ❺

Rooms George, Zambelíou 30 ☎08210/88 715. Old building with steep stairs and eccentric antique furniture; basic rooms vary in price according to position and size. ❶

Lucia, Aktí Koundouriótou ☎08210/90 302, ⓕ91 834. Harbourfront hotel with balcony rooms; less expensive than you might expect for one of the best views in town. ❷

Pension Lena, Theotokopoúlou 60 ☎ & ⓕ 08210/86 860, ⓦwww.lena@travelling-crete.com. Charming rooms in an old wooden Turkish house

restored by friendly German proprietor. Pleasant breakfast café below. ❷

Meltemi, Angélou 2 ☎08210/92 802. First of a little row of pensions in a great situation on the far side of the harbour; perhaps noisier than its neighbours, but excellent views and a good café downstairs. ❷

Rooms Stella, Angélou 10 ☎08210/73 756. Creaky, eccentric old house above a ceramics shop, close to the *Lucia*, with plain, clean rooms. ❷

Thereza, Angélou 8 ☎ & ⓕ 08210/92 798. Beautiful old house in a great position, with stunning views from roof terrace and some of the rooms; classy decor, too. A more expensive pension than its neighbours but deservedly so; unlikely to have room in season unless you book. ❸

The old town: east of Halídhon

In the eastern half of the old town rooms are far more scattered, usually cheaper, and in the height of the season your chances are much better over here. **Kastélli**, immediately east of the harbour, has some lovely places with views from the heights. Take one of the alleys leading left off Kanevárou if you want to try these, but don't be too hopeful since they are popular and often booked up.

To Dhiporto, Betólo 41, one block north of Skridhlóf ☎08210/53 430. A very good-value rooms place with economical doubles and trebles. Recommended. ❶

Fidias, Kalinákou Sarpáki 8 ☎08210/52 494. Signposted from the cathedral, this favourite backpackers' meeting place is rather bizarrely run, but is a friendly pension and has the real advantage of offering single rooms or fixing shares. Its dormitory rooms are the cheapest in town (€5.50). ❶

Kastelli, Kanevárou 39 ☎08210/57 057, ⓕ45 314. Not in the prettiest of locations, but a comfortable, modern, reasonably priced pension and very quiet at the back. All rooms come with fans and anti-mosquito machines. The owner is exceptionally helpful and also has a few apartments and a beautiful house (for up to five people) to rent. ❷

Monastiri, Ayíou Márkou 18, off Kanevárou ☎08210/54 776. Pleasant rooms, some with a sea view in the restored ruins of a Venetian monastery. ❷

Nikos, Dhaskaloyiánnis 58 ☎08210/54 783. One of a few down here near the inner harbour; good-value, relatively modern rooms, all with shower. Same owner has economical studios nearby with kitchen and fridge. ❷

Vranas Studios, Ayíon Dhéka and Kalinákou Sarpáki, near the cathedral ☎ & ⓕ 08210/58 618. Pleasant, spacious studio-style rooms with TV, air-con, fridge and kitchenette. ❹

The City

Haniá has been occupied almost continuously since Neolithic times, so it comes as a surprise that a city of such antiquity should offer little specifically to see or do. It is, however, a place which is fascinating simply to wander around, stumbling upon surviving fragments of city wall, the remains of **ancient Kydonia** which are being excavated, and odd segments of Venetian or Turkish masonry.

Kastélli and the harbour

The **port** area is as ever the place to start, the oldest and the most interesting part of town. It's at its busiest and most attractive at night, when the lights from bars and restaurants reflect in the water and crowds of visitors and locals turn out to promenade. By day, things are quieter. Straight ahead from Platía Syndriváni (also known as Harbour Square) lies the curious domed shape of the **Mosque of the Janissaries**, built in 1645 (though heavily restored since) and the oldest Ottoman building on the island. It has recently reopened as a gallery to house temporary exhibitions.

The little hill that rises behind the mosque is **Kastélli**, site of the earliest habitation and core of the Minoan, Venetian and Turkish towns. There's not a great deal left, but archeologists believe that they may have found the remains of a Minoan palace (logically, there must have been one at this end of the island) in the **excavations** being carried out – and open to view – along Kanevárou. It's also here that you'll find traces of the oldest **walls**; there were two rings, one defending Kastélli alone, a later set encompassing the whole of the medieval city. Beneath the hill, on the inner (eastern) harbour, the arches of sixteenth-century **Venetian arsenals** survive alongside remains of the outer walls; both are currently undergoing restoration.

Following the esplanade around in the other direction leads to a hefty bastion which now houses Crete's **Naval Museum** (daily 9am–4pm; €1.80). The collection is not exactly riveting, although a recently added section on the 1941 **Battle of Crete** with fascinating artefacts, and poignant photos depicting the suffering here under the Nazis, perhaps justifies the entry fee. You might want to wander in anyway for a (free) look at the seaward fortifications and the platform from which the modern Greek flag was first flown on Crete (in 1913). Walk around the back of these restored bulwarks to a street heading inland and you'll find the best-preserved stretch of the outer walls. Just behind the Naval Museum at the top of Theotokopolou lies the new **Byzantine Museum** (Tues–Sun 8.30am–3pm; free) with a small but interesting collection of mosaics, icons and jewellery from the various periods of Byzantine rule.

The old city

Behind the harbour lie the less picturesque but more lively sections of the old city. First, a short way up Halídhon on the right, is Haniá's **Archeological Museum** (Tues–Sun 8.30am–2.30pm; €1.50) housed in the Venetian-built church of San Francesco. Damaged as it is, especially from the outside, this remains a beautiful building and it contains a fine little display, covering the local area from Minoan through to Roman times. In the garden, a huge fountain and the base of a minaret survive from the period when the Turks converted the church into a mosque; around them are scattered various other sculptures and architectural remnants.

The **cathedral**, ordinary and relatively modern, is just a few steps further up Halídhon on the left. Around it are some of the more animated shopping areas, particularly **Odhós Skrídhlof** ("Leather Street"), lined with the shops of traditional leathermakers plying their trade, with streets leading up to the back of the market beyond. In the direction of the Spiántza quarter are ancient alleys with tumbledown Venetian stonework and overhanging wooden balconies; though gentrification is spreading apace, much of the quarter has yet to feel the effect of the city's modern popularity. There are a couple more **minarets** too, one on Dhaliáni, and the other in Platía-1821, which is a fine traditional platía to stop for a coffee.

The new town

Once out of the narrow confines of the maritime district, the broad, traffic-choked streets of the **modern city** have a great deal less to offer. Up Tzanakáki, not far from the market, you'll find the **public gardens**, a park with strolling couples, a few caged animals (including a few krí-krí or Cretan ibex) and a café under the trees; there's also an open-air auditorium which occasionally hosts live music or local festivities. Beyond here, you could continue to the **Historical Museum**, Sfakianáki 20 (Mon–Fri 9am–2pm; free), but the effort would be wasted unless you're a Greek-speaking expert on the subject; the place is essentially a very dusty archive with a few photographs on the wall. Perhaps more interesting is the fact that the museum lies on the fringes of Haniá's desirable residential districts. If you continue to the end of Sfakianáki and then go down Iróön Polytekhníou towards the sea, you'll get an insight into how Crete's other half lives. There are several (expensive) garden restaurants down here and a number of fashionable café-bars where you can sit outside.

The beaches

Haniá's beaches all lie to the west of the city. For the packed **city beach**, this means no more than a ten-minute walk following the shoreline from the naval museum, but for good sand you're better off taking the local bus out along the coast road. This leaves from the east side of Platía-1866 and runs along the coast road as far as **Kalamáki beach**. Kalamáki and the previous stop, **Oásis beach**, are again pretty crowded but they're a considerable improvement over the beach in Haniá itself. In between, you'll find emptier stretches if you're prepared to walk: about an hour in all (on sandy beach virtually all the way) from Haniá to Kalamáki, and then perhaps ten minutes from the road to the beach if you get off the bus at the signs for *Aptera Beach* or *Camping Hania*. Further afield there are even finer beaches at **Ayía Marína** to the west, or **Stavrós** (see p.265) out on the Akrotíri peninsula (reached by KTEL buses from the main station).

Eating

You're never far from something to **eat** in Haniá: in a circle around the harbour is one restaurant, taverna or café after another. All have their own character, but there seems little variation in price or what's on offer. Away from the water, there are plenty of slightly cheaper possibilities on Kondhiláki, Kanevárou and most of the streets off Halídhon. For snacks or lighter meals, the cafés around the harbour on the whole serve cocktails and fresh juices at exorbitant prices, though breakfast (especially "English") can be good value. For more-traditional places, try around the market and along Dhaskaloyiánnis (*Synganaki* here is a good traditional bakery serving *tyrópitta* and the like, with a cake shop next door). Fast food is also increasingly widespread, with numerous *souvláki* places on Karaolí; at the end of the outer harbour, near the naval museum; and around the corner of Plastíra and Yiannári, across from the **market** (see "Listings" p.265, for details of the market and supermarkets).

Anaplous, Sífaka 37. A couple of blocks west of Platía-1821, this is a popular new open-air restaurant inside a stylishly "restored" ruin of a Turkish mansion bombed in the war. Serves both mezédhes and full meals to live guitar music.

Aroma, Aktí Tombázi 4, next to the Mosque of the Janissaries. Pleasant café with great harbour view to savour over lazy breakfasts or late drinks.

Dino's, inner harbour by bottom of Sarpidhónos. One of the best choices for a pricey seafood meal with a harbour view. The nearby *Faka* is also good.

Ela, top of Kondhiláki. Standard taverna food with live Greek music accompaniment to enliven your meal in yet another roofless taverna townhouse.

Iordanis Bougatsa, Kydhonias 96, opposite the bus station. This place serves little except the traditional creamy *bougátsa*, a sugar-coated cheese pie to eat in or take away.

Karnayio, Platía Kateháki 8. Set back from the inner harbour near the port police. Not right on the water, but one of the best harbour restaurants nonetheless.

Meltemi, Angélou 2. Slow, relaxed terrace bar

beneath the rooms place of the same name; good for breakfast, and where locals (especially expats) sit whiling the day away or playing *tavli*.

Nea Vouli, Yiannári 27, just west of Platía-1866. Excellent and stylish restaurant popular with locals, serving high-quality standards at modest prices. Closed Sun.

Rudi's Bierhaus, Sífaka 24. Haniá's beer shrine: Austrian Rudi Riegler's bar stocks more than a hundred of Europe's finest beers to accompany very tasty mezédhes.

Tamam, Zambelíou just before Renieri Gate. Young, trendy place with adventurous Greek menu including much vegetarian food. Unfortunately only a few cramped tables outside, and inside it can get very hot. Slow service.

Tasty Souvlaki, Halídhon 80. Always packed despite being cramped, which is a testimonial to the quality and value of the *souvláki*. Better to take away.

Tholos, Ayíon Dhéka 36. Slightly north of the cathedral, *Tholos* is another "restaurant in a ruin", this time Venetian/Turkish, with a wide selection of Cretan specialities.

Bars and nightlife

Haniá's **nightlife** has more than enough venues to satisfy the most insomniac night-owls. Most of the clubs and disco bars are gathered in the area around the inner harbour, whilst there are plenty of terrace bars along both harbourfronts, with more scattered throughout the old quarter.

The smartest and newest places to sit out and be seen in the evening are on and around **Sarpidhónos**, in the far corner of the inner harbour, a good example of which is *Ta Dhyo Lux*, one of a line of bars here and the place to try an expensive but sublime lemon *graníta*. The nearby *Fraise* is another popular venue. Heading from here around towards the outer harbour, you'll pass others including the *Four Seasons*, a very popular bar by the port police, and then reach a couple of the older places including *Scorpio* behind the Plaza bar complex on the harbour. To the southeast of the inner harbour running along the **Aktí Miaoúli** seafront just outside the eastern wall are a string of terrace cafés catering almost exclusively to a local under-thirty clientele, and this is currently *the* place to be seen for Haniote late drinkers. At the opposite or **western end of the harbour** *Fagotto*, Angélou 16, is a pleasant, laid-back jazz bar, often with live performers. Other music bars near here are *Mythos* and *Street* on the outer harbour, playing rock and modern Greek sounds until the early hours. **Disco clubs** proper include *Ariadni* on the inner harbour (opens 11.30pm, but busy later), and *Millennium*, a big, bright place on Tsoudherón behind the market, which doesn't really get going until 2am. West of here along Skalídhi (no. 39) *Titanic* is another dance place which is a late starter, and, not far away, tucked down a passage near the Schiavo Bastion (Skalídhi and Halídhon), *N.R.G* is a new place that becomes frenetic after midnight.

A venue offering more traditional entertainment is the *Café Kriti*, Kalergón 22, at the corner of Andhroyíou, basically an old-fashioned kafenío where there's **Greek music** and **dancing** virtually every night. It's also worth checking for events at the open-air auditorium in the public gardens, and for performances in restaurants outside the city, which are the ones the locals will go to. Look for posters, especially in front of the market and in the little platía across the road from there.

For **films**, you should also check the hoardings in front of the market. There are open-air screenings at Attikon, on Venizélou out towards Akrotíri, about 1km from the centre, and occasionally in the public gardens.

Listings

Airlines Olympic, with scheduled daily flights between Haniá and Athens plus frequent flights to Thessaloníki, has an office at Tzanakáki 88 (Mon–Fri 9am–4pm; ☏ 08210/57 701, 57 702 or 57 703) opposite the public gardens. Other airlines running daily scheduled services to the mainland are Aegean-Cronus, Venizélou 12 (☏ 08210/51 100) and Axon, Haniá airport (☏ 08210/20 928). For airport information call ☏ 08210/63 264.

Banks and exchange The main branch of the National Bank of Greece is directly opposite the market with two cash dispensers. Convenient smaller banks for exchange are next to the bus station, at the bottom of Kanevárou just off Platía Syndriváni, or at the top of Halídhon. There are also a couple of exchange places on Halídhon, open long hours.

Bike and car rental Possibilities everywhere, especially on Halídhon, though these are rarely the best value. For bikes, try Kavroulakis, Halídhon 91 (☏ 08210/43 342) or Summertime, Daskaloyiánnis

7, slightly northeast of the market (☏ 08210/98 918); for cars, two reliable local companies are Hermes, Tzanakáki 52 (☏ 08210/54 418) or Tellus Rent a Car, Kanevárou 9, east of Platía Syndriváni (☏ 08210/50 400). Good deals for *Rough Guide* readers are available from El Greco Cars at the *El Greco* hotel (see "Accommodation" p.260; ☏ 08210/91 818, ✉ cars@elgreco.gr), where readers showing this guide will receive a 25 percent discount.

Boat trips Various boat trips are offered by travel agents around town, mostly to Soúdha Bay or out to beaches on the Rodhópou peninsula. Stavros Cruises (mobile ☏ 094/4914045) in the Old Harbour or Domenico's (☏ 08210/55 019), on Kanevárou, offers some of the best of these. The *Angela* sails daily in summer at 1.30pm from the Old Harbour to the offshore island of Áyii Theódori, for swimming and *kri-kri* (ibex) spotting. The *Evagelos* glass-bottomed boat sails three times daily from the Old Harbour to Theodorou with an extension on Saturdays to the Rodhópou peninsula

3

(for information call the mobile number ℡094/5874283).

Ferry tickets The ANEK line office is on Venizélou, right opposite the market (℡08210/27 500).

Internet Haniá has three internet cafés: *Sante* on the outer harbour at Aktí Koundouriótou 55–56 (€3 per hr); the more tranquil *Vranas* (€1.50; 30min), just north of the cathedral and beneath *Vranas Studios* (see "Accommodation" p.260); *E-Café*, Theotokopólou 53 near the *El Greco* hotel (€1.50; 30min) is a relaxed and friendly newcomer.

Laundry There are five laundries, the best of which is Speedy Laundry (℡08210/88 411; 9am–9pm), junction of Koronéou and Korkidi, just west of Platía-1866 charging €6 for a load; they will also collect and deliver. Others are Laundry Express at Kanevárou 38 (Mon–Sat 9am–10pm) and Fidias, Sarpaki 6 (next to the pension of the same name, see p.260; Mon–Sat 9am–9pm). All do service washes.

Left luggage The bus station has a left-luggage office open 6am–8.30pm; €0.90/1.50 per item per day depending on size.

Market and supermarkets To buy food, head for the entertaining market which has fresh fruit and vegetables, meat and fish, bakers, dairy stalls and general stores for cooked meats, tins, etc. Several small stores by the harbour platía sell cold drinks and food, which are expensive but open late. Small supermarkets can be found on Platía-1866 and the larger Marinopolos supermarket is at the top of Pireos, outside the western wall, close to the Schiavo Bastion.

Post office The main post office is on Tzanakáki (Mon–Fri 7am–8pm, Sat 8am–2pm).

Taxis The main taxi ranks are in Platía-1866. For radio taxis try ℡08210/98 700 or 94 300.

Telephones Cardphones (all over town) are the best bet for overseas calls.

Tourist police Inconveniently located at Iraklíou 23 in the southern suburb of Koubés (℡08210/53 333).

Travel agencies El Greco Travel, on Kidhonías near the bus station (℡08210/86 015), and Interkreta, on Platía Eleftherías in the new town (℡08210/27 222), are both good for inexpensive bus tickets, flights and standard excursions. For cheap tickets home try Bassías Travel, Halídhon 69 (℡08210/44 295), very helpful for regular tickets too. They also deal in standard excursions. Other travel agents for tours and day-trips are everywhere.

Around Haniá: the Akrotíri and Rodhópou peninsulas

Just north of Haniá, the **Akrotíri peninsula** loops around to protect the Bay of Soúdha and a NATO military base and missile-testing area. In an ironic twist, the peninsula's northwestern coastline is fast developing into a luxury suburb; the beach of Kalathás, near Horafákia, long popular with jaded Haniotes is surrounded by villas and apartments. **STAVRÓS**, further out, has not yet suffered this fate, and its **beach** is absolutely superb if you like the calm, shallow water of an almost completely enclosed lagoon. It's not very large, so it does get crowded, but rarely overpoweringly so. There's a makeshift taverna/*souvláki* stand on the beach, and a couple of tavernas across the road, but for accommodation you need to search slightly south of here, in the area around **Blue Beach**, where there are plenty of apartment buildings but no low budget accommodation in summer whatsoever. On Blue Beach you could try *Zorba's Rooms* (attached to a taverna of the same name) which rents out apartments (℡08210/39 010; ❷).

Inland are the **monasteries** of **Ayía Triádha** (daily 9am–7pm; €1.20) and **Gouvernétou** (daily 7am–2pm & 4–7.30pm; €1.45). The former is much more accessible and has a beautiful seventeenth-century church inside its pink-and-ochre cloister, though ongoing renovations – the latest has turned one building into an olive-oil factory where the monks produce and bottle their own oil – on occasions make the normally peaceful enclosure more like a building site. Four kilometres north of Gouvernétou – which is in a far better state of preservation and where traditional monastic life can still be observed –

you can clamber down a craggy path to the amazing and abandoned ruins of the **monastery of Katholikó**, built into a craggy ravine, and the remains of its narrow (swimmable) harbour.

West to Rodhópou

The coast to the west of Haniá was the scene of most of the fighting during the German invasion in 1941. As you leave town, an aggressive, monumental diving eagle commemorates the slain German parachutists, and at Máleme there's a big German cemetery; the Allied cemetery is in the other direction, on the coast just outside Soúdha. There are also beaches and considerable tourist development along much of this shore. At **Ayía Marína** there's a fine sandy beach and an island offshore said to be a sea monster petrified by Zeus before it could swallow Crete. Seen from the west, its "mouth" still gapes open.

Between **Plataniás** and **Kolymvári** an almost unbroken strand unfurls, by no means all sandy, but deserted for long stretches between villages. The road here runs through mixed groves of calamus reed (Crete's bamboo) and oranges; the windbreaks fashioned from the reeds protect the ripening oranges from the *meltémi*. At Kolymbári, the road to Kastélli cuts across the base of another mountainous peninsula, **Rodhópou**. Just off the main road here is a monastery, **Goniá** (daily 8am–12.30pm & 4–8pm; free; respectable dress required), with a view most luxury hotels would envy. Every monk in Crete can tell tales of his proud ancestry of resistance to invaders, but here the Turkish cannon balls are still lodged in the walls to prove it, a relic of which the good fathers are far more proud than any of the icons.

South to the Samarian Gorge

From Haniá the **Gorge of Samariá** (May–Oct; €3.60 for entry to the national park) can be visited as a day-trip or as part of a longer excursion to the south. At 18km, it's Europe's longest gorge and is startlingly beautiful. In the June to August period (ring Haniá tourist office for other times) **buses** leave Haniá bus station for the top at 6.15am, 7.30am, 8.30am and 1.30pm (this latter service changes to 4.30pm outside school term time), depositing you at the gorge entrance and then collecting you at the port of Hóra Sfakíon for the return trip to Haniá. Should you take the last bus you will need to spend a night at Ayía Rouméli (the end of the gorge) as you will not get through the gorge in time for the last boat. For the three early buses you'll normally be sold a return ticket (valid from Hóra Sfakíon at any time). It's well worth catching the earliest bus to avoid the full heat of the day while walking through the gorge, though be warned that you will not be alone – there are often as many as five coachloads setting off before dawn for the nail-biting climb into the White Mountains. There are also direct early-morning buses from Iráklion and Réthymnon and bus tours from virtually everywhere on the island, adding up to a couple of thousand plus walkers on most days during high season.

Despite all the crowds, the walk *is* hard work, especially in spring when the stream is a roaring torrent. Early and late in the season, there is a danger of **flash floods**, which are not to be taken lightly: in 1993, a number of walkers perished when they were washed out to sea. For this reason the first and last three weeks of the season are entirely dependent on the weather and you will

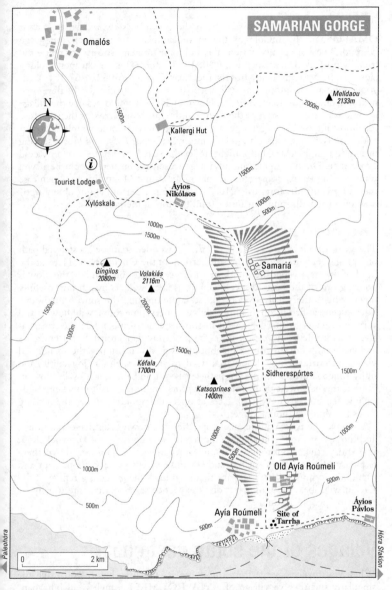

only be allowed into the gorge if the authorities deem it safe. If in doubt (and to save yourself a wasted journey), phone the Haniá Forest Service's **gorge information number** (☎08210/67 140) or the gorge office (☎08210/67 179) for information. Should you arrive after 4pm you will only be allowed into the first couple of kilometres from each end of the gorge and the wardens ensure that no one remains in the gorge overnight, where camping is strictly forbidden.

Omalós

One way to avoid an early start from the north coast would be to stay at **OMALÓS**, in the middle of the mountain plain from which the gorge descends. There are plenty of **tavernas** and some ordinary **rooms** for rent – the friendly no-frills Samaria pension (☎08210/67 168; ❶) is the cheapest – plus a clutch of surprisingly fancy **hotels**; the *Hotel Gingilos* (☎08210/67 181; ❶) is good value and its proprietor will drive you the 5km to the top of the gorge next morning if you stay overnight. However, if you're on foot, since the village is some way from the start of the path, and the first buses arrive as the sun rises, it's almost impossible to get a head start on the crowds. Some people sleep out at the top (where there's a bar-restaurant in the *Tourist Lodge* and kiosks serving drinks and sandwiches), but a night under the stars here can be a bitterly cold experience. The one significant advantage to staying up here would be if you wanted to undertake some other climbs in the White Mountains, in which case there's a **mountain hut** (☎08210/54 560; €6 per person) about ninety minutes' hike (signed) from Omalós or from the top of the gorge.

The gorge

The **gorge** itself begins at the *xylóskala*, or "wooden staircase", a stepped path plunging steeply down from the southern lip of the Omalós plain. Here, at the head of the track, opposite the sheer rock face of Mount Gíngilos, the crowds pouring out of the buses disperse rapidly as keen walkers march purposefully down while others dally over breakfast, contemplating the sunrise for hours. You descend at first through almost alpine scenery: pine forest, wild flowers and very un-Cretan greenery – a verdant shock in the spring, when the stream is also at its liveliest (and can at times be positively dangerous). Small churches and viewpoints dot the route, and about halfway down you pass the abandoned village of **Samariá**, now home to a wardens' station, with picnic facilities and filthy toilets. Further down, the path levels out and the gorge walls close in until at the narrowest point (the *sidherespórtes* or "iron gates") one can practically touch both tortured rock faces at once, and, looking up, see them rising sheer for almost a thousand feet.

At an average pace, with regular stops, the walk down takes five or six hours, and the upward trek considerably longer. It's strenuous (you'll know all about it next day), the path is rough, and solid shoes are vital. On the way down, there is plenty of water from springs and streams (except some years in Sept and Oct), but nothing to eat. The park that surrounds the gorge is a refuge of the Cretan wild ibex, the *kri-kri*, but don't expect to see one; there are usually far too many people around.

Villages of the southwest coast

When you finally emerge from the gorge, it's not long before you reach the singularly unattractive village of **AYÍA ROUMÉLI**, which is all but abandoned until you reach the beach, a mirage of iced drinks and a cluster of tavernas with **rooms** for rent. If you want to get back to Haniá, buy your boat tickets now, especially if you want an afternoon on the beach; the last boat (connecting with the final 6.30pm bus from Hóra Sfakíon) tends to sell out first. If you plan to stay on the south coast, you should get going as soon as possible for the best chance of finding a room somewhere nicer than Ayía Rouméli.

Loutró

For tranquillity, it's hard to beat **LOUTRÓ**, two-thirds of the way to Hóra Sfakíon, and accessible only by boat or on foot. The chief disadvantage of Loutró is its lack of a real beach; most people swim from the rocks around its small bay. If you're prepared to walk, however, there are **deserted beaches** along the coast to the east which can also be reached by hired **canoe**. Indeed, if you're really into walking there's a **coastal trail** through Loutró which covers the entire distance between Ayía Rouméli and Hóra Sfakíon, or you could take the daunting zigzag path up the cliff behind to the mountain village of **Anópoli**. Loutró itself has a number of **tavernas** and **rooms**, though not always enough of the latter in peak season. Call the *Blue House* (☎08250/91 127, ⓦwww.delftmarkt.nl; ❶) if you want to book ahead; this is also the best place to eat. Slightly more upmarket accommodation is on offer at the nearby *Hotel Porto Loutro* (☎08250/91 433; ❷), which also hires out canoes and runs full-day **cruises** on its own boat to "Palm Beach" (p.256) and the island of Gávdhos (p.273); prices should be posted outside. There's space to **camp** out on the cape by a ruined fort, but due to a long history of problems, you should be aware that campers are not very popular in the village. If you're determined to camp, head for the **beaches** and coves to the east (such as Sweetwater) and west (Mármara) of the resort which can be reached on foot, or more comfortably by canoe or daily boats from the harbour.

Hóra Sfakíon and beyond

HÓRA SFAKÍON is the more usual terminus for walkers traversing the gorge, with a regular boat service along the coast to and from Ayía Rouméli. Consequently, it's quite an expensive and not an especially welcoming place; there are plenty of **rooms** and some decent **tavernas**, but for a real beach you should jump straight on a bus (currently running at 11am and 6pm April–Sept) going toward Plakiás. Plenty of opportunities for a dip present themselves en route, one of the most memorable at **Frangokástello**, named after a crumbling Venetian attempt to bring law and order to a district that went on to defy both Turks and Germans. The foursquare, crenellated and imposing thirteenth-century **castle**, isolated a few kilometres below a chiselled wall of mountains, looks like it's been spirited out of the High Atlas or Tibet. The place is said to be haunted by ghosts of Greek rebels massacred here in 1829: every May, these *dhrossoulítes* (dewy ones) march at dawn across the coastal plain and disappear into the sea near the fort. The rest of the time Frangokástello is peaceful enough, with a superb beach and a number of tavernas and rooms, but is somewhat stagnant if you're looking for things to do. A new and stylish **pool-bar** *Eiscafe*, a little west and inland from the castle has livened things a little and the proprietors here can advise on **accommodation** possibilities should you want to stopover. Slightly further east, and less influenced by tourism or modern life, are the attractive villages of **Skalotí** and **Rodhákino**, where basic lodging and food can be found in the villages proper or their seafront offshoots a couple of kilometres to the south.

Soúyia

In quite the other direction from Ayía Rouméli, less regular boats also head to **SOÚYIA** and on to Paleohóra. Soúyia, until World War II merely the anchorage for Koustoyérako inland, is low key, with a long, grey pebble beach and mostly modern buildings (except for a church with a sixth-century Byzantine mosaic as the foundation). Since the completion in 1990 of the paved road to Haniá, the village has started to expand; even so, except in the very middle of summer, it continues to make a good fall-back for finding a room or a place to camp, eating cheaply and enjoying the beach when the rest of the island is seething with visitors.

Of the **rooms** places try the seafront *Hotel Santa Irene* (℡08230/51 342, ℉51 182, ✉nanadakis@cha.forthnet.gr; ●), where en-suite rooms come with view; cheaper en-suite rooms are on offer at the friendly *Lissos* (℡08230/51 244; ●), reached by turning east along the seafront and then inland. An excellent source of **information** on rooms and lots more is Polifimos Travel (℡ & ℉ 08230/51 022, ✉polifim@otenet.gr) on the main street just in from the seafront; they keep piles of information on everything to do in the area – including **gorge walks** in the beautiful Ayía Iríni gorge and a fine hike to the nearby ancient site of **Lissós**. They can also advise on the latest bus and ferry **timetables**, **change money**, **rent cars** and have a couple of screens for **internet** access. For **food**, the nearby *Rembetiko* has a pleasant garden terrace. At the eastern end of the seafront the German-run *Omikron* taverna has a more northern-European ambience and offers some **vegetarian** choices. Finally, as petrol is scarce in these parts, it's worth noting that there is **no pump station** and a full tank would be a wise precaution.

Kastélli and the western tip

Apart from being Crete's most westerly town, and the end of the main E65 coastal highway, **KASTÉLLI** (Kíssamos, or Kastélli Kissámou as it's variously known) has little obvious attraction. It's a busy town with a rocky central **beach** (although there's an excellent sandy beach to the west) visited mainly by people using the boat that runs twice weekly to the island of Kýthira and the Peloponnese. The very ordinariness of Kastélli, however, can be attractive: life goes on pretty much regardless of outsiders, and there's every facility you might need. The town was important in antiquity and a number of recently excavated **mosaics** are visible around the centre (follow the signs) and finds from these digs and others nearby are to be displayed in the town's new **museum** (due to open in 2002) located in the refurbished former Venetian governor's residence on the main square.

A round trip

If you have transport, a circular drive from Kastélli, taking the coast road in one direction and the inland route through Élos and Topólia, makes for a stunningly scenic circuit. Near the sea, villages cling to the high mountainsides, apparently halted by some miracle in the midst of calamitous seaward slides. Around them, olives ripen on the terraced slopes, the sea glittering far below. Inland, especially at **ÉLOS**, the main crop is the chestnut, whose huge old trees shade the village streets.

South of **TOPÓLIA**, the chapel of Ayía Sofía is sheltered inside a cave which has been used as a shrine since Neolithic times. Cutting south just before Élos, a spectacular paved road continues through the high mountains towards Paleohóra. On a motorbike, with a sense of adventure and plenty of fuel, it's great: the bus doesn't come this way, villagers still stare at the sight of a tourist, and a host of small, seasonal streams cascade beside or under the asphalt.

As regards practicalities, the **ferry agent's office** in Kastélli is one block inland from the main square, Platía Kastellíou (Xirouxákis; ℡08220/22 655). The **ferry dock** lies 2km west of town – a significant walk if you're heavily laden, or an inexpensive taxi ride. For **rooms**, *Vergerakis* (aka *Jimmy's*; ℡08220/22 663; ❶) has clean and simple rooms on the main square, but the more attractive option is the excellent *Hotel Galini Beach* (℡08220/23 288, ℱ23 388, ⓦwww.galinibeach .com; ❷) at the east end of the seafront near the sports stadium, or *Maria Beach* (℡08220/22 610 ℱ23 626; ❷) with some much cheaper rooms which you need to ask for on the town's sandy western beach. Heading north from the main square brings you to the beach promenade where there are a number of **tavernas** – *To Kelari* is worth a try – and late-night drinking and music **bars** popular with the local younger set, particularly at weekends.

Falásarna to Elafonísi

To the west of Kastélli lies some of Crete's loneliest, and, for many visitors, finest coastline. The first place of note is ancient and modern **Falásarna**, which has city ruins meaning little to the non-specialist, but overlooking some of the best beaches on Crete, wide and sandy with clean water. There's a handful of **tavernas** and an increasing number of **rooms** for rent: try the seafront *Sun Set* (℡08220/41 204; ❶) near the archeological site. Otherwise, you may have to sleep out, as many people do; make sure to take any rubbish away with you. This can mean that the main beaches are dirty, but they remain beautiful, and there are plenty of others within walking distance. The nearest real town is **Plátanos**, 5km up a paved road, along which there are a couple of daily buses.

Further south, the western coastline is still less discovered and there's little in the way of official accommodation. **SFINÁRI** has a few houses which rent rooms, and a quiet pebble beach a little way below the village where there's a small **campsite** next to the reliable *Captain Fidias's* taverna. **KÁMBOS** is similar, but even less visited, its beach a considerable walk down a hill. However, **accommodation** is available at the good-value *Rooms Hartzulakis* (℡08220/44 445; ❶) on the edge of a long gorge which also leads down to the sea; the same place has a terrace **taverna** with great views, and the proprietor can advise on **walking** hereabouts. Beyond them both is the **monastery of Khryssoskalítissa** increasingly visited by tours from Haniá and Paleohóra now the road has been sealed, but well worth the effort for its isolation and nearby beaches; the bus gets as far as Váthy, from where the monastery is another two-hours' walk away, although you could try hitching – with a fair chance of success – as many of the tourist cars are bound to be heading for the same destination.

Five kilometres beyond Khryssoskalítissa, another stretch of newly laid asphalt has replaced the former cratered nightmare of a track leading to the coast, opposite the tiny uninhabited islet of **Elafonísi**, marooned in a gloriously scenic turquoise lagoon. It's almost too easy now as you glide effortlessly down to the sea, and the increasing number of visitors and almost total lack of facilities to cater for them when they arrive is proving a major problem which no one seems to want to tackle.

You can easily wade out to the islet with its sandy beaches and rock pools, and the shallow lagoon is warm and crystal clear. It looks magnificent, but daily boat trips from Paleohóra and coach tours from elsewhere on the island have attracted a cluster of beach stalls renting loungers and selling tourist tat, which ensures that, in the middle of the day at least, it's far from deserted. To cope with the resulting sanitary problems, a single and totally inadequate portable toilet has been installed by the authorities next to the beach. If you want to stay, and really appreciate the place, there are a couple of seasonal tavernas, but bring some supplies unless you want to be wholly dependent on them.

Kándanos and Paleohóra

Getting down to Paleohóra by the main road which leaves the north coast at Tavronítis, 22km west of Haniá, is a lot easier, and several daily buses from Haniá make the trip. But although this route also has to wind through the western outriders of the White Mountains, it lacks the excitement of the routes to either side. **KÁNDANOS**, at the 58-kilometre mark, has been entirely rebuilt since it was destroyed by the Germans for its fierce resistance to their occupation. The original sign erected when the deed was done is preserved on the war memorial in the central square: "Here stood Kándanos, destroyed in retribution for the murder of 25 German soldiers, and never to be rebuilt again." The pleasantly easy-going and once-again-substantial village had the last laugh.

When the beach at **PALEOHÓRA** finally appears below it is a welcome sight. The little town is built across the base of a peninsula, its harbour and a beach known as Pebble Beach on the eastern side, the wide sands ("Sandy Beach") on the other. Above, on the outcrop, Venetian ramparts stand sentinel. These days Paleohóra has developed into a significant resort, but it's still thoroughly enjoyable, with a main street filling with tables at night as diners spill out of the restaurants, and with a pleasantly chaotic social life. You'll find a helpful **tourist office** (Mon & Wed–Sun 10am–1pm & 6–9pm; ☎08230/41 507) in the town hall on Venizélos, the official name of the main street; they have full accommodation lists and a provide a decent **map** which is useful for finding food and accommodation locations.

There are plenty of **places to stay** (though not always many vacancies in high season) – try the basic *Dolphin Rooms* (☎08230/41 703; ❶), below the Venetian fort, or *Castello Rooms* (☎08230/41 143; ❷), at the southern end of Sandy Beach, for a little more en-suite luxury. *Savas Rooms* (☎08230/41 075; ❶), near the bus station at the north end of town, does balcony en-suite rooms with kitchenette, fridge and fan for a very reasonable price. There's also a fair-sized **campsite** 2km north of Pebble Beach; if you are tempted to sleep on the main Sandy Beach – one of the best on the south coast, with showers, trees and acres of sand – be prepared for trouble from police and local residents who are no longer willing to tolerate this; your best bet is to get as far away from the town as possible if you want to be left in peace. When you tire of Paleohóra and the excellent **windsurfing** in the bay (boards for hire from Happy Surf on the beach), there are excursions up the hill to Prodhrómi, for example, or along a five- to six-hour coastal path to Soúyia.

For **eating** and **drinking**, tavernas, bars and cafés are to be found throughout the resort, particularly along the roads behind the two beaches. A good place to try for some imaginative **vegetarian** specials is *The Third Eye*, just out of the centre towards Sandy Beach. Other decent in-town eating places include *Pizzeria Niki*, off the south side of Kondekáki, and *The Wave* at the south end of Pebble Beach, serving good fish on a seaside terrace. As Paleohóra publicizes itself as a "family" resort there's an unwritten curfew around 11pm when the bars lower their sounds, so if you're looking for some untamed nightlife you've definitely come to the wrong place. The only raucous sounds after this hour are at the **dance club** *Palehora Club* at the extreme north end of the Pebble Beach and close to the campsite, where you can boogie beneath the stars on a dance floor overlooked by palms. An open-air **cinema**, Cine Attikon, tucked away in the northern backstreets is also worth knowing about; most of their films are in English and programmes (which change daily) are posted in the tourist office.

Almost everything else you're likely to need is located in the centre of town. **Banks** (with cash dispensers), **travel agents**, a **laundry**, **mountain bike** and **car hire** companies and **internet** access (at PC Corner above the *Alaloom* cocktail bar) are all along Venizélos, while the **post office** is on the road behind Sandy Beach. There are two **pharmacies** on Kontekáke, the road running from east to west at the south end of Venizélou, and there's a **health centre** in the street parallel to Venizélos to the west. **Boats** run from here to Elafonísi, the island of Gávdhos and along the coast to Soúyia and Ayía Rouméli; the travel agency Interkreta Travel (℡08230/41 393, ℻41 050), close to the junction of Venizélos and Kondekáki, is the best source for information and tickets. They also have information about trips to walk the **Gorge of Samariá**, see p.266, from here, with a bus leaving daily at 6am throughout the summer.

Gávdhos

The island of **Gávdhos**, some fifty kilometres of rough sea south of Paleohóra, is the most southerly landmass in Europe. Gávdhos is small (about 10km by 7km) and barren, but it has one major attraction: the enduring **isolation** which its inaccessible position has helped preserve. It is possible to turn up on spec and find a bed, but travel agents in Paleohóra such as Interkreta (see above) will arrange a room if you want one and also provide current ferry information. There's a semi-permanent community of campers and would-be "Robinson Crusoes" resident on the island throughout the summer – in addition to the six indigenous families who live here year round. Largely because water is often difficult to obtain most people choose to base themselves near to one of the three largest beaches and at the most popular of all, **SARAKINÍKO**, there are at least seven beachfront **tavernas** – *Taverna Gerti & Manolis* have **rooms** (℡08230/41 103; ❶) – in addition to a squatters' community spreading a shanty town of unsightly breezeblock summer dwellings behind the beach. Providing you avoid the crowds in August, if all you wanted is a beach to yourself and a taverna to grill your fish, this remains the place for you.

Travel details

Buses

For the latest timetables and complete route and fare information visit KTEL's website at ⓦ http://bus-service-crete-ktel.com/timetables2.html
Áyios Nikólaos–Sitía (4 daily 7am–4.30pm; 2hr).
Haniá–Hóra Sfakíon (3 daily 8.30am–2pm; 2hr).
Haniá–Paleohóra (4 daily 8.30am–3.30pm; 2hr).
Haniá–Réthymnon–Iráklion (17 daily, 2 via old road 5.30am–8.30pm; 3hr total).
Iráklion–Ayía Galíni (8 daily 6.30am–6.30pm; 2hr 15min).

Iráklion–Áyios Nikólaos (20 daily 6.15am–8.30pm; 1hr 30min).
Iráklion–Festós (8 daily 7.30am–4.30pm; 1hr 30min).
Iráklion–Ierápetra (8 daily 6.30am–7.30pm; 2hr 30min).
Kastélli–Haniá (14 daily 6am–7pm; 1hr 30min).
Réthymnon–Spíli–Ayía Galíni (3 daily 7am–2.15pm; 45min–1hr 30min).

Ferries

For the latest timetables for domestic and international ferries from and to Crete visit ⓦ www.greekislands.gr or ⓦ www.ferries.gr
Áyios Nikólaos and Sitía 5 sailings a week to

Pireás (12hr), 4 ferries a week to Kásos, Kárpathos, Hálki and Rhodes; 4 weekly to Mílos.
Haniá 1 or 2 ferries daily to Pireás (9hr).
Hóra Sfakíon 5 ferries daily to Loutró/Ayía

Rouméli; 4 weekly to Gávdhos in season.
Iráklion 2 ferries daily to Pireás (12hr); 1 daily
fast ferry to Pireás (6hr); 2 ferries weekly to
Thessaloníki; 1 daily ferry to Thíra (4hr), also fast
boats and hydrofoils (2hr 30min); daily ferries to
Páros in season; 1–2 weekly to Mýkonos and Íos;
weekly to Náxos, Tínos, Skýros, Skíathos.

Kastélli (Kíssamos) 2 ferries weekly to Pireás
(11hr); 1–4 ferries weekly to Kýthira; 1 ferry weekly
to Yíthio (8hr); 1 ferry weekly to Kalamáta (9hr).
Paleohóra 3 boats a week in season to Gávdhos.
Also daily sailings to Elafonísi and Soúyia.
Réthymnon daily ferries to Pireás (12hr); seasonal
day-trips to Thíra.

Flights

Flights are on Olympic unless otherwise stated.
Haniá–Athens (4 daily on Olympic; 4 daily on
Aegean-Cronus; 2 daily on Axon)
Haniá–Thessaloníki (2 weekly on Olympic; 3
daily on Aegean-Cronus)
Iráklion–Athens (5–7 daily on Olympic; 6 daily on
Aegean-Cronus; 3 daily on Axon)

Iráklion–Rhodes (2 weekly, summer only, on
Olympic; 1–2 daily on Aegean-Cronus)
Iráklion–Thessaloníki (2 weekly on Olympic; 3
daily on Aegean-Cronus)
Iráklion–Thíra (2 weekly)
Sitía–Athens (1 weekly, Fri all year)

The Dodecanese

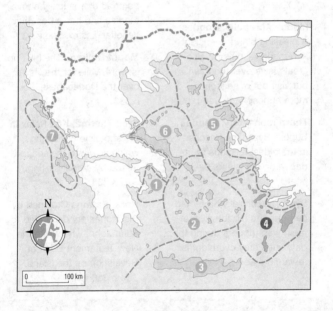

CHAPTER 4   # Highlights

✳ **Northern Kárpathos** Old
walking trails take you
between traditional villages.
See p.287

✳ **Ródhos old town** Superbly
preserved medieval streets,
inextricably linked with the
Knights of Saint John. See
p.292

✳ **Lindos Acropolis, Rhodes**
A pleasing blend of ancient
and medieval culture; also
great views over the town,
but visit out of season for
more atmosphere. See p.299

✳ **Thárri monastery, Rhodes**
Superb Byzantine frescoes
in the oldest religious foundation on the island. See
p.303

✳ **Sými** The officially protected
harbour and hillside village
teem with trippers during the
day, but a stay overnight is
rewarding. See p.312

✳ **Volcano on Níssyros** The
craters of the dormant volcano still hiccup, though the
most recent – producing
ash, steam and earthquakes
– was in 1933. See p.322

✳ **Hóra, AstypFálea** The
windswept island "capital" is
perched dramatically above
the sea and has a beautiful
Venetian *kástro*. See p.339

✳ **Mount Dhíkeos** The hike up
is worthwhile for the views
over the Dodecanese. See
p.333

✳ **Brós Thermá, Kós** Relax in
the shoreline hot springs,
which flow into the sea, protected by a boulder ring.
See p.333

✳ **Hóra, Pátmos** Crowned by
the monastery dedicated to
Saint John, who wrote the
New Testament Book of
Revelation on the island.
See p.356

The Dodecanese

T he furthest Greek island group from the mainland, the **Dodecanese** (Dhodhekánisos) lie close to the Turkish coast – some of the islands, like Kós and Kastellórizo, almost within hailing distance of Anatolia. Because of this position, and their remoteness from Athens, the islands have had a turbulent history: they were the scene of ferocious battles between German and British forces in 1943–44, and were only finally included in the modern Greek state in 1948 after centuries of occupation by Crusaders, Ottomans and Italians. Even now the threat (real or imagined) of invasion from Turkey is very much evident in the form of numerous military bases and smaller watch-points. Despite certain high-level civilian rapprochements which have taken place between Greece and Turkey in recent years, the Greek army and air force clearly prefer to keep their powder dry.

Whatever the rigours of the various occupations, their legacy includes a wonderful blend of architectural styles and of Eastern and Western cultures. Medieval Rhodes is the most famous, but almost every island has some Classical remains, a Crusaders' castle, a clutch of traditional villages and abundant grandiose public buildings. For these last the Italians, who occupied the Dodecanese from 1912 to 1943, are mainly responsible. In their determination to beautify the islands and turn them into a showplace for fascism they undertook public works, excavations and reconstruction on a massive scale; if historical accuracy was often sacrificed in the interests of style, only an expert is likely to complain. A more sinister aspect of the Italian administration was the

Accommodation price codes

Throughout the book we've categorized accommodation according to the following **price codes**, which denote the cheapest available double room in high season. All prices are for the room only, except where otherwise indicated. Many hotels, especially those in category ❹ and over, include breakfast in the price; you'll need to check this when booking. During low season, rates can drop by more than fifty percent, especially if you are staying for three or more nights. Exceptions are during the Christmas and Easter weeks when you'll pay high-season prices. Single rooms, where available, cost around seventy percent of the price of a double.

❶ Up to €24	❹ €43–58
❷ €24–33	❺ €59–72
❸ €34–42	❻ €73 and upwards

Note: Youth hostels typically charge €7–9 for a dormitory bed.
For more accommodation details, see pp.52–54.

attempted forcible Latinization of the populace: spoken Greek and Orthodox observance were banned in public from 1923 to 1943. The most tangible reminder of this policy is the (rapidly dwindling) number of older people who can still converse – and write – more fluently in Italian than in Greek.

Aside from this bilingualism, the Dodecanese themselves display a marked topographic and economic schizophrenia. The dry limestone outcrops of **Kastellórizo**, **Sými**, **Hálki**, **Kássos** and **Kálymnos** have always been forced to rely on the sea for their livelihoods, and the wealth generated by this maritime culture – especially during the nineteenth century – fostered the growth of attractive port towns. The sprawling, relatively fertile giants, **Rhodes**

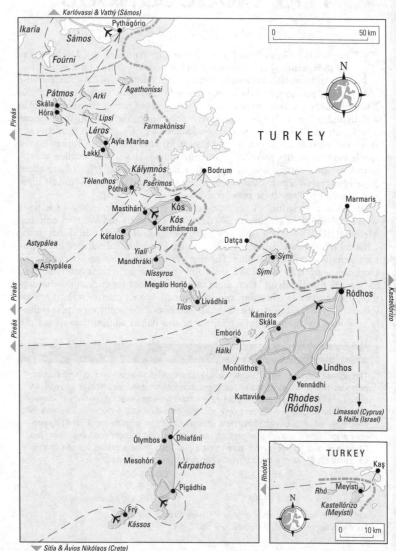

(Ródhos) and **Kós**, have recently seen their traditional agricultural economies almost totally displaced by a tourist industry grown up around good beaches and nightlife, as well as some of the most exciting historical monuments in the Aegean. **Kárpathos** lies somewhere in between, with a lightly forested north grafted on to a rocky limestone south; **Tílos**, despite its lack of trees, has ample water, though the green volcano-island of **Níssyros** does not. **Léros** shelters softer contours and more amenable terrain than its map outline would suggest, while **Pátmos** and **Astypálea** at the fringes of the archipelago offer architecture and landscapes more typical of the Cyclades.

The largest islands in the group are connected by regular **ferries**, and none (except for Kastellórizo, Astypálea and sometimes Tílos) is hard to reach. Rhodes is the main transport hub, with services to Turkey, Israel and Cyprus, as well as connections with Crete, the northeastern Aegean, the Cyclades and the mainland. Kálymnos and Kós are jointly an important secondary terminus, with a useful ferry based on Kálymnos, hydrofoil services using Kós as a focus and transfer point, and excursion boats based on Kós providing a valuable supplement to larger ferries arriving at uncivil hours.

Kássos

Like Psará islet in the northeast Aegean, **Kássos** contributed its large fleet to the Greek revolutionary war effort, and likewise suffered appalling consequences. In late May 1824, an Ottoman army sent by Ibrahim Pasha, Governor of Egypt, besieged the island; on June 7, aided perhaps by a traitor's tip as to the weak point in Kássos's defences, the invaders descended on the populated north-coastal plain, slaughtered most of the inhabitants and put houses, farms and trees to the torch.

Barren and depopulated since then, Kássos attracts few visitors, despite regular air links with Rhodes and Kárpathos, and being a port of call on ferry lines from those isles to Crete. Numerous sheer gorges slash through lunar terrain, with fenced smallholdings of midget olive trees providing the only permanent relief. Springtime grain crops briefly soften the usually empty terraces, and livestock somehow survives on a thin furze of thornbush. What remains of the population is grouped together in five villages facing Kárpathos, leaving most of the island uninhabited and uncultivated. Until very recently, there was little sign here of the wealth brought into other islands by diaspora Greeks or – since Kássos hasn't much to offer them – tourists; amidst the occasional new concrete monster, crumbling houses and disused hillside terraces poignantly recall better days. A long pattern of serving as roving pilots, or residence in Egypt (Kassiots were instrumental in digging the Suez Canal), has been eclipsed by subsequent emigration to the US. Thus American logo-T-shirts and baseball caps are *de rigueur* summer fashion, and the conversation of vacationing expatriates is spiked with Americanisms.

Kássos can be a nuisance to reach, and matters are unlikely to improve as two companies have gone bust attempting to build a new harbour, with the third contractor looking to follow suit. The existing jetty just west of Boúka fishing port in the capital, Frý (pronounced "free"), is so poor that passing ferries won't stop if any appreciable wind is up. In such cases, you disembark at Kárpathos and fly the remaining distance in a light, nineteen-seater aircraft. The air ticket plus a taxi fare to Kárpathos airport isn't much more than the fare charged by Finíki (Kárpathos)-based excursion boats which can manoeuvre into Boúka in most weathers. The airport lies 1km west of Frý, an easy enough walk, otherwise a cheap (€1.50) ride on one of the island's three taxis. Except in July and August, when a few rental motorbikes and boat excursions are offered, the only method of exploring the island's remoter corners is by hiking along fairly arduous, shadeless paths and roads. Place-name signposting tends to be in Greek only, and in Kassiot dialect at that – clearly the islanders aren't expecting many non-Kassiot visitors.

Frý and Emboriós

Most of the appeal of the capital, **FRÝ**, is confined to the immediate environs of the wedge-shaped fishing port of **Boúka**, protected from the sea by two crab-claws of breakwater and overlooked by the cathedral of Áyios Spyrídhon. Inland, Frý is engagingly unpretentious, even down-at-heel; there are no concessions to tourism, and little attempt has been made to prettify an essentially scruffy little town that's quite desolate out of season. Somewhat overpriced **accommodation** is found at the seafront hotels *Anagenissis* (℡02450/41 495, Ⓕ41 036, Ⓦwww.kassos-island.gr; ❷) and, just behind with fewer views, the less expensive, all-en-suite *Anessis* (℡02450/41 201, Ⓕ41 730; ❷). The manager of the *Anagenissis* also has a few pricier apartments, and runs the all-in-one travel agency just below (though Olympic has its own premises two doors down). Both hotels tend to be noisy owing to morning bustle on the waterfront – and the phenomenal number of small but lively fast-food joints and café-bars in town, some right underneath. During high season a few **rooms** operate; these tend to be more expensive and mostly located in the suburb of Emboriós, fifteen-minute's walk east.

Outside of peak season, Frý can support only one full-service **taverna**: *O Mylos*, overlooking the intermittent harbour works. Luckily it's excellent and reasonable, with a good variety of daily-special *mayireftá* at lunch and sometimes fish grills by night. From late June to early September you can also try *Iy Oraia Bouka*, perched above Boúka, or *To Meltemi* ouzerí, on the way to Emboriós. In Emboriós itself, only *Ta Tessera Adherfia* by the palm-tree church shows any sign of life outside of summer. Shops in Frý, including two fruit stalls, are fairly well stocked for self-catering.

Local beaches

Frý's town **beach**, if you can call it that, is at **Ammouá** (Ammoudhiá), a thirty-minute walk beyond the airstrip along the coastal track. This sandy cove, just before the landmark chapel of Áyios Konstandínos, is often caked with seaweed and tar, but persevere five minutes more and you'll find much cleaner pea-gravel coves. The determined can swim off the little patch of sand at **Emboriós**, along with the half-dozen resident ducks, and there's a more private pebble stretch off to the right. But having got this far, you may as well continue ten to fifteen minutes along the shore, first along an old track, then on a path past the last house, for a final scramble to the base of the **Gaïdhouropoúli** ravine, where there's another secluded pebble cove. Otherwise, it's worth shelling out for high-season boat excursions to far better beaches on a pair of islets visible to the northwest, **Armathiá** and **Makrá**. There are no amenities (or shade) on either islet, so come prepared.

The interior

At the edges of the agricultural plain just inland from Frý cluster a number of villages, linked to each other by road; all are worth a passing visit, and can be reached by foot in a single day.

Larger in extent and more rural than Frý, **AYÍA MARÍNA**, 1500m inland and uphill, is most attractive seen from the south, arrayed above olive groves; one of its two belfried churches is the focus of the island's liveliest festival, on July 17. Some fifteen minutes beyond the hamlet of Kathístres, a further 500m southwest, the cave of **Ellinokamára** is named for the late Classical, polygonal wall completely blocking the entrance; its ancient function is uncertain, perhaps a cult shrine or tomb complex. To reach it, turn south at the two restored windmills in Ayía Marína, then right (west) at the phone-box junction; carry on, straight and down (not level and left) until you see a red-dirt path going up the hillside to a crude, stone-built pastoral hut. Some modern masonry walls enclose the start of this path, but once at the hut (the cave is more or less underneath it) you're compelled to hop a fence to visit – there are no gates. From Ellinokamára another, fainter path – you'll probably need a guide – continues within ninety minutes in the same direction to the larger, more natural cave of **Seláï**, with impressive stalactites in the rear chamber.

Generally, walking opportunities on Kássos are poor – trails are few, unmarked and in poor condition, with no shade and few reliable water sources. An exception is the forty-minute path from Arvanitohóri to Póli, which is clearly walled in and enjoyable, shortcutting the road effectively – it starts at the base of the village, where two trees occupy planter wells. **PÓLI**, somewhat impoverished and resolutely agricultural, is the site of a badly deteriorated ancient and medieval acropolis – a few stretches of fortification remain – and marks the start of a four-kilometre road leading southeast to **Áyios Mámas**, signposted in dialect as "**Áï Mámas**", one of two important rural monasteries, perched spectacularly overlooking the sea. Alternatively, from Póli you can descend – again on walled-in path for the first twenty minutes, then dirt track – to **PANAYIÁ**, famous for its now-neglected mansions – many of Kássos's wealthiest ship captains hailed from here – and for the oldest surviving church on the island, the eighteenth-century **Panayía tou Yióryi**.

Between Ayía Marína and Arvanitohóri, another road, that used to be just a dirt track and was only recently paved over, veers off southwest from the road linking the two villages towards the rural monastery of **Áyios Yeóryios Hadhión**. The pleasure of walking this route, however, has been somewhat diminished by the paving over of the road, so you'll probably want to hire a taxi, rent a bike if available or hitch a lift in at least one direction. At the beginning of the route you skirt the narrows of a fearsome gorge, and from there on you are unlikely to see another living thing aside from goats, sheep or an occasional Eleonora's falcon. After about an hour, the Mediterranean appears to the south, a dull expanse ruffled only by the occasional ship bound for Cyprus and the Middle East. When you finally reach a fork, adopt the upper, right-hand turning, following derelict phone lines towards Áyios Yeóryios Hadhión (signed as "**Áï Yeóryi**"), 12km (3hr on foot) from Frý. This is busiest at its late-April festival time, but during the warmer months there's a resident caretaker who runs a small snack/drinks bar. There are a few open guest cells (ask nicely, donation expected) and cistern water here if you need to fill up canteens; the only other water en route is a well at the route's high point.

From the monastery it's another 3km on dirt track – motorbikes can make it most of the way – to **Hélatros** ("Hélathros" on older maps), a lonely cove at the mouth of one of the larger, more forbidding Kassiot canyons. The sand-and-gravel beach itself is small and mediocre, but the water is pristine and – except for the occasional fishing boat – you'll probably be alone. The lower, left-hand option at the fork is the direct track to Hélatros, but this is only 2km shorter and, following severe 1995 storm damage, impassable to any vehicle and all but the most energetic hikers; since the paving of the upper road to Áï Yeóryi, it is likely to have got even worse.

Kárpathos

A long, narrow island marooned between Rhodes and Crete, wild **Kárpathos** has always been something of an underpopulated backwater, although it is the third largest of the Dodecanese. An habitually cloud-capped mountainous spine rises to over 1200m, and divides the more populous, lower-lying south from an exceptionally rugged north. A magnificent, windswept coastline of cliffs and promontories has begun to attract significant numbers of Scandinavian and German package tourists, who arrive on several direct international charters weekly. Since the 1990s, these clients have more or less monopolized several resorts in the southern part of the island, pushing independent travellers up to the remote north of the island. Despite this development, Kárpathos remains saddled with a deficient road system – only partly paved, unspeakable otherwise – and expensive taverna food, which offsets reasonable room prices. Most island-hoppers come here for a glimpse of the traditional village life in the far north, and for the numerous superb, secluded beaches.

The island's interior isn't the most alluring: the central and northern uplands were badly scorched by forest fires in the 1980s, and agriculture plays a slighter role than on any other Greek island of comparable size. The Karpathians are too well off to bother much with farming; massive emigration to America and the resulting remittance economy has transformed Kárpathos into one of the wealthiest Greek islands.

Kárpathos's four Classical cities figure little in ancient chronicles. Alone of the major Dodecanese, the island was held by the Genoese and Venetians after the Byzantine collapse and so has no castle of the crusading Knights of St John, nor any surviving medieval fortresses of consequence. The Ottomans couldn't be bothered to settle or even garrison it; instead they left a single judge or *kadi* at the main town, making the Greek population responsible for his safety during the many pirate attacks.

Pigádhia (Kárpathos Town)

The island capital of **PIGÁDHIA**, often known simply as Kárpathos, nestles at the south end of scenic **Vróndi Bay**, whose sickle of sand extends 3km northwest. The town itself, curling around the jetty and quay where ferries and excursion boats dock, is as drab as its setting is beautiful; an ever-increasing number of concrete blocks contributes to the air of a vast building site, making the Italian-era port police and county governmental buildings seem like heirlooms by comparison. Although there's nothing special to see, Pigádhia does offer just about every facility you might need, albeit with a definite package-tourism slant.

Getting around

Olympic Airways (book a week minimum in advance – planes to Rhodes have just nineteen seats) is at the west end of Apodhímon Karpathíon, the "Street of the Overseas Karpathians", at the corner of Platía 5-Oktovríou. Possi Travel (℡02450/22 235) are sole agents for LANE, currently the only shipping line to call at Pigádhia, and also sell air tickets when Olympic is shut. The **post office** is on Ethnikís Andístasis, while all three **banks** have cash dispensers.

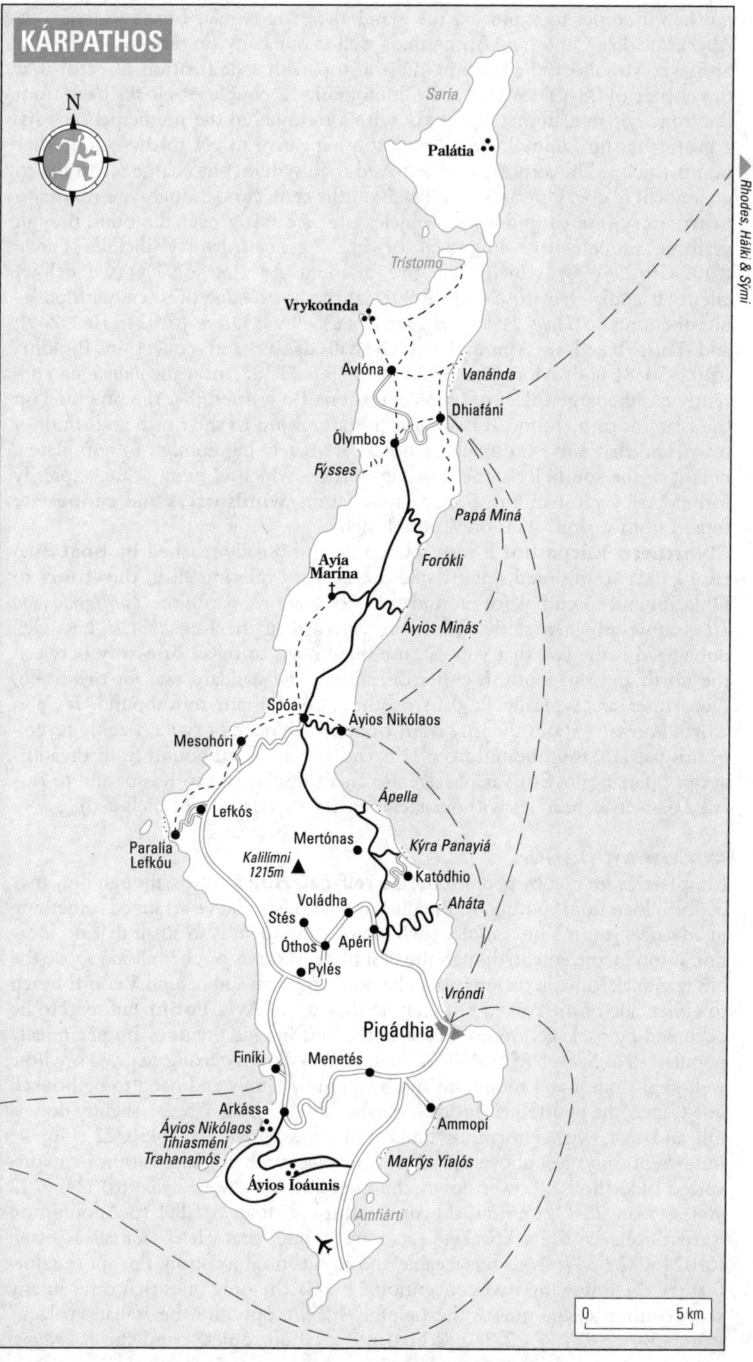

KÁRPATHOS

N

Saría

Palátia

Trístomo

Vrykoúnda

Avlóna — *Vanánda*

Dhiafáni

Ólymbos

Fýsses

Papá Miná

Ayía Marína † *Forókli*

Áyios Minás

Spóa — Áyios Nikólaos

Mesohóri

Ápella

Lefkós

Mertónas *Kýra Panayiá*

Paralía Lefkóu ▲ *Kalilímni 1215m* Katódhio

Voládha *Aháta*

Stés

Óthos Apéri

Pylés

Vróndi

Pigádhia

Finíki Menetés

Arkássa

Áyios Nikólaos Tihiasméni Trahanamós Ammopí

Áyios Ioáunis *Makrýs Yialós*

Amfiárti

✈

0   5 km

When it comes to exploring the island, there are regular **buses** to Pylés, via Apéri, Voládha, Óthos and Ammopí, as well as one daily (in term time only) to Spóa via Mesohóri; the "station" (just a stop with a destination-placard) is at the corner of 28-Oktovríou and Dhimokratías, a couple of blocks back from the front. Set-rate, unmetered **taxis**, with a terminal in the municipal car park a bit further up Dhimokratías, aren't too expensive to get to these and other points (such as the airport) on the paved road system, but charge a fortune to go anywhere else. Upwards of a dozen outfits **rent cars**, though you may have to try every one to find a free vehicle; rates are vastly over the odds, though available models have improved of late. Agencies to try include Circle (☎02450/22 690), which may give discounts to *Rose Studios* (see below) clients; friendly *Avis* (☎02450/22 702), at the north edge of town, with possible discounts to *Hotel Panorama* guests (see below); Drive (☎02450/61 249); and Trust, based in Ammopí, which will deliver and collect in Pigádhia (☎02450/81 060). Moto Carpathos (☎02450/22 382), near the *dhimarhío*, currently has the largest fleet of scooters for rent. Be warned that the only fuel on the island is to be found at two pairs of stations just to the north and south of town, and that tanks on smaller scooters are barely big enough to complete a circuit of the south, let alone head up north – which is, in any case, expressly forbidden by most outfits. For seagoing jaunts, **windsurfers** and **canoes** are rented from various stalls on Vróndi beach.

Northern Kárpathos is most pleasantly and usually reached **by boat**. Two rival kaïkia are moored side by side on the jetty, offering all-in **day-tours** to Dhiafáni and Ólymbos for around €13.20 (pay on board); the *Chrisovalandou III* is more attractive and stable in heavy sea than the *Karpathos II*. Less well publicized is the fact that you can use these boats to travel **one-way** between the north and the south in either direction – the standard rate for this is €6. Departures are typically 8.30am northbound, 4.30pm southbound. It's also worth knowing about the tiny **mail boat** which once or twice weekly reverses this pattern: southbound from Dhiafáni at 8am, northbound from Pigádhia at 3pm (fare again €6). Various agents can also offer trips to Kássos and to isolated east-coast beaches without facilities (bring lunch if not included).

Accommodation

Most ferries are met by people offering **self-catering studios**, though they may be forbidden from touting on the quay itself. Unless you've arranged something in advance, you might consider such offers – the town is so small that no location is too inconvenient, though the best place to stay is on the hillside above the bus terminal. More luxurious places lie north, towards and behind **Vróndi** beach to either side of the ruined fifth-century basilica of **Ayía Fotiní**, but tend to be occupied by package groups. Three of the best hillside premises are perennially popular *Rose Studios* (☎02450/22 284, ✉reservations@mailgate.gr; ❶), whose well-kept studios and rooms are run by a kindly family and need to be booked in advance; the courteous *Amaryllis Studios* (☎02450/22 375; ❷), slightly downhill and east, with enormous units; and *Elias Rooms* (☎02450/22 446; ❶; June–Sept only) just above the *Hotel Karpathos*, with en-suite rooms in a converted older house. Lower down, the rambling, en-suite *Konaki* (☎02450/22 908; ❶) on 28-Oktovríou, the upper through-road parallel to Apodhímon Karpathíon, is a backpackers' standby, while the *Hotel Karpathos* itself (☎02450/22 347; ❶) is serviceable and in a central location. For more comfort try the following two conventional hotels, the only ones that cater in any way to nonpackage guests: the helpful *Atlantis*, opposite the Italian "palace" (☎02450/22 777, ☏22 780, ✉htatlantis@yahoo.com; ❹) and the *Panorama*, in a quiet inland lane at the start of the Vróndi beach road (☎02450/23 262, ℻23 021; ❸).

Eating and drinking

Most of Pigádhia's waterfront **tavernas** are undistinguished – *yíros* and chips reign supreme – and overpriced, though quality and value improves significantly as you head east towards the ferry dock. Towards the end of the strip are clustered three worthy choices: *To Perigiali*, a fairly genuine ouzerí with good bread and home-made desserts; *To Kyma*, good for nonfarmed fish; and the best all-rounder, *Iy Orea Karpathos*, with palatable local bulk wine, *trahanádhes* soup, sausages and great spinach pie. One block inland, the clear winner is *To Ellinikon*, a *mezedhopolío* that caters all year round to a local clientele with hot and cold *orektiká*, meat and good desserts. Live **music** can be heard nightly (June–Sept) at the *Kafenio Life of Angels*, one of the few surviving old buildings next to the church on Apodhímon Karpathíon, though the sessions here are not by any means the best on the island. More trendy **bars** such as *Art Café-Bar*, *Rocks* and *Escape* offer taped sounds from perches overlooking the bay. Pigádhia's main **internet café** is *Café Galileo* (ⓦwww.caffegalileo.gr), two doors down from Olympic on Apodhímon Karpathíon. At Vróndi there are two serviceable lunchtime tavernas at the southerly, town end: *To Limanaki* and the *Seaside Snack Bar*.

Southern and western Kárpathos

The southern extremity of Kárpathos, towards the airport, is extraordinarily desolate and windswept. There's a couple of relatively undeveloped sandy beaches – in particular **Makrýs Yialós** – on the southeast coast in the region known as Amfiárti, but they're only really attractive to foreign windsurfers who come to take advantage of the prevailing northwesterlies. Most people go no further in this direction than **AMMOPÍ**, just 7km from Pigádhia. This, together with the development at Vróndi and Arkássa (see below), is the closest thing on Kárpathos to a purpose-built beach resort. The two sand-and-gravel, tree-fringed coves are bordered by half a dozen **tavernas** and increasing numbers of **hotels** and **rooms** – recommendable among these, not dominated by packages, are the *Votsalakia Rooms* (☎02450/22 204; ❷) and the *Sunflower Studios* (☎ & ℻ 02450/81 019; ❷). West out of Pigádhia the road climbs steeply 9km up to **MENETÉS**, an appealing ridgetop village with handsome old houses, a tiny folklore museum and a spectacularly sited church. There are two **tavernas** here (*Koula* and *Ta Dhyo Adhelfia*) and a World War II memorial with sweeping views north.

Beyond Menetés, you descend to **ARKÁSSA**, on the slopes of a ravine draining to the west coast, with excellent views to Kássos en route. Despite just one good nearby beach interrupting a mostly rocky shore, Arkássa has been heavily developed, with hotels and restaurants sprouting in clusters. Much of the **accommodation** is aimed squarely at the package market, but independent travellers could try the en-suite *Hotel Dimitrios* (☎02450/61 353, ℻61 249; ❷ including breakfast), or the *Seaside Studios* (☎02450/61 421; ❷) above **Áyios Nikólaos** beach signposted just south, a 600-metre stretch of sand – rare hereabouts – with a single taverna. Most other **tavernas** lie north of the ravine in the village centre, for example the durable *Petaloudha* on the dead-end access street.

A few hundred metres south of where the ravine meets the sea, a signposted cement side road leads briefly to the whitewashed chapel of **Ayía Sofía**, marooned amidst various remains of Classical and Byzantine Arkessia. These consist of several mosaic floors with geometric patterns, including one running diagonally under the floor of a half-buried chapel, emerging from the walls on either side. The Paleókastro headland beyond was the site of Mycenaean Arkessia; the walk up is again signposted, but scarcely worth it for the sight of a few stretches of polygonal wall and a couple of tumbled columns.

The tiny fishing port of **FINÍKI**, just a couple of kilometres north, offers a minuscule beach, fairly regular excursions to Kássos, half a dozen **tavernas** and several **rooms/studios** establishments. Accommodation includes *Giavasis Studios* (☎02450/61 365; ❷), on the road to the jetty, or for more comfort and value the well-designed and -built *Arhontiko Studios* up on the main bypass road (☎02450/61 473, ℱ61 054; ❸). *Iy Marina* and *To Dhelfíni* are currently the most salubrious eateries in Finíki, though there's another well-loved one, *Kostas*, 500m north under two tamarisks at reefy Kamarákia beach.

The west-coast road is asphalted all the way to the turning for the attractive resort of **PARALIÁ LEFKOÚ**, shore annexe of the inland hamlet of Lefkós. Although this is a delightful place for flopping on the beach, only three week-ly buses call, and Paralía Lefkoú marks the furthest point you can reach from Pighádhia on a small motorbike and return safely without running out of fuel. However, any effort will be rewarded by the striking topography of cliffs, hills, islets and sandspits surrounding a triple bay. There are now over two dozen places to stay, and perhaps half as many tavernas, but package companies tend to monopolize the better **accommodation** from June to September. Exceptions include the *Akroyiali Studios* (☎02450/71 178; ❶), on a stonier, fourth bay just south off the access road, and the spartan but en-suite *Sunweek Studios* (☎02450/71 025; ❶), above *Zorbas* taverna on the seaward promonto-ry. On the said promontory you'll find the most authentic eating option, the seafood-rich *Steki tou Kalymnou*.

Back on the main road, you climb northeast through one of the few sections of Karpathian pine forest not scarred by fire to **MESOHÓRI**. The village tumbles down towards the sea around narrow, stepped alleys, coming to an abrupt halt at the edge of a flat-topped bluff dotted with three tiny, ancient chapels and separated from the village proper by a vast oasis of orchards. These are nurtured by the fountain (best water on the island) underneath the church of **Panayía Vryssianí**, wedged against the mountainside just east and invisible from the end of the access road. On the stair-street leading to this church is an excellent taverna, the *Dhramoundana*, remarkably reasonable for Kárpathos, and featuring local capers, sausages and marinated "sardines" (really a larger fish, *menoúla*). The paved main road continues over the island's watershed to Spóa, overlooking the east coast (see opposite).

Central Kárpathos

The **centre** of Kárpathos supports a quartet of villages blessed with superb hillside settings, ample running water – and a cool climate, even in August. Nearly everyone here has "done time" in North America, then returned home with their nest eggs. New Jersey, New York and Canadian car plates tell you exactly where repatriated islanders struck it rich – often fabulously so (the area has the highest per capita income in Greece). West-facing **PYLÉS** is the most attractive, set above another spring-fed oasis, while **ÓTHOS**, noted for its red wine and a private ethnographic museum, is the highest (approx 400m) and chilliest, on the flanks of 1215-metre Mount Kalilímni. Among several **taver-nas** here, try *Toxotis*, basically a bar with mezédhes and a couple of cooked dishes of the day, plus the excellent bread the village is noted for. On the east side of the ridge you find **VOLÁDHA** with its tiny Venetian citadel and a pair of tavernas. From **APÉRI**, the largest, lowest and wealthiest settlement, you can drive 6km along a very rough road to the dramatic pebble beach of **Aháta**, with just a rather modest snack bar.

Beyond Apéri, the road up the **east coast** is extremely rough in places, passing above beaches most easily accessible by boat trips from Pigádhia. **Kyrá Panayiá** is the first encountered, reached via a paved but twisty side road through Katódhio hamlet; there's a surprising number of villas and rooms and a few tavernas in the ravine behind the 150m of fine gravel and sheltered, turquoise water. **Ápella** is the best of the beaches you can reach by road, though there's a final short path from the single taverna-rooms (the only facility) at the road's end to the scenic 300-metre gravel strand. The end of this route is **SPÓA**, high above the shore just east of the island's spine, with a snack bar and more reliable kafenío at the edge of the village which might make better meal stops than the overpriced *Votsalo* down at **Áyios Nikólaos**, 5km below, a small hamlet with an average beach and the overgrown ruins of a Paleo-Christian basilica to explore.

Northern Kárpathos

Although connected by dirt road with Spóa, much the easiest (and usual) way to get to northern Kárpathos is by sea. Inter-island ferries call at Dhiafáni two or three times a week in season, or there are the above-cited smaller tour kaḯkia from Pigádhia daily. The journey time on the smaller boats is about ninety minutes, with boats met at Dhiafáni by buses for the eight-kilometre transfer up to the traditional village of Ólymbos, the main attraction in this part of the island.

Ólymbos and around

Originally founded as a pirate-safe refuge in Byzantine times, windswept **ÓLYMBOS** straddles a long ridge below slopes studded with mostly ruined windmills. Two restored ones, beyond the main church, grind wheat and barley during late summer only, though one is kept under sail most of the year. Its basement houses a small ethnographic museum (odd hours; free), while a small shop nearby sells locally produced farm products. The village has long attracted foreign and Greek ethnologists, who treat it as a living museum of peasant dress, crafts, dialect and music long since gone elsewhere in Greece. It's still a very picturesque place, yet traditions are vanishing by the year. Nowadays it's only the older women and those working in the several tourist shops who wear the striking and magnificently colourful traditional dress – an instant photo opportunity in exchange for persistent sales pitches for the trinkets, many of them imported.

After a while you'll notice the prominent role that the women play in daily life: tending gardens, carrying goods on their shoulders or herding goats. Nearly all Ólymbos men emigrate or work outside the village, sending money home and returning only on holidays. The long-isolated villagers also speak a unique dialect, said to maintain traces of its Doric and Phrygian origins – thus "Ólymbos" is pronounced "Élymbos" locally. Live vernacular music is still heard regularly and draws crowds of visitors at festival times, in particular Easter and August 15, when you've little hope of finding a bed.

Among places to **stay**, the friendly *Rooms Restaurant Olymbos* (℡02450/51 252; ❶), near the village entrance, has rooms with baths or unplumbed ones with traditional furnishings, while the *Café-Restaurant Zefiros*, near the centre and run by two sisters, manages the en-suite *Hotel Astro* (℡02450/51 378; ❷).

There are a few other places to **eat**; one of the best and most obvious is *O Mylos*, occupying one of the restored mills and offering locally made wine and home-style specialities.

From the village the superb west-coast beach at **Fýsses** is a sharp 35-minute drop below, first cross-country, later by path. Most **local hikes**, however, head more gently north or east, many of them on waymarked paths, though you'll have to stay overnight in the area to enjoy them. The easiest option is the ninety-minute walk back down to Dhiafáni, beginning just below the two working windmills. The way is well marked, with water en route. It eventually drops to a ravine amidst extensive forest, though the last half-hour is mostly over bulldozed riverbed. You could also tackle the trail north to the ruins and beach at **Vrykoúnda** ("Vrougoúnda" in dialect), via sparsely inhabited **Avlóna**, set on a high upland devoted to grain. *Rooms Olymbos* plans to open an annexe soon at the edge of this hamlet, but it's best to take food and ample water to make a day of it, as it's just under three-hours' walk one way to Vrykoúnda, which offers traces of Hellenistic/Roman Brykous, the remote cave-shrine of John the Baptist on the promontory and good swimming. Trístomo, a Byzantine anchorage in the far northeast of Kárpathos, can also be reached on a magnificent cobbled way beginning above Avlóna; the return is by the same way. There's also a fine ninety-minute marked path from Avlóna down to Vanánda beach (see below).

Dhiafáni

Although its popularity is growing – especially since the 1996 completion of a new dock for large ferries – rooms in **DHIAFÁNI** are still inexpensive, and the pace of life slow outside of August. There are plenty of places at which to stay and eat, shops that will change money and even a small travel agency, Orfanos Travel (℗02450/51 410), which has its own en-suite hotel (②). The obvious *Mayflower Hotel* (℗02450/51 228; ②) opposite the quay is to be refurbished for comfort in 2002; otherwise try the non-en-suite *Pansion Delfini* (℗02450/51 391; ①), up on the southern hillside, though it ain't the same since life-and-soul of the place Kalliopi Lioreisi died in 2000. On the front, the most reliable, year-round **tavernas** are Italian-run *Iy Gorgona/L'Angolo* and the *Mayflower*.

Boat trips are offered to various nearby **beaches**, as well as to the Byzantine site of Palátia on the uninhabited islet of **Saría** or through the narrow strait to Trístomo anchorage and the ruins of Vrykoúnda. There are several coves within walking distance. Closest is **Vanánda**, a stony beach with an eccentrically managed campsite-snack bar in the oasis behind. To get there, follow the pleasant signposted path north through the pines, but don't believe the signs that say ten minutes – it's over thirty minutes away, shortcutting the more recent road. **Papá Miná**, with a few trees and cliff-shade, lies an hour's walk away via the cairned trail taking off from the road to the ferry dock.

Rhodes (Ródhos)

It's no accident that **Rhodes** is among the most visited of the Greek islands. Not only is its east coast lined with numerous sandy beaches, but the capital's nucleus is a beautiful and remarkably preserved medieval city, the legacy of the crusading Knights of St John who used the island as their main base from 1309 until 1522. Unfortunately this showpiece is jammed to capacity with over a million tourists in a good year, as against about 111,000 permanent inhabitants (including many foreigners). Of transient visitors, Germans, Brits, Swedes,

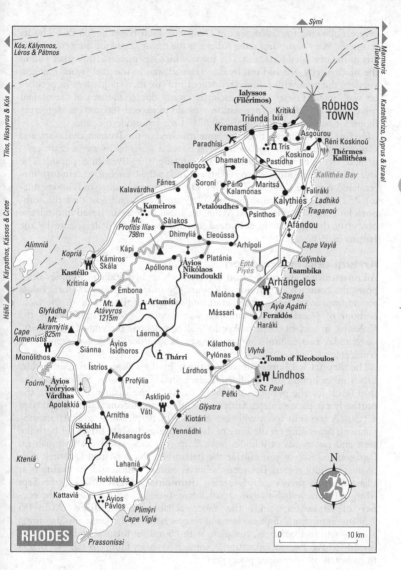

Italians and Danes predominate in that order, though they tend to arrive in different months of the year.

Blessed with an equable climate and strategic position, Rhodes was important from earliest times despite a lack of good harbours. The best natural port spawned the ancient town of Lindos which, together with the other city-states Kameiros and Ialyssos, united in 408 BC to found the new capital of Rhodes at the northern tip of the island. At various moments the cities allied themselves with Alexander, the Persians, Athenians or Spartans as prevailing conditions suited them, generally escaping retribution for backing the wrong side by a combination of seafaring audacity, sycophancy and burgeoning wealth as a trade centre. Following the failed siege of Demetrios Polyorketes in 305 BC, Rhodes prospered even more, displacing Athens as the major venue for rhetoric and the arts in the east Mediterranean. The town, which lies underneath virtually all of the modern city, was laid out by one Hippodamus in the grid layout much in vogue at the time, with planned residential and commercial quarters. Its perimeter walls totalled nearly 15km, enclosing nearly double the area of the present town, and the Hellenistic population was said to exceed 100,000 – a staggering figure for late antiquity, as against 50,631 at the last modern census.

Decline set in when Rhodes became involved in the Roman civil wars, and Cassius sacked the city; by late imperial times, it was a backwater, a status confirmed by numerous barbarian raids during the Byzantine period. The Byzantines were compelled to cede the island to the Genoese, who in turn surrendered it to the Knights of St John. The second great siege of Rhodes, during 1522–23, saw Ottoman Sultan Süleyman the Magnificent oust the stubborn knights, who retreated to Malta; the town once again lapsed into relative obscurity, though heavily colonized and garrisoned, until its seizure by the Italians in 1912.

Arrival and information

All international and inter-island **ferries** dock at the middle of Rhodes' three ports, the commercial harbour of Kolóna; the only exceptions are local **boats** to and from Sými, all excursion craft, and the **hydrofoils**, which use the yacht harbour of Mandhráki. Its entrance was supposedly once straddled by the Colossus, an ancient statue of Apollo built to celebrate the end of the 305 BC siege; today two columns surmounted by bronze deer are less overpowering replacements.

The **airport** is 13km southwest of town, by the village of Paradhísi; public urban buses bound for Paradhíssi, Kalavárdha, Theológos or Sálakos pass the stop (look for the perspex-and-wood kiosk) on the main road opposite the northerly car-park entrance fairly frequently between 6am and midnight (fare €1.50). A taxi into town will cost €10.30–19.10, plus bags and airport supplement, depending on the time of day. Orange-and-white **buses** for both the west and east coasts of Rhodes leave from two almost adjacent terminals on Papágou and Avérof, just outside the Italian-built New Market (a tourist trap, to miss without regret). Between the lower eastern station and the **taxi** rank at Platía Rimínis there's a fairly useless **municipal tourist office** (June–Sept Mon–Sat 9am–9pm, Sun 9am–3pm), while some way up Papágou on the corner of Makaríou stands the more reliable **EOT office** (Mon–Fri 7.30am–3pm); both dispense bus and ferry schedules, the latter also providing a list of standard taxi fares, complete with complaint form. Rhodes taxi drivers don't have a good reputation – some have been found to take kickbacks from hotels or overcharge passengers.

Ródhos Town

RÓDHOS TOWN divides into two unequal parts: the compact old walled city, and the New Town which sprawls around it in three directions. The latter dates from the Ottoman occupation, when Greek Orthodox natives – forbidden to dwell in the old city – founded several suburb villages or *marásia* in the environs, which have since merged. Commercialization is predictably rampant in the walled town, and in the modern district of Neohóri ("Niohóri" in dialect), west of Mandhráki yacht harbour; the few buildings which aren't hotels are souvenir shops, car-rental or travel agencies and bars – easily sixty to seventy in every category. The pointy bit of Neohóri is surrounded by a continuous **beach**, complete with deckchairs, parasols and showers, particularly on the more sheltered east-facing section called **Élli**. At the northernmost point of the island an **Aquarium** (daily: April–Sept 9am–9pm; Oct–March 9am–4.30pm; €1.75), officially the "Hydrobiological Institute", offers some diversion with its subterranean maze of seawater tanks. Upstairs is a less enthralling collection of half-rotten stuffed sharks, seals and even a whale. Some 200m southeast stand the **Murad Reis mosque**, an atmospherically neglected Muslim cemetery, and the equally dilapidated **Villa Cleobolus**, where Lawrence Durrell lived from 1945 to 1947.

Just a few paces northwest of this, the Italian-built Albergo delle Rose (*Hotel Rodon*) was refurbished and pressed into service in 1999 as the **Casino of Rhodes**, Greece's third largest, and unusually, open to locals as well as visitors. Admission is €15, the minimum age is 23 and ID is required.

Accommodation

Hotels and pensions at all price levels abound in the Old Town, mostly in the quad bounded by Omírou to the south, Sokrátous to the north, Perikléous to the east and Ippodhámou to the west. There are also a few possibilities worth considering in Neohóri, especially if you're bound for the airport or to Sými at an early hour. During crowded seasons, or late at night, it's prudent to either ring ahead or be prepared to accept the offers of proprietors meeting the ferries and change base next day if necessary – as it frequently is, since standards amongst quay-touted premises tend to be low.

Old Town

Andreas, Omírou 28D ☏02410/34 156, ℱ74 285, ☻www.hotelandreas.com. Perennially popular (reservations needed) and under new dynamic management, this is one of the more imaginative old-house restoration-pensions, refurbished in 2000. Rooms in a variety of formats (including family-size) and plumbing arrangements (most en-suite). Terrace view-bar for breakfast and evenings, two-night minimum stay, credit cards accepted, indeed vital for advance booking. Open March 15–Oct 31. ❸

Apollo, Omírou 28C ☏02410/63 894. Basic – cold-water sinks in rooms, baths in halls – but clean and friendly rooms place, under new management since 2001 and lightly refurbished; the self-catering kitchen makes it good for longer stays. ❶

La Luna, Ierokléous 21 ☏ & ℱ 02410/25 856. Clean, wood-trimmed if plain (no en suites) pension in a converted old Turkish house, complete with still-functioning *hamam* (Turkish bath). Garden bar for breakfast, by the citrus and banana trees. ❹

Marco Polo Mansion, Ayíou Fanouríou 42 ☏ & ℱ 02410/25 562, ☻www.marcopolomansion.web. Superb 1999 conversion of an old Turkish mansion, again with a *hamam* on site, but here all rooms are en suite and exquisitely furnished with antiques

from the nearby eponymous gallery, plus cotton pillows and handmade mattresses. Large buffet breakfasts provided by ebullient manageress Efi, and adjoining café after hours. One-week minimum stay, book ahead; part open in winter, breakfast included. ❻

Niki's, Sofokléous 39 ☏02410/25 115. Some rooms can be on the small side, but almost all are en suite, and upper-storey ones have fine views. There's a washing machine, common terrace and friendly management to round things off. ❸

Pink Elephant/Roz Elefandas, officially Irodhótou 42 but actually on Timahídhas ☏ & ℱ 02410/22 469. Simple but clean rooms occupying several levels of a modernized old building, near the traditional red-light district; roof deck with sunning and covered sections. Discount for singles. ❸

S. Nikolis, Ippodhámou 61 ☏02410/34 561, ℱ32 034, ☻www.s-nikolis.gr. A variety of premises in the west of the Old Town. Hotel/honeymoon-suite rates of €44 (low) and €147 (high) include breakfast, TV and air-con; the self-catering apartments (€59–88) are among the finest restoration results in the Old Town, and interconnect to accommodate groups/families. Booking essential, and accepted only with credit-card number. Open April–Nov.

Spot, Perikléous 21 ☏ & Ⓕ 02410/34 737. Yet another old-town hotel under a new generation of management, this modern building has cheerfully painted en-suite rooms of varying formats with textiles on the walls, and air-con or fans, representing superb value. Internet facilities and free luggage storage. Open March–Nov. ❸

Via-Via, Lysipoú 2, alley off Pythagóra ☏ & Ⓕ 02410/77 027, Ⓔ viavia@rho.forthnet.gr. Efficiently but congenially French-run hotel; most 1–4-person rooms are en suite but two share a

bath, all simply but tastefully furnished, with ongoing improvements. Self-catering kitchen, roof terrace for breakfast with an eyeful of the Ibrahim Pasha mosque opposite. Credit card or giro-cheque required for reservations. Open March to early Jan. ❸

Youth Hostel, Eryíou 12 ☏ 02410/30 491. Both 3–5-bunk dorms and doubles (€23.50) in this courtyarded house with kitchen facilities; €7.50 for a bunk, but non-YHA-affiliated.

Neohóri

Hotel Capitol, Dhilberáki 65–67 ☏ & Ⓕ 02410/28 645. Another old house with fairly large, en-suite, terrazo-floored rooms; some family-size quads upstairs. Breakfast served in back garden by young managing couple (Greek/German). ❹

Casa Antica, Amarándou 8 ☏ 02410/26 206. Double and quad studios in a madeover 150-year-old house, with clean, white-tile decor, courtyard, roof terrace. Near some of the better Neohóri tavernas. ❹

Hotel Esperia, Yeoryíou Gríva 7 ☏ 02410/23 941, Ⓕ 23 164, Ⓔ esperia@esperia-hotels.gr. Well-

priced, well-run B-class hotel in a quiet location overlooking a little plaza. Small-to-medium size, though salubrious and tasteful rooms with showers, not tubs. Open all year. ❹

New Village Inn, Konstanopédhos 10 ☏ 02410/34 937, Ⓔ newvillageinn@rho. forthnet.gr. Whitewashed, somewhat grotto-like en-suite rooms "refreshed" yearly, air conditioning planned. Friendly Greek and American management; singles available at a good rate. Open most of the year. ❸

The Old Town

Simply to catalogue the principal monuments and attractions cannot do full justice to the infinitely more rewarding **medieval city**. There's ample gratification to be derived from slipping through the eleven surviving gates and strolling the streets, under flying archways built for earthquake resistance, past the warm-toned sandstone and limestone walls painted ochre or blue, and over the *hokhláki* (pebble) pavement.

Dominating the northernmost sector of the city's fourteenth-century fortifications is the **Palace of the Grand Masters** (summer Mon 2.30–9pm, Tues–Fri 8.30am–9pm; winter Mon 12.30–3pm, Tues–Sun 8.30am–3pm; €6). Largely destroyed by an ammunition depot explosion set off by lightning in 1856, it was reconstructed by the Italians as a summer home for Mussolini and Victor Emmanuel III ("King of Italy and Albania, Emperor of Ethiopia"), neither of whom ever visited Rhodes. The exterior, based on medieval engravings and accounts, is passably authentic, but inside, free rein was given to Fascist delusions of grandeur: a marble staircase leads up to rooms paved with Hellenistic mosaics from Kós, and the ponderous period furnishings rival many a northern European palace. The ground floor is home to the splendid **Medieval Exhibit** and **Ancient Rhodes, 2400 Years** gallery (same hours and admission ticket), together the best museums in town. The medieval collection highlights the importance of Christian Rhodes as a trade centre, with exotic merchandise placing the island in a trans-Mediterranean context. The Knights are represented with a display on their sugar-refining industry and a gravestone of a Grand Master; precious manuscripts and books precede a wing of post-Byzantine icons, moved here permanently from Panayía Kástrou (see p.294). Across the courtyard in the north wing, "Ancient Rhodes" overshadows the official archeological museum by explaining the everyday life of the ancients, arranged topically (beauty aids, toys, cookware, worship and so on); highlights

RÓDHOS TOWN

ACCOMMODATION

Andreas	14
Apollo	11
Casa Antica	2
Hotel Capitol	4
Hotel Esperia	3
La Luna	5
Marco Polo Mansion	8
New Village Inn	1
Niki's	10
Pink Elephant/Roz Elefandas	13
S. Nikolis	12
Spot	9
Via-Via	7
Youth Hostel	6

RESTAURANTS, BARS & CLUBS

Anatolikes Nostimies	U
Anthony's Souvlaki on Coals	R
Araliki	M
L'Auberge Bistrot	Q
Café Besara	N
Blue Lagoon Pool Bar	E
Christos' Garden/To Dhiporto	C
Colorado Entertainment Centre	B
El Divino	G
Khristos Ouzeri Inomayerio (O Vlahos)	a
Mango Bar	P
Metaxi Mas	b
Mikes	I
Niohori	A
O Meraklis	J
O'Reilly's	D
Palia Istoria	Y
Resalto	K
Iy Rogmi tou Khronou	L
Rolóï	H
Sakis	Z
Sea Star	O
Sheftalies	S
Stani	W
To Steki tou Tsima	X
To Steno	V
Sticky Fingers	F
Vassilis (Kova)	T

include a Hellenistic floor mosaic and a household idol of Hecate, goddess of the occult. On Tuesday and Saturday afternoons, there's a supplementary tour of the **city walls** (one hour starting at 2.45pm; €6), beginning from a gate next to the palace and finishing at the Koskinoú gate.

The heavily restored **Street of the Knights** (Odhós Ippotón) leads due east from the Platía Kleovoúlou in front of the Palace; the "Inns" lining it housed the Knights of St John, according to linguistic and ethnic affiliation, until the Ottoman Turks compelled them to leave for Malta after a six-month siege in which the defenders were outnumbered thirty to one. Today the Inns house various government offices and cultural institutions vaguely appropriate to their past, with occasional exhibitions, but the whole effect of the Italians' renovation is predictably sterile and stagey (indeed, nearby streets were used in the 1987 filming of *Pascali's Island*).

At the bottom of the hill, the Knights' Hospital has been refurbished as the **Archeological Museum** (Tues–Sun 8.30am–3pm; €2.40), though the arches and echoing halls of the building somewhat overshadow the appallingly labelled and presented contents – largely painted pottery dating from the sixth and seventh centuries BC. Behind the second-storey sculpture garden, the Hellenistic statue gallery is more accessible; in a rear corner stands the so-called "Marine Venus", beloved of Lawrence Durrell, but lent a rather sinister aspect by her sea-dissolved face – in contrast to the friendlier *Aphrodite Bathing*. Virtually next door is the **Decorative Arts Collection** (Tues–Sun 8.30am–3pm; €1.50), gleaned from old houses across the Dodecanese; the most compelling artefacts are carved cupboard doors and chest lids painted in naive style with mythological or historical episodes.

Across the way stands the **Byzantine Museum** (Tues–Sun 8.30am–3pm; €1.50), housed in the old cathedral of the Knights, who adapted the Byzantine shrine of Panayía Kástrou for their own needs. Medieval icons and frescoes lifted from crumbling chapels on Rhodes and Hálki, as well as photos of art still *in situ*, constitute the exhibits; it's worth a visit since most of the Byzantine churches in the Old Town and outlying villages are kept locked. The highlight of the collection is a complete fresco cycle from the domes of Thárri monastery (see p.303) dating from 1624, removed in 1967 to reveal much older work beneath.

If instead you head south from the Palace of the Grand Masters, it's hard to miss the most conspicuous Turkish monument in Rhodes, the rust-coloured **Süleymaniye mosque**. Rebuilt in the nineteenth century on foundations three hundred years older, it's currently closed and under scaffolding like most local Ottoman monuments, though it's soon to emerge from its lengthy refit in all its candy-striped glory. The Old Town is in fact well sown with mosques and *mescids* (the Islamic equivalent of a chapel), many of them converted from Byzantine shrines after the 1522 conquest, when the Christians were expelled from the medieval precinct. A couple of these mosques are still used by the sizeable **Turkish-speaking minority** here, some of them descended from Muslims who fled Crete between 1898 and 1913. Their most enduring civic contributions are, opposite the Süleymaniye, the **Ottoman Library** (Mon–Fri 7.30am–2.30pm & 6–9pm, Sat & Sun 8am–noon; tip to custodian), with a rich collection of early medieval manuscripts and Korans, and the imposing, stillfunctioning **hamam**, or Turkish bath, on Platía Ariónos up in the southwest corner of the medieval city (often shut for "repairs", specimen hours Tues 1–6pm, Wed–Fri 11am–6pm, Sat 8am–6pm; €1.50, but €0.90 Wed & Sat).

Heading downhill from the Süleymaniye mosque, you come to **Odhós Sokrátous**, once the heart of the Ottoman bazaar, and now the "Via Turista", packed with fur and jewellery stores pitched at cruise-ship tourists. Beyond the tiled central fountain in Platía Ippokrátous, Odhós Aristotélous leads into the Platía tón Evréon Martýron (Square of the Jewish Martyrs), named in memory of the large local community that was almost totally annihilated during the summer of 1944. Of the four synagogues which once graced Rhodes, only the ornate, arcaded **Kal Kadosh Shalom** (daily 10am–5pm; donation) on Odhós Simíou just to the south survives. It's maintained essentially as a memorial to the approximately 1800 Jews of Rhodes and Kós sent from here to the concentration camps; plaques in French – the language of educated Ottoman Jews across the east Aegean – commemorate the dead. At the rear of the building, a one-room **museum**, set up by a Los Angeles attorney of Jewish Rhodian descent, features archival photos of the community's life on Rhodes and in its far-flung diaspora in the Americas and Africa.

About 2km southwest of Mandhráki, the sparse, unenclosed remains of **Hellenistic Rhodes** – a restored theatre and stadium, plus a few columns of an Apollo temple – perch atop Monte Smith, the hill of Áyios Stéfanos renamed after a British admiral who used it as a watchpoint during the Napoleonic wars. The wooded site is popular with joggers and strollers, but for summer shade and greenery the best spot is probably **Rodhíni Park**, nearly 2km south of town on the road to Líndhos, and served by city bus route #3. The wooded Zimboúli ravine here, fed by natural springs, is home to ducks, peacocks and (in special pens) the native miniature Rhodian deer. Hellenistic **rock-cut tombs**, signposted via a separate side road at the south end of the park, constitute a final possible diversion.

Eating and drinking

Eating well for a reasonable price in and around Ródhos Town is a challenge, but not an insurmountable one. As a general rule, the remoter and further south you go, the better value you'll find – so touristy, alas, has the Old Town become. Unless otherwise stated, the following restaurants are open all year round.

Old Town

Anthony's Souvlaki on Coals, cnr Omírou and Pythagóra. Exactly as the sign says, superbly executed *souvláki* for a mostly local clientele. A few salads and starters too; supper only; inexpensive.

Araliki, Aristofánous 45. Bohemian expatriates and travellers tired of standard resort grub seek out this old-style *kafenío* on the ground floor of a medieval house. Small plates of exquisitely original *mezédhes* are provided from a perennial menu by Italian proprietors Miriam (the savouries) and Valeria (the sweets), and there are also (often more compelling) daily specials. Reckon on €16.20 per person with drinks, which include Nissyrot *soumádha* or mainland wine. Open March–Dec daily except Sun from 11.30am until late; also closed two random weeks July & Aug.

L'Auberge Bistrot, Praxitélous 21. Genuine, popular, French-run bistro with excellent Frenchified food: allow €17.70 per person for three hefty courses plus wine from a well-selected Greek list, jazz soundtrack included. Summer seating in the courtyard of this restored medieval inn; inside under the arches during cooler months. Open late March to late Dec for supper daily except Mon.

O Meraklis, Aristotélous 30. A *patsatzídhiko* (tripe-soup kitchen) that's only open 3–8am for a motley clientele of post-club lads, Turkish stallholders, nightclub singers and travellers just stumbled off an overnight ferry. Great free entertainment, including famously rude staff, and the soup – the traditional Greek hangover cure – is good too.

Mikes (pronounced "mee-kess"), nameless alley behind Sokrátous 17. Inexpensive (for Rhodes, anyway) hole-in-the-wall, serving only grilled fish, salads and wine.

Sea Star (aka *Pizanias*), Sofokléous 24, cnr of the square ☏ 02410/22 117. A three-decades-old institution, where Pizanias mans the grill himself. Not only fresh scaly fish – staff show you the pink gills – but shellfish like *kydhónia* (cockles) and *petalídhia* (limpets), grilled octopus and squid. With two bottles of expensive wine, starters and loads of seafood, four can eat for €85–88 – elsewhere in the Old Town it'd be double that. Reservations recommended.

Neohóri

Anatolikes Nostimies, Kapodhistríou 60, Akándia port. The name means "Anatolian Delicacies", and that's what's on offer at this Rhodian Turkish-run grill: Turkish/Middle Eastern dips and starters, plus sixteen variations of kebab. Not much atmosphere, but friendly and reasonable; post-prandial hubble-bubble provided on request. Open 11am–midnight.

Khristos Ouzeri Inomayerio (O Vlahos), Klavdhíou Pépper 165, at the big bend, Zéfyros beach. As the name implies, ouzerí fare – marinated fish or peppers, *gávros*, great *tzatzíki* – accompanying a vast oúzo list, plus vegetable-strong *mayireftá* (cuttlefish with spinach, fish soup, eggplant *imam*) that sell out quickly. Not as cheap (€10.30–11.80) or big-portioned as formerly, but still worth the trek out.

Metaxi Mas, Klavdhíou Pépper 115, Zéfyros beach. No sign or menu in English – look for the elevated boat – at this seafood ouzerí purveying various exotic titbits; count on €32.40–35.30 per couple with booze, slightly cheaper per person in a group – but still 25 percent less than in the Old Town. Daily lunch and supper except Sun, lunch only.

Niohori, Ioánni Kazoúli 29, by the Franciscan monastery. Also known as "Kiki's" after the jolly proprietress, this homey, inexpensive local serves lunch and supper; best for grills, sourced from their own butcher/farm.

Palia Istoria, Mitropóleos 108, cnr Dhendhrínou, Ámmos district ✆02410/32 421. Reckoned to be the best *kultúra* taverna in town, but predictably expensive for such dishes as celery hearts in egg-lemon sauce and scallops with mushrooms and artichokes, washed down by a hundred-strong wine list. Supper only, closed Sun; reservations essential.

Sakis, Ipsilándou 27, Áyios Nikólaos. Genuine taverna with pleasant patio seating, equally popular with Rhodians and savvy expats. Excellent seafood and starters; it's possible to have three courses (including modest fish) and a beer for €11.50. Supper only.

Sheftalies, Tsaldhári 21, south of Monte Smith past Marinopoulos Supermarket. Direct antithesis to *Palia Istoria*, since you can fill up for €7.40. Zero atmosphere, but a genuine charcoal griller featuring the namesake *sheftaliés*, dioxin-free chicken (some find this too peppery) and *kokorétsi*, plus a few daily *mayireftá* plates.

Stani, Ayías Anastasías 28, cnr Paleón Patrón Yermanoú, south of the Koskinoú Gate. Most central outlet of a chain of Rhodian Turkish confectioners, scooping out two dozen flavours of the best ice cream on the island, publicity for rival *Mike's* notwithstanding.

To Steki tou Tsima, Peloponnísou 22, around cnr from preceding. Very reasonable seafood ouzerí, with the stress on aficionados' shellfish titbits (*foúskes, spiníalo*) and small fish not prone to farming. No airs or graces, just patently fresh materials, and open Sun too.

To Steno, Ayíon Anaryíron 29, 400m southwest of the Ayíou Athanasíou Gate. A genuinely welcoming ouzerí, with outdoor seating during the warmer months and limited but superb menu (chickpea soup, courgette croquettes, sausages) at eminently reasonable prices.

Vassilis (Kova), Kolokotróni, 80m east of Kanadhá, south of Akándia commercial port. Another place to go when you're down to your last euro: a friendly working-man's canteen, busiest from noon to 2pm, with several *mayireftá* dishes to choose from and shady glass-conservatory seating between the auto-repair shops. Also opens evenings.

Nightlife

The Old Town formerly had a well-deserved reputation for being tomb-silent at night; this has changed drastically since the late 1990s, with an entire alley (Miltiádhou) off Apéllou given over to a half-dozen loud music bars and clubs, frequented almost exclusively by Greeks. This is just appetizers for the estimated two hundred foreigner-patronized bars and clubs in Neohóri, where theme nights and various other gimmicks predominate. They are found mostly along the streets and alleys bounded by Alexándhrou Dhiákou, Orfanídhou, Lohagoú Fanouráki and Nikifórou Mandhilará.

Sedate by comparison, Ministry of Culture-approved folk dances (June–Oct Mon, Wed, Fri 9.20pm; €10.30) are presented with live accompaniment by the Nelly Dimoglou Company, performed in the landscaped "Old Town Theatre" off Andhroníkou, near Platía Ariónos. More of a technological extravaganza is the **Sound and Light** show, spotlighting sections of the city walls, staged in a garden just off Platía Rimínis. There's English-language narration nightly except Sunday, its screening time varying from 8.15pm to 10.15pm (€3.50).

Thanks to a large contingent from the local university, there are several year-round **cinemas** showing first-run fare indoors or open-air according to season and air-con capabilities. Choose from among the summer-only outdoor cinema by the Rodon Municipal Theatre, next to the town hall in Neohóri; the Metropol multiplex, southeast of the Old Town opposite the stadium, refurbished in 2001; and the nearby Pallas multiplex on Dhimokratías, refurbished in 1999.

Blue Lagoon Pool Bar, 25-Martíou 2, Neohóri. One of the better theme bars, in this case a "desert island" with palm trees, waterfalls, live turtles and parrots, a shipwrecked galleon – and taped music. Open March–Oct 8.30am–3am.

Café Besara, Sofokléous 11–13, Old Town. Congenial breakfast café/low-key boozer run by an Australian lady, with interesting mixed clientele and live music some nights.

Christos' Garden/To Dhiporto, Dhilberáki 59, Neohóri. This combination art-gallery/bar/café occupies a carefully restored old house and courtyard with pebble-mosaic floors throughout. Incongruously classy for the area.

Colorado Entertainment Centre, Orfanídhou 57, cnr Aktí Miaoúli, Neohóri. Triple venue: "pub" with live in-house band (rock covers), "club" with taped sounds, and quiet upstairs chill-out bar.

El Divino, Alexándhrou Dhiákou 5, Neohóri. Very classy, Greek-frequented "music bar" with garden seating and the usual range of coffees and alcohol. Open June–Oct.

Mango Bar, Platía Dhoriéos 3, Old Town. Piped music and a variety of drinks at this durable bar

on an otherwise quiet plaza; also a good source of breakfast after 8am, served under a plane tree.

O'Reilly's, Apolloníou Rodhíou 61, Neohóri. Irish theme pub which serves Irish draught and claims to have live music nightly.

Resalto, Plátonos 6, opposite the mosque. Live Greek rebétika and laïkó sounds, rather cheaper than nearby rival *Café Chantant*. Weekends only in low season.

Iy Rogmi tou Khronou, Platía Ariónos. Taped music (not house or techno) at a reasonable level and a congenial crowd make this newly opened bar worth a look.

Rolóï, Orféos 1, Old Town. The Baroque clocktower erected by Ahmet Fetih Pasha in 1857 is now the focus of possibly the most exclusive café-bar in the Old Town. Admission charge to climb the tower, and steeply priced drinks, but you are paying for the terrific view.

Sticky Fingers, Anthoúla Zérvou 6, Neohóri. Long-lived music bar with reasonable drinks; live rock several nights weekly from 10pm onwards. Fri & Sat only off-season.

Listings

Airlines Olympic, Iérou Lóhou 9 ☎02410/24 571. Cronus-Aegean Airlines, Ethelondón Dhodhekanisíon 20 ☎02410/24 400 or 25 444.

Bookshop Second Storey Books, Amarándou 24, Neohóri, has a large stock of used English paperbacks; open all year, normal shop hours. For new books, try News Stand at Grigoríou Lambráki 23.

Car rental Prices at non-international chains are fairly standard at €41–44 per day, but can be bargained down to about €32–35 a day, all-inclusive, out of peak season and/or for long periods. More flexible outfits, all in the New Town, include Alamo/National, 28-Oktovríou 18 ☎02410/73 570; Drive, Avstralías 2 ☎02410/68 243; Just/Ansa, Mandhilará 70 ☎02410/31 811; Kosmos, Papaloúka 31 ☎02410/74 374; Orion, Yeoryíou Leóndos 36 ☎02410/22 137; and Payless, Íonos Dhragoúmi 29 ☎02410/26 586.

Exchange Most conventional bank branches are near Platía Kýprou in Neohóri, plus there are

various exchange bureaux keeping long hours. At other times use the cash dispensers of the Commercial Bank (branch in the Old Town too), Alpha Bank or National Bank (also Old Town branch).

Ferry agents DANE, Avstralías 92 ☎02410/43 150, to Pireás via select Dodecanese; Dodhekanisos Navtiliaki, Avstralías 3, by Shell station ☎02410/70 590, for catamaran to most Dodecanese islands; Inspiration, Aktí Sakhtoúri 4 ☎02410/24 294 (base of main ferry dock), for most G&A boats to Dodecanese and Cyclades, plus DANE sailings; Kyriakoulis Maritime, Neoríon dock ☎02410/78 052, for hydrofoils to Kós and all intervening islands; Kouros, Karpáthou ☎02410/24 377, and Kydon, Ethelondón Dhodhekanisíon 14 ☎02410/23 000, between them act for both companies plying routes to Cyprus; LANE, Alexándhrou Dhiákou 38 ☎02410/33 607, to Crete via Hálki, Kárpathos, Kássos. Weekly tourist office departure-schedule handouts are deeply unreliable, and even get the addresses shown above wrong; authoritative sailing information is available at the *limenarhío* (port police), on Mandhráki esplanade near the post office.

Internet cafés The most central and competitive of several are *Rock Style*, Dhimokratías 7, opposite the stadium ⓦ www.rockstyle.gr, and *Mango Bar* (see "Nightlife" overleaf) ⓔ karelas@rho.forthnet.gr.

Laundries House of Laundry, Erythroú Stavroú 2, Neohóri; Star, Kostí Palamá 4–6, behind New Market; Wash & Go, Plátonos 33, Old Town.

Motorbike rental Low-volume scooters will make little impact on Rhodes; sturdier Yamaha 125s, suitable for two people, start at about €20 a day. In the Old Town, Mandar Moto at Dhimosthénous 2, cnr Platía Evréon Martýron, has a large stable of medium-sized scooters suitable for short jaunts. Recommended outlets in Neohóri include Margaritis, Ioánni Kazoúli 23, with a wide range of late models up to 500cc, plus mountain bikes; or (to roll out in style) Rent a Harley at 28-Oktovríou 80 – classic models for two riders start at a whopping €97 per day.

Post office Main branch with outgoing mail and poste restante on Mandhráki harbour; open Mon–Fri 7.30am–8pm.

Scuba diving Waterhoppers, Trident and Dive Med all tout for business at Mandhráki quay; however, days out are expensive (€39.70 for boat transfer and one dive, €20.60 for second dive) and you're restricted to one small site at Thérmes Kallithéas.

Travel agencies Recommended in the Old Town is Castellania, Evripídhou 1–3, cnr Platía Ippokrátous ☎ 02410/75 860, which can arrange all domestic air tickets, both domestic and international ferries, and also discount scheduled and charter flights abroad. In Neohóri, Visa Travel Club at Grigóri Lambráki 54 ☎ 02410/33 282, ⓦ www.visatravelclub.gr, and Contours at Ammohóstou 9 ☎ 02410/36 001 are also worth contacting. There is no central outlet for hydrofoil tickets to Marmaris in Turkey – comparison shopping is recommended.

The east coast

Heading down the coast from the capital you have to go some way before you escape the crowds from local beach hotels, their numbers swollen by visitors using the regular buses from town or on boat tours out of Mandhráki. You might look in at the decayed, abandoned spa of **Thérmes Kallithéas**, a prize example of enjoyable mock-orientalia dating from the Italian period. Located 3km south of Kallithéa resort proper, down a paved track through pines, the buildings are set in a palm grove, though an EU-funded restoration begun in 1999 proceeds at a snail's pace. Nearby are several secluded coves framed by rock formations which often interpose themselves between the water and the sand, the latter furnished with sunbeds and (in most cases) snack bars. The former fishing village of **FALIRÁKI**, which primarily draws a youngish package clientele, is all too much in the mould of a Spanish *costa* resort, while the scenery just inland – arid, scrubby sandhills at the best of times – has been made that much bleaker by late 1980s fire damage that stretches way beyond Líndhos. The cape to the south, **Ladhikó** (45-minute path from Faliráki), shelters the more scenic bay of "Anthony Quinn", named in honour of the late actor whom Greeks took to their hearts following his roles in *Zorba the Greek* and *The Guns of Navarone* (the latter filmed locally).

The enormous mass of **Tsambíka**, 26km south of town, is the first place at which most nonpackage visitors will seriously consider stopping. Actually the very eroded flank of a once much-larger mountain, this promontory has a monastery on top offering unrivalled views along some 50km of coastline. From the main highway, a steep, 1500-metre cement drive leads to a small car park and a snack bar, from which steps take you to the summit. The little monastery here is unremarkable except for its September 8 festival: childless women climb up – sometimes on their hands and knees – to be relieved of their barrenness, and any children born afterwards are dedicated to the Virgin with the names Tsambikos or Tsambika, which are particular to the Dodecanese. From the top you can survey **Kolýmbia** just to the north, a small beach to one side of a tiny, rock-girt cove, backed by a dozen, low-rise hotels. Shallow **Tsambíka** Bay on the south side of the headland warms up early in the spring, and the excellent beach, though protected by the forest service from development – all it has is a taverna and a half-dozen *kantína* caravans – teems with people all summer.

The next beach south is gravelly **Stegná** with its mix of summer cottages for locals and accommodation for Germans. It has at least two **tavernas** (*Kozas* and *Pitropos*) which attract a Greek clientele. Stegná is reached by a steep road east from the less rewarding village of **ARHÁNGELOS**, just inland and over-looked by a crumbling castle. Though you can disappear into the warren of alleys between the main road and the citadel, the place is now firmly caught up in package tourism, with a full complement of banks, tavernas, minimarts and jewellery stores. Another overnight base on this stretch of coast, English-dominated this time, is **HARÁKI**, a pleasant if undistinguished two-street fishing port with mostly self-catering accommodation (generally ③) overlooked by the stubby ruins of **Feraklós castle**, the last stronghold of the Knights to fall to the Turks. You can swim off the town beach if you don't mind an audience from the handful of waterfront cafés and tavernas, but most people head west out of town, then north 800m along a marked dirt track to the secluded **Agáthi beach**. The (marginally) best taverna near Haráki is *Efterpi*, 200m south at so-called Massári beach.

Líndhos

LÍNDHOS, the island's second-ranking tourist attraction, erupts from barren surroundings 12km south of Haráki. Like Ródhos Old Town, its charm is heavily undermined by commercialism and crowds: up to half a million visitors in a typical year. At midday dozens of coaches park nose-to-tail on the narrow southerly access road, with even more on the drives down to the beaches. Back in the village itself, those few vernacular houses not snapped up by package operators have, since the 1960s, been bought up and refurbished by wealthy British, Germans and Italians. The old agora or serpentine high street presents a mass of fairly indistinguishable bars, creperies, mediocre restaurants and travel agents. Although high-rise hotels and all vehicular traffic have been prohibited inside the municipal boundaries, the result is a relentlessly commercialized theme park – hot and airless in August, but deserted and quite ghostly in winter.

Nonetheless, if you arrive before or after peak season, when the pebble-paved streets between the immaculately whitewashed houses are relatively empty of both people and droppings from the donkeys shuttling up to the acropolis (see below), you can still appreciate the beautiful, atmospheric setting of Líndhos. The most imposing fifteenth-to eighteenth-century **captains' residences** are built around *hokhláki* courtyards, their monumental doorways often fringed by intricate stonework, with the number of braids or cables supposedly corresponding to the number of ships owned. A few are open to the public, most notably the **Papakonstandis Mansion**, the most elaborate and now home to an unofficial museum; entrance to the "open" mansions is free but some pressure will probably be exerted on you to buy something, especially lace and embroidery.

On the bluff looming above the town, the ancient acropolis with its Doric **Temple of Athena** (restorations ongoing) and imposing **Hellenistic stoa** is found inside the Knights' **castle** (summer Tues–Sun 8am–7pm, Mon 12.30–7pm; rest of year Tues–Sun 8.30am–3pm; €6) – a surprisingly felicitous blend of ancient and medieval culture. Though the ancient city of Lindos and its original temple dated from at least 1100 BC, the present structure was begun by local ruler Kleoboulos in the sixth century BC after a fourth-century fire.

Líndhos's north beach, once the main ancient harbour, is overcrowded and occasionally polluted; if you do base yourself here, cleaner, quieter **beaches** are to be found one cove beyond at Pállas beach (with a nudist annexe around the headland), or 5km north at **Vlyhá Bay**. South of the acropolis huddles the small, perfectly sheltered **St Paul's harbour**, where the apostle is said to have landed in 58 AD on a mission to evangelize the island.

Practicalities

It used to be tempting fate to just turn up and hope for **accommodation** vacancies on spec, but since certain British tour companies pulled out of Líndhos in the late 1990s, it's something of a buyers' market. If you're not met at the bus stop under the giant fig tree by proprietors touting rooms, Pallas Travel (℡02440/31 494, ℻31 595) can arrange a room or even a whole villa for a small fee. The oft-cited backpackers' standbys, 1970s-vintage *Pension Electra* (℡02440/31 226; ❷) and *Pension Katholiki* (℡02440/31 445; ❷), next door to each other on the way to the north beaches, are both low standard (shared baths) and overpriced.

Local **restaurants** tend to be exploitive and serve bland fare; one of the better ones, *Agostino's*, by the southerly car park, has the important virtues of bulk Émbonas wine and real country sausages (not imported hot dogs), but goes and spoils it by serving tinned veg as accompaniment. You may as well push the boat out at *Mavrikos* on the fig-tree square, founded in 1933 and in the same family ever since. Mezédhes like *manoúri* cheese with basil and pine-nuts are accomplished, as are quasi-French main courses like cuttlefish in wine sauce; dipping into the excellent (and expensive) Greek wine list as well will add €17.50 a bottle to the typical food charge of €20.50–23.50 per person. If your wallet won't stretch that far, try the *Panorama* up on the main road, 2km towards Vlyhá, which does good fish, though – like *Agostino's* – it's not hugely less expensive than *Mavrikos* these days. For snacks and desserts, try *Il Forno*, an Italian-run bakery, and *Gelo Blu*, still the best of several gelaterie here despite the departure of its Italian founders. There are currently three **internet cafés** operating in Líndhos. Local **car-rental** rates tend to be cheaper than in Ródhos Town, though you've less choice in models, and vehicles may be less roadworthy. There are two proper **banks**, working normal hours, each with cash dispensers. And finally, Lindos Suntours (℡02440/31 333) has metred phones (call boxes tend to have huge queues) and a nice line in unclaimed one-way charter seats back to Britain, as does Village Holidays (℡02410/31 486).

The west coast

Rhodes' west coast is the windward flank of the island, so it's damper, more fertile and more forested; most beaches, however, are exposed and decidedly rocky. None of this has deterred development, and as in the east the first few kilometres of the busy shore road down from the capital have been surrendered entirely to tourism. From Neohóri's aquarium down to the airport, the shore is fringed by an almost uninterrupted line of Miami-Beach-style hotels, though such places as Triánda, Kremastí and Paradhísi are still nominally villages, with real centres. This was the first part of the island to be favoured by the package operators, and tends to be frequented by a decidedly sedate, middle-aged/family clientele that doesn't stir much from the poolside.

There's not much inducement to stop until you reach the important archeological site of **KAMEIROS**, which together with Líndhos and Ialyssos was one of the three Dorian powers that united during the fifth century BC to found the powerful city-state of Rhodes. Soon eclipsed by the new capital, Kameiros was abandoned and only rediscovered in 1859. As a result it is a particularly well-preserved Doric townscape, doubly worth visiting for its beautiful hillside site (summer Tues–Sun 8am–7pm, winter 8.30am–3pm; €3). While none of the individual remains is spectacular, you can make out the foundations of two small temples, the re-erected pillars of a Hellenistic house, a Classical fountain, and the stoa of the upper agora, complete with a water cistern. Because of the gentle slope of the site, there were no fortifications, nor was there an acropolis. On the beach below Kameiros there are several tavernas, highly commercialized but acceptable while waiting for one of the two daily buses back to town (if you're willing to walk 4km back to Kalavárdha you'll have a better choice of service).

At the tiny anchorage of **KÁMIROS SKÁLA** (aka Skála Kamírou) 15km south, there are five more-touristy restaurants, which somewhat inexplicably have become the target of coach tours. Less heralded is the daily **kaïki** which leaves for the island of **Hálki** at 2.30pm, weather permitting, returning early the next morning; on Wednesdays and Sundays there are day-trips departing at 9am and returning at 4pm. For a better **meal**, skip the circus here and proceed 400m southwest to off-puttingly named **Paralía Kopriá** ("Manure Beach"), where *Psarotaverna Johnny's* has good non-farmed fish and *orektiká*, especially on Sundays when own-made *dolmádhes* and (seasonally) squash blossoms may be on the menu with the usual standards; it's been "discovered" and so is pricier than it used to be, but still worth a stop.

A couple of kilometres south of Skála, the "Kastello", signposted as **Kástro Kritinías**, is from afar the most impressive of the Knights' rural strongholds, and the paved access road is too narrow and steep for tour buses. Close up it proves to be no more than a shell, but a glorious shell, with fine views west to assorted islets and Hálki. You make a "donation" to the formidable old woman at the car park in exchange for fizzy drinks, seasonal fruit or flowers.

Beyond Kritinía itself, a quiet hillside village with a few rooms and tavernas, the main road winds south through the dense forests below mounts Akramýtis and Atávyros to **SIÁNNA**, the most attractive mountain settlement on the island, famous for its aromatic pine-sage honey and *soúma*, a grape-residue distillate similar to Italian *grappa* but far smoother. The tiered, flat-roofed farmhouses of **MONÓLITHOS**, 4km southwest at the end of the public bus line, are scant justification for the long trip out here, and food at the four **tavernas** is indifferent owing to the tour-group trade, but the view over the bay is striking and you could use the village as a base by staying in rooms or at the *Hotel Thomas* (☎02410/22 741 or 02460/61 291; €26.50), which has fair-sized rooms belying a grim exterior, and due for a refit in 2002. Diversions in the area include yet another **Knights' castle** 2km west of town, photogenically perched on its own pinnacle but enclosing even less inside than Kástro Kritinías, and the sand-and-gravel beaches (no facilities) at **Foúrni**, five paved but curvy kilometres below the castle. In the headland between the first and second beaches are some caves that were hollowed out by early Christians fleeing persecution.

The interior

Inland Rhodes is hilly, and the northern two-thirds still mostly wooded, despite the depredations of arsonists. You'll need a vehicle to see its highlights, especially as enjoyment resides in getting away from it all; no single site justifies the tremendous expense of a taxi or the inconvenience of trying to make the best of sparse bus schedules.

Ialyssos and the Valley of the Butterflies

Starting from the west-coast highway, turn inland at the central junction in Tríanda for the five-kilometre uphill ride to the scanty acropolis of ancient **Ialyssos** (Tues–Sun 8am–7pm; €3) on flat-topped, strategic Filérimos hill; from its Byzantine castle Süleyman the Magnificent directed the 1522 siege of Rhodes. Filérimos means "lover of solitude", after the tenth-century settlement here by Byzantine hermits. The existing **Filérimos monastery**, restored successively by Italians and British, is the most substantial structure here. As a concession to the Rhodian faithful, the church alone is usually open to pilgrims after the stated hours. Directly in front of the church sprawl the foundations of third-century **temples to Zeus and Athena**, built atop a far older Phoenician shrine. Below this, further towards the car park, lies the partly subterranean church of **Aï-Yeórgis Hostós**, a simple, barrel-vaulted structure with fourteenth- and fifteenth-century frescoes, not as vivid or well preserved as those at Thárri or Asklipió (see p.305). A little way southeast of the parking area, a hillside **Doric fountain** with a columned facade was only revealed by subsidence in 1926 – and is now off-limits owing to another landslip which has covered it again. Southwest of the monastery and archeological zone, a "Way of the Cross", with the fourteen stations marked out in copper plaques during the Italian era, leads to an enormous concrete crucifix, a recent replacement of an Italian-built one; you're allowed to climb out onto the cross-arms for a supplement to the already amazing view. Illuminated at night, the crucifix is clearly visible from the island of Sými and – perhaps more pertinently – infidel Turkey across the way.

The only highly publicized tourist "attraction" in the island's interior, **Petaloúdhes** or the **Butterfly Valley** (May–Sept daily 8.30am–sunset; spring/autumn €1.50, June 15–Sept 15 €2.20), reached by a seven-kilometre paved side road bearing inland from the west-coast highway between Paradhíssi and Theológos, is actually a rest stop for Jersey tiger moths (*Panaxia quadripunctaria*). Only in summer do these creatures congregate here, attracted for unknown reasons by the abundant *Liquidambar orientalis* trees. In season, the moths roost in droves on the tree trunks; they cannot eat during this final phase of their life cycle, must rest to conserve energy and die of starvation soon after mating. When sitting in the trees, the moths are a well-camouflaged black and yellow, but flash cherry-red overwings in flight.

There's a popular **taverna** partway up the valley, by the roadside, but for even better fare continue up the road to the edge of **PSÍNTHOS** village, where the friendly *Piyi Fasouli* serves excellent grills and appetizers at seating overlooking plane trees and the namesake spring.

Eptá Piyés to Profítis Ilías

Heading inland from Kolýmbia junction on the main east-coast highway, you've a four-kilometre walk or drive to **Eptá Piyés** (Seven Springs), a superb oasis with a tiny dam created by the Italians for irrigation. A shaded streamside **taverna**, immensely popular at weekends with islanders and visitors alike, serves hearty grills at fairly normal prices, though a recent refit suggests changes in style. A trail, or a rather claustrophobic Italian aqueduct-tunnel, both lead from the vicinity of the springs to the reservoir.

Continuing inland, you reach the Italian governor's crumbling, Art Deco summer residence at Eleoússa after another 9km, in the shade of the dense forest at the east end of Profítis Ilías ridge. Two other undisturbed villages, Platánia and Apóllona, nestle on the south slopes of the mountain overlooking the start of an area bereft of trees, but most people keep straight on 3km further from Eleoússa to the late Byzantine church of **Áyios Nikólaos Foundoúkli** (St Nicholas of the Hazelnuts). The partly shaded site has a fine view north over cultivated valleys, and locals descend in force for picnics on weekends. The frescoes inside, dating from the thirteenth to the fifteenth centuries, could do with a good clean, but various scenes from the life of Christ are recognizable.

Heading west from the church along mostly paved roads gets you finally to **Profítis Ilías**, where the Italian-vintage chalet-hotels *Elafos* and *Elafina* (now hosting childrens' summer camps) hide in deep woods just north of the 798-metre peak, Rhodes' third-highest point but out of bounds as a military area. However, there's good, gentle strolling below and around the summit, and a snack bar on the through road is generally open in season.

Atávyros villages

All tracks and roads west across Profítis Ilías converge on the main road from Kalavárdha bound for **ÉMBONA(S)**, a large and architecturally nondescript village backed up against the north slope of 1215-metre **Mount Atávyros**. Émbona, with its two *dhomátia* places and half-dozen meat-oriented **tavernas** (try *Savvas*), is more geared to handling tourists than you might expect, since it's the venue for summer "folk-dance tours" from Ródhos Town. The village also lies at the heart of the island's most important wine-producing districts, and CAÏR – the Italian-founded vintners' co-operative – produces a choice of acceptable mid-range varieties. However, products of the smaller, family-run Emery winery (☎02460/41 208; daily 9am–4.30pm for tasting tours) at the northern outskirts are more esteemed. To get some idea what Émbona would be like without tourists, carry on clockwise around the peak past the Artamíti monastery, to less celebrated **ÁYIOS ISÍDHOROS**, with nearly as many vines and tavernas, a more open feel, and the **trailhead** for the five-hour return **ascent of Atávyros**. This path, beginning at the northeast edge of the village at a wooden placard and well-marked with paint splodges, is the safest and easiest way up the mountain, which has extensive foundations of a Zeus temple on top.

Thárri monastery

The road from Áyios Isídhoros to Siánna is paved; not so the perennially rough one that curves for 12km east to Láerma, but it's worth enduring if you've any interest in Byzantine monuments. The **monastery of Thárri**, lost in pine forests 5km south, is the oldest religious foundation on the island, re-established as a living community of half a dozen monks in 1990 by the charismatic abbot Amfilohios. The striking *katholikón* (open daily, all day) consists of a long nave and short transept surmounted by barrel vaulting. Various recent cleanings have restored damp-smudged frescoes dating from 1300 to 1450 to their former exquisite glory. The most distinct, in the transept, depict the Evangelists Mark and Matthew, plus the Archangel Gabriel, while the nave boasts various acts of Christ, including such scenes as the *Storm on the Sea of Galilee*, *Meeting the Samaritan Woman at the Well* and *Healing the Cripple*.

The far south

South of a line connecting Monólithos and Lárdhos, you could easily begin to think you had strayed onto another island. Gone are most of the five-star hotels and roads to match, and with them the bulk of the crowds. Gone too are most other tourist facilities and public transport. Only one or two daily buses (in season) serve the depopulated villages here (except for Yennádhi), approaching

△ Painting in shop, Rhodes

along the east coast; tavernas grace the more popular stretches of sand, but aside from the growing package enclaves of Lárdhos, Péfki and Kiotári, there are few places to stay.

Despite the shelving of plans for a second island airport in the area, new beachfront development mushrooms to either side of **LÁRDHOS**, itself solidly on the tourist circuit despite an inland position between Láerma and the peninsula culminating in Líndhos. The beach 2km away is gravelly and dull, so it's best to continue 3km to **Glýstra** cove, a small but delightful crescent, with umbrellas and a snack bar. Four kilometres east of Lárdhos, **PÉFKI** (Péfkos on some maps) began life as the garden annexe and overflow for Líndhos, but is now a burgeoning package resort in its own right; the sea is clearer than at Lárdhos, with small, well-hidden beaches which are getting harder to find with all the new development on the clifftop.

Asklipió

Nine kilometres beyond Lárdhos, a paved side road heads 3.5km inland to **ASKLIPIÓ**, a sleepy village guarded by a crumbling castle and graced by the Byzantine church of **Kímisis Theotókou** (daily 9am–6pm; free). The building dates from 1060, with a ground plan nearly identical to Thárri's, except that two subsidiary apses were added during the eighteenth century, supposedly to conceal a secret school in a subterranean crypt. The frescoes within are in better condition than those at Thárri owing to the drier local climate; they are also a bit later, though some claim that the final work at Thárri and the earliest here were executed by the same hand, a master from Híos.

The format and subject matter of the frescoes are equally rare in Greece: didactic "cartoon strips" which extend completely around the church in some cases, featuring extensive Old Testament stories in addition to the more usual lives of Christ and the Virgin. There's a complete sequence from Genesis, from the Creation to the Expulsion from Eden; note the comically menacing octopus among the fishes in the panel of the Fifth Day, and Eve subsequently being fashioned from Adam's rib. A *Revelation of John the Divine* takes up most of the east transept; pebble-mosaic flooring decorates both the interior and the vast courtyard. Two adjacent buildings house separate museums: an ecclesiastical exhibit (donation requested) and a more interesting folklore gallery full of rural craft tools.

To the southern tip

Back on the coast road, the beachfront hamlet of **KIOTÁRI** has mushroomed as a package venue for Germans and Italians since the mid-1990s, when the Orthodox Church elected to sell up its vast holdings here. You could sample the **tavernas** *Il Ponte* and *Lighthouse*, at opposite ends of the developed strip, and have a swim. But there's little local character remaining, so you'll most likely choose to continue 4km to **YENNÁDHI**, the only sizeable settlement on this coast, served by up to six buses daily. The older village core inland offers various amenities including **car rental**, a **post office**, some rooms (try *Betty Studios* by the pharmacy; ☎02440/43 020; ❹) and a few **tavernas**; best of these is *Klimis*, one of three behind the seemingly endless sand-and-gravel beach, with good house wine, *mayireftá* and occasional fish grills.

Some 10km south of Yennádhi, and 2km inland, **LAHANIÁ** village with its eponymous **hotel** (☎02440/43 089; ❷) and smattering of private rooms makes another possible base. Abandoned after a postwar earthquake, since the 1980s its older houses have been mostly occupied and renovated by Germans on long-term lease agreements. On the main platía at the lower, eastern end of the village, the *Platanos* taverna has decent food and seating between the church and two wonderful fountains, one with an Ottoman inscription.

You can go directly from Lahaniá to **Plimýri**, an attractive sandy bay backed by dunes heaped up by strong afternoon winds; so far the only facility is the **taverna** *Plimirri Beach* with mostly farmed fish on the menu, next to the church of Zoödhóhou Piyís which has ancient columns upholding its vaulted porch. Beyond Plimýri the road curves inland to **KATTAVIÁ**, over 100km from the capital, marooned amidst grain fields; the village, like so many in the south, is three-quarters deserted, the owners of the closed-up houses off working in Australia or North America.

There are a few **rooms** to rent, a vital **filling station** and several **tavernas** at the junction that doubles as the platía – most interesting of these are the brightly coloured *Martine's Bakaliko / Mayeriko* (closed Thurs), run by folk from Lahanía, which has some vegetarian dishes and attempts to use local organic ingredients when possible.

From Kattaviá a paved road leads on to **Prassoníssi**, Rhodes' southernmost extremity and a mecca for European **windsurfers**. The sandspit which tethers Prassoníssi ("Leek Island") to Rhodes was partially washed away by storms early in 1998, but enough remains to create flat water on the east side and up to two-metre waves on the west, ideal for different ability levels. Of the two windsurfing centres operating here, Swiss-run Procenter (April–Oct; ☏02440/91 045, ✉procenter.prasonisi@EUnet.at) is the more professional, with hourly rates from €13.50, and a ten-hour card (valid over several days) from €112. They're geared for one-week packages, including jeeps and lodged in rooms above the *Lighthouse Restaurant*, one of a half-dozen food and accommodation outfits here; the UK agent is Sportif (☏012730/844919, ✉Sportif@compuserve.com).

The far southwest

From Lahaniá it's also possible to head 9km northwest along a narrow paved road to the picturesque hilltop village of **MESANAGRÓS**. This already existed in some form by the fifth century AD, if foundations of a ruined basilica at the village outskirts are anything to go by. A smaller thirteenth-century chapel squats amidst mosaic-floor patches of the larger, earlier church, with a *hokhláki* floor and stone barrel arches (key from the nearby kafenío).

The onward road to Skiádhi monastery, 6km distant, is shown incorrectly on most maps. Take the Kataviá-bound road initially, then bear right onto an unsigned dirt track after about 2km; the last 4km are quite badly surfaced. Known formally as Panayía Skiadhení, **Skiádhi monastery** – despite its undistinguished modern buildings – was founded in the thirteenth century to house a miraculous icon of the Virgin; in the fifteenth century a heretic stabbed the painting, and blood flowed from the wound in the Mother of God's cheek. The offending hand was, needless to say, instantly paralyzed; the fissure, and intriguing brown stains around it, are still visible. The immediate surroundings of the monastery are rather dreary since a fire in 1992, but the views west are stunning. Tiny Khténia islet is said to be a petrified pirate ship, rendered into stone by the Virgin in answer to prayers from desperate locals. Except on September 7–8, the festival of the icon, you can stay the night by arrangement with the caretaker.

West of Kataviá, the completely paved island loop road emerges onto the deserted, sandy southwest coast; Skiádhi can also be reached from this side as well, by another dirt road. Only strong swimmers should venture far offshore here, as it's exposed and tricky currents are the rule.

The nearest village is nondescript, agricultural **APOLAKKIÁ**, 7km north of the Skiádhi turning and equipped with a bona fide **hotel**, **tavernas**, popular with bike-tourers, and shops. Northwest, the road leads to Monólithos, while the northeasterly bearing leads quickly and pleasantly back to Yennádhi via Váti. Due north, just below an irrigation reservoir, the tiny frescoed chapel of **Áyios Yeóryios Várdhas** (unlocked) is worth the short detour if you have your own transport.

Hálki

Hálki, a tiny (20 square kilometres), waterless, limestone speck west of Rhodes, is a fully fledged member of the Dodecanese, though all but about three hundred of the former population of three thousand emigrated (mostly to Rhodes or to Florida) in the wake of a devastating sponge blight during the early 1900s. Despite a renaissance through tourism in recent years, the island is tranquil compared with its big neighbour, with a slightly weird, hushed atmosphere owing to foreigners in their villas vastly outnumbering locals for much of the year. The big event of the day is the arrival of the regular afternoon kaïki from Kámiros Skála on Rhodes.

Hálki first attracted outside attention in 1983, when UNESCO designated it the "isle of peace and friendship" and the seat of regular international youth conferences. Some 150 crumbling houses were to be restored at UNESCO's expense as accommodation for delegates, but by 1987 just one hotel had been completed, and the only sign of "peace and friendship" was a stream of UNESCO and Athenian bureaucrats staging musical binges under the rubric of "ecological seminars". Confronted with an apparent scam, the islanders sent UNESCO packing and contracted two UK package operators to complete restorations and bring in paying guests. There is now in fact a third tour company present, and most of the ruins have been refurbished.

Emborió

The skyline of **EMBORIÓ**, the island's port and only habitation, is pierced by the tallest freestanding clocktower in the Dodecanese and, a bit further north, the belfry of Áyios Nikólaos church. Emborió's restored houses are pretty much block-booked from April to October by the tour companies mentioned; independent travellers will be lucky to find anything at all on spec, even early or late in the season. Non-package **accommodation**, all requiring advance reservations, includes the delightful, en-suite *Captain's House* (T02460/45 201; ❷), which has the feel of an old French country hotel and whose English manageress Christine can point you in likely directions if she's full; *Pension Keanthi* (T02460/45 334; ❷) near the school, offering bland, pine-furnished rooms with high ceilings plus a few galleried studios (❸); and the municipally-owned *Hotel Halki* (T02460/49 390; ❸) in the old sponge factory on the south side of the bay, indifferently managed and beset by creeping damp, but likely to have a vacancy. Of the half-dozen **tavernas** along the field-stoned, pedestrianized waterfront, *Remezzo* (aka *Takis*) is excellent for *mayireftá* and pizzas, *Maria* behind the post office has good grills, while *Houvardas*, near the north end of the quay has proven reliable for *mayireftá* over the years. Amongst a similar number of bars and cafés, the standout has to be *Soula's* (aka "The Parrot Bar" after resident birds), near the base of the jetty, with puddings and own-made ice cream to die for. There's a **post office**, four well-stocked stores, two good bakeries cranking out a range of bread and pies, plus two **travel agencies** which sell boat tickets and change money (there's no bank); one of them, Zifos Travel (℡02460/45 028, ✆zifos-travel@rho.forthnet.gr) often has a few vacancies amongst studios which they hold back from the UK companies.

The rest of the island

Three kilometres west lies the old pirate-safe village of **HORIÓ**, abandoned in the 1950s but still crowned by the Knights' castle. Except during the major August 14–15 festival, the church here is kept securely locked to protect its frescoes. Across the valley, the little monastery of **Stavrós** is the venue for the other big island bash on September 14. There's little else to see or do inland, though you can spend three hours **walking** across the island on the 1998-vintage dirt track, the extension of the cement "Tarpon Springs Boulevard" donated by the expatriate community in Florida. At the end of the road (best arrange a ride out, and walk back) you'll come to the monastery of **Ayíou Ioánnou Prodhrómou**; the caretaker there can put you up in a cell (except around August 29, the other big festival date), but you'll need to bring supplies. The terrain en route is monotonous, but compensated by views over half the Dodecanese and Turkey.

Longish but narrow **Póndamos**, fifteen-minutes' walk west of Emborió, is the only sandy beach on Hálki, and even this has had to be artificially supplemented. The sole facility is the somewhat pricey *Nick's Póndamos Taverna*, serving lunch daily, plus supper four evenings weekly. Small and pebbly **Yialí**, west of and considerably below Horió via a jeep track, lies an hour's hike away from Póndamos. A thirty-minute walk north of Emborió lies **Kánia**, with a rocky foreshore and a rather industrial ambience from both power lines and the island's only petrol pump to one side.

Since these three coves are no great shakes, it's worth signing on at Emborió quay for **boat excursions** to more remote beaches. More or less at the centre of Hálki's southern shore, directly below Horió's castle, **Trahiá** consists of two coves to either side of an isthmus; you can (just) reach this overland by rough path from Yialí, and this trail is scheduled to be bulldozed into a track soon. North-coast beaches figuring as excursion-boat destinations include the pretty fjord of **Aréta**, **Áyios Yeóryios** just beyond, and the remote double bay of **Dhýo Yialí**. Of these, Aréta is the most attractive, and the only one accessible overland (in ninety minutes one-way) by experienced hillwalkers equipped with the *Chalki, Island of Peace and Friendship* map based on the old Italian topographical survey products.

Alimniá (Alimiá) islet

One of the more promoted local boat excursions visits **Alimniá (Alimiá) islet**, roughly halfway between Hálki and Rhodes. Despite more well-water and greenery and a better harbour than Hálki's, the deserted village here, overlooked by a few palm trees and yet another Knights' castle, was completely abandoned by the 1960s. The locals were initially deported during World War II after they admitted to assisting British commandos sent in April 1944 to sabotage the enemy submarines who used the deep harbour here. The seven commandos themselves were captured on the spot by the Nazis, bundled off first to Rhodes, then to Thessaloníki, where six were summarily executed as spies rather than regular prisoners of war; future Austrian premier and UN Secretary General Kurt Waldheim allegedly countersigned their death sentences.

Interesting history acknowledged, Alimniá is probably not a place you'd want to be stuck for an entire day. Excursions on offer are pricey (about €20.50, picnic lunch included), beach space very limited, the castle a hot, 45-minute walk up (the best thing to do here) and the crumbling village behind its salt marsh unedifying. If you snorkel in the outer bay beyond little Áyios Mínas monastery, you might glimpse outlines of the Italian-built submarine pens to one side of the deep bay. The former inhabitants only show up to graze livestock, or on the date of the annual festival (Áyios Yeóryios).

Kastellórizo (Meyísti)

Kastellórizo's official name, Meyísti (biggest), seems more an act of defiance than a statement of fact. While the largest of a tiny group of islands, it is actually the smallest of the Dodecanese, over seventy nautical miles from its nearest Greek neighbour (Rhodes) but barely more than a nautical mile off the Turkish coast at the narrowest straits. At night its lights are quite outnumbered by those of the Turkish town of Kaş, which lies across the bay and with whom Kastellórizo generally has excellent relations.

Until the early 1900s there were almost 14,000 people here, supported by a fleet of schooners that transported goods, mostly timber, from the Greek towns of Kalamaki (now Kalkan) and Andifelos (Kaş) on the Anatolian mainland opposite. But the withdrawal of island autonomy after the 1908 "Young Turk" revolution, the Italian seizure of the other Dodecanese in 1912 and an inconclusive 1913–1915 revolt against the Turks sent the island into decline. A French occupation of 1915–21 prompted destructive shelling from the Ottoman-held mainland, a harbinger of worse to come (see below). Shipowners failed to modernize their fleets upon the advent of steam power, preferring to sell ships to the British for the Dardanelles campaign, and the new frontier between the island and republican Turkey, combined with the expulsion of all Anatolian Greeks in 1923, deprived any remaining vessels of their trade. During the 1930s the island enjoyed a brief renaissance when it became a major stopover point for French and Italian seaplanes, but events at the close of World War II put an end to any hopes of the island's continued viability.

When Italy capitulated to the Allies in the autumn of 1943, a few hundred Commonwealth commandos occupied Kastellórizo, departing of their own accord in spring 1944 – leaving the island deserted and vulnerable to the attentions of pirates. In early July, a harbour fuel dump caught (or was set on) fire and an adjacent arsenal exploded, taking with it more than half of the two thousand houses on Kastellórizo. Even before these events most of the population had left for Rhodes, Athens, Australia (especially Perth) and North America. Today there are just 342 official residents here by the last census (with only 250 actually living permanently on Kastellórizo), largely maintained by remittances from over 30,000 emigrants and by subsidies from the Greek government, which fears that the island will revert to Turkey should their numbers diminish any further.

Yet Kastellórizo has a future of sorts, thanks to expat "Kassies" who have begun renovating their crumbling ancestral houses as retirement or holiday homes. Each summer, the population is swelled by returnees of Kassie ancestry. Occasionally they celebrate traditional weddings in the **Áyios Konstandínos** cathedral at Horáfia, which incorporates ancient columns from Patara in Asia Minor. Access has also improved since the late 1980s: an airport (domestic flights only) was completed, and the harbour dredged to accommodate larger ferries, though the island has yet to be designated an official port of entry to Greece, which causes problems for both yachties and conventional travellers crossing from Turkey.

You will either love Kastellórizo and stay a week, or crave escape after a day; its detractors dismiss the island as a human zoo maintained by the Greek government for the edification of nationalists, while partisans celebrate an atmospheric, barely commercialized outpost of Hellenism.

Kastellórizo Town

The current population is concentrated in the northern town of **KASTELLÓRIZO** – supposedly the finest natural harbour between Beirut and Fethiye on the Turkish coast – and its little "suburb" of **Mandhráki**, just over the fire-blasted hill with its half-ruined Knights' castle. Its outer bulwark now houses the worthwhile local **museum** (Tues–Sun 7am–2.30pm; free), with displays including plates from a Byzantine shipwreck, frescoes rescued from decaying rural churches and a reconstruction of an ancient basilica on the site of today's gaudy Ayíou Yeoryíou Santrapé church at Horáfia. Just below and beyond the museum, in the cliff-face opposite Psorádhia islet, is Greece's only **Lycian house-tomb**; it's well signposted from the shoreline walkway, up some steps beside the first wooden lamp standard.

Most of the town's surviving mansions are ranged along the waterfront, their tiled roofs, wooden balconies and blue or green shutters on long, narrow windows having obvious counterparts in the originally Greek-built houses of Kalkan and Kaş just across the water. Just one or two streets back, however, many properties are derelict – abandonment having succeeded where the World War I shelling, a 1926 earthquake and the 1944 explosions failed; sepia-toned posters and black-and-white postcards on sale of the town in its prime are poignant evidence of its later decline.

Practicalities

Kastellórizo is not really geared up for large numbers of visitors, though **pensions** in the old houses have been upgraded to en-suite status, and prices have climbed in recent years. If you're not met off the boat, the best budget en-suite options include the large-roomed *Pension Caretta* (⊕ & ⓕ02460/49 028, ⓦwww.kastellorizo.de; ❷), which also has a fine restored apartment (❹); the nearly adjacent *Kristallo* (⊕02460/41 209; ❷); and the *Pension Asimina*, behind the arcaded market (⊕02460/49 361; ❷). More luxury is available at the recently-built, air-conditioned *Kastellorizo Hotel Apartments* (⊕02460/49 044, ⓕ49 279, ⓦwww.kastellorizohotel.gr; ❺–❻), on the opposite side of the bay from the ferry jetty, offering quality-fitted studios or galleried maisonettes, some with sea view.

Apart from fish, goat meat and wild-fig preserves, plus whatever can be smuggled over from Kaş, Kastellórizo has to import foodstuffs and drinking water from Rhodes; prices when eating out can consequently be higher than usual, with the further pretext of the island's celebrity status. It's best to continue past the two most conspicuous waterfront **tavernas**, which do average fare only, and continue a few steps to *To Mikro Parisi* for reliably fresh and affordable seafood and meat grills. Other good quayside choices include *Iy Ipomoni* (supper only), two doors left from the arcaded market, featuring simple but wholesome grills and unusual dishes like sea-snails; *Kaz-Bar*, to the right of the Italian market, where chef Colin and his mother serve up fine grills, vegetable dishes and cold mezédhes nightly except perhaps Thursday in off-season; and the inexpensive but savoury *Akrothalassi*, purveying decent grills and salads near the west end of the quay, by the church. Two to recommend inland are *Iy Orea Meyisti* and *Ta Platania* (June–Sept), opposite Áyios Konstandínos in Horáfia, good for daily-changing *mayireftá* and desserts, often home-made. There are more puddings, and good breakfasts at *Zaharoplastio Iy Meyisti*, back on the waterfront. **Nightlife** spills out of the half-dozen *barákia* lining the quay.

A single **bank**, with handy cash dispenser, stands on the east quay; the **post office** is found on the far side of the bay. Better of the town's two travel agencies is Papoutsis (☎02410/70 830), which represents all boats calling here, and sells Olympic tickets. A public transfer van shuttles between town and airstrip at flight times; Damian Mavrothalassitis of *Pension Caretta* is the airport agent and can also sell tickets in a pinch.

It is possible to arrange a ride over **to Turkey** on one of four local boats, most reliably on Monday or Friday. The standard day-return fee is €14.70 (one-way €11.80), and you have to leave your passport with the authorities the day before. Although Kastellórizo is not yet a legal port of entry to Greece – it lacks a proper Schengen database computer, and customs stamps – police here cannot legally deny disembarkation to EU nationals arriving **from Kaş**, which is an official entry–exit point for Turkey.

The rest of the island

Kastellórizo's austere hinterland is predominantly bare rock, flecked with stunted vegetation; incredibly, two or three generations ago much of the countryside was carefully tended, producing wine of some quality and in quantity. A rudimentary paved road system links points between Mandhráki and the airport, but there aren't many specific places on it to visit and no scooters for rent. Karstic cliffs drop sheer to the sea, offering no anchorage for boats except at the main town, Mandhráki and Návlakas fjord (see overleaf).

Rural monasteries and ruins

Heat permitting, you can hike up the obvious, zigzag stair-path, then south through desolate fire-charred scrub to the rural **monastery of Áyios Yeóryios toú Vounioú**, 35 minutes away. The sixteenth- to eighteenth-century church boasts fine rib-vaulting and a carved *témblon*, but its highlight is a crypt, with the frescoed, subterranean chapel of **Áyios Harálambos** off to one side; access is via a steep, narrow passage descending from the church floor – bring a torch and grubby clothes, and get the key first from Kostas the keeper, who lives behind the *Little Paris* taverna. Alternatively, a fifteen-minute track-walk west of the port leads to the peaceful monastery of **Ayías Triádhas**, perched on the saddle marked by the OTE tower, and an army base (off-limits) – one of many strongpoints which have sprouted here since the Ímia crisis (see p.553).

The onward path arrives after twenty minutes at the ancient citadel of **Paleókastro**, where you'll find masonry from Classical to medieval times, a warren of vaulted chambers, tunnels, cisterns plus another little monastery with a *hokhláki* courtyard. From any of the heights above town there are tremendous views north over sixty kilometres of Anatolian coast.

The shoreline and Rhó

Swimming is complicated by a total absence of decent beaches and an abundance of sea urchins and razor-sharp limestone reefs; the safest entry near town lies beyond the graveyard at Mandhráki, or people just dive from the lidos on the northwest quay (incidentally, it's illegal to swim across the harbour mouth).

Once away from the shore, you're rewarded by clear waters with a rich variety of marine life. From Áyios Yeóryios toú Vounioú, you can continue 45 minutes further on foot, first on a useless new bulldozer track, then on the original, French-built *kalderími*, to the multi-lobed fjord of **Návlakas**, a favourite mooring spot for yachts and fishing boats. The French built this cobbled way to facilitate offloading supplies here during World War I, safe from Ottoman artillery. Uniquely on Kastellórizo, this bay is sea-urchin-free, with freshwater seeps keeping the temperature brisk; there's superb snorkelling to 25-metre depths off the south wall.

Over on the southeast coast, accessible only by a 45-minute boat ride from town, the grotto of **Perastá** (Galázia Spiliá) deserves a look for its stalactites and strange blue-light effects; the low entrance, negotiable only by inflatable raft, gives little hint of the enormous chamber within, with monk seals occasionally nesting in another adjacent cave. Ninety-minute rubber-raft trips (€6 minimum per person) visit only the cave, or for a minimum of €15 on a larger kaïki, you can take it in as part of a five-hour tour that includes Rhó islet.

Should you make the trip out to **Rhó**, the tomb of *Iý Kyrá tís Rhó* (**The Lady of Rhó**), aka Dhespina Akhladhiotis (1898?–1982) – who resolutely hoisted the Greek flag each day on that islet in defiance of the Turks on the mainland – is the first thing you see when you dock at the sandy, northwestern harbour. From here a path heads southeast for 25 minutes to the islet's southerly port, past the side trail up to the intact Hellenistic fortress on the very summit. The islet has no facilities – just a few soldiers to prevent Turkish military landings or poachings of the hundreds of goats – so bring your own food and water.

Sými

Sými's most pressing problem, lack of fresh water, is in many ways also its saving grace. As with so many dry, rocky Dodecanese islands, water must be imported at great expense from Rhodes, pending completion of a reservoir in the distant future. Consequently, the island can't hope to support more than a handful of large hotels; instead, hundreds of people are shipped in daily during the season from Rhodes, relieved of their money and sent back. This arrangement suits both the Symiots and those visitors lucky enough to stay longer; many foreigners return regularly, or even own houses here.

Once beyond the inhabited areas, you'll find a surprisingly attractive island that has retained some of its original forest cover of junipers, valonea oaks and even a few pines – ideal walking country in spring or autumn (though not midsummer, when temperatures are among the highest in Greece). Another prominent feature of the landscape are dozens of tiny monasteries, usually locked except on their patron saint's day, though their cisterns with a can on a string for fetching water are usually accessible.

Sými Town

SÝMI, the island's capital and only proper town, consists of **Yialós**, the excellent natural port, and **Horió**, on the hillside above. Incredibly, less than a hundred years ago the place was richer and more populous (25,000) than Ródhos Town, its wealth generated by shipbuilding and sponge-diving, skills nurtured since pre-Classical times. Under the Ottomans, Sými, like most of the smaller Dodecanese, enjoyed considerable autonomy in exchange for a yearly tribute in sponges to the sultan; but the Italian-imposed frontier, the 1919–22 Greco-

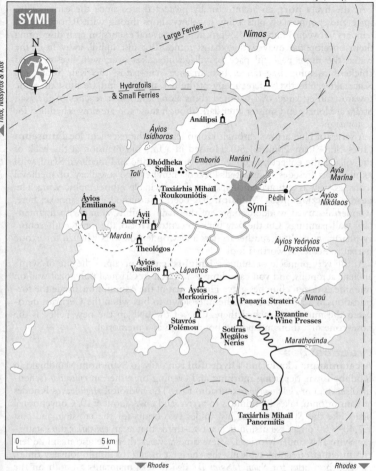

Turkish war, the advent of synthetic sponges and the gradual replacement of the crews by Kalymniots spelt doom for the local economy. Vestiges of past nautical glories remain in still-active boatyards at Pédhi and Haráni, but today the souvenir-shop sponges come entirely from overseas and, the recent boom notwithstanding, a significant fraction of the magnificent nineteenth-century mansions stands roofless and empty.

The approximately twenty-five hundred remaining Symiots are scattered fairly evenly throughout the mixture of Neoclassical and more typical island dwellings; despite the surplus of properties, many outsiders have preferred to build anew, rather than restore derelict shells accessible only by donkey or on foot. As on Kastellórizo, a wartime ammunition blast – this time set off by the retreating Germans – levelled hundreds of houses up in Horió. Shortly afterwards, the official Axis surrender of the Dodecanese to the Allies was signed here on May 8, 1945: a plaque marks the spot at the present-day *Restaurant Les Catherinettes*.

At the lively **port**, an architecturally protected area since the early 1970s, spice and sponge stalls plus a few jewellery shops throng with Rhodes-based trippers between 11am and 3.30pm, and the several excursion craft disgorging them envelop the quay with exhaust fumes. But just uphill, away from the water, the more peaceful pace of village life takes over, with livestock and chickens roaming free-range. Two massive stair-paths, the Kalí Stráta and Katarráktes, effectively deter many of the day-trippers and are most dramatic towards sunset; large, owl-haunted ruins along the lower reaches of the Kalí Stráta are lonely and sinister after dark, though these too are now scheduled for restoration.

A series of blue arrows through Horió leads to the excellent local **museum** (Tues–Sun 10am–2pm; €1.50). Housed in a fine old mansion at the back of the village, the collection concentrates on Byzantine and medieval Sými, with exhibits on frescoes in isolated, locked churches and a gallery of medieval icons, as well as antiquarian maps and the inevitable ethnographic wing. The nearby **Hatziagapitos Mansion** has been refurbished as an annexe; here, wonderful carved wooden chests are the main exhibits, along with fragmentary wall-paintings. On the way back to central Horió, the nineteenth-century pharmacy, with its apothecary jars and wooden drawers labelled for exotic herbal remedies, is worth a look.

At the very pinnacle of things, a **Knights' castle** occupies the site of Sými's ancient acropolis, and you can glimpse a stretch of Classical polygonal wall on one side. A dozen churches grace Horió; that of the Assumption, inside the fortifications, is a replacement of the one blown to bits when the Germans detonated the munitions cached there. One of the bells in the new belfry is the nose-cone of a thousand-pound bomb, hung as a memorial.

Practicalities

A **catamaran**, a **kaïki** and a **hydrofoil** run daily to Sými from Mandhráki in Ródhos Town, departing morning and evening on either an *epivatikó* (scheduled service) or *ekdhromikó* (excursion) basis. The hydrofoil *Aigli* leaves Rhodes at 9am or 6pm, takes 55 minutes to arrive, and costs about €10. Conventional boats like the *Symi I* require just under two hours for the crossing, and cost €7.40–8.80 on an excursion ticket, two-thirds that as an *epivatikó*; the catamaran Symi II is similarly priced. A few times a week there are also mainline ferries in either direction, typically the cheapest of all (1hr 40min journey time). ANES, the outlet for *Symi I/Symi II/Aigli* tickets, maintains a booth on the quay and an office in the marketplace lanes (☎02460/71 444). Among **ferry** agents, Sunny Land, also in the market, is the agent for ANEK (the *Nissos Kalymnos*), while DANE Lines and the Dodecanese Express catamaran is handled by Symi Tours nearby (☎02460/71 307).

There's no official tourism bureau, but the island's English-language advertiser-newsletter, *The Symi Visitor* (free; ⓦwww.symivisitor.com), is literate and has current island gossip with informative features. The **post office** in the official Italian "palace" is open standard hours; of the two **banks**, the Alpha/Ionian is more efficient and has a cash dispenser. During the season a small green bus (€0.60 flat fare) shuttles between Yialós and Pédhi via Horió on the hour (returning at the half-hour) until 11pm. There are also six **taxis** (allow €3 Yialós–Horió with baggage), and one or two pricey outlets for **motor-scooter rental** (€20.50 and up daily), though this is a perfect island for boat and walking excursions. A **laundry** operates in the grid of market lanes, resorted to by those whose hosts forbid clothes-washing in rooms.

Accommodation

Accommodation for independent travellers is somewhat limited and proprietors tend not to meet arriving boats, though the situation isn't nearly so bad as on Hálki. Studios, rather than simple rooms, predominate, and package operators control most of these, though curiously you may have an easier time finding spots in July/August than during spring/autumn, considered the most pleasant season here. Despite asphyxiating summer heat, air conditioning and ceiling fans are rarely found – go for north-facing and/or balconied units when possible. If you're planning in advance, the Symi Visitor website (see opposite) is worth consulting.

Albatros, marketplace ℡02460/71 707 or 71 829. Partial sea views from this exquisite, small hotel; pleasant second-floor breakfast salon, air-con. ❹

Aliki, Haráni quay ℡02460/71 665, ℻71 655, ⓦwww.simi-hotelaliki.gr. A complete overhaul of an 1895 mansion, and Sými's poshest hotel: tasteful rooms with wood floors and some antique furnishings, and large bathrooms, though only some have sea views. Breakfast included in price. ❻

Anastasia, behind the post office ℡02460/71 364. Pleasantly set hotel, though with limited harbour views, this has parquet-floored rooms plus a couple of studios, with some package allotment however. ❸

Egli Rooms, base of the Kalí Stráta ℡02460/71 392. Basic (non-en-suite), but clean enough rooms, and usually has vacancies when everyone else is full. ❷

Fiona, at the top of the Kalí Stráta ℡02460/72 088. Mock-traditional hotel building whose large airy rooms have double beds and stunning views; breakfast in mid-air on common balcony. ❹

Jean Manship, c/o *Jean & Tonic Bar* ℡ & ℻02460/71 819 8pm–1am Greek time. Jean manages two traditional houses in Horió, both suitable for couples and with stunning views. ❸–❹

Katerina Tsakiris Rooms Horió ℡02460/71 813. Just a handful of very plain en-suite rooms with shared kitchen and grandstand view; reserva-

tions essential. ❷–❹

Les Catherinettes, above eponymous restaurant, north quay ℡02460/72 698, ℮marina-epe@rho.forthnet.gr. Creaky but spotless en-suite pension in a historic building with painted ceilings and seaview balconies for most rooms. ❸

Symi Visitor Accommodation ℡02460/72 755, ℮symi-vis@otenet.gr. Managed by affable returned Greek–Australian Nikos Halkitis and partner Wendy Wilcox, who offer a variety of houses restored as double-occupancy studios in prime locations of Horió. Rates range from €35.30 at *The Cottages* to €103 at *The Mule House*, by way of €53 at *The Windmills*; they also have pricier units suitable for 4–5 persons.

Taxiarhis Apartments, edge of Horió overlooking Pédhi ℡02460/72 012, ℻72 013. Secluded, well-designed row of studios and one-bedroom apartments with common areas and balconies, though some package groups. Breakfast on request. ❹–❺

Titika Rooms, rear of platía, Yialós (enquire at sponge shop left of National Bank, or ℡02460/71 501). No views, but quiet and well-equipped rooms with fridge and air-con; tiny common kitchen and shared terrace with tables. ❷–❹

Villa Symeria up the Kalí Stráta (contact *Albatros Hotel*). Restored mansion comprising two apartments with either air-con or fans, suitable for up to four and six persons respectively. ❻

Eating and drinking

You're best off avoiding most **eateries** on the north and west quays of the port, where menus, ingredients, prices and attitudes have been terminally warped by the day-trip trade. Away from these areas, you've a fair range of choice among *kultúra* tavernas, old-style *mayireftá* places, a few genuine ouzerís and even a traditional kafenío or two.

To Amoni, inland side of main platía, Yialós. An excellent, inexpensive, authentic ouzerí, where big helpings of liver, sausage and seafood titbits accompany the usual fried vegetarian starters and mainland bulk wine. Open most of the year, though supper only low season; seating indoors and out.

Dhimitris, south quay, on the way out of town. Excellent, family-run seafood-stressing ouzerí with

exotic items such as *hokhlióalo* (sea snails), *fouskes* (mock oysters), *spinóalo* (pinna-shell flesh) and the indigenous miniature shrimps, along with the more usual dishes and lots of vegetarian starters.

Ellinikon, south side main platía, Yialós. The most prominent of the *kultúra* tavernas, where host Nikos Psarros will escort you to the cooled wine cellar to choose from among 140 varieties of top Greek wine. Food portions aren't huge, but recipes – squid-ink pasta, seafood moussakás, roasts, ice cream with mulberry sauce – are rich. Budget €25 per head plus the cost of wine.

O Ilios, west quay. British-run, with "English" or healthy full breakfasts, plus vegetarian meals and own-made cakes. Also does picnic hampers for beach outings – notify them the previous day. Open 8am–10.30pm.

To Kantirimi, north side main square, Yialós. A good source of pancake or waffle breakfasts under the trees; becomes a snack café/bar later in the day.

O Meraklis, rear of the bazaar. Polite service and fair portions of well-priced *mayireftá* and mezéd-hes make this a reliable bet April–Dec. Sample meal: beans, beets, dips, and roast lamb with potatoes as a tender main course. Allow €13–14 each.

Mythos, south quay between bus/taxi stop, Yialós. Superb, supper-only ouzerí that's reckoned among the best, and best-value, cooking on the island. There is a menu, but why not let chef Stavros hit you with his Frenchified medley which includes salad, seafood starters (squid in basil sauce), duck with juniper berries, lamb slices, and own-made desserts. Budget €20.50 a head before dipping into the decent wine list. Roof terrace annexe opening soon.

Pahos, west quay, beside *O Ilios* (no sign). The old-boys' kafenío, in operation since World War II, and still a classic spot for a sundown oúzo and people-watching.

Yiorgos, near top of Kalí Stráta in Horió. Jolly, much-loved institution maintaining consistent food quality since 1977, with summer seating on a pebble-mosaic courtyard. Service can be slip-shod, but perennial recipes include feta-stuffed peppers, spinach-rice, chicken in mushroom-wine sauce, and grilled fish when available. Open random lunchtimes in season, supper only indoors in winter.

Nightlife

Nightlife continues into the early hours and is sometimes abusively loud, with a number of bars owned by expatriates. Up in Horió, convivial *Jean & Tonic* is the heart and soul of the bar scene, catering to a mixed clientele (visitors and expats until 3am, Greek restaurateurs 3am until dawn) most of the year; a short way down the Kalí Stráta, *Kali Strata* is a low-key place with unbeatable views and excellent, wide-ranging music. Down at Yialós, the *Harani Club* has the nicest interior and a mix of Greek and international music depending on the crowd, until 2am; its neighbours in the noisy alley nicknamed "the Gaza strip" have lapsed into high-volume aural assaults aimed at empty tables. Elsewhere, *Katoi* on the south quay is a no-touts, no-hassle bar favoured by locals, whilst *The Club* on the platía functions between midnight and dawn, and has a pool table.

Around the island

Sými has no big sandy beaches, but there are plenty of pebbly stretches at the heads of the deep, protected bays which indent the coastline. **PÉDHI**, a 45-minute walk from Yialós, retains some of its former identity as a fishing hamlet, with enough water in the plain behind – the island's largest – to support a few vegetable gardens. The beach is poor, though, and patronage from yachts and the giant, overpriced *Pedhi Beach* hotel (☎02460/71 981, ℻71 982; ◉) has considerably bumped up prices at several local **tavernas**, of which the most reasonably priced and authentic is *Iy Kamares* at the far south end. Many will opt for another twenty minutes of walking via a rough but obvious path along the south shore of the almost landlocked bay to **Áyios Nikólaos**. The only all-sand beach on Sými, this offers sheltered swimming, tamarisks for shade and a mediocre taverna. Alternatively, a paint-splodge-marked path on the north side of the inlet leads in just over half an hour to **Ayía Marína**, where there's a minuscule beach, a shingle lido with sunbeds, another snack bar and a monastery-capped islet to which you can easily swim.

Around Yialós, you'll find tiny **NOS (Navtikós Ómilos Sýmis)** "beach" ten minutes past the boatyards at Haráni, but there's sun here only until lunchtime and it's usually packed with day-trippers. You can continue along the cement-paved coast road, or cut inland from the Yialós platía past the abandoned desalination plant, to appealing **Emborió** (Nimborió) Bay, with a poor **taverna** (*Metapontis*) and an artificially sand-strewn beach a bit beyond. Inland from this are Byzantine mosaic fragments under a protective shelter, and, nearby, a catacomb complex known locally as **Dhódheka Spília**.

Plenty of other, more secluded coves are accessible by energetic walkers with sturdy footwear, or those prepared to pay a modest sum for the taxi-boats (daily in season 10am–1pm, returning 4–5pm; one-way fares available to the nearer bays cited above). These are the best method of reaching the southern bays of **Marathoúnda** and **Nanoú**, and the only method of getting to the spectacular fjord of **Áyios Yeóryios Dhyssálona**. Dhyssálona lacks a taverna and lies in shade after 1pm, while unalluring Marathoúnda is fringed by coarse, slimy pebbles, making Nanoú the most popular destination for day-trips. The 200-metre beach there consists of gravel, sand and small pebbles, with a scenic backdrop of pines and a reasonable taverna (menu of squid, chips and salad) behind. It's also possible to reach Nanoú overland, via Panayía Straterí chapel up on the main trans-island road, descending a scenic, forested gorge for some 45 minutes; most of the old path from Horió to Panayía Straterí still exists, making a marvellous traverse of about three hours in total, leaving time for a meal and swim at Nanóu before the boat trip back to Yialós.

For more hiking adventures, you can cross the island from Horió in ninety minutes to **Áyios Vassílios**, the most scenic of the gulfs with its Lápathos beach; in about the same time to **Tolí**, a deserted, west-facing cove, also accessible from Emborió; or in three hours, partly through forest, from Yialós to **Áyios Emilianós** at the island's extreme west end, where a little monastery is tethered to the body of Sými by a causeway. On the way to the latter you should look in at the monastery of **Taxiárhis Mihaïl Roukouniótis** (daily 9am–2pm & 4–8pm), Sými's oldest, with naive eighteenth-century frescoes and a peculiar ground plan: the current *katholikón* is actually superimposed on a lower, thirteenth-century structure abandoned after being burnt and pillaged by pirates during the 1400s, though a fine fresco of St Lawrence (Áyios Lavréntios) survives behind the altar screen. Resident, trilingual Father Amfilohios will gladly tell you anything else you might possibly wish to know about the place.

The Archangel is also honoured at the huge monastery of **Taxiárhis Mihaïl Panormítis** near the southern tip of the island, Sými's biggest rural attraction and generally the first port of call for the excursion boats from Rhodes (confirm the itinerary if you wish to proceed direct to Yialós – some craft do). These allow only a quick thirty-minute tour; if you want more time, you'll have to come by scooter from Yialós (though the still-unpaved road down from the central escarpment is terrible, with nine hairpin bends), or arrange to stay the night (€9 minimum donation) in the **xenónas** (inn) set aside for pilgrims. There are large numbers of these in summer, as Mihaïl has been adopted as the patron of sailors in the Dodecanese.

Like many of Sými's monasteries, Panormítis is of recent (eighteenth-century) vintage and was thoroughly pillaged during World War II, so don't expect too much of the building or its treasures. An appealing pebble-mosaic court surrounds the central *katholikón*, tended by the monk Gabriel and lit by an improbable number of oil lamps. It's also graced by a fine *témblon*, though the frescoes are recent and mediocre. One of the two small museums (€1.50 admits to both) contains a strange mix of precious antiques, exotic junk (stuffed crocodiles and koalas, elephant tusks), votive offerings, models of ships and a chair piled with messages-in-bottles brought here by Aegean currents – the idea being that if the bottle or toy boat arrived, the sender got their prayer answered. There's a small beach, a shop/kafenío, a bakery and a **taverna** (*Panormio*) popular with passengers of the many yachts calling in. Near the taverna stands a memorial commemorating three Greeks, including the monastery's abbot, executed in February 1944 by the Germans for aiding British commandos.

Tílos

The small, blissfully quiet island of **Tílos**, with an official population of about five hundred (dwindling to eighty in winter), is one of the least frequented and worst connected of the Dodecanese, though it can (in theory) be visited on a day-trip by hydrofoil or catamaran once or twice a week. Why anyone would want to come for just a few hours is unclear: while it's a great place to rest on the beach or go walking, there is nothing very striking at first glance. After a few days, however, you may have stumbled on several of the seven small castles of the Knights of St John which stud the crags, or found some of the inconspicuous medieval chapels clinging to the hillsides.

Tílos shares the characteristics of its closest neighbours: limestone mountains resembling those of Hálki, plus volcanic lowlands, pumice beds and red-lava sand as on Níssyros. Though rugged and scrubby on its heights, the island has ample water – from springs or pumped up from the agricultural plains – and clusters of oak and terebinth near the cultivated areas. From many points on the island you've startling views across to Kós, Sými, Turkey, Níssyros, Hálki, Rhodes and even (weather permitting) Kárpathos.

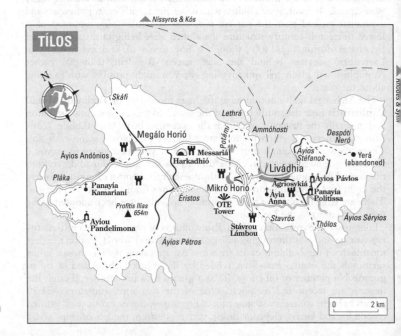

Since the mid-1990s, however, development on Tílos has threatened to reverse the conditions which many visitors have historically come to enjoy; besides the Dodge City atmosphere of Livádhia (see below), a hyperactive bull-dozing programme has scarred virtually every mountain in the east of the island. A 1998-vintage road from the telecom-tower hill, heading east along the summit ridge, is intended to facilitate a proposed fish farm at Áyios Séryios, which will finish that cove as a leisure beach.

Tílos's main road, widened and repaved in 1999–2000, runs 7km from Livádhia, the port village, to Megálo Horió, the capital and only other significant habitation. A public **minibus** links the two, and services are theoretically scheduled to coincide with ferry arrivals; at other times the bus makes up to six runs daily along the Livádhia–Éristos stretch. There are also two **taxis**, or you can rent a **car** from two outlets in Livádhia (Stefanakis Travel and Tilos Travel). Stefanakis currently has a monopoly on ferry tickets; Tilos Travel is arguably the more helpful, however (☎ & ☎02460/44 294, ⓦwww.tilostrav-el.co.uk), offering a full accommodation booking service, money exchange, boat excursions all season – providing there are sufficient passenger numbers – and scooter rental. The island's single filling station lies between Livádhia and Megálo Horió.

Many visitors come specifically to **walk**, assisted by the extremely accurate **map** prepared by Baz "Paris" Ward and sold locally – or by certified walking **guides** Iain and Lyn Fulton (☎02460/44 128 or 094/6054593, ⓔfulton@otenet.gr), who may take you on unusual itineraries not described or mapped in existing literature. A half-dozen critical sections of deteriorating trail or *kalderími* have been surveyed in preparation for cleaning and rebuilding in the near future, so quality walking opportunities may have stabilized and should improve in the future.

Livádhia

With its unpaved streets, unfinished building sites and higgledy-piggledy lay-out, **LIVÁDHIA** makes a poor introduction to the island, but it remains the better equipped of the two settlements to deal with tourists, and is closer to the majority of remaining path-hikes. There are generally enough beds in the various **rooms** and **hotels** to go around, but in peak season it's certainly worth phoning ahead. Budget options include a few adjacent outfits on the shore just beyond the Italian "palace", for example *Paradise* (aka *Stamatia's*; ☎02410/44 341; ❶) or two studios next door at *Galini* (aka *Paraskevi* ☎02410/44 280; ❷). Further along the bay are some newer, better-appointed options: *Anastasia* (☎02460/44 111; ❶), just behind the *Armenon* taverna, where a usual willing-ness to bargain offsets slightly small rooms, or *Pavlos and Nina* (☎02460/44 011; ❷), overlooking the sea near the friendly *Eleni Beach Hotel* about halfway around the bay (☎02460/44 062, ☎44 063; ❹), with large airy rooms requir-ing advance booking. The *Faros Hotel* (☎02460/44 068; ❸) at the extreme end of the bay is widely praised for calm and its hospitable managing family, and also has a decent restaurant.

Inland, go for the well-appointed *Studios Irinna* (☎02410/44 366; ❷), alias *Kula's*, above the ironmonger's which runs it; the *Hotel Irini* (☎02410/44 293, ☎44 238; ❹), 200m inland from mid-beach, with a pool, all mod cons and generally a few on-spec vacancies in amongst the Laskarina package clients here; or, tops on the island and only really available outside peak season, the B-class *Hotel Tilos Mare* (☎02460/44 100, ☎44 105; ❸).

There must be a dozen-plus **tavernas** operating around Livádhia in peak sea-son, of which perhaps half merit consideration. Among the more authentic spots for a no-nonsense Greek feed are *Irina* (alias *Stefanos and Maria*), doling out inexpensive *mayireftá* right on the shore near the church; *Psistaria Kritikos* in the village centre, well regarded by carnivores for its goat chops, sausages and chicken; *To Armenon* (alias Nikos') on the shore road, an excellent and salubrious beach-taverna-cum-ouzerí, with octopus salad, white beans and the like; and inland on the way to *Armenon*, the *Pantelis Souvla Maria's Pizza* (sic), doing just those things superbly, despite zero atmosphere courtesy of plastic chairs and a purple bug-zapper. The best place for reliably fresh grilled fish with mezédhes is *Blue Sky*, an unmissable eyrie perched above the ferry dock.

For **breakfast** (plus evening pizzas and home-made desserts), Anglo-Italian *Joanna's Café*, just inland from *Kritikos*, is hard to beat, also with a long list of strong cocktails. *Iy Omonia*, under trees strung with light bulbs, near the post office, is the enduringly popular "traditional" alternative for a sundowner, breakfast or while waiting for a ferry, and also does inexpensive, savoury mezédhes. Livelier, organized **nightlife** in or near Livádhia is limited to three bars: *Cafe Ino* on the shore near *Irina* for the trendy set, the *Bozi* at the far east end of the bay (nightly in summer, weekends otherwise) and a durable music pub in Mikró Horió (see below).

There's a **post office**, but as yet no bank or cash dispenser, so come with sufficient Greek cash or apply to either travel agency (Tilos Travel will do cash advances on plastic for a small commission). A **bakery** and several well-stocked **supermarkets** round out the roster of amenities.

Around the island

From Livádhia you can walk an hour north along the obvious trail to the pebble bay of **Lethrá**, or in about the same time south on separate itineraries to the secluded coves of **Stavrós** or **Thólos**. The track to the former begins between the *Tilos Mare Hotel* and the *Castellania Apartments*, becoming a trail at the highest new house in the village; once up to the saddle with its new road, you've a sharp drop to the beach – ignore over-eager cairning in the bed of the descending ravine, the true path is up on the right bank, indicated by red-paint surveyor's marks. The route to Thólos begins by the cemetery and the chapel of **Áyios Pandelímon** with its Byzantine *hokhláki* court, then curls around under the seemingly impregnable castle of **Agriosykiá**; from the saddle overlooking the descent to Thólos (again, surveyed in preparation for refurbishment), a route marked with cairns leads northwest to the citadel in twenty minutes. It's less than an hour's walk west, with some surviving path sections shortcutting the road curves, up to the ghost village of **Mikró Horió**, whose 1200 inhabitants left for Livádhia during the 1950s. The only intact structures are the church (locked except for the August 15 festival) and an old house which has been restored as a small-hours **music pub** and operates only during July and August, with a variable formula of Greek/foreign music, and a shuttle van laid on from the port.

Megálo Horió and Éristos

The rest of Tílos's inhabitants live in or near **MEGÁLO HORIÓ**, which has an enviable perspective over the vast agricultural *kámbos* stretching down to Éristos (see opposite), and is overlooked in turn by the vast castle of the Knights, which encloses a sixteenth-century chapel. The castle was built on the site of ancient Tílos – with recycled masonry evident – and is reached by a stiff, thirty-minute climb that begins on the lane behind the Ikonomou supermarket before threading its way through a vast jumble of cisterns, house foundations and derelict chapels – the remains of the much-larger medieval Megálo Horió. Two more flanking fortresses stare out across the plain: the easterly one of **Messariá** helpfully marks the location of the **Harkadhió** cave (closed for ongoing excavations), where Pleiocene midget-elephant bones were discovered in 1971. A signposted 500-metre track goes there from the road, ending near a spring and modern amphitheatre (to be used in a new summer festival) just below the cave-mouth, which was hidden for centuries until a World War II artillery barrage exposed it. The bones themselves have been transferred to a tiny, not very compelling **museum** in Megálo Horió, on the ground floor of the town hall (open Mon–Fri 8am–2.30pm on application upstairs to the warden).

Your choices for **accommodation** in the village are the *Pension Sevasti* (℡02410/44 237; ❶) at the lower end of town, the central *Milios Apartments* (℡02410/44 204; ❷) or, best of the lot, *Studios Ta Elefandakia* (℡02410/44 213; ❷), set among attractive gardens by the car park. Of the two **tavernas**, the *Kali Kardhia*, next to the *Pension Sevasti*, is more reliably open and has the best view; there's a traditional **kafenío** by historic Taxiárhis church, and further up, the Athenian-run *Kafenío Ilakati* (late May to Sept only), with cakes and drinks.

South of and below Megálo Horió, signs direct you towards the three-kilometre paved side road to the long, pink-grey-sand **Éristos** beach, allegedly the island's best, though summer rubbish piles from campers can be disconcerting, and a reefy zone must be crossed entering the water. The far south end, where the reef recedes, is also a designated nudist zone, as are the two secluded, attractive coves at Kavliáris south beyond the headland (accessible by path only). About halfway down the road on the right amongst the orchards is *Taverna-Rooms Tropikana* (℡02410/44 020; ❶), nothing special in either respect, but the most reliable all-season venue for a snack near the beach. For more comfort, there's the 1998-built *Eristos Beach Hotel* (℡02460/44 024; ❷) – the rooms are good value, though the management can be less than welcoming.

The far northwest

The main road beyond Megálo Horió hits the coast again at dreary **Áyios Andónios**, whose one bright spot is a single **taverna**, the *Dhelfíni*, open much of the time for the benefit of local fishermen. At low tide on the exposed, average beach you can find more lava-trapped skeletons strung out in a row – human this time, presumably tide-washed victims of a Nissyrian eruption in 600 BC, and discovered by the same archeologists who found the miniature pachyderms.

There's better swimming at isolated **Pláka** beach, 2km west of Áyios Andónios, where people camp rough despite a total lack of facilities. The paved road finally ends 8km west of Megálo Hório at the fortified **monastery of Ayíou Pandelímona**, founded in the fifteenth century for the sake of its miraculous spring. The settlement hosts the island's major festival from July 25 to 27, and lately a friendly Serbian family has been in residence, acting as caretakers and operating a small snack/drinks *kantína*. The monastery's tower-gate and oasis setting, more than two hundred forbidding metres above the west coast, are the most memorable features, though an eminently photogenic inner courtyard boasts a *hokhláki* surface, and the church a fine marble floor. On the *katholikón* wall, an early eighteenth-century fresco shows the founder-builder holding a model of the monastery, while behind the ornate altar screen hides another fresco of the Holy Trinity.

The public minibus calls in here perhaps once or twice a day. To vary the **return to Megálo Horió**, you can walk back much of the way on a signposted path; it's shown correctly on Baz Ward's map, and ends at the minor monastery of Panayía Kamarianí near Áyios Andónios. Committed and experienced hill-walkers can tackle the challenging path which curls around the southwest flank of Profítis Ilías, Tílos's highest mountain, finishing three hours later at **Éristos**. This begins, as signposted, beside the monastery; it's a well-surveyed route, with no real exposure or sharp drops, but there's only one spring along the way, rather disheartening scree at the start, and the wild feel of a remote traverse on a much larger island.

Níssyros

Volcanic **Níssyros** is noticeably greener than its southern neighbours Tílos and Hálki, and unlike them has proven wealthy enough to retain over eight hundred of its population year-round (down, though, from 10,000 in 1900). While remittances from abroad (particularly Astoria, New York) are significant, most of the island's income is derived from the offshore islet of Yialí, where a vast lump of **pumice** is slowly being quarried away by Lava Ltd. The concession fee collected from Lava by the municipality has engendered a huge public payroll and vast per-capita sums available to spend, making Níssyros something of a mini-Kuwait. Under the circumstances, the Nissyrians bother little with agriculture other than keeping cows and pigs; the hillside terraces meticulously carved out for grain and grapes lie fallow, and wine is no longer made locally.

The main island's peculiar geology is potentially a source of other benefits: DEI, the Greek power company, spent the years between 1988 and 1992 sinking exploratory **geothermal** wells and attempting to convince the islanders of the benefits of cheap electricity. In 1993, a local referendum went massively against the project, and DEI, together with its Italian contractor, took the hint and packed up. The desalination plant, reliant on an expensive fuel-oil generator, scarcely provides enough fresh water to spur a massive growth in package tourism. The relatively few tourists (mostly German) who stay the night, as opposed to the day-trippers from Kós, still find peaceful villages with a minimum of concrete eyesores and a friendly if rather tight-knit population.

Níssyros also offers good **walking** opportunities through a countryside planted with oak and terebinth, on a network of trails fitfully marked and maintained with EU money; wherever you stroll you'll hear the contented grunting of pigs as they gorge themselves on acorns from the many oak trees. Autumn is a wonderful time, especially when the landscape has perked up after the first rains, though the late-January almond-blossoming no longer occurs, as the trees have unhappily died out.

Mandhráki

MANDHRÁKI is the deceptively large port and island capital, with blue patches of sea visible at the end of narrow streets lined with tightly-packed houses, whose brightly painted balconies and shutters are mandated by law. Except for the tattier fringes near the ferry dock, where multiple souvenir shops and bad tavernas pitched at day-trippers leave a poor first impression, the bulk of the place is cheerful and villagey, arrayed around the community orchard or *kámbos* and overlooked by two ancient fortresses.

Into a corner of the nearer of these, the fourteenth-century Knights' castle, is wedged the little monastery of **Panayía Spilianí**, built on this spot in accordance with instructions from the Virgin, who appeared in a vision to one of

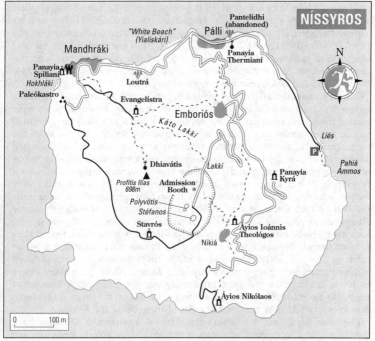

Map labels:
Pantelídhi (abandoned)
Páli
"White Beach" (Yialiskári)
Panayía Thermianí
Mandhráki
Panayía Spiliani
Hokhláki
Paleókastro
Loutrá
Evangelístra
Emboriós
Káto Lakkí
Liés
P
Pahiá Ámmos
Dhiavátis
Lakkí
Profítis Ilías 698m
Admission Booth
Panayía Kyrá
Polyvótis Stéfanos
Stavrós
Nikiá
Áyios Ioánnis Theológos
Áyios Nikólaos
N
0   100 m

the first Christian islanders. The monastery's prestige grew after raiding Saracens failed to discover the vast quantities of silver secreted here in the form of a rich collection of Byzantine icons. During 1996–97, the Langadháki area just below was rocked by a series of earthquakes, damaging a score of venerable houses (mostly repaired now), and rendering the small folklore museum homeless, though it was never really worth the admission fee for a couple of mannequins in traditional dress. A new combination archeological–ethnographical-historical museum has been built on the *kámbos* with money donated by the Nissyrian founder of the Vitex paint company, and should be ready for visitors by the end of 2001.

As a defensive bastion, the seventh-century BC Doric **Paleókastro** (unrestric-ted access), twenty-minutes' well-signposted walk out of the Langadháki district, is infinitely more impressive than the Knights' castle, and ranks as one of the more underrated ancient sites in Greece. You can clamber up onto the massive, polygonal-block walls by means of a broad staircase beside the still-intact gateway.

Practicalities

You'll see a handful of port **hotels** on your left as you disembark; cheapest of these is the waterfront *Three Brothers* (☎02420/31 344; ①) and the *Romantzo* (☎02420/31 340; ①) across the way, with partial sea views, and fridges in the simple but well-kept rooms; they also run the *Studios Volcano* (③) in town. For slightly more comfort, try the municipally run *Xenon Polyvotis* (☎02420/31 011, ℻31 204; ②) just beyond, whose biggish, neutral-decor rooms have fans and (mostly) knockout sea views. In the town proper, the main budget option is the small, very simple, hillside *Hotel Ypapandi* (☎02420/31 485 or visit *Taverna Panorama*; ❶), near Mandhráki's most comfortable accommodation, the *Hotel Porfyris* (☎02420/31 376, ℻31 176; ❹), also overlooking the sea and *kámbos*, with gardens and a large swimming pool. There's little actually on the shore aside from *Studios Sunset-Iliovasilema* (☎02420/31 159 or 097/2141344; ❸), adequate and quiet, near the converted windmill.

Culinary **specialities** include pickled caper greens, honey, *pittiá* (chickpea croquettes) and *soumádha*, an almond–syrup drink widely sold in recycled wine bottles, though it's now made from imported almonds and must be consumed within three months of purchase. When eating out, it's best to give all of the commercialized, shoddy shoreline **tavernas** a miss – simple, old-fashioned *Manolis Papatsou* is the honourable exception, often with fresh fish – in favour of more genuine haunts inland. Top of the heap is evening-only, musical ouzerí *Iy Fabrika* (closed Thurs), with indoor/outdoor tables by season and family recipes from founder Patti preserved by second owner Manolis, also the miners' chef on Yialí. On their days off, the staff here go to eat at resolutely simple *Panayiotis* (no sign) in Langadháki, open on summer evenings only, and serving lovingly prepared home-style dishes at a half-dozen outside tables. Pricier runners-up include *Panorama*, with bean and mushroom salad and suckling pig on offer, or *Irini* on lively, ficus-shaded Platía Ilikioméni, with more involved *mayireftá* unavailable elsewhere. Finally, little *Taverna Nissiros*, the oldest eatery in town, is always busy despite predictably average grill quality. Focuses of **nightlife** are Platía Ilikioméni and a string of *barákia* on the shore at Lefkándio district west of *Manolis*, the most popular of these being the *Enallax*.

The most useful of Mandhráki's three **travel agencies** is Dhiakomihalis, which acts as a representative for most ferries and hydrofoils, rents cars and exchanges money. Kentris, near the town hall, does G&A ferries and Olympic Airways tickets. There's a **post office** at the port and a single **bank** in town, but it has no cash dispenser and levies stiff commissions, as does Dhiakomihalis. At the base of the jetty is the **bus stop**, with (theoretically) up to four daily departures to the hill villages and five to Pálli; otherwise, there are two set-rate **taxis** and three outlets for **scooter rental**, among which Alfa and John and John (branch also in Pálli) provide the best service – rates begin at €10.30 per day.

Beaches and Pálli

Beaches on Níssyros are in even shorter supply than water, so much so that tour agencies here occasionally peddle excursions to a sandy cove on **Áyios Andónios** islet, opposite the Yialí mines. Closer at hand, the short, black-rock beach of **Hokhláki**, behind the Knights' castle, is unusable if the wind is up, and the town "beach" of **Miramáre** at the eastern edge of the harbour is merely a lido filled with sand in high season, a last resort in any weather. It's best to head east along the main road, passing the refurbished spa of **Loutrá** (hot mineral water only by doctor's referral) and the smallish "**White Beach**" (properly Yialiskári), 2km along and dwarfed by an ugly hotel. The Loutrá spa, though itself sporadically shut for restoration, is well worth a stop for its "snack bar" at the far end of the building, really an **ouzerí** with generous portions of reasonably priced salads, fried appetizers, seafood and meat.

A kilometre or so further, 4km in total from Mandhráki, the fishing village of **PÁLLI** makes an excellent hangout at lunchtime, when the port fills with trippers. Tavernas are multiplying, but stick with the two long-term favourites: the less expensive *Ellinis*, with spit-roasted meat by night, grilled fish in season and simple rooms upstairs (☎02420/31 453; ❷), or the adjacent *Afroditi* (aka *Nikos &*

Tsambika), with big portions of grills and *mayireftá*, Cretan bulk wine and excellent own-made desserts. They've also a house to rent, all or in part (☎02420/31 242; €41 for the entire house). The scooter-rental outlet, an excellent bakery cranking out brown bread and fine pies (branch in Mandhráki), and modest nightlife make Pálli also worth considering as a base. A tamarisk-shaded, dark-sand **beach**, kept well groomed of late, extends east of Pálli, to the abandoned Pantelídhi spa, behind which the little grotto-chapel of **Panayía Thermianí** is tucked inside the vaulted remains of a Roman baths complex. To reach Níssyros's best beaches, continue in this direction for an hour on foot (or twenty minutes by bike along the road), past an initially discouraging seaweed- and cowpat-littered shoreline, to the delightful cove of **Liés**, with a snack bar, *Oasis* (June 15–Sept 15). Just beyond here the now-dirt road ends at a car park. Walking a further fifteen minutes along a trail over the headland brings you to the idyllic, 300-metre expanse of **Pahiá Ámmos**, with grey-pink sand heaped in dunes, limited shade at the far end and a large colony of "freelance" campers in summer.

The interior

Níssyros's central, dormant **volcano** gives the island its special character and fosters the growth of the abundant vegetation – and no stay would be complete without a visit. When excursion boats arrive from Kós, several agency coaches and usually one of the public buses are pressed into service to take customers into the interior. These tours tend to monopolize the crater floor between 11am and 2pm, so if you want solitude, use early-morning or late-afternoon scheduled buses to Nikiá (three daily continue to the crater floor), a scooter or your own two feet to get there.

The road up from Pálli winds first past the virtually abandoned village of **EMBORIÓS**, where pigs and free-ranging cattle (a major driving hazard) far outnumber people, though the place is slowly being bought up and restored by Athenians and foreigners. New owners are often surprised to discover natural saunas, heated by volcano steam, in the basements of the crumbling houses; at the outskirts of the village there's a signposted public **steam bath** in a grotto, its entrance outlined in white paint. If you're descending to Pálli from here, an old cobbled way starting at the sharp bend below the sauna offers an attractive short cut of the four-kilometre road, while another *kalderími* drops from behind *To Balkoni tou Emboriou* **taverna** (sporadically May–Sept, limited menu) to within a quarter-hour's walk of the craters.

NIKIÁ, the large village on the east side of the volcano's caldera, is, with seventy inhabitants, more of a going concern, and its spectacular situation 14km from Mandhráki offers views out to Tílos as well as across the volcanic caldera. There are three places to **drink** (and, modestly, **eat**) here: *Porta* (summer eves only) and *Platia* on or near the engagingly round *hokhláki* plaza, or *Nikia*, at the entrance to the village. By the bus turnaround area, signs point to the 45-minute **trail** descending to the crater floor; a few minutes downhill, you can detour briefly to the eyrie-like **monastery of Áyios Ioánnis Theológos**, which only comes to life at the September 25 festival. To **drive** directly to the volcanic area you must use the road which veers off just past Emboriós.

However you approach the **volcano**, a sulphurous stench drifts out to meet you as fields and scrub gradually give way to lifeless, caked powder. The sunken main crater of **Stéfanos** is extraordinary, a moonscape of grey, brown and sickly yellow; there is another, less-visited double crater (dubbed **Polyvótis**) to the west, equally dramatic, with a clear trail leading up to it from the access road. The perimeters of both are pocked with tiny blowholes from which jets of steam puff constantly and around which form little pincushions of pure sulphur crystals. The whole floor of the larger crater seems to hiss, and standing in the middle you can hear something akin to a huge cauldron bubbling away below you. According to legend this is the groaning of Polyvotis, a Titan crushed here by Poseidon under a huge rock torn from Kós. When there are tour groups around, a small, tree-shaded snack bar operates in the centre of the wasteland, and a booth on the access road sporadically charges admission (€1.50) to the volcanic zone.

Since the 1991 destruction of the old direct *kalderími* between the volcano and Mandhráki, finding pleasant options for **walking** back to town requires a bit of imagination and possession of Beate and Jürgen Franke's locally available, GPS-drawn topographical map (free). First choice involves backtracking along the main crater access road for about 1km from the admission booth to find the start of a clear, crudely marked path which passes the volcanic gulch of **Káto Lákki** and the monastery of **Evangelístra** on its two-hour-plus course back to the port. You can lengthen the trip by detouring from Evangelístra south to **Profítis Ilías**, the island's summit, a two-hour round-trip – the route is well marked with cairns or white paint and was cleaned in 1998. An alternative approach to Evangelístra requires returning to Emboriós and leaving from the top of the vil-lage, near the cemetery and small castle, on a 45-minute course to the monastery – an enjoyable link, despite haphazard marking and cleaning. From Evangelístra, the onward route to Mandhráki briefly follows the now mostly paved road down before the marked path resumes, handily shortcutting hairpin bends.

Kós

After Rhodes, **Kós** is the second largest and most popular island in the Dodecanese, and there are superficial similarities between the two. Here also the harbour is guarded by an imposing castle of the Knights of St John; the streets are lined with grandiose Italian public buildings; and minarets and palm trees punc-tuate extensive Hellenistic and Roman remains. Although its hinterland for the most part lacks the wild beauty of Rhodes' interior, acre for acre Kós is the most fertile of the Dodecanese, blessed with rich soil and abundant ground water.

Mass tourism has largely displaced the old agrarian economy amongst the pop-ulation of just over 28,000, and outside the main town and Kardhámena this is very much a family-holiday isle, where you can turn the kids loose on pushbikes. Except for Kós Town and Mastihári, there aren't many independent travellers, and from early July to early September you'll be lucky to find any sort of room at all without reservations far in advance, or a prebooked package. The tourist industry is juxtaposed rather bizarrely with cows munching amidst baled hay, and Greek Army tanks exercising in the volcanic badlands around the airport. All these pecu-liarities acknowledged, Kós is still definitely worth a few days' time while island-hopping: its handful of mountain villages are appealing, the tourist infrastructure excellent (including such amenities as regular city buses and cycle paths) and swimming opportunities are limitless – virtually the entire coast is fringed by beaches of various sizes, colours and consistencies.

Kós Town

The town of **KÓS**, home to over half of the island's population, spreads in all directions from the harbour, with most of its charm residing in scattered ancient and medieval antiquities. Apart from the Knights' castle, the first thing you see on arrival, there's a wealth of Hellenistic and Roman remains, many of which

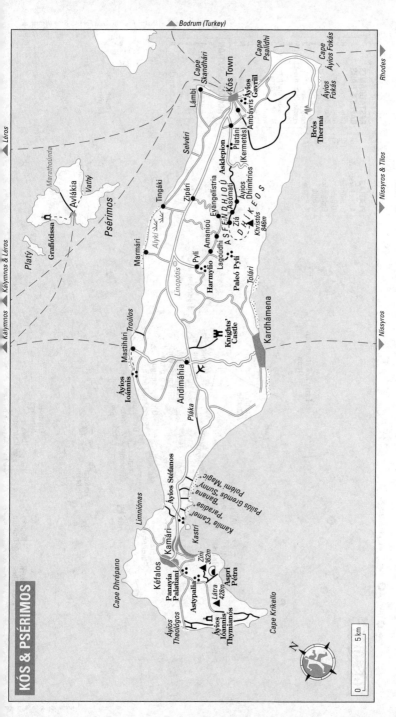

KÓS & PSÉRIMOS

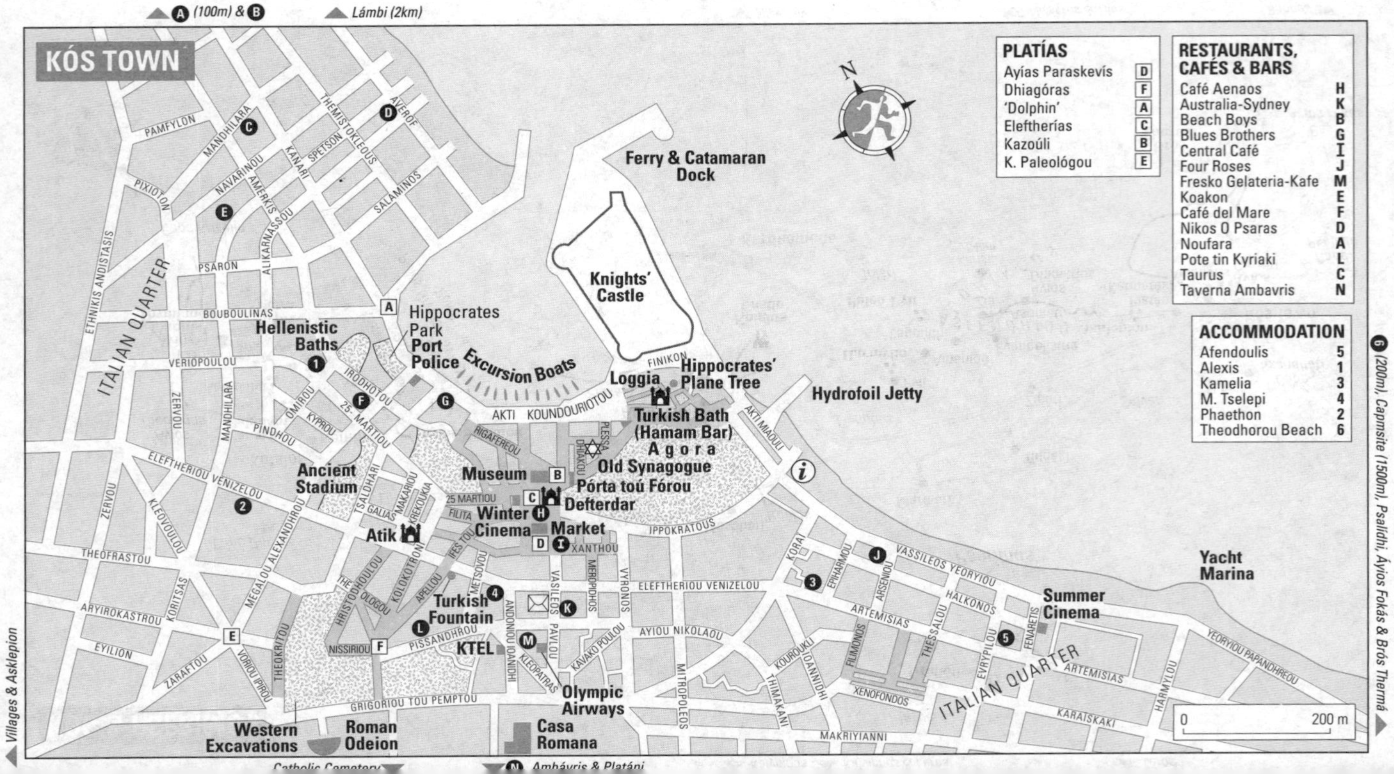

KÓS TOWN

PLATÍAS

Ayías Paraskevís	D
Dhiagóras	F
'Dolphin'	A
Eleftherías	C
Kazoúli	B
K. Paleológou	E

RESTAURANTS, CAFÉS & BARS

Café Aenaos	H
Australia-Sydney	K
Beach Boys	B
Blues Brothers	G
Central Café	I
Four Roses	J
Fresko Gelateria-Kafe	M
Koakon	E
Café del Mare	F
Nikos O Psaras	D
Noufara	A
Pote tin Kyriaki	L
Taurus	C
Taverna Ambavris	N

ACCOMMODATION

Afendoulis	5
Alexis	1
Kamelia	3
M. Tselepi	4
Phaethon	2
Theodhorou Beach	6

0   200 m

(200m), Capmsite (1500m), Psalídhi, Áyios Fokás & Brós Thermá

Villages & Asklepíon

were only revealed by an earthquake in 1933, and excavated subsequently by the Italians, who also planned and laid out the "garden suburb" extending east of the central grid. Elsewhere, vast areas of open space alternate with a hotchpotch of Ottoman monuments and later mock-medieval and Art Deco buildings.

The **castle** (Tues–Sun 8am–2.30pm; €2.40) is reached via a causeway over its former moat, now filled in and planted with palms (hence the avenue's Greek name, Finíkon). The existing double citadel, which was built in stages between 1450 and 1514, replaced an original fourteenth-century fort deemed not capable of withstanding advances in medieval artillery. A fair proportion of ancient Koan masonry has been recycled into the walls, where the escutcheons of several Grand Masters of the Knights of St John can also be seen.

Immediately opposite the castle entrance stands the riven trunk of Hippocrates' plane tree, its branches now propped up by scaffolding instead of the ancient columns of yore; at seven hundred years of age, it's not really elderly enough to have seen the great healer, though it has a fair claim to being one of the oldest trees in Europe. Adjacent are two Ottoman fountains (a dry hexagonal one and a working one in an ancient sarcophagus) and the eighteenth-century **mosque of Hassan Pasha**, also known as the Loggia Mosque after the portico on one side; its ground floor – like that of the **Defterdar mosque** on Platía Eleftherías – is taken up by rows of shops.

Opposite the latter stands the Italian-built **Archeological Museum** (Tues–Sun 8am–2.30pm; €2.40), with a predictable Latin bias in the choice of exhibits. Four rooms of statuary are arrayed around an atrium with a mosaic of Hippocrates welcoming Asklepios to Kós; the most famous item, purportedly a statue of Hippocrates, is indeed Hellenistic, but most of the other highly regarded works (such as Hermes seated with a lamb) are Roman.

The largest single section of ancient Kós is the **agora**, a sunken, free-access zone containing a confusing jumble of ruins, owing to repeated earthquakes between the second and sixth centuries AD. More comprehensible are the so-called western excavations, lent definition by two intersecting marble-paved streets and the **Xystos** or restored colonnade of a covered running track. In the same area lie several floor mosaics, such as the famous one of Europa being carried off by Zeus in the form of a bull, though these tend to be off-limits or hidden under protective gravel. To the south, across Grigoríou toú Pémptou, are a garishly restored Roman-era odeion and the **Casa Romana** (Tues–Sun 8.30am–3pm; €1.50), a third-century-AD house built around three atria with surviving patches of mosaic floors showing panthers and tigers, plus assorted sea creatures.

Kós also retains a thoroughly commercialized **old town**, lining the pedestrianized street running from behind the market hall on Platía Eleftherías as far as Platía Dhiagóras and the isolated minaret overlooking the western archeological zone. One of the few areas of town to survive the 1933 earthquake, today it's crammed with expensive tourist boutiques, cafés and snack bars. About the only genuinely old thing remaining here is a capped **Turkish fountain** with a calligraphic inscription, found where the walkway cobbles cross Odhós Venizélou.

Practicalities

Large **ferries and catamarans** anchor just outside the harbour at a special jetty by one corner of the castle; **excursion boats** to neighbouring islands sail right in and dock all along Aktí Koundouriótou. **Hydrofoils** tie up south of the castle at their own berth, on Aktí Miaoúli. Virtually all ferry and excursion boat agents sit within 50m of each other at the intersection of pedestrianized Vassiléos Pávlou and the waterfront. Among the more helpful and genuinely representative of ferries and hydrofoils, not just expensive excursions, are Adris

Nissia at Vassiléos Pávlou 2, and Exas at Andóni Ioannídhi 4 (☎02420/29 900). If you just want to clear out, Aeolos Travel at Annéttas Laoumtzí 8 (☎02420/26 203) often has stray one-way charter seats back to the UK.

The **airport** is 24km southwest of Kós Town in the centre of the island; an Olympic Airways shuttle bus (€3) meets Olympic flights for a transfer to the town terminal, but if you arrive on any other flight you'll have to either take a taxi or head towards the giant roundabout outside the airport gate and find an orange-and-cream-coloured KTEL bus – they run from here to Mastihári, Kardhámena and Kéfalos as well as Kós Town. The **KTEL terminal** in town is a series of stops around a triangular park 400m back from the water, with an info booth adjacent at Kleopátras 7 (tickets on the bus). The municipality also runs a frequent **local bus** service, DEAS, through the beach suburbs and up to the Asklepion, with a ticket and information office at Aktí Koundouriótou 7. Push- or **mountain-bike** rental are popular options for getting around, given the island's relative flatness; if you want a **motor scooter**, try Moto Harley at Kanari, corner Neomartýrou Khrístou, while Autorent/Helen's at Apostólou Pávlou 31 (☎02420/28 882 or 094/4450062) or in Psalídhi suburb, at both the *Ramira* and *Okeanis* hotels, has a reputation for good-condition **cars**, as does Marion at Vasiléos Yeoryíou 1 (☎02420/26 293).

The municipal **tourist office** at Vassiléos Yeoryíou 3 (July & Aug daily 8am–9pm; May & June, Sept & Oct Mon–Fri 9am–8pm, Sat 8am–3pm; Nov–April Mon–Fri 8am–3pm) keeps stocks of local maps, bus timetables and ferry schedules (the latter not to be trusted implicitly). For more involved information, head for the News Stand book store and newsagent just behind the archeological museum on Platía Kazoúli. No fewer than six **banks** have cash dispensers, while the **post office** is at Vassiléos Pávlou 14. **Internet cafés** include *Café del Mare* at Megálou Alexándhrou 4 (the best equipped), or *Taurus* at Mandhilará 9. **Laundries** include Happy Wash at Mitropóleos 20, Laundry Center on Mandhilará 56 and Laundromat Center at Alikarnassoú 124.

Accommodation

If you're just in transit, you're virtually obliged to **stay** in Kós Town, and even if you plan a few days on the island, it still makes a sensible base, as it is the public transport hub and has the greatest concentration of vehicle rental and nightlife. Be wary of the touts which besiege most arriving sea-craft – their rooms are apt to be unlicensed, inconveniently remote and of dubious cleanliness.

Good, licensed, budget choices in the centre include the deservedly popular *Pension Alexis* (☎02420/25 594; ❷; March–Nov), Irodhótou 9 at the corner of Omírou, across from the Roman agora, with wood-floored, non-en-suite rooms and a self-catering kitchen; the same welcoming family runs the *Hotel Afendoulis* (☎02420/25 321; ❸; April–Nov), about 600m south at Evripýlou 1, with large, balconied en-suite rooms and breakfast available. If they're full, try the nearby *Hotel Kamelia* at Artemisías 3 (☎02420/28 983, ☏27 391; ❸), claimed open all year, with winter heating; the rear rooms have an orchard view. Other quiet possibilities include the air-conditioned *Hotel Phaethon* at Venizélou 75 (☎02420/228 901; ❹) and the self-catering rooms let by Moustafa Tselepi (☎02420/28 896; ❸) at Metsóvou 8 (enquire at Venizélou 35). For more comfort and a small private beach, the *Hotel Theodhorou Beach*, 1200m from the centre at the end of town towards Psalídhi (☎02420/22 280, ☏23 526; ❹) has generous-sized rooms not completely monopolized by packages and attractive common areas. The well-appointed **campsite** (☎02420/23 275; May to early Oct) lies another 1300m out towards Cape Psalídhi, and can be reached by either the DEAS bus service or its own minibus (which meets ferrries).

Despite an overwhelming first impression of Euro-bland cuisine, it's easy to **eat** well and even reasonably in Kós Town, as long as you search inland, away from the harbour. The *Australia-Sydney* on Vassiléos Pávlou opposite the post office is a cheap and cheerful hole-in-the wall with a limited menu of daily dishes where two can eat for under €15; the *Koakon*, on Ieroú Lóhou, at the corner of Amerikís, offers *mayireftá* in a more salubrious environment without the usual multinational flags and photo-menus; while *Noufara* at Kanári 67 is carnivore heaven with roast chicken, *kondosoúvli* and the like. Moving up in the world, the nearby *Nikolaos O Psaras*, on the corner of Alikarnassoú and Avérof, is the most genuine fish taverna in town, with good *orektiká* preceding mildly pricey seafood. Kos's sole real ouzerí is tiny *Pote tin Kyriaki* at Pissándhrou 9 (closed Sun, as the name says), which neither wants nor gets many tourists – there's only a Greek sign out, and no menu per se – proprietor Angelos recites the day's fare. Equal to any of these is *Ambavris* (May–Oct), 800m south out of town by the road from near Casa Romana, in the eponymous village. To order from their English-only à la carte menu is to miss the point of the place; take the hint about "Mezedes" and let the house bring on their best – this changes seasonally but won't much exceed €19 for six plates, drinks extra.

For **breakfast**, the *Central/Kentriko Cafe* on Platía Ayía Paraskevís behind the market hall does American pancakes with fresh fruit juices, while you can join the largely Greek crowd at *Café Aenaos*, right under the Defterdar mosque, and people-watch while refilling your Greek coffee from the traditional *bríki* used to brew it up. For **snacks** or **dessert**, *Fresko Gelateria-Café*, on the corner of Kleopátras and Ioannídhi, serves crepes and waffles in the morning, sticky cakes or decadent own-made ice cream later on. For a convivial **drink** on the water, try long-lived *Blues Brothers* on Aktí Koundouriótou, near the port police; equally durable music bars with dance floors include *Four Roses* on the corner of Arseníou and Vassiléos Yeoryíou, and *Beach Boys* at Kanári 57. If you prefer loud techno and house, look no further than the "Pub Lanes", officially Nafklírou and Dhiákou; every address is a bar, whose identity tends to change each season, so just choose according to the crowd and the noise level. Otherwise there is one active **cinema**, the Orfeas, with summer and winter (Oct–May) premises as shown on the map; the indoor premises also hosts concerts and other special events.

The Asklepion and Platáni

Native son **Hippocrates** is justly celebrated on Kós; not only does he have a tree, a street, a park, a statue and an international medical institute named after him, but the **Asklepion** (summer Tues–Sun 8am–7pm, earlier closure winter; €2.35) 4km south of town, one of just three in Greece, is a major tourist attraction. DEAS buses run to the site via Platáni 8am–6pm and to Platáni only 7–11.45pm; otherwise it's a 45-minute walk. There is a small snack bar at the Asklepion, or pause for lunch in Platáni (see overleaf) en route.

The Asklepion was actually founded just after the death of Hippocrates, but it's safe to assume that the methods used and taught here were his. Both a temple to Asklepios (god of medicine, son of Apollo) and a renowned curative centre, its magnificent setting on three artificial hillside terraces overlooking Anatolia reflects early recognition of the importance of the therapeutic environment. Until recently, two fountains provided the site with a constant supply of clean, fresh water, and extensive stretches of clay piping are still visible, embedded in the ground.

Hippocrates

Hippocrates (c. 460–370 BC) is generally regarded as the father of scientific medicine, though the Hippocratic oath probably has nothing to do with him and is in any case much altered from its original form. Hippocrates was certainly born on Kós, probably at Astypalia near present-day Kéfalos, but otherwise details of his life are few and disputed; what seems beyond doubt is that he was a great physician who travelled throughout the Classical Greek world, but spent at least part of his career teaching and practising at the Asklepion on his native island. A vast number of medical writings have been attributed to Hippocrates, only a few of which he could have actually written; *Airs, Waters and Places*, a treatise on the importance of environment on health, is widely thought to be his, but others were probably a compilation from a medical library kept on Kós, which later appeared in Alexandria during the second century BC. This emphasis on good air and water, and the holistic approach of ancient Greek medicine, now seems positively contemporary.

Today very little remains standing above ground, owing to the chronic earthquakes and the Knights' use of the site as a quarry. The lower terrace in fact never had many structures, being instead the venue for the observance of the *Asklepieia* – quadrennial celebrations and athletic/musical competitions in honour of the healing god. Sacrifices to Asklepios were conducted at an **altar**, the oldest structure on the site, whose foundations can still be seen near the middle of the second terrace. Just to its east, the Corinthian columns of a second-century AD **Roman temple** were partially re-erected by nationalistically minded Italians. A monumental **staircase** leads from the altar to the second-century BC Doric temple of Asklepios on the topmost terrace, the last and grandest of a succession of the deity's shrines at this site.

About halfway to the Asklepion, the village of **PLATÁNI** (also Kermetés, from the Turkish name *Germe*) is, along with Kós Town, the remaining place of residence for the island's dwindling community of ethnic Turks. Until 1964 there were nearly three thousand of them, but successive Cyprus crises and the worsening of relations between Greece and Turkey prompted mass emigration to Anatolia, and a drop in the Muslim population to currently under a thousand. Several excellent, Turkish-run tavernas are to be found at and around the main crossroads junction, with a working Ottoman fountain: *Arap* (summer only), the slightly less touristy *Asklipios* and *Sherif* across the way (summer only) and *Gin's Palace* (all year), each offering Anatolian-style *mezédhes* (fried vegetables with yogurt, *bourekákia*, and so on) and kebabs better than most in Kós Town.

Just outside Platáni on the road back to the port, the island's neglected **Jewish cemetery** lies in a dark conifer grove, 300m beyond the well-kept Muslim graveyard. Dates on the Hebrew-Italian-script headstones stop after 1940, after which none of the local Jews were allowed the luxury of a natural death prior to their deportation in summer 1944. Their former synagogue, a wonderfully orientalized Art Deco specimen at Alexándhrou Dhiákou 4, was refurbished in 1991 as a municipal events hall.

Eastern Kós

If you're looking for anything resembling a deserted **beach** near the capital, you'll need to make use of the DEAS bus line connecting the various resorts to either side of town, or else rent a vehicle; pedal-bikes can take advantage of the cycle paths extending as far east as Cape Psalídhi. Closest is **Lámbi**, 3km north towards Cape Skandhári with its military watchpoint, the last vestige of a vast army camp which has deferred to the demands of tourism – and supposed intra-NATO amity.

The bus line usually terminates at Áyios Fokás, 8km southeast of Kós Town, but sometimes continues an extra 4km to unusual and remote **Brós Thermá** (last service around 6pm); if you make the trip with your own transport be prepared to negotiate a rough dirt track for the final kilometre. Brós Thermá is known for its **hot springs** – best experienced at sunset or after – which issue from a grotto and flow through a trench into a shoreline pool protected by boulders, heating the seawater to an enjoyable temperature. Winter storms typically disperse the boulder wall, rebuilt every April, so that the pool changes from year to year. Just adjacent, the long-running *Psarotaverna Therma* does affordable seafood – especially parrotfish, swordfish and tuna, though the rest of the menu is unmemorable.

Tingáki and Marmári

The two neighbouring beach resorts of Tingáki and Marmári are separated from each other by the salt marsh of **Alykí**, which retains water until June after a wet winter. Between January and April Alykí is host to hundreds of migratory birds, and most of the time you'll find tame terrapins to feed near the outlet to the warm, shallow sea, though the drought of recent years means you're unlikely to see any of this until the next rainy winter. There's almost always a breeze along this coast, which means plenty of windsurfers for hire at either resort. The profiles of Kálymnos, Psérimos and Turkey's Bodrum peninsula all make for spectacular scenery. If you're aiming for either of these resorts from town, especially on a bike of any sort, it's safest and most pleasant to go by the obvious **minor road** which takes off from the southwest corner of town; the entire way to Tingáki is paved, and involves the same distance as using the main trunk road and marked turn-off. Similarly, a grid of paved rural lanes links the inland portions of Tingáki and Marmári.

TINGÁKI, a busy beachside resort popular with Brits, lies 12km west of the harbour. Oddly, there's very little accommodation near the beach in the dozen or so medium-sized hotels and more numerous studios; most of these are scattered inland through fields and cow pastures. One of the better choices, if heavily subscribed to by packages, is the family-oriented *Hotel Constantinos Ilios* (T02420/69 411; ⑤), a well-designed bungalow complex. The best local taverna here is *Ambeli* (supper only), well signposted 2.5km east of the main beachfront crossroads. Among car-rental outfits, Sevi (T02420/69 076) can be recommended, and will even deliver vehicles on request to Kós Town. The beach itself is white sand, long and narrow – it improves, and veers further away from the traffic of the frontage road, as you head southwest.

MARMÁRI, 15km from town, has a smaller built-up area than Tingáki, and the beach itself is broader, especially to the west where it forms little dunes. Most hotels here are monopolized by German tour groups, but you might hit on an on-spec vacancy at the B-class, 1997-built *Esperia* on the main access road down from the island trunk road (T02420/42 010, F42 012; ④), in grassy surroundings. Just inland on the same street stands a pair of adjacent noteworthy **tavernas**: *Apostolis* and the currently superior *Dimitris*, offering *mezedhákia*, seafood and meat grills at reasonable prices and usually also open weekends November to April.

The Asfendhioú villages

The main interest of inland Kós resides in the villages on **Mount Dhíkeos**, a handful of settlements collectively referred to as **Asfendhioú**, nestled amidst the island's only natural forest. Together they give a good idea of what Kós looked like before tourism and ready-mix concrete arrived, and all are now severely depopulated by the mad rush to the coast. They are accessible via the curvy side road from Zipári, 8km from Kós Town; a badly marked but paved minor road to Lagoúdhi; or by the shorter access road for Pylí.

The first Asfendhioú village you reach up the Zipári road is Evangelístria, where a major crossroads by the parish church leads to Lagoúdhi and Amanioú (west), Asómati (east) and Ziá (uphill). ZIÁ's spectacular sunsets make it the target of up to six evening tour buses daily, though the village has barely a dozen families still resident, and its daytime tattiness seems to increase each tourist season. Best of the dozen **tavernas** here is the *Olympia*, at the start of the pedestrian walkway up to the church, open all year with such dishes as chickpeas, bulgur pilaf, *spédzofaï* (sausage and pepper stew), dark bread and good bulk wine; there's a good *pikilía* of mezédhes "off-menu", especially at weekends when a local clientele predominates. Ziá is also the trailhead for the ascent of 846-metre **Dhíkeos peak**, a two-and-a-half-hour round-trip, initially on track but mostly by path. The route is fairly obvious, and the views from the pillbox-like summit chapel of Metamórfosis are ample reward for the effort. Up top, you can also ponder the esoteric symbolism of a giant crucifix fashioned out of PVC sewer pipe and filled with concrete.

East of Ziá or Evangelístria, roads converge at **ASÓMATI**, home to about thirty villagers and numbers of outsiders restoring abandoned houses; the evening view from the church of Arhángelos with its pebble mosaic rivals that of Zía, though there are no reliable facilities here. **ÁYIOS DHIMÍTRIOS**, 2km beyond along a fairly rough track, is marked by its old name of Haïhoúdhes on some maps, and is today completely abandoned except for a single house next to the attractive church; you can continue from here on 3.5km of more rough road to the junction with the paved road linking Platáni with the municipal rubbish tip.

Pylí

PYLÍ can be reached via the paved road through Lagoúdhi and Amanioú, or from the duck-patrolled Linopótis pond on the main island trunk road. In the upper of its two neighbourhoods, 100m west of the partly pedestrianized square and church, the simple *Iy Palia Piyi* taverna serves inexpensive but appetizing grills and mezédhes in a superb setting, beside a giant cistern-fountain (*piyí*), decorated with carved lion-head spouts. Pylí's other attraction is the so-called **Harmýlio** (Tomb of Harmylos), signposted near the top of the village as "Heroon of Charmylos". This consists of a subterranean, niched vault (fenced off), probably a Hellenistic family tomb; immediately above, traces of an ancient temple have been incorporated into the medieval chapel of Stavrós.

Paleó (medieval) **Pylí**, roughly 3km southeast of its modern descendant, was the Byzantine capital of Kós. Head there via Amanioú, keeping straight at the junction where signs point left to Ziá and Lagoúdhi. In any case, the castle should be obvious on its rock, straight ahead; the deteriorating road ends next to a spring, opposite which a stair-path leads within fifteen minutes to the roof of the fort. En route you pass the remains of the abandoned town tumbling southwards down the slope, as well as three fourteenth-century chapels with fresco fragments within; the first one encountered, Arhángelos, has the best-preserved scenes, though the third church (Ipapandí) is the most architecturally interesting.

Western Kós

Near the arid, desolate centre of the island, well sown with military installations, a pair of giant, adjacent roundabouts by the airport funnels traffic northwest towards Mastihári, northeast back towards town, southwest towards Kéfalos, and southeast to Kardhámena.

Mastihári and Andimáhia

The least developed, least "packaged" and least expensive of the northern shore resorts, **MASTIHÁRI** has a shortish, broad beach extending west, and a less attractive one at **Troúlos** 1.5km east. At the end of the westerly beach, inside a partly fenced enclosure, lie remains of the fifth-century basilica of **Áyios Ioánnis**, one of several on the island. If you want to **stay**, try quieter digs overlooking the west beach such as the simple *Hotel Kyma* (℡02420/59 045; ❶) or the *Hotel Fenareti* (℡02420/59 024) further up the grade, with rooms (❶) and studios (❷) in a peaceful garden environment. *O Makis*, one street inland from the quay, and *Kali Kardia*, at the base of the jetty, are the best of a half-dozen tavernas, both well regarded for fresh fish, mezédhes and (at *Kali Kardia*) *mayireftá*. Mastihári is also the port for small ro-ro **ferries** to Kálymnos; there are three well-spaced departures in each direction most of the year, timed more or less to coincide with Olympic Airways' flight schedules – though KTEL buses to or from Kós Town don't (perhaps deliberately) always dovetail well.

The workaday village of **ANDIMÁHIA**, 5km southeast of Mastihári, straggles over several ridges; the only concession to tourism is a much-photographed windmill on the main street, operating as a working museum (typically 8.30am–6pm) with its unfurled sails. If open, for a token fee you can climb up to the mast loft and observe its workings – which incidentally point downwind, not into the wind as popularly imagined. East of Andimáhia, reached via a marked, three-kilometre side road, an enormous, triangular **Knights' castle** overlooks the straits to Níssyros. Once through the imposing north gateway (unrestricted access), you can follow the well-preserved west parapet, and visit two interior chapels: one with a fresco of Áyios Khristóforos (St Christopher) carrying the Christ Child, the other with fine rib-vaulting. Work is underway to provide electricity and unsafe masonry is being consolidated with an eye to using the castle grounds for nocturnal spectacles, so you can expect opening hours and an admission fee in the future.

Kardhámena

KARDHÁMENA, on the southeast coast 31km from Kós Town, is the island's largest package resort after the capital itself, with locals outnumbered twenty to one in season by visitors (mostly young Brits) intent on getting as drunk as possible as cheaply as possible. Runaway local development has banished whatever redeeming qualities the place may once have had, reducing it to a seething mass of bottle-shops, bars, trinket shops and excursion agencies. Pubs named the *Black Swan* or *Slug and Lettuce* dispense imported beer, and you can even find fish and chips. A hefty sand beach stretches to either side of the town, hemmed in to the east with ill-concealed military bunkers and a road as far as Tolári, home to the massive *Norida Beach* all-inclusive complex.

Kardhámena is most worth knowing about as a place to catch a **boat to Níssyros**. There are supposedly two daily sailings in season: the morning tourist excursion kaïki at either 9am or 9.30am, and another, less expensive, barely publicized one – the *Chrissula* – at 2.30pm, but in practice the afternoon departure (typically Mon, Wed, Thurs & Fri) can occur any time between 1.30pm and 6.30pm, depending on when the Nissyrians have finished their shopping.

Outside high season, there are generally a few **rooms** not taken by tour companies, and prices are not outrageous. For more comfort, the *Hotel Rio* (℡02420/91 627; ❹) gets good reviews, and like most accommodation here is underpriced for its class. **Tavernas** are not very numerous, and predictably poor, though the longest-lived and most reasonable one is *Andreas*, right of the jetty as you face the sea.

South-coast beaches

The thinly populated portion of Kós southwest of the airport and Andimáhia boasts the most scenic and secluded beaches on the island, plus a number of minor ancient sites. Though given fanciful English names and shown as separate extents on tourist maps, the south-facing **beaches** form essentially one long stretch at the base of a cliff, most with sunbeds and a jet-ski franchise. **Magic**, officially Polémi, is the longest, broadest and wildest. **Sunny/Markos**, signposted as Psilós Gremós and easily walkable from Magic, has a taverna. **Langádha** is the cleanest and most picturesque, with junipers tumbling off its dunes. **Paradise**, often dubbed "Bubble Beach" because of volcanic gas vents in the tidal zone, is small and oversubscribed, with wall-to-wall sunbeds. **Camel** (Kamíla) is the smallest and loneliest, protected somewhat by the steep drive in.

Uninterrupted beach resumes at **Áyios Stéfanos**, overshadowed by a huge Club Med complex, and extends 5km west to Kamári (see below). A marked public access road leads down to the beach just west of a small peninsula, crowned with the exquisite remains of two triple-aisled, sixth-century basilicas. Though the best preserved on the island, several columns have been toppled since the 1980s, and wonderful bird mosaics languish under a permanent layer of "protective" gravel. The basilicas overlook tiny but striking Kastrí islet with its little chapel; in theory it's an easy swim (sometimes wading) across from the westerly beach, with some of the best snorkelling on Kós around the rock formations, but you must run the gauntlet of boats from the local water-ski school.

The far west

Essentially the shore annexe of Kéfalos (see below), **KAMÁRI** is a sprawling package resort of rapidly multiplying breeze-blocks, pitched a few notches above Kardhámena; it's a major watersports centre and an alternative departure point for Níssyros (up to five days weekly in season). *Stamatia*, near the main roundabout, is the oldest and (relatively) most authentic **taverna** hereabouts; one independent **hotel** that can be recommended is the simple *Maria* (☎02420/71 308; ❷), on the seafront west of the main road up to **KÉFALOS**, 43km from Kós Town. Squatting on a bluff looking down the length of the island, this is the end of the line for buses: a dull village but worth knowing about for its post office and as a staging point for expeditions into the rugged peninsula terminating dramatically at Cape Kríkello.

Main highlights of a half-day tour here, beginning along the widened ridge road south, are: a Byzantine church incorporating an ancient temple, 1km beyond the village; the late Classical theatre (unrestricted access), with two rows of seats remaining, and Hellenistic temple of **ancient Astypalia**, 500m further at the side-path signposted "Palatia"; and the cave of **Áspri Pétra** (inhabited during the Neolithic period), marked rather vaguely off the ridge road and requiring a half-hour walk to reach. A paved road west from just after Astypalia leads to an often windy beach and small chapel at **Áyios Theológos**, 7km from Kéfalos; the *Sunset Wave* taverna is a reliable option for a home-made sweet and coffee, though the fare in recent years has tended towards the hamburger-and-chips variety. Keeping to the main paved road until the end of the line brings you to the appealing (but usually locked) monastery of **Áyios Ioánnis Thymianós**, also 7km from the village.

About 1.5km north of Kéfalos on the road tracing the island's summit ridge, a paved side road covers the 2.7km to **Limniónas**, the only north-facing beach and fishing anchorage on this part of Kós. Of the two fish **tavernas** here, higher, hillside *Miltos* is preferable for excellent *orektiká*, home-made bread, and very fresh fish. Two compact sandy beaches sit either side of the peninsula.

Psérimos

Psérimos could be an idyllic little island were it not so close to Kós and Kálymnos. Throughout the season, both of these larger neighbours dispatch daily excursion boats, which compete strenuously to dock at the small harbour village of **AVLÁKIA**. In midsummer, day-trippers blanket the main sandy beach which curves around the bay in front of Avlákia's thirty-odd houses and huge communal olive grove; even during May or late September you're guaranteed at least a hundred outsiders daily (versus a permanent population of 25). There's a couple of other, somewhat less-attractive beaches to hide away on during the day: clean **Vathý** (sand and gravel), a well-marked, thirty-minute path-walk east, starting from behind the *Taverna Iy Pserimos*, or grubbier **Marathoúnda** (pebble), a 45-minute walk north on the main trans-island track. Nowhere on Psérimos, including the monastery of Grafiótissa (big festival Aug 15), is much more than an hour's walk away.

Even during the season there won't be too many other overnighters, since there's a limited number of beds available, and your reception at some of the more put-upon snack bars may become warmer once it's clear that you're **staying**. Pick of the several small pensions is *Tripolitis* (☏02430/23 196; ❶), over English-speaking *Nick and Anna's* café-snack bar, or the rooms above *Taverna Manola* on the opposite end of the beach (☏02430/51 540; ❶), who also keep the plusher *Studios Kalliston* next door (❷). There's just one small, limited-stock **store**, since most of the island's supplies are brought in daily from Kálymnos. Eating out however, won't break the bank, and there's often fresh fish in the handful of **tavernas**; many of these have contracts with the tour boats, but *Taverna Manola* doesn't, and despite modest appearances proves very adept at ouzerí fare and seafood.

Nearly all the **boats** based on Kós and Kálymnos harbour operate triangle tours (approximately €17.50), which involve departure between 9.30am and 10am, followed by a stop for swimming on either Platý islet or adjacent Psérimos, lunch in Avlákia, or Póthia, the port of Kálymnos (or even on board), and another swimming stop at whichever islet wasn't visited in the morning. If you want to spend the entire day on Psérimos, you're much better off departing Póthia at 9.30am daily on the tiny *Nissos Pserimos*, returning at 4pm (€6 round-trip). The islanders themselves use this boat to visit Kálymnos for shopping and administrative business; with just a bare handful of children, there is no longer a school on the island.

Astypálea

Geographically, historically and architecturally, **Astypálea** (alias Astropália) would be more at home among the Cyclades – on a clear day you can see Anáfi or Amorgós (to the southwest and northwest respectively) far more easily than any of the other Dodecanese. Moreover, Astypálea's inhabitants are descendants

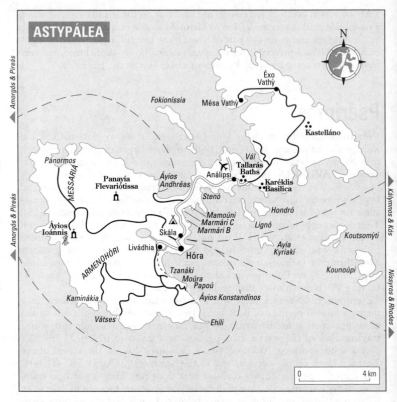

of medieval colonists from the Cyclades, and the island looks and feels more like these than its neighbours to the east.

Despite an evocative butterfly shape, Astypálea does not immediately impress you as the most beautiful of islands. The heights, which offer modest walking opportunities, are windswept and covered in thornbush or dwarf juniper. Yet the herb *alisfakiá*, brewed as a tea, flourishes too, and hundreds of sheep and goats manage to survive – as opposed to snakes, which are (uniquely in the Aegean) entirely absent. Lush citrus groves and vegetable patches in the valleys signal a relative abundance of water, hoarded in a reservoir. The various beaches along the bleak, heavily indented coastline often have reef underfoot and suffer periodic dumpings of seaweed.

In antiquity the island's most famous citizen was Kleomedes, a boxer disqualified from an early Olympic Games for causing the death of his opponent. He came home so enraged that he demolished the local school, killing all its pupils. Things have calmed down a bit in the intervening 2500 years, and today Astypálea is renowned mainly for its honey, fish and lobster (which finds its way into the local dish of *astakomakaronádha*); the abundant local catch has only been shipped to Athens since the late 1980s, a reflection of the traditionally poor ferry links in every direction. These have improved recently with the introduction of extra services towards Piréas via select Cyclades, and high-season links with Rhodes via a few intervening islets, but outside July or August you still risk being marooned here for a day or two longer than intended. There is, curiously, no conventional package tourism here since Laskarina Holidays deleted the island from their list in 1995, frustrated by chronically unreliable connections to Kós and its airport.

Despite this relative isolation, plenty of people find their way to Astypálea during the short, intense midsummer season (mid-July to the first Sept Sun before school starts), when the 1500 permanent inhabitants are all but over-run by upwards of 7000 guests a day. Most arrivals are Athenians, French or Italians, supplemented by large numbers of yachties and foreign owners of holiday homes in the understandably popular Hóra. At such times you won't find a bed without reserving well in advance, and camping rough is expressly frowned upon.

Skála and Hóra

The main harbour of **SKÁLA** or Péra Yialós dates from the Italian era (Astypálea was the first island the Italians occupied in the Dodecanese) and most of the settlement between the quay and the line of nine windmills is even more recent. Its only real bright spot is a 1998-inaugurated **archeological museum** (June–Sept Tues–Sun 8am–2pm & 6pm–midnight, Oct–May Tues–Sun 8am–2pm; free), a single well-lit room crammed with the best local finds spanning all historical periods from the Bronze Age to medieval times.

As you climb up beyond the port towards **HÓRA**, however, the neighbour-hoods get progressively older and more attractive, their steep streets enlivened by the photogenic *poúndia*, or colourful wooden balconies-with-stairways of the whitewashed houses, which owe much to the building styles of Mýkonos and Tínos, the origins of the colonists brought to repopulate the island in 1413. The whole culminates in the thirteenth-century **kástro**, one of the finest in the Aegean, erected not by the Knights but by the Venetian Quirini clan and sub-sequently modified by the Ottomans after 1537. Until well into the twentieth century over three hundred people lived inside the *kástro*, but depopulation and a severe 1956 earthquake combined to leave only a desolate shell today. The fine rib vaulting over the main west gate supports the church of Evangelístria Kastrianí, one of two intact here, the other being Áyios Yeóryios (both usually locked). Currently the *kástro* grounds are in the throes of a consolidation and restoration project undertaken by the Byzantine antiquities authority, designed to keep the perimeter fortifications from crumbling further.

Skála, and to a lesser extent Hóra, have **accommodation** ranging from spar-tan, 1970s-vintage rooms to new luxury studios; proprietors tend not to meet ferries unless arrangements have been made, even if they have vacancies. Owing to high-season harbour noise – particularly the sound of ferries drop-ping anchor at 3am – you might prefer more atmospheric restored studios or entire houses (€73.50 for 2 peak season, but just €29.40 low) up in Hóra if uninterrupted sleep is a priority; enquire at Kostas Vaïkousis' antique shop on the quay or reserve in advance on ☎02430/61 430. Rather plusher are the 2000-built *Kilindra Studios* on the quiet west slope of Hóra (☎02430/61 966, ⓕ61 131, ⓦhttp://astypalea.com/kilindra; open all year), offering luxury amenities including a swimming pool – units accommodate two to four peo-ple, with the smallest at €88 (€59 low season).

Otherwise, the obvious, bog-standard port **hotels** are the 1993-refurbished *Astynea* (☎02430/61 040, ⓕ61 209; ❸) and the elderly but fairly well-kept *Paradisos* (☎02430/61 224, ⓕ61 450; ❸), both en-suite with sea views. Of two backpackers' standbys on the east shore of the bay, *Akti Rooms* (☎02430/61

281; ❹) are much better equipped and maintained than the misnamed *Karlos Studios* (☎02460/61 330; ❸), actually large rooms which are only worth it if you get a seaview unit. A small, basic, seasonal **campsite** operates amongst calamus reeds and tamarisks behind Dhéftero Marmári Bay (see opposite), about 4km along the road to Análipsi, but it can be mosquito-plagued any year after a wet winter (an increasingly rare occurrence).

During August, upwards of 25 **tavernas** and beach snack-bars operate across the island, few of them memorable and many concerned primarily with turning a quick profit. Among the more reliable Skála options, *Iy Monaxia* (aka *Viki's*), one block inland from the ferry jetty by the old power plant, has excellent home-style cooking and is open all year round. The *Astropalia* (closes end Sept) on the hillside above the street up to Hóra, does good, if somewhat pricey, fish and not much else; there's even better seafood, and superbly prepared own-grown vegetable dishes, at the homey *Australia* (open all year), just inland from the head of the bay. Behind the *Hotel Paradhisos*, you'll find more careful cooking, polished presentation (and much higher prices) at *Aitherio* and *Maïstrali* (both open into Oct); it's pot-luck as to which is better any given night. Under the *Astynea* you'll find two more worthy options: *To Steki* for grills, and the *Dapia Café*, for full breakfasts, midday crepes and homemade ice cream.

Most **nightlife** happens up in more atmospheric Hóra, where the esplanade between the windmills and the base of the *kástro* seems to be one solid café-bar. Of these, the favourites are the unsigned *Tou Nikola* (*Iy Mylí*) on the corner, with the island's characters in residence, and the all-purpose *Aigaion* on the opposite side, which does snacks in season. All these are joined in season by music bars such as long-lived *Kastro*, best for conversation-level music, and the newer *Panorama* where the island's youth hang out until dawn. The **post office** and most shops are here, though the island's only **bank** (Emboriki/Commercial), complete with cash dispenser, is down in Skála by the port police.

Two **buses** run along the paved road between Hóra, Skála, Livádhia and Análipsi, frequently in July and August from 8am until 11pm, much less regularly out of season. There are only two official **taxis**, far too few to cope with passenger numbers in season; several places rent out **scooters**, the most reliable being Lakis and Manolis (☎02430/61 263), with branches at Hóra and Skála dock, and also renting out a few cars and jeeps. The island **map** sold locally is grossly inaccurate, even by lenient Greek-island standards, though in compensation rural junctions are adequately signposted.

Around the island

A twenty-minute walk (or a short bus journey) from Hóra brings you to **LIVÁDHIA**, a fertile valley with a popular, good beach with a variable collection of restaurants and cafés immediately behind. You can rent a **room or studio** just inland – for example at *Studios O Manganas* (☎02430/61 68; ❺), on the frontage road, representing the highest standard here, or *Venetos Studios & Bungalows* (☎02430/61 490; ❹), on the westerly hillside. Among the half-dozen **tavernas**, *To Yerani* is about the most consistently open (until Oct) and renowned for its excellent *mayireftá*; they also keep simple rooms adjacent (☎02430/61 484; ❸).

If the busy beach here doesn't suit, continue southwest fifteen minutes on foot to three small single coves at **Tzanáki**, packed out with naturists in midsummer. The third large bay beyond Livádhia, more easily reached by motorbike, is **Áyios Konstandínos**, a partly shaded, sand-and-gravel cove with a good seasonal taverna. Around the headland, the lonely beaches of **Vátses** and **Kaminákia** are more usually visited by excursion boat from Skála, subject to weather and captain's whim. By land, Vátses has the easier dirt road in, some twenty minutes by scooter from Livádhia; it's one of the sandier island beaches but prone to wind. The track to Kaminákia is atrocious in its final moments, but the sheltered, clean scenic cove makes the effort worthwhile; like Vátses it has a simple *kantína*, staying open into September.

A favourite outing in the west of the island is the two-hour walk or half-hour motorbike trip from Hóra to the oasis of **Áyios Ioánnis**, just under 10km distant. Proceed northwest along the signposted paved road beginning from the windmills, then keep left when a side-track goes right to Panayía Flevariotíssas monastery. Beyond this point the main track, briefly dampened by a spring seeping across the road surface, curls north towards farming cottages at Messariá before reaching a junction with gates across each option. Take the left-hand one, and soon the walled orchards of the uninhabited farm-monastery of Áyios Ioánnis come into view. From the balcony of the church, a steep, faint path leads down to the base of a ten-metre waterfall, though alas, after several dry years, the bathing pools here have dried up.

Northeast of the harbour are three coves known as **Próto** (First), **Dhéftero** (Second) and **Tríto** (Third) **Mármari**, and marked as **Marmári A'**, **B'** and **C'** respectively on some maps. The first is home to the power plant and boatyards; the next hosts the campsite (see opposite); while the third, reasonably attractive, also marks the start of the path east to the perfectly decent coves of unfortunately named **Mamoúni** ("Bug" or "Critter" in Greek). Beyond Tríto Marmári, the middle beach at **Stenó** ("narrow", after the isthmus here), with sandy shore and shallows, a few tamarisks and a seasonal *kantína*, is the best.

ANÁLIPSI, widely known as **Maltezána** after medieval Maltese pirates, is a ten-kilometre bus trip or taxi ride from town. Although the second-largest settlement on Astypálea, there's surprisingly little for outsiders save a narrow, sea-urchin-speckled beach (there are better ones east of the main bay) and a nice view south to some islets. Despite this, blocks of **rooms** (open only July & Aug) sprout in ranks well back from the sea, spurred by the proximity of the airport, 700m away. Among a handful of tavernas, the most reliably open (Feb–Christmas) is *Analipsi* (aka *Irini's*, after the proprietress) by the jetty, which doubles as the kafenío for the local fishermen and seemingly every passing worker on the island. The food – fish fry-ups, or *kakaviá* (fish soup) for those willing to wait – is simple but excellent and normally priced. At a somewhat higher mark-up, but also high-quality, is *Ovelix* a few hundred yards inland, where you have to pre-order your fish (✆02430/61 260; closes mid-Sept). Behind calamus reeds and eucalyptus near the fishing jetty lie the best-preserved mosaic floors on the island: those of the Byzantine **Tallarás baths**, with somewhat crude figures of zodiacal signs, the seasons personified, and a central androgynous figure (Time or Fortune) holding the cosmic orb.

The motorable dirt track ends 23km from Hóra at **MÉSA VATHÝ** (invariably and erroneously shown on most maps as Éxo Vathý), a sleepy fishing village with a single **taverna** (*Iy Galini*) and superb small-craft anchorage in what's an almost landlocked inlet. Frankly, though, it's not really worth the long, bumpy trip out unless you're a yachtie, and to rub salt in the wound, the fish on the menu is usually frozen (if local). Following several accidents, this is no longer the **backup ferry port** in winter, when Skála is buffeted by the prevailing southerlies; foot passengers (but no vehicles) are transferred ashore to the unlit quay at **Áyios Andhréas**, just west of Tríto Marmári.

Kálymnos

Most of the 17,000-strong population of **Kálymnos** lives in or around the large port of Póthia, a wealthy but not conventionally beautiful town, famed for its sponge industry. Unfortunately, almost all of the eastern Mediterranean's sponges were devastated by a mysterious disease in 1986, related to freak warm currents, and only three or four of the fleet of thirty-odd boats are still in use. In response to this catastrophe (and a smaller repeat outbreak in 1999), the island established a tourist industry – confined to one string of beach resorts – and also retro-fitted most of its sponge boats for deep-sea fishing. Warehouses behind the harbour still process and sell sponges all year round, though most of these are imported from Asia and the Caribbean. There are also still numbers of elderly gentlemen about who rely on two canes, walking frames or even wheelchairs, stark evidence of the havoc wrought in their youth by nitrogen embolism (the "bends"), long before divers understood its crippling effects. The departure of the remaining sponge fleet, usually just after Easter, is preceded by a festive week known as *Yprogrós*, with food, drink and music; the fleet's return, approximately six months later, has historically also been the occasion for more uproarious, male-oriented celebration in the port's bars.

Kálymnos essentially consists of two cultivated and inhabited valleys sandwiched between three limestone ridges, harsh in the full glare of noon but magically tinted towards dusk. The climate, especially in winter, is alleged to be drier and healthier than that of neighbouring Kós or Léros, since the quick-draining limestone strata, riddled with many caves, doesn't retain as much moisture. The rock does, however, admit seawater, which has tainted Póthia's wells; drinking water must be brought in by tanker truck from the Vathýs valley, and there are also potable springs at Dhámos, Potamí district of Póthia and Hóra.

Since Kálymnos is the home port of the very useful local namesake ferry (see p.360), a minor hub for Kyriakoulis Maritime hydrofoils, and moreover where the long-distance ferry lines from the Cyclades and Astypálea join up with the main Dodecanesian routes, many travellers arrive unintentionally, and are initially most concerned with how to move on quickly. Yet Kálymnos has sufficient attractions to justify a stay of several days while island-hopping – or even longer, as the package industry at the western beaches suggests.

Póthia

PÓTHIA (sometimes pronounced Pothiá), without being obviously picturesque, is colourful and authentically Greek, its houses marching up the valley inland or arrayed in tiers up the sides of the mountains framing it. Your first and overwhelming impression will be of the phenomenal amount of noise engendered by motorbike traffic and the cranked-up sound systems of the half-dozen waterfront cafés. This is not entirely surprising, since with nearly 16,000 inhabitants, Póthia recently overtook Kós Town as the second-largest municipality in the Dodecanese, after Ródhos Town.

Perhaps the most rewarding way to acquaint yourself with Póthia is by wandering the backstreets, where elegant Neoclassical houses are surrounded by surprisingly large gardens, and craftsmen ply their trade in a genuine workaday bazaar. The Pothians particularly excel in iron-working, and all but the humblest dwellings in the eastern Evangelístria district are adorned by superbly ornate banisters, balcony railings and fanlights. During the Italian occupation, many local houses were painted blue and white to irritate the colonial overlords, and though the custom has all but died out, the Greek national colours still appear amongst more traditional pink and ochre buildings.

Of the two local museums, priority should be given to the **Municipal Nautical and Folklore Museum** (Mon–Fri 8am–1.30pm, Sat–Sun 10am–12.30pm; €1.50), on the seaward side of Khristós cathedral. A large photo in the foyer shows Póthia as it was in the 1880s, with no quay, jetty, roads or sumptuous mansions, and with most of the population still up in Hóra, while other photos document sponge-fishing and the Allied liberation of 1945. Three-dimensional exhibits include horribly primitive divers' breathing apparatuses, and "cages" designed to keep propellers from cutting air lines, a constant fear. The local **archeological museum** (Tues–Sun 10am–2pm; free guided tours only) is installed in a grand former residence of the Vouvallis family of sponge magnates. A rather eclectic collection, including a kitsch-furnished Second Empire parlour and small troves from the island's several caves, it's not exactly required viewing.

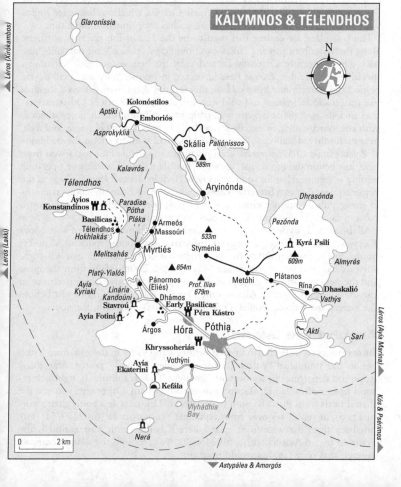

Practicalities

Accommodation is rarely a problem, since *dhomátia* proprietors usually meet the ferries (though many of the premises touted are substandard, unlicensed or remote, often all three). The town's best, and quietest **hotel**, near the Vouvalis museum, is the garden-set *Villa Themelina* (℡02430/22 682, ℉23 920, 🅦www.griechenland.com/io2/reisen/302.html; ❸; open all year but no breakfast Oct–Easter), housed in an early-twentieth-century mansion (another Vouvalis property) plus modern studio annexes (❹), with breakfast patio and a large swimming pool. The high-ceiling, bug-screened, wood-floored rooms in the main house make this Kálymnos's most elegant accommodation. Next niche down, on the west quay but fairly quiet, is occupied by the *Arhondiko* (℡02430/24 051, ℉24 149; ❸), another refurbished mansion whose somewhat plain rooms have TV and fridge; some also have balconies, though promised heating/air-con has not materialized. Two places in Amoudhára district (west of the harbour) are worth contacting in advance: the en-suite *Pension Greek House* (℡02430/29 559; ❶; open most of year) with volubly friendly management and kitsch decor; and considerably above this, the well-signposted, well-kept *Hotel Panorama* (℡02430/22 917, ℉23 138; April–Oct; ❸), which has balconied rooms with views and a pleasant breakfast salon; studios are planned in the future.

The best place for **eating out** used to be the line of fish tavernas northeast along the waterfront past the Italian-built municipal "palace", but standards here have dipped recently. Currently far and away the best seafood and Kalymnian specialties are found at *Taverna Pandelis*, tucked inconspicuously into a cul-de-sac behind the waterfront *Olympic Hotel*; this features daily, fresh-gathered shellfish like *foúskes* and *kalógnomes* and wild scaly fish at reasonable prices. Other alternatives include *mayireftá* at *Xefteris*, well signposted inland from Khristós cathedral, with courtyard seating, or excellent wood-fired pizzas at *Porto Kalymnos* and *Imia*, near each other at mid-quay. Sticky-cake fans will want to attend the traditional *Zaharoplastiki O Mihalaras* back on restaurant row, while four paces west from here, just before the municipal "palace", *Apothiki* is an old warehouse operating reliably as a musical bar for some years now. Back by *Taverna Pandelis*, *Nefeli* is the better equipped of two **internet cafés**, while adjacent *Escape* functions as another music pub. A summer **cinema**, Cine Oasis, operates behind the traditional, column-facaded café-tearoom *Ai Musai*, on the front.

All **boat** and **hydrofoil** agents, including the headquarters of the *Nissos Kalymnos*, plus a municipal **tourist information** booth (sporadic Mon–Fri hours), line the waterfront as you bear right out of the pier-area gate. Olympic Airways has an office at Patriárhou Maxímou 12, 200m inland from the quay, and the new airport near Árgos village is supposed to commence operations in late 2002 (flights to/from Athens only). Finally, four **banks** on or just behind the waterfront (Ethniki, Alpha, Emboriki, Agrotiki) have cash dispensers.

Around the island

Buses run as far as Emborió in the northwest and Vathý in the east, from a stop beside the municipal "palace", with schedules helpfully posted near many stops, and departures in season fairly frequent. Tickets must be bought beforehand from authorized kiosks, and cancelled on board. Otherwise, you can use shared **taxis** from Platía Kýprou (more than KTEL rates, less costly than a normal taxi), or rent a **scooter** from reputable Scootermania (℡02430/51 780), just back from the waterfront, near where it bends south. **Car rental** is also available (eg an Avis franchise, ℡02430/28 990), though the island's compact enough that only families would need one.

The castles and basilicas

Just over 1km northwest of Póthia, in the suburb of Mýli, is a castle of the Knights of Saint John, **Kástro Khryssoheriás** (unrestricted access). From the whitewashed battlements there are wonderful views southeast over town to Kós, and north towards Hóra and Péra Kástro. The former Kalymnian capital of **HÓRA** (aka Horió), 1.5km further along the main road, is still a village of nearly three thousand inhabitants, and guards a critical pass in local geography, focus of settlement in every era. Steep steps lead up from its eastern edge to the Byzantine citadel-town of **Péra Kástro** (daily May–Oct 10am–2pm; tip to guide), appropriated by the Knights of Saint John and inhabited until late in the eighteenth century. Inside the imposing gate the former heaps of rubble are slowly being re-pieced together; a guided tour by the warden visits five well-maintained, whitewashed chapels, containing late medieval fresco fragments.

Some 200m past the turning for Árgos en route to the northwest coast from Horió, you can detour briefly left to visit two early Byzantine basilicas which are fairly representative, and among the easiest to find, of a vast number on Kálymnos. The more impressive of the two, accessed by whitewashed steps on the left just as the highway begins to descend, is that of **Khristós tís Ierousalím**, probably dating from the late fourth century, with its apse fully preserved; the three-aisled **Limniótissa** church in an adjacent field is larger but considerably less intact.

West coast resorts

From the basilicas, the road dips into a tree-shaded valley leading to the con-secutive **beach resorts** of Kandoúni, Myrtiés and Massoúri, collectively referred to as "Brostá" by islanders. **KANDOÚNI**, some 200m of brown, hard-packed sand favoured by the locals, is the shore annexe of the rich agricultur-al valley-village of **Pánormos** (aka Eliés). Accommodation closest to the water here is monopolized by tour companies, and for both bathing and staying you're better off at **Linária**, the north end of the same bay. A smaller cove set apart from Kandoúni proper by a rock outcrop, this has better sand and the possibility of **staying** at *Skopellos Studios* (T02430/47 155; ❸), on the slope below the church. For **eating**, the best option is *Ouzeri Giannis/Ta Linaria* on the shore, with leisurely service but abundant portions of grills and seafood.

The next beach north, **PLATÝ-YIALÓS**, though again a bit shorter than Kandoúni, is arguably the best on the island: cleaner than its southern neigh-bours, more secluded, and placed scenically at the base of a cliff, opposite Ayía Kyriakí islet. A lone **taverna** (*Kyma*), right behind the sand at road's end, will do for lunch (closes at sunset). Among a handful of choices for **staying** on spec, long-time favourite is the Vavoulas family's *Pension Plati Gialos* (T02430/47 029, Wwww.pension-plati-gialos.de), actually overlooking Linária, recently improved with extended balconies, mosquito nets and a breakfast terrace; choose between rooms (❷) or two apartments for four (€44).

The main road climbs from Pánormos up to a pass, where the *Hotel Kamari* (T02430/47 278, F48 130; ❷) is another non-packaged possibility, with views from most rooms, before descending in zigzags to meet the sea again 8km from Póthia at **MYRTIÉS**. Together with **MASSOÚRI** (1km north) and **ARMEÓS** (2km north and end of the line for most buses), it sees the lion's share of Kálymnos tourism: all too many neon-lit music bars, "special menus", souvenir shops and the other accoutrements of the package trade. The beach at Myrtiés is narrow, pebbly and cramped by development, though it does improve as you approach Massoúri. The closest all-sand beach to Myrtiés lies 500m south, at **Melitsahás** cove (Melitsáhas in dialect), which also has the only locally patronized **taverna** at its fishing anchorage, *Iy Dhrossia* (all year), best for oysters, lobster and shrimp as well as scaly fish at affordable rates. Most local **accommodation** is block-booked by overseas companies; remote exceptions enjoying spectacular views include the largish *Maria's Studios* (☎02430/48 135 or 28 528; ❷), above Melitsahás, or *Studios Niki's* (☎02430/47 201; ❷), up on the higher one-way bypass road between Myrtiés and Massoúri. Possibly this coast's most appealing feature is its position opposite the evocatively shaped islet of Télendhos (see below), which frames some of the most dramatic sunsets in Greece. It's also possible to go from Myrtiés directly to Xirókambos on Léros aboard the daily early-afternoon **kaïki**.

Some 5km beyond Massoúri, **ARYINÓNDA** has a clean pebble beach backed by a single **rooms** outfit (*Arginonta Beach* ☎02430/40 000; ❶), with a friendly proprietor, and a few beach **tavernas**. It is also the trailhead for the spectacular two-and-a-half-hour walk inland and over two gentle passes to Metóhi in the Vathý valley. From the bus-stop and gravelled car-park area and small spring, head southeast on a path between rock walls which soon climbs the south flank of the ravine here, sporadically marked by paint dots. Don't believe sources which show the route emerging at Styménia, and be aware that in the future the municipality intends to bulldoze a road from just above the *Arginonta Beach* to Styménia, which may disrupt the first half-hour or so of the trail. You'll need a sun hat, stout shoes and a litre or so of water, as the next source is in Plátanos hamlet, beyond Metóhi.

The end of the bus line, **EMBORIÓS**, 20km from the port, offers a gravel-and-sand beach, which improves as you head west, **accommodation** (much of it taken up by Laskarina Holidays) and a number of **tavernas**, including the long-running *Harry's Paradise*, with attached, air-conditioned garden apartments (☎02430/40 061; ❹) in bland white-and-pine decor, and *Kapetan Kostas*, closer to the sea. If the twice-daily bus service fails you, there is usually a shuttle boat back to Myrtiés at 4pm (leaving the latter at 10am).

Télendhos

The trip across the strait to the striking, volcanic-plug islet of **TÉLENDHOS** is arguably the best reason to come to Myrtiés; little boats shuttle to and fro constantly throughout the day and late into the night. According to local legend, Télendhos is a petrified princess, gazing out to sea after her errant lover; the woman's-head profile is most evident at dusk. The hardly less pedestrian geological explanation has the islet sundered from Kálymnos by a cataclysmic earthquake in 554 AD; traces of a submerged town are said to lie at the bottom of the straits.

Home to about fifteen permanent inhabitants, Télendhos is car-free and blissfully tranquil, though even here package tourism has arrived in a fairly big way. For cultural edification you'll find the ruined thirteenth-century **monastery of Áyios Vassílios** and an enormous, 1997-excavated **basilica of Ayía Triádha** up on the ridge, part way along the flagstoned, ten-minute path to **Hokhlakás** pebble beach, which is small but very scenic, with sunbeds for rent.

There are about eight places to **eat** and a roughly equal number of **accommodation** establishments, most (but not all) linked to the tavernas. Establishments that get uniformly positive reviews include *Barba Stathis* taverna en route to Hokhlakás; *Pension Studios Rita* (☎02430/47 914, ℱ47 927; ❷), rooms and renovated-house studios managed by the namesake snack-bar/café; the simple but en-suite rooms above the worthy *Zorba's* (☎02430/48 660; ❶) or, north beyond Áyios Vassílios, the Greek-Australian-run *On the Rocks*. This combines the functions of superbly appointed rooms with double glazing, mosquito nets and so on

(☎02430/48 260, ℱ48 261, ⓦwww.telendos.com/otr; ❹), full-service taverna with lovely home-made desserts, and a bar that's the heart and soul of local **nightlife** (including Mon & Fri "Greek Nights"). At one corner of the premises you can visit yet another Byzantine monument, the chapel of Áyios Harálambos, occupying a former bathhouse. If you want more (relative) luxury on Télendhos, you'll have to squeeze in between packages at the *Hotel Porto Potha* (☎02430/47 321, ℱ48 108, ⓔportopotha@klm.forthnet.gr; ❷), set rather bleakly at the very edge of things but with a large pool and friendly managing family.

Vathýs

The first four kilometres east from Póthia seem vastly unpromising (power plant, rubbish tip, multiple gasworks and quarries), until you round a bend and the ten-kilometre ride ends dramatically at **VATHÝS**, a long, fertile valley, carpeted with orange and tangerine groves, whose colour provides a startling contrast to the mineral greys and oranges higher up on Kálymnos. At the simple fjord port of **RÍNA**, more ruined basilicas flank the bay; near the southerly one is the best accommodation option, the helpful *Rooms Manolis* (☎02430/41 300; ❶). Some of the five tavernas are pricier than you'd expect, owing to patronage from the numerous yachts which call here; currently the best choice, with shambolic service but good grilled fish, is *The Harbor*, first place on the right at road's end.

The steep-sided inlet has no beach to speak of, so people swim off the artificial lido on the far right; the closest pebble-coves reachable overland are **Aktí**, about 3km back towards Póthia, a functional pebble strand with sunbeds and a single snack bar, and **Pezónda**, a little further north, reached by steep track (and then a 45-minute walk northwest) starting from Metóhi hamlet. At track's end another path heads east in fifteen minutes to the amazingly set little **monastery of Kyrá Psilí**, frequented only on August 15.

Boat excursions sometimes visit the stalactite cave of **Dhaskalió**, inhabited in Neolithic times, out towards the fjord mouth on its north flank, and the remoter, tiny beaches of **Almyrés** and **Dhrasónda**, accessible only by sea.

It's possible to **walk** back to Póthia along the old direct *kalderími* which existed before the coastal highway – a two-hour jaunt which begins in Plátanos hamlet. The route is tricky to find in this direction, however, so most people start in Póthia, at the church of Ayía Triádha behind the *Villa Themelina* hotel – the way is marked initially by red paint splodges.

The southwest

Some 6km southwest of Póthia, the small bay of **Vlyhádhia** is reached via a narrow ravine draining from the nondescript village of Vothýni. The sand-and-pebble beach here isn't really worth a special trip, since the bay is apt to be sumpy and at least some of the locals (who have blotted out all Roman-alphabet road signs) are resentful of foreigners. If you're interested in **scuba diving**, the Vlyhádhia area is one of the limited number of legal diving areas in Greece. Stavros Valsamidhes, the local divemaster, has also assembled an impressive **Museum of Submarine Finds** (Mon–Sat 9am–7pm, Sun 10am–2pm; free), which in addition to masses of sponges and shells offers a reconstructed ancient wreck with amphorae and World War II debris. Depending on your ability, dives (arrange in advance on ☎02430/50 662; €30 for one dive, €53 for two) may visit ancient wrecks *in situ*, as well as seal caves.

Póthia-based kaïkia make well-publicized excursions to the cave of **Kefála** just west of Vlyhádhia, the most impressive of half a dozen caverns around the island. You have to walk thirty minutes from where the boats dock, but the vividly coloured formations repay the effort; the cave was inhabited before recorded history, and later served as a sanctuary of Zeus (who is fancifully identified with a particularly imposing stalagmite in the biggest of six chambers).

Léros

Léros is so indented with deep, sheltered anchorages that during World War II it harboured, in turn, the entire Italian, German and British Mediterranean fleets. Unfortunately, many of these magnificent fjords and bays seem to absorb rather than reflect light, and the island's relative fertility can seem scraggly and unkempt when compared with the crisp lines of its more barren neighbours. These characteristics, plus the island's lack of spectacularly good beaches, meant that until the late 1980s just a few thousand foreigners (mostly Italians who grew up on the island), and not many more Greeks, came to visit each year, mostly in August.

Such a pattern is now history, with German, Dutch, Danish and British package operators at the vanguard of those "discovering" Léros and the company of

islanders unjaded by mass tourism. Foreign-visitor numbers have, however, levelled off since the late 1990s, with matters unlikely to change until and unless the tiny airport is expanded to accommodate jets.

Not that Léros needs, or strenuously encourages, mass tourism; various **prisons and sanatoriums** have dominated the Lerian economy since the 1950s, directly or indirectly employing about a third of the population. During the junta era, the island hosted a notorious detention centre at Parthéni, and today the mental hospital on Léros remains the repository for many of Greece's more intractable psychiatric cases; another asylum is home to hundreds of mentally handicapped children. The island's domestic image problem is compounded by its name, the butt of jokes by mainlanders who pounce on its similarity to the word *lerá*, connoting rascality and unsavouriness.

In 1989, a major scandal emerged concerning the administration of the various asylums, with EU maintenance and development funds found to have been embezzled by administrators and staff, and the inmates kept in degrading and inhumane conditions. Since then, an influx of EU inspectors, foreign psychiatrists and extra funding have resulted in drastic improvements in patient treatment, including the establishment of halfway houses across the island.

More obvious is the legacy of the **Battle of Léros** on November 12–16, 1943, when overwhelming German forces displaced a Commonwealth division which had landed on the island following the Italian capitulation. Bomb nose-cones and shell casings still turn up as gaily painted garden ornaments in the courtyards of churches and tavernas, or have been pressed into service as gateposts. Each year for three days following September 26, memorial services and a naval festival commemorate the sinking of the Greek battleships *Queen Olga* and *Intrepid* during the German attack.

Unusually for a small island, Léros has abundant ground water, channelled into potable cisterns at several points. These, plus low-lying ground staked with the avenues of eucalyptus trees planted by the Italians, make for an unusually active mosquito contingent, so come prepared. The island is compact enough to walk around, with sufficient hills to give mountain-bikers a good work-out. There is a reasonable bus service, plus several scooter- and bicycle-rental outfits, of which Motoland (branches at Álynda and Pandélli) have proven the most reliable.

Lakkí and Xirókambos

All large **ferries** arrive at the main port of **LAKKÍ**, once the headquarters of a bustling, purpose-built Italian naval base. Boulevards far too wide for today's paltry amount of traffic are lined with some marvellous Art Deco edifices, including the round-fronted cinema (closed since 1985), the primary and secondary schools, a shopping centre with a round atrium and the defunct *Leros Palace Hotel*.

Buses don't meet the ferries – instead there's a taxi squadron that charges set fares to standard destinations. Few people stay willingly at any of the handful of moribund hotels in Lakkí, preferring to head straight for the resorts of Pandélli, Álynda or Vromólithos (see overleaf). There's just one bona fide **taverna**, *To Petrino*, inland next to the **post office**, two cash dispensers attached to the National/Ethniki and Commercial/Emboriki **banks**, and Gribelos/Leros Travel, the island's sole G&A Ferries agent. The nearest approximation of a **beach** is at sand-and-gravel **Koulóuki**, 500m west, where there's a seasonal taverna and some pines for shade, though it's too close to the ferry jetty for most tastes. You can carry on another kilometre or so to **Merikiá**, which is a slight improvement and also has a taverna.

XIRÓKAMBOS, nearly 5km from Lakkí in the far south of the island, is the point of arrival for the afternoon kaïki from Myrtiés on Kálymnos (it goes back very early the following morning). Though billed as a resort, it's essentially a fishing port where folk also happen to swim – the beach here is poor to mediocre, improving as you head west. **Accommodation** is available at *Villa Maria* (✆02470/22 827; ❷) on the beach or, for a higher standard, the *Hotel Efstathia* (✆02470/24 099; ❹), actually studio apartments with huge, well-furnished doubles as well as family fourplexes, plus a large pool. **Meals** can be had at *Taverna Tzitzifies*, just by the jujube trees at the east end of things, where the road hits the shore. The island's **campsite** (✆02470/23 367), with an in-house scuba-diving centre, is in an olive grove at the village of **LEPÍDHA**, 750m back up the road to Lakkí. Just north of the site, an access drive on the far side of the road leads up a tiny acropolis with stretches of ancient masonry and sparse patches of early Christian mosaics.

Pandélli and Vromólithos

Just less than 3km north of Lakkí, Pandélli and Vromólithos together form the fastest-growing resort on the island – and are certainly two of the more attractive and scenic places to stay, if not eat.

PANDÉLLI is still very much a working port, the cement jetty benefiting local fishermen as well as an increasing number of yachts which call here. A negligible beach is compensated for by a relative abundance of non-package **accommodation**, such as the *Pension Happiness* (✆02470/23 498; ❷) where the road down from Plátanos meets the sea, or, for a higher standard, the *Niki Studios* (✆02470/25 600; ❸) at the base of the road to the castle, airy, Aussie-run and with partial sea views. Up on the ridge dividing Pandélli from Vromólithos, the *Pension Fanari* (✆02470/23 152; ❷) would seem a good choice for its calm setting below the road and views across to the castle, though hot-water provision was defective at our last stay. Further south along the ridge road, the en-suite *Hotel Rodon* (✆02470/23 524; ❷) is another possibility, though a potentially noisy (but recommended; see below) restaurant operates right next door, as does the musical *Beach Bar*, perched on a rock terrace below, facing Vromólithos. The other long-lived local **bar** is the civilized *Savana*, at the opposite end of Pandélli, beyond the row of waterfront **tavernas** which, alas, have in recent years mostly become tourist traps of the first order. Exceptions include *Psaropoula*, with good fish and *mayireftá*; *Kafenio tou Tzouma*, a seafood ouzerí; and the taverna adjacent to *Hotel Rodon*, *Dimitris*, which scores highly for its stuffed squash blossoms (in autumn) and chunky, herby Lerian sausages.

VROMÓLITHOS boasts the best easily accessible **beach** on the island, car-free and hemmed in by hills studded with massive oaks. The shoreline is gravel and coarse sand, and the sea here is clean, but as so often on Léros you have to cross a nasty, sharp reef at most points before reaching deeper water. Two **tavernas** behind the beach trade more on their location than their cuisine, but the standard of **accommodation** here is higher than at Pandélli, with the result that much of it tends to be monopolized by package companies.

Plátanos and Ayía Marína

The Neoclassical and vernacular houses of **PLÁTANOS**, the island capital 1km west of Pandélli, are draped gracefully along a saddle between two hills, one of them crowned by the inevitable Knights' castle. Known locally as the **Kástro**, this is reached either by a paved but potholed road peeling off the Pandélli road, or via a more scenic stair-path from the central square; the battlements, and the views from them, are dramatic, especially near sunrise or sunset. The medieval church of **Panayía toú Kástrou** inside the gate houses a small museum (daily 8am–1pm & 4–7.30pm; €1.50), though its carved *témblon* and naive oratory are more remarkable than the sparse exhibits, which are mostly icons and other liturgical items.

Except for *Hotel Eleftheria* (☎02470/23 550; ❷), with a peaceful hillside location, Plátanos is not really a place to stay or eat, although it's well sown with **shops** and **services**. The latter include Olympic Airways, south of the turning for Pandélli, a **post office**, down the road towards Ayía Marína, and two **banks** (one with a cash dispenser). The single **bus** (schedule posted at the stop, opposite the island's main **taxi** rank) plies four to six times daily between Parthéni in the north and Xirókambos in the south.

Plátanos merges seamlessly with **AYÍA MARÍNA**, 1km north on the shore of a fine bay, still graced by a small, Italian-built public market building. If you're travelling to Léros on an excursion boat, catamaran or hydrofoil, this will be your port of entry. Although accommodation here is very limited, it's arguably the best place to **eat** on the island. Just west of the police station, on the water, *Mezedhopolio tou Kapaniri* is a good, reasonable ouzerí, at its best after dark, featuring plenty of fried vegetable first courses. Just inland opposite the Agrotiki Trapeza in a little alley, the *Kapetan Mihalis* ouzerí claims to be open all day and offers a range of inexpensive local specialities, including various fish marinated in salt (*pastós*). Further west, the *Ouzeri Neromylos*, out by the marooned windmill, serves a wide variety of dishes. A semblance of **nightlife** is provided by a half-dozen bars, such as *Enallaktiko*, with a few **internet** terminals, and *Harama* on the quay. Kastis Travel nearby (☎02470/22 140) is about the most useful travel agency on the island, plus there's a stand-alone **cash dispenser** on the quay.

Álynda and the north

ÁLYNDA, 3km northwest of Ayía Marína, ranks as the longest-established resort on Léros, with development just across the road from a long, narrow strip of pea-gravel beach. It's also the first area for accommodation to open in spring, and the last to shut in autumn. Many of the half-dozen **hotels** and **pensions** here are block-booked by tour companies, but you may have better luck at two outfits overlooking the war cemetery: *Hotel Gianna* (☎02470/23 153; ❸), with fridge-equipped rooms plus a few studios, or the nearby *Studios Diamantis* (☎02470/23 213; ❸) just inland, with large balconied units, though not the pleasantest management. At Krithóni, 1.5km south, more comfort is available at the island's top-flight accommodation: the *Crithoni Paradise* (☎02470/25 120, ℱ24 680; ❻), a mock-traditional low-rise complex with buffet breakfast, a large pool and all mod cons in the rooms. **Restaurant** options aren't brilliant, except for *To Steki* next to the war cemetery, open year round with good grills and rich mezédhes attracting a local clientele.

The **Allied War Graves Cemetery**, mostly containing casualties of the November 1943 battle, occupies a walled enclosure at the south end of the beach; immaculately maintained, it serves as a moving counterpoint to the holiday hubbub outside. The other principal sight at Álynda is the privately run **Historical and Ethnographic Museum** (May–Sept only, daily 10am–1pm & 6–9pm; €3), housed in the unmistakable castle-like mansion of Paris Bellinis (1871–1957). Most of the top floor is devoted to the Battle of Léros: relics from the sunken *Queen Olga*, a wheel from a Junkers bomber, a stove made from a bomb casing. There's also a rather grisly mock-up clinic (mostly gynecological tools) and assorted rural impedimenta, costumes and antiques.

Alternative beaches near Álynda include **Panayiés**, a series of gravel coves (one naturist) at the far northeast of the bay, and **Goúrna**, the turning for which lies 1km or so off the trans-island road. The latter, Léros's longest sandy beach, is hard-packed and gently shelving; it's also wind-buffeted, bereft of any nearby facilities, and permanently fringed by an impromptu car park and dumped construction rubble. A separate road beyond the Goúrna turning leads to **Kokálli**, no great improvement beach-wise, but flanked to one side by the scenic islet of **Áyios Isídhoros**, which is tethered to the mainland by a causeway, its eponymous chapel perched on top.

Seven kilometres from Álynda along the main route north, a marked sidetrack leads left to the purported **Temple of Artemis**, on a slight rise just west of the airport runway. In ancient times, Léros was sacred to the goddess, and the temple here was supposedly inhabited by guinea fowl – the grief-stricken sisters of Meleager, metamorphosed thus by Artemis following their brother's death. All that remains now are some jumbled, knee-high walls, which may in fact have been an ancient fortress, but the view is superb. The onward road skims the shores of sumpy, reed-fringed Parthéni Bay, with its dreary army base (formerly the political prison), until the paved road ends 11km along at **Blefoútis**, a rather more inspiring sight with its huge, virtually landlocked bay. The beach (the rough Lerian norm) has tamarisks to shelter under and an adequate taverna, *Iy Thea Artemi*, for *kalamári*-and-chips-type lunch.

Pátmos

Arguably the most beautiful and certainly the best known of the smaller Dodecanese, **Pátmos** has a distinctive, immediately palpable atmosphere. It was in a cave here that St John the Divine (in Greek, *O Theológos* or "The Theologian"), received the New Testament's Book of Revelation and unwittingly shaped the island's destiny. The monastery honouring him, founded here in 1088 by the Blessed Khristodhoulos (1021–93), dominates Pátmos both physically – its fortified bulk towering high above everything else – and, to a considerable extent, politically. While the monks inside no longer run the island as they did for more than six centuries, their influence has nonetheless stopped Pátmos going the way of Rhodes or Kós.

Despite vast numbers of visitors and the island's firm presence on the cruise, hydrofoil and yacht circuits, tourism has not been allowed to take Pátmos over completely. While there is a number of clubs and even one disco around Skála, drunken rowdiness is virtually unknown, and this is one island where you do risk being ticked off for nudism on all but the most isolated beaches. Package clients have only since the 1990s begun to outnumber independent visitors, and are pretty much confined to Gríkou and a handful of larger hotels at Skála and Kámbos. Day-trippers still exceed overnighters, and Pátmos seems an altogether different place once the last cruise ship has gone at sunset. Away from Skála, development is appealingly subdued if not deliberately retarded, thanks to the absence of an airport.

Skála and around

SKÁLA, with most of the island's population of about three thousand, seems initially to contradict any solemn, otherworldly image of Pátmos. The water-

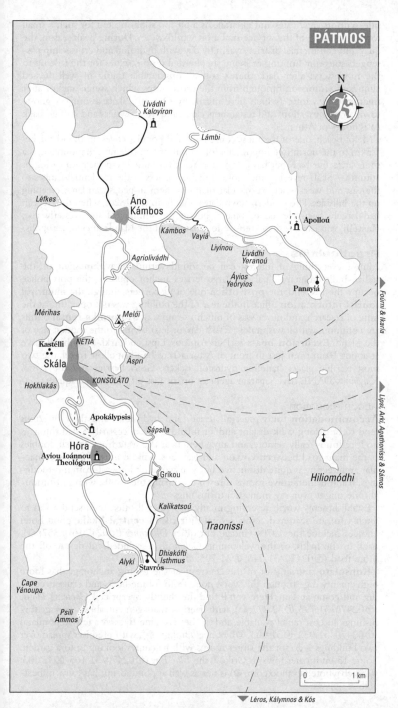

PÁTMOS

N

Livádhi
Kaloyíron

Lámbi

Léfkes

Áno
Kámbos

Apolloú

Kámbos   Vayiá

Liyínou

Agriolivádhi   Livádhi
Yeranoú

Áyios
Yeóryios   Panayiá

Mérihas

Meloï

Kastélli   NETIÁ

Skála   Áspri

Hokhlakás   KONSOLÁTO

Apokálypsis

Sápsila

Hóra
Ayíou Ioánnou
Theológou

Grikou   Hiliomódhi

Kalikatsoú

Traoníssi

Dhiakófti
Isthmus

Alykí   Stavrós

Cape
Yénoupa

Psilí
Ámmos

0   1 km

side, with its ritzy cafés and clientele, is a bit too sophisticated for such a small town, and some of the service staff a bit world-weary. During peak season, the quay and commercial district swarm by day with hydrofoil and cruise-ship passengers souvenir-hunting or being shepherded onto coaches for the ride up to the monastery; after dark there's still a considerable traffic in well-dressed cliques of visitors on furlough from the cruise ships which weigh anchor after midnight. In winter (which here means by Oct 10), Skála assumes a ghost-town air as most shops and restaurants close, and their owners and staff go back to Rhodes or Athens.

Melóï beach, one of the most convenient and popular coves on the island, lies 1.5km to the north (see opposite); Hóra, a bus or taxi ride up the mountain, is a more attractive base, but has few rooms. Yet given time – especially in spring or autumn – Skála reveals some more enticing corners in the residential fringes to the east and west, where vernacular mansions hem in pedestrian lanes creeping up the hillsides. The modern town dates only from the 1820s, when the Aegean had largely been cleared of pirates, but at the summit of the westerly rise, **Kastélli**, you can see the extensive foundations of the island's ancient acropolis.

Practicalities

Almost everything of interest can be found within, or within sight of, the Italian-built municipal "palace": large ferries anchor opposite, the port police occupy the east end, the **post office** one of its corners, though the municipal **tourist information** office in the rear of the building was not operating at the time of research, and never was of much use anyway. **Motorbike rental** outfits are common, with lowish rates (€10 a day or less) owing to the modest size of the island. **Excursion boats** to Psilí Ámmos, Lipsí and Arkí/Maráthi all leave at about 10am from just in front of Astoria Travel and Apollon Travel, the two most reliable places handling hydrofoil tickets. G&A Ferries and the *Nissos Kalymnos*/DANE have separate agencies on, or just off, the central square.

Accommodation

Accommodation touts meet all ferries and hydrofoils, and their offerings tend to be a long walk distant and/or inland – not necessarily a bad thing, as no location is really remote, and anywhere near the waterfront, which doubles as the main road between Gríkou and Kámbos, will be noisy. Pátmos vernacular architecture is quite distinctive, but you wouldn't know it from most lodgings, bland if inoffensive rooms thrown up during the 1980s, with institutional (one might even say monastic) furnishings.

Establishments worth reserving in advance (they'll often then send a van to fetch you) are scattered across several districts. In **central Skála**, good hotel choices include the 1970s-vintage but quiet *Dhiethnes* (T02470/31 357; ❸), back in the fields, or the welcoming *Galini*, in a secluded cul-de-sac off the Hóra road (T02470/31 240, F31 705; ❹).

Konsoláto district, east of the centre near the fishing anchorage, has more high-quality digs, though the worst noise from fishing boats and cruisers coming and going at 4am. Here you'll find the slightly overpriced *Captain's House* (T02470/31 793, F32 277; ❻), with friendly management, above-average furnishings and car rental available, and the better-value *Byzance* a few steps inland (T02470/31 052, F31 663, ✉byzance@hol.gr; ❹), with premises spread over two buildings – go for the larger rooms with balconies looking onto a garden. Some 150m further towards Gríkou, the *Blue Bay* (T02470/31 165, F32 303, ✉bluebayhotel@yahoo.com; ❺) is not as well appointed, but has calm, unbeatable sea views.

Netiá, the unglamorous area northwest between the power plant and Mérihas cove, is actually a good choice as a base. Various members of a Greek-Australian family run clustered establishments: the *Hotel Australis* (☎02470/31 576; ❹), with full breakfast for the price and myriad small kindnesses that guarantee repeat clientele; and the adjacent *Villa Knossos* (☎02470/32 189, ℉32 284; ❹), whose rooms all have attractive terraces, or the simpler *Pension Sydney* (☎02470/31 139; ❸). But the best standard in this area is provided by the *Hotel Asteri* (☎02470/32 465, ℉31 347, ✉pasca@otenet.gr; ❹), unimprovably set on a knoll overlooking the bay, in a well-landscaped environment that's also a working farm – guests have own-produced honey, eggs and tomatoes at breakfast.

Pebbly **Hokhlakás** Bay, just a ten-minute walk southwest of the central market street, is perhaps the quietest district, with wonderful sunset views. Comfortable options here include the hillside *Summer* (☎02470/31 769, ℉31 170; ❺); the *Maria* down in the flatlands (☎02470/31 201, ℉32 018; ❺), where air conditioning and big seaview balconies make up for tiny bathrooms; the budget en-suite rooms, right on the water, above the *Cactus Restaurant* (☎02470/33 059; ❷); and Skála's top accommodation, the *Romeos* (☎02470/31 962, ℉31 070, ✉romeos@w12.gr; ❻) on the southerly slope, with a pool, large common areas, and sizeable units numerous enough that there's usually a vacancy. Hokhlakás isn't very swimmable; if you're keen to stay nearer a proper beach, head for the well-run, pleasantly set **campsite** (*Stefanos-Flowers*) at **MELÓÏ**, just down the slope from Pátmos's most exclusive digs: the *Porto Scoutari Hotel* (☎02470/33 124, ℉33 175; ❻), a self-catering bungalow complex open all year, furnished with mock antiques and original art, and arrayed around a pool and enjoying sea views.

Eating and drinking

Restaurant options are surprisingly limited in Skála; there are altogether too many *souvláki/yíros* joints and not enough good-value, sit-down places. Easily the town's best and most distinctive is seafood-only *Ouzeri To Hiliomodhi*, just off the start of the Hóra road, with its vegetarian *mezédhes* and delicacies such as limpets (served live, be warned), grilled octopus and salted anchovies. Honourable mentions go to *Pandelis*, one lane inland behind Astoria Travel, where a wide-ranging menu of reliably good *mayireftá* make up for famously dour, if efficient, service; *Ostria*, a new ouzerí at the west end of the front; and *Cactus* on the beach at Hokhlakás, doing *nouvelle-minceur* Italian snacks (don't show up too hungry) accompanied by Italian wines and aperitifs.

Aside from that, you're best off heading a bit out of town. Melóï has an excellent *mayireftá* taverna, *Melloi* (alias *Stefanos*), reasonably priced and open early or late in the season; just over the hill at **Áspri** cove are two summer-only fish tavernas, *Aspri* and *Kyma* with in-your-face views of the Hóra; the former is reckoned better, pricier and opens at lunch too. At Sápsila Bay, 2km southeast of Skála, *Benetos* (June–Sept; reserve on ☎02470/33 089) has since 1998 established a reputation as one of the best spots on the island for seafood and generic Mediterranean dishes. Back in town, the most reliable **breakfast** venue is the second, smaller platía beyond the main one, where *La Frianderie* serves hot drinks and croissants under medieval arches, and the adjacent bakery turns out terrific turnovers. The biggest and most durable **café-bar** is the wood-panelled, barn-like *Café Arion* on the waterside, where local youth play cards; others include open-air *Kafe Aman* in Konsoláto, with music and snacks, and the livelier, indoor *Consolato* disco, almost next door. Skála has two **internet cafés**: one inside the *Blue Bay Hotel*, the other – *Millennium* – on the main lane to Hokhlakás cove.

The monasteries and Hóra

Top of your sightseeing agenda is likely to be the monastery of Ayíou Ioánnou Theológou (St John), sheltered behind massive defences in the hilltop capital of Hóra. There is a regular KTEL bus up, or you can do a forty-minute walk by a beautiful old cobbled path. To find its start, proceed through Skála towards Hokhlakás, and once past the telecoms building and the *Millennium Internet Café* bear left onto a lane starting opposite an ironmonger's; follow this uphill to its end on the main road – immediately opposite you'll see the cobbled path. Just over halfway, you might pause at the **monastery of Apokálypsis** or Apocalypse (Mon, Wed, Fri & Sat 8am–1pm, Tues & Thurs 8am–1pm & 4–6pm, Sun 8am–noon & 4–6pm; free) built around the cave where St John heard the voice of God issuing from a cleft in the rock, and where he sat dictating his words to a disciple. In the cave wall, the presumed nightly resting place of the saint's head is fenced off and outlined in beaten silver.

This is merely a foretaste of the monastery of **Ayíou Ioánnou Theológou** (St John) (same hours and admission as Apokálypsis). In 1088, the soldier-cleric Ioannis "The Blessed" Khristodhoulos was granted title to Pátmos by Byzantine Emperor Alexios Komnenos; within three years he and his followers had completed the essentials of the existing monastery, the threats of piracy and the Selçuk Turks dictating a heavily fortified style. A warren of interconnecting courtyards, chapels, stairways, arcades, galleries and roof terraces, it offers a rare glimpse of a Patmian interior; hidden in the walls are fragments of an ancient Artemis temple which stood here before being destroyed by Khristodhoulos. Off to one side, the **treasury** (same hours; €3.50) justifies its hefty entrance fee with its magnificent array of religious treasure, mostly medieval icons of the Cretan school, but pride of place goes to an unusual mosaic icon of Áyios Nikólaos, and the eleventh-century parchment chrysobull (edict) of Emperor Alexios Komnenos, granting the island to Khristodhoulos.

Hóra

The promise of security afforded by St John's stout walls spurred the growth of **HÓRA** immediately outside the fortifications. It remains architecturally homogeneous, with cobbled lanes sheltering dozens of shipowners' mansions from the island's seventeenth- to eighteenth-century heyday. High, windowless walls and imposing wooden doors betray nothing of the opulence within: painted ceilings, pebble-mosaic terraces, flagstoned kitchens, and carved furniture. Inevitably, touristic tattiness disfigures the main approaches to the monastery gate, but away from the principal thoroughfares are lanes that rarely see traffic, and by night, when the monastery ramparts are floodlit to startling effect, it's hard to think of a more beautiful Dodecanesian village. Neither should you miss the **view** from Platía Lódza (named after the remnant of an adjacent Venetian *loggia*), particularly at dawn or dusk. Landmasses to the north, going clockwise, include Ikaría, Thýmena, Foúrni, Sámos with its brooding mass of Mount Kérkis, Arkí, and the double-humped Samsun Dağ (ancient Mount Mykale) in Turkey.

Among several tavernas in Hóra, *Vangelis* on the inner square has a wonderful old jukebox, friendly service and view seating on various levels, but alas the cooking has declined since the late 1990s; you'll probably eat better at *Balkoni* near the monastery. Again on the square, *Kafeteria Stoa* is minimally touristy despite its showcase interior, still functioning as the village kafenío. There are, however, very few places to **stay**; foreigners here are mostly long-term occupants, who have bought up and restored almost a third of the crumbling mansions since the 1960s. Getting a short-term room can be a pretty thankless task, even in spring or autumn; the best strategy is to contact *Vangelis* taverna early in the day, or phone ahead for reservations to Yeoryia Triandafyllou (✆02470/31 963; ❸) or Marouso Kouva (✆02470/31 026; ❸).

The rest of the island

Pátmos, as a locally published guide once memorably proclaimed, "is immense for those who know how to wander in space and time". Lesser mortals may find it easier to get around on foot, or by bus. There's still scope for **walking** despite a dwindling network of paths; otherwise a single **bus** offers surprisingly reliable service between Skála, Hóra, Kámbos and Gríkou – the main stop, with a posted timetable, is right in front of the main ferry dock.

After its extraordinary atmosphere and magnificent scenery, **beaches** are Patmos's principal attraction. From Hóra, a paved road (partly shortcut by a path) winds east to the sandiest part of rather overdeveloped and cheerless **GRÍKOU**, the main venue for Patmian package tourism – and shut tight as a drum come late September. The beach itself, far from the island's best, forms a narrow strip of hard-packed sand giving way to large pebbles towards the south. En route you pass the hillside *Flisvos* (aka *Floros*) taverna, going since the 1960s with a limited choice of inexpensive, savoury *mayireftá*, served on the terrace; they also have simple rooms (❶) and fancier apartments (❹) – reserve on ✆02470/31 380, ℉32 094. Another good **accommodation** option here, open late in the year and not monopolized by packages, is the hillside *Hotel Golden Sun* (✆02470/32 318, ℉34 019; ❺), with most rooms facing the water.

From Hóra, you can ride a scooter over as far as the Dhiakoftí isthmus, beyond which a thirty-minute walk southwest leads to **Psilí Ámmos** beach. This is the only pure-sand cove on the island, with shade lent by tamarisks, nudism galore at the far south end and a good lunchtime **taverna** that occasionally does roast goat, freshly shot on the surrounding hills. There's also a summer kaïki service here from Skála, departing by 10am and returning at 5pm.

More good beaches are to be found in the north of the island, tucked into the startling eastern shoreline (west-facing bays are uniformly unusable owing to wind and washed-up debris); most are accessible from side roads off the main route north from Skála. **Melói** is handy and quite appealing, with tamarisks behind the slender belt of sand, and good snorkelling offshore. The first beach beyond Méloï, **Agriolivádhi (Agriolívadho)**, has mostly sand at its broad centre, kayak rental, and two tavernas: one at mid-beach, the other (*O Glaros*, doing fish) on the south hillside. Hilltop Kámbos is the only other real village on the island, the focus of scattered farms in little oases all around; **Kámbos** beach, 600m downhill, is popular with Greeks, and the most developed remote resort on the island, with seasonal watersports facilities and tavernas (best of these *Ta Kavourakia*), though its appeal is diminished by the road just inland and a rock shelf in the shallows.

East of Kámbos are several less-frequented coves, including pebble **Vayiá**, nudist **Liyínou** and sand-and-gravel **Livádhi Yeranoú**, the latter with more tamarisks, an excellent namesake taverna doing simple but clean grills and salads, and an islet to swim out to. From lower Kámbos you can also journey north to the bay of **Lámbi**, best for swimming when the prevailing wind is from the south, and renowned for an abundance of multicoloured volcanic stones – as well as one of the best beach **tavernas** on the island, *Lambi-Leonidas*, open May to October, with a wide range of fish, mezédhes and grilled meat.

Lipsí

Of the various islets to the north and east of Pátmos, **LIPSÍ** is the largest, most interesting and most populated, and the one that has the most significant summer tourist trade. The presence of a British package company, on-spec French and Italian travellers, and the island's appearance on both main-line and off-line ferry routes, mean that it's unwise to show up in peak season without a reservation (though rooms proprietors meet arrivals at other times).

During quieter months, however, Lipsí still makes an idyllic halt, its sleepy pace making plausible a purported link between the island's name and that of Calypso, the nymph who legendarily held Odysseus in thrall. Deep wells provide water for many small farms, but there is only one flowing spring, and pastoral appearances are deceptive – four times the relatively impoverished full-time population of about seven hundred live overseas (many in Tasmania, for some reason). Most of those who remain cluster around the fine harbour, as does the majority of food and lodging.

A prime **accommodation** choice in all senses is Nikos' and Anna's welcoming *Apartments Galini* (☎02470/41 212, ℱ41 012; ❸), the first building you see above the ferry jetty; Nikos may take guests for fishing trips on request. Equally sought after, though less airy, are the *Studios Kalymnos* in a garden on the road north out of "town" (☎02470/41 141, ℱ41 343, ℯstudios_kalymnos@lipsi-island.gr; ❷), run by Laid Back Holidays (see below). Other good options not monopolized by package clients include *Rena's Rooms* (☎02470/41 363 or 41 120; ❷), overlooking Liendoú beach, the *Flisvos Pension* at the east end of the port (☎02470/41 261; ❷); the *Glaros* (☎02470/41 360; ❷) on the hillside behind the *Kalypso Hotel/Restaurant*; and *Studios Paradise* (☎02470/41 125; ❸), up on the ridge north of the *Dhelfini* restaurant which manages it. Top of the heap is the 1997-built *Aphrodite Hotel* (☎02470/41 000 or 41 394; ❺), a studio-bungalow complex designed to accommodate package clients, though they're not adverse to walk-ins at slow times.

Among eight or so **tavernas**, mostly on or just behind the quay, *To Dhelfini* next to the police station and *O Yiannis* next to the eponymous rooms are the best all-rounders, with a good range of grilled items, appetizers and often local bulk wine (white or rosé). Salubrious *Tholari*, at the east end of the bay, opens all year, while *Theologos Fish Restaurant* on the quay is reliably fresh – he only opens when he's caught something. On the waterfront to either side of the *Kalypso*, kafenía and ouzerís with idiosyncratic decor (especially *Asprakis*) offer mezédhes outdoors – an atmospheric and almost obligatory pre-supper ritual, where an ouzo & octopus titbit runs to €1.20. Later on, *The Rock* is the clear winner amongst a handful of **bars** for a congenial crowd and good taped music. Two licensed **travel agents** (Paradhisis ☎02470/41 120 and Laid Back; phone as above) organize excursions and change money, though there's a freestanding Emboriki/Commercial **cash dispenser** near the former. The **post office** is up a stairway on the attractive cathedral platía, opposite a hilariously indiscriminate **ecclesiastical museum** (theoretically Mon–Fri 9.30am–1.30pm & 4–8pm, Sat/Sun 10am–2pm, best chances of admission 10am–1pm daily; free) featuring such "relics" as oil from the sanctuary on Mount Tabor and water from the Jordan River, as well as archeological finds and two letters from Greek revolutionary hero Admiral Miaoulis.

The island's **beaches** are rather scattered, though none is more than an hour's walk distant. Closest to town, and sandiest, are **Liendoú** and **Kámbos**, but many visitors prefer the attractive duo of **Katsadhiá** and **Papandhriá**, adjacent sand-and-pebble coves 2km south of the port, with an extremely basic taverna,

Andonis (May–Sept), just inland from a musical snack-café-bar run by Andonis' son, *Dilaila* (June–Sept), which dominates the main bay here and runs an informal pine-grove campsite (free but you must buy a meal from them daily).

An hour's walk along the paved road leading west from town brings you to protected **Platýs Yialós**, a small, shallow, sandy bay with a single taverna (mid-June to late Sept only). During these periods a pair of adapted transit vans provides a **minibus** service from the port to all the points cited above; otherwise you can rent a **scooter** from one of two outlets and point them towards isolated east-coast beaches. Of these, **Hokhlakoúra** consists of rather grubby shingle with no facilities, though nearby **Turkómnima** is better. A final ten-minute path scramble gets you from a rough track's end to **Monodhéndhri**, on the northeast coast, notable only for its lone juniper tree and nudist practice – though there's a superior, nameless cove just to the right.

A growing network of roads, paved or otherwise, rather limit opportunities for genuine path-**walks** through the undulating countryside, dotted with blue-domed churches. The most challenging route heads west from the pass between Kámbos and Platýs Yialós to the bay of **Kímisi** (3hr round-trip), where Filippos the octogenarian religious hermit used to dwell in a tiny monastery above the shore, next to the single island spring. A particularly ugly road has been bull-dozed in from the north, and paved; Filippos is ill now and living back in town.

Arkí, Maráthi and Agathónissi

About two-thirds the size of Lipsí, **Arkí** is considerably more primitive, lacking drinking water, dynamo electricity (there are solar panels), ferry anchorage or much in the way of a village centre. Just 45 permanent inhabitants eke out a living here, mostly engaged in fishing, though catering for yacht parties attracted here by the superb anchorage is increasingly important. Arkí is an elective, once-weekly stop on the *Nissos Kalymnos* and Miniotis Lines routes: if you want to disembark here, you must warn the captain well in advance, so he can radio for the shuttle service from the island. Most visitors arrive by the more reliable supply boat from Pátmos, which actually docks at the quay. Of the three tavernas on the round harbourside platía, the better two – *Nikolas* (☎02470/32 477) and *O Trypas* (☎02470/32 230) – each control a handful of rooms (❷), but avoid August when Italians and Greeks snap up every vacancy in advance. *Nikolas* is more food-oriented, with homemade puddings, while *O Trypas* doubles as the happening music pub, courtesy of the owner's enormous collection of CDs and tapes.

You can swim at the "Blue Lagoon" of **Tiganákia** at the southeast tip of the island – excursions from Lipsí stop there – but there are no real beaches to speak of on Arkí. The nearest sandy, tamarisk-shaded one is just offshore on the islet of **Maráthi**, where another pair of **tavernas** caters to day-trippers who come at least several times a week from Pátmos or Lipsí. *Marathi* (☎02470/31 580; ❶), run by the engaging Mihalis Kavouras, is the more traditional, cosy outfit, with waterside seating and simple, adequate rooms; *Pantelis* (☎02470/32 609; ❷) is plusher but more commercially minded, and only open June to October.

The small, steep-sided, waterless islet of **Agathoníssi (Gaïdharo)** is too remote – much closer to Turkey than Pátmos, in fact – to be a target of day-excursions, though a few are advertised on Sámos. Intrepid German and Italian backpackers (some of whom return annually) form its main clientele, along with a steady trickle of yachts. Even though hydrofoil connections dovetail fairly well with appearances of the *Nissos Kalymnos* or a Miniotis Line boat, you should count on staying for three days, especially if the wind's up. Despite the lack of springs (cisterns are ubiquitous, topped up by tanker shipments from Rhodes), the island is greener and more fertile than apparent from the sea; mastic, carob and scrub oak on the heights overlook two arable plains in the west. Just 146 people live here, down from several hundred before World War II, but those who've opted to stay seem determined to make a go of raising goats or fishing (more accurately, fish-farming), and there are virtually no abandoned or neglected dwellings.

Most of the population lives in the hamlet of **MEGÁLO HORIÓ**, just visible on the ridge above the harbour of **ÁYIOS YEÓRYIOS**, and level with tiny **Mikró Horió**. Except for two café-restaurants (*Dhekatria Adherfia* being the more reliable) and the *Katsoulieri Pension* (✆02470/29 035; ❷) in Megálo Horió, all amenities are in the port. Here the choice is between *Rooms Theoloyia Yiameou* (✆02470/29 005; ❶), the vine-patioed *Hotel Maria Kamitsi* (✆02470/29 003; ❶), *George's Rooms* behind and inland (✆02470/29 064; ❶), or the 1999-built *Yiannis Rooms* (✆02470/29 062; ❷), of a slightly higher standard. Worthy **eating/drinking** options in Áyios Yeóryios include *George's* (he of the rooms) near the jetty, local hangout *Limanaki*, with fish grills, and *Glaros*, perhaps the best all-rounder sharing management with *Yiannis Rooms*.

With no wheeled transport for rent, exploring involves **walking** along the cement- or dirt-road network, or following a limited number of tracks and paths. If you don't swim at the port, which has the largest beach, you can walk twenty minutes southwest along a track to shingle-gravel **Spiliás**, or continue another quarter-hour along a faint path over the ridge to **Gaïdhourávlakos**, where nudists enjoy a gravel-and-sand cove. Bays in the east of the island, all served by the paved road system (occasionally shortcut by trails), tend to be dominated by fish farms; **Pálli** is the most pristine of these, though usually visited by boat trip. At **Thóli** in the far southeast, an hour-plus trek away, you can see an arcaded Byzantine structure, probably a combination granary and trading post, and by far the most venerable sight on Agathoníssi.

Travel details

To simplify the lists below, several companies/boats have been left out. DANE provides a once-weekly link between Rhodes, Kós, Sámos and Thessaloníki in each direction, while NEL also plies once weekly (north, then south) between Rhodes, Kós, Sámos, Híos, Lésvos, Límnos and Alexandhroúpoli.

Nissos Kalymnos

The small, slow but reliable Nissos Kalymnos (cars carried) is the most regular lifeline of the smaller islands (aside from Kárpathos and Kássos) – it visits them all twice a week between mid-March and mid-Jan. This ship can be poorly publicized on islands other than its home port; if you encounter difficulties obtaining information, you should phone the central agency on Kálymnos (✆02430/29 612). Specimen schedules, observed for some years now, are as follows:

Mid-March to April and mid-Sept to mid-Jan: Mon and Fri 7am, leaves Kálymnos for Kós, Níssyros, Tílos, Sými, Rhodes; out to Kastellórizo late afternoon, turns around at midnight. Tues and Sat 9am, departs Rhodes for Sými, Tílos, Níssyros,

Kós, Kálymnos, with a Tues evening return trip to Astypálea. Wed and Sun departs Kálymnos 7am for Léros, Lipsí, Pátmos, Arkí (Wed only), Agathónissi, Pythagório (Sámos), returning from Sámos at 2.30pm bound for Kálymnos via the same islands. Thurs 7am from Kálymnos to Astypálea, returns immediately.

May to mid-June: Mon and Fri 7am, leaves Kálymnos for Kós, Níssyros, Tílos, Sými, Rhodes; out to Kastellórizo late afternoon, turns around at midnight. Tues and Sat 9am, departs Rhodes for Sými, Tílos, Níssyros, Kós, Kálymnos, with an evening return trip both days to Astypálea. Wed and Sun departs Kálymnos 7am for Léros, Lipsí, Pátmos, Arkí (Wed only), Agathónissi, Pythagório

(Sámos), returning from Sámos at 2.30pm bound for Kálymnos via the same islands. Thurs, idle. **Mid-June to mid-Sept**: Mon and Thurs 7am, leaves Kálymnos for Kós, Níssyros, Tílos, Sými, Rhodes; out to Kastellórizo late afternoon, turns around at midnight. Tues and Fri 9am, departs Rhodes for Sými, Tílos, Níssyros, Kós, Kálymnos, with an evening return trip both days to Astypálea. Wed and Sun departs Kálymnos 7am for Léros, Lipsí, Pátmos, Arkí (Wed only), Agathónissi, Pythagório (Sámos), returning from Sámos at 2.30pm bound for Kálymnos via the same islands. Sat, 7am from Kálymnos to Astypálea, returning immediately,

Large ferries

Note that the following frequencies are only valid for the period mid-June to mid-Sept; in spring or autumn some of the more esoteric links, such as Astypálea to Níssyros, or Foúrni to Kós, do not operate.

Agathoníssi 1 weekly on Miniotis Lines to Arkí, Lipsí, Pátmos, Sámos (Pythagório).

Astypálea 3–5 weekly to Amorgós, Náxos, Páros and Pireás, 1 weekly to Sýros, on one of two companies; 1–2 weekly to Kós, Kálymnos, Rhodes and Níssyros on DANE or G&A.

Hálki 2 weekly to Ródhos Town, Kárpathos (both ports), Kássos, Crete and Mílos on LANE, all subject to cancellation in bad weather. Once-daily kaïki (6am) to Rhodes (Kámiros Skála).

Kálymnos Similar ferry service to Kós, plus 3 daily ro-ro ferries, well-spaced, to Mastihári; daily morning kaïki to Psérimos; and a daily kaïki (1pm) from Myrtiés to Xirókambos on Léros.

Kárpathos (both ports) and **Kássos** 2–3 weekly with each other, Crete (Áyios Nikólaos and/or Sitía), Milos and Ródhos Town, on LANE; 1–2 weekly to Hálki on LANE.

Kastellórizo (Méyisti) 1 weekly to Rhodes, then Pireás indirectly, via select Dodecanese and Cyclades.

Kós 7–14 weekly to Rhodes, Kálymnos, Léros, Pátmos and Pireás on G&A or DANE; 3 weekly to Ikaría (Áyios Kírykos) on G&A; 1–2 weekly to Foúrni and Lipsí on G&A; 1 weekly to Tílos, Níssyros, Astypálea and Sými on DANE and G&A; 1 weekly to Náxos, Páros, Sýros on G&A; 3 daily ro-ro ferries year-round from Mastihári to Kálymnos; 4–7 weekly excursion kaïkia to Níssyros; 4 weekly islanders' kaïki from Kardhámena to Níssyros.

Léros 7–14 weekly to Pireás, Pátmos, Kálymnos,

Kós and Rhodes on G&A or DANE; 3 weekly to Ikaría (Áyios Kírykos); 2 weekly to Foúrni; 1 weekly to Sými, Tílos on DANE; 1 weekly to Lipsí on G&A; seasonal daily excursion boats from Ayía Marína to Lipsí and Pátmos (2pm), and from Xirókambos to Myrtiés on Kálymnos (7.30am).

Lipsí 1 weekly to Léros, Kós, Pátmos, Ikaría (Áyios Kírykos), Tílos, Níssyros on G&A; 1 weekly to Sámos (Vathý) on Hellas Ferries.

Níssyros and Tílos Same as for Sými, plus excursion boats between Níssyros and Kós as follows: to Kardhámena nearly daily at 3.30–4pm; 4–7 weekly to Kós Town (all of these are seasonal). The islanders' somewhat less expensive "shopping" kaïki, the *Chrissula*, leaves 4–5 times weekly at 7am. Unless you're bound for the airport it's not really cheaper to use Kardhámena services when you consider the bus to Kós Town – €7.50 to Kardhámena on an excursion boat, versus €9 to Kós.

Pátmos Similar ferry service to Léros, with the addition of 1 weekly to Sámos (Vathý) on Hellas Ferries, 1 weekly to Arkí, seasonal tourist boats to Sámos (Pythagório), Lipsí, Arkí and Maráthi on a daily basis; Mon–Thurs only to Arkí in low season.

Rhodes 7–14 weekly to Kós, Kálymnos and Pireás on G&A or DANE; at least 1 daily to Léros and Pátmos on G&A or DANE; 2 weekly to Kárpathos, Kássos, Hálki, Crete (Sitía or Áyios Nikólaos), Mílos on LANE; 2 weekly to Foúrni and Ikaría (Áyios Kírykos) on G&A; 1–2 weekly to Sými, Lipsí, Tílos, Níssyros, Astypálea on G&A or DANE; 1 weekly to Náxos, Páros, Sýros.

Sými 1–2 weekly to Rhodes, Tílos, Níssyros, Kós, Kálymnos, Léros, Pátmos and Pireás on G&A Ferries or DANE; at least daily catamaran or hydrofoil run by ANES to Rhodes.

Catamarans

Two high-speed **catamarans** ply the Dodecanese: The *Dodecanese Express*, also known as *O Spanos* after the supermarket chain which owns it, and the *Sea Star*. The *Dodecanese Express*, based on Rhodes, can carry 4–5 cars and a slightly larger number of two-wheelers; it's a sleek, new, Norwegian-built craft, with a limited amount of deck space (but no deck chairs). The *Sea Star* does not carry vehicles, and is the much less reliable of the two, fitfully serving the line Tilos–Rhodes with occasionally other nearby islands thrown in.

2001 was the *Dodecanese Express*'s second season, and departure patterns seem to have settled down as follows: daily 8.30am departure from Rhodes to Kós, Kálymnos, Léros and Pátmos, calling at Lipsí 4 days weekly (usually northbound) and Tílos and Níssyros once weekly, both inbound and outbound, usually Wed; returns from Pátmos shortly after 1pm, arrives Rhodes

6.30–7.30pm. In spring or autumn it may call at Lipsí just once or twice weekly, serving Sými and Kastellórizo instead twice weekly. It has never called at Astypálea, Agathoníssi, Hálki, Kárpathos or Sámos (Pythagório) and is unlikely to in the future.

Hydrofoils

Two hydrofoil companies, Kyrakoulis Maritime and Laoumtzis Flying Dolphins, serve the Dodecanese between mid-May and mid-October, operating out of Rhodes, Kálymnos and Sámos (Kirakoulis only), plus Kós (both companies). Kyrakoulis Maritime has ten craft in theory, inherited from the amalgamation of previously existing companies Samos Hydrofoils and Dodecanese Hydrofoils, but only about six of these are active at any given time. Schedules are complicated but fairly predictable. In peak season, there is a daily link Rhodes–Kós and back, north in the morning and south in the evening; on successive weekend days it may detour via Sými or Níssyros. Another craft leaves Kálymnos between 7 and 11am for Kós and a selection of islands north to Pythagório on Sámos, returning between 12.30 and 2pm; while the third craft, based in Pythagório, leaves Kós between 1 and 2pm, returning to Sámos via Kálymnos, Léros, Lipsí and Pátmos. Several days a week, this craft calls at Foúrni as well, and twice a week Agathoníssi is served. Still another craft based on Kálymnos

leaves at dawn for Rhodes via Kós, returning between 4 and 6pm; once or twice a week it will call at Hálki and Tílos either direction. There is also a nominal Saturday service from Kálymnos to Astypálea, but owing to weather conditions and lack of passenger demand this tends to run at most three times in any summer. Some of the unusual runs to the smaller islands can get completely booked by transfers of package-tour groups. For current routes and schedules, phone ☎02420/25 920 (Kós), ☎02410/78 052 (Rhodes) or ☎02730/80 620 (Sámos). Laoumtzis Flying Dolphins, based in Kós, has two craft with a fairly set pattern. One craft always leaves Kós at around 8am for Rhodes, returning shortly after 5pm. Twice weekly there are diversions via Sými in each direction, and on Sat there's the "milk run" via Níssyros, Tílos and Hálki, designed to get package patrons to/from their weekend charters. Twice a week the other craft provides an express run up to Pátmos in the morning, returning in the late afternoon. For exact details ring ☎02420/26 388.

International ferries

Kós 2–14 weekly to Bodrum, Turkey (45min). Greek boat or Laoumtzis hydrofoil leaves 9am, returns 4pm; €29.50 return, Greek tax inclusive; no cheap day-return or one-ways, no Turkish port tax. Identically priced Turkish boat (*Fahri Kaptan*) or hydrofoil, departs Bodrum 9am or so, leaves Kós 4.30pm; this provides the only service in winter.
Rhodes Daily in summer to Marmaris, Turkey (1hr)

by Greek hydrofoil; €29.40 one-way, €41.20 return, plus $10 Turkish port tax. There is no longer a regularly scheduled Turkish car ferry; this must be arranged specially and will work out expensive, so drivers may be better off going to Kós and using the *Fahri Kaptan* to Bodrum. Also 2–3 weekly to Limassol, Cyprus (18hr) and Haifa, Israel (39hr).

Flights

Note: All are on Olympic Aviation/Olympic Airways unless stated otherwise.
Kárpathos 1–2 daily to Rhodes; 3 weekly to Kássos; 3–5 weekly to Athens.
Kássos 3 weekly to Kárpathos; 5 weekly to Rhodes.
Kastellórizo (Meyísti) 1 daily to Rhodes June–Sept, 3 weekly otherwise.

Kós 3 daily to Athens.
Léros 4–6 weekly to Athens.
Rhodes On Olympic, 5 daily to Athens; 2 weekly to Iráklion (April–Oct); 2–5 weekly to Thíra; 3 weekly to Thessaloníki; 2 weekly to Mýkonos (June–Sept). On Aegean-Cronus, 5 daily to Athens; 1–2 daily to Iráklion; 1 daily to Thessaloníki.

5

The East and North Aegean

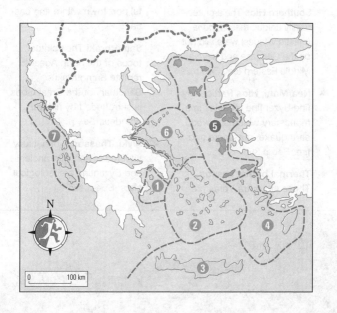

CHAPTER 5

Highlights

* **Vathý, Sámos** The two-wing archeological museum is among the best in the islands; the star is the huge kouros from the local shrine of Hera. See p.370

* **Ikaría** Western Ikaría has superb beaches and an idio-syncratic life-style. See p.381

* **Southern Híos** The architecturally unique *mastihohoriá* (mastic villages) were laid out by the Genoese and have a Middle Eastern feel. See p.394

* **Néa Moní, Híos** Particularly fine Byzantine mosaics in a monastery which survived earthquake, massacre and fire. See p.396

* **Thermal baths, Lésvos** Those at Loutrá Yéras are especially well-kept and ideal for relaxing after a lengthy journey. See p.408

* **Mólyvos, northern Lésvos** This castle-crowned resort village is arguably the most beautiful on the island. See p.414

* **Mýrina, Límnos** A character-ful port town with a fine castle. See p.420

* **Samothráki** The spiritual focus of the north Agean, remote Samothráki's Sanctuary of the Great Gods is surrounded by natural grandeur. See p.427

* **Alykí, Thássos** A beautifully situated beach with ancient and Byzantine archeological sites. See p.435

5

The East and North Aegean

he seven substantial islands and four minor islets scattered off the
north Aegean coast of Asia Minor and northeastern Greece form a
rather arbitrary archipelago. Although there are some passing similarities in architecture and landscape, the strong individual character
of each island is far more striking. Despite their proximity to modern
Turkey, members of the group bear few signs of an Ottoman heritage, especially when compared with Rhodes and Kós. There's the occasional
mosque, often shorn of its minaret, but by and large the enduring
Greekness of these islands is testimony to the four-millennium-long
Hellenic presence in Asia Minor, which ended only in 1923. This heritage
is regularly referred to by the Greek government in an intermittent propaganda war with Turkey over the sovereignty of these far-flung outposts.
Tensions here have often been worse than in the Dodecanese, aggravated
by potential undersea oil deposits in the straits between the islands and the
Anatolian mainland. The Turks have also persistently demanded that
Límnos, astride the sea lanes to and from the Dardanelles, be demilitarized,
but so far Greece has shown no signs of giving in.

Accommodation price codes

Throughout the book we've categorized accommodation according to the following
price codes, which denote the cheapest available double room in high season. All
prices are for the room only, except where otherwise indicated. Many hotels, especially those in category ❹ and over, include breakfast in the price; you'll need to
check this when booking. During low season, rates can drop by more than fifty percent, especially if you are staying for three or more nights. Exceptions are during the
Christmas and Easter weeks when you'll pay high-season prices. Single rooms,
where available, cost around seventy percent of the price of a double.

❶ Up to €24	❹ €43–58
❷ €24–33	❺ €59–72
❸ €34–42	❻ €73 and upwards

Note: Youth hostels typically charge €7–9 for a dormitory bed.
For more accommodation details, see pp.52–54.

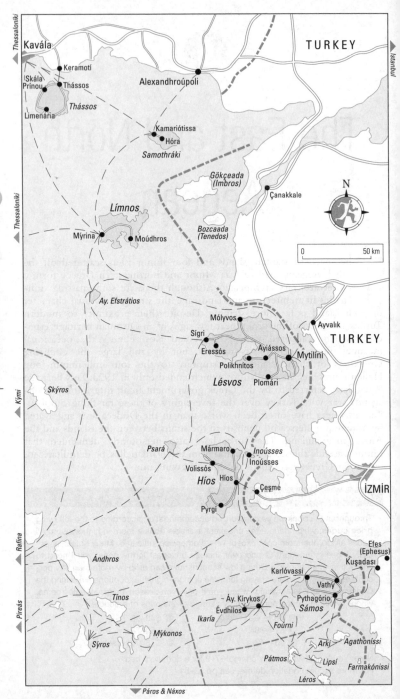

Thessaloníki ▲

Kavála

Keramotí

Skála
Prínou   Thássos

Limenária   *Thássos*

Alexandhroúpoli

Kamariótissa
Hóra

Samothráki

TURKEY

Gökçeada
(Ímbros)

Çanakkale

N

0   50 km

Límnos

Mýrina   Moúdhros

*Bozcaada
(Tenedos)*

Ay. Efstrátios

Mólyvos

Sígri   Ayiássos

Eressós

Polikhnítos

Lésvos   Plomári

Ayvalık

TURKEY

Mytilíni

Skýros

Psará

Mármaro   *Inoússes*
             Inoússes
Volissós

Híos   Híos

Pyrgí   Çeşme

İZMİR

Ándhros

Efes
(Ephesus)

Karlóvassi   Kuşadası

Vathý

Tínos   Pythagório
                 Sámos

- Áy. Kírykos

Évdhilos

Ikaría   *Foúrni*

Mýkonos   *Arkí*   *Agathoníssi*

Sýros   *Pátmos*   *Lipsí*   *Farmakónissi*

                              Léros

▼ Páros & Náxos

Istanbul ►

The heavy military presence can be disconcerting, and despite the growth of tourism, large tracts of land remain off-limits as army or air force bases. But as in the Dodecanese, local tour operators do a thriving business shuttling passengers for inflated tariffs between the easternmost islands and the Turkish coast with its amazing archeological sites and busy resorts. Most of these islands' main ports and towns are not quaint, picturesque spots, but urbanized administrative, military and commercial centres. In most cases you should suppress any initial impulse to take the next boat out, and press on into the interiors.

Sámos ranks as the most visited island of the group, but if you can leave the crowds behind, is still arguably the most verdant and beautiful, even after a devastating July 2000 fire. **Ikaría** to the west remains relatively unspoiled, if a minority taste, and nearby **Foúrni** is a haven for determined solitaries, as are the Híos satellites **Psará** and **Inoússes**, neither of which have any package tourism. **Híos** proper offers far more cultural interest than any neighbours to the south, but its natural beauty has been ravaged by fires, and the development of tourism was until the late 1980s deliberately retarded. **Lésvos** may not impress initially, though once you get a feel for its old-fashioned, Anatolian ambience, you may find it hard to leave. By contrast virtually no foreigners and few Greeks visit **Áyios Efstrátios**, and with good reason. **Límnos** to the north is much livelier, but its appeal is confined mostly to the area immediately around the attractive port town. To the north, Samothráki and Thássos are totally isolated from the others, except via the mainland ports of Kavála or Alexandhroúpoli, and remain easier to visit from northern Greece, which administers them. **Samothráki** (officially in Thrace) has one of the most dramatic seaward approaches of any Greek island, and one of the more important ancient sites. **Thássos** (technically belonging to eastern Macedonia) is more varied, with sandy beaches, mountain villages and minor archeological sites.

Sámos

The lush and seductive island of Sámos was formerly joined to Asia Minor, until sundered from Mount Mykale opposite by Ice Age cataclysms; the resulting 2500-metre strait is now the narrowest distance between Greece and Turkey in the Aegean, except at Kastellórizo. There's little tangible evidence of it today, but Sámos was also once the **wealthiest island** in the Aegean and, under the patronage of the tyrant Polykrates, home to a thriving intellectual community: Epicurus, Pythagoras, Aristarchus and Aesop were among the residents. Decline set in as the star of Classical Athens was in the ascendant, though Sámos's status was improved somewhat in early Byzantine times when it constituted its own *theme* (imperial administrative district). Towards the end of the fifteenth century, the Genoese abandoned the island to the mercies of pirates; following their attacks, Sámos remained **almost uninhabited** until 1562, when an Ottoman admiral received permission from the sultan to repopulate it with Greek Orthodox settlers recruited from various corners of the empire.

The heterogeneous descent of today's islanders largely explains an enduring identity crisis and a rather thin topsoil of indigenous culture. Most of the village names are either clan surnames, or adjectives indicating origins elsewhere – constant reminders of **refugee descent**. Consequently there is no genuine Samiote music, dance or dress, and little that's original in the way of cuisine and architecture. The Samiotes compensated somewhat for this deracination by fighting fiercely for independence during the 1820s, but despite their accomplishments in sinking a Turkish fleet in the narrow strait and annihilating a landing army, the Great Powers handed the island back to the Ottomans in 1830, with the consoling proviso that it be **semi-autonomous**, ruled by an appointed Christian prince. This period, referred to as the *Iyimonía* (Hegemony), was marked by a mild renaissance in fortunes, courtesy of the hemp and (especially) tobacco trades. However, union with Greece in 1912, the ravages of a bitter World War II occupation and mass emigration effectively reversed the recovery until tourism appeared on the horizon during the 1980s.

Today the Samian economy is increasingly dependent on package **tourism**, far too much of it in places; the eastern half of the island, and a large part of the south coast, has pretty much surrendered to the onslaught of holiday-makers, although the more rugged northwestern part has retained some of its undeveloped grandeur. The clientele is rather sedate and couples-oriented; the absence of an official campsite on such a large island, tame nightlife a world away from that in the Cyclades, and phalanxes of self-catering villas hint at the sort of custom expected.

The heavily developed areas have unsurprisingly been the most afflicted by **repeated wildfires**, in particular one which lasted a week in July 2000, destroying twenty percent of the island's forest and orchards, and over ninety dwellings. If you mention Sámos to other Greeks, they say "Ah, tó nisí poú kaïke" ("Oh, the island that burned"), and if you take into account other areas that had been torched since 1987, Sámos is indeed about half-scorched. The trees will be a half-century in returning, and the tourist market a good few years in overcoming this stigma. Volunteer fire-lookouts have now sprouted at critical points, but it does seem a case of locking the stable after the horse has bolted.

Getting there and getting around

Sámos **airport** lies 14km southwest of Vathý and 3km west of Pythagório; an ambitious terminal expansion should be complete by 2003. There are no fewer than three **ferry ports**: Karlóvassi in the west, plus Vathý and Pythagório in the east, making the island a major hub for travel in every direction, though traditional sailing routes seem to have been altered slightly by the wreck of the *Express Samina* (see p.42). All ferries between Pireás, Sýros, Mýkonos, Ikaría and Sámos call at both Karlóvassi and Vathý (except for the high-speed catamaran which serves only Vathý), as do the smaller Miniotis Line ferries linking the island with Híos and, at high season, Foúrni and Ikaría. There was, however, no reliable link with Páros and Náxos for most of summer 2001, and this situation may continue in future years. Vathý also receives the weekly NEL sailing between northern Greece and the Dodecanese, via most intervening islands, the weekly DANE ferry between Thessaloníki and Rhodes, plus small boats from Kuşadası. Pythagório siphons off a bit of the Turkey shipping in high season, and additionally sees two regular weekly ferry connections from as far south as Kós in the Dodecanese, plus a seasonal Miniotis service to Lipsí, Foúrni and Agathoníssi. Both ports host **hydrofoil services** (Kyriakoulis Maritime): Vathý is the start-point base of pretty-undependable hydrofoils to Híos, northern Ikaría and Lésvos, while Pythagório has the lion's share of traffic, with more reliable services to all the Dodecanese down to Kós, plus forays over to Foúrni and southern Ikaría.

The **bus terminals** in Pythagório and Vathý lie within walking distance of the ferry dock; at Karlóvassi, you must make your own way the 3km into town from the port. There is no airport bus service; **taxi** fares to various points are stipulated on prominent placards, and in high season taxis to the airport or docks must be booked several hours in advance. The KTEL service itself is

5

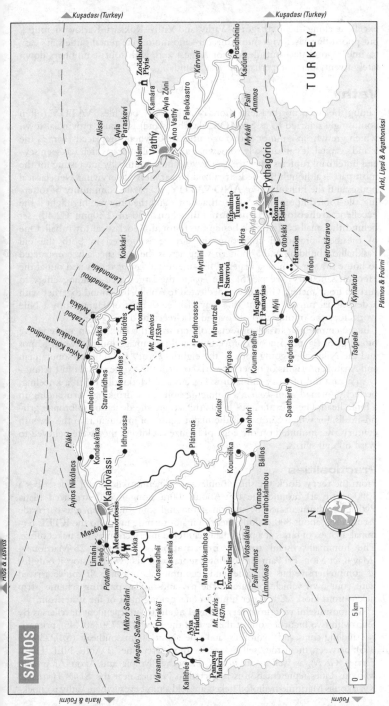

Kuşadası (Turkey)

Kuşadası (Turkey)

TURKEY

Zoödhóhou Piyís

Kérveli

Posidhónio

Kamára

Ayía Zóni

Kadúna

Ayía Paraskeví

Paleókastro

Psilí Ámmos

Nissí

Kalámi

Áno Vathý

Vathý

Mykáli

Pythagório

Efpalínio Tunnel

Roman Baths

Glyfádha

Kokkári

Hóra

Potokáki

Heraíon

Petrokáravo

Myríini

Iréon

Tsamádhou

Timíou Stavroú

Megális Panayías

Mýli

Kyriakoú

Lemonákia

Vrondianís

Vourliótes

Pándhrossos

Mavratzéi

Tzaboú

Aviákia

Mt Ámbelos
1153m

Pyrgos

Koumaradhéi

Pagóndas

Tsópela

Pnáka

Avlákia

Platanákia

Ayíos Konstandínos

Manolátes

Stavrinídhes

Ámbelos

Idhroússa

Plátanos

Neohóri

Spatharéi

Piáki

Kondakéíka

Koútsi

Ayíos Nikólaos

Karlóvassi

Kouméika

Bállos

Meséo

Metamórfosis

Límáni

Paleó

Lékka

Marathókambos

Órmos
Marathokámbou

Kosmadhéi

Kastaniá

Votsalákia

Evangelístrias

Psilí Ámmos

Mikró Seïtáni

Dhrakéi

Límniónas

Megálo Seïtáni

Ayía Triádha

Mt Kérkis
1437m

Vársamo

Kallithéa

Panayía
Makriní

N

Ikaría & Foúrni

Arkí, Lipsí & Agathoníssi

Pátmos & Foúrni

Fríos & Lésvos

Foúrni

0   5 km

excellent along the Pythagório–Vathý and Vathý–Kokkári–Karlóvassi routes, but poor otherwise; with numerous car- and motorbike-rental outlets, it's easy to find a good deal outside July or August and, with tourist numbers down lately twenty percent, perhaps all year round.

Vathý

Lining the steep northeastern shore of a deep bay, beachless **VATHÝ** (often confusingly referred to as **SÁMOS**, like the island) is a busy provincial town which grew from a minor anchorage after 1830, when it replaced Hóra as the island's capital. It's an unlikely, somewhat ungraceful resort, which has seen several hotel bankruptcies since the late 1990s, and is minimally interesting for the most part – although the pedestrianized bazaar, tiers of surviving Neoclassical houses and the hill suburb of **ÁNO VATHÝ**, a separate community of tottering, tile-roofed houses have some attraction – and the only real highlight is the excellent **archeological museum** (Tues–Sun 8.30am–2.30pm; €2.40), set behind the small central park beside the restored Neoclassical town hall. One of the best provincial collections in Greece is housed in both the old Paskhallion building and a modern wing across the way, specially constructed to house the star exhibit: a majestic, five-metre-tall *kouros*, discovered out at the Heraion sanctuary (see p.375). The *kouros*, the largest free-standing effigy to survive from ancient Greece, was dedicated to Apollo, but found together with a devotional mirror to Mut (the Egyptian equivalent of Hera) from a Nile workshop, one of only two discovered in Greece to date.

In the compelling **small-objects collection** of the Paskhallion, more votive offerings of Egyptian design prove trade and pilgrimage links between Sámos and the Nile valley going back to the eighth century BC. The Mesopotamian and Anatolian origins of other artwork confirm the exotic trend, most tellingly in a case full of ivory miniatures: Perseus and Medusa in relief, a kneeling, perfectly formed mini-*kouros*, a pouncing lion and a drinking horn ending in a bull's head. The most famous local artefacts are the dozen or so bronze griffin-heads, for which Sámos was the major centre of production in the seventh century BC; mounted on the edge of bronze cauldrons, they were believed to ward off evil spirits.

Practicalities

From the **ferry dock** the shore boulevard – Themistoklí Sofoúli – describes a 1300-metre arc around the bay. About 400m along is pedestrianized Platía Pythagóra, distinguished by its lion statue and some ugly concrete-barricade "sculpture"; about 800m along there's a major turning inland to the **KTEL** terminal, a chaos of buses at a perennially cluttered intersection by the ticket office. The minimally useful **tourist information** office is at 25-Martíou 4 (May–Oct Mon–Fri 9am–2pm; winter sporadic hours), worth a stop, if only for its comprehensive bus schedules and accommodation listings. If you've arrived with your own vehicle, beware of the pay-and-display **parking** scheme (strip tickets from kiosks €0.30 per hour) in effect along most of the waterfront.

The most useful waterfront **ferry/travel agent** for independent travellers is By Ship, with two branches: one at the base of the jetty (℡02730/80 445), primarily handling ships and hydrofoils, and one about 300m southeast (℡02730/25 065); between them they sell tickets for most ferry lines (DANE, NEL, Hellas Ferries, G&A), as well as air tickets on both Olympic and Axon. At present Miniotis Lines representation is restricted to Nautica near the *Samos Hotel*, and Kyriakoulis Maritime hydrofoil tickets are sold almost everywhere. Vathý is chock-

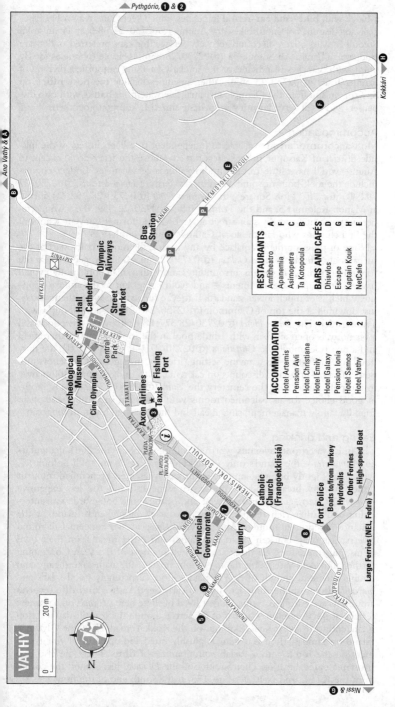

VATHÝ

0 ——— 200 m

N

Pythgório, **1** & **2**

Ano Vathy & **A**

Kokkári

Nissí & **G**

B

H

F

E

D

C

MYKALIS

SMYRNIS

Town Hall

Cathedral

Olympic
Airways

Bus
Station

Street
Market

Archeological
Museum

Cine Olympia

ALEX PASHALI

KAYTEVENI

Central Park

KAYTEVENI

VIANASTASIOU

STAMATI

Fishing
Port

Taxis

Axon Airlines

★

3

ℹ

PLATIA
PYTHAGORA

PLAYOU
NIKOLAOU

AREOS

MOUAGIOU

ENDREKAYDU

GRAMMOU

6

5

Provincial
Governorate

4

KANARI

KALOMIRI

MAVILI

LYKOURGOU

LOGOTHETI

THEMISTOKLI SOFOULI

Laundry

Catholic
Church
(Frangoekklisiá)

7

Port Police

Boats to/from Turkey

Hydrofoils

Other Ferries

High-speed Boat

8

Large Ferries (NEL, Fedra)

KEFALOPOULOU

THEMISTOKLI SOFOULI

P

P

P

RESTAURANTS

Amfitheatro   A
Apanemia   F
Asimopetra   C
Ta Kotopoula   B

BARS AND CAFÉS

Dhiavlos   D
Escape   G
Kaptain Kouk   H
NetCafe   E

ACCOMMODATION

Hotel Artemis   3
Pension Avli   4
Hotel Christiana   1
Hotel Emily   6
Hotel Galaxy   5
Pension Ionia   7
Hotel Samos   8
Hotel Vathý   2

---

a-block with **bike-** and **car-rental** franchises, which keeps rates reasonable, especially off-season. For motorbikes, try Aramis (☎02730/22 682) at Themistoklí Sofoúli 5, with a large fleet and recovery service; for cars, preferred outlets are Budget at Themistoklí Sofoúli 31 (☎02730/28 856), Reliable (phone as for By Ship), with branches islandwide, or the similarly far-flung Autoplan, a division of Samina Tours (☎02730/23 555). Other amenities include the **post office** on Smýrnis, inland from the Olympic terminal, five waterfront **banks** with cash dispensers and a self-serve **laundry** on pedestrianized Lykoúrgou Logothéti.

Accommodation

Most **accommodation** available to independent travellers clusters in the hillside district of Katsoúni, more or less directly above the ferry dock; except in August, you'll have little trouble finding affordable vacancies. Budget choices include the rock-bottom, somewhat noisy waterfront *Hotel Artemis* (☎02730/27 792; ●) just off "Lion Square"; the *Pension Ionia* (☎02730/28 782; ●), inland at Manoli Kalomíri 5; and the *Pension Avli* (☎02730/22 939; ●), a wonderful period piece up a nearby stair-street at Áreos 2, the former convent school of the French nuns who ran the local Catholic church until 1973.

None of these outfits is a palace by any means; for more luxury start at the surprisingly affordable *Hotel Galaxy* (☎02730/22 665; ●), at Angéou 1 near the top of Katsoúni, set in garden surroundings and with a small pool, though you'll have to dodge package allotments – and avoid being sent to the annexe opposite, which is of much lower standard. If they're full, try the sympathetic *Emily*, just downhill at the top of Grámmou (☎02730/24 691; ●), a small outfit with a roof garden. The *Samos Hotel* (☎02730/28 377; ●) right by the ferry dock and a bit noisy, is open all year, with a little pool in the roof garden. Further afield and a taxi ride uphill, the *Christiana* (☎02730/27 149 or 23 084; ●), the only hotel in Áno Vathý, has a ravine setting, friendly management, an enormous pool and a tie-in, giving discounts on car rental with Budget. Some 400m away in Neápoli district near the cemetery, the *Vathy* (☎02730/28 124; ●) is another good choice for its balconied rooms with bay view, small pool and again friendly family management; ring ahead and they may fetch you in their van.

Eating and drinking

The only waterfront **tavernas** worth a second glance are the 2001-inaugurated *Asimopetra* – the island's only *kultúra* taverna – at Themistoklí Sofoúli 97, which has slightly bumped-up prices but well-presented Frenchified minceur dishes, novelty breads and an impressive wine list; and the less expensive *Apanemia Ouzeri*, at the far southwest end of the shore boulevard, with interesting and rather rich recipes, so starve yourself beforehand. Inland, at the Plátanos junction en route to Áno Vathý, *Ta Kotopoula* is a congenial all-round taverna featuring chicken (as in the name) and other meat from their own farms, plus mezédhes. All three are open all or most of the year. Continuing further into Áno Vathý, *Amfitheatro* – right next to the namesake theatre and double medieval church of Aï Yiannáki – does surprisingly good salads and *mayireftá* dishes (dinner only, late June to early Sept). Vathý's **nightlife** revolves around its waterfront bars, the longest lived of these being *Escape*, on a seaview terrace at Kefalopoúlou 9 (north of the jetty), though the real till-dawn action is currently at *Kaptain Kouk*, 2km out on the Kokkári road. The Cine Olympia, inland on Yimnasiárhou Katevéni, is plushly fitted and operates all year (summers on the roof), with a variable programme of **films**. There are also two **internet cafés**, both on Themistoklí Sofoúli: *Dhiavlos* just around the corner from the KTEL, and *NetCafe* at no. 175, at the south end of the front.

Around Vathý

The immediate environs of Vathý offer some modest beaches and small hamlets, though you'll usually need your own transport to visit them. Two kilometres east and uphill spreads the vast inland plateau of **Vlamarí**, devoted to vineyards and supporting the hamlets of Ayía Zóni and Kamára (plus an increasing number of bad-taste modern villas); from Kamára you can climb up a partly cobbled path to the clifftop **monastery of Zoödhóhou Piyís**, for superb views across the end of the island to Turkey.

Heading north out of Vathý, the narrow road ends after 7km at the pebble bay and fishing port of **AYÍA PARASKEVÍ** (or Nissí), with good swimming. There are, alas, no longer any reliable facilities here other than a fitfully working snack-bar, *Aquarius* (typically July & Aug only).

As you head southeast from Vathý along the main island loop road, the triple chapel at **Trís Ekklisíes** marks an important junction, with another fork 100m along the left-hand turning. Bearing left twice takes you through the hilltop village of Paleókastro, 3km beyond which is another junction. Forking left yet again, after another 3km you reach the quiet, striking bay of **Kérveli**, with a small beach, a pair of tavernas (the friendly *Sea and Dolphins* has good mezédhes and *soúma*, the local spirit, but mains have declined in quality and climbed in price lately) by the water and another characterful favourite with simple grills only, *Iy Kryfí Folia*, about 500m uphill along the access road. Taking the right fork leads to **Posidhónio**, with an even smaller beach and another pair of tavernas: the right-hand one, *Kerkezos*, takes its cooking more seriously, though it's expensive. A right turn at the junction before Paleókastro leads to the beaches of Mykáli and Psilí Ámmos, the only spots in this section with a bus service. **Mykáli**, a kilometre of windswept sand and gravel, has been encumbered with three package hotels; the best place to try on spec here is *Villa Barbara* (☎02730/25 192; ④), which has apartments behind the *Sirenes Beach* hotel. Far and away the best **eating** on this coast is at *Kalypso*, which has excellent and well-priced *mayireftá* and is reached by its own dead-end access road off the main Mykáli-bound route. **Psilí Ámmos**, further east around the headland, is a crowded, sandy cove backed by several commercialized tavernas, none worth recommending; if you swim to the islet beware of strong currents which sweep through the narrow straits.

Pythagório and around

Most traffic south of Vathý heads for **PYTHAGÓRIO**, the island's premier resort, renamed in 1955 to honour native son Pythagoras, ancient mathematician, philosopher and mystic. Until then it was known as Tigáni (Frying Pan) – in midsummer you'll learn why. The sixth-century BC tyrant Polykrates had his capital here, now subject to sporadic excavations which have forced modern Pythagório to expand northeast and uphill. The village core of cobbled lanes and thick-walled mansions abuts a small **harbour**, fitting almost perfectly into the confines of Polykrates' ancient port, but today devoted almost entirely to pleasure craft and overpriced cocktail bars.

Sámos's most complete **castle**, the nineteenth-century *pýrgos* of local chieftain Lykourgos Logothetis, overlooks both the town and the shoreline. Logothetis, together with a certain "Kapetan Stamatis" and Admiral Kanaris, chalked up decisive victories over the Turks in the summer of 1824. The final battle was won on Transfiguration Day (August 6), and accordingly the church inside the castle precinct is dedicated to this festival. More antiquities include the fairly dull **Roman baths**, signposted as "Thermai", 400m west of town

(Tues–Sun 8.30am–2.30pm; free) and a minuscule **archeological collection** in the town hall on Platía Irínis (Tues–Thurs & Sun 9am–2pm, Fri & Sat 10am–2pm; free). Considerably more interesting is the **Efpalínio tunnel** (Tues–Sun 8.30am–2.30pm; €1.50), a 1040-metre aqueduct bored through the mountain just north of Pythagório at the behest of Polykrates. To get there, take the signposted path from the shore boulevard at the west end of town, which meets the vehicle access road toward the end of a twenty-minute walk.

Further subterranean experience can be had at the monastery of **Panayía Spilianí**, high on the hillside over town. Though most of this has been insensitively restored and touristified, behind the courtyard lies a cool, hundred-metre-long grotto, at one end of which is a shrine to the Virgin (open daylight hours; free). This was the presumed residence of the ancient oracular priestess Fyto, and a pirate-safe hideout in medieval times.

Practicalities

If there are any **accommodation** vacancies – more likely of late, with local package tourism down twenty percent – rooms proprietors meet all incoming ferries and hydrofoils. The **tourist information booth** (June–Sept daily 8am–10pm; ☎02730/62 274), on the main thoroughfare, Lykoúrgou Logothéti, can help in finding rooms and sells tickets for the *Nissos Kalymnos* ferryboat. Quietly located at the seaward end of Odhós Pythagóra, south of Lykoúrgou Logothéti, the modest *Tsambika* (☎02730/61 642; ❷) or the more comfortable *Dora*, a block west (☎02730/61 456; ❸), are two pensions worth considering. Some 50m inland from the north side of the harbour past the customs house, *Lambis Rooms* on Odhós Íras (☎02730/61 396; ❷) is another backpackers' transit stop. Another peaceful area is the hillside north of Platía Irínis, where *Studios Galini* (☎02730/61 167 or 010/98 42 248 in winter; ❹) has high-quality self-catering units with ceiling fans, balconies and kind English-speaking management. The *Evelin* (☎02730/61 124, Ⓕ61 077; ❸) isn't brilliantly located out by the traffic lights – convenient only for the airport – but it's comfortable, good value and friendly and has a swimming pool, double glazing against noise and on-site motorbike rental.

Eating out can be frustrating in Pythagório, with value for money often a completely alien concept. For waterside dining, you're best off at the far east end of the quay, beyond the shut-down hotel, where the *Remataki* (open all year) features vegetarian dishes such as *angináres ala políta* (stewed artichokes with veg), and the adjacent *Psaropoula* (April–Oct) offers reliably fresh and affordable fish as well as *orektiká* – these are the only two spots the locals themselves will be seen in. Night-owls gather at the *Mythos Club* on Platía Irínis, while all-year **Cine Rex** in Mytiliní village, 7km northwest, screens standard first-run fare.

Buses serving the local area leave from the **stop** that lies just west of the intersection of Lykoúrgou Logothéti and the road to Vathý. Two **banks** (both with cash dispensers) and the **post office** are also on Lykoúrgou Logothéti. The flattish country to the west is ideal for cycling, a popular activity, and if you want to rent a **motorbike** several outfits on Logothéti will oblige you.

Around Pythagório

The main local beach stretches for several kilometres west of the Logothetis "castle", punctuated about halfway along by the end of the airport runway, and the cluster of nondescript hotels known as **POTOKÁKI**. Just before the turn-off to the heart of the beach sprawls the ultra-luxurious *Doryssa Bay* complex (☎02730/61 360, Ⓕ61 463, ⓦwww.doryssabay.gr; ❸), which includes a meticulously concocted fake village, guaranteed to confound archeologists of future eras. No two of the units, joined by named lanes, are alike, and there's even a platía with a café. Although you'll have to contend with the hotel crowds and low-flying jets, the sand-and-pebble **beach** here is well groomed and the water clean; for more seclusion you'll have to head out to the end of the road.

The Potokáki access road is a dead end, with the main island loop road pressing on past the turn-off for the airport and Iréon hamlet. Under layers of alluvial mud, plus today's runway, lies the processional Sacred Way joining the ancient city with the **Heraion**, the massive shrine of the Mother Goddess (Tues–Sun 8.30am–2.30pm; €2.40). Much touted in tourist literature, this assumes humbler dimensions – one surviving column and assorted foundations – upon approach. Yet once inside the precinct you sense the former grandeur of the temple, never completed owing to Polykrates' untimely death at the hands of the Persians. The site chosen, near the mouth of the still-active Imvrassós stream, was Hera's legendary birthplace and site of her trysts with Zeus; in the far corner of the fenced-in zone you glimpse a large, exposed patch of the paved Sacred Way.

The modern resort of **IRÉON** nearby is a nondescript grid of dusty streets behind a coarse-shingle beach, attracting a slightly younger and more active clientele than Pythagório. Here you'll find more nonpackage rooms and a small **hotel**, *Venetia* (℡02730/95 295; ❸) within sight of the water. The oldest and most authentic **taverna** is the *Ireon*, at the far west end by the fishing harbour, also with namesake, basic rooms upstairs (℡02730/95 361; ❷).

Southern Sámos

Since the circumisland bus only passes through or near the places below once or twice daily, you really need your own vehicle to explore them. Some 5km west of Hóra, a well-marked side road leads up and right to **MAVRATZÉÏ**, one of two Samian "pottery villages", which lost 49 houses to the fire in 2000. The few surviving local potteries specialize in the *Koúpa tou Pythagóra* or "Pythagorean cup", supposedly designed by the sage to leak over the user's lap if they are overfilled. Slightly more practical wares can be found in **KOUMARADHÉÏ**, back on the main road, another 2km along.

From here you can descend a paved road to the sixteenth-century monastery of **Megális Panayías** (theoretically daily 9am–noon & 5–7pm), containing the finest frescoes on the island. This route continues to **MÝLI**, submerged in citrus groves and also accessible from Iréon. Four kilometres above Mýli sprawls **PAGÓNDAS**, a large hillside community with a splendid main square and an unusual communal fountain house on the south hillside. From here, a scenic paved road curls 9km around the hill to **SPATHARÉÏ** – its surroundings sadly devastated by repeated fires – set on a natural balcony offering the best sea views this side of the island. From Spatharéï, the road loops back 6km to **PÝRGOS**, at the head of a ravine draining southwest and the centre of Samian honey production; the most reliable local **taverna** (June–Oct) lies 3km west, in the plane-shaded Koútsi ravine which just escaped the July 2000 blaze.

The rugged and beautiful coast south of the Pagóndas–Pýrgos route is largely inaccessible, glimpsed by most visitors for the first and last time from the descending plane bringing them to Sámos. **Tsópela**, a highly scenic sand-and-gravel cove at a gorge mouth, is the only beach here with marked track access and a good seasonal taverna; you'll need a sturdy motorcycle (not a scooter) or jeep to get down there. The western reaches of this shoreline, which suffered comprehensive fire damage in 1994, are approached via the small village of **KOUMÉÏKA**, with a massive inscribed marble fountain and a pair of kafenía on its square. Below extends the long, pebble bay at **BÁLLOS**, with sand, a cave and naturists at the far east end. Bállos itself is merely a sleepy collection of summer houses, several simple places to stay and a few tavernas, all on the shore road. The best **accommodation** for walk-ins is the *Hotel Amfilisos* (☎02730/31 669, ℗31 668; ❷), while far and away the finest **dining** is found at *Akrogiali* nearby, with an honourable mention for humbler *Iy Paralia* off to the east. Returning to Kouméïka, the dubious-looking side road just before the village marked "Velanidhiá" is in fact partly paved and usable by any vehicle – a very useful short cut if you're travelling towards the beaches beyond Órmos Marathokámbou (see p.380).

Kokkári and around

Leaving Vathý on the north coastal section of the island loop road, you've little to stop for until **KOKKÁRI**, Sámos's third major tourist centre after Pythagório and the capital. Sadly, while lower Vathý and Pythagório had little beauty to sacrifice, much has been irrevocably lost here. The town's profile, covering two knolls behind twin headlands, remains unaltered, and one or two families still doggedly untangle their fishnets on the quay, but in general its identity has been altered beyond recognition, with constant inland expansion over vineyards and the abandoned fields of boiling onions that gave the place its name. Since the exposed, rocky beaches here are buffeted by near-constant winds, the promoters have made a virtue of necessity by developing the place as a successful windsurfing resort.

Practicalities

As in Vathý and Pythagório, a fair proportion of Kokkári's **accommodation** is block-booked by tour companies; establishments not completely devoted to such trade include *Lemos* (☎02730/92 250; ❹), near the north end of the west beach, and the more modest *Vicky* (☎02730/92 231; ❸), facing the same strand. For a guaranteed view of the fishing port, try the *Pension Alkyonis* (☎02730/92 225; ❷) or the *Pension Angela* (☎02730/92 052; ❷). Otherwise Yiorgos Mihelios has a range of rooms and flats to rent (☎02730/92 456; ❷–❹), including the *Pension Green Hill*. If you get stuck, seek assistance from the seasonal **EOT post** (☎02730/92 217), housed in a Portakabin near the main church. If money's no object, then it has to be the A-class *Arion* (☎02370/92 020, ℗92 006, ⓦwww.diavlos.gr/samos/arion/arion1.html; ❻), a well-designed bungalow complex on an unburnt patch of hillside 2km west.

Most **tavernas** line the north waterfront, and charge above the norm, though they're steadily losing ground to breakfast or cocktail bars. At the far east end of things, *Ta Adhelfia/The Brothers* is a good-value place strong on grilled fish and meat, but with a few oven dishes daily; adjacent and further west, *To Avgo tou Kokora* is another good (if pricier) all-rounder, while *Piccolo Porto* still further west does excellent Italian dishes, including wood-fired pizzas. The co-managed *Barino*, also here at mid-strip, is the best breakfast place, with various fresh-squeezed juices, waffles and crepes. Most (noisy) **bars** ring the little square just west of where the concreted stream (with its family of ducks) meets the sea, but there's also the more elaborate and well-established disco, *Cabana Beach Club*, on the west beach, drawing clubbers from across the island.

Other amenities include an Emboriki/Commercial Bank **cash dispenser** on the through road, a **post office** in a Portakabin on a seaward lane and next door, a long-hours, self-service **laundry**; there are also branches of the major Vathý **travel agents**, and a newsstand.

West of Kokkári: the coast

The closest sheltered beaches are thirty- to forty-minutes' walk away to the west, all with sunbeds and permanently anchored umbrellas. The first, **Lemonákia**, is a bit too close to the road, with an obtrusive café, though many *Arion* patrons like it; 1km beyond, the graceful crescent of **Tzamadhoú** figures in virtually every EOT poster of the island. With path-only access, it's a bit less spoiled, and each end of the beach (saucer-shaped pebbles) is by tacit consent a nudist/gay zone. There's one more pebble bay, 7km west beyond Avlákia, called **Tzaboú**, but it's not worth a special detour when the prevailing northwest wind is up.

The next spot of any interest along the coast road is **Platanákia**, essentially a handful of tavernas and rooms for rent at a bridge by the turning for Manolátes (see p.378); best of the tavernas is *Iy Apolavsis*, with a limited choice of very good *mayireftá*. Platanákia is actually the eastern suburb of **ÁYIOS KONSTANDÍNOS**, whose surf-pounded esplanade has been prettified. However, there are no usable beaches within walking distance, so the collection of warm-toned stone buildings, with few modern intrusions, constitutes a peaceful alternative to Kokkári. In addition to modest 1970s-vintage **rooms**, such as the *Four Seasons* (☎02730/94 287; ❷) or the *Atlantis* (☎02730/94 329; ❶) just above the highway, there's a new generation of more modern rooms below the road, such as *Maria's* (☎02730/94 460; ❸). **Eating** out, you're spoilt for choice; besides *Iy Apolavsis*, there's *To Kyma* at the east end of the quay, with good bulk wine and *mayireftá*; *To Akroyiali* at mid-quay, where the food's cheaper and better than the plastic menu-photos suggest; or (best of all) the *Aeolos* at the far west end of the esplanade (June–Sept), with terrific fish or grilled meat and a few well-chosen baked dishes.

Once past "Áyios", as it's locally abbreviated, the mountains hem the road in against the sea, and the terrain doesn't relent until **Kondakéïka**; its diminutive shore annexe of **Áyios Nikólaos** has an excellent venue for fish meals in *Iy Psaradhes* (☎02730/32 489; Easter–Oct), with a terrace lapped by the waves – booking in season is mandatory as it's appeared (deservedly) in so many guides. There's also the reasonable beach of **Piáki**, ten-minutes' walk east past the last studio units, evidence of a mild explosion in package development here since 1995.

Hill villages

Inland between Kokkári and Kondakéïka, an idyllic landscape of pine, cypress and orchards is overawed by dramatic mountains; except for some streaks of damage reaching the sea between Lemonákia and Tzaboú, it miraculously escaped the July 2000 fire. Despite destructive nibblings by bulldozers, some of the trail system linking the various **hill villages** is still intact, and walkers can return to the main highway to catch a bus home. Failing that, most of the communities can provide a bed at short notice.

The monastery of **Vrondianís** (Vrónda), directly above Kokkári, was once a popular destination, but between severe fire damage in 2000 and the army's use of it as a barracks, the place only really comes alive during its annual festival (Sept 7–8). **VOURLIÓTES**, 2km west of the monastery, has beaked chimneys and brightly painted shutters sprouting from its typical tile-roofed houses. Restaurateur greed has ruined the formerly photogenic central square, by cutting down two ancient mulberries, and it's best to pass over the tavernas here in favour of *Iy Pera Vrysi*, at the village entrance, or (even better) the *Piyi Pnaka* taverna, in the idyllic eponymous hamlet just off the ascending Vourliótes road.

MANOLÁTES, further uphill and an hour-plus walk away via a deep river canyon, also has several simple tavernas (the pick of these being *Iy Filia* near the village entrance), and is the most popular trailhead for the five-hour round-trip up **Mount Ámbelos** (Karvoúnis), the island's second-highest summit. From Manolátes you can no longer easily continue on foot to Stavrinídhes, the next village, but should plunge straight down, partly on a cobbled path, through the shady valley known as **Aïdhónia** (Nightingales), towards Platanákia. Manolátes has accommodation with *Studios Angela* at the edge of town (☎02730/94 478; ❸), but by far the most characterful base in the area is down in Aïdhónia at the *Hotel Aidonokastro* (☎02730/94 686, ☞94 404; ❹). Here the kindly, English-speaking Yannis Pamoukis has renovated half the abandoned hamlet of **Valeondátes** as a unique cottage-hotel, each former house comprising a pair of two- or four-person units with traditional touches.

5 Karlóvassi

KARLÓVASSI, 35km west of Vathý and the second town of Sámos, is decidedly sleepier and more old-fashioned than the capital, despite having roughly the same population. Though lacking in distinction, it's popular as a base for exploring western Sámos's excellent beaches and walking opportunities. The name, despite a vehement denial of Ottoman legacy elsewhere on Sámos, appears to be a corruption of the Turkish for "snowy plain" – the plain in question being the conspicuous saddle of Mount Kérkis overhead. The town divides into four straggly neighbourhoods: Néo, well inland, whose untidy growth was spurred by the influx of post-1923 refugees; Meséo, across the usually dry riverbed, tilting appealingly off a knoll towards the shore; and postcard-worthy Paleó (or Áno), above Limáni, the small harbour district.

Most tourists stay at or near **Limáni**, the part of town with most of the tourist facilities. Hotels tend to have road noise and not much view; **rooms**, all on the inland pedestrian lane behind the through road, are quieter – try those of Vangelis Feloukatzis (☎02730/33 293; ❷). The port itself is an appealing place with a working boatyard at the west end and all the **ferry-ticket agencies** grouped at the middle; a shuttle-bus service operates from Néo Karlóvassi, timed to coincide with boat arrivals and departures. Tavernas and bars are abundant on the quay, though the only remarkable ones are *Rementzo* (April–Oct), tellingly the locals' hangout, with good fish in season plus *mayireftá*, and the more touristy *Boussoulas* next door, which stays open year-round, with consistent quality. The local university contingent (a maths and computer science faculty is based here) keeps **nightlife** surprisingly lively; try *Popcorn* on the quay.

Immediately overhead is the partly hidden hamlet of **Paleó**, its hundred or so houses draped on either side of a leafy ravine, but no reliable tourist facilities. **Meséo**, just east, is a conceivable alternative base to Limáni, with the *Hotel Aspasia* (☎02730/31 201; ❹), well sited 100m west of the wood-fired bakery, with a pool and air-conditioning. Following the street linking the central square to the waterfront, you pass one of the improbably huge, early twentieth-century churches, topped with twin belfries and a blue-and-white dome, which dot the coastal plain here. Just at the intersection with the shore road you'll find the friendly, good-value, sunset-view *To Kyma* ouzerí (April–Oct), where the Sudanese proprietress adds a welcome Middle Eastern touch to the broad variety of dishes – most days you'll fight for a table.

Néo has little to recommend it besides a wilderness of derelict stone-built warehouses and mansions down near the river mouth, reminders of the long-vanished leather industry which flourished here during the first half of the twentieth centry. However, if you're staying at Limáni, you'll almost certainly visit one of the three **banks** (with cash dispensers), the **post office** or the **bus stop** on the main lower square. There are virtually no **eateries** except the popular, year-round *Dionysos Psistaria*, on the west side of town at the start of the Marathókambos road.

Western Sámos

Visitors tolerate dull Karlóvassi for the sake of western Sámos's excellent **beaches**. Closest of these is **Potámi**, forty-minutes' walk away via the coast road from Limáni or an hour by a more scenic, high trail from Paleó. This broad arc of sand and pebbles gets crowded at summer weekends, when virtually the entire population of Karlóvassi descends on the place. Near the end of the trail from Paleó stands *To Iliovasilema*, a friendly if oversubscribed *psistariá* with fish and meat; there are also a very few **rooms** signposted locally, and many folk camp rough along the lower reaches of the river which gives the beach its name.

A streamside path leads twenty minutes inland, past the eleventh-century church of **Metamórfosis** – the oldest on Sámos – to a point where the river disappears into a small gorge (a new, guardrailed but still vertiginous stairway takes you up and left here). Otherwise, you must swim and wade 100m in heart-stoppingly cold water through a sequence of fern-tufted rock pools before reaching a low but vigorous waterfall; bring shoes with good tread and perhaps even rope if you want to explore above the first cascade. You probably won't be alone until you dive in, since the canyon is well known to locals and tour agencies. Just above the Metamórfosis church, a clear if precipitous path leads up to a small, contemporaneous **Byzantine fortress**. There's little to see inside other than a subterranean cistern and badly crumbled lower curtain wall, but the views out to sea and up the canyon are terrific, while in October the place is carpeted with pink autumn crocuses.

The coast beyond Potámi ranks among the most beautiful and unspoiled on Sámos; since the early 1980s it has served as a protected refuge for the rare monk seal. The dirt track at the west end of Potámi bay ends after twenty minutes on foot, from which you backtrack 100m or so to find the well-cairned side trail running parallel to the water. After twenty minutes along this you'll arrive at **Mikró Seïtáni**, a small pebble cove guarded by sculpted rock walls. A full hour's walk from the trailhead, through partly fire-damaged olive terraces, brings you to **Megálo Seïtáni**, the island's finest beach, at the mouth of the intimidating Kakopérato gorge. You'll have to bring food and water, though not necessarily a swimsuit – there's no dress code at either of the Seïtáni bays.

Southwestern beach resorts

The first place you reach on the island loop road south of Karlóvassi is **MARATHÓKAMBOS**, a pretty, amphitheatrical village overlooking the eponymous gulf; there's a taverna or two, but no short-term accommodation. Its port, **ÓRMOS MARATHOKÁMBOU**, 18km from Karlóvassi, has recently emerged as a tourist resort, though some character still peeks through in its backstreets. The port has been improved, with kaïkia offering day-trips to Foúrni and the nearby islet of Samiopoúla, while the pedestrianized quay has become the focus of attention, home to several **tavernas** – best of these, by a nod, *Kyra Katina*, with a good range of seafood. Among the few nonpackaged **accommodation** outfits, try *Studios Avra* (☎02730/37 221; ③), unimprovably perched above the jetty.

The beach immediately east from Órmos is hardly the best; for better ones continue 2km west to **VOTSALÁKIA** (officially signposted as "Kámbos"), Sámos's fastest-growing resort, straggling a further 2km behind the island's longest (if not its most beautiful) beach. But for most, Votsalákia is still a vast improvement on the Pythagório area, and the mass of 1437-metre Mount Kérkis overhead rarely fails to impress (see below). As for **accommodation**, Emmanuil Dhespotakis (℡02730/31 258; ❸) has numerous premises towards the quieter, more scenic western end of things. Also in this vicinity is *Loukoullos*, an unusual *kultúra* **taverna** overlooking the sea where all fare is prepared in a wood oven. Other facilities include branches of nearly all the main Vathý travel agencies, offering **vehicle rental** (necessary, as only two daily buses call here) and money exchange.

If Votsalákia doesn't suit, you can continue 3km past to the 600-metre beach of **Psilí Ámmos**, more aesthetic and not to be confused with its namesake beach in the southeast corner of Sámos. The sea shelves very gently here, and cliffs shelter clusters of naturists at the east end. Surprisingly there is still little development: just three small studio complexes in the pines at mid-beach, and two tavernas back up on the road as you approach, either of these fine for a simple lunch. Access to **Limniónas**, a smaller cove 2km further west, passes the *Limnionas Bay Hotel* (℡02730/37 057; ❻), much the highest-standard accommodation locally with its tiered units arrayed around a garden and pool. Yachts and pleasure kaïkia occasionally call at the protected bay, which offers decent swimming away from a rock shelf at mid-strand, especially at the east end where there's a simple **taverna**.

Mount Kérkis and around

Gazing up from a supine seaside position, you may be inspired to climb **Mount Kérkis**. The classic route begins at the west end of the Votsalákia strip, along the bumpy jeep track leading inland towards Evangelistrías convent. After thirty minutes on the track system, through fire-damaged olive groves and past charcoal pits (a major local industry), the path begins, more or less following power lines up to the convent. A friendly nun may proffer an oúzo in welcome and point you up the paint-marked trail, continuing even more steeply up to the peak. The views are tremendous, though the climb itself is humdrum once you're out of the trees. About an hour before the top there's a chapel with an attached cottage for sheltering in emergencies, and just beyond, a welcome spring. All told, it's a seven-hour outing from Votsalákia and back, not counting rest stops.

Less ambitious walkers might want to circle the flanks of the mountain, first by vehicle and then by foot. The road beyond Limniónas to Kallithéa and Dhrakéï, truly back-of-beyond villages with views across to Ikaría, is paved most of the way to Dhrakéï, making it possible to venture out here on an ordinary motorbike. The bus service is better during the school year, when a vehicle leaves Karlóvassi (Mon–Fri 1pm) bound for these remote spots; during summer it only operates two days a week at best (typically Mon & Fri).

From **DHRAKÉÏ**, the end of the line with just a pair of very simple kafenía to its credit, a lovely trail, minimally damaged by a track, descends ninety minutes through forest to Megálo Seïtáni, from where it's easy enough to continue on to Karlóvassi within another two-and-a-half hours. People attempting to reverse this itinerary often discover to their cost that the bus (if any) returns from Dhrakéï early in the day, at about 2.30pm, compelling them to stay at one of two unofficial **rooms** establishments (summer only) in Dhrakéi, and dine at one of four taverna-kafenía. In **KALLITHÉA**, there's only a simple *psistariá* on the square. From Kallithéa, a newer track (from beside the cemetery) and an older trail both lead up within 45 minutes to a spring, rural chapel and plane tree on the west flank of Kérkis, with path-only continuation for another thirty minutes to a pair of cave-churches. **Panayía Makriní** stands detached at the mouth of a high, wide but shallow grotto, whose balcony affords terrific views of Sámos's west tip. By contrast, **Ayía Triádha**, a ten-minute scramble overhead, has most of its structure made up of cave wall; just adjacent, another long, narrow, volcanic cavern can be explored with a torch some hundred metres into the mountain.

After these subterranean exertions, the closest spot for a swim is **Vársamo** (Válsamo) cove, 4km below Kallithéa and reached via a well-signposted dirt road. The beach here consists of multicoloured volcanic pebbles, with two caves to shelter in and a single very friendly **taverna** just inland, run by three generations of women.

Ikaría

Ikaría, a narrow, windswept landmass between Sámos and Mýkonos, is little visited and invariably underestimated. The name supposedly derives from the legendary Icarus, who fell into the sea just offshore after the wax bindings on his wings melted. For years the only substantial tourism was generated by a few **hot springs** on the south coast, some reputed to cure rheumatism and arthritis, some to make women fertile, though others are so highly radioactive that they've been closed for decades.

Ikaría, along with Thessaly on the mainland and Lésvos, has traditionally been one of the Greek Left's strongholds. This tendency dates from the long decades of right-wing domination in Greece, when (as in past ages) the island was used as a place of **exile** for political dissidents. Apparently the strategy backfired, with the Communist transportees favourably impressing and proselytizing their hosts; at the same time, many Ikarians emigrated to North America, and ironically their regular capitalist remittances help keep the island going. It can be a bizarre experience to be treated to a monologue on the evils of US imperialism, delivered by a retiree in perfect Alabaman English. Of late, the Ikarians tend to embrace any vaguely Left cause; posters urge you variously to attend rallies on behalf of Turkish political prisoners or contribute to funding a Zapatista teacher-training school in Chiapas. Athens has historically reacted to this contrarian stance with long periods of punitive neglect, which has only made the islanders even more profoundly self-sufficient and idiosyncratic, and supportive (or at least tolerant) of the same in others. Local pride dictates that outside opinion matters not a bit, and until very recently Ikarians seemed to have little idea what "modern tourists" expected. A lack of obsequiousness, and a studied eccentricity, are often mistaken for hostility.

These are not the only Ikarian quirks, and for many the place is an acquired taste, contrasting strongly (for better or worse) with Sámos. Except for forested portions in the northwest (now much fire-denuded near the shore to clear land for hotels), it's not a strikingly beautiful island, with most of the terrain consisting of scrub-covered schist put to good use as building material. The mostly desolate south coast is overawed by steep cliffs, while the north face is less sheer but nonetheless furrowed by deep canyons creating hairpin bends extreme even by Greek-island standards. Neither are there many postcard-picturesque villages, since the rural schist-roofed houses are generally scattered so as to be next to their famous apricot orchards, vineyards and fields.

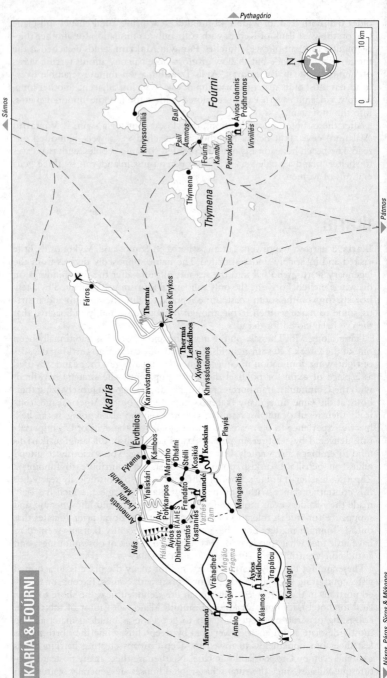

IKARÍA & FOÚRNI

Until the mid-1990s, the Ikarians resisted most attempts to develop their island for conventional tourism; charter flights still don't land here, as the northeastern airport can't accommodate jets. Since then, however, there's been a slow but steady increase in the quantity and quality of tourist facilities in and around Armenistís, the only resort of consequence.

Áyios Kírykos and around

Passing ferries on the Páros–Náxos–Foúrni–Dodecanese line call at the south-coast port and capital of **ÁYIOS KÍRYKOS**, about 1km southwest of the island's main thermal resort. Because of the spa trade, beds are at a premium in town; arriving in the evening from Sámos, accept any reasonable offers of rooms at the jetty, or – if in a group – proposals of a taxi ride to the north coast, which shouldn't cost more than €22 per vehicle to Armenistís. A cream-and-green **bus** sets out across the island from the main square (summer Mon–Fri only at noon) to Évdhilos, usually changing vehicles there at 1.30pm, for the onward trip to Armenistís.

The baths (daily 8am–1pm) in **Thermá** are rather old-fashioned stone tubs, with preference given to those under medical care. A better bet for a less formal soak are the more natural, shoreline hot springs at **Thermá Lefkádhos**, 3km southwest of Áyios Kírykos, below a cluster of villas. Here the seaside spa is derelict, leaving the water to boil up right in the shallows, mixing with the sea between giant volcanic boulders to a pleasant temperature.

A more conventional beach – the largest on the south coast – is found at **Fáros**, 10km northeast of Áyios Kírykos along a good paved road (which also serves the airport). A considerable colony of summer cottages shelters under tamarisks fringing the mixed sand-and-gravel strand, with a reefy zone to cross before deep water; this rather end-of-the-world place looks across to Foúrni and Thýmena, whose beaches (and landscape) it strongly resembles. But the best reason to make the trip out is an excellent, inexpensive and quick-serving **fish taverna**, *Leonídas*, with grilled or fried seafood plus bulk wine (excellent, as it usually is on Ikaría), better than anything in Áyios itself and accordingly popular.

Practicalities

Hydrofoils, the small Miniotis Lines ferries and kaïkia for Foúrni use the small east jetty; large ferries and catamarans dock at the main west pier. There are several **hotels**, such as the *Isabella* (℡02750/22 839; ❷–❸) above the National Bank, or the friendly, basic but spotless *Akti* (℡02750/22 694; ❶–❸), on a knoll east of the hydrofoil and kaïki quay, with views of Foúrni from the garden; both have rooms with and without bathrooms. Otherwise, **pensions** and **rooms** are not especially cheap. Directly behind the base of the ferry jetty and a little to the west there's the well-appointed *Pension Maria-Elena* (℡02750/22 835, ℻22 223; ❸), with sea views. All in a row to the east and suffering some noise from the several kafenía and snack bars below are the *Pension Ikaria* (℡02750/22 804; ❷), the studios above the *Snack Bar Dedalos* (℡02750/22 276; ❸) and the clean *dhomátia* run by Ioannis Proestos (℡02750/23 176; ❷).

Eating out, you've even less choice than in lodging. It's best to give the obvious quayside eateries a miss in favour of the grilled dishes served up at the *Estiatorio Tzivaeri*, just inland from Ioannis Proestos's rooms, or *Iy Klimataria* just around the corner for less distinguished but year-round *mayireftá*. The front is more glitzy, with *Casino* the last remaining traditional kafenío; for further entertainment there's a **summer cinema**, the Rex, with first-run fare. Three **banks** with cash dispensers, a **post office** on the road out of town and three ferry/hydrofoil **agents** round up the list of essentials. You can **rent** motorbikes and cars here, too, but both are typically cheaper in Armenistís.

Évdhilos and around

The twisting, 41-kilometre road from Áyios Kírykos to Évdhilos is one of the most hair-raising on any Greek island (especially as a taxi passenger), and the long ridge extending the length of Ikaría often wears a streamer of cloud, even when the rest of the Aegean is clear. Karavóstamo, with its tiny, scruffy port, is the first substantial north-coast place, beyond which a series of three beaches leads up to **ÉVDHILOS**. Although this is the island's second town and a daily ferry stop on the Sámos–Mýkonos–Sýros line, it's far less equipped to deal with visitors than Áyios Kírykos. Évdhilos offers just two **hotels** – the *Evdoxia* on the slope southwest of the harbour (℡02750/31 502; ❺) and the low-lying *Atheras* (℡02750/31 434, ℻31 926; ❹) with a small pool – plus a few **rooms**, the best of which are run by Apostolos Stenos (℡02750/31 365; ❶) just west of town. A **post office** up towards the *Evdoxia*, a pair of **cash dispensers**, and two good **beaches** just to the east, are also worth knowing about, though the nearer beach will be blighted in the coming years by a new, much-needed harbour jetty. Among several waterfront **restaurants**, the wood-signed "*Kafestiatório*" between *O Flisvos* and the Blue Nice **boat-ticket agency** is the most reliable and reasonable option, but for more interesting fare head 1km west of the harbour to **Fýtema** hamlet, where just on the roadside *To Inomayerio tis Popis*, alias *To Fytema* (Easter–Sept), has lots of options for vegetarians, excellent local wine, low prices and pleasant terrace seating, though portions are on the small side.

KÁMBOS, 1.5km west of Fýtema, offers a small hilltop museum with finds from nearby **ancient Oinoe**; the twelfth-century church of Ayía Iríni lies just below, with the remains of a fourth-century Byzantine basilica serving as the entry courtyard. Lower down still are the sparse ruins of a Byzantine palace (just above the road) used to house exiled nobles, as well as a 250-metre-long sandy beach with a musical drinks *kantína*. *Rooms Dhionysos* are available from the store run by Vassilis Kambouris (℡02750/31 300 or 31 688; ❷), who also acts as the unofficial and enthusiastic tourism officer for this part of Ikaría, keeping the keys for the church and museum.

By following the road heading inland from the large church in Évdhilos, you can also visit the Byzantine **castle of Koskiná** (Nikariás), just over 15km south. The road signposted for Manganítis is paved through Kosikiá, just over 9km away, and for 2km more to the marked side track. You can get a bike or jeep along this to within a short walk of the tenth-century castle, perched on a distinctive conical hill, with an arched gateway and a fine vaulted chapel.

Beyond this turning, the road creeps over the island watershed and drops precipitously in hairpins towards the south coast; most of this is paved, and with your own vehicle offers an alternative (and much less curvy) way back to Áyios Kírykos in much the same time as via Karavóstomo.

Armenistís and around

Most people carry on to **ARMENISTÍS**, 57km from Áyios Kírykos, and with good reason: this little resort lies below Ikaría's finest (if much diminished) forest, with two enormous, sandy beaches battered by near-constant surf – **Livádhi** and **Mesakhtí** – five- and fifteen-minutes' walk to the east respectively. The waves, which attract Athenian surfers, are complicated by strong lateral currents (as signs warn), and regular summer drownings have prompted the institution of that Greek rarity, lifeguard service. Armenistís itself is spectacularly set, looking northeast along the length of Ikaría towards sun- and moonrise, with Mount Kérkis on Sámos closing off the horizon on a clear day. A dwindling proportion of older, schist-roofed buildings, plus fishing boats hauled up in a sandy cove, lend Armenistís the air of a Cornish fishing village. Despite gradual growth it remains a manageable place, reminiscent of similar youth-oriented, slightly "alternative" spots in southern Crete, though gentrification (and a strong package presence) has definitely set in, and the islanders' tolerance doesn't extend to nude bathing. The long-running, semi-official campsite behind Livádhi beach closed in 2001 – a sign of the times – and probably won't reopen; a few free-lance tents still sprout in the rivermouth greenery behind Mesakhtí. Several "music bars", often with live Greek gigs, operate seasonally behind Livádhi and at the quay's north end, but for most visitors **nightlife** takes the form of extended sessions in the tavernas and cafés overlooking the anchorage, or the *zaharoplastía* (especially *En Plo*) at the village entrance.

There are easily a score of rooms establishments in the Armenistís area, as well as four bona fide **hotels**. Among the latter, the 1999-built *Erofili Beach*, right at the entrance to "town" (☎02750/71 058, ⓕ71 483, ⓦwww.erofili.gr; ⓞ) is considered the best on the island and has a small pool perched dramatically over Livádhi beach. Runners-up include the *Messakhti Village* complex (☎02750/71 331, ⓕ71 330, ⓦwww.messakti-village.gr; ⓞ) just above Mesakhtí beach, with a larger pool, its common areas and private terraces making up for the slightly minimalist self-catering units suitable for families of three to six, or – on the western edge of Armenistís – the *Daidalos* (☎02750/71 390, ⓕ71 393, ⓔdaidalos@aegean-exodus.gr; ⓞ), the less impersonal and less package-dominated of two adjacent hotels, with another eyrie-pool, unusually appointed rooms and a shady breakfast terrace. If your budget doesn't run to the *Erofili Beach*, the adjacent *Kirki Rooms* (☎02750/71 254, ⓕ71 083; ❷) are spartan but en suite, with large private balconies and sea views; on the opposite side of the road, but at the top of the hill, the similar-decor *Armena Inn* (☎02750/71 320; ❸) has private parking, seclusion, unobstructed views and cooking facilities in the rooms. Along the shore lane, the *Paskhalia* **rooms** (☎0275/71 302 or 010/24 71 411 in winter; ❶) are on the small side but are en suite and good value, with great views east, while at the far end of Livádhi beach, the *Atsahas Apartments* (☎ & ⓕ 02750/71 226; ❸) offer the best standard and setting outside of the hotels.

Discounting the *zaharoplastía* and *souvláki* stalls (a pair each), there are five full-service **tavernas** in Armenistís, of which three have a consistently good reputation. *Dhelfini*, its terrace hovering right above the fishing cove, is the cheap-and-cheerful favourite – come early or very late for a table, and a mix of grills or *mayireftá*. *Paskhalia* (aka *Vlahos* after the helpful managing family) also serves similar fare at its seaview terrace up the hill, and is the most reliable venue for both breakfast and off-season travellers, open until mid-October. Down on the quay itself, *Symposio* is pricier but well worth it for its creative recipes and rich ingredients reflecting the German co-management and chef. Further afield, the *Atsahas*, attached to the namesake apartments, is pretty good as a beach taverna, with generous portions but occasionally undercooked and over-oiled fare. Just east of Mesakhtí in the fishing settlement of **Yialiskári**, looking out past pines to a picturesque church on the jetty, there's another cluster of tavernas overlooking the boat-launching slips, of which *Tramountana* and *Kelari* are the most popular, the former purveying superb parrotfish fry-ups if you strike lucky. Yialiskári is also home to the area's only **internet café**, *Ic@rian-Sea*.

There are now at least four **scooter/mountain-bike rental** agencies in Armenistís; among a like number of **car-rental** outlets, Aventura (☎02750/71

117) is the most prominent, with a branch in Évdhilos which could be handy for ferry departures at an ungodly hour (typically 4am), when the buses aren't yet running. Indeed getting away when you need to is the main drawback to staying in Armenistís, since both taxis and buses can be elusive, though predictability has improved slightly over the years. Theoretically, **buses** head for Évdhilos three times daily mid-June to mid-September, fairly well spaced (typically 7.15am, noon & 7pm, returning an hour or so later) and designed to coincide with ferries; Áyios Kírykos has only one through service year-round at 7.15am, though this can be full with school kids in term-time. If you've a ferry to catch, it's far easier on the nerves to prebook a **taxi**: ring Kostas Stroupas (☎02750/41 132), or Yiannis Tsantiris (☎02750/41 322).

Ráhes

Armenistís is actually the shore annexe of four inland hamlets – Áyios Dhimítrios, Áyios Polýkarpos, Kastaniés and Khristós – collectively known as **RÁHES**. Despite the modern, mostly paved access roads through the pines (trails shortcut them, see below), the settlements retain a certain Shangri-La quality, with the older residents speaking a positively Homeric dialect. On an island not short of foibles, Khristós (Khristós Rahón in full) is particularly strange inasmuch as the locals sleep until 11am or so, shop and educate their kids until about 4pm, then have another nap until 9pm, whereupon they rise and spend the entire night shopping, eating and drinking until almost dawn. In fact most of the villages west of Évdhilos adhere to this schedule, defying central government efforts to bring them in line with the rest of Greece.

Near the pedestrianized *agorá* of Khristós, paved in schist and studded with gateways fashioned from the same rock, there's a **post office** and a **hotel/restaurant** (☎02750/71 269; ❸), but in accordance with the above diurnal schedule, lunchtime can offer pretty slim pickings. The most reliable venue (strictly after 1pm) are the unmarked premises of Vassilis Yiakas, at the far southeast end of the pedestrian way – you'll know it from the enormous Victrola and the bare wood floors. The slightly spaced-out demeanour of those serving – plus numbers of old boys shambling around in dirty clothes, with their flies unzipped – may be attributable to overindulgence in the excellent home-brewed **wine** which everyone west of Évdhilos makes. The local festival is August 6, though better ones take place further southwest in the woods at the Langádha valley (August 14–15) or at the Áyios Isídhoros monastery (May 14).

Since the early 1990s, **walking** between Ráhes and the coastal resorts has rocketed in popularity, and there are finally locally produced, accurate if somewhat chatty map-guides widely available. The black-and-white *Road & Hiking Map of Western Ikaria* (€1.20) shows most asphalt roads, tracks and trails in the west-centre of the island; the more closely focused, colour *Round of Rahes on Foot* (€3) details a loop hike taking in the best the Ráhes villages have to offer. The route sticks mostly to surviving paths, and is well marked; the authors suggest a full day for the circuit, with ample rests, though total walking time won't be more than six hours. More advanced outings involve descending the Hálaris canyon, with its historic bridge, to Nás, or crossing the island to Manganítis via Ráhes.

Nás

By tacit consent, Greek or foreign hippies and beachside naturists have been allowed to shift 3km west of Armenistís by paved road to **Nás**, a tree-clogged river canyon ending in a small but deceptively sheltered sand-and-pebble beach. This little bay is almost completely enclosed by weirdly sculpted rock formations, but for the same reasons as at Mesakhtí it's unwise to swim outside the cove's natural limits. The crumbling foundations of the fifth-century temple of **Artemis Tavropoleio** (Patroness of Bulls) overlook the permanent deep pool at the mouth of the river. If you continue inland along this past colonies of freelance campers defying prohibition signs, you'll find secluded rock pools for freshwater dips. Back at the top of the stairs leading down to the beach from the road are six tavernas, most of them offering rooms. Among the **tavernas**, *O Nas* doesn't abuse its prime position, operating Easter to October, with a good range of lunchtime *mayireftá*; among **rooms**, the *Artemis* (☎02750/71 485; ❸) overlooks the river canyon, while *Thea* (☎02750/71 491; ❸) faces out to sea, both places halving the rates out of season.

Satellite islands: Thýmena and Foúrni

The straits between Sámos and Ikaría are speckled with a mini-archipelago of three islets, of which the inhabited ones are Thýmena and Foúrni. More westerly **Thýmena** has one tiny hillside settlement; a regular kaïki calls at the quay below on its way between Ikaría and Foúrni, but there are no tourist facilities, and casual visits are explicitly discouraged. Foúrni is home to a huge fishing fleet and one of the more thriving boatyards in the Aegean; thanks to these, and the improvement of the jetty to receive car ferries, its population is stable, unlike so many small Greek islands. The islets were once the lair of Maltese pirates, and indeed many of the islanders have a distinctly North African appearance.

The aforementioned **kaïki** leaves Ikaría at about 1pm several days weekly, stays overnight at Foúrni and returns the next morning; another twice-weekly kaïki from Karlóvassi, and the larger car ferries which appear every few days, are likewise not tourist excursion boats but exist for the benefit of the islanders. The only practical way to visit Foúrni on a day-trip is by using the tourist kaïki *Ayios Nikolaos*, which leaves Áyios Kírykos daily in season at 10am, and returns from Foúrni at 5pm, or on one of the summer morning **hydrofoils** out of Sámos (Vathý or Pythagório).

Foúrni

Apart from the remote hamlet of **Khryssomiliá** in the north, where the island's longest (and often roughest) road goes, most of Foúrni's inhabitants are concentrated in the **port** and Kambí hamlet just to the south. The harbour community is larger than it seems from the sea, with a friendly ambience reminiscent of 1970s Greece. Among several **rooms** establishments, the most popular are the various premises run by Manolis and Patra Markakis (☎02750/51 268), immediately to your left as you disembark; there are simple rooms, some with balconies (❶), and superb hilltop studios (❷). If they're full you can head inland to the modern block of Evtyhia Amoryianou (☎02750/51 364; ❶), whose father Nikos Kondylas meets all boats and is a mine of information about the island.

There are two full-service waterfront **tavernas**: local favourite *Rementzo*, better known as *Nikos'*, where, if you're lucky, the local *astakós* or Aegean lobster may be on the menu until mid-August; or the cheaper, less polished *Miltos*, also with good seafood. For breakfast and desserts, repair to the tamarisk terrace at the Markakis family's *To Arhondiko tis Kyras Kokonas*, under their inn. There's surprisingly lively **nightlife** at a half-dozen music bars, clubs and ouzerís, often until 5am.

The central "high street", fieldstoned and mulberry-shaded, ends well inland at a little platía with more traditional kafenía under each of two plane trees;

between them stands a Hellenistic sarcophagus found in a nearby field, and overhead is a conical hill, site of the ancient acropolis. There's a **post office**, plus several surprisingly well-stocked shops, but at the time of writing no functioning cash machine or other money-changing facilities, so come prepared.

A fifteen-minute trail-walk south from the school, skirting the cemetery and then slipping over the windmill ridge, brings you to **KAMBÍ**, a scattered community overlooking a pair of sandy, tamarisk-shaded coves which you may share with chickens and hauled-up fishing boats. There are two cheap, comparable and sustaining **tavernas**: the *Kambi* with tables on the sand, and *O Yiorgos* clinging to the side of a valley inland. A path continues to the next bay south which, like Kambí cove, is a preferred anchorage for wandering yachts.

Heading north from the harbour via steps, then a trail, you'll find another **beach**: **Psilí Ámmos** in front of a derelict fish-processing plant, with shade at one end. At the extreme north of the island, remote **KHRYSSOMILIÁ** is still best approached by the taxi-boat *Evangelistria* rather than the atrocious eighteen-kilometre road. The village, split into a shore district and a hillside settlement, has a decent beach flanked by better but less accessible ones. Simple **rooms** and **meals** can be arranged on the spot, though the locals can be less than forthcoming with outsiders. The hamlet and monastery of **Áyios Ioánnis Pródhromos** in the far south of Foúrni is probably a better day-trip target on foot, taxi-boat or by scooter (available for rent), with some good, secluded beaches just below.

Híos

"Craggy Híos", as **Homer** aptly described his putative birthplace, has a turbulent history and a strong identity. It has always been relatively prosperous: in medieval times through the export of mastic **resin** – a trade controlled by Genoese overlords between 1346 and 1566 – and later by the **Ottomans**, who dubbed the place Sakız Adası ("Resin Island"). Since union with Greece in 1912, several shipping dynasties have emerged here, continuing the pattern of wealth. Participation in the maritime way of life is widespread, with someone in almost every family spending time in the merchant navy.

The more powerful ship-owning families and the military authorities did not encourage tourism until the late 1980s, but the worldwide shipping crisis and the saturation of other, more obviously "marketable" islands eroded their resistance. Increasing numbers of foreigners are discovering a Híos beyond its rather daunting port capital: fascinating villages, important Byzantine monuments and a respectable, if remote, complement of beaches. While unlikely ever to be dominated by tourism, the local scene has a distinctly modern flavour – courtesy of numerous returned Greek-Americans and Greek–Canadians – and English is widely spoken.

Unfortunately, the island has suffered more than its fair share of **catastrophes** during the past two centuries. The Turks perpetrated their most infamous, if not their worst, anti-revolutionary atrocity here in March 1822, massacring 30,000 Hiots and enslaving or exiling even more. In 1881, much of Híos was destroyed by a violent **earthquake**, and throughout the 1980s the natural beauty of the island was markedly diminished by devastating forest fires, compounding the effect of generations of tree-felling by boat-builders. Nearly two-thirds of the majestic pines are now gone, with substantial patches of woods persisting only in the far northeast and the centre of Híos.

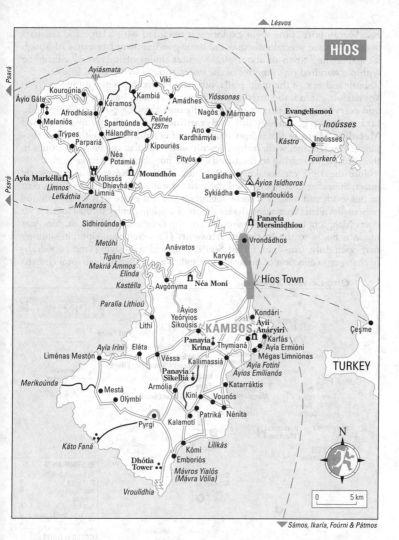

In 1988 the first charters from northern Europe were instituted, signalling potentially momentous changes for the island. But there are still fewer than four thousand guest beds on Híos, the vast majority of them in the capital or the nearby beach resorts of Karfás and Ayía Ermióni. Further expansion, however, is hampered by the lack of direct flights from most countries (including Britain), and the refusal of property owners to part with land for the extension of the airport runway.

Híos Town

HÍOS, the harbour and main town, will come as a shock after modest island capitals elsewhere; it's a bustling, concrete-laced commercial centre, with little predating the 1881 quake. Yet in many ways it is the most satisfactory of the east Aegean ports; time spent exploring is rewarded with a large and fascinating marketplace, several museums and some good, authentic tavernas. Although it's a sprawling town of about 30,000, most things of interest to visitors lie within a hundred or so metres of the water, fringed by Leofóros Egéou.

South and east of the main platía, officially Plastíra but known universally as Vounakíou, extends the marvellously lively tradesmen's **bazaar**, where you can find everything from parrots to cast-iron woodstoves. Opposite the Vounakíou **taxi rank**, the grandiosely titled "**Byzantine Museum**", occupying the old **Mecidiye Mosque** (Tues–Sun 10am–1pm; free), is little more than an archeological warehouse, with Turkish, Jewish and Armenian marble gravestones in the courtyard testifying to the island's varied population in past centuries.

Until the 1881 earthquake, the Byzantine–Genoese **Kástro** was completely intact; thereafter developers razed the seaward walls, filled in much of the moat to the south and made a fortune selling off the real estate thus created around present-day Platía Vounakíou. Today the most satisfying entry to the citadel is via Porta Maggiora behind the town hall. The top floor of a medieval mansion just inside is home to the **Justiniani Museum** (Tues–Sun 9am–3pm, in summer may open daily 9am–7pm; €1.50, Sun €0.90), with a satisfying (and periodically changing) collection of unusual icons and mosaics rescued from local church-

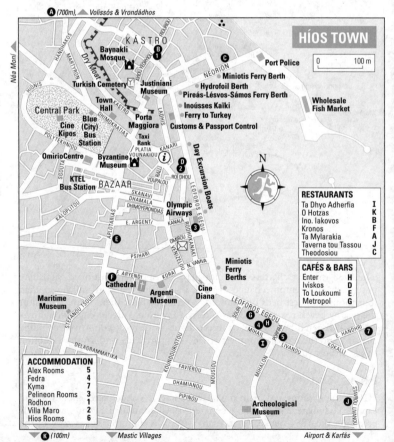

HÍOS TOWN

0   100 m

RESTAURANTS
Ta Dhyo Adherfia	I
O Hotzas	K
Ino. Iakovos	B
Kronos	F
Ta Mylarakia	A
Taverna tou Tassou	J
Theodosiou	C

CAFÉS & BARS
Enter	H
Iviskos	D
To Loukoumi	E
Metropol	G

ACCOMMODATION
Alex Rooms	5
Fedra	4
Kyma	7
Pelineon Rooms	3
Rodhon	1
Villa Maro	2
Hios Rooms	6

es. The small dungeon adjacent briefly held 75 Hiot hostages before their execution by the Ottomans in 1822. The old residential quarter inside the surviving castle walls, formerly the Muslim and Jewish neighbourhoods, is well worth a wander; among the wood and plaster houses you'll find assorted Ottoman monuments in various states of decay: a Muslim cemetery, a small minaretless mosque, a ruined *hamam* (Turkish bath) and several inscribed fountains.

Further afield, three other museums beckon. The **Maritime Museum** at Stefánou Tsoúri 20 (Mon–Sat 10am–1pm; free) consists principally of model ships and oil paintings of various craft, Greek and foreign, all rather overshadowed by the mansion containing them. In the foyer are enshrined the knife and glass-globe grenade of Admiral Kanaris, who partly avenged the 1822 massacre by ramming and sinking the Ottoman fleet's flagship. In the centre of town, the **Argenti Folklore Museum** (Mon–Thurs 8am–2pm, Fri 8am–2pm & 5–7.30pm, Sat 8am–12.30pm; €1.50), on the top floor of the Koráï Library at Koráï 2, features ponderous genealogical portraits of the endowing family, an adjoining wing of costumes and rural impedimenta, plus multiple replicas of Delacroix's *Massacre at Hios*, a painting which did much to arouse sympathy for the cause of Greek independence.

The **Archeological Museum** on Mihálon (June–Sept daily 8am–7pm; Oct–May Tues–Sun 8am–2.30pm; €1.50) finally reopened in late 1999 after an eight-year overhaul. The wide-ranging and well-lit collection, arranged both thematically and chronologically from Neolithic to Roman times, demands at least an hour or so of one's attention. Highlights include limestone column bases from the Apollo temple at Faná in the shape of lion's claws; numerous statuettes and reliefs of Cybele (the Asiatic goddess was especially honoured here); Archaic faïence miniatures from Emborió in the shape of a cat, a hawk and a flautist; terracottas from various eras of a dwarf riding a boar; and figurines (some with articulated limbs) of *hierodouloi* or sacred prostitutes, presumably from an Aphrodite shrine. Most famous of all is an inscribed edict of Alexander the Great from 322 BC, commanding local political changes and setting out relations between himself and the Hiots.

Arrival, information and services

Ferries large and small, plus the infrequent **hydrofoil**, dock at various points as shown on the town map. The **airport** lies 4km south along the coast at Kondári, a €3.50 taxi-ride away; otherwise any blue urban bus labelled "Kondári Karfás" departing from the terminal on the north side of the park passes the airport gate, opposite which is a conspicuous stop with shelter. **Ferry** agents cluster to either side of the customs building, towards the north end of the waterfront Egéou and its continuation Neoríon: NEL (℡02710/23 971) is a few paces south of customs, while Miniotis Lines, at Neoríon 21–23 (℡02710/24 670) or Egéou 11 (℡02710/21 463), operates small, slow ferries to many neighbouring islands. Hiona Travel at Neoríon 13 is the central agent for Hellas Ferries, though Hellas (and the few weekly hydrofoils to Lésvos or Sámos, plus air tickets) are also handled by competent Serafim Travel at Kanári 24 (℡02710/23 558). The Turkish evening ferry to Çeşme as well as the most regular boat to Inoússes (see 401), is represented by Faros Travel at Egéou 18 (℡02710/27 240). The helpful municipal **tourist office** (May–Sept daily 7am–10pm; Oct–April Mon–Fri 7am–3pm; ℡02710/44 389) is at Kanári 18, near the Alpha Bank.

The standard green-and-cream **KTEL buses** leave from a parking area beside their ticket office on the south side of the park, behind the Omirio Cultural Centre. While services to the south of Híos are adequate, those to the centre and northwest of the island are almost nonexistent, and to explore there you'll need to rent a powerful **motorbike** or a car, or share a **taxi** (which are bright red here, not grey as in most of Greece). Three independent or small-chain **car-rental** agencies sit in a row at Evyenías Handhrí 5–7, behind the eyesore *Chandris Hotel*; of these, Vassilakis/Reliable Rent a Car (☎02710/29 300 or 094/4334898), with a branch at Mégas Limniónas, is particularly recommended. The **post office** is on Omírou, while numerous **banks** all have cash dispensers. A final Hiot idiosyncrasy is afternoon **shopping hours** limited to Monday and Thursday in summer.

Accommodation

Híos Town has a fair bit of affordable **accommodation**, rarely completely full. Most places line the water or the perpendicular alleys and parallel streets behind, and almost all are plagued by traffic noise to some degree – listed are the more peaceful establishments.

Alex Rooms, Mihaïl Livanoú 29 ☎02710/26 054. The friendly proprietor often meets late-arriving ferries; otherwise ring the bell. There's a roof garden above the well-furnished rooms, some en-suite. ❶

Fedra, Mihaïl Livanoú 13 ☎02710/41 130, ℱ41 128. Well-appointed pension in an old mansion, with stone arches in the downstairs winter bar; in summer the bar operates outside, so ask for a rear room to avoid nocturnal noise. ❹

Hios Rooms, Kokáli 1, cnr Egéou ☎02710/20 198 or 097/2833841. Wood-floored, high-ceilinged rooms, mostly with shared bath but relatively quiet for a seafront location, lovingly restored by proprietors Don (New Zealander) and Dina (Greek), who live on-site. ❶

Kyma, east end of Evyenías Handhrí ☎02710/44 500, ℱ44 600, ⊛http://chios.proodos.gr/kyma. En-suite hotel rooms in a Neoclassical mansion or a modern extension, with TV, huge terraces on the sea-facing side and jacuzzis in some rooms. Splendid service and big breakfasts really make

the place. The old wing saw a critical moment in modern Greek history in September 1922, when Colonel Nikolaos Plastiras commandeered it as his HQ after the Greek defeat in Asia Minor, and announced the deposition of King Constantine I. ❺ Aug, ❸ otherwise.

Pelineon Rooms, Omírou 9, cnr Egéou ☎02710/28 030. Choose between light, airy and noisy seaview rooms (most en suite), or quiet, pokey ones at the back, though these are affected by cooking fumes from the *souvláki* bar below. ❷

Rodhon, Platéon 10 ☎02710/24 335. The owners can be awkward, and the rooms are not en suite, but it's just about the only place inside the *kástro*, and pretty quiet. ❸

Villa Maro, Roïdhou 15 ☎02710/27 003. Modern pension tucked onto a tiny plaza just inland from the water; rear rooms unfortunately overlook the public toilets, but all are en-suite, tile-floored and well equipped, plus there's a pleasant breakfast/snack bar on the ground floor. ❹

Eating

Eating out in Híos Town can be more pleasurable than the fast-food joints, touristy tavernas and multiple *barákia* on the waterfront (and American-style pizza parlours inland) would suggest; it is also usually a lot cheaper than on neighbouring Sámos or Lésvos.

Ta Dhyo Adherfia, cnr Mihalón and Mihaïl Livanoú. No-nonsense, competent *mayireftá* and grills, served in the garden during warmer months. Open Sun too.

O Hotzas, Yeoryíou Kondhýli 3, cnr Stefánou Tsoúri, off map. Oldest (and arguably best) taverna in town, with chef Ioannis Linos, the fourth generation of his family, presiding. Menu varies seasonally, but expect a mix of vegetarian dishes (*mavromátika*, cauliflower, stuffed red peppers), and sausages, baby fish and *mydhopílafo* (rice and mussels) washed down by own-brand oúzo or retsina. Allow €12 each. Dinner only, garden in summer; closed Sun.

Inomayerio Iakovos, Ayíou Yeoryíou Frouríou 20, Kástro. A good balance of well-executed fishy dishes, grilled titbits, cheese-based recipes and vegetables; local white bulk wine or oúzo. Atmospheric garden seating in a vine-cloaked ruin opposite, or inside during winter. Budget €10–12 each. Closed Sun, and no lunch Sept–June.

Kronos, Filíppou Aryéndi 2, cnr Aplotariás. The island's best, and own-made ice cream, purveyed since 1929; limited seating or take away.

Ta Mylarakia, by three restored windmills in Tambákika district, on the road to Vrondádhos (☎02710/40 412). A large, well-priced seafood selection, every kind of Hiot oúzo and limited waterside seating make reservations advisable in summer. Dinner all year, lunch also Oct–April.

Tavernaki tou Tassou, Stávrou Livanoú 8, Bella Vista district. Superb all-rounder with creative salads, better-than-average bean dishes, dolmádhes, snails, properly done chips, and a strong line in seafood; a bit pricier than usual – allow €15 each – but Tassos' and Tsambika's cooking is worth it.

Good barrel wine; open lunch and supper most of the year, with seaview garden seating during warmer months.

Theodhosiou Ouzeri, Neoríon 33. The genuine article, with a large, reasonable menu, moved in 2001 to large, quieter, arcaded premises from its old spot opposite the main ferry berth. Dinner only; closed Sun.

Drinking, nightlife and entertainment

The 1400 or so students at the local technical schools and economics/business management faculties of the University of the Aegean help keep things lively, especially along the portion of the waterfront between the two "kinks" in Egéou.

Cine Kipos, in central park from June to mid-Sept only. Quality/art-house first-run fare, two screenings nightly; watch for flyers around town or enquire at *Pension Fedra*. During winter, the action shifts to *Cine Diana*, under the eponymous hotel.

Enter, seaward from the *Faidra* hotel. The best-equipped internet café with ten or so terminals upstairs.

Iviskos, about halfway along Egéou. This tasteful café is the most popular daytime hangout on the quay, with a range of juices, coffees and alcoholic drinks.

To Loukoumi, alley off Aplotariás 27/c. Old warehouse refitted as a café (8am–2pm), ouzerí (7pm–2am) and occasional events centre. Well executed and worth checking out, but closes May–Oct & Sun.

Metropol, Egéou. The longest-lived and most civilized of the music bars on this stretch of the front.

Omirio, south side of the central park. Cultural centre and events hall with frequently changing exhibitions; foreign musicians often come here after Athens concerts to perform in the large auditorium.

Beaches near Híos Town

Híos Town itself has no beaches worth mentioning; the closest decent one is at **KARFÁS**, 7km south beyond the airport and served by frequent blue buses. Once there you can **rent cars** at MG (☏02710/32 222) or bikes from Rabbit Moto (☏02710/32 501) both uphill from the bus stop. Most large Hiot package hotels are planted here, to the considerable detriment of the 500-metre-long beach itself, sandy only at the south end, where all watersports are offered. The main bright spot is a unique **pension**, *Markos' Place* (☏02710/31 990, ⓦwww.marcos-place.gr; ❶–❷; April–Nov), installed in the disestablished **monastery of Áyios Yeóryios and Áyios Pandelímon**, on the hillside south of the bay. Markos Kostalas, who leases the premises from Thymianá municipality, has created a uniquely peaceful, leafy environment much loved by special-activity groups. Guests are lodged in the former pilgrims' cells, with a kitchen available; individuals are more than welcome (there are several single "cells"), though advance reservations are advisable and a minimum stay of four days is required. Visitors should also like cats (there are usually about twenty in residence).

Shoreline **eating** quality has declined so much that it's better to strike inland. *Ouzeri To Apomero* (open daily), in hillside Spiládhia district west of the airport (go around the runway and follow the many luminous green signs) has lovely terrace seating, live music a few nights weekly in summer, and such delights as pancetta with cumin, *garídhes saganáki* and *sheftalyés* (Cypriot-style meat rissoles). Inland, between Thymianá and Neohóri, *Fakiris Taverna* (open all year but weekends only in winter) offers home-marinated aubergine and artichokes, goat baked in tomato sauce and excellent wood-fired pizzas along with well-executed seafood and pork-based *bekrí mezé* in big portions. Until a sign is put up, the easiest way to find it is to head south on the road to Kalimassiá and then turn west onto Ayíou Trýfonos road, just before Neohóri, and proceed about a kilometre.

Some 2km further along the coast from Karfás, **AYÍA ERMIÓNI** is not a beach but a fishing anchorage surrounded by a handful of tavernas (again, none standing out) and apartments to rent. The nearest beach is at **Mégas Limniónas**, a few hundred metres further, smaller than Karfás but more scenic where low cliffs provide a backdrop. Both Ayía Ermióni and Mégas Limniónas are served by extensions of the blue-bus route to either Karfás or Thymianá, the nearest inland village. The coast road loops up to Thymianá, from where you can (with your own transport only) continue 3km south towards Kalimassiá to the turning for **Ayía Fotiní**, a 700-metre pebble beach with exceptionally clean water. There's no shade, however, unless you count shadows from the numerous blocks of rooms contracted out to Scandinavian tour operators; a few tavernas cluster around the point where the side road meets the sea, but there's better eating at the south end of the strand, in the **restaurant** operating in the grounds of **Áyios Emilianós monastery**.

Southern Híos

Besides olive groves, the gently rolling countryside in the south of the island is also home to the **mastic bush** (*Pistacia lentisca*), found across much of Aegean Greece but only here producing an aromatic resin of any quality or quantity. For centuries it was used as a base for paints, cosmetics and the chewable jelly beans, which became a somewhat addictive staple in the Ottoman harems. Indeed, the interruption of the flow of mastic from Híos to Istanbul by the revolt of spring 1822 was one of the root causes of the brutal Ottoman reaction.

The wealth engendered by the mastic trade supported twenty *mastihohoriá* (mastic villages) from the time the Genoese set up a monopoly in the substance during the fourteenth and fifteenth centuries, but the end of imperial Turkey and the development of petroleum-based products knocked the bottom out of the mastic market. Now it's just a curiosity, to be chewed – try the sweetened Elma-brand gum – or drunk as a liqueur called *mastíha*, though it has had medicinal applications since ancient times. These days, however, the *mastihohoriá* live mainly off their tangerines, apricots and olives.

The towns themselves, the only settlements on Híos spared by the Ottomans in 1822, are architecturally unique, laid out by the Genoese but retaining a distinct Middle Eastern feel. The basic plan consists of a rectangular warren of tall houses, with the outer row doubling as the town's perimeter fortification, and breached by a limited number of arched gateways.

The mastic villages

ARMÓLIA, 20km from town, is the smallest and least imposing of the mastic villages. Its main virtue is its pottery industry; the best workshop, selling useful kitchenware as well as the usual kitsch souvenirs, is Yeoryios Sfikakis, the third outfit on the right as you head southwest. **PYRGÍ**, 5km further south, is the most colourful of these communities, its houses elaborately embossed with *xystá*, geometric patterns cut into whitewash, revealing a layer of black volcanic sand underneath; strings of sun-drying tomatoes add a further splash of colour in autumn. On the northeast corner of the central square the twelfth-century Byzantine church of **Áyii Apóstoli** (Tues–Thurs & Sat 10am–1pm), embellished with much later frescoes, is tucked under an arcade. Of late, vast numbers of postcard racks and boutiques have sprung up on every main thoroughfare, detracting somewhat from the atmosphere. Pyrgí has a handful of **rooms**, many of them bookable through the Women's Agricultural and Tourist Cooperative (☎02710/72 496; ❷) – the office is on the left as you walk up from the bus stop. In the medieval core you'll find a **bank** (with cashpoint), a **post office** and a few *souvláki* grills, but no real tavernas. **OLÝMBI**, 7km further west along the bus route serving Armólia and Pyrgí, is the least visited of the mastic villages, but not devoid of interest. The characteristic tower-keep, which at Pyrgí stands half-inhabited away from the modernized main square, here looms bang in the middle of the platía, its ground floor occupied by the community kafenío on one side, and *Estiatorio Pyrgos* on the other, with more elaborate main dishes.

Sombre, monochrome **MESTÁ**, 4km west of Olýmbi, is considered the finest example of the genre; despite more snack bars and trinket shops than strictly necessary on the outskirts, Mestá remains just the right side of twee as most people here still work the land. From its main square, dominated by the **church of the Taxiárhis** (the largest on the island), a bewildering maze of cool, shady lanes with anti-seismic buttressing and tunnels, leads off in all directions. Most streets end in blind alleys, except those leading to the six gates; the northeast one still has its original iron grate. If you'd like to stay, there are half a dozen **rooms** in restored traditional dwellings managed by Dhimitris Pipidhis (☎02710/76 319; ❸) and Dhespina Karambela (☎02710/76 065 or 22 068, or ask at *O Morias sta Mesta* taverna, below; ❸). Alternatively, three separate premises managed by Anna Floradhi (☎02710/76 455; ❸) are somewhat more modernized, and like the other two outfits are open year-round, with heating. Of the two **tavernas** on the main platía, *O Morias sta Mesta* is renowned for tasty rural specialities like pickled *krítamo* (rock samphire) and locally produced raisin wine, which is heavy, semi-sweet and sherry-like. However, portions have shrunk of late, and *Mesaionas* – whose tables share the square – is better value and has perhaps the more helpful proprietor (she also has rooms: ☎02710/76 494; ❸).

The south coast
One drawback to staying in Mestá is a lack of good beaches nearby; the closest candidate is surf-battered, facility-less **Merikoúnda**, 4km west of Mestá by dirt track. Reached by a seven-kilometre side road starting just west of Pyrgí, the little cove of **Káto Faná** is also bereft of amenities (save for a spring), but more sheltered; by the roadside 400m above the shore, the fragmentary remains of an Apollo temple surround a medieval chapel.

Pyrgí is actually closest to the two major beach resorts in this corner of the island. The nearest, 6km distant, is **EMBORIÓS**, an almost landlocked harbour with four passable **tavernas** (*Porto Emborios* has the edge with homemade desserts and *atherína*-and-onion fry-up); there's a scanty, British-excavated acropolis on the hill to the northeast, vaguely signposted 1km along the road to Kómi – all finds are displayed in Híos Town's archeological museum. For swimming, follow the road to its end at an oversubscribed car park and the beach of **Mávros Yialós** (Mávra Vólia), then continue by flagstoned walkway over the headland to another, more dramatic pebble strand (part nudist) of purpley-grey volcanic stones, twice as long and backed by impressive cliffs.

If you want sand you'll have to go to **KÓMI**, 3km northeast, also accessible from Armólia via Kalamotí; there are just a few tavernas (most reliably open of these are *Nostalgia* and *Bella Mare*), café-bars and summer apartments behind the pedestrianized beachfront. The bus service is fairly good in season, often following a loop route through Pyrgí and Emboriós.

Central Híos

The portion of Híos extending west and southwest from Híos Town matches the south in terms of interesting monuments, and good roads (being improved still further with EU funding) make touring under your own power an easy matter. There are also several beaches on the far shore of the island which, though not necessarily the best on Híos, are fine for a dip at the middle or end of the day.

The Kámbos

The **Kámbos**, a vast fertile plain carpeted with citrus groves, extends southwest from Híos Town almost as far as the village of Halkió. The district was originally settled by the Genoese during the fourteenth century, and remained a preserve of the local aristocracy until 1822. Exploring it by bicycle or motorbike is less frustrating than going by car, since the web of narrow, poorly marked lanes sandwiched between high walls guarantee disorientation and frequent backtracking. Behind the walls you catch fleeting glimpses of ornate old mansions built from locally quarried sandstone; courtyards are paved in pebbles or alternating light and dark tiles, and most still contain a pergola-shaded irrigation pond filled by a *mánganos* or donkey-powered water-wheel, used before the age of electric pumps to draw water up from wells up to 30m deep.

Many of the sumptuous three-storey dwellings, constructed in a hybrid Italo-Turco-Greek style, have languished derelict since 1881, but an increasing number are being converted for use as private estates or unique **accommodation**. The best and most consistently attended of these is *Mavrokordatiko* (℡02710/32 900, ℱ32 902, ⓦwww.mavrokordatiko.com; ❹–❻), about 1.5km south of the airport, with enormous heated, wood-panelled rooms and breakfast (included) served by the *mánganos* courtyard.

Not strictly speaking in Kámbos, but most easily reached from it en route to the *mastihohoriá*, is an outstanding rural Byzantine monument. The thirteenth-century **church of Panayía Krína**, isolated amidst orchards and woods, is well worth the challenge of negotiating a maze of paved but poorly marked lanes beyond Vavýli village, 9km from town. It's currently closed indefinitely for snail's-pace restoration, but a peek through the apse window will give you a fair idea of the finely frescoed interior, sufficiently lit by a twelve-windowed drum. All of the late medieval frescoes which overlay the Byzantine work have been removed, and are sometimes displayed in Híos Town's Byzantine and Justiniani museums (see p.390). The alternating brick and stonework of the exterior alone justifies the trip here, though architectural harmony is marred by the later addition of a clumsy lantern over the narthex, and the visibly unsound structure is kept from collapse by cable-binding at the roofline.

Néa Moní

Almost exactly in the middle of the island, the **monastery of Néa Moní** was founded by the Byzantine Emperor Constantine Monomahos ("The Dueller") IX in 1042 on the spot where a wonder-working icon had been discovered. It ranks among the most beautiful and important monuments on any of the Greek islands; the mosaics, together with those of Dháfni and Ósios Loukás on the mainland, are among the finest surviving art of their age in Greece, and the setting – high up in still partly forested mountains 15km west of the port – is no less memorable.

Once a powerful and independent community of six hundred monks, Néa Moní was pillaged in 1822 and most of its residents (including 3500 civilians sheltering here) put to the sword; since then many of its outbuildings have languished in ruins, though a recent EU grant has prompted massive restoration work. The 1881 tremor caused comprehensive damage, while exactly a century later a forest fire threatened to engulf the place until the resident icon was paraded along the perimeter wall, miraculously repelling the flames. Today the monastery, with its giant refectory and vaulted water cisterns, is inhabited by just a couple of lay workers.

Bus excursions (around €12) are provided by the KTEL on Tuesday and Friday mornings, continuing to Anávatos, Lithí and Armólia; otherwise come by motorbike, or walk from Karyés, 7km northeast, to which there is a regular blue-bus service. **Taxis** from town, however, are not prohibitive, at about €15 round-trip per carload, including a wait while you look around.

Just inside the main gate (daily 8am–1pm & 4–8pm) stands a **chapel/ossuary** containing some of the bones of those who met their death here in 1822; axe-clefts in children's skulls attest to the savagery of the attackers. The **katholikón**, with the cupola resting on an octagonal drum, is of a design seen elsewhere only in Cyprus; the frescoes in the exonarthex are badly damaged by holes allegedly left by Turkish bullets, but the **mosaics** are another matter. The narthex contains portrayals of the various saints of Híos sandwiched between *Christ Washing the Disciples' Feet* and the *Betrayal of Christ*, in which Judas's kiss has unfortunately been obliterated, but Peter is clearly visible lopping off the ear of the high priest's servant. In the dome of the sanctuary (currently hidden by scaffolding), which once contained a complete life-cycle of Christ, only the *Baptism*, part of the *Crucifixion*, the *Descent from the Cross*, the *Resurrection* and the Evangelists *Mark* and *John* survived the earthquake.

The west coast

With your own transport, you can proceed 5km west of Néa Moní to **AVGÓNYMA**, a cluster of dwellings on a knoll overlooking the coast; the name means "Clutch of Eggs", an apt description when it's viewed from the ridge above. Since the 1980s, the place has been almost totally restored as a summer haven by descendants of the original villagers, though the permanent population is just seven. A returned Greek-American family runs a reasonable, simple-fare **taverna**, *O Pyrgos* (open all year), in an arcaded mansion on the main square; co-managed *To Arhondiko* and *To Asteria* at the outskirts have far less reliable cooking and opening hours. The classiest **accommodation** option here is *Spitakia*, a cluster of small restored houses for up to five people (☎02710/20 513 or 094/5569787, ℱ02710/43 052, ✉missetzi@otenet.gr; ④).

A paved side road continues another 4km north to **ANÁVATOS**, whose empty, dun-coloured dwellings, soaring above pistachio orchards, are almost indistinguishable from the 300-metre-high bluff on which they're built. During the 1822 insurrection, some four hundred inhabitants and refugees threw themselves over this cliff rather than surrender to the besieging Ottomans, and it's still a preferred suicide leap. Anávatos can now only muster two permanent inhabitants, and given a lack of accommodation, plus an eerie, traumatized atmosphere, it's no place to be stranded at dusk – though there's a very good **taverna**, *Anavatos*, at the village entrance (open for lunch most of the year, plus dinner in summer).

West of Avgónyma, the main road descends 6km to the sea in well-graded loops. Turning right (north) at the junction leads first to the beach at **Elínda**, alluring from afar but rocky and murky up close; it's better to continue towards more secluded, mixed sand-and-gravel coves to either side of Metóhi (best of these are **Tigáni** and **Makriá Ámmos**, the latter nudist), or to **SIDHI-**

ROÚNDA, the only village hereabouts (with a summer taverna), which enjoys a spectacular hilltop setting overlooking the coast.

All along this coast, as far southwest as Liménas Mestón, are round **watch-towers** erected by the Genoese to look out for pirates – the first swimmable cove you reach by turning left from the junction has the name **Kastélla** (officially Trahíli), again mixed sand and gravel. A sparse weekday-only bus service resumes 9km south of the junction at **LITHÍ**, a friendly village of whitewashed buildings perched on a wooded ledge overlooking the sea. There are tavernas and kafenía near the bus turnaround area, but most visitors head 2km downhill to **Paralía Lithíou**, a popular weekend target of Hiot townies for the sake of its large but hard-packed, windswept beach. The better of two tavernas here is *Ta Tria Adherfia*; the other, *Kyra Despina*, has a few rooms (☎02710/73 373; ●).

Some 5km south of Lithí, the valley-bottom village of **VÉSSA** is an unsung gem, more open and less casbah-like than Mestá or Pyrgí, but still homogeneous. Its honey-coloured buildings are arrayed in a vast grid punctuated by numerous belfries; there's a simple taverna (*Snack Bar Evanemos*) installed in a tower-mansion on the main through road.

Northern Híos

Northern Híos never really recovered from the 1822 massacre, and the desolation left by fires in 1981 and 1987 will further dampen inquisitive spirits. Since the early 1900s the villages have languished all but deserted much of the year, which means correspondingly sparse bus services. About one-third of the former population now lives in Híos Town, venturing out here only during major festivals or to tend smallholdings; others, based in Athens or the US, visit their ancestral homes for just a few intense weeks in midsummer, when marriages are arranged between local families.

The road to Kardhámyla

Blue city buses run north from Híos Town up to **VRONDÁDHOS**, an elongated coastal suburb that's a favourite residence of the island's many seafarers. Homer is reputed to have lived and taught here, and in the terraced parkland just above the little fishing port and pebble beach you can visit his purported lectern, more probably an ancient altar of Cybele. Accordingly many of the buses out here are labelled "Dhaskalópetra", the Teacher's Rock.

Some 15km out of town, just past the tiny bayside hamlet of Pandoukiós, a side road leads to stony **Áyios Isídhoros** cove, home to the rather inconveniently located (and sporadically open – ring first to check) island **campsite**, *Chios Camping* (☎02710/74 111), though the site itself is shaded and faces Inoússes islet across the water. **LANGÁDHA**, just beyond, is probably the first point on the eastern coast road where you'd be tempted to stop, though there is no proper beach nearby. Set at the mouth of a deep valley, this attractive little harbour settlement looks across its bay to a pine grove, and beyond to Turkey. There are a couple of **rooms** outfits, but most evening visitors come for the sustaining seafood at two adjacent **tavernas** on the quay: *Tou Kopelou*, better known as *Stelios'*, and second-choice *Paradhisos*.

Just beyond Langádha an important side road leads 5km up and inland to **PITYÓS**, an oasis in a mountain pass presided over by a tower-keep; people come here from some distance to **dine** at *Makellos* on the west edge of the village, a shrine of local cuisine (June–Sept daily; Oct–May Fri–Sun evenings only). Continuing 4km more brings you to a junction allowing quick access to the west of the island and the Volissós area (see opposite).

Kardhámyla and around

Most traffic proceeds to **ÁNO KARDHÁMYLA** and **KÁTO KARDHÁMYLA**, the latter 37km out of the main town. Positioned at opposite edges of a fertile plain rimmed by mountains, they initially come as welcome relief from Homer's crags. Káto, better known as **MÁRMARO**, is larger, indeed the island's second town, with a bank, post office and filling station. However, there is little to attract a casual visitor other than some Neoclassical architecture; the port, mercilessly exposed to the *meltémi*, is strictly businesslike, and there are few tourist facilities. An exception is *Hotel Kardamyla* (☎02720/23 353; ❺ Aug, ❹ otherwise), co-managed with Híos Town's *Hotel Kyma*. It has the bay's only pebble beach, and its restaurant is a reliable source of lunch (July & Aug) if you're touring. Worthwhile independent **tavernas** include *"Snack Bar" Irini Tsirigou*, by the port authority, or *Iy Vlyhadha*, facing the eponymous bay west over the headland, with locally produced suckling pig and squid.

For better swimming head west 5km to **Nagós**, a gravel-shore bay at the foot of an oasis, which is where the summertime bus service sometimes terminates. Lush greenery is nourished by active springs up at a bend in the road, enclosed in a sort of grotto overhung by tall cliffs. The place name is a corruption of *naos*, after a large Poseidon temple that once stood near the springs, but centuries of orchard-tending, antiquities-pilfering and organized excavations after 1912 mean that nothing remains visible. Down at the shore the swimming is good, if a bit chilly; there are two mediocre **tavernas** and a few **rooms** to rent. Your only chance of relative solitude in July or August lies 1km west at **Yióssonas**; this is a much longer beach, but less sheltered, rockier and with no facilities.

Volissós and around

VOLISSÓS, 42km from Híos Town by the most direct road (44km via the much easier Avgónyma route), was once the market town for a dozen remote hill villages beyond, and its old stone houses still curl appealingly beneath the crumbling hilltop Byzantine fort. The towers were improved by the Genoese, from whose era also dates the utterly spurious "House of Homer" signposted near the top of town. Volissós can seem depressing at first, with the bulk of its 250 mostly elderly permanent inhabitants living in newer buildings around the main square, but opinions improve with longer acquaintance. The upper quarters are in the grip of a restoration mania, most of it done in admirable taste, with ruins changing hands for stratospheric prices.

Grouped around the platía you'll find a **post office**, a **bank** with cashpoint, two well-stocked shops and three mediocre **tavernas**; there's a better one up in Pýrgos district by the castle car-park, the vegetarian *Kafenio E* (April–Sept), run by Nikos Koungoulios; reservations (☎02740/21 480) are advised. A filling station operates 2.5km out of town, the only one hereabouts; you should plan on overnighting since the bus only comes out here on Sundays on a day-trip basis, or on Monday, Wednesday and Friday in the early afternoon (unless you care to travel at 4am). This should cause no dismay, since the area has the best beaches and some of the most interesting **accommodation** on Híos. The most reliably available and staffed of a few restoration projects are sixteen old houses, mostly in Pýrgos district, available through Omiros Travel (☎02740/21 413, ℗21 521; ❸). Units usually accommodate two people – all have terraces, fully equipped kitchens and features such as tree trunks upholding sleeping lofts.

LIMNIÁ, (sometimes Limiá), the port of Volissós, lies 2km south, with a small ferry coming from and going to Psará (theoretically Mon, Wed & Fri most of the year). The most consistent **tavernas** here are the long-established

Ta Limnia on the jetty for *mayireftá*, or summer-only *To Limanaki* at the rear of the cove, best for fish. At Limniá you're not far from the fabled beaches either. A 1.5-kilometre walk southeast over the headland brings you to **Managrós**, a seemingly endless sand-and-pebble beach. More intimate, sandy **Lefkáthia** lies just a ten-minute stroll along the cement drive threading over the headland north of the harbour; amenities are limited to a seasonal snack shack on the sand, and Ioannis Zorbas's apartments (T02740/21 436, F21 720; ❸), beautifully set in a garden where the concrete track joins an asphalt road down from Volissós. This is bound for **Límnos** (not to be confused with Limniá), the next protected cove, 400m east of Lefkáthia, where *Taverna Akroyiali* provides salubrious food and professional service, and the spruce *Latini Apartments* (T02740/21 461, F21 871; ❹) are graced with multiple stone terraces.

Ayía Markélla, 5km further northwest of Límnos, stars in many local postcards: a long, stunning beach fronting the monastery of Híos's patron saint, the latter not especially interesting or useful for outsiders, since its cells are reserved for Greek pilgrims. In an interesting variation on the expulsion of the money-changers from the temple, only religious souvenirs are allowed to be sold in the holy precincts, while all manner of plastic junk is on offer just outside. There's a single, rather indifferent taverna to hand as well, and around July 22 – the local saint's **festival** and biggest island bash – the "No Camping" signs are doubtless unenforced.

The dirt road past the monastery grounds is passable to any vehicle, with care, and emerges up on the paved road running high above the northwest coast. Turn left and proceed to the remote village of **ÁYIO GÁLA**, whose claim to fame is a **grotto-church** complex, built into a stream-lapped palisade at the bottom of the village. Signs ("Panayía Ayiogaloúsena") point to a lane crossing the water, but for access, except at the festival on August 23, you'll need to find the key-keeper (ask at the central kafenío), and descend via a flight of stairs starting beside a eucalyptus tree. Of the two churches inside the cavern, the larger one near the mouth of the grotto dates from the fifteenth century but seems newer owing to a 1993 external renovation. Inside, however, a fantastically intricate *témblon* vies for your attention with a tinier, older chapel, built entirely within the rear of the cavern. Its frescoes are badly smudged, except for a wonderfully mysterious and mournful Virgin, surely the saddest in Christendom, holding a knowing Child.

Satellite islands: Psará and Inoússes

There's a single settlement, with beaches and an isolated rural monastery, on both of Híos's satellite isles, but each is surprisingly different from the other, and of course from their large neighbour. Inoússes, the nearer and smaller islet, has a daily kaïki or hydrofoil service from Híos Town in season; Psará has less regular services subject to weather conditions (in theory daily from either Híos or Limniá), and is too remote to be done justice on a day-trip.

Psará

The birthplace of revolutionary war hero Admiral Kanaris, **Psará** devoted its merchant fleets – the third largest in 1820s Greece after those of Ídhra and Spétses – to the cause of independence, and paid dearly for it. Vexed beyond endurance, the Turks landed overwhelming forces in 1824 to stamp out this nest of resistance. Perhaps 3000 of the 30,000 inhabitants escaped in small boats which were rescued by a French fleet, but the majority retreated to a hilltop powder magazine and blew it (and themselves) up rather than surrender. The nationalist poet Dhionysios Solomos immortalized the incident in famous stanzas:

On the Black Ridge of Psará,
Glory walks alone.
She meditates on her heroes
And wears in her hair a wreath
Made from a few dry weeds
Left on the barren ground.

Today, it's a sad, stark place fully living up to its name ("the grey things" in Greek), which never really recovered from the holocaust. The Turks burned whatever houses and vegetation the blast had missed, and the permanent population barely exceeds four hundred. The only positive recent development was a 1980s revitalization project instigated by a French-Greek descendant of Kanaris and a Greek team. The port was improved, mains electricity and pure water provided, a secondary school opened, and cultural links between France and the island established, though so far this has not been reflected in increased tourist numbers.

Arrival can be something of an ordeal: the regular small ferry from Híos Town can take up to four hours to cover the 57 nautical miles of habitually rough sea. Use the port of Limniá to sail in at least one direction if you can; this crossing takes just over an hour at just over half the price.

Since few buildings in the east-facing harbour community predate the twentieth century, it's a strange hotchpotch of ecclesiastical and secular architecture that greets the eye on disembarking. There's a distinctly southern feel, more like the Dodecanese or the Cyclades, and some peculiar churches of which no two are alike in style.

If you **stay overnight**, there's a choice between a handful of fairly basic rooms and three more professional outfits: *Psara Studios* (☏02740/61 233; ❹) and *Apartments Restalia* (☏02740/61 000, ℻61 201; ❺ August, ❸ otherwise), both a bit stark but with balconies and kitchens, or the EOT *xenónas* (☏02740/61 293; ❶) in a restored prison. For **eating**, the best and cheapest place is the EOT-run *Spitalia*, housed in a renovated medieval hospital at the north edge of the port. A **post office**, bakery and shop complete the list of amenities; there is no full-service bank.

Psará's **beaches** are decent, improving the further northeast you walk from the port. You quickly pass Káto Yialós, Katsoúni and Lazarétta with its off-putting power station, before reaching **Lákka** ("narrow ravine"), fifteen minutes along, apparently named after its grooved rock formations in which you may have to shelter – much of this coast is windswept, with a heavy swell offshore. **Límnos**, 25 minutes from the port along the coastal path, is big and attractive, but there's no reliable taverna here, or indeed at any of the other beaches. The only other thing to do on Psará is to walk north across the island – the old track there has now been paved – to the **monastery of the Kímisis (Assumption)**; uninhabited since the 1970s, this comes to life only in the first week of August, when its revered icon is carried in ceremonial procession to town and back on the eve of August 5.

Inoússes

Inoússes has a permanent population of about three hundred – less than half its prewar figure – and a very different history from Psará. For generations this medium-sized islet has provided the Aegean with many of her wealthiest shipping families: various members of the Livanos, Lemos and Pateras clans (with every street or square named after the last-named family) were born here. This helps explain the large villas and visiting summer yachts in an otherwise sleepy Greek backwater – as well as a **maritime museum** (daily 10am–1pm; €1.20) near the quay, endowed by various shipping magnates. At the west end of the quay, the bigwigs have also funded a large nautical academy, which trains future members of the merchant navy.

On Sundays in season can you make an inexpensive **day-trip** to Inoússes from Híos with the locals' ferry *Inousses*; on most other days of the week this arrives at 3pm, returning early the next morning. One or two days weekly in summer there's an unreliable hydrofoil service as well, leaving Híos at about 9.30am, and returning from Inoússes at about 3pm. Otherwise, during the tourist season you must participate in the pricier excursions offered from Híos, typically on the *Maria*, with return tickets running up to three times the cost of the regular ferry.

Two church-tipped islets, each privately owned, guard the unusually well-protected harbour (whose jetty is currently being expanded); the **town** of Inoússes is surprisingly large, draped over hillsides enclosing a ravine. Despite a wealthy reputation, its appearance is unpretentious, the houses displaying a mix of vernacular and modest Neoclassical style. There is just one, fairly comfortable **hotel**, the *Thalassoporos* (☎02720/51 475; ❷), on the main easterly hillside lane, but no licensed pensions or rooms. **Eating out** is similarly limited; every season a few simple ouzerís off towards the nautical academy try their luck, but the most reliable option is the simple good-value *Taverna Pateronissia*, conspicuous at the base of the disembarkation jetty. Otherwise, be prepared to patronize one of the three shops (one on the waterfront, two up the hill). Beside the museum is a **post office** and a **bank**.

The rest of this tranquil island, at least the southern slope, is surprisingly green and well tended; there are no springs, so water comes from a mix of fresh and brackish wells, as well as a reservoir. The sea is extremely clean and calm on the sheltered southerly shore; among its beaches, choose from **Zepánga**, **Biláli** or **Kástro**, respectively five-, twenty- and thirty-minutes' walk west of the port. More secluded **Fourkeró** (Farkeró in dialect) lies 25 minutes east: first along a cement drive ending at a seaside chapel, then by path past pine groves and over a ridge. As on Psará, there are no reliable facilities at any of the beaches.

At the end of the westerly road, beyond Kástro, stands the somewhat macabre convent of **Evangelismoú**, endowed by a branch of the Pateras family. Inside reposes the mummified body of the lately canonized daughter, Irini, whose prayers to die of cancer in place of her terminally ill father Panagos were answered early in the 1960s on account of her virtue and piety; he's entombed here also, having outlived Irini by some years. The abbess, presiding over about twenty nuns, is none other than the widowed Mrs Pateras; only women are allowed admission, and even then casual visits are not encouraged.

Lésvos (Mytilíni)

Lésvos, the third-largest Greek island after Crete and Évvia, is not only the birthplace of Sappho, but also of Aesop, Arion and – more recently – the Greek primitive artist Theophilos, the Nobel laureate poet Odysseus Elytis and the novelist Stratis Myrivilis. Despite these artistic associations, Lésvos may not at first strike the visitor as particularly beautiful or interesting; much of the landscape is rocky, volcanic terrain, dotted with thermal springs and alternating

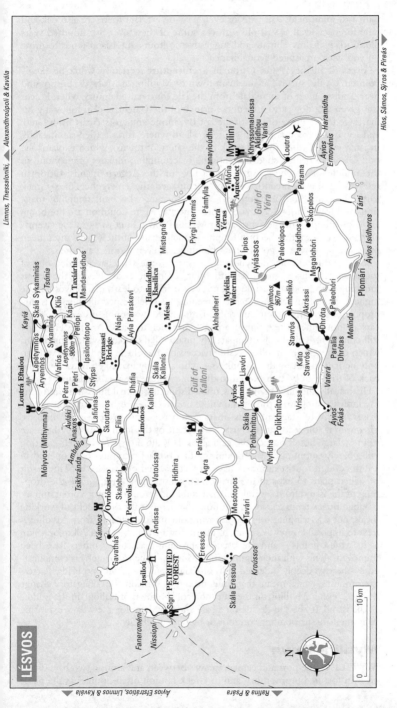

5

THE EAST AND NORTH AEGEAN | LÉSVOS

403

Mólyvos (Míthymna)
Tsikhránda
Kámbos
Gavathás
Ándissa
Ipsiloú
PETRIFIED FOREST
Sígri
Faneroméni
Nissiopi
Skála Eressoú
Eressós
Mesótopos
Tavári
Kroússos
Ovriókastro
Skalohóri
Perivólis
Vatoússa
Hídhira
Ágra
Parákila
Nyfídha
Polikhnítou
Skála
Polikhnítou
Áyios
Fókas
Áyios Ioánnis
Lisvóri
Vrissa
Áyios Ioánnis
Polikhnítos
Vaterá
Paralía
Dhrótas
Melínda
Dhróta
Paleohóri
Akrássi
Ambelikó
Olymbos, 967m ▲
Stavrós
Káto Stavrós
Megalohóri
Paleohóri
Papádhos
Plomári
Áyios Isídhoros
Skópelos
Pérama
Loutrá
Áyios Ermoyénis
Aklidhiou
Variá
Khryssoloússa
Mytilíni ✈
Panayioúdha
Pámfylla
Móira
Aqueduct
Loutrá Yéras
Gulf of Yéras
Tárti
Haramídha
Panayioúdha
Pýrgi Thermís
Mistegná
Ípios
Ayiássos
Mylélia Watermill
Akhladherí
Mésa
Halinádhou Basilica
Ayía Paraskeví
Nápi
Dháfia
Kalloní
Limónos
Filía
Skoutáros
Lafiónas
Anaxos
Avláki
Pétri
Pétra
Vafiós
Lepétymnos 968m ▲
Ipsilométopo
Stýpsi
Kremastí Bridge
Skála Kallonís
Gulf of Kallóni
Lepétymnos
Aryenos
Loutrá Eftaloú
Sykaminiá
Skála Sykaminiás
Kayiá
Kápi
Pélopi
Mandamádhos
Taxiárhis
Klió
Tsónia

N

0   10 km

with vast grain fields, salt pans or even near-desert. But there are also oak and pine forests as well as vast olive groves, some of these over five hundred years old. With its balmy climate and suggestive contours, the island tends to grow on you with prolonged acquaintance.

Lovers of medieval and Ottoman **architecture** certainly won't be disappointed. Castles survive at the main town of Mytilíni, at Mólyvos, Eressós and near Ándissa; most of these date from the late fourteenth century, when Lésvos was given as a dowry to a Genoese prince of the Gateluzzi clan following his marriage to the niece of one of the last Byzantine emperors. Apart from Crete and Évvia, Lésvos was the only Greek island where Turks settled significantly in rural villages (they usually stuck to the safety of towns), which explains the odd Ottoman bridge, shed-like mosque or crumbling minaret often found in the middle of nowhere. Again unusually for the Aegean islands, Ottoman reforms of the eighteenth century encouraged the emergence of a Greek Orthodox land- and industry-owning aristocracy, who built rambling mansions and tower-houses, a few of which survive. More common are the bourgeois townhouses of the worthies in Mytilíni town, built early in the twentieth century to French Second Empire models; many of these have often been pressed into service as government buildings or even restored as hotels.

Social and economic idiosyncrasies persist: anyone who has attended one of the extended village *paniyíria*, with hours of music and tables in the streets groaning with food and drink, will not be surprised to learn that Lésvos has the highest alcoholism rate in Greece. Breeding livestock, especially horses, is disproportionately important, and traffic jams caused by mounts instead of parked cars are not unheard of – signs reading "Forbidden to Tether Animals Here" are still common, as are herds of apparently unattended donkeys wandering about. Much of the acreage in olives is still inaccessible to vehicles, and the harvest can only be hauled out by those donkeys – who are duly loaded en masse onto the back of trucks to be transported to the point where the road fizzles out.

Historically, the olive plantations, oúzo distilleries, animal husbandry and fishing industry supported those who chose not to emigrate, but with these enterprises relatively stagnant, mass-market tourism has made visible inroads. However, it still accounts for just five percent of the local economy: there are still few large hotels outside the capital, Skála Kalloní or Mólyvos; self-catering villas barely outnumber rooms, and the first official campsites only opened in 1990. Foreign tourist numbers have in fact levelled out since 1996, the result of stalled plans to expand the airport, unrealistic hotel pricing and the dropping of the island from several German and Dutch tour operators' programmes.

Public **buses** tends to radiate out from the harbour for the benefit of working locals, not day-tripping tourists. Carrying out such excursions from Mytilíni is next to impossible anyway, owing to the size of the island – about 70km by 45km at its widest points – and the last few appalling roads (most others have been improved, along with their signposting). Moreover, the topography is complicated by the two deeply indented gulfs of Kalloní and Yéra, with no bridges across their mouths, which means that going from A to B involves an obligatory change of bus at either Mytilíni, on the east shore, or the town of Kalloní, in the middle of the island. It's best to decide on a base and stay there for a few days, exploring its immediate surroundings on foot or by rented vehicle.

Mytilíni Town

MYTILÍNI, the port and capital, sprawls between and around two bays divided by a fortified promontory, and in Greek fashion often doubles as the name

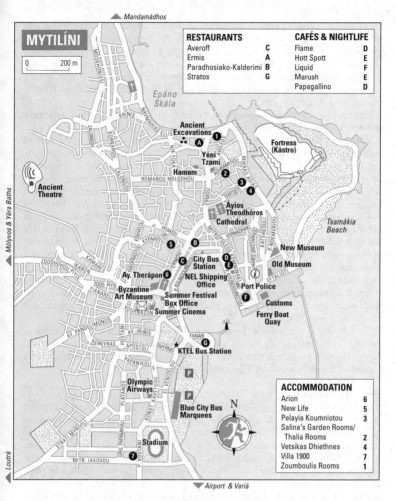

▲ Mandamádhos

MYTILÍNI

0   200 m

Epáno
Skála

RESTAURANTS	
Averoff	C
Ermis	A
Paradhosiako-Kalderimi	B
Stratos	G

CAFÉS & NIGHTLIFE	
Flame	D
Hott Spott	E
Liquid	F
Marush	E
Papagallino	D

Ancient
Excavations   **1**

Fortress
(Kástro)

Yéni
Tzamí   **2**

Hamam

3

4

Ancient
Theatre

Áyios
Theodhóros
Cathedral

Tsamákia
Beach

Móllyvos & Yéra Baths

5

City Bus
Station

New Museum

Ay. Therápon   **6**

Byzantine
Art Museum

NEL Shipping
Office

Old Museum

Summer Festival
Box Office

Port Police

Summer Cinema

Customs

Ferry Boat
Quay

FANARI

KTEL Bus Station

P

Olympic
Airways

P

N

Blue City Bus
Marquees

ACCOMMODATION	
Arion	6
New Life	5
Pelayia Koumniotou	3
Salina's Garden Rooms/	
Thalia Rooms	2
Vetsikas Dhiethnes	4
Villa 1900	7
Zoumboulis Rooms	1

Stadium   **7**

Loutrá

▼ Airport & Variá

of the island. Many visitors are put off by the combination of urban bustle and (in the traditionally humbler northern districts) slight seediness, and contrive to leave as soon as possible; the town returns the compliment by being a fairly impractical and occasionally expensive place to base yourself.

Nonetheless, Mytilíni has enough to justify a layover of a few hours. On the promontory sits the Byzantine-Genoese-Ottoman **fortress** (Tues–Sun 8am–2.30pm; €1.50), comprising ruined structures from all these eras and an Ottoman inscription above a Byzantine double-headed eagle at the south gate. Further inland, the town skyline is dominated in turn by the Germanic-Gothic belfry spire of **Áyios Theodhóros** and the mammary dome of **Áyios Therápon**, both expressions of the post-Baroque taste of the nineteenth-century Ottoman Greek bourgeoisie. They stand more or less at opposite ends of the bazaar, whose main street, Ermoú, links the town centre with the little-used north harbour of Páno Skála. On its way there Ermoú passes several expensive but rather picked-over antique shops near the roofless, derelict **Yéni Tzamí** at the heart of the old Muslim quarter, just a few steps east of a superb Turkish **hamam**, currently being restored to its former glory and due to function again as a bathhouse by late 2002. Between Ermoú and the castle lies a maze of atmospheric lanes lined with grandiose Belle Époque mansions and elderly vernacular houses, though most of the ornate townhouses are to be found in the southerly districts of Sourádha and Kióski, on the way to the airport.

Mytilíni's excellent **archeological collection** is housed in **two separate galleries** (May–Sept daily 8am–7pm; Oct–April Tues–Sun 8.30am–3pm; €1.50), a few hundred metres apart. The newer, upper museum, at the base of 8-Noemvríou, is devoted to finds from wealthy Roman Mytilene, in particular three rooms of well-displayed mosaics from second/third-century AD villas – highlights are a crude but engaging scene of Orpheus charming all manner of beasts, and two fishermen surrounded by clearly recognizable (and edible) sea creatures. Earlier eras are represented in the older wing (Tues–Sun 8.30am–3pm; same ticket as Roman wing), housed in a former mansion just behind the ferry dock. The ground floor has Neolithic finds from Áyios Vartholoméos cave and Bronze Age Thermí, but the star, late-Classical exhibits upstairs include minutely detailed terracotta figurines: a pair of acrobats, two *kourotrophoi* figures (goddesses suckling infants, predecessors of all Byzantine Galaktotrofoússa icons), children playing with a ball or dogs, and Aphrodite riding a dolphin. A specially built annexe at the rear contains stone-cut inscriptions of various edicts and treaties, plus a Roman sculpture of a drunken satyr asleep on a wineskin.

There's also a worthwhile **Byzantine Art Museum** (no regular hours at present; apply to church office adjacent Mon–Fri 9am–noon) just behind Áyios Therápon, containing various icons rescued from rural churches, plus a canvas of the *Assumption* by Theophilos (see p.408).

Practicalities

There's no bus link with the **airport**, so a shared taxi for the 7km into Mytilíni Town is the usual shuttle method; Olympic Airways is southwest of the main harbour at Kavétsou 44. As on Híos, there are two **bus stations**: the *iperastykó* (standard KTEL) buses leave from a small station near Platía Konstandinopóleos at the southern end of the harbour, while the *astykó* (blue bus) service departing from one corner of the enormous free public **car park** nearby (which you should use if driving, as there are no other easily available spaces in the centre). If you're intent on getting over to Ayvalık in Turkey on the Turkish **boats** *Cunda Express* or *Jalehan*, book tickets through either Dimakis Tours at Koundouriótou 73 (℡02510/27 865) or Picolo Travel at no. 73a (℡02510/27 000). NEL Ferries has its own agency at Koundouriótou 47 (℡02510/28 480), though tickets (including the high-speed service) are also sold through Dimakis Tours, while Hellas Ferries and the occasional hydrofoil south are handled by Picolo Travel.

Car rental is best arranged through reputable local-chain franchises like Payless/Auto Moto at Koundouriótou 49 (℡02510/43 555, ✉automoto@otenet.gr), Budget next door (℡02510/29 600), Egeon at Híou 2 (℡02510/29 820), Just at no. 47 (℡02510/43 080) or Alpha in the alley off Koundouriótou 83 (℡02510/26 113) – though it's often cheaper to rent at the resort of your choice. Other amenities include the **post office** on Vournázou, behind the central park, and at least five **banks** along Koundouriótou with cash dispensers, plus a free-standing booth on the quay. Before leaving town, you might visit the **EOT** regional headquarters at James Aristárhou 6

(Mon–Fri 8am–2.30pm) to get hold of their excellent town and island maps, plus other brochures.

Accommodation

Finding **accommodation** can be initially daunting: the waterfront hotels are noisy and exorbitantly priced, with few single rooms to speak of. If you need to stay, it's preferable to hunt down better-value rooms in the backstreets, especially between the castle and Ermoú, with supply usually exceeding demand. Yeoryíou Tertséti street in particular has two possibilities: the friendly if basic *Pelayia Koumniotou* at no. 6 (☏02510/20 643; ❶), or the fancier, en-suite *Vetsikas/Dhiethnes* at no. 1 (☏02510/24 968; ❷). Two other quiet establishments sit between the north harbour and fortress: *Salina's Garden Rooms*, behind the Yéni Tzamí at Fokéas 7 (☏02510/42 073; ❶), co-managed with the *Thalia Rooms* across the street (☏02510/24 640; ❶). Moving slightly upmarket, *Zoumbouli Rooms*, facing the water on Navmahías Ellís (☏02510/29 081; ❸), are en-suite and air conditioned, but may get more noise from traffic and the ouzerí below. *New Life* at the end of Olýmbou, a cul-de-sac off Ermoú (☏02510/42 650 or 093/2279057; ❸), offers wood-floored, en-suite rooms in an old mansion, or similarly priced ones, but with bizarre modern murals, in the co-managed *Arion* down the street at Árionos 4. *Villa 1900*, another restored mansion in the south of town at P. Vostáni 24 (☏02510/23 448, ℗28 034; ❹), has en-suite, variable-sized units with fridges, air conditioning and sometimes traditional ceiling murals.

Eating, drinking and nightlife

Dining options in Mytilíni have improved since a late-1990s nadir, when several of the more characterful old-style ouzerís and tavernas shut down in favour of fast-food joints. The obvious, if blatantly touristy, venue for a seafood blowout is the cluster of tavernas on the southerly quay known as Fanári; *Stratos* at the far end is marginally the best, and the only one that doesn't tout aggressively. For *mayireftá* (including early-morning *patsás*), look no further than the *Averoff* on the west quay, a popular place for lunch before an afternoon ferry departure. Finally, there are two recently refurbished, traditional ouzerís at opposite ends of the bazaar. *Paradhosiako-Kalderimi* (closed Sun) occupies two premises around Thássou 2, with seating under the shade of vines; the fare is large-portioned if a bit plainly presented for about €12 per head. For the same or even less (and with friendlier service), you might be better off at the *Ermis* (open daily), best of a cluster of ouzerís up at Páno Skála; a recent refit hasn't much affected its century-old decor (panelled ceiling, giant mirrors, faded oil paintings), or its claimed two centuries of purveying titbits to a jolly, mixed crowd in the pleasant courtyard.

For **snacks**, **breakfast and drinks**, try either *Liquid*, Koundouriótou 79, which does omelettes, or *Papagallino* nearby at no. 59, which offers crepes and pricey smoothies, and a magnificent interior atrium occasionally hosting exhibits. With an important university in residence, Mytilíni can offer decent **nightlife and entertainment**, especially along the northeast quay, which the student contingent have claimed as their own. Here, all in a row between Budget car rental and the NEL agency, you'll find *Flame* (with bowling upstairs), *Papagallino* (see above), *Marush* (with video games) and the durable *Hott Spott*. Formal live events constitute the *Lesviakó Kalokéri*, held in the castle or other venues from mid-July to late August, while the summer cinema *Pallas* is between the post office and the park on Vournázon.

Around Mytilíni

Beyond the airport and Krátigos village, the paved road loops around to **Haramídha**, 14km from town and the closest decent (pebble) beach (the fee-entry town "beach" at Tsamákia is mediocre); the eastern bay has several tavernas. The double cove at **Áyios Ermoyénis**, 3km west, is more scenic and sandy but small and crowded at weekends, with no full-service taverna, just a snack bar. The latter is more directly accessible from Mytilíni via Loutrá village. For other pleasant immersions near Mytilíni, make for **Loutrá Yéras**, 8km along the main road to Kallóni. These public baths (daily: June–Sept 7am–7pm; April–May & Oct 8am–6pm; Nov–March 9am–5pm; €2) are just the thing if you've spent a sleepless night on a ferry, with ornate spouts that feed 38°C water to marble-lined pools in vaulted chambers; there are separate facilities for men and women.

The Variá museums

The most rewarding single targets near Mytilíni are a pair of museums at **VARIÁ**, 5km south of town (half-hourly buses). The **Theophilos Museum** (May–Sept Tues–Sun 9am–2pm & 6–8pm; Oct–April may open 9am–2pm only; €1.50 includes key-catalogue) honours the painter, born here in 1873, with four rooms of wonderful, little-known compositions specifically commissioned by his patron Thériade (see below) during the years leading up to Theophilos' death in 1934. A wealth of detail is evident in elegiac scenes of fishing, reaping, olive-picking and baking from the pastoral Lésvos which Theophilos obviously knew best; there are droll touches also, such as a cat slinking off with a fish in *The Fishmongers*. In classical scenes – *Sappho and Alkaeos*, a landscape series of Egypt, Asia Minor and the Holy Land, and episodes from wars historical and contemporary – Theophilos was clearly on shakier ground. In *Abyssinians Hunting an Italian Horseman*, the subject has been conflated with New World Indians chasing down a conquistador.

The adjacent, imposing **Thériade Museum** (Tues–Sun 9am–2pm & 5–8pm; €1.50) is the brainchild of another native son, Stratis Eleftheriades (1897–1983). Leaving the island at an early age for Paris, he gallicized his name to Thériade and went on to become a renowned avant-garde art publisher, convincing some of the leading artists of the twentieth century to participate in his ventures. The displays – slightly depleted by a recent burglary – consist of lithographs, engravings, wood-block prints and watercolours by the likes of Miró, Chagall, Picasso, Matisse, Le Corbusier, Léger, Rouault and Villon, either annotated by the painters themselves or commissioned as illustrations for the works of prominent poets and authors – an astonishing collection for a relatively remote Aegean island.

Southern Lésvos

The southernmost portion of the island is indented by two great inlets, the gulfs of **Kallóni** and **Yéra**, the first curving in a northeasterly direction, the latter northwesterly, creating a fan-shaped peninsula at the heart of which looms 967-metre Mount Ólymbos. Both shallow gulfs are almost landlocked by virtue of very narrow outlets to the open sea, which don't have – and probably never will have – bridges spanning them. This is the most verdant and productive olive-producing territory on Lésvos, and the stacks of pressing-mills stab the skyline.

With its disused industrial warehouses, **PÉRAMA** is one of the larger places on the Gulf of Yéra, and has a regular **kaïki-ferry** service (no cars) linking it with Koundoroudhiá and blue city buses to/from Mytilíni on the far side. A more likely reason to show up is to patronize one of the better **taverna-ouzerís** in the region: *Balouhanas*, northernmost of a line of eateries on the front, with a wooden, cane-roofed balcony jutting out over the water. The name's a corruption of *balıkhane* or "fish-market" in Turkish, and seafood is a strong point, whether grilled or made into croquettes, as are regional starters like *giouzlemés* (cheese-stuffed fried crepe) and own-made desserts. They're open all year (lunch & dinner); count on €15 per head.

Plomári and around

Due south of Mount Ólympos, at the edge of the "fan", **PLOMÁRI** is the only sizeable coastal settlement in the south, and indeed the second largest municipality on Lésvos. It presents an unlikely juxtaposition of scenic appeal and its famous oúzo industry, courtesy of several local distilleries. Despite a resounding lack of good beaches within walking distance, it's besieged in summer by hordes of Scandinavian tourists, but you can usually find a **room** (they are prominently signposted) at the edge of the old, charmingly dilapidated town, or (better) 1km west in **Ammoudhélli** suburb, which has a small pea-gravel beach. Your best bet for an on-spec vacancy is the welcoming *Pension Lida* above the inland Platía Beniamín (T & F 02520/32 507; ❷), a fine restoration inn occupying adjacent old mansions, with seaview balconies for most units. Rustling up a decent meal presents more difficulties, with the dinner-only *Platanos* taverna at the central plane tree often unbearably busy, and nothing special at that. Better to stick to the east end of the harbour park-square, where *Bacchus* is reliable and long-established. Ammoudhélli can offer shambolic but friendly *Tó Ammoudhelli*, perched unimprovably over the beach and open at lunch too; skip the touristy printed menu and ask for the dishes of the day (which can be anything from *ambelofásola* to sardines) and *orektiká* like *tyrokafterí* and grilled octopus – budget €9 each.

Áyios Isídhoros, 3km east, is where most tourists actually stay; pick of the hotels here, not completely overrun with package tours, is the *Pebble Beach* (T02520/31 651, F31 566; ❹), with most of the large rooms overlooking a slightly reefy section of beach. Eating out here, try *Iy Mouria*, where the road turns inland to cross the creek draining to the long, popular pebble beach, or (1km inland from this) *Tou Panaï*, with seating in an olive grove.

Melínda, another 700-metre sand-and-shingle beach at the mouth of a canyon, lies 6km west of Plomári by a mostly paved road. Here you'll find three inexpensive **taverna-rooms** outfits, of which *Maria's* (T02520/93 239; ❶) is an endearingly ramshackle place with simple but reasonably priced food and lodging, with *Paradhisos* (T02520/93 220; ❶) of similar standard; *Melinda* (aka Dhimitris Psaros; T02520/93 234; ❶) at the west end of the strand has a more elaborate menu and en-suite rooms. Even more unspoiled (thanks to a formerly dreadful ten-kilometre side road in, now sixty percent paved), **Tárti**, some 22km in total from Plomári, is a 400-metre-wide cove where Lésvos hoteliers and restaurant owners take *their* holidays. There are three beachfront **tavernas**, plus **rooms** lining the final stretch of road should you want to stay.

The **bus** into Plomári travels via the attractive villages of Paleókipos and Skópelos (as well as Áyios Isídhoros); the road north from Plomári to Ayiássos has paving and public transport only as far as Megalohóri.

Ayiássos and Mylélia

AYIÁSSOS, nestled in a remote, wooded valley under the crest of Mount Ólymbos, is the most beautiful hill town on Lésvos, its narrow cobbled streets lined by ranks of tiled-roof houses. On the usual, northerly approach, there's no clue of the enormous village until you see huge knots of parked cars at the southern edge of town (where the bus leaves you after the 26-kilometre run from Mytilíni).

Don't be put off by endless ranks of kitsch wooden and ceramic souvenirs or carved "Byzantine" furniture, aimed mostly at Greeks, but continue past the central **church of the Panayía Vrefokratoússa**, originally built in the twelfth century to house an icon supposedly painted by the Evangelist Luke, to the **old bazaar**, with its kafenía, yoghurt shops and butchers' stalls. With such a venerable icon as a focus, the local August 15 *paniyíri* is one of the liveliest in Greece, let alone Lésvos. Ayiássos also takes Carnival very seriously; there's a club dedicated to organizing it, opposite the post office. The best **restaurants** are *Dhouladhelli*, on your left as you enter the village from the extreme south (bus stop) end, or the idiosyncratic nocturnal ouzerí *To Stavri*, at the extreme north end of the village in Stavrí district. At either of these spots you can eat for a fraction of the prices asked at the coastal resorts.

If you're headed for Ayiássos with your own transport, you might visit the **Mylélia water mill**, whose inconspicuously signposted access track takes off 1km west of the turning for Ípios village. The name means "place of the mills", and there were once several hereabouts, powered by a spring, up-valley at Karíni. The last survivor (open daily 9am–6pm), restored to working order, has not been made twee in the least; the keeper will show you the millrace and paddle-wheel, as well as the flour making its spasmodic exit, after which you're free to buy gourmet pastas at the adjacent shop.

Vaterá, Skála Polikhnítou – and spas en route

A different bus route from Mytilíni leads to Vaterá beach via the inland villages of Polikhnítos and Vríssa. **VRÍSSA** itself has just opened a new **natural history museum** (daily 9.30am–7pm; €0.90) dedicated to local paleontological finds – it's not exactly required viewing at present, but a new, more extensive gallery is promised. Until 20,000 years ago, Lésvos (like all other east Aegean islands) was joined to the Asian mainland, the gulf of Vaterá was a subtropical lake, and all manner of creatures flourished here, their fossilized bones constituting the star exhibits.

If you're after a hot bath, head for the small, vaulted **spa-house** 1.5km east of Polikhnítos, well restored by an EU programme (daily: July–Aug 6–11am & 3–6pm; spring/autumn 7–11am & 4–6pm; €1.50); there are separate, pink-tinted chambers for each sex. Alternatively there are more **hot springs** at **Áyios Ioánnis**, signposted 3km below the village of Lisvóri. On the far side of the stream here are two pools housed in whitewashed, vaulted chambers (€1.50 fee payable when adjacent snack bar attended); the left-hand one's nicer, and there's no gender segregation or dress code.

VATERÁ, 9km south of Polikhnítos, is a huge, seven-kilometre-long sand beach, backed by vegetated hills; the sea here is delightfully calm and clean, the strand itself rated as one of the best in Greece. If you intend to stay here you'll probably want your own transport (there's **car rental** locally through Alpha, ℡02520/61 132), as the closest well-stocked shops are 4km away at Vríssa, and the bus appears only a few times daily. Development straggles for several kilometres to either side of the central T-junction, consisting mostly of seasonal villas and apartments for locals; at the west end of the strip is one of the very few consistently attended and professionally run hotels, the Greek- and American-owned *Vatera Beach* (℡02520/61 212, ℱ61 164, ℗www.our-lesvos.com; ⑤), whose rooms have air-con and fridges. It also has a good attached restaurant with own-grown produce and shoreline tables from where you can gaze on the cape of **Áyios Fokás** 3km to the west, where only foundations remain of a temple of Dionysos and a superimposed early Christian basilica. The little tamarisk-shaded anchorage here has an acceptable fish **taverna**, *Akrotiri/Agelerou*; it's better than most eateries east of the T-junction at Vaterá, many of which only operate July and August, but not so good as the half-dozen tavernas at **SKÁLA POLIKHNÍTOU**, 4km northwest of Polikhnítos itself, where *T'Asteria* and *Exohiko Kendro Tzitzifies* can both be recommended, staying open most of the year. Skála itself is pleasantly workaday, with only a short, narrow beach but one unusual accommodation option, "Soft Tourism" run by Lefteris and Erika (℡ 02520/42 678 or 093/7925435; ❷), who also have the concession to run the Polikhnítos spa. They generally host special-interest groups April to June and September, but welcome independent travellers during July and August.

East from Vaterá, a partly paved road leads via Stavrós, and then Akrássi (this stretch will be the last to be improved) to either Ayiássos or Plomári within ninety minutes. When leaving the area going north towards Kalloní, use the short cut via the naval base and seashore hamlet at Akhladherí – it's completely paved, despite appearing otherwise on obsolete maps.

Western Lésvos

The main road west of Loutrá Yéras is surprisingly devoid of settlement, with little to stop for before Kalloní other than the traces of an ancient **Aphrodite temple** at **Mésa** (Méson), 1km north of the main road, and signposted just east of the Akhladherí turn-off. At the **site** (Tues–Sun 8am–2.30pm; free) just eleventh-century BC foundations and a few column stumps remain, plus the ruins of a fourteenth-century Genoese-built basilica wedged inside; it was once virtually on the sea but a nearby stream has silted things up in the intervening millennia. All told, it's not worth a special trip, but certainly make the short detour if passing by. With more time and your own transport, you can turn northeast towards **Ayía Paraskeví** village, midway between two more important monuments from diverse eras: the Paleo-Christian **basilica of Halinádhou**, and the large **medieval bridge** of Kremastí.

KALLONÍ itself is an unembellished agricultural and market town more or less in the middle of the island, with various shops and services (including pharmacies, a post office and three banks with cash dispensers). Some 3km south lies **SKÁLA KALLONÍS**, a somewhat unlikely package resort backing a long but coarse-sand beach on the lake-like gulf. It's mainly distinguished as a bird-watching centre, attracting hundreds of twitchers for the March–May nesting season in the adjacent salt marshes. Pick of a half-dozen **hotels** is the human-scale bungalow complex *Malemi* (℡ 02530/22 594, ℻ 22 838, ⓦ www.hit360.com/malemi; ❺), with a variety of units from doubles to family suites, attractive grounds, tennis court and a large pool. **Tavernas** lining the quay with its fishing fleet are generally indistinguishable – though most offer the gulf's celebrated *sardhélles pastés*, or salt-cured sardines; the locals themselves tend to favour *Mimi's*, on the square just inland.

Inland monasteries and villages

West of Kalloní, the road winds 4km uphill to the **monastery of Limónos**, founded in 1527 by the monk Ignatios, whose actual cell is maintained in the surviving medieval north wing. It's a huge, rambling complex, with just a handful of monks and lay workers to maintain three storeys of cells around a vast, plant-filled courtyard. The *katholikón*, with its ornate carved-wood ceiling and archways, is built in Asia Minor style and is traditionally off-limits to women; a sacred spring flows from below the south foundation wall. A former abbot established a **museum** (daily 9.30am–6.30pm, may close 3pm off-season; €1.50) on two floors of the west wing; the ground-floor ecclesiastical collection is, alas, the only wing open as of writing, with the more interesting upstairs ethnographic gallery off-limits indefinitely. Content yourself with an overflow of farm implements stashed in a corner storeroom below, next to a chamber where giant *pithária* (urns) for grain and olive oil are embedded in the floor.

The main road beyond passes through **VATOÚSSA**, a landlocked and beautiful settlement in the heart of Lésvos's westernmost landmass. Besides unspoilt architecture it can offer two sterling examples of the endangered traditional oúzo-mezédhes kafenío in the upper platía: *Tryfon* and *Mihalis*.

Some 8km beyond Vatoússa, a short track leads down to the sixteenth-century **monastery of Perivolís** (daily 8am–1hr before sunset; donation, no photos), built in the midst of a riverside orchard (*perivóli*). Feeble electric light is available to view the narthex's fine if damp-damaged frescoes. In an apocalyptic panel worthy of Bosch (*The Earth and Sea Yield up their Dead*) the Whore of Babylon rides her chimera and assorted sea-monsters disgorge their victims; just to the right, towards the main door, the Three Magi approach the Virgin enthroned with the Christ Child. On the north side you see a highly unusual iconography of *Abraham, the Virgin, and the Penitent Thief of Calvary in Paradise*, with the Four Rivers of Paradise gushing forth under their feet; just right are assembled the Hebrew kings of the Old Testament.

ÁNDISSA, 3km further on, nestles under the arid west's only pine grove; at the edge of the village a sign implores you to "Come Visit Our Square", not a bad idea for the sake of several kafenía sheltering under three enormous plane trees. For more substantial fare, however, follow the paved road from directly below Ándissa 6km north to **GAVATHÁS**, a fishing hamlet with a narrow, partly protected beach (there's a bigger, surf-buffeted one at Kámbos just to the east) and a few places to eat and stay – among these are *Rooms Restaurant Paradise* (☎02530/56 376; ❷), serving good fish and locally grown vegetables.

Just west of Ándissa there's an important junction. Keeping straight leads you past the still-functioning **monastery of Ipsiloú**, founded in 1101 atop an outrider of the extinct volcano of Órdhymnos. The *katholikón*, tucked in one corner of a large, irregular courtyard, has a fine wood-lattice ceiling but had its frescoes repainted to detrimental effect in 1992; more intriguing are portions of Iznik tile stuck in the facade, and the handsome double gateway. Upstairs you can visit a fairly rich **museum** of ecclesiastical treasure (sporadically open; small donation). Ipsiloú's patron saint is John the Theologian, a frequent dedication for monasteries overlooking apocalyptic landscapes like the surrounding parched, boulder-strewn hills.

Signposted just west is the paved, five-kilometre side road to the main concentration of Lésvos's rather overrated **petrified forest** (daily 8am–sunset; €1.50), a fenced-in "reserve" which is toured along 3km of walkways. For once, contemporary Greek arsonists cannot be blamed for the state of the trees, created by the combined action of volcanic ash from Órdhymnos and hot springs some fifteen to twenty million years ago. The mostly horizontal sequoia trunks average a metre or less in length, save for a few poster-worthy exceptions; another more accessible (and free) cluster is found south of Sígri (see opposite), plus there is a fair number of petrified logs strewn about the courtyard of Ipsiloú.

Sígri

SÍGRI, near the western tip of Lésvos, has an appropriately end-of-the-line feel; the bay here is guarded both by an Ottoman castle, and the long island of Nissiopí, which protects the place somewhat from prevailing winds. Accordingly it's an important NATO naval base, with one or two weekly NEL **ferries** to Rafina, Psará, Áyios Efstrátios and Límnos obliged to dodge numbers of battleships often anchored here. The eighteenth-century **castle** (built atop the ruins of an earlier one) sports the sultan's monogram over the entrance, something rarely seen outside Istanbul, and a token of the high regard in which this productive island was held. The vaguely Turkish-looking **church of Ayía Triádha** is in fact a converted mosque, while the town itself presents a drab mix of vernacular and cement dwellings. The town beach, south of the castle headland, is narrow and hemmed in by the road; there are much better beaches at **Faneroméni**, 3.5km north by coastal dirt track from the northern outskirts of town, plus another 2km south, just below the fifteen-kilometre dirt track to Eressós; neither beach has any facilities.

Most **accommodation** is monopolized by British tour company Direct Greece, but you might try *Nelly's Rooms and Apartments* (☎02530/54 230; ❸), overlooking the castle, or the nearby *Rainbow Studios* (☎02530/54 310; ❸). Among several **tavernas**, the best all-rounder, just inland, is Italian-run, ultra-hygienic *Una Fatsa Una Ratsa*, with lovely grilled garlicky vegetables, pizza, pasta, grills and an Italian wine list; *Remezzo* further back is good for lobster. *Kavo Doro* opposite the jetty gets first pick of the fishermen's catch, but is no longer nearly as cheap as it was.

Skála Eressoú

Most visitors to western Lésvos park themselves at the resort of **SKÁLA ERESSOÚ**, accessible via the southerly turning between Ándissa and Ipsiloú. The three-kilometre beach here runs a close second in quality to Vaterá's, and consequently the place rivals Plomári and Mólyvos for numbers of visitors, who form an odd mix of Brits, Germans, Scandinavians, Greek families, neo-hippies and lesbians. Behind stretches the largest and most attractive agricultural plain on Lésvos, a welcome green contrast to the volcanic ridges above.

There's not much to Skála – just a roughly rectangular grid of perhaps five streets by eight, angling up to the oldest cottages on the slope of **Vígla hill**. The waterfront pedestrian zone (officially Papanikolí) is divided by a café-lined round platía midway along dominated by a bust of **Theophrastos**, the renowned botanist who hailed from ancient Eressós. This was not, as you might suppose, on the site of the modern inland village, but atop Vígla hill at the east end of the beach; some of the remaining citadel wall is still visible from a distance. On top, the ruins prove scanty, but it's worth the scramble up for the views – you can discern the ancient jetty submerged beyond the modern fishing anchorage.

Another famous reputed native of ancient Eressós was **Sappho** (c. 615–562 BC), the ancient poetess and reputed lesbian. There are usually appreciable numbers of gay women here paying homage, particularly at the two hotels devoted to their exclusive use (see overleaf), and in the clothing-optional zone of the beach west of the river mouth. Ancient Eressós endured into the Byzantine era, the main legacy of which is the **basilica of Áyios Andhréas** behind the modern church, merely foundations and an unhappily covered floor mosaic; the adjacent museum of local odds and ends is even less compelling.

Skála has countless **rooms and apartments**, but ones near the sea fill early in the day or are block-booked by tour companies; in peak season often the

5

best and quietest you can hope for is something inland overlooking a garden or fields. Even following a recent decline in tourist numbers (Direct Greece has dropped the resort, citing a lack of commitment to "family values"), it's wise to entrust the search to Sappho Travel (☎02530/52 140, ☏52 000). Jo and Joanna are switched-on and helpful, also serving as the local Budget car-rental station, ferry agent and air-ticket source; they are happy to place walk-ins in accommodation (②–④), but suggest you consult their UK-based website, ⓦwww.lesvos.co.uk, in advance. Otherwise, there are just three bona fide **hotels** in the village, and two of these – the remote *Antiopi* (☎02530/53 311; ① rooms, ③ studios) and the seafront *Sappho the Eressia* (☎02530/53 495, ☏53 174, ⓔSappho_sarani@hotmail.com; ③) – are run exclusively by and for lesbians. The alternative is the central, air-conditioned *Galini* (☎02530/53 138, ☏53 137; ④), slightly inland.

Most **tavernas**, with elevated wooden dining platforms, crowd the beach; none is utterly awful – they wouldn't survive the intense competition from falling tourist numbers – but some stand out. The *Blue Sardine* at the far west end of the front is an excellent seafood ouzerí with good bread, clearly identified frozen items, unusual salads and extra touches to the fish. By contrast, adjacent, grossly overpriced *Adonis* is best avoided in favour of *Soulatsos* a couple of doors further east, a good full-on taverna with meat and fish dishes. East of the platía, *Zephyros* makes a good account of itself for grills, while Canadian-run *Yamas* is the place for pancake breakfasts, veggie burgers, wholemeal bread and decadent chocolate desserts. The gay-women's contingent favours *Dhekati Mousa/Tenth Muse*, on the Theophrastos platía, though everyone is made welcome; a summer **cinema** further inland rounds up the nightlife. Skála has a **post office** and a coin-op **laundry** near the church, but **no bank** or cash dispenser; come prepared or pay travel agency commissions.

If you're returning to the main island crossroads at Kallóní, you can complete a loop from Eressós along the western shore of the Gulf of Kallóní via the hill villages of Mesótopos and Ágra; this route is now entirely paved, despite obsolete maps showing it as a track.

Northern Lésvos

The main road north of Kallóní winds up a piney ridge and then down the other side into increasingly attractive country, stippled with poplars and blanketed by olive groves. Long before you can discern any other architectural detail, the cockscomb silhouette of **Mólyvos castle** indicates your approach to the oldest established tourist spot on Lésvos.

Mólyvos (Míthymna)

MÓLYVOS (officially Míthymna), 61km from Mytilíni, is arguably the most beautiful village on Lésvos. Tiers of sturdy, red-tiled houses, some standing defensively with their rear walls to the sea, mount the slopes between the picturesque harbour and the **Genoese castle** (Tues–Sun 8am–2.30pm; €1.50), which provides interesting rambles around its perimeter walls and views of Turkey across the straits. Closer examination reveals a score of weathered Turkish fountains along flower-fragrant, cobbled alleyways, a reflection of the fact that before 1923 Muslims constituted over a third of the local population and owned most of the finest dwellings. You can try to gain admission to the **Krallis and Yiannakos mansions**, or the **municipal art gallery** occupying the former residence of local author Argyris Eftaliotis, which hosts temporary exhibitions. The small **archeological museum** (Tues–Sun 8am–2.30pm;

free), in the basement of the town hall, features finds from the ancient town, including blue Roman beads to ward off the evil eye (belief in this affliction is age-old and pan-Mediterranean). Archival photos depict the Greek conquest of the island in November–December 1912, with Ottoman POWs being dispatched afterwards from Mólyvos port to Anatolia. Barely excavated **ancient Mithymna** to the northwest is of essentially specialist interest, though a necropolis has been unearthed next to the bus stop.

Modern dwellings and hotels have been banned from the municipal core, but this hasn't stopped a steady drain of all the authentic life from the upper bazaar; just one lonely tailor still plies his trade amongst souvenir shops vastly surplus to requirements, and the last traditional locals' ouzerí shut in 1989. Cast as an upmarket resort in the early 1980s, Mólyvos is now firmly middle of the road, with the usual silly T-shirts and other shoddy souvenirs carpeting every vertical surface of yet another, however intrinsically attractive, stage-set for mass tourism.

Practicalities

The **town beach** is mediocre, improving somewhat as you head towards the southern end and a clothing-optional zone. Advertised **boat excursions** to bays as remote as Ánaxos and Tsónia (see p.416–417) seem a frank admission of this failing; there are also five to seven daily minibus shuttles in season, linking all points between Ánaxos and Eftaloú.

The main sea-level thoroughfare, straight past the tourist office, heads towards the harbour; along or just below it stand a number of bona fide **hotels** or **pensions** not completely taken over by packages. These include the *Hermes* very near the beach (℡02530/71 250; ❹), with large airy rooms; the *Molyvos I* next door (℡02530/71 496, ℱ71 640; ❺); the humble *Poseidon* just down from the tourist office (℡02530/71 981; ❸); and the *Adonis* inland and northwest of these (℡02530/71 866, ℱ71 636; ❺), which has heating and is thus the only all-year hotel here. For rooms, seek out the modern studio units of Khryssi Bourdhadonaki (℡02530/72 193; ❸), towards Ayía Kyriakí; those of Panayiotis Baxevanellis (℡02530/71 558 or call at the *El Greco* cake shop; ❶), with a preponderance of double beds and a communal kitchen; *Studios Voula* below the castle car park (℡02530/72 017 or 71 305), which has studios (❸) or a restored four-person house (❹), both with knockout views; and the quiet, exceedingly simple rooms of Varvara Kelesi (℡02530/71 460; ❷), way up by the castle. Otherwise, rooms can be reserved through the municipal **tourist office** by the bus stop (daily: summer theoretically 8am–3pm & 6.30–8.30pm; spring and autumn 8.30am–3pm; ℡02530/71 347). The official **campsite**, *Camping Methymna*, lies 2km northeast of town on the Eftaloú road.

The sea-view **tavernas** on the lower market lane of 17-Noemvríou are all much of a muchness, where you pay primarily for the view; it's far better to either head for outlying villages or descend to the fishing port, where *The Captain's Table* (with green chairs) combines the virtues of fresh seafood, meat grills and vegetarian mezédhes, while *To Khtapodhi*, in the old customs house by the port entrance, has fairly consistent quality and treats such as *sardhélles pastés*. Many consider the five-kilometre trip east to Vafiós worth it to patronize either *To Petrino*, *Taverna Vafios* or *Taverna Ilias*, especially the last of them with its wonderful bread and bulk wine – but avoid deep-fried dishes at any of these places. Also highly recommended, and open all year, is *Iy Eftalou*, 4km northeast near the eponymous spa (see p.416), where the food (mostly grills) and tree-shaded setting are splendid. For dessert, try the pudding and cake shop *El Greco* on the lower market lane, where proprietor Panayiotis is a wonderful raconteur (in several languages).

Midsummer sees a short **festival of music and theatre** up in the castle, and there's also a well-regarded summer **cinema** next to the taxi rank. Night-owls are well catered for with a selection of music bars: *Music Bazaar* near the harbour for loud, danceable sounds; *Skala* just up the hill from the port, with live music three nights weekly; the disco and young-things' hangout *Congas Bar* (shuts mid-Sept) below the shore road; and the all-season *Gatelousi Piano Bar* near the *Olive Press Hotel*, a more genteel branch of state-of-the-art outdoor disco *Gatelousi*, 3km towards Pétra, the place to be seen on a Saturday night (June–Aug only). Around the tourist office you'll find two **bank** autotellers, plus numerous **motorbike and car rental** places, including Kosmos (℡02530/71 650). The main **post office** is near the top of the upper commercial street, with a seasonal branch on the shore road Mihaïl Goútou.

Pétra and Ánaxos

Since there are political and practical limits to the expansion of Mólyvos, many package companies have shifted emphasis to **PÉTRA**, 5km due south. The place has sprawled untidily behind its broad sand beach and seafront square, but the core of old stone houses, many with Levantine-style balconies overhanging the street, remains. Pétra takes its name from the giant **rock monolith** located some distance inland and enhanced by the eighteenth-century **church of the Panayía Glykofiloússa**, reached via 103 rock-hewn steps. Other local attractions include the sixteenth-century **church of Áyios Nikólaos**, with three phases of well-preserved frescoes, and the intricately decorated **Vareltzídhena mansion** (Tues–Sun 8.30am–7pm, may close earlier off-season; free), with naive wall paintings of courting couples and a stylized view of a naval engagement at Constantinople.

Most small hotels and studios are block-booked, so on-spec arrivals should make a beeline for the Women's Agricultural Tourism Cooperative on the south side of the seafront square (℡02530/41 238, ℉41 309, ⒠womes@otenet.gr), formed by Pétra's women in 1984 to offer something more unusual for visitors. In addition to operating an excellent, inexpensive restaurant on the square, with both grills and *mayireftá* served at rooftop seating, they arrange rooms or studios (❶–❷) in a number of scattered premises. Aside from the co-operative's eatery, most tavernas lack distinction, though some people like *Iy Dhrosia* and *To Khrysso Petalo* behind the beach. You're probably better off out of town – either at the *Taverna Petri* in the *Petri* village 3km inland, with superb home-recipe *mayireftá* and a view terrace, or at Avláki, 1.5km southwest en route to Ánaxos, where there's a competent, signposted eponymous taverna/ouzerí behind a tiny beach.

ÁNAXOS, 3km south of Pétra, is a higgledy-piggledy package resort fringing by far the cleanest beach in the area: a kilometre of sand cluttered with sunbeds, pedalos and a handful of tavernas that are an improvement on the unmemorable snack bars of yore. From anywhere along here you enjoy beautiful sunsets between and beyond three offshore islets.

Around Mount Lepétymnos

East of Mólyvos, the villages of 968-metre **Mount Lepétymnos**, marked by tufts of poplars, provide a day's rewarding exploration. The first stop, though not exactly up the hill, might be **Loutrá Eftaloú**, some thermal baths 5km along the road passing the campsite. Insist on patronizing the hot pool under the Ottoman-era domed structure, not the sterile modern tub-rooms (daily 8am–noon & 2–6pm; €2.40). Nearby, there is a considerable number of fancy hotels and bungalow complexes, friendliest and best value (though tour-dominated like the others) being the *Eftalou* (☎02530/71 584; ❹), with a pool, well-tended garden and loyal repeat clientele.

The main road around the mountain first heads 6km east to **VAFIÓS**, with its three aforementioned tavernas (see p.415), before curling north around the base of the peaks. This route is entirely paved, but the twice-daily bus service back towards Mytilíni does not resume until Áryennos, 6km before the exquisite hill village of **SYKAMINIÁ** (**Sykamiá**), birthplace of the novelist Stratis Myrivilis. Below the "Plaza of the Workers' First of May", with its two traditional kafenía and views north to Turkey, one of the imposing basalt-built houses is marked as his childhood home. A marked trail shortcuts the twisting road down to **SKÁLA SYKAMINIÁS**, easily the most picturesque fishing port on Lésvos. Myrivilis used it as the setting for his best-known work, *The Mermaid Madonna*, and the tiny rock-top chapel at the end of the jetty will be instantly recognizable to anyone who has read the book.

On a practical level, Skála has a few pensions, such as the central *Gorgona* (☎02530/55 301; ❷), and four **tavernas**. The most durable of these is *Iy Skamnia* (aka *Iy Mouria*), with seating under the mulberry tree in which Myrivilis used to sleep on hot summer nights, though newer *Anemoessa* (closest to the chapel) has overtaken it quality-wise. The only local beach is the extremely stony one of **Kayiá** 1.5km east, where *Psarotaverna Kayia* near its east end does lots of dishes besides fish.

Continuing east from upper Sykaminiá, you soon come to **KLIÓ**, whose single main street (marked "kentrikí agorá") leads down to a platía with a plane tree, fountain, kafenía and more views across to Turkey. The village is set attractively on a slope, down which a six-kilometre dirt road, marked in English or Greek and passable with care in an ordinary car, descends to **Tsónia beach**, 600m of beautiful pink volcanic sand.

South of Klió, the route forks at Kápi, from where you can complete a loop of the mountain by bearing west along a road completely paved except for a few hundred metres before Stýpsi. **PELÓPI** is the ancestral village of unsuccessful 1988 US presidential candidate Michael Dukakis (who finally visited the island in 2000), and sports a former mosque, now used as a warehouse, on the main square. **IPSILOMÉTOPO**, 5km further along, is punctuated by a minaret (but no mosque) and hosts revels on July 17, the feast of Ayía Marína. By the time you reach sprawling **STÝPSI**, you're just 4km shy of the main Kalloní–Mólyvos road; it's also not a bad start-point for rambles along Lepétymnos's steadily dwindling network of trails (a locally sold guide by Mike Maunder, *17 Walks Around Pétra and Mólyvos*, details some).

Mandamádhos and Taxiárhis monastery

The main highway south from Klió and Kápi leads back to the capital through **MANDAMÁDHOS**. This attractive inland village is famous for its pottery, including the Ali Baba-style *pithária* (olive oil urns) seen throughout Lésvos, but more so for the "black" icon of the Archangel Michael, whose enormous **monastery of Taxiárhis** (daily: summer 6am–10pm; winter 6.30am–7pm), in a valley just northeast, is the powerful focus of a thriving cult. The image – supposedly made from a mixture of mud and the blood of monks slaughtered in a massacre – is really more idol than icon, both in its lumpy three-dimensionality and in the former rather pagan manner of veneration. First there was the custom of the coin-wish, whereby you pressed a coin to the Archangel's forehead – if it stuck, your wish would be granted. Owing to wear and tear on the image, the practice is now forbidden, with supplicants referred to an alternative icon by the main entrance.

5

THE EAST AND NORTH AEGEAN | Northern Lésvos

It's further believed that while carrying out his various errands on behalf of the faithful, the Archangel gets through more footwear than Imelda Marcos. Accordingly the icon used to be surrounded not by the usual *támmata* (votive medallions) but by piles of miniature gold and silver shoes. The ecclesiastical authorities, embarrassed by such "primitive" practices, removed all the little shoes in 1986. Since then, a token substitute has reappeared: several pairs of tin slippers which can be filled with money and left in front of the icon. Just why his devotees should want to encourage these perpetual peripatetics is unclear, since in Greek folklore the Archangel Michael is also the one who fetches the souls of the dying, and modern Greek attitudes towards death are as bleak as those of their pagan ancestors.

5 Límnos

Límnos is a sizeable agricultural and garrison island whose remoteness and peculiar ferry schedules have until recently protected it from the worst excesses of the holiday trade. Most summer visitors are Greek, particularly from Thessaloníki, though the locals are becoming increasingly used to numbers of German and British visitors. Accommodation tends to be comfortable if a bit overpriced, with a strong bias towards self-catering units, and **backpackers** are explicitly **discouraged**. The bucolic island has been getting trendy of late: there are upscale souvenir shops, village houses restored by Thessalonians as weekend retreats, some sort of noon-to-small-hours musical bar at every beach, and a fairly significant gay scene.

Límnos's traditional role is as an army posting. Its **military presence** ran to 25,000 soldiers at the nadir of Greco-Turkish relations in the late 1980s, though it is now down to about 10,000; conventional tourism was slow in coming because the islanders made a reliable living off the soldiers and family members coming to visit them. Since the 1960s, the island has been the focus of periodic disputes between the Greek and Turkish governments; Turkey has a long-standing demand that Límnos should be demilitarized, and Turkish aircraft regularly intrude Greek air space overhead, prompting immediate responses from the Greek Air Force squadron here.

The bays of **Bourniá** and **Moúdhros**, the latter one of the largest natural harbours in the Aegean, almost divide Límnos in two. The west of the island is dramatically bare and hilly, with abundant basalt put to good use as street cobbles and house masonry. Like most volcanic islands, Límnos produces excellent wine from westerly vineyards – good dry whites, rosés and excellent retsina – plus oúzo at Kondiás. The east is low-lying and speckled with marshes popular with duck-hunters, where it's not occupied by cattle, combine harvesters and vast corn fields.

Despite off-islander slander to that effect, Límnos is not flat, barren or treeless; much of the countryside consists of rolling hills, well vegetated except on their heights, and with substantial clumps of almond, jujube, myrtle, oak, poplar and mulberry trees. The island is, however, extremely dry, with irrigation water pumped from deep wells, and a limited number of potable springs. Yet various terrapin-haunted creeks bring sand to several long, **sandy beaches** around the coast, where it's easy to find a stretch to yourself – though there's no escaping the stingless jellyfish which occasionally pour out of the Dardanelles and die here in the shallows (they've fortunately decreased in recent years). On the plus side, beaches shelve gently, making them ideal for children and quick to warm up in early summer, with no cool currents except near the river mouths.

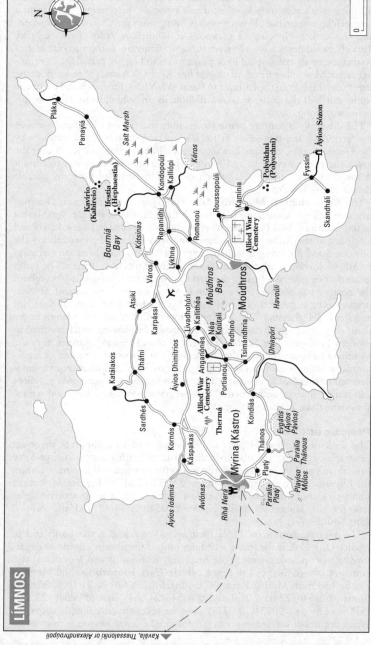

LÍMNOS

▼ Rafína, Áyios Efstrátios, Lésvos & Híos

▼ Kavála, Thessaloníki or Alexandhroúpoli

Pláka

Panayiá

Salt Marsh

Kéros

Kondopoúli

Kalliópi

Kavírio (Kabírio)

Ifestía (Hephaestia)

Bourniá Bay

Kótsinas

Repanídhi

Romanoú

Roussopoúli

Polyókhni (Polyochni)

Kamínia

Fyssíni

Áyios Sózon

Skandháli

Város

Lýkhna

Atsikí

Karpássi

Moúdhros Bay

Néa Koútali

Livadhohóri

Kallithéa

Pedhinó

Tsimándhria

Moúdhros

Havoúli

Dhapóri

Allied War Cemetery

Dháfni

Áyios Dhimítrios

Angariónes

Portianoú

Allied War Cemetery

Thermá

Katálakos

Sardhés

Kornós

Káspakas

Kondiás

Kóndiás

Thános

Áyios Ioánnis

Avlónas

Rihá Nerá

Mýrina (Kástro)

Platý

Paralía Platý

Playíso Mólos

Paralía Thánous

Evgátis (Áyios Pávlos)

N

0   5 km

Mýrina

MÝRINA (Kástro), the capital and port on the west coast, has the atmosphere of a provincial market town rather than of a resort. With about five thousand inhabitants, it's pleasantly low-key, if not especially picturesque, apart from a core neighbourhood of old stone houses dating from the Ottoman occupation, and the ornate Neoclassical mansions at Romeïkós Yialós. Few explicitly Turkish monuments have survived, though a fountain at the harbour end of Kýdha retains its calligraphic inscription and is still highly prized for its drinking water. Most other things of interest line Kydhá/Karatzá, the main shopping street stretching from the harbour to Romeïkós Yialós, the beach and esplanade to the north of the castle, or Garoufalídhou, its perpendicular offshoot, roughly halfway along.

The originally Byzantine **castle** (access unrestricted), on a headland between the ferry dock and Romeïkós Yialós, is quite ruined despite later additions by the Genoese and Ottomans, but warrants a climb at sunset for views over the town, the entire west coast and – in exceptional conditions – over to Mount Athos, 35 nautical miles west (which can also be glimpsed from any suitable height east of town).

The **Archeological Museum** (daily 8am–7pm; €1) occupies an Ottoman mansion behind Romeïkós Yialós, not far from the site of Bronze Age Myrina in the suburb of Rihá Nerá. Finds are assiduously labelled in Greek, Italian and English, and the entire premises are exemplary in terms of presentation – the obvious drawback being that many of the best items have been spirited away to Athens, leaving a collection that's essentially of specialist interest. The south ground-floor gallery is mainly devoted to pottery from Polyókhni (Polychni); the north wing contains more of the same, plus items from ancient Myrina; upstairs features galleries of post-Bronze Age artefacts from Kavírio (Kabireio) and Ifestía (Hephaestia). The star upper-storey exhibits are votive lamps in the shape of sirens, found in an Archaic sanctuary at Hephaestia, much imitated in modern local jewellery. Rather less vicious than Homer's creatures, they are identified more invitingly as the "muses of the underworld, creatures of superhuman wisdom, incarnations of nostalgia for paradise". Another entire room is devoted to metalwork, of which the most impressive items are gold jewellery and bronze objects, both practical (cheese graters, door-knockers) and whimsical-naturalistic (a snail, a vulture).

Practicalities

The sleek new civilian **airport** is 19km east of Mýrina, almost at the exact geographic centre of the island, sharing a runway with an enormous air-force base; there's an Olympic-run shuttle bus between town and airport – consult the Olympic office for departure times (℡02540/22 078). **Ferries** dock at the southern end of the town, in the shadow of the castle; there are separate agencies for the sailings of NEL boats (℡02540/22 460) and the *Saos II* (℡02540/29 571).

The **bus station** is on Platía Eleftheríou Venizélou, at the north end of Kydhá. One look at the sparse schedules (only a single daily afternoon departure to most points, slightly more frequently to Kondiás and Moúdhros) will convince you of the need to rent a vehicle. **Cars**, **motorbikes** and **bicycles** can be had from Myrina Rent a Car (℡02540/24 476 or 24 100), Petridou Tours (℡02540/22 039), Holiday (℡02540/24 357), Best (℡02540/22 127) or Auto Europe (℡02540/23 777); rates for bikes are only slightly above the island norm, but cars are expensive. A motorbike (most obviously from Moto

Lemnos, ☎02540/25 002) is generally enough to explore the coast and the interior, as there are few steep gradients but many perilously narrow village streets.

All five **banks** have cash dispensers; the **post office** and Olympic airlines terminal are adjacent to each other on Garoufalídhou, with a **laundry** across the way by the Hotel Paris. There are **internet** facilities at *Excite Club*, just behind the port roundabout, and at *Joy*, by the post office.

Accommodation

Despite Límnos's steady gentrification, you may still be met off the boat with offers of a **room**; there are officially a couple dozen licensed establishments. The most durable budget establishment is the welcoming *Apollo Pavillion*, hidden away in a peaceful cul-de-sac off Frýnis (☎02540/24 315, ℱ23 712, ℮apollo47@otenet.gr), with multibed rooms in the basement (€26.50 for a standard double) and more comfortable self-catering units upstairs (❹). Otherwise, try the *Hotel Lemnos* (☎02540/22 153, ℱ23 329; ❹), by the harbour, with air-con, fridges and balconies offsetting small-hours ferry noise, or the quiet *Hotel Ifestos* in Andhróni district (☎02540/24 960, ℱ23 623; ❹), with similar amenities but a mix of sea and mountain views, a pleasant bar-lounge and professional service (something of a rarity in town).

Romeïkós Yialós has a few **pensions and small hotels** housed in its restored houses, though all are affected by evening noise from the bars below. Best value is *Blue Waters* (☎02540/24 403, ℱ25 004, ℮bwkon@otenet.gr; ❹), with smallish but decently appointed rooms; one block inland at Sakhtoúri 7, *Pension Romeïkos Yialos* (☎02540/23 787; ❹) in a stone mansion may be quieter. Just north of Romeïkós Yialós, the areas of Rihá Nerá and Áyios Pandelímonas are likely bets for self-catering units. Finally, the *Akti Myrina* (☎02540/22 681, ℱ22 947, ⓦwww.ventaglio-com) is a self-contained **luxury** complex of wood-and-stone bungalows (avoid the awful modern annexe) at the north end of Romeïkós Yialós, with all conceivable diversions and comforts. It is run by, and mainly caters for Italians, and is off-limits from late June through August, but during low season (May/Sept) you can squeeze in for €235 per couple per night, all meals and sports facilities included.

There's **no official campsite** on Límnos; Greek caravanners and campers have been banished from the north end of Platý beach, though a few tents still sprout furtively at Paralía Thánous (see overleaf) and at Kéros (see p.423).

Eating and drinking

About halfway along Kydhá, *O Platanos* serves traditional *mayireftá* to big crowds on an atmospheric little square under two plane trees; for affordable seaside dining, look no further than *Ostria* at the town end of Toúrkikos Yialós beach, which offers a mix of grills, fish and ouzomezédhes from noon until late. Seafood is excellent on Límnos owing to its proximity to the Dardanelles and seasonal fish migrations; accordingly there are no fewer than five tavernas arrayed around the little fishing port. There's little to distinguish their prices or menus, though *O Glaros* at the far end is considered the best – and works out slightly more expensive.

Not too surprisingly given the twee setting, the restaurants and bars on Romeïkós Yialós are pretty poor value, except for a drink in sight of the castle. The tree-shaded tables of *Iy Tzitzifies* on Rihá Nerá, the next bay north, are a far better option; most of the extensive menu of fish, mezédhes and *mayireftá* is likely to be available on any given day.

Western Límnos

As town **beaches** go, Romeïkós Yialós and Toúrkikos Yialós are not at all bad; Rihá Nerá is even better, with watersports craft on offer. But if you're looking for more pristine conditions, head 3km north past the *Akti Myrina* to Avlónas, unspoiled except for the *Porto Marina Palace* luxury complex flanking it on the south. Some 6km from town you work your way through **KÁSPAKAS**, its north-facing houses in pretty, tiled tiers, before plunging down to **Áyios Ioánnis**. Here, the island's most unusual taverna (late June to Aug) features seating in the shade of piled-up volcanic boulders, with a serviceably sandy beach just north of the fishing anchorage. If it's shut, *Taverna Iliovasilemata* to the south is welcoming, with good (if slightly pricey) fish.

PLATÝ, 2km southeast of Mýrina, has had its profile spoiled by the kind of modern villa construction that is blighting many Limnian villages latterly, but it does have two nocturnally popular **tavernas**. By far the better of these is *O Sozos*, just off the main platía, where you'll have to show up early for a table (groups should reserve on ☎02540/25 085). Fine *orektiká*, lamb chops, steamed mussels, grilled *biftéki*, *tsípouro* and local bulk wine are strong points; the bill shouldn't exceed €9. The long sandy beach, 700m below, is popular and usually jellyfish-free, with watersports available; except for the unsightly Mark Warner compound at the south end, the area is still pretty rural, with sheep parading to and fro at dawn and dusk. The single **hotel**, low-rise *Plati Beach* (☎02540/23 583 or 094/4965189; ❷), has an enviable position in the middle of the beach, but get a room towards the back if you don't fancy noise from the ground-floor bar/restaurant; there are more basic **rooms**, though with fridges and proper showers, available through *Tzimis Taverna* (☎02540/24 142; ❶), which divides the lunchtime trade with its neighbour *Grigoris* near the south end of the beach, though both lose out in the evenings to the village-centre tavernas. The highest standard of **studios** in the area, if not the island, is the tastefully landscaped *Villa Afroditi* (☎02540/23 141, ℉25 031, winter ☎01/96 33 488; ❸), with a pleasant pool bar, weekly barbecue nights for guests, and one of the best buffet breakfasts in Greece. The South African management also offers a lovely restored house in Kondiás village, which sleeps four – €73.50 per night for a week's stay.

THÁNOS, 2km further southeast, seems a bigger, more architecturally characterful version of Platý village, with a well-regarded central-platía taverna (evenings only) and high-standard mock-trad bungalows at the east edge (☎02540/23 162; ❸). **Paralía Thánous**, 1.5km on a paved road below the village, is perhaps the most scenic of the southwestern beaches, flanked by weird volcanic crags and with views on a clear afternoon out to Áyios Efstrátios island. Of two tavernas, one, *O Nikos* (☎02540/22 787; ❶), rents a handful of basic rooms. Beyond Thános, the road curls over to the enormous beach at **Evgátis** (Áyios Pávlos), reckoned to be the island's best, with more igneous pinnacles on the west. Despite this rating, there's so far just the regulation music bar/*kantína* on the sand, and a full-service taverna across the road.

Some 3km further along (11km from Mýrina), **KONDIÁS** is the island's third largest settlement, cradled between two hills tufted with Limnos's only pine forest. Stone-built, red-tiled houses combine with the setting to make Kondiás the most attractive inland village, a fact not lost on the urban Greeks restoring old houses with varying degrees of taste. Short-term facilities are limited, and aren't much better at the shore annexe of **Dhiapóri**, 2km east. The beach is unappealing (and backed by a huge, fenced-off minefield), the tavernas listless, with the main interest lent by the narrow isthmus dividing the bays of Kondiás and Moúdhros.

Eastern Límnos

The shores of **Moúdhros Bay**, glimpsed south of the trans-island road, are muddy and best avoided unless you're a clam-digger. The bay itself enjoyed considerable importance during World War I, culminating in the Ottoman surrender aboard the British warship HMS *Agamemnon* here on October 30, 1918. The port of **MOÚDHROS**, the second-largest town on Límnos, is a dreary place, with only a wonderfully kitsch, two-belfried church to recommend it. The closest decent beach is at **Havoúli**, 4km south by dirt track and still far from the open sea. Despite this, there are three hotels here; best of these, if overpriced, is *Kyma* (℡02540/71 333, ℱ71 484; ❹), whose more reasonable restaurant is well placed for a lunch break if you're visiting the archeological sites and beaches of eastern Límnos.

About 800m along the Roussopoúli road, you pass an **Allied military cemetery** (unlocked) maintained by the Commonwealth War Graves Commission; its neat (if rather dry) lawns and rows of white headstones seem incongruous in such parched surroundings. In 1915, Moúdhros Bay was the principal staging area for the disastrous Gallipoli campaign. Of the roughly 36,000 Allied dead, 887 – mainly battle casualties who died after having been evacuated to the base hospital at Moúdhros – are buried here, with 348 more at another signposted graveyard behind the church in Portianoú.

Indications of the most advanced Neolithic civilization in the Aegean have been unearthed at **Polyókhni** (**Polyochni**), 3km from the gully-hidden village of Kamínia (7km east of Moúdhros). The site occupies a bluff overlooking a long, narrow rock-and-sand beach flanked by stream valleys. Since the 1930s, Italian excavations have uncovered five layers of settlement, the oldest from late in the fourth millennium BC, predating Troy on the Turkish coast opposite. The town met a sudden, violent end from war or earthquake in about 2100 BC. The actual **ruins** (daily 8am–7pm; free) are of essentially specialist interest, though a *bouleuterion* (assembly hall) with bench seating, a mansion and the landward fortifications are labelled. During August and September the Italian excavators are about, and may be free to show you around the place; at other times you should obtain the useful TAP brochure from the Mýrina museum to make any sense of the place.

Ifestía and Kavírio, the other significant **ancient sites** on Límnos, are reached via the village of Kondopoúli, 7km northeast of Moúdhros. Both sites are rather remote, and only reachable with your own transport. **Ifestía** (**Hephaestia**), 4km from Kondopoúli by rough, signposted track, has little to offer nonspecialists. **Kavírio** (**Kabireio**), on the opposite shore of Tigáni Bay and accessed by the same road built to serve the now-bankrupt and derelict Kaviria Palace luxury complex, is more evocative. The **ruins** (daily 8am–7pm; free) are those of a sanctuary connected with the cult of the Samothracian Kabiroi (see p.427), though the site here is probably older. Little survives other than the ground plan, but the setting is undeniably impressive. Eleven column stumps stake out a stoa, behind eight spots marked as column bases in the *telestirio* or shrine where the cult mysteries took place. More engaging, perhaps, is a nearby sea grotto identified as the Homeric **Spiliá toú Filoktíti**, where the Trojan war hero Philoctetes was abandoned by his comrades-in-arms until his stinking, gangrenous leg had healed. Landward access to the cave is via steps leading down from the caretaker's shelter, though final access (from a little passage on the right as you face the sea) involves some wading.

The beach at **Kéros**, 2.5km by dirt road below **KALLIÓPI** (which has two snack bar/**tavernas**, and smart **rooms** at the edge of town – ℡02540/41 730,

❸), is the best in this part of the island. A 1500-metre stretch of sand with dunes and a small pine grove, plus shallow water, it attracts a number of Greek tourists and foreigners with camper vans and windsurfers; a small snack *kantína* operates near the parking area during July and August only.

On the other side of Kondopoúli, reached via Repanídhi village, the often dirty, hard-packed beach of **Kótsinas** is set in the protected western limb of Bourniá Bay. The nearby anchorage (follow signs to "Kótsinas Fortress") offers a pair of **tavernas**; the better of these is *To Korali* by the water, which is reliably open at lunch, with a wide range of mezédhes and affordable fish. Up on a knoll overlooking the jetty, there's a corroded, sword-brandishing statue of Maroula, a Genoese-era heroine who delayed the Ottoman conquest by a few years, and a large **church of Zoödhóhou Piyís** (the Life-Giving Spring). This is nothing extraordinary, but beside it 63 steps lead down through an illuminated tunnel in the rock to the potable (if slightly mineral) spring in question, oozing into a cool, vaulted chamber.

Áyios Efstrátios (Aï Strátis)

Áyios Efstrátios is without doubt one of the quietest and loneliest islands in the Aegean. Historically, the only outsiders to stay here were compelled to do so – it served as a place of exile for political prisoners under both the Metaxas regime of the 1930s and the various right-wing governments that followed the civil war. It's still unusual for foreign travellers to visit the island, and, if you do, you might be asked why you've shown up.

You may initially ask yourself the same question, for **ÁYIOS EFSTRÁTIOS** village – the only habitation on the island – must be one of the ugliest in Greece. Devastation caused by an earthquake in February 1968, which killed half the population, was compounded by the reconstruction plan: the contract went to a company with junta connections, who prevented the survivors from returning to their old homes and used army bulldozers to raze even those structures that could have been repaired. From the hillside, some two dozen surviving houses of the old village overlook its replacement, whose grim rows of prefabs constitute a sad monument to the corruption of the junta years. If you're curious, there's a pre-earthquake photograph of the village in the kafenío by the port.

Architecture apart, Áyios Efstrátios still functions as a traditional fishing and farming community, with the prefabs set at the mouth of a wooded stream valley draining to the sandy harbour beach. Tourist amenities consist of just two basic **tavernas** (a third may open in midsummer), plus a total of three **pensions**. Best of these, in one of the surviving old houses, is the *Xenonas Aï-Stratis* (☎02540/93 329; ❸); Andonis Paneras (☎02540/93 209; ❸) and Apostolos Paneras (☎02540/93 343; ❸) have more conventional rooms in the prefabs. These relatively stiff prices for such an out-of-the-way place reflect Aï Strátis' increasing popularity with Greeks, and you may have to ring all three spots for a vacancy in season.

As you walk away from the village – there are few cars and no real roads – things improve rapidly. The landscape, dry hills and valleys scattered with a surprising number of oak trees, is deserted apart from wild rabbits, sheep, an occasional shepherd, and some good beaches where you can camp in seclusion. **Alonítsi**, on the north coast – a ninety-minute walk from the village following a track up the north side of the valley – is a two-kilometre stretch of sand with rolling breakers and views across to Límnos.

South of the village, there's a series of greyish sand beaches, most with wells and drinkable water, although with few real paths in this part of the island, getting to them can be something of a scramble. **Lidharío**, at the end of an attractive wooded valley, is the first worthwhile beach, but again it's a ninety-minute walk, unless you can persuade a fisherman to take you by boat. Some of the caves around the coast are home to the rare Mediterranean monk seal, but you're unlikely to see one.

Ferries on the Kavála–Límnos–Rafína line call at Áyios Efstrátios twice weekly most of the year; in summer a small Límnos-based ferry, the *Aiolis*, sails every weekday (Mon–Fri) at 3pm from Límnos, returning the next morning. Despite recent harbour improvements, this is still a very exposed anchorage, and in bad weather you could end up stranded here far longer than you bargained for. If an indefinite stay does not appeal, it's best to visit from Límnos on the day-trip offered by the *Aiolis* (usually on Sun).

Samothráki (Samothrace)

Samothráki has one of the most dramatic profiles of all the Greek islands, second only to Thíra's: its dark mass of granite rises abruptly from the sea, culminating in the 1611-metre **Mount Fengári**. Seafarers have always been guided by its imposing outline, clearly visible from the mainland, and in legend its summit provided a vantage point for Poseidon to watch over the siege of Troy. The mostly forbidding coastline provides no natural anchorage, but in ancient times the island was colonized by settlers from Thrace, with more recent migrations from Anatolia and Lésvos swelling the population. Landing is still very much subject to the vagaries of the notoriously unpredictable weather, but it did not deter pilgrims who, for hundreds of years, journeyed to the island to visit the **Sanctuary of the Great Gods** and were initiated into its mysteries. The Sanctuary remains the main archeological attraction of the island

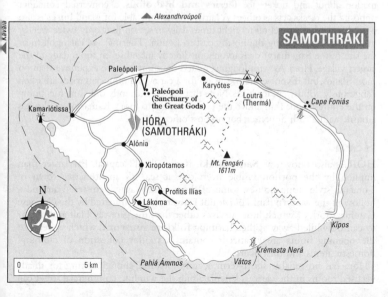

which, too remote for most tourists, combines earthy simplicity with natural grandeur. The tourist season is relatively short-lived – essentially (late) July and August – but you will find some facilities open as early as Easter and one or two all year round.

Kamariótissa

All ferries and hydrofoils dock at the dull village of **KAMARIÓTISSA**, where you're unlikely to want to spend much time. That said it could be your most convenient base, since some of Samothráki's best **hotels** lie along or just behind the tree-lined seafront and various **rooms** for rent, many them more than acceptable, can be found in the maze of streets behind; owners often meet incoming vessels. As on most islands with a short season, accommodation can be pricey for what you get, and bargaining is not always productive, especially in midsummer. Along the shore, some way east of your point of arrival, is the recently refurbished *Kyma* (☎05510/41 263; ❸); be aware that rooms overlooking the pebbly beach can get noise from the string of *barákia* which constitutes Samothráki's main nightlife, and avoid the hotel restaurant – the taverna (see below) is much better. Calmer, but somewhat pricier, is the *Niki Beach* (☎05510/41 561; ❹) beyond the far north end of the quay. Above, occupying a bluff and visible from out to sea, is the slightly impersonal *Aeolos* (☎05510/41 595, ☞41 810; ❺); with a large pool and quiet, spacious rooms, it's the island's most comfortable accommodation and offers good half-board deals out of season. Bars and cafés on the harbourfront serve snacks and breakfasts, but the only commendable **taverna** is the *Limanaki*, at the southern end, beyond the docks: excellent Limniot wine from the barrel is perfect with the fish and seafood on offer, which you can virtually watch being unloaded by local fishermen as you order.

Motorbikes and **cars** are in short supply, so it's worth grabbing one immediately on disembarkation – or even reserving a bike in advance from Hanou Brothers (☎05510/41 511) or a car from Niki Tours (☎05510/41 465), which sells plane tickets as well; also try Kyrkos car rental (☎097/4371122). For information about and tickets for **ferries and hydrofoils**, a converted container opposite the docks acts as offices. A fairly reliable timetable for island **buses** is also posted here; these travel up to eight times daily in season (but only twice weekly in deepest winter) along the north coast to Loutrá (Thermá) via Paleópoli (near the site of the Sanctuary) or Karyótes, or directly inland seven times daily to the largest village, Hóra. As with lodging, rented transport is more expensive than on most islands, but if you've the means go for a car as Samothracian roads are often dangerously windswept for bikes. Note that there is currently only one fuel pump on the entire island, 1km above the port, en route to Hóra. Kamariótissa also has a **bank** with a cash dispenser, but no post office.

Hóra

HÓRA, also known as **Samothráki**, is the island's capital. Far larger than implied by the portion visible from out at sea, it's an attractive town of Thracian-style stone houses, some of them whitewashed, clustered around a hollow in the western flanks of Mount Fengári. It is dominated by the Genoese Gateluzzi fort, of which little survives other than the gateway. Half an hour or so can be whiled away at the charming **folklore museum**, which is free, but the opening hours are erratic; it contains a motley collection of clothing, domestic items and miscellany.

Hóra has no reliable short-term accommodation, though asking for unadvertised rooms in the various kafenía along the winding commercial street can be productive. On the atmospheric, irregularly shaped platía, a couple of **tavernas**, *Iy Platia* and the more down-to-earth *To Kastro*, provide the best suppers on the island, with such delicacies as stuffed squid and *mýdhia saganáki* (mussels with cheese). There have been mutterings of moving the administrative capital down to Kamariótissa, but until further notice the island's **post office** is here.

The Sanctuary of the Great Gods

From Hóra it is 3km to the hamlet of Paleópoli (see below) and, in a stony but thickly wooded ravine between it and the plunging northwestern ridge of Mount Fengári, lie the remains of the **Sanctuary of the Great Gods**. Buses from Kamariótissa stop nearby, opposite a small car park on the seashore. From the late Bronze Age until the early Byzantine era, the mysteries and sacrifices of the cult of the Great Gods were performed on Samothráki, indeed in ancient Thracian dialect until the second century BC. The island was the spiritual focus of the northern Aegean, and its importance in the ancient world was comparable (although certainly secondary) to that of the Mysteries of Eleusis.

The religion of the Great Gods revolved around a hierarchy of ancient Thracian fertility figures: the Great Mother Axieros, a subordinate male deity known as Kadmilos, and the potent and ominous twin demons the *Kabiroi*, originally the local heroes Dardanos and Aeton. When the Aeolian colonists arrived (traditionally c.700 BC) they simply syncretized the resident deities with their own – the Great Mother became Cybele, her consort Hermes and the *Kabiroi* were fused interchangeably with the *Dioskouroi* Castor and Pollux, patrons of seafarers. Around the nucleus of a sacred precinct the newcomers made the beginnings of what is now the Sanctuary.

Despite their long observance, the mysteries of the cult were never explicitly recorded, since ancient writers feared incurring the wrath of the *Kabiroi* (who could brew up sudden, deadly storms), but it has been established that two levels of initiation were involved. Both ceremonies, in direct opposition to the elitism of Eleusis, were open to all, including women and slaves. The lower level of initiation, or *myesis*, may, as is speculated at Eleusis, have involved a ritual simulation of the life, death and rebirth cycle; in any case, it's known that it ended with joyous feasting, and it can be conjectured, since so many clay torches have been found, that it took place at night. The higher level of initiation, or *epopteia*, carried the unusual requirement of a moral standard (the connection of theology with morality, so strong in the later Judeo-Christian tradition, was rarely made by the early Greeks). This second level involved a full confession followed by absolution and baptism in bull's blood.

The only **accommodation** near the Sanctuary is in the tiny hamlet of **PALEÓPOLI**, where the old and basic *Xenia Hotel* (☎05510/41 166 or 41 230; ❹) offers a downmarket alternative to the smart but overpriced *Kastro Hotel* (☎05510/89 400, ℱ41 001, ⓦwww.kastro.hotel.gr; ❻), which comes with pool, restaurant and sea views; there are also some basic but en-suite rooms (❸) down on the seashore below the *kastro*.

The site

The **site** (Tues–Sun 8.30am–8.30pm, or dusk if earlier; €1.50 combined ticket with museum but no charge for site when museum is closed) is well labelled, simple to grasp and strongly evokes its proud past, while commanding views of the mountains and the sea. You might like to visit the **archeological museum** first (Tues–Sun 8.30am–3pm), and its exhibits spanning all eras of habita-

△ Sanctuary of the Great Gods, Samothráki

tion, from the Archaic to the Byzantine, since it explains the significance of the Sanctuary. Highlights include a **frieze** of dancing girls from the propylon of the Temenos, entablatures from different buildings, and Roman votive offerings such as coloured glass vials from the necropolis of the ancient town east of the Sanctuary. You can also see a reproduction of the exquisitely sculpted marble statue, the *Winged Victory of Samothrace*, which once stood breasting the wind at the prow of a marble ship in the Nymphaeum (see below). Discovered in 1863 by a French diplomat to the Sublime Porte it was carried off to the Louvre, where it is a major draw, and the well-crafted copy, visible here, was graciously donated to this museum a mere century later.

The **Anaktoron**, or hall of initiation for the first level of the mysteries, dates in its present form from Roman times. Its inner sanctum was marked by a warning stele, now in the museum, and at the southeast corner you can make out the **Priestly Quarters**, an antechamber where candidates for initiation donned white gowns. Next to it is the **Arsinoeion**, the largest circular ancient building known in Greece, used for libations and sacrifices. Within its rotunda are the fourth-century BC walls of a double precinct where a rock altar, the earliest preserved ruin on the site, has been uncovered. A little further south, on the same side of the path, you come to the **Temenos**, a rectangular area open to the sky where the feasting probably took place, and, edging its rear corner, the conspicuous **Hieron**, the site's most immediately impressive structure. Five columns and an architrave of the facade of this large Doric edifice, which hosted the higher level of initiation, have been re-erected; dating in part from the fourth century BC, it was heavily restored in Roman times. The stone steps have been replaced by modern blocks, but Roman benches for spectators remain *in situ*, along with the sacred stones where confession was heard. To the west of the path you can just discern the outline of the theatre, while just above it, tucked under the ridge is the **Nymphaeum (Fountain) of Nike**, which the *Winged Victory* used to preside over. West of the theatre, occupying a high terrace, are remains of the main stoa; immediately north of this is an elaborate medieval fortification made entirely of antique material.

The north coast

With its running streams, giant plane trees and namesake hot springs, **LOUTRÁ** (aka **THERMÁ**), 6km east of Paleópoli, is a pleasant place to stay, although less so when it's packed in late July and August, mainly with an incongruous mixture of foreign hippies and elderly Greeks, here to take the sulphurous waters. You have a Hobson's choice of three facilities: the sterile, junta-era main baths (in theory, daily 8am–1pm & 5–7pm; often closed out of season; €1.50), the *psarováthres* or "fish ponds" – a trio of pleasantly rustic open-air pools with a wooden sun-shade, and a ramshackle hut with a very hot pool (keys from the warden of the main baths). These last two are free with no fixed opening hours, and they're reached by a dirt road starting above and to the right as you face the "improved" spa. For a cold-water but far more appealing contrast, the low waterfalls and rock pools of **Gría Váthra** are signposted 1.5km up the paved side road leading east from the main Thermá access drive.

Loutrá is also the prime base for the tough, six-hour climb up the 1611-metre **Mount Fengári** (known to the ancients as **Sáos**, a name found on some maps to this day), the highest peak in the Aegean islands; the path starts at the top of the village, beside a concrete water tank and a huge open-boled plane tree. Tell your accommodation proprietors that you're going, but no one else, as the police may try to stop you – army teams have been summoned on occasion to rescue ill-prepared climbers on what can be an unforgiving mountain. Fengári is Greek for "moon" and, according to legend, if you reach the top on the night of a full moon your wish will come true – most of those foolhardy enough to attempt this will just hope to get back down safely.

Loutrá is a rather dispersed place, with its winding dead-end streets, all ghostly quiet in winter, and its white-elephant miniharbour – built as an alternative to Kamariótissa, but never used. **Accommodation** includes the *Kaviros Hotel* (℡05510/98 277; ❹), just east of the "centre", and, further downhill, 700m from the beach, the *Mariva Bungalows* (℡05510/98 258; ❹). None of the tavernas is very inspired, a possible result (or cause) of a predominance in self-catering rooms; *Paradhisos* has the best setting, up under the trees, and charges accordingly. About halfway along the track to Gría Váthra, *Safki*, a summer-only café-bar, occupies the delightful old schoolhouse.

Beyond Loutrá and a ford, on the wooded coastline and reached by a road initially signposted "military camp", are two municipal **campsites**: the first, 1.5km from the village, although large, has no facilities except toilets, while the second, 3km from the village, is more expensive but has hot water, electricity, a small shop, restaurant and bar. The Loutrá bus sometimes goes to either site if you ask nicely.

Beaches on Samothráki's north shore are mostly clean but uniformly pebbly and exposed, but it's still worth continuing along the road east from Loutrá for the views and one or two minor sights. At **Cape Foniás** there's a ruined Gateluzzi watchtower and, 45-minutes' walk inland along the stream, there are **waterfalls** and cold pools much more impressive than those at Gría Váthra, though the sign-posted description of "canyon" is exaggerated. Some 15km from Loutrá along a fine corniche road is **Kípos beach**, a long strand facing the Turkish-held island of Gökçeada (Ímvros to the Greeks) and backed by open pasture and picturesque crags. The water is clean and there's a rock overhang for shelter at one end, a spring, shower and seasonal drinks *kantína*, but no food available.

The south coast

From the warmer south flank of the island, with its fertile farmland dotted with olive-groves, there are fine views out to sea – as far as Gökçeada on a clear day. Up to three daily buses go from Kamariótissa via the sleepy village of Lákoma as far as **PROFÍTIS ILÍAS**, an attractive hill village with a number of good **tavernas** – the best being *Paradhisos*, with a wonderful terrace – but no accommodation to speak of, except for some basic **rooms** (❷–❸). From Lákoma it is 8km east to aptly named **Pahiá Ámmos** ("coarse sand"), a long, clean beach with a taverna-rooms place (℡05510/94 235; ❸) at the west end. The nearest (meagre) supplies are in Lákoma, but this doesn't deter big summer crowds who also arrive by excursion kaïkia. These also continue east to **Vátos**, a secluded and sometimes nudist beach also accessible by land, the **Kremastá Nerá** coastal waterfalls, and finally round to Kípos beach.

Thássos

Just 12km from the mainland, **Thássos** has long been a popular resort island for northern Greeks, and since the early 1990s has also attracted a cosmopolitan variety of tourists, in particular Romanians, Serbs, Bulgarians and Hungarians holidaying a tank or so of petrol away from home, plus plenty of the usual Germans and Brits on packages. Far from unspoiled – vast numbers of rural *bouzoúkia* (music halls) and tavernas lay on music at weekends with

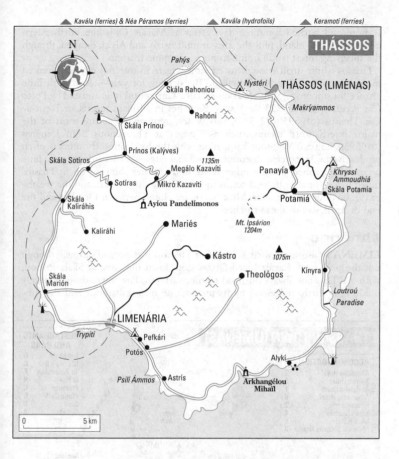

5

THE EAST AND NORTH AEGEAN | Thássos

cheerful vulgarity – it has, however, some areas of outstanding natural beauty and the island's ordinary rural industries have somehow managed to survive.

Thássos still makes a substantial living from the pure-white marble which constitutes two-thirds of the landmass, found only here and quarried at dozens of sites (legal and unlicensed) in the hills between Liménas and Panayía. Olives, honey, fruit and nuts (often sold candied) are also important products. The spirit *tsípouro*, rather than wine, is the main local tipple; pear extract, onions or spices like cinnamon and anise are added to home-made batches.

Inhabited since the Stone Age, Thássos was settled by Parians in the seventh century BC, attracted by gold deposits between modern Liménas and Kínyra. Buoyed by revenues from these, and from silver mines under Thassian control on the mainland opposite, the ancient city-state here became the seat of a medium-sized seafaring empire. Commercial acumen did not spell military invincibility however; the Persians under Darius swept the Thassian fleets from the seas in 492 BC, and in 462 BC Athens permanently deprived Thássos of its autonomy after a three-year siege. The main port continued to thrive into Roman times, but lapsed into Byzantine and medieval obscurity.

Sadly, the salient fact of more recent history has been a series of devastating, deliberately set **fires** in the 1980s and 1990s; the worst one, in 1989, began near

Rahóni and burned for three days as far as Mariés. Only the northeastern quadrant of the island, plus the area around Astrís and Alykí, escaped, though the surviving forest is still home to numerous pine martens.

Thássos is just small enough to circumnavigate in one full day on a rented motorbike or car. The KTEL will do the driving for you – albeit with little chance for stopping – some four times daily. **Car rental** is dominated by Potos Car Rental (☎05930/23 969), with branches in all main resorts, or Rent-a-Car Thassos (☎05930/22 535), also widely represented, as are most of the major international chains, such as Budget at Theagénous 2 in Liménas (☎05930/23 050). Vigorous bargaining with the local one-off outfits is often productive of 35-percent discounts on official rates – particularly in early June or mid-September. On the other hand, don't bother showing up in Thássos much before or after these dates, as most facilities will be shut, and the weather can be dodgy in any case. Most hotels are closed between October and the end of April, so call ahead to check.

Liménas

LIMÉNAS (also signposted as Limín or Thássos) is the island's capital, though not the only port. Kavála-based ferries stop down the coast at Skála Prínou, with a KTEL bus always on hand to meet arrivals. The town, though largely modern, is partly redeemed by its picturesque fishing harbour and the sub-

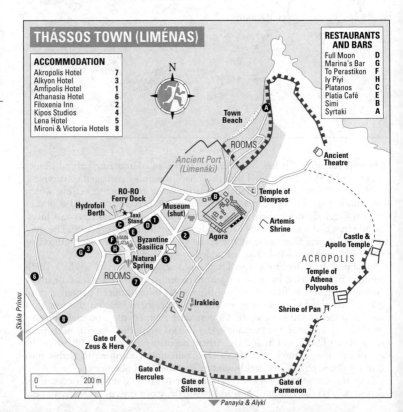

THÁSSOS TOWN (LIMÉNAS)

ACCOMMODATION

Akropolis Hotel	7
Alkyon Hotel	3
Amfipolis Hotel	1
Athanasia Hotel	6
Filoxenia Inn	2
Kipos Studios	4
Lena Hotel	5
Mironi & Victoria Hotels	8

RESTAURANTS AND BARS

Full Moon	D
Marina's Bar	G
To Perastikon	F
Iy Piyi	H
Platanos	C
Platia Café	E
Simi	B
Syrtaki	A

stantial remains of the ancient city which appear above and below the streets.

With its mineral wealth and safe harbour, **ancient Thassos** prospered from Classical to Roman times. The largest excavated area is the agora, a little way back from the fishing harbour. The site (free) is fenced but not always locked, and is most enjoyably seen towards dusk. Two Roman stoas are prominent, but you can also make out shops, monuments, passageways and sanctuaries from the remodelled Classical city. At the far end of the site (away from the sea) a fifth-century BC passageway leads through to an elaborate sanctuary of Artemis, a substantial stretch of Roman road and a few seats of the odeion. The nearby archeological museum is closed indefinitely for extensive expansion.

From a **temple of Dionysos** behind the fishing port, a path curls up to a **Hellenistic theatre**, fabulously positioned above a broad sweep of sea. It's currently open, but is a chaos of excavation, with summer-festival performances set to resume in the distant future. On the same corner of the headland as the theatre, you can still see the old-fashioned kaïkia being built, and gaze across to the uninhabited islet of Thasopoúla. It's possible to rent boats from the fishing harbour, self-skippered or not, to take you there and elsewhere.

From just before the theatre, the trail winds on to the **acropolis**, where a Venetian-Byzantine-Genoese fort arose between the thirteenth and fifteenth centuries, constructed from recycled masonry of an Apollo temple which stood here. You can continue, following the remains of a massive circuit of fifth-century walls to a high terrace supporting the foundations of the Athena Polyouhos (Athena Patroness of the City) temple, with Cyclopean walls. An artificial cavity in the rock outcrop just beyond was a shrine of Pan, shown in faint relief playing his pipes. From behind the summit, a rock-hewn stairway provided a discreet escape route to the Gate of Parmenon, the only gate in the fortifications to have retained its lintel; it's named from an ancient inscription ("Parmenon Made Me") on a nearby wall slab. From here a track, then a paved lane descend through the southerly neighbourhoods of the modern town, for a satisfying one-hour circuit.

Practicalities

Given the cheap-and-cheerful-package ethos, cuisine is not Liménas's strong point, and eateries are generally overpriced. The picturesque **tavernas** around the old harbour are predictably touristy – sophisticated *Simi* is marginally the best, and serves memorably good wine. Another good option is *Syrtaki*, at the far eastern end of the overly popular town beach. In the town centre, greasy fast food is all too abundant, though a dependable favourite for *mayireftá* is *Iy Piyi*, up at the south corner of the main square, next to the natural sunken spring of the name. *Platanos*, with a pleasant terrace opposite the ferry docks, is the place to head for breakfast, be it English style or ambrosia-like yoghurt and honey, and its coffee is highly drinkable. Finally, *To Perastikon* at the northwest corner of the square near *Iy Piyi*, serves the best ice cream on the island. By contrast, there's plenty of choice in local **bars**: *Full Moon* near the *Hotel Amfipolis* is the main Anglophile watering-hole, and comes with a paperback-swap library. *Platia Cafe Bar* on yet another corner of the basilica square, has good music, while *Marina's Bar* near the *Hotel Alkyon* is the best waterfront nightspot, attracting a mainly Greek clientele.

Mountain and motorbikes can be rented from Billy's Bikes (☎05930/22 490), Thomai Tsipou (☎05930/22 815) or Babis (☎05930/22 129). The KTEL office is on the front, virtually opposite the ferry mooring; the service is good, with several daily **buses** to Panayía and Skála Potamiás, Limenária via Potós, Theológos, Kínyra and Alykí. The **taxi** rank is just in front of the bus stop. Thassos Tours (℡05930/23 250), at the east end of the waterfront, is the principal airline agent (the closest airport is Kavála's Alexander the Great, 14km from Keramotí on the mainland). Several **banks** have cash dispensers.

Accommodation

At first glance Liménas – plagued with vehicle traffic and often noisy bars – seems an unlikely resort, with many **hotels** enjoying little in the way of calm or views. Despite this, there are some worthy finds; if none from the list below suits, there are also areas in the southwest of town, and some relatively quiet rooms (②–③) just behind the town beach. Note that most of the town hotels are shut from October to early May. The closest **campsite** to town is at Nystéri cove, 2.5km west; the beach is OK, and its snack bar has tables out on a lawn, but the site is small, basic and on hard ground.

Akropolis ℡05930/22 488, ℻22 441. Occupying a fine traditional house with flagstone floors and a rear garden-bar, though it can get traffic noise; worth a try now that package companies don't use it. ②

Alkyon ℡05930/22 148, ℻23 662. Certainly the most pleasant of the harbour hotels; English tea and breakfast, plus friendly, voluble management make it a home from home for independent British travellers. Open most of the year; ask also about their cottage in Sotíras and beach villa at Astrís. ③

Amfipolis ℡05930/23 101, ℻22 110. Housed in a folly, this atmospheric hotel is the town's most exclusive accommodation outfit – and you pay dearly for the privilege; some package commitment. ⑤

Athanasia ℡05930/23 247. Giant and eccentrically furnished rooms with balconies; take the lane inland from behind the *Xenia Hotel* to reach it. Run by a friendly fisherman, this place takes the overflow from the *Alkyon*. ②

Filoxenia Inn ℡05930/23 331, ℻22 231. Quietly situated behind the archeological museum, this has immaculate new rooms with fridges, designated breakfast areas and a garden with a small pool. ③

Kipos Studios ℡05930/22 469. In a quiet cul-de-sac near *Iy Piyi* taverna, this has cool lower-ground-floor doubles (③) and four-person galleried apartments of a fair standard (④); a pool has been installed in the garden, ostensibly to make the premises attractive to package companies.

Lena ℡05930/23 565. Good-value hotel, lightly refurbished in 1998, near the post office, with English-speaking management; no packages. ③

Myroni ℡05930/23 256, ℻22 132. Excellent value, well run and allergic to package companies. It's co-managed with the more modest *Victoria* (℡05930/23 556; ③) next door, with which it shares a common breakfast room. ④

Around the coast

Whether you plan to circumnavigate the island clockwise, or in the opposite direction, plan on a lunch stop at **Alykí**, roughly a third of the way along in the circuit described below, and the most photogenic spot along the coast.

Panayía, Potamiá and Mount Ipsárion

The first beach east of Liménas, **Makrýammos**, is a purpose-built, controlled-access compound for package tourists, so carry on to **PANAYÍA**, the attractive hillside village overlooking Potamiá Bay. It's a large, thriving place where life revolves around the central square with its large plane trees, multispouted fountain and slate-roofed houses. Top **accommodation** choice in both senses is the *Hotel Thassos Inn* (℡05930/61 612, ℻61 027; ④), up in the Trís Piyés district near the Kímisis church, with fine views over the rooftops. Second choice, slightly lower down, is the vine-shrouded *Hotel Theo* (℡05930/61 284; ③), more old-fashioned but with a nice ground-floor bar. Down on the main road, beside the municipal car park, the newish, clean *Pension Stathmos* (℡05930/61 666; ④) is the quietest of several nearby, with stunning views out the back; there are also high-standard rooms (℡05930/61 981; ③) below the school basketball courts. Some readers have complained about high-pressure touting tactics from the hotly competing tavernas on the square; for a more low-key approach, try *Iy Thea*, a view-terrace *psistariá* at the southeast edge of town en route to Potamiá.

POTAMIÁ, much lower down in the river valley, is far less prepossessing – with modern red tiles instead of slates on the roofs – and thus little visited, though it has a lively winter carnival. It also offers the **Polygnotos Vayis Museum** (Tues–Sat 9.30am–12.30pm, summer also 6–9pm, Sun 10am–1pm; free), devoted to the locally born sculptor; though Vayis emigrated to America when young, he bequeathed most of his works to the Greek state. Potamiá also marks the start of the commonest route up to the 1204-metre summit of **Mount Ipsárion**. Follow the bulldozer track to the big spring near the head of the valley extending west of the village (last water here), where you'll see the first red-painted arrows on trees. Beyond this point, cairns mark the correct turnings in a modern track system; forty minutes above the spring, take an older, wide track, which ends ten minutes later at a narrow ravine with a stream and the current trailhead. The path is steep, strenuous and unmaintained, and you'll be dependent on cairns and painted arrows. Go early in the day or season, and allow four hours up from Potamiá, and nearly as much for the descent.

Skála Potamiás and Khryssí Ammoudhiá

The onward road from Potamiá is lined with *dhomátia*- and apartment-type accommodation, popular with Germans. A side road some 12km from Liménas takes you down to **SKÁLA POTAMIÁS**, at the southern end of the bay, where some fairly uninspired **tavernas** line the harbour front; a road off to the left brings you to sand dunes extending all the way to the far northern end of the bay. An honourable exception amongst the tavernas is *Flor International* (no sign), at the corner where the bus (hourly 7am–8pm to Liménas) turns around; the *Afrodite*, a short way along, is also acceptable for *mayireftá*. Worth a mention also is *Eric's Bar* on the approach road, where one Stratos Papafilippou has made a career of his uncanny resemblance to footballer Eric Cantona; full English breakfast (of course) available. The best places to **stay** are either above the plane-shaded traffic turnaround area by the port, beyond the tavernas – where the *Hera* (☎05930/61 467; ❶), just on the left looking inland, or the *Delfini* (☎05930/61 275; ❶), 200m straight back, are peaceful but basic – or, if you're prepared to pay rather more, there's the *Miramare* (☎05930/77 209; ❺), which has a swimming pool among well-manicured gardens, further up the same lane. Alternatively, head north along the shore towards the sandy beach, for **rooms**, to either side of the *Arion* (☎05930/61 486; ❸) and *Anna* (☎05930/61 070; ❷) hotels, which represent the best value hereabouts. The north end of this beach is called **Khryssí Ammoudhiá** ("golden sands"), merely another cluster of tavernas, hotels and a campsite; a direct road (no bus service) spirals the 5km down from Panayía. Once there, you can choose between the self-catering *Villa Emerald* (☎05930/61 979; ❺) or the *Golden Sand* (☎05930/61 771 or 61 209; ❹), nearer the sands. The *Golden Beach* campsite (☎05930/61 472) is the only official one on this side of the island.

Kínyra and Alykí

The dispersed hamlet of **KÍNYRA**, some 24km south of Liménas, marks the start of the burnt zone which overlooks it, though incipient greenery suggests that recovery is underway; it's endowed with a poor beach, a couple of grocery stores and several small hotels. Those not block-booked include *Villa Athina* (☎05930/41 214; ❷) at the north end of things, whose top-floor rooms see the water over the olive trees, and the welcoming *Pension Marina* (☎05930/31 384; ❷). The *Faros* is about the only independent taverna here. Kínyra is convenient for the superior **beaches** of Loutroú (1km south) and partly nudist Paradise (3km along) – officially called Makrýammos Kinýron – both of which can be reached down poorly signposted dirt tracks. The latter ranks as most scenic of all Thassian beaches, with still-forested cliffs inland and a namesake islet offshore beyond the extensive shallows, with much cleaner water than at Khryssí Ammoudhiá, though a couple of ugly buildings have sprung up over the past year or so. So far the only place for food and drink is a mediocre snack bar that exploits its monopoly.

The south-facing coast of Thássos has the balance of the island's best beaches. **ALYKÍ** hamlet, 35km from Liménas and just below the main road, faces a perfect double bay which almost pinches off a headland. Alone of Thassian seaside settlements, it retains its original whitewashed, slate-roofed architecture, because the presence of extensive antiquities here has led to a ban on any modern construction. The ruins include an ancient temple to an unknown deity, and two exquisite early-Christian basilicas out on the headland, with a few columns re-erected. The sand-and-pebble west bay gets oversubscribed in peak season, though you can always stalk off to the less crowded, rocky east cove, or snorkel in the crystal-clear waters off the marble formations on the headland's far side. A row of water-edge **tavernas** compete for your custom, with *To Limanaki/The Little Mole* winning, if only for its varied menu. Ask around for **rooms** (❸).

Arhangélou Mihaïl to Potós

Some 5km west of Alykí, the **convent of Arhangélou Mihaïl** (open reasonable daylight hours) clings spectacularly to a cliff on the seaward side of the road. Though founded in the twelfth century above the spot where a spring had gushed forth, it has been hideously renovated by the nuns, resident here since 1974. A dependency of Filothéou on Mount Áthos, its prize relic is a purported nail from the Crucifixion.

At the extreme south tip of Thássos, 9km further west, **ASTRÍS** (Astrídha) can muster two uninspiring medium-sized hotels, a few rooms and a good beach. Just 1km west is another better but crowded beach, Psilí Ámmos, with watersports on offer. A few kilometres further, **POTÓS** is the island's prime Germanophone package venue, its centre claustrophobically dense, with the few non-block-booked rooms overlooking cramped alleys. However, the kilometre-long beach is still unspoiled. For a less touristy place to eat, the **taverna** *Iy Mouria* remains one of the cheaper and better places and is tucked away at the southern end of the seafront, in a semi-pedestrianized street; next door, *Michael's Place* has great ice cream and breakfasts. Along the harbourfront a string of varyingly trendy **bars and cafés** offer viable alternatives. There are plenty of rental outlets for **cars**, scooters and mountain bikes, including the headquarters of Potos Rent a Car. **Pefkári** with its manicured beach and namesake pine-grove, 1km west, is essentially an annexe of Potós, with a few mid-range **accommodation** options such as *Prasino Veloudho* (☎05930/52 001, ℱ51 232; ❸) and the rather more upmarket *Thassos* (☎05930/51 596, ℱ51 794; ❻). The **campsite**, the *Pefkari* (☎05930/51 190; June–Sept), with its attractive wooded location and clean facilities, is one of the best on Thássos.

Limenária and the west coast

LIMENÁRIA, the island's second town, was built to house German mining executives brought in by the Ottomans at the turn of the 19th/20th centuries. Their remaining mansions, scattered on the slopes above the harbour, lend some character, but despite attempts at prettifying the waterfront, it's not the most attractive place on Thássos though it is handy for its **banks** and cash dispensers, **post office** and seasonal hydrofoil connections. The best **accommodation**, should you take a shine to the place is the hotel *George* (☎05930/51 413, ⓕ52 530; ❹), a relative newcomer with bright and modern rooms at the lower end of the main street leading down to the harbourfront. At the east end of the quay, in some 1960s blocks, are a cluster of very basic hotels such as the *Sgouridis* (☎05930/51 241; ❸) and the towering *Papayioryiou* (☎05930/51 205; ❷–❸), with mostly Greek clientele. There are also plenty of **rooms** on offer (❶–❸). For eating and drinking, choose from among half-a-dozen each of bars and eateries along the front.

The closest good beach is **Trypití**, a couple of kilometres west – turn left into the pines at the start of a curve right. All development – mostly package villas – is well inland from the broad, 800-metre-long strand, although there are umbrellas and sun loungers for rent. The cleft which the name refers to (literally "pierced" in Greek), is a slender tunnel through the headland at the west end of the beach, leading to a tiny three-boat anchorage.

Continuing clockwise from Limenária to Thássos Town, there's progressively less to stop off for as the western coast is the most exposed and scenically least impressive. The various *skáles* such as Skála Kaliráhis and Skála Sotíros – stop-offs for ferries – are bleak, straggly and windy. **Skála Marión**, 13km from Limenária, is the exception that proves the rule: an attractive little bay, with fishing boats hauled up on the sandy foreshore, and the admittedly modern low-rise village arrayed in a U-shape all around. There are **rooms** available (❷–❸), a few tavernas, and, most importantly, two fine beaches on either side. **Skála Prínou** has little to recommend it, other than ferry connections to Kavála. Buses are usually timed to coincide with the ferries, but if you want to stay, there are several hotels, numerous rooms, quayside tavernas and an EOT **campsite** (☎05930/71 171; June–Sept) 1km south of the ferry dock. **Skála Rahoníou**, between here and Liménas, has more accommodation (including the *Perseus* campsite) and fish restaurants, as well as proximity to **Pahýs beach**, 9km short of Liménas, by far the best strand on the northwest coast. Narrow dirt tracks lead past various tavernas through surviving pines to the sand, partly shaded in the morning.

The interior

Few people get around to exploring inland Thássos – with the post-fire scrub still barely waist-high, it's not always rewarding – but there are several worthwhile excursions to or around the **hill villages**, besides the aforementioned trek up Mount Ipsárion from Potamiá (see p.435).

From Potós you can head 10km along a well-surfaced but poorly signposted road to **THEOLÓGOS**, founded in the sixteenth century by refugees from Constantinople and the island's capital under the Ottomans (the last Muslims only departed after 1923). Its houses, most with oversized chimneys and slate roofs, straggle in long tiers to either side of the main street, surrounded by generous kitchen gardens or walled courtyards. A stroll along the single high street, with its couple of kafenía, a soldiers' bar, sandalmaker and traditional bakery, is rewarding and quickly dispels the off-putting effect of vigorous advertising at the outskirts for "Greek Nights" at local tavernas. Two that eschew musical gimmicks and rely on their good fare are the long-running *Psistaria Lambiris*, near the edge of town, and *Kleoniki/Tou Iatrou*, in the very centre, on the right-hand side past the bus stop and police station. They're at their best in the evening when the *soúvles* loaded with goat and suckling pig start turning.

Despite its proximity as the crow flies, there's no straightforward way from Theológos to **KÁSTRO**, the most naturally protected of the anti-pirate redoubts; especially with a car, it's best to descend to Potós before heading up a rough, seventeen-kilometre dirt track from Limenária. Thirty ancient houses and a church surround a rocky pinnacle, fortified by the Byzantines and the Genoese, which has a sheer drop on three sides. Summer occupation by shepherds is becoming the norm after total abandonment in the nineteenth century, when mining jobs at Limenária proved irresistible. There's only one kafenío on the ground floor of the former school, one telephone therein, no mains electricity and far more sheep than people.

From Skála Marión an unmarked but paved road (slipping under the main highway bridge to the north) proceeds 11km inland through gnarled, old olive-trees, to well-preserved **MARIÉS** at the top of a wooded stream valley; of two tavernas here, the well-signed one to the right, *Bethel*, is more of a going concern. From Skála Sotíros, a very steep road heads 3.5km up to **SOTÍRAS**, the only interior village with an unobstructed view of sunset over the Aegean and thus popular with foreigners who've bought up about half of the houses for restoration. On the ridge opposite are exploratory shafts left by the miners, whose ruined lodge looms above the church. On the plane-shaded square below the old fountain, *O Plátanos* taverna is congenially run by Maria and Manolis, who offer grills plus one *mayireftá* dish-of-the-day, good bulk wine and sometimes their potent, home-made *tsípouro*.

From Prínos (Kalýves) on the coast road, you've a six-kilometre journey inland to the Kazavíti villages, shrouded in greenery that escaped the fires; they're (poorly) signposted and mapped officially as Megálo and Mikró Prínos but still universally known by their Ottoman name. **MIKRÓ KAZAVÍTI** marks the start of the track south for the convent of Ayíou Pandelímona, and **MEGÁLO KAZAVÍTI**, 1km beyond, was once the architectural showcase of the island, a fact apparently lost on many of the outsiders who bought holiday homes here and proceeded to carry out appallingly vandalistic renovations. On the magnificent platía, arguably the prettiest spot on the whole island, are a couple of decent, normal-priced **tavernas**, while *Vassilis*, below in a beautifully restored house, is regarded as a cut above. Some 4km up from its *skála*, **RAHÓNI** is well set at the head of its denuded valley, paired with the small village of Áyios Yeóryios across the way. The road up to the square has plenty of simple tavernas, for example *Iy Dhrosia*.

Travel details

To simplify the lists that follow we've excluded two regular sailings in a generally north-to-south direction. These are the weekly DANE sailing between Rhodes, Kós, Sámos and Thessaloníki (23hr for the full run, usually over the weekend), and the NEL sailing linking Alexandhroúpoli with Límnos, Lésvos, Híos, Sámos, Kós and Rhodes (one-way trip through all ports, total 30hr).

We've also omitted the more convoluted long-distance schedules kept by the small ferries of Miniotis Lines, based on Híos. These slow and often tardy craft link Híos with Sámos (both northern ports) twice a week year-round, usually Sun & Thurs evening, returning Tues & Fri evening. Twice weekly (usually Mon & Fri), they venture from Sámos (Karlóvassi and Pythagório respectively) to Foúrni and Ikaría (Áyios Kírykos) and back, and twice weekly (typically Tues & Fri am) there's an out-and-back run from Pythagório to Agathoníssi, Arkí, Lipsí and Pátmos – these additional services are reliably available June to Oct, though year-round departures are foreseen as of late 2001.

Áyios Efstrátios 2 weekly on NEL Lines to Límnos, Rafína and Kavála; 5 weekly by small local ferry to Límnos; 1 weekly to Lésvos (Sígri) and Psará.

Foúrni 2–3 weekly ferries to Sámos (northern ports), Náxos, Páros and Pireás; 2–3 weekly to Pátmos, Kós, Rhodes; morning kaïki to Ikaría on Mon, Wed, Fri; twice weekly (usually Mon & Thurs) morning kaïki to Karlóvassi (Sámos).

Híos 11 weekly on NEL Lines to Pireás (10hr slow ferry, 4hr high-speed) and Lésvos (3hr 30min/1hr 30min); 4 weekly to Pireás and Lésvos on Hellas Ferries; 1–2 weekly to Límnos on NEL, usually with a long layover at Mytilíni; 1 weekly to Lésvos, Sámos, Sýros on Hellas Ferries. Daily 2pm kaïki to Inoússes except Sun morning, and Tues in off-season; 4 weekly on Miniotis Lines – usually Tues, Thurs, Sat & Sun – from Híos Town to Psará (3hr 30min), 3 weekly on Miniotis from Limniá to Psará, usually Mon, Wed, Fri pm (1hr 30min).

Ikaría At least daily from either Áyios Kírykos or Évdhilos to Sámos (both northern ports) and Pireás, on Hellas Ferries, G&A or NEL's catamaran; 3 weekly to Rhodes, Kós, Pátmos, Foúrni, Náxos and Páros from Áyios Kírykos; 5–6 weekly to Mýkonos from Évdhilos; 3 weekly to Sýros from Évdhilos; 3 weekly to Mýkonos and Sýros, from Áyios Kírykos; daily kaïki from Áyios Kírykos to Foúrni; 3 weekly kaïkia, usually Mon, Wed, Fri am, from Manganítis to Áyios Kírykos.

Lésvos 10–12 weekly on NEL Lines from Mytilíni to Pireás (11hr direct, 13hr 30min via Híos, 7hr 30min on high-speed craft; 16hr 30min via Mýkonos/Sýros); 9–11 weekly to Híos (3hr 30min, or 1hr 30min high-speed); 4 weekly to Híos and Pireás on Hellas Ferries; 3–4 weekly to Límnos (6hr from Mytilíni, 5hr from Sígri); 2 weekly to Thessaloníki (14hr); 1–3 weekly to Kavála on NEL (12hr from Mytilíni, 10hr from Sígri); 1 weekly to Rafína on NEL (8hr, from Sígri only); 1 weekly to Áyios Efstrátios on NEL (4hr, from Sígri only); 1 weekly to Psará on NEL (4hr, from Sígri only); 1 weekly to Mýkonos and Sýros on NEL; 1 weekly to

Sámos and Sýros on Hellas Ferries.

Límnos 5–6 weekly on NEL Lines to Lésvos (Mytilíni or Sígri); 4 weekly to Kavála, 2 weekly to Lávrio, and 1 weekly to Thessaloníki, Samothráki direct on the *Saos II*; 3 weekly to Kavála and Rafína on NEL; 2 weekly to Thessaloníki, Pireás and Híos on NEL.

Psará 1 weekly on NEL Lines to Lésvos (Sígri) Áyios Efstrátios, Límnos, Kavála; 1 weekly direct to Pireás (8hr).

Sámos (Karlóvassi) As for Vathý, but no NEL catamaran service; also 2 weekly kaïki departures, usually early Mon and Thurs afternoon, to Foúrni.

Sámos (Pythagório) 2 weekly (Wed and Sun afternoon) with the *Nissos Kalymnos* to Agathónissi, Lipsí, Pátmos, Léros and Kálymnos, with onward connections to all other Dodecanese (see p.360 for the full schedule).

Sámos (Vathý) 1–2 daily, on G&A or Hellas Ferries, to Ikaría (Áyios Kírykos or Évdhilos) and Pireás (13–14hr); 5 weekly to Pireás by NEL high-speed boat (6hr); 4–6 weekly to Mýkonos and Sýros; 2 weekly to Foúrni, Páros and Náxos on G&A; 1 weekly to Pátmos and Lipsí on Hellas Ferries.

Samothráki 2–3 daily ferries to/from Alexandhroúpoli (2hr 30min) in season, dropping to 5–6 weekly out of season. Also 2 weekly late spring and early autumn, up to 4 weekly in peak season, to Kavála (and thence other north Aegean islands). During July & Aug, 1 weekly (usually Fri) direct to Límnos; 4 other days there is tedious indirect service via Kavála.

Thássos 8–10 ferries daily, in summer months only (1 daily Oct–May), between Kavála and Skála Prínou (1hr 15min; 7am–10pm, 6am–9pm to Kavála from the island); 10 daily all year round between Keramotí and Liménas (40min; 7am–10pm, 6am–8.30pm from Thássos).

Hydrofoils

Just one company, Kyriakoulis Maritime, operates in the east Aegean. Based on Sámos and Kós, this offers (late May to late Sept) nearly daily early morning and early afternoon service from Pythagório to Pátmos, Lipsí, Léros, Kálymnos and Kós (in the Dodecanese), returning from Kós in the late afternoon, and conversely morning service from Kós through the same ports, returning from Pythagório at mid-afternoon. Ikaría and Foúrni are called at 5–6 times weekly (sometimes from Vathý instead), with Agathónissi served twice weekly. In 2001 there were also 3 weekly nominal high-season links between Sámos (Vathý), Híos, Inoússes and Lésvos, departing in the morning and returning early afternoon, but these are deeply unreliable

owing to weather and typically run once weekly at best. From Easter to mid-May, and late Sept to late Oct, official frequencies fall to 4–5 weekly to the Dodecanese cited (but 2 to Lipsí, 1 to Agathóníssi); 2 weekly to Foúrni/Ikaría; and 1 weekly to Híos/Inoússes/Lésvos.

Samothráki is served by hydrofoil from Alexandhroúpoli April–Nov 4–7 times weekly, usually at 8am (1hr); mid-June to mid-Sept there are 1–2 extra daily departures at 1 and/or 5pm. Two to four times weekly the morning or early afternoon sailing may continue on to Límnos, but don't rely on this.

Thássos (Liménas) used to be served all year by hydrofoils from Kavála, but the service is now limited to the summer: 8–15 times daily, 7am–9pm

(6am–8pm from Thássos); in the high season there may also be 2–3 daily departures from Kavála to the west-coast resorts of Skála Kaliráhon, Skála Marión and Limenária.

International ferries

Híos–Çeşme (Turkey) 2–13 boats weekly, depending on season. Spring/autumn, about 7 weekly; Thurs evening (Turkish boat) and Sat morning (Greek boat) services tend to run year-round. Passenger fares on the Greek boat (*Psara*, Miniotis Lines) are €47 one-way, €59 open return (no day-return fare), including Greek taxes; no Turkish taxes. These are the "rack rates", which can often be beaten by comparison shopping and bargaining; it's also about twenty percent less expensive to travel *from* Turkey. Turkish boat (typically *Ertürk II*) is usually cheaper going from Híos, at €33 one-way, €44 return, Greek taxes inclusive. Small cars €73.50 each way, taken on either morning or evening boats. Journey time 45min.

Mytilíni (Lésvos)–Ayvalık (Turkey) 4–8 weekly May–Oct; winter link unreliable. One of two Turkish craft, the *Cunda Express* and the *Jalehan*, departs Mytilíni 8am most days; the *Jalehan* (carries two cars) may also do an evening trip Tues, Thurs, Sat. Passenger rates €38 one-way, €47 round trip, all taxes inclusive. Small cars €58 each way. Journey time 1hr 40min.

Vathý (Sámos)–Kuşadası (Turkey) At least 1 daily, late April to late Oct; otherwise a small Turkish boat only by demand in winter, usually Fri or Sat. Morning Greek boat, 4–5 weekly (passengers only); afternoon Turkish boats (usually 2 daily in season taking two cars apiece). Rates are €38 one-way including taxes on both the Greek and Turkish sides, €43 open return; no day-return rate. Small cars €50 one-way. Journey time 1hr 30min. Also occasional (2–3 weekly) services in season from Pythagório, passengers only (journey time 2hr 15min).

Flights

NB All flights on Olympic Airways/Aviation unless otherwise specified. Frequencies are for the period May–Oct only.

Híos–Athens (4–5 daily on Olympic; 1hr)
Híos–Thessaloníki (3 weekly, 1 via Lésvos; 1hr 30min–2hr)
Lésvos–Athens (4–5 daily on Olympic; 55min; 3 daily on Aegean-Cronus; 45min)
Lésvos–Híos (1 weekly; 30min)

Lésvos–Thessaloníki (6–8 weekly on Olympic, 1 daily on Aegean-Cronus; 1hr 10min–2hr)
Límnos–Athens (3–4 daily; 1hr)
Límnos–Lésvos (4 weekly; 40min)
Límnos–Thessaloníki (6 weekly; 45min)
Sámos–Athens (4–5 daily on Olympic; 1hr; 2 daily on Axon; 40min)
Sámos–Thessaloníki (3 weekly on Olympic; 1hr 20min

The Sporades and Évvia

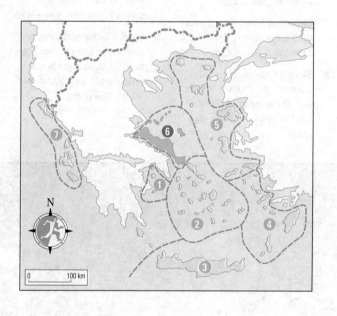

N

0   100 km

6

THE SPORADES AND ÉVVIA

CHAPTER 6

Highlights

* **Laláxria beach, Skiáthos** A
  beautiful beach covered with
  smooth white stones, with
  steep cliffs rising behind it.
  See p.449

* **Glóssa** An unspoiled,
  authentic Greek town, set
  high above the port of
  Loutráki. See p.450

* **Skópelos Town** One of the
  prettiest towns in the
  Sporades. See p.450

* **Skýros** Only recently "discovered" by tourism, this is
  one of the most traditional
  islands in the Aegean. See
  p.457

* **The goat dance** One of
  Greece's liveliest and most
  outrageous festivals. See
  p.458

* **The convent of Ayíou
  Nikoláou Galatáki** Superbly
  set on the wooded slopes of
  Mount Kandhíli and decorated with vivid sixteenth-
  century frescoes. See p.470

* **Loutrá Edhipsoú** Greece's
  biggest spa town, with plenty of Belle Époque hotels
  (many well restored) to marvel at. See p.472

The Sporades and Évvia

he three northern **Sporades**, Skiáthos, Skópelos and Alónissos, are scattered (as their Greek name suggests) just off the mainland, their mountainous terrain betraying their origin as extensions of Mount Pílio in Thessaly. They are archetypal holiday islands, with a wide selection of good beaches, transparent waters and thick pine forests. All are very busy in season, with Skiáthos attracting by far the most package tours.

Skiáthos has the best beaches, and is still the busiest island in the group, though these days **Skópelos** gets very crowded, too. **Alónissos** is the quietest of the three, and has the wildest scenery, so it's really more for nature lovers than night-owls. **Skýros**, further southeast, retains more of its traditional culture than the other three islands, though development is now well under way. The main town doesn't yet feel like a resort, but its main street is not without its fast-food and souvenir shops. Unlike on the other three islands, the best beaches are those closest to the main town. To the south, the huge island of **Évvia** (or Euboea) runs for 150km alongside the mainland. It is one of the most attractive Greek islands, with a forested mountain spine and long stretches of rugged, largely undeveloped coast. Perhaps because it lacks any impressive ruins or real

Accommodation price codes

Throughout the book we've categorized accommodation according to the following **price codes**, which denote the cheapest available double room in high season. All prices are for the room only, except where otherwise indicated. Many hotels, especially those in category ❹ and over, include breakfast in the price; you'll need to check this when booking. During low season, rates can drop by more than fifty percent, especially if you are staying for three or more nights. Exceptions are during the Christmas and Easter weeks when you'll pay high-season prices. Single rooms, where available, cost around seventy percent of the price of a double.

❶ Up to €24	❹ €43–58
❷ €24–33	❺ €59–72
❸ €34–42	❻ €73 and upwards

Note: Youth hostels refuges typically charge €7–9 for a dormitory bed.
For more accommodation details, see pp.52–54.

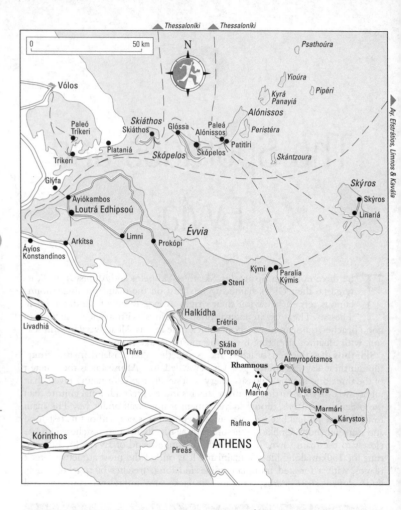

island feel owing to its proximity to the mainland, Évvia is explored by few foreign tourists, though Athenians and Thessalians visit the island in force and have erected holiday homes around half a dozen of its major resorts.

The Sporades are well connected by **bus** and **ferry** with Athens (via Áyios Konstandínos or Kými), Thessaloníki and Vólos, and it's easy to island-hop in the northern group. The only ferry connection to Skýros is from Kými, plus a Flying Dolphin hydrofoil service in summer from Vólos via the other Sporades. Évvia is linked to the mainland by a bridge at its capital Halkídha, and by a series of shuttle ferries. Both Skiáthos and Skýros have airports.

Skiáthos

The commercialization of **Skiáthos** is legendary among foreigners and Greeks: it's a close fourth to that of Corfu, Mýkonos and Rhodes. But if you've some time to spare, or a gregarious nature, you might still break your journey here to sample the best, if most overcrowded, **beaches** in the Sporades. Along the south and southeast coasts, the road serves an almost unbroken line of villas, hotels and restaurants, and although this doesn't take away the island's natural beauty, it makes it difficult to find anything unspoiled or particularly Greek about it all. As almost the entire population lives in Skiáthos Town, a little walking soon pays off. However, camping outside official sites is strongly discouraged, since summer turns the dry pine-needles to tinder.

Skiáthos Town

Skiáthos Town, where the ferries dock, looks great from a distance, but as you approach, tourist development becomes very apparent, especially to the east side of the port and around Alexándhrou Papadhiamándi, where most of the services, the tackier shops, "English" pubs and eateries are located. But tucked into the alleys on the western, older side of town, it is still possible to find some pockets of charm: older houses, gardens and flowers galore. Skiáthos boasts some good restaurants and nightclubs, and can be fun, in a crowded, boisterous way.

The few sights comprise the **Papadhiamándi museum** (Tues–Sun 9.30am–1pm & 5–8pm; free) – housed in the nineteenth-century home of one of Greece's best-known novelists – and two antique shops, Archipelago two blocks in from the waterfront, and the enduring Galerie Varsakis (open usual shop hours), on Platía Trión Ierarhón near the fishing port. The latter has one of the best **folklore displays** in Greece, and many of the older items would do the Benaki Museum proud; the proprietor neither expects, nor wants, to sell the more expensive of these, which include antique textiles, handicrafts and jewellery.

Arrival, transport and other facilities

Buses and **taxis** ply from the area around the **ferry harbour**. To Koukounariés, the bus is the cheapest option (€0.80); it runs at least hourly in summer (every fifteen minutes at peak times), the last bus returning at 1am.

A large number of competing **rental outlets** in town, most on the front behind the ferry harbour, offer bicycles, motorbikes, cars and motorboats. For bikes, good rates can be had from Makis Dimas, whose workshop is signposted at the far end of Papadhiamándi. The cheapest, smallest cars go for around €45 a day, as do motorboats. Several travel agents organize "round-the-island" **mule trips** (€18 a day), and there's **horseriding** at the Pinewood Riding Club (no phone) at Koukounariés. Most other facilities are on Alexándhrou Papadhiamándi, including the **post office**, **banks** and a branch of American Express.

Accommodation

Much of the island's accommodation is in Skiáthos Town. The few reasonably priced **hotels** or **pensions** are heavily booked in season, though you can usually find a room, albeit at a slightly more elevated price than on most islands. At other times, supply exceeds demand and you can find very cheap **rooms** with a little bargaining. Try for locations in the older quarters to the west; avoid lodgings in the flatlands to the north, as they tend to be noisy. There is a room-owners' association kiosk on the quay that opens fitfully in high season, but at other times bookings can be made through several tourist agencies. For an honest and helpful approach, try the Mare Nostrum at Papadhiamándi 21 (☎04270/21 463) or the efficient Heliotropio (☎04270/22 430, ☎21 952) on the seafront. A more direct option is Adonis Stamelos's rooms just outside town at Megáli Ámmos (☎04270/22 962; ⑥). Good, small hotels include the *Bourtzi* (☎04270/22 694; ⑥) and *Pothos* (☎04270/21 304; ⑥), both immaculate with delightful gardens, and the *Orsa* (☎04270/22 430; ❻), a remodelled house overlooking the sea on the west side of the port which can be booked through Heliotropio. Other fine options are the *Alkyon Hotel*, on the seafront at the commercial port end (☎04270/22 981; ❻), or the *Meltemi Hotel*, on the front near the taxi rank (☎04270/22 493; ❻).

The island has three official **campsites**. Koukounariés and Asélinos are fairly decent with standard facilities. Xanémos beach is 3km northeast of Skiáthos Town, right next to the airport runway, and, apart from being within walking distance of the town, has little to recommend it.

Eating, drinking and nightlife

You're spoiled for choice for **eating places**, but nothing is particularly cheap apart from the few burger/*yíros* joints. One of the best of the cheaper tavernas is *Zorba's*, opposite the taxi rank, while *Mesogeia*, above and to the west of Plátia Trión Ierarkhón, has excellent moussaka and home-cooked dishes. *Ellinikon*, up in the backstreets above the west seafront, also has home-style cooking and good wine in a secluded garden, while *Cuba*, set in a leafy square east of Papadhiamándi, has a huge range of grilled meat, fish and starters. For more elegant dining, head for *Agnantio*, at the start of the road to Evangelístria, for superlative Greek cuisine and views; *The Windmill* at the top of the hill above Áyios Nikólaos, for nouvelle cuisine and views; and *Calypso*, on the east waterfront, for genuine Italian food. Back on the west side, above the flat rocks where people sunbathe, *Tarsanas* is a converted boatbuilders' yard with a picturesque veranda – the best place in town for an evening drink as the harbour lights come on.

Nightlife centres on the clubs on or near Polytekhníou. The best places are *Borzoi*, the oldest club on the island, *Stones* and the *Apothiki Music Hall* for Greek music and a good atmosphere, while on the seafront *BBC* pulses till

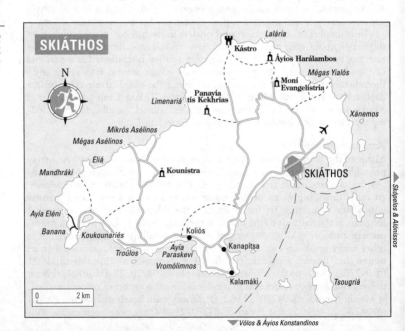

dawn. In the bars in the backstreets around Polytekhníou you can hear a wider range of music; places like the *Banana* are pop-oriented and popular with British beer-drinkers, the old and much-loved *Kentavros* plays jazz and blues, *Adagio* has classical music in the evenings, and *Blue Chips* is a stylish, upmarket place. On the east shore, the chic *Remezzo* with its maritime motifs is a perennial favourite, while *Kavos* and *Kalua* rival it for pumping out the loudest disco sounds.

Skiáthos's outdoor **cinema**, *Refresh Paradiso*, on the ring road, shows new releases in their original language. Another source of entertainment is the little offshore Boúrtzi fortress, transformed into an outdoor **theatre** and home to occasional plays and musical performances during the summer.

Around the island

Other than using the buses or the various rental outlets in town (for which see p.445), you could also get your bearings on a **boat trip** around the island. These cost about €15 per person and leave at around 10am. Or try a boat trip to the islet of **Tsougriá** (opposite Skiáthos Town), where there's a good beach and a taverna. Boats leave from the fishing harbour beyond the Boúrtzi, and not the yacht anchorage to the north of the ferry harbour; east-coast boats leave from the quay area in front of the bus station.

If you're interested in seeing more of Skiáthos on foot, the locally produced guide to **walks** (by Rita and Dietrich Harkort; available in larger tourist shops) has detailed instructions and maps for trails all over the island.

The monasteries and Kástro

The **Evangelístria monastery** (daily 8am–noon & 4–8pm) is more than an hour on foot out of Skiáthos Town. Founded in the late eighteenth century, it is exceptionally beautiful, even beyond the grandeur of isolation you find in all Greek monasteries. The Greek flag was raised here in 1807, and heroes of the War of Independence such as Kolokotronis pledged their oaths to fight for freedom here. To reach the monastery, walk 500m out of the centre of town on the road towards the airport until, at the point where the asphalt veers to the right, you take a prominently signposted paved side road that veers left; be careful to stick to this and not to wander off onto the dirt roads.

Beyond Evangelístria, a mule track continues to the abandoned **Áyios Harálambos monastery**, from where it's possible to walk across the island to the ruined capital of Kástro along another dirt road; this takes about two hours. To reach Kástro from Skiáthos Town, it's quicker to take the direct paved road towards it on a motorbike, or take a kaïki ride round the island and get off at the beach below Kástro.

Just over halfway between Evangelístria and Kástro, a well-used dirt track (signposted) turns left and heads towards the abandoned fifteenth-century monastery of **Panayía tís Kekhriás**, three-hours' walk from town. It's said to be the oldest on the island and has a colony of bats inside. It's a beautiful walk (or organized donkey-ride), and there are two pebbly beaches below, one with a welcoming stream that provides a cool shower. Back on the paved road, you can continue to within a thirty-minute walk of **Kástro** – a spectacular spot, built on a windswept headland. In the past, the entrance was only accessible by a drawbridge, which has been replaced by a flight of steps. The village was built in the sixteenth century, when the people of the island moved here for security from pirate raids. It was abandoned three hundred years later in 1830, following independence from Turkey, when the population moved back to build the modern town on the site of ancient Skiáthos. The ruins are largely over-grown, and only three churches survive intact, the largest still retaining some original frescoes. From outside the gates, a path leads down the rocks to a good pebble **beach**; with a stream running down from the hills and a daytime café (with slightly overpriced food and drinks), it makes a good place to camp. For an apparently inaccessible spot though, it does attract a surprising number of people. All the island excursion boats call here, and even when they've gone, there's little chance of having the ruins or beach to yourself.

Finally, the seventeenth-century **Kounístra monastery** can be reached by turning right off the paved road that runs north across the island from Tróulos to Asélinos (see below for these). It's very pretty spot, with a beautiful carved icon screen, splendid icons, a grape arbour and a taverna.

The beaches

The real business of Skiáthos is **beaches**. There are reputed to be more than sixty of them, but that's hardly enough to soak up the hordes of summer visitors: at the height of the season, the local population of four thousand can be swamped by up to fifty thousand visitors. The beaches on the northeast coast aren't easily accessible unless you pay for an excursion kaïki: reaching them on foot requires treks more arduous than those described above. The bus, though, runs along the entire south coast, and from strategic points along the way you can easily reach a good number of beaches. The prevailing summer *meltémi* wind blows from the north, so the beaches on the south coast are usually better protected. Most of the popular beaches have at least a drinks/snacks stall; those at Vromólimnos, Asélinos and Tróulos have proper tavernas.

The beaches before the **Kalamáki peninsula** (where English and rich Greeks have their villas) are unexciting, but on the promontory itself are the highly rated **Ayía Paraskeví** and **Vromólimnos beaches**, close to Koliós hamlet; Vromólimnos offers windsurfing and waterskiing. For scuba enthusiasts, there is the Dolphin Diving Centre (☎04270/22 599) at the *Nostos* hotel, on the eastern side of the Kalamáki peninsula by Kanapiítsa hamlet.

Just before Tróulos beach, the last on the south coast before Koukounariés, you can turn right up a paved road, which runs 4km north to **Mégas Asélinos**, a very good beach with a campsite, beach bar and a reasonable taverna. A daily bus and excursion boats call here, so it's crowded in season. A fork in the paved road leads to Kounístra monastery (see above) and continues to **Mikrós Asélinos**, just east of its larger neighbour and somewhat quieter.

The bus only goes as far as **KOUKOUNARIÉS**, a busy resort with wooden walkways traversing the sand to a series of *kantínas* selling drinks and light snacks, though the three beaches are excellent if you don't mind the crowds. There's a majestic sandy bay of clear, gradually deepening water, backed by acres of pines, which despite its popularity merits at least one visit if only to assess the claim that it's the best beach in Greece. The road runs behind a small lake at the back of the pine trees, and features a string of **hotels, rooms** and **restaurants**, as well as a good campsite. Here, the *Strofilia* apartments which sleep four (☎04270/49 251, ⓕ49 585, ⓔstrophilia@n-skiathos.gr; ⓪) are particularly nicely furnished. The smart *Limni Hotel*, right opposite the lake itself, is also decent value (☎04270/49 362; ④). Jet-skis, motorboats, windsurfing and waterskiing are all available off the beach.

"**Banana beach**" (also known as Krassá), the third cove on the far side of Poúnda headland, is one of the trendiest beaches with watersports, a couple of bars and tolerance of nude bathing. For the less adventurous, the turning for

Ayía Eléni, 1km from the road, leads to a pleasant beach with a drinks kiosk. Further north, **Mandhráki** and **Eliá** beaches have similar facilities, and are accessible by scooter along dirt tracks.

The famed **Laláría beach**, almost at the northernmost point of Skiáthos, can be reached by taxi-boats from the town. Covered with smooth white stones, it's beautiful, with steep cliffs rising behind it; the swimming is excellent, but beware of the undertow. The island's three natural grottoes – Skotiní, Galázia and Halkiní – are nearby, and are included in many of the "round-the-island" trips. East of Evangelístria are the greyish sands of **Mégas Yialós**, one of the less crowded beaches, and **Xánemos**, another nudist beach; both suffer from airport noise.

Skópelos

Bigger, more rugged and better cultivated than Skiáthos, **Skópelos** is almost as busy, but its concessions to tourism are lower key and in better taste than in Skiáthos. Most of the larger beaches have sunbeds, umbrellas and some watersports, though smaller, secluded coves do exist. Inland, the island is a well-watered place, growing olives, plums, pears and almonds. **Glóssa** and **Skópelos**, its two main towns, are also among the prettiest in the Sporades, clambering uphill along paved steps, their houses distinguished by attractive wooden balconies and grey slate roofs. A number of **nationalities** have occupied the island at various stages of its history, among them the Romans, Persians, Venetians, French and, of course, the Ottomans. The Ottoman pirate-admiral Barbarossa (Redbeard) – actually a Greek renegade from Lésvos – had the entire population of the island slaughtered in the sixteenth century.

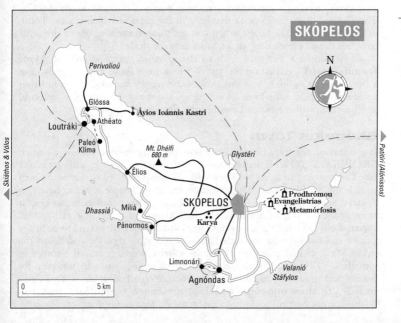

Loutráki, Glóssa and the west

Most boats and hydrofoils call at both ends of Skópelos, stopping first at the small port of **LOUTRÁKI** ("Glóssa" on schedules) with its narrow pebble beach, small hotels and rooms for rent. The village has been spoiled a little by development at either end, but it's not a bad place to stay if you're after peace and quiet; try *O Stelios* (☎04240/33 412; ❸), a simple pension above the *Vrahos* taverna, the *Avra* (☎04240/33 550; ❹) or any of the rooms advertised just in from the seafront. Though most of the quayside tavernas don't offer value for money, there are exceptions: the *Orea Ellas* taverna by the harbour is shaded by beautiful chestnut trees and sells a highly recommended, home-made retsina, while the *Flisvos* is a friendly place with decent pasta dishes.

High above Loutráki, **GLÓSSA** would be perhaps a preferable base if it had more places to stay. It is a sizeable and quite beautiful, totally Greek town, with several kafenía, a taverna and a few rooms to let, some of which are hot and musty, with erratic water pressure. *Kostas and Nina's* place (☎04240/33 686; ❸) has simple, clean rooms, some with a view; they also rent out studios longer term, or you could stay at the *Selinounda Apartments* (☎04240/33 570; ❹) on the road between Loutráki and Glóssa. The one central taverna, popular *To Agnandi*, serves excellent, innovative food and has a roof terrace with wonderful views, while *Iy Kali Kardhia*, east of town on the road out towards Élios, also serves good food in a pleasant setting. Incidentally, it's a good idea to accept offers of a taxi ride up to Glóssa from Loutráki; it's a stiff walk up even if you know the path shortcuts, and taxi drivers will know if there are any vacancies. If it's really high season, though, and even Glóssa is packed, two nearby villages, **Athéato** and **Paleó Klíma**, have rooms, while Élios on the coast below has two big hotels, bungalows and rooms.

Ninety-minutes' walk from Glóssa, up to the north coast, will bring you to the **beach** called **Perivolioú**. The walk itself is worthwhile, passing a **monastery** next to a stone cairn containing masses of human bones and skulls. There's also a huge hollow oak tree here, in the heart of which is a small tank of drinking water. The beach, when you get there, is nothing out of the ordinary, but there's pure spring water and a cave for shade.

East of Glóssa, a dirt road leads to the splendidly sited church of **Áyios Ioánnis Kastrí**, perched on the top of a rock high above a small sandy cove where you can swim. A new unsightly house nearby has spoiled the isolation somewhat, but the walk from Glóssa (again, about ninety minutes) is beautiful and peaceful, with hawks and nightingales for company.

Skópelos Town

If you stay on the ferry beyond Loutráki – probably the best plan – you reach **SKÓPELOS TOWN**, sloping down one corner of a huge, almost circular bay. The best way to arrive is by sea, with the town revealed slowly as the boat rounds the final headland. Though more and more people seem to have discovered Skópelos Town, the locals are making a tremendous effort to keep it from going the way of Skiáthos. The harbour area is practically wall-to-wall tavernas and cafés, but the shops and eateries in the back alleys tend to be imaginative and tasteful, with wooden, hand-painted name signs. Spread below the oddly whitewashed ruins of a Venetian **kástro** is an enormous number of churches – 123 reputedly, though some are small enough to be mistaken for houses and most are locked except for their annual festival day. Other sights include a **folklore museum** (Wed–Fri 10am–2pm & 6–8pm, Sat 6–9pm, Sun 11am–1pm & 6–9pm) and photography exhibitions in summer.

Outside town, perched on the slopes opposite the quay, are two convents, worth visiting for their seclusion and views: **Evangelístrias** (daily 8am–1pm & 4–7pm), which is within view of the town, and **Prodhrómou** (daily 8am–1pm & 5–8pm). The monastery of **Metamórfosis**, also on this promontory, was abandoned in 1980, but is now being restored by the monks and is open to visitors. Access is simplest by following an old road behind the line of hotels along the bay to Evangelístria (an hour's walk). From there it's an extra half-hour's scramble over mule tracks to Pródhromos, the remotest and most beautiful of the three. Ignore the new road that goes part way – it's longer, and misses most of the beauty of the walk.

Practicalities

The **ferry quay** is at the western end of a long promenade, lined with an array of boutiques, bars, stores and restaurants. The local hydrofoil agency is Skopelos Shipping (℡04240/22 767). To get to the **bus station**, turn left where the quay meets the main road, and follow the sea until you pass the children's swings and the second *períptero*, at the point where the road divides around a car park. Opposite the bus station entrance, a short road leads into a maze of lanes and signposts to the **post office**. There are **banks** (with cash dispensers) about 50m from the quay. Among the several **motorbike rental** outlets, friendly service can be had at Panos Bikes (℡04240/23 696), near the start of the road towards Glóssa. For around €15, day-long **boat cruises** offer to take you around the island or to Alónissos and the marine park.

In the main part of the town there are dozens of **rooms** for rent. These can be arranged through the Association of Room Owners office (℡ & ℱ 04240/24 567; daily 9am–noon & 6–8pm), on the seafront 100m from the ferry dock. Alternatively, there are a few pleasant small hotels such as *Andromache* (℡04240/22 940, or enquire at Madro Travel by the quay ℡04240/22 145; ❹), in a quiet old house near the post office, and the relaxed and casual *Kyr Sotos* (℡04240/22 549, ℱ23 668; ❹) nearby. The old-style *Georgios* (℡04240/22 308; ❹), right by the quay, is a fair standby and the gaily painted *Adonis* (℡04240/22 231, ℱ23 239; ❺), just above the mid-seafront is also good though noisy. For larger, more **expensive hotels** with pools higher up from the port, you're unlikely to find a space without having booked through a tour operator, but if you fancy the likes of the cosy *Elli* (℡04240/22 943, ℱ23 284; ❻) on the east side of town, the modern *Aperitton* (℡04240/22 256, ℱ22 976; ❻) on the ring road above the town, or the first-rate, neo-rustic *Dionyssos* (℡04240/23 210, ℱ22 954; ❻), also on the ring road – ask about vacancies at Madro Travel on the quay.

There's a wide variety of **places to eat**, ranging from the acceptable to the truly excellent. Those at the near end of the harbour, like *Angelos-Ta Kymata*, *Molos* and *Klimataria*, all offer decent meals, as does *To Aktaion*, with exceptionally pleasant staff and large, delicious and reasonably priced portions. At the far end of the front *Stergios* has tasty dishes like chicken in white-wine sauce. A little way inland, two *souvláki* places, both named *O Platanos*, compete for the distinction of having the best *yíros*; the one with blue chairs also has a much wider menu. If you're sick of Greek food, then *Perivoli*, above the two *souvladzídhika* at the east end of town, is the place for an "international-cuisine" gourmet blowout – fairly affordable at about €19 apiece.

Nightlife in Skópelos is on the increase, but is more of the late-night bar than the nightclub variety, apart from the *Cocos* disco out of town. That said, *Metro*, *Ano Kato* and *Panselinos,* which form a cluster on Dhoulídhis, are pretty

THE SPORADES AND ÉVVIA | Skópelos

jumping on a hot summer evening. Among bars, look out for the classy *Vengera*, in a restored house that compares favourably with the town's folk art museum, and the small, atmospheric *Nemesis*. The *bouzoúki* joint *Meintani* is housed in an old olive press near Souvlaki Square, while the *Skopelitissa* and *Anatoli* on top of the *kástro* play Greek music till the early hours.

Around the rest of the island

Buses cover the island's main paved road between Skópelos Town and Loutráki via Glóssa (around 6–8 times daily 7am–10.30pm), stopping at the paths to all the main beaches and villages. **Stáfylos**, 4km south of town, is the closest beach, though rather small and rocky. It's getting increasingly crowded, but the *Terpsis* taverna, just inland at a spot shaded by a vast pine tree, is famous for its quality grilled meat (especially chicken). Among the new room ventures, *Mando* (℡04240/23 917; ⑤) is friendly and quiet.

When Stáfylos gets too busy, it's better to go to **Velanió** beach, a short walk east along the coast, to have a chance of escaping the crowds. Nudity is acceptable and although the official campsite has long since closed, you shouldn't be hassled if you stay a night or two. There's spring water and a *kantína* too.

Further around the coast to the west, the tiny horseshoe-shaped harbour of **AGNÓNDAS** (with its three fish tavernas and rooms) is the start of a fifteen-minute path (2km by road) or half-hourly kaïki trip to **LIMNONÁRI**, 300m of fine sand set in a closed, rocky bay. The *Limnonari Beach* restaurant serves delicious spiral-shaped local *tyrópittes* and rents rooms (℡04240/23 046; ④).

PÁNORMOS is very much a full-blown, commercial resort, with rooms, tavernas, a campsite, yacht anchorage and watersports. The beach here is gravelly and steeply shelving, but there are small secluded bays close by. The thirty-room *Panormos Beach Hotel* (℡04240/22 711, ℱ23 366; ⑥) has a beautiful garden and fine views, and is lovingly looked after; beyond it, the *Adrina Beach* (℡04240/23 373; ⑥) is one of the most attractive and most expensive hotels in the Sporades. Slightly further on at **MILIÁ**, there is a tremendous, 1500m sweep of tiny pebbles beneath a bank of pines, facing the islet of Dhassía. There's one taverna and the *Milia Apartments* (℡04240/23 998; ④) in this languid setting; nudist swimming is possible at a lovely five-hundred-metre-long beach a little way north. The shore beyond is indented with many tiny coves, ranging from individual- to family-size.

Further north, **ÉLIOS**, 9km short of Glóssa, is a medium-sized, fairly new resort settled by residents of the earthquake-damaged villages above it, with nothing special to offer besides a pleasant beach. If you want to stay, try the *Hotel Apartments Zanneta* (℡04240/33 140, ℱ33 717; ⑥). Beyond here, the renovated village of Paleó Klíma marks the start of a beautiful forty-minute **trail** to Glóssa, via the empty hamlet of Áyii Anáryiri and the oldest village on the island, **Athéato** (Mahalás).

West of Skópelos Town, various jeep tracks and old paths wind through olive and plum groves towards **Mount Dhélfi** and the Vathiá forest, or skirt the base of the mountain northeast to Revýthi hill with its fountains and churches, and the site of **Karyá**, with its *sendoúkia*: ancient rock-cut tombs which may be early Christian. To the northwest of Skópelos Town, **Glystéri** is a small pebble beach with no shade, whose taverna is much frequented by locals on Sundays. A fork off the Glystéri and Mount Dhélfi tracks can – in theory – be followed across the island to Pánormos within ninety minutes; it's a pleasant walk, though the route isn't always obvious.

Alónissos and some minor islets

The most remote of the Sporades, **Alónissos** is also, at first sight, the least attractive, owing to an unfortunate recent history. The vineyards were wiped out by disease in 1950, and the *hóra* was damaged by an earthquake in 1965. Although its houses were mostly repairable, lack of water, combined with corruption and the social control policies of the new junta, were instrumental in the transfer of virtually the entire population down to the previously unimportant anchorage of Patitíri. The result is a little soulless, but what charm may be lacking in the built environment on the coast is made up for by the hospitality of the islanders.

Patitíri and the old town

PATITÍRI is not a good introduction to the island, though it's trying hard to rectify that. The port, a pretty cove flanked by pine trees, is marred by rows of flat-roofed concrete buildings rising up behind it. Nevertheless, the line of near-identical bars and restaurants that runs along the waterfront is pleasant enough. Alónissos attracts fewer visitors than Skíathos or Skópelos; most of those who do come stay in Patitíri, and from mid-July to the end of August it can get very crowded. It's easy, though, to pick up connections here for beaches and the old town, and there are several good hotels to choose from. The most interesting place to visit is the **Monk Seal Information Centre** (daily 10am–1pm & 7–10pm) on the first floor of a building halfway along the seafront. The displays include models, photos, video and slide shows; see box on p.455.

PALEÁ ALÓNISSOS is a fine but steep fifty-minute walk via the traditional *kalderími* – signposted on the left just outside Patitíri. Alternatively, there's a frequent bus service in the mornings and afternoons. Although some houses are still derelict, much of the village has been painstakingly restored, mainly by the English and Germans who bought the properties at knock-down rates. Only a few local families continue to live here, which gives the village a rather odd and un-Greek atmosphere, but it is picturesque, and the views make the trip worthwhile.

Practicalities

All the important facilities are in Patitíri; **buses** and **taxis** have adjacent terminals. The **post office** is on the Hóra road, while kaïkia leave from the quay beside the *Pension Flisvos*. You can rent a scooter or larger motorbike at Dhyo Trohi or even a car (check with Ikos Travel, overleaf) at reasonable prices. The roads between Patitíri, Stení Vála and the northernmost point on the island are paved, and the dirt roads down to the beaches are in good condition: not half as dangerous as the twisting, busy roads on Skiáthos and Skópelos. A couple of the rental places on the waterfront also rent out motorboats and dinghies.

Rooms are easy to find here, as you'll probably be approached with offers as you get off the ferry, sometimes by older women wearing traditional blue-and-white costumes. The local room-owners' association (℡ & ℻ 04240/65 577), on the front, can also find you a room (mostly ❸) in Patitíri or nearby Vótsi. Other options include the *Ioulieta* pension (℡04240/65 463; ❸), *Haravyi* (℡04240/65 090, ℻65 189; ❺) and *Pantheon* (℡04240/65 139; ❹). Best in the higher price range are *Liadromia* (℡04240/65 521, ℻65 096, ✉liadromia@alonissos.com; ❺), above the port, *Niirides* (℡04240/65 643; ❺),

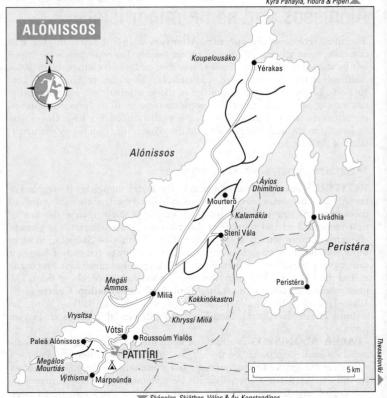

ALÓNISSOS

N

Koupelousáko

Yérakas

Alónissos

*Áyios
Dhimítrios*

Mourteró

Kalamákia

Livádhia

Steni Vála

Peristéra

*Megáli
Ammos*

Miliá

Kokkinókastro

Peristéra

Vrysítsa

Khryssí Miliá

Vótsi

Paleá Alónissos

Roussoúm Yialós

*Megálos
Mourtiás*

PATITÍRI

Wýthisma Marpoúnda

0   5 km

Thessaloníki

comprising studio apartments with pool, and *Paradise* (☎04240/65 160; ⑤),
on the promontory east of the port with a pool overlooking the sea. Ikos
Travel, the hydrofoil agent (☎04240/65 320), can do bookings for a limited
number of rooms and apartments in the old town, though accommodation
here is in short supply, so expect to pay well over the odds, particularly in season. Otherwise, ask around; few people put up "room for rent" signs, but try
the simple and clean *Fadasia House* (☎04240/65 186; ③), at the entrance to
Hóra.

The **restaurants** on the front of Patitíri are reasonably priced, but for the
most part the food is nothing special. One exception is the *Pleiades*, its tables
set in a peaceful courtyard, and with well-executed dishes from a limited menu.
Recommended ouzerís include *To Kamaki*, two blocks up towards the post
office from the waterfront, with an amazing selection of seafood. Two other
ouzerís worth a try on the same road are *Kala Krassa* and *Kapetan Spyros*. The
Tzimakis grill has good food in a splendid setting on the promontory. Up in
the old town, *Astrofengia* has breathtaking terrace seating, a German take on
Greek recipes, and decadent desserts.

Nightlife is low-key. The best of the seafront bars is *Pub Dennis*, whose ice-
cream concoctions are divine, though both *En Plo* and *La Vie* are popular.
Club-wise, *Borio* and *Enigma* are fairly European, while *Rembetika*, on the road
to the old town, specializes in Greek music.

The island's beaches

Alónissos has some of the cleanest water in the Aegean, but it's lacking in sandy beaches. There's only two really – Výthisma and Vrysítsa. The rest vary from rough to fine pebbles. There's a very limited bus service along the Hóra–Patitíri–Stení Vala route, but kaïkia run half-hourly from Patitíri north to Khryssí, Miliá, Kokkinókastro, Stení Vála, Kalamákia and Áyios Dhimítrios, and south around the coast to Marpoúnda, Výthisma and Megálos Mourtiás. Kaïkia also sail occasionally to Livádhia and Peristéra islet.

At Patitíri there's decent swimming from the rocks around the promontory to the north; pick your way along a hewn-out path past the hotels and you're there (ladder provided). To the north, above the headlands, Patitíri merges into two adjoining settlements, **Roussoúm Yialós** and **Vótsi**. For better beaches, you'll have to get in a boat or on a bike.

Khryssí Miliá, the first good beach, has pine trees behind the sand and a taverna; there's a couple of new hotels on the hillside above, such as the posh *Milia Bay* (☎04240/66 035, ⓕ66 037, ⓔmilia-bay@forthnet.gr; ⓞ), and it

6

The Mediterranean monk seal

The **Mediterranean monk seal** has the dubious distinction of being the European mammal most in danger of extinction. Fewer than eight hundred survive worldwide, the majority around the Portuguese Atlantic island of Madeira. A large colony off the coast of the West African state of Mauritania was decimated early in 1997: an estimated two hundred seals died, possibly poisoned by algae. Small numbers survive in the Ionian and Aegean seas; the largest population here, of around thirty seals, lives around the deserted islands north of Alónissos.

Monk seals can travel up to 200km a day in search of food, but they usually return to the same places to rear their **pups**. They have one pup every two years, and the small population is very vulnerable to disturbance. Originally, the pups would have been reared in the open, but with increasing disturbance by man, they have retreated to isolated sea caves, with partly submerged entrances, particularly around the coast of the remote islet of Pipéri.

Unfortunately, the seals compete with fishermen for limited stocks of fish, and, in the overfished Aegean, often destroy nets full of fish. Until recently it was common for seals to be killed by fishermen. This occasionally still happens, but in an attempt to protect the seals, the seas around the northern Sporades have been declared a **marine wildlife reserve**: fishing is restricted in the area north of Alónissos and prohibited within 5km of Pipéri. On Alónissos, the conservation effort and reserve have won a great deal of local support, mainly through the efforts of the Hellenic Society for the Protection of the Monk Seal (HSPMS), based at Stení Vála. The measures have been particularly popular with local fishermen, as tight restrictions on larger, industrial-scale fishing boats from other parts of Greece should help restore local stocks, and eventually benefit the fishermen financially.

Despite this, the government has made no serious efforts to enforce the restrictions, and boats from outside the area continue to fish around Pipéri. There are also government plans to reduce the prohibited area around Pipéri to 500m. On a more positive note, the HSPMS, in collaboration with the Pieterburen Seal Creche in Holland, has reared several abandoned seal pups, all of which have been successfully released in the seas north of Alónissos.

For the moment, your chances of actually seeing a seal are remote, unless you plan to spend a few weeks on a boat in the area. It's recommended that you shouldn't visit Pipéri – this is officially prohibited in any case – or approach sea caves on other islands which might be used by seals, or try to persuade boat-owners to do so.

can get crowded in summer. At **Kokkinókastro**, over the hill to the north, excavations have revealed the site of ancient Ikos and evidence of the oldest known prehistoric habitation in the Aegean. There's nothing much to see, but it's a beautiful spot with a good red-pebble beach, and, in July and August, a daytime bar.

STENÍ VÁLA, opposite the island of Peristéra, a haven for the yachts and flotillas that comb the Sporades, has almost become a proper village, with two shops, several houses, a bar, rooms and five tavernas, one of which stays open more or less throughout the year. The Monk Seal Treatment and Rehabilitation Centre, housed in a small hut on the beach, can provide information and insight into the HSPMS's work. There's an unofficial campsite (℡04240/65 258) in an olive grove by the harbour, a long pebble beach – Glýfa, where boats are repaired – and some stony beaches within reasonable walking distance in either direction. **KALAMÁKIA**, to the north, also has a couple of tavernas and a few rooms.

If you want real solitude, **Áyios Dhimítrios**, **Megáli Ámmos**, and **Yérakas** (an old shepherds' village at the northernmost point of Alónissos) are possibilities. However, before committing yourself to a Robinson Crusoe existence, check it out by scooter or take one of the round-the-island trips available, and return the next day with enough food for your stay: there are no stores outside the port and Stení Vála. West of Patitíri, **Marpoúnda** features a large hotel and bungalow complex and a rather small beach. It's better to turn left after the campsite towards **Megálos Mourtiás**, a pebble beach with several tavernas linked by dirt track with Paleá Alónissos, 200m above. **Výthisma**, the lovely beach just before Megálos Mourtiás, can only be reached by boat, the path here having been washed out. Further north, visible from Paleá Alónissos, **Vrysítsa** is tucked into its own finger-like inlet. There's sand and a taverna, but little else.

Beyond Alónissos: some minor islets

Northeast of Alónissos, half a dozen tiny **islets** speckle the Aegean. Virtually none of these has any permanent population, or a ferry service, and the only way you can reach them – at least Peristéra, Kyrá Panayía and Yioúra – is by excursion kaïki (ask at Ikos Travel), weather permitting. No boats are allowed to take you to the other, more remote islets, as they are protected areas within the Sporades National Marine Park. But though it is possible to be left for a night or more on any of the closer islands, be sure to bring more supplies than you need: if the weather worsens you'll be marooned until such time as small craft can reach you.

Peristéra is the closest islet to Alónissos, to which it was once actually joined, but subsidence (a common phenomenon in the area) created the narrow straits between the two. It is graced with some sandy beaches and there is rarely anyone around, though some Alonissans do come over for short periods to tend the olive groves, and in season there are regular evening "barbecue boats" from the main island. As on Alónissos, a few unofficial campers are tolerated, but there is only one spot, known locally as "Barbecue Bay", where campfires are allowed.

Kyrá Panayiá (also known as Pelagós) is the next islet out and is equally fertile. It's owned by the Meyístis Lávras monastery of Mount Athos and there are two monasteries here, one still inhabited. Boats call at a beach on the south shore, one of many such sandy stretches and coves around the island. There's no other permanent population besides wild goats.

Nearby **Yioúra** boasts a stalactite cave reputed to be the previous abode of Polyphemus, the Cyclops who imprisoned Odysseus, but you won't be able to check its credentials. No one is allowed within 500m of the island, since, like Pipéri, it lies inside the restricted zone of the Marine Park.

Pipéri, near Yioúra, is a seabird and monk-seal refuge, and permission from a ministry of the environment representative (in Alónissos) is required for visits by specialists; nonscientists are not allowed. Tiny, northernmost **Psathoúra** is dominated by its powerful modern lighthouse, the tallest in the Aegean, although here, as around many of these islands, there's a submerged ancient town, brought low by the endemic subsidence. Roughly halfway between Alónissos and Skýros, green **Skántzoura**, with a single empty monastery and a few seasonal shepherds, is a smaller version of Kyrá Panayiá.

Skýros

Despite its proximity to Athens, **Skýros** remained a very traditional and idiosyncratic island until recently. Any impetus for change had been neutralized by the lack of economic opportunity (and even secondary schooling), forcing the younger Skyrians to live in Athens and leaving behind a conservative gerontocracy. A high school was finally provided in the mid-1980s, and the island has

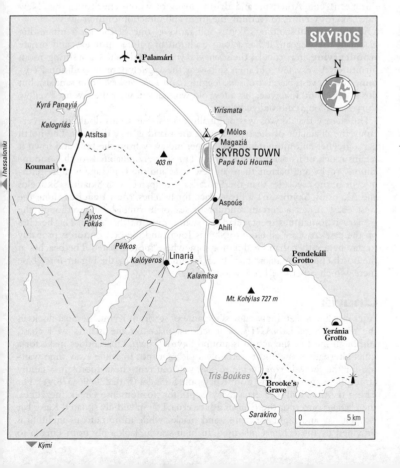

Skýros has some particularly lively, even outrageous, festivals. The *Apokriátika* (pre-Lenten) Carnival here is structured around the famous **goat dance**, performed by masked revellers in the village streets. The foremost character in this is the Yéros, a menacing figure concealed by a goatskin mask and weighed down by garlands of sheep bells. Accompanying him are Korélles and Kyriés ("Maidens" and "Ladies" – who are transvestites, as only the men participate) and Frangi (maskers in "Western" garb). For further details, read Joy Koulentianou's *The Goat Dance of Skyros*, available in Athens and occasionally on the island.

The other big annual event takes place near Magaziá beach on August 15, when children race domesticated members of the **wild pony** herd, native to Skýros and said to be related to the Shetland pony (if so, it must be very distantly). They are thought, perhaps, to be the diminutive horses depicted in the Parthenon frieze, and at any time of the year you might find some of the tame individuals tethered and grazing near Skýros Town.

been somewhat "discovered" since that time. It's now the haunt of continental Europeans, chic Athenians and British, many of whom check into the "New Age" Skýros Centre, to "rethink the form and direction of their lives".

All this notwithstanding, Skýros still ranks as one of the most interesting places in the Aegean. It has a long tradition of painted **pottery** and ornate **woodcarving**, in particular the *salonáki skyrianó* (handmade set of sitting-room furniture). A very few old men still wear the vaguely Cretan traditional costume of cap, vest, baggy trousers, leggings and *trohádhia* (Skýrian sandals), but this is dying out. Likewise, just a few old women still wear the favoured yellow scarves and long embroidered skirts.

The theory that Skýros was originally two islands seems doubtful, but certainly the character of the two parts of the island is very different. The north has a greener and more gentle landscape, and away from the port and town it retains much of its original pine forest. The sparsely inhabited south is mountainous, rocky and barren; there are few trees and the landscape is more reminiscent of the Cyclades than the Sporades. Compared with Skiáthos, Skópelos and Alónissos, Skýros isn't a great place for beaches. Most **beaches** along the west coast attract a certain amount of seaborne rubbish, and, although the scenery is sometimes spectacular, the swimming isn't that good. The beaches on the east coast are all close to Skýros Town, and the best option is probably to stay here rather than heading for somewhere more isolated. The beaches at the north end of the island have been commandeered by the big air-force base there, which otherwise keeps a low profile.

Linariá

After crossing a seemingly endless expanse of sea from Kými, the boat docks at the tiny port of **LINARIÁ**, a functional place on the island's west coast. Although most of the action is around Skýros Town, Linariá does make for a quiet alternative base and is certainly a pleasant spot to while away time waiting for the ferry. If you decide to stay, you can rent cheap rooms in a family atmosphere above the bay from Khrysoula Strandzi (☎02220/96 378; ②). For eating try the *Almyra* taverna (May–Sept), for no-nonsense Greek mezédhes, the *Psariotis* ouzerí or the *Filippos* fish taverna. The splendidly situated *Kavos* bar is open day and night for drinks and snacks, while more raucous nightlife is provided by the *Castro Club* disco. In high season, kaïkia ply from Linariá to the Pentekáli and Yeránia **grottoes**, and to the islet of **Sarakíno**, which has a cave and a very few Skyrian wild ponies – almost extinct in the wild. There's a reasonable sandy **beach** called **Kalóyeros** a few minutes' walk along the main road from Linariá, where you can camp.

An asphalt road connects Linariá to Skýros Town, 10km away, and then continues round past the airport to Atsítsa, where the Skyros Centre has its main branch; **buses** to **Skýros Town** and **Magaziá**, on the coast below, leave from the quay. Midway up the Linariá–Skýros Town route, a paved side road goes to Ahíli and Kalamítsa. Most other roads are passable by scooter, apart from the direct track between Skýros Town and Atsítsa.

Skýros Town

SKÝROS TOWN (also known as Horió), with its decidedly Cycladic architecture, sits on the landward side of a high rock rising precipitously from the coast. According to legend, King Lycomedes pushed Theseus to his death from its summit. The town doesn't feel like a resort, with its workaday atmosphere, but away from the tattier outskirts is decidedly picturesque. The older and more intriguing parts of town are higher up, climbing towards the **kástro**, a mainly Byzantine building, built on the site of the ancient **acropolis**. There are few traces of the acropolis, although remains of the Classical city walls survive below on the seaward side of the rock. The *kástro* is open to visitors; to reach its upper parts you pass through a rather private-looking gateway into the monastery, then through an attractive shaded courtyard and up a whitewashed tunnel. There's little to see at the top, apart from a few churches in various states of ruin, but there are great views over the town and the island, and the climb up takes you through the quieter and more traditional part of town, with glimpses into traditionally decorated houses. With their gleaming copper pots, porcelain plates and antique embroideries decorating the hearth, these dwellings are a matter of intense pride among the islanders, who are often found seated in their doorways on tiny carved chairs.

At the northern end of town is the striking and splendidly incongruous **memorial to Rupert Brooke**. It takes the form of a bronze statue of "Immortal Poetry" and its nakedness caused a scandal among the townspeople when it was first erected. Brooke, who visited the south of the island very briefly in April 1915, died shortly afterwards of blood poisoning on a French hospital ship anchored offshore and was buried in an olive grove above the bay of Trís Boúkes. (The site can be reached on foot from Kalamítsa, by kaïki, or, less romantically, by taxi.) Brooke, who became something of a local hero, despite his limited acquaintance with Skýros, was adopted as the paragon of patriotic youth by Kitchener and later Churchill, who conveniently overlooked his forthright socialist and internationalist views.

Just below the Brooke statue are two museums. The **Archeological Museum** (Tues–Sun 8am–2pm; €1.50) has a modest collection of pottery and statues from excavations on the island, and a reconstruction of a traditional Skýros house interior. The privately run **Faltaïts Museum** (daily 10am–1pm & 5.30–8pm/6–9pm in summer; free), in a nineteenth-century house built over one of the bastions of the ancient walls, is more interesting, with a collection of domestic items, costumes, embroideries, porcelain and rare books.

Practicalities

The **bus** from Linariá leaves you by the school, 200m below the main platía; in season, schedules are guaranteed to meet the ferries, but otherwise it can be

△ Skópelos Town

limited, in which case you might be better off getting a taxi. The **post office** and **bank** are both near the platía. Skýros Travel (☎02220/91 600 or 91 123), on the main street above the platía, can provide **information** or advice, and can find a room or hotel; in high season it's a good idea to telephone them in advance. Of the **motorbike and bicycle** rental places in the area around the platía, the most prominent and efficient is Trahanas (☎02220/92 032).

You'll probably be met off the bus with offers of **rooms**, which it's as well to accept. If you'd like to stay in a traditional Skyrian house, those of Anna Stergiou (☎02220/91 657; ❸) and Maria Mavroyiorgi (☎02220/91 440; ❸) are both clean and cosy. Or you could try the pleasant, if rather overpriced, *Nefeli* hotel (☎02220/91 964, ℱ92 061; ❻) on the main road before the platía. A more basic option is the *Elena* (☎02220/91 738; ❷) next to the post office, which has very cheap singles with shared bath. There's a picturesque **campsite** nearer the beach, at the bottom of the steps below the archeological museum, with basic amenities but a good bar and friendly management.

The platía and the main street running by it are the centre of village life, with a few noisy pubs and a wide choice of kafenía, tavernas and fast-food places. There are just a few outstanding **places to eat**: most are overpriced, or serve undistinguished fare. *Maryetis* has the best grilled fish and stewed goat, *O Papous ki Ego* is Hóra's best ouzerí, with a mix of fried plates and grilled cuttlefish, while the *Sweets Workshop* does some wonderful cakes. For a special occasion, try *Kristina's* restaurant below the taxi rank (signposted); its Australian owner has an imaginative menu featuring great desserts. The *Panorama*, in the lower town, towards Magaziá, is also good for its home cooking with a view.

The town's **nightlife** is mostly bar-based until very late, when the few clubs get going. The most popular **bars** are the trendy *Kalypso* which plays jazz and blues, dance-oriented *Kata Lathos* and the rockier *Iroön* and *Rodon*. Later on, *Iy Stasis* is one of the most popular places. The best clubs include the *Skyropoula, Mylos* and the *Stone Club*. Some bars also serve good breakfasts; here the favourite is *Anemos*, followed by *Kalypso*, which has tasty Danish pastries. Another fine supper-only wine-bar with an extensive range of generic Mediterranean snacks is *Anatolikos Anemos*, near the museum, with sweeping views across the bay.

Magaziá and Mólos and nearby beaches

A path leads down past the archeological museum towards the small coastal village of **MAGAZIÁ**, coming out by the official campsite. From Magaziá, an 800-metre-long sandy beach stretches to the adjacent village of **MÓLOS**. In recent years, a sprawl of new development between the road and the beach has more or less joined the two villages together. Despite this, the beach is still good, and there are lots of **rooms** down here for the young crowd that uses the beach's watersports and volleyball facilities. *Stamatis Marmaris* (☎02220/91 672; ❸) beyond Mólos, and *Manolis Balotis* (☎02220/91 386; ❸) near the campsite, are both excellent choices. More upmarket hotels include the *Paliopyrgos* (☎02220/91 014, ℱ92 185; ❹), halfway between the beach and town, with a wonderful view, and the *Angela* (☎02220/91 764; ❺), garden-set bungalows in Mólos. The beachfront **tavernas** often compare favourably with those in town: on the Magaziá side *Stefanos* taverna is reliable, while the *Koufari* ouzerí near the *Xenia Hotel* has excellent food for higher prices. At Mólos try *Tou Thoma To Magazi,* the *Maryetis* garden restaurant and the ouzerí at *Balabani's Mill*, all at the end of the beach. It's worth sampling lobster in Skýros: it's a local speciality, often served flaked into pasta as *astakomakaronádha*.

For quieter beaches, carry on past Mólos, or try the excellent and undeveloped (unofficial nudist) beach, **Papá toú Houmá**, directly below the *kástro*. The path down to the beach starts 150m beyond the *Skyropoula* disco, and isn't obvious from above. However, further along the road south of here, the beaches are disappointing until **Aspoús**, which has a couple of tavernas and rooms to rent, as well as the smart *Ahillion* hotel (☎02220/93 300, ℱ93 303; ⑤). Further south, **Ahíli**, had one of the best beaches on the island until the construction of its new marina. Southeast of Ahíli, the coast is rocky and inaccessible, although you can take a kaïki trip down to the bay of **Trís Boúkes**, passing some picturesque sea caves on the way.

Around the rest of the island

In summer, the whimsical bus service visits the more popular beaches. But if you want to branch out on your own, rent a scooter. Tracks and footpaths diverge from the main circle road, leading inward and seaward. Among the most interesting places to head for is **Palamári**, the neglected site of an early Bronze Age settlement and a spectacular beach. Turn right after the road has begun to descend to the airport plain.

For a taste of the wooded interior, a hike on the dirt track from Skýros Town to **ATSÍTSA** is well worth the effort; it takes three to four hours, and is too rough for a scooter. Atsítsa is an attractive bay with pine trees down to the sea (tapped by the Skyrian retsina industry), a very good fish **taverna** (*O Andonis*) and an increasing number of rooms, in addition to the Skyros Centre buildings. The beach here is rocky and isn't great for swimming, but there are small sandy beaches fifteen- and twenty-minutes' walk to the north at **Kalogriás** and **Kyrá Panayiá**, with its eponymous taverna, though they are nothing out of the ordinary.

Elsewhere in the coniferous north, **Áyios Fokás** and **Péfkos** bays are easiest reached by a turning from the paved road near Linariá, while access from Atsítsa is via a reasonable dirt road. Both are in the process of being discovered by villa companies, but they have few rooms. Though quite primitive, Áyios Fokás has a very basic, excellent taverna; Péfkos has two, of which *Barba Mitsos* is the more appealing (these are only open in high season, as are all the other tavernas away from Linariá, Skýros Town, Magaziá and Mólos). The bay is beautiful, and the beach reasonable but not that clean – the beaches around Skýros Town are much better for swimming.

As for exploring the great southern mountain of **Kohýlas**, this is best attempted only if you have a four-wheel-drive vehicle, as the tracks are poor away from the main west-coast road via Kalamítsa to the naval base at Trís Boúkes (where Rupert Brooke is buried). **Kalamítsa** beach, just east of Linariá but tricky to get to from there, lacks character, but the *Mouries* taverna between it and Linariá is worth a stop, as is the remote beach halfway to Trís Boúkes, which has no facilities.

Évvia (Euboea)

Évvia is the second-largest Greek island (after Crete), and seems more like an extension of the mainland to which it was in fact once joined. At **Halkídha**, the gateway to the island, the curious old drawbridge has only a forty-metre channel to span, the island reputedly having been split from Attica and Thessaly by a blow from Poseidon's trident (earthquakes and subsidence being the more

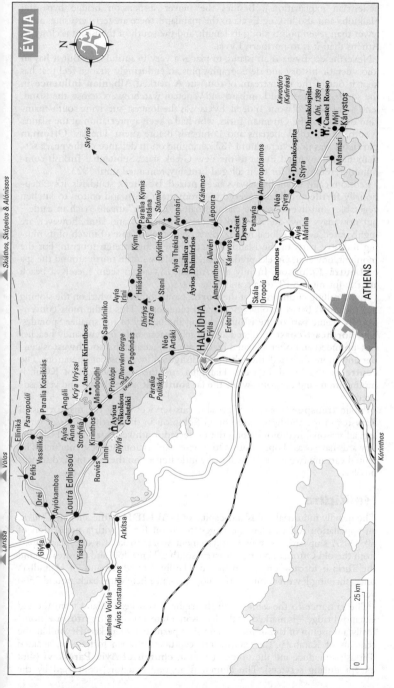

pedestrian explanations). Besides the newer suspension bridge bypassing Halkídha and also linking Évvia to the mainland, there are ferry crossings at no fewer than seven points along its length, and the south of the island is closer to Athens than it is to northern Évvia.

Nevertheless, Évvia *is* an island, in places a very beautiful one. But it has an idiosyncratic history and demography, plus an enduringly strange feel that has kept it out of the mainstream of tourism. A marked **Albanian influence** in the south, and scattered Lombard and Venetian watchtowers acrosss the island, lend a distinctive flavour. Indeed, Évvia was the longest-surviving south-mainland outpost of the Ottoman Turks, who had a keen appreciation of the island's wealth, as did the Venetians and Lombards before them. The last **Ottoman garrison** was not evicted until 1833, hanging on in defiance of the peace settlement that awarded Évvia to the new Greek state. Substantial Turkish communities, renowned for their alleged brutality, remained until 1923.

Economically, Évvia has always been prized. By Greek standards, it's exceptionally **fertile**, producing everything from grain, corn and cotton to kitchen vegetables and livestock. The classical name "Euboea" means "rich in cattle", but nowadays cows are few and far between; its kid and lamb, however, are highly rated, as is the local retsina. Because of the collapse of much of its mining industry, parts of the island are actively seeking foreign tourism. For the moment, however, Greeks predominate, especially in the north around the spa of **Loutrá Edhipsoú**. In July and August, Évvia can seem merely a beach annexe for much of Thessaly and Athens.

In the rolling countryside of the **north**, grain combines whirl on the sloping hay meadows between olive groves and pine forest. This is the most conventionally scenic part of the island, echoing the beauty of the smaller Sporades. The **northeast coast** is rugged and largely inaccessible, its few sandy beaches surf-pounded and often plagued by flotsam and jetsam; the **southwest** is gentler and more sheltered, though much disfigured by industrial operations. The **centre** of the island, between Halkídha and the easterly port of Kými, is mountainous and dramatic, while the far **southeast** is mostly dry and very isolated.

Public **transport** consists of passable bus services along the main roads to Kárystos in the southeast, and Loutrá Edhipsoú in the northwest. As of writing, all seasonal hydrofoils along the protected southwest coast from Halkídha upwards have ceased operations. Otherwise, explorations are best conducted by rented car; any two-wheeler will make little impact on the enormous distances involved.

Halkídha

The heavily industrialized island-capital of **HALKÍDHA** (the ancient *Chalkis*, an appellation still used) is the largest town on Évvia, with a population of 50,000. A shipyard, rail sidings and cement works make it a dire place, apart from the old Ottoman quarter, **Kástro**, south of Venizélou, and the area around the Turkish fortress on the mainland. Hardly a trace remains of Halkídha's once-thriving Jewish community, whose presence here dates back around 2500 years.

The entrance to the *kástro* – on the right as you head inland from the old Euripos bridge – is marked by the handsome fifteenth-century **mosque**, nominally a museum of Byzantine artefacts, but permanently locked. Beyond lie the remains of Karababa, the seventeenth-century Ottoman fortress, an arcaded Turkish aqueduct and the unique basilican **church of Ayía Paraskeví** (shut except during services). The church is an odd structure, converted by the

Crusaders during the fourteenth century into a Gothic cathedral. In the opposite direction, in the new town, an **archeological museum** at Venizélou 13 (Tues–Sun 8am–2.30pm; €1.50) has a good display of prehistoric, Hellenic and Roman finds from all over the island. The waterside overlooks the **Évripos**, the narrow channel dividing Évvia from the mainland, whose strange currents have baffled scientists for centuries. You can stand on the bridge that spans the narrowest point and watch the water swirling by like a river. Every few hours the current changes and the "tide" reverses. Aristotle is said to have thrown himself into the waters in despair at his inability to understand what was happening, so if you're puzzled you're in good company; there is still no entirely satisfactory explanation.

Practicalities

For most visitors, though, such activities are strictly time-fillers, with much the best view of the place to be had from the bus or train on the way out. **Trains** arrive on the mainland side of the channel, beneath the old fortress; given numerous, quick rail links with Athens, there's little reason to stay overnight. Should you want to, the basic *Kentrikon* hotel (☎02210/22 375; ❸) is a far better deal than the huge waterfront establishments it backs onto. Most other services of interest lie within sight of the old Évripos bridge. The **bus station** is 400m from the bridge along Kótsou, then 50m right; you should get a connection for any corner of the island as long as you show up by 2pm, later for Kými or Límni.

Halkídha is noted for its superior seafood and ouzerís; the waterfront **restaurants** are popular at weekends with Athenians but not necessarily the best-value options. Two to try are *Ta Pende Fi* at Evvías 61, a classic fish taverna in a peaceful setting, or the more central, long-running *Ouzeri Tsaf* at Papanastasíou 3, off Platía Agorás, again strong on seafood titbits. For the truly impecunious or time-pressured, there's also a handful of acceptable grills serving adequate lunches in the immediate vicinity of the bus station.

Halkídha to Kými

The coast road heading east out of Halkídha is an exceptionally misleading introduction to the interior of Évvia. The industrial zone gives way to nondescript hamlets, which are succeeded between Erétria and Amárynthos by sequestered colonies of Athenian second homes, rather bleak beaches and large hotels frequented by British and German package-tour companies. There are some intriguing **Frankish towers** at **Fýlla**, worth a detour inland from Vasilikó if you have a car, but little else.

Modern **ERÉTRIA** is a rather dreary resort laid out on a grid plan; for non-package travellers its main asset is a well-advertised ferry service across to Skála Oropoú in Attica. The site of **ancient Eretria** is more distinguished, though much of it lies under the town. A few scanty remains are dotted around the town centre, most conspicuously an **agora** and a **temple of Apollo**, but more interesting are the excavations in the northwest corner, behind the excellent small museum (Tues–Sun 8am–2.30pm; €1.50), opened in 1991 in collaboration with the Swiss School of Archeology. Here a **theatre** has been uncovered; steps from the orchestra descend to an underground vault used for sudden entrances and exits. Beyond the theatre are the ruins of a **gymnasium** and a **sanctuary**. The museum guard will be happy to unlock the fourth-century BC **House of Mosaics**, five-minutes' walk from the museum. Of the dozen or so hotels in town one of the more affordable and interesting options is the municipal tourist complex *Dreams Island* (☎02290/61 224, ℻61 268; ❹), which occupies a tiny offshore island, linked by causeway to the end of the bay. For a beachside, self-contained complex, try the B-class, 1998-renovated *Grand Bleu* (☎02290/61 012, ℻61 090; ❹), 2km from the centre.

Nine kilometres further along, **AMÁRYNTHOS** is a smaller and more pleasant resort to stay in. Though the town boasts nothing of particular interest, the seafront square is picturesque enough and there is an ample selection of good eateries, such as *Stefanos* fish taverna right by the square and *To Limenaki* a few minutes west of it. Two good accommodation options are *Iliaktidhes Hotel Apartments* (☎02290/37 605; ❹), just off the main road, and the B-class *Stefania Hotel* (☎02290/38 382, ℻38 384; ❺), right on the beach.

Just before **Alivéri**, an enormous modern power plant and a virtually intact medieval castle seem incongruously juxtaposed, and more Frankish towers look down from nearby hills. Though Alivéri itself is dreary, the nearby fishing harbour of **Káravos** has several pleasant watering holes, among them the *Vlahos* taverna. Thereafter, the route heads inland. Beyond Lépoura, where the road branches north and south, the scenery improves drastically. Take the north fork towards Kými, and cross some of the most peaceful countryside in Greece. With your own vehicle you can detour east after 5km at Neohóri to the excellent beaches at **Kálamos** and **Korasídha**. There is a growing selection of rooms and tavernas at Kálamos.

Twelve kilometres north of Lépoura, at Háni Avlonaríou, stands the Romanesque thirteenth- or fourteenth-century **basilica of Áyios Dhimítrios**, Évvia's largest and finest (ask for the key at the café next door). **AVLONÁRI** proper, 2km east, is dominated by a hill that commands most of the island's centre. At its crown is a huge Lombard or Venetian tower, rearing above the Neoclassical and vernacular houses that tier the lower slopes. There's a single taverna below the platía, though no accommodation.

This part of Évvia is particularly well endowed with Byzantine chapels, since Avlonári was an archiepiscopal see from the sixth century onwards. Back on the road to Kými, a left fork just north of Háni Avlonaríou (the bus goes this way) leads past the hamlet of **Ayía Thékla**, where a small, shed-like **chapel** of that saint, probably slightly later than Áyios Dhimítrios, hides in a lush vale below the modern church. Inside, enough fresco fragments remain with their large-eyed faces to suggest what has been lost over time. The right fork leads towards the coast and takes you past Oxýlithos, with its somewhat more elaborate chapels of **Áyios Nikólaos** and **Ayía Ánna**, both at least a hundred years older than Áyios Dhimítrios.

The road hits the coast at the fine beach of **Stómio** (known also as just Paralía, or "Beach"), some 1500m of sand closing off the mouth of a river, which is deep, swimmable and often cleaner than the sea. To the north and east you glimpse the capes enclosing the broad bay of Kými. Up on the road, there are a couple of cafés and a small pension; most facilities, however, are further round the coast at **PLATÁNA**, where another river is flanked by a line of older houses, many with rooms or flats to rent.

Despite its name, the extremely functional port of **PARALÍA KÝMIS** has no real beach, and is not a particularly congenial place to be stuck overnight waiting for a ferry to Skýros. The most substantial and traditional **taverna** is *Spanos/To Egeo*, at the south end of the front, while *To Valanti* is also reasonable and the sweet little *Rock Club* plays eclectic sounds; there are just two **hotels**, *Coralli* (☎02220/22 212, ℻23 355; ❹) and *Beis* (☎02220/22 604, ℻22 870; ❹).

Most travellers get to **KÝMI** (the main ferry port to Skýros) by bus, which takes the inland route via Ayía Thékla. The upper part of town is built on a green ridge overlooking both the sea and Paralía Kými, 4km below. Note that all buses deposit you in the upper town except for the one or two daily that connect with the ferry. At the bottom of the town, on the harbour-bound road, you can visit the **Folklore Museum**, which has an improbably large collection of costumes, household and agricultural implements and old photos recording the doings of Kymians both locally and in the US, where there's a huge community. Among the emigrants was Dr George Papanikolaou, deviser of the "Pap" cervical smear test, and there's a statue honouring him up in the upper-town platía, where you might ask about **rooms**. There are some good **tavernas** like *To Balkoni*, on the main road towards the shore, with its superb view, where you can sample the products of the local vineyards.

To get up into the rugged country west of Kými, you must negotiate jeep tracks through the forest, or return to Halkídha for the bus service up to **STENÍ**, a large and beautiful village at the foot of Mount Dhírfys. The village has a few cheap *psistariés* and two **hotels**, the *Dirfys* (☎02280/51 217; ❸) and the *Steni* (☎02280/51 221; ❸). It's a good area for hiking, most notably up the peaks of Dhírfys and Xirovoúni, and beyond to the isolated beach hamlets of Hiliádhou and Ayía Iríni, though you'll need a specialist hiking guide to do this (see "Books", p.607).

Southeast Évvia

The extension of Évvia southeast of Lépoura, so narrow that you can sometimes glimpse the sea on both sides, has a flavour very distinct from the rest of the island. Often bleak and windswept, it forms a geological unit with neighbouring Ándhros, with shared slates and marble. Ethnically, the south also has much in common with that northernmost Cyclade: both were heavily settled by Albanian immigrants from the early fifteenth century onwards, and Arvanítika – a **medieval dialect** of Albanian – was until recently the first language of the remoter villages here. Even non-Arvanítika speakers often betray their ancestry by their startlingly fair colouring and aquiline features. For a place so close to Athens, the south is often surprisingly untouched by modernity; some of the houses have yet to lose their original slate roofs. Others still lack electricity, and the few fields on the steep slopes are far more often worked by donkeys and horses than by farm machinery.

Immediately southeast of Lépoura, most maps persist in showing the lake of Dhýstos in bright blue. In fact, the lake area has been almost totally drained and reclaimed as rich farmland, much to the detriment of the migratory birds who used to stop off here, and to the annoyance of Greek and foreign environmentalists who would prefer that they still did so. Atop the almost perfectly conical hill in the centre of the flat basin are the sparse fifth-century BC ruins of **ancient Dystos** and a subsequent medieval citadel, hard to explore because the surroundings are so swampy.

Beyond the Dhýstos plain, the main road continues along the mountainous spine of the island to Kárystos at the southern end of the paved road system and bus line. If you have your own transport, it's worth stopping off at **STÝRA**, above which are a cluster of **Dhrakóspita** (Dragon Houses), signposted at the north edge of the village and reached by track, then trail. They are so named because only mythological beings were thought capable of shifting into place their enormous masonry blocks. Their origins and uses have yet to be definitively established. The most convincing theory suggests that they are sixth-century BC temples built by immigrants or slaves from Asia Minor working in the nearby marble and slate quarries.

The shore annexe of **NÉA STÝRA**, 5km downhill from the hill village, is a fairly standard package resort, worth knowing about only for its handy ferry connection to Ayía Marína (which gives access to ancient Ramnous) on the Attic peninsula. Much the same can be said for **MARMÁRI**, 19km south, except in this case the ferry link is with Rafina. Here the smart *Hotel Delfíni* (☏02240/31 296, ⓕ32 300; ❸) is surprisingly good value and there are a few decent places to eat; try the *Zygos mezedhopolío,* which serves cheap fish in a nice atmosphere. The road between Marmári and Kárystos is now more or less finished, completing the "superhighway" and allowing you to enjoy the nether reaches of the island as you cruise down to its last major settlement.

Kárystos and around

At first sight **KÁRYSTOS** is a rather boring grid (courtesy of nineteenth-century Bavarian town-planners), which ends abruptly to east and west and is studded with modern buildings. King Otho liked the site so much that he contemplated transferring the Greek capital here, and there are still some graceful Neoclassical buildings dating from that period. Kárystos improves with prolonged acquaintance, though you're unlikely to stay for more than a few days. What it can offer is the superb (if often windy) beach to the west, the smaller, sandier **Psilí Ámmos** ten-minutes' walk to the east and a lively, genuine working-port atmosphere. Only one plot of fenced-in foundations, in the central bazaar, bears out the town's ancient provenance, and the oldest obvious structure is the fourteenth-century Venetian **Bourtzi** (locked except for occasional summer-evening art exhibitions) on the waterfront. This small tower is all that remains of once-extensive fortifications. Every evening the shore road is blocked with a gate at this point to allow an undisturbed promenade by the locals. There is a small but interesting **archeological museum** (Tues–Sun 8am–3pm; €1.50) inside the Cultural Centre opposite the Bourtzi, displaying finds from the local area – mostly statues and temple carvings, plus a few smaller votive objects.

Practicalities

Rafina-based **ferries** and **hydrofoils** also serve Kárystos, though services via Marmári are more frequent; **buses** arrive inland, above the central platía and below the National Bank, near a tiny combination grill/ticket office labelled KTEL. This has information on the extremely infrequent (once daily at best) departures to the remote villages of the Kavodóro (Kafiréas) cape to the east. Information on the August wine festival and sightseeing in the region, including walking routes, is provided by the friendly tourist office in a kiosk near the quay.

Finding affordable **accommodation** is not a big problem. The most central is the *Als* (☏02240/22 202, ⓕ25 002; ❸), right opposite the quay, although it may get noisy in high season. Other options are the big *Galaxy* (☏02240/22 600, ⓕ22 463; ❹) on the west side of the waterfront, the plush *Apollon Suite* (☏02240/22 045, ⓕ22 049, ⓔapollon-suite@yahoo.com; ❺) on Psilí Ámmos beach, and the excellent *Karystion* (☏02240/22 391, ⓕ22 727; ❹), which does mouthwatering breakfasts and is situated in the park beyond the Bourtzi on the shore road. Another strategy is to follow up signs in restaurant windows advertising **rooms** inland.

You're also spoilt for choice when **eating out**, as Kárystos must have more restaurants than the rest of Évvia put together. Good choices include the *Kavo Doro*, a friendly and reasonable taverna on Párodos Sakhtoúri one block west of the square, serving *mayireftá; Ta Kalamia*, at the west end of the esplanade by the start of the beach, a cheap, filling and popular lunchtime option; and English-speaking *Ta Ovreïka*, in the old Jewish quarter at Sakhtoúri 114, with both Greek and "international" cuisine as well as breakfasts. On the road running up from the *Als* there are several fine *psistariés,* serving the local lamb and goat for which Kárystos is renowned.

Mount Óhi

The obvious excursion from Kárystos is inland towards **Mount Óhi** (1399m) Évvia's highest peak after Dhírfys and Xirovoúni. **MÝLI**, a fair-sized village around a spring-fed oasis, 3km straight inland, makes a good first stop, with its few tavernas. Otherwise, the medieval castle of **Castel Rosso** beckons above, a twenty-minute climb up from the main church (longer in the frequent, howling gales). Inside, the castle is a total ruin, except for an Orthodox **chapel of Profítis Ilías** built over the Venetians' water cistern, but the sweeping views over the sea and the town make the trip worthwhile.

Behind, the ridges of Óhi are as lunar and inhospitable as the broad plain around Kárystos is fertile. From Mýli, it's a three-hour-plus hike up the largely bare slopes, mostly by a path cutting across the new road, strewn with unfinished granite columns, abandoned almost two thousand years ago. The path passes a little-used alpine club shelter (fed by spring water) and yet another **dhrakóspito**, even more impressive than the three smaller ones at Stýra. Built of enormous schist slabs, seemingly sprouting from the mountain, this one is popularly supposed to be haunted.

From Halkídha to Límni

The main road due north from Halkídha crosses a few kilometres of flat farmland and salt marsh on either side of the refugee settlement of Néa Artáki, after which it climbs steeply through forested hills and the **Dhervéni gorge**, gateway to the north of Évvia. With your own transport, you can take a pleasant detour along the road left before Psákhna to the long pebbly beach of **Paralía Politikón**, dotted with places to stay or eat.

The village of **PROKÓPI** lies beyond the narrows, in a valley defined by the rich and beautiful woods that make it famous. A counterpoint, in the village itself, is the ugly 1960s pilgrimage church of **Saint John the Russian**, which holds the saint's relics. The "Russian" was actually a Ukrainian soldier, captured by the Ottomans in the early eighteenth century and taken to Turkey where he died. According to locals, his mummified body began to promote miracles, and the saint's relics were brought here by Orthodox Greeks from Cappadocian Prokópi (today Ürgüp) in the 1923 population exchange – Évvian Prokópi is still referred to by the locals as Akhmétaga, the name of the old Turkish fiefdom here that was bought by an English nobleman, Edward Noel, a cousin of Lord Byron's, right after the War of Independence. His descendants the Noel-Bakers now run summer courses in various crafts, based in the manor house.

Following a shady, stream-fed glen for the 8km north of Prokópi, you suddenly emerge at **Mandoúdhi**, much the biggest village in the north of the island, though now squarely in the doldrums following the collapse of the local magnesite industry; ignore signs or depictions on certain maps of a beach at Paralía Mandoúdhi, which is nothing more than abandoned quarries and crushing plants. The closest serviceable beach is at **Paralía Kírinthos**, better known as **Krýa Vrýssi** (take a right-hand turning off the main road, 3km beyond Mandoúdhi). At the coast, a river and an inlet bracket a small beach, with the headland south of the river supporting the extremely sparse remains of **ancient Kirinthos**. The hamlet of Kírinthos, just past Mandoúdhi, has some visitors, owing to the craft school there.

Back on the main road, a fork at Strofyliá, 8km north of Mandoúdhi, offers a choice of routes: continue north to the coastal resorts that curl round the end of the island (see opposite), east to Pýli and then south to some unspoiled beaches on the way to Cape Sarakíniko, or head west for Límni.

Límni

If you're hunting for a place to stay, **LÍMNI**, on the west coast 19km from Strofiliá, is by far the most practical and attractive base north of Halkídha. The largely Neoclassical, tile-roofed town, built from the wealth engendered by nineteenth-century shipping prowess, is the most appealing on the island, with serviceable beaches and a famous convent nearby. A small **folk art museum** features pottery, coins and sculpture fragments, as well as local costumes, fabrics and furniture.

Buses from Halkídha stop at the north side of the quay. Límni has a **post office** and **two banks**, all inland just off the main through-road into town from Strofiliá.

As yet, Límni gets few package tours, and **accommodation** is usually available in its rooms or hotels, except during August. At the extreme southern, quieter, end of the waterfront, the *Límni* (℡02270/31 316; ❷) is good value, with singles and doubles; the *Plaza* (℡02270/31 235; ❷), beside the bus stop, is very similar, but has no singles and gets some noise from nocturnal revels outside. Smarter rooms with TV can be rented at *Livaditis* (℡02270/31 640; ❹), above *Pyrofanis*, an ouzerí beyond the *Plaza*. The best **place to eat** in terms of setting, menu and popularity is *O Platanos* (under the enormous quayside plane tree) with the adjacent *Avra* not far behind. Other local favourites are *Kallitsis* inland from the waterfront, and *Lambros* and *O David* on the way to Katoúnia beach to the south of town.

Around Límni

There are no recommendable beaches in Límni itself, though if you continue 2.5km northwest from the town you reach the gravel strand of **Kohýli**, with a basic but leafy **campsite** out on the cape, 500m beyond mid-beach. Here there are some congenial places to stay, most notably *Denis House* (℡02270/31 787; ❺) and the more luxurious *Ostria* (℡02270/32 247; ❺), which has a pool and includes breakfast.

ROVIÉS, some 14km west of Límni, doesn't really stand out, but with its medieval tower, rooms, hotels, grid of weekenders' apartments and services, it's the last place of any sort along the scenic coast road to Loutrá Edhipsoú.

The outstanding excursion from Límni is 7km south (under your own steam) to the **convent of Ayíou Nikoláou Galatáki**, superbly set on the wooded slopes of Mount Kandhíli, overlooking the north Evvian Gulf. To get there, veer up and left at the unsigned fork off the coast road; there's no formal scheme for visiting, but don't show up in the early afternoon or around sunset as the gates will be shut. Though much rebuilt since its original Byzantine foundation atop a Poseidon temple, the convent retains a thirteenth-century tower built to guard against pirates, and a crypt. One of a dozen or so nuns will show you frescoes in the *katholikón* dating from the principal sixteenth-century renovation. Especially vivid, on the right of the narthex, is the *Entry of the Righteous into Paradise*: the righteous ascend a perilous ladder to be crowned by angels and received by Christ, while the wicked miss the rungs and fall into the maw of Leviathan.

Below Ayíou Nikoláou Galatáki, and easily combined with it to make a full half-day outing, are the pebble-and-sand beaches of **Glýfa**, arguably the best on this part of Évvia's southwest-facing coast. There are several in succession, leading up to the very base of Mount Kandhíli, some reachable by paths, the last few only by boat. The shore is remarkably clean, considering the number of summer campers who pitch tents here for weeks on end; a single roadside spring, 2km before the coast, is the only facility in the whole zone.

Northern coastal resorts

Returning to the junction at Strofiliá, take the main road north for 8km to **AYÍA ÁNNA** (locally and universally elided to *Ayiánna*), which has long enjoyed the unofficial status of Évvia's most **folkloric village**, by virtue of traditional costumes worn by the older women and an assiduous local ethnographer, Dimitris Settas, who died in 1989. The place itself is nothing extraordinary, and most passers-by are interested in the prominently marked turn-off for **Angáli beach**, 5km east. This is billed as the area's best, and it's sandy enough, the low hills behind lending a little drama, but like this entire coast it's exposed and can gather rubbish. A frontage road, set back 200m or so, is lined by a few kilometres of anonymous villas and apartments, with the "village" at the north end. The *Agali Hotel* (T02270/97 104, F97 067; ❺) is a congenial place to stay, and there is also a campsite. Horseriding on the beach is a well-advertised and popular diversion.

Ten kilometres north of Ayía Ánna, a side road heads downhill for 6km, past the village of Kotsikiá, to **Paralía Kotsikiás**. The small cove with its taverna and rooms serves primarily as a fishing-boat anchorage, and its tiny, seaweed-strewn beach is of little interest. **Psaropoúli beach**, 2km below Vassiliká village (13km north of the Kotsikiá turn-off), is more useable in its three-kilometre length, but like Ayía Ánna it is scruffy and shadeless, with a smattering of rooms, self-catering units and tavernas not imparting much sense of community. If you choose to stay, you can't do much better than *Motel Canadiana* (T02260/43 274; ❷), where the road down meets the seafront. **Ellinká**, the next signposted beach, lies just 800m below its namesake village inland; it's far smaller than Angáli or Psaropoúli, but cleaner and certainly the most picturesque spot on this coast, with a church-capped islet offshore as a target to swim to. The approach driveway has a very limited number of facilities: a minimarket, one taverna and a few studios. *Motel Aigaio* (T02260/42 262; ❸) is as good as any for a stay.

Beyond Ellinká, the road (and bus line) skirts the northern tip of Évvia to curl southwest towards **PÉFKI**, a seaside resort mobbed with Greeks in summer, which straggles for some 2km along a mediocre beach. The best **restaurants**, near the north end of this strip, include *Ouzeri Ta Thalassina* and *Psitopolio O Thomas*, while *Zaharoplastio O Peristeras* proffers decadent desserts. **Accommodation** is the usual Évvian mix of self-catering units and a few seaside hotels such as *Galini* (T02260/41 208, F41 650; ❹) and *Myrtia* (T02260/41 202; ❸), all resolutely pitched at mainlanders; the **campsite**, *Camping Pefki*, is 2km north of town behind the beach, rather pricey and geared to people with caravans. Hydrofoils for the Sporades depart from here at most once daily in the morning during summer only.

The next resort (14km southwest), **OREÍ**, is a low-key fishing village, whose cafés are favoured by those in the know as the best places to watch the sunset. It has a fine statue of a Hellenistic bull, hauled up from the sea in 1965. Nearby Néos Pýrgos beach has a selection of rooms and restaurants. Some 7km further along the coast, **AYIÓKAMBOS** has a frequent ferry connection to Glýfa on the mainland opposite, from where there are buses to Vólos. Ayiókambos is surprisingly pleasant considering its port function, with a patch of beach, two or three tavernas and a few rooms for rent.

The trans-island bus route ends 14km south of Ayiókambos at **LOUTRÁ EDHIPSOÚ**, which attracts older Greeks, who come to bathe at the **spas** renowned since antiquity for curing everything from gallstones to depression. The spas themselves are cheap (€1 for 20min) and quite an experience. The vast number of hotels, some old and creaky, which service the summer influx means good deals can be had off-season. The classy 1920s-vintage *Egli* (℡02260/22 215, ℉22 886; ❸) on the seafront is a good choice, while you can really push the boat out at the 1897-built *Thermae Sylla* (℡02260/60 100, ℉22 055, ⓦwww.thermaesylla.gr; ❻), a French-style monument atop what's claimed to be the best thermal spring in Greece, thoroughly overhauled in 1998. More affordable options in the side streets near the port are *Valar's* (℡02260/22 278, ℉23 419; ❸) and the more modern *Lito* (℡02260/22 081; ❸). There is an abundance of tavernas strung along the front; try the leafy restaurant of the *Egli* or the traditional *To Fagadhiko tou Barous*, which offers a wide selection of mezédhes.

There are less-regimented **hot springs** at **Yiáltra**, 15km west around the head of Edhipsós bay, where the water boils up on the rocky beach, warming the shallows to comfortable bath temperature. From Loutrá Edhipsoú, the coast road heads southeast to Límni.

Travel details

Following the recent shake-ups in the Greek sea-transport industry, all ferry services out of Vólos and Áyios Konstandínos to the northern Sporades, as well as hydrofoils, are run solely by Hellas (Minoan) Flying Dolphins or its subsidiaries. Hydrofoils – and the catamaran between Áyios Konstandínos and Thessaloníki, via the islands – only run reliably between early June and mid-September. These craft are, as ever, pricier than the ferries, but cut journey times virtually in half. Kými-to-Skýros is another, over-priced monopoly sailing served by a single ferry.

Skiáthos, Skópelos and Alónissos

Ferries

NB Departure frequencies given are for the June-to-mid-Sept period, and are valid in reverse sense. Áyios Konstandínos to: Skiáthos (2–3 daily; 3hr); Skópelos (1–2 daily; 5hr); Alónissos (1 daily, 6hr).

Vólos to: Skiáthos (3–4 daily; 3hr); Skópelos (2–3 daily; 4hr); Alónissos (1–2 daily; 5hr). NB This is the most consistent service out of season, and always the cheapest.

Catamaran

Daily from July to mid-Sept, and 5 times weekly in June, there's a catamaran which typically leaves Thessaloníki at 1.45pm, calls at Alónissos, Skópelos and Skiáthos between 4.20 and 5.20pm, doubling back from Áyios Konstandínos at 6.30pm through all these islands in reverse, arriving back in Thessaloníki just before midnight. This is a small "Flying Cat" and no vehicles are carried.

Hydrofoils

Áyios Konstandínos to: Skiáthos, Glóssa, Skópelos and Alónissos (1 daily at 10am; sets off from Alónissos same day at 6.30am). Tríkeri (Pílion) to: Vólos, Skiáthos, Skópelos (both ports) and Alónissos (1–2 daily).

Paleó Tríkeri Island to: Vólos, Skiathos, Skópelos (both ports) and Alónissos (1 daily) Vólos to: Skiáthos, Skópelos Town (4–5 daily); Glóssa, Alónissos (2–3 daily).

Flights

Athens to: Skiáthos (mid-June to mid-Sept 1 daily, otherwise 3 weekly; 50min).

Skýros

Ferries

Skýros is served from Kými (2hr) by conventional ferry, the *Lykomidis*. Services are at least twice daily mid-June to mid-Sept (usually at around 11am and 5–6pm), once daily (6–7pm) the rest of the year; there may be an additional 9pm boat at summer weekends – ☎02220/22 522 for current information. There is a connecting bus service for the late-afternoon boat, from the Liossíon 260 terminal in Athens (departs 10am & 2.45pm). Once or twice a week in July and Aug only, there is a rather useful long-haul ferry connecting Skýros with Skiáthos and Thessaloníki to the north, and Iráklio (Crete) to the far south, via Sýros, Páros, Mýkonos and Thíra in the Cyclades; this is typically run by G&A Ferries.

Flights

Athens to: Skýros (mid-June to mid-Sept 2 weekly; 40min).

Évvia

Buses

Athens (Liossíon 260 terminal) to: Halkídha (every 30min 5.30am–9.30pm; 1hr 30min); Kými (5 daily; 3hr 15min).

Halkídha to: Kárystos (2 daily; 3hr); Kými (8 daily; 1hr 45min); Límni (5 daily; 1hr 30min); Loutrá Edhipsoú (4 daily; 3hr).

Trains

Athens (Laríssis station) to: Halkídha (19 daily; 1hr 30min).

Ferries

Arkítsa to: Loutrá Edhipsoú (at least hourly July–Sept 15, every 1–2hr otherwise, last at 10–11pm/8–9pm; 45min).
Ayía Marína to: Néa Stýra (summer 12–14 daily; 45min); Alymyropótamos dock (summer 1 daily; 45min).

Glýfa to: Ayiókambos (8–11 daily summer, 4 in winter; last sailing at 8.30pm/5pm; 30min).
Rafína to: Kárystos (Mon–Fri 1 daily in evening, Sat & Sun 2 daily; 1hr 15min); Marmári (8–9 daily; 45min).
Skála Oropoú to: Erétria (March–Oct every 30min 6.45am–7.45pm, then hourly to 11pm; 30min).

Hydrofoils

Péfki to: Skiáthos, Skópelos and Alónissos (June 4 weekly, July to mid-Sept 1 daily, in the evening). NB Connecting buses from Athens run to Rafína (every 30min; 1hr), Ayía Marína (5 daily; 1hr 15min) and Skála Oropoú (hourly; 1hr 30min) all from the Mavromatéon terminal, and to Arkítsa and Glýfa from the Liossíon 260 terminal.

The Ionian Islands

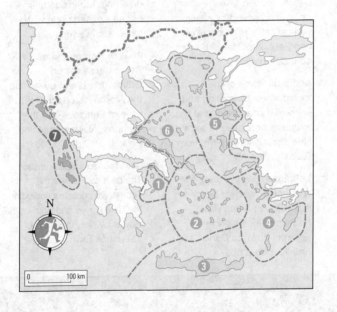

CHAPTER 7

Highlights

* **Kérkyra (Corfu) Town**
Venetian fortresses, beautiful
churches, fine museums and
appealing architecture,
Corfu's capital is the cultural
heart of the Ionians. See
p.479

* **Perouládhes, Corfu** This
beach, shaded till early afternoon and backed by sheer
vertical cliffs, is an excellent
hang-out, especially off season. See p.490

* **Andípaxi** Some of the
Ionian's best swimming and
snorkelling can be had at the
exquisite beaches of Paxi's
little sister on a day-trip from
Gaïos. See p.500

* **Lefkádha's west coast** The
archipelago's finest beaches
run from Ai Nikítas via
Káthisma, Yialós and
Egremní down to Pórto
Katsíki. See p.505

* **Mount Énos, Kefalloniá** The
highest point in the Ionians
boasts its own species of fir
and has stunning vistas of sea
and distant land. See p.507

* **Melissáni Cave, Kefalloniá**
See dappled sunlight on the
water amid rock formations
on a boat trip inside this
once-enclosed underwater
cave. See p.510

* **Ith́áki's Homeric sites**
Relive the myths on
Odysseus's island by visiting
the Arethoússa Spring, the
cave of Eumaeus and the
Nymphs, Alalkomenae and
Pelikáta Hill. See p.517

* **Boat tour round Zákynthos**
The best way to see the
impressive coastline, including
the Blue Caves and Shipwreck
Bay, is by daily cruise from
Zákynthos Town. See p.522

7

The Ionian Islands

T he six **Ionian** islands, shepherding their satellites down the west coast of the mainland, float on the haze of the Adriatic, their green, even lush, silhouettes coming as a shock to those more used to the stark outlines of the Aegean. The fertility of the land is a direct result of the heavy rains that sweep over the archipelago – and especially Corfu – from October to March, so if you visit at this time, come prepared.

The islands were the Homeric realm of Odysseus, centred on Ithaca (modern Itháki) and here alone of all modern Greek territory (except for Lefkádha) the Ottomans never held sway. After the fall of Byzantium, possession passed to the **Venetians** and the islands became a keystone in Venice's maritime empire from 1386 until its collapse in 1797. Most of the population must have remained immune to the establishment of Italian as the official language and the arrival of Roman Catholicism, but Venetian influence remains evident in the architecture of the island capitals, despite damage from a series of earthquakes.

On Corfu, the Venetian legacy is mixed with that of the **British**, who imposed a military "protectorate" over the Ionian islands at the close of the Napoleonic Wars, before ceding the archipelago to Greece in 1864. There is, however, no question of the islanders' essential Greekness: the poet Dhionyssios Solomos, author of the national anthem, hailed from the Ionians, as did Nikos Mantzelos, who provided the music, and the first Greek president, Ioannis Kapodhistrias.

Accommodation price codes

Throughout the book we've categorized accommodation according to the following **price codes**, which denote the cheapest available double room in high season. All prices are for the room only, except where otherwise indicated. Many hotels, especially those in category ④ and over, include breakfast in the price; you'll need to check this when booking. During low season, rates can drop by more than fifty percent, especially if you are staying for three or more nights. Exceptions are during the Christmas and Easter weeks when you'll pay high-season prices. Single rooms, where available, cost around seventy percent of the price of a double.

① Up to €24	④ €43–58
② €24–33	⑤ €59–72
③ €34–42	⑥ €73 and upwards

Note: Youth hostels typically charge €7–9 for a dormitory bed.
For more accommodation details, see pp.52–54.

Today, **tourism** is the dominating influence, especially on **Corfu** (Kérkyra), which was one of the first Greek islands established on the package-holiday circuit. Parts of its coastline are among the few stretches in Greece with development to match the Spanish *costas*, and in summer even its distinguished old capital, Kérkyra Town, wilts beneath the onslaught. However, the island is large enough to retain many of its charms and is perhaps the most scenically beautiful of the group. Parts of **Zákynthos** (Zante) – which with Corfu has the Ionians' most oversubscribed beaches – have also

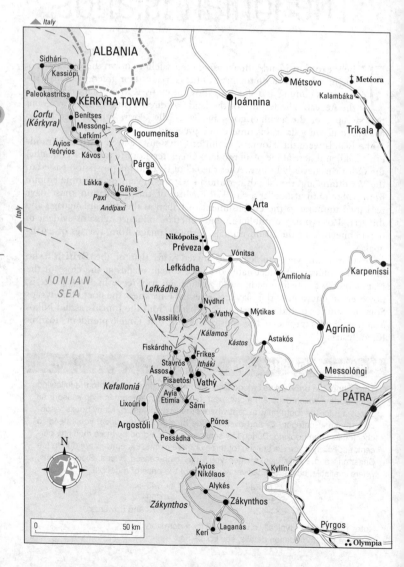

gone down the same tourist path, but elsewhere the island's pace and scale of development is a lot less intense. Little **Páxi** is rather tricky to reach and lacks the water to support large-scale hotels, but still gets surprisingly packed in August, while **Lefkádha** – which is connected to the mainland by a causeway and "boat bridge" – has, so far at least, quite a low-key straggle of tourist centres and only two major resorts, despite boasting some excellent beaches. Perhaps the most rewarding duo for island-hopping are **Kefalloniá** and **Itháki**, the former with a series of "real towns" and a life in large part independent of tourism, the latter, Odysseus's rugged capital, protected by an absence of sand. The Ionian islands' claims to Homeric significance are manifested in the countless bars, restaurants and streets named after characters in the *Odyssey*, including the "nimble-witted" hero himself, Penelope, Nausicaa, Calypso and Cyclops.

Corfu (Kérkyra)

Between the heel of Italy and the west coast of mainland Greece, green, mountainous **Corfu (Kérkyra)** was one of the first Greek islands to attract mass tourism in the 1960s. Indiscriminate exploitation turned parts into eyesores, but much of the island still consists of olive groves, mountain or woodland. The majority of package holidays are based in the most developed resorts, but unspoiled terrain is often only a few minutes' walk away.

Corfu is thought to have been the model for Prospero's and Miranda's place of exile in Shakespeare's *The Tempest*, and was certainly known to writers like Spenser and Milton and – more recently – Lear and Miller, plus Gerald and Lawrence Durrell. Lawrence Durrell's *Prospero's Cell* evokes the island's "delectable landscape", still evident in some of the best beaches of the whole archipelago.

The staggering amount of accommodation (over 5000 places) on the island means that competition keeps prices down even in high season, at least in many resorts outside of Kérkyra Town. Prices at restaurants and in shops also tend to be a little lower than average for the Ionians.

Kérkyra (Corfu) Town

The capital, **KÉRKYRA (CORFU) TOWN**, was renovated for an EU summit in 1994, and is now one of the most elegant island capitals in the whole of Greece. Although many of its finest buildings were destroyed by Nazi bombers in World War II, its two massive forts, the sixteenth-century church of Áyios Spyrídhon and buildings dating from French and British administrations remain intact. As the island's major port of entry by ferry or plane, Kérkyra Town is packed in summer.

Arrivals, information and services

Ferries and hydrofoils to and from Italy, the mainland (Igoumenítsa and Pátra) and Paxí dock at the New Port (Néo Limáni) west of the Néo Froúrio (New Fort). The Old Port (Paleó Limáni), east of the New Port, is used for day-excursions. Most of the ferry offices are on the main road opposite the New Port; ferries to Italy or south towards Pátra become very busy in summer and booking is advisable. The port authority (✆06610/32 655) can advise on services.

CORFU (KÉRKYRA)

Erikoussa

Italy

ALBANIA

Mathráki & Othoní

Sidhári

Perouládhes

Astrakeri

Almyrós

Cape Áyias
Ekaterínis

Avliótes

Karousádhes

Ródha

Aharávi

Loútses

Kassiópi

Áyios Stéfanos

Maghouládhes

Períthia

Avláki

Áyios Stéfanos
Kerasiá
Kouloúra
Kalámi

Aríllas

Agrafí

Epískepsi

Kraviá

Afiónas

Strinýlas

Mt.
Pandokrátor

Áy. Yeóryios

Spartýlas

Agní

Makrádhes

Troumpéta

Nissáki

Angelókastro

Lákones

Pyrgi

Paleokastrítsa

Skriperó

Ípsos

Barbáti

Liapádhes

Dhassiá
Dhafníla

Vídhos

Gouviá
Kondókali

Érmones

Vátos

Potamós

KÉRKYRA
TOWN

Myrtiótissa
Glyfádha

Pélekas

Kanóni
Pondikoníssi
Pérama

Achillion

Gastoúri

Áyios Górdhis

Áyii
Dhéka

Benítses

Pendáti

Paramónas

Ano
Moraïtika

Moraïtika
Messongí

Pendanísia

Áyios Matthéos

Prasoúdhi

Ano
Messongí

Boúkari

Gardhíki
Pýrgos

Halikoúna

Korissía
Lagoon

Línia

Petrití

Aryirádhes

Lefkími

Issós

Áyios
Yeóryios

Perivóli

Ayía Varvára

Kritiká

Neohóri

Sparterá

Kávos

Ay. Górdhis
Paleohoríou

Arkoudhílas

Cape
Asprókavos

Igoumenítsa

Igoumenítsa

Paxí & Pátra

N

0   10 km

The **airport** is 2km south of the city centre. There are no airport buses, although local **blue buses** #5 and #6 can be flagged at the junction where the airport approach meets the main road (500m). It's a thirty-minute walk on flat terrain into town (follow the road running beside the *Hotel Bretagne* opposite the junction for the shortest route or turn right then follow the sea road). **Taxis** charge around €6 (but agree the fare in advance) or phone ☎06610/33

811 for a radio cab.

The **tourist office** (Mon–Fri 8am–2pm; ☎06610/37 520) on the corner of Vouleftón and Mantzárou has accommodation and transport details. The **post office** is on the corner of Alexándhras and Zafiropoúlou (Mon–Fri 7.30am–8pm). Of the town's several internet cafés, the best value are *Recorder*, P. Konstandá 1 (Mon–Sat 9am–2pm & 6–11pm; ☎06610/46 549), just off Platía San Rocco, and *Hobby Net*, Solomoú 32 (daily 10am–11pm; ☎06610/44 475), near the Old Port.

Getting around

Corfu's **bus** service radiates from the capital. There are **two** terminals: the islandwide green bus service is based on Avramíou, and the suburban blue bus system, which also serves nearby resorts such as Benítses and Dhassiá, is based in Platía San Rocco (Platía G. Theotóki). Islandwide services stop between 6 and 8pm, suburban ones at around 10pm. Printed English timetables are available for both and can be picked up at the tourist office. Avramíou also serves Athens and Thessaloníki, and sells combined bus-and-ferry tickets. Major **ferry** lines have franchises on Ethnikís Andistásis opposite the New Port: Minoan (☎06610/25 000, ☎46 555), Strintzis (☎06610/81 222, ☎26 660), ANEK (☎06610/24 504, ☎36 935), Fragline (☎06610/38 089, ☎35 416), Ventouris (☎06610/32 664) and Adriatica (☎06610/38 089). The Petrakis agency (☎06610/38 690, ☎26 555) runs the **hydrofoil** service to Paxí and Igoumenítsa, as well as tours to Albania, Párga and other Ionian islands, which it sells at much cheaper rates than the travel agents in the resorts.

Cars can also be rented from international agencies at the airport or in town; try Avis, Ethnikís Andistásis 42 (☎06610/24 404), Budget, Venízelou 22 (☎06610/49 100; airport ☎06610/44 017) or Hertz (☎06610/33 547). Among local companies, Sunrise, Ethnikís Andistásis 14 (☎06610/44 325) rents out cars, and **bikes** can be rented from Easy Rider, I. Theotóki 128 (☎06610/43 026), both in the New Port.

Accommodation

Accommodation in Kérkyra Town is busy all year round, and fairly expensive. Room owners often meet mainland and international ferries, or you can try the Room Owners' Association, near the tourist office at Polylá 24 (Mon–Fri 9am–1.30pm & 6–8pm; ☎06610/26 133, ☎23 403). Budget travellers might best head straight for the nearest **campsite** at Dhassiá (see p.487).

Arcadion, Kapodhistríou 44 ☎06610/37 670, ☎45 087, ☎arcadion@otenet.gr. Has moved upmarket after renovation. In a central setting so street noise can be a problem. ⑥

Astron, Dónzelot 15 ☎06610/39 505, ☎33 708, ☎hotel_astron@hol.gr. Tastefully renovated hotel in the Old Port. Good deals available outside the short peak season. All rooms with fan and optional air-con. ⑥

Atlantis, Xenofóndos Stratigoú 48 ☎06610/35 560, ☎46 480, ☎atlanker@mail.otenet.gr. Large and spacious air-conditioned hotel but rather lacking in character. ⑥

Bella Venezia, Zambéli 4 ☎06610/46 500, ☎20 708, ☎belven@hol.gr. Smart, yellow Neoclassical

building just behind the *Cavalieri*, with all the *Cavalieri*'s comforts, but cheaper. ⑤

Cavalieri, Kapodhistríou 4 ☎06610/39 041, ☎39 283. Smart and friendly, with all mod cons, great views and a roof bar open to the public. ⑥

Europa, Yitsiáli 10 ☎06610/39 304. Small family hotel one block back from the New Port. One of the best deals around. Some rooms have TV. ❸

Hermes, Markorá 14 ☎06610/39 268. An old favourite in a busy part of town. The cheapest rooms have shared bathrooms. Overlooks the noisy market. ❸

Ionion, Xenofóndos Stratigoú 46 ☎06610/39 915, ☎44 690. Conveniently located in the New Port, this is a large, functional, friendly and very reasonably priced hotel. Ceiling fans in all rooms. ❹

Phoenix, Khryssostómou Smýrnis 2, Garítsa

ⓣ 06610/42 290, ⓕ 42 990. Small, stylish hotel between the airport and the seafront. Good value, with complimentary breakfast. ❹

The Town

Kérkyra Town comprises a number of distinct areas. The **Historic Centre**, the area enclosed by the Old Port and the two forts, consists of several smaller districts: **Campiello**, the oldest, sits on the hill above the harbour; **Kofinéta** stretches towards the Spianádha (Esplanade); **Áyii Apóstoli** runs west of the Mitrópolis (orthodox) cathedral; while tucked in beside the Néo Froúrio are **Ténedos** and what remains of the old **Jewish quarter**. These districts form the core of the old town, and their tall, narrow alleys conceal some of Corfu's most beautiful architecture. **Mandoúki**, beyond the Old Port, is the commercial and dormitory area for the port, and is worth exploring as a living quarter of the city, away from the tourism racket. The town's **commercial area** lies inland from the Spianádha, roughly between Yeoryíou Theotóki, Alexándhras and Kapodhistríou streets, with shops and boutiques around Voulgaréos and Yeoryíou Theotóki and off Platía Theotóki. Tucked behind Platía San Rocco and Odhós Theotóki is the old morning **market** which sells fish and farm produce.

The most obvious sights are the forts, the **Paleó Froúrio** and **Néo Froúrio**, whose designations (*paleó* – "old", *néo* – "new") are a little misleading, since what you see of the older structure was begun by the Byzantines in the mid-twelfth century, just a hundred years before the Venetians began work on the newer citadel. They have both been damaged and modified by various occupiers and besiegers, the last contribution being the Neoclassical shrine of **Saint George**, built by the British in the middle of Paleó Froúrio during the 1840s. Looming above the Old Port, the Néo Froúrio (daily 9am–10pm; €1.50) is the more interesting of the two architecturally. The entrance, at the back of the fort, gives onto cellars, dungeons and battlements, with excellent views over the town and bay; there's a small gallery and café at the summit. The Paleó Froúrio (daily 9am–7pm; €2.40) is not as well preserved and contains some incongruous modern structures, but has an interesting Byzantine museum just inside the gate, and even more stunning views from the central Land Tower. It also hosts daily son et lumière shows.

Just west of the Paleó Froúrio, the **Listón**, an arcaded street built during the French occupation by the architect of the Rue de Rivoli in Paris, and the green **Spianádha** (Esplanade) it overlooks, are the focus of town life. The cricket pitch, still in use at the northern end of the Spianádha, is another British legacy, while at the southern end the **Maitland Rotunda** was built to honour the first British High Commissioner of Corfu and the Ionian islands. The neighbouring statue of Ioannis Kapodhistrias celebrates the local hero and statesman (1776–1831) who led the diplomatic efforts for independence and was made Greece's first president in 1827. At the far northern end of the Listón, the nineteenth-century **Palace of SS Michael and George**, a solidly British edifice built as the residence of their High Commissioner (one of the last of whom was the future British prime minister William Gladstone), and later used as a palace by the Greek monarchy. The former state rooms house the **Asiatic Museum** (Tues–Sun 8.30am–3pm; free) which is a must for aficionados of Oriental culture, although it's currently undergoing some reorganization. Amassed by Corfiot diplomat Gregorios Manos (1850–1929) and others, it includes Noh theatre masks, woodcuts, wood and brass statuettes, samurai weapons and art works from Thailand, Korea and Tibet. Opened in 1996, the adjoining **Modern Art**

Museum (daily 9am–9pm; €1.50) holds a small collection of contemporary Greek art. It's an interesting diversion, as are the gardens and café-bar secreted behind the palace.

In a nearby backstreet off Arseníou, five minutes from the palace, is the museum dedicated to modern Greece's most famous nineteenth-century poet, **Dhionysios Solomos** (Mon–Fri 5–8pm; €0.60). Born on Zákynthos, Solomos was author of the poem *Ímnos stín Eleftheria* (*Hymn to Liberty*), which was to become the Greek national anthem. He studied at Corfu's Ionian Academy, and lived in a house on this site for much of his life.

Up a short flight of steps on Arseníou, the **Byzantine Museum** (Tues–Sun 9am–3pm; €1.50) is housed in the restored church of the Panayía Andivouniótissa. It houses church frescoes and sculptures and sections of mosaic floors from the ancient site of Paleópolis, just south of Kérkyra Town. There are also some pre-Christian artefacts, and a collection of icons dating from the fifteenth to nineteenth centuries.

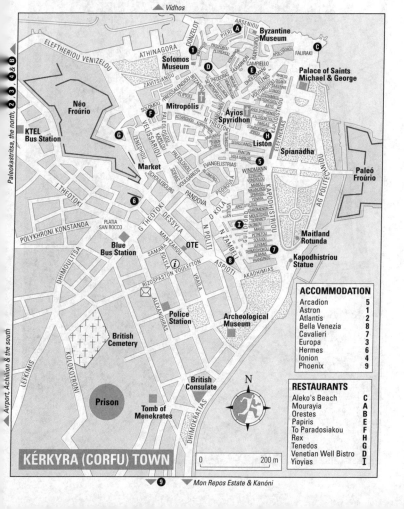

KÉRKYRA (CORFU) TOWN

ACCOMMODATION	
Arcadion	5
Astron	1
Atlantis	2
Bella Venezia	8
Cavalieri	7
Europa	3
Hermes	6
Ionion	4
Phoenix	9

RESTAURANTS	
Aleko's Beach	C
Mourayia	A
Orestes	B
Papiris	E
To Paradosiakou	F
Rex	H
Tenedos	G
Venetian Well Bistro	D
Yioyias	I

△ Stairs in Kérkyra (Corfu) old town

A block behind the Listón, down Spyrídhonos, is the sixteenth-century **church of Áyios Spyrídhon**, whose maroon-domed campanile dominates the town. Here you will find the silver-encrusted coffin of the island's patron saint, **Spyrídhon** – Spyros in the diminutive – after whom about half the male population is named. Four times a year (Palm Sunday and the following Sat, Aug 11 and the first Sun in Nov), to the accompaniment of much celebration and feasting, the relics are paraded through the streets of Kérkyra Town. Each of the days commemorates a miraculous deliverance of the island credited to the saint – twice from plague during the seventeenth century, from a famine of the sixteenth century and (a more blessed release than either of those for any Greek) from the Turks in the eighteenth century.

The next most important of the town's many churches, the **Mitrópolis** (orthodox cathedral), perched at the top of its own square opposite the Old Port, also houses the remains of a saint, in this case Saint Theodora, the ninth-century wife of Emperor Theophilus. The building dates from 1577 and the plain exterior conceals a splendid iconostasis, as well as some fine icons, including a fine sixteenth-century image of *Saint George Slaying the Dragon* by the Cretan artist Mihail Dhamaskinos, and three dark, atmospheric Italianate paintings.

Kérkyra Town's **Archeological Museum** (Tues–Sun 8.30am–3pm; €2.35), just south round the coast, is the best in the archipelago. The most impressive exhibit is a massive (17m) gorgon pediment excavated from the Doric temple of Artemis at Paleópolis, just south of Kérkyra Town ; this dominates an entire room, the gorgon flanked by panthers and mythical battle scenes. The museum also has fragments of Neolithic weapons and cookware, and coins and pots from the period when the island was a colony of ancient Corinth.

Just south of Platía San Rocco and signposted on the corner of Methodhíou and Kolokotróni, the well-maintained **British cemetery** features some elaborate civic and military memorials. It's a quiet green space away from the madness of San Rocco, and in spring and early summer is alive with dozens of species of orchids and other exotic blooms.

The outskirts

Each of the following sights on the outskirts of the city is easily seen in a morning or afternoon, and best visited from the town rather than outlying resorts.

Around the bay from the Rotunda and Archeological Museum, tucked behind Mon Repos beach, the **Mon Repos** estate (8am–7pm; free) contains the most accessible archeological remains on the island. Thick woodland conceals two **Doric temples**, dedicated to Hera and Artemis. The Neoclassical Mon Repos **villa**, built by British High Commissioner Frederic Adam in 1824 and handed over to Greece in 1864, is the birthplace of Britain's Prince Philip and was finally opened fully to the public in summer 2001 (daily 9am–3pm; €1.50).

The most famous excursion from Kérkyra Town is to the islets of **Vlahérna** and **Pondikoníssi**, 2km south of town below the hill of Kanóni, named after the single cannon trained out to sea atop it. A dedicated bus (#2) leaves San Rocco square every half-hour, or it's a pleasant walk of under an hour. Reached by a short causeway, the tiny white convent of Vlahérna is one of the most photographed images on Corfu. Pondikoníssi ("Mouse Island") can be reached by a short boat trip from the dock at Vlahérna (€1.50 return). Tufted with greenery and a small chapel, Vlahérna is identified in legend with a ship from Odysseus's fleet, petrified by Poseidon in revenge for the blinding of his son Polyphemus, the Homeric echoes somewhat marred by the thronging masses and low-flying aircraft from the nearby runway. A quieter destination is

Vídhos, the wooded island visible from the Old Port, reached from there by an hourly shuttle kaïki (€0.90 return).

Four kilometres further to the south, past the resort sprawl of Pérama, is a rather more bizarre attraction: the **Achillion** (daily 9am–3pm; €2.35), a palace built in a (fortunately) unique blend of Teutonic and Neoclassical styles in 1890 by Elizabeth, Empress of Austria. Henry Miller considered it "the worst piece of gimcrackery" that he'd ever laid eyes on and thought it "would make an excellent museum for surrealistic art". The house is predictably grandiose, but the gardens are pleasant to walk around and afford splendid views in all directions.

Eating and drinking

Although there are the inevitable tourist traps, Kérkyra Town offers some excellent, quality restaurants. As well as those listed below, there are several decent *psarotavérnes* on the Garítsa seafront, though you need to be careful of the fish prices.

Aleko's Beach, Faliráki jetty. Set in the tiny harbour below the palace with great views, this place offers simple, mostly grilled meat and fish dishes at good prices.

Mourayia, Arseníou 15–17. This unassuming, good-value ouzerí near the Byzantine Museum does a range of tasty mezédhes, including sausage and seafood such as mussels and shrimp. One of the best seafront establishments.

Orestes, Xenophóndos Stratigoú, in Mandoúki. Probably the best fish and seafood restaurant in town, and better priced than the central or Garítsa equivalents.

Papiris, Ayías Theodóras 25. A well-concealed Campiello restaurant serving fine family cooking such as meats in rich sauces. Justifiably popular with locals.

To Paradosiakon, Solomoú 20. Behind the Old Port, this friendly place serves good fresh food, especially home-style oven dishes like *stifádho* and *kokkinistó*.

Rex, Zavitsiánou behind the Listón. Pricey owing to its location, but some of the best food in the centre, mixing Greek with north European.

Tenedos, 1st Párodhos Solomoú 1, Spiliá. At the foot of the steps to the Néo Froúrio, this place offers an excellent range of mezédhes, eg courgette fritters and *yígandes* plus succulent meat dishes to the accompaniment of subtle live guitar music.

Venetian Well Bistro, Platía Kremásti. A well-kept secret, tucked away in a tiny square a few alleys to the south of the cathedral, this is the nearest you're likely to get to Greek *nouvelle cuisine*, with large portions, and exotica such as wild boar in red wine sauce and Albanian calves' livers done in oúzo. Very expensive.

Yioyias, Guildford St. The best all-round-value taverna in town, set in an atmospheric pedestrianized road. Wonderful range of mezédhes, meat – try the *sofríto* – and fish dishes, all washed down with fine (and cheap) barrelled wine.

Nightlife

Kérkyra Town has plenty to offer in the way of **bars** and nightlife. On the Listón, avoid the mark-ups at the *Magnet* and follow the locals to *Aegli*, *Europa* or *Olympia*, or drink in one of the hotels; the *Cavalieri* rooftop bar can be heaven at night and stays open till the wee hours. For local atmosphere, try *Dirty Dick's*, on the corner of Arseníou and Zavitsiánou, or the expat hangout *Mermaid*, on Ayíon Pandón off the Listón, which will give you a different spin on island culture.

Corfu's self-proclaimed **disco** strip lies a couple of kilometres north of town, past the New Port. Here, at nightclubs like *Symplegma*, the *Hippodrome* (the town's biggest disco, with its own pool), and the bizarrely decorated *Apokalypsis* and *Coca*, party animals dress up for wild and fairly expensive nights out. In some clubs, women travelling without male partners should beware of *kamákia* – slang for Greek males "spearfishing" for foreign women. Somewhat calmer and smaller watering holes on the same strip include *Ethnik* and *Pagoda*. Kérkyra Town's two **cinemas** – the winter Orfeus on the corner of Akadhimías and Aspióti and the open-air summer Phoenix down the side street opposite – both show mostly English-language films.

The northeast and the north coast

The northeast, at least beyond the immediate suburbs, is the most typically Greek part of Corfu – it's mountainous, with a rocky coastline chopped into pebbly bays and coves, above wonderfully clear seas. Green **buses** between Kérkyra Town and Kassiópi serve all resorts, along with some blue suburban buses as far as Dhassiá.

Kérkyra Town to Ípsos

The landscape just north of Kérkyra Town is an industrial wasteland, and things don't improve much at the first village you come to, **KONDÓKALI**, overrun by holiday developments. The old town consists of a short street with a number of bars and traditional *psistariés*, the best of which are *Gerekos* and *Takis*, an international restaurant, *Flags*, and the pricey *Lithari* fish taverna.

Neighbouring **GOUVIÁ** is also Corfu's largest yachting marina. The village boasts a couple of small **hotels**, notably the *Hotel Aspa* (☎06610/91 409; ❸) and great-value *Gouvia View* by the beach (☎06610/91 167). For **rooms**, try Maria Lignou (☎06610/91 348; ❸) or Karoukas Travel (☎06610/91 596, ℱ91 943, ⓔkaroukas@otenet.gr). There's a number of decent **restaurants**, including *The Captain's* taverna and *Steki psistariá*, and a couple of pizzerias, *La Bonita* and *Palladium*. The very narrow shingle **beach**, barely 5m wide in parts, shelves into sand; given the sea traffic, the water quality is doubtful.

Two kilometres beyond Goúvia the coastline begins to improve at **DHAFNÍLA** and **DHASSIÁ**, set in wooded bays with pebbly beaches. Two large and expensive **hotels**, the *Dassia Chandris* and *Corfu Chandris* (both ☎06610/97 100–3, ℱ93 458, ⓔchandris@ker.forthnet.gr; ❻), dominate Dhassiá, with extensive grounds, pools and beach facilities. The more reasonable *Hotel Amalia* (☎06610/93 523; ❹) has pleasant en-suite rooms and its own pool and garden. **Rooms** are scarce, although Spyros Rengis's minimarket in Dhassiá has a few (☎06610/90 282; ❸) and the Dafnilas supermarket has some of the cheapest going (☎06610/90 282; ❶). Dhafníla does, however, have the best **campsite** on the island, *Dionysus Camping Village* (☎06610/91 417, ℱ91 760); tents are pitched under terraced olive trees. *Dionysus* also has simple bungalow huts, a pool, shop, bar and restaurant, and the friendly, multilingual owners offer a ten-percent discount to Rough Guide readers.

ÍPSOS, 2km north of Dhassiá, can't really be recommended to anyone but hardened bar-hoppers. There is hardly room to swing a cat on the thin pebble beach, right beside the busy coast road, and the resort is pretty tacky. Most **accommodation** is prebooked by package companies, although Premier/Ípsos Travel (☎06610/93 661, ℱ93 637) can offer rooms. *Corfu Camping Ípsos* (☎06610/93 579, ℱ93 741) has a bar and restaurant, and offers standing tents. Ípsos is also home to one of the island's major **diving centres**, Waterhoppers (☎06610/93 867, ⓔdiverclub@hotmail.com). **Eating** on the main drag is dominated by fast food, though a more traditional meal and a quieter setting can be found in the *Akrogiali* and *Asteria* tavernas, by the marina to the south of the strip. The northern end is largely devoted to competing bars and discos.

North to Áyios Stéfanos

Ípsos has now engulfed the neighbouring hamlet of Pyrgí, which is the main point of access for the villages and routes leading up to **Mount Pandokrátor**; the road, signposted Spartílas, is 200km beyond the junction in Pyrgí. A popular base for walkers is the village of **STRINÝLAS**, 16km from Pyrgí. Accommodation is basic but easy to come by: the *Elm Tree Taverna*, a long-time favourite with walkers, can direct you to rooms. In summer the main routes are busy, but there are quieter walks taking in the handsome Venetian village of Epískepsi, 5km northwest of Strinýlas – anyone interested in walking the Pandokrátor paths is advised to get the **map** of the mountain by island-based cartographer Stephan Jaskulowski or Hilary Whitton-Paipeti's walking book, both available locally.

The coast road beyond Ípsos mounts the slopes of Pandokrátor towards **BARBÁTI**, 4km further on. Here you'll find the best beach on this coast, though its charm has been somewhat diminished recently by the initial construction of the gargantuan *Riviera Barbati* complex. The beach is a favourite with families, and much **accommodation** is prebooked in advance. However, there are some rooms available on spec – *Paradise* (☎06630/91 320, ℉91 479; ❸) and *Roula Geranou* (☎06630/92 397; ❷), both on the main road.

The mountainside becomes steeper and the road higher beyond Barbáti, and the population thins drastically. **NISSÁKI** is a sprawling roadside settlement rather than a village, with a number of coves, the first and last accessible by road, the rest only by track – the furthest dominated by the gigantic, expensive and rather soulless *Nissaki Beach Hotel* (☎06630/91 232, ℉22 079, ✉nissaki@otenet.gr; ❺ half-board). There's a couple of shops and a bakery, and a few travel and **accommodation agencies**. The British-owned Falcon Travel (☎06630/91 318, ℉91 070, ✉falcontr@otenet.gr; ❸) rents out apartments above the first beach, a tiny, white-pebble cove with a trio of fine tavernas – try the quayside *Mitsos*. The *Nissaki Holidays Center* (☎06630/91 166, ℉91 206), up by the junction, may have some cheaper rooms.

Three pebbly coves no one visiting this coast should miss are Agní, not far past the *Nissaki Beach Hotel*, Kalámi and neighbouring Kouloúra: the first for its trio of fine tavernas, the second for its Durrell connection, the third for its exquisite bay. Crowds flock to **AGNÍ** for the fine eating – *Nicolas* is the oldest taverna and just pips *Toula* and *Agni* for quality. **KALÁMI** is on the way to being spoiled, but the village is still small and you can imagine how it would have looked in the year Lawrence Durrell spent here on the eve of World War II. The **White House**, where Durrell wrote *Prospero's Cell*, is now split in two: the ground floor is an excellent taverna; the upper floor is let through CV Travel (see p.15). Sunshine Travel (☎06630/91 170, ℉91 572, ✉info@sunshineclub.gr) and Kalami Tourist Services (☎06630/91 062, ℉91 369, ✉kalamits@otenet.gr) both have a range of rooms on their books, or ask at *Matella's* restaurant (☎06630/91 371; ❷). The **restaurant** at the White House is recommended, as is *Matella's*, the *Kalami Beach Taverna* and *Pepe's*, all on the beach. Two cocktail bars compete for the happy-hour trade.

The tiny harbour of **KOULOÚRA** has managed to keep its charm intact, set at the edge of an unspoiled bay with nothing to distract from the pine trees and kaïkia. The fine **taverna** here has to be the most idyllic setting for a meal in the whole of Corfu.

Around the coast to Aharávi

Two kilometres beyond Kouloúra down a shady lane, the large pebble cove of **Kerasiá** shelters the family-run *Kerasia Taverna*. The most attractive resort on this stretch of coast, however, 3km down a lane from Agnitsíni on the main road, is **ÁYIOS STÉFANOS**. Most **accommodation** here is of the upmarket prebooked villa sort, and the village has yet to succumb to any serious development; so far only the *Kochili* taverna has independent rooms and apartments (☎06630/81 522; ❸). Recommended are the *Galini* and *Kaparelli* **tavernas**, and the pricier *Eucalyptus* over by the village's small beach. The *Waves* café and *Damianos* cocktail bar are the main spots to idle with a drink.

A thirty-minute walk from the coastguard station above Áyios Stéfanos, along a newly surfaced road, stretches the beach of **Avláki**, a pebble bay that provides lively conditions for the **windsurfers** who visit the beach's windsurf club. There are two **tavernas**, the *Barbaro* and *Avlaki*, and some **rooms** a few hundred yards back from the beach – Mortzoukos (℡06630/81 196; ❸), and *Tsirimiagos* (℡06630/81 522; ❸).

Further round the coast is **KASSIÓPI**, a fishing village that's been transformed into a major party resort. The Roman emperor Tiberius had a villa here, and the village's sixteenth-century church is said to stand on the site of a temple of Zeus once visited by Nero. Little evidence of Kassiópi's past survives, apart from an abandoned Angevin *kástro* on the headland – many visitors come for the nightlife and the five pebbly beaches. Most **accommodation** in Kassiópi is through village agencies; the largest, Travel Corner (℡06630/81 220, ℱ81 108, ⓔinfo@kassiopi.com), on the main road near the square, is a good place to start. An independent alternative, the smart *Kastro* café-pension, overlooks the beach behind the castle (℡06630/81 045; ❺), and Elli Tsiliani (℡06630/81 483; ❸) offers bargain rooms behind Kalamíonas beach. International cuisine dominates **eating** in Kassiópi – try the tasty Italian at *Little Italy*, the Tex-Mex at *Poco loco* or the *Sze Chuan* Chinese – but for something more traditional, head for the *Three Brothers* taverna on the harbour, or the neighbouring *Porto* fish restaurant. At night, Kassiópi rocks to the cacophony of its music and video bars: the flashiest is the gleaming hi-tech *Eclipse*, which also shows DVDs, closely followed by the *Baron*, *Angelos* and *Jasmine*, all within falling-over distance of the small town square. The *Axis Club* boasts imported British DJs, and frolics sometimes extend onto the beach until dawn. The village is also home to one of the most reliable diving operations, Corfu Divers (℡06630/81 218, ⓔcorfudivers@yahoo.com), which is partly British-run. Internet facilities are available at the *Pallace* bar (℡06630/81 719), off the main road.

The coastline beyond Kassiópi is overgrown and marshy until you get to little-used **Almyrós beach**, one of the longest on the island. It is also the least-developed beach, with only a few apartment buildings under construction at the hamlet of **Almyrós**. For a peaceful stay you could try *Villa Maria* (℡06630/63 359; ❸) and eat at *Liberty's* grill a little further along the beach. The Andinióti lagoon, smaller than Korissía (see p.494), but still a haven for birds and twitchers, backs Cape Áyias Ekaterínis to the east. With its wide main road, **AHARÁVI**, the next stop west on the main coast road, resembles an American Midwest truck stop, but the village proper is tucked behind this in a quiet crescent of old tavernas, bars and shops. Aharávi makes a quieter beach alternative to the southerly strands, and should also be considered by those seeking alternative routes up onto **Mount Pandokrátor**. Roads to small hamlets such as Áyios Martínos and Láfki continue onto the mountain, and even a stroll up from the back of Aharávi will find you on the upper slopes in under an hour.

Accommodation isn't easy to find, but a good place to start is Castaway Travel (℡06630/63 541, ℱ63 376, ⓔcastaway@otenet.gr) or HN Travel (℡06630/63 458, ℱ63 454). One independent hotel is *Dandolo* (℡06630/63 557, ℱ63 457; ❹), set in lush grounds towards the old village. There's a number of **restaurants** on Aharávi's main drag; go for the *Pump House* steak and pasta joint, the traditional tavernas *Chris's* and *George's*, or the *Young Tree*, which specializes in Corfiot dishes such as *sofríto* (veal stew with vinegar seasoning) and *pastitsádha* (a variation on *pastítsio*). The bar-restaurants tend to get quite rowdy at night, although the light and airy *Captain Aris* is a pleasant watering hole. For a quieter evening, head for the excellent *Theritas* taverna, the friendly *Mitsouras* kafenío or the cosy *Hole in the Wall* pub, all in the old village.

Ródha, Sidhári and Avliótes

Just to the west, **RÓDHA** has tipped over into overdevelopment, and can't be wholeheartedly recommended for those after a quiet time. Its central crossroads have all the charm of a service station, and the beach is rocky in parts and swampy to the west. "Old Ródha" is a small warren of alleys between the main road and the seafront, where you'll find the best **restaurants** and **bars**: the *Taverna Agra* is the oldest in Ródha and the best place for fish, and the *Rodha Star Taverna* and *New Port* are also good. For bars, try *Big Ben* or *Five Roses*, both with Sky Sports, or the trendier bar-club *Skouna*. For **accommodation**, the friendly seafront *Roda Inn* (☏06630/63 358; ❸) has decently priced en-suite rooms. Both the Anglo-Greek NSK UK Travel (☏06630/63 471, ℻63 274) on the main drag and Nostos Travel on the seafront (☏06630/64 602, ℻64 601) rent rooms and handle car rental. The smart *Roda Beach Camping* (☏06630/93 120) is a little way east of the resort, while even pleasanter *Karoussades Camping* (☏ & ℻ 06630/31 415) is to the west towards Sidhári. Myron's good-rate motorbike rental (☏06630/63 477) and Kostas horse-riding are also based in Ródha. Several kilometres inland from Ródha, just east of Agrafí, the Angonari *mezedhopolío* serves an excellent range of dishes and great barrelled wine in a relaxed garden with subtle live music.

The next notable resort, **SIDHÁRI**, is expanding rapidly and is totally dominated by British-package tourists; it has a small but pretty town square, with a bandstand set in a small garden, but this is lost in a welter of bars, boutiques and snack joints. The beach is sandy but not terribly clean, and many people tend to head just west to the curious coves, walled by wind-carved sandstone cliffs, around the vaunted Canal d'Amour. The best sources of **rooms** are Maria Fakiola (☏06630/95 369; ❷) and Nikolaos Korakianitis's minimarket on the main road (☏06630/95 058; ❷). The biggest accommodation agency is run by young tycoon Philip Vlasseros, whose Vlasseros Travel (☏06630/95 695, ℻95 969) also handles car rental, horse-riding and excursions, including a once-weekly trip to the Dhiapóndia islands (see p.496). Sidhári's **campsite**, *Dolphin Camping* (☏06630/31 846), is some way inland from the junction at the western end of town. Most **restaurants** are pitched at those looking for a great night out rather than a quiet meal in a taverna. The pricey *Olympic* is the oldest taverna here; also recommended are the *Diamond* and *Sea Breeze* tavernas or *Kavvadias* on the eastern stretch of beach. Ethnic cuisine and cheap full-on English breakfasts are also readily available. There are no quiet bars in Sidhári, and two **nightclubs** vie for late custom, the *Remezzo* and *Caesar's*. Sidhári also has its own waterpark with free entry, a good place to keep the kids happy.

The Sidhári bus usually continues to **AVLIÓTES**, a handsome hill town with several bars and tavernas but few concessions to tourism. The town is noteworthy for two reasons: its accessibility to the stunning beach, bordered by vertical cliffs and shady in the mornings, below the quiet village of Perouládhes, just over 1km away, and the fact that **Áyios Stéfanos** (see p.492) is under thirty-minutes' walk from here, downhill through lovely olive groves.

Paleokastrítsa and the northwest coast

The northwest conceals some of the island's most dramatic coastal scenery, the violent interior mountainscapes jutting out of the verdant countryside. The area's honeypot attraction, **Paleokastrítsa**, is the single most picturesque resort on Corfu, but is suffering from its popularity. Further down the west coast, the terrain opens out to reveal long sandy beaches, such as delightful **Myrtiótissa** and the backpackers' haven of **Áyios Górdhis**. Public **transport** along the west coast is difficult: virtually all buses ply routes from Kérkyra Town to single destinations, and rarely link resorts.

Paleokastrítsa

PALEOKASTRÍTSA, a small village surrounded by dramatic hills and cliffs, has been identified as the Homeric city of Scheria, where Odysseus was washed ashore and escorted by Nausicaa to the palace of her father Alcinous, king of the Phaeacians. It's a stunning site, as you would expect, though one that's long been engulfed by tourism. The focal point of the village is the car park on the seafront, which backs onto the largest and least attractive of three **beaches**, home to sea taxis and kaïkia. The second beach, to the right and signed by flags for Mike's Ski Club, is stony with clear water, and the best of the three is a small unspoiled strand reached along the path by the *Astakos Taverna*. Protected by cliffs, it's undeveloped apart from the German-run Korfu-Diving Centre (☎06630/41 604) at the end of the cove. From the beach in front of the main car park, you can get a **boat trip** to some nearby seawater caves, known as the "blue grottoes" (€5.85 for a half-hour trip, €8.80 for drop-off and later pick-up), a trip worth taking for the spectacular coastal views. Boats also serve as a taxi service to three neighbouring beaches, Áyia Triánda, Platákia and Alípa, which all have snack bars.

On the rocky bluff above the village, the **Theotókou monastery** (7am–1pm & 3–8pm; free, although donations invited) is believed to have been established in the thirteenth century. There's also a museum, resplendent with icons, jewelled Bibles and other impedimenta of Greek Orthodox ritual, though the highlight is the gardens, with spectacular coastal views. Paleokastrítsa's ruined castle, the **Angelókastro**, is around 6km up the coast; only approachable by path from the hamlet of Kríni, it has stunning, almost circular views of the surrounding sea and land. For a drink or snack with tremendous views, it's worth stopping at either the *Bella Vista* or *Golden Fox* tavernas on the way up, between Lákones and Makrádhes.

Unfortunately, perhaps owing to the pressure of commerce in such a small space, there's a rather mercenary air about tourism here. **Accommodation** is at a premium, and you may be expected to commit yourself for three to seven days in some places. A good **hotel** is the family-run *Odysseus* (☎06630/41 209, ☞41 342; ⑤), on the road into town, while the nearby modern *Akrotiri Beach* (☎06630/41 237, ☞41 277, ✉belvenht@hol.gr; ⑤) is friendly and unpretentious. There are good-value **rooms** for rent above Alípa beach on the road down into Paleokastrítsa: try at the *Dolphin Snackbar* (☎06630/41 035; ④), the *Green House* (☎06630/41 311; ③) or Michalas tourist bureau (☎06630/41 113, ☞41 298, ✉michalastravel@ker.forthnet.gr). Above the village, past Nikos' Bikes, the friendly Korina family also have rooms (☎06630/44 064; ③). *Paleokastritsa Camping* (☎06630/41 204, ☞41 104) is just off the main road into town, a ten-minute walk from the centre.

There isn't a huge choice of **restaurants** in the centre of Paleokastrítsa. The *Astakos Taverna* and *Corner Grill* are two traditional places, while *Il Pirata* offers a variety of Italian and Greek dishes, including local fish and seafood, and the seafront *Smurfs* has a good seafood menu despite the name. Also recommended are the very smart *St Georges on the Rock*, and the shady *Calm*, which has internet facilities. **Nightlife** hangouts include the restaurant-bars in the centre, and those straggling up the hill towards Lákones. By the Lákones turning is Paleokastrítsa's one nightclub, *The Paleo Club*, a small disco-bar with a garden.

Áyios Yeóryios and Áyios Stéfanos

Like many of the west-coast resorts, **ÁYIOS YEÓRYIOS**, 6km north of Paleokastrítsa, isn't actually based around a village. The resort has developed in response to the popularity of its large sandy bay, and it's a major **windsurfing** centre, busy even in low season. There is one particularly good-value **hotel**, the *Alkyon Beach* (℡06630/56 204, ℻96 206; ❸), some rooms at the Arista supermarket (℡06630/96 350; ❶) or *Studio Eleana* (℡ & ℻ 06630/96 366; ❸) and the *San George* campsite (℡06630/51 759), nearly 1km back from the beach towards Kavvadhádhes. On the way north towards Áyios Stéfanos, the pleasant sandy beach of **Aríllas** has given rise to gradual development, including several tavernas – try *Kostas on the Beach*. Accommodation can be arranged through Arillas Travel (℡06630/51 280, ℻51 381, ✉arillast@otenet.gr) or there is the smart *Akti Arilla* hotel (℡06630/51 201, ℻51 221, ✉aktiarill@otenet.gr; ❹ half-board).

The northernmost of the west-coast's resorts, **ÁYIOS STÉFANOS** is low-key, popular with families and a quiet base from which to explore the northwest and the Dhiapóndia islands, visible on the horizon. Day-trips to Mathráki, Othoní and Eríkoussa (see p.496) run every Thursday in season, and range from €14.65 to €23.50 per person. Áyios Stéfanos's oldest **hotel**, the *Nafsika* (℡06630/51 051, ℻51 112; ❸), has a large restaurant, a favourite with villagers, and gardens with a pool and bar. In recent years it has been joined by the upmarket *Thomas Bay* (℡06630/51 767, ℻51 913; ❺) and *Hotel San Stefano* (℡06630/51 053, ℻51 202; ❸), attached to the *Golden Beach* taverna. For those on a budget, Pelis and Maria's gift shop offers bargain **rooms** (℡06630/51 424; ❷) and the *Restaurant Evinos* (℡ & ℻ 06630/51 766; ❷) has apartments above the village. A number of travel agencies handle accommodation, among them San Stefanos (℡06630/51 910, ℻51 771, ✉steftrav@otenet.gr) in the centre. Besides the above-mentioned hotels, good options for **eating** include the *Waves* and very reasonable *Mistral* tavernas above the beach, while *O Manthos* taverna serves Corfiot specialities like *sofríto* and *pastitsádha*. For **nightlife**, there's a couple of lively music bars, *Magnet* and *Athens*, plus the small *Enigma* nightclub.

Central and southern Corfu

Two natural features divide the centre and south of Corfu. The first is the **plain of Rópa**, whose fertile landscape backs on to some of the best beaches on this coast. Settlements and development stop a little to the south of Paleokastrítsa and only resume around **Érmones** and **Pélekas** – a quick bus ride across the island from Kérkyra Town. Down to the south, a second dividing point is the **Korissía lagoon**, the sandy plains and dunes that skirt this natural feature being great places for botanists and ornithologists. Beyond, a single road trails the interior, with sporadic side roads to resorts on either coast. The landscape here is flat, an undistinguished backdrop for a series of increasingly developed beaches and, in the far south, **Kávos**, Corfu's big youth resort.

Érmones to the Korissía lagoon: the west coast

ÉRMONES, south of Paleokastrítsa, is one of the busiest resorts on the island, its lush green bay backed by the mountains above the Rópa River. The resort is dominated by the upmarket *Ermones Beach* **hotel** (℡06610/94 241, ℻94 248; ❻ half-board), which provides guests with a funicular railway down to the beach. More reasonably-priced accommodation can be found at the *Pension Katerina* (℡06610/94 615; ❷) and *Georgio's Villas* (℡06610/94 950; ❸), on the hillside above the road that leads to the beach. Both the *Maria* and *Nafsica* **tav-**

ernas above the beach provide good, filling mezédhes and main dishes. Just inland is the Corfu Golf and Country Club (℡06610/94 220), the only golf club in the archipelago, and said to be the finest in the Mediterranean.

The nearby small village of **VÁTOS** has a couple of tavernas, a disco and rooms, and is on the Glyfádha bus route from Kérkyra Town. Spyros Kousounis, owner of the *Olympic Restaurant and Grill* (℡06610/94 318; ❸) on the main road has rooms and apartments, as does Prokopios Himarios (℡06610/94 503; ❸), next to the Doukakis café–minimarket up in the village. The Myrtiótissa **path** is signposted just beyond the extremely handy, if basic, *Vatos Camping* (℡06610/94 393).

Far preferable to the gravelly sand of Érmones are the sandy beaches just south of the resort, at Myrtiótissa and Glyfádha. In *Prospero's Cell*, Lawrence Durrell described **Myrtiótissa** as "perhaps the loveliest beach in the world"; it was until recently a well-guarded secret but now gets very busy in the summer and supports three *kantínas*, so it's best visited either at the end of the day or out of high season. Above the beach is the tiny whitewashed **Myrtiótissa monastery**, dedicated to Our Lady of the Myrtles.

The sandy bay of **GLYFÁDHA**, walled in by cliffs, is dominated by the *Louis Grand* hotel. There's a far better **accommodation** option at the extreme north end of the beach, the *Glifada Beach* (℡06610/94 258; ❹), whose owners, the Megas family, also have a fine taverna. The resort's other accommodation is likely to be block-booked, though the *Gorgona* pool bar and *Restaurant Michaelis* might have rooms. Nightlife centres on two music bars, the *Kikiriko* and *Aloha*, which pump out heavy-duty sounds all day, as the beach is popular with young Greek and Italian trendies.

PÉLEKAS, inland and 2km south of Glyfádha, has long been popular for its views – the **Kaiser's Throne** viewing tower, along the road to Glyfádha, was Wilhelm II's favourite spot on the island. New developments are beginning to swamp the town, but there are some good **room** deals here, including the friendly *Pension Paradise* (℡06610/94 530; ❸) on the way in from Vátos, and the *Alexandros* taverna (℡06610/94 215, ℻94 833, ✉axel@hol.gr; ❸) and *Thomas* (℡06610/94 491; ❸) both on the way towards Kaiser's Throne. Agatha's Tours (℡06610/94 283, ℻94 602) may have some even cheaper rooms. Among the **tavernas**, the *Alexandros* and *Roula's Grill House* are highly recommended. The colourful *Zanzibar* is a pleasant spot for a drink by the diminutive square, whose Odhigitria church, renovated in 1884, is worth a peek. Pélekas's sandy **beach** is reached down a short path. Here you'll find *Maria's Place*, an excellent family-run **taverna/rooms** place (℡06610/94 601; ❸), with fish caught daily by the owner's husband. Sadly, the beach has been rather spoilt by the monstrous *Pelekas Beach* hotel that now looms over it.

Around 7km south of Pélekas, **ÁYIOS GÓRDHIS** is one of the key play beaches on the island, largely because of the activities organized by the startling **Pink Palace** complex (℡06610/53 103, ℻53 025, ✉Pink-Palace@ker.forth-net.gr) which dominates the resort. It has pools, games courts, restaurants, a shop and a disco. Backpackers cram into communal rooms for up to ten (smaller rooms and singles are also available) for €23.50 a night, including breakfast and evening meal. Other accommodation is available on the beach, notably at the quieter *Michael's Place* taverna (℡06610/53 041; ❸); the neighbouring *Alex-in-the-Garden* **restaurant** is also a favourite.

Inland from the resort is the south's largest prominence, the humpback of **Áyii Dhéka** (576m), reached by path from the hamlet of Áno Garoúna; it is the island's second-largest mountain after Pandokrátor. The lower slopes are wooded, and it's possible to glimpse buzzards wheeling on thermals over the higher slopes.

Around 5km south by road from Áyios Górdhis, the fishing hamlet of **PENDÁTI** is still untouched by tourism. There is no accommodation here, but *Angela's* café and minimarket and the *Strofi* grill cater to villagers and the few tourists who wander in. Another 4km on, **PARAMÓNAS** affords excellent views over the coastline, and, being rather low-key, offers some of the best **accommodation** deals on the island: the panoramic *Sunset* (T06610/75 149, F75 686; ❶), right above the beach, and the *Paramonas Bridge* restaurant (T06610/75 711; ❶), a little further inland, are both extremely good value, as is the *Areti Studios* (T06610/75 838; ❷), on the road in from Pendáti.

The town of **ÁYIOS MATTHÉOS**, 3km inland, is still chiefly an agricultural centre, although a number of kafenía and tavernas offer a warm if bemused welcome to passers-by: head for the *Mouria* snack bar-grill, or the modern *Steki*, which can rustle up tasty mezédhes. On the other side of Mount Áyios Matthéos, 2km by road, is the **Gardhíki Pýrgos**, the ruins of a thirteenth-century castle built in this unlikely lowland setting by the despots of Epirus. The road continues on to the northernmost tip of splendid and deserted **Halikoúna** beach on the sea edge of the **Korissía lagoon**, which, if you don't have your own transport, is most easily reached by walking from the village of Línia (on the Kávos bus route) via Íssos beach; other, longer routes trail around the north end of the lagoon from Áno Messongí and Khlomotianá. Over 5km long and 1km wide at its centre, Korissía is home to turtles, tortoises, lizards and numerous indigenous and migratory birds. For one of the quietest stays on the island, try *Marin Christel Apartments* (T06610/75 947; ❹), just north of Halikoúna beach, or *Logara Apartments* (T06610/76 477; ❹), 500m inland.

Benítses to Petríti: the east coast

South of Kérkyra Town, there's nothing to recommend before **BENÍTSES**, a once notorious bonking-and-boozing resort, whose old town at the north end is now reverting to a quiet bougainvillea-splashed Greek village. There's really little to see here, beyond the ruins of a Roman bathhouse at the back of the village, and the tiny **Shell Museum**, part-exhibit, part-shop. **Rooms** are plentiful: try Best Travel (T06610/72 037, F71 036; ❸) and All Tourist (T06610/72 223; ❸). Visitor numbers have picked up again after a serious decline, and some hotels can offer good deals. The *Corfu Maris* (T06610/72 035; ❹), on the beach at the southern end of town, has modern en-suite rooms with balconies and views, while the friendly *Hotel Benitsa* and neighbouring *Agis* in the centre (both T06610/39 269; ❷) offer quiet rooms set back from the main road. Benítses has its fair share of decent if not particularly cheap **tavernas**, notably *La Mer de Corfu* and the Corfiot specialist *Spiros*, as well as the plush *Marabou*. The **bars** at the southern end of town like *Happy Dog* and *Tribal Club* are fairly lively, despite new rules controlling all-night partying, and the *Stadium* **nightclub** is still going strong. If you're looking for a quiet drink head for the north end of the village, away from the traffic.

MORAÏTIKA's main street is an ugly strip of bars, restaurants and shops, but its beach is the best between Kérkyra Town and Kávos. Reasonable beach-side **hotels** include the *Margarita Beach* (T & F 06610/76 267; ❹) and the *Three Stars* (T06610/75 862; ❹). The Budget Ways agency (T06610/76 768, F75 664; ❸) offers a range of accommodation and there are **rooms** between the main road and beach, and up above the main road: try Alekos Bostis (T06610/75 637; ❸) or Kostas Vlahos (T06610/55 350; ❷). Much of the main drag is dominated by souvenir shops and minimarkets, as well as a range of **bars**, including the village's oldest, *Charlie's*, which opened in 1939, and the lively *Very Coco* nightclub. The *Rose Garden* **restaurant** is just off the main road and has a fair mix of vegetarian, Greek and international food, as does the unfortunately named beach restaurant *Crabs*, where the seafood and special salads are excellent. The village proper, **ÁNO MORAÏTIKA**, is signposted a few minutes' hike up the steep lanes inland, and is virtually unspoiled. Its tiny houses and alleys are practically drowning in bougainvillea, among which you'll find two **tavernas**: the *Village Taverna* and the *Bella Vista*, which has a basic menu but justifies its name with a lovely garden, sea views and breezes.

Barely a hundred metres on from the Moraïtika seafront, **MESSONGÍ** continues this stretch of package-tour-oriented coast. The sandy beach is dominated by the vast *Messonghi Beach* **hotel** complex (℡06610/76 684, ℻75 334; ⑥), plush but impersonal and rather disorganized. Both the *Hotel Gemini* (℡06610/75 221, ℻ 75 213; ⑥ half-board) and great-value *Pantheon Hall* (℡06610/75 802, ℻75 801; ②) have pools and gardens, and en-suite rooms with balconies. Messongí has a number of good **restaurants**: notably the *Memories* taverna, which specializes in Corfiot dishes and serves its own barrel wine, and the upmarket *Castello*. An alternative is to head for the beachside *Bacchus* and *Spanos* tavernas a short walk south on the road to Boúkari. Try the *Dimensions* bar for a relaxed seaside drink.

The quiet road from Messongí to **BOÚKARI** follows the seashore for about 3km, often only a few feet above it. Boúkari itself comprises little more than a handful of tavernas, a shop and a few small, family-run hotels; the *Boukari Beach* is the best of the **tavernas**, offering fresh fish and live lobster. The very friendly Vlahopoulos family who run the taverna also manage two small hotels nearby, the *Penelopi* and newer *Villa Alexandra* (℡06620/51 269, ℻51 792; ③), as well as good rooms (②) attached to the taverna. Boúkari is out of the way, but an idyllic little strip of unspoiled coast for anyone fleeing the crowds elsewhere on the island, and inland from here is the unspoiled wooded region around **Aryirádhes**, rarely visited by tourists and a perfect place for quiet walks.

Back on the coastline, the village of **PETRITÍ** fronts onto a small but busy dirt-track harbour, but is mercifully free of noise and commerce; its beach is rock, mud and sand, set among low olive-covered hills. The *Pension Egrypos* (℡06620/51 949; ③) has **rooms** and a **taverna**. At the harbour, three tavernas serve the trickle of sea traffic: the smart *Limnopoula* guarded by caged parrots, and the more basic but friendly *Dimitris* and *Stamatis*. Back from the village, near the hamlet of Vassilátika, is the elegant *Regina* **hotel**, with gardens and pool (℡06620/52 132, ℻52 135; ④).

Southern Corfu

Across the island on the west coast, the beach at **ÁYIOS YEÓRYIOS** spreads as far south as Ayía Varvára, and north to encircle the edge of the Korissía lagoon, around 12km of uninterrupted sand. The village itself, however, is an unprepossessing sprawl. British package operators have arrived in force, with bars competing to present bingo, quizzes and video nights. The smart *Golden Sands* (℡06620/51 225, ℻51 140; ④) has a pool, open-air restaurant and gardens, but the best **hotel** bargain is the smaller *Blue Sea* (℡06620/51 624, ℻51 172, ✉bluesea@otenet.gr; ③); both are situated midway along the seafront road. The easiest place to look for good **rooms** is at Stork Tours (℡ & ℻ 06620/51 168; ②), halfway along the seafront. Áyios Yeóryios has a number of good **restaurants** on the seafront: *La Perla's* which serves Greek and north European food in a walled garden; the *Napoleon psistariá*; and the *Dario* Italian joint. **Nightlife** centres around music and pool bars like the *Gold Hart* and *Traxx*, although the best bar in Áyios Yeóryios is the sea-edge *Panorama*, which has views as far south as Paxí.

A few minutes' walk north of Áyios Yeóryios, **Íssos** is a far better and quieter beach; the dunes north of Íssos are an unofficial nude-bathing area. Facilities around Íssos are sparse: one **taverna**, the *Rousellis Grill* (which sometimes has rooms), a few hundred metres from the beach on the lane leading to Línia on the main road, and the *Friends* snack bar in Línia itself. An English-run **windsurfing school** operates on the beach.

Anyone interested in how a Greek town works away from the bustle of tourism shouldn't miss **LEFKÍMI**, on the island's east coast. The second-largest town after Corfu, it's the administrative centre of the south of the island as well as the alternative ferry port to/from Igoumenítsa, with half a dozen daily crossings in summer, and has some fine architecture, including two striking churches: **Áyios Theódoros**, on a mound above a small square, and **Áyios Arsénios**, with a vast orange dome that can be seen for miles. There are some **rooms** at the *Cheeky Face* taverna (☎06620/22 627; ❷), by the bridge over the canal that carries the Hímaros River through town, and the *Maria Madalena* apartments (☎06620/22 386; ❸) further up. A few **bars** and **restaurants** sit on the edge of the canal – try the home cooking at *Maria*. Away from the centre, the *Hermes* bar has a leafy garden, and there's a number of other good local places where tourists are rare enough to guarantee you a friendly welcome, including the *Mersedes* and *Pacific* bars, and, notably, the *Kavouras* and *Fontana* tavernas.

There are no ambiguities in **KÁVOS**, directly south of Lefkími: either you like 24-hour drinking, clubbing, bungee-jumping, go-karts, video bars named after British sitcoms and chips with almost everything, or you should avoid the resort altogether. Kávos stretches over 2km of decent sandy beach, with watersports galore. This is very much package-tour territory; if you want independent **accommodation**, try Pandis Travel (☎06620/61 400, 🖷61 401) or Island Holidays (☎06620/61 357, 🖷61 426), and the nearest to genuine Greek **food** you'll find is at the *Two Brothers psistariá*, at the south end of town. Fast food and British-style ethnic cuisine are much easier to come by. *Future* is the biggest **club**, with imported north European DJs, followed by *Whispers*, *42nd St* and *Buzz*. Favourite **bars** include *JCs*, *Jungle*, *The Face*, *Fire* and *Bonkers*, and at night the main drag is one unbroken crowd of young revellers.

Beyond the limits of Kávos, where few visitors stray, a path leaving the road south to the hamlet of Spartwill heads through unspoiled countryside; after around thirty minutes of walking it reaches the cliffs of **Cape Asprókavos** and the crumbling **monastery of Arkoudhílas**. The cape looks out over the straits to Paxí, and down over deserted **Arkoudhílas beach**, which can be reached from Sparterá, 5km by road but only 3km by the signed path from Kávos. Even wilder is **Áyios Górdhis Paleohoríou beach**, 3km further on from Sparterá, one of the least visited on the island and not to be confused with the eponymous beach further north.

Corfu's satellite islands

Corfu's three inhabited satellite islands, **Eríkoussa**, **Othoní** and **Mathráki**, in the quintet of **Dhiapóndia islands**, are scattered up to 20km off the northwest coast. Some travel agencies in the northern resorts offer **day-trips** to Eríkoussa only, often with a barbecue thrown in – fine if you're happy to spend the day on the beach. A trip taking in all three islands from Sidhári or Áyios Stéfanos is excellent value: they are between thirty and sixty minutes apart by boat, and most trips allow you an hour on each (longer on sandy Eríkoussa).

Locals use day-trip boats between the islands, so it's possible to pay your way between them. There is also a thrice-weekly **ferry** from Kérkyra Town, the *Alexandros II*, which brings cars and goods to the islands, but given that it has to sail halfway round Corfu first, it's the slowest way to proceed.

Mathráki

Hilly, densely forested and with a long empty beach, beautiful **Mathráki** has the fewest inhabitants of the three islands. Portelo beach begins at the edge of the tiny harbour, and extends south for 3km of fine, dark-red sand, a nesting site for the endangered **loggerhead turtle** (see box on p.525). It's important therefore not to camp anywhere near the beach – and not to make any noise there at night.

A single road rises from the harbour into the interior and the scattered village of **KÁTO MATHRÁKI**, where just one friendly taverna-kafenío-shop overlooks the beach and Corfu. The views are magnificent, as is the sense of isolation. However, Mathráki is gradually gearing up towards visitors, and islander Tassos Kassimis (☎06630/71 700; ❸) already rents **rooms**. The road continues to the village of **Áno Mathráki**, with its single, old-fashioned kafenío next to the church, but this is beyond walking distance on a day-visit.

Othoní

Six kilometres north, **Othoní** is the largest, and at first sight the least inviting of Corfu's satellite islands. The island has a handful of good tavernas and rooms for rent in its port, **ÁMMOS**, but the reception from islanders who aren't in the tourism trade is rather cool. Ámmos has two beaches, both pebbly, one in its harbour. The village kafenío serves as a very basic shop, and there's one smart **restaurant**, *La Locanda dei Sogni*, which also has **rooms** (☎06630/71 640; ❸) – though these tend to be prebooked by Italian visitors. Three tavernas, *New York*, *Mikros* and tiny *Rainbow*, offer decent but fairly limited menus; the owner of the *New York* also offers rooms for rent (☎06630/71 581; ❸). The island's interior is dramatic, and a path up out of the village leads through rocky, tree-covered hills to the central hamlet, **Horió**, after a thirty-minute walk. Horió, like other inland villages, is heavily depopulated – only about sixty people still live on the island through the winter – but it's very attractive, and the architecture is completely traditional.

Eríkoussa

East of Othoní, **Eríkoussa** is the most popular destination for day-trippers. It's invariably hyped as a "desert island" trip, although this is a desert island with a medium-sized hotel, rooms, tavernas and a year-round community. In high season, it gets very busy: Eríkoussa has a large diaspora living in America and elsewhere who return to family homes in their droves in summer, so you may find your *yiá soú* or *kaliméra* returned in a Brooklyn accent.

Eríkoussa has an excellent golden sandy beach right by the harbour, with great swimming, and another, quieter, beach reached by a path across the wooded island interior. The island's cult following keeps its one **hotel**, the *Erikoussa* (☎06630/71 110, ☏71 555; ❹), busy through the season; rooms are en suite with balconies and views. Simpler rooms are available from the *Anemomilos* **taverna** (☎06630/71 647; ❸). If you're hoping to stay, phoning ahead is essential, as is taking anything you might not be able to buy – the only shop is a snack bar selling basic groceries.

Paxí (Paxos) and Andípaxi

Verdant, hilly and still largely unspoiled, **Paxí (Paxos)** is the smallest of the main Ionian islands. Barely 12km by 4km, it has no sandy beaches, no historical sites, only two hotels and a serious water shortage, yet is so popular it is best avoided in high season. It's a particular favourite of yachting flotillas, whose spending

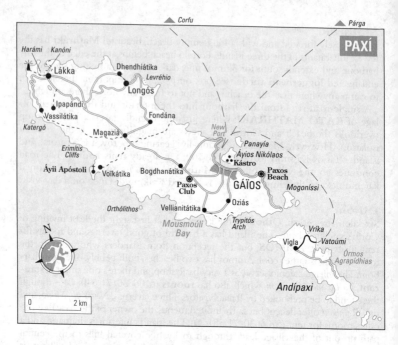

habits have brought the island an upmarket reputation, making it just about the most expensive place to visit in the Ionian islands and lending it a rather cliquey air. Pockets of unauthorized camping, however, are tolerated after the closure of the official site. Most accommodation is block-booked by travel companies, though there are local tour operators whose holiday deals are often a fraction of the price. The capital, **Gáïos**, is quite cosmopolitan, with delis and boutiques, but northerly **Lákka** and tiny **Longós** are where hardcore Paxophiles head.

Gáïos

Most visitors arrive at the New Port 1km north of **GÁÏOS**, a pleasant town built around a small square on the seafront overlooking two islands, Áyios Nikólaos and Panayía. Room owners often meet ferries, although it's advisable to phone ahead: try Gáïos Travel (☎06620/32 033, ⒻP32 175, Ⓔgaiostrv@otenet.gr) or Bouas Tours (☎06620/32 401, ⒻP32 610, Ⓔinfo@bouastours.gr), both situated on the seafront. Paxí's two seasonal **hotels** are both near Gáïos: the *Paxos Beach Hotel* (☎06620/31 211, ⒻP32 695, Ⓔzerbas1@otenet.gr; ❻ half-board) which has smart en-suite bungalows on a hillside above a pebbly beach 2km south of town, and the fairly luxurious *Paxos Club Hotel* (☎06620/32 450, ⒻP32 097; ❻), 2km inland from Gáïos.

Gáïos boasts a number of decent **tavernas**, most of which are on the pricey side. One exception is the friendly family-run *Acropol*, on a side street off the square, which serves wholesome meat, fish and veg dishes at very reasonable rates. Also recommended are *Dodo's*, set in a garden inland from the Anemoyiannis statue; the *Volcano*, which is the best of those on the square; and *Vassilis*, which has the best selection and prices of the trio to the left of the road up towards the bus stop. *The Cellar* at the top of the square is the best place for a tasty *souvláki*. Other options include the *Blue Grotto*, in an alleyway off the square, or *Carcoleggio's*, 1.5km out of town towards Bogdhanátika, popular with locals for its grills. The two kafenía, the *Gonia* by the old ferry ramp and the unnamed one opposite the *Acropol* are the traditional places for a coffee or drink. Trendier bars include *Carnayo* near the square and *Deep Blue* round the quay towards the new port. The *Phoenix* disco out by the new port opens sporadically after midnight and has a terrace for sublunar fun, while the inland *Tango*, beyond the bus stop, is a more regular disco.

Inland are some of the island's oldest settlements, such as Oziás and Vellianitátika, in prime walking country, but with few if any facilities. Noel Rochford's book, *Landscapes of Paxos* (Sunflower), lists dozens of walks, and cartographers Elizabeth and Ian Bleasdale's *Paxos Walking Map* is on sale in most travel agencies.

The rest of the island

Paxí's one main road runs along the spine of the island, with a turning at the former capital Magaziá, leading down to the tiny port of Longós. The main road continues to Lákka, the island's funkiest resort, set in a breathtaking horseshoe bay. Two buses ply the road between Gáïos and Lákka six times a day, most diverting to swing through Longós. The Gáïos–Lákka bus (30min) affords panoramic views, and the route is an excellent walk of under three hours (one-way). A taxi between the two costs around €8–9.

Approached from the south, **LÁKKA** is an unprepossessing jumble of buildings, but once in its maze of alleys and neo-Venetian buildings, or on the quay with views of distant Corfu, you do get a sense of its charm. Lákka's two **beaches**, Harámi and Kanóni, are the best on the island, although there have been complaints in high season of pollution from the yachts that cram the bay. The terraced olive grove behind Kanóni is a favourite with campers but has no facilities. **Accommodation** is plentiful (except in high season) from the island's two biggest agencies: Planos Holidays (☏06620/31 744, ℱ31 010, ℮planos@otenet.gr) or Routsis (☏06620/31 807, ℱ31 161, ℮routsis-holidays@ker.forthnet.gr), both on the seafront. The latter runs two bargain rooming houses, *Ilios* and *Lefcothea* (both ❷). There's an embarrassment of good tavernas, such as the friendly *Nionios* and its new neighbour *Pounendes*, or the more upmarket *Pergola* and exotic *Rosa di Paxos*. There's a similar wealth of bars: the seafront *Romantica* cocktail bar, *Serano* in the square, or the friendly *To Ariston* kafenío – the hub of village life. Lákka is also well situated for **walking**: up onto either promontory, to the lighthouse or Vassilátika, or to Longós and beyond. One of the finest walks – if combined with a bus or taxi back – is an early evening visit to the **Erimítis cliffs**, near the hamlet of Voïkátika: on clear afternoons, the cliffs change colour at twilight like a seagoing Uluru (Ayers Rock).

LONGÓS is the prettiest village on the island, and perfectly sited for morning sun and idyllic alfresco breakfasts. The village is dominated by the upmarket villa crowd, but the Planos office here (☏ & ℱ 06620/31 530) is the best place to look for accommodation. Longós has some of the island's best restaurants: the seafront *Vassilis*, which does terrific fish dishes, *Kakarantzas*, with a wide variety of fish and seafood, and *Iy Gonia*, a much simpler and cheaper *psitariá*. *To Taxidhi* on the quay is a nice spot for coffee or an early drink, while *Four Seasons* and *Ores* pander to the night-owls.

Longós has a small, scruffy beach, with sulphur springs favoured by local grannies, but most people swim off Levréhio beach in the next bay south, which gets the occasional camper. (Islanders are touchy about camping for fear of fires; it's politic to ask at the beach taverna if it's acceptable to camp.) Longós is at the bottom of a steep winding hill, making **walking** a chore, but the short circle around neighbouring **Dhendhiátika** provides excellent views, and the walk to **Fondána** and **Magaziá** can be done to coincide with a bus back to Longós.

Andípaxi

A mile south, Paxí's tiny sibling **Andípaxi** has scarcely any accommodation and no facilities beyond several beach tavernas open during the day in season. It is most easily reached by the frequent shuttle kaïkia from Gáios (€3–4).The sandy, blue-water coves have been compared with the Caribbean, but you'll have to share them with kaïkia and sea taxis from all three villages, plus larger craft from Corfu (boats from Paxí may also take you to its sea stacks and caves, the most dramatic in the Ionian islands).

Boats basically deposit you either at the sandy **Vríka beach** or the longer pebble beach of **Vatoúmi**.Vríka has a taverna at each end, of which *Spiros* (☎06620/31 172) has good food and can arrange self-catering accommodation up in **Vígla**, the island's hilltop settlement, on a weekly basis.Vatoúmi's only facility is the justifiably named *Bella Vista*, perched on a cliff high above the beach, although a taverna was under construction behind the beach at the time of writing.

For a swim in quieter surroundings the trick is to head south away from the pleasure-craft moorings, although path widening has made even the quieter bays more accessible. Paths also lead inland to connect the handful of homes and the southerly lighthouse, but there are no beaches of any size on Andípaxi's western coastline and thick thorny scrub makes it difficult to approach. In low season, there's also the risk of bad weather keeping pleasure craft in port and stranding you on the island.

Lefkádha (Lefkas)

Lefkádha is an oddity. Connected to the mainland by a long causeway through lagoons, it barely feels like an island, at least on the busier eastern side – and historically in fact it isn't. It is separated from the mainland by a canal cut by Corinthian colonists in the seventh century BC, which has been re-dredged (after silting up) on various occasions since, and today is spanned by a thirty-metre boat-drawbridge built in 1986. Lefkádha was long an important strategic base, and approaching the causeway you pass a series of fortresses, climaxing in the fourteenth-century castle of **Santa Maura** – the Venetian name for the island. These defences were too close to the mainland to avoid an Ottoman tenure, which began in 1479, but the Venetians wrested back control a couple of centuries later.They were in turn overthrown by Napoleon in 1797 and then the British took over as Ionian protectors in 1810. It wasn't until 1864 that Lefkádha, like the rest of the Ionian archipelago, was reunited with Greece.

At first glance Lefkádha is not overwhelmingly attractive, although it is a substantial improvement on the mainland just opposite.The whiteness of its rock strata – *lefkás* has the same root as *lefkós*, "white" – is often brutally exposed by road cuts and quarries, and the highest ridge is bare except for ugly military and telecom installations.With the marshes and sumpy inlets on the east coast, mosquitoes can be a midsummer problem. On the other hand, the island is a fertile place, supporting cypresses, olive groves and vineyards, particularly on the western slopes, and life in the mountain villages remains relatively untouched, with the older women still wearing traditional local dress – two skirts (one forming a bustle), a dark headscarf and a rigid bodice.

Lefkádha has been the home of various literati, including two prominent Greek poets, Angelos Sikelianos and Aristotelis Valaoritis, and the British writer Lafcadio Hearn. Support for the arts continues in the form of a well-attended international **festival** of theatre and folk-dancing, now extended throughout the summer, with most events staged in the Santa Maura castle. On a smaller scale, frequent village celebrations accompanied by *bouzoúki* and clarinet ensure that the strong local wine flows well into the early hours.

LEFKÁDHA

Lefkádha remains relatively undeveloped, with just two major resorts: **Vassilikí**, in its vast bay in the south, claims to be Europe's biggest windsurf centre; **Nydhrí**, on the east coast, overlooks the island's picturesque archipelago, and is the launching point for the barely inhabited island of **Meganíssi**.

Lefkádha Town and around

Lefkádha Town sits at the island's northernmost tip, hard by the causeway. Like other southerly capitals, it was hit by the earthquakes of 1948 and 1953, and the town was devastated, with the exception of a few **Italianate churches**. As a precaution against further quakes, little was rebuilt above two storeys, and most houses acquired second storeys of wood, giving the western dormitory area an unintentionally quaint look. The town is small – you can cross it on foot in little over ten minutes – and despite the destruction, still very attractive, especially around the main square, Platía Ayíou Spyridhónos, and the arcaded high street of Ioánnou Méla. Much of Lefkádha Town is pedestrian-only, mainly because of the narrowness of its lanes. The centre boasts over half a dozen richly decorated private family churches, usually locked and best visited around services. Many contain gems from the Ionian School of painting, including work by its founder, Zakynthian Panayiotis Doxaras.

The folklore museum was closed for renovation at the time of writing, but you can catch a glimpse of the old way of life at the quaint little **Phonograph Museum** (daily 9am–1pm & 6–11pm; free), which is dedicated to antique phonographs and bric-a-brac, and sells cassettes of rare traditional music. On the northwestern seafront a new Cultural Centre houses the newly expanded **archeological museum** (Tues–Sun 8.30am–3pm; €1.50), which contains interesting, well-labelled displays on aspects of daily life, religious worship and funerary customs in ancient times, as well as a room on prehistory dedicated to the work of eminent German archeologist Wilhelm Dörpfeld.

Practicalities

The **bus station** is on Dhimítri Golémi opposite the small yacht marina. It now has services to almost every village on the island, and Nydhrí, Vassilikí and west-coast beaches such as Káthisma have extensive daily services. Car and motorbike rental is useful for exploring; try EuroHire, Golémi 5 (℡06450/26 776), near the bus station or I Love Santas (℡06450/25 250) next to the *Ionian Star* hotel. Most resorts have bicycle-rental outlets, although you'll need stamina to do anything more than local touring.

Hotels have actually dwindled in Lefkádha Town, and currently number just six. All are in busy areas, but the more expensive ones are glazed against the noise and heat. Now in private hands and renamed, the *Ionian Star* (℡06450/24 672, Ⅎ25 125; ❻) has become the plushest hotel with brand-new fittings and a pool. The other smart hotels are the stylish seafront *Nirikos*, Ayías Mávras (℡06450/24 132, Ⅎ23 756; ❻), the cosy *Santa Maura*, Spyridhónos Viánda 2 (℡06450/21 308–9, Ⅎ26 253; ❹) and the large *Lefkas*, Pétrou Filípa Panáyou (℡06450/23 916, Ⅎ24 579; ❻). The *Patras*, Platía Ayíou Spyridhónos (℡06450/22 359; ❷) is a bargain, as is the *Byzantio*, Dörpfeld 40 (℡ & Ფ 06450/21 315; ❷); both are small and basic, in noisy areas of town and are only guaranteed to open in high season. There are simple **rooms** in the dormitory area west of Dörpfeld: the Lefkádha Room Owners Association (℡06450/21 266) can help, or try the *Pinelopis Rooms* (℡06450/24 175; ❷) in Odhós Pinelópis, off the seafront two short blocks from the pontoon bridge. Lefkádha Town has no campsite, although there are decent sites at Karyótes and Epískopos, a few kilometres to the south.

The best **restaurants** are hidden in the backstreets: the *Regantos* taverna, on Dhimárhou Venióti is the local favourite, but opening hours can be erratic. If it's closed, head for the *Lighthouse*, in its own small garden on Filarmonikís. The *Romantika* on Mitropóleos has nightly performances of Lefkadhan *kantádhes*, while the smartest place in town is the *Adriatica*, Faneroménis and Merarhías, where people tend to dress up to eat.

Of the **bars** in the main square, the *Serano* ouzerí/café is the cheapest, with occasional evening entertainment from buskers, jugglers and even fire-eaters. Further from the action the best is the *Cafe Karfakis*, on Ioánnou Melá, an old-style kafenío with splendid *mezédhes*, or the real local hangout *Theofilos* further along. The trendiest bars such as *Excess* and *Il Posto* line the seafront west of the bridge. The town's outdoor **cinema**, Eleni, on Faneroménis, has two showings and programmes change daily.

Around Lefkádha Town

The town has a decent and fairly large shingle beach west of the lagoon at **Yíras**, a forty-minute walk from the centre. In season there's also a bus (hourly 10am–2pm) from the bus station. Roughly 4km long, the beach is often virtually deserted even in high season; there's a **taverna** at either end, and at the western end a couple of **bars** in the renovated windmills, as well as the trendy *Club Milos*.

The uninhabited **Faneroméni monastery** (daily 8am–2pm & 4–8pm; free) is reached by any of the west-coast buses, or by a steep hike on foot from town (30min) through the hamlet of Fríni. There's a small museum and chapel, and an ox's yoke and hammer, used when Nazi occupiers forbade the use of bells. There are wonderful views over the town and lagoon from the Fríni road.

The island's **interior**, best reached by bus or car from Lefkádha Town, offers imposing mountainscapes and excellent walking between villages only a few kilometres apart. **KARYÁ** is its centre, with a hotel, the *Karia Village Hotel* (℡06450/41 004; ❹), tucked away above the village, and some rooms: try the Kakiousis family (℡06450/61 136; ❷), Olga Lazari (℡06450/61 547; ❷) or Michael Halikias (℡06450/61 026; ❶). The leafy town square has a popular taverna, *Iy Klimataria*, just off the platía and two *psistariés* on it, *Ta Platania*, and the smarter *O Rousos*. Karyá is the centre of the island's lace and weaving industry, with a fascinating small **museum** set in a lacemaker's home. The historic and scenic villages of **Vafkerí** and **Englouví** are within striking distance, with the west-coast hamlets of **Dhrymónas** and **Exánthia** a hike over the hills.

The east coast to Vassilikí

Lefkádha's east coast is the most accessible and the most developed part of the island. Apart from the campsites at Karyótes (*Kariotes Beach*, ℡ & ℻ 06450/71 103) and Epískopos (*Episcopos Beach*, ℡06450/71 388), there's little point stopping before the small fishing ports of **LIYIÁ**, which has some rooms and the hotel *Konaki* (℡06450/71 127, ℻71 125; ❻), or **NIKIÁNA**, where you'll find the hotel *Pegasus* (℡06450/71 766, ℻25 290; ❻) and the smarter but considerably cheaper *Ionion* (℡06450/71 721, ℻71 852; ❺), as well as the *Porto Fino* pension (℡06450/71 389; ❸). In addition, Nikiána has a selection of fine tavernas, notably the *Pantazis*, which also has rooms to let, and the *Lefko Akroyiali*, a good fish restaurant further south. Beaches here tend to be pebbly and small.

Most package travellers will find themselves in **NYDHRÍ**, the coast's biggest resort, with ferry connections to Meganíssi and myriad **boat trips** around the nearby satellite islands. The German archeologist Wilhelm Dörpfeld believed

THE IONIAN ISLANDS | The east coast

Nydhrí, rather than Itháki, to be the site of Odysseus's capital, and did indeed find Bronze Age tombs on the plain nearby. His theory identifying ancient Ithaca with Lefkádha fell into disfavour after his death in 1940, although his obsessive attempts to give the island some status over its neighbour are honoured by a statue on Nydhrí's quay. Dörpfeld's tomb is tucked away at Ayía Kyriakí on the opposite side of the bay, near the house in which he once lived, visible just above the chapel and lighthouse on the far side of the water.

Nydhrí is an average resort, with some good pebble beaches and a lovely setting, but the centre is an ugly strip with heavy traffic. The best place to stay is the *Hotel Gorgona* (℡06450/92 197, ℻92 268; ❸), set in a lush garden away from the traffic a minute along the Ráhi road, which leads to Nydhrí's very own **waterfall**, a 45-minute walk inland. There are also rooms in the centre – try Emilios Gazis (℡06450/92 703; ❷) and Athanasios Konidharis (℡06450/92 749; ❸). The town's focus is the Aktí Aristotéli Onássi quay, where most of the rather ritzy **restaurants** and **bars** are found. The *Barrel* and *Il Sappore* restaurants are pricey but recommended, as is the *Agra* on the beach, slightly less so *George's*. However, eating is better value on the noisy main drag – try *Agrabeli* or *Ta Kalamia*. Nightlife centres around bars like *No Name* and *Byblos*, and the late-night *Status* or *Tropicana*.

Nydhrí sits at the mouth of a deep inlet stretching to the next village, somnolent **VLYHÓ**, with a few good tavernas and mooring for yachts. Over the Yéni peninsula across the inlet is the large **Dhessími Bay**, home to two campsites: *Santa Maura Camping* (℡06450/95 007, ℻95 493), and *Dessimi Beach Camping* (℡06450/95 374, ℻95 190), one at each end of the beach but often packed with outsized mobile homes. The *Pirofani* beach taverna in between them is excellent.

The coast road beyond Vlyhó turns inland and climbs the foothills of Mount Stavrotás, through the hamlets of Katohóri and Paliokatoúna to **Póros**, a quiet village with few facilities. Just south of here is the increasingly busy beach resort of **MIKRÓS YIALÓS**, boasting a handful of **tavernas**, a few rooms at *Oceanis Studios* (℡ & ℻ 06450/95 095; ❹); plus the posh *Poros Beach Camping* (℡06450/95 452, ℻95 152), which has bungalows (❹), shops and a pool. For food, try the *Rouda Bay* taverna opposite the beach, which also has rooms (℡ & ℻ 06450/95 634, ✉manolitsis@otenet.gr; ❺).

A panoramic detour off the main road to quiet **Vournikás** and **Sývros** is recommended to walkers and drivers (the Lefkádha–Vassilíki bus also visits); both places have tavernas and some private rooms. It's around 14km to the next resort, the fjord-like inlet of **SÝVOTA**, 2km down a steep hill (bus twice daily). There's no beach except for a remote cove, but some fine fish tavernas: the *Ionion* is the most popular, but the *Delfinia* and *Kavos* are also good. Ask at the *Delfinia* or the adjacent Yiannis supermarket for **rooms** (℡06450/31 180, ℻31 050; ❸), or there's a basic unofficial campsite by the bus stop at the edge of the village.

Beyond the Sývota turning, the mountain road dips down towards Kondárena, almost a suburb of **VASSILIKÍ**, the island's premier watersports resort. Winds in the huge bay draw vast numbers of windsurfers, with light morning breezes for learners and tough afternoon blasts for advanced surfers. Booking your **accommodation** ahead is mandatory in high season. Hotels are not cheap: *Pension Hollidays* (℡06450/31 011; ❹), round the corner from the ferry dock, is a reasonable option with air conditioning and TV in all rooms. Also good value for its rating is slightly more upmarket *Hotel Apollo* (℡06450/31 122, ℻31 142; ❹) nearby. In the centre of town, the two main hotels are the smart and reasonably priced *Vassiliki Bay Hotel* (℡06450/21 567,

Ⓕ23 567; ④) and the *Hotel Lefkatas* (Ⓣ06450/31 801, Ⓕ31 804; ⑤), a large, modern building overlooking the busiest road in town. Rooms and apartments are available along the beach road to Póndi: *Billy's House* (Ⓣ06450/31 418; ③) and *Christina Politi's Rooms* (Ⓣ06450/31 440; ③) are smart and purpose-built or ask at the central Samba Tours (Ⓣ06450/31 520). The largest of the three beach windsurf centres, *Club Vassiliki*, offers all-in **windsurf tuition** and accommodation deals. Vassilikí's only **campsite**, the large *Camping Vassiliki Beach* (Ⓣ06450/31 308, Ⓕ31 458), is about 500m along the beach road; it has its own restaurant, bar and shop.

Vassilikí's pretty quayside is lined with **tavernas** and bars, notably the *Dolphin Psistaria*, the glitzier *Restaurant Miramare*, specializing in fish, the *Penguin* and *Alexander*, which has pizza, as well as the *Jasmine Garden* Chinese. The best place for a **drink** is *Livanakis* kafenío (next to the bakery), now modernized but still genuine and cheap.

The beach at Vassilikí is stony and poor, but improves 1km on at tiny **PÓNDI**; most non-windsurfers, however, use the daily kaïki trips to nearby Ayiófili or around Cape Lefkátas to the superior beaches at Pórto Katsíki and Egremní on the sandy west coast. There's a gradually increasing number of places to stay at Póndi, some with great views of the bay and plain behind, particularly from the terrace of the *Ponti Beach Hotel* (Ⓣ06450/31 572, Ⓕ31 576; ⑤), which is very popular with holidaying Greeks, and has a decent restaurant and bar. The *Nefeli* (Ⓣ06450/31 515; ③), right on the beach, is much better value though.

The west coast

Tsoukaládhes, just 6km from Lefkádha, is developing a roadside tourism business, but better beaches lie a short distance to the south, so there's very little reason to stay here. Four kilometres on, the road plunges down to the sand-and-pebble **Pefkoúlia beach**, one of the longest on the island, with two tavernas at the north end, one of which, *Mesoyios*, has rooms (Ⓣ06450/97 070, Ⓕ97 170; ④) and unofficial camping down at the other end, about 2km away.

Jammed into a gorge between Pefkoúlia and the next beach, Mýlos, is **AÏ NIKÍTAS**, the prettiest resort on Lefkádha, a jumble of lanes and small wooden buildings. The back of the village is a dust-blown car park, which detracts from the appeal of the pleasant, if basic, *O Aï Nikitas* **campsite** (Ⓣ06450/97 301, Ⓕ21 173), set in terraced olive groves. The most attractive **accommodation** is in the *Pension Ostria* (Ⓣ06450/97 483, Ⓕ97 300; ④), a beautiful blue-and-white building above the village decorated in a mix of beachcomber and ecclesiastical styles. The *Villa Milia* (Ⓣ06450/97 475; ③), by the junction, or the *Elena patisserie* (Ⓣ06450/97 385; ③) offer better rates than most. Other options are in the alleys that run off the main drag; the best bets are the small *Hotel Selene* (Ⓣ06450/97 369; ④) and quieter *Olive Tree* (Ⓣ06450/97 453, Ⓕ97 153; ④), which is also signposted from the main road. The best tavernas include the *Sapfo* fish taverna by the sea and the *T'Agnantia*, just above the main street, which serves excellent traditional cuisine. *Captain's Corner* near the beach is the liveliest drinking venue.

Sea taxis (€1.50 one-way) ply between Aï Nikítas and **Mýlos** beach, or it's a 45-minute walk (or bus ride) to the most popular beach on the coast, **Káthisma**, a shadeless kilometre of fine sand, which becomes nudist and a lot less crowded beyond the large jutting rocks halfway along. There are two tavernas on the beach: the barn-like *Kathisma Beach* (Ⓣ06450/97 050, Ⓕ97 335; ⑤), with smart apartments, and the expensive and unfriendly *Akroyiali*. Above the beach the *Sunset* has **rooms** (☎06450/97 488; ❹) and the *Balkoni* restaurant commands fine views. Beyond Káthisma, hairpin bends climb the flank of Mount Méga towards the small village of **KALAMÍTSI**, a much cheaper base for this area: Spyros Karelis (☎06450/99 214; ❷) and Spyros Veryinis (☎06450/99 411; ❷) have rooms. *Hermes* (☎06450/99 417; ❷), the *Blue and White House* (☎06450/99 413; ❸) and *Pansion Nontas* (☎06450/99 451; ❸) have larger rooms and apartments. There are also three good tavernas: the *Paradeisos* in its own garden with fountain, the more basic *Ionio* and, just north of the village, the aptly titled *Panoramic View*. Three kilometres down a newly paved road is the village's quiet sandy beach.

South of Kalamítsi, past the hamlets of Hortáta, which boasts the excellent *Lygos* taverna with rooms (☎06450/33 395; ❷), and Komíli, the landscape becomes almost primeval. At 38km from Lefkádha Town, **ATHÁNI** is Lefkádha's most remote spot to stay, with a couple of good tavernas which both have great-value rooms: the *Panorama* (☎06450/33 291, Ⓕ33 476; ❷) and *O Alekos* (☎06560/33 484; ❷), the latter only open in high season. Three of the Ionian's choicest **beaches**, each with basic refreshment facilities, are accessible from Atháni: the nearest, reached by a 4km paved road is **Yialós**, followed by **Egremní**, down a steep incline unpaved for the last 2km. Further south an asphalted road leads to the dramatic and popular twin beach of **Pórto Katsíki**, where there are several better-stocked *kantínas* on the cliff above.

Keeping to the main road for 14km from Atháni will bring you to barren **Cape Lefkátas**, which drops abruptly 75m into the sea. Byron's Childe Harold sailed past this point, and "saw the evening star above, Leucadia's far projecting rock of woe: And hail'd the last resort of fruitless love". The fruitless love is a reference to Sappho, who in accordance with the ancient legend that you could cure yourself of unrequited love by leaping into these waters, leapt – and died. In her honour the locals termed the place *Kávos tís Kyrás* ("Lady's Cape"), and her act was imitated by the lovelorn youths of Lefkádha for centuries afterwards. And not just by the lovelorn, for the act (known as *katapondismós*) was performed annually by scapegoats – always a criminal or a lunatic – selected by priests from the Apollo temple whose sparse ruins lie close by. Feathers and even live birds were attached to the victims to slow their descent and boats waiting below took the chosen one, dead or alive, away to some place where the evil banished with them could do no further harm. The rite continued into the Roman era, when it degenerated into little more than a fashionable stunt by decadent youth. These days, in a more controlled modern re-enactment, Greek hang-gliders hold a tournament from the cliffs every July.

Lefkádha's satellites

Lefkádha has four satellite islands clustered off its east coast, although only one, **Meganíssi**, the largest and most interesting, is accessible. **Skorpiós**, owned by the Onassis family, fields armed guards to deter visitors. **Madhourí**, owned by the family of poet Nanos Valaorítis, is private and similarly off-limits, while tiny **Spárti** is a large scrub-covered rock. Day-trips from Nydhrí skirt all three islands, and some stop to allow swimming in coves.

Meganíssi

Meganíssi, twenty minutes by frequent daily ferries from Nydhrí, is a large island with limited facilities but a magical, if bleak landscape. Ferries stop first at **Spiliá**, below **SPARTOHÓRI**, an immaculate village with whitewashed buildings and an abundance of bougainvillea. The locals – many returned émigrés from Australia – live from farming and fishing and are genuinely welcoming. You arrive at a jetty on a pebble beach with a few tavernas and a primitive but free (for a night or two only) campsite behind the excellent *Star Taverna*. The village proper boasts three restaurants: a pizza place called the *Tropicana*, which can direct you to **rooms** (T06450/51 486; ❶–❸), the *Gakias* and the traditional taverna *Lakis*. Further west round the coast at Áyios Yiánnis there is a good beach with the *Il Paradiso* taverna and a makeshift campsite, a great spot to unwind in.

The attractive inland village of **KATOMÉRI** is an hour's walk through magnificent country. It has the island's one **hotel**, the *Meganissi*, a comfortable place with a restaurant and pool (T06450/51 240, F51 639; ❹), and a few café-bars. Ten-minutes' walk downhill is the main port of **VATHÝ**, with some accommodation (*Different Studios*: T06450/22 170; ❸) and several highly-rated restaurants, notably the waterside taverna, *Porto Vathi*, which Lefkádhans flock to on ferries for Sunday lunch, and the *Rose Garden*. After the high-season madness of Nydhrí, Meganíssi's unspoiled landscape is a tonic, and it's easy to organize a **day-trip** from Nydhrí, getting off at Spiliá, walking via Spartohóri to Katoméri for lunch at the *Meganissi* or down at Vathý, from where you can catch the ferry back. Paths lead from Katoméri to remote beaches, including popular **Ambelákia**, but these aren't realistic on a day-trip.

Kefalloniá

Kefalloniá is the largest of the Ionian islands – a place that has real towns as well as resorts. Like its neighbours, Kefalloniá was overrun by Italians and Germans in World War II; the "handover" after Italy's capitulation in 1943 led to the massacre of over five thousand Italian troops on the island by invading German forces. These events form a key episode in Louis de Bernières' novel, *Captain Corelli's Mandolin*, a tragicomic epic of life on the island, which takes place mostly during the occupation and whose film version was made on the island in 2000.

Until the late 1980s, the island paid scant regard to tourism; perhaps this was partly due to a feeling that Kefalloniá could not easily be marketed. Virtually all of its towns and villages were levelled in the 1953 earthquake, and these masterpieces of Venetian architecture had been the one touch of elegance in a severe, mountainous landscape. A more likely explanation, however, for the island's late emergence on the Greek tourist scene is the Kefallonians' legendary reputation for insular pride and stubbornness, and a good measure of eccentricity.

Having decided on the advantages of an easily exploitable industry, however, Kefalloniá is at present in the midst of a tourism boom. Long favoured by Italians, it has begun attracting British package companies, for whom an airport terminal was constructed in the mid-Nineties, while virtually every decent beach has been endowed with restaurants. There are definite attractions here, with some **beaches** as good as any in the Ionian islands, and a fine (if pricey) local wine, the dry white *Rombola*. Mercifully, the anticipated Corelli factor has not so far led to the island becoming either oversubscribed or overexpensive. Moreover, the island seems able to soak up a lot of people without feeling at all crowded, and the magnificent scenery speaks for itself, the escarpments culminating in the 1632-metre bulk of **Mount Énos**, declared a national park to protect the fir trees (*Abies cephalonica*) named after the island.

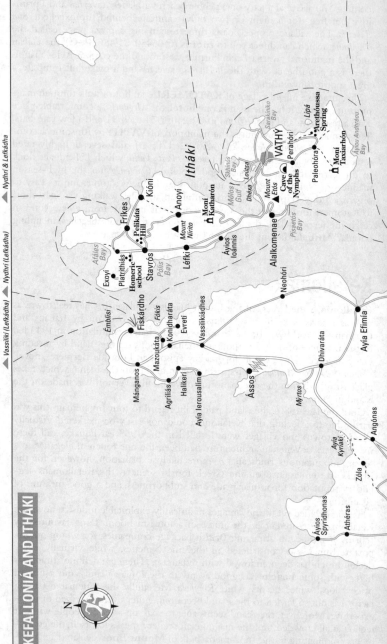

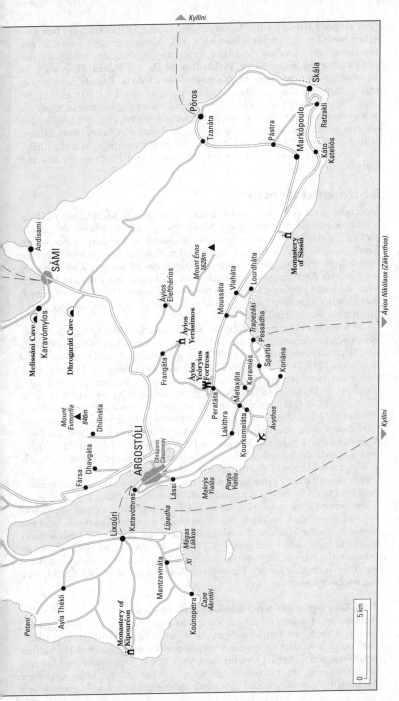

▲ *Kyllíni*

▼ *Áyios Nikólaos [Zákynthos]*

▼ *Kyllíni*

For **airport** arrival see the Argostóli section on p.513. Kefalloniá's **bus** system is basic but expanding, and with a little legwork it can be used to get you almost anywhere on the island. Key routes connect Argostóli with the main tourist centres of **Sámi**, **Fiskárdho**, **Skála** and **Póros**. There's a useful connection from Sámi to the tiny resort of **Ayía Efimía**, which also attracts many package travellers. If you're using a motorbike, take care, as the terrain is very rough in places – although an increasing number of roads are being surfaced – and the gradients can sometimes be a bit challenging for underpowered machines. The island has a plethora of **ferry** connections, principally from Fiskárdho to Lefkádha and Itháki, and from Sámi to Itháki, Pátra and Italy, as well as links from Argostóli and Póros to Kyllíni and Pessádha to Zákynthos.

Sámi and around

Most boats dock at the large and functional port town of **SÁMI**, built and later rebuilt near the south end of the Itháki straits, more or less on the site of ancient Sami. This was the capital of the island in Homeric times, when Kefalloniá was part of Ithaca's maritime kingdom: today the administrative hierarchy is reversed, Itháki being considered the backwater. With the only ferry link to Pátra, frequent connections to Itháki and direct links to Italy, the town is clearly preparing itself for a burgeoning future. The long sandy beach that stretches round the bay is quite adequate; 2km beyond ancient Sami, lies a fine pebble beach, **Andísami**.

The town has three big **hotels**: the *Sami Beach* (☎06740/22 802, ⓕ22 846, ⓔsamibeach@otenet.gr; ⑥) and friendly *Athina Beach* (☎06740/23 066, ⓕ23 040; ⑨), both actually situated at the far end of the beach in Karavómylos, and the *Pericles* (☎06740/22 780, ⓕ22 787; ⑨), over 1km along the Argostóli road, which has extensive grounds, two pools and sports facilities. The best mid-range bet is the *Ionion* (☎06740/22 035; ③), followed by the *Melissani* (☎ & ⓕ 06740/22 464; ④), both behind the seafront; on the front itself the *Kastro* (☎06740/22 282, ⓕ23 004; ④) is very comfortable. Both *períptera* on the quay offer rooms, as do a variety of private homes a few blocks back from the front. Sámi's **campsite**, *Camping Karavomilos Beach* (☎06740/22 480, ⓕ22 932), has over 300 well-shaded spaces, a taverna, shop and bar, and opens onto the beach. It is by far the better of the island's two official sites.

Sámi doesn't have a great many **tavernas** beyond those on the seafront; visitors tend to go to the slightly touristic *Adonis* or the *Dolphins*, but cheaper and more genuine choices are *Gorgona* and *O Faros*, both with a good selection of veg and meat dishes, including the famous local meat pie. Better still, head further towards the beach to the *Akroyiali*, where you can sample fresh seafood, succulent meat dishes and good local wine. The *Riviera* and *Aqua Marina* are the favourite **bars** in the evenings, while the best place for a snack breakfast or ice cream is *Captain Jimmy's*. The seafront Sami Center (☎06740/22 254) rents out **motorbikes** at fair rates.

The Dhrogaráti and Melissáni caves

Another good reason to stay in Sámi is its proximity to the Drogharáti and Melissáni caves; the former is 5km out of town towards Argostóli, the latter 3km north towards Ayía Efimía. A very impressive stalagmite-bedecked chamber, **Dhrogaráti** (April–Oct daily 8am–9pm; €3) is occasionally used for concerts thanks to its marvellous acoustics – Maria Callas once sang here. **Melissáni** (8am–sunset; €4.70) is partly submerged in brackish water, which, amazingly, emerges from an underground fault which leads the whole way under the island to a point near Argostóli. At that point, known as Katavóthres, the sea gushes endlessly into a subterranean channel – and, until the 1953 earthquake disrupted it – the current was used to drive sea mills. That the water, now as then, still ends up in the cave has been shown with fluorescent tracer dye. The beautiful textures and shades created by the light pouring through the collapsed roof of the cave make it a must.

Ayía Efimía

AYÍA EFIMÍA, 9km north of Sámi, is a friendly little fishing harbour popular with package operators, yet with no major developments. Its two drawbacks are its beaches – the largest, Paradise beach, is around 20m of shingle, although there are other coves to the south – and its poor transport connections (only two daily buses to Sámi and Fiskárdho). **Accommodation** here is good at two small, smart **hotels**: *Pyllaros* (☎06740/61 800, ℱ61 801; ❻) and the better-value *Moustakis* (☎ & ℱ 06740/61 030; ❹) or the apartments of Yerasimos Raftopoulos (☎06740/61 233, ℱ61 216; ❹). The *Dendrinos* **taverna**, round the headland past the harbour, is the place for island cuisine; the *Pergola* also has a wide range of island specialities and standard Greek dishes. Predictably, the café-bar where the film crew and actors used to hang out has been renamed *Captain Corelli's*. The town's nightclub is *Paranoia*, 700m out of town towards Fiskárdho. The *Strawberry zaharoplastío* is the place for a filling breakfast.

Southeast Kefalloniá

Travel **southeast from Sámi** has been made a lot easier by the completion of the asphalt road to **Póros** and the consequent addition of a twice-daily bus route between the two. Another route links Póros to **Skála** along the recently paved coastal road.

Póros

PÓROS was one of the island's earliest developed resorts, and definitely gives the impression of having seen better days. The town's small huddle of hotels and apartment blocks is almost unique on Kefalloniá, and not enhanced by a scruffy seafront and thin, pebbly beach.

Póros does, however, have a regular ferry link to **Kyllíni** on the mainland, a viable alternative to Sámi–Pátra. Póros is actually made up of two bays: the first, where most tourists are based, and the actual harbour, a few minutes over the headland. There's plenty of rooms, apartments and a few **hotels**. The best deal is at the cosy *Santa Irina* (☎06740/72 017, ℱ72 117, ✉maki@otenet.gr; ❸), by the crossroads inland, while the nearby *Odysseus Palace* (☎06740/72 036, ℱ72 148; ❻) often gives good discounts. The *Kefalos* (☎06740/72 139; ❹) has en-suite rooms on the seafront. Among **travel agents**, Poros Travel by the ferry dock (☎06740/72 476, ℱ72 069) offers a range of accommodation, as well as services such as car rental and ferry bookings. The main seafront has the majority of the **restaurants** and **bars**. The *Fotis Family* taverna serves good food in a pleasant setting and the *Mythos* café has internet access. At night, however, the old port is quieter and has more atmosphere, with tavernas such as *Tzivas* and the *Dionysus*, which are strong on local seafood.

The aforementioned road twists 12km around the rocky coastline from Póros to Skála at the southern extremity of the island. It's a lovely, isolated route, with scarcely a building on the way, save for a small chapel, 3km short of Skála, next to the ruins of a **Roman temple**.

Skála

In total contrast to Póros, the resort of **SKÁLA** is a low-rise development set among handsome pines above a few kilometres of good sandy beach. A **Roman villa** and some mosaics were excavated here in the 1950s, near the site of the *Golden Beach Palace* rooms, and are open daily to the public.

Its faithful return crowd keep Skála busy until well after Póros has closed for the season, and accommodation can be hard to find. There are studios and apartments at *Dionysus Rooms* (☎06710/83 283; ❸), a block south of the high street, and rooms can be found at the *Golden Beach Palace* (☎06710/83 327; ❹) above the beach or through Etam Travel Service (☎06710/83 101, ⓕ83 142). The more upmarket *Tara Beach Hotel* (☎06710/83 250, ⓕ83 344, ⓔtarabeach@tarabeach.gr; ❻) has rooms and individual bungalows in lush gardens on the edge of the beach. Skála boasts a number of good **restaurants**: the *Pines*, the *Flamingo* and, on the beach, the *Paspalis* and *Sunset*. Drinkers head for *The Loft* cocktail **bar** and the beachside *Pikiona* pool-bar.

Skála to Lourdháta

Some of the finest sandy beaches on the island are just beyond Skála below the village of Ratzákli, and around the growing microresort of **KÁTO KATELIÓS**, which already has a couple of hotels: the smart *Odyssia* (☎06710/81 615, ⓕ81 614; ❺) and the *Galini Resort* (☎06710/81 582, ⓔniko-P-@hotmail.com; ❺), which has good deals on **apartments** for four. There are also some rooms and apartments available through the *Lighthouse* taverna (☎06710/81 355; ❷) and *Jimmy's* (☎06710/81 363; ❹). Of the half a dozen restaurants and cafés at the seafront, the *Blue Sea* taverna is renowned for the freshness and quality of its fish, the *Arbouro* offers a wide selection of dishes, while the *Cozy* bar is the prime drinking location. The coast around Káto Kateliós is also Kefalloniá's key breeding ground for the loggerhead **turtle** (see box, p.525). Camping on the nearby beaches is discouraged.

The inland village of **MARKÓPOULO**, claimed by some to be the birthplace of homophonous explorer Marco Polo, witnesses a bizarre snake-handling ritual every year on August 15, the **Assumption of the Virgin festival**. The church where this ritual is enacted stands on the site of an old convent. The story goes that when the convent was attacked by pirates, the nuns prayed to be transformed into snakes to avoid being taken prisoner. Their prayers were supposedly answered, and each year the "return" of a swarm of small, harmless snakes is meant to bring the villagers good luck. As Mother Nature is unlikely to keep to such a schedule, some discreet snake-breeding on the part of the village priests must be suspected.

The coastline is largely inaccessible until the village of **VLAHÁTA**, which has some rooms and restaurants, but there's little point in staying up here, when you can turn 2km down to **LOURDHÁTA**, which has a kilometre-long shingle beach, mixed with imported sand. *Adonis* (☎06710/31 206; ❹) and *Ramona* (☎06710/31 032; ❸) have **rooms** just outside the village on the approach road, while the one **hotel**, the *Lara* (☎06710/31 157, ⓕ31 156, ⓔlarab@hol.gr; ❺), towards the beach, has en-suite rooms with sea views and a pool. There's a couple of **tavernas** on the tiny plane-shaded village square – *Alexia's* and the *Diamond* – as well as the smarter *Spiros* steak and grill house above and *Dionysus*, closer to Vlaháta, while at the beach itself *Mangas* is good, if a little costly. The beachside *Astrabar* is friendly and plays a good mix of English and Greek music into the wee hours. Another fine beach, reached by a turning from Moussáta, west of Vlaháta, is **Trapezáki**, an attractive strand with just one restaurant by the small jetty.

Argostóli and around

ARGOSTÓLI, Kefalloniá's capital, is a large and thriving town, virtually a city, with a marvellous site on a bay within a bay. The stone bridge, connecting the two sides of the inner bay, was initially constructed by the British in 1813. A small obelisk remains, but the plaque commemorating "the glory of the British Empire" has disappeared. The town was totally rebuilt after the earthquake, but has an enjoyable streetlife that remains defiantly Greek, especially during the evening *vólta* around **Platía Metaxá** – the nerve centre of town – and along the pedestrianized Lithóstrotou, which runs parallel to the seafront.

The **Korgialenio History and Folklore Museum** (Mon–Sat 9am–2pm; €3), on Ilía Zervoú behind the Municipal Theatre, has a rich collection of local religious and cultural artefacts, including photographs taken before and after the 1953 quakes. Insight into how the island's nobility used to live can be gained from a visit to the new **Focas-Cosmetatos Foundation**, on Valianoú opposite the provincial government building. It contains elegant furniture and a collection of lithographs and paintings, including works by nineteenth-century British artists Joseph Cartwright and Edward Lear. The newly refurbished **Archeological Museum** (Tues–Sun 8.30am–3pm; €1.50), on nearby R. Vergóti, has a sizeable collection of pottery, jewellery, funerary relics and statuary from prehistoric, through Mycenaean to late Classical times. It is well laid out and labelled, rivalling Kérkyra Town's (see p.485) as the best such museum in the Ionians.

Practicalities

Argostóli's shiny new **Kefalloniá airport** lies 7km south of town. There are no airport buses, and suburban bus services are so infrequent or don't go close enough that a taxi (at an inflated flat rate of around €10) is the only dependable connection. Those arriving in Argostóli by bus from Sámi or elsewhere will wind up at the KTEL **bus station**, a minute from the Dhrápano causeway and ten-minutes' walk south of the main square, Platía Metaxá. Argostóli's friendly **tourist office** (summer Mon–Fri 7.30am–2.30pm & 5–10pm, Sat 9am–1pm; rest of year Mon–Fri 7.30am–2.30pm; ℡06710/22 248, ℻24 466), on Andoníou Trítsi at the north end of the seafront, next to the port authority, has information about rooms, piles of brochures and trail guides, and can advise on transport, sites and all resorts around the island. The islandwide Sunbird agency (℡06710/23 723, ℻25 484) is a reliable outlet for car or motorbike rental. Excelixis (℡06710/25 530) at Minoos 3, behind the church on Lithóstrotou, has internet facilities.

Hotels around Platía Metaxá stay open all year, but tend to be pricey: the best bet here is the *Ionian Plaza* (℡06710/25 581, ℻25 585; ◉). A good mid-range option away from the square is the *Fokas*, Yeroulánou 1–3 (℡06710/22 566, ℻23 109; ◉), while the partly British-run *Mouikis*, Výronos 3 (℡06710/23 454, ℻24 528, ✉hotel@mouikis.com; ◉) is classy but not cheap; one of the best deals going, if you don't mind sharing a bathroom, is the friendly *Chara* (℡06710/22 427; ◉), set in a lovely shady courtyard at the corner of G. Vergóti and Dhevossétou near Dhrápano bridge. The newly upgraded pension attached to the *Tsíma Cavo* cafeteria (℡06710/23 941; ◉), opposite the Lixoúri ferry ramp, is good value, with TV in all the air-conditioned rooms. In a working town with a large permanent population, **private rooms** aren't too plentiful, but you can call the Roomowners Association (℡06710/29 109) to see what's on offer. Some of the best bargains can be found through waterfront tavernas, such as the *Kalafatis* (℡06710/22 627; ◉–◉), not far from the Dhrápano bridge on the Metaxá waterfront or the *Tzivras* (℡06710/24 259; ◉–◉), on Vandórou, just off the centre of the waterfront. A number of travel agencies also offer rooms, apartments and villas: try Ainos Travel (℡06710/22 333, ℻24 608), opposite the Archeological Museum, or Myrtos at A. Trítsi 117 (℡06710/25 895, ℻24 230, ✉Myrtostr@compulink.gr; ③–⑤). The town's **campsite**, *Argostóli Camping* (℡06710/23 487), lies 2km north of the centre, just beyond the Katovóthres sea mills; there's only an infrequent bus service in high season, so you'll probably have to walk and it's rather basic and limited in shade.

The aforementioned *Tzivras Estiatório* (only open until 5pm) is one of the best places to try Kefallonian cuisine; the upmarket *Captain's Table* **taverna** just off the main square is worth a splurge for its live *kantádhes* (see p.575), though they can just about as easily be heard from the far more reasonable *To Steki* next door. Of the seafront eateries, the *Maistrato* ouzerí near the square has a good selection of seafood and mezédhes and also features gentle live music. For a change of diet, try the *Queen Vic*, 50m towards the front from the square, a non-tacky British pub, serving excellent Indian food in the garden. Local posers hang out at *Central* café-bar and the *Flonitiko* café, both on the square, and the nearby *My Way* club-bar; the *Space Girls* bar, round the corner from *My Way*, is rather more esoteric and *Cinema* is a late-night indoor disco by the museum. The quay bars, particularly the *Aristofanis* kafenío by the Dhrápano bridge, are quiet, cheap and have the best views.

South of Argostóli: beaches and Áyios Yeóryios

Many package travellers will find themselves staying in **LÁSSI**, a short bus ride or twenty-minute walk from town. Lássi sprawls unattractively along a busy main road, but it does have good sandy beaches, particularly at **Makrýs Yialós** and **Platýs Yialós**, although they're right under the airport flight path. **Beaches** such as **Ávythos** are well worth seeking out, although if you're walking beyond **Kourkomeláta** there is a real if occasional risk of being attacked by farm dogs, particularly during the hunting season (Sept 25–Feb 28). There is very little accommodation in the region, and precious few shops or bars. **Pessádha** has a twice-daily ferry link with Zákynthos in summer, but little else, and be warned that the pathetic bus service from Argostóli is no good for connecting with the boats. You'll have to hitch or take an expensive taxi in most cases.

With a scooter, the best inland excursion is to **ÁYIOS YEÓRYIOS**, the medieval Venetian capital of the island. The old town here supported a population of 15,000 until its destruction by an earthquake in the seventeenth century: substantial ruins of its **castle** (Tues–Sat 8am–8pm, Sun 8am–2pm; €1.50), now reopened after extensive renovations, churches and houses can be visited on the hill above the modern village of Peratáta. Byron lived for a few months in the nearby village of Metaxáta and was impressed by the view from the summit in 1823; sadly, as at Messolóngi, the house where he stayed no longer exists. Two kilometres south of Áyios Yeóryios is a fine collection of religious icons and frescoes kept in a restored church that was part of the nunnery of Áyios Andhréas.

Mount Énos

At 15km from a point halfway along the Argostóli–Sámi road, **Mount Énos** isn't really a walking option, but roads nearly reach the official 1632-metre summit. The mountain has been declared a national park, to protect the *Abies cephalonica* firs (named after the island) which clothe the slopes. There are absolutely no facilities on or up to the mountain, but the views from the highest point in the Ionian islands out over its neighbours and the mainland are wonderful. In low season, watch the weather, which can deteriorate with terrifying speed. Not far before the mountain turning, taking a detour towards Frangáta is doubly rewarded by the huge and lively **Áyios Yerásimos**

monastery, which hosts two of the island's most important festivals (Aug 15 and Oct 20), and right behind it the **Robola winery** (8am–8pm in summer), which offers a free self-guided tour and generous wine-tasting.

Lixoúri

Half-hourly ferries (hourly in winter) ply between the capital and **LIXOÚRI** throughout the day until midnight. The town was flattened by earthquakes, and hasn't risen much above two storeys since. It's a little drab, but has good restaurants, quiet hotels and is favoured by those who want to explore the eerie quakescapes left in the south and the barren north of the peninsula. **Hotels** are not especially plentiful or cheap, but two comfortable air-conditioned options are the *La Cité* (☎06710/92 701, ℗92 702; ❹), four blocks back from the front, and a beach hotel just south of town, *Summery* (☎06710/91 771, ℗91 062; ❹). Two agencies offer cheaper accommodation in town: A. D. Travel (☎06710/93 142, ℗92 663; from ❶) on the main road through town, and Perdikis Travel (☎06710/91 097, ℗92 503; from ❸) on the quay. Among the tavernas, *Akrogiali* on the seafront is excellent and cheap, drawing admirers from all over the island. *Iy Avli*, on the block behind, serves a variety of dishes in a leafy garden, while *Adonis* is a good basic *psistariá* at the back of the square. *Adagio* is the trendy place to drink on the square, but the seafront has a couple of much more genuine kafenía.

Lixoúri's nearest beach is **Lípedha**, a two-kilometre walk south. Like the **Xí** and **Mégas Lákkos** beaches (served by bus from Lixoúri and both with restaurants and accommodation), it has rich-red sand and is backed by low cliffs. Those with transport can also strike out for the monastery at **Kipouréon**, and north to the spectacular beach at **Petaní**, where there are two reasonable restaurants, the further of which, *Xougras*, should have rooms by 2002, courtesy of Greek-American Dina (☎06710/97 128; ❸), and should make a tremendous place for a relaxed stay.

The west coast and the road north

The journey between Argostóli and Fiskárdho, by regular bus or rented vehicle, is the most spectacular ride in the archipelago. Leaving town, the road rises into the Evmorfía foothills and, beyond Agónas, clings to near-sheer cliffs as it heads for Dhiváráta, which has a smattering of rooms and is the stop for **Mýrtos beach**. It's a four-kilometre hike down on foot (you can also drive down), with just one taverna on the beach, but from above or below this is the most dramatic beach in the Ionian islands – a splendid strip of pure-white sand and pebbles. Sadly, it's shadeless and gets mighty crowded in high season.

Six kilometres on is the turning for the atmospheric village of **ÁSSOS**, clinging to a small isthmus between the island and a huge hill crowned by a ruined fort. Accommodation is scarce – villagers invariably send you to Andhreas Rokos' rooms (☎06740/51 523; ❶) on the approach road, which are great value, or you can opt for the posher *Kanakis Apartments* opposite (☎06740/51 631, ℗51 660; ❺). Ássos has a small pebble beach, and three tavernas, notably the *Nefeli* and the *Platanos Grill*, on a plane-shaded village square backed by mansions, mostly now restored after being ruined in the quake. It can get a little claustrophobic, but there's nowhere else like it in the Ionian islands.

Fiskárdho

FISKÁRDHO, on the northernmost tip of the island, sits on a bed of limestone that buffered it against the worst of the quakes. Two **lighthouses**, Venetian and Victorian, guard the bay, and the ruins on the headland are believed to be from a twelfth-century chapel begun by Norman invader

Robert Guiscard, who gave the place his name. The nineteenth-century harbour frontage is intact, nowadays occupied by smart restaurants and chic boutiques. There is a small new **Environmental and Nautical Museum**, with free entry but erratic opening hours, near the quay.

The island's premier resort, Fiskárdho is very busy through to the end of October, with accommodation at a premium. The cheapest rooms are those of Sotiria Tselenti (℡06740/41 204; ❸), 50m back from the tiny square, followed by *Regina's* (℡06740/41 125; ❸) with its own café at the back of the village, next to the car park. *Theodora's Café Bar* has rooms in whitewashed houses on the quay (℡06740/41 297; ❸), and another reasonable option is the small *Erissos* pension (℡06740/41 327; ❹), just off the seafront. Pama Travel (℡06740/41 033, ℻41 032), on the seafront furthest away from the ferry quay, is another source of rooms and costlier apartments. There's a wealth of good restaurants. Two to try on the seafront are the *Tassia,* which has a vast range of seafood, and the *Captain's Table,* serving succulent Greek and Kefallonian fare. On the sqaure, *Alexis* serves pizzas and pastas, while *Lagoudera,* just off the square, specializes in tasty oven food. *Sirenes*, on the seafront, near the square, is the favoured bar, although the seafront kafenío's mezédhes are the finest to be had anywhere. The dance spot is *Kastro Club* up at the back of the village. There are two good pebble beaches – **Émblisi** 1km back out of town and **Fókis** just to the south – and a nature trail on the northern headland. Daily **ferries** connect Fiskárdho to Itháki and Lefkádha in season.

Itháki

Rugged **Itháki**, Odysseus's legendary homeland, has yielded no substantial archeological discoveries, but it fits Homer's description to perfection: "There are no tracks, nor grasslands . . . it is a rocky severe island, unsuited for horses, but not so wretched, despite its small size. It is good for goats." In Constantine Cavafy's splendid poem *Ithaca*, the island is symbolized as a journey to life:

> *When you set out on the voyage to Ithaca*
> *Pray that your journey may be long*
> *Full of adventures, full of knowledge.*

Despite the romance of its name, and its proximity to Kefalloniá, very little tourist development has arrived to spoil the place. This is doubtless accounted for in part by a dearth of beaches, though the island is good walking country, with a handful of small fishing villages and various pebbly coves to swim from. In the north, apart from the ubiquitous drone of scooters, the most common sounds are sheep bells jangling and cocks (a symbol of Odysseus) crowing.

Its beaches are minor, mainly pebbly with sandy seabeds, but relatively clean and safe; the real attractions are the interior and sites from the **Odyssey**. Some package travellers will find themselves flying into Kefalloniá and being bused to Fiskárdho (sit on the left for the bus ride of your life), for a short ferry crossing to **Fríkes** or the premier resort **Kióni**. Most visitors, however, will arrive at **Vathý**, the capital.

Vathý

Ferries from Pátra, Astakós and a minority of those from Kefalloniá land at the main port and capital of **VATHÝ** (Itháki Town), a bay within a bay so deep that few realize the mountains out "at sea" are actually the north of the island. This snug town is compact, relatively traffic-free and boasts the most idyllic seafront setting of all the Ionian capitals. Like its southerly neighbours, it was damaged by the 1953 earthquake, but some fine examples of pre-quake architecture remain here and in the northern port of **Kióni**. Vathý has a small **archeological museum** on Odhós Kalliníkou (Tues–Sun 8am–2.30pm; free), a short block back from the quay. There are banks, a post office, police and a medical centre in town.

Vathý now has three **hotels**: the old but air-conditioned *Mentor* (☎06740/32 433, ℉32 293; ⑤) at the left end of the seafront, the newer *Omirikon* (☎06740/33 598, ℉33 596; ⑥) further on round the bay, and much better-value *Captain Yiannis* (☎06740/33 173, ℉32 849; ④), complete with pool. Room owners meet ferries until the end of the season, but you can also call ahead to Vassiliki Vlassopoulou (☎06740/32 119; ③), whose rooms are in pleasant gardens by the church above the quay. The town's two main quayside travel agents, Polyctor Tours (☎06740/33 120, ℉33 130, ℮polyctor@otenet.gr) and Delas Tours (☎06740/32 104, ℉33 031, ℮delas@otenet.gr) both offer a range of accommodation throughout the island.

Even though it's tiny, Vathý has a wealth of **tavernas** and **bars**. Many locals head off south around the bay towards *Gregory's*, popular for its lamb and fish, and the more traditional *Tziribis* and *O Vrachos*. In town, the excellent *O Nikos* fills early, while *To Kohili* is the best of the half-dozen harbourside tavernas. The *Sirenes Ithaki Yacht Club* is upmarket with a nautical theme, but as usual the town's ancient kafenío one street back from the front is the spot for a quiet and inexpensive tipple with the locals.

There are two reasonable pebble **beaches** within fifteen-minutes' walk of Vathý: **Dhéxa**, over the hill above the ferry quay, and tiny **Loútsa**, opposite it around the bay. Better beaches at **Sarakíniko** and **Skhinós** to the south are an hour's trek along recently improved roads leaving the opposite side of the bay. In season, daily kaïkia ply between the quay and remote coves.

Odysseus sights

Three of the main **Odysseus** sights are just within walking distance of Vathý: the Arethoússa Spring, the Cave of the Nymphs and ancient Alalkomenae, although the last is best approached by **bus** or **taxi** (no more than €12 round-trip).

The Arethoússa Spring

The walk to the **Arethoússa Spring** – allegedly the place where Eumaeus, Odysseus's faithful swineherd, brought his pigs to drink – is a three-hour round trip along a track signposted next to the seafront OTE. The unspoiled landscape and sea views are magnificent, but the walk crosses slippery inclines and might best be avoided if you're nervous of heights. The route is shadeless, so take a hat and plenty of water.

Near the top of the lane leading to the spring path, a signpost points up to what is said to have been the **Cave of Eumaeus**. The route to the spring continues for a few hundred metres, and then branches off onto a narrow footpath through gorse-covered steep cliffs. Parts of the final downhill track involve scrambling across rock fields (follow the splashes of green paint), and care should be taken around the small but vertiginous ravine that houses the **spring**. The spring is sited at the head of a small ravine below a crag known as **Korax** (the raven), which matches Homer's description of the meeting between Odysseus and Eumaeus. In summer it's just a dribble of water.

The spring is a dead end – the only way out is back the way you came. If weather and time allow, you might swim in a small cove a short scramble down from the spring. If you're uneasy about the gradients involved, it's still worth continuing along the track that runs above it, which loops round and heads back into the village of **Perahóri** above Vathý, which has views as far as Lefkádha to the north. On the way, you'll pass **Paleóhora**, the ruined medieval capital abandoned centuries ago, but with vestiges of houses fortified against pirate attacks and some churches still with Byzantine frescoes.

The Cave of the Nymphs

The **Cave of the Nymphs** (Marmarospíli) is about 2.5km up a rough but navigable road signposted on the brow of the hill above Dhéxa beach. The cave is atmospheric, but it's underwhelming compared to the caverns of neighbouring Kefalloniá, and these days is illuminated by coloured lights. The claim that this is the *Odyssey*'s Cave of the Nymphs, where the returning Odysseus concealed the gifts given to him by King Alcinous, is enhanced by the proximity of Dhéxa beach, although there is some evidence that the "true" cave was just above the beach, and was unwittingly demolished during quarrying many years ago.

Alalkomenae and Pisaetós

Alalkomenae, Heinrich Schliemann's much-vaunted "Castle of Odysseus", is signposted on the Vathý–Pisaetós road, on the saddle between Dhéxa and Pisaetós, with views over both sides of the island. The actual site, however, some 300m uphill, is little more than foundations spread about in the gorse. Schliemann's excavations unearthed a Mycenaean burial chamber and domestic items such as vases, figurines and utensils (displayed in the archeological museum), but the ruins actually date from three centuries after Homer. In fact, the most likely contender for the site of Odysseus's castle is above the village of Stavrós (see below).

The road (though not buses) continues to the harbour of **Pisaetós**, about 2km below, with a large pebble beach that's good for swimming and popular with local rod-and-line fishermen. There is just one *kantína* here serving the regular ferries from Sámi on Kefalloniá.

Northern Itháki

The main road out of Váthy continues across the isthmus and takes a spectacular route to the northern half of Itháki, serving the villages of **Léfki**, **Stavrós**, **Fríkes** and **Kióni**. There are only two daily **buses**, though the north of Itháki is excellent scooter country; the close proximity of the settlements, small coves and Homeric interest also make it good rambling country. Once a day a kaïki also visits the last two of those communities – a cheap and scenic ride used by locals and tourists alike to meet the mainline ferries in Vathý. As with the rest of Itháki there is only a limited amount of accommodation.

Stavrós and around

STAVRÓS, the second-largest town on the island, discounting Perahóri, is a steep two kilometres above the nearest beach (Pólis Bay). It's a pleasant enough town nonetheless, with kafenía edging a small square dominated by a rather fierce statue of Odysseus. There is even a tiny **museum** (Tues–Sun 9.30am–2.30pm; free) off the road to Platrithiás, displaying local archeological finds. Stavrós's Homeric site is on the side of **Pelikáta Hill**, where remains of roads, walls and other structures have been suggested as the possible site of Odysseus's castle. Stavrós is useful as a base if both Fríkes and Kióni are full up, and is an obvious stopping-off point for exploring the northern hamlets and the road up to the medieval village of Anoyí (see below). Both Polyctor and Delas handle **accommodation** in Stavrós; the traditional *Petra* taverna (☎06740/31 596; ❸) offers rooms, or there's the *Porto Thiaki* pension (☎06740/31 245, ☞31 638; ❸) above the pizzeria. The oldest and best taverna is *Fatouros*, and the *Margarita zaharoplastío* is a good place for a drink or to sample the local sweet *rovaní* (syrupy rice cakes).

A scenic mountain road leads 5km southeast from Stavrós to **ANOYÍ**, which translates roughly as "upper ground". Once the second-most important settlement on the island, it is almost deserted today. The centre of the village is dominated by a free-standing Venetian campanile, built to serve the (usually locked) church of the **Panayía**, which comes alive for the annual *paniyíri* on August 14, the eve of the Virgin's Assumption; at other times enquire at the kafenío about access to the church, the Byzantine frescoes of which have been heavily restored following centuries of earthquake damage. On the outskirts of the village are the foundations of a ruined **medieval prison**, and in the surrounding countryside are some extremely strange rock formations, the biggest being the eight-metre-high Iraklís (Hercules) rock, just east of the village. The **monastery of Katharón**, 3km further south along the road, has stunning views down over Vathý and the south of the island, and houses an icon of the *Panayía* discovered by peasants clearing scrubland in the area. Byron is said to have stayed here in 1823, during his final voyage to Messolóngi. The monastery celebrates its festival on September 8 with services, processions and music.

Two roads push north of Stavrós: one, to the right, heads 2km down to Fríkes, while the main road, to the left, loops below the hill village of **Exoyí**, and on to **Platrithiás**. Just off the start of the road up to Exoyí a signpost points about 1km along a rough track to the supposed **School of Homer**, where excavations still in progress have revealed extensive foundations, a well and ancient steps. The site is unfenced and well worth a detour for its views of **Afáles Bay** as much as the remains. On the outskirts of Platrithiás a track leads down to Afáles, the largest bay on the entire island, with an unspoiled and little-visited pebble beach. The landscape around here, thickly forested in parts and dotted with vineyards, is excellent walking terrain.

Fríkes

At first sight, tiny **FRÍKES** doesn't appear to have much going for it. Wedged in a valley between two steep hills, it was only settled in the sixteenth century, and emigration in the nineteenth century almost emptied the place – as few as two hundred people live here today – but the protected harbour is a natural year-round port. Consequently, Fríkes stays open for tourism far later in the season than neighbouring Kióni, and has a smart range of tavernas. There are no beaches in the village, but plenty of good, if small, pebble strands a short walk away towards Kióni. When the ferries and their cargoes have departed, Fríkes falls quiet and this is its real charm: a downbeat but cool place to lie low.

Fríkes' one **hotel** is the smart but pricey *Nostos* (☎06740/31 644, ☞31 716; ❺) or you can try the equally comfy *Aristotelis Apartments* (☎06740/31 079, ☞31 179; ❸). Kiki Travel (☎ & ☞06740/31 387; from ❷) has **rooms** and other accommodation, as do the adjacent souvenir shop (☎06740/31 735; ❷) and *Ulysses* taverna (☎06740/31733; ❸). Phoning ahead is advisable and in peak season chances are slim. Fríkes has a quartet of good seafront **tavernas**: the *Symposium*, the *Rementzo*, the *Penelope* and aforementioned *Ulysses*. Tucked in the corner of the harbour, *Café Bemenis* often springs into life late at night as the north's main meeting place for youngsters.

Kióni

KIÓNI sits at a dead end 5km southeast of Fríkes. On the same geological base as the northern tip of Kefalloniá, it avoided the very worst of the 1953 earthquakes, and so retains some fine examples of pre-twentieth-century architecture. It's an extremely pretty village, wrapped around a tiny harbour, and tourism here is dominated by British blue-chip travel companies and visiting yachts.

The bay has a small **beach**, 1km along its south side, a sand and pebble strand below a summer-only snack bar. Better pebble beaches can be found within walking distance towards Fríkes. While the best **accommodation** has been snaffled by the Brits, some local businesses have rooms and apartments to let, among them *Captain's Apartments* (☎06740/31 481, ℱ31 090; ❹), K. Raftopulos (☎06740/31 654; ❸) and *Kioni Vacations* (☎06740/31 668; ❸). A quieter option, a short walk uphill on the main road in the hamlet of Ráhi, are the rooms and studios run by Captain Theofilos Karatzis and his family (☎06740/31 679; ❸), which have panoramic views.

Kióni's **restaurants** are dotted around the picturesque harbour, but compare unfavourably with those in Fríkes; *Mythos* has a wide selection and is the best of the bunch, the *Avra* fish taverna and *Kioni* pizzeria are adequate, while the upmarket *Calypso* taverna has interesting dishes but is overpriced. Village facilities stretch to two well-stocked shops, a post office and a couple of bars and cafés.

Zákynthos (Zante)

Zákynthos, southernmost of the six core Ionian islands, currently teeters between underdevelopment and indiscriminate commercialization. Much of the island is still green and unspoiled, but the development in some resorts is threatening to spill over into the quieter parts.

The island has three distinct zones: the barren, mountainous northwest; the fertile central plain; and the eastern and southern coasts which house the resorts. The big resort – rivalling the biggest on Corfu – is **Laganás**, on Laganás Bay in the south, a 24-hour party venue that doesn't give up from Easter until the last flight home in October. There are smaller, quieter resorts north and south of the capital, and the southerly Vassilikós peninsula has the best countryside and beaches, including exquisite **Yérakas**.

Although half-built apartment blocks are spreading through the central plain, this is where the quieter island begins: farms and vineyards, ancient villages and the ruins of Venetian buildings levelled in the 1948 and 1953 earthquakes. The island still produces fine wines, such as the white Popolaro, as well as sugar-shock-inducing *mandoláto* nougat, whose honey-sweetened form is best. Zákynthos is also the birthplace of *kantádhes*, the hybrid of Cretan folk song and Italian opera ballad that can be heard in tavernas in Zákynthos Town and elsewhere. It also harbours one of the key breeding sites of the endangered **loggerhead sea turtle** at Laganás Bay. The loggerhead (see box on p.525) is the subject of a continuing dispute between tourism businesses and environmentalists, which has caused an international political scandal and even provoked a bomb attack against the environmentalists.

Zákynthos Town

The town, like the island, is known as both **ZÁKYNTHOS** and Zante. This former "Venice of the East" (*Zante, Fior di Levante*, "Flower of the Levant", in

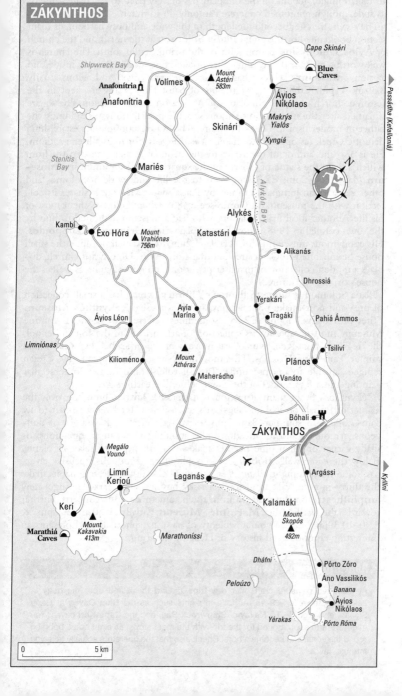

ZÁKYNTHOS

Cape Skinári

Shipwreck Bay

Blue Caves

Mount Astéri 583m

Volímes

Anafonítria

Anafonítria

Áyios Nikólaos

Makrýs Yialós

Skinári

Xyngiá

Stenítis Bay

Mariés

Alykés

Kambí

Éxo Hóra

Katastári

Mount Vrahiónas 756m

Alikanás

Dhrossiá

Yerakári

Ayía Marína

Tragáki

Pahiá Ámmos

Áyios Léon

Limniónas

Tsiliví

Kiliómeno

Mount Athéras

Plános

Maherádho

Vanáto

Bóhali

ZÁKYNTHOS

Megálo Vounó

Limní Kerioú

Laganás

Argássi

Kerí

Mount Kakavakia 413m

Kalamáki

Marathiá Caves

Marathoníssi

Mount Skopós 492m

Dháfni

Pórto Zóro

Áno Vassilikós

Peloúzo

Banana

Áyios Nikólaos

Yérakas

Pórto Róma

0   5 km

an Italian jingle), rebuilt on the old plan, has bravely tried to re-create some of its style, though reinforced concrete can only do so much.

The town stretches beyond the length of the wide and busy harbour, its main section bookended by the grand **Platía Solomoú** at the north, and the church of **Áyios Dhionýsios**, patron saint of the island, at the south. The church is well worth a visit for the dazzling giltwork and fine modern murals inside, and a new **museum**, which has some fine paintings and icons (daily 8.30am–11pm; €0.90). The vestments of Saint Dhionýsios are kept in the restored church of Áyios Nikólaos tou Mólou on Platía Solomoú. The square is named after the island's most famous son, the poet Dhionysios Solomos, the father of modernism in Greek literature, who was responsible for establishing demotic Greek (as opposed to the elitist *katharévousa* form) as a literary idiom. He is also the author of the lyrics to the national anthem, an excerpt from which adorns the statue of Liberty in the square. There's an impressive **museum** (daily 9am–2pm; €2.35) devoted to the life and work of Solomos and other Zakynthian luminaries in nearby Platía Ayíou Márkou. It shares its collection with the museum on Corfu (see p.483), where Solomos spent most of his life. Another local man of letters, who had a museum dedicated to him by the town council in 1998, is novelist and playwright **Grigorios Xenopoulos**. His eponymous museum (Mon–Fri 9am–2pm; free), which occupies the small house he inhabited in Gaïta street, not far from Áyios Dhionýsios church, displays a modest collection of manuscripts, books and photographs, as well as the house's original furniture.

Platía Solomoú is home to the town's **library**, which has a small collection of pre- and post-quake photography, and the massive **Zákynthos Museum** (Tues–Sun 8am–2.30pm; €2.35), sometimes referred to as the Byzantine Museum, most notable for its collection of artworks from the Ionian School, the region's post-Renaissance art movement, spearheaded by Zakynthian painter Panayiotis Doxaras. The movement was given impetus by Cretan refugees, unable to practise under Turkish rule. It also houses some secular painting and a fine model of the town before the earthquake.

Zákynthos's other main attraction is its massive **kástro**, brooding over the hamlet of **Bóhali** on its bluff above the town. The ruined Venetian fort (daily 8am–7.30pm in summer, 8am–2pm in winter; €1.50) has vestiges of dungeons, armouries and fortifications, plus stunning views in all directions. Its shady carpet of fallen pine needles makes it a great spot to relax or picnic. Below the *kástro* walls, **Bóhali** has a couple of good though expensive tavernas, some hosting nightly *kantádhes*, although Zakynthian driving habits make the thirty-minute walk from town a risky business after dark. The ugly new **amphitheatre** on the road up from town sometimes hosts concerts. Further towards the *kástro* the **Maritime Museum** (daily 9.30am–2.30pm & 6.30–10.30pm; €2.35) contains plenty of naval paraphernalia and presents an interesting chronological history of Hellenic seafaring.

Boat trips from Zákynthos

At least ten pleasure craft offer **day-trips** around the island from the quay in Zákynthos town for €9–15. All take in sights such as the **Blue Caves** at Cape Skinári, and moor in **Tó Naváyio (Shipwreck Bay)** and the **Cape Kerí** caves. You might want to shop around for the trip with the most stops, as eight hours bobbing round the coast can become a bore. Check also that the operators actually take you into the caves.

Zákynthos is a working town with limited concessions to tourism, although there are hotels and restaurants aplenty, and it's the only place to stay if you want to see the island by public transport. The **bus** station is one block back from the seafront, about halfway along it. On the front nearby, the **tourist police** have a fairly welcoming office (daily 7.30am–9.30pm; ☎06950/27 367) in the main police station, which can supply basic information and help people find accommodation. The Roomowners Association (☎06950/49 498) can also be contacted for accommodation around town and all over the island. Of the central **hotels**, the *Egli*, on Loútzi (☎06950/28 317; ❸) is the bargain, tucked in beside the gargantuan and more expensive *Strada Marina* (☎06950/42 761, ℱ28 733; ❻). There are quieter hotels in the Répara district beyond Platía Solomoú: try either the *Plaza* (☎06950/48 909, ℱ45 733; ❺) or the classy *Palatino*, Kolokotróni 10 (☎06950/27 780, ℱ45 400, ℰpalatzak@otenet.gr; ❺), both near the municipal lido. Cheaper options at the back of town include the functional *Apollo*, Tertséti 30 (☎06950/42 838; ❸), opposite the post office, and the cosier *Haravyi* pension, Xanthopoúlou 4 (☎06950/23 629; ❷) further south. Most of the **restaurants** and bars on the seafront and Platía Ayíou Márkou are bedevilled by traffic, although the seafront *Psaropoula* does fine meat and fish, and the pricey but elegant *Komis*, across the quay from Áyios Dhionýsios, serves unusual seafood dishes and is far enough away from the bustle. First stop though, should be the friendly *Arekia* beyond the lido, which offers succulent taverna staples and nightly *kantádhes*. The neighbouring *Alivizos* also specializes in island cuisine and music, and the *Green Boat* further along serves up quality fare at a snip. When the bored teens get off their bikes, they go **clubbing** to bars like *Base* on Ayíou Márkou, which plays anything from Miles Davis to Philip Glass, or the *Jazz Café*, on Tertséti which, despite plundering the London jazz club's logo, is actually a techno bar with DJ and token cover charge.

The south and west

The road heading southeast from Zákynthos passes through **ARGÁSSI**, the busiest resort on this coast, but with a beach barely a few feet wide in parts. Although independent travellers would be better off basing themselves at one of the places further down, it could be used as a jumping-off point for the Vassilikós peninsula; there are rooms at the *Pension Vaso* (☎06950/44 599; ❸) and *Soula* (☎06950/44 864; ❸) just off the main road entering the village, and the seafront boasts some smart hotels, among them the *Locanda* (☎06950/45 386, ℱ23 769; ❹) and the joint *Chryssi Akti/Paradise Beach* (☎06950/28 679, ℱ28 699; ❺). Beyond a few indigenous tavernas – try *Three Brothers* or *The Big Plate* restaurant – culture is mainly low-brow with set-piece "Greek nights", one notable exception being the *Venetsiana*, which accompanies traditional food with nightly *kantádhes*. Argássi is also home to some of the island's biggest and most popular discos on the town side, such as *Vivlos* and *Barrage*, and a host of cheap and cheerful bars in the village.

The Vassilikós peninsula

The peninsula that stretches southeast of Argássi is one of the most attractive parts of the island, with a happy blend of development and natural beauty. Various maps vaguely identify different inland spots as **Vassilikós** villages, but the real interest lies in the series of small beach resorts, mainly situated on the east coast. The first two are recently developed **Kamínia**, with the comfortable *Levantino* rooms (℡ & ℗ 06950/35 366; ❹), and the more established **Pórto Zóro**, a better strand with the good-value eponymous hotel (℡06950/35 304, ℗35 087; ❹) and restaurant. The only real facilities away from the coast are to be found at the sprawling village of **Áno Vassilikós**, which serves the nearby beaches of **Iónio** and **Banana**. Among accommodation possibilities are the *Vassilikos Apartments* (℡06950/35 280; ❹), on the main road, and *Angelika* (℡06950/35 201; ❸), by the church just off it. Among the **tavernas**, on the main road, *O Adherfos tou Kosta* is well worth a try, as is the *Logos Rock Club*. Isolated **Áyios Nikólaos** has a good beach and lures day-trippers from Argássi, Kalamáki and Laganás with a **free bus** service in season; its expanding *Vasilikos Beach* (℡06950/35 325, ℗35 327, ✉stnicks@otenet.gr; ❺) complex is the focal point of a fast-emerging hamlet with a few restaurants and rooms – the neat white *Christina's* (℡06950/39 474; ❷) is one of the best deals on the island.

At the very tip of the peninsula is its star: **Yérakas**, a sublime crescent of golden sand. It's also a key loggerhead turtle breeding ground, and is therefore off-limits between dusk and dawn; the excellent open-air **Turtle Info Centre** provides interesting background on these and other sea creatures. Otherwise, there's little here beyond two tavernas back from the beach and some pleasant, if remote, cabin accommodation at *Liuba Apartments* (℡06950/35 372; ❸). The beach does draw crowds, but the 6am bus out of Zákynthos Town should secure you a few hours of Yérakas to yourself. Compared with Yérakas, **Pórto Róma**, back on the east coast, is a disappointment, a small sand-and-pebble bay with a taverna and bar, some rooms on the approach road and occasional hardy campers, although there is a more genuinely Greek flavour to it. Beaches on the west coast, like **Dháfni**, require your own transport and have few facilities, but are worth a visit, especially in the quieter months.

Laganás and Kalamáki

The majority of the 400,000 people or so who visit Zákynthos each year find themselves in **LAGANÁS**. The nine-kilometre beach in the bay is good, if trampled, and there are entertainments from watersports to ballooning, and even an occasional funfair. Beachfront bars and restaurants stretch for well over a kilometre, the bars and restaurants on the main drag another kilometre inland. Some stay open around the clock; others just play music at deafening volume until dawn. The competing video and music bars can make Laganás at night resemble the set of *Bladerunner*, but that's how its predominantly English visitors like it. If this is your bag, there's no place better; if it isn't, flee. **Accommodation** is mostly block-booked by package companies. There's a basic campsite on the southern edge of town, where there are also quietish private rooms, or you can contact the Union of Room Owners (daily 8.30am–2pm & 5–8pm; ℡06950/51 590). As for hotels, try the old-fashioned *Byzantio* (℡06950/51 136; ❸), near the crossroads, *Pension Tasoula* (℡06950/51 560; ❹), between the beach and the campsite, or the larger *Ionis* (℡06950/51 141, ℗51 601, ✉ionishtl@otenet.gr; ❺), on the main drag towards the beach. *Nefeli* and *Zougras* are among the more authentic **tavernas**, the former hosting nightly *kantádhes*, and respectable Chinese/Indian food can be had at *Bee Garden* or *Taj Mahal*. Favourite **bars** include *Kamikazi*, *Must*, *Potters Bar* and *Zeros* nightclub.

Neighbouring **KALAMÁKI** has a better beach than Laganás, and is altogether quieter, although both resorts suffer from airport noise. There are several sizeable, mostly package-oriented hotels, but the upmarket *Crystal Beach*

Loggerhead turtles

The Ionian islands harbour the Mediterranean's main concentration of **loggerhead sea turtles** (*Caretta caretta*). These creatures, which lay their eggs at night on sandy coves, are under direct threat from the tourist industry in Greece. Each year, many turtles are injured by motorboats, their nests are destroyed by bikes ridden on the beaches, and the newly hatched young die entangled in deckchairs and umbrellas left out at night on the sand. The turtles are easily frightened by noise and lights, too, which makes them uneasy cohabitants with freelance campers and late-night discos.

The Greek government has passed laws designed to protect the loggerheads, including restrictions on camping at some beaches, but local economic interests tend to prefer a beach full of bodies to a sea full of turtles.

On Laganás, nesting grounds are concentrated around the fourteen-kilometre bay, but Greek marine zoologists striving to protect and study the turtles are in angry dispute with locals and the burgeoning tourist industry. Other important locations include the turtles' nesting ground just west of Skála on Kefalloniá, although numbers have dwindled to half their former strength in recent years, and now only about 800 remain. Ultimately, the turtles' main hope of survival may rest in their being appreciated as a unique tourist attraction in their own right.

While capitalists and environmentalists are still at, well, loggerheads, the **World Wildlife Fund** has issued guidelines for visitors:

1. Don't use the beaches of Laganás and Yérakas between sunset and sunrise.
2. Don't stick umbrellas in the sand in the marked nesting zones.
3. Take your rubbish away with you – it can obstruct the turtles.
4. Don't use lights near the beach at night – they can disturb the turtles, sometimes with fatal consequences.
5. Don't take any vehicle onto the protected beaches.
6. Don't dig up turtle nests – it's illegal.
7. Don't pick up the hatchlings or carry them to the water, as it's vital to their development that they reach the sea on their own.
8. Don't use speedboats in Laganás Bay – a 9kph speed limit is in force for vessels in the bay.

(☎06950/42 788, ℉42 917; ◑) keeps some rooms aside and the islandwide Spring Tours agency (☎06950/43 795) can also arrange accommodation. The two *Stanis* tavernas have extensive menus of Greek and international dishes, although the beachside version is geared more to lunches and its sibling more to evening meals. Alternatives include *Afrodite* and *Merlis* or the *Guru* curry house. **Nightlife** centres around bars like *Harvest* and *Down Under* on the Laganás road, and the *Cave Club* or *Vyzantio* discos on the hillside above the village, which play foreign and Greek dance music respectively.

Kerí

The village of **KERÍ** is hidden in a fold above the cliffs at the island's southernmost tip. The village retains a number of pre-quake, Venetian buildings, including the church of the **Panayía Kerioú**; the Virgin is said to have saved the island from marauding pirates by hiding it in a sea mist. Kerí is also famous for a geological quirk, a series of small tar pools mentioned by both Pliny and Herodotus, but these have mysteriously dried up in recent years. A rough path leaving the southern end of the village leads 1km on to the lighthouse, with spectacular views of the sea, rock arches and stacks and a taverna. The beach next to **Límni Kerioú** at the southwestern end of Laganás Bay has developed into a laid-back and picturesque resort and is home to the Turtle Beach Diving Centre (☎ & ℉ 06950/48 768). **Rooms** can be found at the friendly *Pension*

Limni (℡06950/48 716; ➌) or through the local Roomowners Association (℡ & ℗ 06950/45 105). For **food** there is the *Pirates of Kastello* overlooking the bay from the far end and the *Keri* restaurant, which has good daily specials.

Maherádho, Kilioméno and Kambí

The bus system does not reach the wild western side of the island, but a rental car or sturdy motorbike will get you there. **MAHERÁDHO** boasts impressive pre-earthquake architecture set in beautiful arable uplands, surrounded by olive and fruit groves. The church of **Ayía Mávra** has an impressive free-standing campanile, and inside a splendid carved iconostasis and icons by Zakynthian painter Nikolaos Latsis. The town's major festival – one of the biggest on the island – is the saint's day, which falls on the first Sunday in June. The other notable church in town, that of the Panayía, commands breathtaking views over the central plain.

KILIOMÉNO is the best place to see surviving pre-earthquake domestic architecture, in the form of the island's traditional two-storey houses. The town was originally named after its church, **Áyios Nikólaos**, whose impressive campanile, begun over a hundred years ago, still lacks a capped roof. The *Alitzerini* taverna still occupies a cave-like house that dates from 1630. The road from Kilioméno passes through the nondescript village of Áyios Léon, from where two turnings lead through fertile land and down a newly-paved loop road to the impressive rocky coast at **Limniónas**, where there is a tiny bay and a taverna.

Further along the main road another turning leads to the tiny clifftop hamlet of **KAMBÍ**, popular with day-trippers, who come to catch the sunset over the sea. And indeed, there are extraordinary views to be had of the 300-metre-high cliffs and western horizon from Kambí's three clifftop **tavernas**. The best of the three is named after the imposing concrete **cross** above the village, constructed in memory of islanders killed here during the 1940s, either by nationalist soldiers or Nazis. The tiny village of **Mariés**, 5km to the north and set in a wooded green valley, has the only other coastal access on this side of Zákynthos, a seven-kilometre track leading down to the rocky inlet of **Stenítis Bay**, where there's a taverna and yacht dock, and another road to the uninspiring **Vrómi Bay**, from where speedboats run trips to Shipwreck Bay (see below).

The north

North and inland from Zákynthos Town, the roads thread their way through luxuriantly fertile farmland, punctuated with tumulus-like hills. **Tsiliví**, 5km north of the capital, is the first beach resort here, which has now effectively merged with the hamlet of **PLÁNOS** and matches Argássi for development. Unfortunately, this part of the coastline suffers from occasional oil pollution, with nothing but the winter storms to clear it. There's a good, basic **campsite**, *Zante Camping* (℡06950/61 710), beyond Plános, and, for a prime package-tour location, a surprising variety of accommodation – try the beachside *Anetis Hotel* (℡06950/44 590, ℗28 758; ➍), which has air-conditioning and TV in all rooms; *Gregory's* rooms (℡06950/61 853; ➌); or contact Tsilivi Travel (℡06950/44 194, ℗22 655), on the inland road in from town. *The Olive Tree* taverna is the best of a touristy bunch, while the *Mandarin* Chinese is fairly authentic. Pubs such as *The Local* and *Red Lion* tend to be Brit-oriented.

The beaches further along this stretch of coast become progressively quieter and pleasanter, and they all have at least a smattering of accommodation and restaurants to choose from. Good choices include **Pahiá Ámmos**, with the

Pension Petra (☎06950/61 175; ❸) and *Porto Roulis* fish taverna. Also recommended is **Dhrossiá**, where you can find the *Avouris* (☎06950/61 716; ❸) and *Drosia* apartments (☎06950/62 256; ❹) and eat at another popular fish taverna, *Andreas*.

Alykés and its bay

Ormós Alykón, 12km north of Tsiliví, is a large sandy bay with lively surf and two of the area's largest resorts. The first, **ALIKANÁS**, is a small but expanding village, much of its accommodation being overseas villa rentals; the second, **ALYKÉS**, named after the spooky salt pans behind the village, has the best beach north of the capital. There are **rooms** near the beach and a number of **hotels** set back from it, but with sea views – try the *Ionian Star* (☎06950/83 416, ℱ83 173; ❹) or the *Montreal* (☎06950/83 241, ℱ83 342, ℯmontreal@montreal.gr; ❺), although the best deal is off the crossroads at the *Picadilly* (☎06950/83 606; ❷). There are many eating joints, among the best the *Anatolikos*, *Fantasia* and *Golden Dolphin* tavernas. Alykés is the last true resort on this coast, and the one where the bus service largely gives out. **Xyngiá** beach, 4km north, has sulphur springs flowing into the sea – follow the smell – which provide the odd sensation of swimming in a mix of cool and warm water. The next small beach of **Makrýs Yialós**, which has a good taverna, makeshift campsite and a diving school, also makes for an extremely pleasant break on a tour of the north.

Áyios Nikólaos, 6km on, is a small working port serving daily ferries to and from Pessádha on Kefalloniá. From here another good trip is a ride by **kaïki** (around €6) to the extreme northern tip of the island, where the **Blue Caves** are some of the more realistically named of the many contenders in Greece. They're terrific for snorkelling, and when you go for a dip here your skin will appear bright blue. The road snakes onwards through a landscape of gorse bushes and dry-stone walls until it ends at the lighthouse of **Cape Skinári**. With only a taverna and a cafeteria, and a view of the mountainous expanse of Kefalloniá, it's a good spot for unofficial camping, or you could stay in the unique setting of the converted windmill rented out by *To Faros* taverna (☎06950/31 132; ❹).

Katastári, Ayía Marína and Volímes

The northern towns and villages are accessible only to those with cars or sturdy motorbikes, and although there are guided coach tours from the resorts, none is really geared to tourism. Two kilometres inland from Alykés, **KATASTÁRI** is the largest settlement after the capital. Precisely because it's not geared towards tourism, it's the best place to see Zákynthian life as it's lived away from the usual racket. Its most impressive edifice is the huge rectangular church of Iperáyia Theotókos, with a twin belfry and small new amphitheatre for festival performances.

AYÍA MARÍNA, a few kilometres south of Katastári, has a church with an impressive Baroque altar screen, and a belfry that's being rebuilt from the remnants left after the 1953 earthquake. As in most Zákynthos churches, the bell tower is detached, in Venetian fashion. Just above Ayía Marína is the *Parthenonas* taverna, rightly boasting one of the best views on the island. From here you can see the whole of the central plain from beyond Alykés in the north to Laganás Bay in the south.

VOLÍMES is the centre of the island's embroidery industry – with your own transport, you could make it to the **Anafonítria monastery**, 3km south, thought to have been the cell of the island's patron saint, Dhionysios, whose festivals are celebrated on August 24 and December 17. A newly paved road leads on to the cliffs overlooking **Shipwreck Bay** (Tó Naváyio), with hair-raising views down to the shipwreck (a cargo ship which ran aground in the Sixties) and a taverna to recover your composure in.

Kýthira island

Isolated at the foot of the Peloponnese, the island of **Kýthira** traditionally belongs to the Ionian islands, and shares their history of Venetian, and later, British rule; under the former it was known as Cerigo. Administratively it is part of Pireás in mainland Attica – like the Argo-Saronic islands. For the most part, similarities end there. The island architecture of whitewashed houses and flat-roofs looks more like that of the Cyclades, albeit with a strong **Venetian** influence. The landscape is different, too: wild scrub- and gorse-covered hills, or moorland sliced by deep valleys and ravines.

Depopulation has left the land underfarmed and the abandoned fields over-grown, for, since World War II, most of the islanders have left for Athens or Australia, giving Kýthira a reputation of being the classic emigrant island; it is known locally as "Australian Colony" or "Kangaroo Island", and Australia is referred to as "Big Kýthira". Many of the villages are deserted, their platías empty and the schools and kafenía closed. Kýthira was never a rich island, but, along with Monemvasiá, it did once have a military and economic significance – which it likewise lost with Greek independence and the opening of the Corinth Canal. These days, tourism has brought prosperity (and a few luxury hotels), but most summer visitors are Greeks and especially Greek Australians. For the few foreigners who reach Kýthira, it remains something of a refuge, with its undeveloped **beaches** a principal attraction. However, Theo Angelopoulos' film *Taxidhi sta Kýthira* ("Journey to Kythira"), and, to a much greater extent, a 1998 popular Greek television serial filmed on the island, have attracted a huge amount of domestic attention and, consequently, holiday-makers from the mainland. Much of the accommodation is now fully booked by Christmas for the entire Greek school-summer-holiday period; outside of this period some accommodation does not open until June and closes early in September. The Association of Rental Room Owners (℡ & ℻ 07360/31 855) have a list of places to stay: in addition to the following, there is accommodation in the villages of Aroniádhika, Dhókana, Dhrymónas, Frátsia, Frilingiánika, Goudhiánika, Kálamos, Kalokerinés, Karvounádhes, Káto Livádhi, Kondoliánika, Mitáta, Mylopótamos, Strapódhi and Travasariánika.

Arrival and getting around

Arrival on the island has changed in recent years. In 1997 a huge new all-weather **harbour** was opened at Dhiakófti, and now all hydrofoils and most ferries dock here instead of Ayía Pelayía or Kapsáli. The airport is deep in the interior, 8km southeast of Potamós; recent expensive refurbishment did not include extension of the short runway, therefore many of the facilities languish unused due to lack of flights. Further expenditure is unlikely in the near future as governing Pireás concentrates its resources on infrastructure for the 2004 Olympic Games at the expense of the periphery. The few Olympic Airways flights are met by taxis, as are most high-season boats. Sadly, there is no other **public transport** at the time of writing, with the

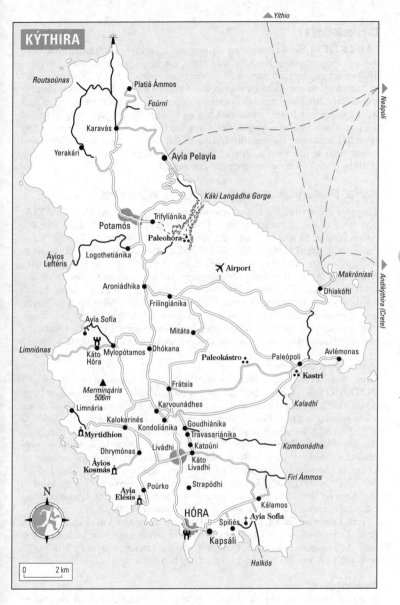

island buses being only used for school runs, although locals are pressing for the implementation of, at the least, bus services to meet ferries. The only alternative to often overcharging taxis is to hitch or, more advisedly, hire a **car** or **scooter**. The roads are now well surfaced all over the island and there are reliable petrol stations on the central road at Potamós, Kondoliánika and Livádhi.

Dhiakófti

DHIAKÓFTI, until recently an unsung and relatively inaccessible backwater towards the bottom of the northeast coast, has been catapulted into the fore-front of activity by the opening of the harbour, constructed by joining the islet of Makrónisi to the shore by a causeway. Perched on nearby Prasónisi island – and slightly disconcerting when arriving by sea – is a Greek container ship that went aground in 1999. Dhiakófti has a nice sandy beach, and exploitation of the tourist potential is currently fairly low key and seasonal; there are just a few **tavernas**, including the friendly *Notaras* by the causeway, and **apartments** and rooms such as the *Porto Diakofti* (☎07360/33 041; April–Oct; ④–⑥). Active (☎07360/33 207) have an office for **car rental**.

Ayía Pelayía and northern Kýthira

There's a reasonable choice of **rooms** and **tavernas** in **AYÍA PELAYÍA**; best value of the upmarket hotels is *Venardos* (☎07360/34 205, ⑥33 850; ⑥), which is open all year and can offer very good deals off season. The clean and comfortable *Hotel Kytherea* (☎07360/33 321; ⑤; open all year) is more luxu-rious, as are the more recent *Filoxenia Apartments* (☎07360/33 100, ⑥33 610; April–Oct; ⑤), with striking blue shutters and an imaginative layout around small courtyards. The *Moustakias* taverna, amongst the seafront eating places north of the jetty, has good, fresh food, including fish, while the *Paleo* ouzerí is also recommended. The main beaches are small, rather scruffy and disap-pointing, despite the provision of blue-and-white-striped changing huts; the beach at Kalamítsa, a short dirt track about 2km away to the south, is better.

Potamós and around

From Ayía Pelayía, the main road winds up the mountainside towards **POTAMÓS**, Kýthira's largest village – a pleasant and unspoiled place which, if you a rented vehicle, makes a good base for exploring the island. It has a few **rooms** with kitchens, such as those at the *Xenonas Porfyra* (☎07360/33 329, ⑥33 924; ④) which have TV, and a pretty terrace and courtyard, and the *Alevizopoulos* (☎07360/33 245; ④) with air conditioning. In addition to **tav-ernas**, a **bank**, a **post office** and **petrol stations**, facilities include an Olympic Airways office (☎07360/33 688) and the Sirene Travel Club (☎07360/34 371, ⑥34 372), the island's agents for the Neápoli ferry. Most of the shops on the island are here, too, as is the **Sunday market**, Kýthira's liveli-est regular event. The *Selana* café can provide **internet** facilities.

From **Logothetiánika**, just south of Potamós, an unpaved road leads down to Áyios Leftéris, where you can **swim** from rocks on the west coast, backed by high cliffs. At Logothetiánika itself, there is a popular taverna, *Karydies* (☎07360/33 664) with live music Thursday to Saturday, when booking is advisable.

Paleohóra

The main reason for visiting Potamós is to get to **PALEOHÓRA**, the ruined **medieval capital** (then called Áyios Dhimítrios) of Kýthira, 3km to the east of the town. Few people seem to know about or visit these remains, though they constitute one of the best Byzantine sites around. The most obvious com-parison is with Mystra, and although Paleohóra is much smaller – a fortified village rather than a town – its natural setting is perhaps even more spectacu-lar. Set on a hilltop at the head of the **Káki Langádha gorge**, it is surround-ed by a sheer hundred-metre drop on three sides.

The site is lower than the surrounding hills and invisible from the sea and most of the island, something which served to protect it from the pirates that plagued Paleohóra through much of its history. The town was built in the thirteenth century by Byzantine nobles from Monemvasiá, and when Mystra fell to the Turks, many of its noble families also sought refuge here. Despite its seemingly impregnable and perfectly concealed position, the site was discovered and sacked in 1537 by Barbarossa, commander of the Turkish fleet, and the island's seven thousand inhabitants were killed or sold into slavery.

The town was never rebuilt, and tradition maintains that it is a place of ill fortune, which perhaps explains the emptiness of the surrounding countryside, little of which is farmed today. The hills are dotted with Byzantine **chapels**, which suggests that, in its heyday, the area must have been the centre of medieval Kýthira; it is rumoured to have once had eight hundred inhabitants and 72 churches. Now the principal remains are of the surviving churches, some still with traces of frescoes (but kept firmly locked), and the castle. The site is unenclosed and has never been seriously investigated.

If you have your own transport, there's a road to Paleohóra, signposted off the main road from Potamós just north of Aroniádhika: the first 2.4km is asphalt, the remainder driveable gravel. By foot, it's more interesting to take the path from the tiny village of Trifyliánika, just outside Potamós – look out for a rusting sign to the right as you enter the village. The path is overgrown in parts and not easy to follow; the ruins only become visible when you join the road above the gorge.

Karavás

KARAVÁS, 6km north of Potamós, has architecture and a setting – above a deep, partly wooded valley with a stream – which are more reminiscent of the Ionian islands. There is nowhere to stay, but there is a popular **restaurant**, *Amir Ali*, providing a large range of mezédhes (and sometimes live music) in a shady, streamside setting at the northern end of the village, off the road to Platiá Ámmos; food is also available at the German-run *Maina* ("mynah").

Platiá Ámmos, at the end of the valley, and en route to the lighthouse at the island's northern tip, is a sandy beach with a seasonal fish **taverna**. There is also an ouzerí, café, the *Modeas* restaurant, and several **rooms** establishments of which the best is the *Akrotiri* (☎07360/33 216; ④). Winter storm damage in late 2000 washed away part of the access road, which awaits repair. The little pebble beach at **Foúrni**, 2km south by dirt road, is more attractive.

Kapsáli

KAPSÁLI, in addition to its harbour function, is the one place on Kýthira largely devoted to tourism although much of it closes down from September to June. Most foreign visitors to Kýthira in summer stay here, and it's a popular port of call for yachts heading from the Aegean to the Ionian islands and Italy, particularly since it is sheltered from the strong north winds of summer. Set behind double pebble-and-sand bays, overlooked by Hóra castle, and backed by high grey cliffs on which the tiny white monastery of Áyios Ioánnis Éngremmos perches, it is certainly picturesque. The larger of its two bays has a line of **tavernas**; *Vlastos* is one of the earliest to open in the season, with fish, local dishes, and its speciality, cockerel (*kókoras*) in wine; *Venetsianiko*, halfway along the front, has good food at reasonable prices, but the best is *Hydragogio* at the Hóra end of the beach which serves up good veggie options. For nightlife the liveliest place is *Shaker*, playing the standard mix of Greek and foreign hits.

The best **accommodation** is in high demand and expensive. Top of the tree is the *Porto Delfino* (℗07360/31 940; April–Oct; ⑥); a few hundred metres above the bay are *Kalokerines Katikies* (℗ & ℱ 07360/31 265; May–Oct; ⑥) and *Hotel Raïkos* (℗07360/31 629, ℱ31 801; May–Sept; ⑥). The *Afroditi Apartments* (℗07360/31 328; ⑥) have slightly more reasonable rates, as do *Megaloudi* rooms (℗07360/31 340; ⑤). A very basic **campsite** (June–Sept) nestles in the pine trees behind the village.

There's a mobile **post office** in summer, and Panayiotis (℗07360/31 600, ℱ31 789, ℮panayoti@otenet.gr) rents **cars**, **motorbikes** and **scooters**, as well as canoes and pedalboats; you can call off-season (℗094/4263757) and get wheels when most places are closed.

Hóra

HÓRA (or Kýthira Town), a steep 2km haul above Kapsáli, has an equally dramatic site, its Cycladic-style houses tiered on the ridge leading to the Venetian **castle**. Access to the fortress is up a modern pathway, but, to the right of this, the original narrow tunnel entrance is still usable. Within the walls, most of the buildings are in ruins, except the paired churches of Panayía Myrtidhiótissa and the smaller Panayía Orfáni (these were Catholic and Orthodox respectively, under the Venetian occupation), and the office of the archives of Kýthira opposite. There are spectacular views down to Kapsáli and out to sea to the striking chunk of inaccessible islet known as Avgó (Egg), legendary birthplace of Aphrodite. On the cliffs grow the yellow-flowered everlasting (*sempreviva*), used locally for making small dried flower arrangements. Below the castle are both the remains of older Byzantine walls and, in Mésa Vouryó, numerous well-signed but securely locked Byzantine churches. A small **museum** (Tues–Sun 8.30am–3pm; free) at the junction of the Hóra–Kapsáli road, houses modest remnants (labelled only in Greek) of the island's numerous occupiers, in particular Minoan finds from excavations at Paleópoli and an Archaic stone lion, as well as a telling selection of gravestones from the English cemetery. The Stavros bookshop, almost opposite, sells a book of walks (mainly in the southern half of the island; a walk book in German has more complete coverage).

Compared with Kapsáli, Hóra stays quiet and many places are closed out of season. Kythira Travel (℗07360/31 390) are agents for the hydrofoils. Other facilities include a couple of **banks**, a **post office** and a branch of Panayiotis vehicle rental (℗07360/31 004). A few **tavernas** open in summer, of which *Zorba* is by far the best, but the climb from Kapsáli discourages the crowds. A popular bar is *Mercato*, which stays open in the winter and also has exhibitions of local art. **Accommodation** is slightly easier to find than in Kapsáli. Options include the *Castello Studios* (℗07360/31 069; ④), and the *Hotel Margarita* (℗07360/31 711, ℱ31 325; ⑥) in a beautiful 1840s house, with air conditioning and TV in the rooms. The *Xenonas Keiti/Keti/Kaiti* (℗07360/31 318; April–Oct; ⑥) has non-smoking rooms in a large 240-year-old characterful house which has seen General Metaxas and George Papandreou as visitors. At **MANITOHÓRI**, 2km further inland, is the more basic *Pension Kythera* (℗07360/31 563; June–Aug; ③).

The southeast coast

The beach at Kapsáli is decent but not large and gets very crowded in July and August. For quieter, undeveloped beaches, it's better to head out to the east coast, towards Avlémonas.

Firí Ámmos, Kombonádha and Halkós beaches, and Spiliés cave

Firí Ámmos, the nearest good sand beach to Kapsáli, is popular but not over-crowded, even in summer. To get there, you can follow paved roads from Kapsáli or Livádhi as far as the *Filio* taverna (June–Sept; with good traditional food and local specialities) in the scattered settlement of Kálamos; the onward road becomes a four-kilometre dirt track to the beach. Firí Ámmos can also be reached by a second dirt track off the Livádhi–Kálamos road, while another, longer, dirt track, off the Káto Livádhi–Frátsia road leads to **Kombonádha**, the next beach north. There are summer canteens at both beaches. Much smaller, but prettier **Halkós** beach near the southeast corner of the island is signpost-ed from the crossroads at the entrance to Kálamos. Between Kálamos and Kapsáli, a short surfaced road leads south to **Spiliés** village; immediately before the village a signed earth road leads down to a small gorge and a large stalag-mite cave with an open-roofed church dedicated to Ayía Sofía (not to be con-fused with the sea cave near Mylopótamos).

Paleópoli and Avlémonas

PALEÓPOLI, a hamlet of a few scattered houses, is accessible by asphalt roads from Aroniádhika, Frátsia and Kondoliánika. The area is the site of the ancient city of **Skandia**, and excavations on the headland of **Kastrí** have revealed remains of an important Minoan colony. There's little visible evidence, apart from shards of pottery in the low crumbling cliffs, but happily, tourist devel-opment in the area has been barred because of its archeological significance. Consequently, there's just one solitary **taverna**, the *Skandia* (June–Oct), on the two-kilometre sand-and-pebble **beach** that stretches to either side of the headland. This place has recently been taken over by seven hippieish Anglo-Greek siblings and has a great atmosphere with home cooking and frequent spontaneous musical evenings.

Paleokástro, the mountain to the west, is the site of ancient Kýthira where there was a sanctuary of Aphrodite, but again, there's little to be seen today. Heading west from Paleópoli, and crossing the river bridge onto the Kondoliánika road, an unpaved road off to the left leads up to a tiny, white-washed church. From there, a rougher track leads down to **Kaladhí**, a beauti-ful cliff-backed pebble beach with caves, and rocks jutting out to sea.

AVLÉMONAS, on a rocky shoreline 2km east of Paleópoli beach, is a small fishing port with a bleak end-of-the-world feel as you approach from a dis-tance. It becomes much more attractive once reached, and has a remarkable co-ordination of colour schemes throughout the village. There is a small, unimpressive Venetian fortress, and two **tavernas**, of which *Sotiris* is particu-larly recommended for a wide selection of fresh, well-prepared and reason-ably-priced fish dishes. There are a number of **rooms**, including the swish new apartments of Popi Kastrisiou (℡07360/33 735; ⑤), and the older, air-conditioned *Schina* studios (℡07360/33 060; ④). The Petrohilos family has a number of rooms or studios, including those of Evdokhia (℡07360/34 069; ④) opposite the *Sotiris*.

North and west of Hóra

LIVÁDHI, 4km north of Hóra, has **rooms** and, on the main road, the *Hotel Aposperides* (℡07360/31 656, ℻31 688; ⑤) which, together with the adequate *Toxotis* restaurant opposite, would make a good base if you had transport. Livádhi is also home to the most efficient travel agency on the island, Porfyra

Travel, which is the main ANEK/ANEN and Olympic agent (☎07360/31 888, ⑤31 889, ⓔporfyra@kythira.com), with exchange and car rental; they can also arrange accommodation or transfers.

At **Káto Livádhi**, a kilometre to the east of Livádhi, there is a small museum of Byzantine and post-Byzantine art (Tues–Sun 8.30am–2pm; free) next to the large central church. It contains (labelled in Greek only) frescoes, painstakingly removed from island churches, dating from the twelfth to the eighteenth centuries, a seventh-century mosaic floor and some portable icons. Not far away there is also a co-operative pottery workshop (open all day except 2–4pm) and, on the road to Katoúni, a multiple-arched bridge, said to be the longest stone bridge in Greece and a legacy of the nineteenth century when all the Ionian islands were a British protectorate; like others on the island it was built by a Scottish engineer called McPhail. The best view of it is from beside *Rena's zaharoplastío* in Livádhi. A popular **taverna** nearby is the *Theofilos*.

From Livádhi, a side road heads west to Kalokerinés, and continues 3.6km further to the island's principal monastery, **Myrtidhíon**, set above the wild and windswept west coast, among a dead forest of pines burned in June 2000. The monastery's main icon is said to date from 1160. Beyond the monastery, a track leads down to a small anchorage at **Limnária**; there are few beaches along this rocky, forbidding shore. An early left fork off the Myrtidhíon road out of Livádhi brings you through the hamlet of Poúrko and past the unusual Byzantine church of Áyios Dimítrios. From Poúrko, an increasingly steep road leads up to the **Ayía Elésis**, a nineteenth-century monastery marking the martyrdom of the saint on the hilltop in 375 AD, an event depicted in recent wall-paintings inside the church. For many visitors, however the breathtaking view from the western side of the courtyard is the main reason to visit.

Mylopótamos, Káto Hóra and the Ayía Sofía cave

North of Livádhi, just beyond Dhókana, it is worth making a detour off the main road for **MYLOPÓTAMOS**, a lovely traditional village and an oasis in summer, set in a wooded valley occupied by a small stream. The shady *Platanos* kafenío makes a pleasant stop for a drink above the village's springs and *Tó Kamari*, in an old restored building, serves snacks and drinks on a lower waterside terrace. Follow the signs for "Katarraktis Neraidha" to find a waterfall, hidden from view by lush vegetation, next to a long-closed café. The valley below the falls is overgrown but contains the remains of the watermill that gave the village its name.

Káto Hóra (Kástro Mylopotamoú), 500m down the road, was Mylopótamos's predecessor, and remains half-enclosed within the walls of a Venetian fortress. The fortress is small, full of locked, well-labelled churches, and has a rather domestic appearance: unlike the castle at Hóra, it was built as a place of refuge for the villagers in case of attack, rather than as a base for a Venetian garrison. All the houses within the walls are abandoned – as are many outside – but are open and accessible. Beyond here, a surfaced but briefly precipitous road continues 5km through spectacular cliffscapes to **Limniónas**, a rocky inlet with a small sand beach, but a fire in June 2000 has left the surrounding countryside unattractive and bereft of vegetation.

The reason most visitors come to Mylopótamos is to see the **cave of Ayía Sofía**, the largest and most impressive of a number of caverns on the island. A half-hour signposted walk from the village, or a short drive by a new dirt road being constructed off the Limniónas road, the cave is open regularly from mid-

June to mid-September (Mon–Fri 3–8pm, Sat & Sun 11am–5pm; €2.50). When the cave is closed, you can probably find a guide in Mylopótamos; ask at the village, giving a day's notice if possible. The cave is worth the effort to see: the entrance has been used as a church and has an iconostasis carved from the rock, with important Byzantine frescoes on it. Beyond, the cave system comprises a series of chambers which reach 250m into the mountain, although the thirty-minute guided tour (in Greek and English) only takes in the more interesting outer chambers. These include some startling formations like the "shark's teeth", but you have to ask to be shown "Aphrodite's chambers". A minute new species of disc-shaped insect has been discovered there.

Andikýthira island

Thirteen kilometres to the south of Kýthira, the tiny, wind-blown island of **ANDIKÝTHIRA** has, theoretically, a twice-weekly connection with Crete on the Kýthira–Kastélli–Kýthira run; landings are often impossible due to adverse weather. There are attempts to organize a ferry from Kýthira on August 17 for the festival of Áyios Mýron, returning the following day, but these are frequently thwarted by the wind. Rocky and poor, the island only received electricity in 1984. Attractions include good birdlife and flora, but it's not the place if you want company: with only seventy or so inhabitants divided among a scattering of settlements – mainly in **Potamós**, the harbour, and **Sohória**, the village – people are rather thin on the ground. A resident doctor and a teacher serve the dwindling community (there are three children at the village school, compared with nearly forty in the 1960s). The only official accommodation is the set of **rooms** run by the local community (☎07360/31 390, ℻33 471) at Potamós, which also has the sole **taverna**, but you'd be recommended to bring plenty of supplies with you. In Sohória the only provisions available are basic foodstuffs at the village shop.

Travel details

Corfu (Kérkyra)

There are 4 or 5 daily flights between Corfu and Athens (1hr) on Olympic, plus 2 daily on Aegean-Cronus, and 3 weekly except Sun to Thessaloníki (1hr). Several ferries (Port Authority ☎06610/32 655) per hour (5.15am–10pm) run between Corfu and Igoumenítsa (1hr 15min) in high season. Also 6 daily between Igoumenítsa and Lefkími (40min). Additionally, many ferries between Italy (Brindisi, Bari, Ancona and Venice) and Pátra stop at Corfu; stopover is free if specified in advance and there is no problem buying Corfu–Pátra tickets. Although there is only a twice-weekly ferry to Paxí, there are up to 5 hydrofoils daily in season, either direct (1hr) or via Igoumenítsa (1hr 30min). The twice-weekly (Wed & Sat) tour hydrofoil does sometimes take one-way passengers to Kefalloniá. Buses to Athens via the Igoumenítsa ferry depart 3 or 4 times daily, twice daily to Thessaloníki.

Eríkoussa, Mathráki and Othoní

A car ferry, the *Alexandros II*, runs from Kérkyra Town to all the islands 3 times weekly (Tues &

Thurs 7.30am; Sun 9am) and to Othoní only on Sat (4pm). The ferry leaves from near the BP station on the seafront, midway between the Old and New Ports, although it involves sailing halfway round the island. Quicker access, favoured by islanders without vehicles, is via daily excursions from Sidhári or Áyios Stéfanos run by Nearchos Seacruises (☎06630/95 248).

Itháki (Ithaca)

Seasonal ferries from Fríkes to: Fiskárdho (Kefalloniá; 1 daily; 1hr); Nydhrí (Lefkádha; 1 daily; 1hr 45min). Pisaetós to: Sámi (Kefalloniá; 3 daily; 45min). Váthý to: Astakós (1 daily; 2hr 30min); Pátra (2 daily; 5hr); Sámi (Kefalloniá; 2 daily; 1hr). Off-season, there is 1 daily service on each route, weather permitting – check with Port Authority (☎06740/32 909).

Kefalloniá

1–2 daily flights to and from Athens (1hr). Ferries in season from Sámi to: Astakós (1 daily; 4hr); Pátra (4 daily;1hr 40min–2hr 30min);

Pisaetós (Itháki; 3 daily; 45min); Vathý, (Itháki; 2 daily; 1hr). Also ferries from Póros to Kyllíni (3 daily; 1hr 15min). Fiskárdho to: Fríkes (Itháki; 1 daily; 1hr); Nydhrí (Lefkádha; 1 daily; 2hr 45min); Vassilikí (Lefkádha; 3 daily; 1hr 15min). Argostóli to: Kyllíni (2 daily; 2hr 30min); Lixoúri (every 30min; 20min). Pessádha to: Áyios Nikólaos (Zákynthos; 2 daily; 1hr 30min). Most routes maintain 1 daily service in winter – check with Port Authorities (Argostóli ☎06710/22 224; Sámi ☎06740/22 031; Póros ☎06740/72 460). The twice-weekly tour hydrofoils from Sámi to Corfu will usually take one-way passengers.

5 daily buses from Argostóli to Athens (6–7hr). 1 daily from Lixoúri, Póros and Sámi.

Lefkádha

5 buses daily to and from Athens (6–7hr), and 5 buses daily to the Áktio ferry (30min) for Préveza, passing Áktio airport (25min). 7 ferries daily in season from Nydhrí to Meganíssi; daily connections (several in summer and 1 all year) from Nydhrí or Vassilikí to Kefalloniá (Fiskárdho) and Itháki (Fríkes). The weekly cruise boat *Ikaros* will take one-way passengers to Párga or Paxí.

Paxí

Ferry connections to Paxí (Port Authority ☎06620/32 259) have stabilized in the last couple of years. To Corfu, there is a twice-weekly service throughout the year, plus up to 5 hydrofoils daily. There are 1–3 daily ferries to/from Igoumenítsa. In summer 2 kaïkia connect daily with Párga.

Zákynthos

Zákynthos Town to: Kyllíni (5 daily all year, up to 8 in season; 1hr 30min). Áyios Nikoláos to: Pessádha (Kefalloniá; 2 daily May–Sept; 1hr 30min).

Buses from Zákynthos Town to Athens (3–8 daily, according to season; 6hr).

Flight (on Olympic) from Zákynthos Town to Athens (1–2 daily; 1hr).

contexts

contexts

The historical framework 539–566

Mythology, an A to Z 567–576

Music 577–583

Wildlife 584–593

Books 594–609

CONTEXTS

The historical framework

This section is intended just to lend some perspective to travels around the Greek islands, and is heavily weighted towards the era of the modern, post-independence nation – especially the twentieth century. More detailed accounts of particular periods are to be found in the relevant sections of the guide.

Neolithic, Minoan and Mycenaean ages

Other than the solitary discovery of a fossilized Neanderthal skull near Thessaloníki, the earliest evidence of **human settlement** in Greece is to be found at Néa Nikomedhía, near Véria. Here, traces of large, rectangular houses dated to around 6000 BC have been excavated.

It seems that people originally came to this eastern Mediterranean territory in fits and starts, predominantly from Anatolia. These **pre-Hellenes** settled in essentially peaceful farming communities, made pottery and worshipped earth/fertility goddesses – clay statuettes of which are still found on the sites of old settlements. This simple way of life eventually disappeared, as people started to tap the land's resources for profit and to compete and trade.

Minoans and Mycenaeans

The years between around **2000** and **1100 BC** were a period of fluctuating regional dominance, based at first upon sea power, with vast **royal palaces** serving as centres of administration. Particularly important were those at **Knossos** on Crete, and **Mycenae**, **Tiryns** and **Pylos** in the Peloponnese.

Crete monopolized the eastern Mediterranean trade routes during an era subsequently called the **Minoan Age**, with the palace at Knossos surviving two earthquakes and a massive volcanic eruption on the island of Thíra (Santoríni), at some indefinite point between 1500 and 1450 BC. The most obvious examples of Minoan culture can be seen in frescoes, in jewellery and in pottery, the distinctive red-and-white design on a dark background marking the peak period of Minoan achievement. When Knossos finally succumbed to disaster, natural or otherwise, around 1400 BC, it was the flourishing centre of **Mycenae** that assumed the leading role (and gave its name to the civilization of this period), until it in turn collapsed around 1200 BC.

This is a period whose history and remains are bound up with its legends, recounted most famously by Homer and his disciples. Knossos was the home of King Minos, while the palaces of Mycenae and Pylos were the respective bases of Agamemnon and Nestor; Menelaos and Odysseus hailed from Sparta and Ithaca. The **Homeric and other legends** relating to them almost certainly reflect the growing prevalence of violence, revenge and war, instigated and aggravated by trade rivalry. The increasing scale of conflict and militarization is exemplified by the massive Mycenean fortifications of the Peloponnese and central mainland that were built around many of the palaces and dubbed

Cyclopean by later ages, after the only beings thought capable of hefting the huge stones.

The Greece of these years was by no means a united nation – as the Homeric legend reflects – and its people were divided into what were in effect a series of splinter groups, defined in large part by sea and mountain barriers and by access to **pasture**. Settlements flourished according to their proximity to and prowess on the sea and the fertility of their land; most were self-sufficient, specializing in the production of particular items for **trade**. Olives, for example, were associated with the region of Attica, and minerals with the island of Mílos.

The Dorian and Classical eras

The Mycenaean-era Greek states had also to cope with and assimilate periodic influxes of new peoples and trade. The traditional view of the collapse of the Mycenaean civilization has it that a northern "barbarian" people, the **Dorians**, "invaded" from the north, devastating the existing palace culture and inaugurating a "dark age"; a competing theory has the so-called "Sea Peoples", probably based in southwestern Anatolia, conducting a series of raids over several decades. These days, archeologists see the influx more in terms of shifting trade patterns, though undoubtedly there was major disruption of the palace cultures and their sea power during the eleventh century.

Two other trends are salient in the period: the almost total supplanting of the mother goddesses by **male deities** (a process begun under the Mycenaeans), and the appearance of an **alphabet** still recognizable by modern Greeks, which replaced the so-called "Linear A" and "Linear B" Minoan/Mycenaean scripts.

City-states: Sparta and Athens

The ninth century BC ushered in the beginnings of the Greek **city-state** (*polis*). Citizens – rather than just kings or aristocrats – became involved in government, took part in community activities and organized industry and leisure. Colonial ventures increased, as did commercial dealings, and a consequent rise in the import trade was gradually to create a new class of manufacturers.

The city-state was the life of the people who dwelt within it, and each state retained both its independence and a distinctive style, with the result that the sporadic attempts to unite in a league against an external enemy were always pragmatic and temporary. The two most powerful states to emerge were Athens and Sparta, who were to become rivals over the next five centuries.

Sparta was associated with the Dorians, who had settled in large numbers on the fertile Eurotas (Évrotas) river plain. The society of Sparta and its environs possessed a hierarchical ethos – the majority of the population, the helots, existed in a state of serfdom and worked to support the elite. Sparta was also highly militaristic, accentuated by the need to defend the exposed and fertile land on which it stood. Rather than build intricate fortifications, the people of Sparta relied upon military prowess and a system of laws decreed by the (semi-legendary) **Lycurgus**. Males were subjected to military instruction between the ages of seven and thirty. Weak babies were known periodically to "disappear". Girls too had to perform athletic feats of sprinting and wrestling, and even dwellings were more like barracks than houses.

Athens, the fulcrum of the state of Attica, was dynamic and exciting by contrast, though here too slavery was vital to the economy. Home to the administrations of **Solon** and **Pericles**, the dramatic talents of Sophocles and Aristophanes, the oratory of Thucydides and Demosthenes, and the philosophical power of Socrates and Plato, it made up in cultural achievement what it lacked in Spartan virtue. Yet Sparta did not deserve all the military glory. The Athens of the sixth and fifth centuries BC, the so-called **Classical period** in Greek history, played the major part in repelling the armies of the Persian king Xerxes at Marathon (490 BC) and Salamis (480 BC), campaigns later described by Aeschylus in *The Persians*.

Athens also gave rise to a tradition of **democracy** (*demokratía*), literally "control by the people" – although at this stage "the people" did not include either women or slaves. In Athens there were three organs of government. The Areopagus, composed of the city elders, exercised steadily decreasing authority and eventually dealt solely with murder cases. Then there was the Council of Five Hundred (men), elected annually by ballot to prepare the business of the Assembly and to attend to matters of urgency. The Assembly gave every free man a political voice; it had sole responsibility for law-making and provided an arena for the discussion of important issues. It was a genuinely enfranchised council of citizens.

This was a period of intense creativity, particularly in Athens, whose actions and pretensions were fast becoming imperial in all but name. Each city-state had its **acropolis**, or high town, where religious activity was focused. In Athens, Pericles endowed the acropolis with a complex of buildings, whose climax was the temple of the Parthenon. Meanwhile, the era saw the tragedies of Sophocles performed, and the philosophies of Socrates and Plato expounded.

Religion at this stage was polytheistic, ordering eleven main gods under the aegis of Zeus. Urban temples tended to be dedicated to Zeus, Athena or Poseidon; in the countryside the proliferation of names and sanctuary finds suggests a preference for Apollo, Hera, Dionysos and Artemis.

The Peloponnesian wars

The power struggles between Athens and Sparta, allied with various networks of city-states, eventually culminated in the **Peloponnesian wars** of 431–404 BC. After these conflicts, superbly recorded by Thucydides and nominally won by Sparta, the city-state ceased to function so effectively.

This was in part due to drained resources and political apathy, but to a greater degree a consequence of the increasingly commercial and complex pressures on everyday life. Trade, originally spurred by the invention of **coinage** in the sixth century BC, continued to expand; a revitalized Athens, for example, was exporting wine, oil and manufactured goods, getting corn in return from the Black Sea and Egypt.

The amount of time each man had to devote to the affairs of government decreased, and a position in political life became a professional job rather than a natural assumption. Democracy had changed, while in philosophy there was a shift from the idealists and mystics of the sixth and fifth centuries BC to the Cynics, Stoics and Epicureans – followers, respectively, of Diogenes, Zeno and Epicurus.

Hellenistic and Roman Greece

The most important factor in the decline of the city-states was meanwhile developing outside their sphere, in the kingdom of Macedonia to the north.

The Macedonian empire

Ruling from the Macedonian capital of Pella, **Philip II** (359–336 BC) was forging a strong military and unitary force, extending his territories into Thrace and finally establishing control over Athens and southern Greece. His son, **Alexander the Great**, in a brief but glorious thirteen-year reign, extended these gains into Persia and Egypt and parts of modern India and Afghanistan.

This unwieldy empire splintered almost immediately upon Alexander's death in 323 BC, to be divided into the three Macedonian dynasties of **Hellenistic Greece**: the Antigonids in Macedonia, the Seleucids in Syria and Persia, and the Ptolemies in Egypt. Each was in turn conquered and absorbed by the new Roman empire, the Ptolemies – under their queen Cleopatra – last of all.

Roman Greece

Mainland and island Greece were subdued by the Romans over some seventy years of campaigns, from 215 to 146 BC. Once in control, however, **Rome** allowed considerable autonomy to the old territories of the city-states. Greek remained the official language of the eastern Mediterranean and its traditions and culture coexisted fairly peacefully with that of the overlords during the next three centuries.

In central Greece both **Athens** and **Corinth** remained important cities but the emphasis was shifting north – particularly to towns, such as **Salonica** (Thessaloníki), along the new Via Egnatia, a military and civil road engineered between Rome and Byzantium via the port of Brundisium (modern Brindisi in Italy). Out among the islands, Rhodes had declined since Hellenistic times but Kós, Lésvos, Thássos and Gortys on Crete remained important centres.

The Byzantine empire and Medieval Greece

The shift of emphasis northwards was given even greater impetus by the decline of the Roman empire and its division into eastern and western empires. In the year 330 AD Emperor Constantine moved his capital to the Greek city of Byzantium, and here emerged Constantinople (modern Istanbul), the "new Rome" and spiritual and political capital of the **Byzantine empire**.

While the last western Roman emperor was deposed by barbarian Goths in 476, this eastern portion was to be the dominant Mediterranean power for some seven hundred years; only in 1453 did it collapse completely.

Christianity

Christianity had been introduced under Constantine, and by the end of the fourth century was the official state religion, its liturgies (still in use in the Greek Orthodox Church), Creed and New Testament all written in Greek. A distinction must be drawn though, between perceptions of Greek as a language or culture, and as a concept. The Byzantine empire styled itself Roman, or

Romios, rather than Hellenic, and moved to eradicate all remaining symbols of pagan Greece. The Delphic Oracle was forcibly closed, and the Olympic Games discontinued, by the emperor Theodosius at the end of the fourth century. Schools of philosophy, especially neo-Platonic ones, did however survive until 529.

The seventh century saw **Constantinople** besieged by Persians, and later Arabs, but the Byzantine empire survived, losing only Egypt, the least "Greek" of its territories. From the ninth to the early eleventh centuries it enjoyed an archetypal "golden age" in culture, confidence and security. Bound up with the Orthodox Byzantine faith was a sense of spiritual superiority, and the emperors saw Constantinople as a "new Jerusalem" for their "chosen people". It was the beginning of a diplomatic and ecclesiastical conflict with the Catholic West that was to have disastrous consequences over the next five centuries. In the meantime the Eastern and Western patriarchs mutually excommunicated each other.

From the seventh until the eleventh centuries **Byzantine Greece**, certainly in the islands, became something of a provincial backwater. Administration was absurdly top-heavy, and imperial taxation led to semi-autonomous provinces ruled by military generals, whose lands were usually acquired from bankrupted peasants. This alienation of the poor provided a force for change, with a disaffected populace ready to turn towards or cooperate with the empire's enemies if the terms on offer were an improvement.

Waves of **Slavic raiders** needed no encouragement to sweep down from the north Balkans throughout this period. At the same time other tribal groups moved down more peaceably from **central Europe** and were absorbed with little difficulty. According to one theory, the nomadic **Vlachs** from Romania eventually settled in the Píndhos mountains, and later, from the thirteenth century onwards, immigrants from **Albania** repopulated the islands of Spétses, Ídhra, Angístri, Salamína, Ándhros and Évvia, as well as parts of Attica and the Peloponnese.

The crusades: Frankish and Venetian rule

From the early years of the eleventh century, less welcome and less assimilable Western forces began to appear. The **Normans** landed first at Corfu in 1085, and returned again to the mainland with papal sanction a decade later on their way to liberate Jerusalem.

These were only a precursor, though, for the forces that were to descend en route for the **Fourth Crusade** of 1204, when Venetians, Franks and Germans turned their armies directly on Byzantium to sack and occupy Constantinople. These Latin princes and their followers, intent on new lands and kingdoms, settled in to divide up the best part of the empire. All that remained of Byzantium were four small peripheral kingdoms, or **despotates**: the most powerful in Nicaea in Asia Minor, less significant ones at Trebizond on the Black Sea, and (in present-day Greece) in Epirus and around Mystra in the Peloponnese (known in those times as the Moreás).

There followed two extraordinarily involved centuries of manipulation and struggle between Franks, Venetians, Genoese, Catalans and Turks. The Paleologos dynasty at Nicaea recovered the city of Constantinople in 1261, but little of its former territory and power. Instead, the focus of Byzantium shifted to the Peloponnese, where the autonomous **despotate of Mystra**, ruled by members of the imperial family, eventually succeeded in wresting most of the peninsula from Frankish hands. At the same time this despotate enjoyed an intense cultural renaissance, strongly evoked in the churches and shells of cities seen today at modern Mystrás and Monemvasiá.

Ottoman occupation

Within a generation of driving out the Franks, the Byzantine Greeks faced a much stronger threat in the expanding empire of the **Ottomans**. "Turks" is the common term used for them in Greece, but the Ottomans were in fact a motley, assimilative crew, who included large numbers of Albanian, Arab and Kurdish Muslims, as well as Christian renegades from Venice, Hungary and the territory of Greece. Torn apart by internal struggles between their own ruling dynasties, the **Palaeologi** and **Cantacuzenes**, and unaided by the Catholic West, they were to prove no match for the Ottomans. On Tuesday, May 29, 1453, a date still solemnly commemorated by the Orthodox Church, Constantinople fell to the besieging Sultan Mehmet II.

Mystra was to follow within seven years, and Trebizond within nine, by which time virtually all of the old Byzantine empire lay under Ottoman domination. Only the **Ionian islands, Crete** and the **Cyclades**, which remained Venetian for two more centuries (or longer), and a few scattered and remote enclaves – like the Máni in the Peloponnese and Soúli in Epirus – were able to resist the "Turkish" advance.

Ottoman rule

Under what Greeks refer to as the *turkokratía* or era of **Ottoman rule**, the lands of present-day Greece passed into rural provincialism, taking refuge in a self-protective mode of village life that was only substantially disrupted by World War II. Taxes and discipline, sporadically backed up by the massacre of dissenting communities, were inflicted by Istanbul (as Constantinople was renamed), but large areas passed into the hands of local chieftains who often had considerable independence. On the larger, more fertile islands such as Crete, Lésvos and Évvia, rule was inevitably stricter, with larger garrisons and more onerous taxes; small islands too impoverished to be exploited were left pretty much to their own devices.

Greek identity, meanwhile, was preserved through the offices of the **Orthodox Church** which, despite instances of enforced conversion, the sultans allowed to continue. The **monasteries**, sometimes secretly, organized schools and became the trustees of Byzantine culture, though this had gone into stagnation after the fall of Constantinople and Mystra, whose scholars and artists emigrated west, adding impetus to the Renaissance.

As Ottoman administration became progressively decentralized and inefficient, individual Greeks rose to local positions of considerable influence, and a number of communities achieved a degree of autonomy. Sými was granted an empire-wide monopoly on sponge-diving in return for a yearly tribute to the sultan. Sámos was declared a "Muslim-free" zone and enjoyed special tax exemptions for two centuries. And on the Albanian-repopulated islands of Ídhra and Spétses, as well as Kássos and Psará, a **Greek merchant fleet** came into being in the eighteenth century, permitted to trade throughout the Mediterranean. Greeks, too, were becoming organized overseas in the sizeable expatriate colonies of central Europe, which often had affiliations with the semi-autonomous village clusters of Zagóri (in Epirus), Ambeláki (Thessaly) and Mount Pílion.

The struggle for independence

Despite these privileges, by the eighteenth century opposition to Ottoman rule was becoming widespread on the mainland, exemplified most obviously by the **klephts** (brigands) of the mountains. It was not until the nineteenth century, however, that a resistance movement could muster sufficient support and firepower to prove a real challenge to the Ottomans. In 1770 a Russian-backed uprising had been easily and brutally suppressed, but fifty years later the situation was different.

In Epirus the Ottomans were overextended, subduing the expansionist campaigns of local ruler **Ali Pasha**. The French Revolution had given impetus to "freedom movements", and the Greek fighters were provided with financial and ideological underpinnings by the Filikí Etería, or "Friendly Society", a secret group recruited among the exiled merchants and intellectuals of central Europe.

This somewhat motley coalition of klephts and theorists launched their insurrection at the monastery of **Ayía Lávra** near Kalávryta in the Peloponnese, where on March 25, 1821, the Greek banner was openly raised by the local bishop, Yermanos.

The War of Independence

To describe in detail the course of the **War of Independence** is to provoke unnecessary confusion, since much of the rebellion consisted of local and fragmentary guerrilla campaigns. What is important to understand is that Greeks, though fighting for liberation from the Ottomans, were not fighting as and for a nation. Motives differed enormously: landowners assumed their role was to lead and sought to retain and reinforce their traditional privileges, while the peasantry saw the struggle as a means towards land redistribution.

Outside Greece, the prestige of and publicity for the insurrection were promoted by the arrival of a thousand or so European **Philhellenes**, almost half of them German, though the most important was the English poet, **Lord Byron**, who died while training Greek forces at Mesolóngi in April 1824.

Though it was the Greek guerrilla leaders, above all **Theodhoros Kolokotronis**, "the old man of the Morea", who brought about the most significant military victories of the war, the death of Byron had an immensely important effect on public opinion in the West. Aid for the Greek struggle had come neither from Orthodox Russia, nor from the Western powers of France and Britain, both still ravaged by the Napoleonic wars. But by 1827, when Mesolóngi fell again to the Ottoman Turks, these three "Great Powers" finally agreed to seek autonomy for certain parts of Greece and sent a combined fleet to put pressure on the sultan's Egyptian army and fleet, then ransacking and massacring in the Peloponnese. Events took over, and an accidental naval battle in **Navarino Bay** resulted in the destruction of almost the entire Turkish-Egyptian fleet. The following spring Russia itself declared war on the Ottomans, and Sultan Mahmud II was forced to accept the existence of an autonomous Greece.

At a series of conferences from 1830 to 1832, Greek independence was confirmed by the Western powers and **borders** were drawn in 1832. These included just 800,000 of the six million Greeks living within the Ottoman empire, and territories which were for the most part the poorest of the Classical and Byzantine lands: Attica, the Peloponnese and the islands of the Argo-Saronic, Sporades and Cyclades. The rich agricultural belt of Thessaly, Epirus in the west, and Macedonia in the north, remained in Ottoman hands. Meanwhile, the Ionian islands were controlled by a British protectorate and the Dodecanese by the Ottomans (and after 1913 by recently unified Italy).

The emerging state

Modern Greece began as a republic, and **Ioannis Kapodistrias**, its first president, concentrated his efforts on building a viable central authority and government in the face of diverse protagonists from the Independence struggle. Almost inevitably he was assassinated – in 1831, by two chieftains from the ever-disruptive Máni – and perhaps equally inevitably the three powers stepped in. They created a monarchy, gave limited aid and set on the throne a Bavarian prince, **Otho (Otto)**.

The new king proved an autocratic and insensitive ruler, bringing in fellow Germans to fill official posts and ignoring all claims by the landless peasantry for redistribution of the old estates. In 1862 he was forced from the country by a popular revolt, and the Europeans produced a new prince, this time from Denmark, who requested that Britain cede the Ionian islands as a condition of his accession to the throne. **George (Yeoryios) I**, in fact, proved more capable and popular: he had the first railways and roads built, introduced limited land reforms in the Peloponnese and oversaw the first expansion of the Greek borders.

The Megáli Idhéa and expansionist wars

From the very beginning, the unquestioned motive force of Greek foreign policy was the **Megáli Idhéa** (Great Idea) of liberating Greek populations outside the country and incorporating the old territories of Byzantium into the kingdom. In 1878 **Thessaly**, along with southern Epirus up to Árta, was ceded to Greece by the Ottomans.

Less illustriously, the Greeks failed in 1897 to achieve *énosis* (union) with **Crete** by attacking Ottoman forces on the mainland, and in the process virtually bankrupted the state. The island was, however, placed under a high commissioner, appointed by the Great Powers, and in 1913 did become a part of Greece.

It was from Crete, also, that the most distinguished modern Greek statesman emerged. **Eleftherios Venizelos**, having led a civilian campaign for his island's liberation, was elected as Greek prime minister in 1910. Two years later he organized an alliance of Balkan powers to fight the **Balkan wars** (1912–13), campaigns that saw the Ottomans virtually driven from Europe. With Greek borders extended to include the northeast Aegean islands, northern Thessaly, central Epirus and parts of Macedonia, the Megáli Idhéa seemed to be approaching reality. At the same time Venizelos proved himself a shrewd manipulator of domestic public opinion by revising the constitution and introducing a series of liberal social reforms.

Division, however, was to appear with the outbreak of **World War I**. Venizelos urged Greek entry on the Allied side, seeing in the conflict possibilities for the "liberation" of Greeks in Thrace and Asia Minor, but the new king, Constantine (Konstandinos) I, who was married to a sister of the German Kaiser, imposed a policy of neutrality. Eventually Venizelos set up a revolutionary government in Thessaloníki, and in 1917 Greek troops entered the war to join the French, British and Serbians in the **Macedonian campaign**. Upon the capitulation of Bulgaria and Ottoman Turkey, the Greeks occupied **Thrace**, and Venizelos presented demands at Versailles for the predominantly Greek region of Smyrna on the Asia Minor coast.

The Katastrofí and its aftermath

This was the beginning of one of the most disastrous episodes in modern Greek history, the so-called **Katastrofí** ("Catastrophe"). Venizelos was authorized to move forces into Smyrna in 1919, but in Turkey itself a new nationalist movement was coming to power under Mustafa Kemal, or **Atatürk** as he came to be known. In 1920 Venizelos lost the elections and monarchist factions took over, their aspirations unmitigated by the Cretan's skill in foreign diplomacy. Despite Allied support for such ventures now having completely evaporated, Greek forces were ordered to advance upon Ankara in an attempt to bring Atatürk to terms.

This so-called **Anatolian campaign** ignominiously collapsed in summer 1922 when Ottoman troops forced the Greeks back to the coast and into a hurried evacuation from **Smyrna**. As they left Smyrna, the Ottomans moved in and systematically massacred much of the Armenian and Greek population before burning most of the city to the ground.

Although an entire Greek army remained intact in eastern Thrace, Britain, hitherto Greece's only backer, let it be known that Greece should accept Atatürk's terms, formalized by the 1923 Treaty of Lausanne, which ordered the **exchange of religious minorities** in each country – in effect, the first large-scale regulated ethnic cleansing. Turkey was to accept 390,000 Muslims resident on Greek soil. Greece, mobilized almost continuously for the last decade and with a population of under five million, was faced with the resettlement of over 1,400,000 Christian refugees. Many of these had already read the writing on the wall after 1918 and arrived of their own accord, from Bulgaria and revolutionary Russia as well as Asia Minor; significant numbers were settled on Thássos, Límnos, Lésvos, Híos, Sámos, Évvia and Crete, as well as around Athens and in the northern mainland. The Megáli Idhéa had ceased to be a viable blueprint.

Changes, inevitably, were intense and far-reaching. The great agricultural estates of Crete, Évvia, Lésvos and Thessaly were finally redistributed, both to Greek tenants and refugee farmers, and huge shanty towns grew into new quarters around Athens, Pireás and other cities, a spur to the country's then almost nonexistent industry.

Politically, too, reaction was swift. By September 1922, a group of Venizelist army officers under **Colonel Nikolaos Plastiras**, assembled after the retreat from Smyrna, "invited" King Constantine to abdicate, and in November they executed six of his ministers held most responsible for the debacle. Democracy was nominally restored with the proclamation of a republic, but for much of the next decade changes in government were brought about by factions within the armed forces. Meanwhile, among the urban refugee population, unions were being formed and the Greek Communist Party (KKE) was established.

Venizelos's last gasp — and the rise of Metaxas

Elections in 1928 **returned Venizelos** to power, but his freedom to manoeuvre was restricted by the Great Crash of the following year. He had borrowed heavily abroad and was unable to renegotiate loan terms in 1931. Late 1932 saw a local crash caused by England's abandonment of the gold standard, with Greek currency heavily devalued and Venizelos forced from office. His supporters under Plastiras tried to reinstate him by force in March 1933, but their coup was quashed and Venizelos fled to Paris, where he died in 1936.

By 1936 the Communist Party had enough electoral support to hold the balance of power in parliament, and would have done so had not the army and the by-then restored king decided otherwise. **King George (Yeoryios) II** had been returned by a plebiscite held – and almost certainly manipulated – the previous year, and so presided over an increasingly factionalized parliament. In April 1936 George II appointed **General Ioannis Metaxas** as prime minister, despite the latter's being supported by only six elected deputies. A series of KKE-organized strikes broke out immediately and the king, ignoring attempts to form a broad liberal coalition, dissolved parliament without setting a date for new elections. It was a blatantly unconstitutional move and opened the way for five years of ruthless and at times absurd dictatorship.

Metaxas averted a general strike with military force and proceeded to set up a state based on **fascist** models of the era. Left-wing and trade union opponents were imprisoned or forced into exile, a state youth movement and efficient secret police set up, and rigid censorship, extending even to passages of Thucydides, imposed. But it was at least a Greek dictatorship, and though Metaxas was sympathetic to Nazi organizational methods and economics he completely opposed German or Italian domination.

World War II and the Greek civil war

Using a submarine based on Léros in the Dodecanese, the Italians tried to provoke the Greeks into prematurely entering **World War II** by surreptitiously torpedoing the Greek cruiser *Elli* in Tínos harbour on August 15, 1940, but they met with no immediate response. However, when Mussolini occupied Albania and sent an ultimatum on October 28, 1940, demanding passage for his troops through Greece, Metaxas responded to the Italian foreign minister with the apocryphal one-word answer **"óhi"** (no). (In fact, his response, in the mutually understood French, was "*C'est la guerre*".) The date marked the entry of Greece into the war, and the gesture is still celebrated as a national holiday. Galvanized into brief unity by the crisis, the Greeks drove Italian forces from the country, and managed moreover to take control of the long-coveted and predominantly Greek-populated northern Epirus (southern Albania). However, the Greek army subsequently frittered away its strength in the snowy mountains of northern Epirus rather than consolidating its gains or defending the Macedonian frontier, and the proposed coordination with the British never materialized.

Occupation and resistance

In April of the following year Nazi mechanized columns swept through Yugoslavia and across the Greek mainland, effectively reversing the only Axis defeat to date, and by late May 1941 airborne and seaborne **German invasion** forces had completed the occupation of Crete and the other islands. Metaxas had died before their arrival, while King George and his new self-appointed ministers fled into exile in Cairo; few Greeks, of any political persuasion, were sad to see them go.

The joint Italian–German–Bulgarian Axis **occupation** of Greece was among the bitterest experiences of the European war. Nearly half a million Greek civilians starved to death over the winter of 1941–42, as all available food was requisitioned, principally by the Germans, to feed occupying armies. In addition, entire villages throughout the mainland and especially on Crete were burned at the least hint of resistance activity. In their northern sector, which included Thássos and Samothráki, the Bulgarians desecrated ancient sites and churches to support a future bid to annexe "Slavic" Macedonia.

After the Italians capitulated in September 1943, the Jewish communities in Rhodes, Kós, Crete, Corfu, Vólos, Évvia and Zákynthos in particular were exposed to the full force of Nazi racial doctrine; in the last three places, however, cooperation between courageous church or municipal authorities and the budding Resistance (see below) ensured that most local Jews survived.

With a quisling government in Athens – and an unpopular, discredited royalist government in exile in Cairo – the focus of Greek political and military action over the next four years passed largely to the **EAM**, or National Liberation Front. By 1943 it was in virtual control of most areas of the country, including Sámos and Lésvos (but not Crete), working with the British on tactical operations, with its own army (**ELAS**) and navy and both civil and secret police forces. Initially it commanded widespread popular support and appeared to offer an obvious framework for the resumption of postwar government.

However, most of its highest-ranking members were Communists, and the British prime minister, **Winston Churchill**, was determined to reinstate the monarchy. Even with two years of the war to run, it became obvious that there could be no peaceable post-liberation regime other than a republic. Accordingly, in August 1943, representatives from each of the main Resistance movements (including two non-Communist groups) flew clandestinely to Cairo to request that the king not return unless a plebiscite had first voted in his favour. Both the Greek and British authorities refused to consider the proposal, and the best possibility of averting civil war was lost.

The EAM contingent returned divided, as perhaps the British had intended, and a conflict broke out between those who favoured taking peaceful control of any government imposed after liberation, and the hard-line Stalinist ideologues, who forbade participation in any "bourgeois" regime.

In October 1943, with fears of an imminent British landing force and takeover, ELAS launched a full-scale attack upon its Greek rivals on the mainland; by the following April, they had wiped out all but the EDES, their most right-wing rival, suspected of collaboration with the Germans. ELAS's ferocity was spurred by the failure of the Egyptian conference and by half-true reports that British and American agents were being infiltrated into Greece to prevent the establishment of a Communist government when the Germans began withdrawing their forces.

In fact, as the Germans began to leave in October 1944, most of the EAM leadership agreed to join a British-sponsored "official" **interim government**. It quickly proved a tactical error, however. With almost ninety percent of the provinces under their control, the Communists were eventually given only one-third representation in Athens, and a new regular army began to form, relying on right-wing extremists rather than the ELAS officer corps. The king showed no sign of renouncing his claims, and, in November, Allied forces ordered ELAS to disarm. On December 3 all pretences of civility or neutrality were dropped; the police fired on an EAM demonstration in Athens, killing at least sixteen, and fighting broke out between ELAS and **British troops**, in the so-called **Dhekemvriana** events. Though ELAS quickly quashed all opposition in the countryside, they failed to drive the British and right-wing Greeks from Athens, thus losing their best chance of seizing power. In their fury at being thwarted, ELAS rounded up their most influential and wealthiest opponents in the largest towns, and marched them out to rural areas in conditions that guaranteed their death.

A truce of sorts was negotiated at Várkiza near Athens in February 1945, but the agreement was never implemented. The army, police and civil service remained in right-wing hands, and, while collaborationists were often allowed to retain their positions, left-wing sympathizers, many of whom were merely Venizelist Republicans and not Communists, were systematically excluded. The elections of 1946 were won by the right-wing parties (the Left, perhaps unwisely, boycotted them), followed by another rigged plebiscite in favour of the king's return. By 1947 guerrilla activity had again reached the scale of a full **civil war**, with ELAS reorganized into the Democratic Army of Greece (**DSE** in Greek).

In the interim, King George had died and been succeeded by his brother Paul (with his consort Frederika), while the **Americans** had taken over the British role, and begun implementing the cold-war **Truman doctrine**. In March 1947 they took virtual control of Greece, their first significant postwar experiment in anti-Communist intervention. Massive economic and military aid was given to a client Greek government, and official decrees had to be countersigned by the American Mission chief in order to become valid.

In the mainland mountains US military advisers trained the nationalist army for **campaigns against the DSE**, and in the cities there were mass arrests, courts martial and imprisonments – a kind of "White Terror" – lasting until 1951. Over three thousand executions were recorded, including (for their pacifist stance and refusal to swear loyalty oaths) a number of Jehovah's Witnesses, "a sect proved to be under Communist domination", according to US Ambassador Grady. To deny the DSE local support, over 700,000 civilians were forcibly evacuated from mountain villages and dumped in squalid internment camps near towns, a move which helped destroy any hope of postwar rural existence.

In the autumn of 1949, with the Yugoslav–Greek border closed after Tito's rift with Stalin, the last DSE guerrillas finally admitted defeat, retreating into Albania from their strongholds on Mount Grámmos. Atrocities had been committed on both sides, including, from the Left, considerably more than three thousand executions, widescale vandalization of monasteries and the dubious evacuation of children from "combat areas" (as told in Nicholas Gage's virulently anti-Communist book *Eleni*). Such actions, as well as the hopelessness of lightly armed guerrillas fighting an American-backed army equipped with aircraft and heavy artillery, almost certainly doomed the DSE's efforts from the start.

Reconstruction American style 1950–67

After a decade of war that had shattered much of Greece's infrastructure (supposedly not one bridge was left standing by 1948), it was a demoralized country that emerged into the Western political orbit of the 1950s. Greece was also perforce American-dominated, enlisted into the Korean War in 1950 and NATO the following year. In domestic politics, the US Embassy – still giving the orders – foisted upon the Greeks a winner-takes-all electoral system, which was to ensure victory for the Right over the next twelve years. Overt leftist activity was banned (though a "cover" party for Communists was soon founded); those individuals who were not herded into political "re-education" camps on barren islands, or dispatched by firing squads, legal or vigilante, went into exile throughout eastern Europe, to return only after 1974.

The American-backed, highly conservative **"Greek Rally"** party, led by General Papagos, won the first decisive post-civil-war elections in 1952. After the general's death, the party's leadership was taken over – and to an extent liberalized – by **Constantine (Konstandinos) Karamanlis**. Under his rule, stability of a kind was established and some economic advances registered, particularly after the revival of Greece's traditional German markets. Health and life expectancy improved dramatically, as the age-old scourges of tuberculosis and malaria were finally confronted with American-supplied food and pesticides. Less commendable was Karamanlis's encouragement of the law of **andiparohí**, whereby owners of small refugee shanties or Neoclassical mansions alike could offer the site of their property to apartment-block developers in exchange for two flats (out of eight to ten) in the finished building. This effectively ripped the heart out of most Greek towns, and explains their baleful aesthetics half a century on.

The 1950s was also a decade that saw wholesale **depopulation** of remote villages as migrants sought work in Australia, America and western Europe, or the larger Greek cities. This was most pronounced on the remoter islands of Kýthira, Kefalloniá, the northeast Aegean and the Dodecanese, where the longed-for union with Greece in 1948 had ironically conferred the right to emigrate, mostly denied under the Ottomans and Italians.

The main crisis in foreign policy throughout this period was **Cyprus**, where a long terrorist campaign was waged by Greek-Cypriots opposing British rule, and there were sporadic threats of a new Greco–Turkish war. An ultimately unworkable compromise was forced on the island by Britain in 1960, granting independence without the possibility of self-determination (ie union with Greece). Much of the traditional Greek–British goodwill was destroyed by the issue, with Britain seen to be acting with regard primarily for its two military bases (over which, incidentally, it still retains sovereignty).

By 1961 unemployment, the Cyprus issue and the imposition of US nuclear bases on Greek soil were changing the political climate, and when Karamanlis was again elected there was strong suspicion of a fraud arranged by the king and army. Strikes became frequent in industry and even agriculture, while King

Paul and autocratic, fascist-inclined Queen Frederika were openly attacked in parliament and at protest demonstrations. The far Right grew uneasy about **"communist resurgence"** and, losing confidence in their own electoral influence, arranged the **assassination** of left-wing deputy **Grigoris Lambrakis** in Thessaloníki in May 1963. (The murder, and its subsequent cover-up, is the subject of Vassilis Vassilikos's thriller *Z*, filmed by Costa-Gavras.) It was against this volatile background that Karamanlis dissolved parliament, lost the subsequent elections and left the country.

The new government – the first controlled from outside the Greek Right since 1935 – was formed by **George Papandreou's Centre Union Party**, and had a decisive majority of nearly fifty seats. It was to last, however, for under two years as conservative forces conspired to thwart its progress. In this the chief protagonists were army officers and their constitutional commander-in-chief, the new king, 23-year-old **Constantine II**.

Since power in Greece depended on a pliant military as well as a network of political appointees, Papandreou's most urgent task in order to govern securely and effectively was to reform the armed forces. His first minister of defence proved incapable of the task and, while he was investigating the right-wing plot suspected of rigging the 1961 election, "evidence" was produced of a leftist conspiracy connected with Papandreou's son Andreas (also a minister in the government). When the allegations grew to a crisis, George Papandreou assumed the defence portfolio himself, a move which the king refused to sanction. He then resigned in order to gain a fresh mandate at the polls but the king would not order new elections, instead persuading members of the Centre Union – chief among them **Constantine Mitsotakis** – to defect and organize a coalition government. Punctuated by strikes, resignations and mass demonstrations, this lasted for a year and a half until new elections were eventually set for May 28, 1967. They failed to take place.

The colonels' junta 1967–74

It was a foregone conclusion that Papandreou's party would win the polls against the discredited coalition partners. And it was equally certain that there would be some anti-democratic action to prevent it from reassuming power. Disturbed by the party's leftward shift, King Constantine was said to have briefed senior generals for a coup d'état, to take place ten days before the elections. However, he was caught by surprise, as was nearly everyone else, by the coup of April 21, 1967, staged by a group of "unknown" colonels. It was, to quote Andreas Papandreou, "the first successful CIA military putsch on the European continent".

The colonels' junta, having taken control of the means of power, was sworn in by the king and survived the half-hearted counter-coup which he subsequently attempted to organize. It was an ostensibly fascist regime, absurdly styling itself as the true "Revival of Greek Orthodoxy" against Western "corrupting influences", though in reality its ideology was nothing more than warmed-up dogma from the Metaxas era mixed with ultra-nationalism.

All political activity was banned, independent trade unions were forbidden to recruit or meet, the press was so heavily censored that many papers stopped printing, and thousands of "Communists" were arrested, imprisoned and often tortured. Among the persecuted were both the Papandreous, the composer

Mikis Theodhorakis (deemed "unfit to stand trial" after three months in custody) and Amalia Fleming (widow of Alexander Fleming). While relatively few people were killed outright, thousands were permanently maimed physically and psychologically in the junta's torture chambers. The best-known Greek actress, Melina Mercouri, was stripped of her citizenship in absentia, and thousands of prominent Greeks joined her in exile.

Culturally, the colonels put an effective end to popular music (banning, for example, bagpipes on Mýkonos lest visitors think Greece too "primitive", and closing many Pláka clubs), while inflicting ludicrous censorship on literature and the theatre, including (as under Metaxas) a ban on production of the Classical tragedies. By contrast, chief colonel Papadapoulos's rambling, illiterate speeches became a byword for bad grammar, obfuscation and Orwellian Newspeak.

The colonels lasted for seven years, opposed (especially after the first two years) by the majority of the Greek people, officially excluded from the Council of Europe, but propped up and given massive aid by US presidents **Lyndon Johnson** and **Richard Nixon**. To them and the CIA the junta's Greece was an ideal client state: human rights considerations were then thought trivial; orders were placed for sophisticated military technology; and foreign investment on terms highly unfavourable to Greece was made available to multinational corporations – a fairly routine scenario of exploitation of an underdeveloped nation.

Opposition was voiced from the beginning by exiled Greeks in London, the United States and western Europe, but only in 1973 did demonstrations break out openly in Greece – the colonels' secret police had done too thorough a job of infiltrating domestic resistance groups and terrifying everyone else into docility. On November 17 the students of **Athens Polytechnic** began an occupation of their buildings. The ruling clique lost its nerve; armoured vehicles stormed the Polytechnic gates and a still-undetermined number of students (estimates range from tens to hundreds) were killed. Martial law was tightened and junta chief Colonel Papadopoulos was replaced by the even more noxious and reactionary General Ioannides, head of the secret police.

The return to civilian rule 1975–81

The end of the ordeal, however, came within a year as the dictatorship embarked on a disastrous political adventure in **Cyprus**, essentially the last playing of the Megáli Idhéa card. By attempting to topple the Makarios government and impose *énosis* (union with Greece) on the island, they provoked a Turkish invasion and occupation of forty percent of Cypriot territory. The army finally mutinied, and **Karamanlis** was invited to return from Paris to take office again. He swiftly negotiated a ceasefire (but no durable solution) in Cyprus, withdrew temporarily from NATO and warned that US bases would have to be removed except where they specifically served Greek interest.

In November 1974 Karamanlis and his **Néa Dhimokratía (New Democracy) Party** were rewarded by a sizeable majority in **elections**, with a centrist and socialist opposition. The latter was the **Panhellenic Socialist Movement (PASOK)**, a new party led by Andreas Papandreou.

The election of Néa Dhimokratía was in every sense a safe conservative option, but to Karamanlis's enduring credit it oversaw an effective and firm return to democratic stability, even legitimizing the KKE (Communist Party) for the first time in its history. Karamanlis also held a **referendum on the monarchy**; 59 percent of Greeks rejected the return of Constantine II, so he instituted in its place a French-style presidency, a post which he himself occupied from 1980 to 1985, and again from 1990 to 1995. Economically there were limited advances, although these were more than offset by inflationary defence spending (the result of renewed tension with Turkey), hastily negotiated entrance into the EC and the decision to let the drachma float after decades of its being artificially fixed at thirty to the US dollar.

Most crucially, Karamanlis failed to deliver vital reforms in bureaucracy, social welfare and education; and while the worst figures of the junta were brought to trial and jailed indefinitely, the face of Greek political life and administration was little changed. By 1981 inflation was hovering around 25 percent, and it was estimated that tax evasion was depriving the state of one-third of its annual budget. In foreign policy the US bases remained, and it was felt that Greece, back in NATO, was still acting as little more than an American satellite. The traditional Right had proved demonstrably inadequate to the task at hand.

PASOK 1981–89

"Change" (*Allayí*) and "Out with the Right" (*Ná Fíyi íy Dhexiá*) were the slogans of the election campaign that swept **PASOK** and Andreas Papandreou to power on October 18, 1981.

This victory meant a chance for Papandreou to form the first socialist government in Greek history and to break a half-century monopoly of authoritarian right-wing rule. With so much at stake the campaign had been passionate even by Greek standards, and PASOK's victory was greeted with euphoria both by the generation whose political voice had been silenced in the civil war, and by a large proportion of the young. Their hopes ran naively, perhaps dangerously, high.

The electoral margin, at least, was conclusive. PASOK won 174 of the 300 parliamentary seats and the Communist KKE – though not part of the new government – returned thirteen deputies, one of them composer Mikis Theodhorakis, while Néa Dhimokratía moved into unaccustomed opposition. There appeared to be no obstacle to the implementation of a **radical programme**: devolution of power to local authorities, the effective nationalization of heavy industry, improvement of the woefully skeletal social services, a purge of bureaucratic inefficiency and malpractice, the end of bribery and corruption as a way of life, an independent and dignified foreign policy following closure of the US bases and finally withdrawal from NATO and the European Community.

A change of style was promised, too, replacing the country's long traditions of authoritarianism and bureaucracy with openness and dialogue. Even more radically, given that Greek political parties had long been the personal followings of charismatic leaders, PASOK was to be a party of ideology and principle, dependent on no single individual member. Or so, at least, thought some of the youthful PASOK cadres.

The new era started with a bang. ELAS was officially recognized; hitherto they hadn't been allowed to take part in any celebrations, wreath-layings or other ceremonies commemorating the wartime Resistance. Peasant women were granted pensions for the first time – 3000 drachmas a month (about

US$55 in 1982), the same as their outraged husbands – and wages were indexed to the cost of living. In addition, civil marriage was introduced, family law reformed in favour of wives and mothers, and equal rights legislation was put on the statute book.

These quick, low-cost and popular reformist moves seemed to mark a break with the past, and the atmosphere had indeed changed. Greeks no longer lowered their voices to discuss politics in public or wrapped their opposition newspaper in the respectably conservative *Kathimerini*. At first there were real fears that the climate would be too much for the military who would once again intervene to choke a dangerous experiment in democracy, especially when Andreas Papandreou, imitating his father, briefly assumed the defence portfolio himself. But he went out of his way to soothe military susceptibilities, increasing their salaries, buying new weaponry and being fastidious in his attendance at military functions. In reality, the resistance of the Polytechnic students to the 1967–74 junta was mythologized, and PASOK activists could be counted on to form human cordons around party headquarters at the least sign of unrest in the armed forces.

The end of the honeymoon

Papandreou promised a populist bonanza which he must have known, as an academically trained economist, he could not deliver; as a result he pleased nobody. He could not fairly be blamed for the inherited lack of investment, low productivity, deficiency in managerial and labour skills and other chronic problems besetting the Greek economy. However, he certainly aggravated the situation early in his first term by allowing his supporters to indulge in violently anti-capitalist rhetoric and by the prosecution and humiliation of the Tsatsos family, owners of one of Greece's few competitive businesses (Hercules Cement), for the illegal export of capital, something of which every Greek with any savings was guilty. These were cheap victories, not backed by any rational public investment programme, and the only nationalizations were of hopelessly lame-duck companies.

Faced with a sluggish economy and burdened with the additional expense of (marginally) improved social benefits and wage-indexing, Papandreou's government also had to cope with the effects of **world recession**. **Shipping**, the country's main foreign-currency earner, was devastated. Remittances from emigré workers fell off as they became unemployed in their host countries, and tourism diminished under the dual impact of recession and US President Ronald Reagan's warning to Americans to stay away from allegedly terrorist-vulnerable Athens airport.

With huge quantities of imported goods continuing to be sucked into the country in the absence of significant domestic production, the **foreign debt** topped £10 billion in 1986, while inflation remained at 25 percent and the balance of payments deficit approached £1 billion. Greece also began to experience the social strains of unemployment for the first time. Not that it didn't exist before, but it had always been concealed as underemployment because of numerous family-run businesses and the rural/seasonal nature of the economy – as well as by the absence of reliable statistics.

The second term

A modest spending spree, transparently intended to buy votes, continued satisfaction at the discomfiture of the Right, plus the popularity of his Greece-for-the-Greeks foreign policy, gave Papandreou a second term with a **June 1985** electoral victory scarcely less decisive than the first. But his complacent and frankly dishonest slogan was "Vote PASOK for Even Better Days". By October PASOK had imposed a two-year wage freeze and import restrictions, abolished the wage-indexing scheme and devalued the drachma by fifteen percent. Papandreou's fat was pulled out of the fire by none other than his *bête noire*, the European Community, which offered a huge two-part loan on condition that an IMF-style **austerity programme** was maintained.

The political price of such classic monetarist strategies, accompanied by shameless soliciting for foreign investment, was the alienation of the Communists and most of PASOK's own core constituency. Increasingly autocratic (ironic, given his earlier pledges of openness), Papandreou's response to **dissent** was to fire recalcitrant trade union leaders and expel some three hundred members of his own party. Assailed by strikes, the government stumbled badly, losing ample ground in the municipal elections of October 1986 to Néa Dhimokratía, including the mayoralties of the three major cities – Athens, Thessaloníki and Pátra – the first two retained by them ever since. Papandreou assured the nation that he had taken the message to heart, but all that followed were two successive cabinet reshuffles, which saw the departure of most remaining PASOK veterans; the new cabinet was so unsocialist that even the right-wing press called it "centrist".

Similar about-faces took place in foreign policy. The first-term anti-US, anti-NATO and anti-EC rhetoric had been immensely popular, and understandable for a people shamelessly bullied by bigger powers since 1830. There was some high-profile nose-thumbing, like refusing to join EC partners in condemning Jaruzelski's Polish regime or the Soviet downing of a Korean airliner. The "realistic" policies that Papandreou increasingly pursued during his second term were far more conciliatory towards his big Western brothers. Not least was the fact that **US bases** remained in Greece until 1994, largely owing to the fear that snubbing NATO would lead to Greece being exposed to Turkish aggression, still the only issue that unites the main parties to any degree. As for the once-reviled **European Community** (soon to become the European Union), Greece had by now become an established beneficiary, and its leader was hardly about to bite the hand that feeds.

Scandal

Even as late as **mid-1988**, despite the many betrayals and failings of Papandreou, it seemed unlikely that PASOK would be toppled in the following year's elections. This was due mainly to the lack of a credible alternative. Constantine Mitsotakis, a bitter personal enemy of Papandreou's since 1965, when his defection had brought down his father's government and set in motion the events that culminated in the junta, was an unconvincing and unlikeable character at the helm of Néa Dhimokratía. Meanwhile, the liberal centrist parties had disappeared, and the main Communist party, the KKE, seemed trapped in a Stalinist timewarp under the leadership of Harilaos Florakis. Only the **Ellenikí Aristerá (Greek Left)**, the Euro-Communist party spun off from the KKE, seemed to offer any sensible alternative, but they had a precariously small following.

However, a combination of spectacular blunders, plus perhaps a general shift to the Right influenced by the cataclysmic events in Eastern Europe, conspired against PASOK. First came the extraordinary **cavortings of the prime minister** himself. Late in 1988, 70-year-old Papandreou was flown to Britain for open-heart surgery. He took the occasion, with fear of death presumably rocking his judgement, to make public a year-long liaison with a 34-year-old Olympic Airways hostess, **Dimitra "Mimi" Liani**. Widespread media images of an old man shuffling about after a young, large-chested blonde, to the public humiliation of Margaret, his American-born wife, and his family, were not helpful (Papandreou soon divorced Margaret and married Mimi). His integrity was further dented when he missed important public engagements in order to relive his youth in flashy nightspots with Mimi.

The real damage, however, was done by a series of **economic scandals**, ranging from illegal arms deals to fraudulent farm-produce sales by assorted ministers. The most serious of these involved a self-made, Greek-American con-man, **Yiorgos Koskotas**, director of the Bank of Crete, who embezzled £120m (US$190m) of deposits and, worse still, slipped through the authorities' fingers on a private jet back to the US, where he had begun his career as a housepainter. Certain PASOK ministers and even Papandreou himself were implicated in this scandal.

United in disgust at this corruption, the other left-wing parties – KKE and Ellinikí Aristerá – formed a coalition, **Synaspismós**, siphoning off still more support from PASOK.

Three bites at the cherry

In this climate, an inconclusive result to the **June 1989 election** was unsurprising. Less predictable, however, was the formation of a bizarre "**kathársis" (purgative) coalition** of conservatives and Communists, expressly to cleanse PASOK's Augean stables.

Synaspismós would have formed a government with PASOK, but set an imposible condition for doing so – that Papandreou step down as prime minister. In the deal finally cobbled together between the Left and Néa Dhimokratía, Mitsotakis was denied the premiership, too, in favour of **Ioannis Tzanetakis**, a popular former naval officer who had led a mutiny against the junta.

During the three months that the coalition lasted, *kathársis* turned out to be largely a matter of burying the knife as deeply as possible into the ailing body of PASOK. Andreas Papandreou and three other ministers were officially indicted of involvement in the Koskotas affair – though there was no time to try them before the Greek people returned once again to the polls. In any case, the chief witness and protagonist, Koskotas himself, was still imprisoned in America, awaiting extradition proceedings.

Contrary to the Right's hope that publicly accusing Papandreou and his cohorts of criminal behaviour would pave the way for a Néa Dhimokratía victory, PASOK actually recovered slightly in the **November 1989 elections**, though the result was again inconclusive. This time the Left refused to do deals with anyone, resulting in a caretaker government under the neutral aegis of Xenophon Zolotas, reluctantly dragged into the prime minister's office from the rectorship of Athens University. His only mandate was to keep the country on the rails while preparations were made for yet another election.

These took place in **April 1990** with the same party leaders in situ, and with Synaspismós having completed its about-turn to the extent that in the five single-seat constituencies (the other 295 seats are drawn from multiple-seat constituencies in a complex system of reinforced proportional representation), they supported independent candidates jointly with PASOK. Greek Communists are good at about-turns, though; after all, composer Mikis Theodhorakis, musical

Women's right to vote wasn't universally achieved in Greece until 1956 and, until the mid-1970s, adultery was still a punishable offence. The socialist party, PASOK, had a strong theoretical programme for women's rights, and their women's council review committees, set up in the early, heady days, effected a landmark reform with the 1983 Family Law. This prohibited requiring dowry (though custom still demands it) and stipulated equal legal status and shared property rights between husband and wife.

Subsequently however, the PASOK governments did little to follow through on practical issues, like improved childcare, health and family planning. Contraception is not available as part of the skeletal Greek public health service, leaving many women to fall back on abortion as the preferred method of birth control – still running (as for many years past) to an estimated 70,000–80,000 a year.

By far the largest women's rights organization is the Union of Greek Women. Founded in 1976, this espouses an independent feminist line and is responsible for numerous consciousness-raising activities across the country, though it remains too closely linked to PASOK for the comfort of many. Indeed, Margaret Papandreou felt compelled to resign from the Union following her well-publicized divorce from Andreas, leaving it without her effective and vocal leadership. Other, more autonomous groups have been responsible for setting up advice and support networks, highlighting women's issues within trade unions and campaigning for changes in media representation.

None of this is easy in a country as socially variable as Greece. In many rural areas women rely heavily on traditional extended families for security, and are unlikely to be much affected by legislative reforms or city politics. Yet Greek men of all classes and backgrounds are slowly becoming used to the notion of women in positions of power and responsibility and are taking a substantial share in child-rearing – both developments utterly unthinkable two decades ago, and arguably one of the few positive legacies with which PASOK can at least in part be credited.

torch-bearer of the Left during the dark junta years, and formerly a KKE MP, was now standing for Néa Dhimokratía, prior to his resignation from politics altogether.

On the night, Néa Dhimokratía scraped home with a majority of one, later doubled with the defection of a centrist, and Mitsotakis finally realized his long-cherished dream of becoming prime minister. The only other memorable feature of the election was the first parliamentary representation for an independent member of the Turkish minority in Thrace, and for the Greens in Attica – a focus for many disaffected PASOK voters.

A return to the Right: Premier Mitsotakis

On assuming power, Mitsotakis prescribed a course of **austerity measures** to revive the chronically ill economy. Little headway was made, though given the world recession that was hardly surprising. Greek inflation was still approaching twenty percent annually, and at nearly ten percent, unemployment remained chronic. Other measures introduced by Mitsotakis included laws to combat strikes and **terrorism**. The latter had been a perennial source of worry for Greeks since the appearance in 1974 of a group called **Dhekaeftá Novemvríou** ("November 17", the date of the colonels' attack on the Polytechnic in 1973). Since 1974 they (and one or two copycat groups) have killed 24 industrialists, politicians and NATO military personnel and have attacked buildings of foreign corporations in Athens; the lack of any significant arrests to date fuels continued speculation that they were a rogue faction from within PASOK itself. It hardly seemed likely that Mitsotakis's laws, however, were the solution. They stipulated that the typically long-winded, ideologically contorted statements of the group could no longer be published, which led to one or two newspaper editors being jailed for a few days for defiance – much to everyone's embarrassment. The **anti-strike laws** threatened severe penalties but were equally ineffectual, as breakdowns in public transport, electricity and rubbish collection all too frequently illustrated.

As for the Koskotas scandal, the man himself was eventually extradited and gave evidence for the prosecution against Papandreou and various of his ministers. The trial was televised and proved as popular as any soap opera, given its twists of high drama – which included one of the defendants, Agamemnon "Menios" Koutsoyiorgas, dying in court of a heart attack in front of the cameras. The case against Papandreou gradually ran out of steam and he was officially acquitted (by a margin of one vote on the tribunal panel) in early 1992. The two other surviving ex-ministers, Tsovolas and Petsos, were convicted, given jail sentences (bought off with a heavy fine) and barred from public office for a time.

The great showcase trial thus went out with a whimper and did nothing to enhance Mitsotakis's position. If anything, it served to increase sympathy for Papandreou, who was felt to have been unfairly victimized. The indisputable villain of the piece, Koskotas, was eventually convicted of major fraud and is serving a lengthy sentence at the high-security Korýdhallos prison.

The Macedonian question

The last thing the increasingly unpopular Mitsotakis needed was a major foreign policy headache. That is exactly what he got when, in 1991, one of the breakaway republics of the former Yugoslavia named itself **Macedonia**, thereby injuring Greek national pride and sparking off vehement protests at home and abroad. Diplomatically, the Greeks fought tooth and nail against anyone's recognizing the breakaway state, let alone its use of the name "Macedonia", but their position became increasingly isolated, and by 1993 the new country had gained official recognition from both the EU and the UN – albeit under the provisional title of the Former Yugoslav Republic of Macedonia (FYROM).

Salt was rubbed into Greek wounds when the FYROM started using the "Star of Vergina" (and of the ancient Macedonian kings) as a national symbol on their new flag, allegedly printed a banknote portraying the White Tower of Thessaloníki (Solun in Macedonian) and retained passages in its constitution referring to "unredeemed" Aegean territories. Greece still refuses to call its neighbour Macedonia, instead referring to it as Proín Yugoslavikí Dhimokratía Makedhonás, or *Tá Skópia* after its capital; for quite some time you couldn't go anywhere in Greece without coming across officially placed stickers proclaiming that "Macedonia was, is and always will be Greek and only Greek!"

The ongoing argument for legitimacy hinges mostly on whether the ancient Macedonian kings were pure-bred Hellenes (the Greek position), Hellenized barbarians (the neutral conclusion) or proto-Slavs (the Macedonian claim).

The pendulum swings back

The Macedonian problem effectively led to Mitsotakis's **political demise**. Mitsotakis had also been plagued for many months by accusations of phone-tapping and theft of antiquities to stock his large private collection in Crete, plus links with a complicated contracts scandal focused on the national cement company. In the early summer of 1993 his ambitious and disaffected foreign minister, **Andonis Samaras**, jumped on the bandwagon of resurgent Greek nationalism to set up his own party, **Politikí Ánixi (Political Spring)**. His platform, still right-wing, was largely based on action over Macedonia, and during the summer of 1993 more **Néa Dhimokratía** (ND) MPs defected, making Politikí Ánixi a force to be reckoned with. When parliament reconvened in September to approve severe new budget proposals, it became clear that the government lacked sufficient support, and early **elections** were called for **October 1993**.

On October 11, Papandreou romped to election victory; ND lost in 85 percent of the constituencies and the Synaspismós was replaced as the third party in parliament by Samaras's Politikí Ánixi and the unreconstructed Communists, now under Aleka Papariga. The youthful Miltiades Evert, ex-mayor of Athens, replaced Mitsotakis as head of Néa Dhimokratía, so that – along with ex-KKE head Florakis – two of the dinosaurs of post-junta politics had passed from the scene.

The morning after

And so a frail-looking Papandreou, now well into his seventies, became prime minister for the third time. He soon realized that he was not going to have nearly so easy a ride as in the 1980s.

PASOK immediately fulfilled two of its pre-election promises by removing restrictions on the reporting of terrorists' communiques and de-privatizing the Athens city bus company. The new government also set about improving the health system, and began proceedings for Mitsotakis to be tried for his purported misdemeanours, though all charges were mysteriously dropped in January 1995, prompting allegations of an under-the-table deal between Papandreou and his old nemesis.

The root of popular dissatisfaction remained **the economy**, still in dire straits. Nor could PASOK claim to have won any diplomatic battles over Macedonia, despite a lot of tough posturing. The only concrete move was the imposition in October 1993 of a **trade embargo** on the FYROM, which merely landed the Greeks in trouble with the European Court of Justice – and succeeded in virtually shutting down the port of Thessaloníki. By contrast, alone among NATO members, Greece was conspicuous for its open **support of Serbia** in the wars wracking ex-Yugoslavia, ostentatiously breaking that particular embargo with supply trucks to Belgrade via Bulgaria.

In autumn 1994, for the first time ever, in a PASOK-sponsored reform, provincial governors were directly elected in regional elections, rather than appointed from Athens. The following spring, **presidential elections** were held in parliament to designate a successor to the 88-year-old Karamanlis, who enjoyed just three years of well-deserved retirement before his death in spring 1998. The winner, supported by Politikí Ánixi and PASOK, was Kostis Stefanopoulos, ex-head of the dissolved party **DIANA** (Democratic Renewal).

Untainted by scandal, if a bit of a nonentity, he had been nominated by Samaras and accepted by Papandreou in a deal that would allow PASOK to see out its term without ructions.

The prime recurring scandal for 1995 had to do with the high-security **prison of Korýdhallos**, home to Koskotas, the former junta figures – and Colombian-style rackets. Two mass breakout attempts bracketed the discovery of an extensive drug-dealing ring controlled from inside; a call girl was detected in Koskotas's cell, as were large quantities of guns, ammunition and narcotics in the office of the head warden (subsequently arrested).

In November, Greece lifted its embargo on "Macedonia", opening the borders for tourism and trade in return for the FYROM suitably editing its constitution and removing the offending emblem from their flag. Relations, in fact, were instantly almost normalized, with only the name still a moot point; perennial possibilities include "New Macedonia" or "Upper Macedonia", though as of the time of writing the place was still being referred to as the FYROM by most outsiders.

The end of an era

However, the emerging critical issue was the 76-year-old Papandreou's obstinate clinging to power despite obvious signs of dotage. Numerous senior members of PASOK became increasingly bold and vocal in their criticism, no longer fearing expulsion or the sack as in the past.

By late 1995, Papandreou was desperately ill in intensive care at the Onassis hospital, dependent on life-support machinery. As there was no constitutional provision for replacing an infirm (but alive) prime minister, the country was essentially rudderless for two months, until the barely conscious old demagogue finally faced up to his own mortality and signed a letter **resigning** as prime minister (though not as party leader) in January 1996. The "palace clique" of "Mimi" Liani and cohorts was beaten off in the parliamentary replacement vote in favour of the allegedly colourless but widely respected technocrat **Kostas Simitis**, who seemed to be just what the country needed after years of incompetent flamboyance.

Upon assuming office, Simitis indicated that he wouldn't necessarily play to the gallery as Papandreou had with (for a Greek politician) this remarkable statement:

"Greece's intransigent nationalism is an expression of the wretchedness that exists in our society. It is the root cause of the problems we have had with our Balkan neighbours and our difficult relations with Europe."

These beliefs were immediately put to the test by a tense armed stand-off with Turkey over the uninhabited Dodecanese double-islet of **Ímia**, which very nearly degenerated into a shooting war. Simitis eventually bowed to US and UN pressure and ordered a withdrawal of Greek naval forces, conceding "disputed" status to the tiny goat-grazed outcrops – in hindsight a wise decision, but one for which at the time he was roundly criticized in parliament by fire-eating ND MPs and the media.

Andreas finally succumbed to his illness on June 22, 1996, prompting a moving display of national mourning; it was genuinely the end of an era, with only Karamanlis (who died less than two years later) and junta colonel Papadopoulos (who died, still incarcerated, in June 1999) as the last remaining "dinosaurs" of postwar Greek politics. His canonization process proceeds apace already, with a spate of streets renamed to honour him in provincial towns where he was always revered, but the long-term **verdict of history** is likely to be harsher. Papandreou the Younger valued sycophancy over ability, and in his declining years was completely manipulated by the "Palace Clique" around "Mimi" (styled as the Empress Theodora reincarnated by many observers). Alleged Bank of Crete transactions aside, he also enjoyed indubitable success as a "common cheat" (as described by Karamanlis in his tart memoirs), dying with a huge fortune which he could not possibly have amassed on a public servant's salary.

Simitis two, ND nil

Papandreou's demise was promptly followed by PASOK's summer conference, where Simitis ensured his survival as party leader by co-opting his main internal foe, Papandreou's former head of staff, Akis Tsohadzopoulos, with a promise of future high office (minister of defence at the time of writing). Following the summer congress, Simitis cleverly rode the wave of pro-PASOK sympathy caused by Papandreou's death and called **general elections** a year early in **September 1996**.

The **results** were as hoped for: 162 seats for PASOK versus 108 for Néa Dhimokratía despite a margin of only three percentage points, the winner's strength artificially inflated by a convoluted electoral law. Given that the two main parties' agendas were virtually indistinguishable, the core issues boiled down to which was better poised to deliver results – and whether voters would be swayed by ND chief Evert's strident Slav- and Turk-baiting nationalism (they weren't). The biggest surprise was the collapse of Samaras's Politikí Ánixi, which failed to clear the three-percent nationwide hurdle for parliamentary representation, but three leftist splinter parties did well: eleven seats and just over five percent for Papariga's KKE; ten seats (including one Thracian Muslim deputy) with about the same tally for the Synaspismós under new chief Nikos Konstantopoulos; and nine seats at just under five percent for the Democratic Social Movement (DIKKI), founded early in the year by rehabilitated ex-minister Tsovolas to push for 1980s-vintage leftist policies. Evert resigned as ND leader, and was succeeded by Karamanlis's nephew Kostas. Néa Dhimokratía was down but by no means out; in the **June 1999** Euro-elections the party finished first nationwide and sent forty percent of Greece's Euro MPs to Strasbourg.

Simitis's first-term problems arose mainly from the economic squeeze caused by continuing **austerity measures**. In December 1996, protesting farmers closed off the country's main road and rail arteries for several weeks, before dismantling the blockades in time for people to travel for the Christmas holidays. Much of 1997 saw teachers or students (or both) on strike over proposed educational reforms – essentially about imposing some discipline on the notoriously lax school regimens. September 1997 also saw a timely boost to national morale and economic prospects with the awarding of the 2004 **Olympic Games** to Athens. Simitis sensibly warned against people treating it as an excuse merely for unbridled money-making projects, and hopefully more substantial and long-lasting benefits will accrue. The new airport at Spáta and (after a fashion) the Athens metro have been completed, but worryingly, much of the infrastructure for the Games has yet to materialize.

Simitis, by nature far more pro-European than his maverick predecessor, devoted himself to the unenviable task of getting the Greek economy in sufficiently good shape to meet the criteria for **monetary union**. The *Eforía*, or Greek Inland Revenue, has made some highly publicized headway in curbing the largest **black economy** in the EU, by requiring meticulous documentation of transactions and by publicly "outing" the more flagrant tax-dodgers.

After some initial success with his "hard drachma" policy (often propping it up by dumping foreign currency reserves), Simitis was obliged to devalue it upon Greece's **entry to the ERM** in March 1998; however, with other internationally traded currencies badly exposed in the Far East economic crises, the drachma had regained prior levels by October 1998. The fact that inflation stays consistently down in single figures for the first time in decades is testament to Simitis's ability as an accountant; indeed his nickname, amongst both foes and supporters, is *o loyistís*, or "the book-keeper". Simitis has also had the sense to delegate to the capable, and to refrain from meddling, such that his finance minister, Yannos Papantoniou, has had an unprecedented six years in the job.

Increasingly amicable relations with its Balkan neighbours – Greece is the principal foreign investor in Bulgaria and the FYROM, for example – promise to generate jobs and trim unemployment, currently just over nine percent officially (though among recent graduates it is more like twenty percent). But the most dramatic **improvement in international relations** has occurred with old nemesis Turkey, brought about by the severe **earthquake** which struck northern Athens on September 7, 1999, killing scores and rendering almost one hundred thousand homeless (and immobilizing two of the three national mobile phone networks). It came less than a month after the devastating tremor in northwest Turkey, and ironically proved to be the spur for a thaw between the two historic rivals. Greeks donated massive amounts of blood and foodstuffs to the Turkish victims, and were the earliest foreign rescue teams on hand in Turkey; in turn they saw Turkish disaster-relief squads among the first on the scene in Athens. Soon afterwards**, Foreign Minister George (Yeoryios) Papandreou** (son of Andreas) announced that Greece had dropped its long-time opposition to EU financial aid to Turkey in the absence of a solution to the outstanding Cyprus and Aegean disputes, and further indicated that Greece would not at present oppose Turkish candidacy for accession to the EU.

With his handling of the Turkish détente and progress towards EMU the main campaign issues, Simitis called **elections** five months earlier than required, on **April 9, 2000**. In the event, PASOK squeaked into office for an unprecedented third consecutive term by a single percentage point, 43.7 to ND's 42.7, with 158 seats against 125. The crucial factor that swung the cliffhanger – not decided until 1am the day after – was voters' mistrust of Karamanlis the Younger's manifest inexperience. The KKE held steady at just over five percent and eleven seats, but Synaspismós barely cleared the three-percent hurdle for its six seats, while DIKKI didn't.

Simitis capped his narrow victory by announcing Greece's official **entry into the euro currency zone** on June 20, at an EU summit in Portugal. He needed this bit of good news, as the country's international reputation had again taken a battering on June 8, when the terror group November 17 emerged from a couple of years' quiescence by assassinating **Brigadier Stephen Saunders**, the UK military attaché, while his car was stalled in Athens traffic. There were various mutterings abroad (again, especially in the US) that adequate security could not be guaranteed for the forthcoming, Greece-hosted Olympics. In July, the Orthodox Church mounted a last-ditch attack on the

new-style national identity cards, which omitted to state the bearer's religion; government spokesman proclaimed that the old-style cards were illegal under EU regulations, and an ND-sponsored bill to allow for optional citation of religious faith was defeated in parliament.

Tourism, the most important foreign-exchange earner for the country, had had a pretty good year in 1999 (after a rocky spring occasioned by the Kosovo war, roundly condemned by most, traditionally pro-Serbian Greeks), but a well-publicized spate of forest fires during an unusually hot summer, plus the *Express Samina* shipwreck (see box pp.42–3) conspired to make 2000 an *annus horribilis* for tourist arrival numbers. 2001 was another bad season, ending on the double sour notes of the September 11 US terror incidents (which means no significant American arrivals for the foreseeable future) and Virgin Atlantic's announcement that it was abandoning its London–Athens routes as of October 28.

In the run-up to the Olympics, Greece has mounted a renewed public relations campaign for the return of the **Elgin marbles** from the British Museum. A new museum for the Parthenon relics is finally being built south of the Acropolis, with a large wing pointedly reserved for the eventual return of the marbles, which, as Greece broadly hints, it would be a nice gesture to have back in time for the Games. The long-standing British argument that the Greeks were incompetent barbarians not fit to curate the precious friezes was rather undercut by the 1999 revelation that heavy-handed "cleaning" in 1937–38, with wire brushes and harsh solvents, had damaged the sculptures irreparably. Foreign Minister Papandreou travelled to London in June 2000 to state the Greek case and was heard sympathetically by Labour and Lib-Dem MPs (the Tories walked out), but was ultimately rebuffed by Tony Blair's announcement that the UK had no intention of budging on the issue.

Greek society today

The following account concentrates on recent, salient events and can only give a flavour of the massive, ground-level changes which have occurred in Greece since the late 1980s. First and foremost, it's a conspicuously wealthier, more **consumerist society** than before, with vast disparities in income, imbued with rampant Thatcherism (in particular a mania for privatizing) long after that ideology has largely subsided in its homeland. Athens, Thessaloníki and most large towns have their legions of **yuppies**, addicted to gourmet wines, properly made cappuccinos, designer accessories, fast cars and **travel**; even small-town agencies promote junkets to Thailand and Cuba (the current trendy favourites). Greek domestic tourism is also heavily marketed, in particular weekend breaks to "name" islands like Corfu, Santoríni, and Rhodes, or outdoor expeditions to the mountains; there are numerous Greek-language travel magazines, Sunday supplements and bound guides, advising the yuppies where to spend their cash.

Mobile phones are ubiquitous – along with Italy and Cyprus, Greece has the highest per-capita use in Europe – and the success of the two private networks has forced partly privatized OTE to offer its own mobile network at reasonable prices, and in general sharpen up. You can walk into an OTE phone shop and get any high-tech device or network service more or less instantly, unlike the bad old days – as recently as 1994 – when OTE was a national disgrace and provision of a simple analogue line could take years.

In tandem with this increased materialism, the **Orthodox Church** has declined from "guardian of the nation" to something of a **national embarrassment**. Rather than address the pressing social problems and hidden poverty occasioned by Greece's immigrant crisis (see below), its version of moral leadership has been to organize demos against the new secularized ID cards (as above), and (more understandably) to extract from Pope John Paul II during his May 2001 visit an apology for the 1204 sacking of Constantinople. But the Church's medieval mindset has really come to the fore in its continuing ban on cremation, and near-hysteria on the subject of bar codes. Greece is the only EU country where cremation is forbidden; every summer there's a malodorous backlog of corpses to be interred at the overcrowded cemeteries, whilst some people relatively surreptitiously cart their relatives' remains to be burnt in more accommodating Bulgaria or Romania, under threat of excommunication – Orthodox doctrine is adamant that immolation would compromise the Resurrection, and that the bones of a saint (still revered as relics) might inadvertently be destroyed. But it's bar codes on ID cards and hand- or forehead-stamping for casino patrons and bank employees that have really exercised the Athonite monks in particular (and made them something of a laughing-stock). They (and a considerably number of the lay faithful) see this as a Jewish–Masonic conspiracy in fulfilment of Revelation 13:16–17 and 14:9, which relates to the Mark of the Beast; vast stacks of printed leaflets are distributed on the subject.

The clergy's rantings notwithstanding, bar-coded Greece is now firmly locked into the **global economy**, and not just in the matter of cross-border shipment of the dead. International franchises such as McDonalds, Next, Haagen Däzs and The Body Shop proliferate in most larger towns; consumer interest rates have plunged, the Athens stock exchange burgeoned (before crashing spectacularly, prompting a wave of suicides by those who lost their savings), and foreign or multinational companies have flocked to invest. It is they who are funding and carrying out massive infrastructure improvements designed to long outlast the 2004 Olympics: the airport at Spáta, metros in Athens and Thessaloníki, the Río-Andírrio bridge over the Gulf of Corinth, and the Via Egnatia expressway across Epirus, Macedonia and Thrace. **Overseas companies** are also quietly **acquiring** more (or less) productive elements of the Greek economy; Britain's Blue Circle, for example, in 1998 purchased Hercules Cement from Italian interests, while Cyprus Airways and an Australian holding group were among contenders to buy out troubled flag-carrier Olympic Airways (at time of writing it seems that Axon Airlines, one of several private airlines to emerge since air travel was deregulated in 1994, will get the nod). The 2003 end of cabotage – whereby only Greek companies have been allowed to provide ferry services within Greece – should weed out the flakier shipping companies and have the others pulling their socks up, under threat of possibly being challenged by the likes of P&O or Fred Olsen. Matters can only get better since the *Express Samina* sinking, which fully exposed the weaknesses in safety, pricing and personnel training of Greek Aegean transport – and most of all the oligopolies which have resulted from domestic companies following overseas examples and engaging in extensive **corporate takeovers**. Minoan (now Hellas) Flying Dolphins, the responsible party in the shipwreck, had acquired Ceres Hydrofoils, several smaller steamship outfits and a majority interest in an airline, to become the largest domestic transport company; Alpha Bank absorbed the troubled Ionian/Ioniki Bank in early 1999 and instantly became the second largest banking/insurance group in the country.

It used to be that a lifetime sinecure with the civil service was the goal for most graduates, but no longer – now young people crave a **career** in the private sector, with unlimited salary prospects, and will initially work for low pay which older, less qualified professionals with families – who often must cobble together part-time jobs – simply can't live on. Yet most Greeks have now become too grand for menial jobs; the late Andreas once grumbled that Greece shouldn't remain "a nation of waiters", though it seems he needn't have worried.

Greece may continue to occupy the EU's economic cellar with Portugal, but it's still infinitely wealthier (and more stable) than any of its neighbours, and this has acted as a magnet for **a permanent underclass of immigrants**. Since 1990 they have arrived in numbers estimated variously at 800,000 to over a million, a huge burden for a not especially rich country of just over ten million (it would be the equivalent of Britain having six million refugees rather than a few hundred thousand). These days your waiter, hotel desk clerk or cleaning lady is most likely to be Albanian, Ukrainian or Bulgarian, to cite the three largest groups of arrivals. There are also significant communities of Russians, Poles, Filipinos, Romanians, Sudanis, Kurds, equatorial Africans and Georgians (not to mention ethnic Greeks from the Caucasus) – a striking change in what had hitherto been a homogeneous, parochial culture.

The **Greek response** to this has been decidedly mixed; the Albanians, making up roughly half the influx, are almost universally detested (except for the ethnic-Greek northern Epirots), and blamed for all manner of social ills. They have also prompted the first anti-immigration measures with teeth in a country whose population is more used to being on the other side of such laws; Greece is a member of the Schengen visa scheme and sees itself, as in past ages, as the first line of defence against the barbarian hordes from the Orient. All of the east Aegean islands regularly receive boatloads of people fleeing from every country in Asia, and the country's few refugee camps (near Athens) are grossly inadequate. In June 2001, as an attempt to cope, legal residence was offered to illegals who could demonstrate two years' presence in Greece and pay a hefty amount for retroactive social security contributions; yet when this **amnesty period** ended in early September, only about 350,000 individuals had applied to be "regularized", leaving the remainder still subject to arrest and deportation.

On a positive note, these diverse groups, increased travel abroad by the Greeks themselves, touring bands or dance companies and programmes on the private television channels have created a taste for **exotic music and foods**. One doesn't always have to wait for the summer festivals to see name jazz, blues or soul acts in Thessaloníki or Athens, and there are now decent foreign-cuisine restaurants there as well as in many of the major resorts. All of these factors, however, have had the effect of making Greece less identifiably Greek and, it must be said, of making the native Greeks themselves rather less welcoming and more self-absorbed than formerly.

Mythology, an A to Z

While all ancient cultures had their **myths**, those of ancient Greece have had the greatest influence on Western civilization. The Trojan War, the wanderings of Odysseus, the adventures of Herakles – these and many other stories have inspired some of the finest literature, music and art.

Homer and his followers were the first bards to codify some of the stories in around 800 BC, but they had existed in the oral tradition for many years, and it was another few centuries before Homeric epics were actually written down and other legends set forth in **Hesiod's** *Theogeny*. With the ritual enactment of the myths in their religious festivals and ceremonies, along with their representation in designs on their pots and the performances of the stories at theatre and drama competitions, Greek myth and culture became inextricably blended.

Many versions of the myths exist, some of which are contradictory and confusing. Below is a summary of the principal **gods** and **heroes**. For further reading Pierre Grimal's *Dictionary of Classical Mythology* is a good reference, but perhaps the best starting point and a way into feeling how the myths might have been told is to read Homer's epics *The Iliad* and *The Odyssey*.

Agamemnon, see Atreus, House of; Trojan War.

Aphrodite When Kronos castrated Ouranos and threw his testicles into the sea off Cyprus, the water spumed and produced Aphrodite, which means "born from sea foam". Her most famous shrines were at Paphos on Cyprus, Knidos on the Anatolian coast and on Lésvos. Aphrodite's magic girdle made people fall in love with the wearer, but her famed adultery with Ares ended badly when she became ensnared in the nets that Hephaistos, her husband, had made to expose her infidelity. She restored her virginity, but later had an affair with Hermes which produced a double-sexed offspring – Hermaphroditos. She particularly favoured the mortal Paris, instigator of the Trojan War.

Apollo, the illegitimate son of Zeus and the nymph Leto, was god of the sun, of plagues and, conversely, of healing. He killed the Python snake that terrorized the land around Delphi, a location with which he subsequently had great associations (his other two main precincts were on the islet of Delos, his purported birthplace, and at Letoön in Asia Minor). His shrine at Delphi was, with Olympia, considered one of the centres of the Hellenic world, and through the priestess of the oracle here, the god gave prophecies to pilgrims. Outstandingly beautiful, Apollo represented music and poetry, and was usually depicted with either a bow and arrow or a lyre, which was a gift to him from Hermes. He was not generally unlucky in love, but was famously spurned by Daphne.

Ares, the god of war and the only legitimate son of Zeus and Hera, had few associations with myths or temples – not surprisingly, given Zeus's famous utterance that Ares was the most hateful of all his offspring. Usually attended by his demon henchmen Deimos (Terror) and Phobos (Fear), Ares was not, however, uniformly victorious – in *The Iliad* he was more than once outwitted by Athena.

Argonauts, see Jason and the Argonauts.

Ariadne, see Theseus, Ariadne and the Minotaur.

Artemis, Apollo's twin sister, was the goddess of hunting, the moon, unmarried maidens and indeed all of nature beyond the city. Her epithet was "Mistress of the Animals" and she was typically attended by trains of nymphs and lions. Artemis was always described as a virgin endowed with perpetual youth; she also had a dark aspect that involved human sacrifice at some of her rites. Furthermore, she killed the huntsman Orion, who had tried to rape her, and instigated the death of Actaeon, who had seen her bathe naked, by changing him into a stag and setting his own hounds upon him. Her most important shrines were at Brauron in Attica, at Sparta and at Ephesos in Asia Minor.

Athena did not have a conventional birth – she sprang fully formed out of the head of Zeus, ready for battle with armour, helmet and spear. Hephaistos had split Zeus's forehead for the "birth" to occur, and then attempted to ravish her; she remained a virgin, but some of his semen which he flicked off her thigh fell to earth, where it grew up as her son Ericthonius/Erechtheus, legendary first king of Athens. She was accordingly the protectress and namesake of that city and by extension all others, and was regarded as the goddess of both war and certain more peaceable crafts and trades vital to civilized life: olive culture, wool-gathering, spinning, ship-building, chariots and horse tackle. Her many temples are typically on city acropoles or centres; she was ever ready to intervene on behalf of favourite mortals, particularly Odysseus and Herakles.

Atlas, see Herakles.

Atreus, House of A dynasty haunted by revenge, murder, incest and tragedy. Atreus hated his younger brother Thyestes, and when their separate claims for the kingship of Mycenae were voiced, the gods promoted Atreus. Atreus banished Thyestes, but learning that his wife had had an affair with him, Atreus feigned forgiveness and recalled him from exile. He then had Thyestes' sons murdered, cut up, cooked and fed to Thyestes. When Thyestes had finished eating, Atreus showed him the heads of his children, clarifying the true nature of the meal. He again banished Thyestes, who took refuge at Sikyon and, sanctioned by the gods, fathered Aegisthus by his daughter, Pelopia. Pelopia then married Atreus, her uncle, and Aegisthus (who did not know who his real father was) was brought up and cared for by Atreus. When Aegisthus came of age, Atreus instructed him to kill Thyestes, but Aegisthus found out the truth, returned to Mycenae and killed Atreus. Atreus's two sons were Agamemnon and Menelaos. Agamemnon paid for his father's crimes by dying at the hands of his wife Clytemnestra (who had committed adultery with Aegisthus while Agamemnon was fighting at Troy). She ensnared him in a net while he took a bath and stabbed him to death. She in turn was killed by her son Orestes, who was pursued by the Furies before being absolved of matricide by Athena.

Bacchus, see Dionysos.

Centaurs and Lapiths The centaurs were monstrous beings with the heads and torsos of men and the lower bodies of horses. They lived a debauched life, feeding on raw flesh and enjoying the pleasures of wine, but were also considered particularly skilled in sorcery and herbal healing. There are tales of centaurs battling with Herakles on his quest to complete the Twelve Labours, but the most famous story is of the fight that broke out between them and the Lapiths, a race of heroes and warriors who were the descendants of the river god Pineos (the Piniós still flows near Mount Olympus). Pirithous, a Lapith of partial centaurean descent, invited them all to his wedding. At the feast the centaurs tried to abduct all the women, including the bride. A bloody brawl followed, of which the Lapiths were the victors; it is depicted on the pediment reliefs at Olympia, as a metaphor for the triumph of reason over barbarism.

Daphne The nymph Daphne was one of the daughters of the river god Pineos. Apollo took a fancy to her and chased her through the woods, but just as he caught up with her, she prayed to her father to save her. He took pity and turned her into a laurel tree, and she became rooted to the spot. Apollo loved her even as a tree and made the laurel sacred, dedicating wreaths of its leaves as a sign of honour. Her name, to this day, is the Greek word for the laurel tree.

Demeter was the goddess of agriculture, in particular corn, grain and pigs, as well as of death and regeneration. Both her origins and rites were shadowy, though we do know that women were her particular devotees. She exercised her power by making the whole Earth sterile after her daughter Persephone's abduction by Hades. The mother-and-daughter duo were usually revered together, particularly at their major sanctuary at Eleusis.

Dionysos, also known as Bacchus, was the god of wine and mystic ecstasy. He was the son of Zeus by Semele, who during conception was consumed by the god in the form of a lightning-bolt; Zeus rescued the unborn child and sewed him up in his thigh for the full gestation period. On birth, he was conveyed by Hermes to a far-off realm to be reared by the nymphs, and as a small boy he was disguised as a girl to hide him from Hera. As a youth, he was abducted by pirates; Dionysos caused the ship to be overgrown with ivy and vines (henceforth his symbols) and in panic the pirates dived overboard to become the first dolphins. Thus at his festivals a commemorative miniature ship was carried or propelled on wheels, suitably decorated. In art he is often shown riding in a chariot drawn by panthers, and followed by a coterie of satyrs, sileni and mortal followers brandishing *thyrsoi* (wands topped with pine cones). Dionysos' semi-mythical women followers, the maenads, roamed the countryside at certain seasons in a state of madness; more usually, he was revered in the form of a bearded mask on a column, the antecedent of the comic and tragic masks of theatre. He rescued Ariadne from Náxos following her abandonment there by Theseus.

Eurydice, see Orpheus and Eurydice.

Golden Fleece, see Jason and the Argonauts.

Hades was the brother of Zeus and Poseidon, and when the cosmos was divided between them he was allotted the underworld. His name means "the invisible", because in the battle with Kronos and the Titans he concealed himself by wearing a magic helmet given to him by the Cyclops. To refer to him as Hades was thought to bring about his awesome anger, so the Greeks called him by his surname Pluto, which means "the rich" and alludes to the wealth that lies hidden underground. His wife was Persephone, daughter of Demeter (see above). Rather than temples, he had suitably mysterious oracles, most notably at Ephyra in Epirus and that of Trophonios at Levadia.

Helen was the daughter of Zeus, who appeared in the form of a swan to her mother Leda. She was believed to be the most beautiful woman in the world. Her husband Menelaos, king of Sparta, entertained the Trojans Paris and Aeneas and was foolish enough to leave them alone with her; Paris abducted her. Some sources say she went willingly, impressed by his beauty and wealth; others say she was raped. In either event her departure from Sparta was the cause of the Trojan War.

Hephaistos was the god of fire and a master craftsman. In his workshop on volcanic Límnos, where he was especially revered, he fashioned everything from jewellery to armour. Elsewhere his cult was less elaborated, except at Athens, where he had a sumptuous temple in honour of his role in siring Erechtheus (see Athena). He was made lame, and there are two conflicting versions of how he sustained his injuries: either they were inflicted when Zeus threw him from Olympus because he had defended Hera in a quarrel, or alternatively when Hera, who bore him, tossed him down to Límnos in disappointment at his ugliness. Clever as well as unprepossessing, he was married to Aphrodite, the most beautiful of the goddesses.

Hera was Zeus's sister, wife and the most powerful of the goddesses – she wreaked her vengeance and jealousy on anyone whom Zeus seduced and the offspring of most of his encounters (see Io, opposite). Zeus punished her heavily for her anger against Herakles by suspending her from her wrists from Mount Olympus, weighing her ankles down with anvils and whipping her. Despite her vindictive and irascible Homeric portrayal, she was the protecting deity of wives and marriage. Her totems and sacrificial animals were the cow, cuckoo and peacock; her four principal temples were on Sámos, near Argos, at modern Perahóra on the Gulf of Corinth and at Olympia.

Herakles (Hercules) was the superhero of the ancient world. A mighty hunter and sacrificer, Herakles appealed to young men in particular. His mother was the mortal Alcmene, and his father Zeus. Jealous Hera sent two snakes to kill Herakles while he was still in his cradle, which he duly strangled, all good preparation for his Twelve Labours.

These were commanded by King Eurystheus of the Argolid, who was under the thrall of Hera. These tasks took him to the fringes of the known world, even involving his supporting it on his shoulders while Atlas took a break to lend him a hand in his final task. The Labours were: to kill the Nemean lion; to slay the many-headed Hydra monster at Lerna; to bring back the wild boar of Erymanthus alive; to hunt the Keryneian hind that was sacred to Artemis; to kill the man-eating birds at the lake of Stymphaleia; to clean the stables of King Augeas; to bring back the untameable Cretan bull alive; to capture the flesh-eating horses of Diomedes; to fetch the girdle of the Amazon warrior queen; to fetch the herds of Geryon from beyond the edge of the ocean; to capture Cerberus the guard dog of the underworld gates; and finally to fetch the golden apples from the garden of the Hesperides.

Curiously for such a macho figure, Herakles spent a certain amount of time as a slave, or in drag, or both. During a fit of madness sent by Hera, he slew his wife and children at Thebes; in atonement he passed some years dressed as a woman in the court of Queen Omphale of Lydia.

His death was as dramatic as his life. Deianeira, his second wife, gave him a garment that she thought had magic powers and would prevent him from being unfaithful to her. When he put it on, it burned into his flesh; the cloak had, it seemed, been steeped in the blood of the centaur Nessos, who had been slain by Herakles in the act of attempting to rape Deianeira. (With his dying breath, Nessos ensured posthumous revenge by telling Deianeira that his blood was a love-philtre rather than poisonous.) Unable to bear the pain, Herakles built a funeral pyre and immolated himself. He was fully deified by Zeus – the only mortal or demigod to be so honoured.

Hermes was the son of Zeus and Maia, the daughter of Atlas. He was born in the Kyllene mountains of Arcadia, where his only major temple existed at Pheneos. A trickster figure, Hermes showed his mettle by inventing the lyre on the day of his birth, then stealing Apollo's sacred cattle, denying the deed to his brother. Zeus effected a reconciliation, and Hermes gave Apollo the lyre in exchange for the cattle and a golden staff. Hermes was the god of commerce, thievery, herdsmen, travel and boundaries; rather than shrines he had herms, stone cairns or boundary markers. In his role as Conductor of Souls, Hermes regularly crossed between the living and underworld. He was often depicted wearing winged shoes, a wide-brimmed hat and carrying the herald's staff which showed his position as the messenger of the gods.

Hippolytos and Phaedra Hippolytos, son of the hero Theseus and the Amazon Hippolyta, was an accomplished hunter who revered Artemis and scorned Aphrodite. Aphrodite sought to teach him a lesson and conspired for Phaedra, the new wife of Theseus, to fall in love with the young man. When she was spurned by Hippolytos she feared he might reveal her advances and so accused him of rape. When Theseus heard this, he called upon Poseidon to kill his son; Hippolytos was then flung from his chariot and torn apart by his horses. Phaedra in shame and remorse hanged herself.

Io, a priestess of Hera at Argos, was only one of the many mortals who caught Zeus's eye, but before he could get to know her better, Hera got wind of his interest and Zeus hastily transformed Io into a cow. Hera demanded her as a present, and placed her under the guard of the hundred-eyed monster Argos. But Hermes, presumably at the behest of Zeus, killed Argos, enabling Io to escape. Unfazed by this setback, Hera then proceeded to torment poor Io in her cow shape by sending a stinging gadfly to goad her on her travels. She made first for the Ionian Sea, which was named after her, and then crossed the straits into Asia at the Bosporus (literally, the "Cow Ford"). Before settling in Egypt, she wandered all over Asia, even visiting Prometheus, while he was chained to the Caucasus mountain range.

Jason and the Argonauts Jason, a Greek hero from Iolkos (present-day Vólos), was the legitimate heir to the Thessalian throne, which had been usurped by his uncle Pelias. The latter received a prophecy that he would die at the hands of a one-sandalled man. When Jason appeared in his court, shod accordingly, the frightened Pelias attempted to get rid of him by sending him on what he hoped would be a fatal quest to the remote Black Sea kingdom of Colchis for the Golden Fleece. Jason assembled his crew, assorted heroes of the ancient Greek world, and commissioned a ship, called the *Argo* after its maker Argos and built with the help of Athena and Hera – its prow had the remarkable gift of speech and prophecy. A long, incident-filled journey followed, including landfall at Límnos where the crew repopulated the island, the local women having previously murdered their menfolk. Some of the crew didn't complete the voyage, among them Herakles who missed the boat because he was searching for his favourite, Hylas, a beautiful boy who had been abducted by the nymphs. Hera instructed the sea-nymphs (nereids) to carry the *Argo* past the dangerous Wandering Rocks, which would otherwise have smashed the ship. When Jason and his crew finally arrived in Colchis, King Aeëtes would not hand over the Golden Fleece unless Jason completed various labours. The king's daughter, the sorceress Medea (see below), fell in love with Jason and undertook to help him; they stole the fleece and fled, pursued by Aeëtes. Medea slowed down their pursuers by tearing up her brother Apsyrtus and casting his body parts into the sea, obliging Aeëtes to collect the pieces. Zeus was greatly angered by this heinous crime and the *Argo* spoke to the crew, telling them that they would have to purify themselves at Circe's island. After more wanderings through treacherous seas, the crew arrived at Iolkos, where Medea fulfilled the prophecy by doing away with Pelias, and then proceeded to Corinth where Jason dedicated the Golden Fleece to Poseidon.

Judgement of Paris The goddess Eris (Strife) began a quarrel between Athena, Hera and Aphrodite by throwing a golden apple between them and saying that it belonged to whichever goddess was the most beautiful. All the gods were too frightened to judge the contest, so Hermes took the goddesses to the top of Mount Ida for Paris, the son of King Priam of Troy, to decide. Each used bribery to win his favour: Athena offered him wisdom and victory in combat, Hera the kingdom of Asia, but Aphrodite, the winner of the contest, offered him the love of Helen of Sparta.

Kronos The Titan Kronos was the youngest son of the pre-Olympian deities Gaia and Ouranos, who seized power in the heavens by castrating his father. Once on the throne, Kronos lived in perpetual fear of the prediction that one of his offspring would one day overthrow him, and so he swallowed all of his children except Zeus, Zeus's mother Rhea having substituted a stone for the bundle that Kronos thought was his baby. Kronos and his Titan brothers were defeated in a cosmic battle by Zeus and his Olympian supporters.

Lapiths, see Centaurs and Lapiths.

Maenads The maenads were the possessed or intoxicated female followers of Dionysos. They wore scanty clothes, had wreaths of ivy around their heads and played upon tambourines or flutes in their processions. They had power over wild animals, and in their frenzy they believed they drank milk or honey from freshwater springs. In their orgiastic ecstasies they tore limb from limb those who offended them, did not believe or who spied upon their rites – including Orpheus (see opposite).

Medea exacted gruesome revenge on any who stood against her. She persuaded the daughters of Pelias (see Jason and the Argonauts) to cut their father up and put him in a boiling cauldron, having convinced them that if they did so she could rejuvenate him. To their extreme disappointment, his body parts did not come back together. Akastos, Pelias's son, banished her and Jason as a punishment; they went together to Corinth, where Jason abandoned her to marry Kreusa the daughter of the local king, Kreon. In revenge, Medea orchestrated a gruesome death for Kreusa by sending her a tunic which burst into flames when it was put on, and then murdered her own two young sons by Jason.

Minotaur, see Theseus, Ariadne and the Minotaur.

Muses The Muses were the result of nine nights of lovemaking between Mnemosyne (Memory) and Zeus. They were primarily singers and the inspiration for music (to which they gave their name), but also had power over thought in all its forms: persuasion, eloquence, knowledge, history, mathematics and astronomy. Apollo conducted their singing around the Hippocrene fountain on Mount Helikon or on Mount Olympus itself.

Nymphs There were various subspecies of nymph: meliads were the nymphs of the ash trees; naïads lived in the springs and streams; nereids in the ocean; dryads were individual tree nymphs; oreads were the mountain nymphs; and the alseids lived in the groves. They were thought to be the daughters of Zeus and attended certain deities, particularly Artemis and Poseidon.

Odysseus Our word "odyssey" derives from Odysseus's ten-year journey home, which was no less fraught with danger, adventure and grief than the ten-year war against the Trojans which preceded it. Shipwrecked, tormented by the gods, held against his will by bewitching women, almost lured to his death by the hypnotic Sirens, witnessing his comrades devoured by the giant one-eyed Cyclops Polyphemos and all the time missing and desiring his faithful wife Penelope, Odysseus proved himself to be a great and scheming hero. At the end of his arduous journey he arrived in disguise at his palace on Ithaca to find suitors pestering his wife. He contrived a cunning trap and killed them all with a bow which only he could flex.

Oedipus was a man profoundly cursed. The Delphic Oracle said that Laius, King of Thebes, should not father any children, for if he did one would kill him. When Oedipus was born Laius abandoned the baby, piercing his ankles with a nail and tying them together: hence the name, which means "swollen foot". But the baby was discovered and brought up at the court of the neighbouring king, Polybos, at Corinth. The same oracle revealed to the adult Oedipus that he would kill his father and marry his mother. When he heard this news he resolved not to return home to Corinth, but east of Delphi he met with Laius, who was heading west to consult the oracle as to how to rid Thebes of the Sphinx. Because the road was narrow, Laius ordered Oedipus to get out of the way, and when one of the guards pushed him, Oedipus drew his sword in anger and, not knowing that Laius was his father, killed him and most of his entourage. He then made his way to Thebes, where Laius had been king, and solved the riddle of the Sphinx. As a reward and in thanks, he was crowned king and offered Laius's widow Iocaste (his mother) in marriage. Plague then fell upon Thebes, because of the crimes of patricide and incest at the heart of the city. The Delphic Oracle instructed Oedipus to expel the murderer of Laius, and in his ignorance he ordered the guilty party cursed and banished. The seer and prophet Teiresias then revealed the full nature of the crime to Iocaste and Oedipus; she hanged herself and he put out his own eyes. He left the city as a vagabond accompanied by his daughter Antigone, and only at his death was granted peace. Attica, the country that received his dead body, became blessed.

Olympus, **Mount**, see Zeus.

Orpheus and Eurydice Orpheus was a great musician who received his lyre from Apollo himself. He played and sang so beautifully that wild beasts were charmed, trees would uproot themselves to come closer, and even the very rocks were moved. He enlisted in the crew of Argonauts and sang for them to row their oars in time. On his return from the *Argo's* voyage he married the nymph Eurydice. She was bitten by a snake on the banks of the river Pineos (Piniós) and died, and Orpheus was so distraught that he went to the underworld to bring her back to life. His wish was granted by Hades on condition that during the return journey he did not look back at her. As the couple approached daylight, however, his mind became consumed with doubt and, turning around to see if she was behind him, he lost her forever. He preached that Apollo was the greatest god, much to the anger of Dionysos, who set the maenads on him. They tore him apart and cast his head, still singing, into the Thracian river Hebrus; it was finally washed up on the shores of the island of Lésvos, supposedly conferring great musical gifts on the local population.

Ouranos was the personification of the sky and by his union with Gaia (Earth) fathered many children, including Kronos and the Titans. Gaia became so exhausted by her husband's continual advances that she sought protection from her sons. Kronos was the only one to assist; he cut off Ouranos' testicles with a sickle and threw them into the sea, giving rise to Aphrodite.

Pan The patron of shepherds and flocks, Pan was the son of Hermes and a nymph and, with his beard, horns, hairy body and cloven hooves, was said to be so ugly that his own mother ran from him in fear. He had an insatiable libido, energetically pursuing both sexes. Apollo learned the art of prophecy from Pan, and hunters looked to him for guidance. He enjoyed the cool woodland shade and streams of Arcadia and relished his afternoon naps so much that he wreaked havoc if he was disturbed.

Pandora, see Prometheus.

Pegasus, see Poseidon.

Penelope, see Odysseus.

Persephone, also known as Kore (the Maiden), was out picking flowers one day when the Earth opened up and swallowed her; she had been abducted by Hades riding his chariot. Her mother Demeter was distraught and when she found out the truth, she left Olympus in protest and made the Earth sterile so that it produced no crops. Zeus ordered Hades to return Persephone, but because she had eaten pomegranate seeds in the underworld she was bound to him. As a compromise, she would be allowed to return to Earth for two thirds of the year and had to reside with Hades for the remaining third. Thus Demeter divided the year into seasons, so that while Persephone was with Hades the Earth would be wintry and sterile, and while she was on Earth the ground would be fertile for spring, summer and autumn.

Perseus A son of Zeus, and believed to be a direct ancestor of Herakles, Perseus was cast out to sea in a trunk with his mother Danae, because his grandfather feared a prophecy that Perseus would one day kill him. Danae and Perseus were washed up on Sérifos island, where they were discovered by a fisherman who looked after them. When Perseus came of age, the king of Sérifos demanded that he bring back the head of Medusa the gorgon, whose gaze could turn people to stone. Perseus acquired some special aids from Hermes and Athena to perform the task, including a helmet which made him invisible and winged sandals to fly through the air. He cut off Medusa's head while looking at her reflection in Athena's polished shield. On his return flight he saw and fell in love with Andromeda, who was being offered as a sacrifice to a sea-monster. He rescued her and returned home to find his mother had been raped by the king. He held up the gorgon's head, turned the king to stone and then presented the head as a gift to Athena, who placed it in the middle of her shield. Perseus went on to participate in the king of Lárissa's celebratory games; he competed in the discus-throwing competition, but his throw went off course and killed his grandfather, who was a spectator, thus fulfilling the prophecy.

Phaedra, see Hippolytos and Phaedra.

Poseidon was the god of the sea, earthquakes and storms, and patron of fishermen. In the battle with Kronos and the Titans, Poseidon, the brother of Zeus, wielded the trident which he later used to shake both sea and land. After the victory he was awarded, by lot, the realm of the ocean, where he dwelt in the depths. He produced some strange offspring, including the Cyclops Polyphemos who had it in for Odysseus, and mated with the gorgon Medusa – which resulted in the winged horse Pegasus. He quarrelled frequently with the other gods, competing with them for power over some of the major cities including Athens, Corinth and Argos. Although he helped destroy Troy, as recounted in *The Iliad*, he also persecuted Odysseus mercilessly on his return home. Among his numerous temples, the most important were those at Isthmía, Soúnio and Póros near Athens; Mykale in Asia Minor; and an oracle at Cape Ténaro.

Prometheus For someone whose name means "forethought", Prometheus showed a distinct lack of it. In his desire to help mankind, he stole fire from the heavens and was immediately punished by Zeus, who bound him in chains, tied him to the Caucasus mountains and then sent an eagle to peck perpetually at his liver. Zeus then dealt with mankind by sending Pandora to Prometheus' brother Epimetheus, whose name means "afterthought". Her curiosity about the contents of his box got the better of her and, peeping inside, she unleashed all the evils and one good (hope) on the world. Prometheus gave some useful advice to Herakles when he passed by on one of his labours and Herakles rewarded him by setting him free.

Theseus, Ariadne and the Minotaur Theseus' father, Aegeus of Athens, sent him as a child away from Athens for his own safety. At sixteen the hero returned, in full strength and with the weapons that his father had set aside for him. Theseus was destined for a life of action, and his greatest adventure was to kill the Minotaur on Crete. As tribute from Athens, King Minos demanded six men and six women every nine years for sacrifice to the Minotaur – a gruesome beast, half-man half-bull, born from the bestial copulation of the queen Pasiphae with the huge bull sent by Poseidon. The Minotaur was kept in the labyrinth at Crete. Ariadne, Minos's daughter, had fallen in love with Theseus and contrived to help him kill the Minotaur. She gave him a ball of thread so that he would not lose his way in the labyrinth and then accompanied him in his flight from the island, only to be abandoned later on the island of Náxos. Dionysos saw her disconsolate on the shore, took pity on her and married her.

Theseus, meanwhile, on his return to Athens forgot to change the black sails to white as a signal to his father that he was alive, and Aegeus – thinking that his son had been killed by the Minotaur – threw himself into the sea which took his name: the Aegean.

Titans The Titans were the six male children of Ouranos and Gaia. Their six sisters, who helped them father numerous gods, were called the Titanides. Kronos was the youngest Titan, and after he had overthrown his father he helped his brothers to power. The Titans lost their grip when they were toppled by the upstart Olympians, led by Zeus, in the cataclysmic battle called the Titanomachia.

Trojan War When Menelaos of Sparta realized that the Trojan Paris had made off with his wife Helen, he called on his brother Agamemnon of Mycenae. Together they roused the might of Greece to get her back. With just about every hero (Ajax, Achilles, Troilus, Hector, Paris, Odysseus, Priam, Diomedes, Aeneas) making an appearance in this epic, the story of the Trojan War is arguably the greatest tale from the ancient world. Homer's *Iliad* dealt with only one aspect of it, the wrath of Achilles. The ten-year war, fought over a woman and which sent many heroes' souls down to Hades, was finally won by the trickery of the Greeks, who used a huge wooden horse, left ostensibly as a gift to the Trojans, to smuggle an armed platoon inside the city walls. The cunning plan was thought to be the work of Odysseus, who, like many of the surviving heroes, had a less-than-easy journey home.

Zeus was the supreme deity, king of gods and men, but did not get to this position without a struggle. His father, the Titan Kronos, seized power in the heavens by castrating Ouranos the sky god, and in turn lived in fear that one of his own offspring would one day overthrow him. So he swallowed all of his children except Zeus, whose mother, Rhea, came to the rescue and hid him in a cave on the island of Crete, where the warrior Kouretes concealed his cries by clashing their swords and shields together. When he came of age, Zeus poisoned Kronos so that he vomited up all Zeus's siblings; with their help, and the assistance of the Cyclops, he cast Kronos and the Titans from Mount Olympus, the home of the gods. The Cyclops gave Zeus the thunderbolt as a weapon to use in the battle and it became his symbol of power, and emblem of his role as deity of weather and rain. Zeus used his position to maintain cosmic order, control the other gods and men and to get his way with whomever he fancied. Numerous myths tell of his metamorphoses to mate with a variety of mortals out of sight of his jealous wife Hera; all of his liaisons resulted in offspring, which included Herakles, Perseus and Helen.

Music

Although **music** is central to Greek culture, it is possible to travel through the islands and hear only the most modern versions of older songs and tunes, or pieces composed since 1990 or so, rendered in a style barely resembling the *nisiótika* (island music) of even the 1970s. Much of the live music performed in public places has been dramatically altered over the past three decades by contact with Western pop (and a simultaneous rejection by Greeks of their own traditional music).

A good case in point is Náxos, an island which until the 1970s supported a beautiful, unique musical tradition featuring a large number of fine violinists, some of whom played in the older style, but then went "modern". Although some superb recordings of traditional music have been issued recently, you'll no longer hear this kind of music in Náxos's public places or on local radio stations. At **live-music events** such as *paniyíria* (saints'-day festivals), you may well have your ears blasted by overwhelming amplification, coupled with excessive reverb that radically alters the natural tone of the violin. The use of a pickup on the *laoúto*, the plucked-string instrument still played with the violin on most islands, makes it sound far too much like an electric guitar (and sometimes an electric or acoustic guitar will indeed be substituted). The *bouzoúki*, more at home in Greek urban musical genres, will also often be heard in a band alongside the *laoúto*, as well as *kroustá* (percussion) – anything from the lap-drum known as *toumbéleki* to a modern rock/jazz drum set. Although this commercialized instrumentation is typical nowadays, there are exceptions (see below) which can be found by luck and knowing what to look for.

The social context

Instrumental music, dance and song have been an essential part of Greek life from ancient times to the present, and it's difficult to exaggerate its significance for those who have grown up with it. Music and dance form an integral part of weddings, betrothals, baptisms, elections, saint's days observed at local churches or monasteries, name-days (for those who share the name of the saint) observed at private homes or tavernas, Easter and the pre-Lenten Carnival.

Many pieces, which vary from island to island, are specifically associated with **weddings**. Some are processional songs/tunes (*patinádhes*), sung/played while going to fetch the bride from her home, or as the wedding couple leave the church, plus there are specific dances associated with different stages of a wedding ritual. It was common in the past (and in places even today) for the music and dancing that followed a wedding feast to last for up to three days. Some songs are sung only at **pre-Lenten Carnivals** (*Apókries* in Greek), accompanied by the shaking of large goat-bells roped together and, in some places, such as Skýros, the wearing of animal skins. Such rituals, widespread across Europe, date back to pre-Christian times. Music also accompanies informal, unpublicized **private gatherings** in homes, kafenía, and tavernas with facilities (eg a stage and dance-floor) for musicians and patrons.

Don't be shy about asking people where you can hear *tá paradhosiaká* (traditional music); a few words of Greek go a long way towards inclining locals to help foreign travellers. Learn the Greek names of the instruments you would like to hear, or find someone to translate for you if necessary. Once it's clear that you're a budding *meraklís* (untranslatable, but roughly, aficionado) and past the Zorba-soundtrack stage, people will be flattered by the respect paid to "real" music, and doors will open for you.

The older tradition

Island musical tradition is wonderfully diverse, so only a general overview will be attempted here. Each archipelago has its dances, songs and customs which vary between islands and even between towns on the same island. Different dances go by the same name from place to place (eg *syrtós*), while different lyrics are set to many of the same melodies and vice versa. The same tune can be played so idiosyncratically between neighbouring island groups as to be barely recognizable to an outsider. Compared to western styles, island music is far less linear and more circuitous, as would be expected from its Byzantine origins and later Ottoman influences. As in all "folk music", pieces are learned by ear. Though transcriptions exist, and there are some who teach with written notes, folk tradition is primarily an aural, hands-on one.

In Crete, **rhymed couplets** called *mantinádhes* are sung in alteration with instrumental interludes; similar satirical couplets are sung in the Dodecanese (eg *pismatiká* on Kálymnos), while on Náxos such couplets are called *kotsákia*, and the short repeating melody to which they are set is called a *kotsátos*. Singers improvise such rhymed couplets on the spot, thinking of new lines during the short instrumental breaks and coming in again when ready with new lines. These often tease the wedding couple, praise the in-laws, lament the loss of a community member or chide a politician. There are also "set" couplets which have entered the traditional canon, sometimes mixed in with newly improvised material.

Many songs (except for the slow table songs, or *epitrapézia*) are in **dance rhythm**, with a vital interaction between dancers and musicians/singers. Dancers and listeners may also join in the song (solo or as a chorus), or even initiate verses. It is customary for the lead dancer to tip the musicians, often requesting a particular tune and/or dance rhythm for his party to dance to.

An excellent introduction to the subject is Yvonne Hunt's *Traditional Dance in Greek Culture* (Centre for Asia Minor Studies, Athens 1996), which, though primarily about dance, also covers important festivals and customs and the social role of music and musicians. A fine bibliography lists works of significant Greek musicological researchers, anthropologists and travellers. This book can be purchased at the Folk Art Museum, Kydhathinéon 17, at the **Museum of Greek Popular Musical Instruments** at Dhioyénous 1–3 in the Pláka district of Athens. This latter museum, in addition to stocking a good selection of folk recordings, also features displays of instruments from every region of Greece. Headphones provided allow you to listen to brief samples of music played on them.

The instruments
The violin (**violí** in Greek) supposedly appeared in Greece during the seventeenth century, migrating from western Europe (followed some decades later by the clarinet, played mainly in mainland Greek music). Although the violin is also played on the Greek mainland, it is the main melody instrument of the islands, with the striking exceptions of Crete, Kárpathos, Kássos and Hálki in the southern Aegean, where two kinds of *lýra* still prevail (see below). The violin bridge may be sanded in Greece to a less highly arched form than that used for Western classical music (this is also done in Western folk traditions). An

alternate **tuning** known as "*álla Toúrka*", more widespread in the past, is still used by some musicians on certain islands (eg Sífnos, Kýthnos and Kós). From high to low, its string values are D, A, D, and G, with a fourth between the two higher-pitched strings instead of the typical all-fifths arrangement. The lowered high string is slacker and "sweeter", and the violin's tonality altered by the modified tuning. Some violinists have reported being pressured to tune "*álla Fránga*", ie the standard European tuning with "E" on top.

Playing **styles** vary widely within island groups (or even between villages) but Greek violin technique in general differs radically from that of the classical violin (as well as from more familiar Western folk styles). Modes (related to both the Byzantine and Ottoman systems) are used rather than Western scales, there's a range of possible ornamentation techniques (vibrato being only one of them and used very infrequently), and, in some places, unmetered solos (called *taxímia*) based upon the mode of the melody and subject to modulation into other modes. Some very idiosyncratic violin styles are still found on Sífnos or Kýthnos in the Cyclades, and on Kálymnos or Kós in the Dodecanese, with a few of the finest old-fashioned performers only recently deceased (eg Andonis Xanthakis and Andonis Mougadhis Komis in Sífnos). Bowing patterns in these places can be swift and angular, resulting in a more "fiddle"-like sound than styles that rely on smoother, longer bow-strokes.

The **laoúto** is a member of a family of instruments generally referred to as long-necked lutes. It has a fat, gourd-like back like the oud (*oúti* in Greek, *al-ud* in Arabic) from which the *laoúto* (and lute) derives its name and basic form, but a long fretted neck (the oud has a short, unfretted one) and four sets of double metal strings (the oud has gut ones). The Greek *laoúto* is tuned in fifths (C, G, D, A from "lowest" to highest), but the G actually has the lowest pitch, since the C is anomalously tuned a fourth higher than the G. On some islands (Sífnos, Kýthnos) the heavier of the lowest-pitched doublet is removed to accentuate the treble end, and make the *laoúto*'s sound less "thunderous".

In most of the Aegean, the *laoúto* is played with the *violí* or *lýra* and sometimes also with the island bagpipe, the *tsamboúna* (see below). Typical duos are *violí/laoúto* in the Cyclades or *lýra/laoúto* in Crete and the Dodecanese. In north Aegean islands (such as Lésvos and Samothráki) the *laoúto* may be played with violin and *sandoúri* or even in large ensembles which include brass instruments and accordion. In the hands of a competent player, the *laoúto* is not merely "accompanying" a *violí* or *lýra*, but forms part of a true duo, or *ziyiá*, by virtue of well-chosen rhythmic patterns and melody notes/phrases, that make the whole more dynamic. Conversely, good violin- or *lýra*-playing can be ruined by the slick modern *laoúto* style, much more mechanical even compared to that of the early 1980s, with more frequent chord changes and abrupt attack. The use of electric pickup (see above) alters the instrument's unique tone, and makes open chords impossible as they become "boomy". To make matters worse, the *laoúto* is often drowned out in modern recordings by drums and electric bass. The larger, more deeply pitched Cretan *laoúto* will play melody as well as chords to accompany violin or *lýra* more often than in other island groups, as well as solo melodies or *taxímia*. In any duo with *violí* or *lýra* and *laoúto*, at least one (and often both) of the musicians sings while the *laoúto* chords continue, the verses alternating with instrumental passages.

The **sandoúri** is a member of the zither family, resembling the hammered dulcimer and played with the *violí* (or *violí* plus *laoúto*) in many of the Dodecanese and also the northeast Aegean islands, where it may also appear in much larger ensembles. It entered these island groups from nearby Asia Minor, principally after 1923 when it was (re)introduced by refugees, especially on

All of the following are available on CD unless specified otherwise; similarly, all are Greek label pressings except for the Ziyia entries.

If you're stopping over in Athens en route to the islands, the best record stores – Musiki Gonia, Xylouris and Metropolis – are within a few hundred metres of each other on Odhós Panepistimíou, between the university and Omónia square. In the UK the best source is Trehantiri, 367 Green Lanes, London N4 (℡020/8802 6530), which also operates a worldwide mail-order service. In North America, try Down Home Music, 10341 San Pablo Avenue, El Cerrito, CA (℡510/525-2129).

Avthentika Nisiotika tou Peninda (Lyra CD 0168). Good Cretan and Pontic material from the 1950s, with the Dodecanese also represented, from the collection of the late Ted Petrides, musician and dance master.

Dhodhekanisa (Hellenic Music Archives CD AEM 012). Representative songs and dances from the Dodecanese with native *lýra*, *violí* and *tsamboúna* players.

Ellines Akrites (FM Records). FM's folk pressings are generally to be approached with caution, but Vol. 1 of this series (FM 801, "Híos, Mytilíni, Sámos, Ikaría") and Vol. 2 (FM 802, "Límnos, Samothráki, Ímvros, Ténedhos") feature excellent local musicians *(violí/lýra)* and singers such as Strais Rallis of Lésvos, as well as violinist Kyriakos Gouvendas of Thessaloníki.

Emilia Hatzidhaki *Thalassina Tragoudhia* (LP: Panvox 16311, reissued as CD by MBI). The sole easily available collection dedicated to this artist, who otherwise appears only on *nisiótika* anthologies.

Nikos Ikonomidhis *Perasma stin Amorgo/Passage to Amorgos* (Keros Music CD 101). From the islet of Skhinoússa southeast of Náxos, violinist and *lautiéris* Ikonomidhis sings traditional pieces from nearby Amorgós on this 2001-issued recording. His 1991 *Perasma sta Kythira /Passage to Kythera* Keros1982 disc of songs from that lesser-known island is also worth a listen, as is *Anatolika tou Egeou/East of the Aegean* (Verso CD 101). Despite a persistent, annoying electric bass, Ikonomidhis's playing is so clean and spirited that it is difficult not to enjoy this recording.

Kalimera Theia-Samothrakiki Skopi ke Tragoudia #1/*Good Morning Auntie – Tunes and Songs of Samothraki #1* (Hellenic Archives-AEM 014). First in a two-CD set (second CD pending) featuring the local repertoire from this north Aegean island, as well as pieces from neighbouring islands and from Asia Minor.

Anna Karabessini & Effi Sarri CD reissues from old LP's: *Yialo Yialo Piyeno* (Lyra 0102067), *Tis Thalassas* (Lyra 10777) and *Ena Glendi* (Lyra 10717). Two singing sisters from the island of Kós, who were for the Dodecanese what the Konitopoulos family (see below) was for the Cyclades; the fact that they performed only for private gatherings added to their status.

Kassos: Skopi tis Lyras/Lyra Tunes (Lyra 0113). A recent collection from the bleakest, but one of the more musical, of the Dodecanese.

Kastellorizo (Syrtos 561). Studio production of musicologist Manolis Karpathios; of the collected-and-remastered variety, but the only thing easily available for this island.

Irini Konitopoulou-Legaki *Athanata Nisiotika 1* (Tzina-Astir 1020). A 1978 warhorse, beloved of bus drivers across the islands. *Anefala Thalassina* (Lyra 4693) from 1993 is far less commercial and one of the finest recordings from Náxos, featuring fellow Naxian *lautiéris* Dhimitris Fyroyenis and Yiannis Zevgolis, one the last old-style island violinists. Age 61, Irini sings her heart out in a richer, deeper voice than she was known for on club stages.

Yiorgos Konitopoulos & Clan *Sto Diava tou Egeou* (Minos EMI 77) and *Yiorgos ke Irini Konitopoulou-Legaki: Apo Limani se Limani* (EMI 107243480859231). CD reissues of early recordings made by violinist Yiorgos with sister Irini (as above), of a famous (and numerous) Náxos family musically active for the past four decades.

Kritiki Mousiki Paradhosi, Iy Protomastores 1920–1953/Cretan Musical Tradition, the First Masters (Aerakis, 10 CDs). The whole set's prohibitively pricey, and some titles are of specialist interest, but luckily discs are available individually; go for No. 1 (Baxevanis, *lýra* and small orchestra); No. 4 (Stelios Foustalieris, the last master of the *voúlgari*, knowledge of which died with him); No. 5 (Yiannis Demirtzoyiannis, guitarist and epic singer) and No. 6 (Yiorgis Koutsourelis, on melodic *laoúto*).

Tis Lerou ta Tragoudhia/Songs of Leros (Politistikós ké Morfotikós Sýllogos Néon Lérou/Instructive & Cultural Lerian Youth Society), double CD produced by Music Folklore Archive. Live field recordings from 1996 and 1998 of island musicians and singers; *violí*, *sandoúri*, *laoúto* and bagpipes in various combinations, plus unaccompanied singing. Each disc finishes with an archival track of bygone greats Emilia Hatzidhaki and Manolis Skoumbouridis, both Lerian.

Lesvos Aiolis: Tragoudhia ke Hori tis Lesvou/Songs & Dances of Lesvos (University Press of Crete, double CD 9/10). Two decades (1974–96) of field recordings of the last traditional music extant on the island, a labour of love supervised by musicologist Nikos Dhionysopoulos. Pricey, but the quality and uniqueness of the instrumental festival tunes and dances especially, and the illustrated booklet, merit the expense (typically over £20 equivalent).

Lesvos: Mousika Stavrodhromia sto Egeo/Musical Crossroads of the Aegean (University of the Aegean 5-CD set with an enormous book accompanying it (with photos). Everything from Asia Minor music played in Lésvos to carols and wedding songs. Very pricey but worth it.

Seryiani sta Nisia Mas, Vol 1 (CD, MBI 10371). An excellent retrospective of various *nisiótika* hits and artists, mostly from the 1950s. The highlight of Vol. 1 (2 doesn't exist) is Emilia Hatzidhaki's rendering of "Bratsera".

Skopi tis Kalymnou/Kalymnian Folk Music (Lykio ton Ellinidhon E2-276-97). Double CD with excellent notes and song translations. Traditional Kalymnian repertoire and native musicians features Mikes Tsounias, 78, on violin, his young grandson playing unison violin on some pieces, plus good *tsamboúna* accompaniment.

Skopi kai Tragoudhia apo tin Apirantho tis Naxou (Aperathitikos Syllogos TC-CP957). 1983 recording from the famous Náxos mountain village of Apíranthos featuring native Yiannis Zevgolis (violin) with singer Koula Klironomou-Sidheri, Yiorgos Karapatis on *laoúto*, plus others on guitar and *tsamboúna*. Beautiful renditions of traditional Náxos music, with many wistful and nostalgic songs from an era now past.

Songs of...(Society for the Dissemination of National Music, Greece). A thirty-disc-plus series of field recordings from the 1950s–70s, each covering traditional music of one region or type. Lyrics in English, all available in Athens in LP, cassette or CD form, especially at the Museum of Greek Popular Instruments (address on p.578). Best island discs to date are *Mytilene and Chios* (SDNM 110); *Mytilene and Asia Minor* (SDNM 125); *Rhodes, Chalki and Symi* (SDNM 104); *Kassos and Karpathos* (SDNM 103); and *Amorgos, Kythnos and Sifnos* (SDNM105).

Thalassa Thymisou/Sea of Memories: Tragoudhia ke Skopi apo tis Inousses (Navtiko Mousio Inousson-En Khordais CD 1801/1802). The result of a "field trip" by the En Khordais traditional music school of Thessaloníki to Inoússes, a small islet northeast of Híos, to rescue vanishing traditional material with the help of the islanders' long memories; the result's superb, a mix of live sessions in Inoussan tavernas and some studio recordings. Thorough and intelligent notes, but no translations of the lyrics.

continued overleaf

Discography continued

Tragoudhia ke Skopi tis Patmou/Songs and Melodies of Patmos (CD, Politistikon Idhryma Dhodhekanisou 201). Live 1995 field recordings of well-edited pieces, as raw but compelling as you'd hear them at an old-time festival. Local singers and instrumentalists on *violí*, *tsamboúna* and *sandoúri*.

Nikos Xylouris *O Arkhangelos tis Kritis*,1958–1968 (MBI 10376); *Ta Khronia stin Kriti* (2CD, MBI 10677/78). The best two retrospectives of the sweet-voiced Cretan singer, with copious notes; the first covers his initial decade of recordings, previously unavailable, with self-accompaniment on the *lýra*.

Ziyia Fine arrangements and singing of music from across Greece, by a five-member, bi-coastal group from the US. Their first outing, *From the Mountains to the Islands* (AgaRhythm, self-produced, 1993) has more island music than *Travels with Karaghiozis* (AgaRhythm, self-produced, 1995), which does however include a fine piece from Kálymnos.

Lésvos. The *sandoúri* plays both chords and melody, as well as introductory *taxímia*. While at times only basic chords are played on it to complement the violin, it can fill in with arpeggios, scale runs or melodic tags. It occasionally serves as a solo instrument, and has been recorded as such on the island of Lésvos.

The term **lýra** applies to a family of small, pear- or bottle-shaped instruments which are held upright on the player's thigh with strings facing forward and bowed with the palm facing away from the body. Greek island types are pear-shaped and have three metal strings, with notes played by pressing the finger-nails laterally against the strings. The **Dodecanesian lýra** has a drone string in the middle which fills out the sound, and is bowed continually while play-ing on either of the outer strings; the bow in some cases has little bells on it which provide rhythmic accompaniment. Its tonal range matches that of the *tsamboúna* played in the Dodecanese and can be played alone, with *laoúto*, with *tsamboúna*, or both of these together, often accompanying vocalists. The **Cretan lýra** is a relatively modern instrument, having supplanted the Dodecanesian type which was used on the island before the 1930s. The con-temporary *lýra* is larger and fatter, lacks a drone string and is tuned lower and in successive fifths, thus extending the melodic range by a fifth beyond that of the older instrument. The old belled bow was abandoned, both because it was too heavy for the quick and elaborate tunes now possible, but also because its rhythmic function was replaced by the *laoúto* (and earlier by a lute-family member, the *boúlgari*). A fingerboard was added to make fingering easier, as well as a longer, narrow neck, and a modern violin bow replaced the older, more convex bow. Yet despite all these violin-like innovations, the *lýra* retains a tone quality very different from that of the violin; even a skilled violinist can never entirely imitate its sound.

The **tsamboúna** (in Crete, *askomandoúra*) is the Greek-island bagpipe made of goatskin, with no drone and two chanters made of calamus reed. The left chanter does not vary between island groups, having five holes which allow an incomplete diatonic scale from 'do' to 'fa'. The right chanter is of three types, with anywhere from two to five holes depending on the island. In the Dodecanese this bagpipe may be played alone, with another *tsamboúna*, or with a *laoúto* and *lýra*; many songs are accompanied by these various combinations. In the Cyclades (and formerly Híos) the *tsamboúna* is (or was) played with a **toumbáki** or two-headed drum, only one side of which is struck with two wooden (or bone) drumsticks. It is suspended to one side of the player's torso by a strap. The *tsamboúna* and *toumbáki* are quintessential shepherds' instruments, their skins taken from their flocks. Along with the *lýra*, they are the oldest of the instruments played on the islands, though rare now except in some of the places mentioned above. On Náxos the *tsamboúna-toumbáki* duo is still much in demand during the pre-Lenten *Apokriátika* festivities.

Accordion, clarinet, guitar and *bouzoúki*, all **imported** from the Greek mainland or urban traditions, are sometimes played along with the more traditional instruments on the islands. Alone of all modern Greek territory, the **Ionian islands** (except for Lefkádha) were never occupied by the Ottomans, but instead by the Venetians, and thus have a predominantly Western musical tradition. The indigenous song-form is both Italianate in name (*kantádhes*) and instrumentation (guitar and mandolin – as in Captain Corelli's).

Susan Raphael, with Marc Dubin

Wildlife

For anyone who has first seen the smaller Greek islands at the height of summer with their brown parched hillsides and desert-like ambience, the richness of the wildlife – in particular the flora – may come as a surprise. As winter changes to spring, the countryside (and urban waste ground) transforms itself from green to a mosaic of coloured flowers, which attract a plethora of insect life, followed by birds. Isolated areas have had many thousands of years to develop their own individual species. Overall, Greece has around six thousand species of native flowering plants, nearly four times that of Britain but in the same land area. Many are unique to Greece, and make up about one third of Europe's endemic plants.

Some background

In early antiquity Greece, including the islands, was thickly forested: Aleppo and Calabrian pines grew in coastal regions, giving way to fir or black pine up in the hills and low mountains. But this **native woodland** contracted rapidly as human activities expanded. By Classical times, a pattern had been set of forest clearance, followed by agriculture, abandonment to scrub and then a resumption of cultivation or grazing. Huge quantities of timber were consumed in the production of charcoal, pottery and smelted metal, and for ships and construction work. Small patches of virgin woodland have remained on the largest islands, but even these are under threat from loggers and arsonists.

Greek **farming** often lacks the rigid efficiency of northern European agriculture. Many peasant farmers still cultivate little patches of land, and even town-dwellers travel at weekends to collect food plants from the countryside. Wild greens under the generic term *hórta* are gathered to be cooked like spinach, and grape-hyacinth bulbs are boiled as a vegetable. The buds and young shoots of capers, and the fruit of wild figs, carobs, plums, strawberry trees, cherries and sweet chestnuts are harvested. Emergent snails and mushrooms are collected after wet weather. The more resilient forms of wildlife can coexist with these land-uses, but for many Greeks only those species that have practical application are regarded as having any value.

Now, however, increased access to heavier earth-moving machinery means farmers can sweep away an ancient meadow full of orchids in an easy morning's work – often to clear a field that is used for forage for a year or two and then abandoned to coarse thistles. Increasingly, the pale scars of dirt tracks criss-cross once intact hill- and mountain-sides, allowing short-termist agricultural destruction of previously undisturbed upland habitats.

During the 1950s a policy of draining **wetlands** was instituted in order to increase agriculture, and many important areas were lost to wildlife completely. Those lakes, lagoons and deltas that remain on the larger islands are, in theory, now protected for their fragile bio-diversity and their environmental and scientific value – but industrial and sewage pollution, disturbance and misuse are unchecked. Local 4WD vehicles and noisy motorbikes race through dunes, destroying the surface stability and decimating nesting species; Greek military planes practise low-altitude flight over flocks of flamingos; rows of illegally overnighting camper vans disfigure the beaches; and locals drive out here to dump unwanted televisions and fridges. On Lésvos, one of the island's main

△ Goats on a cliff

tourist attractions, the Kalloní salt pans, once beloved by rare birds, are being poisoned by sewage. The **Church**, whose lands once often provided wildlife with a refuge from hunters, now looks to capitalize on their value for major tourist developments, with plans to develop mass tourism and golf courses around the Toploú monastery in eastern Crete, already one of Greece's most water-deficient areas.

Since the 1970s, **tourist developments** have ribboned out along coastlines, sweeping away both agricultural plots and wildlife havens as they do so. These expanding resorts increase local employment, often attracting inland workers to the coast; the generation that would have been shepherds on remote hillsides now works in tourist bars and tavernas. Consequently, the pressure of domestic animal grazing, particularly in the larger islands, has been significantly reduced, allowing the regeneration of tree seedlings. Crete, for example, now has more woodland than at any time in the last five centuries. Fires since 1980 have destroyed much of the tree cover in Thássos, southern Rhodes, Kárpathos, Híos and, in 2000, Sámos; the trees may well regenerate eventually, but by then the complex shade-dependent ecology is irrecoverably lost.

Despite an often negative attitude to wildlife, Greece was probably the first place in the world where it was an object of study. Theophrastos (372–287 BC) was the first recorded **botanist** and a systematic collector of general information on plants, while his contemporary, Aristotle, studied the animal world. During the first century AD the distinguished physician Dioscorides compiled a herbal that remained a standard work for over a thousand years.

Flowers

Whereas in temperate northern Europe plants flower from spring until autumn, the arid summers of Greece confine the main **flowering period** to the spring-time, a climatic window when the days are bright, the temperatures not too high and the ground-water supply still adequate. **Spring** starts in the the southeast Aegean during early March, and then travels progressively westwards and north-wards. Rhodes, Kárpathos and eastern Crete are at their best in March, western Crete in early April, the eastern Aegean mid-April to late April, and the Ionian islands in early May, though a cold dry winter can cause several weeks' delay. In the higher mountains the floral spring is held back until the chronological sum-mer, with the alpine zones of central and western Crete in full flower in June.

The delicate flowers of early spring – orchids, fritillaries, anemones, cycla-men, tulips and small bulbs – are replaced as the season progresses by more robust shrubs, tall perennials and abundant annuals, but many of these close down completely for the fierce **summer**. A few tough plants, like shrubby thyme and savory, continue to flower through the heat and act as magnets for butterflies.

Once the worst heat is over, and the first showers of **autumn** arrive, so does a second "spring", on a much smaller scale but no less welcome after the brown drabness of summer. Squills, autumn cyclamen, crocus in varying shades, pink or lilac colchicum, yellow sternbergia and other small bulbs all come into bloom, while the seeds start to germinate for the following year's crop of annu-als. By the new year, early spring bulbs and orchids are flowering in the south.

Seashore

Plants on the **beach** tend to be hardy species growing in a difficult environ-ment where fresh water is scarce. Feathery tamarisk trees are adept at surviving this habitat, and consequently are often planted to provide shade. On hot days or nights you may see or feel them sweating away surplus saltwater from their foliage.

Sand dunes in the southern and eastern islands may support the low gnarled trees of the prickly **juniper**. These provide shelter for a variety of colourful small plants like pink campions, yellow restharrow, white stocks, blue alkanet and violet sea-lavender. The flat sandy areas or slacks behind the dunes can be home to a variety of plants, where they have not been illegally ploughed for cultivation. Open stretches of beach sand usually have fewer plants, particular-ly nowadays in resort areas where the bulldozed "spring cleaning" of the beach removes the local flora along with the winter's rubbish.

Watercourses

Large areas of **freshwater** are scarce, particularly on the smaller islands. Many watercourses dry up completely during the hot season, and what seem to be dry river courses are often simply flood-beds, which fill irregularly at times of torrential rain. Consequently, there are few true aquatic plants compared with much of Europe. However, species that survive periodic drying-out can flour-ish, such as the giant reed or **calamus**, a bamboo-like grass reaching up to 6m in height and often cut for use as canes. It often grows in company with the shrubby, pink- or white-flowered and very poisonous **oleander**.

Cultivated land

Arable fields can be rich with colourful weeds: scarlet poppies, blue bugloss, yellow or white daisies, wild peas, gladioli, tulips and grape hyacinths. Small **meadows** can be equally colourful, with slower-growing plants such as orchids in extraordinary quantities. The rather dull violet flowers of the mandrake conceal its celebrated history as a narcotic and surgical anaesthetic. In the absence of herbicides, olive groves can have an extensive underflora. In the presence of herbicides there is usually a yellow carpet of the introduced, weed-killer-resistant *Oxalis pescaprae*, which now occurs in sufficient quantity to show up in satellite photographs.

Lower hillsides

The rocky earth makes cultivation on some hillsides difficult and impractical. Agriculture is often abandoned and areas regenerate to a rich mixture of shrubs and perennials – known as **garigue**. With time, a few good wet winters and in the absence of grazing, some shrubs develop into small trees, intermixed with tough climbers – the much denser **maquis** vegetation. The colour yellow often predominates in early spring, with brooms, gorse, Jerusalem sage the three-metre giant fennel followed by the pink and white of large rockroses (*Cistus* spp.). An abundance of the latter is often indicative of an earlier fire, since they flourish in the cleared areas. Strawberry trees (*Arbutus* spp.) are also fire-resistant; they flower in winter or early spring, producing an orange-red edible (though disappointingly insipid) fruit in the autumn, fermented to make an (unlicensed) liqueur. The Judas tree flowers on bare wood in spring, making a blaze of pink against green hillside.

A third vegetation type is **phrygana** – smaller, frequently aromatic or spiny shrubs, often with a narrow strip of bare ground between each hedgehog-like bush. Many **aromatic herbs** such as lavender, rosemary, savory, sage and thyme are natives to these areas, intermixed with other less tasty plants such as the toxic euphorbias and the spiny burnet or wire-netting bush.

Nearly 160 species of **orchid** are believed to occur in Greece; their complexity blurs species' boundaries and keeps botanists in a state of taxonomic flux. In particular, the *Ophrys* bee and spider orchids have adapted themselves, through subtleties of lip colour and false scents, to seduce small male wasps. These insects mistake the flowers for a potential mate, and unintentionally assist the plant's pollination. Other orchids mimic the colours and scents of honey-producing plants, to lure bees. Though all species are officially protected, many are still picked for decoration – in particular the giant *Barlia* orchid – and fill vases in homes, cafés, tavernas and even on graves.

Irises have a particular elegance and charm. The blue to violet winter iris, as its name suggests, is the first to appear, followed by the small blue *Iris gynan-driris*. The flowers of the latter open after midday and into the night, to wither by the following morning. The widow iris is sombre-coloured in funereal shades of black and green, while the taller, white *Iris albicans*, the holy flower of Islam, is a relic of the Ottoman occupation. On the limestone peaks of Sámos, *Iris suavolens* has short stems, but huge yellow and brown flowers.

Mountains and gorges

The higher **mountains** of the Greek islands have winter snow cover varying with altitude, and cooler weather for much of the year, so that flowering is consequently later than at lower altitudes. The **limestone peaks** of islands such as Corfu, Kefaloniá, Crete, Rhodes, Sámos and Thássos hold rich collections of attractive flowering rock plants whose nearest relatives may be from the Balkan Alps or from the Turkish Toros ranges. Gorges are another spectacular habitat, particularly rich on Crete. Their inaccessible cliffs act as refuges for plants that cannot survive the grazing, competition or more extreme climates of open areas. Many of Greece's endemic plants – bellflowers, knapweeds and *Dianthus* spp. in particular – are confined to cliffs, gorges or mountains.

Much of the surviving **island forest** is in the mountainous areas of Kefaloniá, Évvia, Lésvos and Crete. Depending on the island, the woodland can comprise cypress (widespread at low altitudes), Greek fir (especially on Kefaloniá), oak (on Lésvos, Níssyros, Kéa and Crete) and a few species of pine: Calabrian or Aleppo at lower altitudes, black pine on the summits of Crete and Sámos. The cypress is native to the south and east Aegean, but in its columnar form it has been planted everywhere with a Mediterranean climate. It is sometimes said that the slim trees are the male and the broader, spreading form are female, but female cones on the thin trees prove this wrong. On Kárpathos, Sými and Crete there are extensive stands of juniper, while shady stream canyons of the largest islands shelter plane, oriental sweetgum, chestnut and poplar. The cooler shade of woodland provides a haven for plants which cannot survive full exposure to the Greek summer. Such species include the wonderful red, pink or white peonies found on Sámos, along with helleborine and bird's-nest orchids, and numerous ferns.

With altitude, the forest thins out to scattered individual hardy conifers and kermes oak, before finally reaching a limit ranging from 1000–1200m (Samothráki, Sámos) to 1400m (Kefaloniá), ending at about 1800m (Crete). Above this treeline are limited summer meadows, and then bare rock. If not severely grazed, these habitats are home to many low-growing, gnarled, but often splendidly floriferous plants.

Birds

Migratory species which have wintered in East Africa move north in spring through the eastern Mediterranean from mid-March to mid-May, or later, depending on the season and the weather. Some stop to breed in Greece; others move on into the rest of Europe. The southern islands can be the first landfall after a long sea-crossing, and smaller birds recuperate for a few days before moving on north. Larger birds such as storks and ibis often fly very high, and binoculars are needed to spot them as they pass over. In autumn the birds return, but usually in more scattered groups. Although some species such as quail and turtle dove are shot, there is nothing like the wholesale slaughter that takes place in some other Mediterranean countries.

Swallows, and their relatives the martins, are constantly swooping through the air to catch insects, as are the larger and noisier swifts. Warblers are numerous, with the Sardinian warbler often conspicuous because of its black head, bright red eye and bold habits; the Rüppell's warbler is considerably rarer, and confined to thicker woodland such as occurs on Lésvos. Other small insect-eaters include stonechats, flycatchers and woodchat shrikes.

At **night**, the tiny Scops owl has a very distinct, repeated single-note call, very like the sonar beep of a submarine; the equally diminutive little owl is by contrast also visible by day, particularly on ruined houses, and has a strange repertoire of cries, chortles and a throaty hiss. Certainly the most evocative nocturnal bird is the nightingale, which requires wooded stream valleys and is most audible around midnight in May, its mating season.

Larger **raptors** are rare on the islands but can occur in remoter areas, particularly around mountain gorges and cliffs. Certain Dodecanese islands and Lésvos support populations of Eleonora's falcons, while peregrines visit the Ionian islands. Buzzards are perhaps the most abundant, and mistaken by optimistic birdwatchers for the much rarer, shyer eagles; vultures are also seen in passing on the largest islands. Lesser kestrels are brighter, noisier versions of the common kestrel, and often appear undisturbed by the presence of humans. Also to be seen in the mountains of larger islands are ravens and smaller, colourful birds such as black and white wheatears, wallcreepers and blue rock thrushes.

In lowland areas, hoopoes are a startling combination of pink, black and white, particularly obvious when they fly; they're about the only natural predator of the processionary caterpillar, a major pest in pine forests. The much shyer golden oriole has an attractive song but is rarely seen for more than a few moments before hiding its brilliant colours among the olive trees. Rollers are bright blue and chestnut, while multicoloured flocks of slim and elegant bee-eaters, especially on Tílos in April or May, fill the air with their soft calls as they hunt insects. Brightest of all is the kingfisher, more commonly seen sea-fishing than in northern Europe.

In those areas of **wetland** that remain undrained and undisturbed, birds flourish. In salt marshes, coastal lagoons, estuaries and freshwater ponds, herons and egrets, ducks, ospreys, glossy ibises and spoonbills, black storks, white storks, pelicans and many waders can be seen feeding. Greater flamingos sometimes occur as lone individuals or small flocks, particularly in salt pans of the eastern Aegean.

Seashore birds are also notable; the southern Dodecanese are home to a small population of Audoin's gulls, endangered both by human activity and the more versatile yellow-legged gull. Cormorants roost on and dive off coastal cliffs from late summer onwards.

Mammals

The island **mammal** population ranges from small rodents and shrews to hedgehogs, hares and squirrels (a very dark form of the red, seen only on Lésvos). Rats are particularly common on Corfu and Sámos. Medium-sized mammals include badgers and foxes, but one of the commonest is the fast moving, ferret-like, stone (or beech) marten, named for its habit of decorating stones with droppings to mark its territory. In the White Mountains of Crete an endemic ibex, known to Cretan hunters as the *agrími* or *krí-krí*, is occasionally seen running wild but more often as a zoo attraction. When formerly in danger of extinction, a colony of them was established on the offshore islet of Dhía, where they managed in turn to exterminate the rare local flora.

The extremely rare Mediterranean **monk seal** also breeds on some stretches of remote coast in the east Aegean and Sporades; the small world population is now highly endangered since losing many individuals – and most of its main breeding ground – to a toxic algal bloom off Morocco. If spotted, these seals should be treated with deference; they cannot tolerate human disturbance, and on present trends are unlikely to survive long into the new millennium.

Reptiles and amphibians

Reptiles flourish in the hot dry summers of Greece, and there are many species, the commonest being **lizards**. Most of these are small, slim, agile and wary, rarely staying around for closer inspection. They're usually brown to grey, with subtle patterns of spots, streaks and stripes, though in adult males the undersides are sometimes brilliant orange, green or blue. The more robust green lizards, with long whip-like tails, can be 50cm or more in length, but equally shy and fast-moving unless distracted by territorial disputes with each other.

On some islands, mainly in the central and eastern Aegean, lives the angular, iguana-like **agama**, sometimes called the Rhodes dragon. Occasionally reaching a robust 30cm in length, their skin is rough and grey to brown with indistinct patterning. Unlike other lizards, they will often stop to study you, before finally disappearing into a wall or under a rock.

Geckos are large-eyed, semi-transparent, nocturnal lizards, up to 15cm long, with short tails and often rough skins. Their spreading toes have claws and ingenious adhesive pads, allowing them to walk up house walls and onto ceilings in their search for insects. Groups of them lie in wait near bright lights that attract their prey, and small ones living indoors can have very pale, almost transparent skins. Not always popular locally – one Greek name for them, *miaró*, means "defiler" after their outsized faeces – they should be left alone to eat mosquitoes and other bugs. The **chameleon** is a rare, slow-moving, swivel-eyed inhabitant of eastern Crete and some eastern Aegean islands such as Sámos. Although essentially green, it has the ability to adjust its coloration to match the surroundings.

Once collected for the pet trade, **tortoises** can be found on many larger islands, though not on Crete. Usually it is their noisy progress through vegetation on sunny or wooded hills that first signals their presence. They spend their often long lives grazing the vegetation and can reach lengths of 30cm. Closely related **terrapins** are more streamlined, freshwater tortoises which love to bask on waterside mud by streams or ponds on many islands. Shy and nervous, they are usually only seen as they disappear underwater. They are scavengers and will eat anything, including fingers if handled.

Sea turtles occur mostly in the Ionian Sea, but also in the Aegean. The least rare are the loggerhead turtles (*Caretta caretta*), which nest on Zákynthos and Kefalloniá, and occasionally in Crete. Their nesting grounds are disappearing under tourist resorts, although they are a protected endangered species (see box on p.525).

Snakes are abundant in many islands (though Astypálea has none); most are shy and non-venomous. Several species, including the Ottoman and nose-horned **vipers**, do have a poisonous bite, though they are not usually aggressive. They are adder-like and often have a very distinct, dark zigzag stripe down the back. They are only likely to bite if a hand is put in the crevice of a wall or a rock-face where one of them is resting, or if they are attacked. Unfortunately, the locals in some areas attempt to kill any snake they see, and thus greatly increase the probability of their being bitten. Leave them alone, and they will usually do the same for you (but if the worst comes to worst, see the advice on p.33). Most snakes are not only completely harmless to humans, but beneficial in that they keep down populations of pests such as rats and mice. There are also three species of legless lizards – slow-worm, glass lizard and legless skink – all equally harmless, which suffer because they are mistaken for snakes.

Frogs and **toads** are the commonest and most obvious amphibians on many Greek islands, particularly during the spring breeding season. The green toad has green marbling over a pinkish or mud-coloured background and makes a cricket-like trill. Frogs prefer the wettest places, and the robust marsh frog particularly revels in artificial water-storage ponds, where the concrete sides magnify their croaking impressively. **Tree frogs** are tiny jewels, usually emerald green, with huge and strident voices at night. They rest by day in trees and shrubs, and can sometimes be found in quantity plastered onto the leaves of waterside oleanders.

Insects

Greece teems with **insects**. Some, like flies, wasps and mosquitoes, pester, but most are harmless to humans. The huge, slow-flying, glossy black carpenter bee may cause alarm by its size and noise, but is rarely a problem; almost invisible gnats emerge on late summer nights and pack a mighty bite.

Grasshoppers and **crickets** swarm through open areas of vegetation in summer, with several larger species that are carnivorous on the smaller individuals and which can bite strongly if handled. Larger still is the grey-brown locust, which flies noisily before crash-landing into trees and shrubs. The high-pitched and endlessly repeated chirp of house crickets can drive one to distraction on autumn nights when temperatures fall to their liking, as can the summer daytime whirring of cicadas on the trunks of trees. The latter insects are giant relatives of the aphids that cluster on roses.

From spring through to autumn Greece is full of **butterflies**, particularly in late spring and early summer. There are three swallowtail species, named for the drawn-out corners of the hind wings, in shades of cream and yellow, with black and blue markings. Their smaller relatives, the festoons, lack the tails, but add red spots to the palette. The rarer, robust brown and orange pasha is unrelated but is Europe's largest butterfly. In autumn the black and orange plain tiger or African monarch may appear, sometimes in large quantities. In areas of deciduous woodland, look high up and you may see fast-flying large tortoiseshells, while lower down, southern white admirals skim and glide through clearings between the trees. Some of the smallest but most beautiful butterflies are the blues. Their subtle, camouflaging grey and black undersides make them vanish from view when they land and fold their wings.

Some of the Greek **hawkmoths** are equally spectacular, particularly the green and pink oleander hawkmoth. Their large caterpillars can be recognized by their tail horn. The hummingbird hawkmoth, like its namesake, hovers at flowers to feed, supported by a blur of fast-moving wings. Tiger moths, with their black and white forewings and startling bright orange hindwings, are the "butterflies" that occur in huge quantity in sheltered sites of islands such as Rhodes and Páros. The giant peacock moth is Europe's largest, up to 15cm across. A mixture of grey, black and brown, with big eye-spots, it is usually only seen during the day while resting on tree trunks.

Other insects include the camouflaged praying mantis, holding their powerful forelegs in a position of supplication until another insect comes within reach. The females are voracious – and notorious for eating the males during

In case of difficulty obtaining the titles listed below from conventional booksellers, there is a reliable mail-order outlet for wildlife field guides within the UK. **Summerfield Books**, Main Street, Brough, Kirkby Stephen, Cumbria CA17 4AX ⓣ017683/41577, ⓕ41687, ⓔatkins@summerfield-books.com, not only has new botanical titles, but also rare or out-of-print natural history books on all topics. Postage is extra, but they often have special offers on select products. The shop is open Mon–Sat 9.30am–4.30pm.

Flowers

Hellmut Baumann *Greek Wild Flowers and Plant Lore in Ancient Greece* (Herbert Press, UK). Crammed with fascinating ethnobotany, plus good colour photographs.

Marjorie Blamey and Christopher Grey-Wilson *Mediterranean Wild Flowers* (HarperCollins, UK). Comprehensive field guide, with coloured drawings; recent and taxonomically up to date.

Lance Chilton *Plant Check-lists* (Marengo Publications, UK). Small pamphlets, which also include birds, reptiles and butterflies, for a number of Greek islands and resorts. Contact the author directly at ⓣ & ⓕ 01485/532710, ⓦwww.marengo .supanet.com.

Pierre Delforge *Orchids of Britain and Europe* (HarperCollins, UK). A comprehensive guide, with recent taxonomy, though beware small inaccuracies in the translation.

Anthony Huxley and William Taylor *Flowers of Greece and the Aegean* (Hogarth Press, UK, o/p). The only volume dedicated to the islands (and mainland), with colour photos, but now slightly dated for taxonomy.

Oleg Polunin *Flowers of Greece and the Balkans* (Oxford UP, UK). Classic, older field guide (reprinted 1997), also with colour photographs, useful if Huxley and Taylor proves unfindable.

Oleg Polunin and Anthony Huxley *Flowers of the Mediterranean* (Hogarth Press, UK). The larger scope means that many Greek endemics get missed out, but recent printings have a table of taxonomic changes.

Birds

Richard Brooks *Birding in Lesbos* (Brookside Publishing, UK). Superb guide which includes a list of birdwatching sites, detailed maps, colour photos and an annotat-

mating. Ant-lion adults resemble a fluttery dragonfly, but their young are huge-jawed and build pits in the sand to trap ants. Hemispherical carob beetles collect balls of dung and push them around with their back legs, while the huge longhorn beetles of the southern Ionian islands munch their way through tree trunks. Longhorns are named for their absurdly extended, whip-like antennae. Cockroaches of varying species live in buildings, particularly hotels, restaurants and bakeries, attracted by warmth and food scraps.

Corfu is famous for its extraordinary **fireflies**, which loop in quantities across meadows and marshes on May nights, speckling the darkness with bursts of cold light to attract partners. Look carefully in nearby hedges, and you may spot the less flashy, more sedentary glow-worm.

Centipedes are not often seen, but the fast-moving twenty-centimetre *skolópendra* should be treated with respect since they can give very painful bites. Other non-vertebrates of interest include the land crabs, which are found in the south and east. They need water to breed, but can cause sured species-by-species bird list with much useful information. Contact the author directly at ©email/richard-brooks.co.uk.

George Handrinos and T. Akriotis *Birds of Greece* (A&C Black, UK). A comprehensive guide that includes island birdlife.

Heinzel, Fitter and Parslow *Collins Guide to the Birds of Britain and Europe*; **Petersen, Mountfort and Hollom** *Field Guide to the Birds of Britain and Europe* (both Collins, UK; Stephen Green Press, US). Though not specific to Greece, these two field guides have the best coverage of Greek birds outside of Lésvos.

Mammals

Corbet and Ovenden *Collins Guide to the Mammals of Europe* (Collins, UK; Stephen Green Press, US). The best field guide on its subject.

Reptiles

Arnold, Burton and Ovenden *Collins Guide to the Reptiles and Amphibians of Britain and Europe* (Collins, UK; Stephen Green Press, US). A useful guide, though excludes the Dodecanese and east Aegean islands.

Jiri Cihar *Amphibians and Reptiles* (Conran Octopus, UK, o/p). Selective coverage, but includes most endemic species of the Dodecanese and east Aegean isles.

Insects

Michael Chinery *Collins Guide to the Insects of Britain and Western Europe* (Collins, UK; Stephen Green Press, US). Although Greece is outside the geographical scope of the guide, it will provide genus identifications for most insects seen.

Lionel Higgins and Norman Riley *A Field Guide to the Butterflies of Britain and Europe* (Collins, UK; Stephen Green Press, US). A thorough and detailed field guide that illustrates nearly all species seen in Greece.

Marine life

B. Luther and K. Fiedler *A Field Guide to the Mediterranean* (HarperCollins, UK, o/p). Very thorough, includes most Greek shallow-water species.

prise when found walking on remote hillsides. There are plenty of genuine marine creatures to be seen, particularly in shallow seawater sheltered by rocks – sea cucumbers, sea butterflies, octopus, marine worms, starfish and sea urchins.

Lance Chilton, with Marc Dubin

Books

Where separate editions exist in the UK and US, publishers are detailed below in the form UK publisher; US publisher, unless the publisher is the same in both countries. Where books are published in one country – or Athens – only, this follows the publisher's name.

An out-of-print but still highly recommended book is indicated by the abbreviation "o/p"; the recommended Greek-specialist book dealers often have large back-stocks of these. University Press is abbreviated as UP.

Books marked ⊠ are particularly recommended, many of them part of a "Modern Greek Writers" series, numbering over thirty titles, issued by the Athenian company Kedros Publishers.

Travel and general accounts

Modern accounts

⊠ **Kevin Andrews** *The Flight of Ikaros* (Penguin, o/p). An intense and compelling account of an educated, sensitive archeologist loose in the back country during the civil war, including an initial chapter on Páros as it was pre-tourism.

⊠ **Gillian Bouras** *A Foreign Wife* (Penguin Australia). In which a woman who married a Greek-Australian during the 1960s consents to return permanently to the mother country in 1980. An excellent chronicle of cross-cultural/continental angst and the migrant experience in both directions, with penetrating insights into child-rearing, comparative views of leisure, local medicine and general expectations tempered by the grinding Messinian poverty of only a few decades ago. It inaugurates a series of several works: *A Fair Exchange*, the sequel; *Aphrodite and the Others*, in which Bouras explores her always-difficult relations with her formidable mother-in-law; the autobiographical novel

A Stranger Here, in which the widespread ambivalence of being in Greece – never content there, yet not being able to keep away – is teased out still more exquisitely; and *Starting Again* (all Penguin Australia).

Gerald Durrell *My Family and Other Animals* (Penguin, UK). Sparkling, funny anecdotes of Durrell's childhood on Corfu during the 1930s – and his passion for the island's fauna: toads, tortoises, bats, scorpions, the lot.

Lawrence Durrell *Prospero's Cell* (Faber & Faber; Penguin, o/p); *Reflections on a Marine Venus* (Faber & Faber; Penguin); *The Greek Islands* (Faber & Faber; Penguin, both o/p). The elder Durrell lived before World War II with Gerald and the family on Corfu, the subject of *Prospero's Cell*. *Marine Venus* recounts Lawrence's 1945–47 experiences and impressions of Rhodes and other Dodecanese islands.

Sheelagh Kanneli *Earth and Water: A Marriage in Kalamata* (Efstathiadhis, Athens). A classic account of that rare thing – a foreign woman integrating successfully into provincial Greek society. Rich in period detail of pre-tourism and pre-earthquake Kalamáta.

Katherine Kizilos *The Olive Grove: Travels in Greece* (Lonely Planet Journeys, UK). Returned, ambivalent Greek-Australian's musings on the country, and Istanbul, with a good initial section on Sýros, Santoríni, Pátmos, Ikaría and Lésvos.

Elias Kulukundis *Journey to a Greek Island* (Cassell, o/p). More accurately, a journey back through time and genealogy by a diaspora Greek two generations removed from Kássos, poorest of the Dodecanese.

Willard Manus *This Way to Paradise: Dancing on the Tables* (Lycabettus Press, Athens). An American expatriate's memoir of nearly four decades in Líndhos, Rhodes, beginning long before its descent into mass-tourist tattiness. Wonderful period detail, including hippy/bohemian excesses and often hilarious cameos by the likes of S.J. Perelman, Germaine Greer and Martha Gellhorn.

Henry Miller *The Colossus of Maroussi* (Minerva, o/p; New Directions). Corfu, Crete and the soul of Greece in 1939, with Miller, completely in his element, at his most inspired.

James Pettifer *The Greeks: the Land and People since the War* (Penguin; Viking). A useful, if spottily edited and now slightly dated (1994) introduction to contemporary Greece – and its recent past. Pettifer charts the state of the nation's politics, food, family life, religion and tourism.

Patricia Storace *Dinner with Persephone* (Granta; Pantheon). A New York poet, resident for a year in Athens (with forays to the provinces) puts the country's psyche on the couch, while avoiding the same position with various predatory males. Storace has a sly sense of humour, and in showing how permeated – and imprisoned – Greece is by its imagined past, gets it right ninety percent of the time.

William Travis *Bus Stop Symi* (Rapp & Whiting, o/p). Chronicles three years' residence there in the mid-Sixties; fairly insightful (if rather resented on the island itself), though Travis erroneously prophesied that the place would never see tourism.

Faith Warn *Bitter Sea: The Real Story of Greek Sponge Diving* (Guardian Angel Press, UK, but widely available on Kálymnos). Short, photo-illustrated potted history of the traditional Kálymnos livelihood, by a resident English woman.

Sarah Wheeler *An Island Apart* (Abacus, o/p). An entertaining chronicle of a five-month ramble through Évvia, one of the least-visited islands. Wheeler has a sure touch with Greek culture and an open approach to nuns, goatherds and academics; the main quibble is her success in making Évvia seem more interesting than it really is.

Older accounts

★ James Theodore Bent *Aegean Islands: The Cyclades, or Life Among the Insular Greeks* (Argonaut, US, o/p, but available through Hellenic Bookservice in A4 format). Originally published in 1881, this remains the best account of island customs and folklore; it's also a highly readable, droll account of a year's Aegean travel, including a particularly violent Cycladic winter.

Edward Lear *The Corfu Years* (Denise Harvey, Límni, Évvia). Superbly illustrated journals by the nonsense versifier and noted landscape painter, whose watercolours and sketches of Corfu, Paxí and elsewhere offer a rare glimpse of the Ionian archipelago during the nineteenth century. *The Cretan Journal* (same imprint) will also be of interest.

★ Terence Spencer *Fair Greece, Sad Relic: Literary Philhellenism from Shakespeare to Byron* (Denise Harvey, Límni, available in UK; Scholarly Press). Masterfully traces how the scribblings of poets steeped in the classics, culminating in Byron, and the accounts of early travellers to what's now Greece, gradually fuelled European support for the 1821 Revolution – despite the misgivings of many of them about the contemporary Greeks themselves. Also demonstrates just how old the Zorba stereotype is (the feckless, "merrie Greeke" is already described in the 1500s).

Richard Stoneman, ed *A Literary Companion to Travel in Greece* (Getty Centre for the History of Art and the Humanities, US). Ancient and medieval authors, plus Grand Tourists – good for dipping into.

The classics

Many of the classics make excellent companion reading for a trip around Greece – especially the historians Thucydides and Herodotus. Reading Homer's *Odyssey* when you're battling with or resigning yourself to the vagaries of island ferries puts your own plight into perspective.

Most of the standard undergraduate staples are part of the Penguin Classics paperback series. Routledge and Duckworth both also have a huge, steadily expanding backlist of Classical Studies, though many titles are expensive and quite specialized.

Herodotus *The Histories* (Penguin), or A.D. Godley, tr (Cambridge UP). Revered as the father of systematic history and anthropology, this fifth-century BC Anatolian writer chronicled both the causes and campaigns of the Persian Wars, as well as the contemporary, assorted tribes and nations inhabiting Asia Minor.

Homer *The Iliad; The Odyssey*. The first concerns itself, semi-factually, with the late Bronze Age war of the Achaeans against Troy in Asia Minor; the second recounts the hero Odysseus's long journey home, via seemingly every corner of the Mediterranean. For a verse rendition, ▣ Richmond Lattimore's translation (University of Chicago, *Iliad*;

HarperCollins, *Odyssey*) has yet to be bettered. For a prose rendition, ▣ Martin Hammond's *Iliad* (Penguin) and *Odyssey* (Duckworth, UK) currently edge out second-best choices by the father-and-son team of E.V. Rieu (*Iliad*, Penguin) and D.C.H. Rieu (*Odyssey*, Penguin).

Ovid *The Metamorphoses*, A.D. Melville, tr (Oxford UP). Though collected by a first-century AD Roman poet, this remains one of the most accessible renditions of the more piquant Greek myths, involving transformations as divine blessing or curse. Ted Hughes' version, *Tales of Ovid*, catches the poetic flavour (Faber & Faber).

Plutarch *The Age of Alexander*; *On Sparta*; *The Rise and Fall of Athens*

(Penguin). Another ancient author, writing perhaps with the benefit of hindsight, but with the disadvantage of unreliable sources and much conjecture.

▣ **Thucydides** *History of the Peloponnesian War* (Penguin). Bleak month-by-month account of the conflict, by a cashiered Athenian officer whose affiliation and dim view of human nature didn't usually obscure his objectivity; see George Cawkwell's book (below) for a revisionist view.

Xenophon *The History of My Times* (Penguin). Thucydides' account of the Peloponnesian War stops in 411 BC; this work continues events until 362 BC.

Ancient history and interpretation of the classics

▣ **Mary Beard and John Henderson** *The Classics: a Very Short Introduction* (Oxford UP). As it says; an excellent overview.

▣ **A.R. Burn** *History of Greece* (Penguin). Probably the best general introduction to ancient Greece, though for fuller analysis you'll do better with one or other of the following more specialized titles.

Paul Cartlege *Cambridge Illustrated History of Ancient Greece* (Cambridge UP). Large-format, pricey volume packed with information useful for both novices and experts.

George Cawkwell *Thucydides and the Peloponnesian War* (Routledge). Recent, revisionist overview of Thucydides' work and relations with main personalities of the war, challenging previous assumptions of his infallibility.

▣ **M.I. Finley** *The World of Odysseus* (Pimlico, UK). The latest reprint of a 1954 warhorse, pioneering in its investigation of the historicity (or otherwise) of the events and society related by Homer. Breezily readable and stimulating, with prejudices apparent rather than subtle.

Michael Grant and John Hazel *Who's Who in Classical Mythology* (Routledge). A gazetteer of over 1200 mythological personalities, together with historical and geographical background.

▣ **Pierre Grimal, ed** *Dictionary of Classical Mythology* (Penguin). Though translated from the French, still considered to have the edge on the more recent Grant/Hazel title.

Simon Hornblower *The Greek World 479–323 BC* (Routledge). An erudite survey of ancient Greece at its zenith, from the end of the Persian Wars to the death of Alexander; now a standard university paperback text.

John Kenyon Davies *Democracy and Classical Greece* (Fontana; Harvard UP). An established and accessible account of the Classical period and its political developments.

Robin Lane Fox *Alexander the Great* (Penguin). An absorbing study, which mixes historical scholarship with imaginative psychological detail.

Oswyn Murray *Early Greece* (Fontana; Harvard UP). The Greek story from the Mycenaeans and Minoans through to the beginning of the Classical period.

Robin Osborne *Greece in the Making 1200–479 BC* (Routledge). A well-illustrated paperback on the rise of the city-state.

John Purkis *Teach Yourself Classical Civilisation* (Teach Yourself Books). A nice, succinct introduction to the subject.

Tony Spawforth *Greece, an Oxford Archaeological Guide* (Oxford UP). An interpretative guide, by the co-author, with Simon Hornblower, of the also-recommended *Oxford Classical Dictionary* (Oxford UP).

F.W. Walbank *The Hellenistic World* (Fontana; Harvard UP). Greece under the sway of the Macedonian and Roman empires.

Ancient religion

Harry Brewster *River Gods of Greece* (I.B. Tauris; St Martin's). Most ancient rivers had a deity associated with them; here are the cults and legends.

★ **Walter Burkert** *Greek Religion: Archaic and Classical* (Blackwell). A superb overview of deities and their attributes and antecedents, rites, the protocol of sacrifice and the symbolism of major festivals; especially good on relating Greek worship to its predecessors in the Middle East.

Matthew Dillon *Pilgrims and Pilgrimage in Ancient Greece* (Routledge). A pricey hardback exploring not only the main sanctuaries such as Delphi, but also minor oracles, the role of women and children and the secular festivities attending the rites.

Nano Marinatos and Robin Hagg *Greek Sanctuaries: New Approaches* (Routledge). The form and function of the temples, in the light of recent scholarship.

Food and wine

Rosemary Barron *Flavours of Greece* (Grub Street, UK). Probably the leading cookbook among many contenders, by an internationally recognized authority on Greek cui-

sine. Contains over 250 recipes.

Andrew Dalby *Siren Feasts* (Routledge). Subtitled *A history of food and gastronomy in Greece*, this analysis of ancient texts demonstrates just how little Greek cuisine has changed in three millennia; also excellent on the introduction and etymology of common vegetables and herbs.

⭐ **Alan Davidson** *Mediterranean Seafood* (Penguin, o/p). A 1972 classic, periodically reprinted, this amazingly erudite and witty book catalogues (almost) all known edible species, complete with legends, anecdotes, habits, local names and a suggested recipe or two for each.

⭐ **James Davidson** *Courtesans and Fishcakes* (HarperCollins, UK). The politics, class characteristics and etiquette of consumption and consummation – with wine, women, boys and seafood – in ancient Athens, with their bearing on both historical events and modern attitudes.

⭐ **Nico Manessis** *The Illustrated Greek Wine Book* (Olive Press

Publications, Corfu; available at select retailers in Greece or through Ⓦ www.greekwineguide.gr). Covers almost all the wineries, from mass-market to micro, with very reliable ratings; also fascinating features on grape varieties, traditional retsina-making, and even how Greeks were instrumental in introducing vines to the New World. Pricey but worth it.

Nikos Stavroulakis *Cookbook of the Jews of Greece* (Lycabettus Press, Athens; Cadmus Press, US). Tasty recipes interspersed with their rela-tion to the Jewish liturgical year, plus potted histories of the communities which produced them. There have been murmurings, however, that many of the recipes emanate from one sub-group – the ex-Jewish Ma'min of Thessaloníki.

300 Traditional Greek Recipes (Grecocard, Greece). As it says; the best of a huge pile of glossy pictorial cookbooks pitched at the tourist market.

Archeology and art

John Beckwith *Early Christian and Byzantine Art* (Yale UP). Illustrated study placing Byzantine art within a wider context.

William R. Biers *Archeology of Greece: An Introduction* (Cornell UP, US). A 1990s–revised and excellent standard text.

⭐ **John Boardman** *Greek Art* (Thames & Hudson, UK). A very good concise introduction: part of the "World of Art" series.

Reynold Higgins *Minoan and Mycenaean Art* (Thames & Hudson). A clear, well-illustrated round-up.

Sinclair Hood *The Arts in Prehistoric Greece* (Penguin; Yale UP). A sound introduction to the subject.

Roger Ling *Classical Greece* (Phaidon, UK). Another useful illustrated introduction.

Colin Renfrew *The Cycladic Spirit* (Thames & Hudson; Abrams). A fine, illustrated study of the meaning and purpose of Cycladic artefacts.

Gisela Richter *A Handbook of Greek Art* (Phaidon; Da Capo). An exhaustive survey of the visual arts of ancient Greece.

William St Clair *Lord Elgin and the Marbles* (Oxford UP). The latest word on the vicissitudes of the statues whose ownership remains hotly disputed.

R.R.R. Smith *Hellenistic Sculpture* (Thames & Hudson). A modern reappraisal of the art of Greece under Alexander and his successors.

David Talbot Rice *Art of the Byzantine Era* (Thames & Hudson). Talbot Rice was, with Robert Byron, one of the pioneering scholars in the "rediscovery" of Byzantine art; this is an accessible illustrated study.

Peter Warren *The Aegean Civilizations* (Phaidon, o/p; P. Bedrick Books, o/p). An illustrated account of the Minoan and Mycenaean cultures.

"Coffee-table" books

William Abramowicz *The Greek File: Images of a Mythic Land* (Rizzoli). An obstinately nostalgic black-and-white look at the country in the 1980s, by this veteran Condé Nast photographer; the main complaint is it fails to take on board the vast changes that had swept through Greece since Manos's pioneering work (see below).

Chris Hellier *Monasteries of Greece* (Tauris Parke; St Martin's). A magnificently photographed survey of the surviving, active monasteries, including the one on Pátmos, and their treasures, with insightful accompanying essays.

Constantine Manos *A Greek Portfolio* (W. W. Norton). A long-awaited, reasonably priced reissue of a 1972 classic: the fruits of a gifted Greek American photographer's three-year odyssey in the early Sixties through a country on the edge of modernization, still essentially unchanged from the 1930s. The quality and insight you'd expect from a member of the Magnum cooperative, in elegiac black-and-white photos, strong on Crete and Kárpathos.

Mark Ottaway *The Most Beautiful Villages of Greece* (Thames and Hudson, UK). Not exhaustively inclusive, but easily available and with good photos by Hugh Palmer.

Clay Perry *Vanishing Greece* (Conran Octopus; Abbeville Press, both o/p). Well-captioned photos depict the threatened landscapes and relict ways of life in rural Greece; plenty of paperback copies floating around Greece.

Suzanne Slesin et al. *Greek Style* (Thames & Hudson; Crown). Stunning (if sometimes contrived) designer-tweaked interiors from Corfu, Rhodes and Sérifos, among other spots.

Janine Trotereau *Greece from the Air* (Thames & Hudson). A translation of a French-issued work, with photos by Yann Arthus.

CONTEXTS | Books

Byzantine, medieval and Ottoman history

Averil Cameron *The Mediterranean World in Late Antiquity, AD 395–600* (Routledge). Essentially the early Byzantine years.

Nicholas Cheetham *Medieval Greece* (Yale UP, o/p in US). A general survey of the period and its infinite convolutions in Greece, with Frankish, Catalan, Venetian, Byzantine and Ottoman struggles for power.

John Julius Norwich *Byzantium: The Early Centuries; Byzantium: the Apogee* and *Byzantium: The Decline* (all Penguin; Viking-Knopf). Perhaps the main surprise for first-time travellers to Greece is the fascination of Byzantine monuments, above all at Mystrás. This is an astonishingly detailed yet readable trilogy, also available in one fat volume as ✴ *A Short History of Byzantium* (Penguin).

★ **Vangelis Pavlidis** *Rhodes 1306–1522: A Story* (Rodos Image, Rhodes). A caricature-illustrated history of the Knights of St John's occupation of Rhodes, by one of Greece's leading political car-toonists, but this isn't tourist pap – rigorous research and witty text illuminate a little-known era in the Dodecanese.

Michael Psellus *Fourteen Byzantine Rulers* (Penguin). A fascinating contemporary source on the stormy but brilliant period from 976 to 1078.

Steven Runciman ✴ *The Fall of Constantinople, 1453* (Canto-Cambridge UP) is the standard account of the event; *The Great Church in Captivity* (Cambridge UP) follows the vicissitudes of the Orthodox Patriarchate in Constantinople up to the War of Independence. *Byzantine Style and Civilization* (Penguin, o/p in US) and *Mistra* (Thames & Hudson, o/p in US) are more slanted towards art, culture and monuments.

★ **Bishop Kallistos (Timothy) Ware** *The Orthodox Church* (Penguin). A good introduction to what is effectively the established religion of Greece, by the Orthodox bishop resident in Oxford.

Modern Greece

Timothy Boatswain and Colin Nicolson *A Traveller's History of Greece* (Windrush Press; Interlink). Dated (coverage ceases in early 1990s) but well-written overview of the important Greek periods and personalities.

David Brewer *The Flame of Freedom: The Greek War of Independence 1821–1833* (John Murray, UK). A newish history with just a few black-and-white illustrations.

★ **Richard Clogg** *A Concise History of Greece* (Cambridge UP). A remarkably clear and well-illustrated account of Greece, from the decline of Byzantium to 1992, with the emphasis on recent decades; there are numerous maps and lengthy feature captions to the artwork.

Douglas Dakin *The Unification of Greece, 1770–1923* (Ernest Benn; St Martin's, both o/p). A benchmark account of the foundation of the Greek state and the struggle to extend its boundaries.

★ **Oriana Falacci** *A Man* (Arrow; Pocket Books, o/p). A gripping account of the junta years, relating the author's involvement with Alekos Panagoulis, the army officer who attempted to assassinate Colonel Papadopoulos in 1968. Issued ostensibly as a "novel" in response to threats by those who were implicated in Panagoulis's own murder in 1975.

★ **H.A. Lidderdale, trs and ed** *The Memoirs of General Makriyannis, 1797–1864* (Oxford UP, o/p). The "Peasant General", one of the few honest and self-sacrificing protagonists of the Greek uprising, taught himself to write at age 32 to set down this apologia of his conduct, in vivid demotic Greek. It's heartbreaking in its portrayal of the incipient schisms, linguistic and otherwise, that tore the country apart until recently.

★ **Michael Llewellyn Smith** *Ionian Vision, Greece in Asia Minor, 1919–22* (C. Hurst; University of Michigan). A standard work, by the former UK ambassador to Greece, on the disastrous Anatolian campaign, which led to the exchange of populations between Greece and Turkey. His account evinces considerable sympathy for the post-1920 royalist government pursuing an unwanted, inherited war they knew was unwinnable.

Yiannis Roubatis *Tangled Webs: The US in Greece 1947–67* (Pella Publishing, US). Chronicles growing American involvement in Greece during the lead-up to the military coup.

Peter Varoulakis *The Greek War of Independence* (Hellenic International Press). A nice counterweight to the Brewer work, with lots of colour reproductions of famous scenes, with far less text.

C.M. Woodhouse *Modern Greece, A Short History* (Faber & Faber). Woodhouse was active in the Greek Resistance during World War II. Writing from a more right-wing perspective than Clogg, this history (from the foundation of Constantinople in 324 to the 1980s), is briefer and a bit drier, but scrupulous with facts. *The Rise and Fall of the Greek Colonels* (Granada, o/p; Watts) recounts the (horror) story of the dictatorship.

World War II and its aftermath

★ **David H. Close** *The Origins of the Greek Civil War* (Longman, o/p). An excellent, readable study that focuses on the social conditions in 1920s and 1930s Greece that made the country so ripe for conflict. Draws on primary sources, slays a few sacred cows along the way and is relatively objective (though he's no great fan of the Left).

★ **Iakovos Kambanellis** *Mauthausen* (Kedros, Athens; Central Books, UK). Náxos native Kambanellis was active in the Resistance, caught by the Germans and sent to Mauthausen, the concentration camp reserved for those politicians or partisans who had opposed the Nazis' rise to power. Harrowing atrocities in flashback there are a-plenty, but the main thrust of the book is post-liberation, describing the author's awkward romance with a Lithuanian Jew, and how the idealist inmates are slowly disillusioned as they see that the "New World Order" will be scarcely different from the old. The basis of a play and of the Theodhorakis oratorio of the same name.

★ **Mark Mazower** *Inside Hitler's Greece: The Experience of Occupation* 1941–44 (Yale UP). Somewhat choppily organized, but the standard of scholarship is high and the photos alone justify the price, though there's not a great deal specifically on the islands. Demonstrates how the complete demoralization of the country and the incompetence of conventional politicians led to the rise of ELAS and the onset of civil war. The sequel to this is *After the War was Over: Reconstructing the Family and State in Greece, 1943–1960*

(Princeton UP), consisting of scholarly articles on various aspects of Greece in the period specified.

Marion Sarafis and Martin Eve (eds) *Background to Contemporary Greece, vols 1 & 2* (Merlin, UK). Useful, not overly academic essays on a wide variety of subjects, from the death of *katharévoussa* to (especially) the civil war; a mild left-wing bias, not surprising since Sarafis was the (English) widow of DSE commander Stefanos Sarafis.

Adrian Seligman *War in the Islands* (Alan Sutton, UK). Collected oral histories of a little-known Allied unit: a flotilla of kaïkia organized to raid the Axis-held Aegean islands. Boy's Own stuff, with service-jargon-laced prose, but lots of fine period photos and detail.

C.M. Woodhouse *The Struggle for Greece, 1941–49* (Hart-Davis, o/p; Beekman). A masterly and by no means uncritical account of this crucial decade, explaining how Greece emerged without a Communist government.

Ethnography

★ **Juliet du Boulay** *Portrait of a Greek Mountain Village* (Oxford UP, o/p; Denise Harvey, Límni, Évvia). An account of the village of Ambéli, on Évvia, during the 1960s. The habits and customs of an all-but-vanished way of life are observed and evoked in an absorbing narrative.

★ **Loring Danforth and Alexander Tsiaras** *The Death Rituals of Rural Greece* (Princeton UP). Many visitors find Greek funeral customs – the wailing, the

open-casket vigils, the disinterment after three years – the most disturbing aspect of the culture; this book helps make sense of them.

★ **Gail Holst-Warhaft** *Road to Rembetika: Songs of Love, Sorrow and Hashish* (Denise Harvey, Límni, Évvia; available in the UK). The most intriguing Greek urban musical style of the past century, evocatively traced by a Cornell University professor; useful discography has been updated to the mid-1990s.

York; o/p). Exactly as the title states, and still highly applicable a century after its writing; well worth scouring libraries and antiquarian dealers for.

Modern Greek fiction

Roderick Beaton *An Introduction to Modern Greek Literature* (Oxford UP). A chronological survey of fiction and poetry from Independence to the early 1990s, with a useful discussion on the "Language Question".

✩ **Maro Douka** *Fool's Gold* (Kedros, Athens; Central Books, UK). Describes an upper-class young woman's involvement, and subsequent disillusionment, with the clandestine resistance to the junta.

✩ **Apostolos Doxiades** *Uncle Petros and the Goldbach Conjecture* (Faber & Faber, UK). Self-translated from the Greek; an excellent read despite the mathematical puzzle at the heart of the novel.

Eugenia Fakinou *The Seventh Garment* (Serpent's Tail). Greek history, from the War of Independence to the colonels' junta, told through the life stories (interspersed in counterpoint) of three generations of women; a rather more successful experiment than Fakinou's *Astradeni* (Kedros, Athens; Central Books, UK), in which a young girl – whose slightly irritating narrative voice is adopted throughout – leaves the island of Sými, with all its traditional values, for Athens.

Nikos Kazantzakis Whether in intricate Greek or translated into inadequate English, Kazantzakis can be hard going, yet the power of his writing still shines through. *Zorba the Greek* is a surprisingly dark, nihilistic work, worlds away from the two-dimensional characters of the film. On the other hand, the movie version of *The Last Temptation of Christ* provoked riots amongst Orthodox fanatics in Athens in 1989. *Christ Recrucified* (published in the US as *The Greek Passion*) resets the Easter drama against the backdrop of Christian/Muslim relations on nineteenth-century Crete, while *Freedom or Death* (published in the US as *Captain Michalis*) chronicles the rebellions of late nineteenth-century Crete. The *Fratricides* portrays a family riven by the civil war, while *Report to Greco* – perhaps the most accessible of his works – is an autobiographical exploration of his Cretanness/Greekness (all Faber & Faber; Touchstone).

✩ **Artemis Leontis, ed** *Greece: A Traveller's Literary Companion* (Whereabouts Press, San Francisco, US). An overdue idea, brilliantly executed: various regions of the country as portrayed in (very) short fiction or essays by modern Greek writers. A recommended antidote to the often condescending Grand Tourist accounts.

Stratis Myrivilis ⊡ *Life in the Tomb* (Quartet; New England UP). A harrowing and unorthodox war memoir, based on the author's experience on the Macedonian front during 1917–18, well translated by Peter Bien. Completing a kind of trilogy are two later novels, set on the north coast of Lésvos, Myrivilis's homeland: *The Mermaid Madonna* and *The Schoolmistress with the Golden Eyes*

(Efstathiadis, Athens). Translations of these are not so good, and tend to be heavily abridged.

Alexandhros Papadiamantis *The Murderess* (Writers & Readers). A landmark novel set on the island of Skiáthos at the beginning of the last century, in which an old woman, appalled by the fate that awaits them in adulthood, concludes that little girls are better off dead. Also available is a collection of short stories, *Tales from a Greek Island* (Johns Hopkins UP).

★ **Nick Papandreou** *Father Dancing* (Penguin). Thinly veiled roman à clef by the late Andreas's younger son. Papandreou Senior, not too surprisingly, comes across as a gasbag and petty domestic tyrant.

Yannis Ritsos *Iconostasis of Anonymous Saints* (Kedros, Athens; Central Books, London). The first three instalments of a projected nine-volume autobiographical novel. The "anonymous saints" are the characters of these vaguely sequential vignettes. Book 1, *Ariostos the Observant*, written during World War II, is, depending on your viewpoint, either a surrealist masterpiece or self-indulgent rubbish; Book 2, *Such Strange Things*, and Book 3, *With a Nudge of the Elbow*, are more straightforwardly based on Ritsos's peers and life events.

★ **Dido Sotiriou** *Farewell Anatolia* (Kedros, Athens; Central Books, London). A perennial favourite since its initial appearance in 1962, this epic chronicles the traumatic end of Greek life in Asia Minor, from World War I to the catastrophe of 1922, as narrated by a fictionalized version of the author's father. In the finale, he escapes across the narrow strait of Mykale to Sámos, as so many did during those turbulent years.

★ **Stratis Tsirkas** *Drifting Cities* (Kedros, Athens; Central Books, London). Set by turns in the Jerusalem, Cairo and Alexandria of World War II, this unflinchingly honest and humane epic of a Greek army hero secretly working for the leftist Resistance got the author expelled from the Communist Party.

Vassilis Vassilikos *Z* (Four Walls Eight Windows). A novel based closely enough on events – the 1963 political assassination of Gregoris Lambrakis in Thessaloníki – to be banned under the colonels' junta, and brilliantly filmed by Costa-Gavras in 1968.

★ **Alki Zei** *Achilles' Fiancée* (Kedros, Athens; Central Books, London). An often moving portrait of the friendships and intrigues amongst a collection of Communist exiles floating between Athens, Rome, Moscow, Paris and Tashkent in the years between the civil war and the colonels' junta. Largely autobiographical, it captures the flavour of the illusions, nostalgia and party-line schisms endemic in this community.

Greece in foreign fiction

★ **Louis de Bernières** *Captain Corelli's Mandolin* (Minerva; Random House). Set on Kefalloniá during the World War II occupation, this accomplished 1994 tragicomedy quickly acquired cult, then word-of-mouth bestseller status, but has lately become a *succès de scandale*. When the islanders, Greek Left intellectuals and surviving Italian partisans woke up to its virulent anti-Communism and disparaging portrayal of ELAS, there was a furore, with de Bernières eventually obliged to eat large quantities of humble pie in the UK press. It also seems the novel is closely based on the experiences of still-alive-and-kicking Amos Pampaloni, an artillery captain on Kefalloniá in 1942–44 who later joined ELAS, and who accuses de Bernières of distorting the roles of both Italians and ELAS on the island. The Greek translation has been suitably abridged to avoid causing offence, and the Big Movie (starring Nicholas Cage and Penelope Cruz), watered down to a pallid love story as a condition for filming on the island, sank without trace after a few weeks in 2001.

John Fowles *The Magus* (Vintage; Dell). Fowles's biggest and best novel: a tale of mystery and manipulation – plus Greek island life –

inspired by his stay on Spétses as a teacher in the 1950s.

Mary Renault *The King Must Die*; *The Last of the Wine*; *The Mask of Apollo* (Sceptre; Random House) and others (all Penguin). Mary Renault's imaginative reconstructions are more than the adolescent's reading they're often taken for, with impeccable research and tight writing. The trio above retell, respectively, the myth of Theseus, the life of a pupil of Socrates and that of a fourth-century BC actor. The life of Alexander the Great is told in *Fire from Heaven*, *The Persian Boy* and *Funeral Games*, available separately or in one economical volume.

Evelyn Waugh *Officers and Gentleman* (Penguin). This volume of the wartime trilogy includes an account of the Battle of Crete and subsequent evacuation.

Modern Greek poetry

With two Nobel laureates in recent years – George Seferis and Odysseus Elytis – modern Greece has an extraordinarily intense and dynamic poetic tradition. Translations of all of the following are excellent.

C.P. Cavafy *Collected Poems* (Chatto & Windus; Princeton UP). The complete works, translated by Edmund Keeley and Philip Sherrard, of perhaps the most accessible modern Greek poet, resident for most of his life in Alexandria. For some, *The Complete Poems of Cavafy* (Harcourt Brace Jovanovich), translated by Rae Dalven, or *The Poems of C.P. Cavafy* by John Mavrogordato (Chatto & Windus, UK) are superior versions.

Odysseus Elytis *The Axion Esti* (Anvil Press; Pittsburgh UP); *Selected Poems* (Anvil Press; Viking Penguin, o/p); The *Sovereign Sun* (Bloodaxe

Books; Temple UP, Philadelphia, o/p). The major works in good English versions. Easier to find is *Collected Poems* (Johns Hopkins UP), which includes virtually everything except *The Axion Esti*.

Modern Greek Poetry (Efstathiadis, Athens). Despite the publisher's reputation for shoddy work, this in fact is a decent anthology of translations, predominantly of Seferis and Elytis.

Yannis Ritsos *Exile and Return, Selected Poems 1967–1974* (Anvil Press; Ecco Press). A fine volume of

Greece's foremost leftist poet, from the junta era when he was internally exiled on Sámos.

George Seferis *Collected Poems, 1924–1955* (Anvil Press, o/p; Princeton UP, o/p). Virtually the complete works of the Nobel laureate, with Greek and English verses on facing pages. More recent, but lacking the parallel Greek text, is *Complete Poems* (Anvil Press; Princeton UP).

Specific guides

Archeology

★ **A.R. and Mary Burn** *The Living Past of Greece: A Time Traveller's Tour of Historic and Prehistoric Places* (Herbert Press; HarperCollins). Unusual in extent, this covers sites from Minoan through to Byzantine and Frankish, with good clear plans and lively text.

★ **Paul Hetherington** *The Greek Islands: Guide to Byzantine and Medieval Buildings and their Art* (Quiller, UK). Equally good follow-up to his mainland-only *Byzantine and Medieval Greece: Churches, Castles and Art* (John Murray), with more illustrations.

Evi Melas, ed *Temples and Sanctuaries of Ancient Greece: A Companion Guide* (Thames & Hudson, o/p). An excellent collection of essays on the main sites, written by archeologists who have worked at them.

Alexander Paradissis *Fortresses and Castles of Greece* (Efstathiadis, Athens). Three exhaustive and extremely prolix volumes, widely available in Greek bookshops.

Hiking

★ **Lance Chilton** Various walking pamphlets (Marengo Publications, UK). Small but thorough guides to the best walks at various mainland and island charter resorts, accompanied by three-colour maps. Areas covered to date include: Áyios Yeóryios, Corfu; Yeoryioúpolis and Plakiás, Crete; Stoúpa, Peloponnese; the central Pelion peninsula; the Párga area; Líndhos, Rhodes; Kokkári, Sámos; and Sými. In specialist UK shops or by mail order; catalogue from 17 Bernard Crescent, Hunstanton PE36 6ER (☎ & ℻ 01485/532710, ℮ marengo@supanet.com).

Marc Dubin *Trekking in Greece* (Lonely Planet; o/p). Though many sections are showing their age (and the depredations of bulldozers), still an excellent walkers' guide, expanding on the hikes covered in this book. Includes day-hikes and longer treks, plus extensive preparatory and background information.

Loraine Wilson *The White Mountains of Crete* (Cicerone Press; Hunter). Nearly sixty walks and treks from easy to gruelling by the doyenne of foreign trekking guides in Crete; implicitly trustworthy directions and prudent warnings. Marred only by rudimentary maps (buy the Harms series) and rather bizarre transliterations of Greek phrases.

Regional guides

Johan de Bakker *Across Crete* (World Discovery Guide Books, Netherlands). A superb first volume (central Crete) of three-part coverage of Crete, assessing the modern sites in comparison with accounts by eighteenth- and nineteenth-century travellers. Vols. 2/3, East/West Crete, due late 2002.

Marc Dubin *The Rough Guide to the Dodecanese and the East Aegean* (Penguin). Exhaustive coverage of the islands described in Chapters Nine and Ten of this book, by a part-time resident of Sámos.

John Fisher and Geoff Garvey *The Rough Guide to Crete* (Penguin). An expanded and practical guide to the island by two Cretophiles, who contributed the Crete chapter to this book.

Lycabettus Press Guides (Athens, Greece). This series takes in several of the more popular islands; most volumes, despite decade-long intervals between revisions, pay their way in interests and usefulness – in particular those on Páros, Kós, Pátmos, Ídhra and the travels of Saint Paul.

Oliver Rackham and Jennifer Moody *The Making of the Cretan Landscape* (Manchester UP; St Martin's). It's hard to classify this academic-press product written for the casual visitor. As the title says, but much more, taking in geology, natural history, agricultural practices, place names, architecture and demography, all arranged by topic. Not error-free – nothing this ambitious could be – but impressive.

Nikos Stavroulakis *Jewish Sites and Synagogues of Greece* (Talos Press, Athens). A lavishly illustrated alphabetical gazetteer of all Jewish monuments in Greece, with town plans and full histories of the communities that created them. A few have been demolished since publication, however.

Bookshops

Athens has a number of excellent bookshops, at which many of the recommendations above should be available (at fifty percent mark-up for foreign-published titles). In London, the Hellenic Bookservice, 91 Fortess Rd, Kentish Town, London NW5 1AG (☎020/7267 9499, ℗7267 9498, 🌐www.hellenicbookservice.com), is the UK's premier walk-in Greek bookshop: knowledgeable and well-stocked specialist dealers in new, secondhand and out-of-print books. Rivals Zeno's have premises at 57A Nether St, North Finchley, London N12 7NP (☎020/8446 1985, 🌐www.the-greekbookstore.com).

Yachting

H.M. Denham *The Aegean; The Ionian Islands to the Anatolian Coast* (John Murray, UK, o/p). Long the standard references if you were out yachting; still found in secondhand bookshops, but a bit obsolete.

Rod Heikell *Greek Waters Pilot* (Imray, Laurie, Norrie and Wilson, UK). Rather better than the preceding, which it has superseded.

language

language

Learning basic Greek..613

Greek alphabet: transliteration..614

Greek words and phrases...615

A food and drink glossary...619

Katharévoussa, dhimotikí and dialects...................................622

A glossary of recurrent words and terms 624

Language

So many Greeks have lived or worked abroad in North America, Australia and, to a much lesser extent, Britain, that you will find someone who speaks English in the tiniest island village. Add to that the thousands attending language schools or working in the tourist industry – English is the lingua franca of most resorts, with German second – and it is easy to see how so many visitors come back having learned only half a dozen restaurant words.

You can certainly get by this way, but it isn't very satisfying, and the willingness and ability to say even a few words will transform your status from that of dumb *tourístas* to the more honourable one of *xénos/xéni*, a word which can mean foreigner, traveller and guest all rolled into one.

Learning basic Greek

Greek is not an easy language for English-speakers – translators' unions in the UK rate it as harder than German, slightly less complex than Russian – but it is a very beautiful one, and even a brief acquaintance will give you some idea of the debt owed to it by Western European languages.

Language-learning materials

Teach-yourself Greek courses

Breakthrough Greek (Pan Macmillan; book and four cassettes). Excellent, basic teach-yourself course; no Greek lettering, but good for classicists who need to unlearn bad habits.

Greek Language and People (BBC Publications, UK; book and two cassettes available). More limited in scope but good for acquiring the essentials, and the confidence to try them.

Anne Farmakides *A Manual of Modern Greek* (Yale UP; McGill UP; 3 vols). If you have the discipline and motivation, this is one of the best for learning proper, grammatical Greek; indeed, mastery of just the first volume will get you a long way.

Hara Garoufalia *Teach Yourself Holiday Greek* (Hodder & Stoughton, UK; book and cassette available). Unlike many quickie courses, this provides a good grammatical foundation, but you'll need a dictionary (see below) to supplement the scanty vocabulary lists.

Niki Watts *Greek in Three Months* (Hugo, Dorling Kindersley; book and four cassettes). Delivers as promised; equals or exceeds *Breakthrough Greek*.

Phrasebooks

Greek, a Rough Guide Phrasebook (Penguin, UK & US). Up-to-date and accurate pocket phrasebook not full of "*plume de ma tante*"-type expressions. The English-to-Greek section is sensibly transliterated, though the Greek-to-English part requires basic mastery of the Greek alphabet. Feature boxes fill you in on dos and don'ts and cultural know-how.

The Oxford Dictionary of Modern Greek (Oxford UP, UK & US). A bit bulky in its wide format, but generally considered the best Greek–English, English–Greek paperback dictionary.

Collins Pocket Greek Dictionary (HarperCollins, UK & US). Very nearly as complete as the Oxford and probably better value for money. The inexpensive Collins Gem Greek Dictionary (UK only) is palm-sized but exactly the same in contents – the best day-pack choice.

Oxford Greek–English, English–Greek Learner's Dictionary (Oxford UP, UK & US). If you're planning a prolonged stay, this pricey, hardbound, two-volume set is unbeatable for usage and vocabulary. There's also a more portable one-volume Learner's Pocket Dictionary.

The Greek alphabet: transliteration

On top of the usual difficulties of learning a new language, Greek presents the additional problem of an entirely separate **alphabet**. Despite initial appearances, this is in practice fairly easily mastered – a skill that will help enormously if you are going to get around independently. In addition, certain combinations of letters have unexpected results. This book's transliteration system should help you make intelligible noises, but you have to remember that the correct **stress** (marked throughout the book with an acute accent or sometimes dieresis) is crucial. With the right sounds but the wrong stress people will either fail to understand you, or else understand something quite different from what you intended – there are numerous pairs of words with the same spelling and phonemes, distinguished only by their stress (the classic, naughty example is *gámo*, "a wedding", versus *gamó*, "I fuck").

Set out below is the Greek alphabet, the system of transliteration used in this book and a brief aid to pronunciation.

Greek	Transliteration	Pronounced
Α, α	a	a as in father
Β, β	v	v as in vet
Γ, γ	y/g	y as in yes except before consonants or a, o or oi when it's a breathy g, approximately as in gap
Δ, δ	dh	th as in then
Ε, ε	e	e as in get
Ζ, ζ	z	z sound
Η, η	i	i as in ski
Θ, θ	th	th as in theme
Ι, ι	i	i as in ski
Κ, κ	k	k sound
Λ, λ	l	l sound
Μ, μ	m	m sound
Ν, ν	n	n sound
Ξ, ξ	x	x sound, never z
Ο, ο	o	o as in toad
Π, π	p	p sound
Ρ, ρ	r	r sound

Σ, σ, ς	s	s sound, except z before m or g; note that single sigma has the same phonic value as double sigma
T, τ	t	t sound
Y, υ	y	y as in barel*y*
Φ, φ	f	f sound
X, χ	h before vowels, kh before consonants	harsh h sound, like ch in lo*ch*
Ψ, ψ	ps	ps as in li*ps*
Ω, ω	o	o as in t*o*ad, indistinguishable from o

Diphthongs and combinations

AI, αι	e	e as in h*e*y
AY, αυ	av/af	av or af depending on following consonant
EI, ει	i	long i, exactly like i or h
EY, ευ	ev/ef	ev or ef, depending on following consonant
OI, οι	i	long i, exactly like i or h
OY, ου	ou	ou as in t*ou*rist
ΓΓ, γγ	ng	ng as in a*ng*le; always medial
ΓΚ, γκ	g/ng	g as in *g*oat at the beginning of a word, ng in the middle
ΜΠ, μπ	b/mb	b at the beginning of a word, mb in the middle
NT, ντ	d/nd	d at the beginning of a word, nd in the middle
ΤΣ, τσ	ts	ts as in hi*ts*
ΤΖ, τζ	tz	dg as in ju*dg*e, j as in *j*am in some dialects

Note on diereses

The dieresis is used in Greek over the second of two adjacent vowels to change the pronunciation that you would expect from the preceding table; often in this book it can function as the primary stress. In the word *kaïki* (caique), the presence of the dieresis changes the pronunciation from "cake-key" to "ka-ee-key" and additionally the middle "i" carries the primary stress. In the word *païdhákia* (lamb chops), the dieresis again changes the sound of the first syllable from "pay" to "pah-ee", but in this case the primary stress is on the third syllable. It is also, uniquely among Greek accents, used on capital letters in signs and personal-name spellings in Greece, and we have followed this practice on our maps.

Greek words and phrases

Greek **grammar** is more complicated still: nouns are divided into three genders, all with different case endings in the singular and in the plural, and all adjectives and articles have to agree with these in gender, number and case. (All adjectives are arbitrarily cited in the neuter form in the boxed lists.) Verbs are even more complex; they come in two conjugations, in both active and passive voices, with passively constructed verbs often having transitive sense (and you thought learning the alphabet was bad). To begin with at least, the best thing is simply to say what you know the way you know it, and never mind the niceties. "Eat meat hungry" should get a result, however grammatically incorrect. If you worry about your mistakes, you'll never say anything.

Yes - Né
Certainly - Málista
No - Óhi
Please - Parakaló
Okay, agreed - Endáxi
Thank you (very much) - Efharistó (polý)
I (don't) understand - (Dhén) Katalavéno
Excuse me, do you speak English? - Parakaló, mípos miláte angliká?
Sorry/excuse me - Signómi
Today - Símera
Tomorrow - Ávrio
Yesterday - Khthés
Now - Tóra
Later - Argótera
Open - Anikhtó
Closed - Klistó
Day - Méra
Night - Nikhta
In the morning - Tó proï
In the afternoon - Tó apóyevma
In the evening - Tó vrádhi

Here - Edhó
There - Ekí
This one - Aftó
That one - Ekíno
Good - Kaló
Bad - Kakó
Big - Megálo
Smal - Mikró
More - Perisótero
Less - Ligótero
A little - Lígo
A lot - Polý
Cheap - Ftinó
Expensive - Akrivó
Hot - Zestó
Cold - Krýo
With (together) - Mazí (mé)
Without - Horís
Quickly - Grígora
Slowly - Sigá
Mr/Mrs - Kýrios/Kyría
Miss - Dhespinís

To eat/drink - Trógo/píno
Bakery - Foúrnos, psomádhiko
Pharmacy - Farmakío
Post office - Tahydhromío
Stamps - Gramatóssima
Petrol station - Venzinádhiko

Bank - Trápeza
Money - Leftá/Khrímata
Toilet - Toualéta
Police - Astynomía
Doctor - Yiatrós
Hospital - Nosokomío

To ask a question, it's simplest to start with *parakaló*, then name the thing you want in an interrogative tone.

Where is the bakery? - Parakaló, o foúrnos?
Can you show me the road to . . . ? - Parakaló, ó dhrómos yiá . . . ?
We'd like a room for two - Parakaló, éna dhomátio yiá dhýo átoma
May I have a kilo of oranges? - Parakaló, éna kiló portokália?
Where? - Poú?
How? - Pós?

How many? - Póssi, pósses or póssa?
How much? - Póso?
When? - Póte?
Why? - Yiatí?
At what time . . . ? - Tí óra . . . ?
What is/Which is . . . ? - Tí íne/pió íne . . . ?
How much (does it cost)? - Póso káni?
What time does it open? - Tí óra aníyi?
What time does it close? - Tí óra klíni?

Talking to people

Greek makes the distinction between the informal (*essý*) and formal (*essís*) second person, as French does with "tu" and "vous". Young people, older people and country people often use *essý* even with total strangers, though if you greet someone familiarly and they respond formally, it's best to adopt their usage as the conversation continues, to avoid offence. By far the most common greeting, on meeting and parting, is *yiá sou/yiá sas* – literally "health to you". Incidentally, as across most of the Mediterranean, the approaching party utters the first greeting, not those seated at sidewalk kafenío tables or doorsteps – thus the silent staring as you enter a village.

Hello - **Hérete**
Good morning - **Kalí méra**
Good evening - **Kalí spéra**
Good night - **Kalí níkhta**
Goodbye - **Adío**
How are you? - **Tí kánis/Tí kánete?**
I'm fine - **Kalá íme**
And you? - **Ké essís?**
What's your name? - **Pós se léne?**
My name is . . . - **Mé léne . . .**

Speak slower, please - **Parakaló, miláte pió sigá**
How do you say it in Greek? - **Pós léyete stá Elliniká?**
I don't know - **Dhén xéro**
See you tomorrow - **Thá sé dhó ávrio**
See you soon - **Kalí andhámosi**
Let's go - **Páme**
Please help me - **Parakaló, ná mé voithíste**

Greek's Greek

There are numerous words and phrases which you will hear constantly, even if you rarely have the chance to use them. These are a few of the most common.

Éla! - Literally, Come, but also Speak to me! You don't say! etc
Oríste! - Literally, Indicate!; in effect, What can I do for you?
Embrós! or Léyete! - Standard phone responses
Tí néa? - What's new?
Tí yínete? - What's going on (here)?
Étsi k'étsi - So-so

Ópa! - Whoops! Watch it!
Po-po-po! - Expression of dismay or concern, like French "O là là!"
Pedhí moú - My boy/girl, sonny, friend, etc
Maláka(s) - Literally, wanker, but often used (don't try it!) as an informal term of address
Sigá sigá - Take your time, slow down
Kaló taxídhi - Bon voyage

Accommodation

Hotel - **Xenodhohío**
Inn - **Xenón(as)**
Youth hostel - **Xenónas neótitos**
A room . . . - **Éna dhomátio . . .**
　for one/two/three people - **yiá éna/dhýo/tría átoma**
　for one/two/three nights - **yiá mía/dhýo/trís vradhiés**
　with a double bed - **mé megálo kreváti**
　with a shower - **mé doús**

Hot water - **Zestó neró**
Cold water - **Krýo neró**
Air conditioning - **Klimatismós**
Fan - **Anamistíra**
Can I see it? - **Boró ná tó dhó?**
Can we camp here? - **Boroúme na váloume ti skiní edhó?**
Campsite - **Kámping/Kataskínosi**
Tent - **Skiní**

On the move

Aeroplane – Aeropláno
Bus, coach – Leofório, púlman
Car – Aftokínito, amáxi
Motorbike, scooter – Mihanáki, papáki
Taxi – Taxí
Ship – Plío/vapóri/karávi
High-speed catamaran – Tahýplio
Hydrofoil – Dhelfíni
Bicycle – Podhílato
Hitching – Otostóp
On foot – Mé tá pódhia
Trail – Monopáti
Bus station – Praktorío leoforíon, KTEL
Bus stop – Stássi
Harbour – Limáni
What time does it leave? – Ti óra févyi?
What time does it arrive? – Ti óra ftháni?
How many kilometres? – Póssa hiliómetra?
How many hours? – Pósses óres?

Where are you going? – Poú pás?
I'm going to . . . – Páo stó . . .
I want to get off at . . . – Thélo ná katévo stó . . .
The road to . . . – O dhrómos yiá . . .
Near – Kondá
Far – Makriá
Left – Aristerá
Right – Dhexiá
Straight ahead – Katefthía, ísia
A ticket to . . . – Éna isitírio yiá . . .
A return ticket – Éna isitírio mé epistrofí
Beach – Paralía
Cave – Spiliá
Centre (of town) – Kéndro
Church – Ekklissía
Sea – Thálassa
Village – Horió

Numbers

1 – énas/éna/mía
2 – dhýo
3 – trís/tría
4 – tésseres/téssera
5 – pénde
6 – éxi
7 – eftá
8 – okhtó
9 – ennéa (or more slangy, enyá)
10 – dhéka
11 – éndheka
12 – dhódheka
13 – dhekatrís
14 – dhekatésseres
20 – íkossi
21 – íkossi éna (all compounds written separately thus)

30 – triánda
40 – saránda
50 – penínda
60 – exínda
70 – evdhomínda
80 – ogdhónda
90 – enenínda
100 – ekató
150 – ekatón penínda
200 – dhiakóssies/dhiakóssia
500 – pendakóssies/pendakóssia
1000 – hílies/hília
2000 – dhýo hiliádhes
1,000,000 – éna ekatomírio
first – próto
second – dhéftero
third – tríto

The time and days of the week

Sunday – Kyriakí
Monday – Dheftéra
Tuesday – Tríti
Wednesday – Tetárti
Thursday – Pémpti
Friday – Paraskeví
Saturday – Sávato
What time is it? – Tí óra íne?

One/two/three o'clock – Mía óra, dhýo/trís (óres)
Twenty minutes to four – Tésseres pará íkossi
Five minutes past seven – Eftá ké pénde
Half past eleven – Éndheka ké misí
In half an hour – Sé misí óra
In a quarter-hour – S'éna tétarto

Months and seasonal terms

NB You may see *katharévoussa*, or hybrid, forms of the months written on schedules or street signs; these are the spoken demotic forms.

January - Yennáris
February - Fleváris
March - Mártis
April - Aprílis
May - Maïos
June - Ioúnios
July - Ioúlios

August - Ávgoustos
September - Septémvris
October - Októvrios
November - Noémvris
December - Dhekémvris
Summer schedule - Therinó dhromolóyio
Winter schedule - Himerinó dhromolóyio

A food and drink glossary

Basics

Aláti - Salt
Avgá - Eggs
(Horís) Ládhi - (Without) oil
Hortofágos - Vegetarian
Katálogo/Lísta - Menu
Kréas - Meat
Lahaniká - Vegetables
O logariasmós - The bill
Méli - Honey

Neró - Water
Olikís - Wholemeal bread
Psári(a) - Fish
Psomí - Bread
Sikalísio - Rye bread
Thalassiná - Seafood
Tyrí - Cheese
Yiaoúrti - Yoghurt
Záhari - Sugar

Cooking terms

Akhnistó - Steamed
Pastó - Marinated in salt
Psitó - Roasted
Saganáki - Cheese-based red sauce; also any fried cheese
Skáras - Grilled

Sti soúvla - Spit-roasted
Stó foúrno - Baked
Tiganitó - Pan-fried
Tís óras - Grilled/fried to order
Yakhní - Stewed in oil and tomato sauce
Yemistá - Stuffed (squid, vegetables, etc)

Soups and starters

Avgolémono - Egg and lemon soup
Dolmádhes - Stuffed vine leaves
Fasoládha - Bean soup
Florínes - Canned red sweet Macedonian peppers
Hortópita - Turnover or pie stuffed with wild greens
Kafterí - Cheese dip with chilli added
Kápari - Pickled caper leaves
Kopanistí/Khtypití - Pungent, fermented cheese purée
Krítamo - Rock samphire

Mavromátika - Black-eyed peas
Melitzanosaláta - Aubergine/eggplant dip
Revythokeftédhes - Chickpea/garbanzo patties
Skordhaliá - Garlic dip
Soúpa - Soup
Taramosaláta - Cod roe paté
Tyrokafterí - Cheese dip with chilli, different from *kopanistí*
Tzatzíki - Yoghurt and cucumber dip
Tzirosaláta - Cured mackerel dip

Vegetables

Angináres - Artichokes
Angoúri - Cucumber
Ánitho - Dill
Bámies - Okra/ladies' fingers
Bouréki, bourekákia - Courgette/zucchini, potato and cheese pie
Briám - Ratatouille
Domátes - Tomatoes
Fakés - Lentils
Fasolákia - French/green beans
Horiátiki (saláta) - Greek salad (with olives, féta etc)
Hórta - Greens (usually wild), steamed
Kolokythákia - Courgette/zucchini
Koukiá - Broad/fava beans

Maroúli - Lettuce
Melitzánes imám - Aubergine/eggplant slices baked with onion, garlic and copious olive oil
Patátes - Potatoes
Piperiés - Peppers
Pligoúri/pinigoúri - Bulgur wheat
Radhíkia - Wild chicory – a common *hórta*
Rýzi/Piláfi - Rice (usually with *sáltsa* – sauce)
Rókka - Rocket greens
Saláta - Salad
Spanáki - Spinach
Vlíta - Notchweed – another common *hórta*
Yígandes - White haricot beans

Fish and seafood

Astakós - Aegean lobster
Atherína - Sand smelt
Bakaliáros - Cod
Barbóuni - Red mullet
Fangrí - Common bream
Galéos - Dogfish, hound shark
Garídhes - Shrimp, prawns
Gávros - Mild anchovy
Glóssa - Sole
Gópa - Bogue
Kalamarákia - Baby squid
Kalamária - Squid
Karavídhes - Crayfish
Kefalás - Axillary bream
Koliós - Chub mackerel
Koutsomoúra - Goatfish (small red mullet)
Kydhónia - Cockles
Lakérdha - Light-fleshed bonito, marinated

Marídhes - Picarel
Melanoúri - Saddled bream
Ménoula - Sprat
Mýdhia - Mussels
Okhtapódhi - Octopus
Pandelís - Corvina; also called *sykiós*
Platý - Skate, ray
Sardhélles - Sardines
Sargós - White bream
Seláhi - Skate, ray
Synagrídha - Dentex
Skathári - Black bream
Skoumbrí - Atlantic mackerel
Soupiá - Cuttlefish
Tsipoúra - Gilt-head bream
Vátos - Skate, ray
Xifías - Swordfish
Yermanós - Leatherback

Meat and meat-based dishes

Arní - Lamb
Biftéki - Hamburger
Brizóla - Pork or beef chop
Hirinó - Pork
Keftédhes - Meatballs
Kokorétsi - Liver/offal roulade, spit-roasted
Kopsídha - (Lamb) shoulder chops
Kotópoulo - Chicken
Kounélli - Rabbit
Loukánika - Spicy homemade sausages

Moskhári - Veal
Moussakás - Aubergine, potato and lamb-mince casserole with bechamel topping
Païdhákia - Rib chops (lamb or goat)
Papoutsákia - Stuffed aubergine/eggplant "shoes" – like *moussakás* without bechamel
Pastítsio - Macaroni "pie" baked with minced meat
Patsás - Tripe and trotter soup

Salingária - Garden snails
Soutzoukákia - Minced meat rissoles/beef patties
Stifádho - Meat stew with tomato and boiling onions

Sykóti - Liver
Tzigeros armás - Lamb's liver in cabbage
Youvétsi - Baked clay casserole of meat and *kritharáki* (short pasta)

Sweets and dessert

Baklavás - Honey and nut pastry
Bougátsa - Salt or sweet cream pie served warm with sugar and cinnamon
Galaktobóureko - Custard pie
Halvás - Sweetmeat of sesame or semolina
Karydhópita - Walnut cake
Kréma - Custard

Loukoumádhes - Dough fritters in honey syrup and sesame seeds
Pagotó - Ice cream
Pastélli - Sesame and honey bar
Ravaní - Spongecake, lightly syruped
Ryzógalo - Rice pudding

Fruit and nuts

Akhládhia - Big pears
Aktinídha - Kiwis
Fistikia - Pistachio nuts
Fráoules - Strawberries
Karpoúzi - Watermelon
Kerásia - Cherries
Krystália - Miniature pears
Kydhóni - Quince

Lemónia - Lemons
Míla - Apples
Pepóni - Melon
Portokália - Oranges
Rodhákino - Peach
Stafýlia - Grapes
Sýka - Figs

Cheese

Ayeladhinó - Cow's-milk cheese
Féta - Salty, white cheese
Graviéra - Gruyère-type hard cheese
Kasséri - Medium-sharp cheese

Katsikísio - Goat cheese
Myzíthra - Sweet cream cheese
Próvio - Sheep cheese

Drinks

Alisfakiá - Island sage tea
Boukáli - Bottle
Býra - Beer
Gála - Milk
Galakakáo - Chocolate milk
Gazóza - Generic fizzy drink
Kafés - Coffee
Krasí - Wine
  áspro - white
  kokkinélli/rozé - rosé

kókkino/mávro - red
Limonádha - Lemonade
Metalikó neró - Mineral water
Portokaládha - Orangeade
Potíri - Glass
Stinyássas! - Cheers!
Tsáï - Tea
Tsáï vounoú - "Mountain" (mainland) sage tea

Katharévoussa, dhimotikí and dialects

Greek may seem complicated enough in itself, but problems are multiplied when you consider that since the early 1800s there has been an ongoing dispute between two versions of the language: **katharévoussa** and **dhimotikí**.

When Greece first achieved independence in the nineteenth century, its people were almost universally illiterate, and the language they spoke – **dhimotikí**, "demotic" or "popular" Greek – had undergone enormous change since the days of the Byzantine empire and Classical times. The vocabulary had assimilated countless borrowings from the languages of the various invaders and conquerors, namely the Turks, Venetians, Albanians and Slavs.

The finance and inspiration for the new Greek state, as well as its early leaders, came largely from the diaspora – Greek families who had been living in the sophisticated cities of central and eastern Europe, in Constantinople or in Russia. With their European notions about the grandeur of Greece's past and their lofty conception of Hellenism, they set about obliterating the memory of subjugation to foreigners in every possible field. And what better way to start than by purging the language of its foreign accretions and reviving its Classical purity?

They accordingly set about creating what was in effect a new form of the language, *katharévoussa* (literally "cleansed" Greek). The complexities of Classical grammar and syntax were reinstated, and Classical words, long out of use, were reintroduced. To the country's great detriment, *katharévoussa* became the language of the schools and the prestigious professions, government, business, the law, newspapers and academia. Everyone aspiring to membership in the elite strove to master it, and to speak it – even though there was no consensus on how many of the words should be pronounced.

The *katharévoussa/dhimotikí* debate remained a highly contentious issue until the early 1980s. Writers – from Solomos and Makriyiannis in the nineteenth century to Seferis, Kazantzakis and Ritsos in the twentieth – have all championed the demotic, or some approximation of it, in their literature. Advocacy of demotic became increasingly linked to left-wing politics, while crackpot right-wing governments forcibly (re)instated *katharévoussa* at every opportunity. Most recently, the **colonels' junta** of 1967–74 reversed a decision of the previous government to teach using *dhimotikí* in the schools, bringing back *katharévoussa*, even on sweet wrappers, as part of their ragbag of notions about racial purity and heroic ages.

Dhimiotikí returned once more after the fall of the colonels and now seems here to stay; perhaps the final blow to the classicizers was the official decision, in 1981, to do away with breath marks (which in fact no longer signified anything) and abolish the three different stress accents in favour of a **single acute accent** (though there are still plenty of left-over road signs displaying the older system). *Dhimotikí* is used in schools, on radio and TV, and after a fashion in newspapers (with the exception of the extreme right-wing *Estia*). The only institutions which refuse to bring themselves up to date are the Church and the legal professions – so beware rental contracts and official documents.

This is not to suggest that there is now any less confusion. The Metaxas dictatorship of the 1930s changed scores of village names from Slavic to Classical forms, and these official **place names** still hold sway on most road signs and maps – even though the local people may use the *dhimotikí* form. Thus you will see "Plomárion" or "Spétsai" written, while everyone actually says "Plomári" or "Spétses".

Dialects and minority languages

If the lack of any standard Greek were not enough, Greece still offers a rich field of linguistic diversity, both in its regional dialects and minority languages. Island **dialects** are alive and well in many a remote area, and some of them are quite incomprehensible to outsiders (which can mean inhabitants of the next island). The dialect of Sfákia in Crete is one such; those of Náxos and Lésvos are other strong Aegean dialects, which owe much to migration from Crete and influences from Asia Minor respectively. The dialect of Sámos and that of adjacent Híos are completely different from one another, Híos being considered a more pure "Ionian" (and this thousands of years after the Ionians arrived from the mainland), while the rough "Samian" variant owes much to the diverse origins of its settlers. *Arvanítika* – a dialect of medieval Albanian – was until well into the twentieth century the first language of many villages of southern Évvia, northern Ándhros and much of the Argo–Saronic area; it is still spoken (and sung) among the oldest generation. On Rhodes and Kós there is a dwindling Turkish-speaking population, probably not in excess of seven thousand persons as of writing.

A glossary of recurrent words and terms

acropolis – Ancient, fortified hilltop.

agora – Market and meeting place of an ancient Greek city; also the commercial "high street" of a modern village (**agorá** in modern Greek).

amphora – Tall, narrow-necked jar for oil or wine.

áno – Upper; common prefix element of village names.

apse – Polygonal or curved recess at the altar end of a church.

Archaic period – Late Iron Age period, from around 750 BC to the start of the Classical period in the fifth century BC.

architrave – Horizontal masonry atop temple columns; same as **entablature**.

arhondikó – A lordly stone mansion, as in Kastoriá, Pílion or Zagóri.

astykó – (Intra) city, municipal, local; adjective applied to phone calls and bus services.

atrium – Open, inner courtyard of an ancient house, usually Roman.

áyios/ayía/áyii – Saint or holy (m/f/plural). Common place-name prefix often spelled **agios** or **aghios** (abbreviated Ag or Ay).

basilica – Colonnaded, "hall-" or "barn-" type church adapted from Roman models, most common in northern Greece.

bema – Rostrum for oratory (and later the chancel) of a church.

bouleuterion – Auditorium for meetings of an ancient town's deliberative council.

Byzantine empire – Created by the division of the Roman empire in 395 AD, this, the eastern half, was ruled from Constantinople (modern Istanbul). In Greece, Byzantine culture peaked twice: in the eleventh century, and again at Mystra in the early fifteenth century.

capital – The flared top, often ornamented, of a column.

cella – Sacred room of a temple, housing the cult image.

Classical period – Essentially from the end of the Persian wars in the fifth century BC

until the unification of Greece under Philip II of Macedon (338 BC).

Corinthian – Decorative columns, festooned with acanthus florettes; a temple built in this order.

dhimarhío – Town hall.

dhomátia – Rooms for rent in purpose-built blocks or (seldom these days) private houses.

Dorian – Northern civilization that displaced and succeeded the Mycenaeans and Minoans through most of Greece around 1100 BC.

Doric – Minimalist, unadorned columns, dating from the Dorian period; a temple built in this order.

drum – Cylindrical or faceted vertical section, usually pierced by an even number of narrow windows, upholding a church cupola.

entablature – The horizontal linking structure atop the columns of an ancient temple.

eparhía – Greek Orthodox diocese, also the smallest subdivision of a modern province, analogous to a county.

exedra – Display niche for statuary.

exonarthex – The outer vestibule or entrance hall of a church, when a true **narthex** is present.

forum – Market and meeting place of a Roman-era city.

frieze – Band of sculptures around a temple. Doric friezes consist of various tableaux of figures (**metopes**) interspersed with grooved panels (**triglyphs**); Ionic ones have continuous bands of figures.

froúrio – Medieval castle; nowadays, usually means a modern military headquarters.

garsoniéra/es – Studio villa/s, self-catering apartment/s.

Geometric period – Post-Mycenaean Iron Age era named for the style of its pottery; begins in the early eleventh century BC with the arrival of Dorian peoples. By the eighth century BC, with the development of representational styles, it becomes known as the Archaic period.

Hellenistic period – The last and most unified "Greek empire", created in the wake of Alexander the Great's Macedonian empire and finally collapsing with the fall of Corinth to the Romans in 146 BC.

heroön – Shrine or sanctuary, usually of a demigod or mortal; war memorials in modern Greece.

hokhláki – Mosaic of coloured pebbles, found in church or house courtyards of the Dodecanese and Spétses.

hóra – Main town of an island or region; literally it means "the place". An island hóra is often known by the same name as the island.

ierón – Literally, "sacred" – the space between the altar screen and the apse of a church, reserved for priestly activities.

ikonostási – Screen between the nave of a church and the altar, supporting at least three icons.

Ionic – Elaborate, decorative development of the older Doric order; Ionic temple columns are slimmer, with deeper "fluted" edges, spiral-shaped capitals and ornamental bases.

iperastykó – Inter-city, long-distance – as in phone calls and bus services.

kafenío – Coffee house or café; in a small village the centre of communal life and probably serving as the bus stop, too.

kaïki – (plural kaïkia) Caique, or medium-sized boat, traditionally wooden and used for transporting cargo and passengers; now refers mainly to island excursion boats.

kalderími – A cobbled mule-track or footpath.

kámbos – Fertile agricultural plain, usually near a river mouth.

kantína – Shack, caravan or even a disused bus on the beach, serving drinks and perhaps sandwiches or quick snacks.

kástro – Any fortified hill (or a castle), but most often the oldest, highest, walled-in part of an island hóra.

katholikón – Central chapel of a monastery.

káto – Lower; common prefix element of village names.

kendrikí platía – Central square.

kouros – Nude Archaic statue of an idealized young man, usually portrayed with one foot slightly forward of the other.

Macedonian empire – Empire created by Philip II in the mid-fourth century BC.

megaron – Principal hall or throne room of a Mycenaean palace.

meltémi – North wind that blows across the Aegean in summer, starting softly from near the mainland and hitting the Cyclades, the Dodecanese and Crete full on.

metope – see frieze

Minoan – Crete's great Bronze Age civilization, which dominated the Aegean from about 2500 to 1400 BC.

moní – Formal term for a monastery or convent.

Moreás – Medieval term for the Peloponnese; the outline of the peninsula was likened to the leaf of a mulberry tree, moreá in Greek.

Mycenaean – Mainland civilization centred on Mycenae and the Argolid from about 1700 to 1100 BC.

naos – The inner sanctum of an ancient temple; also, any Orthodox Christian shrine.

narthex – Western vestibule of a church, reserved for catechumens and the unbaptized; typically frescoed with scenes of the Last Judgement.

Neolithic – Earliest era of settlement in Greece, characterized by the use of stone tools and weapons together with basic agriculture. Divided arbitrarily into Early (c 6000 BC), Middle (c 5000 BC) and Late (c 3000 BC).

néos, néa, néo – New; a common prefix to a town or village name.

nomós – Modern Greek province – there are more than fifty of them. Village bus services are organized according to their borders.

odeion – Small theatre in Classical times, used for musical performances, minor dramatic productions or councils.

orchestra – Circular area in an ancient theatre where the chorus would sing and dance.

palaestra – Gymnasium for athletics and wrestling practice in Classical times.

paleós, paleá, paleó – Old; again, a common prefix in town and village names.

Panayía – Virgin Mary.

Pandokrátor – Literally, The Almighty; generally refers to the stern portrayal of Christ in Majesty frescoed or in mosaic in the dome of many Byzantine churches.

paniyíri – Festival or feast – the local celebration of a holy day.

paralía – Beach or seafront promenade.

pediment – Triangular, sculpted gable below the roof of a temple.

pendentive – Any of four triangular sections of vaulting with concave sides, positioned at a corner of a rectangular space to support a circular or polygonal dome; in churches, often adorned with frescoes of the four Evangelists.

períptero – Street kiosk.

peristereónes – Pigeon towers, in the Cyclades.

peristyle – Gallery of columns around a temple or other building.

pinakothíki – Picture gallery, ancient or modern.

pithos – (plural **pithoi**) Large ceramic jar for storing oil, grain etc. Very common in Minoan palaces and used in almost identical form in modern Greek homes.

platía – Square, plaza.

polygonal masonry – Wall-building technique of the Classical and Hellenistic period, which used unmortared, closely joined stones; often called "Lesbian polygonal" after the island where the method supposedly originated. The much-(ab)used term "Cyclopean" refers only to Mycenaean/Bronze Age mainland sites such as Tiryns, Glas and Mycenae itself.

propylaion – Monumental columned gateway of an ancient building; often used in the plural, **propylaia**.

pýrgos – Tower or bastion; also tower-mansions found in the Máni or on Lésvos.

skála – The port of an inland island settlement, nowadays often larger and more important than its namesake, but always younger since built after the disappearance of piracy.

squinch – Small concavity across a corner of a columnless interior space, which supports a superstructure such as a dome.

stele – Upright stone slab or column, usually inscribed with an edict; also an ancient tombstone, with a relief scene.

stoa – Colonnaded walkway in Classical-era marketplace.

taverna – Restaurant; see "Eating and Drinking" in *Basics*, p.58, for details of the different types of specialist eating places.

témblon – Wooden altar screen of an Orthodox church, usually ornately carved and painted and studded with icons; more or less interchangeable with **ikonostási**.

temenos – Sacred precinct of ancient temple, often used to refer to the sanctuary itself.

theatral area – Open area found in most of the Minoan palaces with seat-like steps around. Probably a type of theatre or ritual area, though this is not conclusively proven.

tholos – Conical or beehive-shaped building, especially a Mycenaean tomb.

triglyph – see **frieze**

tympanum – The recessed space, flat or carved in relief, inside a pediment.

Acronyms

ANEK – Anónymi Navtiliakí Etería Krítis (Shipping Co of Crete, Ltd), which runs most ferries between Pireás and Crete, plus many to Italy.

DANE – Dhodhekanisiakí Anónymi Navtiliakí Etería (Dodecanesian Shipping Company Ltd), which runs many ferries between Rhodes and Pireás via intervening islands.

DIKKI – Democrat Social Movement, a more left-leaning spinoff from **PASOK**.

EAM – National Liberation Front, the political force behind **ELAS**.

ELAS – Popular Liberation Army, the main Resistance group during World War II and the basis of the Communist army (DSE or "Democratic Army of Greece") during the civil war.

ELTA – Postal service.

EOT – Ellinikós Organismós Tourismoú, the National Tourist Organization.

FYROM – Former Yugoslav Republic of Macedonia (Greek initials are PGDM, for Proín Yugoslavikí Dhimokratía Makedhonías).

KKE – Communist Party, unreconstructed.

KTEL – National syndicate of bus companies; also used to refer to individual bus stations.

LANE – Lasithiakí Anónymi Navtiliakí Etería (Lasithian Shipping Company Ltd), based in eastern Crete, which runs ferries between Rhodes, Hálki, Kárpathos, eastern Crete and Pireás.

ND – Conservative (Néa Dhimokratía) party.

NEL – Navtiliakí Etería Lésvou (Lesvian Shipping Co), which runs most of the northeast Aegean ferries.

OTE – Telephone company.

PASOK – Socialist party (Pan-Hellenic Socialist Movement).

index

and small print

Index

Map entries are in colour.

A

Abrámi 173
accommodation 52
Achillion 486
acronyms, Greek ..626–627
Adhámas 132
Aegina – see Égina
Afáles 519
Agáthi 299
Agathoníssi
    (Gaïdharo) 359
Agathopés 158
Agístri – see Angístri
Agnóndas 452
Agriolivádhi
    (Agriolívadho) 357
Agriosykiá 320
Aharávi 489
Aháta 287
Ahíli 462
Aï Nikítas 505
Aï Strátis – see Áyios
    Efstrátios
Aïdhónia (Ándhros) 141
Aïdhónia (Sámos) 378
airlines
    in Australasia 24
    in Greece 11, 46
    in North America.............. 21
    in UK & Ireland 12
Akhládhi 159
Akrotíri (Thíra) 196
Aktí (Kálymnos) 347
Alalkomenae 518
Albanian immigrants ..566
alcoholic drinks 61, 62
Alexander the Great 542
Alikanás 527
Alimiá (Iráklia) 179
Alimniá (Alimiá),
    Dodecanese 308
Allied military
    cemeteries 351, 423
Almyrés (Kálymnos) 347
Almyrós (Corfu) 489
Almyrós (Skhinoússa) ..178
Alónissos 453
Alónissos 454
Alonítsi 424
Aloprónia 187
Alykés (Zákynthos) 527
Alykí (Kímolos) 137

Alykí (Kós) 333
Alykí (Páros) 164
Alykí (Thássos) 436
Álynda 351
Amárynthos 466
Ambelákia (Meganíssi) ..507
Ambelás (Páros) 163
Ambéli (Folégandhros) ..190
Ámbelos, Mount 378
Amíti 175
Ammopí 285
Ammouá 280
Ammoudhélli 409
Ammoúdhi (Thíra) 194
Amorgós 179
Amorgós 180
amphibians 590
Anáfi 197
Anáfi 198
Anafonítria monastery ..527
Análipsi (Astypálea) 341
Anávatos 397
Ánaxos 416
Ándhros 137
Ándhros 138
Andikýthira 535
Andimáhia 335
Andíparos 165
Andípaxi (Antipaxos) ..500
Andísami 510
Ándissa 412
Angáli (Folégandhros) ..190
Angáli beach (Évvia) 471
Angelokástro 491
Angístri 98
Angístri 99
Animals – see fauna
Áno Méra (Mýkonos) ..151
Áno Meriá
    (Folégandhros) 190
Áno Moraïtika 495
Áno Sýros 155
Áno Vathý (Sámos) 370
Anoyí 519
Antipaxos – see Andípaxi
Apalírou 172
Apáno Kástro (Náxos) ..173
Ápella 287
Apéri 287
Aphaia, Temple of
    (Égina) 96
Aphrodite temple
    (Lésvos) 411
Apikía 141

Apíranthos 174
Apocalypse – see
    Apokálypsis
Apokálypsis monastery
    (Pátmos) 356
Apokoftó 130
Apókroussi 119
Apolakiá 307
Apóllon (Náxos) 175
Apollonía (Sífnos) 127
Apróvato, Káto/Áno 140
archeological sites,
    opening hours 69
Aréta 308
Arethoússa spring 517
Aretí (Mílos) 134
Argássi 523
Argo-Saronic 92
Argostóli 513
Arhángelos (Rhodes) ..299
Arhangélou Mihaïl convent
    (Thássos) 436
Arkássa 285
Arkessini, ancient 182
Arkessíni village 182
Arkhoudhílas
    beach/monastery 496
Arkí 359
Armathiá 280
Arméni 194
Armenistís 384
Armeós (Sýros) 158
Armólia 394
Arní 140
Artemis temple (Ikaría) ..387
Artemis temple (Léros) ..352
Artemónas 128
Aryinónda 346
Aryirádhes 495
Asélinos, Mikró/Megálo
   448
Asfendhioú villages 333
Asfodhilítis 182
Asklepion (Kós) 331
Asklipió (Rhodes) 305
Asómati 334
Aspoús 462
Áspri Pétra 336
Ássos 515
Astrís (Astrídha) 436
Astypálea 337
Astypálea 338
Astypalia, ancient
    (Kós) 336

Atávyros, Mount 303
Aténi 139
Atháni 506
Athéato 450
Athéato 452
Athens, quick guide
...........................25–27
ATMs – see cash
dispensers
Atsítsa 462
Avgónyma 397
Avláki 489
Avlákia 337
Avlémonas 533
Avliótes 490
Avlóna 288
Avlonári 466
Ávythos 513
Axis occupation 549
Ayiá (Náxos) 175
Ayía Ánna (Amorgós) ..181
Ayía Ánna (Évvia) 471
Ayía Ánna (Mýkonos) ..151
Ayía Ánna (Náxos) 170
Ayía Efimía 511
Ayía Efpraxía 105
Ayía Eléni (Skiáthos) 449
Ayía Ermióni 394
Ayía Fotiní 394
Ayía Iríni (Páros) 161
Ayía Marína (Égina) 97
Ayía Marína (Kássos) ..281
Ayía Marína (Kéa) 118
Ayía Marína (Léros) 351
Ayía Marína
(Spétses) 108
Ayía Marína (Sými) 316
Ayía Marína
(Zákynthos) 527
Ayía Markélla 400
Ayía Paraskeví
(Sámos) 373
Ayía Paraskeví
(Skiáthos) 448
Ayía Paraskeví
(Spétses) 109
Ayía Pelayía 530
Ayía Sofía cave
(Kýthira) 534
Ayía Theodhóti 186
Ayía Triádha (Ídhra) 106
Ayía Triádha (Sámos) ..381
Ayía Triádha
(Télendhos) 346
Ayías Triádhas
(Kastellórizo) 311
Ayiássos (Lésvos) 409
Ayiássos (Náxos) 172
Áyii Anáryiri (Páros) 160

Áyii Anáryiri (Spétses) 109
Áyii Apóstoli (Náxos) ..173
Áyii Dhéka (Corfu) 493
Áyii Theodhóri (Páros) ..165
Áyio Gála 400
Ayiókambos 471
Áyios Andhréas
(Astypálea) 341
Áyios Andhréas
(Sífnos) 130
Áyios Andónios
(Níssyros) 324
Áyios Andónios (Páros)..164
Áyios Andónios (Tílos) ..321
Áyios Athanásios
(Iráklia) 178
Áyios Dhimítrios
(Alónissos) 456
Áyios Dhimítrios
(Évvia) 466
Áyios Dhimítrios (Kós) ..334
**Áyios Efstrátios
(Aï Strátis)** 424
Áyios Emilianós (Híos) ..394
Áyios Emilianós (Sými) 317
Áyios Ermoyénis 408
Áyios Fokás (Lésvos) ..411
Áyios Fokás (Skýros) ..462
Áyios Górdhis (central
Corfu) 493
Áyios Górdhis Paleohoríou
(S. Corfu) 496
Áyios Harálambos
(Skiáthos) 447
Áyios Ioánnis (Kós) 335
Áyios Ioánnis (Límnos) 422
Áyios Ioánnis
(Mýkonos) 150
Áyios Ioánnis (Sérifos) ..123
Áyios Ioánnis cave
(Iráklia) 178
Áyios Ioánnis Kastrí 450
Áyios Ioánnis Pródhromos
(Foúrni) 388
Áyios Ioánnis spa
(Lésvos) 410
Áyios Ioánnis Theológos
(Níssyros) 325
Áyios Ioánnis
Thymianós 336
Áyios Isídhoros (Híos) ..398
Áyios Isídhoros (Léros) ..352
Áyios Isídhoros
(Lésvos) 409
Áyios Isídhoros
(Rhodes) 303
Áyios Kírykos 383
Áyios Konstandínos
(Astypálea) 340

Áyios Konstandínos
(Sámos) 377
Áyios Mámas/Aï Mámas
...................................281
Áyios Matthéos (Corfu) ..494
Áyios Matthéos
(Náxos) 172
Áyios Minás (Páros) 164
Áyios Nektários convent
(Égina) 96
Áyios Nikólaos (Anáfi) 197
Áyios Nikólaos (Crete)
– see under Crete
Áyios Nikólaos
(Folégandhros) 190
Áyios Nikólaos (Ídhra) ..106
Áyios Nikólaos (N
Kárpathos) 287
Áyios Nikólaos (S
Kárpathos) 285
Áyios Nikólaos (N
Zákynthos) 527
Áyios Nikólaos (S
Zákynthos) 524
Áyios Nikólaos
(Sámos) 377
Áyios Nikólaos
(Síkinos) 188
Áyios Nikólaos (Sými) 316
Áyios Nikólaos
Foundouklí 303
Áyios Pandelímonas
(Síkinos) 188
Áyios Pétros (Ándhros) ..140
Áyios Prokópios 170
Áyios Sóstis (Sérifos) ..123
Áyios Stéfanos
(NE Corfu) 488
Áyios Stéfanos
(NW Corfu) 492
Áyios Stéfanos (Kós) ..336
Áyios Stéfanos
(Kýthnos) 122
Áyios Stéfanos
(Mýkonos) 150
Áyios Theológos (Kós) ..336
Áyios Vassílios (Sými) 317
Áyios Vassílios
(Télendhos) 346
Áyios Yeóryios
(Agathoníssi) 360
Áyios Yeóryios
(Andíparos) 165
Áyios Yeóryios
(N Corfu) 492
Áyios Yeóryios
(S Corfu) 495
Áyios Yeóryios (Hálki) ..308
Áyios Yeóryios (Iráklia) ..178

Áyios Yeóryios
  (Kefalloniá) 514
Áyios Yeóryios (Náxos)..170
Áyios Yeóryios
  (Síkinos) 188
Áyios Yeóryios
  Dhyssálona 317
Áyios Yeóryios
  Hadhión 281
Áyios Yeóryios toú
  Vounioú 311
Áyios Yeóryios
  Várdhas 307
Áyios Yerásimos 514
Ayíou Ioánnou
  Khryssostómou
  (Náxos) 175
Ayíou Ioánnou Prodhrómou
  (Hálki) 308
Ayíou Ioánnou Theológou
  monastery (Pátmos) ..356
Ayíou Nikoláou
  Galatáki 470
Ayíou Pandelímona
  monastery (Tílos) 321

B

Balkan Wars 546
Bállos 376
Banana beach (Kós) 283
Banana beach
  (Skiáthos) 448
Banana beach
  (Zákynthos) 524
banks 35
Barbáti 488
bars 62
basketball 74
Batsí 139
Baxédhes 194
BBC World Service 68
beer 62
Benítses 494
Biláli 402
birds 588
Bísti 106
Blefoútis 352
Blue Caves 527
Bóhali 522
Bonátsa 137
books 594–609
  archeological
    guidebooks 599
  archeology and art ...591
  classics, the 588
  "coffee-table" books ..592
  ethnography 595

fiction by foreign writers ..597
food and wine 590
hiking guides 599
history, ancient 589
history, Byzantine–Ottoman
 593
history, modern Greek ...593
literature, modern Greek ..596
poetry, modern Greek 598
regional guidebooks 600
religion, ancient 590
travel/general accounts ...586
yachting guides 601
Boúka 280
Boúkari 495
breakfast 56, 62
Brooke, Rupert 459
Brós Thermá 333
buses, local 47
business hours 69
Byron, Lord 545
Byzantine Greece 542

C

cafés 61
Camel Beach 336
camping 55
car rental 49
cash dispensers 36
Castel Rosso 469
catamarans 45
Catholics 142, 154
Cave of the Nymphs ..518
Cephallonia – see
  Kefalloniá
chemists – see pharmacies
children, travelling with ..83
Chios – see Híos
cinema 73
civil war 550
Classical era 540
coffee 61, 62
colonels' junta 544
Constantine II, King 552
consumer protection 79
Corfu (Kérkyra) 479
Corfu 480
costs 34
credit cards 36
creepy-crawlies 33
CRETE (KRíTI)
  Crete 208–209
Akrotíri peninsula 265
Almyrídha 254
Amári valley 256
Ammoúdhi 255
Anemospiliá 222
Anóyia 235
Arhánes 222

Arkádhi monastery 253
Árvi 247
Aryiroúpolis 253
Ayía Galíni 256
Ayía Marína 266
Ayía Pelayía 233
Ayía Rouméli 268
Ayía Triádha 225
Ayía Triádha monastery ...265
Áyii Dhéka 223
Áyios Ioánnis 225
Áyios Nikólaos 237
Áyios Nikólaos 238
Balí 234
Blue Beach 265
climate 206
Dhamnóni 255
Dhiktean Cave 237
Elafonísi 232
Élos 270
Eloúnda 240
Falásarna 271
Faneroméni monastery 241
Festós/Phaestos 224
Festós 225
Fódhele 234
Frangokástello 269
Gávdhos 273
Goniá monastery 266
Gorge of Samariá 266
Górtys 223
Goúrnes 228
Gourniá, ancient 242
Gouvernétou monastery ...265
Goúves 228
Haniá 257–265
Haniá 258–259
Hersónissos/Limín
  Hersoníssou 228
history 205
Hóra Sfakíon 269
Idhéon Ándhron 235
Ierápetra 246
Iráklion 207–219
Iráklion 210–211
Ítanos 208
Kalamáki 227
Kalí Liménes 227
Kalýves 254
Kamáres 236
Kámbos 271
Kándanos 272
Kastélli/Kíssamos 270
Katholikó monastery 266
Kefalás 254
Keratókambos 247
Khryssoskalítissa
  monastery 271
Kíssamos – see Kastélli
Knossós 219
Knossós 220
Kókkino Horió 254
Kolymvári 266
Kómmos 227
Kournás, Lake 254
Kritsá 241
Lasíthi plateau 236

Lató, ancient 241
Lebena, ancient 228
Léndas 227
Loutró 269
Makryialós 246
Mália, palace 232
Mália palace 231
Mália, resort 230
Mátala 226
Mathés 254
Mílatos 232
Minoans 205
Míres 224
Mókhlos 242
Mýrthios 255
Mýrtos 247
Myrtiá 222
Neápoli 236
Nídha plateau 235
Oloús 240
Omalós 268
Pahiá Ámmos 242
Palékastro 245
Paleohóra 272
"Palm beach" 256
Panayía Kyrá 241
Pánormos 234
Phaestos – see under Crete,
  Festós
Pitsídhia 227
Pláka 241
Pláka 254
Plakiás 255
Plataniás 266
Plátanos 271
Préveli monastery 256
Psilorítis, Mount 235
Psykhró 237
Réthymnon 248
Réthymnon 249
Rodhákino 269
Rodhopoú peninsula 266
Samarian Gorge 266
Samarian Gorge 267
Sfinári 271
Sísi 232
Sitía 242
Sitía 243
Skalotí 269
Skotinó cave 228
Soúyia 269
Spíli 256
Spinalónga 240
Stalídha 230
Stavrós 265
Toploú monastery 244
Topólia 270
Tsoútsouros 248
Týlissos 235
Tzermiádho 236
Vái beach 244
Vathýpetro 223
Vorízia 236
where to go 206
Yeoryoúpoli 254
Zákros palace 245
Zákros, Áno/Káto 245

Crete 208–209
Crusades 543
cultural festivals 73
Cyclades 114–115
cycling 48
Cyprus crises 551, 553

D

Dárga 152
Delos 152
Delos 153
departure tax 84
desserts 62
Dháfni 524
Dhafníla 487
Dhapóri 422
Dhaskalió cave 347
Dhassiá 487
Dhekaeftá Noemvríou ..559
Dhekemvrianá (Battle of
  Athens) 550
Dhelfíni (Sýros) 158
Dhervéni gorge 469
Dhessími bay 504
Dhéxa 517
Dhiafáni 288
Dhiakófti 530
Dhiapóndia islands 496
Dhílos – see Delos
dhimotikí 622
Dhódheka Spília 317
Dhodhekánisos – see
  Dodecanese
dhomátia 53
Dhonoússa 179
Dhragonéra 99
Dhrakéï 380
dhrakóspita (dragon
  houses) 467, 469
Dhrasónda 347
Dhrogaráti cave 510
Dhrossiá 527
Dhrymónas 503
Dhryopídha 121
Dhryós 165
Dhýo Horiá 146
Dhýo Yialí 308
dialects 622
directory 84
disabled travellers 79
discography 580–582
disrespect (lese-majesty)
 78
doctors 34
Dodecanese 278
Dorian era 540

driving in Greece 50
driving to Greece from
  Britain 18
drug laws 78
DSE (Democratic Army of
  Greece) 550
Dystos, ancient 467

E

EAM (National Liberation
  Front) 549–550
Eándio 93
East and North
  Aegean 366
Easter 70
Efpalínio tunnel 374
Eftaloú 416
Égina (Aegina) 94
Égina 95
Égina Town 94
Egremní 506
ELAS (Popular Liberation
  Army) 549–550
electrical supply 84
Elgin Marbles dispute ..564
Eliá (Mýkonos) 151
Eliá (Skiáthos) 449
Elínda 397
Élios 452
Elliniká (Évvia) 471
Elliniká (Kímolos) 137
Ellinokamára 281
email 66
embassies and consulates,
  Greek 30
Émblisi 516
Émbona(s) 303
Emborió (Hálki) 307
Emborió (Sými) 317
Emboriós (Híos) 395
Emboriós (Kálymnos) ..346
Emboriós (Kássos) 237
Emboriós (Mílos) 135
Emboriós (Níssyros) 325
emergency numbers 78
employment
  documentation 76
Englouví 503
Énos, Mount 514
Episkopí (Ídhra) 106
Episkopí (Kýthnos) 119
Episkopí (Síkinos) 188
Eptá Piyés 302
Eressós – see Skála
  Eressoú
Erétria 465
Eríkoussa 497

INDEX

Erimítis cliffs 499
Éristos 321
Érmones 492
Ermoúpoli 154
Ermoúpoli 156
estiatória 58
Euboea – see Évvia
Eumaeus, Cave of 517
euro, the 36
Evangelismoú (Inoússes) 402
Evangelístria (Skiáthos) 447
Evangelistrías (Skópelos) 451
Évdhilos 384
Evgátis (Áyios Pávlos) 422
Évvia (Euboea) 462
Évvia 463
Exánthia 503
Exóbourgo 145
Exoyí 519
Eyiáli 182

F

Faliráki 298
Faneroméni (Lefkádha)..503
Faneroméni (Lésvos) ..413
Faneroménis (Náxos) ..175
Fáros (Sífnos) 129
Fengári, Mount 429
Feraklós 299
ferries
cross-Channel 18
from Greek mainland ...28–29
from Italy 20–21
within Greece 44
Ferry, hydrofoil & catamaran routes 86
festival calendar, religious 71–73
field guides, flora/fauna 592
Filérimos 302
film, photographic 84
Filóti 174
Fínikas (Koufoníssi) 177
Fínikas (Sýros) 158
Finíki (Kárpathos) 286
Finikiá (Thíra) 194
Firá (Folégandhros) 190
Firá (Thíra) 192
Firáyia 130
Firí Ámmos 533
Firipláka 135
Firostefáni 193
fish 59
Fiskárdho 515
Flamboúri 122
Flério 173
flights
from Australasia 23
from North America 20
from UK & Ireland 11
within Greece 46
flora/flowers 586
Flying Dolphins – see hydrofoils
Fókis 516
Folégandhros 188
Foniás, Cape 430
food and drink 56
football 74
Fourkeró 402
Fourkovoúni 134
Foúrni 387
Foúrni (Kýthira) 531
Foúrni (Rhodes) 301
Frankish rule 543
Fríkes 519
Frý 280
Fýlla (Évvia) 465
Fýsses 288
Fylakopí 135

G

Gaïdhourávlakos 360
Gaïdhouropoúli 280
Gáïos 498
galaktopolía 62
Galanádho 172
Galaní 125
Galissás 158
Gánema 126
Gardhíki Pýrgos 494
Gavathás 412
Gávrio 139
gay/lesbian travellers 82
George I, King 546
George II, King 548
getting around 42
Glinádho 172
Glóssa 450
glossary of recurrent terms 624–626
Glýfa (Andíparos) 165
Glýfa (Évvia) 471
Glýstra 305
Glyfádha (Corfu) 493
Glyfó (Sífnos) 130
Glystéri 452
goat dance, Skyrian 458
Goúrna 352
Gouviá 487
Gramvoússa (Amorgós) 180
Greece and the islands ....ii–iii
Greek alphabet 614
Greek language ..613–627
Gría Váthra 429
Gríkou 357

H

Hálakas 135
Halikádha 99
Halikoúna 494
Halinádhou 411
Hálki 307
Halkí (Náxos) 173
Halkídha 464
Haniá (Crete) – see under Crete
Haráki 299
Harakópou 177
Haramídha 408
Harkadhió cave 321
Harmýlio 334
Havoúli 422
health 32
Hélatros 281
Hellenistic Greece 541
Hephaestia, ancient 423
Heraion, ancient.......... 375
Herónissos (Sífnos) 128
hiking
maps 39
walking holiday companies ..16
Híos 388
Híos 389
Híos Town 389–393
Híos Town 390
Hippocrates 332
history 539–566
hitching 52
Hivadholímni 134
Hokhlakás (Télendhos)..346
Hokhláki (Níssyros) 324
Hokhlakoúra (Lipsí) 359
“Homer’s” tomb 186
Hóra (Amorgós) 181
Hóra (Anáfi) 197
Hóra (Ándhros) 140
Hóra (Astypálea) 339
Hóra (Folégandhros) ..189
Hóra (Íos) 185
Hóra (Kálymnos) 345
Hóra (Kímolos) 136
Hóra (Koufoníssi) 177
Hóra (Kýthira) 532
Hóra (Kýthnos) 121

Hóra (Pátmos) 356
Hóra (Samothráki) 426
Hóra (Sérifos) 124
Hóra (Skhinoússa) 177
Horió (Hálki) 308
Horió (Sými) 314
hospitals 34
hot-water systems 53
hotels 53
Hozoviotíssa
  monastery 181
Hydra – see Ídhra
hydrofoils 45

I

Ía 194
Ialyssos, ancient 302
ice cream 62
Ídhra (Hydra) 103
Ídhra 103
Ídhra Town 103
Ifestía 423
Ikaría 381
Ikaría & Foúrni 382
Imerovígli 194
Ímia crisis 561
immigration crisis 566
Independence, War of ..545
information 38
Inoússes 401
insect pests 33
insects 591
insurance 30
internet cafés 66
internet sites, Greek 41
Ionian islands 478
Iónio 524
Íos 183
Íos 184
Ioulídha 118
Ipsárion, Mount 435
Ipsilométopo 417
Ipsiloú monastery 412
Ípsos 487
Iráklia 178
Iráklion – see under Crete
Iréon 375
Íssos 496
Istérnia 144
Itháki (Ithaca) 516

J

jellyfish 32

Jews 295, 332, 549
junta, colonels' 552

K

Kabireio, ancient 423
kafenía 61
kaïkia 46
Kaládhi 533
Kalafáti 151
Kalamáki (Skiáthos) 448
Kalamáki (Zákynthos) ..524
Kalamákia (Alónissos) ..456
Kalámi (Corfu) 488
Kalamiótissa 199
Kalamítsi (Lefkádha) 427
Kálamos (Évvia) 466
Kálamos (Íos) 186
Kálandou 174
Kalávria 102
Kalliópi 423
Kallithéa (Sámos) 380
Kállitsos 125
Kalloní 411
Kaló Livádhi (Mýkonos)..151
Kalogriás (Skýros) 462
Kalotarítissa 179
Kalóyeros (Andíparos) ..165
Kalóyeros (Skýros) 459
Kálymnos 342
Kálymnos 343
Kamáres (Sífnos) 127
Kamári (Amorgós) 182
Kamári (Kós) 336
Kamári (Thíra) 195
Kamariótissa 426
Kambí (Foúrni) 388
Kambí (Kéa) 119
Kambí (Zákynthos) 526
Kámbos (Híos) 396
Kámbos (Ikaría) 384
Kámbos (Pátmos) 357
Kámbos (Sýros) 158
Kameiros, ancient 301
Kaméni islets (Thíra) 196
Kaminákia 340
Kamíni (Ídhra) 105
Kámiros Skála 301
Kanála 122
Kandoúni 345
Kánia (Hálki) 308
Kapariá 141
Kapodistrias, Ioannis ..546
Kapsáli 531
Karamanlis,
  Constantine 551, 553
Karavás 531

Karávi (Sérifos) 123
Káravos (Évvia) 466
Karavostássi 188
Kardhámena 335
Kardhámyla, Áno/Káto ..400
Kardhianí 144
Karfás 393
Karlóvassi 378
Kárpathos 282
Kárpathos 283
Kárpathos Town 282
Karterádhos 193
Karthaia, ancient 119
Karyá (Lefkádha) 503
Karyá (Skópelos) 452
Kárystos 468
Káspakas 422
Kassiópi 489
Kássos 279
Kastélla (Híos) 398
Kastélli (Anáfi) 198
Kastellórizo (Meyísti) ..309
Kastellórizo Town 310
Kastráki (Náxos) 172
Kastrí (Kýthira) 533
Kástro (Inoússes) 402
Kástro (Léros) 350
Kástro (Mílos) 133
Kástro (Sífnos) 129
Kástro (Skíathos) 447
Kástro (Thássos) 438
Kástro Khryssoheriás ..345
Kástro Kritinías 301
Kástro–Hóra (Síkinos) ...187
Katákilos, Áno/Káto 139
Katápola 180
Katastári 527
katastrofí (Asia Minor,
  1922) 547
Katelímatsa 199
Katergó 189
katharévoussa 622
Katharón monastery 519
Káthisma 505
Káto Faná 395
Káto Hóra (Kýthira) 534
Káto Kateliós 512
Káto Lákki 326
Káto Livádhi (Kýthira) ..534
Katoméri 507
Katoúni (Kýthira) 534
Katsadhiá 358
Kattaviá 306
Kavírio 423
Kávos 496
Kayiá 417
Kazavíti, Mikró/Megálo ..438
Kéa (Tzía) 116
Kéa 117

INDEX

Kea, lion of 118
Kefála cave 347
**Kefalloniá
(Cephallonia)** 507
Kefalloniá &
Itháki 508–509
Kéfalos (Kós) 336
Kekhrovouníou 146
Kéndarhos 125
Kéndros (Dhonoússa) ..179
Kerasiá 488
Kerí 524
Kérkis, Mount 380
Kérkyra (Corfu) Town ..479
Kérkyra Town 483
Kérkyra – see Corfu
Kermetés – see Platáni
Kéros (Náxos) 177
Kéros (Límnos) 423
Kérveli 373
Khíos – see Híos
Khristós tís Ierousalím ..345
Khristoú stoú
Dhássous 161
Khryssí Aktí (Páros) 165
Khryssí Ammoudhiá 435
Khryssí Miliá
(Alónissos) 455
Khryssomiliá (Foúrni) ..388
Khryssopiyís
monastery 130
Kilioméno 526
Kímisi (Lipsí) 359
Kímisis (Thirassía) 197
Kímisis monastery
(Psará) 401
Kímolos 136
Kíni 158
Kínyra 435
Kióni (Itháki) 520
Kiónia (Tínos) 144
Kiotári 305
Kípos (Mílos) 135
Kípos (Samothráki) 430
Kipouréon 515
Kirinthos, ancient 470
Kíthnos – see Kýthnos
Kléftiko 135
Klíma (Mílos) 134
Klió 417
Klisídhi 198
Kohýlas, Mount 462
Kohýli (Évvia) 470
Kokálli 352
Kokkári 376
Kokkinókastro 456
Kolofána 182
Kolokotronis,
Theodhoros 545

Kolóna (Kýthnos) 119
Kolýmbia 298
Kolymbíthra (Tínos) 145
Kolymbíthres (Páros) ..163
Kombonádha 533
Kómi 395
Komiakí 174
Kondakéïka 377
Kondiás 422
Kondókali 487
Korasídha (Évvia) 466
Kórfos (Thirassía) 196
Korissía (Corfu) 494
Korissía (Kéa) 116
Korthí 141
Kós 326
Kós & Psérimos 327
Kós Town 326
Kós Town 328
Koskiná 384
Koskotas, Yiorgos 557
Kóstos 164
Kótsinas 424
Koufoníssi, Áno/Káto ..177
Koukounariés 448
Kouloúki 349
Kouloúra 488
Koumaradhéï 375
Koumbára 185
Kouméïka 375
Koúndouros 119
Kounístra 448
Koutalás 126
Krémastá Nerá 430
Kremastí bridge
(Lésvos) 411
Kríkellos, Mount 183
Kríti – see Crete
Krýa Vrýssi 469
Ktikádhos 144
Kykládhes – see Cyclades
Kými 466
Kyrá Panayiá
(Kárpathos) 287
Kyrá Panayiá (Skýros) ..462
Kyrá Panayiá (Sporades
islet) 456
Kýthira 528–535
Kýthira 529
Kýthnos (Thermiá) 119
Kýthnos 120

L

Ladhikó 298
Laganás 524
Lahaniá 305

Lákka (Paxí) 499
Lákka (Psará) 401
Lakkí 349
Lalária 449
Lámbi (Kós) 332
Lámbi (Pátmos) 357
Lambrakis, Grigoris 552
Langádha (Amorgós) ..183
Langádha (Híos) 398
Langéri 163
language learning
materials 613
Lárdhos 305
Lássi 514
laundries 84
Lefkádha (Lefkas) 500
Lefkádha 501
Lefkádha Town 502
Lefkátas, Cape 506
Lefkáthia 400
Léfkes 164
Lefkími 496
Lefkós – see Paralía Lefkoú
Lemonákia 377
Lepétymnos, Mount 416
Lepídha 350
Léros 348
Léros 348
Lésvos (Mytilíni) 402
Lésvos 403
Lethrá 320
Liá (Mýkonos) 151
Liani, Dimitra
"Mimi" 549, 554
Lidharió 424
Liendoú 358
Liés (Níssyros) 325
Limenária (Angístri) 99
Limenária (Thássos) 436
Liménas 432
Liménas 432
Limín – see Liménas
Limiónas (Kýthira) 534
Límni (Évvia) 470
Límni Kerioú 524
Limniá (Híos) 339
Limniónas (Kós) 337
Limniónas (Sámos) 380
Limniónas (Zákynthos) ..526
Limnióniza (Ídhra) 106
Limniótissa 345
Limnonári 452
Límnos 418
Límnos 419
Límnos (Híos) 400
Límnos (Psará) 401
Limónos monastery 411
Linária (Kálymnos) 345
Linariá 458

636

Líndhos 299
Lindos, ancient 299
lion of Kéa 118
Liónas 174
Lípedha 515
Lipsí 358
Lithí 398
Livadhákia (Sérifos) 122
Livádhi (Ikaría) 384
Livádhi (Iráklia) 178
Livádhi (Kýthira) 533
Livádhi (Sérifos) 122
Livádhi Yeranoú 357
Livádhia (Astypálea) 340
Livádhia (Tílos) 319
Lixoúri 515
Liyiá 503
Liyínou 357
Logarás 164
Longós 499
Lourdháta 512
Loustriá 189
Loutrá (Kýthnos) 121
Loutrá (Níssyros) 324
Loutrá (Samothráki) 429
Loutrá (Tínos) 145
Loutrá Eftaloú 416
Loutrá Ehipsoú 472
Loutrá Yéras 408
Loutráki (Skópelos) 450
Loútsa 517

M

Magaziá 461
magazines 68
Magic Beach 336
Maherádho 526
mainland ports
  Alexandhroúpoli 28
  Ástakos 28
  Áyios Konstandínos 29
  Igoumenítsa 28
  Kavála 28
  Lávrio 28
  Neápoli (Peloponnese) 28
  Párga 28
  Pátra (Patras) 28
  Pireás (Piraeus) 27
  Rafína 29
  Thessaloníki 29
  Vólos 29
  Ýithio (Gythion) 29
Makrá 281
Makriá Ámmos (Híos) ..397
Makrýs Yialós
  (Kefalloniá) 514
Makrýs Yialós
  (Lefkádha)..................285

Makrýs Yialós
  (Zákynthos) 527
Maltezána – see Análipsi
  (Astypálea)
Maltézi 181
mammals 589
Mamoúni 341
Managrós 400
Mandamádhos 417
Mandhráki (Ídhra) 105
Mandhráki (Níssyros) ..322
Mandhráki (Skiáthos) ..449
Mandhrákia (Mílos) 135
Manganári 186
Manitohóri 532
Manolás 196
Manolátes 378
map sources 40
maps 38
Maráthi 359
Maráthi (Páros) 164
Marathókambos 379
Marathónas (Égina) 97
Marathoúnda
  (Psérimos) 337
Marathoúnda (Sými) ...317
Mariés (Thássos) 438
Mariés (Zákynthos) 526
Markópoulo 512
Mármara (Páros) 163
Marmári (Évvia) 468
Marmári (Kós) 333
Marmári coves
  (Astypálea) 341
Mármaro (Híos) 399
Márpissa 164
Marpoúnda 456
Massoúri 345
mastic villages (Híos) ..394
Mastihári 335
Mastihohoriá (Híos) 394
Mathráki 497
Mávra Vólia – see Mávros
  Yialós
Mavratzéï 375
Mávros Yialós 395
meats 59
media 67
Megáli Ámmos
  (Alónissos) 456
Megáli Ámmos
  (Kýthnos) 122
Megáli Ámmos
  (Mýkonos) 150
Megáli Idhéa 546–547
Megális Panayías 375
Megálo Horió
  (Agathoníssi) 360
Megálo Horió (Tílos) 320

Megálo Livádhi
  (Sérifos) 125
Megalohóri (Thíra) 192
Megálos Mourtiás 456
Meganíssi 506
Mégas Lákkos 515
Mégas Limniónas 394
Mégas Yialós
  (Skiáthos) 449
Mégas Yialós (Sýros) ..159
Melínda 409
Melissáni Cave 510
Melitsahás 345
Melóï 355, 357
Melos, ancient 134
Menetés 285
Ménites (Ándhros) 141
**menu guide, food and
  drink** 619–621
Mérihas 119
Merikiá 349
Merikoúnda 395
Mersíni (Dhonoússa) ..179
Mésa (Lésvos) 411
Mésa Vathý
  (Astypálea) 341
Mesakhtí 384
Mesanagrós 306
Mesohóri 286
Messariá (Ándhros) 141
Messariá (Thíra) 196
Messongí 495
Mestá 395
Metamórfosis (Sámos) 379
Metamórfosis
  (Skópelos) 451
Metaxas dictatorship ..548
Metóhi (Angístri) 99
Meyísti – see Kastellórizo
mezédhes 58, 61
mezedhopolía 61
Míkonos – see Mýkonos
Mikró Horió (Tílos) 320
Mikrós Yialós
  (Lefkádha) 504
Miliá (Skópelos) 452
Mílos 131
Mílos & Kímolos 131
Minoa, ancient 181
Minoan era 539
Minor Cyclades 176
Míthymna – see Mólyvos
Mitsotakis, Constantine
  ....552, 558–559
mobile phones 65
Mólos (Páros) 163
Mólos (Skýros) 461
Mólyvos (Míthymna) 414
Mon Repos 485

monarchy, deposition
of 554
monasteries
staying in 55
visits 69
Monastíri (Anáfi) 199
Monastíri (Páros) 163
money transfers 37
Moní (Égina) 98
Moní (Náxos) 173
Monodhéndhri 359
Monólithos (Rhodes) ..301
Monólithos (Thíra) 195
Moraïtika 494
Moúdhros 423
Moúros 182
Moutsoúna 174
movies 73
museums, opening
hours 70
music 577–583
Muslims 294, 332
Mýkonos 146
Mýkonos & Delos 149
Mýkonos Town 146
Mýkonos Town 147
Mýli (Évvia) 469
Mýli (Sámos) 375
Mýlos (Angístri) 99
Mýlos (Lefkádha) 505
Mýrina 420
Mýrtos (Kefalloniá) 515
Mýtikas 158
Mycenaean era 539
Mykáli 373
Mylélia 410
Mylopótamos (Íos) 186
Mylopótamos (Kýthira) 534
Mylópotas – see
Mylopótamos (Íos)
Myrtiés 345
Myrtiótissa,
monastery/beach 493
**mythology, ancient
Greek** 567–576
Mytilíni Town 404
Mytilíni Town 405

Nagós 399
Nanoú 317
Náoussa (Páros) 162
Nás 387
Návlakas 312
Náxos 166
Náxos 167

Náxos Town 167
Néa Dhimokratía (New
Democracy) 553
Néa Moní 396
Néa Stýra 468
Neolithic Greece 539
newsletters, Greece-
specific 67
newspapers 67
Nikiá 325
Nikiána 503
Nikouriá 182
Nissáki 488
Níssyros 322
Níssyros 323
NOS (Sými) 316
Notiná 182
nude bathing 77
Nydhrí 503

O

Odysseus sites (Itháki) ..517
Óhi, Mount 469
Oía – see Ía
Olýmbi 395
Ólymbos (Kárpathos) ..287
opening hours 69
Oreí 471
Órmos Athniós 192
Órmos Marathokámbou
......................................379
Ornós 150
Óros, Mount (Égina) 97
OTE (Greek telecom
corporation) 63
Otho, King 546
Othoní 497
Óthos 286
Otto – see Otho, King
Ottoman rule 544
Otziás 118
ouzerís 61
oúzo 61

P

package specialists
in Australasia 25
in North America 23
in UK 15–16
Pagóndas 375
Páhena 135
Pahiá Ámmos
(Níssyros) 325

Pahiá Ámmos
(Samothráki) 430
Pahiá Ámmos
(Zákynthos) 526
Pahiá Ráhi 97
Pahýs (Thássos) 437
Palamári 462
Paleá Alónissos 453
Paleó Klíma 450
Paleó Pylí (Kós) 334
Paleohóra (Égina) 97
Paleóhora (Itháki) 518
Paleohóra (Kýthira) 530
Paleohóri (Mílos) 134
Paleokastrítsa 491
Paleókastro (Ándhros) 141
Paleókastro
(Kastellórizo) 311
Paleókastro (Kímolos) ..137
Paleókastro (Síkinos) ..188
Paleókastro monastery
(Mýkonos) 152
Paleópoli (Kýthira) 533
Paleópoli (Samothráki) ..427
Paleópolis (Ándhros) ..140
Pálli (Agathoníssi) 360
Pálli (Níssyros) 324
Paloúkia 93
Panakhrándou 141
Panayía (Iráklia) 178
Panayiá (Kássos) 281
Panayiá (Sérifos) 125
Panayía (Thássos) 434
Panayía Dhrossianí 173
Panayía Kastrianí (Kéa)..118
Panayía Krína 396
Panayía Makriní 381
Panayía Myrtidhíon 534
Panayía Panohorianí ..183
Panayía Spilianí 374
Panayía Thermianí 325
Panayía tís Kekhriás 447
Panayía Tourlianí 152
Panayiés 352
Pandéli 350
Pandokrátor, Mount
..........................487, 489
Pánormos (Kálymnos) ..345
Pánormos (Mýkonos) ..151
Pánormos (Náxos) 174
Pánormos (Skópelos) ..452
Pánormos (Tínos) 145
Papá Miná 288
Papá toú Houmá 462
Papafránga 135
Papandhriá 358
Papandreou,
Andreas 553–562
Papandreou, George ..552

Paradise (Mýkonos) 151
Paradise beach (Kós) ..336
Paralía Kírinthos 469
Paralía Kopriá 301
Paralía Kotsikiás
    (Évvia) 471
Paralía Kýmis 466
Paralía Lefkoú 286
Paralía Lithíou 398
Paralía Politikón 469
Paralía Thánous 422
Paramónas 494
Paránga 151
Paraspóros 161
Parikía 160
Páros 159
Páros & Andíparos 159
PASOK 553, 554–555
pastries 62
Patitíri 453
Pátmos 352
Pátmos 353
Paxí (Paxos) 497
Paxí 498
Paxos – see Paxí
Pédhi 316
Pefkári (Thássos) 436
Péfki (Évvia) 471
Péfki (Rhodes) 305
Péfkos (Skýros) 462
Pefkoúlia 505
Pélekas 493
Pelópi 417
Peloponnesian Wars ..541
Pendáti 494
Péra Kástro
    (Kálymnos) 345
Perahóri (Itháki) 518
Pérama 408
Perastá 312
Pérdhika (Égina) 98
períptera (kiosks) 84
Périssa 195
Peristéra (Sporades) ..456
Perivolioú 450
Perivolís monastery 412
Pessádha 514
Petaloúdhes (Páros) 161
Petaloúdhes
    (Rhodes) 302
Petáni 515
Pétra 416
petrified forest
    (Lésvos) 412
Petrití 495
Pezónda 347
pharmacies 33
Philip II of Macedon 542
phone codes, changing ..65

phone codes, useful 64
phones 63
photographic film 84
phrases and words,
    useful 615–619
Phylakope – see Fylakopí
Piáki 377
picnic fare 56
Pigádhia (Kárpathos) ..282
Pipéri (Páros) 163
Pipéri (Sporades) 457
Pisaetós 518
Píso Livádhi 164
Písses 119
Pityós 398
Pláka (Mílos) 133
Pláka (Náxos) 172
Pláka (Tílos) 321
Plákes (Amorgós) 180
Plános 526
Platána (Évvia) 466
Platanákia (Sámos) 377
Platáni (Kós) 332
Plátanos (Léros) 350
Pláthiena 134
Platiá Ámmos
    (Kýthira) 531
Platiá Ámmos (Páros) ..163
Platý (Límnos) 422
Platý Yialós
    (Kálymnos) 345
Platýs Yialós
    (Kefaloniá) 514
Platýs Yialós (Lipsí) 359
Platýs Yialós
    (Mýkonos) 150
Platýs Yialós (Sérifos) 125
Platýs Yialós (Sífnos) ..129
Plimýri 306
Plomári 409
Póli 281
police 78
Politikí Ánixi (Political
    Spring) 560
Pollónia (Mílos) 135
Polykhnítos spa 410
Polyókhni/Polyochni ..423
Polytechnic revolt 553
Polyvótis crater 325
Póndamos 308
Póndi 505
Pondikoníssi 485
ponies, Skyrian 458
Porí 177
Póros (Kefaloniá) 511
Póros (Lefkádha) 504
Póros 100
Póros 100
Póros Town 100

Pórtes (Égina) 97
Pórto (Tínos) 144
Pórto Katsíki 506
Pórto Róma 524
Pórto Zóro 524
Poseidon temple
    (Póros) 102
Posidhónio (Sámos) 373
Possidhonía (Sýros) 158
postal services 63
poste restante 63
Potámi (Sámos) 379
Potamiá (Thássos) 435
Potamiá villages
    (Náxos) 174
Potamós (Amorgós) 182
Potamós (Kýthira) 530
Póthia 342
Potokáki 374
Potós 436
Poulopódhi 182
Poúnda 164
Prassoníssi 306
Pródhromos (Páros) 164
Prodhrómou
    (Skópelos) 451
Profítis Ilías (Ídhra) 105
Profítis Ilías
    (Níssyros) 326
Profítis Ilías (Rhodes) 303
Profítis Ilías
    (Samothráki) 430
Profítis Ilías (Sífnos) 130
Profítis Ilías (Thíra) 196
Prokópi 469
Provatás 134
Psará 400
Psaralíki 165
Psaropoúli 471
Psaroú 150
Psathí (Íos) 186
Psathí (Kímolos) 136
Psathoúra 457
Psérimos 337
Psilí Ámmos (Foúrni) ..388
Psilí Ámmos (Náxos) ..174
Psilí Ámmos (Pátmos) 357
Psilí Ámmos
    (E Sámos) 373
Psilí Ámmos
    (W Sámos) 380
Psilí Ámmos (Sérifos) ..123
Psínthos 302
psistariés 58
public holidays 69
Pýrgos (Sámos) 375
Pýrgos (Thíra) 196
Pýrgos (Tínos) 145
Pýrgos Himárou 174

ⓘ

Pylés (Kárpathos) 286
Pylí (Kós) 334
Pyrgáki (Náxos) 172
Pyrgí 394
Pythagório 373

R

radio 68
Ráhes 386
Rahóni 438
reptiles 590
residence visas 76
restaurants 57
Rhó islet 312
Rhodes (Ródhos) 288
Rhodes island 289
Rína 347
Ródha 490
Ródhos Town 290–298
Ródhos Town 293
Roman Greece 542
rooms 53
Roúkounas 198
Roussoúm Yialós 455
Roviés 470

S

sailing 74
Salamína (Salamis) 93
Salamína Town 93
Salamis – see Salamína
Samaras, Andonis 560
Sámi 510
Sámos 367
Sámos 369
Sámos Town – see Vathý
   (Sámos)
Samothrace – see
   Samothráki
Samothráki (Corfu islet)
   – see Mathráki
**Samothráki
   (Samothrace)** 425
Samothráki 425
**Sanctuary of the Great
   Gods** 427
Sangrí, Áno/Káto 173
Sánta Margaríta 146
Sánta María 163
Santa Maura castle 500
Santoríni – see Thíra
Sarakíniko (Itháki) 517
Sarakíniko (Mílos) 135

Sarakíno (Skýros) 459
Saría 288
**scooter and motorbike
   rental** 47
scuba diving 74
sea urchins 32
seafood 59
seals, Mediterranean
   monk 455
Seïtáni, Mikró/Megálo
  379
Seláï 281
Selínia 93
senior travellers 81
Sérifos 122
Sérifos 123
sexual harassment 78
Shipwreck Bay 528
shops, opening hours ..69
Siánna 301
Sidhári 490
Sidhiroúnda 397
Sífnos 126
Sífnos 126
Sígri 413
Síkinos 186
Síkinos &
   Folégandhros 187
Simitis, Kostas 561–563
Síros – see Sýros
Skála (Angístri) 98
Skála (Astypálea) 339
Skála (Kefalloniá) 512
Skála (Kímolos) 137
Skála (Pátmos) 352
Skála Eressoú 413
Skála Kallonís 411
Skála Marión 437
Skála Polikhnítou 411
Skála Potamiás 435
Skála Prínou 437
Skála Rahoníou 437
Skála Sykaminiás 417
Skantzoúra 457
Skhinós 517
Skhinoússa 177
Skiádhi monastery 306
Skiáthos 444
Skiáthos 446
Skiáthos Town 445
Skinári, Cape 527
Skíros – see Skýros
Skópelos 449
Skópelos 449
Skópelos Town 450
Skýros 457
Skýros 457
Skýros Town 459
snack food 57

soccer 74
Sorós 165
Sotíras (Thássos) 438
soúma 61
Spartohóri 506
Spatharéï 375
Spétses (Spetsai) 106
Spétses 106
Spétses Town 107
Spiliá toú Filoktíti 423
Spiliás 360
Spóa 287
Sporades 444
**sports and outdoor
   pursuits** 74
St John monastery,
   Pátmos – see Ayíou
   Ioánnou Theológou
   (Pátmos)
St Paul's harbour 300
Stáfylos 452
stamps 63
Stavrós (Dhonoússa) ..179
Stavrós (Hálki) 308
Stavrós (Itháki) 518
Stavrós (Tílos) 320
Stéfanos crater 325
Stegná 299
Stení 467
Stení Vála 456
Steniés 141
Stenítis Bay 526
Stenó 341
stingrays 32
Stómio 466
Strinýlas 487
Stýpsi 417
Stýra 467
Sunny/Markos Beach 336
Super Paradise 151
sweets 62
Sými 312
Sými 313
Sýros 154
Sýros 155
Sývota 504
Sývros 504
Sykamiá – see Sykaminiá,
   Lésvos
Sykaminiá (Lésvos) 417
Sykaminiá (Sérifos) 125
Syríngas 158

T

Tallarás baths 341
Tarsaná (Mýkonos) 151

Tárti 409
tavernas 58
taxi boats 46
Taxiárhis Mihaïl
  Panormítis 317
Taxiárhis Mihaïl
  Roukouniótis 317
Taxiárhis monastery
  (Lésvos) 417
Taxiarhón (Serifós) 125
taxis 52
Télendhos 346
telephones 63
television 68
Thános (Koufoníssi) 177
Thános (Límnos) 422
Thapsaná 164
Thárri monastery 303
Thássos 430
Thássos 431
Thássos Town, see
  Liménas
Theológos (Amorgós) ..183
Theológos (Thássos)....437
Theophilos Museum ..408
Theotókou monastery ..491
Thériade Museum 408
Thermá (Ikaría) 383
Thermá (Samothráki) ..429
Thérmes Kallithéas 298
Thermiá – see Kýthnos
Thíra (Santoríni) 190
Thíra (Santoríni) 191
Thira, ancient 195
Thirassía islet 196
Tholária 183
Thóli (Agathoníssi) 360
Thólos (Tílos) 320
Thýmena 387
Tiganákia (Arkí) 359
Tigáni (Híos) 397
Tílos 318
Tílos 318
time differences 84
Tingáki 333
Tínos 142
Tínos 143
Tínos Town 142
toilets 85
Tolí 317
topless sunbathing 78
topographical maps 39
tourist information 38
Toúrlos 150
Tragéa region 173
Tragoníssi 151
Trahiá 308
trains
  rail passes 17

to Greece from Britain 16
transliteration scheme ..614
travel agents
  in Australasia 24
  in Iráklion (Crete) 219
  in North America 22
  in Ródhos Town (Rhodes) ..298
  in UK & Ireland 15
travellers' cheques 35
Triádhes 135
Triandáros 146
Triovássalos 133
Trípodhes 172
Tripótamos 145
Trís Boúkes 462
Troúllos 335
Truman Doctrine 550
Trypití (Mílos) 133
Trypití (Thássos) 437
Tsambíka,
  beach/monastery 298
Tsigoúri 178
Tsigrádho 135
tsikoudhiá 61
Tsiliví 526
Tsónia 417
Tsópela 375
Tsougriá 447
Tsoukaládhes 505
Turkey
  entry from Dodecanese
    islands 12, 362
  entry from north and east
    Aegean islands 12, 439
Turkómnima 359
turtles, loggerhead 525
2004 Olympic Games 562
Tzaboú 377
Tzamadhoú 377
Tzanáki 340
Tziá – see Kéa

V

Vafiós 415
Vafiós 417
Vafkerí 503
Valeondátes 378
Vanánda 288
Vardhiá 189
Vári 159
Variá 408
Vársamo (Válsamo) 381
Vassilikí (Lefkádha) 504
Vassilikós, villages/penin-
  sula (Zákynthos) 523
Vaterá 410
Vathý (Itháki) 516

Vathý (Meganíssi) 507
Vathý (Psérimos) 337
Vathý (Sámos) 370
Vathý 371
Vathý (Sífnos) 130
Vathýs (Kálymnos) 347
Vátos (Corfu) 493
Vátos (Samothráki) 430
Vatoúmi 500
Vatoússa 412
Vátses 341
Vayiá 357
Velanió 452
Venetian rule 543
Venizelos,
  Eleftherios 546–548
Véssa 398
Vídhos 486
Vígla 500
villa rental 55
visas 29
Vlaháta 512
Vlahérna 485
Vlamarí 373
Vlyhá (Rhodes) 300
Vlyhádhia 347
Vlyhó (Lefkádha) 504
Vlyhós (Ídhra) 105
Voládha 286
Vólakas 145
Vólax 145
Volímes 527
Volissós 399
Votsalákia 380
Vótsi 455
Voúdhia 135
Vourkári 117
Vourliótes 377
Vournikás 504
Vréllos 109
Vríka 500
Vríssa 410
Vrómi Bay 526
Vromólimnos 448
Vromólithos 350
Vrondádhos 398
Vróndi 282
Vrondianís (Vrónda) 377
Vrykoúnda 288
Vrysítsa 456
Výthisma 456

W

walking 74
War of Independence ..537
watersports 74

weever fish 32
"White Beach" 324
wildlife 584–593
windsurfing 74
wine 60
wiring money 37
women's organizations ..558
words and phrases,
  useful 615–619
work visas 76
working in Greece 75
World War I 547
World War II 548

X

Xánemos 449
Xí 515
Xinára 145
Xirókambos 350
Xyngía 527

Y

Yennádhi 305
Yérakas (Alónissos) 456
Yérakas (Zákynthos) ..524
Yiali (Hálki) 308
Yialiskári (Ikaría) 385
Yialiskári (Kéa) 117
Yialós (Íos) 184
Yialós (Lefkádha) 506
Yialós (Sými) 313
Yiáltra 472
Yióssonas 399
Yioúra 456
Yíras 503
youth hostels 55

Z

zaharoplastía 62

Zákynthos (Zante) 520
Zákynthos 521
Zákynthos Town 520
Zante – see Zákynthos
Zefyría 134
Zepánga 402
Ziá 334
Zogeriá 109
Zoödhóhou Piyís
  (Anáfi) 199
Zoödhóhou Piyís
  (Ándhros) 141
Zoödhóhou Piyís
  (Límnos) 424
Zoödhóhou Piyís
  (Póros) 102
Zoödhóhou Piyís
  (Sámos) 373
Zoödhóhou Piyís
  (Síkinos) 188
Zourvás 106

Twenty Years of Rough Guides

In the summer of 1981, Mark Ellingham, Rough Guides' founder, knocked out the first guide on a typewriter, with a group of friends. Mark had been travelling in Greece after university, and couldn't find a guidebook that really answered his needs.There were heavyweight cultural guides on the one hand – good on museums and classical sites but not on beaches and tavernas – and on the other hand student manuals that were so caught up with how to save money that they lost sight of the country's significance beyond its role as a place for a cool vacation. None of the guides began to address Greece as a country, with its natural and human environment, its politics and its contemporary life.

Having no urgent reason to return home, Mark decided to write his own guide. It was a guide to Greece that tried to combine some erudition and insight with a thoroughly practical approach to travellers' needs. Scrupulously researched listings of places to stay, eat and drink were matched by careful attention to detail on everything from Homer to Greek music, from classical sites to national parks and from nude beaches to monasteries. Back in London, Mark and his friends got their Rough Guide accepted by a far-sighted commissioning editor at the publisher Routledge and it came out in 1982.

The Rough Guide to Greece was a student scheme that became a publishing phenomenon. The immediate success of the book – shortlisted for the Thomas Cook award – spawned a series that rapidly covered dozens of countries. The Rough Guides found a ready market among backpackers and budget travellers, but soon acquired a much broader readership that included older and less impecunious visitors. Readers relished the guides' wit and inquisitiveness as much as the enthusiastic, critical approach that acknowledges everyone wants value for money – but not at any price.

Rough Guides soon began supplementing the "rougher" information – the hostel and low-budget listings – with the kind of detail that independent-minded travellers on any budget might expect. These days, the guides – distributed worldwide by the Penguin group – include recommendations spanning the range from shoestring to luxury, and cover more than 200 destinations around the globe. Our growing team of authors, many of whom come to Rough Guides initially as outstandingly good letter-writers telling us about their travels, are spread all over the world, particularly in Europe, the US and Australia. As well as the travel guides, Rough Guides publishes a series of dictionary phrasebooks covering two dozen major languages, an acclaimed series of music guides running the gamut from Classical to World Music, a series of music CDs in association with World Music Network, and a range of reference books on topics as diverse as the Internet, Pregnancy and Unexplained Phenomena. Visit **www.roughguides.com** to see what's cooking.

Rough Guide credits

Text editors: Ruth Blackmore and Alison Murchie
Series editor: Mark Ellingham
Editorial: Martin Dunford, Jonathan Buckley, Jo Mead, Kate Berens, Ann-Marie Shaw, Helena Smith, Judith Bamber, Orla Duane, Olivia Eccleshall, Geoff Howard, Claire Saunders, Gavin Thomas, Alexander Mark Rogers, Polly Thomas, Joe Staines, Richard Lim, Duncan Clark, Peter Buckley, Lucy Ratcliffe, Clifton Wilkinson, Matthew Teller, Andrew Dickson (UK); Andrew Rosenberg, Stephen Timblin, Yuki Takagaki, Richard Koss, Hunter Slaton (US)
Production: Susanne Hillen, Andy Hilliard, Link Hall, Helen Prior, Julia Bovis, Michelle Draycott, Katie Pringle, Mike Hancock, Zoë Nobes, Rachel Holmes, Andy Turner
Cartography: Melissa Baker, Maxine Repath, Ed Wright, Katie Lloyd-Jones
Picture research: Louise Boulton, Sharon Martins, Mark Thomas
Online: Kelly Cross, Anja Mutic-Blessing, Jennifer Gold, Audra Epstein, Suzanne Welles, Cree Lawson (US)
Finance: John Fisher, Gary Singh, Edward Downey, Mark Hall, Tim Bill
Marketing & Publicity: Richard Trillo, Niki Smith, David Wearn, Chloë Roberts, Demelza Dallow, Claire Southern (UK); Simon Carloss, David Wechsler, Kathleen Rushforth (US)
Administration: Tania Hummel, Julie Sanderson

Publishing information

This fourth edition published February 2002 by Rough Guides Ltd, 62–70 Shorts Gardens, London WC2H 9AH. Penguin Putnam, Inc. 375 Hudson Street, NY 10014, USA.
Distributed by the Penguin Group
Penguin Books Ltd,
80 Strand, London WC2R ORL
Penguin Putnam, Inc.
375 Hudson Street, NY 10014, USA
Penguin Books Australia Ltd,
487 Maroondah Highway, PO Box 257,
Ringwood, Victoria 3134, Australia
Penguin Books Canada Ltd,
10 Alcorn Avenue, Toronto, Ontario,
Canada M4V 1E4
Penguin Books (NZ) Ltd,
182–190 Wairau Road, Auckland 10,
New Zealand
Typeset in Bembo and Helvetica to an original design by Henry Iles.

Printed in Italy by LegoPrint S.p.A

680pp includes index
A catalogue record for this book is available from the British Library

ISBN 1-85828-867-3

The publishers and authors have done their best to ensure the accuracy and currency of all the information in The Rough Guide to The Greek Islands, however, they can accept no responsibility for any loss, injury, or inconvenience sustained by any traveller as a result of information or advice contained in the guide.

Help us update

We've gone to a lot of effort to ensure that the fourth edition of The Rough Guide to The Greek Islands is accurate and up to date. However, things change – places get "discovered", opening hours are notoriously fickle, restaurants and rooms raise prices or lower standards. If you feel we've got it wrong or left something out, we'd like to know, and if you can remember the address, the price, the time, the phone number, so much the better.

We'll credit all contributions, and send a copy of the next edition (or any other Rough Guide if you prefer) for the best letters. Everyone who writes to us and isn't already a subscriber will receive a copy of our full-colour twice-yearly newsletter. Please mark letters: "Rough Guide Greek Islands Update" and send to: Rough Guides, 62–70 Shorts Gardens, London WC2H 9AH, or Rough Guides, 4th Floor, 345 Hudson St, New York, NY 10014. Or send an email to: mail@roughguides.co.uk or mail@roughguides.com.

Acknowledgements

Andrew Benson thanks Peter Mackridge in Oxford for his invaluable advice on just about everything; Peter Bowen and everyone on the Akrotíri for Easter festivities and hospitality; Denise and the boys for May Day fun, serious discussions and Athonite wisdom; Brian Donovan for a special insight into the Olympian pantheon, all kinds of insider information and ice-cold beers. At Rough Guides, Kate Berens for her continuing confidence, and editor Ruth Blackmore for keeping very calm – congratulations to her, too!

John Bozman thanks Kostas Zissis, Nansy, Thanos, Christos, Suzanna, Sakis, Kostas, Maria and George in Athens; Dimitris and Soula Ghikas on Páros; Despina Kitini and Stavros on Náxos; Artemis on Amorgós; Aris and Loucas Ziras, Markos Karvounis and Sharen Treutel on Santorini; Nik Panou on Angístri; Michael Journtos on Ídhra; David Ewens and Bunny on Ándhros; Sharon Turner on Tínos; John and Koula Kladis on Íos; John van Lerberghe and Maria Paoula on Mýkonos; Aphrodite Depasta, Apostolos Dimopoulos and Apostolis Diareme on Sífnos; Kostas Krinas and Stavros on Sérifos; Sharon Mathiodakis on Mílos; Apostolis on Kímolos; Adonis on Kýthnos; Alkestis in Égina; George on the Express Dionyssos; Shirley Watson in Dallas; Kyle McCarthy in New York; Marc Dubin, Ruth Blackmore and Carolyn in London.

Lance Chilton thanks wife Hilary; Chris and Dave Windell in Pyrgiótika; Yiannis Katranis in Spárti; Julia Tzanidou-Zuberer of Porfyra Travel in Kýthira; Babis Doufexis and Nicola Dyas of Doufexis Travel in Stoúpa; Chrissy Papavasilopoulos in Iráklion, and Sue Carr in Bury St Edmunds.

Marc Dubin thanks Thanos, Nancy and Susanna in Athens; Roy & Effi Hounsell in Koukouli; the Khristodoulis family in Papingo; George & Barbara Ballis, and George & Effi Kapsalis on Lésvos; Markos Kostalas, and Theodhore and Güher Spordhilis on Híos; Alexis and Dhionysia Zikas on Kós; David, Iain, Lynn, Joanna and Andrea on Tílos, plus Nigel Gardner for the loan of his lovely house; Paul and Stella, plus Efi, Spyros, Sotiris and Marianne (again) on Rhodes; Nikos, Wendy and Jean on Sými; Christine and Alex Sakellaridis on Hálki; Nikos and Anna on Lipsí; Bruno in Galaxídhi; Kostas and Marianthi Pappas in Lykiádhes; Thanasis and Toula Nakas in Kastráki; Nick Gekas in Kalambáka for that vital map; Jill Sleeman in Moúressi; Panayiotis and Aphrodite Papasotiriou on Límnos; Mark and Clovis for the necessary "time out" on Paxí; and last but not least to Pamela for over-eating once again for science, minding the farm in London and cheerfully island-hopping from Ikaría to Kós when we were supposed to be on Lésvos.

Nick Edwards would like to thank the following: the staff of the Corfu and Kefallonia OTE offices; Yiorgia & Catherine and the Zoupanos clan for hospitality in Corfu; Spyros Hytiris for advice and musical sustenance in Corfu; Panayiotis Vandoros for *filoxenía*, friendship and constant *kafedhákia* in Argostóli; June Kalogeratou for the homely nest in Zákynthos; Steve & Yiota for the Patra overnight; Steve T, Yiannis K and Klaes K for good times in various spots; and finally Maria for continuing support.

In addition, the editors would like to thank all those involved in producing this book, in particular Katie Pringle for her expert typesetting and lay-out, Katie Lloyd-Jones for an excellent job with the maps, Sharon Martins for picture research and Jennifer Speake for proofreading.

SMALL PRINT

Readers' letters

Our thanks to readers of the previous edition who sent in comments and suggestions. In particular:

Gale Mead, Julia Newell and David Piper, Sue Carr, Liz Fogarty, Ian Gates, Gavin Breeze, Ceri Bygrave, Daniel Brook, Phil Davis, Jeff Evans, Anne Galos, Betty Garscia, Letta Gassiou, Eirik Gjonnes, Peter Harmston, Dylan Harris, Andy Kirk, David Lee, Charles Manton, Peter Marsh, Jutta Mistelbacher, Kevin Mitchell, Espen Naevestad, Anne Parker, Joy Rawlin, Ruth A. Cookson, David Burt, Barbara Goulden, J. H. Martin, Anne Parker, Chloe Britton, Peter Marsh.

Photo credits

SMALL PRINT

The ideas expressed in this code were developed by and for independent travellers.

Learn About The Country You're Visiting

Start enjoying your travels before you leave by tapping into as many sources of information as you can.

The Cost Of Your Holiday

Think about where your money goes - be fair and realistic about how cheaply you travel. Try and put money into local peoples' hands; drink local beer or fruit juice rather than imported brands and stay in locally owned accommodation. Haggle with humour and not aggressively. Pay what something is worth to you and remember how wealthy you are compared to local people.

Embrace The Local Culture

Open your mind to new cultures and traditions - it will transform your experience. Think carefully about what's appropriate in terms of your clothes and the way you behave. You'll earn respect and be more readily welcomed by local people. Respect local laws and attitudes towards drugs and alcohol that vary in different countries and communities. Think about the impact you could have on them.

Exploring The World – The Travellers' Code

Being sensitive to these ideas means getting more out of your travels - and giving more back to the people you meet and the places you visit.

Minimise Your Environmental Impact

Think about what happens to your rubbish - take biodegradable products and a water filter bottle. Be sensitive to limited resources like water, fuel and electricity. Help preserve local wildlife and habitats by respecting local rules and regulations, such as sticking to footpaths and not standing on coral.

Don't Rely On Guidebooks

Use your guidebook as a starting point, not the only source of information. Talk to local people, then discover your own adventure!

Be Discreet With Photography

Don't treat people as part of the landscape, they may not want their picture taken. Ask first and respect their wishes.

We work with people the world over to promote tourism that benefits their communities, but we can only carry on our work with the support of people like you. For membership details or to find out how to make your travels work for local people and the environment, visit our website.

www.tourismconcern.org.uk

TourismConcern
Campaigning for Ethical and Fairly Traded

Don't bury your head in the sand!

Take cover!

with Rough Guide Travel Insurance

Worldwide cover, for Rough Guide readers worldwide

UK Freefone **0800 015 09 06**

US Freefone **1 866 220 5588**

Worldwide **(+44) 1243 621 046**

Check the web at

www.roughguides.com/insurance

ROUGH GUIDES

Insurance organized by Torribles Insurance Brokers Ltd, 21 Prince Street, Bristol, BS1 4PH, England